THE WORLD'S CLASSICS
THE FRENCH REVOLUTION

THOMAS CARLYLE was born in 1795 in Ecclefechan, a small market village in Dumfriesshire. He studied for the ministry, enrolled in law classes, and taught briefly before deciding on a career as a writer. During the 1820s, his essays and translations helped to introduce German literature and thought to a British audience. *Sartor Resartus*, his one full-scale work of imaginative fiction, was first published periodically in 1833–4. In 1826 Carlyle had married Jane Welsh. In 1834 they moved from Scotland to London and settled at Cheyne Row, Chelsea. It was here that Carlyle wrote the works that confirmed his position as the most influential of the Victorian cultural leaders: *The French Revolution* (1837), *On Heroes and Hero-Worship* (1841), *Past and Present* (1843), *Latter-Day Pamphlets* (1850), and the six-volume history of *Frederick the Great* (1858–65). His *Reminiscences* were published shortly after his death, in 1881.

KENNETH FIELDING is Emeritus Professor at the University of Edinburgh. He is joint editor of the Duke–Edinburgh edition of the *Carlyle Letters*, has edited Charles Dickens's *Speeches*, been a joint editor of the Pilgrim edition of the *Dickens Letters*, and published critical books and essays, chiefly on Dickens and Carlyle.

DAVID SORENSEN is Assistant Professor of English Literature at St Joseph's University, Philadelphia. He is writing a book on Thomas Carlyle and British Historiography, and has written and published on other Victorians.

THE WORLD'S CLASSICS

——

THOMAS CARLYLE

The
French Revolution
A History

——

Edited by

K. J. FIELDING and DAVID SORENSEN

Μέγα ὁ ἀγών ἔστι, θεῖον γὰρ ἔργον· ὑπὲρ βασιλείας ὑπὲρ
ἐλευθερίας, ὑπὲρ εὐροίας, ὑπὲρ ἀταραξίας. ARRIANUS *

Δόγμα γὰρ αὐτῶν τίς μεταβάλλει; χωρὶς δὲ δογμάτων μεταβολῆς,
τί ἄλλο ἢ δουλεία στενόντων καὶ πείθεσθαι προσποιουμένων;
ANTONINUS *

Oxford   New York
OXFORD UNIVERSITY PRESS

Oxford University Press, Walton Street, Oxford OX2 6DP

Oxford New York Toronto
Delhi Bombay Calcutta Madras Karachi
Kuala Lumpur Singapore Hong Kong Tokyo
Nairobi Dar es Salaam Cape Town
Melbourne Auckland Madrid

and associated companies in
Berlin Ibadan

Oxford is a trade mark of Oxford University Press

Introduction, Note on the Text, Select Bibliography,
Chronologies © K. J. Fielding 1989
Explanatory Notes © David Sorensen 1989

First published as a World's Classics paperback 1989

British Library Cataloguing in Publication Data

Data available

Library of Congress Cataloging in Publication Data
Carlyle, Thomas, 1795-1881.
The French Revolution: a history/edited by K. J. Fielding and David Sorensen.
p. cm.—(The world's classics)
Bibliography: p. Includes index.
1. France—History—Revolution, 1789-1795. 2. France—History—Louis XVI,
1774-1793. I. Fielding, K. J. II. Sorensen, David. III. Title. IV. Series.
944.04—dc19 DC161.C3 1989 88-31861

ISBN 0-19-281843-0

5 7 9 10 8 6 4

Printed in Great Britain by
BPC Paperbacks Ltd
Aylesbury, Bucks

CONTENTS

CONTENTS

INTRODUCTION

Carlyle and the passage of time have made for many difficulties in reading *The French Revolution*. He does not try to give a dispassionate idea of what happened but asks for participation. He provokes and bewilders; his language jostles the reader with irony and allusion; and, while involving us in sharing his sympathy or outrage, he does not give an unbuttoned outpouring of personal comment, but challenges the accepted decorous 'dignity of history'. Stylistically his targets are admired historians who have adopted its established, superior, measured tone, such as Hallam, James Mill, Archibald Alison, Gibbon, Hume, and Bolingbroke. As a result, the work can appear mannered and eccentric, as he strives to achieve a way of writing that will suit his subject, with methods which may still seem disturbing. For, in giving his account, Carlyle is repeatedly disputing the assumption that history can faithfully tell us what happened and pass judgements based on current assumptions; and unless we understand what he is doing, his method and remarks about other historians must look as captious as, for example, they always seemed to the assertive and rational Macaulay.[1]

It would have been better if Carlyle had made his position clear from the first, but his readers are challenged to follow him. The opening is particularly abrupt and bewildering, though it evidently makes the point that Louis XV's court was as remote from ordinary life as the palace of Tasso's voluptuous Armida, or the Domdaniel of the

[1] They disagreed, with outward restraint, on history and politics whenever they met. Macaulay refused to review TC's *Chartism* (1840), found his 'Latterday something or other' 'trash . . . beneath contempt' (4 Apr. 1851); meeting him, he was 'that ass Carlyle who talked more nonsense than I ever heard' (30 June 1851); and, at the Malvern water-cure: 'If he goes away writing common sense in good English, I shall declare myself a convert to hydropathy. At present I believe that Doctor and patient are quacks alike' (24 Aug. 1851).

Arabian tales and Southey's *Thalaba*. Louis the *Bien-aimé* appalled Carlyle when he first read about 'the five Mademoiselles of Nesle' in Lacretelle's *Histoire de France pendant le dix-huitième siècle*, noting that 'The Swine had *four* of them for mistresses, partly in succession, partly simultaneously. The Chateauroux was the last . . . a fifth refused him. Pompadour, Du Barry, the Parc-aux-cerfs: how *strange* is all this!' Louis 'took to debauchery, and let the Devil do his own way with everything.'[2] Yet though at the start he flings down information, he challenges us to make sense of it. Newton and his dog Diamond probably saw a similar 'pair of Universes' (i.7), but understood them differently!— 'For ours is a most fictile world; and man is the most fingent plastic of all creatures' (i.8); philosophers assure us that even the material world is, strictly speaking, 'made by these outward senses of ours'; and just as Church and King, for example, are among countless 'realised ideals' or symbols made by men (i.8), so are all religions, including the Old Testament, which are the product of men's art as well as their beliefs (i.10).

Yet if history is essentially fictitious, how can it be told, how does 'accuracy' matter, and why should we take pains with it? There are several answers, but two belong to Carlylean orthodoxy. The first is that if everything perceived is a matter of appearances, this only increases the need to seek the reality behind them:[3] all of which had just been expounded in *Sartor Resartus*, still buried for most readers of

[2] J. C. D. de Lacretelle (Paris, 1819) ii.182–92, cf. *FR* i.6, and Journal. After this references to *FR* and *Works* are bracketed in the text. For abbreviations, see ii.455.

[3] Explained throughout TC's writings, as: 'How impressive the smallest historical *fact* may become, as contrasted with the grandest *fictitious* event' ('Biography' xxviii.54); 'Truth, Fact, is the life of all things, "fiction" . . . is certain to be death' (*Latter-Day Pamphlets*, xxi.325), ' "Imagination" . . . except as the vehicle for truth, or *fact* of some sort,—which surely a man should first try other ways of vehiculating, and conveying safe,—what is it?' (*Past and Present*, x.46); 'I am very anxious to be perfectly accurate' (*CL*, viii.25); 'I grow daily to honour Facts more and more . . . A Fact seems to me a great thing; a Sentence printed if not by God, then at least by the Devil' (*CL* viii.336).

1837 in back numbers of *Fraser's Magazine*. The second, related problem, is that perhaps we can see the ultimate reality of God repeated in recorded events, for 'Is not Man's History . . . a perpetual Evangel?' (i.202). As Carlyle was to write later, 'All History . . . is an inarticulate Bible . . . The loud-roaring Loom of Time, with all its French Revolutions, Jewish revelations, "weaves the vesture thou seest Him by" ' (xx.325–6). So whatever 'facts' can be recovered from the past have an almost sacred value, though necessarily subject to interpretation. There is therefore a duality in Carlyle's thought and writing in *The French Revolution*; and his effort to combine a searching sense of actuality with a distrust of appearances made strong demands on his technique.

His style was always provocative. His old friend, Lord Jeffrey, had steadily advised against it, complaining it was unlike that of 'my friend Macaulay' who, with 'several others', though 'struck with the force and originality of the writing', had rightly 'laughed at' Carlyle's brilliant essay 'Characteristics' and 'some of the ravings about the ravings of your German novelists'. Jeffrey's reception of the new work was the same: his admiration for its 'Genius' struggled with disapproval of 'the style . . . too odd, broken and ostentatiously irregular—But what I most object to, is the tone of *mockery*—and Mephistophelic *humour*.'[4] The manner of the 'dignified' historians of the Enlightenment was not to be mocked. History, as they taught, should be abstract and inductive; a historian must avoid details, 'vulgarity' and first-person documentation, and (as Sir James Mackintosh once explained) be neither 'a jester or a satirist', 'sneer or laugh at men', or 'jest at human nature', but maintain 'the dignity of man'.[5] His aim should be to show 'philosophy

[4] Jeffrey's earlier remarks come from letters to TC of 1 Mar. 1830 and 16 May 1831 and, on receipt of the *FR*, 18 May 1837, MS:NLS. In spite of his good nature, his letters to TC (many unpublished) often show an aloof superior whiggism which makes TC seem mild and humane.

[5] In his review of J. C. L. Sismondi, *Histoire des Français*, 3 vols. (Paris and London, 1821) in the *Edinburgh Review*, 35 (1821), 491.

teaching by experience',[6] to instruct rather than amuse, and show the record of man's gradual progress, which was thus subject to history's retrospective judgement.[7]

Such history often had the drawback of being suffocatingly dull: yet Carlyle objected less to this than to the way that the result was untrue to life. For if history lies largely in subjective record, then the way it was seen and felt at the time it happened was itself 'fact'. Details *were* essential to give the sense of what happened, and often best conveyed through personal accounts, hard as such records might be to reconcile. Because it involved a whole people, the French Revolution introduced almost a new kind of history, involving named participants of every class. The very doctrine that there was an accepted superior style and tone to be adopted by judicious historians was one Carlyle scorned with a ferocity based on principle even more than on his personal tone and feeling. Hence, he made himself a verbal 'terrorist',[8] and joined new movements challenging the old. Even his friend John Sterling criticized the language of *Sartor* as a 'lawless defiance', often 'barbarous and repulsive', questioning Carlyle's use of such words as 'environment', 'visualized', and 'talented' (a 'newspaper and hustings word'); while Carlyle—already writing *The French Revolution*—replied, 'do you reckon this really a time for Purism of Style . . . with whole ragged battallions of Scott's-Novel Scotch, with Irish, German, French, and even Newspaper Cockney . . . storming in on us, and the whole structure of our Johnsonian English breaking up from its foundations—revolution *there* as visible as anywhere else!' (*CL*, viii.135).

[6] Bolingbroke's remark, taken from earlier writers, borrowed by later historians, often anathematized by TC; also found in Livy ('in history you behold the lessons of every kind of experience', preface Bk. 1), French school-texts, and French historians.

[7] A deep distrust of this widespread faith in progress and often ridiculous hope of perfectibility is probably the chief underlying pre-conception of the *FR*.

[8] G. H. Hartman's expression, *Criticism in the Wilderness* (1980), 151; but hardly 'unconscious', as he suggests.

Before long Carlyle's public was to learn how to read him without too much difficulty; but, for the moment, Sterling's warning that Carlyle's language would turn readers against him was justified. It was not only staider reviewers, such as Herman Merivale in the *Edinburgh Review*, who disliked Carlyle for 'his bastard English'. In the *Athenaeum* the popular novelist, Lady Morgan, attacked Carlyle's 'whimsical coxcombry', inexcusable in what she called an 'English writer', however understandable in misguided revolutionary French and Germans. Thackeray was fairer in *The Times*, clearly fascinated by Carlyle's language, though aware that it was offensive to 'those who love history as it gracefully runs in Hume, or struts pompously in Gibbon'. He was unwilling to involve himself with the 'philosophy', but found that the work showed 'most extraordinary powers', if 'disfigured by grotesque conceits and images'.[9]

It is not necessary to give many examples of Carlyle's linguistic 'barbarity', which is obvious enough, though his aim may be misunderstood. Yet it can be curiously 'vulgar' at times, including the grotesque Anglicizing of French and clumsy French intrusions accompanied by indifference to what the reader can make of lengthy epigraphs in untranslated Greek and German. They are 'shock tactics', as in the strange irruption into World History of 'Mrs. Momoro', temporary Goddess of Reason in spite of her bad teeth (ii.358) or the landlady of the *Bras D'Or* at Varennes, the fair, young 'Mrs. Le Blanc' who takes to the woods like the Scotch Bessy Bell (ii.142) before the advance of the Duke of Brunswick. Yet most contemporary readers were well aware that Carlyle first won a reputation as an accomplished translator.

In a similar fashion the headlong narrative forces us, in an egalitarian way, to mix with as varied an assortment as Anarchasis Clootz's 'tag-rag-and-bobtail' specimens of *le*

---

[9] *Thomas Carlyle, The Critical Heritage*, ed. J. P. Seigel (1971), from the *Athenaeum*, 20 May 1837; *Edinburgh Review*, 71 (1840), 411–45; *The Times*, 3 Aug. 1837.

Genre Humain (i.354–6). To some extent this is an inescapable feature of Revolutionary history itself, with its basis in bureaucratic archives, memoirs, and newspapers, and is common to many histories of the period. But Carlyle seizes on this feature and exploits it, re-enacting the experience of the Revolution through details, names, occupations, and characteristic touches as of the weather and all kinds of personal observations. It is both foreign and familiar, and everything is based on reported but not unquestioned fact.

There are other shocks. Though the French Revolution was a popular subject, it was often gently handled. Hedva Ben-Israel is in fact wrong in saying that Mignet does not refer to the guillotine in his History,[10] but Mignet and others play it down while Carlyle brings it to the fore. His account of the massacres is as unpleasant as the subject. It is true that he may not explain what the bloody *grands-lèvres* were (ii.152), but they are not expurgated; Danton's language is softened; and Carlyle does not directly say what unmentionable diseases various figures suffered from, but they are mentioned after all. His account is disinfected with irony. But though we are often asked to compare *The French Revolution* with Scott's novels, in this respect they belong to different worlds. Carlyle's work was deliberately bold: for ourselves, he wrote authorially, it means 'the open violent Rebellion, and Victory, of disimprisoned Anarchy against corrupt worn-out Authority ... till the frenzy' burn 'itself out' and 'the Uncontrollable be got, if not reimprisoned, yet harnessed' (i.221). He told Sterling, 'It is a wild savage Book, itself a kind of French Revolution ... born in blackness whirlwind and sorrow' (*CL*, ix.116).

However much we may want, like Thackeray, to shun the philosophy of historical narrative, it is essential to an understanding of Carlyle's method. For though Carlyle read widely to authenticate his history, he was constantly aware that in the nature of things no account could ever exactly correspond with the events. He frequently speaks

[10] *English Historians on the French Revolution* (Cambridge, 1968), 60; a valuable and important study.

about this; and though it may worry us when we find discrepancies in his accounts from time to time, as it worried Carlyle, it may matter less than we think. He has often been blamed for relying too much on personal memoirs (with all their drawbacks) written soon after the Revolution, but he knew perfectly well that they were biased and possibly mistaken; that even contemporary reports were not authentic; and that recorded speeches in whatever form are almost certainly unreliable.

His point is that, with all their faults, such records are broken reflections of reality. In fact, Carlyle had a particular attraction to half-legendary or flawed accounts even in contemporary history. Historians, for example, have disputed whether de Sombreuil's daughter was forced to drink 'Aristocrats' blood' to save her father (ii.153), but Carlyle accepted it—as a report; it is the same with the tanned human skins of Meudon (ii.376); and even the 'whiff of grapeshot', now apparently dubious. They were attempts at the truth and, if possibly mistaken, were once believed and often acted on. Carlyle is usually careful, by current standards, to note the *kind* of sources he is using, as in such instances as these; and though, after 150 years, his account is no substitute for a modern history—and is not just different in detail but of a different kind—it is essentially true.

So, when he discovered that the story of the sinking of the *Vengeur* (see ii.371 and the Note on the Text) was just a French propaganda victory, the fact was briefly mentioned in the next edition but dealt with in detail only in an article for *Fraser's Magazine* in June 1839. It proved his point: the tale was 'Founded, like the World itself, on *Nothing*'. He made only a minimal addition to the text. It is like Admiral Nesham's sword (i.323), where he kept the wrong name in his narrative with no more than a footnote explanation: that was how 'history' had told it, and necessary corrections were just footnoted in passing.[11]

[11] As the Note shows this had to be added in 1857. TC's practical and theoretical method can be contrasted with C. L. R. Fletcher's, who edited

Although we can admit some laziness in Carlyle's reluctance to revise, it fitted into his general scheme. Nowhere can this be seen more remarkably than in the curious ending. From time to time throughout his work Carlyle introduces self-quotation, again perhaps to show that we are reading a fallible writer rather than a dispassionately accurate observer. But at the end of *The French Revolution* he returns to a fictitious 'discourse', put into the mouth of his favourite imposter Cagliostro (see i.59). Without explanation, it is taken from the end of Carlyle's account of 'The Diamond Necklace', in which though Cagliostro was an historical figure his speech declaring that 'Reality rests on a dream' is entirely Carlyle's invention. This is rather like the opening of *The French Revolution*, but if this comes with the assurance of an arch-liar, is it meant to be true?

It can hardly be so. It is part of the 'duality' in his outlook on history. Yet we may note that the most remarkable alteration to later editions was the addition of a long, closely-printed 'Chronological Summary' in 1857. It was as if he believed that once readers had discovered how to read his work, he also wanted them to accept it as a genuine history of the revolution as faithful as could be expected. Though replaced in the present edition by a shorter version, the chronology made for Carlyle was precise and closely keyed into the text. His riddle remains, therefore, of how history should be told.

There are other peculiarities which may present problems, among them Carlyle's use of images with a classical colouring. It was not meant as a dignified veneer but in ironic mockery, echoing the inflated rhetoric of the *philosophes* and revolutionaries. He satirizes their naïve longing for a lost 'age of gold' (i.31, 33, 358–64), or for the time of Astraea

---

TC's history with painstaking corrections, which are often wrong. But TC's system later broke down with revisions for later editions of his *Cromwell*, which he had unfortunately claimed would give a complete and accurate collection. For TC's general accuracy see John D. Rosenberg, *Carlyle and the Burden of History* (Oxford, 1985), 41, 103.

Redux when truth and justice will return (i.28–35, 46–50). He ridicules the Rousseauistic classical festivals of Reason and the Supreme Being (ii.395–7). He ironically describes the adoption of new names, like the Parisian section of Mutius-Scaevola presided over by someone with the same legendary name (ii.335); the way that Tallien can whisk out a dagger—'the Steel of Brutus we call it' (ii.409); the revolutionary red nightcaps (ii.59); and the affectation of simple ways of speech (ii.132). Yet this is authentically historical, and except in selection never merely Carlylean.

Other references run alongside, less obviously absurd but made faintly ridiculous by repetition: like those to Lafayette, curiously styled 'Scipio Americanus' by contemporaries, who retires 'Cincinnatus-like' (ii.10) in a contemporary cliché borrowed by Carlyle; or his exaggerated fantasy that France confronted by democracy was like the nymph Semele consumed by fire in the presence of Jove (ii.189). There are the chapters on 'Loménie's Thunderbolts', 'Mercury de Brézé', and 'Broglie the War God'. Simpler classical allusions may be half serious and yet often made tongue-in-cheek. For there is an underlying scorn for the manner in which the classical historians themselves, such as Plutarch, had withdrawn from unpleasant reality, and the way the French had gone even further in transforming ancient heroes into virtuous abstractions. Carlyle was also not alone in noticing how the Romans imitated by the revolutionaries had never existed outside Livy.[12]

Yet these fictions are shadowed by myths, such as the war of the Titans, the destructive passions of the Maenads, the abyss of Tartarus, and possibly by Christian myth, as in Louis' supper of bread and wine after his recapture at Varennes, which express profound truths through their serious resonance. And distinct from all these is the use made of Homer and, to a lesser extent, Greek tragedy.

[12] See Harold T. Parker, *The Cult of Antiquity and the French Revolutionaries* (New York, 1965). TC's 'heroes' are never classical, but were to be such figures as Odin, Mahomet, Dante, Burns, and even Rousseau: men who saw into the nature of reality.

Homer's influence and the use Carlyle made of him came
from a deep enjoyment of his epic power and poetry, his
account of great events, and the way he went 'to the heart of
human nature'. Homer, too, though he may have believed
'his story to be a fiction' had 'no doubt of its truth',
repeating 'what survived in tradition and records', and
expecting 'his hearers to believe them as he did'. Carlyle's
own epic consciously imitates Homer and Greek tragedy,
not only through allusive phrases, but by attempting to
convey their 'depth of feeling' in the same way, the success
of which partly depends on our seeing his intention.[13] His
letters show how clear about it he was, and readers and
reviewers such as Emerson and Mill were quick to see the
work as a Homeric epic, 'the history of the French
Revolution, and the poetry of it, both in one' (Seigel, 52,
219). Hence the attempt to note such allusions in the
present edition.

With some misgivings we have included many of
Carlyle's allusions to the Bible. With Milton and Shakespeare it was the only source in common culture he could
rely on readers to recognize; but the allusions can be
misleading. As a general rule the truth of the Bible was like
Homer, with which he often compared it. It gave general
truths of men and nature, both mythical and based on
human traditions, intensely believed. But it should not be
thought that the familiar echoes imply a literal belief in a
personal God. Carlyle rejected ordination in the Church
and his parents' religion, held aloof from family prayers,
and gave up attending church. Nor is it to be supposed that
we can sensibly classify him as a kind of 'Calvinist' except
in a peculiar national sense. In particular, references to
God's judgement are mythical or metaphorical: any idea
that Carlyle really believed that a Hebrew Jehovah
punished innocent victims of the Terror for misconduct at
the court of Louis the *Bien-aimé* would be absurd. To
Carlyle, God's judgement, Nemesis, and the Aeschylean

[13] See his *Lectures on the History of Literature*, ed. J. Reay Greene (1892),
given 1838, 20–5.

'Furies', are all parts of a belief in the necessary consequences of human action; though he, perhaps wrongly, leaves this for the reader to deduce.

Readers who are historians are sometimes puzzled by Carlyle's use of the dramatic present tense, but this is another device to bring events into prominence, as Archibald Alison recognized in his *History of Europe from the Commencement of the French Revolution* ([1833], i.427–8): 'the intellect, all powerful in reviewing the past, is seldom felt in judging of the present' which is ruled by passion, so that a true account should show not only what happened but also men's feelings as part of the happening. The present tense allows this, giving a running commentary on the conflict, and a dramatic form to the action, which is essential to Carlyle's method as he described it to Sterling: a method not of '*hearsays*' but of 'recording the *presence*, bodily concrete coloured prescence of things' (*CL*, ix.15). It is a method triumphantly justified by such great scenes as the taking of the Bastille, Louis' execution, and Danton's trial.

Always present is Carlyle's voice, or 'voices' if we allow for the flexibility and variety of tone which take their authority from his energy, style, and apparent confidence. There is no need for *Sartor*'s array of narrative personae, its Teufelsdröckh, the Hofrath, Editor, and Sauerteig. It was the first book to be published over his name, and, as well as being his own act of revolution, rings with an aggressively personal Scottish accent, much as in his lectures, 'gollying', or roaring, in what he called his 'Annandale voice' (*CL*, viii.94). The vocabulary deliberately includes such words as 'shifty' (active), *brool*, *dirl*, cadger, melly, and whinstone. Scottish characters figure in the allusions: Knox, Wallace, Douglas Bell-the-Cat, the Covenanters, Renwick, the Cameronians, the Western Scotch Whigs, the *Lords of the Articles*, and Bessy Bell. And Carlyle uses this voice to comment, for example, on the topicality of the work: how current British radicals are mere Girondins, how the factory child is worse off even than the Dauphin in the Temple prison, how 'starvation is starvation' in Ireland as in France, how democracy is on the march, and how revolution and counter-revolution will go on. Within the account there is discussion of the causes of the Revolution, the extent and nature of the Terror, about the Sansculottes, the French themselves, debate about leading figures, and the morality of men's actions, which to Carlyle's contempt were so often passed over by historians such as Thiers. His techniques are all means to an end. Though provoking, he is thought-provoking, and he wants us to understand as well as to experience.

Two hundred years after the fall of the Bastille, most readers will judge for themselves whether the book is fair about the ideals of the French Revolution, and whether they really lead to liberty, equality, and fraternity. We are asked to decide in the conflict between reality and idealism, representation and responsibility. Here, too, Carlyle speaks for himself—if we allow him to. There is prejudice against him, some of which he brought on himself; yet it was his misfortune not his fault to have provided, in *Frederick the Great*, a work with which Goebbels tried to console Hitler in the Berlin bunker.

The French Revolution has nothing to do with this. Its teaching can be as well be linked with two very different companions, Joseph Conrad and Bertrand Russell. Deeply impressed by Conrad, Russell wrote of his 'philosophy':

I felt . . . that he thought of civilized and morally tolerable human life as a dangerous walk on a thin crust of barely cooled lava which at any moment might break and let the unwary sink into fiery depths. He was very conscious of the various forms of passionate madness to which men are prone, and it was this that gave him such a passionate belief in the importance of discipline. His point of view . . . was the antithesis of Rousseau's: 'Man is born in chains, but he can become free.' He becomes free, so I believe Conrad would have said . . . by subduing wayward impulse to a dominant purpose . . . Conrad adhered to the older tradition, that discipline should come from within. He despised indiscipline, hated discipline that was merely external.[14]

---

[14] *Portraits from Memory* (1956), 83.

All Carlyleans will recognize the thin volcanic earth-rind, man's inner madness, and the scorn for mere idealism and sentiment; they may see a likeness in their regard for duty and the work ethic, for action rather than talk, and in their ironic disbelief in absolutes. The dualities in the insight of such writers may also remind us that *The French Revolution* is not only 'a history', but as Carlyle says a vision of 'the depth and height . . . revealed in man', and an inspired attempt to confront and contemplate it, 'with just sympathy and just antipathy, with clear eye and open heart' (ii.443).

Edinburgh   K. J. F.

NOTE ON THE TEXT

The work was published, in three volumes, on 9 May 1837, in an edition of 1,000 copies, by James Fraser; then in an edition of three volumes, and 1,000 copies, prompted by Emerson, published by Little and Brown, of Boston, 25 December 1837. There were further editions before one of two volumes, in 1857, published by Chapman and Hall in Carlyle's *Collected Works*. It is this edition from which the two-volume World's Classics edition (Oxford University Press, 1907) was taken, with an introduction by C. R. L. Fletcher. The text of the present edition is reproduced from that of 1907, less the introduction and a 'Chronological Summary', of seventeen pages added in 1857, and with a new chronology and new and more complete index. The 1857 chronology was apparently added by Vernon Lushington as 'Philo', to whom Carlyle wrote: 'I remember feeling, when the Book first came out, that it *wd* be better for a Chronological Summary: ("Book I, Chap. 1", and then the main points it handles, dated, clearly signified,— and with extreme *brevity*, the *chaff ALL* blown away): Suppose you considered this a little?' (K. J. Fielding, 'Vernon Lushington: Carlyle's Friend and Editor,' *Carlyle Newsletter* 8 [1987]:10). The second edition (James Fraser: 1839), first briefly corrected the story of the sinking of the *Vengeur* (ii.371-2). As Carlyle's accuracy has wrongly been questioned by such historians as G. P. Gooch, it should be noted that an Admiral Griffiths had written recalling the actual event in which he had taken part, and that his remarks were widely discussed in the press. Carlyle wrote about it for *Fraser's Magazine* (July, 1839); and his 'On the Sinking of the *Vengeur*' was added to his *Miscellanies* (1840); see *Works*, xxix.208–25, and *CL*, x.236–40. Notes were added on Admiral Nesham (i.323) in 1857, and on Frederick I (i.296) in 1868, though the text was otherwise unchanged. Much can be learned about the actual writing of the work from the Duke–Edinburgh *Collected Letters*, including the story of the loss of the whole of the manuscript of the first volume, burnt while in the care of John Stuart Mill and Harriet Taylor. Jane Carlyle noted that the rewritten version was 'less vivacious perhaps but better *thought* and put together' (*CL*, viii.194), and Carlyle wrote that he made many changes in proof, including the division into chapters. Some scraps of manuscript remain, mainly but not all listed by Barbara Rosenbaum and Pamela White, *Index of English Literary Manuscripts* (1982), iv.380–1. There have been editions with historical notes by J. Holland Rose (1902) and C. R. L. Fletcher (1902). An edition, by Fred Kaplan, with full apparatus, will be published in *The Essential Carlyle* (1990). The present edition is jointly edited, the introduction by K. J. Fielding and the Explanatory Notes mainly by David Sorensen.

SELECT BIBLIOGRAPHY

The following list is highly selective. There are standard biographies by J. A. Froude (1882, 1884), D. A. Wilson (1923–34), and Fred Kaplan (Cambridge, 1983). Useful introductions can be found in G. B. Tennyson's *A Carlyle Reader* (New York, 1969; Cambridge, 1984), and by Ian Campbell (1974) and A. L. LeQuesne (Oxford, 1982). Carlyle's *Reminiscences* (1881 and later editions) gives an enjoyable account of some of his life.

Earlier collections of letters are being superseded by the Duke-Edinburgh edition, eds. C. R. Sanders, K. J. Fielding, C. de L. Ryals, assoc. eds. I. Campbell, A. Christianson, and H. J. Smith: vols. 1–18 to 1844 (1970, in progress). A useful work showing Carlyle's reception is J. P. Seigel (ed.), *Carlyle, The Critical Heritage* (1971). Two general works particularly recommended are G. B. Tennyson, *Sartor Called Resartus* (Princeton, 1965), and Ruth apRoberts *The Ancient Dialect, Thomas Carlyle and Comparative Religion* (Berkeley and Los Angeles, 1988).

There are also studies by A. J. LaValley, *Carlyle and the Idea of the Modern* (New Haven, 1968), and Philip Rosenberg, *The Seventh Hero: Thomas Carlyle and the Theory of Radical Activism* (Cambridge, Mass., 1974). Two important works on Carlyle and the French Revolution are the relevant chapter in Hedva Ben-Israel, *English Historians and the French Revolution* (Cambridge, 1968), and John D. Rosenberg, *Carlyle and the Burden of History* (Oxford, 1984). For further inquiry, see Helen C. Flint, 'Indications in Carlyle's *French Revolution* of the Influence of Homer and the Greek Tragedians', *Classical Journal*, 5 (1910): 118–26; C. F. Harrold, 'Carlyle's General Method in *The French Revolution*,' PMLA 43 (1928), 1150–1169, and 'Carlyle's Sources for "The French Revolution" ', appendix II in Isaac W. Dyer, *A Bibliography of Thomas Carlyle's Writings and Ana* (Portland, Maine, 1928); also the chapter on Carlyle in John Holloway,

The Victorian Sage (1953), and John Clubbe, 'Epic Heroes in *The French Revolution*', in *Thomas Carlyle 1981* ed. H. W. Drescher (Frankfurt, 1983), 165–85, and 'Carlyle as Epic Historian,' in *Victorian Literature and Society*, ed. J. R. Kincaid and A. J. Kuhn (Columbus, 1984).

Relevant essays in Carlyle's *Critical and Miscellaneous Essays* include 'On History', 'History Again', 'Biography', 'Sir Walter Scott', 'The Diamond Necklace', and 'Parliamentary History of the French Revolution'. There are also important comments on the writing of history in *Oliver Cromwell's Letters and Speeches* and *Frederick the Great*, and in published and unpublished drafts for *Cromwell*; see K. J. Fielding, 'Carlyle and Cromwell: the Writing of History and Dryasdust', *Strouse Lectures on Carlyle & His Era* (Santa Cruz, Calif., 1985), ii.44–57. A number of recent articles on Carlyle's narrative technique, which can be found in specialist journals, have gone in the same direction as Hayden White, *Metahistory* (1977) and *Tropics of Discourse* (1978), and are interesting but not conclusive.

For further guidance: up to 1972, see G. B. Tennyson in *Victorian Prose, A Guide to Research*, ed. D. J. DeLaura (New York, 1973), 33–104, and later the annual bibliographies in *Victorian Studies*; also, R. L. Tarr, *Thomas Carlyle: A Bibliography of English Language Criticism 1824–1974* (Charlottesville, 1976).

A CHRONOLOGY OF
THOMAS CARLYLE

1835   Destruction of first volume of *The French Revolution* while in Mill's possession. Rewritten with great effort by August

1836   April: finishes second volume of *The French Revolution*; *Sartor Resartus* published in Boston

1837   *The French Revolution* finished, revised, and published by the end of May; 'Mirabeau', 'The Diamond Necklace', and 'Parliamentary History of the French Revolution'

1838   First British edition of *Sartor*; first American edition of *Critical and Miscellaneous Essays*; 'Scott'; April: Lectures on the Revolutions of Modern Europe (various lectures are given, 1837–40)

1839   'On the Sinking of the Vengeur'; first British edition of the *Essays*; *Chartism*

1840   Work for the foundation of the London Library (1841), and attention turns to the Cromwellian period

1841   *Heroes and Hero-Worship*

1842   *Past and Present*; continues work on Cromwell

1845   *Oliver Cromwell's Letters and Speeches*

1848   Articles on France and Ireland

1849   First meets Froude; tour in Ireland; 'Occasional Discourse on the Nigger Question'

1850   *Latter-Day Pamphlets*

1851   *Life of Sterling*; 4–7 Oct.: 'Excursion to Paris' (pub. *Last Words*, 1892)

1854   Turns to writing about Frederick the Great

1857   May: death of Lady Harriet Ashburton, after long friendship and consequent jealousy of Jane Carlyle

1858–65   *History of Frederick the Great*, vols. 1 and 2 (1858), vol. 3 (1863), vol. 4 (1864), vols. 5 and 6 (1865)

1866   Inaugural Address as Rector of Edinburgh University; Jane Carlyle's death

1867   'Shooting Niagara: and After?'; continued writing of the *Reminiscences* followed by collecting and editing the *Letters and Memorials of Jane Welsh Carlyle* (1883)

1875   *Early Kings of Norway* and *The Portraits of John Knox*

1881   5 February, death

A CHRONOLOGY OF THE FRENCH REVOLUTION

1774 Death of Louis XV; Maurepas prime minister; Turgot controller of finances

1776 Turgot dismissed and Necker appointed

1781 Necker dismissed

1783 Replaced by Calonne who

1787 convokes Assembly of Notables, but replaced by Loménie de Brienne. Struggle with Parlement of Paris (PP)

1788 8 August: Estates-General (EG) called for 1 May 1789; 24–26th: Loménie de Brienne replaced by Necker

1789 5 May: opening session of EG
17 June: Third Estate constitutes itself as National Assembly, and 9 July Constituent Assembly (CA). 20th: Tennis Court oath
11 July: Necker dismissed, riots, and (14th): fall of Bastille; Necker recalled. Municipalities and citizen guards formed in provinces. July–August: the Great Fear (brigands) and peasant uprisings. 4 August: abolition of feudalism; 27th: Declaration of the Rights of Man; August–September: 'Patrollotism v. Patriotism'
5 October: Insurrection of Women; 6th: King brought to Paris from Versailles. October–December: first emigration

1790 4 February: King visits CA; National Oath
21 May: Paris divided into 48 sections
14 July: Federation ceremony or 'Feast of Pikes'
31 August: Bouillé suppresses mutiny at Nancy; Mirabeau has interviews with Queen

1791 2 April: death of Mirabeau
20 June: royal flight to Varennes; 25th: return to Paris
17 July: Champs de Mars massacre
5 August: France renounces foreign conquest, but met by declaration of Pilnitz (27th)
13 September: Louis XVI accepts new constitution and CA dissolved

1 October: first session of Legislative Assembly (LA); its ineffective debates; changes of War minister

1792 20 April: France declares war on Hungary and Bohemia
20 June: Paris sections growing more violent demonstrate in procession, and invade Tuileries confronting King
6 July: 'Baiser l'amourette', reconciliation in LA; 22nd: proclamation of 'la Patrie en danger'; 24–25th: Prussian declaration of war and Duke of Brunswick's manifesto; 29th: arrival in Paris of 500 Marseillais who 'know how to die', invited by Barbaroux
10 August: Constitution of the revolutionary commune of Paris, Tuileries stormed and Swiss guards killed; royal family imprisoned in the Temple. 23rd: Longwy surrenders. 29th: Dumouriez occupies passes of Argonne
2–5 September: Massacres in Paris prisons; 20th: French victory at Valmy; 21st: NC meets; monarchy abolished, Year 1 begins; 28 September–8 October: Siege of Lille, followed by Prussian retreat
19 November: French offer of 'freedom and succour' to European countries seeking freedom
10 December: Louis's trial by the NC begins

1793 21 January: Louis guillotined
1 February: France declares war on England and Holland; 23rd: the NC conscripts 300,000 men
March–July: struggle between Girondins and the Mountain; 18 March: Dumouriez defeated at Neerwinden; defects, 3 April
6 April: Committee of Public Safety (CPS) formed
4 May: Law of Maximum prices; 31st: Parisian uprising against Girondins
2 June: Girondin deputies arrested; 'Federalist' up-risings
10 July: Reorganization of the CPS (Great Committee); 13th: Charlotte Corday kills Marat; republican vengeance; 26th: surrender of Valenciennes; 27th: Robespierre elected to CPS
1 August: The NC orders systematic assault on La Vendée; renewed allied attack; 23rd: Barrère proclaims *levée en masse*
17 September: Law of Suspects
5 October: new Calendar adopted; republicans recapture Lyons; 16th: execution of Marie-Antoinette; 17th: defeat of Vendéans at Cholet; 22nd: Girondins guillotined
November–December: Reign of Terror, plunder of churches

6 November: execution of d'Orléans Egalité; 8th: of Mme Roland; 10th: Festival of Reason celebrated in Notre-Dame; 18th December: Toulon recaptured. Noyades

1794 4 February: NC decrees abolition of slavery
24 March: execution of the Hébertists
5 April: execution of the Dantonists. Dechristianization
7 May: NC decrees recognition of Supreme Being, and holds Festival (8 June)
1 June: Howe's naval victory, and the fable of the *Vengeur*
27 July: Robespierre fails to be given a hearing in the NC, arrested and guillotined with his supporters (28th). Committees reorganized
5 August: release of many prisoners
12 November: Jacobin Club closed
8 December: 73 Girondin deputies return; 16th: execution of Carrier; 24th: abolition of the 'maximum'

1795 January: Continued downfall of Sansculottism; rise of the *jeunesse dorée*
4 February: arrest of Baboeuf
1 April: insurrection of 12 Germinal; 2nd: ended by Pichegru with 'two blank cannon shot'; 5th: peace of Basle between France and Prussia
4 May: massacre of Jacobin prisoners at Lyons; 20–23rd: insurrection of Prairial, results in end of Sansculottism
21 July: French victory at Quiberon Bay; rekindling, then ultimate suppression of, revolt of Vendée
22 August: NC adopts new constitution
5 October: (13 Vendémiaire) Royalist insurrection crushed by Barras and Napoleon; the revolution ends

THE FRENCH
REVOLUTION

Diesem Ambos vergleich' ich das Land, den Hammer dem Herrscher;
    Und dem Volke das Blech, das in der Mitte sich krümmt.
Wehe dem armen Blech, wenn nur willkürliche Schläge
    Ungewiss treffen, und nie fertig der Kessel erscheint!

Goethe.*

CONTENTS
OF THE FIRST VOLUME

PART I
THE BASTILLE

BOOK I
DEATH OF LOUIS XV

BOOK II
THE PAPER AGE

BOOK III
THE PARLEMENT OF PARIS

BOOK IV

STATES-GENERAL

BOOK V

THE THIRD ESTATE

BOOK VI

CONSOLIDATION

BOOK VII

THE INSURRECTION OF WOMEN

PART II

THE CONSTITUTION

BOOK I

THE FEAST OF PIKES

BOOK II

NANCI

BOOK III

THE TUILERIES

BOOK IV

VARENNES

CONTENTS
OF THE SECOND VOLUME

PART II

THE CONSTITUTION

(*Continued*)

BOOK V

PARLIAMENT FIRST

BOOK VI

THE MARSEILLESE

PART III

THE GUILLOTINE

BOOK I

SEPTEMBER

BOOK II

REGICIDE

BOOK III

THE GIRONDINS

BOOK IV

TERROR

BOOK V

TERROR THE ORDER OF THE DAY

BOOK VI

THERMIDOR

BOOK VII

VENDÉMIAIRE

VOLUME I

PART I
THE BASTILLE

BOOK I

DEATH OF LOUIS XV

CHAPTER I

LOUIS THE WELL-BELOVED

PRESIDENT HÉNAULT,* remarking on royal Surnames of Honour how difficult it often is to ascertain not only why, but even when, they were conferred, takes occasion in his sleek official way to make a philosophical reflection. ' The Surname of *Bien-aimé* (Well-beloved)', says he, ' which Louis XV bears, will not leave posterity in the same doubt. This Prince, in the year 1744, while hastening from one end of his kingdom to the other, and suspending his conquests in Flanders that he might fly to the assistance of Alsace, was arrested at Metz by a malady which threatened to cut short his days. At the news of this, Paris, all in terror, seemed a city taken by storm : the churches resounded with supplications and groans ; the prayers of priests and people were every moment interrupted by their sobs : and it was from an interest so dear and tender that this Surname of *Bien-aimé* fashioned itself,—a title higher still than all the rest which this great Prince has earned '.[1]

So stands it written ; in lasting memorial of that year 1744. Thirty other years have come and gone ; and ' this great Prince ' again lies sick ; but in how altered circumstances now ! Churches resound not with excessive groanings ; Paris is stoically calm : sobs interrupt no prayers, for indeed none are offered ; except Priests' Litanies, read or chanted at fixed money-rate per hour, which are not liable to interruption. The shepherd of the people has been carried home from Little Trianon,*

---

[1] Abrégé Chronologique de l'Histoire de France (Paris, 1775), p. 701.

heavy of heart, and been put to bed in his own Château
of Versailles : the flock knows it, and heeds it not.   At
most, in the immeasurable tide of French Speech (which
ceases not day after day, and only ebbs towards the
short hours of night), may this of the royal sickness
emerge from time to time as an article of news.   Bets
are doubtless depending ; nay, some people ' express
themselves loudly in the streets '.[1]   But for the rest,
on green field and steepled city, the May sun shines
out, the May evening fades ; and men ply their useful
or useless business as if no Louis lay in danger.

Dame Dubarry,* indeed, might pray, if she had a
talent for it ; Duke d'Aiguillon* too, Maupeou* and the
Parlement Maupeou : these, as they sit in their high
places, with France harnessed under their feet, know
well on what basis they continue there.   Look to it,
D'Aiguillon ; sharply as thou didst, from the Mill of
St. Cast, on Quiberon and the invading English ; thou
' covered if not with glory yet with meal ' !   Fortune
was ever accounted inconstant : and each dog has but
his day.

Forlorn enough languished Duke d'Aiguillon, some
years ago ; covered, as we said, with meal ; nay with
worse.   For La Chalotais, the Breton Parlementeer,
accused him not only of poltroonery and tyranny, but
even of *concussion* (official plunder of money) ; which
accusations it was easier to get ' quashed ' by backstairs
Influences than to get answered : neither could the
thoughts, or even the tongues, of men be tied.   Thus,
under disastrous eclipse, had this grand-nephew of the
great Richelieu* to glide about ; unworshipped by the
world ; resolute Choiseul,* the abrupt proud man, dis-
daining him, or even forgetting him.   Little prospect
but to glide into Gascony, to rebuild Châteaus there,[2]
and die inglorious killing game !   However, in the year

[1] Mémoires de M. le Baron Besenval (Paris, 1805), ii. 59–
90.
[2] Arthur Young, Travels during the years 1787-8-9
(Bury St. Edmund's, 1792), i. 44.

1770, a certain young soldier, Dumouriez* by name,
returning from Corsica, could see ' with sorrow, at
Compiègne, the old King of France, on foot, with doffed
hat, in sight of his army, at the side of a magnificent
phaeton, doing homage to the—Dubarry '.[1]

Much lay therein ! Thereby, for one thing, could
D'Aiguillon postpone the rebuilding of his Château, and
rebuild his fortunes first. For stout Choiseul would
discern in the Dubarry nothing but a wonderfully
dizened Scarlet-woman ; and go on his way as if she
were not. Intolerable : the source of sighs, tears, of
pettings and poutings ; which would not end till 'France'
(La France, as she named her royal valet) finally mus-
tered heart to see Choiseul ; and with that ' quivering
in the chin ' (tremblement du menton) natural in such
case,[2] faltered out a dismissal : dismissal of his last
substantial man, but pacification of his Scarlet-woman.
Thus D'Aiguillon rose again, and culminated. And with
him there rose Maupeou, the banisher of Parlements ;
who plants you a refractory President ' at Croe in Combrailles on the top of steep rocks, inaccessible except by
litters ', there to consider himself. Likewise there rose
Abbé Terray,* dissolute Financier, paying eightpence in
the shilling,—so that wits exclaim in some press at the
playhouse, ' Where is Abbé Terray, that he might reduce us to two-thirds ! ' And so have these individuals
(verily by black-art) built them a Domdaniel,* or enchanted Dubarrydom ; call it an Armida-Palace,* where
they dwell pleasantly ; Chancellor Maupeou ' playing
blind-man's-buff ' with the scarlet Enchantress ; or gallantly presenting her with dwarf Negroes ;—and a Most
Christian King has unspeakable peace within doors,
whatever he may have without. ' My Chancellor is
a scoundrel ; but I cannot do without him '.[3]

Beautiful Armida-Palace, where the inmates live

[1] La Vie et les Mémoires du Général Dumouriez (Paris,
1822), i. 141.
[2] Besenval, Mémoires, ii. 21.
[3] Dulaure, Histoire de Paris (Paris, 1824), vii. 328.

enchanted lives; lapped in soft music of adulation;
waited on by the splendours of the world;—which
nevertheless hangs wondrously as by a single hair.
Should the Most Christian King die; or even get
seriously afraid of dying! For, alas, had not the fair
haughty Chateauroux*to fly, with wet cheeks and flaming heart, from that Fever-scene at Metz, long since;
driven forth by sour shavelings? She hardly returned,
when fever and shavelings·were both swept into the
background. Pompadour*too, when Damiens wounded
Royalty ' slightly, under the fifth rib ', and our drive to
Trianon went off futile, in shrieks and madly shaken
torches,—had to pack, and be in readiness: yet did
not go, the wound not proving poisoned. For his
Majesty has religious faith; believes, at least in a Devil.
And now a third peril; and who knows what may be
in it! For the Doctors look grave; ask privily, If his
Majesty had not the small-pox long ago?—and doubt
it may have been a false kind. Yes, Maupeou, pucker
those sinister brows of thine, and peer out on it with
thy malign rat-eyes: it is a questionable case. Sure
only that man is mortal; that with the life of one
mortal snaps irrevocably the wonderfullest talisman,
and all Dubarrydom rushes off, with tumult, into infinite Space; and ye, as subterranean Apparitions are
wont, vanish utterly,—leaving only a smell of sulphur!

These, and what holds of these may pray,—to Beelzebub, or whoever will hear them. But from the rest
of France there comes, as was said, no prayer; or
one of an *opposite* character, ' expressed openly in
the streets '. Château or Hôtel, where an enlightened
Philosophism scrutinizes many things, is not given
to prayer: neither are Rossbach* victories, Terray
Finances, nor, say only ' sixty thousand *Lettres de
Cachet* '*(which is Maupeou's share), persuasives towards
that. O Hénault! Prayers? From a France smitten
(by black-art) with plague after plague; and lying
now, in shame and pain, with a Harlot's foot on its
neck, what prayer can come? Those lank scarecrows,

that prowl hunger-stricken through all highways and
byways of French Existence, will they pray ? The dull
millions that, in the workshop or furrowfield, grind fore-
done at the wheel of Labour, like haltered gin-horses,
if blind so much the quieter ? Or they that in the
Bicêtre Hospital,* 'eight to a bed', lie waiting their
manumission ? Dim are those heads of theirs, dull
stagnant those hearts : to them the great Sovereign
is known mainly as the great Regrater of Bread.* If
they hear of his sickness, they will answer with a dull
Tant pis pour lui ; or with the question, Will he die ?

Yes, will he die ? that is now, for all France, the
grand question, and hope ; whereby alone the King's
sickness has still some interest.

CHAPTER II

REALIZED IDEALS

Such a changed France have we ; and a changed
Louis. Changed, truly ; and further than thou yet
seest !—To the eye of History many things, in that
sick-room of Louis, are now visible, which to the Courtiers there present were invisible. For indeed it is well
said, ' in every object there is inexhaustible meaning ;
the eye sees in it what the eye brings means of seeing'.*
To Newton and to Newton's Dog Diamond,* what a different pair of Universes ; while the painting on the
optical retina of both was, most likely, the same ! Let
the Reader here, in this sick-room of Louis, endeavour
to look with the mind too.

Time was when men could (so to speak) of a given
man, by nourishing and decorating him with fit appliances, to the due pitch, *make* themselves a King,
almost as the Bees do ; and, what was still more to the
purpose, loyally obey him when made. The man so
nourished and decorated, thenceforth named royal, does
verily bear rule ; and is said, and even thought, to be,

for example, 'prosecuting conquests in Flanders', when
he lets himself like luggage be carried thither : and no
light luggage ; covering miles of road. For he has his
unblushing Chateauroux, with her bandboxes and rouge-
pots, at his side ; so that, at every new station, a wooden
gallery must be run up between their lodgings. He
has not only his *Maison-Bouche*, and *Valetaillé* without
end, but his very Troop of Players, with their pasteboard coulisses, thunder-barrels, their kettles, fiddles,
stage-wardrobes, portable larders (and chaffering and
quarrelling enough) ; all mounted in wagons, tumbrils,
second-hand chaises,—sufficient not to conquer Flanders, but the patience of the world. With such a flood
of loud jingling appurtenances does he lumber along,
prosecuting his conquests in Flanders : wonderful to
behold. So nevertheless it was and had been : to some
solitary thinker it might seem strange ; but even to him,
inevitable, not unnatural.

For ours is a most fictile world ; and man is the
most fingent plastic of creatures. A world not fixable ;
not fathomable ! An unfathomable Somewhat, which is
Not we ;* which we can work with, and live amidst,—
and model, miraculously in our miraculous Being, and
name World.—But if the very Rocks and Rivers (as
Metaphysic teaches) are, in strict language, *made* by
those Outward Senses of ours, how much more, by the
Inward Sense, are all Phenomena of the spiritual kind :
Dignities, Authorities, Holies, Unholies ! Which inward sense, moreover, is not permanent like the outward ones, but for ever growing and changing. Does
not the Black African take of Sticks and Old Clothes
(say, exported Monmouth-Street cast-clothes) what will
suffice ; and of these, cunningly combining them, fabri-
cate for himself an Eidolon (Idol, or *Thing Seen*), and
name it *Mumbo-Jumbo* ; which he can thenceforth pray
to, with upturned awestruck eye, not without hope ?
The white European mocks ; but ought rather to consider ; and see whether he, at home, could not do the
like a little more wisely.

So it *was*, we say, in those conquests of Flanders,

thirty years ago : but so it no longer is. Alas, much
more lies sick than poor Louis : not the French King
only, but the French Kingship ; this too, after long
rough tear and wear, is breaking down. The world is
all so changed ; so much that seemed vigorous has sunk
decrepit, so much that was not is beginning to be !—
Borne over the Atlantic, to the closing ear of Louis,
King by the Grace of God, what sounds are these ;
muffled-ominous, new in our centuries ? Boston Harbour is black with unexpected Tea : behold a Penn-
sylvanian Congress gather ; and ere long, on Bunker
Hill, DEMOCRACY announcing, in rifle-volleys death-
winged, under her Star Banner, to the tune of Yankee-
doodle-doo, that she is born, and, whirlwind-like, will
envelop the whole world !

Sovereigns die and Sovereignties ; how all dies, and
is for a Time only ; is a ' Time-phantasm, yet reckons
itself real ' !* The Merovingian Kings,* slowly wending
on their bullock-carts through the streets of Paris, with
their long hair flowing, have all wended slowly on,—
into Eternity. Charlemagne* sleeps at Salzburg, with
truncheon grounded ; only Fable expecting that he will
awaken. Charles the Hammer, Pepin Bow-legged,*
where now is their eye of menace, their voice of command ? Rollo* and his shaggy Northmen cover not the
Seine with ships ; but have sailed off on a longer voyage.
The hair of Towhead*(*Tête d'étoupes*) now needs no
combing ; Iron-cutter (*Taillefer*)*cannot cut a cobweb ;
shrill Fredegonda, shrill Brunhilda* have had out their
hot life-scold, and lie silent, their hot life-frenzy cooled.
Neither from that black Tower de Nesle descends now
darkling the doomed gallant, in his sack, to the Seine
waters ; plunging into Night : for Dame de Nesle* now
cares not for this world's gallantry, heeds not this
world's scandal ; Dame de Nesle is herself gone into
Night. They are all gone ; sunk,—down, down, with
the tumult they made ; and the rolling and the trampling of ever new generations passes over them ; and
they hear it not any more for ever.

And yet withal has there not been realized somewhat ? Consider (to go no further) these strong Stone-
edifices, and what they hold ! Mud-Town of the Bor-
derers (*Lutetia Parisiorum* or *Barisiorum*) has paved
itself, has spread over all the Seine Islands, and far and
wide on each bank, and become City of Paris, sometimes boasting to be ' Athens of Europe ', and even
' Capital of the Universe '. Stone towers frown aloft ;
long-lasting, grim with a thousand years. Cathedrals
are there, and a Creed (or memory of a Creed) in them ;
Palaces, and a State and Law. Thou seest the Smoke-
vapour ; *un*extinguished Breath as of a thing living.
Labour's thousand hammers ring on her anvils : also a
more miraculous Labour works noiselessly, not with the
Hand but with the Thought. How have cunning workmen in all crafts, with their cunning head and right-
hand, tamed the Four Elements to be their ministers ;
yoking the Winds to their Sea-chariot, making the very
Stars their Nautical Timepiece ;—and written and collected a *Bibliothèque du Roi* ;* among whose Books is
the Hebrew Book ! A wondrous race of creatures :
these have been realized, and what of Skill is in these :
call not the Past Time, with all its confused wretched-
nesses, a lost one.

Observe, however, that of man's whole terrestrial
possessions and attainments, unspeakably the noblest
are his Symbols, divine or divine-seeming ; under which
he marches and fights, with victorious assurance, in
this life-battle : what we can call his Realized Ideals.
Of which realized Ideals, omitting the rest, consider
only these two : his Church, or spiritual Guidance ;
his Kingship, or temporal one. The Church : what a
word was there ; richer than Golconda and the trea-
sures of the world ! In the heart of the remotest
mountains rises the little Kirk ; the Dead all slumbering round it, under their white memorial-stones, ' in
hope of a happy resurrection ' :—dull wert thou, O
Reader, if never in any hour (say of moaning midnight, when such Kirk hung spectral in the sky, and
Being was as if swallowed up of Darkness) it spoke

to thee—things unspeakable, that went to thy soul's
soul. Strong was he that had a Church, what we can
call a Church : he stood thereby, though ' in the centre
of Immensities, in the conflux of Eternities '* yet man-
like towards God and man ; the vague shoreless Universe had become for him a firm city, and dwelling
which he knew. Such virtue was in Belief ; in these
words, well spoken : *I believe.* Well might men prize
their *Credo*, and raise stateliest Temples for it, and
reverend Hierarchies, and give it the tithe of their
substance ; it was worth living for and dying for.

Neither was that an inconsiderable moment when
wild armed men first raised their Strongest aloft on the
buckler-throne ; and, with clanging armour and hearts,
said solemnly : Be thou our Acknowledged Strongest !
In such Acknowledged Strongest (well named King,
Kön-ning, Can-ning, or Man that was Able) what a Symbol
shone now for them,—significant with the destinies of
the world ! A Symbol of true Guidance in return for
loving Obedience ; properly, if he knew it, the prime
want of man. A Symbol which might be called sacred ;
for is there not, in reverence for what is better than we,
an indestructible sacredness ? On which ground, too,
it was well said there lay in the Acknowledged Strongest
a divine right ; as surely there might in the Strongest,
whether Acknowledged or not,—considering *who* it was
that made him strong. And so, in the midst of confusions and unutterable incongruities (as all growth is
confused), did this of Royalty, with Loyalty environing
it, spring up ; and grow mysteriously, subduing and
assimilating (for a principle of Life was in it) ; till it
also had grown world-great, and was among the main
Facts of our modern existence. Such a Fact, that
Louis XIV, for example, could answer the expostulatory
Magistrate with his ' *L'Etat c'est moi* (The State ? I am
the State) ' ; and be replied to by silence and abashed
looks. So far had accident and forethought ; had your
Louis Elevenths, with the leaden Virgin in their hatband, and torture-wheels and conical *oubliettes* (man-
eating !) under their feet ; your Henri Fourths,* with

their prophesied social millennium, 'when every peasant should have his fowl in the pot'; and on the whole, the fertility of this most fertile Existence (named of Good and Evil),—brought it, in the matter of the King-ship. Wondrous! Concerning which may we not again say, that in the huge mass of Evil, as it rolls and swells, there is ever some Good working imprisoned; working towards deliverance and triumph?

How such Ideals do realize themselves; and grow, wondrously, from amid the incongruous ever-fluctu-ating chaos of the Actual: this is what World-History, if it teach any thing, has to teach us. How they grow; and, after long stormy growth, bloom out mature, supreme; then quickly (for the blossom is brief) fall into decay; sorrowfully dwindle; and crumble down, or rush down, noisily or noiselessly disappearing. The blossom is so brief; as of some centennial Cactus-flower, which after a century of waiting shines out for hours! Thus from the day when rough Clovis,* in the Champ de Mars, in sight of his whole army, had to cleave retributively the head of that rough Frank, with sudden battle-axe, and the fierce words, 'It was thus thou clavest the vase' (St. Remi's and mine) 'at Soissons', forward to Louis the Grand and his *L'Etat c'est moi*, we count some twelve hundred years: and now this the very next Louis is dying, and so much dying with him!—Nay, thus too if Catholicism, with and against Feudalism (but *not* against Nature and her bounty), gave us English a Shakespeare and Era of Shakespeare, and so produced a blossom of Catholicism —it was not till Catholicism itself, so far as Law could abolish it, had been abolished here.

But of those decadent ages in which no Ideal either grows or blossoms? When Belief and Loyalty have passed away, and only the cant and false echo of them remains; and all Solemnity has become Pageantry; and the Creed of persons in authority has become one of two things: an Imbecility or a Machiavelism? Alas, of these ages World-History can take no notice; they have to become compressed more and more, and finally

suppressed in the Annals of Mankind ; blotted out as
spurious,—which indeed they are. Hapless ages :
wherein, if ever in any, it is an unhappiness to be born.
To be born, and to learn only, by every tradition and
example, that God's Universe is Belial's and a Lie ;
and 'the Supreme Quack' the hierarch of men ! In
which mournfullest faith, nevertheless, do we not see
whole generations (two, and sometimes even three successively) live, what they call living ; and vanish,—
without chance of reappearance ?

In such a decadent age, or one fast verging that
way, had our poor Louis been born. Grant also that
if the French Kingship had not, by course of Nature,
long to live, he of all men was the man to accelerate
Nature. The blossom of French Royalty, cactus-like,
has accordingly made an astonishing progress. In those
Metz days, it was still standing with all its petals,
though bedimmed by Orleans Regents and *Roué* Ministers and Cardinals ; but now, in 1774, we behold it
bald, and the virtue nigh gone out of it.

Disastrous indeed does it look with those same
'realized Ideals', one and all ! The Church, which
in its palmy season, seven hundred years ago, could
make an Emperor wait barefoot, in penance-shirt,* three
days, in the snow, has for centuries seen itself decaying ;
reduced even to forget old purposes and enmities, and
join interest with the Kingship : on this younger
strength it would fain stay its decrepitude ; and these
two will henceforth stand and fall together. Alas, the
Sorbonne*still sits there, in its old mansion ; but mum-
bles only jargon of dotage, and no longer leads the
consciences of men : not the Sorbonne ; it is *Encyclopédies, Philosophie,* and who knows what nameless
innumerable multitude'of ready Writers, profane Singers,
Romancers, Players, Disputators, and Pamphleteers,
that now form the Spiritual Guidance of the world.
The world's Practical Guidance too is lost, or has glided
into the same miscellaneous hands. Who is it that the
King (*Able-man,* named also *Roi, Rex,* or Director) now
guides ? His own huntsmen and prickers : when there

is to be no hunt, it is well said, ' *Le Roi ne fera rien*
(To-day his Majesty will do *nothing*) '.[1] He lives and
lingers there, because he is living there, and none has
yet laid hands on him.

The Nobles, in like manner, have nearly ceased either
to guide or misguide ; and are now, as their master is,
little more than ornamental figures. It is long since
they have done with butchering one another or their
king : the Workers, protected, encouraged by Majesty,
have ages ago built walled towns, and there ply their
crafts ; will permit no Robber Baron to ' live by the
saddle ', but maintain a gallows to prevent it. Ever
since that period of the *Fronde*,* the Noble has changed
his fighting sword into a court rapier ; and now loyally
attends his King as ministering satellite ; divides the
spoil, not now by violence and murder, but by soliciting
and finesse. These men call themselves supports of
the throne : singular gilt-pasteboard *caryatides* in that
singular edifice ! For the rest, their privileges every
way are now much curtailed. That Law authorizing
a Seigneur, as he returned from hunting, to kill not
more than two Serfs, and refresh his feet in their warm
blood and bowels, has fallen into perfect desuetude,—
and even into incredibility ; for if Deputy Lapoule can
believe in it, and call for the abrogation of it, so cannot
we.[2] No Charolois, for these last fifty years, though
never so fond of shooting, has been in use to bring down
slaters and plumbers, and see them roll from their roofs ;[3]
but contents himself with partridges and grouse. Close-
viewed, their industry and function is that of dress-
ing gracefully and eating sumptuously. As for their
debauchery and depravity, it is perhaps unexampled
since the era of Tiberius and Commodus.* Nevertheless,
one has still partly a feeling with the lady Maréchale :

[1] Mémoires sur la Vie privée de Marie Antoinette, par
Madame Campan (Paris, 1826), i. 12.

[2] Histoire de la Révolution Française, par Deux Amis de
la Liberté (Paris, 1792), ii. 212.

[3] Lacretelle, Histoire de France pendant le 18me Siècle
(Paris, 1819), i. 271.

' Depend upon it, Sir, God thinks twice before damning
a man of that quality '.[1]   These people, of old, surely
had virtues, uses ; or they could not have been there.
Nay, one virtue they are still required to have (for
mortal man cannot live without a conscience): the
virtue of perfect readiness to fight duels.

Such are the shepherds of the people : and now how
fares it with the flock ? With the flock, as is inevitable,
it fares ill, and ever worse. They are not tended, they
are only regularly shorn. They are sent for, to do
statute-labour, to pay statute-taxes ; to fatten battle-
fields (named 'bed of honour') with their bodies, in
quarrels which are not theirs ; their hand and toil is in
every possession of man ; but for themselves they have
little or no possession. Untaught, uncomforted, unfed ; to pine stagnantly in thick obscuration, in squalid
destitution and obstruction : this is the lot of the millions ; *peuple taillable et corvéable*d merci et miséricorde.
In Brittany they once rose in revolt at the first introduction of Pendulum Clocks ; thinking it had something to do with the *Gabelle.*[*] Paris requires to be cleared
out periodically by the Police ; and the horde of hunger-
stricken vagabonds to be sent wandering again over
space—for a time. 'During one such periodical clearance', says Lacretelle, 'in May, 1750, the Police had
presumed withal to carry off some reputable people's
children, in the hope of extorting ransoms for them.
The mothers fill the public places with cries of despair ;
crowds gather, get excited ; so many women in distraction run about exaggerating the alarm : an absurd
and horrid fable rises among the people ; it is said that
the Doctors have ordered a Great Person to take baths
of young human blood for the restoration of his own,
all spoiled by debaucheries. Some of the rioters', adds
Lacretelle, quite coolly, ' were hanged on the following
days ': the Police went on.[2] O ye poor naked wretches'!
and this then is your inarticulate cry to Heaven, as of

[1] Dulaure, vii. 261.
[2] Lacretelle, iii. 175.

a dumb tortured animal, crying from uttermost depths
of pain and debasement ? Do these azure skies, like
a dead crystalline vault, only reverberate the echo of it
on you ?   Respond to it only by 'hanging on the following days' ?—Not so: not for ever! Ye are heard in
Heaven.   And the answer too will come,—in a horror
of great darkness,* and shakings of the world, and a cup
of trembling* which all the nations shall drink.

Remark, meanwhile, how from amid the wrecks and
dust of this universal Decay new Powers are fashioning
themselves, adapted to the new time, and its destinies.
Besides the old Noblesse, originally of Fighters, there is
a new recognized Noblesse of Lawyers ; whose gala-day
and proud battle-day even now is.   An unrecognized
Noblesse of Commerce ; powerful enough, with money
in its pocket.   Lastly, powerfullest of all, least recognized of all, a Noblesse of Literature ; without steel on
their thigh, without gold in their purse, but with the
' grand thaumaturgic faculty of Thought '*in their head.
French Philosophism has arisen ; in which little word
how much do we include !   Here, indeed, lies properly
the cardinal symptom of the whole wide-spread malady.
Faith is gone out ; Scepticism is come in.   Evil abounds
and accumulates ; no man has Faith to withstand it, to
amend it, to begin by amending himself ; it must even
go on accumulating.   While hollow languor and vacuity
is the lot of the Upper, and want and stagnation of the
Lower, and universal misery is very certain, what other
thing is certain ?   That a Lie cannot be believed ! Philosophism knows only this : her other Belief is mainly,
that in spiritual supersensual matters no Belief is possible.   Unhappy!   Nay, as yet the Contradiction of
a Lie is some kind of Belief ; but the Lie with its Contradiction once swept away, what will remain ?   The
five unsatiated Senses will remain, the sixth insatiable
Sense (of Vanity) ; the whole *daemonic* nature of man
will remain,—hurled forth to rage blindly without rule
or rein ; savage itself, yet with all the tools and weapons
of civilization : a spectacle new in History.

In such a France, as in a Powder-tower, where fire

unquenched and now unquenchable is smoking and
smouldering all round, has Louis XV lain down to die.
With Pompadourism and Dubarryism, his Fleur-de-lis
has been shamefully struck down in all lands and on
all seas ; Poverty invades even the Royal Exchequer,
and Tax-farming can squeeze out no more ; there is
a quarrel of twenty-five years' standing with the Parlement ; everywhere Want, Dishonesty, Unbelief, and
hotbrained Sciolists for state-physicians : it is a portentous hour.

Such things can the eye of History see in this sick-
room of King Louis, which were invisible to the Courtiers there.   It is twenty years, gone Christmas-day,
since Lord Chesterfield,*summing up what he had noted
of this same France, wrote, and sent off by post, the
following words, that have become memorable : ' In
short, all the symptoms which I have ever met with in
History, previous to great Changes and Revolutions in
Government, now exist and daily increase in France '.[1]

CHAPTER III

VIATICUM

For the present, however, the grand question with
the Governors of France is : Shall extreme unction, or
other ghostly viaticum (to Louis, not to France), be
administered ?

It is a deep question.   For, if administered, if so
much as spoken of, must not, on the very threshold of
the business, Witch Dubarry vanish ; hardly to return
should Louis even recover ?   With her vanishes Duke
d'Aiguillon and Company, and all their Armida-Palace,
as was said ; Chaos swallows the whole again, and there
is left nothing but a smell of brimstone.   But then, on
the other hand, what will the Dauphinists and Choiseul-

[1] Chesterfield's Letters, December 25, 1753.

ists say ?   Nay, what may the royal martyr himself say,
should he happen to get deadly-worse, without getting
delirious ?   For the present, he still kisses the Dubarry
hand ; so we, from the anteroom, can note : but afterwards ?   Doctors' Bulletins may run as they are ordered,
but it is ' confluent small-pox ',—of which, as is whispered too, the Gatekeeper's once so buxom Daughter
lies ill : and Louis XV is not a man to be trifled with
in his viaticum.   Was he not wont to catechize his very
girls in the *Parc-aux-cerfs,*[*] and pray with and for them,
that they might preserve their—orthodoxy ?[1] A strange
fact, not an unexampled one ; for there is no animal so
strange as man.

For the moment, indeed, it were all well, could Archbishop Beaumont but be prevailed upon—to wink with
one eye !   Alas, Beaumont would himself so fain do it :
for singular to tell, the Church too, and whole posthu-
mous hope of Jesuitism, now hangs by the apron of this
same unmentionable Woman.   But then ' the force of
public opinion ' ?   Rigorous Christophe de Beaumont,
who has spent his life in persecuting hysterical Jansenists*and incredulous Non-confessors ; or even their dead
bodies, if no better might be,—how shall he now open
Heaven's gate, and give Absolution with the *corpus de-
licti* still under his nose ?   Our Grand-Almoner Roche-
Aymon,[*] for his part, will not higgle with a royal sinner
about turning of the key : but there are other Church-
men ; there is a King's Confessor, foolish Abbé Moudon;
and Fanaticism and Decency are not yet extinct.   On
the whole, what is to be done ?   The doors can be well
watched ; the Medical Bulletin adjusted ; and much, as
usual, be hoped for from time and chance.

The doors are well watched, no improper figure can
enter.   Indeed, few wish to enter ; for the putrid infection reaches even to the *Œil de Bœuf* ;[*] so that ' more
than fifty fall sick, and ten die '.   Mesdames the Princesses alone wait at the loathsome sick-bed ; impelled
by filial piety.   The three Princesses, *Graille, Chiffe,*

---

[1] Dulaure (viii. 217] ; Besenval, &c.

Coche (Rag, Snip, Pig, as he was wont to name them),
are assiduous there ; when all have fled. The fourth
Princess, *Loque* (Dud), as we guess, is already in the
Nunnery, and can only give her orisons. Poor *Graille*
and Sisterhood, they have never known a Father ; such
is the hard bargain Grandeur must make. Scarcely at
the *Débotter* (when Royalty took off its boots) could
they snatch up their ' enormous hoops, gird the long
train round their waists, huddle on their black cloaks
of taffeta up to the very chin ' ; and so, in fit appearance of full dress, ' every evening at six ', walk majestically in ; receive their royal kiss on the brow ; and
then walk majestically out again, to embroidery, small-
scandal, prayers, and vacancy. If Majesty came some
morning, with coffee of its own making, and swallowed
it with them hastily while the dogs were uncoupling for
the hunt, it was received as a grace of Heaven.[1] Poor
withered ancient women ! in the wild tossings that yet
await your fragile existence, before it be crushed and
broken ; as ye fly through hostile countries, over tempestuous seas, are almost taken by the Turks ; and
wholly, in the Sansculottic* Earthquake, know not your
right hand from your left,* be this always an assured
place in your remembrance : for the act was good and
loving ! To us also it is a little sunny spot, in that
dismal howling waste, where we hardly find another.

Meanwhile, what shall an impartial prudent Courtier
do ? In these delicate circumstances, while not only
death or life, but even sacrament or no sacrament, is
a question, the skilfullest may falter. Few are so happy
as the Duke d'Orleans and the Prince de Condé* ; who
can themselves, with volatile salts, attend the King's
antechamber ; and, at the same time, send their brave
sons (Duke de Chartres,* *Egalité* that is to be ; Duke
de Bourbon, one day Condé too, and famous among
Dotards) to wait upon the Dauphin.* With another few,
it is a resolution taken ; *jacta est alea.* Old Richelieu,
when Archbishop of Beaumont, driven by public opinion,

---

[1] Campan, i. 11-36.

is at last for entering the sick-room,—will twitch him
by the rochet, into a recess ; and there, with his old
dissipated mastiff-face, and the oiliest vehemence, be
seen pleading (and even, as we judge by Beaumont's
change of colour, prevailing) 'that the King be not
killed by a proposition in Divinity '. Duke Fronsac,
son of Richelieu, can follow his father : when the Curé
of Versailles whimpers something about sacraments, he
will threaten to ' throw him out of the window if he
mention such a thing '.

Happy these, we may say ; but to the rest that hover
between two opinions, is it not trying ? He who would
understand to what a pass Catholicism, and much else,
had now got ; and how the symbols of the Holiest have
become gambling-dice of the Basest,—must read the
narrative of those things by Besenval,*and Soulavie, and
the other Court Newsmen of the time. He will see the
Versailles Galaxy all scattered asunder, grouped into
new ever-shifting Constellations. There are nods and
sagacious glances ; go-betweens, silk dowagers mysteriously gliding, with smiles for this constellation, sighs
for that : there is tremor, of hope or desperation, in
several hearts. There is the pale grinning Shadow of
Death, ceremoniously ushered along by another grinning Shadow, of Etiquette : at intervals the growl of
Chapel Organs, like prayer by machinery ; proclaiming, as in a kind of horrid diabolic horse-laughter, *Vanity
of vanities, all is Vanity !**

CHAPTER IV

LOUIS THE UNFORGOTTEN

POOR LOUIS ! With these it is a hollow phantasmagory, where like mimes they mope and mowl, and utter
false sounds for hire ; but with thee it is frightful
earnest.

Frightful to all men is Death ; from of old named

King of Terrors.* Our little compact home of an Existence, where we dwelt complaining, yet as in a home,
is passing, in dark agonies, into an Unknown of Separation, Foreignness, unconditioned Possibility. The Heathen Emperor asks of his soul : Into what places art
thou now departing ? The Catholic King must answer :
To the Judgement-bar of the Most High God ! Yes, it
is a summing up of Life ; a final settling, and giving-
in the ' account of the deeds done in the body ' : they
are done now ; and lie there unalterable, and do bear
their fruits, long as Eternity shall last.

Louis XV had always the kingliest abhorrence of
Death. Unlike that praying Duke of Orleans, *Egalité's*
grandfather,—for indeed several of them had a touch of
madness,—who honestly believed that there was no
Death ! He, if the Court Newsmen can be believed,
started up once on a time, glowing with sulphurous contempt and indignation on his poor Secretary, who had
stumbled on the words, *feu roi d'Espagne* (the late King
of Spain) : ' *Feu roi, Monsieur ?* '—' Monseigneur ',
hastily answered the trembling but adroit man of business, ' *c'est une titre qu'ils prennent* ('tis a title they
take) '.[1] Louis, we say, was not so happy ; but he did
what he could. He would not suffer Death to be spoken
of ; avoided the sight of churchyards, funereal monuments, and whatsoever could bring it to mind. It is
the resource of the Ostrich ; who, hard hunted, sticks
his foolish head in the ground, and would fain forget
that his foolish unseeing body is not unseen too. Or
sometimes, with a spasmodic antagonism, significant of
the same thing, and of more, he *would* go ; or stopping
his court carriages, would send into churchyards, and
ask ' how many new graves there were to-day ', though
it gave his poor Pompadour the disagreeablest qualms.
We can figure the thought of Louis that day, when, all
royally caparisoned for hunting, he met, at some sudden
turning in the Wood of Senart, a ragged Peasant with
a coffin : ' For whom ? '—It was for a poor brother

[1] Besenval, i. 199.

slave, whom Majesty had sometimes noticed slaving in
those quarters: 'What did he die of?'—'Of hunger' :—the King gave his steed the spur.[1]

But figure his thought, when Death is now clutching
at his own heart-strings; unlooked for, inexorable!
Yes, poor Louis, Death has found thee. No palace
walls or life-guards, gorgeous tapestries or gilt buckram
of stiffest ceremonial could keep him out; but he is here,
here at thy very life-breath, and will extinguish it.
Thou, whose whole existence hitherto was a chimera
and scenic show, at length becomest a reality: sumptuous Versailles bursts asunder, like a Dream, into void
Immensity; Time is done, and all the scaffolding of
Time falls wrecked with hideous clangour round thy
soul: the pale Kingdoms yawn open; there must thou
enter, naked, all unking'd, and await what is appointed
thee! Unhappy man, there as thou turnest, in dull
agony, on thy bed of weariness, what a thought is thine!
Purgatory and Hellfire, now all too possible, in the
prospect: in the retrospect,—alas, what thing didst
thou do that were not better undone; what mortal
didst thou generously help; what sorrow hadst thou
mercy on? Do the 'five hundred thousand' ghosts,
who sank shamefully on so many battle-fields from
Rossbach to Quebec,* that thy Harlot might take
revenge for an epigram,*—crowd round thee in this
hour? Thy foul Harem; the curses of mothers, the
tears and infamy of daughters? Miserable man! thou
'hast done evil as thou couldst': thy whole existence
seems one hideous abortion and mistake of Nature;
the use and meaning of thee not yet known. Wert thou
a fabulous Griffin, *devouring* the works of men; daily
dragging virgins to thy cave;—clad also in scales that
no spear would pierce: no spear but Death's? A Griffin
not fabulous but real! Frightful, O Louis, seem these
moments for thee.—We will pry no further into the
horrors of a sinner's deathbed.

[1] Campan, iii. 39.

And yet let no meanest man lay flattering unction* to his soul. Louis was a Ruler ; but art not thou also one ? His wide France, look at it from the Fixed Stars (themselves not yet Infinitude), is no wider than thy narrow brickfield, where thou too didst faithfully, or didst unfaithfully. Man, ' Symbol of Eternity imprisoned into Time ! '* it is not thy works, which are all mortal, infinitely little, and the greatest no greater than the least, but only the Spirit thou workest in, that can have worth or continuance.

But reflect, in any case, what a life-problem this of poor Louis, when he rose as *Bien-Aimé* from that Metz sick-bed, really was ! What son of Adam could have swayed such incoherences into coherence ? Could he ? Blindest Fortune alone has cast *him* on the top of it : he swims there ; can as little sway it as the drift-log sways the wind-tossed moon-stirred Atlantic. ' What have I done to be so loved ? ' he said then. He may say now : What have I done to be so hated ? Thou hast done nothing, poor Louis ! Thy fault is properly even this, that thou didst *nothing*. What could poor Louis do ? Abdicate, and wash his hands of it,—in favour of the first that would accept ! Other clear wisdom there was none for him. As it was, he stood gazing dubiously, the absurdest mortal extant (a very Solecism Incarnate) into the absurdest confused world ;—wherein at last nothing seemed so certain as this, That he, the incarnate Solecism, had five senses ; that there were Flying Tables (*Tables Volantes*, which vanish through the floor, to come back reloaded), and a *Parc-aux-cerfs*.

Whereby at least we have again this historical curiosity : a human being in an original position ; swimming passively, as on some boundless ' Mother of Dead Dogs ',* towards issues which he partly saw. For Louis had withal a kind of insight in him. So when a new Minister of Marine, or what else it might be, came announcing his new era, the Scarlet-woman would hear from the lips of Majesty at supper : ' Yes, he spread out his ware like another ; promised the beautifullest things in the world ; not a thing of which will come :

he does not know this region ; he will see '. Or again :
' 'Tis the twentieth time I have heard all that ; France
will never get a Navy, I believe '. How touching also
was this : ' If *I* were Lieutenant of Police, I would
prohibit those Paris cabriolets '.[1]

Doomed mortal ;—for is it not a doom to be Solecism
incarnate ! A new *Roi Fainéant*, King Donothing ; but
with the strangest new *Mayor of the Palace* :* no bow-
legged Pepin now for *Mayor*, but that same cloud-capt,
fire-breathing Spectre of DEMOCRACY ; incalculable,
which is enveloping the world !——Was Louis, then, no
wickeder than this or the other private Donothing and
Eatall ; such as we often enough see, under the name
of Man of Pleasure, cumbering God's diligent Creation,
for a time ? Say, wretcheder ! His Life-solecism was
seen and felt of a whole scandalized world ; him endless
Oblivion cannot engulf, and swallow to endless depths,
—not yet for a generation or two.

However, be this as it will, we remark, not without
interest, that ' on the evening of the 4th ', Dame Dubarry issues from the sick-room, with perceptible ' trouble
in her visage '. It is the fourth evening of May, year of
Grace 1774. Such a whispering in the Œil-de-Bœuf !
Is he dying then ? What can be said, is that Dubarry
seems making up her packages ; she sails weeping
through her gilt boudoirs, as if taking leave. D'Aiguillon
and Company are near their last card ; nevertheless
they will not yet throw up the game. But as for the
sacramental controversy, it is as good as settled without
being mentioned ; Louis sends for his Abbé Moudon
in the course of next night ; is confessed by him, some
say for the space of ' seventeen minutes ', and demands
the sacraments of his own accord.

Nay already, in the afternoon, behold is not this
your Sorceress Dubarry with the handkerchief at her
eyes, mounting D'Aiguillon's chariot ; rolling off in his
Duchess's consolatory arms ? She is gone : and her

---

[1] Journal de Madame de Hausset, p. 293, &c.

place knows her no more.* Vanish, false Sorceress; into
Space! Needless to hover at neighbouring Ruel; for
thy day is done. Shut are the royal palace-gates for
evermore; hardly in coming years* shalt thou, under
cloud of night, descend once, in black domino, like a
black night-bird, and disturb the fair Antoinette's
music-party in the Park; all Birds of Paradise flying
from thee, and musical windpipes growing mute.[1] Thou
unclean, yet unmalignant, not unpitiable thing! What
a course was thine: from that first trucklebed (in
Joan of Arc's country) where thy mother bore thee,
with tears, to an unnamed father; forward, through
lowest subterranean depths, and over highest sunlit
heights, of Harlotdom and Rascaldom—to the guillotine-
axe, which sheers away thy vainly whimpering head!
Rest there uncursed; only buried and abolished; what
else befitted thee?

Louis, meanwhile, is in considerable impatience for
his sacraments; sends more than once to the window,
to see whether they are not coming. Be of comfort,
Louis, what comfort thou canst: they are under way,
these sacraments. Towards six in the morning, they
arrive. Cardinal Grand-Almoner Roche-Aymon is here
in pontificals, with his pyxes and his tools: he approaches the royal pillow; elevates his wafer; mutters
or seems to mutter somewhat;—and so (as the Abbé
Georgel, in words that stick to one, expresses it) has
Louis 'made the *amende honorable* to God'; so does
your Jesuit construe it.—'*Wa, Wa*', as the wild
Clotaire groaned out, when life was departing, 'what
great God is this that pulls down the strength of the
strongest kings!'[2]

The *amende honorable*, what 'legal apology' you
will, to God:—but not, if D'Aiguillon can help it, to
man. Dubarry still hovers in his mansion at Ruel;
and while there is life, there is hope. Grand-Almoner
Roche-Aymon, accordingly (for he seems to be in the

[1] Campan, i. 197.
[2] Gregorius Turonensis, Histor. lib. iv. cap. 21.

secret), has no sooner seen his pyxes and gear repacked,
than he is stepping majestically forth again, as if the
work were done ! But King's Confessor Abbé Moudon
starts forward; with anxious acidulent face, twitches
him by the sleeve ; whispers in his ear. Whereupon
the poor Cardinal has to turn round ; and declare
audibly, ' that his Majesty repents of any subjects of
scandal he may have given (*a pu donner*) ; and purposes, by the strength of Heaven assisting him, to
avoid the like—for the future ! ' Words listened to
by Richelieu with mastiff-face, growing blacker ; and
answered to, aloud, ' with an epithet ',—which Besenval
will not repeat. Old Richelieu, conqueror of Minorca,
companion of Flying-Table orgies, perforator of bedroom walls,[1] is thy day also done ?

Alas, the Chapel organs may keep going ; the Shrine
of Sainte Genevieve be let down, and pulled up again,
—without effect. In the evening the whole Court,
with Dauphin and Dauphiness, assist at the Chapel :
priests are hoarse with chanting their ' Prayers of Forty
Hours ' ; and the heaving bellows blow. Almost frightful ! For the very heaven blackens ; battering rain-
torrents dash, with thunder ; almost drowning the
organ's voice : and electric fire-flashes make the very
flambeaux on the altar pale. So that the most, as we
are told, retired, when it was over, with hurried steps
' in a state of meditation (*recueillement*) ', and said little
or nothing.[2]

So it has lasted for the better half of a fortnight ;
the Dubarry gone almost a week. Besenval says, all
the world was getting impatient *que cela finît* ; that
poor Louis would have done with it. It is now the
10th of May, 1774. He will soon have done now.

This tenth May day falls into the loathsome sick-
bed ; but dull, unnoticed there : for they that look out
of the windows are quite darkened ; the cistern-wheel

[1] Besenval, i. 159–72. Genlis ; Duc de Levis, &c.
[2] Weber, Mémoires concernant Marie-Antoinette (London, 1809), i. 22.

moves discordant on its axis ; Life, like a spent steed,
is panting towards the goal. In their remote apartments, Dauphin and Dauphiness stand road-ready ; all
grooms and equerries booted and spurred : waiting for
some signal to escape the house of pestilence.[1] And,
hark ! across the Œil-de-Bœuf, what sound is that ;
sound ' terrible and absolutely like thunder ' ? It is the
rush of the whole Court, rushing as in wager, to salute
the new Sovereigns : Hail to your Majesties ! The
Dauphin and Dauphiness are King and Queen ! Over-
powered with many emotions, they two fall on their
knees together, and, with streaming tears, exclaim : ' O
God, guide us, protect us ; we are too young to reign ! '
—Too young indeed.

But thus, in any case, ' with a sound absolutely like
thunder ', has the Horologe of Time struck, and an old
Era passed away. The Louis that was, lies forsaken, a
mass of abhorred clay ; abandoned ' to some poor persons, and priests of the *Chapelle Ardente* ',—who make
haste to put him ' in two lead coffins, pouring in abundant spirits of wine '. The new Louis with his Court is
rolling towards Choisy, through the summer afternoon :
the royal tears still flow ; but a word mispronounced by
Monseigneur d'Artois*sets them all laughing, and they
weep no more. Light mortals, how ye walk your light
life-minuet, over bottomless abysses, divided from you
by a film !*

For the rest, the proper authorities felt that no

---

[1] One grudges to interfere with the beautiful theatrical
' candle ', which Madame Campan*(i. 79) has lit on this
occasion, and blown out at the moment of death. What
candles might be lit or blown out, in so large an Establishment as that of Versailles, no man at such distance would
like to affirm : at the same time, as it was two o'clock in
a May Afternoon, and these royal Stables must have been
some five or six hundred yards from the royal sick-room,
the ' candle ' does threaten to go out in spite of us. It
remains burning indeed—in her fantasy ; throwing light
on much in those *Mémoires* of hers.

Funeral could be too unceremonious. Besenval himself
thinks it was unceremonious enough. Two carriages
containing two noblemen of the usher species, and a
Versailles clerical person; some score of mounted pages,
some fifty palfreniers: these, with torches, but not so
much as in black, start from Versailles on the second
evening, with their leaden bier. At a high trot, they
start; and keep up that pace. For the jibes (*brocards*)
of those Parisians, who stand planted in two rows, all
the way to St. Denis, and ' give vent to their pleasantry,
the characteristic of the nation', do not tempt one to
slacken. Towards midnight the vaults of St. Denis
receive their own: unwept by any eye of all these; if
not by poor *Loque* his neglected Daughter's, whose Nunnery is hard by.

Him they crush down, and huddle under-ground, in
this impatient way; him and his era of sin and tyranny
and shame: for behold a New Era is come; the future
all the brighter that the past was base.

BOOK II

THE PAPER AGE

CHAPTER I

ASTRAEA REDUX[*]

A PARADOXICAL philosopher, carrying to the uttermost length that aphorism of Montesquieu's,[*] 'Happy
the people whose annals are tiresome', has said, 'Happy
the people whose annals are vacant':[*] In which saying,
mad as it looks, may there not still be found some grain
of reason ? For truly, as it has been written, 'Silence
is divine';[*] and of Heaven ; so in all earthly things too
there is a silence which is better than any speech. Consider it well, the Event, the thing which can be spoken
of and recorded, is it not, in all cases, some disruption,
some solution of continuity ? Were it even a glad
Event, it involves change, involves loss (of active
Force); and so far, either in the past or in the present,
is an irregularity, a disease. Stillest perseverance
were our blessedness ; not dislocation and alteration,
—could they be avoided.

The oak grows silently, in the forest, a thousand
years; only in the thousandth year, when the woodman
arrives with his axe, is there heard an echoing through
the solitudes ; and the oak announces itself when, with
far-sounding crash, it *falls*. How silent too was the
planting of the acorn ; scattered from the lap of some
wandering wind ! Nay, when our oak flowered, or put
on its leaves (its glad Events), what shout of proclamation could there be ? Hardly from the most observant a word of recognition. These things *befel* not,
they were slowly *done* ; not in an hour, but through
the flight of days : what was to be said of it ? This
hour seemed altogether as the last was, as the next
would be.

It is thus everywhere that foolish Rumour babbles
not of what was done, but of what was misdone or
undone ; and foolish History (ever, more or less, the
written epitomized synopsis of Rumour) knows so little
that were not as well unknown. Attila Invasions,
Walter-the-Penniless Crusades, Sicilian Vespers, Thirty-
Years' Wars :* mere sin and misery ; not work, but
hindrance of work ! For the Earth, all this while, was
yearly green and yellow with her kind harvests ; the
hand of the craftsman, the mind of the thinker rested
not : and so, after all, and in spite of all, we have this
so glorious high-domed blossoming World ; concerning
which, poor History may well ask, with wonder,
Whence *it* came ? She knows so little of it, knows
so much of what obstructed it, what would have rendered it impossible. Such, nevertheless, by necessity
or foolish choice, is her rule and practice ; whereby
that paradox, ' Happy the people whose annals are
vacant ', is not without its true side.

And yet, what seems more pertinent to note here,
there is a stillness, not of unobstructed growth, but of
passive inertness, the symptom of imminent downfall.
As victory is silent, so is defeat. Of the opposing forces
the weaker has resigned itself ; the stronger marches
on, noiseless now, but rapid, inevitable : the fall and
overturn will not be noiseless. How all grows, and has
its period, even as the herbs of the fields, be it annual,
centennial, millennial ! All grows and dies,* each by
its own wondrous laws, in wondrous fashion of its own ;
spiritual things most wondrously of all. Inscrutable,
to the wisest, are these latter ; not to be prophesied of,
or understood. If when the oak stands proudliest
flourishing to the eye, you know that its heart is sound,
it is not so with the man ; how much less with the
Society, with the Nation of men ! Of such it may be
affirmed even that the superficial aspect, that the
inward feeling of full health, is generally ominous. For
indeed it is of apoplexy, so to speak, and a plethoric lazy
habit of body, that Churches, Kingships, Social Institu-

tions, oftenest die. Sad, when such Institution plethori-
cally says to itself, Take thy ease, thou hast goods laid
up ;—like the fool of the Gospel, to whom it was
answered, Fool, *this night* thy life shall be required of
thee !*

Is it the healthy peace, or the ominous unhealthy,
that rests on France, for these next Ten Years ?   Over
which the Historian can pass lightly, without call to
linger : for as yet events are not, much less performances.   Time of sunniest stillness ;—shall we call it,
what all men thought it, the new Age of Gold ?   Call
it at least, of Paper ; which in many ways is the succe-
daneum of Gold.   Bank-paper, wherewith you can still
buy when there is no gold left ; Book-paper, splendent
with Theories, Philosophies, Sensibilities,—beautiful
art, not only revealing Thought, but also of so beautifully hiding from us the want of Thought !   Paper is
made from the *rags* of things that did once exist ; there
are endless excellences in Paper.—What wisest Philosophe, in this halcyon uneventful period, could prophesy
that there was approaching, big with darkness and
confusion, the event of events ?   Hope ushers in a Revolution,—as earthquakes are preceded by bright
weather.   On the Fifth of May, fifteen years hence,
old Louis will not be sending for the Sacraments ; but
a new Louis, his grandson, with the whole pomp of
astonished intoxicated France, will be opening the
States General.

Dubarrydom and its D'Aiguillons are gone for ever.
There is a young, still docile, well-intentioned King ; a
young, beautiful and bountiful, well-intentioned Queen ;
and with them all France, as it were, become young.
Maupeou and his Parlement have to vanish into thick
night ; respectable Magistrates, not indifferent to the
Nation, were it only for having been opponents of the
Court, descend now unchained from their ' steep rocks
at Croe in Combrailles ' and elsewhere, and return singing praises :   the old Parlement of Paris*resumes its
functions.   Instead of a profligate bankrupt Abbé
Terray, we have now, for Controller-General, a virtuous

philosophic Turgot,* with a whole Reformed France in
his head. By whom whatsoever is wrong, in Finance or
otherwise, will be righted,—as far as possible. Is it not
as if Wisdom herself were henceforth to have seat and
voice in the Council of Kings ? Turgot has taken
office with the noblest plainness of speech to that effect ;
been listened to with the noblest royal trustfulness.[1]
It is true, as King Louis objects, ' They say he never
goes to mass ' ; but liberal France likes him little worse
for that ; liberal France answers, ' The Abbé Terray
always went '. Philosophism sees, for the first time,
a Philosophe (or even a Philosopher) in office : she in
all things will applausively second him ; neither will
light old Maurepas*obstruct, if he can easily help it.

Then how ' sweet ' are the manners ; vice ' losing all
its deformity '*; becoming *decent* (as established things,
making regulations for themselves, do) ; becoming
almost a kind of ' sweet ' virtue ! Intelligence so
abounds ; irradiated by wit and the art of conversation.
Philosophism sits joyful in her glittering saloons, the
dinner-guest of Opulence, grown ingenuous, the very
Nobles proud to sit by her ; and preaches, lifted up
over all Bastilles, a coming millennium. From far
Fernay, Patriarch Voltaire gives sign : veterans
Diderot, D'Alembert have lived to see this day ; these
with their younger Marmontels, Morellets, Chamforts,
Raynals,* make glad the spicy board of rich ministering
Dowager, of philosophic Farmer-General.* O nights and
suppers of the gods !* Of a truth, the long-demonstrated
will now be done : ' the Age of Revolutions approaches*'
(as Jean Jacques wrote), but then of happy blessed
ones. Man awakens from his long somnambulism ;
chases the Phantasms that beleaguered and bewitched
him. Behold the new morning glittering down the
eastern steeps ;*fly, false Phantasms, from its shafts of
light ; let the Absurd fly utterly, forsaking this lower
Earth for ever. It is Truth and *Astraea Redux* that

[1] Turgot's Letter : Condorcet, Vie de Turgot (Œuvres de
Condorcet, t. v.), p. 67. The date is 24th August, 1774.

(in the shape of Philosophism) henceforth reign. For
what imaginable purpose was man made, if not to be
' happy ' ?   By victorious Analysis and Progress of
the Species, happiness enough now awaits him.   Kings
can become philosophers ; or else philosophers Kings.
Let but Society be once rightly constituted,—by
victorious Analysis. The stomach that is empty*shall
be filled ; the throat that is dry shall be wetted with
wine. Labour itself shall be all one as rest ; not
grievous, but joyous.* Wheat-fields, one would think,
cannot come to grow untilled ; no man made clayey,
or made weary thereby ;—unless indeed machinery
will do it ?   Gratuitous Tailors*and Restaurateurs may
start up, at fit intervals, one as yet sees not how.   But
if each will, according to rule of Benevolence, have
a care for all, then surely—no one will be uncared for.
Nay, who knows but, by sufficiently victorious Analysis,
' human life may be indefinitely lengthened ', and men
get rid of Death, as they have already done of the
Devil ?   We shall then be happy in spite of Death and
the Devil.—So preaches magniloquent Philosophism
her *Redeunt Saturnia regna.*

The prophetic song of Paris and its Philosophes is
audible enough in the Versailles Œil-de-Bœuf ; and the
Œil-de-Bœuf, intent chiefly on nearer blessedness, can
answer, at worst, with a polite ' Why not ? '   Good
old cheery Maurepas is too joyful a Prime Minister to
dash the world's joy. Sufficient for the day*be its own
evil. Cheery old man, he cuts his jokes, and hovers
careless along ; his cloak well adjusted to the wind, if
so be he may please all persons. The simple young
King, whom a Maurepas cannot think of troubling with
business, has retired into the interior apartments ; taciturn, irresolute ; though with a sharpness of temper at
times : he, at length, determines on a little smith-work ;
and so, in apprenticeship with a Sieur Gamain (whom
one day he shall have little cause to bless), is learning
to make locks. [1]   It appears further, he understood
Geography ; and could read English.   Unhappy young

---

[1] Campan, i. 125.

King, his childlike trust in that foolish old Maurepas
deserved another return. But friend and foe, destiny
and himself have combined to do him hurt.

Meanwhile the fair young Queen, in her halls of
state, walks like a goddess of Beauty, the cynosure of
all eyes ; as yet mingles not with affairs ; heeds not the
future ; least of all, dreads it. Weber* and Campan [1]
have pictured her, there within the royal tapestries, in
bright boudoirs, baths, peignoirs, and the Grand and
Little Toilette ; with a whole brilliant world waiting
obsequious on her glance : fair young daughter of Time,
what things has Time in store for thee ! Like Earth's
brightest Appearance, she moves gracefully, environed
with the grandeur of Earth : a reality, and yet a magic
vision ; for, behold, shall not utter Darkness swallow it !
The soft young heart adopts orphans, portions merito-
rious maids, delights to succour the poor,—such poor
as come picturesquely in her way ; and sets the fashion
of doing it ; for, as was said, Benevolence has now
begun reigning. In her Duchess de Polignac,* in her
Princess de Lamballe,* she enjoys something almost like
friendship : now too, after seven long years, she has
a child, and soon even a Dauphin, of her own ; can
reckon herself, as Queens go, happy in a husband.

Events ? The grand events are but charitable
Feasts of Morals (*Fêtes des mœurs*), with their Prizes
and Speeches ; Poissarde Processions to the Dauphin's
cradle ; above all, Flirtations, their rise, progress, decline and fall. There are Snow-statues raised by the
poor in hard winter, to a Queen who has given them
fuel. There are masquerades, theatricals ; beautifyings
of little Trianon, purchase and repair of St. Cloud ;
journeyings from the summer Court-Elysium to the
winter one. There are poutings and grudgings from
the Sardinian Sisters-in-law*(for the Princes too are
wedded) ; little jealousies, which Court-Etiquette can
moderate. Wholly the lightest-hearted frivolous foam
of Existence ; yet an artfully refined foam ; pleasant

were it not so costly, like that which mantles on the
wine of Champagne !

Monsieur, the King's elder Brother, has set up for
a kind of wit ; and leans towards the Philosophe side.
Monseigneur d'Artois pulls the mask from a fair imper-
tinent ; fights a duel in consequence,—almost drawing
blood.[1] He has breeches of a kind new in this world ;
—a fabulous kind ; ' four tall lackeys ', says Mercier,
as if he had seen it, ' hold him up in the air, that he
may fall into the garment without vestige of wrinkle ;
from which rigorous encasement the same four, in the
same way, and with more effort, have to deliver him at
night '.[2] This last is he who now, as a grey timeworn
man, sits desolate at Grätz*;[3] having winded up his
destiny with the Three Days.* In such sort are poor
mortals swept and shovelled to and fro.

CHAPTER II

PETITION IN HIEROGLYPHS

WITH the working people, again, it is not so well.
Unlucky ! For there are from twenty to twenty-five
millions of them. Whom, however, we lump together
into a kind of dim compendious unity, monstrous but
dim, far off, as the· canaille ; or, more humanely, as
' the masses '. Masses indeed : and yet, singular to
say, if, with an effort of imagination, thou follow them,
over broad France, into their clay hovels, into their
garrets and hutches, the masses consist all of units.
Every unit of whom has his own heart and sorrows ;
stands covered there with his own skin, and if you prick
him, he will bleed.* O purple Sovereignty, Holiness,

---

[1] Besenval, ii. 282–330.
[2] Mercier, Nouveau Paris, iii. 147.
[3] A.D. 1834.

Reverence; thou, for example, Cardinal Grand-
Almoner, with thy plush covering of honour, who hast
thy hands strengthened with dignities and moneys, and
art set on thy world-watchtower solemnly, in sight of
God, for such ends,—what a thought: that every unit
of these masses is a miraculous Man, even as thyself
art; struggling, with vision or with blindness, for *his*
infinite Kingdom (this Life which he has got, once only,
in the middle of Eternities); with a spark of the
Divinity, what thou callest an immortal soul, in him!

Dreary, languid do these struggle in their obscure
remoteness; their hearth cheerless, their diet thin. For
them, in this world, rises no Era of Hope; hardly now
in the other,—if it be not hope in the gloomy rest of
Death, for their faith too is failing. Untaught, uncomforted, unfed! A dumb generation; their voice only
an inarticulate cry: spokesman, in the King's Council,
in the world's forum, they have none that finds credence.
At rare intervals (as now, in 1775), they will fling down
their hoes and hammers; and, to the astonishment of
thinking mankind,[1] flock hither and thither, dangerous,
aimless; get the length even of Versailles. Turgot is
altering the Corn-trade, abrogating the absurdest Corn-
laws; there is dearth, real, or were it even 'factitious';
an indubitable scarcity of bread. And so, on the 2nd
day of May, 1775, these waste multitudes do here, at
Versailles Château, in wide-spread wretchedness, in
sallow faces, squalor, winged raggedness, present, as in
legible hieroglyphic writing, their Petition of Grievances.
The Château-gates must be shut; but the King will
appear on the balcony, and speak to them. They have
seen the King's face; their Petition of Grievances has
been, if not read, looked at. For answer, two of them
are hanged, on a 'new gallows forty feet high'; and
the rest driven back to their dens,—for a time.

Clearly a difficult 'point' for Government, that of
dealing with these masses;—if indeed it be not rather

---

[1] Lacretelle, *France pendant le 18me Siècle*, ii. 455.
Biographie Universelle, § Turgot (by Durozoir).

the sole point and problem of Government, and all
other points mere accidental crotchets, superficialities,
and beatings of the wind!* For let Charter-Chests,
Use and Wont, Law common and special say what they
will, the masses count to so many millions of units;
made, to all appearance, by God,—whose Earth this is
declared to be. Besides, the people are not without
ferocity; they have sinews and indignation. Do but
look what holiday old Marquis Mirabeau,* the crabbed
old Friend of Men, looked on, in these same years, from
his lodging, at the Baths of Mont d'Or : ' The savages
descending in torrents from the mountains ; our people
ordered not to go out. The Curate in surplice and
stole ; Justice in its peruke ; Marechausée sabre in
hand, guarding the place, till the bagpipes can begin.
The dance interrupted, in a quarter of an hour, by
battle ; the cries, the squealings of children, of infirm
persons, and other assistants, tarring them on, as the
rabble does when dogs fight : frightful men, or rather
frightful wild-animals, clad in jupes of coarse woollen,
with large girdles of leather studded with copper nails ;
of gigantic stature, heightened by high wooden-clogs
(*sabots*) ; rising on tiptoe to see the fight ; tramping
time to it ; rubbing their sides with their elbows: their
faces haggard (*figures hâves*), and covered with their
long greasy hair ; the upper part of the visage waxing
pale, the lower distorting itself into the attempt at
a cruel laugh and a sort of ferocious impatience. And
these people pay the *taille* ! And you want further
to take their salt from them ! And you know not what
it is you are stripping barer, or as you call it, governing ;
what, by the spurt of your pen, in its cold dastard
indifference, you will fancy you can starve always with
impunity ; always till the catastrophe come !—Ah
Madame, such Government by Blindman's-buff, stumbling along too far, will end in the General Overturn
(*culbute générale*) '.[1]

[1] Mémoires de Mirabeau écrits par Lui-même, par son
Père, son Oncle et son Fils Adoptif (Paris. 1834-5), ii. 186.

Undoubtedly a dark feature this in an Age of Gold,—
Age, at least, of Paper and Hope ! Meanwhile, trouble
us not with thy prophecies, O croaking Friend of Men :
'tis long that we have heard such ; and still the old
world keeps wagging,* in its old way.

CHAPTER III

QUESTIONABLE

OR is this same Age of Hope itself but a simulacrum ;
as Hope too often is ? Cloud-vapour with rainbows
painted on it,* beautiful to see, to sail towards,—which
hovers over Niagara Falls ? In that case, victorious
Analysis will have enough to do.

Alas, yes ! a whole world to remake, if she could see
it : work for another than she ! For all is wrong, and
gone out of joint ; the inward spiritual, and the outward
economical ; head or heart, there is no soundness in it.
As indeed, evils of all sorts are more or less of kin, and
do usually go together : especially it is an old truth,
that wherever huge physical evil is, there, as the parent
and origin of it, has moral evil to a proportionate extent
been. Before those five-and-twenty labouring Millions,
for instance, could get that haggardness of face, which
old Mirabeau now looks on, in a Nation calling itself
Christian, and calling man the brother of man,—what
unspeakable, nigh infinite Dishonesty (of *seeming* and
not *being*) in all manner of Rulers, and appointed
Watchers, spiritual and temporal, must there not,
through long ages, have gone on accumulating ! It
will accumulate : moreover, it will reach a head ; for
the first of all Gospels is this, that a Lie cannot endure
for ever.

In fact, if we pierce through that rosepink vapour
of Sentimentalism, Philanthropy, and Feasts of Morals,
there lies behind it one of the sorriest spectacles. You
might ask, What bonds that ever held a human society
happily together, or held it together at all, are in force
here ? It is an unbelieving people ;* which has supposi-

tions, hypotheses, and froth-systems of victorious
Analysis; and for *belief* this mainly, that Pleasure is
pleasant. Hunger they have for all sweet things; and
the law of Hunger: but what other law? Within
them, or over them, properly none!

Their King has become a King Popinjay*: with his
Maurepas Government, gyrating as the weather-cock
does, blown about by every wind. Above them they
see no God; or they even do not look above, except
with astronomical glasses. The Church indeed still is;
but in the most submissive state; quite tamed by
Philosophism; in a singularly short time; for the hour
was come. Some twenty years ago, your Archbishop
Beaumont would not even let the poor Jansenists get
buried: your Loménie Brienne*(a rising man, whom
we shall meet with yet) could, in the name of the
Clergy, insist on having the Antiprotestant Laws, which
condemn to death for preaching, 'put in execution'.[1]
And alas, now not so much as Baron Holbach's*Atheism
can be burnt,—except as pipe-matches by the private
speculative individual. Our Church stands haltered,
dumb, like a dumb ox; lowing only for provender
(of tithes); content if it can have that; or, with dumb
stupor, expecting its further doom. And the Twenty
Millions of 'haggard faces'; and, as finger-post and
guidance to them in their dark struggle, 'a gallows
forty feet high'! Certainly a singular Golden Age;
with its Feasts of Morals, its 'sweet manners', its sweet
institutions (*institutions douces*); betokening nothing
but peace among men!—Peace? O Philosophe-
Sentimentalism, what hast thou to do with peace, when
thy mother's name is Jezebel?* Foul Product of still
fouler Corruption, thou with the corruption art
doomed!

Meanwhile it is singular how long the rotten will
hold together, provided you do not handle it roughly.
For whole generations it continues standing, 'with a
ghastly affectation of life', after all life and truth has

[1] Boissy d'Anglas, Vie de Malesherbes, i. 15-22.

fled out of it : so loth are men to quit their old ways ;
and, conquering indolence and inertia, venture on new.
Great truly is the Actual ; is the Thing that has rescued
itself from bottomless deeps of theory and possibility,
and stands there as a definite indisputable Fact, whereby men do work and live, or once did so. Wisely shall
men cleave to that, while it will endure ; and quit it
with regret, when it gives way under them. Rash
enthusiast of Change, beware ! Hast thou well considered all that Habit does in this life of ours ; how all
Knowledge and all Practice hang wondrous over
infinite abysses of the Unknown, Impracticable ; and
our whole being is an infinite abyss, *overarched* by
Habit, as by a thin Earth-rind, laboriously built together ?

But if ' every man ', as it has been written, ' holds
confined within him a *mad*-man ',* what must every
Society do ;—Society, which in its commonest state is
called ' the standing miracle of this world ' ! ' Without
such Earth-rind of Habit ', continues our Author, ' call
it System of Habits, in a word, *fixed ways* of acting
and of believing,—Society would not exist at all.
With such it exists. better or worse. Herein too, in
this its System of Habits, acquired, retained how you
will, lies the true Law-Code and Constitution of a
Society ; the only Code, though an unwritten one,
which it can in no wise *dis*obey. The thing we call
written Code, Constitution, Form of Government, and
the like, what is it but some miniature image, and
solemnly expressed summary of this unwritten Code ?
Is,—or rather, alas, is *not* ; but only should be, and
always tends to be ! In which latter discrepancy lies
struggle without end '. And now, we add in the same
dialect, let but, by ill chance, in such ever-enduring
struggle,—your ' thin Earth-rind ' be once *broken* !
The fountains of the great deep boil forth; fire-fountains,
enveloping, engulfing. Your ' Earth-rind ' is shattered,
swallowed up ; instead of a green flowery world there
is a waste wild-weltering chaos ;—which has again, with
tumult and struggle, to *make* itself into a world.

On the other hand, be this conceded : Where thou findest a Lie that is oppressing thee, extinguish it. Lies exist there only to be extinguished ; they wait and cry earnestly for extinction. Think well, meanwhile, in what spirit thou wilt do it : not with hatred, with headlong selfish violence ; but in clearness of heart, with holy zeal, gently, almost with pity. Thou wouldst not *replace* such extinct Lie by a new Lie, which a new Injustice of thy own were ; the parent of still other Lies ?* Whereby the latter end of that business were worse than the beginning.*

So, however, in this world of ours, which has both an indestructible hope in the Future, and an indestructible tendency to persevere as in the Past, must Innovation and Conservation* wage their perpetual conflict, as they may and can. Wherein the ' daemonic element ', that lurks in all human things, *may* doubtless, some once in the thousand years,—get vent ! But indeed may we not regret that such conflict,—which, after all, is but like that classical one of ' hate-filled Amazons with heroic Youths ', and will end in *embraces*,—should usually be so spasmodic ? For Conservation, strengthened by that mightiest quality in us, our indolence, sits for long ages, not victorious only, which she should be ; but tyrannical, incommunicative. She holds her adversary as if annihilated ; such adversary lying, all the while, like some buried Enceladus ; who, to gain the smallest freedom, has to stir a whole Trinacria with its Aetnas.

Wherefore, on the whole, we will honour a Paper Age too ; an Era of Hope ! ' For in this same frightful process of Enceladus Revolt ; when the task, on which no mortal would willingly enter, has become imperative, inevitable,—is it not even a kindness of Nature that she lures us forward by cheerful promises, fallacious or not ; and a whole generation plunges into the Erebus Blackness, lighted on by an Era of Hope ? It has been well said : ' Man is based on Hope ;* he has properly no other possession but Hope ; this habitation of his is named the Place of Hope '.

CHAPTER IV

MAUREPAS

BUT now, among French hopes, is not that of old
M. de Maurepas one of the best-grounded; who hopes
that he, by dexterity, shall contrive to continue
Minister ? Nimble old man, who for all emergencies
has his light jest; and ever in the worst confusion will
emerge, corklike, unsunk ! Small care to him is Perfectibility, Progress of the Species, and *Astraea Redux*:
good only, that a man of light wit, verging towards
fourscore, can in the seat of authority feel himself
important among men. Shall we call him, as haughty
Châteauroux was wont, of old, ' *M. Faquinet* (Dimi-
nutive of Scoundrel) ' ? In courtier dialect, he is now
named ' the Nestor of France '; such governing Nestor
as France has.

At bottom, nevertheless, it might puzzle one to say
where the Government of France, in these days, specially is. In that Château of Versailles, we have Nestor,*
King, Queen, ministers and clerks, with paper-bundles
tied in tape: but the Government ? For Government
is a thing that *governs*, that guides; and if need be,
compels. Visible in France there is not such a thing.
Invisible, inorganic, on the other hand, there is: in
Philosophe saloons, in Œil-de-Bœuf galleries; in the
tongue of the babbler, in the pen of the pamphleteer.
Her Majesty appearing at the Opera is applauded; she
returns all radiant with joy. Anon the applauses wax
fainter, or threaten to cease; she is heavy of heart, the
light of her face has fled. Is Sovereignty some poor
Montgolfier*; which, blown into by the popular wind,
grows great and mounts; or sinks flaccid, if the wind
be withdrawn ? France was long a ' Despotism tempered by Epigrams '*; and now, it would seem, the
Epigrams have got the upper hand.

Happy were a young ' Louis the Desired ' to make
France happy; if it did not prove too troublesome, and
he only knew the way. But there is endless discre-

pancy round him; so many claims and clamours; a
mere confusion of tongues.* Not reconcilable by man;
not manageable, suppressible, save by some strongest
and wisest man ;—which only a lightly-jesting lightly-
gyrating M. de Maurepas can so much as subsist amidst.
Philosophism claims her new Era, meaning thereby
innumerable things. And claims it in no faint voice;
for France at large, hitherto mute, is now beginning to
speak also; and speaks in that same sense. A huge,
many-toned sound*; distant, yet not unimpressive. On
the other hand, the Œil-de-Bœuf, which, as nearest,
one can hear best, claims with shrill vehemence that
the Monarchy be as heretofore a Horn of Plenty;
wherefrom loyal courtiers may draw,—to the just support of the throne. Let Liberalism and a New Era,
if such is the wish, be introduced; only no curtailment
of the royal moneys! Which latter condition, alas, is
precisely the impossible one.

Philosophism, as we saw, has got her Turgot made
Controller-General; and there shall be endless reformation. Unhappily this Turgot could continue only
twenty months. With a miraculous *Fortunatus'* *Purse*
in his Treasury, it might have lasted longer; with such
Purse indeed, every French Controller-General, that
would prosper in these days, ought first to provide
himself. But here again may we not remark the bounty
of Nature in regard to Hope ? Man after man advances
confident to the Augean Stable,* as if *he* could clean it;
expends his little fraction of an ability on it, with such
cheerfulness; does, in so far as he was honest, accomplish something. Turgot has faculties; honesty, insight, heroic volition; but the Fortunatus' Purse he
has not. Sanguine Controller-General! a whole pacific
French Revolution may stand schemed in the head of
the thinker; but who shall pay the unspeakable 'in-
demnities' that will be needed ? Alas, far from that:
on the very threshold of the business, he proposes that
the Clergy, the Noblesse, the very Parlements be sub-
jected to taxes like the People! One shriek of indignation and astonishment reverberates through all the

Château galleries ; M. de Maurepas has to gyrate : the
poor King, who had written few weeks ago, '*Il n'y a
que vous et moi qui aimions le peuple* (There is none
but you and I that has the people's interest at heart)',
must write now a dismissal ;[1] and let the French Revolution accomplish itself, pacifically or not, as it can.

Hope then is deferred ?* Deferred ; not destroyed,
or abated. Is not this, for example, our Patriarch
Voltaire, after long years of absence, revisiting Paris ?
With face shrivelled to nothing ; with 'huge peruke *à
la Louis Quatorze*, which leaves only two eyes visible,
glittering like carbuncles '* the old man is here.[2] What
an outburst ! Sneering Paris has suddenly grown reverent ; devotional with Hero-worship. Nobles have
disguised themselves as tavern-waiters to obtain sight
of him : the loveliest of France would lay their hair
beneath his feet. 'His chariot is the nucleus of a
Comet ; whose train fills whole streets ' : they crown
him in the theatre, with immortal vivats ; finally
'stifle him under roses ',—for old Richelieu recommended opium in such state of the nerves, and the excessive Patriarch took too much. Her Majesty herself
had some thought of sending for him ; but was dis-
suaded. Let Majesty consider it nevertheless. The
purport of this man's existence has been to wither up
and annihilate all whereon Majesty and Worship for
the present rests : and is it *so* that the world recognizes
him ? With Apotheosis ; as its Prophet and Speaker,
who has spoken wisely the thing it longed to say ? Add
only that the body of this same rose-stifled, beatified
Patriarch cannot get buried except by stealth. It is
wholly a notable business ; and France, without doubt,
is *big* (what the Germans call ' Of good Hope ') : we
shall wish her a happy birth-hour, and blessed fruit.

Beaumarchais too has now winded up his Law-
Pleadings (*Mémoires*) ;[3] not without result, to himself

[1] In May 1776.   [2] February 1778.
[3] 1773-6. See Œuvres de Beaumarchais ; where they,
and the history of them, are given.

and to the world.   Caron Beaumarchais*(or de Beaumarchais, for he got ennobled) had been born poor, but
aspiring, esurient ; with talents, audacity, adroitness ;
above all with the talent for intrigue : a lean, but also
a tough indomitable man.   Fortune and dexterity
brought him to the harpsichord of Mesdames, our good
Princesses *Loque, Graille* and Sisterhood.   Still better,
Pâris Duvernier, the Court-Banker, honoured him with
some confidence ; to the length even of transactions
in cash.   Which confidence, however, Duvernier's Heir,
a person of quality, would not continue.   Quite otherwise ; there springs a Lawsuit from it : wherein tough
Beaumarchais, losing both money and repute, is, in the
opinion of Judge-Reporter Goezman, of the Parlement
Maupeou, and of a whole indifferent acquiescing world,
—miserably beaten.   In all men's opinion, only not in
his own !   Inspired by the indignation, which makes,
if not verses, satirical law-papers, the withered Music-
master, with a desperate heroism, takes up his lost
cause in spite of the world ; fights for it, against Reporters, Parlements and Principalities, with light banter,
with clear logic ; adroitly, with an inexhaustible toughness and resource, like the skilfulest fencer ; on whom,
so skilful is he, the whole world now looks.   Three
long years it lasts ; with wavering fortune.   In fine,
after labours comparable to the Twelve of Hercules,
our unconquerable Caron triumphs ; regains his Lawsuit and Lawsuits ; strips Reporter Goezman of the
judicial ermine ; covering him with a perpetual garment
of obloquy instead :—and in regard to the Parlement
Maupeou (which he has helped to extinguish), to Parlements of all kinds, and to French Justice generally,
gives rise to endless reflections in the minds of men.
Thus has Beaumarchais like a lean French Hercules
ventured down, driven by destiny, into the Nether
Kingdoms ; and victoriously tamed hell-dogs there.
He also is henceforth among the notabilities of his
generation.

CHAPTER V

ASTRAEA REDUX WITHOUT CASH

OBSERVE, however, beyond the Atlantic, has not the new day verily dawned! Democracy, as we said, is born; storm-girt, is struggling for life and victory. A sympathetic France rejoices over the Rights of Man; in all saloons, it is said, What a spectacle! Now too behold our Deane, our Franklin,* American Plenipotentiaries, here in person soliciting: [1] the sons of the Saxon Puritans, with their Old-Saxon temper, Old-Hebrew culture, sleek Silas, sleek Benjamin, here on such errand, among the light children of Heathenism, Monarchy, Sentimentalism, and the Scarlet-woman. A spectacle indeed; over which saloons may cackle joyous,—though Kaiser Joseph,* questioned on it, gave this answer, most unexpected from a Philosophe: ' Madame, the trade I live by is that of royalist (*Mon métier à moi c'est d'être royaliste*) '.

So thinks light Maurepas too; but the wind of Philosophism and force of public opinion will blow him round. Best wishes, meanwhile, are sent; clandestine privateers armed. Paul Jones* shall equip his *Bon Homme Richard*: weapons, military stores can be smuggled over (if the English do not seize them); wherein, once more Beaumarchais, dimly as the Giant Smuggler, becomes visible,—filling his own lank pocket withal. But surely, in any case, France should have a Navy. For which great object were not now the time; now when that proud Termagant of the Seas has her hands full? It is true, an impoverished Treasury cannot build ships; but the hint once given (which Beaumarchais says *he* gave), this and the other loyal Seaport, Chamber of Commerce, will build and offer them. Goodly vessels bound into the waters; a *Ville de Paris*, Leviathan of ships.

[1] 1777; Deane somewhat earlier: Franklin remained till 1785.

And now when gratuitous three-deckers dance there at anchor, with streamers flying ; and eleutheromaniac Philosophedom grows ever more clamorous, what can a Maurepas do—but gyrate ? Squadrons cross the ocean : Gateses, Lees, rough Yankee Generals, ' with woollen night-caps under their hats', present arms to the far-glancing Chivalry of France ; and new-born Demo-cracy sees, not without amazement, ' Despotism tem-pered by Epigrams' fight at her side. So, however, it is. King's forces and heroic volunteers ; Rocham-beaus, Bouillés, Lameths, Lafayettes,* have drawn their swords in this sacred quarrel of mankind ;—shall draw them again elsewhere, in the strangest way.

Off Ushant* some naval thunder is heard. In the course of which did our young Prince, Duke de Char-tres, ' hide in the hold ' ; or did he materially, by *active* heroism, contribute to the victory ? Alas, by a second edition, we learn that there was no victory ; or that English Keppel had it.[1] Our poor young Prince gets his Opera plaudits changed into mocking tehees ; and cannot become Grand-Admiral,—the source to him of woes which one may call endless.*

Woe also for *Ville de Paris*, the Leviathan of ships ! English Rodney has clutched it, and led it home, with the rest ; so successful was his ' new manœuvre of breaking the enemy's line '. [2] It seems as if, according to Louis XV, ' France were never to have a Navy '. Brave Suffren must return from Hyder Ally and the Indian Waters ; with small result ; yet with great glory for ' six ' *non-defeats* ;—which indeed, with such seconding as he had, one may reckon heroic. Let the old sea-hero rest now, honoured of France, in his native Cevennes mountains ; send smoke, not of gunpowder, but mere culinary smoke, through the old chimneys of the Castle of Jalès,*—which one day, in other hands, shall have other fame. Brave Lapérouse shall by and

---

[1] 27th July, 1778.
[2] 9th and 12th April, 1782.

by lift anchor, on philanthropic Voyage of Discovery;
for the King knows Geography.[1] But alas this also will
not prosper: the brave Navigator goes, and returns
not; the Seekers search far seas for him in vain. He
has vanished trackless into blue Immensity; and only
some mournful mysterious shadow of him hovers long
in all heads and hearts.

Neither, while the War yet lasts, will Gibraltar*surrender. Not though Crillon, Nassau-Siegen, with the
ablest projectors extant, are there; and Prince Condé
and Prince d'Artois have hastened to help. Wondrous
leather-roofed Floating-batteries, set afloat by French-
Spanish *Pacte de Famille*,* give gallant summons: to
which, nevertheless, Gibraltar answers Plutonically,
with mere torrents of redhot iron,—as if stone Calpé
had become a throat of the Pit; and utters such a
Doom's-blast of a *No*, as all men must credit.[2]

And so, with this loud explosion, the noise of War
has ceased; an Age of Benevolence may hope, for ever.
Our noble volunteers of Freedom have returned, to be
her missionaries. Lafayette, as the matchless of his
time, glitters in the Versailles Œil-de-Bœuf; has his
Bust set up in the Paris Hôtel-de-Ville. Democracy
stands inexpugnable, immeasurable, in her New
World; has even a foot lifted towards the Old;—and
our French Finances, little strengthened by such work,
are in no healthy way.

What to do with the Finances ? This indeed is the
great question : a small but most black weather-symp-
tom, which no radiance of universal hope can cover.
We saw Turgot cast forth from the Controllership, with
shrieks,—for want of a Fortunatus' Purse. As little
could M. de Clugny manage the duty; or indeed do
anything, but consume his wages; attain 'a place in
History', where as an ineffectual shadow thou beholdest

---

[1] August 1, 1785.
[2] Annual Register (Dodsley's), xxv. 258-67. September, October, 1782.

him still lingering ;—and let the duty manage itself.
Did Genevese Necker*possess such a Purse then ?   He
possessed banker's skill, banker's honesty ; credit of all
kinds, for he had written Academic Prize Essays,
struggled for India Companies, given dinners to Philosophes, and ' realized a fortune in twenty years '.   He
possessed further a taciturnity and solemnity; of depth,
or else of dullness.   How singular for Celadon*Gibbon,
false swain as he had proved ; whose father, keeping
most probably his own gig, ' would not hear of such
a union ',—to find now his forsaken Demoiselle Curchod
sitting in the high places of the world, as Minister's
Madame, and ' Necker not jealous ' ! [1]

A new young Demoiselle, one day to be famed as a
Madame and De Staël,*—was romping about the knees
of the Decline and Fall : the lady Necker founds
Hospitals ; gives solemn Philosophe dinner-parties, to
cheer her exhausted Controller-General.   Strange things
have happened : by clamour of Philosophism, management of Marquis de Pezay, and Poverty constraining
even Kings.   And so Necker, Atlas-like, sustains the
burden of the Finances, for five years long.[2]   Without
wages, for he refused such ; cheered only by Public
Opinion, and the ministering of his noble Wife.   With
many thoughts in him, it is hoped ;—which however he
is shy of uttering.   His Compte Rendu,* published by
the royal permission, fresh sign of a New Era, shows
wonders ;—which what but the genius of some Atlas-
Necker can prevent from becoming portents ?   In
Necker's head too there is a whole pacific French
Revolution, of its kind ; and in that taciturn dull depth,
or deep dullness, ambition enough.

Meanwhile, alas, his Fortunatus' Purse turns out to
be little other than the old ' vectigal of Parsimony ":
Nay, he too has to produce his scheme of taxing :
Clergy, Noblesse to be taxed ; Provincial Assemblies,
and the rest,—like a mere Turgot !   The expiring

[1] Gibbon's Letters, date, 16th June, 1777, &c.
[2] Till May 1781.

M. de Maurepas must gyrate one other time. Let
Necker also depart ; not unlamented.

Great in a private station, Necker looks on from the
distance ; abiding his time. ' Eighty thousand copies '
of his new Book, which he calls *Administration des
Finances*, will be sold in few days. He is gone ; but
shall return, and that more than once, borne by a whole
shouting Nation. Singular Controller-General of the
Finances ; once Clerk in Thelusson's Bank !

CHAPTER VI

WINDBAGS

So marches the world, in this its Paper Age, or Era
of Hope. Not without obstructions, war-explosions ;
which however, heard from such distance, are little
other than a cheerful marching-music. If indeed that
dark living chaos of Ignorance and Hunger, five and
twenty million strong, under your feet,—were to begin
playing !

For the present, however, consider Longchamp ;
now when Lent is ending, and the glory of Paris and
France has gone forth, as in annual wont. Not to
assist at *Tenebris**Masses, but to sun itself and show
itself, and salute the young Spring.[1] Manifold, bright-
tinted, glittering with gold ; all through the Bois de
Boulogne, in longdrawn variegated rows ;—like long-
drawn living flower-borders, tulips, dahlias, lilies of the
valley ; all in their moving flower-pots (of newgilt
carriages) : pleasure of the eye, and pride of life ! So
rolls and dances the Procession : steady, of firm assurance, as if it rolled on adamant and the foundations
of the world ; not on mere heraldic parchment,—under
which smoulders a lake of fire. Dance on, ye foolish

[1] Mercier, Tableau de Paris, ii. 51. Louvet, Roman de
Faublas, &c.

ones ; ye sought not wisdom, neither have ye found it.*
Ye and your fathers have sown the wind, ye shall reap
the whirlwind.* Was it not, from of old, written : *The
wages of sin is death ?*

But at Longchamp,* as elsewhere, we remark for one
thing, that dame and cavalier are waited on each by
a kind of human familiar, named *jokei*. Little elf, or
imp ; though young, already withered ; with its
withered air of premature vice, of knowingness, of
completed elf-hood : useful in various emergencies.
The name *jokei* (jockey) comes from the English ; as
the thing also fancies that it does. Our Anglomania,
in fact, is grown considerable ; prophetic of much. If
France is to be free, why shall she not, now when mad
war is hushed, love neighbouring Freedom ? Cultivated men, your Dukes de Liancourt, de la Rochefoucault* admire the English Constitution, the English
National Character ; would import what of it they can.
Of what is lighter, especially if it be light as wind,
how much easier the freightage ! Non-Admiral Duke
de Chartres (not yet d'Orléans or Egalité) flies to and
fro across the Strait ; importing English Fashions : this
he, as hand-and-glove with an English Prince of Wales,
is surely qualified to do. Carriages and saddles ; top-
boots and *rédingotes*, as we call riding-coats. Nay the
very mode of riding : for now no man on a level with
his age but will trot *à l'Anglaise*, rising in the stirrups ;
scornful of the old sitfast method, in which, according to
Shakespeare, ' butter and eggs '*go to market. Also, he
can urge the fervid wheels,* this brave Chartres of ours ;
no whip in Paris is rasher and surer than the unprofes-
sional one of Monseigneur.

Elf *jokeis*, we have seen ; but see now real Yorkshire
jockeys, and what they ride on, and train : English
racers for French Races. These likewise we owe first
(under the Providence of the Devil) to Monseigneur.
Prince d'Artois also has his stud of racers. Prince
d'Artois has withal the strangest horseleech : a moon-
struck, much-enduring individual, of Neuchâtel in

Switzerland,—named *Jean Paul Marat*.* A problematic
Chevalier d'Eon,* now in petticoats, now in breeches,
is no less problematic in London than in Paris; and
causes bets and lawsuits. Beautiful days of international communion! Swindlery and Blackguardism
have stretched hands across the Channel, and saluted
mutually: on the race-course of Vincennes or Sablons,
behold, in English curricle-and-four, wafted glorious
among the principalities and rascalities, an English
Dr. Dodd,[1]*—for whom also the too early gallows gapes.

Duke de Chartres was a young Prince of great
promise, as young princes often are; which promise
unfortunately has belied itself. With the huge Orléans
Property, with Duke de Penthièvre for Father-in-law
(and now the young Brother-in-law Lamballe killed
by excesses),—he will one day be the richest man in
France. Meanwhile, 'his hair is all falling out, his
blood is quite spoiled',—by early transcendentalism of
debauchery. Carbuncles stud his face; dark studs on
a ground of burnished copper. A most signal failure,
this young Prince! The stuff prematurely burnt out
of him: little left but foul smoke and ashes of expiring
sensualities: what might have been Thought, Insight,
and even Conduct, gone now, or fast going,—to confused darkness, broken by bewildering dazzlements;
to obstreperous crotchets; to activities which you may
call semi-delirious, or even semi-galvanic! Paris
affects to laugh at his charioteering; but he heeds not
such laughter.

On the other hand, what a day, not of laughter, was
that, when he threatened, for lucre's sake, to lay sacrilegious hand on the Palais-Royal Garden![2] The flower-
parterres shall be riven up; the Chestnut Avenues shall
fall: time-honoured boscages, under which the Opera
Hamadryads were wont to wander, not inexorable to
men. Paris moans aloud. Philidor,* from his Café de

---

[1] Adelung, Geschichte der menschlichen Narrheit,
§ Dodd.

[2] 1781–2. (Dulaure, viii. 423.]

la Régence, shall no longer look on greenness; the
loungers and losels of the world, where now shall they
haunt? In vain is moaning. The axe glitters; the
sacred groves fall crashing,—for indeed Monseigneur
was short of money: the Opera Hamadryads fly with
shrieks. Shriek not, ye Opera Hamadryads; or not
as those that have no comfort. He will surround your
Garden with new edifices and piazzas: though nar-
rowed, it shall be replanted; dizened with hydraulic
jets, cannon which the sun fires at noon; things bodily,
things spiritual, such as man has not imagined;—and
in the Palais-Royal shall again, and more than ever,
be the *Sorcerer's Sabbath* and *Satan-at-Home* of our
Planet.

What will not mortals attempt? From remote
Annonay in the Vivarais, the Brothers Montgolfier send
up their paper-dome, filled with the smoke of burnt
wool.[1] The Vivarais Provincial Assembly is to be
prorogued this same day: Vivarais Assembly-members
applaud, and the shouts of congregated men. Will
victorious Analysis scale the very Heavens then?
Paris hears with eager wonder; Paris shall ere long
see. From Réveillon's Paper-warehouse there, in the
Rue St. Antoine (a noted Warehouse),—the new Montgolfier air-ship launches itself. Ducks and poultry
have been borne skyward: but now shall men be
borne.[2] Nay, Chemist Charles thinks of hydrogen and
glazed silk. Chemist Charles will himself ascend, from
the Tuileries Garden; Montgolfier solemnly cutting
the cord. By Heaven, this Charles does also mount,
he and another! Ten times ten thousand hearts go
palpitating; all tongues are mute with wonder and
fear;—till a shout, like the voice of seas, rolls after
him, on his wild way. He soars, he dwindles upwards;
has become a mere gleaming circlet,—like some Tur-
gotine snuffbox, what we call '*Turgotine-Platitude*';

---

[1] 5th June, 1783.
[2] October and November 1783.

like some new daylight Moon ! Finally he descends ;
welcomed by the universe. Duchess Polignac, with a
party, is in the Bois de Boulogne, waiting ; though it is
drizzly winter, the 1st of December 1783. The whole
chivalry of France, Duke de Chartres foremost, gallops
to receive him.[1]

Beautiful invention ; mounting heavenward, so
beautifully,—so unguidably ! Emblem of much, and
of our Age of Hope itself ; which shall mount, speci-
fically-light, majestically in this same manner ; and
hover,—tumbling whither Fate will. Well if it do not,
Pilâtre-like,* explode ; and *de*mount all the more
tragically !—So, riding on windbags, will men scale the
Empyrean.

Or observe Herr Doctor Mesmer,* in his spacious
Magnetic Halls. Long-stoled he walks ; reverend,
glancing upwards, as in rapt commerce ; an Antique
Egyptian Hierophant in this new age. Soft music
flits ; breaking fitfully the sacred stillness. Round
their Magnetic Mystery, which to the eye is mere tubs
with water,—sit breathless, rod in hand, the circles
of Beauty and Fashion, each circle a living circular
Passion-Flower : expecting the magnetic afflatus, and
new-manufactured Heaven-on-Earth. O women, O
men, great is your infidel-faith !* A Parlementary
Duport, a Bergasse, D'Espréménil we notice there ;
Chemist Berthollet*too,—on the part of Monseigneur
de Chartres.

Had not the Academy of Sciences, with its Baillys,
Franklins, Lavoisiers,* interfered ! But it did interfere.[2] Mesmer may pocket his hard money, and withdraw. Let him walk silent by the shore of the Bodensee,
by the ancient town of Constance ; meditating on
much. For so, under the strangest new vesture, the
old great truth (since no vesture can hide it) begins again
to be revealed : That man is what we call a miraculous
creature, with miraculous power over men ; and, on

[1] Lacretelle, 18me Siècle, iii. 258.
[2] August 1784.

the whole, with such a Life in him, and such a World round him, as victorious Analysis, with her Physiologies, Nervous-systems, Physic and Metaphysic, will never completely *name*, to say nothing of explaining. Wherein also the Quack shall, in all ages, come in for his share.

CHAPTER VII

CONTRAT SOCIAL*

IN such succession of singular prismatic tints, flush after flush suffusing our horizon, does the Era of Hope dawn on towards fulfilment. Questionable ! As indeed, with an Era of Hope that rests on mere universal Benevolence, victorious Analysis, Vice cured of its deformity ; and, in the long run, on Twenty-five dark savage Millions, looking up, in hunger and weariness, to that *Ecce-signum* of theirs ' forty feet high ',—how could it be but questionable ?

Through all time, if we read aright, sin was, is, will be, the parent of misery. This land calls itself most Christian, and has crosses and cathedrals ; but its High-priest is some Roche-Aymon, some Necklace-Cardinal Louis de Rohan.* The voice of the poor, through long years, ascends inarticulate, in *Jacqueries*, meal-mobs ; low-whimpering of infinite moan : unheeded of the Earth ; not unheeded of Heaven. Always moreover where the Millions are wretched, there are the Thousands straitened, unhappy ; only the Units can flourish ; or say rather, be ruined the last. Industry, all noosed and haltered, as if it too were some beast of chase for the mighty hunters of this world to bait, and cut slices from,—cries passionately to these its well-paid guides and watchers, not, *Guide me* ; but, *Laissez faire*, Leave me alone of *your* guidance ! What market has Industry in this France ? For two things there may be market and demand : for the coarser kind of field-fruits, since the Millions will live : for the finer

kinds of luxury and spicery,—of multiform taste, from
opera-melodies down to racers and courtesans; since
the Units will be amused. It is at bottom but a mad
state of things.

To mend and remake all which we have, indeed,
victorious Analysis. Honour to victorious Analysis;
nevertheless, out of the Workshop and Laboratory,
what thing was victorious Analysis yet known to make?
Detection of incoherences, mainly; destruction of the in-
coherent. From of old, Doubt was but half a magician;
she evokes the spectres which she cannot quell. We
shall have 'endless vortices of froth-logic'; whereon
first words, and then things, are whirled and swallowed.
Remark, accordingly, as acknowledged grounds of
Hope, at bottom mere precursors of Despair, this perpetual theorizing about Man, the Mind of Man, Philosophy of Government, Progress of the Species, and
such like; the main thinking furniture of every head.
Time, and so many Montesquieus, Mablys,* spokesmen
of Time, have discovered innumerable things: and now
has not Jean Jacques promulgated his new Evangel of
a *Contrat Social*; explaining the whole mystery of
Government, and how it is *contracted* and bargained
for,—to universal satisfaction? Theories of Government! Such have been, and will be; in ages of
decadence. Acknowledge them in their degree; as
processes of Nature, who does nothing in vain; as
steps in her great process. Meanwhile, what theory
is so certain as this, That all theories, were they never
so earnest, painfully elaborated, are, and, by the
very conditions of them, must be incomplete, questionable, and even false?* Thou shalt know that this
Universe is, what it professes to be, an *infinite* one.
Attempt not to swallow *it*, for thy logical digestion;
be thankful, if skilfully planting down this and the
other fixed pillar in the chaos, thou prevent its swallowing *thee*. That a new young generation has exchanged
the Sceptic Creed, *What shall I believe?* for passionate
Faith in this Gospel according to Jean Jacques, is a
further step in the business; and betokens much.

Blessed also is Hope; and always from the beginning there was some Millennium prophesied; Millennium of Holiness; but (what is notable) never till this
new Era, any Millennium of mere Ease and plentiful
Supply. In such prophesied Lubberland, of Happiness,
Benevolence, and Vice cured of its deformity, trust not,
my friends! Man is not what one calls a happy animal;
his appetite for sweet victual is so enormous. How, in
this wild Universe, which storms in on him, infinite,
vague-menacing, shall poor man find, say not happiness,
but existence, and footing to stand on, if it be not by
girding himself together for continual endeavour and
endurance? Woe, if in his heart there dwelt no devout
Faith; if the word Duty had lost its meaning for him!
For as to this of Sentimentalism, so useful for weeping
with over romances and on pathetic occasions, it otherwise verily will avail nothing; nay less. The healthy
heart that said to itself, ' How healthy am I! ' was
already fallen into the fatallest sort of disease. Is not
Sentimentalism twin-sister to Cant, if not one and the
same with it? Is not Cant the *materia prima* of the
Devil; from which all falsehoods, imbecilities, abomi-
nations body themselves; from which no true thing *can*
come? For Cant is itself properly a double-distilled
Lie; the second-power of a Lie.

And now if a whole Nation fall into that? In such
case, I answer, infallibly they will return out of it! For
life is no cunningly-devised deception*or self-deception:
it is a great truth that thou art alive, that thou hast
desires, necessities; neither can these subsist and satisfy
themselves on delusions, but on fact. To fact, depend
on it, we shall come back: to such fact, blessed or
cursed, as we have wisdom for. The lowest, least
blessed fact one knows of, on which necessitous mortals
have ever based themselves, seems to be the primitive
one of Cannibalism: That *I* can devour *Thee*. What
if such Primitive Fact were precisely the one we had
(with our improved methods) to revert to, and begin
anew from!

CHAPTER VIII

PRINTED PAPER

In such a practical France, let the theory of Perfectibility say what it will, discontents cannot be wanting :
your promised Reformation is so indispensable ; yet it
comes not ; who will begin it—with himself ?   Discontent with what is around us, still more with what is
above us, goes on increasing ;   seeking ever new vents.

Of Street Ballads, of Epigrams that from of old
tempered Despotism, we need not speak.   Nor of
Manuscript Newspapers (*Nouvelles à la main*) do we
speak.   Bachaumont and his journeymen and followers
may close those ' thirty volumes of scurrilous eaves-
dropping ', and quit that trade ;   for at length if not
liberty of the Press, there is licence.   Pamphlets can be
surreptitiously vended and read in Paris, did they even
bear to be ' Printed at Pekin '.   We have a *Courrier de
l'Europe* in those years, regularly published at London ;
by a De Morande, whom the guillotine has not yet
devoured.   There too an unruly Linguet,* still unguillotined, when his own country has become too hot
for him, and his brother Advocates have cast him out,
can emit his hoarse wailings, and *Bastille Dévoilée*
(Bastille Unveiled).   Loquacious Abbé Raynal, at
length, has his wish; sees the *Histoire Philosophique*,
with its ' lubricity ', unveracity, loose loud eleutheromaniac rant (contributed, they say, by Philosophedom
at large, though in the Abbé's name, and to his glory),
burnt by the common hangman ;—and sets out on his
travels as a martyr.   It was the Edition of 1781 ;
perhaps the last notable Book that had such fire-beati-
tude,—the hangman discovering now that it did not
serve.

Again, in Courts of Law, with their money-quarrels,
divorce-cases, wheresoever a glimpse into the household
existence can be had, what indications !   The Parle-

ments of Besançon and Aix ring, audible to all France,
with the amours and destinies of a young Mirabeau.*
He, under the nurture of a ' Friend of Men ', has, in
State Prisons, in marching Regiments, Dutch Authors'-
garrets, and quite other scenes, ' been for twenty years
learning to resist despotism ' : despotism of men, and
alas also of gods.   How, beneath this rose-coloured veil
of Universal Benevolence and *Astraea Redux*, is the
sanctuary of Home so often a dreary void, or a dark
contentious Hell-on-Earth ! The old Friend of Men
has his own divorce-case too ; and at times, ' his whole
family but one ' under lock and key : he writes much
about reforming and enfranchising the world ; and for
his own private behoof, he has needed sixty *Lettres-de-
Cachet.* A man of insight too ; with resolution, even
with manful principle : but in such an element, inward
and outward ; which he could not rule, but only madden.
Edacity, rapacity ;—quite contrary to the finer sensibilities of the heart ! Fools, that expect your verdant
Millennium, and nothing but Love and Abundance,
brooks running wine, winds whispering music,—with
the whole ground and basis of your existence champed
into a mud of Sensuality ; which, daily growing deeper,
will soon have no bottom but the Abyss !

   Or consider that unutterable business of the Diamond
Necklace. Red-hatted Cardinal Louis de Rohan ;
Sicilian jailbird Balsamo Cagliostro ;* milliner Dame de
Lamotte, ' with a face of some piquancy ' : the highest
Church Dignitaries waltzing, in Walpurgis Dance,* with
quack-prophets, pickpurses and public women ;—a
whole Satan's Invisible World displayed ;* working
there continually under the daylight visible one ; the
smoke of its torment* going up for ever ! The Throne
has been brought into scandalous collision with the
Treadmill. Astonished Europe rings with the mystery
for ten months ; sees only lie unfold itself from lie ;
corruption among the lofty and the low, gulosity,
credulity, imbecility, strength nowhere but in the
hunger. Weep, fair Queen, thy first tears of unmixed
wretchedness ! Thy fair name has been tarnished by

foul breath ; irremediably while life lasts. No more
shalt thou be loved and pitied by living hearts, till a new
generation has been born, and thy own heart lies cold,
cured of all its sorrows.—The Epigrams henceforth
become, not sharp and bitter ; but cruel, atrocious,
unmentionable. On that 31st of May 1786, a miserable
Cardinal Grand-Almoner Rohan, on issuing from his
Bastille, is escorted by hurrahing crowds : unloved he,
and worthy of no love ; but important since the Court
and Queen are his enemies.[1]

How is our bright Era of Hope dimmed ; and the
whole sky growing bleak with signs of hurricane and
earthquake ! It is a doomed world : gone all ' obedience that made men free '* ; fast going the obedience that
made men slaves,—at least to one another. Slaves only
of their own lusts they now are, and will be. Slaves of
sin ; inevitably also of sorrow. Behold the mouldering
mass of Sensuality and Falsehood ; round which plays
foolishly, itself a corrupt phosphorescence, some
glimmer of Sentimentalism ;—and over all, rising, as
Ark of *their* Covenant, the grim Patibulary Fork ' forty
feet high ' ; which also is now nigh rotted. Add only
that the French Nation distinguishes itself among
Nations by the characteristic of Excitability ; with the
good, but also with the perilous evil, which belongs to
that. Rebellion, explosion, of unknown extent is to be
calculated on. There are, as Chesterfield wrote, ' all
the symptoms I have ever met with in History ! '
Shall we say then : Woe to Philosophism, that it
destroyed Religion, what it called ' extinguishing the
abomination (*écraser l'infame*) ' ?* Woe rather to those
that made the Holy an abomination, and extinguish-
able ; woe to all men that live in such a time of world-
abomination and world-destruction ! Nay, answer the
Courtiers, it was Turgot, it was Necker, with their mad

[1] Fils Adoptif, Mémoires de Mirabeau, iv. 325.—See
Carlyle's Biographical Essays, § Diamond Necklace, § Count
Cagliostro.

innovating; it was the Queen's want of etiquette; it
was he, it was she, it was that.   Friends! it was every
scoundrel that had lived, and quacklike pretended to be
doing, and been only eating and *mis*doing, in all provinces of life, as Shoeblack or as Sovereign Lord, each
in his degree, from the time of Charlemagne and earlier.
All this (for be sure no falsehood perishes, but is as
seed sown out to grow) has been storing itself for thousands of years; and now the account-day has come.*
And rude will the settlement be: of wrath laid up
against the day of wrath.* O my Brother, be not thou
a Quack! Die rather, if thou wilt take counsel; 'tis
but dying once, and thou art quit of it for ever. Cursed
is that trade; and bears curses, thou knowest not how,
long ages after thou art departed, and the wages thou
hadst are all consumed; nay, as the ancient wise have
written,—through Eternity itself, and is verily marked
in the Doom-Book of a God!*

Hope deferred maketh the heart sick. And yet, as
we said, Hope is but deferred; not abolished, not abo-
lishable.   It is very notable, and touching, how this
same Hope does still light onwards the French Nation
through all its wild destinies.   For we shall still find
Hope shining, be it for fond invitation, be it for anger
and menace; as a mild heavenly light it shone; as
a red conflagration it shines: burning sulphurous-blue,
through darkest regions of Terror, it still shines; and
goes not out at all, since Desperation itself is a kind of
Hope.   Thus is our Era still to be named of Hope,
though in the saddest sense,—when there is nothing
left but Hope.*

But if any one would know summarily what a Pandora's Box*lies there for the opening, he may see it in
what by its nature is the symptom of all symptoms, the
surviving Literature of the Period.   Abbé Raynal, with
his lubricity and loud loose rant, has spoken *his* word;
and already the fast-hastening generation responds to
another.   Glance at Beaumarchais' *Mariage de Figaro*;
which now (in 1784), after difficulty enough, has issued

on the stage ; and ' runs its hundred nights ', to the admiration of all men.   By what virtue or internal vigour
it so ran, the reader of our day will rather wonder :—
and indeed will know so much the better that it flattered
some pruriency of the time ; that it spoke what all were
feeling, and longing to speak.   Small substance in that
Figaro : thin wiredrawn intrigues, thin wiredrawn sentiments and sarcasms ; a thing lean, barren ; yet which
winds and whisks itself, as through a wholly mad universe, adroitly, with a high-sniffing air : wherein each,
as was hinted, which is the grand secret, may see some
image of himself, and of his own state and ways.   So
it runs its hundred nights, and all France runs with it ;
laughing applause.   If the soliloquizing Barber ask :
' What has your Lordship done to earn all this ? ' and
can only answer : ' You took the trouble to be born
(*Vous vous êtes donné la peine de naître*)',—all men
must laugh : and a gay horse-racing Anglomaniac
Noblesse loudest of all.   For how can small books have
a great danger in them ? asks the Sieur Caron ; and
fancies his thin epigram may be a kind of reason.
Conqueror of a golden fleece, by giant smuggling ; tamer
of helldogs, in the Parlement Maupeou ; and finally
crowned Orpheus in the *Théâtre Français*, Beaumarchais has now culminated, and unites the attributes of
several demigods.   We shall meet him once again, in
the course of his decline.

Still more significant are two Books produced on
the eve of the ever-memorable Explosion itself, and
read eagerly by all the world : Saint-Pierre's*Paul et
Virginie*, and Louvet's* *Chevalier de Faublas*. Noteworthy Books ; which may be considered as the last-
speech of old Feudal France.   In the first there rises
melodiously, as it were, the wail of a moribund world :
everywhere wholesome Nature in unequal conflict with
diseased perfidious Art ; cannot escape from it in the
lowest hut, in the remotest island of the sea.   Ruin and
death must strike down the loved one ; and, what is
most significant of all, death even here not by necessity
but by etiquette.   What a world of prurient corruption

lies visible in that super-sublime of modesty ! Yet, on the whole, our good Saint-Pierre is musical, poetical, though most morbid : we will call his Book the swan-song of old dying France.

Louvet's, again, let no man account musical. Truly, if this wretched *Faublas* is a death-speech, it is one under the gallows, and by a felon that does not repent. Wretched *cloaca* of a Book ; without depth even as a *cloaca* ! What ' picture of French society ' is here ? Picture properly of nothing, if not of the mind that gave it out as some sort of picture. Yet symptom of much ; above all, of the world that could nourish itself thereon.

BOOK III
THE PARLEMENT OF PARIS

CHAPTER I

DISHONOURED BILLS

WHILE the unspeakable confusion is everywhere weltering within, and through so many cracks in the surface sulphur-smoke is issuing, the question arises: Through what crevice will the main Explosion carry itself ? Through which of the old craters or chimneys ; or must it, at once, form a new crater for itself ? In every Society are such chimneys, are Institutions serving as such : even Constantinople is not without its safety-valves ; there too Discontent can vent itself, —in material fire ;* by the number of nocturnal conflagrations, or of hanged bakers, the Reigning Power can read the signs of the times, and change course according to these.

We may say that this French Explosion will doubtless first try all the old Institutions of escape ; for by each of these there is, or at least there used to be, some communication with the interior deep; they are national Institutions in virtue of that. Had they even become personal Institutions, and what we can call choked up from their original uses, there nevertheless must the impediment be weaker than elsewhere. Through which of them then ? An observer might have guessed : Through the Law Parlements ; above all, through the Parlement of Paris.

Men, though never so thickly clad in dignities, sit not inaccessible to the influences of their time ; especially men whose life is business ; who at all turns, were it

even from behind judgement-seats, have come in contact
with the actual workings of the world. The Counsellor of Parlement, the President himself, who has bought
his place with hard money that he might be looked up
to by his fellow-creatures, how shall he, in all Philo-
sophe-soirées, and saloons of elegant culture, become
notable as a Friend of Darkness ? Among the Paris
Long-robes there may be more than one patriotic
Malesherbes, whose rule is conscience and the public
good; there are clearly more than one hotheaded
D'Espréménil, to whose confused thought any loud
reputation of the Brutus sort may seem glorious. The
Lepelletiers, Lamoignons have titles and wealth ; yet,
at Court, are only styled 'Noblesse of the Robe'.
There are Duports of deep scheme ; Fréteaus, Sabatiers,*
of incontinent tongue : all nursed more or less on the
milk of the *Contrat Social.* Nay, for the whole Body,
is not this patriotic opposition also a fighting for oneself ? Awake, Parlement of Paris, renew thy long
warfare ! Was not the Parlement Maupeou abolished
with ignominy ? Not now hast thou to dread a
Louis XIV, with the crack of his whip, and his Olympian looks ; not now a Richelieu and Bastilles : no, the
whole Nation is behind thee. Thou too (O heavens !)
mayst become a Political Power; and with the
shakings of thy horse-hair wig, shake principalities and
dynasties, like a very Jove with his ambrosial curls !*

Light old M. de Maurepas, since the end of 1781,
has been fixed in the frost of death : 'Never more',
said the good Louis, 'shall I hear his step in the room
there overhead'; his light jestings and gyratings are
at an end. No more can the importunate reality be
hidden by pleasant wit, and to-day's evil be deftly
rolled over upon to-morrow. The morrow itself has
arrived; and now nothing but a solid phlegmatic
M. de Vergennes sits there, in dull matter of fact, like
some dull punctual Clerk (which he originally was) ;
admits what cannot be denied, let the remedy come
whence it will. In him is no remedy ; only clerklike

'dispatch of business' according to routine. The
poor King, grown older yet hardly more experienced,
must himself, with such no-faculty as he has, begin
governing; wherein also his Queen will give help.
Bright Queen, with her quick clear glances and impulses;
clear, and even noble; but all-too superficial, vehe-
ment-shallow, for that work! To govern France were
such a problem; and now it has grown wellnigh too
hard to govern even the Œil-de-Bœuf. For if a distressed People has its cry, so likewise, and more audibly,
has a bereaved Court. To the Œil-de-Bœuf it remains
inconceivable how, in a France of such resources, the
Horn of Plenty should run dry: did it not *use* to flow?
Nevertheless Necker, with his revenue of parsimony,
has 'suppressed above six hundred places', before the
Courtiers could oust him; parsimonious finance-pedant
as he was. Again, a military pedant, Saint-Germain,
with his Prussian manœuvres; with his Prussian
notions, as if merit and not coat-of-arms should be
the rule of promotion, has disaffected military men;
the Mousquetaires, with much else are suppressed:
for he too was one of your suppressors; and unsettling
and oversetting, did mere mischief—to the Œil-de-Bœuf.
Complaints abound; scarcity, anxiety: it is a changed
Œil-de-Bœuf. Besenval says, already in these years
(1781) there was such a melancholy (such a *tristesse*)
about Court, compared with former days, as made it
quite dispiriting to look upon.

No wonder that the Œil-de-Bœuf feels melancholy,
when you are suppressing its places! Not a place can
be suppressed, but some purse is the lighter for it; and
more than one heart the heavier; for did it not employ
the working-classes too,—manufacturers, male and
female, of laces, essences; of Pleasure generally, whosoever could manufacture Pleasure? Miserable econo-
mies; never felt over Twenty-five Millions! So, however, it goes on: and is not yet ended. Few years more
and the Wolf-hounds shall fall suppressed, the Bear-
hounds, the Falconry; places shall fall, thick as
autumnal leaves.* Duke de Polignac*demonstrates, to

the complete silencing of ministerial logic, that his
place cannot be abolished; then gallantly, turning to
the Queen, surrenders it, since her Majesty so wishes.
Less chivalrous was Duke de Coigny,* and yet not
luckier: ' We got into a real quarrel, Coigny and I ',
said King Louis; ' but if he had even struck me, I
could not have blamed him '.¹ In regard to such
matters there can be but one opinion. Baron Besenval,
with that frankness of speech which stamps the independent man, plainly assures her Majesty that it is
frightful (*affreux*); you go to bed, and are not sure
but you shall rise impoverished on the morrow: one
might as well be in Turkey'. It is indeed a dog's life.

How singular this perpetual distress of the royal
treasury! And yet it is a thing not more incredible
than undeniable. A thing mournfully true: the stum-
b'ing-block on which all Ministers successively stumble,
and fall. Be it ' want of fiscal genius ', or some far
other want, there is the palpablest discrepancy between
Revenue and Expenditure; a *Deficit* of the Revenue:
you must ' choke (*combler*) the Deficit ', or else it will
swallow you! This is the stern problem; hopeless
seemingly as squaring of the circle. Controller Joly de
Fleury, who succeeded Necker, could do nothing with
it; nothing but propose loans, which were tardily filled
up; impose new taxes, unproductive of money, productive of clamour and discontent. As little could Controller d'Ormesson* do, or even less; for if Joly main-
tained himself beyond year and day, D'Ormesson
reckons only by months: till ' the King purchased
Rambouillet without consulting him ', which he took
as a hint to withdraw. And so, towards the end of
1783, matters threaten to come to a still-stand. Vain
seems human ingenuity. In vain has our newly-devised
' Council of Finances ' struggled, our Intendants of
Finance, Controller-General of Finances: there are
unhappily no Finances to control. Fatal paralysis
invades the social movement; clouds, of blindness or

¹ Besenval, iii. 255-8.

of blackness, envelop us : are we breaking down, then,
into the black horrors of NATIONAL BANKRUPTCY ?

Great is Bankruptcy: the great bottomless gulf
into which all Falsehoods, public and private, do sink,
disappearing ; whither, from the first origin of them,
they were all doomed. For Nature is true and not a
lie. No lie you can speak or act but it will come, after
longer or shorter circulation, like a Bill drawn on
Nature's Reality, and be presented there for payment,—
with the answer, *No effects*. Pity only that it often
had so long a circulation : that the original forger were
so seldom he who bore the final smart of it ! Lies, and
the burden of evil they bring, are passed on ; shifted
from back to back, and from rank to rank ; and so
land ultimately on the dumb lowest rank, who with
spade and mattock, with sore heart and empty wallet,
daily come in *contact* with reality, and can pass the
cheat no further.

Observe nevertheless how, by a just compensating
law, if the lie with its burden (in this confused whirlpool
of Society) sinks and is shifted ever downwards, then
in return the distress of it rises ever upwards and
upwards. Whereby, after the long pining and demi-
starvation of those Twenty Millions, a Duke de Coigny
and his Majesty come also to have their ' real quarrel '.
Such is the law of just Nature ; bringing, though at
long intervals, and were it only by Bankruptcy, matters
round again to the mark.

But with a Fortunatus' Purse in its pocket, through
what length of time might not almost any Falsehood
last ! Your Society, your Household, practical or
spiritual Arrangement, is untrue, unjust, offensive to the
eye of God and man. Nevertheless its hearth is warm,
its larder well replenished : the innumerable Swiss of
Heaven, with a kind of natural loyalty, gather round it ;
will prove, by pamphleteering, musketeering, that it is
a truth ; or if not an unmixed (unearthly, impossible)
Truth, then better, a wholesomely attempered one (as
wind is to the shorn lamb), and works well. Changed
outlook, however, when purse and larder grow empty !

Was your Arrangement so true, so accordant to Nature's ways, then how, in the name of wonder, has Nature, with her infinite bounty, come to leave it famishing there ? To all men, to all women and all children, it is now indubitable that your Arrangement was *false*. Honour to Bankruptcy ; ever righteous on the great scale, though in detail it is so cruel ! Under all Falsehoods it works, unweariedly mining. No Falsehood, did it rise heaven-high and cover the world, but Bankruptcy, one day, will sweep it down, and make us free of it.

CHAPTER II

CONTROLLER CALONNE

Under such circumstances of *tristesse*, obstruction and sick languor, when to an exasperated Court it seems as if fiscal genius had departed from among men, what apparition could be welcomer than that of M. de Calonne ?* Calonne, a man of indisputable genius ; even fiscal genius, more or less ; of experience both in managing Finance and Parlements, for he has been Intendant at Metz, at Lille ; King's Procureur at Douai. A man of weight, connected with the moneyed classes ; of unstained name,—if it were not some peccadillo (of showing a Client's Letter) in that old D'Aiguillon-Lachalotais business, as good as forgotten now. He has kinsmen of heavy purse, felt on the Stock Exchange. Our Foulons, Berthiers*intrigue for him :—old Foulon, who has now nothing to do but intrigue ; who is known and even seen to be what they call a scoundrel ; but of unmeasured wealth ; who, from Commissariat-clerk which he once was, may hope, some think, if the game go right, to be Minister himself one day.

Such propping and backing has M. de Calonne ; and then intrinsically such qualities ! Hope radiates from his face ; persuasion hangs on his tongue. For all

straits he has present remedy, and will make the world
roll on wheels before him. On the 3rd of November
1783, the Œil-de-Bœuf rejoices in its new Controller-
General. Calonne also shall have trial ; Calonne also,
in his way, as Turgot and Necker had done in theirs,
shall forward the consummation ; suffuse, with one
other flush of brilliancy, our now too leaden-coloured
Era of Hope, and wind it up—into fulfilment.

Great, in any case, is the felicity of the Œil-de-
Bœuf. Stinginess has fled from these royal abodes :
suppression ceases ; your Besenval may go peaceably
to sleep, sure that he shall awake unplundered. Smiling
Plenty, as if conjured by some enchanter, has returned ;
scatters contentment from her new-flowing horn. And
mark what suavity of manners ! A bland smile distinguishes our Controller : to all men he listens with an air
of interest, nay of anticipation ; makes their own wish
clear to themselves, and grants it ; or at least, grants
conditional promise of it. ' I fear this is a matter of
difficulty ', said her Majesty.—' Madame ', answered
the Controller, ' if it is but difficult, it is done ; if it is
impossible, it shall be done (*se fera*) '. A man of such
' facility ' withal. To observe him in the pleasure-
vortex of society, which none partakes of with more
gusto, you might ask, When does he work ? And yet
his work, as we see, is never behindhand ; above all,
the fruit of his work : ready-money. Truly a man of
incredible facility ; facile action, facile elocution, facile
thought : how, in mild suasion, philosophic depth
sparkles up from him, as mere wit and lambent spright-
liness ; and in her Majesty's Soirées, with the weight
of a world lying on him, he is the delight of men and
women ! By what magic does he accomplish miracles ?
By the only true magic, that of genius. Men name him
'*the* Minister ' ; as indeed, when was there another such?
Crooked things are become straight by him, rough
places plain ;* and over the Œil-de-Bœuf there rests an
unspeakable sunshine.

Nay, in seriousness, let no man say that Calonne

had not genius : genius for Persuading ; before all
things, for Borrowing. With the skilfullest judicious
appliances of underhand money, he keeps the Stock-
Exchanges flourishing : so that Loan after Loan is filled
up as soon as opened. ' Calculators likely to know ' [1]
have calculated that he spent, in extraordinaries, ' at
the rate of one million daily ' ; which indeed is some
fifty thousand pounds sterling : but did he not procure
something with it ; namely peace and prosperity, for
the time being ?   Philosophedom grumbles and croaks ;
buys, as we said, 80,000 copies of Necker's new Book :
but Nonpareil Calonne, in her Majesty's Apartment,
with the glittering retinue of Dukes, Duchesses, and
mere happy admiring faces, can let Necker and Philosophedom croak.

The misery is, such a time cannot last ! Squander-
ing, and Payment by Loan is no way to choke a Deficit.
Neither is oil the substance for quenching conflagrations ;—alas no, only for assuaging them, *not* permanently ! To the Nonpareil himself, who wanted not
insight, it is clear at intervals, and dimly certain at all
time, that his trade is by nature temporary, growing
daily more difficult ; that changes incalculable lie at no
great distance.   Apart from financial Deficit, the world
is wholly in such a newfangled humour ; all things
working loose from their old fastenings, towards new
issues and combinations.   There is not a dwarf *jokei*,
a cropt Brutus'-head, or Anglomaniac horseman rising
on his stirrups, that does not betoken change.   But
what then ? The day, in any case, passes pleasantly;
for the morrow, if the morrow come, there shall be
counsel too.   Once mounted (by munificence, suasion,
magic of genius) high enough in favour with the Œil-
de-Bœuf, with the King, Queen, Stock-Exchange, and
so far as possible with all men, a Nonpareil Controller
may hope to go careering through the Inevitable, in
some unimagined way, as handsomely as another.

At all events, for these three miraculous years, it

[1] Besenval, iii. 216.

has been expedient heaped on expedient : till now, with
such cumulation and height, the pile topples perilous.
And here has this world's-wonder of a Diamond Necklace brought it at last to the clear verge of tumbling.
Genius in that direction can no more : mounted high
enough, or not mounted, we must fare forth.   Hardly
is poor Rohan, the Necklace-Cardinal, safely bestowed
in the Auvergne Mountains, Dame de la Motte* (un-
safely) in the Salpêtrière, and that mournful business
hushed up, when our sanguine Controller once more
astonishes the world.   An expedient, unheard of for
these hundred and sixty years, has been propounded ;
and, by dint of suasion (for his light audacity, his hope
and eloquence are matchless) has been got adopted,—
Convocation of the Notables.

Let notable persons, the actual or virtual rulers of
their districts, be summoned from all sides of France ;
let a true tale, of his Majesty's patriotic purposes and
wretched pecuniary impossibilities, be suasively told
them ; and then the question put : What are we to
do ?   Surely to adopt healing measures ; such as the
magic of genius will unfold ; such as, once sanctioned
by Notables, all Parlements and all men must, with
more or less reluctance, submit to.

CHAPTER III

THE NOTABLES

HERE then is verily a sign and wonder ; visible to
the whole world ; bodeful of much.   The Œil-de-Bœuf
dolorously grumbles ; were we not well as we stood,—
quenching conflagrations by oil ?   Constitutional Philosophedom starts with joyful surprise ; stares eagerly
what the result will be.   The public creditor, the public
debtor, the whole thinking and thoughtless public have
their several surprises, joyful or sorrowful.   Count
Mirabeau, who has got his matrimonial and other Law-

suits huddled up, better or worse ; and works now in the
dimmest element at Berlin ; compiling *Prussian Monarchies*, Pamphlets *On Cagliostro* ; writing, with pay,
but not with honourable recognition, innumerable
Dispatches for his Government,—scents or descries
richer quarry from afar. He, like an eagle or vulture,
or mixture of both, preens his wings for flight homewards.[1]

M. de Calonne has stretched out an Aaron's Rod
over France ; miraculous ; and is summoning quite
unexpected things. Audacity and hope alternate in
him with misgivings ; though the sanguine-valiant
side carries it. Anon he writes to an intimate friend,
' *Je me fais pitié à moi-même* (I am an object of pity
to myself) ' ; anon, invites some dedicating Poet or
Poetaster to sing ' this Assembly of the Notables, and
the Revolution that is preparing '.[2] Preparing indeed ;
and a matter to be sung,—only not till we have *seen* it,
and what the issue of it is. In deep obscure unrest,
all things have so long gone rocking and swaying : will
M. de Calonne, with this his alchemy of the Notables,
fasten all together again, and get new revenues ? Or
wrench all asunder ; so that it go no longer rocking and
swaying, but clashing and colliding ?

Be this as it may, in the bleak short days, we behold men of weight and influence threading the great
vortex of French Locomotion, each on his several line,
from all sides of France, towards the Château of Versailles : summoned thither *de par le roi*. There, on the
22nd day of February 1787, they have met, and got
installed : Notables to the number of a Hundred and
Thirty-seven, as we count them name by name : [3] add
Seven Princes of the Blood, it makes the round Gross
of Notables. Men of the sword, men of the robe ;
Peers, dignified Clergy, Parlementary Presidents :
divided into Seven Boards (*Bureaus*) ; under our Seven

[1] Fils Adoptif, Mémoires de Mirabeau, t. iv. livv. 4 et 5.
[2] Biographie Universelle, § Calonne (by Guizot).
[3] Lacretelle, iii. 286.   Montgaillard, i. 347.

Princes of the Blood, Monsieur, D'Artois, Penthièvre, and the rest; among whom let not our new Duke d'Orléans (for, since 1785, he is Chartres no longer) be forgotten. Never yet made Admiral, and now turning the corner of his fortieth year, with spoiled blood and prospects; half-weary of a world which is more than half-weary of him, Monseigneur's future is most questionable. Not in illumination and insight, not even in conflagration; but, as was said; 'in dull smoke and ashes of outburnt sensualities', does he live and digest. Sumptuosity and sordidness; revenge, life-weariness, ambition, darkness, putrescence; and, say, in sterling money, three hundred thousand a year,—were this poor Prince once to burst loose from his Court-moorings, to what regions, with what phenomena, might he not sail and drift! Happily as yet he 'affects to hunt daily'; sits there, since he must sit, presiding that Bureau of his, with dull moon-visage, dull glassy eyes, as if it were a mere tedium to him.

We observe finally, that Count Mirabeau has actually arrived. He descends from Berlin, on the scene of action; glares into it with flashing sun-glance; discerns that it will do nothing for him. He had hoped these Notables might need a Secretary. They do need one; but have fixed on Dupont de Nemours; a man of smaller fame, but then of better ;—who indeed, as his friends often hear, labours under this complaint, surely not a universal one, of having 'five kings to correspond with'.[1] The pen of a Mirabeau cannot become an official one; nevertheless it remains a pen. In defect of Secretaryship, he sets to denouncing Stockbrokerage (*Dénonciation de l'Agiotage*); testifying, as his wont is, by loud bruit, that he is present and busy; —till, warned by friend Talleyrand,* and even by Calonne himself underhand, that 'a seventeenth *Lettre-de-Cachet* may be launched against him', he timefully flits over the marches.

And now, in stately royal apartments, as Pictures

[1] Dumont, Souvenirs sur Mirabeau (Paris, 1832), p. 20.

of that time still represent them, our hundred and
forty-four Notables sit organized ; ready to hear and
consider.   Controller Calonne is dreadfully behindhand
with his speeches, his preparatives ; however the man's
' facility of work ' is known to us.   For freshness of
style, lucidity, ingenuity, largeness of view, that opening Harangue of his was unsurpassable :—had not the
subject-matter been so appalling.   A Deficit, concerning
which accounts vary, and the Controller's own account
is not unquestioned ; but which all accounts agree in
representing as ' enormous '.   This is the epitome of our
Controller's difficulties : and then his means ?   Mere
Turgotism ; for thither, it seems, we must come at last :
Provincial Assemblies ; new Taxation ; nay, strangest
of all, new Landtax, what he calls *Subvention Terri-*
toriale, from which neither Privileged nor Unprivileged,
Noblemen, Clergy, nor Parlementeers, shall be exempt !

Foolish enough !   These Privileged Classes have
been used to tax ; levying toll, tribute and custom, at
all hands, while a penny was left : but to be themselves
taxed ?   Of such Privileged persons, meanwhile, do
these Notables, all but the merest fraction, consist.
Headlong Calonne had given no heed to the ' composition ', or judicious packing of them ; but chosen such
Notables as were really notable ; trusting for the issue
to offhand ingenuity, good fortune, and eloquence that
never yet failed.   Headlong Controller-General !   Eloquence can do much, but not all.   Orpheus,* with eloquence grown rhythmic, musical (what we call Poetry),
drew iron tears from the cheek of Pluto : but by what
witchery of rhyme or prose wilt thou, from the pocket
of Plutus, draw gold ?

Accordingly, the storm that now rose and began to
whistle round Calonne, first in these Seven Bureaus,
and then on the outside of them, awakened by them,
spreading wider and wider over all France, threatens to
become unappeasable.   A Deficit so enormous !   Mis-
management, profusion is too clear.   Peculation itself
is hinted at ; nay, Lafayette and others go so far as to
speak it out, with attempts at proof.   The blame of his

Deficit our brave Calonne, as was natural, had endeavoured to shift from himself on his predecessors ; not
excepting even Necker. But now Necker vehemently
denies ; whereupon an ' angry Correspondence ', which
also finds its way into print.

In the Œil-de-Bœuf, and her Majesty's private
Apartments, an eloquent Controller, with his ' Madame,
if it is but difficult ', had been persuasive : but, alas,
the cause is now carried elsewhither. Behold him,
one of these sad days, in Monsieur's Bureau ; to which
all the other Bureaus have sent deputies. He is standing at bay : alone ; exposed to an incessant fire of
questions, interpellations, objurgations, from those
' hundred and thirty-seven ' pieces of logic-ordnance,—
what we may well call *bouches à feu*, fire-mouths literally ! Never, according to Besenval, or hardly ever,
had such display of intellect, dexterity, coolness, suasive
eloquence, been made by man. To the raging play of
so many fire-mouths he opposes nothing angrier than
light-beams, self-possession and fatherly smiles. With
the imperturbablest bland clearness, he, for five hours
long, keeps answering the incessant volley of fiery
captious questions, reproachful interpellations ; in
words prompt as lightning, quiet as light. Nay, the
cross-fire too : such side-questions and incidental interpellations as, in the heat of the main-battle, he (having
only one tongue) could not get answered ; these also
he takes up, at the first slake ; answers even these.[1]
Could blandest suasive eloquence have saved France,
she were saved.

Heavy-laden Controller ! In the Seven Bureaus
seems nothing but hindrance : in Monsieur's Bureau,
a Loménie de Brienne, Archbishop of Toulouse, with
an eye himself to the Controllership, stirs up the Clergy ;
there are meetings, underground intrigues. Neither
from without anywhere comes sign of help or hope,
For the Nation (where Mirabeau is now, with stentor-
lungs, ' denouncing Agio ') the Controller has hitherto

---

[1] Besenval, iii. 196,

done nothing, or less.   For Philosophedom he has done
as good as nothing,—sent out some scientific Lapérouse,
or the like : and is he not in ' angry correspondence '
with its Necker ?   The very Œil-de-Bœuf looks questionable ; a falling Controller has no friends.   Solid M.
de Vergennes, who with his phlegmatic judicious punc-
tuality might have kept down many things, died the
very week before these sorrowful Notables met.   And
now a Seal-keeper, *Garde-des-Sceaux* Miroménil is
thought to be playing the traitor ; spinning plots for
Loménie-Brienne ! Queen's-Reader Abbé de Vermond,
unloved individual, was Brienne's creature, the work of
his hands from the first : it may be feared the backstairs
passage is open, the ground getting mined under our
feet.   Treacherous Garde-des-Sceaux Miroménil, at
least, should be dismissed ; Lamoignon, the eloquent
Notable, a staunch man, with connexions, and even ideas,
Parlement-President yet intent on reforming Parlements, were not he the right Keeper ?   So, for one,
thinks busy Besenval ; and, at dinner-table, rounds the
same into the Controller's ear,—who always, in the
intervals of landlord-duties, listens to him as with
charmed look, but answers nothing positive.[1]

Alas, what to answer ?   The force of private intrigue, and then also the force of public opinion, grows
so dangerous, confused ! Philosophedom sneers aloud,
as if its Necker already triumphed.   The gaping
populace gapes over Wood-cuts or Copper-cuts ; where,
for example, a Rustic is represented convoking the
Poultry of his barnyard, with this opening address :
' Dear animals, I have assembled you to advise me
what sauce I shall dress you with ' ; to which a Cock
responding, ' We don't want to be eaten ', is checked
by ' You wander from the point (*Vous vous écartez
de la question*) '.[2]   Laughter and logic ; ballad-singer,
pamphleteer ; epigram and caricature : what wind of
public opinion is this,—as if the Cave of the Winds

---

[1] Besenval, iii. 203.
[2] Republished in the Musée de la Caricature (Paris, 1834).

were bursting loose! At nightfall, President Lamoignon
steals over to the Controller's; finds him ' walking with
large strides in his chamber, like one out of himself '.[1]
With rapid confused speech the Controller begs M. de
Lamoignon to give him ' an advice '. Lamoignon candidly answers that, except in regard to his own anticipated Keepership, unless that would prove remedial, he
really cannot take upon him to advise.

' On the Monday after Easter ', the 9th of April
1787, a date one rejoices to verify, for nothing can
excel the indolent falsehood of these *Histoires* and
Mémoires,—' On the Monday after Easter, as I, Besenval, was riding towards Romainville to the Maréchal
de Ségur's, I met a friend on the Boulevards, who told
me that M. de Calonne was out. A little further on
came M. the Duke d'Orléans, dashing towards me,
head to the wind ' (trotting *à l'Anglaise*) ' and confirmed
the news '.[2] It is true news. Treacherous Garde-des-
Sceaux Miroménil is gone, and Lamoignon is appointed
in his room : but appointed for his own profit only,
not for the Controller's : ' next day ' the Controller
also has had to move. A little longer he may linger
near ; be seen among the money-changers, and even
' working in the Controller's office ', where much lies
unfinished : but neither will that hold. Too strong
blows and beats this tempest of public opinion, of
private intrigue, as from the Cave of all the Winds ;
and blows him (higher Authority giving sign) out of
Paris and France,—over the horizon, into Invisibility,
or outer Darkness.

Such destiny the magic of genius could not for ever
avert. Ungrateful Œil-de-Bœuf! did he not miraculously rain gold manna on you ; so that, as a Courtier
said, ' All the world held out its hand, and I held out
my hat',—for a time ? Himself is poor ; penniless,
had not a ' Financier's widow in Lorraine ' offered him,
though he was turned of fifty, her hand and the rich
purse it held. Dim henceforth shall be his activity,

---

[1] Besenval, iii. 209.   [2] Ibid. iii. 211.

though unwearied: Letters to the King, Appeals,
Prognostications; Pamphlets (from London), written
with the old suasive facility; which however do not
persuade. Luckily his widow's purse fails not. Once,
in a year or two, some shadow of him shall be seen
hovering on the Northern Border, seeking election as
National Deputy; but be sternly beckoned away.
Dimmer then, far-borne over utmost European lands,
in uncertain twilight of diplomacy, he shall hover,
intriguing for ' Exiled Princes ', and have adventures;
be overset into the Rhine-stream and half-drowned,
nevertheless save his papers dry. Unwearied, but in
vain! In France he works miracles no more; shall
hardly return thither to find a grave. Farewell, thou
facile sanguine Controller-General, with thy light rash
hand, thy suasive mouth of gold: worse men there have
been, and better; but to thee also was allotted a task,
—of raising the wind, and the winds; and thou hast
done it.

But now, while Ex-Controller Calonne flies storm-
driven over the horizon, in this singular way, what has
become of the Controllership? It hangs vacant, one
may say; extinct, like the Moon in her vacant interlunar
cave.* Two preliminary shadows, poor M. Fourqueux,
poor M. Villedeuil, do hold, in quick succession, some
simulacrum of it,[1]—as the new Moon will sometimes
shine out with a dim preliminary old one in her arms.
Be patient, ye Notables! An actual new Controller
is certain, and even ready; were the indispensable
manœuvres but gone through. Long-headed Lamoignon, with Home-Secretary Breteuil, and Foreign Secretary Montmorin have exchanged looks; let these three
once meet and speak. Who is it that is strong in the
Queen's favour, and the Abbé de Vermond's? That
is a man of great capacity? Or at least that has
struggled, these fifty years, to have it thought great;
now, in the Clergy's name, demanding to have Protestant

---

[1] Besenval, iii. 225,

death-penalties ' put in execution ' ; now flaunting it
in the Œil-de-Bœuf, as the gayest man-pleaser and
woman-pleaser ; gleaning even a good word from Philosophedom and your Voltaires and D'Alemberts? That
has a party ready-made for him in the Notables ?—
Loménie de Brienne, Archbishop of Toulouse ! answer
all the three, with the clearest instantaneous concord ;
and rush off to propose him to the King ; ' in such
haste', says Besenval, ' that M. de Lamoignon had to
borrow a *simarre* ', seemingly some kind of cloth apparatus necessary for that.[1]

Loménie-Brienne, who had all his life ' felt a kind
of predestination for the highest offices ', has now therefore obtained them.   He presides over the Finances ;
he shall have the title of Prime Minister itself, and the
effort of his long life be realized.   Unhappy only that it
took such talent and industry to *gain* the place ; that
to *qualify* for it hardly any talent or industry was left
disposable !   Looking now into his inner man, what
qualification he may have, Loménie beholds, not without astonishment, next to nothing but vacuity and
possibility.   Principles or methods, acquirement outward or inward (for his very body is wasted, by hard
tear and wear) he finds none; not so much as a plan, even
an unwise one.   Lucky, in these circumstances, that
Calonne has had a plan !   Calonne's plan was gathered
from Turgot's and Necker's by compilation ; shall become Loménie's by adoption.   Not in vain has Loménie
studied the working of the British Constitution ; for he
professes to have some Anglomania, of a sort.   Why, in
that free country, does one Minister, driven out by Parliament, vanish from his King's presence, and another
enter, borne in by Parliament ?[2]   Surely not for mere
change (which is ever wasteful) ; but that all men may
have share of what is going ; and so the strife of Freedom indefinitely prolong itself, and no harm be done.

[1] Besenval, iii. 224.

[2] Montgaillard, Histoire de France, i. 410-7.

The Notables, mollified by Easter festivities, by the sacrifice of Calonne, are not in the worst humour. Already his Majesty, while the ' interlunar shadows ' were in office, had held session of Notables ; and from his throne delivered promissory conciliatory eloquence: 'the Queen stood waiting at a window, till his carriage came back ; and Monsieur from afar clapped hands to her ', in sign that all was well.[1] It has had the best effect ; if such do but last. Leading Notables meanwhile can be ' caressed ' ; Brienne's new gloss, Lamoignon's long head will profit somewhat ; conciliatory eloquence shall not be wanting. On the whole, however, is it not undeniable that this of ousting Calonne and adopting the plans of Calonne, is a measure which, to produce its best effect, should be looked at from a certain distance, cursorily ; not dwelt on with minute near scrutiny ? In a word, that no service the Notables could now do were so obliging as, in some handsome manner, to—take themselves away ? Their ' Six Propositions' about Provisional Assemblies, suppression of *Corvées* and such like, can be accepted without criticism. The *Subvention* or Landtax, and much else, one must glide hastily over ; safe nowhere but in flourishes of conciliatory eloquence. Till at length, on this 25th of May, year 1787, in solemn final session, there bursts forth what we can call an explosion of eloquence ; King, Loménie, Lamoignon and retinue taking up the successive strain ; in harangues to the number of ten, besides his Majesty's, which last the livelong day ;—whereby, as in a kind of choral anthem, or bravura peal, of thanks, praises, promises, the Notables are, so to speak, organed out, and dismissed to their respective places of abode. They had sat, and talked, some nine weeks : they were the first Notables since Richelieu's, in the year 1626.

By some Historians, sitting much at their ease, in the safe distance, Loménie has been blamed for this

---

[1] Besenval, iii. 220.

dismissal of his Notables : nevertheless it was clearly
time. There are things, as we said, which should not
be dwelt on with minute close scrutiny : over hot coals
you cannot glide too fast. In these Seven Bureaus,
where no work could be done, unless talk were work,
the questionablest matters were coming up. Lafayette,
for example, in Monseigneur d'Artois' Bureau, took
upon him to set forth more than one deprecatory
oration about *Lettres-de-Cachet*, Liberty of the Subject,
Agio, and such like ; which Monseigneur endeavouring
to repress, was answered that a Notable being summoned to speak his opinion must speak it.[1]

Thus too his Grace the Archbishop of Aix perorating once, with a plaintive pulpit-tone, in these words :
' Tithe, that free-will offering of the piety of Chris-
tians '—' Tithe', interrupted Duke la Rochefoucault,
with the cold business-manner he has learned from the
English, ' that free-will offering of the piety of Chris-
tians ; on which there are now forty thousand law-suits
in this realm '. [2] Nay, Lafayette, bound to speak his
opinion, went the length, one day, of proposing to convoke a ' National Assembly '. ' You demand States-
General ? '* asked Monseigneur with an air of minatory
surprise.—' Yes, Monseigneur ; and even better than
that '.—' Write it ', said Monseigneur to the Clerks.[3]—
Written accordingly it is ; and what is more, will be
acted by and by.

---

[1] Montgaillard, i. 360.
[2] Dumont, Souvenirs sur Mirabeau, p. 21.
[3] Toulongeon, Histoire de France depuis la Révolution
de 1789 (Paris, 1803), i. app. 4.

CHAPTER IV

LOMÉNIE'S EDICTS

THUS then have the Notables returned home ; carrying, to all quarters of France, such notions of deficit, decrepitude, distraction ; and that States-General will cure it, or will not cure it but kill it. Each Notable, we may fancy, is as a funereal torch ; disclosing hideous abysses, better left hid ! The unquietest humour possesses all men; ferments, seeks issue, in pamphleteering, caricaturing, projecting, declaiming ; vain jangling*of thought, word and deed.

It is Spiritual Bankruptcy, long tolerated ; verging now towards Economical Bankruptcy, and become intolerable. For from the lowest dumb rank, the inevitable misery, as was predicted, has spread upwards. In every man is some obscure feeling that his position, oppressive or else oppressed, is a false one : all men, in one or the other acrid dialect, as assaulters or as defenders, must give vent to the unrest that is in them. Of such stuff national well-being, and the glory of rulers, is not made. O Loménie, what a wild-heaving, waste-looking, hungry and angry world hast thou, after lifelong effort, got promoted to take charge of !

Loménie's first Edicts are mere soothing ones : creation of Provincial Assemblies, ' for apportioning the imposts ', when we get any ; suppression of *Corvées* or statute-labour ; alleviation of *Gabelle*. Soothing measures, recommended by the Notables; long clamoured for by all liberal men. Oil cast on the waters has been known to produce a good effect. Before venturing with great essential measures, Loménie will see this singular ' swell of the public mind ' abate somewhat.

Most proper, surely. But what if it were not a swell of the abating kind ? There are swells that come of upper tempest and wind-gust. But again there are swells that come of subterranean pent wind, some say ; and even of inward decomposition, of decay that has become self-combustion :—as when, according to Neptuno-Plutonic*Geology, the World is all decayed down into due attritus of this sort; and shall now be *exploded*, and new-made ! These latter abate not by oil.—The fool says in his heart,* How shall not to-morrow be as yesterday :* as all days,—which were once to-morrows ? The wise man, looking on this France, moral, intellectual, economical, sees, ' in short, all the symptoms he has ever met with in history',—*un*abateable by soothing Edicts.

Meanwhile, abate or not, cash must be had ; and for that, quite another sort of Edicts, namely ' bursal ' or fiscal ones. How easy were fiscal Edicts, did you know for certain that the Parlement of Paris would what they call ' register ' them ! Such right of registering, properly of mere *writing down*, the Parlement has got by old wont ; and, though but a Law-Court, can remonstrate, and higgle considerably about the same. Hence many quarrels ; desperate Maupeou devices, and victory and defeat ;—a quarrel now near forty years long. Hence fiscal Edicts, which otherwise were easy enough, become such problems. For example, is there not Calonne's *Subvention Territoriale*, universal, unexempting Landtax ; the sheet-anchor of Finance ? Or, to show, so far as possible, that one is not without original finance talent, Loménie himself can devise an *Edit du Timbre* or Stamptax,—borrowed also, it is true ; but then from America : may it prove luckier in France than there !

France has her resources : nevertheless, it cannot be denied, the aspect of that Parlement is questionable. Already among the Notables, in that final symphony of dismissal, the Paris President had an ominous tone. Adrien Duport, quitting magnetic sleep, in this agitation of the world, threatens to rouse himself into preternatural wakefulness. Shallower but also louder, there is magnetic D'Espréménil, with his tropical heat (he was born at Madras); with his dusky confused violence; holding of Illumination, Animal Magnetism, Public Opinion, Adam Weisshaupt,* Harmodius and Aristogiton,* and all manner of confused violent things: of whom can come no good. The very Peerage is infected with the leaven. Our Peers have, in too many cases, laid aside their frogs, laces, bag-wigs; and go about in English costume, or ride rising in their stirrups, —in the most headlong manner; nothing but insubordination, eleutheromania, confused unlimited opposition in their heads. Questionable: not to be ventured upon, if we had a Fortunatus' Purse! But Loménie has waited all June, casting on the waters what oil he had; and now, betide as it may, the two Finance Edicts must out. On the 6th of July, he forwards his proposed Stamptax and Landtax to the Parlement of Paris; and, as if putting his own leg foremost, not his borrowed Calonne's-leg,—places the Stamptax first in order.

Alas, the Parlement will *not* register: the Parlement demands instead a ' state of the expenditure ', a ' state of the contemplated reductions '; ' states ' enough; which his Majesty must decline to furnish! Discussions arise; patriotic eloquence: the Peers are summoned. Does the Nemean Lion* begin to bristle? Here surely is a duel, which France and the Universe may look upon: with prayers; at lowest, with curiosity and bets. Paris stirs with new animation. The outer courts of the Palais de Justice roll with unusual crowds, coming and going; their huge outer hum mingles with the clang of patriotic eloquence within, and gives vigour to it. Poor Loménie gazes from the distance, little comforted; has his invisible emissaries flying to and fro, assiduous, without result.

So pass the sultry dog-days, in the most electric manner; and the whole month of July. And still, in the Sanctuary of Justice, sounds nothing but Harmodius-Aristogiton eloquence, environed with the hum of crowding Paris; and no registering accomplished, and no ' states ' furnished. ' States ? ' said a lively Parlementeer: ' Messieurs, the states that should be fur-

nished us, in my opinion are the States-General '.
On which timely joke there follow cachinnatory buzzes
of approval. What a word to be spoken in the Palais
de Justice! Old D'Ormesson (the Ex-Controller's
uncle) shakes his judicious head; far enough from
laughing. But the outer courts, and Paris and France,
catch the glad sound, and repeat it; shall repeat it, and
re-echo and reverberate it, till it grow a deafening peal.
Clearly enough here is no registering to be thought of.

The pious Proverb says, ' there are remedies for all
things but death '.* When a Parlement refuses registering, the remedy, by long practice, has become
familiar to the simplest: a Bed of Justice. One complete month this Parlement has spent in mere idle
jargoning, and sound and fury;* the *Timbre* Edict not
registered, or like to be; the *Subvention* not yet so
much as spoken of. On the 6th of August let the whole
refractory Body roll out, in wheeled vehicles, as far as
the King's Château of Versailles; there shall the King,
holding his Bed of Justice,* *order* them, by his own
royal lips, to register. They may remonstrate, in an
undertone; but they must obey, lest a worse unknown
thing befall them.

It is done: the Parlement has rolled out, on royal
summons; has heard the express royal order to register. Whereupon it has rolled back again, amid the
hushed expectancy of men. And now, behold, on the
morrow, this Parlement, seated once more in its own
Palais, with ' crowds inundating the outer courts ', not
only does not register, but (O portent!) declares all
that was done on the prior day to be *null*, and the Bed
of Justice as good as a futility! In the history of
France here verily is a new feature. Nay better still,
our heroic Parlement, getting suddenly enlightened on
several things, declares that, for its part, it is incompe-
tent to register Tax-edicts at all,—having done it by
mistake, during these late centuries; that for such act
one authority only is competent: the assembled Three
Estates of the Realm!

To such length can the universal spirit of a Nation penetrate the most isolated Body-corporate: say rather, with such weapons, homicidal and suicidal, in exasperated political duel, will Bodies-corporate fight! But, in any case, is not this the real death-grapple of war and internecine duel, Greek meeting Greek; whereon men, had they even no interest in it, might look with interest unspeakable ? Crowds, as was said, inundate the outer courts: inundation of young eleu-theromaniac Noblemen in English costume, uttering audacious speeches; of Procureurs, Basoche-Clerks, who are idle in these days ; of Loungers, Newsmongers and other nondescript classes,—rolls tumultuous there. ' From three to four thousand persons', waiting eagerly to hear the *Arrêtés* (Resolutions) you arrive at within ; applauding with bravos, with the clapping of from six to eight thousand hands ! Sweet also is the meed of patriotic eloquence, when your D'Espréménil, your Fréteau, or Sabatier, issuing from his Demosthenic Olympus, the thunder being hushed for the day, is welcomed, in the outer courts, with a shout from four thousand throats ; is borne home shoulder-high ' with benedictions ', and strikes the stars with his sublime head.*

CHAPTER V

LOMÉNIE'S THUNDERBOLTS

ARISE, Loménie-Brienne : here is no case for ' Letters of Jussion ' ; for faltering or compromise. Thou seest the whole loose *fluent* population of Paris (whatsoever is not solid, and fixed to work) inundating these outer courts, like a loud destructive deluge ; the very Basoche of Lawyers' Clerks talks sedition. The lower classes, in this duel of Authority with Authority, Greek throt-tling Greek, have ceased to respect the City-Watch : Police-satellites are marked on the back with chalk (the M signifies *mouchard*, spy); they are hustled,

hunted like *ferae naturae.* Subordinate rural Tribunals
send messengers of congratulation, of adherence.
Their Fountain of Justice is becoming a Fountain of
Revolt. The Provincial Parlements look on, with intent eye, with breathless wishes, while their elder sister
of Paris does battle : the whole Twelve are of one blood
and temper; the victory of one is that of all.

Ever worse it grows : on the 10th of August, there
is ' *Plainte* ' emitted touching the ' prodigalities of
Calonne ', and permission to ' proceed ' against him.
No registering, but instead of it, denouncing : of
dilapidation, peculation ; and ever the burden of the
song, States-General ! Have the royal armories no
thunderbolt, that thou couldst, O Loménie, with red
right-hand, launch it among these Demosthenic theatrical thunder-barrels, mere resin and noise for most
part ;—and shatter, and smite them silent ? On the
night of the 14th of August, Loménie launches his
thunderbolt, or handful of them. Letters named of
the Seal (*de Cachet*), as many as needful, some six score
and odd, are delivered over night. And so, next day
betimes, the whole Parlement, once more set on wheels,
is rolling incessantly towards Troyes in Champagne ;
' escorted ', says History, ' with the blessings of all
people ' ; the very innkeepers and postilions looking
gratuitously reverent.[1] This is the 15th of August
1787.

What will not people bless ; in their extreme need !
Seldom had the Parlement of Paris deserved much
blessing, or received much. An isolated Body-corporate, which, out of old confusions (while the Sceptre
of the Sword was confusedly struggling to become
a Sceptre of the Pen), had got itself together, better
and worse, as Bodies-corporate do, to satisfy some dim
desire of the world, and many clear desires of individuals ; and so had grown, in the course of centuries, on
concession, on acquirement and usurpation, to be what

[1] A. Lameth, Histoire de l'Assemblée Constituante
(Int. 73).

we see it : a prosperous Social Anomaly, deciding Law-suits, sanctioning or rejecting Laws ; and withal dis-posing of its places and offices by sale for ready money, —which method sleek President Hénault, after medi-tation, will demonstrate to be the indifferent-best.[1]

In such a Body, existing by purchase for ready money, there could not be excess of public spirit ; there might well be excess of eagerness to divide the public spoil. Men in helmets have divided that, with swords ; men in wigs, with quill and inkhorn, do divide it : and even more hatefully these latter, if more peaceably ; for the wig-method is at once irresistibler and baser. By long experience, says Besenval, it has been found useless to sue a Parlementeer at law ; no Officer of Justice will serve a writ on one : his wig and gown are his Vulcan's-panoply,*his enchanted cloak-of-darkness.

The Parlement of Paris may account itself an unloved body ; mean, not magnanimous, on the political side. Were the King weak, always (as now) has his Parlement barked, cur-like at his heels ; with what popular cry there might be. Were he strong, it barked before his face ; hunting for him as his alert beagle. An unjust Body ; where foul influences have more than once worked shameful perversion of judgement. Does not, in these very days, the blood of murdered Lally*cry aloud for vengeance ? Baited, circumvented, driven mad like the snared lion, Valour had to sink extin-guished under vindictive Chicane. Behold him, that hapless Lally, his wild dark soul looking through his wild dark face ; trailed on the ignominious death-hurdle ; the voice of his despair choked by a wooden gag ! The wild fire-soul that has known only peril and toil ; and, for threescore years, has buffeted against Fate's obstruction and men's perfidy, like genius and courage amid poltroonery, dishonesty and commonplace; faithfully enduring and endeavouring,—O Parlement of Paris, dost thou reward it with a gibbet and a gag ? [2]

---

[1] Abrégé Chronologique, p. 975.
[2] 9th May 1766 : Biographie Universelle, § Lally.

The dying Lally bequeathed his memory to his boy ; a young Lally* has arisen, demanding redress in the name of God and man.   The Parlement of Paris does its utmost to defend the indefensible, abominable ; nay, what is singular, dusky-glowing Aristogiton d'Espréménil is the man chosen to be its spokesman in that.

Such Social Anomaly is it that France now blesses. An unclean Social Anomaly ; but in duel against another worse !   The exiled Parlement is felt to have ' covered itself with glory '.   There are quarrels in which even Satan, bringing help, were not unwelcome ; even Satan fighting stiffly, might cover himself with glory,—of a temporary sort.

But what a stir in the outer courts of the Palais, when Paris finds its Parlement trundled off to Troyes in Champagne ;   and nothing left but a few mute Keepers of Records ;   the Demosthenic thunder become extinct, the martyrs of liberty clean gone !   Confused wail and menace rises from the four thousand throats of Procureurs, Basoche-Clerks, Nondescripts, and Anglomaniac Noblesse ;   ever new idlers crowd to see and hear ; Rascality, with increasing numbers and vigour, hunts *mouchards*.   Loud whirlpool rolls through these spaces ; the rest of the City, fixed to its work, cannot yet go rolling.   Audacious placards are legible ;   in and about the Palais, the speeches are as good as seditious. Surely the temper of Paris is much changed.   On the third day of this business (18th of August), Monsieur and Monseigneur d'Artois, coming in state-carriages, according to use and wont, to have these late obnoxious *Arrêtés* and Protests ' expunged ' from the Records, are received in the most marked manner.   Monsieur, who is thought to be in opposition, is met with vivats and strewed flowers :   Monseigneur, on the other hand, with silence ;   with murmurs, which rise to hisses and groans ; nay an irreverent Rascality presses towards him in floods, with such hissing vehemence, that the Captain of the Guards has to give order, ' *Haut les armes* (Handle arms) ! '—at which thunder-word, indeed, and the flash of the clear iron, the Rascal-flood recoils, through all avenues, fast enough.[1] New features these. Indeed, as good M. de Malesherbes pertinently remarks, ' it is a quite new kind of contest this with the Parlement ' : no transitory sputter, as from collision of hard bodies ; but more like ' the first sparks of what, if not quenched, may become a great conflagration '.[2]

This good Malesherbes sees himself now again in the King's Council, after an absence of ten years : Loménie would profit if not by the faculties of the man, yet by the name he has. As for the man's opinion, it is not listened to ;—wherefore he will soon withdraw, a second time ; back to his books and his trees. In such King's Council what can a good man profit ? Turgot tries it not a second time : Turgot has quitted France and this Earth, some years ago ; and now cares for none of these things. Singular enough : Turgot, this same Loménie, and the Abbé Morellet were once a trio of young friends ; fellow-scholars in the Sorbonne. Forty new years have carried them severally thus far.

Meanwhile the Parlement sits daily at Troyes, calling cases ; and daily adjourns, no Procureur making his appearance to plead. Troyes is as hospitable as could be looked for : nevertheless one has comparatively a dull life. No crowds now to carry you, shoulder-high, to the immortal gods ; scarcely a Patriot or two will drive out so far, and bid you be of firm courage. You are in furnished lodgings, far from home and domestic comfort : little to do, but wander over the unlovely Champagne fields ; seeing the grapes ripen ; taking counsel about the thousand-times consulted : a prey to tedium ; in danger even that Paris may forget you. Messengers come and go : pacific Loménie is not slack in negotiating, promising ; D'Ormesson and the prudent elder Members see no good in strife.

After a dull month, the Parlement, yielding and retaining, makes truce, as all Parlements must. The

[1] Montgaillard, i. 369. Besenval, &c.
[2] Montgaillard, i. 373.

Stamptax is withdrawn: the *Subvention* Landtax is
also withdrawn; but, in its stead, there is granted,
what they call a ' Prorogation of the Second Twentieth ',
—itself a kind of Landtax, but not so oppressive to the
Influential classes; which lies mainly on the Dumb
class. Moreover, secret promises exist (on the part of
the Elders), that finances may be raised by Loan. Of
the ugly word States-General there shall be no mention.

And so, on the 20th of September, our exiled Parlement returns: D'Espréménil said, ' it went out
covered with glory, but had come back covered with
mud (*de boue*) '. Not so, Aristogiton; or if so, thou
surely art the man to clean it.

CHAPTER VI

LOMÉNIE'S PLOTS

WAS ever unfortunate Chief Minister so bested as
Loménie-Brienne ? The reins of the State fairly in his
hand these six months; and not the smallest motive-
power (of Finance) to stir from the spot with, this way
or that ! He flourishes his whip, but advances not.
Instead of ready money, there is nothing but rebellious
debating and recalcitrating.

Far is the public mind from having calmed; it goes
chafing and fuming ever worse : and in the royal coffers,
with such yearly Deficit running on, there is hardly
the colour of coin. Ominous prognostics ! Malesherbes, seeing an exhausted, exasperated France grow
hotter and hotter, talks of ' conflagration ' : Mirabeau,
without talk, has, as we perceive, descended on Paris
again, close on the rear of the Parlement,[1]—not to quit
his native soil any more.

Over the Frontiers, behold Holland invaded by
Prussia;[2] the French party oppressed, England and

[1] Fils Adoptif, Mirabeau, iv. l. 5.
[2] October 1787. Montgaillard, i. 374. Besenval, iii. 283.

the Stadtholder* triumphing : to the sorrow of War-secretary Montmorin and all men. But without money, sinews of war, as of work, and of existence itself, what can a Chief Minister do ? Taxes profit little : this of the Second Twentieth falls not due till next year ; and will then, with its ' strict valuation ', produce more controversy than cash. Taxes on the Privileged Classes cannot be got registered ; are intolerable to our sup-porters themselves : taxes on the Unprivileged yield nothing,—as from a thing drained dry more cannot be drawn. Hope is nowhere, if not in the old refuge of Loans.

To Loménie, aided by the long head of Lamoignon, deeply pondering this sea of troubles, the thought suggested itself : Why not have a Successive Loan (*Emprunt Successif*), or Loan that went on lending, year after year, as much as needful ; say, till 1792 ? The trouble of registering such Loan were the same : we had then breathing time ; money to work with, at least to subsist on. Edict of a Successive Loan must be proposed. To conciliate the Philosophes, let a liberal Edict walk in front of it, for emancipation of Protestants ; let a liberal Promise guard the rear of it, that when our Loan ends, in that final 1792, the States-General shall be convoked.

Such liberal Edict of Protestant Emancipation, the time having come for it, shall cost a Loménie as little as the ' Death-penalties to be put in execution ' did. As for the liberal Promise, of States-General, it can be fulfilled or not : the fulfilment is five good years off ; in five years much intervenes. But the registering ? Ah, truly, there is the difficulty !—However, we have that promise of the Elders, given secretly at Troyes. Judi-cious gratuities, cajoleries, underground intrigues, with old Foulon, named ' *Ame damnée*, Familiar-demon, of the Parlement ', may perhaps do the rest. At worst and lowest, the Royal Authority has resources,—which ought it not to put forth ? If it cannot realize money, the Royal Authority is as good as dead ; dead of that surest and miserablest death, inanition. Risk and

win ; without risk all is already lost ! For the rest,
as in enterprises of pith,* a touch of stratagem often
proves furthersome, his Majesty announces *a Royal
Hunt*, for the 19th of November next ; and all whom
it concerns are joyfully getting their gear ready.

Royal Hunt indeed ; but of two-legged unfeathered
game ! At eleven in the morning of that Royal-Hunt
day, 19th of November 1787, unexpected blare of trum-
peting, tumult of charioteering and cavalcading dis-
turbs the Seat of Justice : his Majesty is come, with
Garde-des-Sceaux Lamoignon, and Peers and retinue,
to hold Royal Session and have Edicts registered.
What a change, since Louis XIV entered here, in
boots ; and, whip in hand, ordered his registering to
be done,—with an Olympian look, which none durst
gainsay ; and did, without stratagem, in such unceremonious fashion, hunt as well as register ! [1] For Louis
XVI, on this day, the Registering will be enough ; if
indeed he and the day suffice for it.

Meanwhile, with fit ceremonial words, the purpose
of the royal breast is signified :—Two Edicts, for Protestant Emancipation, for Successive Loan : of both
which Edicts our trusty Garde-des-Sceaux Lamoignon
will explain the purport ; on both which a trusty
Parlement is requested to deliver its opinion, each
member having free privilege of speech. And so
Lamoignon too having perorated not amiss, and wound
up with that Promise of States-General,—the Sphere-
music of Parlementary eloquence begins. Explosive,
responsive, sphere answering sphere,* it waxes louder
and louder. The Peers sit attentive ; of diverse sentiment : unfriendly to States-General ; unfriendly to
Despotism, which cannot reward merit, and is suppressing places. But what agitates his Highness
d'Orléans ? The rubicund moonhead goes wagging ;
darker beams the copper visage, like unscoured copper ;
in the glazed eye is disquietude ; he rolls uneasy in

---

[1] Dulaure, vi. 306.

his seat, as if he meant something. Amid unutterable
satiety, has sudden new appetite, for new forbidden
fruit, been vouchsafed him ? Disgust and edacity ;
laziness that cannot rest ; futile ambition, revenge,
non-admiralship :—O, within that carbuncled skin,
what a confusion of confusions* sits bottled !

'Eight Couriers', in the course of the day, gallop
from Versailles, where Loménie waits palpitating ; and
gallop back again, not with the best news. In the
outer Courts of the Palais, huge buzz of expectation
reigns ; it is whispered the Chief Minister has lost six
votes over night. And from within, resounds nothing
but forensic eloquence, pathetic and even indignant ;
heartrending appeals to the royal clemency, that his
Majesty would please to summon States-General forthwith, and be the Saviour of France :—wherein dusky-
glowing D'Espréménil, but still more Sabatier de Cabre,
and Fréteau, since named *Commère* Fréteau (Goody
Fréteau), are among the loudest. For six mortal
hours it lasts, in this manner ; the infinite hubbub
unslackened.

And so now, when brown dusk is falling through
the windows, and no end visible, His Majesty, on hint
of Garde-des-Sceaux Lamoignon, opens his royal lips
once more to say, in brief, That he must have his Loan-
Edict registered.—Momentary deep pause !—See !
Monseigneur d'Orléans rises ; with moon-visage turned
towards the royal platform, he asks, with a delicate
graciosity of manner covering unutterable things :
'Whether it is a Bed of Justice, then, or a Royal
Session ?' Fire flashes on him from the throne and
neighbourhood : surly answer that 'it is a Session'.
In that case, Monseigneur will crave leave to remark
that Edicts cannot be registered by *order* in a Session ;
and indeed to enter, against such registry, his individual humble Protest. '*Vous êtes bien le maître* (You
will do your pleasure)', answers the King ; and thereupon, in high state, marches out, escorted by his Court-
retinue ; D'Orléans himself, as in duty bound, escorting
him, but only to the gate. Which duty done, D'Orléans

returns in from the gate ; redacts his Protest, in the
face of an applauding Parlement, an applauding France ;
and so—has *cut* his Court-moorings, shall we say ?
And will now sail and drift, fast enough, towards Chaos ?

Thou foolish D'Orléans ; Equality that art to be !
Is Royalty grown a mere wooden Scarecrow ; whereon
thou, pert scaldheaded crow, mayst alight at pleasure,
and peck ?   Not yet wholly.

Next day, a Lettre-de-Cachet sends D'Orléans to
bethink himself in his Château of Villers-Cotterets,
where, alas, is no Paris with its joyous necessaries of
life ; no fascinating indispensable Madame de Buffon,
—light wife of a great Naturalist much too old for her.
Monseigneur, it is said, does nothing but walk distractedly, at Villers-Cotterets ; cursing his stars.
Versailles itself shall hear penitent wail from him, so
hard is his doom. By a second, simultaneous Lettre-
de-Cachet, Goody Fréteau is hurled into the Stronghold of Ham, amid the Norman marshes ; by a third,
Sabatier de Cabre into Mont St. Michel, amid the
Norman quicksands. As for the Parlement, it must,
on summons, travel out to Versailles, with its Register-
Book under its arm, to have the Protest *biffé* (expunged);
not without admonition, and even rebuke. A stroke
of authority, which, one might have hoped, would quiet
matters.

Unhappily, no : it is a mere taste of the whip to
rearing coursers, which makes them rear worse ! When
a team of Twenty-five Millions begins rearing, what is
Loménie's whip ? The Parlement will nowise acquiesce
meekly ; and set to register the Protestant Edict, and
do its other work, in salutary fear of these three
Lettres-de-Cachet. Far from that, it begins questioning
Lettres-de-Cachet generally, their legality, endurability ;
emits dolorous objurgation, petition on petition to have
its three Martyrs delivered ; cannot, till that be com-
plied with, so much as think of examining the Protestant Edict, but puts it off always ' till this day week '.[1]

[1] Besenval, iii. 309.

In which objurgatory strain Paris and France joins it, or rather has preceded it; making fearful chorus. And now also the other Parlements, at length opening their mouths, begin to join; some of them, as at Grenoble and at Rennes, with portentous emphasis,— threatening, by way of reprisal, to interdict the very Tax-gatherer.[1] 'In all former contests', as Malesherbes remarks, 'it was the Parlement that excited the Public; but here it is the Public that excites the Parlement'.

CHAPTER VII

INTERNECINE

WHAT a France, through these winter months of the year 1787! The very Œil-de-Bœuf is doleful, uncertain; with a general feeling, among the Suppressed, that it were better to be in Turkey. The Wolf-hounds are suppressed, the Bear-hounds; Duke de Coigny, Duke de Polignac: in the Trianon little-heaven, her Majesty, one evening, takes Besenval's arm; asks his candid opinion. The intrepid Besenval,—having, as he hopes, nothing of the sycophant in *him*,—plainly signifies that, with a Parlement in rebellion, and an Œil-de-Bœuf in suppression, the King's Crown is in danger;—whereupon, singular to say, her Majesty, as if hurt, changed the subject, *et ne me parla plus de rien!* [2]

To whom, indeed, can this poor Queen speak! In need of wise counsel, if ever mortal was; yet beset here only by the hubbub of chaos! Her dwelling-place is so bright to the eye, and confusion and black care darkens it all. Sorrows of the Sovereign, sorrows of the woman, thick-coming sorrows environ her more and more. Lamotte, the Necklace-Countess, has in

---

[1] Weber, i. 266.   [2] Besenval, iii. 264.

these late months escaped, perhaps been suffered to
escape, from the Salpêtrière. Vain was the hope that
Paris might thereby forget her; and this ever-widening
lie, and heap of lies, subside. The Lamotte, with a V
(for *Voleuse*, Thief) branded on both shoulders, has got
to England; and will therefrom emit lie on lie; defiling
the highest queenly name: mere distracted lies; [1]
which, in its present humour, France will greedily
believe.

For the rest, it is too clear our Successive Loan is
not filling. As indeed, in such circumstances, a Loan
registered by expunging of Protests was not the likeliest to fill. Denunciation of *Lettres-de-Cachet*, of
Despotism generally, abates not: the Twelve Parlements are busy; the Twelve hundred Placarders,
Balladsingers, Pamphleteers. Paris is what, in figurative speech, they call 'flooded with pamphlets (*regorgé
de brochures*)'; flooded and eddying again. Hot
deluge,—from so many Patriot ready-writers, all at
the *fervid* or boiling point; each ready-writer, now in
the hour of eruption, going like an Iceland Geyser!
Against which what can a judicious Friend Morellet
do; a Rivarol,* an unruly Linguet (well paid for it),—
spouting *cold*!

Now also, at length, does come discussion of the
Protestant Edict: but only for new embroilment; in
pamphlet and counter-pamphlet, increasing the madness of men. Not even Orthodoxy, bedrid as she
seemed, but will have a hand in this confusion. She
once again in the shape of Abbé Lenfant, 'whom Prelates drive to visit and congratulate',—raises audible
sound from her pulpit-drum.[2] Or mark how D'Espréménil, who has his own confused way in all things,
produces at the right moment in Parlementary harangue
a pocket Crucifix, with the apostrophe: 'Will ye

[1] Mémoires justificatifs de la Comtesse de Lamotte (London, 1788). Vie de Jeanne de St. Remi Comtesse de
Lamotte, &c., &c.—See Diamond Necklace (*ut supra*).
[2] Lacretelle, iii. 343. Montgaillard, &c.

crucify him afresh ?' *Him*, O D'Espréménil, without
scruple ;—considering what poor stuff, of ivory and
filigree, *he* is made of !

To all which add only, that poor Brienne has fallen
sick ; so hard was the tear and wear of his sinful youth,
so violent, incessant is this agitation of his foolish old
age. Baited, bayed at through so many throats, his
Grace, growing consumptive, inflammatory (with
humeur de dartre), lies reduced to milk diet ; in exasperation, almost in desperation ; with ' repose ', precisely the impossible recipe, prescribed as the indispensable.[1]

On the whole, what can a poor Government do, but
once more recoil ineffectual ? The King's Treasury is
running towards the lees ; and Paris ' eddies with
a flood of pamphlets '. At all rates, let the *latter* subside a little ! D'Orléans gets back to Raincy, which
is nearer Paris and the fair frail Buffon ; finally to
Paris itself : neither are Fréteau and Sabatier banished
for ever. The Protestant Edict is registered ; to the
joy of Boissy d'Anglas and good Malesherbes : Successive Loan, all protests expunged or else withdrawn,
remains open,—the rather as few or none come to fill
it. States-General, for which the Parlement has
clamoured, and now the whole Nation clamours, will
follow ' in five years ',—if indeed not sooner. O Parlement of Paris, what a clamour was that ! ' Messieurs ',
said old D'Ormesson, ' you will get States-General, and
you will repent it '. Like the Horse in the Fable,* who,
to be avenged of his enemy, applied to the Man. The
Man mounted ; did swift execution on the enemy ;
but, unhappily, would not dismount ! Instead of five
years, let three years pass, and this clamorous Parlement shall have both seen its enemy hurled prostrate,
and been itself ridden to foundering (say rather, jugu-
lated for hide and shoes), and lie dead in the ditch.

Under such omens, however, we have reached the

spring of 1788. By no path can the King's Government find passage for itself, but is everywhere shamefully flung back. Beleagured by Twelve Rebellious Parlements, which are grown to be the organs of an angry Nation, it can advance nowhither; can accomplish nothing, obtain nothing, not so much as money to subsist on; but must sit there, seemingly, to be eaten up of Deficit.

The measure of the Iniquity,* then, of the Falsehood which has been gathering through long centuries, is nearly full? At least, that of the Misery is! From the hovels of the Twenty-five Millions, the misery, permeating upwards and forwards, as its law is, has got so far,—to the very Œil-de-Bœuf of Versailles. Man's hand, in this blind pain, is set against man :* not only the low against the higher, but the higher against each other; Provincial Noblesse is bitter against Court Noblesse; Robe against Sword; Rochet against Pen. But against the King's Government who is *not* bitter? Not even Besenval, in these days. To it all men and bodies of men are become as enemies; it is the centre whereon infinite contentions unite and clash. What new universal vertiginous movement is this; of Institutions, social Arrangements, individual Minds, which once worked co-operative; now rolling and grinding in distracted collision? Inevitable: it is the breaking up of a World-Solecism, worn out at last, down even to bankruptcy of money! And so this poor Versailles Court, as the chief or central Solecism, finds all the other Solecisms arrayed against it. Most natural! For your human Solecism, be it Person or Combination of Persons, is ever, by law of Nature, uneasy; if verging towards bankruptcy, it is even miserable :—and when would the meanest Solecism consent to blame or amend *itself*, while there remained another to amend?

These threatening signs do not terrify Loménie, much less teach him. Loménie, though of light nature, is not without courage, of a sort. Nay, have we not read of lightest creatures, trained Canary-birds, that could fly cheerfully with lighted matches, and fire

cannon; fire whole powder-magazines? To sit and die
of Deficit is no part of Loménie's plan. The evil is considerable ; but can he not remove it, can he not attack
it ? At lowest, he can attack the *symptom* of it : these
rebellious Parlements he can attack, and perhaps
remove. Much is dim to Loménie, but two things are
clear : that such Parlementary duel with Royalty is
growing perilous, nay internecine ; above all, that
money must be had. Take thought, brave Loménie ;
thou Garde-des-Sceaux Lamoignon, who hast ideas !
So often defeated, balked cruelly when the golden fruit
seemed within clutch,* rally for one other struggle. To
tame the Parlement, to fill the King's coffers : these
are now life-and-death questions.

Parlements have been tamed, more than once. Set to
perch ' on the peaks of rocks inaccessible except by
litters ', a Parlement grows reasonable. O Maupeou,
thou bold bad man, had we left thy work where it was !
—But apart from exile, or other violent methods, is
there not one method, whereby all things are tamed,
even lions ? The method of hunger ! What if the
Parlement's supplies were cut off; namely its Lawsuits !

Minor Courts, for the trying of innumerable minor
causes, might be instituted : these we could call *Grand
Bailliages*. Whereon the Parlement, shortened of its
prey, would look with yellow despair ; but the Public,
fond of cheap justice, with favour and hope. Then for
Finance, for registering of Edicts, why not, from our
own Œil-de-Bœuf Dignitaries, our Princes, Dukes,
Marshals, make a thing we could call *Plenary Court* ;
and there, so to speak, do our registering ourselves ?
Saint Louis had his Plenary Court, of Great Barons ; [1]
most useful to him : our Great Barons are still here (at
least the Name of them is still here); our necessity is
greater than his.

Such is the Loménie-Lamoignon device ; welcome
to the King's Council, as a light-beam in great darkness.
The device seems feasible, it is eminently needful : be

---

[1] Montgaillard, i. 405.

it once well executed, great deliverance is wrought.
Silent, then, and steady; now or never!—the World
shall see one other Historical Scene; and so singular
a man as Loménie de Brienne still the Stage-manager
there.

Behold, accordingly, a Home-Secretary Bréteuil
'beautifying Paris', in the peaceablest manner, in this
hopeful spring weather of 1788; the old hovels and
hutches disappearing from our Bridges: as if for the
State too there were halcyon weather, and nothing to
do but beautify. Parlement seems to sit acknowledged
victor. Brienne says nothing of Finance; or even
says, and prints, that it is all well. How is this; such
halcyon quiet; though the Successive Loan did not
fill? In a victorious Parlement, Counsellor Goeslard
de Monsabert even denounces that 'levying of the
Second Twentieth on strict valuation'; and gets decree
that the valuation shall not be strict,—not on the Privileged classes. Nevertheless Brienne endures it,
launches no Lettre-de-Cachet against it. How is this?

Smiling is such vernal weather; but treacherous,
sudden! For one thing, we hear it whispered, 'the
Intendants of Provinces have all got order to be at
their posts on a certain day'. Still more singular, what
incessant Printing is this that goes on at the King's
Château, under lock and key? Sentries occupy all
gates and windows; the Printers come not out; they
sleep in their work-rooms; their very food is handed
in to them![1] A victorious Parlement smells new
danger. D'Espréménil has ordered horses to Versailles;
prowls round that guarded Printing-Office; prying,
snuffing, if so be the sagacity and ingenuity of man may
penetrate it.

To a shower of gold most things are penetrable.
D'Espréménil descends on the lap of a Printer's Danaë,
in the shape of 'five hundred louis d'or': the Danaë's
Husband smuggles a ball of clay to her; which she
delivers to the golden Counsellor of Parlement. Kneaded

---

[1] Weber, i. 276.

within it, there stick printed proof-sheets:—by Heaven!
the royal Edict of that same self-registering *Plenary
Court*; of those *Grand Bailliages* that shall cut short
our Lawsuits! It is to be promulgated over all France
in one and the same day.

This, then, is what the Intendants were bid wait for
at their posts: this is what the Court sat hatching, as
its accursed cockatrice-egg*; and would not stir, though
provoked, till the brood were out! Hie with it,
D'Espréménil, home to Paris; convoke instantaneous
Sessions; let the Parlement, and the Earth, and the
Heavens know it.

CHAPTER VIII

LOMÉNIE'S DEATH-THROES

On the morrow, which is the 3rd of May 1788, an
astonished Parlement sits convoked; listens speechless
to the speech of D'Espréménil, unfolding the infinite
misdeed. Deed of treachery; of unhallowed darkness,
such as Despotism loves! Denounce it, O Parlement
of Paris; awaken France and the Universe; roll what
thunder-barrels of forensic eloquence thou hast: with
thee too it is verily Now or never!

The Parlement is not wanting, at such juncture. In
the hour of his extreme jeopardy, the lion first incites
himself by roaring, by lashing his sides. So here the
Parlement of Paris. On the motion of D'Espréménil,
a most patriotic Oath, of the One-and-all sort, is sworn,
with united throat;—an excellent new-idea, which, in
these coming years, shall not remain unimitated. Next
comes indomitable Declaration, almost of the rights of
man, at least of the rights of Parlement; Invocation
to the friends of French Freedom, in this and in subsequent time. All which, or the essence of all which, is
brought to paper; in a tone wherein something of
plaintiveness blends with, and tempers, heroic valour.

And thus, having sounded the storm-bell,—which Paris
hears, which all France will hear; and hurled such
defiance in the teeth of Loménie and Despotism, the
Parlement retires as from a tolerable first day's work.

But how Loménie felt to see his cockatrice-egg (so
essential to the salvation of France) broken in this premature manner, let readers fancy! Indignant he
clutches at his thunderbolts (*de Cachet*, of the Seal); and
launches two of them: a bolt for D'Espréménil; a bolt
for that busy Goeslard, whose service in the Second
Twentieth and 'strict valuation' is not forgotten.
Such bolts clutched promptly overnight, and launched
with the early new morning, shall strike agitated Paris
if not into requiescence, yet into wholesome astonishment.

Ministerial thunderbolts may be launched; but if
they do not *hit* ?   D'Espréménil and Goeslard, warned,
both of them, as is thought, by the singing of some
friendly bird, elude the Loménie Tipstaves; escape
disguised through skywindows, over roofs, to their own
Palais de Justice : the thunderbolts have *missed.* Paris
(for the buzz flies abroad) is struck into astonishment
not wholesome.   The two Martyrs of Liberty doff their
disguises ; don their long gowns : behold ! in the space
of an hour, by aid of ushers and swift runners, the Parlement, with its Counsellors, Presidents, even Peers,
sits anew assembled.   The assembled Parlement
declares that these its two Martyrs cannot be given up,
to any sublunary authority ; moreover that the 'session is permanent', admitting of no adjournment, till
pursuit of them has been relinquished.

And so, with forensic eloquence, denunciation and
protest, with couriers going and returning, the Parlement, in this state of continual explosion that shall
cease neither night nor day, waits the issue.   Awakened
Paris once more inundates those outer courts ; boils, in
floods wilder than ever, through all avenues.   Dissonant
hubbub there is ; jargon as of Babel, in the hour when
they were first smitten (as here) with mutual unintel-
ligibility, and the people had not yet dispersed !

Paris City goes through its diurnal epochs, of working and slumbering; and now, for the second time, most European and African mortals are asleep. But here, in this Whirlpool of Words, sleep falls not; the Night spreads her coverlid of Darkness over it in vain. Within is the sound of mere martyr invincibility; tempered with the due tone of plaintiveness. Without is the infinite expectant hum,—growing drowsier a little. So has it lasted for six-and-thirty hours.

But hark! through the dead of midnight, what tramp is this? Tramp as of armed men, foot and horse; Gardes Françaises, Gardes Suisses: marching hither; in silent regularity; in the flare of torchlight! There are Sappers too, with axes and crowbars: apparently, if the doors open not, they will be forced!—It is Captain D'Agoust, missioned from Versailles. D'Agoust, a man of known firmness;—who once forced Prince Condé himself, by mere incessant looking at him, to give satisfaction and fight: [1] he now, with axes and torches, is advancing on the very sanctuary of Justice. Sacrilegious; yet what help? The man is a soldier; looks merely at his orders; impassive, moves forward like an inanimate engine.

The doors open on summons, there need no axes; door after door. And now the innermost door opens; discloses the long-gowned Senators of France: a hundred and sixty-seven by tale, seventeen of them Peers; sitting there, majestic, 'in permanent session'. Were not the man military, and of cast-iron, this sight, this silence re-echoing the clank of his own boots, might stagger him! For the hundred and sixty-seven receive him in perfect silence; which some liken to that of the Roman Senate overfallen by Brennus;* some to that of a nest of coiners surprised by officers of the Police.[2] *Messieurs*, said D'Agoust, *De par le Roi!* Express order has charged D'Agoust with the sad duty of arresting two individuals: M. Duval d'Esprémenil and M. Goeslard de Monsabert. Which respectable indi-

---

[1] Weber, i. 283.   [2] Besenval, iii. 355.

viduals, as he has not the honour of knowing them, are
hereby invited, in the King's name, to surrender themselves.—Profound silence ! Buzz, which grows a murmur : ' We are all D'Espréménils ! ' ventures a voice ;
which other voices repeat. The President inquires,
Whether he will employ violence ? Captain D'Agoust,
honoured with his Majesty's commission, has to execute his Majesty's order ; would so gladly do it without
violence, will in any case do it ; grants an august
Senate space to deliberate which method *they* prefer.
And thereupon D'Agoust, with grave military courtesy,
has withdrawn for the moment.

What boots it, august Senators ? All avenues are
closed with fixed bayonets. Your Courier gallops to
Versailles, through the dewy Night ; but also gallops
back again, with tidings that the order is authentic,
that it is irrevocable. The outer courts simmer with
idle population ; but D'Agoust's grenadier-ranks stand
there as immovable floodgates : there will be no revolting to deliver you. ' Messieurs ! ' thus spoke D'Espréménil, ' when the victorious Gauls entered Rome,
which they had carried by assault, the Roman Senators,
clothed in their purple, sat there, in their curule chairs,
with a proud and tranquil countenance, awaiting
slavery or death. Such too is the lofty spectacle, which
you, in this hour, offer to the universe (*à l'univers*), after
having generously '—with much more of the like, as
can still be read.[1]

In vain, O D'Espréménil ! Here is this cast-iron
Captain D'Agoust, with his cast-iron military air, come
back. Despotism, constraint, destruction sit waving
in his plumes. D'Espréménil must fall silent ; heroically give himself up, lest worse befall. Him Goeslard
heroically imitates. With spoken and speechless
emotion, they fling themselves into the arms of their
Parlementary brethren, for a last embrace : and so
amid plaudits and plaints, from a hundred and sixty-
five throats ; amid wavings, sobbings, a whole forest-
sigh of Parlementary pathos,—they are led through

[1] Toulongeon, i. App. 20.

winding passages, to the rear-gate; where, in the grey
of the morning, two Coaches with *Exempts* stand waiting. There must the victims mount; bayonets
menacing behind. D'Espréménil's stern question to
the populace, 'Whether they have courage?' is
answered by silence. They mount, and roll; and neither the rising of the May sun (it is the 6th morning),
nor its setting shall lighten their heart: but they fare
forward continually; D'Espréménil towards the utmost
Isles of Sainte Marguerite, or Hières (supposed by some,
if that is any comfort, to be Calypso's Island);* Goeslard towards the land-fortress of Pierre-en-Cize, extant
then, near the City of Lyons.

Captain D'Agoust may now therefore look forward
to Majorship, to Commandantship of the Tuileries; [1]
—and withal vanish from History; where nevertheless
he has been fated to do a notable thing. For not only
are D'Espréménil and Goeslard safe whirling southward,
but the Parlement itself has straightway to march out:
to that also his inexorable order reaches. Gathering
up their long skirts, they file out, the whole Hundred
and Sixty-five of them, through two rows of unsympathetic grenadiers: a spectacle to gods and men.* The
people revolt not; they only wonder and grumble: also,
we remark, these unsympathetic grenadiers are *Gardes
Françaises,*—who, one day, will sympathize! In
a word, the Palais de Justice is swept clear, the doors
of it are locked; and D'Agoust returns to Versailles
with the key in his pocket,—having, as was said,
merited preferment.

As for this Parlement of Paris, now turned out to
the street, we will without reluctance leave it there.
The Beds of Justice it had to undergo, in the coming
fortnight, at Versailles, in registering, or rather refusing
to register, those new-hatched Edicts; and how it
assembled in taverns and tap-rooms there, for the
purpose of Protesting; [2] or hovered disconsolate, with
outspread skirts, not knowing where to assemble; and

[1] Montgaillard, i. 404.   [2] Weber, i. 299–303.

was reduced to lodge Protest 'with a Notary'; and
in the end, to sit still (in a state of forced 'vacation'),
and do nothing: all this, natural now, as the burying
of the dead after battle, shall not concern us. The
Parlement of Paris has as good as performed its part;
doing and misdoing, so far, but hardly further, it could
stir the world.

Loménie has removed the evil then? Not at all:
not so much as the symptom of the evil; scarcely the
twelfth part of the symptom, and exasperated the other
eleven! The Intendants of Provinces, the military
Commandants are at their posts, on the appointed 8th
of May: but in no Parlement, if not in the single one
of Douai, can these new Edicts get registered. Not
peaceable signing with ink; but browbeating, blood-
shedding, appeal to primary club-law! Against these
Bailliages, against this Plenary Court, exasperated
Themis everywhere shows face of battle: the Provincial
Noblesse are of her party, and whoever hates Loménie
and the evil time; with her Attorneys and Tipstaves,
she enlists and operates down even to the populace.
At Rennes in Brittany, where the historical Bertrand
de Moleville* is Intendant, it has passed from fatal continual duelling, between the military and gentry, to
street-fighting; to stone-volleys and musket-shot: and
still the Edicts remain unregistered. The afflicted
Bretons send remonstrance to Loménie, by a Deputation of Twelve; whom, however, Loménie, having
heard them, shuts up in the Bastille. A second larger
Deputation he meets, by his scouts, on the road, and
persuades or frightens back. But now a third largest
Deputation is indignantly sent by *many* roads: refused
audience on arriving, it meets to take counsel; invites
Lafayette and all Patriot Bretons in Paris to assist;
agitates itself; becomes the *Breton Club*, first germ of
—the *Jacobins' Society*.[1*]

[1] A. F. de Bertrand-Moleville, Mémoires Particuliers
(Paris, 1816), i. ch. i.   Marmontel, Mémoires, iv. 27.

So many as eight Parlements get exiled: [1] others might need that remedy, but it is one not always easy of appliance. At Grenoble, for instance, where a Mounier, a Barnave*have not been idle, the Parlement had due order (by *Lettres-de-Cachet*) to depart, and exile itself : but on the morrow, instead of coaches getting yoked, the alarm-bell bursts forth, ominous ; and peals and booms all day : crowds of mountaineers rush down, with axes, even with firelocks,—whom (most ominous of all !) the soldiery shows no eagerness to deal with. 'Axe over head', the poor General has to sign capitulation ; to engage that the *Lettres-de-Cachet* shall remain unexecuted, and a beloved Parlement stay where it is. Besançon, Dijon, Rouen, Bordeaux, are not what they should be ! At Pau in Bearn, where the old Commandant had failed, the new one (a Grammont, native to them) is met by a Procession of townsmen with the Cradle of Henri Quatre, the Palladium of their Town ; is conjured as he venerates this old Tortoise-shell, in which the great Henri was rocked, not to trample on Bearnese liberty ; is informed, withal, that his Majesty's cannon are all safe—in the keeping of his Majesty's faithful Burghers of Pau, and do now lie pointed on the walls there ; ready for action ! [2]

At this rate, your Grand Bailliages are like to have a stormy infancy. As for the Plenary Court, it has literally expired in the birth. The very Courtiers looked shy at it ; old Marshal Broglie* declined the honour of sitting therein. Assaulted by a universal storm of mingled ridicule and execration, [3] this poor

---

[1] Montgaillard, i. 308.

[2] Besenval, iii. 348.

[3] La Cour Plénière, héroï-tragi-comédie en trois actes et en prose ; jouée le 14 Juillet 1788, par une société d'amateurs dans un Château aux environs de Versailles ; par M. l'Abbé de Vermond, Lecteur de la Reine : A Bâville (*Lamoignon's Country-house*), et se trouve à Paris, chez la veuve Liberté, à l'enseigne de la Révolution, 1788.—La Passion, la Mort et la Résurrection du Peuple : Imprimé à Jerusalem, &c., &c.—See Montgaillard, i. 407.

Plenary Court met once, and never any second time.
Distracted country !   Contention hisses up, with forked
hydra-tongues, wheresoever poor Loménie sets his
foot. ' Let a Commandant, a Commissioner of the
King ', says Weber, ' enter one of these Parlements to
have an Edict registered, the whole Tribunal will disappear, and leave the Commandant alone with the
Clerk and First President. The Edict registered and
the Commandant gone, the whole Tribunal hastens
back, to declare such registration null. The highways
are covered with *Grand Deputations* of Parlements,
proceeding to Versailles, to have their registers expunged by the King's hand ; or returning home, to
cover a new page with a new resolution still more
audacious '.[1]

Such is the France of this year 1788. Not now
a Golden or Paper Age of Hope ; with its horse-racings,
balloon-flyings, and finer sensibilities of the heart : ah,
gone is that ; its golden effulgence paled, bedarkened
in *this* singular manner,—brewing towards preternatural weather ! For, as in that wreck-storm of *Paul
et Virginie** and Saint-Pierre,—' One huge motionless
cloud ' (say, of Sorrow and Indignation) ' girdles our
whole horizon ; streams up, hairy, copper-edged, over
a sky of the colour of lead '. Motionless itself ; but
' small clouds ' (as exiled Parlements and such like),
' parting from it, fly over the zenith, with the velocity
of birds ' :—till at last, with one loud howl, the whole
Four Winds be dashed together, and all the world
exclaim, There is the tornado ! *Tout le monde s'écria,
Voilà l'ouragan !*

For the rest, in such circumstances, the Successive
Loan, very naturally, remains unfilled ; neither, indeed,
can that impost of the Second Twentieth, at least not
on ' strict valuation ', be levied to good purpose :
' Lenders ', says Weber, in his hysterical vehement
manner, ' are afraid of ruin ; tax-gatherers of hanging '.

[1] Weber, i. 275.

The very Clergy turn away their face: convoked in
Extraordinary Assembly, they afford no gratuitous
gift (*don gratuit*),—if it be not that of advice; here too
instead of cash is clamour for States-General.[1]

O Loménie-Brienne, with thy poor flimsy mind all
bewildered, and now 'three actual cauteries' on thy
worn-out body: who art like to die of inflammation,
provocation, milk-diet, *dartres vives* and *maladie*—(best
untranslated);[2] and presidest over a France with
innumerable *actual cauteries*, which also is dying of
inflammation and the rest! Was it wise to quit the
bosky verdures of Brienne, and thy new ashlar Château
there, and what it held, for *this* ? Soft were those
shades and lawns; sweet the hymns of Poetasters, the
blandishments of high-rouged Graces:[3] and always
this and the other Philosophe Morellet (nothing deem-
ing himself or thee a questionable Sham-Priest) could
be so happy in making happy:—and also (hadst thou
known it), in the Military School hard by, there sat,
studying mathematics, a dusky-complexioned taciturn
Boy, under the name of: NAPOLEON BONAPARTE !—*
With fifty years of effort, and one final dead-lift
struggle, thou hast made an exchange! Thou hast
got thy robe of office,—as Hercules had his Nessus'-
shirt.*

On the 13th of July, of this 1788, there fell, on the
very edge of harvest, the most frightful hailstorm;
scattering into wild waste the Fruits of the Year;
which had otherwise suffered grievously by drought.
For sixty leagues round Paris especially, the ruin was
almost total.[4] To so many other evils, then, there is
to be added, that of dearth, perhaps of famine.

Some days before this hailstorm, on the 5th of July;
and still more decisively some days after it, on the 8th
of August,—Loménie announces that the States-
General are actually to meet in the following month

[1] Lameth, Assemb. Const. (Introd.) p. 87.
[2] Montgaillard, i. 424.   [3] See Mémoires de Morellet.
[4] Marmontel, iv. 30,

of May. Till after which period, this of the Plenary
Court, and the rest, shall remain *postponed*. Further,
as in Loménie there is no plan of forming or holding
these most desirable States-General, ' thinkers are invited ' to furnish him with one,—through the medium
of discussion by the public press !

What could a poor Minister do ? There are still ten
months of respite reserved : a sinking pilot will fling
out all things, his very biscuit-bags, lead, log, compass
and quadrant, before flinging out *himself*. It is on this
principle, of sinking, and the incipient delirium of
despair, that we explain likewise the almost miraculous
' invitation to thinkers '. Invitation to Chaos to be
so kind as build, out of its tumultuous drift-wood, an
Ark of Escape for him ! In these cases, not invitation
but command has usually proved serviceable.—The
Queen stood, that evening, pensive, in a window, with
her face turned towards the Garden. The *Chef de
Gobelet* had followed her with an obsequious cup of
coffee ; and then retired till it were sipped. Her
Majesty beckoned Dame Campan to approach :
' *Grand Dieu !* ' murmured she, with the cup in her
hand, ' what a piece of news will be made public to-day !
The King grants States-General '. Then raising her
eyes to Heaven (if Campan were not mistaken), she
added : ' 'Tis a first beat of the drum, of ill omen for
France. This Noblesse will ruin us '.[1]

During all that hatching of the Plenary Court, while
Lamoignon looked so mysterious, Besenval had kept
asking him one question : Whether they had cash ?
To which as Lamoignon always answered (on the faith
of Loménie) that the cash was safe, judicious Besenval
rejoined that then all was safe. Nevertheless the
melancholy fact is, that the royal coffers are almost
getting literally void of coin. Indeed, apart from all
other things, this ' invitation to thinkers ', and the
great change now at hand are enough to ' arrest the
circulation of capital ', and forward only that of

----

[1] Campan, iii. 104, 111.

pamphlets. A few thousand gold louis are now all of
money or money's worth that remains in the King's
Treasury. With another movement as of desperation,
Loménie invites Necker to come and be Controller of
Finances! Necker has other work in view than con-
trolling Finances for Loménie: with a dry refusal he
stands taciturn; awaiting his time.

What shall a desperate Prime Minister do? He has
grasped at the strongbox of the King's Theatre: some
Lottery had been set on foot for those sufferers by the
hailstorm; in his extreme necessity, Loménie lays
hands even on this.[1] To make provision for the passing day, on any terms, will soon be impossible.—On
the 16th of August, poor Weber heard, at Paris and
Versailles, hawkers, 'with a hoarse stifled tone of voice
(*voix étouffée, sourde*)', drawling and snuffling, through
the streets, an *Edict concerning Payments* (such was
the soft title Rivarol had contrived for it): all Payments at the Royal Treasury shall be made henceforth,
three-fifths in Cash, and the remaining two-fifths—in
Paper bearing interest! Poor Weber almost swooned
at the sound of these cracked voices, with their bodeful
raven-note; and will never forget the effect it had on
him.[2]

But the effect on Paris, on the world generally?
From the dens of Stock-brokerage, from the heights of
Political Economy, of Neckerism and Philosophism;
from all articulate and inarticulate throats, rise hootings and howlings, such as ear had not yet heard.
Sedition itself may be imminent! Monseigneur
d'Artois, moved by Duchess Polignac, feels called to
wait upon her Majesty; and explain frankly what crisis
matters stand in. 'The Queen wept'; Brienne himself wept;—for it is now visible and palpable that he
must go.

Remains only that the Court, to whom his manners
and garrulities were always agreeable, shall make his
fall soft. The grasping old man has already got his

---

[1] Besenval, iii. 360.   [2] Weber, i. 339.

Archbishopship of Toulouse exchanged for the richer one of Sens : and now, in this hour of pity, he shall have the Coadjutorship for his nephew (hardly yet of due age) ; a Dameship of the Palace for his niece ; a Regiment for her husband ; for himself a red Cardinal's-hat, a *Coup de Bois* (cutting from the royal forests), and on the whole ' from five to six hundred thousand livres of revenue ' : [1] finally his Brother, the Comte de Brienne, shall still continue War-minister. Buckled round with such bolsters and huge featherbeds of Promotion, let him now fall as soft as he can !

And so Loménie departs : rich if Court-titles and Money-bonds can enrich him ; but if these cannot, perhaps the poorest of all extant men. ' Hissed at by the people of Versailles ', he drives forth to Jardi ; southward to Brienne,—for recovery of health. Then to Nice, to Italy ; but shall return ; shall glide to and fro, tremulous, faint-twinkling, fallen on awful times : till the Guillotine—snuff out his weak existence ? Alas, worse : for it is *blown* out, or choked out, foully, pitiably, on the way to the Guillotine ! In his Palace of Sens, rude Jacobin Bailiffs made him drink with them from his own wine-cellars, feast with them from his own larder ; and on the morrow morning, the miserable old man lies dead. This is the end of Prime Minister, Cardinal Archbishop Loménie de Brienne. Flimsier mortal was seldom fated to do as weighty a mischief ; to have a life as despicable-envied, an exit as frightful. *Fired*, as the phrase is, with ambition : blown, like a kindled rag, the sport of winds, not this way, not that way, but of all ways, straight towards *such* a powdermine,—which he kindled ! Let us pity the hapless Loménie ; and forgive him ; and, as soon as possible, forget him.

[1] Weber, i. 341.

CHAPTER IX

BURIAL WITH BONFIRE

BESENVAL, during these extraordinary operations, of Payment two-fifths in Paper, and change of Prime Minister, had been out on a tour through his District of Command; and indeed, for the last months, peacefully drinking the waters of Contrexéville. Returning now, in the end of August, towards Moulins, and ‘knowing nothing’, he arrives one evening at Langres; finds the whole town in a state of uproar (*grande rumeur*). Doubtless some sedition; a thing too common in these days! He alights nevertheless; inquires of a ‘man tolerably dressed’, what the matter is ?— ‘How ?’ answers the man, ‘you have not heard the news ? The Archbishop is thrown out, and M. Necker is recalled; and all is going to go well !’ [1]

Such *rumeur* and vociferous acclaim has risen round M. Necker, ever from ‘that day when he issued from the Queen’s Apartments’, a nominated Minister. It was on the 24th of August: ‘the galleries of the Château, the courts, the streets of Versailles; in few hours, the Capital; and, as the news flew, all France, resounded with the cry of *Vive le Roi, Vive M. Necker !*’ [2] In Paris indeed it unfortunately got the length of ‘turbulence’. Petards, rockets go off, in the Place Dauphine, more than enough. A ‘wicker Figure (*Mannequin d'osier*)’, in Archbishop’s stole, made emblematically, three-fifths of it satin, two-fifths of it paper, is promenaded, not in silence, to the popular judgement-bar; is doomed; shriven by a mock Abbé de Vermond; then solemnly consumed by fire, at the foot of Henri’s Statue on the Pont Neuf;—with such petarding and

---

[1] Besenval, iii. 366.   [2] Weber, i. 342.

huzzaing that Chevalier Dubois and his City-watch see good finally to make a charge (more or less ineffectual); and there wanted not burning of sentry-boxes, forcing of guard-houses, and also 'dead bodies thrown into the Seine over-night', to avoid new effervescence.[1]

Parlements therefore shall return from exile: Plenary Court, Payment two-fifths in Paper have vanished; gone off in smoke, at the foot of Henri's Statue. States-General (with a Political Millennium) are now certain; nay, it shall be announced, in our fond haste, for January next: and all, as the Langres man said, is 'going to go'.

To the prophetic glance of Besenval, one other thing is too apparent: that Friend Lamoignon cannot keep his Keepership. Neither he nor War-minister Comte de Brienne! Already old Foulon, with an eye to be war-minister himself, is making underground movements. This is that same Foulon named *âme damnée du Parlement*; a man grown grey in treachery, in griping, projecting, intriguing and iniquity: who once when it was objected, to some finance-scheme of his, 'What will the people do?'—made answer, in the fire of discussion, 'The people may eat grass': hasty words, which fly abroad irrevocable,—and will send back tidings!

Foulon, to the relief of the world, fails on this occasion; and will always fail. Nevertheless it steads not M. de Lamoignon. It steads not the doomed man that he have interviews with the King; and be 'seen to return *radieux*', emitting *rays*. Lamoignon is the hated of Parlements: Comte de Brienne is Brother to the Cardinal Archbishop. The 24th of August has been; and the 14th September is not yet, when they two, as their great Principal had done, descend,—made to fall *soft*, like him.

[1] Histoire Parlementaire de la Révolution Française; ou Journal des Assemblées Nationales depuis 1789 (Paris, 1833 et seqq.), i. 253.—Lameth, Assemblée Constituante, i. (Introd.) p. 89.

And now, as if the last burden had been rolled from its heart, and assurance were at length perfect, Paris bursts forth anew into extreme jubilee. The Basoche rejoices aloud, that the foe of Parlements is fallen; Nobility, Gentry, Commonalty have rejoiced; and rejoice. Nay now, with new emphasis, Rascality itself, starting suddenly from its dim depths, will arise and do it,—for down even thither the new Political Evangel, in some rude version or other, has penetrated. It is Monday, the 14th of September, 1788: Rascality assembles anew, in great force, in the Place Dauphine; lets off petards, fires blunderbusses, to an incredible extent, without interval, for eighteen hours. There is again a wicker Figure, '*Mannequin* of osier': the centre of endless howlings. Also Necker's Portrait snatched, or purchased, from some Printshop, is borne processionally, aloft on a perch, with huzzas;—an example to be remembered.

But chiefly on the Pont Neuf, where the Great Henri, in bronze, rides sublime; there do the crowds gather. All passengers must stop, till they have bowed to the People's King, and said audibly: *Vive Henri Quatre; au diable Lamoignon!* No carriage but must stop; not even that of his Highness d'Orléans. Your coach-doors are opened: Monsieur will please to put forth his head and bow; or even, if refractory, to alight altogether, and kneel: from Madame a wave of her plumes, a smile of her fair face, there where she sits, shall suffice:—and surely a coin or two (to buy *fusées*) were not unreasonable, from the Upper Classes, friends of Liberty? In this manner it proceeds for days; in such rude horse-play,—not without kicks. The City-watch can do nothing; hardly save its own skin: for the last twelvemonth, as we have sometimes seen, it has been a kind of pastime to *hunt* the Watch. Besenval indeed is at hand with soldiers; but they have orders to avoid firing, and are not prompt to stir.

On Monday morning the explosion of petards began: and now it is near midnight of Wednesday; and the 'wicker *Mannequin*' is to be buried,—apparently in the Antique fashion. Long rows of torches, following it, move towards the Hôtel Lamoignon ; but ' a servant of mine ' (Besenval's) has run to give warning, and there are soldiers come. Gloomy Lamoignon is not to die by conflagration, or this night ;—not yet for a year, and then by gunshot (suicidal or accidental is unknown).[1] Foiled Rascality burns its ' Mannikin of osier ', under his windows ; ' tears up the sentry-box ', and rolls off : to try Brienne ; to try Dubois Captain of the Watch. Now, however, all is bestirring itself ; Gardes Françaises, Invalides, Horse-patrol : the Torch Procession is met with sharp shot, with the thrusting of bayonets, the slashing of sabres. Even Dubois makes a charge, with that Cavalry of his, and the cruelest charge of all : ' there are a great many killed and wounded '. Not without clangour, complaint ; subsequent criminal trials, and official persons dying of heartbreak ![2] So, however, with steel-besom, Rascality is brushed back into its dim depths, and the streets are swept clear.

Not for a century and half had Rascality ventured to step forth in this fashion ; not for so long, showed its huge rude lineaments in the light of day. A Wonder and new Thing : as yet gambolling merely, in awkward Brobdingnag sport, not without quaintness ; hardly in anger : yet in its huge half-vacant laugh lurks a shade of grimness,—which could unfold itself !

However, the thinkers invited by Loménie are now far on with their pamphlets : States-General, on one plan or another, will infallibly meet ; if not in January, as was once hoped, yet at latest in May. Old Duke de Richelieu, moribund in these autumn days, opens his eyes once more, murmuring, ' What would Louis Fourteenth ' (whom he remembers) ' have said ! '—then closes them again, for ever, before the evil time.

---

[1] Histoire de la Révolution par Deux Amis de la Liberté, i. 50.

[2] Ibid. p. 58.

BOOK IV

STATES-GENERAL

CHAPTER I

THE NOTABLES AGAIN

THE universal prayer, therefore, is to be fulfilled! Always in days of national perplexity, when wrong abounded and help was not, this remedy of States-General was called for; by a Malesherbes, nay by a Fénelon;[1*] even Parlements calling for it were 'escorted with blessings'. And now behold it is vouchsafed us; States-General shall verily be!

To say, let States-General be, was easy; to say in what manner they shall be, is not so easy. Since the year 1614, there have no States-General met in France, all trace of them has vanished from the living habits of men. Their structure, powers, methods of procedure, which were never in any measure fixed, have now become wholly a vague possibility. Clay which the potter may shape,* this way or that:—say rather, the twenty-five millions of potters; for so many have now, more or less, a vote in it! How to shape the States-General? There is a problem. Each Body-corporate, each privileged, each organized Class has secret hopes of its own in that matter; and also secret misgivings of its own,—for, behold, this monstrous twenty-million Class, hitherto the dumb sheep which these others had

[1] Montgaillard, i. 461.

to agree about the manner of shearing, is now also
arising with hopes! It has ceased or is ceasing to be
dumb; it speaks through Pamphlets, or at least brays
and growls behind them, in unison,—increasing wonderfully their volume of sound.

As for the Parlement of Paris, it has at once declared
for the 'old form of 1614'. Which form had this
advantage, that the *Tiers État*, Third Estate, or
Commons, figured there as a show mainly: whereby
the Noblesse and Clergy had but to avoid quarrel
between themselves, and decide unobstructed what
they thought best. Such was the clearly declared
opinion of the Paris Parlement. But, being met by
a storm of mere hooting and howling from all men,
such opinion was blown straightway to the winds; and
the popularity of the Parlement along with it,—never
to return. The Parlement's part, we said above, was
as good as played. Concerning which, however, there
is this further to be noted: the proximity of dates.
It was on the 22nd of September that the Parlement
returned from 'vacation' or 'exile in its estates'; to
be reinstalled amid boundless jubilee from all Paris.
Precisely next day it was, that this same Parlement
came to its 'clearly declared opinion': and then on
the morrow after that, you behold it 'covered with
outrages'; its outer court, one vast sibilation, and the
glory departed from it for evermore.[1] A popularity
of twenty-four hours was, in those times, no uncommon
allowance.

On the other hand, how superfluous was that invitation of Loménie: the invitation to thinkers! Thinkers
and unthinkers, by the million, are spontaneously at
their post, doing what is in them. Clubs labour:
Société Publicole; Breton Club; Enraged Club, *Club
des Enragés*. Likewise Dinner-parties in the Palais
Royal; your Mirabeaus, Talleyrands dining there, in
company with Chamforts, Morellets, with Duponts and
hot Parlementeers, not without object! For a certain

---

[1] Weber, i. 347.

*Neck*erean Lion's-provider, whom one could name,
assembles them there ; [1]—or even their own private
determination to have dinner does it.   And then as to
Pamphlets—in figurative language, ' it is a sheer
snowing of pamphlets ; like to snow up the Government thoroughfares ! '   Now is the time for Friends of
Freedom ; sane, and even insane.

Count, or self-styled Count, d'Aintrigues,*' the young
Languedocian gentleman ', with perhaps Chamfort the
Cynic to help him, rises into furor almost Pythic ;
highest, where many are high.[2]   Foolish young Languedocian gentleman ; who himself so soon, ' emigrating
among the foremost ', has to fly indignant over the
marches, with the *Contrat Social* in his pocket,—towards outer darkness, thankless intriguings, *ignis-
fatuus* hoverings, and death by the stiletto !   Abbé
Sieyes* has left Chartres Cathedral, and canonry and
book-shelves there ; has let his tonsure grow, and come
to Paris with a secular head, of the most irrefragable
sort, to ask three questions, and answer them : *What
is the Third Estate ?   All.—What has it hitherto been
in our form of government ?   Nothing.—What does it
want ?   To become Something.*

D'Orléans, for be sure he, on his way to Chaos, is in
the thick of this,—promulgates his *Deliberations* ; [3]
fathered by him, written by Laclos* of the *Liaisons
Dangereuses.*   The result of which comes out simply :
' The Third Estate is the Nation '.   On the other hand,
Monseigneur d'Artois, with other Princes of the Blood,
publishes, in solemn *Memorial* to the King, that if such
things be listened to, Privilege, Nobility, Monarchy,
Church, State and Strongbox are in danger.[4]   In

[1] Weber, i. 360.

[2] Mémoire sur les Etats-Généraux. See Montgaillard,
i. 457-9.

[3] Délibérations à prendre pour les Assemblées des Bailliages.

[4] Mémoire présenté au Roi par Monseigneur Comte d'Ar-
tois, M. le Prince de Condé, M. le Duc de Bourbon, M. le
Duc d'Enghien, et M. le Prince de Conti. (Given in Hist.
Parl. i. 256.)

danger truly : and yet if you do not listen, are they out
of danger ?   It is the voice of all France, this sound
that rises.   Immeasurable, manifold ; as the sound of
outbreaking waters : wise were he who knew what to
do in it,—if not to fly to the mountains, and hide
himself ?

How an ideal, all-seeing Versailles Government, sitting there on such principles, in such an environment,
would have determined to demean itself at this new
juncture, may even yet be a question.   Such a Government would have felt too well that its long task was
now drawing to a close ; that, under the guise of these
States-General, at length inevitable, a new omnipotent
Unknown of Democracy was coming into being;   in
presence of which no Versailles Government either
could or should, except in a provisory character, continue extant.   To enact which provisory character, so
unspeakably important, might its whole faculties but
have sufficed ;   and so a peaceable, gradual, well-con-
ducted Abdication and *Domine-dimittas* have been the
issue !

This for our ideal, all-seeing Versailles Government.
But for the actual irrational Versailles Government ?
Alas ! that is a Government existing there only for its
own behoof : without right, except possession ; and
now also without might.   It foresees nothing, sees
nothing ;   has not so much as a purpose, but has only
purposes,—and the instinct whereby all that exists will
struggle to keep existing.   Wholly a vortex ; in which
vain counsels, hallucinations, falsehoods, intrigues,
and imbecilities whirl ;   like withered rubbish in the
meeting of winds !   The Œil-de-Bœuf has its irrational
hopes, if also its fears. Since hitherto all States-
General have done as good as nothing, why should
these do more ?   The Commons, indeed, look dangerous ; but on the whole is not revolt, unknown now
for five generations, an impossibility ?   The Three
Estates can, by management, be set against each other ;
the Third will, as heretofore, join with the King ; will,

out of mere spite and self-interest, be eager to tax and
vex the other two. The other two are thus delivered
bound into our hands, that we may fleece them likewise. Whereupon, money being got, and the Three
Estates all in quarrel, dismiss them, and let the future
go as it can ! As good Archbishop Loménie was wont
to say : ' There are so many accidents ; and it needs
but one to save us '.—Yes ; and how many to destroy
us ?

Poor Necker in the midst of such an anarchy does
what is possible for him. He looks into it with obsti-
nately hopeful face ; lauds the known rectitude of the
kingly mind ; listens indulgent-like to the known per-
verseness of the queenly and courtly ;—emits if any
proclamation or regulation, one favouring the *Tiers
État* ; but settling nothing ; hovering afar off rather,
and advising all things to settle themselves. The grand
questions, for the present, have got reduced to two :
the Double Representation, and the Vote by Head.
Shall the Commons have a ' double representation ',
that is to say, have as many members as the Noblesse
and Clergy united ? Shall the States-General, when
once assembled, vote and deliberate, in one body, or in
three separate bodies ; ' vote by head, or vote by class ',
—*ordre* as they call it ? These are the moot-points
now filling all France with jargon, logic and eleutheromania. To terminate which, Necker bethinks him,
Might not a second Convocation of the Notables be
fittest ? Such second Convocation is resolved on.

On the 6th of November of this year 1788, these
Notables accordingly have reassembled ; after an
interval of some eighteen months. They are Calonne's
old Notables, the same Hundred and Forty-four,—to
show one's impartiality ; likewise to save time. They
sit there once again, in their Seven Bureaus, in the hard
winter weather : it is the hardest winter seen since
1709 ; thermometer below zero of Fahrenheit, Seine
River frozen over.[1] Cold, scarcity and eleuthero-

[1] Marmontel, Mémoires (London, 1805), iv. 33. Hist.
Parl., &c.

maniac clamour : a changed world since these Notables
were ' organned out ', in May gone a year ! They shall
see now whether, under their Seven Princes of the
Blood, in their Seven Bureaus, they can settle the
moot-points.

To the surprise of Patriotism, these Notables, once
so patriotic, seem to incline the wrong way ; towards
the anti-patriotic side. They stagger at the Double
Representation, at the Vote by Head : there is not
affirmative decision ; there is mere debating, and that
not with the best aspects. For, indeed, were not these
Notables themselves mostly of the Privileged Classes ?
They clamoured once ; now they have their misgivings ;
make their dolorous representations. Let them vanish,
ineffectual ; and return no more ! They vanish, after
a month's session, on this 12th of December, year 1788 :
the *last* terrestrial Notables ; not to reappear any other
time, in the History of the World.

And so, the clamour still continuing, and the Pamphlets ; and nothing but patriotic Addresses, louder
and louder, pouring in on us from all corners of France,
—Necker himself, some fortnight after, before the year
is yet done, has to present his *Report* ; [1] recommending
at his own risk that same Double Representation ;
nay almost enjoining it, so loud is the jargon and
eleutheromania. What dubitating, what circumam-
bulating ! These whole six noisy months (for it began
with Brienne in July), has not *Report* followed *Report*,
and one Proclamation flown in the teeth of the
other ? [2]

However, that first moot-point, as we see, is now
settled. As for the second, that of voting by Head or
by Order, it unfortunately is still left hanging. It
hangs there, we may say, between the Privileged
Orders and the Unprivileged ; as a ready-made battle-
prize, and necessity of war, from the very first : which

[1] Rapport fait au Roi dans son Conseil, le 27 Décembre
1788.
[2] 5th July ; 8th August ; 23rd September, &c., &c.

battle-prize whosoever seizes it—may thenceforth bear
as battle-flag, with the best omens !

But so, at least, by Royal Edict of the 24th of
January, [1] does it finally, to impatient expectant
France, become not only indubitable that National
Deputies *are* to meet, but possible (so far and hardly
further has the royal Regulation gone) to begin electing
them.

CHAPTER II

THE ELECTION

UP, then, and be doing !   The royal signal-word flies
through France, as through vast forests the rushing of
a mighty wind.   At Parish Churches, in Townhalls,
and every House of Convocation ; by Bailliages, by
Seneschalsies,* in whatsoever form men convene ; there,
with confusion enough, are Primary Assemblies forming.   To elect your Electors ; such is the form prescribed :   then to draw up your ' Writ of Plaints and
Grievances (*Cahier de plaintes et doléances*) ', of which
latter there is no lack.

With such virtue works this Royal January Edict ;
as it rolls rapidly, in its leathern mails, along these
frost-bound highways, towards all the four winds.   Like
some *fiat*, or magic spell-word ;—which such things do
resemble !   For always, as it sounds out ' at the mar-
ket-cross ', accompanied with trumpet-blast ; presided
by Bailli, Seneschal, or other minor Functionary, with
beef-eaters ; or, in country churches, is droned forth
after sermon, ' *au prône des messes paroissales* ' ; and
is registered, posted and let fly over all the world,—you
behold how this multitudinous French People, so long
simmering and buzzing in eager expectancy, begins
heaping and shaping itself into organic groups.   Which

[1] Réglement du Roi pour la Convocation des Etats-
Généraux à Versailles (Reprinted, wrong dated, in Histoire
Parlementaire, i. 262).

organic groups, again, hold smaller organic grouplets:
the inarticulate buzzing becomes articulate speaking
and acting. By Primary Assembly, and then by
Secondary; by 'successive elections', and infinite
elaboration and scrutiny, according to prescribed process,—shall the genuine 'Plaints and Grievances' be
at length got to paper; shall the fit National Representative be at length laid hold of.

How the whole People shakes itself, as if it had one
life; and, in thousand-voiced rumour, announces that
it is awake, suddenly out of long death-sleep, and will
thenceforth sleep no more!* The long looked-for has
come at last; wondrous news, of Victory, Deliverance,
Enfranchisement, sounds magical through every heart.
To the proud strong man it has come; whose strong
hands shall no more be gyved; to whom boundless
unconquered continents lie disclosed. The weary day-
drudge has heard of it; the beggar with his crust mois-
tened in tears. What! To us also has hope reached;
down even to us? Hunger and hardship are not to be
eternal? The bread we extorted from the rugged
glebe, and, with the toil of our sinews, reaped and
ground, and kneaded into loaves, was not wholly for
another, then; but we also shall eat of it, and be filled?
Glorious news (answer the prudent elders), but all-too
unlikely!—Thus, at any rate, may the lower people,
who pay no money taxes and have no right to vote,[1]
assiduously crowd round those that do; and most
Halls of Assembly, within doors and without, seem animated enough.

Paris, alone of Towns, is to have Representatives;
the number of them twenty. Paris is divided into
Sixty Districts; each of which (assembled in some
church, or the like) is choosing two Electors. Official
deputations pass from District to District, for all is
inexperience as yet, and there is endless consulting.
The streets swarm strangely with busy crowds, pacific

---

[1] Réglement du Roi (in Histoire Parlementaire, as above,
i. 267–307).

yet restless and loquacious; at intervals, is seen the
gleam of military muskets; especially about the Palais,
where the Parlement, once more on duty, sits querulous,
almost tremulous.

Busy is the French world! In those great days,
what poorest speculative craftsman but will leave his
workshop; if not to vote, yet to assist in voting? On
all highways is a rustling and bustling. Over the wide
surface of France, ever and anon, through the spring
months, as the Sower casts his corn abroad upon the
furrows, sounds of congregating and dispersing; of
crowds in deliberation, acclamation, voting by ballot
and by voice,—rise discrepant towards the ear of
Heaven. To which political phenomena add this
economical one, that Trade is stagnant, and also Bread
getting dear; for before the rigorous winter there was,
as we said, a rigorous summer, with drought, and on
the 13th of July with destructive hail. What a fearful
day! all cried while that tempest fell. Alas, the next
anniversary of it will be a worse.[1] Under such aspects
is France electing National Representatives.

The incidents and specialties of these Elections belong
not to Universal, but to Local or Parish History: for
which reason let not the new troubles of Grenoble or
Besançon; the bloodshed on the streets of Rennes,
and consequent march thither of the Breton 'Young
Men' with Manifesto by their 'Mothers, Sisters and
Sweethearts';[2] nor such like, detain us here. It is
the same sad history everywhere; with superficial
variations. A reinstated Parlement (as at Besançon),
which stands astonished at this Behemoth of a States-
General it had itself evoked, starts forward, with more

[1] Bailly, Mémoires, i. 336.
[2] Protestation et Arrêté des Jeunes Gens de la Ville de
Nantes, du 28 Janvier 1789, avant leur départ pour Rennes.
Arrêté des Jeunes Gens de la Ville d'Angers, du 4 Février
1798. Arrêté des Mères, Sœurs, Epouses et Amantes des
Jeunes Citoyens d'Angers, du 6 Février 1789. (Reprinted
in Histoire Parlementaire, i. 290-3.)

or less audacity, to fix a thorn in its nose ;* and, alas,
is instantaneously struck down, and hurled quite out,
—for the new popular force can use not only arguments
but brickbats! Or else, and perhaps combined with
this, it is an order of Noblesse (as in Brittany), which
will beforehand tie up the Third Estate, that it harm not
the old privileges. In which act of tying up, never so
skilfully set about, there is likewise no possibility of
prospering; but the Behemoth-Briareus* snaps your
cords like green rushes. Tie up? Alas, Messieurs!
And then, as for your chivalry rapiers, valour and
wager-of-battle, think one moment, how can that
answer? The plebeian heart too has red life in it, which
changes not to paleness at glance even of you; and
' the six hundred Breton gentlemen, assembled in arms,
for seventy-two hours, in the Cordeliers' Cloister, at
Rennes ',—have to come out again, *wiser* than they
entered. For the Nantes Youth, the Angers Youth, all
Brittany was astir; ' mothers, sisters and sweethearts '
shrieking after them, *March!* The Breton Noblesse
must even let the mad world have its way.[1]

In other Provinces, the Noblesse, with equal goodwill, finds it better to stick to Protests, to well-redacted
' *Cahiers* of grievances ', and satirical writings and
speeches. Such is partially their course in Provence;
whither indeed Gabriel Honoré Riquetti Comte de
Mirabeau has rushed down from Paris, to speak a word
in season. In Provence, the Privileged, backed by
their Aix Parlement, discover that such novelties,
enjoined though they be by Royal Edict, tend to
National detriment; and, what is still more indisputable, ' to impair the dignity of the Noblesse '.
Whereupon Mirabeau protesting aloud, this same
Noblesse, amid huge tumult within doors and without,
flatly determines to expel him from their Assembly.
No other method, not even that of successive duels,
would answer with him, the obstreperous fierce-glaring
man. Expelled he accordingly is.

[1] Hist. Parl. i. 287.   Deux Amis de la Liberté, i. 105–128.

' In all countries, in all times ', exclaims he departing,
' the Aristocrats have implacably pursued every friend
of the People ; and with tenfold implacability, if such
a one were himself born of the Aristocracy. It was
thus that the last of the Gracchi*perished, by the hands
of the Patricians. But he, being struck with the mortal
stab, flung dust towards heaven, and called on the
Avenging Deities ; and from this dust there was born
Marius,—Marius not so illustrious for exterminating
the Cimbri, as for overturning in Rome the tyranny of
the Nobles '.[1] Casting up *which* new curious handful
of dust (through the Printing-press), to breed what it
can and may, Mirabeau stalks forth into the Third
Estate.

That he now, to ingratiate himself with this Third
Estate, ' opened a cloth-shop in Marseilles ', and for
moments became a furnishing tailor, or even the fable
that he did so, is to us always among the pleasant
memorabilities ·of this era. Stranger Clothier never
wielded the ell-wand ; and rent webs for men, or frac-
tional parts of men. The *Fils Adoptif* is indignant at
such disparaging fable,[2]—which nevertheless was
widely believed in those days.[3] But indeed, if Achilles,
in the heroic ages, killed mutton,* why should not
Mirabeau, in the unheroic ones, measure broadcloth ?

More authentic are his triumph-progresses through
that disturbed district, with mob jubilee, flaming
torches, ' windows hired for two louis ', and voluntary
guard of a hundred men. He is Deputy Elect, both
of Aix and of Marseilles ; but will prefer Aix. He has
opened his far-sounding voice, the depths of his far-
sounding soul ; he can quell (such virtue is in a spoken
word) the pride-tumults of the rich, the hunger-tumults
of the poor ; and wild multitudes move under him, as
under the moon do billows of the sea : he has become
a world-compeller, and ruler over men.

[1] Fils Adoptif, v. 256.
[2] Mémoires de Mirabeau, v. 307.
[3] Marat, Ami-du-Peuple Newspaper (in Histoire Parlementaire, ii. 103), &c.

One other incident and specialty we note ; with how
different an interest ! It is of the Parlement of Paris ;
which starts forward, like the others (only with less
audacity, seeing better how it lay), to nose-ring that
Behemoth of a States-General. Worthy Doctor Guillotin,* respectable practitioner in Paris, has drawn up
his little ' Plan of a *Cahier* of *doléances* ' ;—as had he
not, having the wish and gift, the clearest liberty to do ?
He is getting the people to sign it ; whereupon the
surly Parlement summons him to give account of
himself. He goes ; but with all Paris at his heels ;
which floods the outer courts, and copiously signs the
Cahier even there, while the Doctor is giving account of
himself within ! The Parlement cannot too soon dismiss Guillotin, with compliments ; to be borne home
shoulder-high.[1] This respectable Guillotin we hope to
behold once more, and perhaps only once ; the Parlement not even once, but let it be engulfed unseen by us.

Meanwhile such things, cheering as they are, tend
little to cheer the national creditor, or indeed the creditor of any kind. In the midst of universal portentous
doubt, what certainty can seem so certain as money in
the purse, and the wisdom of keeping it there ? Trading
Speculation, Commerce of all kinds, has as far as possible
come to a dead pause ; and the hand of the industrious
lies idle in his bosom. Frightful enough, when now the
rigour of seasons has also done its part, and to scarcity
of work is added scarcity of food ! In the opening
spring, there come rumours of forestalment, there come
King's Edicts, Petitions of bakers against millers ; and
at length, in the month of April,—troops of ragged
Lackalls, and fierce cries of starvation ! These are the
thrice-famed *Brigands* :* an actually existing quotity
of persons ; who, long reflected and reverberated
through so many millions of heads, as in concave multi-
plying mirrors, become a whole Brigand World ; and,
like a kind of Supernatural Machinery, wondrously

---

[1] Deux Amis de la Liberté, i. 141.

move the Epos of the Revolution. The Brigands are
here; the Brigands are there; the Brigands are coming! Not otherwise sounded the clang of Phoebus
Apollo's silver bow, scattering pestilence and pale
terror: for this clang too was of the imagination; preternatural; and it too walked in formless immeasura-
bility, *having made itself like to the Night* (νυκτὶ
ἐοικώς) !*

But remark at least, for the first time, the singular
empire of Suspicion, in those lands, in those days. If
poor famishing men shall, prior to death, gather in
groups and crowds, as the poor fieldfares and plovers
do in bitter weather, were it but that they may chirp
mournfully together, and misery look in the eyes of
misery; if famishing men (what famishing fieldfares
cannot do) should discover, once congregated, that they
need not die while food is in the land, since they are
many, and with empty wallets have right hands: in
all this, what need were there of Preternatural Machinery? To most people none; but not to French
people, in a time of Revolution. These Brigands (as
Turgot's also were, fourteen years ago) have all been
set on; enlisted, though without tap of drum,—by
Aristocrats, by Democrats, by D'Orléans, D'Artois,
and enemies of the public weal. Nay Historians, to
this day, will prove it by one argument: these Brigands,
pretending to have no victual, nevertheless contrive to
drink, nay have been seen drunk.[1] An unexampled
fact! But on the whole, may we not predict that
a people, with such a width of Credulity and of Incredulity (the proper union of which makes Suspicion, and
indeed unreason generally), will see Shapes enough of
Immortals fighting*in its battle-ranks, and never want
for Epical Machinery?

Be this as it may, the Brigands are clearly got to
Paris, in considerable multitudes: [2] with sallow faces,
lank hair (the true enthusiast complexion), with sooty

[1] Lacretelle, 18me Siècle, ii. 155.
[2] Besenval, iii. 385, &c.

rags; and also with large clubs, which they smite
angrily against the pavement! These mingle in the
Election tumult; would fain sign Guillotin's *Cahier*,
or any *Cahier* or Petition whatsoever, could they but
write. Their enthusiast complexion, the smiting of
their sticks bodes little good to any one; least of all to
rich master-manufacturers of the Suburb Saint-Antoine,
with whose workmen they consort.

CHAPTER III

GROWN ELECTRIC

BUT now also National Deputies from all ends of
France are in Paris, with their commissions, what they
call *pouvoirs*, or powers, in their pockets; inquiring,
consulting; looking out for lodgings at Versailles.
The States-General shall open there, if not on the First,
then surely on the Fourth of May; in grand procession
and gala. The *Salle des Menus* is all new-carpentered,
bedizened for them; their very costume has been fixed:
a grand controversy which there was, as to 'slouch-
hats or slouched-hats', for the Commons Deputies, has
got as good as adjusted. Ever new strangers arrive:
loungers, miscellaneous persons, officers on furlough,—
as the worthy Captain Dampmartin,* whom we hope to
be acquainted with: these also, from all regions, have
repaired hither, to see what is toward. Our Paris
Committees, of the Sixty Districts, are busier than
ever; it is now too clear, the Paris Elections will be
late.

On Monday, the 27th day of April, Astronomer Bailly
notices that the Sieur Réveillon* is not at his post.
The Sieur Réveillon, 'extensive Paper Manufacturer
of the Rue Saint-Antoine': he, commonly so punctual,
is absent from Electoral Committee;—and even will
never reappear there. In those 'immense Magazines

of velvet paper', has aught befallen ? Alas, yes !
Alas, it is no Montgolfier rising there to-day; but
Drudgery, Rascality and the Suburb that is rising !
Was the Sieur Réveillon, himself once a journeyman,
heard to say that 'a journeyman might live handsomely on fifteen *sous* a-day' ? Some sevenpence
halfpenny : 'tis a slender sum ! Or was he only
thought, and believed, to be heard saying it ? By this
long chafing and friction, it would appear, the National
temper has got *electric*.

Down in those dark dens, in those dark heads and
hungry hearts, who knows in what strange figure the
new Political Evangel may have shaped itself; what
miraculous ' Communion of Drudges '*may be getting
formed ! Enough : grim individuals, soon waxing to
grim multitudes, and other multitudes crowding to see,
beset that Paper-Warehouse; demonstrate, in loud
ungrammatical language (addressed to the passions too),
the insufficiency of sevenpence halfpenny a-day.   The
City-watch cannot dissipate them; broils arise and
bellowings : Réveillon, at his wits' end, entreats the
Populace, entreats the Authorities.   Besenval, now in
active command, Commandant of Paris, does, towards
evening, to Réveillon's earnest prayer, send some
thirty Gardes Françaises.   These clear the street,
happily without firing; and take post there for the
night, in hope that it may be all over.[1]

Not so : on the morrow it is far worse.   Saint-
Antoine has arisen anew, grimmer than ever ;—reinforced by the unknown Tatterdemalion Figures, with
their enthusiast complexion, and large sticks.   The
City, through all streets, is flowing thitherward to
see : ' two cartloads of paving-stones, that happened
to pass that way', have been seized as a visible god-
send.   Another detachment of Gardes Françaises must
be sent; Besenval and the Colonel taking earnest
counsel.   Then still another; they hardly, with
bayonets and menace of bullets, penetrate to the spot.

[1] Besenval, iii. 385–8.

What a sight! A street choked up, with lumber, tumult and the endless press of men. A Paper-Warehouse eviscerated by axe and fire: mad din of Revolt; musket-volleys responded to by yells, by miscellaneous missiles, by tiles raining from roof and window,—tiles, execrations and slain men!

The Gardes Françaises like it not, but have to persevere. All day it continues, slackening and rallying; the sun is sinking, and Saint-Antoine has not yielded. The City flies hither and thither: alas, the sound of that musket-volleying booms into the far dining-rooms of the Chaussée d'Antin; alters the tone of the dinner-gossip there. Captain Dampmartin leaves his wine; goes out with a friend or two, to see the fighting. Unwashed men growl on him, with murmurs of ' *A bas les Aristocrates* (Down with the Aristocrats)'; and insult the cross of Saint Louis! They elbow him, and hustle him; but do not pick his pocket;—as indeed at Réveillon's too there was not the slightest stealing.[1]

At fall of night, as the thing will not end, Besenval takes his resolution: orders out the *Gardes Suisses* with two pieces of artillery. The Swiss Guards shall proceed thither; summon that rabble to depart, in the King's name. If disobeyed, they shall load their artillery with grape-shot, visibly to the general eye; shall again summon; if again disobeyed, fire,—and keep firing ' till the last man ' be in this manner blasted off, and the street clear. With which spirited resolution, as might have been hoped, the business is got ended. At sight of the lit matches, of the foreign red-coated Switzers, Saint-Antoine dissipates; hastily, in the shades of dusk. There is an encumbered street; there are ' from four to five hundred ' dead men. Unfortunate Réveillon has found shelter in the Bastille; does therefrom, safe behind stone bulwarks, issue plaint, protestation, explanation, for the next month. Bold

---

[1] Evènemens qui se sont passés sous mes yeux pendant la Révolution Française, par A. H. Dampmartin (Berlin, 1799), i. 25-7.

Besenval has thanks from all the respectable Parisian classes; but finds no special notice taken of him at Versailles,—a thing the man of true worth is used to.[1]

But how it originated, this fierce electric sputter and explosion ? From D'Orléans! cries the Court-party: he, with his gold, enlisted these Brigands,—surely in some surprising manner, without sound of drum: he raked them in hither, from all corners; to ferment and take fire; evil is his good.* From the Court! cries enlightened Patriotism: it is the cursed gold and wiles of Aristocrats that enlisted them; set them upon ruining an innocent Sieur Réveillon; to frighten the faint, and disgust men with the career of Freedom.

Besenval, with reluctance, concludes that it came from 'the English, our natural enemies'. Or, alas, might one not rather attribute it to Diana in the shape of Hunger ?* To some twin *Dioscuri*,* OPPRESSION and REVENGE; so often seen in the battles of men ? Poor Lackalls, all betoiled, besoiled, encrusted into dim defacement;—into whom nevertheless the breath of the Almighty has breathed a living soul! To them it is clear only that eleutheromaniac Philosophism has yet baked no bread; that Patriot Committee-men will level down to their own level, and no lower. Brigands or whatever they might be, it was bitter earnest with them. They bury their dead with the title of *Défenseurs de la Patrie*, Martyrs of the good Cause.

Or shall we say: Insurrection has now *served* its Apprenticeship; and this was its proof-stroke, and no inconclusive one ? Its next will be a master-stroke; announcing indisputable Mastership to a whole astonished world. Let that rock-fortress, Tyranny's stronghold, which they name *Bastille*, or *Building*, as if there were no other building,—look to its guns!

But, in such wise, with primary and secondary Assemblies, and *Cahiers* of Grievances; with motions,

[1] Besenval, iii. 389.

congregations of all kinds; with much thunder of
froth-eloquence, and at last with thunder of platoon-
musquetry,—does agitated France accomplish its Elections. With confused winnowing and sifting, in this
rather tumultuous manner, it has now (all except some
remnants of Paris) sifted out the true wheat-grains of
National Deputies, Twelve Hundred and Fourteen in
number; and will forthwith open its States-General.

CHAPTER IV

THE PROCESSION

On the first Saturday of May, it is gala at Versailles;
and Monday, fourth of the month, is to be a still greater
day. The Deputies have mostly got thither, and
sought out lodgings; and are now successively, in long
well-ushered files, kissing the hand of Majesty in the
Château. Supreme Usher de Brézé* does not give
the highest satisfaction: we cannot but observe that
in ushering Noblesse or Clergy into the anointed Presence, he liberally opens *both* his folding-doors; and
on the other hand, for members of the Third Estate,
opens only one! However, there is room to enter;
Majesty has smiles for all.

The good Louis welcomes his Honourable Members,
with smiles of hope. He has prepared for them the
Hall of *Menus*, the largest near him; and often surveyed the workmen as they went on. A spacious Hall:
with raised platform for Throne, Court and Blood-
royal; space for six hundred Commons Deputies in
front; for half as many Clergy on this hand, and half
as many Noblesse on that. It has lofty galleries;
wherefrom dames of honour, splendent in *gaze d'or*;
foreign Diplomacies, and other gilt-edged white-frilled
individuals, to the number of two thousand,—may sit
and look. Broad passages flow through it; and, outside the inner wall, all round it. There are committee-
rooms, guard-rooms, robing-rooms: really a noble

Hall ; where upholstery, aided by the subject fine-arts, has done its best ; and crimson tasselled cloths, and emblematic *fleurs-de-lys* are not wanting.

The Hall is ready : the very costume, as we said, has been settled ; and the Commons are *not* to wear that hated slouch-hat (*chapeau clabaud*), but one not quite so slouched (*chapeau rabattu*). As for their manner of *working*, when all dressed ; for their ' voting by head or by order ' and the rest,—this, which it were perhaps still time to settle, and in few hours will be no longer time, remains unsettled ; hangs dubious in the breast of Twelve Hundred men.

But now finally the Sun, on Monday the 4th of May, has risen ;—unconcerned, as if it were no special day. And yet, as his first rays could strike music from the Memnon's Statue on the Nile, what tones were these, so thrilling, tremulous, of preparation and foreboding, which he awoke in every bosom at Versailles ! Huge Paris, in all conceivable and inconceivable vehicles, is pouring itself forth ; from each Town and Village come subsidiary rills : Versailles is a very sea of men. But above all, from the Church of St. Louis to the Church of Notre-Dame : one vast suspended-billow of Life,— with *spray* scattered even to the chimney-tops ! For on chimney-tops too, as over the roofs, and up thither-wards on every lamp-iron, signpost, breakneck coign of vantage, sits patriotic Courage ; and every window bursts with patriotic Beauty : for the Deputies are gathering at St. Louis Church ; to march in procession to Notre-Dame, and hear sermon.

Yes, friends, ye may sit and look : bodily or in thought, all France, and all Europe, may sit and look ; for it is a day like few others. Oh, one might weep like Xerxes*:—So many serried rows sit perched there ; like winged creatures, alighted out of Heaven : all these, and so many more that follow them, shall have wholly fled aloft again, vanishing into the blue Deep ; and the memory of this day still be fresh. It is the baptism day of Democracy ; sick Time has given it

birth, the numbered months being run. The extreme-
unction day of Feudalism ! A superannuated System
of Society, decrepit with toils (for has it not done much ;
produced *you*, and what ye have and know !)—and
with thefts and brawls, named glorious-victories ; and
with profligacies, sensualities, and on the whole with
dotage and senility,—is now to die : and so, with death-
throes and birth-throes, a new one is to be born. What
a work, O Earth and Heavens, what a work ! Battles
and bloodshed, September Massacres, Bridges of Lodi,*
retreats of Moscow, Waterloos, Peterloos, Tenpound
Franchises, Tarbarrels* and Guillotines ;——and from
this present date, if one might prophesy, some two centuries of it still to fight ! Two centuries ; hardly less ;
before Democracy go through its due, most baleful,
stages of *Quack*ocracy ; and a pestilential World be
burnt up, and have begun to grow green and young
again.

Rejoice nevertheless, ye Versailles multitudes ; to
you, from whom all this is hid, the glorious end of it is
visible. This day, sentence of death is pronounced on
Shams ; judgement of resuscitation, were it but afar
off, is pronounced on Realities. This day, it is declared
aloud, as with a Doom-trumpet, that *a Lie is unbeliev-
able*. Believe that, stand by that, if more there be
not ; and let what thing or things soever will follow it
follow. ' Ye can no other ;· God be your help ! '* So
spake a greater than any of you ; opening *his* Chapter
of World-History.

Behold, however ! The doors of St. Louis Church
flung wide ; and the Procession of Processions advancing towards Notre-Dame ! Shouts rend the air ; one
shout, at which Grecian birds might drop dead.* It is
indeed a stately, solemn sight. The Elected of France,
and then the Court of France ; they are marshalled and
march there, all in prescribed place and costume. Our
Commons ' in plain black mantle and white cravat ' ;
Noblesse, in gold-worked, bright-dyed cloaks of velvet,
resplendent, rustling with laces, waving with plumes ;

the Clergy in rochet, alb, or other best *pontificalibus*:
lastly comes the King himself, and King's Household,
also in their brightest blaze of pomp,—their brightest
and final one. Some Fourteen Hundred Men blown
together from all winds, on the deepest errand.

Yes, in that silent marching mass there lies Futurity
enough. No symbolic Ark, like the old Hebrews, do
these men bear: yet with them too is a Covenant;
they too preside at a new Era in the History of Men.
The whole Future is there, and Destiny dim-brooding
over it; in the hearts and unshaped thoughts of these
men, it lies illegible, inevitable. Singular to think:
they have it in them; yet not they, not mortal, only the
Eye above can read it,—as it shall unfold itself, in fire
and thunder, of siege, and field artillery; in the rustling
of battle-banners, the tramp of hosts, in the glow of
burning cities, the shriek of strangled nations! Such
things lie hidden, safe-wrapt in this Fourth day of May;
—say rather, had lain in some other unknown day, of
which this latter is the public fruit and outcome. As
indeed what wonders lie in every Day,—had we the
sight, as happily we have not, to decipher it: for is
not every meanest Day ' the conflux of two Eternities '!

Meanwhile, suppose we too, good Reader, should,
as now without miracle Muse Clio enables us,—take
our station also on some coign of vantage; and glance
momentarily over this Procession, and this Life-sea;
with far other eyes than the rest do,—namely with
prophetic? We can mount, and stand there, without
fear of falling.

As for the Life-sea, or onlooking unnumbered Multitude, it is unfortunately all-too dim. Yet as we gaze
fixedly, do not nameless Figures not a few, which shall
not always be nameless, disclose themselves; visible or
presumable there! Young Baroness de Staël—she
evidently looks from a window; among older honourable women.[1]   Her father is Minister, and one of the

---

[1] Madame de Staël, Considérations sur la Révolution
Française (London, 1818), i. 114-91.

gala personages ; to his own eyes the chief one. Young
spiritual Amazon, thy rest is not there ; nor thy loved
Father's : ' as Malebranche* saw all things in God, so
M. Necker sees all things in Necker ',—a theorem that
will not hold.

But where is the brown-locked, light-behaved,
fire-hearted Demoiselle Théroigne ?* Brown eloquent
Beauty ; who, with thy winged words and glances,
shalt thrill rough bosoms, whole steel battalions,
and persuade an Austrian Kaiser,—pike and helm lie
provided for thee in due season ; and, alas, also strait-
waistcoat and long lodging in the Salpêtrière ! Better
hadst thou stayed in native Luxemburg, and been the
mother of some brave man's children : but it was not
thy task, it was not thy lot.

Of the rougher sex how, without tongue, or hundred
tongues, of iron, enumerate the notabilities ! Has not
Marquis Valadi*hastily quitted his Quaker broadbrim ;
his Pythagorean Greek in Wapping, and the city of
Glasgow ? [1] De Morande from his *Courrier de l'Europe* ;
Linguet from his *Annales*, they looked eager through
the London fog, and became Ex-Editors,—that they
might feed the guillotine, and have their due. Does
Louvet (of *Faublas*) stand a-tiptoe ? And Brissot,*
hight De Warville, friend of the Blacks ? He, with
Marquis Condorcet,* and Clavière* the Genevese ' have
created the *Moniteur* Newspaper ',* or are about creating
it. Able Editors must give account of such a day.

Or seest thou with any distinctness, low down probably, not in places of honour, a Stanislas Maillard,*
riding-tipstaff (*huissier à cheval*) of the Châtelet ; one
of the shiftiest of men ? A Captain Hulin* of Geneva,
Captain Elie of the Queen's Regiment ; both with an
air of half-pay ? Jourdan,* with tile-coloured whiskers,
not yet with tile-beard ; an unjust dealer in mules ?
He shall be, in few months, Jourdan the Headsman,
and have other work.

---

[1] Founders of the French Republic (London, 1798),
§ Valadi.

Surely also, in some place not of honour, stands or
sprawls up querulous, that he too, though short, may
see,—one squalidest bleared mortal, redolent of soot
and horse-drugs : Jean Paul Marat of Neuchâtel !   O
Marat, Renovator of Human Science, Lecturer on
Optics ;   O thou remarkablest Horseleech, once in
D'Artois' Stables,—as thy bleared soul looks forth,
through thy bleared, dull-acrid, woe-stricken face, what
sees it in all this ?   Any faintest light of hope ;   like
dayspring after Nova-Zembla night ?   Or is it but *blue*
sulphur-light, and spectres ;   woe, suspicion, revenge
without end ?

Of Draper Lecointre,* how he shut his cloth-shop
hard by, and stepped forth, one need hardly speak.
Nor of Santerre,* the sonorous Brewer from the Faubourg St. Antoine.   Two other Figures, and only two,
we signalize there.   The huge, brawny Figure ; through
whose black brows, and rude flattened face (*figure
écrasée*), there looks a waste energy as of Hercules not
yet furibund,—he is an esurient, unprovided Advocate ;
Danton* by name :   him mark.   Then that other, his
slight-built comrade, and craft-brother ;   he with the
long curling locks ;   with the face of dingy blackguardism, wondrously irradiated with genius, as if
a naphtha-lamp burnt within it :   that Figure is Camille
Desmoulins.*   A fellow of infinite shrewdness,* wit, nay
humour ;   one of the sprightliest clearest souls in all
these millions.   Thou poor Camille, say of thee what
they may, it were but falsehood to pretend one did not
almost love thee, thou headlong lightly sparkling man !
But the brawny, not yet furibund Figure, we say, is
Jacques Danton ;   a name that shall be ' tolerably
known in the Revolution '.   He is President of the
electoral Cordeliers District* at Paris, or about to be
it ;   and shall open his lungs of brass.

We dwell no longer on the mixed shouting Multitude :
for now, behold, the Commons Deputies are at hand !

Which of these Six Hundred individuals, in plain
white cravat, that have come up to regenerate France,

might one guess would become their *king*? For a king
or leader they, as all bodies of men, must have: be
their work what it may, there is one man there who, by
character, faculty, position, is fittest of all to do it;
that man, as future not yet elected king, walks there
among the rest. He with the thick black locks, will it
be? With the *hure*, as himself calls it, or black *boar's-
head*, fit to be 'shaken' as a senatorial portent?
Through whose shaggy beetle-brows, and rough-hewn,
seamed, carbuncled face, there look natural ugliness,
small-pox, incontinence, bankruptcy,—and burning
fire of genius; like comet-fire glaring fuliginous through
murkiest confusions? It is *Gabriel Honoré Riquetti de
Mirabeau*, the world-compeller; man-ruling Deputy
of Aix! According to the Baroness de Staël, he steps
proudly along, though looked at askance here; and
shakes his black *chevelure*, or lion's-mane; as if prophetic of great deeds.

Yes, Reader, that is the Type-Frenchman of this
epoch; as Voltaire was of the last. He is French in
his aspirations, acquisitions, in his virtues, in his vices;
perhaps more French than any other man;—and
intrinsically such a mass of manhood too. Mark him
well. The National Assembly were all different without
that one; nay, he might say with the old Despot:
'The National Assembly? I am that'.

Of a southern climate, of wild southern blood: for
the Riquettis, or Arrighettis, had to fly from Florence
and the Guelfs, long centuries ago, and settled in Provence; where from generation to generation they have
ever approved themselves a peculiar kindred: irascible,
indomitable, sharp-cutting, true, like the steel they
wore; of an intensity and activity that sometimes
verged towards madness, yet did not reach it. One
ancient Riquetti, in mad fulfilment of a mad vow, chains
two Mountains together; and the chain, with its ' iron
star of five rays ', is still to be seen. May not a modern
Riquetti *un*chain so much, and set it drifting,—which
also shall be seen?

Destiny has work for that swart burly-headed Mira-

beau ; Destiny has watched over him, prepared him
from afar.   Did not his Grandfather, stout *Col-d'Argent*
(Silver-Stock, so they named him), shattered and
slashed by seven-and-twenty wounds in one fell day,
lie sunk together on the Bridge at Casano ; while Prince
Eugene's cavalry galloped and regalloped over him,—
only the flying sergeant had thrown a camp-kettle over
that loved head ; and Vendôme, dropping his spyglass,
moaned out, ' Mirabeau is *dead*, then ! '   Nevertheless
he was not dead : he awoke to breath, and miraculous
surgery ;—for Gabriel was yet to be.   With his *silver
stock* he kept his scarred head erect, through long years ;
and wedded ; and produced tough Marquis Victor, the
Friend of Men.   Whereby at last in the appointed
year 1749, this long-expected rough-hewn Gabriel
Honoré did likewise see the light : roughest lion's
whelp* ever littered of that rough breed.   How the old
lion (for our old Marquis too was lionlike, most unconquerable, kingly-genial, most perverse) gazed wondering on his offspring ; and determined to train him as
no lion had yet been !   It is in vain, O Marquis !   This
cub, though thou slay him and flay him, will not learn
to draw in dogcart of Political Economy, and be
a *Friend of Men* ; he will not be Thou, but must and
will be Himself, another than Thou.   Divorce lawsuits,
' whole family save one in prison, and three-score
Lettres-de-Cachet ' for thy own sole use, do but astonish
the world.

Our luckless Gabriel, sinned against and sinning,* has
been in the Isle of Rhé, and heard the Atlantic from
his tower ; in the Castle of If, and heard the Mediterranean at Marseilles.   He has been in the Fortress of
Joux ; and forty-two months, with hardly clothing to
his back, in the Dungeon of Vincennes ;—all by *Lettre-
de-Cachet,* from his lion father.   He has been in Pontar-
lier Jails (self-constituted prisoner) ; was noticed
fording estuaries of the sea (at low water), in flight
from the face of men.   He has pleaded before Aix
Parléments (to get back his wife) ; the public gathering
on roofs, to see since they could not hear : ' the clatter-

teeth (*claque-dents*) ! ' snarls singular old Mirabeau ;
discerning in such admired forensic eloquence nothing
but two chattering jaw-bones, and a head vacant,
sonorous, of the drum species.

But as for Gabriel Honoré, in these strange wayfar-
ings, what has he not seen and tried ! From drill-sergeants, to prime ministers, to foreign and domestic
booksellers, all manner of men he has seen. All manner
of men he has gained ; for at bottom it is a social,
loving heart, that wild unconquerable one :—more
especially all manner of women. From the Archer's
Daughter at Saintes to that fair young Sophie
Madame Monnier, whom he could not but ' steal ',
and be beheaded for—in effigy ! For indeed hardly
since the Arabian Prophet lay dead to Ali's admiration,* was there seen such a Love-hero, with the
strength of thirty men. In War, again, he has helped
to conquer Corsica; fought duels, irregular brawls;
horsewhipped calumnious barons. In Literature, he
has written on *Despotism*, on *Lettres-de-Cachet* ; Erotics
Sapphic-Werterean, Obscenities, Profanities ; Books on
the *Prussian Monarchy*, on *Cagliostro*, on *Calonne*, on
the Water Companies of Paris :—each Book comparable,
we will say, to a bituminous alarum-fire ; huge, smoky,
sudden ! The firepan, the kindling, the bitumen were
his own ; but the lumber, of rags, old wood and nameless combustible rubbish (for all is fuel to him), was
gathered from hucksters, and ass-paniers, of every
description under heaven. Whereby, indeed, hucksters
enough have been heard to exclaim : Out upon it, the
fire is *mine* !

Nay, consider it more generally, seldom had man
such a talent for borrowing. The idea, the faculty of
another man he can make his ; the man himself he can
make his. ' All reflex and echo (*tout de reflet et de
réverbère*) ! ' snarls old Mirabeau, who can see, but will
not. Crabbed old Friend of Men ! it is his sociality,
his aggregative nature ; and will now be the quality
of qualities for him. In that forty years' ' struggle
against despotism ', he has gained the glorious faculty

of *self-help*, and yet not lost the glorious natural gift
of *fellowship*, of being helped.   Rare union : this man
can live self-sufficing—yet lives also in the life of other
men ; can make men love him, work with him ; a born
king of men !

But consider further how, as the old Marquis still
snarls, he has ' made away with (*humé*, swallowed) all
Formulas '*;—a fact which, if we meditate it, will in
these days mean much.   This is no man of system,
then ; he is only a man of instincts and insights.   A
man nevertheless who will glare fiercely on any object ;
and see through it, and conquer it : for he has intellect,
he has will, force beyond other men.   A man not with
logic-spectacles ; but with an *eye* !   Unhappily without
Decalogue, moral Code or Theorem of any fixed sort ;
yet not without a strong living Soul in him, and
Sincerity there : a Reality, not an Artificiality, not
a Sham !   And so he, having struggled ' forty years
against despotism ', and ' made away with all formulas ',
shall now become the spokesman of a Nation bent to
do the same.   For is it not precisely the struggle of
France also to cast off despotism ; to make away with
her old formulas,—having found them naught, worn
out, far from the reality ?   She will make away with
such formulas ;—and even go *bare*, if need be, till she
have found new ones.

Towards such work, in such manner, marches he,
this singular Riquetti Mirabeau.   In fiery rough figure,
with black Samson-locks under the slouch-hat, he steps
along there.   A fiery fuliginous mass, which could not
be choked and smothered, but would fill all France
with smoke.   And now it has got *air* ; it will burn its
whole substance, its whole smoke-atmosphere too, and
fill all France with flame.   Strange lot !   Forty years
of that smouldering, with foul fire-damp and vapour
enough ; then victory over that ;—and like a burning
mountain he blazes heaven-high ; and for twenty-three
resplendent months, pours out, in flame and molten
fire-torrents, all that is in him, the Pharos and Wonder-
sign of an amazed Europe ;—and then lies hollow, cold

for ever ! Pass on, thou questionable Gabriel Honoré, the greatest of them all : in the whole National Deputies, in the whole Nation, there is none like and none second to thee.

But now if Mirabeau is the greatest, who of these Six Hundred may be the meanest ?   Shall we say, that anxious, slight, ineffectual-looking man, under thirty, in spectacles ; his eyes (were the glasses off) troubled, careful ; with upturned face, snuffing dimly the uncertain future times; complexion of a multiplex atrabiliar colour, the final shade of which may be the pale sea-green.[1]   That greenish-coloured (*verdâtre*) individual is an Advocate of Arras ; his name is *Maximilien Robespierre.** The son of an Advocate ; his father founded mason-lodges under Charles Edward, the English Prince or Pretender.   Maximilien the first-born was thriftily educated ; he had brisk Camille Desmoulins for school-mate in the College of Louis le Grand, at Paris.   But he begged our famed Necklace-Cardinal, Rohan, the patron, to let him depart thence, and resign in favour of a younger brother.   The strict-minded Max departed ; home to paternal Arras ; and even had a Law-case there and pleaded, not unsuccessfully, ' in favour of the first Franklin thunder-rod '.   With a strict painful mind, an understanding small but clear and ready, he grew in favour with official persons, who could foresee in him an excellent man of business, happily quite free from genius.   The Bishop, therefore, taking counsel, appoints him Judge of his diocese ; and he faithfully docs justice to the people :   till behold, one day, a culprit comes whose crime merits hanging ;   and the strict-minded Max must abdicate, for his conscience will not permit the dooming of any son of Adam to die.   A strict-minded, strait-laced man !   A man unfit for Revolutions ?   Whose small soul, transparent whole-some-looking as small-ale, could by no chance ferment

---

[1] See De Staël, Considérations (ii. 142) ; Barbaroux, Mémoires, &c.

into virulent *alegar*,—the mother of ever new alegar;
till all France were grown acetous virulent ?   We shall
see.

Between which two extremes of grandest and meanest, so many grand and mean roll on, towards their
several destinies, in that Procession !   There is *Cazalès*,
the learned young soldier ; who shall become the eloquent orator of Royalism, and earn the shadow of
a name.   Experienced *Mounier*, experienced *Malouet* ;
whose Presidential Parlementary experience the stream
of things shall soon leave stranded.   A *Pétion*[*]has left
his gown and briefs at Chartres for a stormier sort of
pleading ; has not forgotten his violin, being fond of
music.   His hair is grizzled, though he is still young :
convictions, beliefs placid-unalterable are in that man ;
not hindmost of them, belief in himself.   A Protestant-
clerical *Rabaut-St.-Etienne*,[*] a slender young eloquent
and vehement *Barnave*, will help to regenerate France.
There are so many of them young.   Till thirty the
Spartans did not suffer a man to marry : but how many
men here under thirty ; coming to produce not one
sufficient citizen, but a nation and a world of such !
The old to heal up rents ; the young to remove rubbish :
—which latter, is it not, indeed, the task here ?

Dim, formless from this distance, yet authentically
there, thou noticest the Deputies from Nantes ?   To
us mere clothes-screens, with slouch-hat and cloak, but
bearing in their pocket a *Cahier* of *doléances* with this
singular clause, and more such, in it : ' That the master
wigmakers of Nantes be not troubled with new guild-
brethren, the actually existing number of ninety-two
being more than sufficient ! ' [1] The Rennes people
have elected Farmer *Gérard*, ' a man of natural sense
and rectitude, without any learning '.   He walks there,
with solid step ; unique, ' in his rustic farmer-clothes ' ;
which he will wear always ; careless of short-cloaks
and costumes.   The name Gérard, or ' *Père Gérard*,
Father Gérard ', as they please to call him, will fly far ;

---

[1] Histoire Parlementaire, i. 335.

borne about in endless banter ; in Royalist satires, in
Republican didactic Almanacs.[1]   As for the man
Gérard, being asked once, what he did, after trial of it,
candidly think of this Parlementary work,—' I think ',
answered he, ' that there are a good many scoundrels
among us '.   So walks Father Gérard ; solid in his
thick shoes, whithersoever bound.

And worthy *Doctor Guillotin*, whom we hoped to
behold one other time ?   If not here, the Doctor should
be here, and we see him with the eye of prophecy : for
indeed the Parisian Deputies are all a little late.   Singular Guillotin, respectable practitioner ; doomed by
a satiric destiny to the strangest immortal glory that
ever kept obscure mortal from his resting-place, the
bosom of oblivion !   Guillotin can improve the venti-
lation of the Hall ; in all cases of medical police and
hygiène be a present aid : but, greater far, he can produce his ' Report on the Penal Code ' ; and reveal
therein a cunningly devised Beheading Machine, which
shall become famous and world-famous.   This is the
product of Guillotin's endeavours, gained not without
meditation and reading ; which product popular gratitude or levity christens by a feminine derivative name,
as if it were his daughter : *La Guillotine !* ' With my
machine, Messieurs, I whisk off your head (*vous fais
sauter la tête*) in a twinkling, and you have no pain ' ;
—whereat they all laugh.[2]   Unfortunate Doctor ! For
two-and-twenty years he, unguillotined, shall hear
nothing but guillotine, see nothing but guillotine ; then
dying, shall through long centuries wander, as it were,
a disconsolate ghost, on the wrong side of Styx and
Lethe ; his name like to outlive Caesar's.

See *Bailly*, likewise of Paris, time-honoured Historian
of Astronomy Ancient and Modern.   Poor Bailly, how
thy serenely beautiful Philosophizing, with its soft

---

[1] Actes des Apôtres (by Peltier and others) ; Almanach
du Père Gérard (by Collot d'Herbois), &c. &c.
[2] Moniteur Newspaper, of December 1, 1789 (in Histoire
Parlementaire).

moonshiny clearness and thinness, ends in foul thick
confusion—of Presidency, Mayorship, diplomatic Officiality, rabid Triviality, and the throat of everlasting
Darkness !   Far was it to descend from the heavenly
Galaxy to the *Drapeau Rouge* : beside that fatal dung-
heap, on that last hell-day, thou must ' tremble ', though
only with cold, ' *de froid* '.   Speculation is not practice :
to be weak is not so miserable*; but to be weaker than
our task.   Wo the day when they mounted thee,
a peaceable pedestrian, on that wild Hippogryff of
a Democracy ; which, spurning the firm earth, nay
lashing at the very *stars*, no yet known Astolpho* could
have ridden !

In the Commons Deputies there are Merchants,
Artists, Men of Letters ; three hundred and seventy-
four Lawyers [1] ; and at least one Clergyman : the *Abbé
Sieyes*.   Him also Paris sends, among its twenty.
Behold him, the light thin man ; cold, but elastic, wiry ;
instinct with the pride of Logic ; passionless, or with
but one passion, that of self-conceit.   If indeed that
can be called a passion, which, in its independent concentrated greatness, seems to have soared into transcendentalism ; and to sit there with a kind of god-like
indifference, and look down on passion !   He is the
man, and wisdom shall die with him.   This is the
Sieyes who shall be System-builder, Constitution-
builder General ; and build Constitutions (as many as
wanted) skyhigh,—which shall all unfortunately fall
before he get the scaffolding away.   ' *La Politique* ',
said he to Dumont; ' Polity is a science I think I have
completed (*achevée*) '.[2]   What things, O Sieyes, with
thy clear assiduous eyes, art thou to see !   But were
it not curious to know how Sieyes, now in these days
(for he is said to be still alive [3]), looks out on all that
Constitution masonry, through the rheumy soberness

---

[1] Bouillé, Mémoires sur la Révolution Française (London, 1787), i. 68.

[2] Dumont, Souvenirs sur Mirabeau, p. 64.

[3] A.D. 1834.

of extreme age ?   Might we hope, still with the old
irrefragable transcendentalism ?   The victorious cause
pleased the gods, the vanquished one pleased Sieyes
(*victa Catoni*).*

Thus, however, amid skyrending *vivats*, and blessings
from every heart, has the Procession of the Commons
Deputies rolled by.

Next follow the Noblesse, and next the Clergy ; concerning both of whom it might be asked, What they
specially have come for ?   Specially, little as they
dream of it, to answer this question, put in a voice of
thunder :   What are you doing in God's fair Earth and
Task-garden ; where whosoever is not working is begging or stealing ?   Wo, wo to themselves and to all,
if they can only answer :   Collecting tithes, Preserving
game !—Remark, meanwhile, how *D'Orléans* affects to
step before his own Order, and mingle with the Commons.   For him are *vivats* : few for the rest, though
all wave in plumed ' hats of a feudal cut ', and have
sword on thigh ; though among them is *D'Antraigues*,
the young Languedocian gentleman,—and indeed many
a Peer more or less noteworthy.

There are *Liancourt*, and *La Rochefoucault* ; the
liberal Anglomaniac Dukes.   There is a filially pious
Lally ; a couple of liberal *Lameths*.   Above all, there
is a *Lafayette* ; whose name shall be Cromwell-Gran-
dison,* and fill the world.   Many a ' formula ' has this
Lafayette too made away with ;   yet not *all* formulas.
He sticks by the Washington-formula ;   and by that
he will stick ;—and hang by it, as by sure bower-anchor
hangs and swings the tight war-ship, which, after all
changes of wildest weather and water, is found still
hanging.   Happy for him ;   be it glorious or not !
Alone of all Frenchmen he has a theory of the world,
and right mind to conform thereto ;   he can become
a hero and perfect character, were it but the hero of
one idea.   Note further our old Parlementary friend,
Crispin-Catiline *d'Espréménil*.   He is returned from
the Mediterranean Islands, a redhot royalist, repentant

to the finger ends ;—unsettled-looking ; whose light,
dusky-glowing at best, now flickers foul in the socket ;
whom the National Assembly will by and by, to save
time, ' regard as in a state of distraction '.   Note lastly
that globular *Younger* Mirabeau*; indignant that his
elder Brother is among the Commons : it is *Viscomte*
Mirabeau ; named oftener Mirabeau *Tonneau* (Barrel
Mirabeau), on account of his rotundity, and the quantities of strong liquor he contains.

There then walks our French Noblesse.   All in the
old pomp of chivalry : and yet, alas, how changed from
the old position ; drifted far down from their native
latitude, like Arctic icebergs got into the Equatorial
sea, and fast thawing there !   Once these Chivalry
Duces (Dukes, as they are still named) did actually *lead*
the world,—were it only towards battle-spoil, where
lay the world's best wages then : moreover, being the
ablest Leaders going, they had their lion's share, those
Duces ; which none could grudge them.   But now,
when so many Looms, improved Ploughshares, Steam-
Engines and Bills of Exchange have been invented ;
and, for battle-brawling itself, men hire Drill-Sergeants
at eighteen-pence a-day,—what mean these goldmantled
Chivalry Figures, walking there ' in black velvet cloaks ',
in high-plumed ' hats of a feudal cut ' ?   Reeds shaken
in the wind !*

The Clergy have got up ; with *Cahiers* for abolishing
pluralities, enforcing residence of bishops, better payment of tithes.[1]   The Dignitaries, we can observe,
walk stately, apart from the numerous Undignified,—
who indeed are properly little other than Commons
disguised in Curate-frocks.   Here, however, though by
strange ways, shall the Precept be fulfilled, and they
that are greatest (much to their astonishment) become
least.* For one example, out of many, mark that
plausible *Grégoire* :* one day Curé Grégoire shall be
a Bishop, when the now stately are wandering dis-

[1] Hist. Parl. i. 322-7.

tracted, as Bishops *in partibus.* With other thought,
mark also the *Abbé Maury :** his broad bold face ;
mouth accurately primmed ; full eyes, that ray out
intelligence, falsehood,—the sort of sophistry which is
astonished you should find it sophistical. Skilfullest
vamper up of old rotten leather, to make it look like
new ; always a rising man ; he used to tell Mercier,*
'You will see ; I shall be in the Academy before you '. [1]
Likely indeed, thou skilfullest Maury ; nay thou shalt
have a Cardinal's Hat, and plush and glory ; but alas,
also, in the longrun—mere oblivion, like the rest of us;
and six feet of earth ! What boots it, vamping rotten
leather on these terms ? Glorious in comparison is the
livelihood thy good old Father earns, by making shoes,
—one may hope, in a sufficient manner. Maury does
not want for audacity. He shall 'wear pistols, by and
by ; and, at death-cries of ' *La Lanterne,* the Lamp-
iron ! '—answer coolly, ' Friends, will you see better
there ? '

But yonder, halting lamely along, thou noticest next
Bishop Talleyrand-Perigord, his Reverence of Autun.
A sardonic grimness lies in that irreverend Reverence
of Autun. He will do and suffer strange things ; and
will *become* surely one of the strangest things ever seen,
or like to be seen. A man living in falsehood, and on
falsehood ; yet not what you can call a false man :
there is the specialty ! It will be an enigma for future
ages, one may hope : hitherto such a product of Nature
and Art was possible only for this age of ours,—Age
of Paper, and of the Burning of Paper. Consider
Bishop Talleyrand and Marquis Lafayette as the topmost of their two kinds ; and say once more, looking at
what they did and what they were, *O Tempus ferax
rerum !**

On the whole, however, has not this unfortunate
Clergy also drifted in the Time-stream, far from its
native latitude ? An anomalous mass of men ; of
whom the whole world has already a dim understand-

[1] Mercier, Nouveau Paris.

ing that it can understand nothing. They were once a Priesthood, interpreters of Wisdom, revealers of the Holy that is in Man ; a true *Clerus* (or Inheritance of God on Earth): but now ?—They pass silently, with such *Cahiers* as they have been able to redact ; and none cries, God bless them.

King Louis with his Court brings up the rear : he cheerful, in this day of hope, is saluted with plaudits ; still more Necker his Minister. Not so the Queen ; on whom hope shines not steadily any more. Ill-fated Queen ! Her hair is already grey with many cares and crosses ; her firstborn son is dying in these weeks : black falsehood has ineffaceably soiled her name ; ineffaceably while this generation lasts. Instead of *Vive la Reine*, voices insult her with *Vive d'Orléans*. Of her queenly beauty little remains except its stateliness ; not now gracious, but haughty, rigid, silently enduring. With a most mixed feeling, wherein joy has no part, she resigns herself to a day she hoped never to have seen. Poor Marie Antoinette ; with thy quick noble instincts ; vehement glancings, vision all-too fitful narrow for the work thou hast to do ! O there are tears in store for thee ; bitterest wailings, soft womanly meltings, though thou hast the heart of an imperial Theresa's Daughter. Thou doomed one, shut thy eyes on the future !—

And so, in stately Procession, have passed the Elected of France. Some towards honour*and quick fire-consummation ; most towards dishonour ; not a few towards massacre, confusion, emigration, desperation : all towards Eternity !—So many heterogeneities cast together into the fermenting-vat ; there, with incalculable action, counteraction, elective affinities, explosive developments, to work out healing for a sick moribund System of Society ! Probably the strangest Body of Men, if we consider well, that ever met together on our Planet on such an errand. So thousandfold complex a Society, ready to burst up from its infinite

depths; and these men, its rulers and healers, without
life-rule for themselves,—other life-rule than a Gospel
according to Jean Jacques! To the wisest of them,
what we must call the wisest, man is properly an
Accident under the sky. Man is without Duty round
him; except it be ' to make the Constitution'. He
is without Heaven above him, or Hell beneath him;
he has no God in the world.

What further or better belief can be said to exist
in these Twelve Hundred ? Belief in high-plumed hats
of a feudal cut; in heraldic scutcheons; in the divine
right of Kings, in the divine right of Game-destroyers.
Belief, or what is still worse, canting half-belief, or
worst of all, mere Machiavelic pretence-of-belief,—in
consecrated dough-wafers, and the godhood of a poor
old Italian Man! Nevertheless in that immeasurable
Confusion and Corruption, which struggles there so
blindly to become less confused and corrupt, there is,
as we said, this one salient-point of a New Life discernible: the deep fixed Determination to have done
with Shams. A determination, which, consciously or
unconsciously, is *fixed*; which waxes ever more fixed,
into very madness and fixed-idea; which in such
embodiment as lies provided there, shall now unfold
itself rapidly: monstrous, stupendous, unspeakable;
new for long thousands of years !—How has the Heaven's *light*, oftentimes in this Earth, to clothe itself in
thunder and electric murkiness; and descend as molten
lightning, blasting, if purifying! Nay is it not rather
the very murkiness, and atmospheric suffocation, that
brings the lightning and the light ? The new Evangel,
as the old had been, was it to be born in the Destruction
of a World ?

But how the Deputies assisted at High Mass, and
heard sermon, and applauded the preacher, church as
it was, when he preached politics; how, next day, with
sustained pomp, they are, for the first time, installed
in their *Salle des Menus* (Hall no longer of *Amusements*),
and become a States-General,—readers can fancy for
themselves. The King from his *estrade*, gorgeous as

Solomon in all his glory, runs his eye over that majestic Hall ; many-plumed, many-glancing ; bright-tinted as rainbow, in the galleries and near side-spaces, where Beauty sits raining bright influence. Satisfaction, as of one that after long voyaging had got to port, plays over his broad simple face : the innocent King ! He rises and speaks, with sonorous tone, a conceivable speech. With which, still more with the succeeding one-hour and two-hour speeches of Garde-des-Sceaux and M. Necker, full of nothing but patriotism, hope, faith, and deficiency of the revenue,—no reader of these pages shall be tried.

We remark only that, as his Majesty, on finishing the speech, put on his plumed hat, and the Noblesse according to custom imitated him, our Tiers-État Deputies did mostly, not without a shade of fierceness, in like manner clap on, and even crush on their slouched hats ; and stand there awaiting the issue.[1] Thick buzz among them, between majority and minority of *Couvrez-vous, Découvrez-vous* (Hats off, Hats on) ! To which his Majesty puts end, by taking *off* his own royal hat again.

The session terminates without further accident or omen than this ; with which, significantly enough, France has opened her States-General.

---

[1] Histoire Parlementaire (i. 356]; Mercier, Nouveau Paris, &c.

BOOK V

THE THIRD ESTATE

CHAPTER I

INERTIA

THAT exasperated France, in this same National
Assembly of hers, has got something, nay something
great, momentous, indispensable, cannot be doubted;
yet still the question were: Specially *what*? A question hard to solve, even for calm onlookers at this
distance; wholly insoluble to actors in the middle of
it. The States-General, created and conflated by the
passionate effort of the whole Nation, is there as a thing
high and lifted up. Hope, jubilating, cries aloud that
it will prove a miraculous Brazen Serpent in the Wilderness; whereon whosoever looks, with faith and
obedience,* shall be healed of all woes and serpent-bites.

We may answer, it will at least prove a symbolic
Banner; round which the exasperated complaining
Twenty-five Millions, otherwise isolated and without
power, may rally, and work—what it is in them to
work. If battle must be the work, as one cannot help
expecting, then shall it be a battle-banner (say, an
Italian Gonfalon, in its old Republican *Carroccio*)*; and
shall tower up, car-borne, shining in the wind: and
with iron tongue peal forth many a signal. A thing
of prime necessity; which whether in the van or in
the centre, whether leading or led and driven, must do
the fighting multitude incalculable services. For
a season, while it floats in the very front, nay as it were
stands solitary there, waiting whether force will gather

round it, this same National *Carroccio*, and the signal-peals it rings, are a main object with us.

The omen of the 'slouch-hats clapt on' shows the Commons Deputies to have made up their minds on one thing : that neither Noblesse nor Clergy shall have precedence of them ; hardly even Majesty itself. To such length has the *Contrat Social*, and force of public opinion, carried us. For what is Majesty but the Delegate of the Nation ; delegated, and bargained with (even rather tightly),—in some very singular posture of affairs, which Jean Jacques has not fixed the date of ?

Coming therefore into their Hall, on the morrow, an inorganic mass of Six Hundred individuals, these Commons Deputies perceive, without terror, that they have it all to themselves. Their Hall is also the Grand or general Hall for all the Three Orders. But the Noblesse and Clergy, it would seem, have retired to their two separate Apartments or Halls ; and are there 'verifying their powers', not in a conjoint but in a separate capacity. They are to constitute two separate, perhaps separately-voting Orders, then ? It is as if both Noblesse and Clergy had silently taken for granted that they already were such ! Two Orders against one ; and so the Third Order to be left in a perpetual minority ?

Much may remain unfixed ; but the negative of that is a thing fixed : in the Slouch-hatted heads, in the French Nation's head. Double representation, and all else hitherto gained, were otherwise futile, null. Doubtless, the ' powers must be verified ' ;—doubtless, the Commission, the electoral Documents of your Deputy must be inspected by his brother Deputies, and found valid : it is the preliminary of all. Neither is this question, of doing it separately or doing it conjointly, a vital one : but if it lead to such ? It must be resisted ; wise was that maxim, Resist the beginnings !* Nay were resistance unadvisable, even dangerous, yet surely pause is very natural : pause, with Twenty-five

Millions behind you, may become resistance enough.
—The inorganic mass of Commons Deputies will restrict
itself to a ' system of inertia ',* and for the present remain
inorganic.

Such method, recommendable alike to sagacity and
to timidity, do the Commons Deputies adopt; and,
not without adroitness, and with ever more tenacity,
they persist in it, day after day, week after week. For
six weeks their history is of the kind named barren ;
which indeed, as Philosophy knows, is often the fruit-
fullest of all. These were their still creation-days ;
wherein they sat incubating ! In fact, what they did
was to do nothing, in a judicious manner. Daily the
inorganic body reassembles; regrets that they cannot
get organization, ' verification of powers in common ',
and begin regenerating France. Headlong motions
may be made, but let such be repressed ; inertia alone
is at once unpunishable and unconquerable.

Cunning must be met by cunning ; proud pretension
by inertia, by a low tone of patriotic sorrow ; low, but
incurable, unalterable. Wise as serpents ; harmless as
doves :* what a spectacle for France ! Six Hundred
inorganic individuals, essential for its regeneration and
salvation, sit there, on their elliptic benches, longing
passionately towards life ; in painful durance ; like
souls waiting to be born. Speeches are spoken ; eloquent ; audible within doors and without. Mind
agitates itself against mind ; the Nation looks on with
ever deeper interest. Thus do the Commons Deputies
sit incubating.

There are private conclaves, supper-parties, consulta-
tions ; Breton Club, Club of Viroflay ; germs of many
Clubs. Wholly an element of confused noise, dimness,
angry heat ;—wherein, hówever, the Eros-egg,* kept at
the fit temperature, may hover safe, unbroken till it
be hatched. In your Mouniers, Malouets, Lechapeliers
is science sufficient for that ; fervour in your Barnaves,
Rabauts. At times shall come an inspiration from
royal Mirabeau : he is nowise yet recognized as royal ;

nay he was ' groaned at ', when his name was first mentioned : but he is struggling towards recognition.

In the course of the week, the Commons having
called their Eldest to the chair, and furnished him with
young stronger-lunged assistants,—can speak articulately ; and, in audible lamentable words, declare, as
we said, that they are an inorganic body, longing to
become organic. Letters arrive ; but an inorganic
body cannot open letters ; they lie on the table un-
opened. The Eldest may at most procure for himself
some kind of List or Muster-roll, to take the votes by ;
and wait what will betide. Noblesse and Clergy are
all elsewhere : however, an eager public crowds all
galleries and vacancies ; which is some comfort. With
effort, it is determined, not that a Deputation shall be
sent, for how can an inorganic body send deputations ?
—but that certain individual Commons Members shall,
in an accidental way, stroll into the Clergy Chamber,
and then into the Noblesse one ; and mention there,
as a thing they have happened to observe, that the
Commons seem to be sitting waiting for them, in order
to verify their powers. That is the wiser method !

The Clergy, among whom are such a multitude of
Undignified, of mere Commons in Curates' frocks,
depute instant respectful answer that they are, and
will now more than ever be, in deepest study as to
that very matter. Contrariwise the Noblesse, in
cavalier attitude, reply, after four days, that they, for
their part, are all verified and constituted ; which,
they had trusted, the Commons also were ; such
separate verification being clearly the proper constitutional wisdom-of-ancestors method ;—as they the
Noblesse will have much pleasure in demonstrating
by a Commission of their number, if the Commons will
meet them, Commission against Commission ! Directly
in the rear of which comes a deputation of Clergy,
reiterating, in their insidious conciliatory way, the
same proposal. Here then is a complexity : what will
wise Commons say to this ?

Warily, inertly, the wise Commons, considering that

they are, if not a French Third Estate, at least an
Aggregate of individuals pretending to some title of
that kind, determine, after talking on it five days, to
name such a Commission,—though, as it were, with
proviso not to be convinced : a sixth day is taken up
in naming it ; a seventh and an eighth day in getting
the forms of meeting, place, hour, and the like, settled :
so that it is not till the evening of the 23rd of May that
Noblesse Commission first meets Commons Commission, Clergy acting as Conciliators ; and begins the
impossible task of convincing it. One other meeting,
on the 25th, will suffice : the Commons are inconvin-
cible, the Noblesse and Clergy irrefragably convincing ;
the Commissions retire ; each Order persisting in its
first pretensions.[1]

Thus have three weeks passed. For three weeks,
the Third-Estate Carroccio, with far-seen Gonfalon,
has stood stockstill, flouting the wind ; waiting what
force would gather round it.

Fancy can conceive the feeling of the Court ; and
how counsel met counsel, and loud-sounding inanity
whirled in that distracted vortex, where wisdom could
not dwell. Your cunningly devised Taxing-Machine
has been got together ; set up with incredible labour ;
and stands there, its three pieces in contact ; its two
fly-wheels of Noblesse and Clergy, its huge working-
wheel of Tiers-État. The two fly-wheels whirl in the
softest manner ; but, prodigious to look upon, the huge
working-wheel hangs motionless, refuses to stir ! The
cunningest engineers are at fault. How *will* it work,
when it does begin ? Fearfully, my Friends ; and to
many purposes ; but to gather taxes, or grind court-
meal, one may apprehend, never. Could we but have
continued gathering taxes *by hand* ! Messeigneurs
d'Artois, Conti, Condé (named Court Triumvirate),
they of the anti-democratic *Mémoire au Roi*, has not
their foreboding proved true ? They may wave

---

[1] Reported Debates, 6th May to 1st June 1789 (in Histoire Parlementaire, i. 379–422).

reproachfully their high heads; they may beat their
poor brains; but the cunningest engineers can do
nothing. Necker himself, were he even listened to,
begins to look blue. The only thing one sees advisable
is to bring up soldiers. New regiments, two, and
a battalion of a third, have already reached Paris;
others shall get in march. Good were it in all circumstances, to have troops within reach; good that the
command were in sure hands. Let Broglie be appointed;
old Marshal Duke de Broglie; veteran disciplinarian,
of a firm drill-sergeant morality, such as may be
depended on.

For, alas, neither are the Clergy, or the very Noblesse
what they should be; and might be, when so menaced
from without: entire, undivided within. The Noblesse,
indeed, have their Catiline or Crispin D'Espréménil,
dusky-glowing, all in renegade heat: their boisterous
Barrel-Mirabeau; but also they have their Lafayettes,
Liancourts, Lameths; above all, their D'Orléans, now
cut for ever from his Court-moorings, and musing
drowsily of high and highest sea-prizes (for is not he too
a son of Henri Quatre, and partial potential Heir-
Apparent?)—on his voyage towards Chaos. From
the Clergy again, so numerous are the Curés, actual
deserters have run over: two small parties; in the
second party Curé Grégoire. Nay there is talk of
a whole Hundred and Forty-nine of them about to
desert in mass, and only restrained by an Archbishop
of Paris. It seems a losing game.

But judge if France, if Paris sat idle, all this while!
Addresses from far and near flow in: for our Commons
have now grown organic enough to open letters. Or
indeed to cavil at them! Thus poor Marquis de Brézé,
Supreme Usher, Master of Ceremonies, or whatever
his title was, writing about this time on some ceremonial matter, sees no harm in winding up with
a 'Monsieur, yours with sincere attachment'.—'To
whom does it address itself, this sincere attachment?'
inquires Mirabeau. 'To the Dean of the Tiers-État'.
—'There is no man in France entitled to write that',

rejoins he ; whereat the Galleries and the World will
not be kept from applauding.[1]   Poor De Brézé !
These Commons have a still older grudge at him ; nor
has he yet done with them.

In another way, Mirabeau has had to protest against
the quick suppression of his Newspaper, *Journal of the
States-General* ;—and to continue it under a new name.
In which act of valour, the Paris Electors, still busy
redacting their *Cahier*, could not but support him, by
Address to his Majesty : they claim utmost ' provisory
freedom of the press ' ; they have spoken even about
demolishing the Bastille, and erecting a Bronze Patriot
King on the site !—These are the rich Burghers : but
now consider how it went, for example, with such loose
miscellany, now all grown eleutheromaniac, of Loungers,
Prowlers, social Nondescripts (and the distilled Rascality of our Planet), as whirls for ever in the Palais
Royal ;—or what low infinite groan, fast changing into
a growl, comes from Saint-Antoine, and the Twenty-
five Millions in danger of starvation !

There is the indisputablest scarcity of corn ;—be it
Aristocrat-plot, D'Örléans-plot, of this year ;   or
drought and hail of last year : in city and province,
the poor man looks desolately towards a nameless lot.
And this States-General, that could make us an age
of gold, is forced to stand motionless ; cannot get its
powers verified ! All industry necessarily languishes,
if it be not that of making motions.

In the Palais Royal there has been erected, apparently by subscription, a kind of Wooden Tent (*en
planches de bois*) ; [2]—most convenient ; where select
Patriotism can now redact resolutions, deliver harangues, with comfort, let the weather be as it will.
Lively is that Satan-at-Home ! On his table, on his
chair, in every *café*, stands a patriotic orator ; a crowd
round him within ; a crowd listening from without,
open-mouthed, through open door and window ; with

---

[1] Moniteur (in Histoire Parlementaire, i. 405).
[2] Histoire Parlementaire, i. 429.

'thunders of applause for every sentiment of more
than common hardiness'. In Monsieur Dessein's
Pamphlet-shop, close by, you cannot without strong
elbowing get to the counter : every hour produces its
pamphlet, or litter of pamphlets ; ' there were thirteen
to-day, sixteen yesterday, ninety-two last week'.[1]
Think of Tyranny and Scarcity ; Fervid-eloquence,
Rumour, Pamphleteering ; *Société Publicole*, Breton
Club, Enraged Club ;—and whether every tap-room,
coffee-room, social reunion, accidental street-group,
over wide France, was not an Enraged Club !

To all which the Commons Deputies can only listen
with a sublime inertia of sorrow ; reduced to busy
themselves 'with their internal police'. Surer position
no Deputies ever occupied ; if they keep it with skill.
Let not the temperature rise too high ; break not the
Eros-egg till it be hatched, till it break itself ! An
eager public crowds all Galleries and vacancies ;
'cannot be restrained from applauding'. The two
Privileged Orders, the Noblesse all verified and constituted, may look on with what face they will ; not
without a secret tremor of heart. The Clergy, always
acting the part of conciliators, make a clutch at the
Galleries, and the popularity there ; and miss it.
Deputation of them arrives, with dolorous message
about the ' dearth of grains', and the necessity there is
of casting aside vain formalities, and deliberating on
this. An insidious proposal ; which, however, the
Commons (moved thereto by sea-green Robespierre)
dexterously accept as a sort of hint, or even pledge,
that the Clergy will forthwith come over to them,
constitute the States-General, and *so* cheapen grains ![2]
—Finally, on the 27th day of May, Mirabeau, judging
the time now nearly come, proposes that ' the inertia
cease ' ; that, leaving the Noblesse to their own stiff
ways, the Clergy be summoned, ' in the name of the
God of Peace ', to join the Commons, and begin.[3]   To

---

[1] Arthur Young, Travels, i. 104.
[2] Bailly, Mémoires, i. 114.
[3] Histoire Parlementaire, i. 413.

which summons if they turn a deaf ear,—we shall see !
Are not one Hundred and Forty-nine of them ready to
desert ?

O Triumvirate of Princes, new Garde-des-Sceaux
Barentin, thou Home-Secretary Breteuil, Duchess
Polignac, and Queen eager to listen,—what is now to
be done ?   This Third Estate will get in motion, with
the force of all France in it ; Clergy-machinery with
Noblesse-machinery, which were to serve as beautiful
counterbalances and drags, will be shamefully dragged
after it,—and take fire along with it.   What is to be
done ?   The Œil-de-Bœuf waxes more confused than
ever.   Whisper and counter-whisper ; a very tempest
of whispers !   Leading men from all the Three Orders
are nightly spirited thither ; conjurors many of them ;
but can they conjure this ?   Necker himself were now
welcome, could he interfere to purpose.

Let Necker interfere then ; and in the King's name !
Happily that incendiary ' God-of-Peace ' message is
not yet *answered*.   The Three Orders shall again have
conferences ; under this Patriot Minister of theirs,
somewhat may be healed, clouted up ;—we meanwhile
getting forward Swiss Regiments, and a ' hundred
pieces of field-artillery '.   This is what the Œil-de-
Bœuf, for its part, resolves on.

But as for Necker—Alas, poor Necker, thy obstinate
Third Estate has one first-last word, *verification in
common*, as the pledge of voting and deliberating in
common !   Half-way proposals, from such a tried
friend, they answer with a stare.   The tardy conferences speedily break up : the Third Estate, now
ready and resolute, the whole world backing it, returns
to its Hall of the Three Orders ; and Necker to the
Œil-de-Bœuf, with the character of a disconjured
conjuror there,—fit only for dismissal.[1]

And so the Commons Deputies are at last on their
own strength getting under way ?   Instead of Chair-

[1] Debates, 1st June to 17th June 1789 (in Histoire Parlementaire, i. 422–78).

man, or Dean, they have now got a President: Astronomer Bailly. Under way, with a vengeance! With
endless vociferous and temperate eloquence, borne on
Newspaper wings to all lands, they have now, on this
17th day of June, determined that their name is not
Third Estate, but—*National Assembly!** They then are
the Nation? Triumvirate of Princes, Queen, refractory Noblesse and Clergy, what then are *you*? A most
deep question;—scarcely answerable in living political
dialects.

All regardless of which, our new National Assembly
proceeds to appoint a ' committee of subsistences';
dear to France, though it can find little or no grain.
Next, as if our National Assembly stood quite firm on
its legs,—to appoint ' four other standing committees ';
then to settle the security of the National Debt; then
that of the Annual Taxation: all within eight-and-
forty hours. At such rate of velocity it is going: the
conjurors of the Œil-de-Bœuf may well ask themselves,
Whither?

CHAPTER II

MERCURY DE BRÉZÉ

Now surely were the time for a ' god from the
machine '; there is a *nodus* worthy of one. The only
question is, Which god? Shall it be Mars de Broglie,
with his hundred pieces of cannon?—Not yet, answers
prudence; so soft, irresolute is King Louis. Let it
be Messenger *Mercury*, our Supreme Usher de Brézé!

On the morrow, which is the 20th of June, these
Hundred and Forty-nine false Curates, no longer
restrainable by his Grace of Paris, will desert in a body:
let De Brézé intervene, and produce—closed doors!
Not only shall there be Royal Session, in that Salle
des Menus; but no meeting, nor working (except by

carpenters), till then. Your Third Estate, self-styled
' National Assembly ', shall suddenly see itself extruded
from its Hall, by carpenters, in this dexterous way;
and reduced to do nothing, not even to meet, or articulately lament,—till Majesty, with *Séance Royale* and
new miracles, be ready! In this manner shall De
Brézé, as Mercury *ex machina*, intervene; and, if the
Œil-de-Bœuf mistake not, work deliverance from the
nodus.

Of poor De Brézé we can remark that he has yet
prospered in none of his dealings with these Commons.
Five weeks ago, when they kissed the hand of Majesty,
the mode he took got nothing but censure; and then
his ' sincere attachment ', how was it scornfully whiffed
aside! Before supper, this night, he writes to President Bailly, a new Letter, to be delivered shortly after
dawn to-morrow, in the King's name. Which Letter
however, Bailly, in the pride of office, will merely crush
together into his pocket, like a bill he does not mean
to pay.

Accordingly on Saturday morning the 20th of June,
shrill-sounding heralds proclaim, through the streets of
Versailles, that there is to be *Séance Royale* next
Monday; and no meeting of the States-General till
then. And yet, we observe, President Bailly, in sound
of this, and with De Brézé's Letter in his pocket, is
proceeding, with National Assembly at his heels, to the
accustomed Salle des Menus; as if De Brézé and
heralds were mere wind. It is shut, this Salle; occupied by Gardes Françaises. ' Where is your Captain?'
The Captain shows his royal order: workmen, he is
grieved to say, are all busy setting up the platform for
his Majesty's *Séance*; most unfortunately, no admission; admission, at furthest, for President and Secretaries to bring away papers, which the joiners might
destroy!—President Bailly enters with Secretaries;
and returns bearing papers: alas, within doors, instead
of patriotic eloquence, there is now no noise but hammering, sawing, and operative screeching and rumbling!
A profanation without parallel.

The Deputies stand grouped on the Paris road, on this umbrageous *Avenue de Versailles* ; complaining aloud of the indignity done them. Courtiers, it is supposed, look from their windows, and giggle. The morning is none of the comfortablest : raw ; it is even drizzling a little.[1] But all travellers pause ; patriot gallery-men, miscellaneous spectators increase the groups. Wild counsels alternate. Some desperate Deputies propose to go and hold session on the great outer Staircase at Marly, under the King's windows ; for his Majesty, it seems, has driven over thither. Others talk of making the Château Forecourt, what they call *Place d'Armes*, a Runnymede and new *Champ de Mai* of free Frenchmen : nay of awakening, to sounds of indignant Patriotism, the echoes of the Œil-de-Bœuf itself.—Notice is given that President Bailly, aided by judicious Guillotin and others, has found place in the Tennis-Court of the Rue St. François. Thither, in long-drawn files, hoarse-jingling, like cranes on wing, the Commons Deputies angrily wend.

Strange sight was this in the Rue St. François, Vieux Versailles ! A naked Tennis-Court, as the Pictures of that time still give it : four walls ; naked, except aloft some poor wooden penthouse, or roofed spectators'-gallery, hanging round them :—on the floor not now an idle teeheeing, a snapping of balls and rackets ; but the bellowing din of an indignant National Representation, scandalously exiled hither ! However, a cloud of witnesses looks down on them, from wooden pent-house, from wall-top, from adjoining roof and chimney ; rolls towards them from all quarters, with passionate spoken blessings. Some table can be procured to write on ; some chair, if not to sit on, then to stand on. The Secretaries undo their tapes ; Bailly has constituted the Assembly.

Experienced Mounier, not wholly new to such things, in Parlementary revolts, which he has seen or heard of, thinks that it were well, in these lamentable threaten-

---

[1] Bailly, *Mémoires*, i. 185-206.

ing circumstances, to unite themselves by an Oath.—
Universal acclamation, as from smouldering bosoms
getting vent! The Oath is redacted; pronounced
aloud by President Bailly,—and indeed in such a sonorous tone, that the cloud of witnesses, even out doors,
hear it, and bellow response to it. Six hundred right-
hands rise with President Bailly's, to take God above
to witness that they will not separate for man below,
but will meet in all places, under all circumstances,
wheresoever two or three* can get together, till they
have made the Constitution. Made the Constitution,
Friends! That is a long task. Six hundred hands,
meanwhile, will sign as they have sworn : six hundred
save *one* ; one Loyalist Abdiel,* still visible by this sole
light-point, and nameable, poor 'M. Martin d'Auch,
from Castelnaudary, in Languedoc '. Him they permit
to sign or signify refusal ; they even save him from the
cloud of witnesses, by declaring ' his head deranged '.
At four o'clock, the signatures are all appended ; new
meeting is fixed for Monday morning, earlier than the
hour of the Royal Session ; that our Hundred and
Forty-nine Clerical deserters be not balked : we will
meet ' at the Recollets Church or elsewhere ', in hope
that our Hundred and Forty-nine will join us ;—and
now it is time to go to dinner.

This then is the Session of the Tennis-Court, famed
Séance du Jeu de Paume ; the fame of which has gone
forth to all lands. This is Mercurius de Brézé's appearance as *Deus ex machina* ; this is the fruit it brings!
The giggle of Courtiers in the Versailles Avenue has
already died into gaunt silence. Did the distracted
Court, with Garde-des-Sceaux Barentin, Triumvirate
and Company, imagine that they could scatter six hundred National Deputies, big with a National Constitution, like as much barndoor poultry, big with next to
nothing,—by the white or black rod of a Supreme
Usher ? Barndoor poultry fly cackling : but National
Deputies turn round, lion-faced ; and, with uplifted
right-hand, swear an Oath that makes the four corners
of France tremble.

President Bailly has covered himself with honour ;
which shall become rewards. The National Assembly
is now doubly and trebly the Nation's Assembly ; not
militant, martyred only, but triumphant ; insulted,
and which could not *be* insulted. Paris disembogues
itself once more, to witness, ' with grim looks ', the
Séance Royale : [1] which, by a new felicity, is postponed
till Tuesday. The Hundred and Forty-nine, and even
with Bishops among them, all in processional mass,
have had free leisure to march off, and solemnly join
the Commons sitting waiting in their Church. The
Commons welcomed them with shouts, with embracings, nay with tears ; [2] for it is growing a life-and-death
matter now.

As for the *Séance* itself, the Carpenters seem to have
accomplished their platform ; but all else remains
unaccomplished. Futile, we may say fatal, was the
whole matter. King Louis enters, through seas of
people, all grim-silent, angry with many things,—for
it is a bitter rain too.* Enters, to a Third Estate, likewise grim-silent ; which has been wetted waiting under
mean porches, at back-doors, while Court and Privileged were entering by the front. King and Garde-
des-Sceaux (there is no Necker visible) make known,
not without longwindedness, the determinations of the
royal breast. The Three Orders *shall* vote separately.
On the other hand, France may look for considerable
constitutional blessings ; as specified in these Five-and-
thirty Articles,[3] which Garde-des-Sceaux is waxing
hoarse with reading. Which Five-and-thirty Articles,
adds his Majesty again rising, if the Three Orders most
unfortunately cannot agree together to effect them,
I myself will effect : ' *seul je ferai le bien de mes peuples* ',—which being interpreted may signify, You,
contentious Deputies of the States-General, have probably not long to be here ! But, in fine, all shall now

[1] See Arthur Young (Travels, i. 115–18) ; A. Lameth,
&c.

[2] Dumont, Souvenirs sur Mirabeau, c. 4.

[3] Histoire Parlementaire, i 13.

withdraw for this day ; and meet again, each Order in its separate place, to-morrow morning, for dispatch of business. *This* is the determination of the royal breast : pithy and clear. And herewith King, retinue, Noblesse, majority of Clergy file out, as if the whole matter were satisfactorily completed.

These file out ; through grim-silent seas of people. Only the Commons Deputies file not out ; but stand there in gloomy silence, uncertain what they shall do. One man of them is certain ; one man of them discerns and dares ! It is now that King Mirabeau starts to the Tribune, and lifts up his lion-voice. Verily a word in season*; for, in such scenes, the moment is the mother of ages !* Had not Gabriel Honoré been there, —one can well fancy, how the Commons Deputies, affrighted at the perils which now yawned dim all round them, and waxing ever paler in each other's paleness, might very naturally, one after one, have *glided off* ; and the whole course of European History have been different !

But he is there. List to the *brool* of that royal forest-voice ; sorrowful, low ; fast swelling to a roar ! Eyes kindle at the glance of his eye :—National Deputies were missioned by a Nation ; they have sworn an Oath ; they—But lo ! while the lion's voice roars loudest, what Apparition is this ? Apparition of Mercurius de Brézé, muttering somewhat !—' Speak out ', cry several.—' Messieurs ', shrills De Brézé, repeating himself, ' You have heard the King's orders ! '— Mirabeau glares on him with fire-flashing face ; shakes the black lion's mane : ' Yes, Monsieur, we have heard what the King was advised to say : and you, who cannot be the interpreter of his orders to the States-General ; you, who have neither place nor right of speech here ; *you* are not the man to remind us of it. Go, Monsieur, tell those who sent you that we are here by the will of the People, and that nothing but the force of bayonets shall send us hence ! '[1]   And poor

[1] Moniteur (Hist. Parl. ii. 22].

De Brézé shivers forth from the National Assembly;
—and also (if it be not in one faintest glimmer,
months later) finally from the page of History!—

Hapless De Brézé; doomed to survive long ages, in
men's memory, in this faint way, with tremulent white
rod! He was true to Etiquette, which was his Faith
here below; a martyr to respect of persons.* Short
woollen cloaks could not kiss Majesty's hand as long
velvet ones did. Nay lately, when the poor little
Dauphin lay dead, and some ceremonial Visitation
came, was he not punctual to announce it even to the
Dauphin's *dead body*: 'Monseigneur, a Deputation
of the States-General!' [1] *Sunt lachrymae rerum.*

But what does the Œil-de-Bœuf, now when De Brézé
shivers back thither? *Dispatch* that same force of
bayonets? Not so: the seas of people still hang
multitudinous,* intent on what is passing; nay rush
and roll, loud-billowing, into the Courts of the Château
itself; for a report has risen that Necker is to be
dismissed. Worst of all, the Gardes Françaises seem
indisposed to act: 'two Companies of them *do not fire*
when ordered!' [2] Necker, for not being at the *Séance*,
shall be shouted for, carried home in triumph; and
must not be dismissed. His Grace of Paris, on the
other hand, has to fly with broken coach-panels, and
owe his life to furious driving. The *Gardes-du-Corps*
(Body-Guards), which you were drawing out, had
better be drawn in again.[3] There is no sending of
bayonets to be thought of.

Instead of soldiers, the Œil-de-Bœuf sends—carpenters, to take down the platform. Ineffectual shift! In
few instants, the very carpenters cease wrenching and
knocking at their platform; standing on it, hammer
in hand, and listen open-mouthed.[4] The Third Estate
is decreeing that it is, was, and will be, nothing but
a National Assembly; and now, moreover, an invioi-
able one, all members of it inviolable: 'infamous,

---

[1] Montgaillard, ii. 38.   [2] Histoire Parlementaire, ii. 26.
[3] Bailly, i. 217.   [4] Histoire Parlementaire, ii. 23.

traitorous, towards the Nation, and guilty of capital
crime, is any person, body-corporate, tribunal, court
or commission that now or henceforth, during the present session or after it, shall dare to pursue, interrogate,
arrest, or cause to be arrested, detain or cause to be
detained, any ' &c. &c. ' on *whose part soever* the same
be commanded '.[1] Which done, one can wind up with
this comfortable reflection from Abbé Sieyes : ' Messieurs, you are to-day what you were yesterday'.

Courtiers may shriek ; but it is, and remains, even
so. Their well-charged explosion has exploded *through
the touch-hole* ; covering themselves with scorches, confusion, and unseemly soot ! Poor Triumvirate, poor
Queen ; and above all, poor Queen's Husband, who
means well, had he any fixed meaning ! Folly is that
wisdom which is wise only behindhand. Few months
ago these Thirty-five Concessions had filled France
with a rejoicing, which might have lasted for several
years. Now it is unavailing, the very mention of it
slighted ; Majesty's express orders set at naught.

All France is in a roar ; a sea of persons, estimated
at ' ten thousand ', whirls ' all this day in the Palais
Royal.' [2] The remaining Clergy, and likewise some
Forty-eight Noblesse, D'Orléans among them, have
now forthwith gone over to the victorious Commons ;
—by whom, as is natural, they are received ' with
acclamation '.

The Third Estate triumphs ; Versailles Town shouting round it ; ten thousand whirling all day in the
Palais Royal ; and all France standing a-tiptoe, not
unlike whirling ! Let the Œil-de-Bœuf look to it. As
for King Louis, he will swallow his injuries ; will
temporize, keep silence ; will at all costs have present
peace. It was Tuesday, the 23rd of June, when he
spoke that peremptory royal mandate ; and the week
is not done till he has written to the remaining obstinate
Noblesse, that they also must oblige him, and give in.
D'Espréménil rages his last ; Barrel Mirabeau ' breaks

[1] Montgaillard, ii. 47.   [2] Arthur Young, i. 119.

his sword', making a vow,—which he might as well
have kept. The 'Triple Family' is now therefore
complete ; the third erring brother, the Noblesse, having joined it ;—erring but pardonable ; soothed, so far
as possible, by sweet eloquence from President Bailly.

So triumphs the Third Estate ; and States-General
are become National Assembly ; and all France may
sing *Te Deum*. By wise inertia, and wise cessation of
inertia, great victory has been gained. It is the last
night of June : all night you meet nothing on the
streets of Versailles but 'men running with torches',
with shouts and jubilation. From the 2nd of May
when they kissed the hand of Majesty, to this 30th of
June when men run with torches, we count eight weeks
and three days. For eight weeks the National Carroccio has stood far-seen, ringing many a signal ; and,
so much having now gathered round it, may hope to
stand.

CHAPTER III

BROGLIE THE WAR-GOD

THE Court feels indignant that it is conquered ; but
what then ? Another time it will do better. Mercury
descended in vain ; now has the time come for Mars.—
The gods of the Œil-de-Bœuf have withdrawn into the
darkness of their cloudy Ida ; and sit there, shaping
and forging what may be needful, be it 'billets of a
new National Bank', munitions of war, or things for
ever inscrutable to men.

Accordingly, what means this 'apparatus of troops' ?
The National Assembly can get no furtherance for its
Committee of Subsistences ; can hear only that, at
Paris, the Bakers' shops are besieged ; that, in the
Provinces, people are 'living on meal-husks and boiled
grass'. But on all highways there hover dust-clouds,
with the march of regiments, with the trailing of

cannon: foreign Pandours, of fierce aspect; Salis-Samade, Esterhazy, Royal-Allemand; so many of them foreign; to the number of thirty thousand,—which fear can magnify to fifty: all wending towards Paris and Versailles! Already, on the heights of Montmartre, is a digging and delving; too like a scarping and trenching. The effluence of Paris is arrested Versailles-ward by a barrier of cannon at Sèvres Bridge. From the Queen's Mews, cannon stand pointed on the National Assembly Hall itself. The National Assembly has its very slumbers broken by the tramp of soldiery, swarming and defiling, endless, or seemingly endless, all round those spaces, at dead of night, ' without drum-music, without audible word of command'.[1] What means it?

Shall eight, or even shall twelve Deputies, our Mirabeaus, Barnaves at the head of them, be whirled suddenly to the Castle of Ham; the rest ignominiously dispersed to the winds? No National Assembly can make the Constitution with cannon levelled on it from the Queen's Mews! What means this reticence of the Œil-de-Bœuf, broken only by nods and shrugs? In the mystery of that cloudy Ida, what is it that they forge and shape?—Such questions must distracted Patriotism keep asking, and receive no answer but an echo.

Questions and echo bad enough in themselves:—and now, above all, while the hungry food-year, which runs from August to August, is getting older; becoming more and more a famine-year! With ' meal-husks and boiled grass ', Brigands may actually collect; and, in crowds, at farm and mansion, howl angrily, *Food! Food!* It is in vain to send soldiers against them: at sight of soldiers they disperse, they vanish as under ground; then directly reassemble elsewhere for new tumult and plunder. Frightful enough to look upon; but what to *hear* of, reverberated through Twenty-five Millions of suspicious minds! Brigands and Broglie, open Conflagration, preternatural Rumour are driving mad most hearts in France. What will the issue of these things be?

[1] A. Lameth, Assemblée Constituante, i. 41.

At Marseilles, many weeks ago, the Townsmen have
taken arms ; for ' suppressing of Brigands ', and other
purposes : the military Commandant may make of it
what he will. Elsewhere, everywhere, could not the
like be done ? Dubious, on the distracted Patriot
Imagination, wavers, as a last deliverance, some foreshadow of a *National Guard*. But conceive, above all,
the Wooden Tent in the Palais Royal ! A universal
hubbub* there, as of dissolving worlds : there loudest
bellows the mad, mad-making voice of Rumour ; there
sharpest gazes Suspicion into the pale dim World-
Whirlpool; discerning shapes and phantasms : imminent
bloodthirsty Regiments camped on the Champ-de-
Mars ; dispersed National Assembly ; red-hot cannon-
balls (to burn Paris) :—the mad War-god and Bellona's
sounding thongs. To the calmest man it is becoming
too plain that battle is inevitable.

Inevitable, silently nod Messeigneurs and Broglie :
Inevitable and brief ! Your National Assembly, stopped short in its Constitutional labours, may fatigue the
royal ear with addresses and remonstrances : those
cannon of ours stand duly levelled ; those troops are
here. The King's Declaration, with its Thirty-five too
generous Articles, was spoken, was not listened to ; but
remains yet unrevoked : he himself shall effect it, *seul
il fera !*

As for Broglie, he has his head quarters at Versailles,
all as in a seat of war : clerks writing ; significant
staff-officers, inclined to taciturnity : plumed aides-de-
camp, scouts, orderlies flying or hovering. He himself
looks forth, important, impenetrable ; listens to
Besenval Commandant of Paris, and his warning and
earnest counsels (for he has come out repeatedly on
purpose), with a silent smile.[1] The Parisians resist ?
scornfully cry Messeigneurs. As a meal-mob may !
They have sat quiet, these five generations, submitting
to all. Their Mercier declared, in these very years,
that a Parisian revolt was henceforth ' impossible '.[2]

[1] Besenval, iii. 398.
[2] Mercier, Tableau de Paris. vi. 22.

Stand by the royal Declaration, of the Twenty-third of
June. The Nobles of France, valorous, chivalrous as
of old, will rally round us with one heart ;—and as for
this which you call Third Estate, and which we call
canaille of unwashed Sansculottes, of Patelins, Scrib-
blers, factious Spouters,—brave Broglie, ' with a whiff
of grapeshot (*salve de canons*) ', if need be, will give
quick account of it. Thus reason they: on their
cloudy Ida ; hidden from men,—men also hidden from
them.

Good is grapeshot, Messeigneurs, on one condition :
that the shooter also were made of metal ! But unfortunately he is made of flesh ; under his buffs and bandoleers, your hired shooter has instincts, feelings, even
a kind of thought. It is his kindred, bone of his bone,
this same *canaille* that shall be whiffed ; he has brothers
in it, a father and mother,—living on meal-husks and
boiled grass. His very doxy, not yet ' dead i' the
spital ', drives him into military heterodoxy ; declares
that if he shed Patriot blood, he shall be accursed
among men. The soldier, who has seen his pay stolen
by rapacious Foulons, his blood wasted by Soubises,
Pompadours, and the gates of promotion shut inexor-
ably on him if he were not born noble,—is himself
not without griefs against you. Your cause is not the
soldier's cause ; but, as would seem, your own only,
and no other god's nor man's.

For example, the world may have heard how, at
Béthune lately, when there rose some ' riot about
grains ', of which sort there are so many, and the soldiers stood drawn out, and the word ' Fire ! ' was given,
—not a trigger stirred ; only the butts of all muskets
rattled angrily against the ground ; and the soldiers
stood glooming, with a mixed expression of countenance ;—till clutched ' each under the arm of a patriot
householder ', they were all hurried off, in this manner,
to be treated and caressed, and have their pay increased
by subscription ! [1]

[1] Histoire Parlementaire.

Neither have the Gardes Françaises, the best regiment of the line, shown any promptitude for street-firing lately. They returned grumbling from Réveillon's; and have not burnt a single cartridge since; nay, as we saw, not even when bid. A dangerous humour dwells in these Gardes. Notable men too, in their way! Valadi the Pythagorean was, at one time, an officer of theirs. Nay, in the ranks, under the three-cornered felt and cockade, what hard heads may there not be, and reflections going on,—unknown to the public! One head of the hardest we do now discern there: on the shoulders of a certain Sergeant Hoche. Lazare Hoche, that is the name of him; he used to be about the Versailles Royal Stables, nephew of a poor herbwoman; a handy lad; exceedingly addicted to reading. He is now Sergeant Hoche, and can rise no further: he lays out his pay in rushlights, and cheap editions of books.[1]

On the whole, the best seems to be: Consign these Gardes Françaises to their Barracks. So Besenval thinks, and orders. Consigned to their barracks, the Gardes Françaises do but form a 'Secret Association', an Engagement not to act against the National Assembly. Debauched by Valadi the Pythagorean; debauched by money and women! cry Besenval and innumerable others. Debauched by what you will, or in need of no debauching, behold them, long files of them, their consignment broken, arrive, headed by their Sergeants, on the 26th day of June, at the Palais Royal! Welcomed with vivats, with presents, and a pledge of patriot liquor; embracing and embraced; declaring in words that the cause of France is their cause! Next day and the following days the like. What is singular too, except this patriot humour, and breaking of their consignment, they behave otherwise with 'the most rigorous accuracy'.[2]

---

[1] Dictionnaire des Hommes Marquans, Londres (Paris), 1800, ii. 198.

[2] Besenval, iii, 394-6,

They are growing questionable, these Gardes!
Eleven ringleaders of them are put in the Abbaye
Prison. It boots not in the least. The imprisoned
Eleven have only, ' by the hand of an individual ', to
drop, towards nightfall, a line in the Café de Foy;
where Patriotism harangues loudest on its table. ' Two
hundred young persons, soon waxing to four thousand ',
with fit crowbars roll towards the Abbaye; smite
asunder the needful doors; and bear out their Eleven,
with other military victims :—to supper in the Palais
Royal Garden; to board, and lodging ' in camp-beds,
in the *Théâtre des Variétés* '; other national *Prytaneum*
as yet not being in readiness. Most deliberate! Nay
so punctual were these young persons, that finding one
military victim to have been imprisoned for real civil
crime, they returned him to his cell, with protest.

Why new military force was not called out? New
military force was called out. New military force did
arrive, full gallop, with drawn sabre : but the people
gently ' laid hold of their bridles '; the dragoons
sheathed their swords; lifted their caps by way of
salute, and sat like mere statues of dragoons,—except
indeed that a drop of liquor being brought them, they
' drank to the King and Nation with the greatest
cordiality '![1]

And now, ask in return, why Messeigneurs and
Broglie the great god of war, on seeing these things, did
not pause, and take some other course, any other
course? Unhappily, as we said, they could see nothing.
Pride, which goes before a fall ;* wrath, if not reasonable, yet pardonable, most natural, had hardened their
hearts*and heated their heads : so with imbecility and
violence (ill-matched pair) they rush to seek their hour.
All Regiments are not Gardes Françaises, or debauched
by Valadi the Pythagorean : let fresh undebauched
Regiments come up; let Royal-Allemand, Salis-
Samade, Swiss Château-Vieux come up,—which can
fight, but can hardly speak except in German gutturals ;

[1] Histoire Parlementaire, ii. 32.

let soldiers march, and highways thunder with artillery-wagons : Majesty has a *new* Royal Session to hold,—and miracles to work there ! The whiff of grapeshot can, if needful, become a blast and tempest.

In which circumstances, before the red-hot balls begin raining, may not the Hundred-and-twenty Paris Electors, though their *Cahier* is long since finished, see good to meet again daily, as an ' Electoral Club ' ? They meet first ' in a Tavern ' ;—where ' a large wedding-party' cheerfully gives place to them.[1] But latterly they meet in the *Hôtel-de-Ville*, in the Town-hall itself. Flesselles,* Provost of Merchants, with his Four Echevins (*Scabins*, Assessors) could not prevent it ; such was the force of public opinion. He, with his Echevins, and the Six-and-Twenty Town Councillors, all appointed from Above, may well sit silent there, in their long gowns ; and consider, with awed eye, what prelude this is of convulsion coming from Below, and how they themselves shall fare in that !

CHAPTER IV

TO ARMS !

So hangs it, dubious, fateful, in the sultry days of July. It is the passionate printed *advice* of M. Marat, to abstain, of all things, from violence.[2] Nevertheless the hungry poor are already burning Town Barriers, where Tribute on eatables is levied ; getting clamorous for food.

The twelfth July morning is Sunday : the streets are all placarded with an enormous-sized *De par le Roi*,

---

[1] Dusaulx, Prise de la Bastille (Collection des Mémoires, par Berville et Barrière, Paris, 1821), p. 269.

[2] Avis au Peuple, ou les Ministres dévoilés, 1st July 1789 (in Histoire Parlementaire, ii. 37).

'inviting peaceable citizens to remain within doors', to feel no alarm, to gather in no crowd. Why so? What mean these 'placards of enormous size'? Above all, what means this clatter of military; dragoons, hussars, rattling in from all points of the compass towards the Place Louis Quinze; with a staid gravity of face, though saluted with mere nicknames, hootings and even missiles?[1] Besenval is with them. Swiss Guards of his are already in the Champs Elysées, with four pieces of artillery.

Have the destroyers descended on us, then? From the Bridge of Sèvres to utmost Vincennes, from Saint-Denis to the Champ-de-Mars, we are begirt! Alarm, of the vague unknown, is in every heart. The Palais Royal has become a place of awestruck interjections, silent shakings of the head: one can fancy with what dolorous sound the noontide cannon (which the Sun fires at crossing of his meridian) went off there; bodeful, like an inarticulate voice of doom.[2] Are these troops verily come out 'against Brigands'? Where are the Brigands? What mystery is in the wind?— Hark! a human voice reporting articulately the Job's-news:* *Necker, People's Minister, Saviour of France, is dismissed.* Impossible; incredible! Treasonous to the public peace! Such a voice ought to be choked in the water-works;[3]—had not the news-bringer quickly fled. Nevertheless, friends, make of it what ye will, the news is true. Necker is gone. Necker hies northward incessantly, in obedient secrecy, since yesternight. We have a new Ministry: Broglie the War-god; Aristocrat Breteuil; Foulon who said the people might eat grass!

Rumour, therefore, shall arise; in the Palais Royal, and in broad France. Paleness sits on every face; confused tremor and fremescence; waxing into thunder-peals, of Fury stirred on by Fear.

But see Camille Desmoulins, from the Café de Foy,

---

[1] Besenval, iii. 411.
[2] Histoire Parlementaire, ii. 81.   [3] Ibid.

rushing out, sibylline in face ; his hair streaming, in
each hand a pistol ! He springs to a table : the Police
satellites are eyeing him ; alive they shall not take him,
not they alive him alive. This time, he speaks without
stammering :—Friends ! shall we die like hunted hares ?
Like sheep hounded into their pinfold ; bleating for
mercy, where is no mercy, but only a whetted knife ?
The hour is come ; the supreme hour of Frenchman and
Man ; when Oppressors are to try conclusions with
Oppressed ; and the word is, swift Death, or Deliverance for ever. Let such hour be *well*-come ! Us,
meseems, one cry only befits : To Arms ! Let universal
Paris, universal France, as with the throat of the
whirlwind, sound only : To arms !—' To arms ! ' yell
responsive the innumerable voices ; like one great
voice, as of a Demon yelling from the air : for all faces
wax fire-eyed, all hearts burn up into madness. In
such, or fitter words,[1] does Camille evoke the Elemental
Powers, in this great moment.—Friends, continues
Camille, some rallying-sign ! Cockades ; green ones ;
—the colour of Hope !—As with the flight of locusts,
these green tree-leaves ; green ribands from the neighbouring shops ; all green things are snatched, and
made cockades of. Camille descends from his table ;
' stifled with embraces, wetted with tears ' ; has a bit
of green riband handed him ; sticks it in his hat. And
now to Curtius' Image-shop there ; to the Boulevards ;
to the four winds, and rest not till France be on fire !

France, so long shaken and wind-parched, is probably at the right inflammable point.—As for poor
Curtius, who, one grieves to think, might be but imperfectly paid,—he cannot make two words about his
Images. The Wax-bust of Necker, the Wax-bust of
D'Orléans, helpers of France : these, covered with
crape, as in funeral procession, or after the manner of
suppliants appealing to Heaven, to Earth, and Tartarus

---

[1] Vieux Cordelier, par Camille Desmoulins, No. 5 (reprinted in Collection des Mémoires, par Baudouin Frères,
Paris, 1825), p. 81.

itself, a mixed multitude bears off. For a sign! As
indeed man, with his singular imaginative faculties,
can do little or nothing without signs: thus Turks
look to their Prophet's Banner; also Osier *Mannikins*
have been burnt, and Necker's Portrait has erewhile
figured, aloft on its perch.

In this manner march they, a mixed, continually
increasing multitude; armed with axes, staves and
miscellanea; grim, many-sounding, through the streets.
Be all Theatres shut; let all dancing, on planked floor,
or on the natural greensward, cease! Instead of a
Christian Sabbath, and feast of *guinguette* tabernacles,*
it shall be a Sorcerer's Sabbath; and Paris, gone rabid,
dance,—with the Fiend for piper!

However, Besenval, with horse and foot, is in the
Place Louis Quinze. Mortals promenading homewards,
in the fall of the day, saunter by, from Chaillot or Passy,
from flirtation and a little thin wine; with sadder step
than usual. Will the Bust-Procession pass that way?
Behold it; behold also Prince Lambesc dash forth on
it, with his Royal-Allemands! Shots fall, and sabre-
strokes; Busts are hewed asunder; and, alas, also
heads of men. A sabred Procession has nothing for it
but to *explode*, along what streets, alleys, Tuileries
Avenues it finds; and disappear. One unarmed man
lies hewed down; a Garde Française by his uniform:
bear him (or bear even the report of him) dead and
gory to his Barracks;—where he has comrades still
alive!

But why not now, victorious Lambesc, charge
through that Tuileries Garden itself, where the fugitives
are vanishing? Not show the Sunday promenaders
too how steel glitters, besprent with blood; that it be
told of, and men's ears tingle?—Tingle, alas, they did;
but the wrong way. Victorious Lambesc, in this his
second or Tuileries charge, succeeds but in overturning
(call it not slashing, for he struck with the flat of his
sword) one man, a poor old schoolmaster, most pacifically tottering there; and is driven out, by barricade

of chairs, by flights of ' bottles and glasses ', by execrations in bass-voice and treble. Most delicate is the
mob-queller's vocation ; wherein Too-much may be as
bad as Not-enough. For each of these bass-voices, and
more each treble voice, borne to all parts of the City,
rings now nothing but distracted indignation ; will
ring all night. The cry, *To arms*, roars tenfold; steeples
with their metal storm-voice boom out, as the sun
sinks ; armorers' shops are broken open, plundered ;
the streets are a living foam-sea, chafed by all the winds.

Such issue came of Lambesc's charge on the Tuileries
Garden : no striking of salutary terror into Chaillot
promenaders ; a striking into broad wakefulness of
Frenzy and the three Furies,—which otherwise were
not asleep ! For they lie always, those subterranean
Eumenides*(fabulous and yet so true), in the dullest
existence of man ;—and can dance, brandishing their
dusky torches, shaking their serpent-hair. Lambesc
with Royal-Allemand may ride to his barracks, with
curses for his marching-music ; then ride back again,
like one troubled in mind : vengeful Gardes Françaises,
*sacre*ing, with knit brows, start out on him, from their
barracks in the Chaussé d'Antin ; pour a volley into
him (killing and wounding) ; which he must not answer,
but ride on.[1]

Counsel dwells not under the plumed hat. If the
Eumenides awaken, and Broglie has given no orders,
what can a Besenval do ? When the Gardes Françaises, with Palais-Royal volunteers, roll down, greedy
of more vengeance, to the Place Louis Quinze itself,
they find neither Besenval, Lambesc, Royal-Allemand,
nor any soldier now there. Gone is military order.
On the far Eastern Boulevard, of Saint-Antoine, the
Chasseurs Normandie arrive, dusty, thirsty, after
a hard day's ride ; but can find no billet-master, see
no course in this City of confusions ; cannot get to
Besenval, cannot so much as discover where he is :
Normandie must even bivouac there, in its dust and

[1] Weber, ii. 75–91.

thirst,—unless some patriot will treat it to a cup of liquor, with advices.

Raging multitudes surround the Hôtel-de-Ville, crying: Arms! Orders! The Six-and-twenty Town Councillors, with their long gowns, have ducked under (into the raging chaos);—shall never emerge more. Besenval is painfully wriggling himself out, to the Champ-de-Mars; he must sit there 'in the cruellest uncertainty': courier after courier may dash off for Versailles; but will bring back no answer, can hardly bring himself back. For the roads are all blocked with batteries and pickets, with floods of carriages arrested for examination . such was Broglie's one sole order; the Œil-de-Bœuf, hearing in the distance such mad din, which sounded almost like invasion, will before all things keep its own head whole. A new Ministry, with, as it were, but one foot in the stirrup, cannot take leaps. Mad Paris is abandoned altogether to itself.

What a Paris, when the darkness fell! A European metropolitan City hurled suddenly forth from its old combinations and arrangements; to crash tumultuously together, seeking new. Use and wont will now no longer direct any man; each man, with what of originality he has, must begin thinking; or following those that think. Seven hundred thousand individuals, on the sudden, find all their old paths, old ways of acting and deciding, vanish from under their feet. And so there go they, with clangour and terror, they know not as yet whether running, swimming or flying,—headlong into the New Era. With clangour and terror: from above, Broglie the war-god impends, preternatural, with his red-hot cannon-balls; and from below, a preternatural Brigand-world menaces with dirk and fire-brand: madness rules the hour.

Happily, in place of the submerged Twenty-six, the Electoral Club is gathering; has declared itself a 'Provisional Municipality'. On the morrow, it will get Provost Flesselles, with an Echevin or two, to give help in many things. For the present it decrees one most essential thing: that forthwith a 'Parisian Militia' shall be enrolled. Depart, ye heads of Districts, to labour in this great work; while we here, in Permanent Committee, sit alert. Let fencible men, each party in its own range of streets, keep watch and ward, all night. Let Paris court a little fever-sleep; confused by such fever-dreams, of 'violent motions at the Palais Royal';—or from time to time start awake, and look out, palpitating, in its nightcap, at the clash of discordant mutually-unintelligible Patrols; on the gleam of distant Barriers, going up all too ruddy towards the vault of Night.[1]

CHAPTER V

GIVE US ARMS

On Monday, the huge City has awoke, not to its week-day industry: to what a different one! The working man has become a fighting man; has one want only: that of arms. The industry of all crafts has paused;—except it be the smith's, fiercely hammering pikes; and, in a faint degree, the kitchener's, cooking offhand victuals, for *bouche va toujours*. Women too are sewing cockades;—not now of *green*, which being D'Artois colour, the Hôtel-de-Ville has had to interfere in it; but of *red* and *blue*, our old Paris colours: these, once based on a ground of constitutional *white*, are the famed TRICOLOR,—which (if Prophecy err not) 'will go round the world'.

All shops, unless it be the Bakers' and Vintners', are shut: Paris is in the streets;—rushing, foaming like some Venice wine-glass*into which you had dropped poison. The tocsin, by order, is pealing madly from all steeples. Arms, ye Elector Municipals; thou Flesselles with thy Echevins, give us arms! Flesselles

---

[1] Deux Amis, i. 267-306.

gives what he can: fallacious, perhaps insidious promises of arms from Charleville; order to seek arms
here, order to seek them there. The new Municipals
give what they can; some three hundred and sixty
indifferent firelocks, the equipment of the City-Watch:
'a man in wooden shoes, and without coat, directly
clutches one of them, and mounts guard'. Also as
hinted, an order to all Smiths to make pikes with their
whole soul.

Heads of Districts are in fervent consultation; subordinate Patriotism roams distracted, ravenous for
arms. Hitherto at the Hôtel-de-Ville was only such
modicum of indifferent firelocks as we have seen. At
the so-called Arsenal, there lies nothing but rust, rubbish
and saltpetre,—overlooked too by the guns of the Bastille. His Majesty's Repository, what they call *Garde-
Meuble*, is forced and ransacked: tapestries enough,
and gauderies; but of serviceable fighting-gear small
stock! Two silver-mounted cannons there are; an
ancient gift from his Majesty of Siam to Louis Fourteenth: gilt sword of the Good Henri; antique
Chivalry arms and armour. These, and such as these,
a necessitous Patriotism snatches greedily, for want
of better. The Siamese cannons go trundling, on an
errand they were not meant for. Among the indifferent
firelocks are seen tournay-lances; the princely helm
and hauberk glittering amid ill-hatted heads,—as in
a time when all times and their possessions are suddenly sent jumbling!

At the *Maison de Saint-Lazare*, Lazar-House once,
now a Correction-House with Priests, there was no
trace of arms; but, on the other hand, corn, plainly
to a culpable extent. Out with it, to market; in this
scarcity of grains!—Heavens, will 'fifty-two carts',
in long row, hardly carry it to the *Halle aux Bleds*?
Well truly, ye reverend Fathers, was your pantry
filled; fat are your larders; over-generous your wine-
bins, ye plotting exasperators of the Poor; traitorous
forestallers of bread!

Vain is protesting, entreaty on bare knees: the House of Saint-Lazarus has that in it which comes not out by protesting. Behold, how, from every window, it *vomits* : mere torrents of furniture, of bellowing and hurlyburly;—the cellars also leaking wine. Till, as was natural, smoke rose,—kindled, some say, by the desperate Saint-Lazaristes themselves, desperate of other riddance; and the Establishment vanished from this world in flame. Remark nevertheless that ' a thief ' (set on or not by Aristocrats), being detected there, is ' instantly hanged '.

Look also at the Châtelet Prison. The Debtors' Prison of La Force is broken from without; and they that sat in bondage to Aristocrats go free: hearing of which the Felons at the Châtelet do likewise ' dig up their pavements ', and stand on the offensive; with the best prospects,—had not Patriotism, passing that way, ' fired a volley ' into the Felon-world; and crushed it down again under hatches. Patriotism consorts not with thieving and felony: surely also Punishment, this day, hitches (if she still hitch) after Crime, with frightful shoes-of-swiftness ! ' Some score or two ' of wretched persons, found prostrate with drink in the cellars of that Saint-Lazare, are indignantly haled to prison; the Jailor has no room; whereupon, other place of security not suggesting itself, it is written, ' *on les pendit,* they hanged them '.[1]   Brief is the word; not without significance, be it true or untrue !

In such circumstances, the Aristocrat, the unpatriotic rich man is packing up for departure. But he shall not get departed. A wooden-shod force has seized all Barriers, burnt or not: all that enters, all that seeks to issue, is stopped there, and dragged to the Hôtel-de-Ville: coaches, tumbrils, plate, furniture, ' many meal-sacks ', in time even ' flocks and herds ' encumber the Place de Grève.[2]

---

[1] Histoire Parlementaire, ii. 96.
[2] Dusaulx, Prise de la Bastille, p. 290.

And so it roars, and rages, and brays ; drums beating, steeples pealing ; criers rushing with hand-bells :
' Oyez, oyez, All men to their Districts to be enrolled ! '
The Districts have met in gardens, open squares ; are
getting marshalled into volunteer troops. No red-hot
ball has yet fallen from Besenval's Camp ; on the contrary, Deserters with their arms are continually dropping in : nay now, joy of joys, at two in the afternoon,
the Gardes Françaises, being ordered to Saint-Denis,
and flatly declining, have come over in a body ! It is
a fact worth many. Three thousand six hundred of the
best fighting men, with complete accoutrement ; with
cannoneers even, and cannon ! Their officers are left
standing alone ; could not so much as succeed in
' spiking the guns '. The very Swiss, it may now be
hoped, Château-Vieux and the others, will have doubts
about fighting.

Our Parisian Militia, which some think it were better
to name National Guard,—is prospering as heart could
wish. It promised to be forty-eight thousand ; but
will in few hours double and quadruple that number :
invincible, if we had only arms !

But see, the promised Charleville Boxes, marked
Artillerie ! Here then are arms enough ?—Conceive
the blank face of Patriotism, when it found them filled
with rags, foul linen, candle-ends, and bits of wood !
Provost of the Merchants, how is this ? Neither at
the Chartreux Convent, whither we were sent with
signed order, is there or ever was there any weapon of
war. Nay here, in this Seine Boat, safe under tarpaul-
ings (had not the nose of Patriotism been of the finest),
are ' five thousand-weight of gunpowder ' ; not coming
in, but surreptitiously going out ! What meanest thou,
Flesselles ? 'Tis a ticklish game, that of ' amusing '
us. Cat plays with captive mouse : but mouse with
enraged cat, with enraged National Tiger ?

Meanwhile, the faster, O ye black-aproned Smiths,
smite ; with strong arm and willing heart. This man
and that, all stroke from head to heel, shall thunder
alternating, and ply the great forgehammer, till stithy

reel and ring again; while ever and anon, overhead,
booms the alarm-cannon,—for the City has now got gunpowder. Pikes are fabricated; fifty thousand of them,
in six-and-thirty hours: judge whether the Black-
aproned have been idle. Dig trenches, unpave the
streets, ye others, assiduous, man and maid; cram the
earth in barrel-barricades, at each of them a volunteer
sentry; pile the whinstones in window-sills and upper
rooms. Have scalding pitch, at least boiling water
ready, ye weak old women, to pour it and dash it on
Royal-Allemand, with your old skinny arms: your
shrill curses along with it will not be wanting!—Patrols
of the newborn National Guard, bearing torches, scour
the streets, all that night; which otherwise are vacant,
yet illuminated in every window by order. Strange
looking; like some naphtha-lighted* City of the
Dead, with here and there a flight of perturbed
Ghosts.

O poor mortals, how ye make this Earth bitter for
each other; this fearful and wonderful*Life fearful and
horrible; and Satan has his place in all hearts! Such
agonies and ragings and wailings ye have, and have had,
in all times :—to be buried all, in so deep silence ;* and
the salt sea is not swoln with your tears.

Great meanwhile is the moment, when tidings of
Freedom reach us; when the long-enthralled soul, from
amid its chains and squalid stagnancy, arises, were it
still only in blindness and bewilderment, and swears
by Him that made it, that it will be *free*! Free?
Understand that well, it is the deep commandment,
dimmer or clearer, of our whole being, to be *free*.
Freedom is the one purport, wisely aimed at, or
unwisely, of all man's struggles, toilings and sufferings
in this Earth. Yes, supreme is such a moment (if thou
have known it): first vision as of a flame-girt Sinai,* in
this our waste Pilgrimage,—which thenceforth wants
not its pillar of cloud by day, and pillar of fire by night*!
Something it is even,—nay, something considerable,
when the chains have grown *corrosive*, poisonous,—to
be free ' from oppression by our fellow-man '. Forward,

ye maddened sons of France ; be it towards this destiny
or towards that ! Around you is but starvation, falsehood, corruption and the clam of death. Where ye
are is no abiding.*

Imagination may, imperfectly, figure how Commandant Besenval, in the Champ-de-Mars, has worn out
these sorrowful hours. Insurrection raging all round ;
his men melting away ! From Versailles, to the most
pressing messages, comes no answer ; or once only some
vague word of answer which is worse than none. A
Council of Officers can decide merely that there is no
decision : Colonels inform him, ' weeping ', that they
do not think their men will fight. Cruel uncertainty
is here : war-god Broglie sits yonder, inaccessible in his
Olympus ; does not descend terror-clad, does not produce his whiff of grapeshot ; sends no orders.

Truly, in the Château of Versailles all seems mystery :
in the Town of Versailles, were we there, all is rumour,
alarm and indignation. An august National Assembly
sits, to appearance, menaced with death ; endeavouring
to defy death. It has resolved ' that Necker carries
with him the regrets of the Nation '. It has sent solemn
Deputation over to the Château, with entreaty to have
these troops withdrawn. In vain : his Majesty, with
a singular composure, invites us to be busy rather with
our own duty, making the constitution ! Foreign Pandours, and such like, go pricking and prancing, with
a swashbuckler air ; with an eye too probably to the
Salle des Menus,—were it not for the ' grim-looking
countenances ' that crowd all avenues there.[1] Be
firm, ye National Senators ; the cynosure of a firm,
grim-looking people !

The august National Senators determine that there
shall, at least, be Permanent Session till this thing end.
Wherein however, consider that worthy Lafranc de
Pompignan, our new President, whom we have named
Bailly's successor, is an old man, wearied with many

[1] See Lameth ; Ferrieres, &c.

things. He is the Brother of that Pompignan who
meditated lamentably on the Book of *Lamentations* :

> *Savez-vous pourquoi Jérémie*
> *Se lamentait toute sa vie ?*
> *C'est qu'il prévoyait*
> *Que Pompignan le traduirait !*

Poor Bishop Pompignan withdraws ; having got
Lafayette for helper or substitute : this latter, as nocturnal Vice-President, with a thin house in disconsolate
humour, sits sleepless, with lights unsnuffed ;—waiting
what the hours will bring.

So at Versailles. But at Paris, agitated Besenval,
before retiring for the night, has stept over to old
M. de Sombreuil,* of the *Hôtel des Invalides* hard by.
M. de Sombreuil has, what is a great secret, some
eight-and-twenty thousand stand of muskets deposited
in his cellars there ; but no trust in the temper of his
Invalides. This day, for example, he sent twenty of
the fellows down to unscrew those muskets ; lest Sedition might snatch at them : but scarcely, in six hours,
had the twenty unscrewed twenty gun-locks, or dogs-
heads (*chiens*) of locks,—each Invalide his dogshead !
If ordered to fire, they would, he imagines, turn their
cannon against himself.

Unfortunate old military gentleman, it is your hour,
not of glory ! Old Marquis de Launay too, of the
Bastille, has pulled up his drawbridges long since, ' and
retired into his interior ' ; with sentries walking on his
battlements, under the midnight sky, aloft over the
glare of illuminated Paris ;—whom a National Patrol,
passing that way, takes the liberty of firing at : ' seven
shots towards twelve at night ', which do not take
effect.[1] This was the 13th day of July 1789 ; a worse
day, many said, than the last 13th was, when only hail
fell out of Heaven, not madness rose out of Tophet,*
ruining worse than crops !

In these same days, as Chronology will teach us, hot

---

[1] *Deux Amis de la Liberté*, i. 312.

old Marquis Mirabeau lies stricken down, at Argenteuil,
—*not* within sound of these alarm-guns ; for *he* properly is not there, and only the body of him now lies,
deaf and cold for ever. It was on Saturday night that
he, drawing his last life-breaths, gave up the ghost
there ;—leaving a world, which would never go to his
mind, now broken out, seemingly, into deliration and
the *culbute générale.* What is it to him, departing elsewhither, on his long journey ? The old Château Mirabeau stands silent, far off, on its scarped rock, in that
' gorge of two windy valleys ' ; the pale-fading spectre
now of a Château : this huge World-riot, and France,
and the World itself, fades also, like a shadow on the
great still mirror-sea ; and all shall be as God wills.

Young Mirabeau, sad of heart, for he loved this
crabbed brave old Father ; sad of heart, and occupied
with sad cares,—is withdrawn from Public History.
The great crisis transacts itself without him.[1]

CHAPTER VI

STORM AND VICTORY

But, to the living and the struggling, a new, Fourteenth morning dawns. Under all roofs of this distracted City is the nodus of a drama, not untragical,
crowding towards solution. The bustlings and pre-
parings, the tremors and menaces ; the tears that fell
from old eyes ! This day, my sons, ye shall quit you
like men.* By the memory of your fathers' wrongs,
by the hope of your children's rights ! Tyranny
impends in red wrath : help for you is none, if not in
your own right hands. This day ye must do or die.*

From earliest light, a sleepless Permanent Committee
has heard the old cry, now waxing almost frantic,
mutinous : Arms ! Arms ! Provost Flesselles, or what

[1] Fils Adoptif, Mirabeau, vi. l. 1.

traitors there are among you, may think of those
Charleville Boxes. A hundred-and-fifty thousand of
us ; and but the third man furnished with so much as
a pike ! Arms are the one thing needful :* with arms
we are an unconquerable man-defying National Guard ;
without arms, a rabble to be whiffed with grapeshot. ·

Happily the word has arisen, for no secret can be
kept,—that there lie muskets at the *Hôtel des Invalides*.
Thither will we : King's Procureur M. Ethys de Corny,
and whatsoever of authority a Permanent Committee
can lend, shall go with us. Besenval's Camp is there ;
perhaps he will not fire on us ; if he kill us, we shall
but die.

Alas, poor Besenval, with his troops melting away
in that manner, has not the smallest humour to fire !
At five o'clock this morning, as he lay dreaming, oblivious in the *École Militaire*, a ' figure ' stood suddenly
at his bedside ; ' with face rather handsome ; eyes
inflamed, speech rapid and curt, air audacious ' : such
a figure drew Priam's curtains !* The message and
monition of the figure was, that resistance would be
hopeless ; that if blood flowed, woe to him who shed it.
Thus spoke the figure : and vanished. ' Withal there
was a kind of eloquence that struck one '. Besenval
admits that he should have arrested him, but did not.[1]
Who this figure with inflamed eyes, with speech rapid
and curt, might be ? Besenval knows, but mentions
not. Camille Desmoulins ? Pythagorean Marquis
Valadi, inflamed with ' violent motions all night at
the Palais Royal ' ? Fame names him, ' Young M.
Meillar ' ;[2] then shuts her lips about him for ever.

In any case, behold about nine in the morning, our
National Volunteers rolling in long wide flood, southwestward to the *Hôtel des Invalides* ; in search of the
one thing needful. King's Procureur M. Ethys de

[1] Besenval, iii. 414.
[2] Tableaux de la Révolution, *Prise de la Bastille* (a folio
Collection of Pictures and Portraits, with letter-press, not
always uninstructive,— part of it said to be by Chamfort).

Corny and officials are there; the Curé of Saint-
Etienne du Mont marches unpacific, at the head of his
militant Parish; the Clerks of the Basoche*in red coats
we see marching, now Volunteers of the Basoche; the
Volunteers of the Palais Royal:—National Volunteers,
numerable by tens of thousands; of one heart and
mind. The King's muskets are the Nation's; think,
old M. de Sombreuil, how, in this extremity, thou wilt
refuse them! Old M. de Sombreuil would fain hold
parley, send couriers; but it skills not: the walls are
scaled, no Invalide firing a shot; the gates must be
flung open. Patriotism rushes in, tumultuous, from
grunsel up to ridge-tile, through all rooms and passages;
rummaging distractedly for arms. What cellar, or what
cranny can escape it? The arms are found; all safe
there; lying packed in straw,—apparently with a view
to being burnt! More ravenous than famishing lions
over dead prey, the multitude, with clangour and vociferation, pounces on them; struggling, dashing, clutching:—to the jamming-up, to the pressure, fracture and
probable extinction of the weaker Patriot.[1]   And so,
with such protracted crash of deafening, most discordant Orchestra-music, the Scene is changed; and
eight-and-twenty thousand sufficient firelocks are on
the shoulders of as many National Guards, lifted
thereby out of darkness into fiery light.

Let Besenval look at the glitter of these muskets, as
they flash by! Gardes Françaises, it is said, have
cannon levelled on him; ready to open, if need were,
from the other side of the River.[2]   Motionless sits he;
'astonished', one may flatter oneself, 'at the proud
bearing (*fière contenance*) of the Parisians '.—And now,
to the Bastille, ye intrepid Parisians! There grapeshot
still threatens: thither all men's thoughts and steps
are now tending.
Old De Launay, as we hinted, withdrew 'into his
interior' soon after midnight of Sunday. He remains

---

[1] Deux Amis, i. 302.   [2] Besenval, iii. 416.

there ever since, hampered, as all military gentlemen
now are, in the saddest conflict of uncertainties. The
Hôtel-de-Ville 'invites' him to admit National Soldiers,
which is a soft name for surrendering. On the other
hand, His Majesty's orders were precise. His garrison
is but eighty-two old Invalides, reinforced by thirty-
two young Swiss; his walls indeed are nine feet thick,
he has cannon and powder; but, alas, only one day's
provision of victuals. The city too is French, the poor
garrison mostly French. Rigorous old De Launay,
think what thou wilt do!

All morning, since nine, there has been a cry everywhere: To the Bastille! Repeated 'deputations of
citizens' have been here, passionate for arms; whom
De Launay has got dismissed by soft speeches through
port-holes. Towards noon, Elector Thuriot de la
Rosière gains admittance; finds De Launay indisposed
for surrender; nay disposed for blowing up the place
rather. Thuriot mounts with him to the battlements:
heaps of paving-stones, old iron and missiles lie piled;
cannon all duly levelled; in every embrasure a cannon,
—only drawn back a little! But outwards, behold, O
Thuriot, how the multitude flows on, welling through
every street: tocsin furiously pealing, all drums beating the *générale*: the Suburb Saint-Antoine rolling
hitherward wholly, as one man! Such vision (spectral
yet real) thou, O Thuriot, as from thy Mount of Vision,
beholdest in this moment: prophetic of what other
Phantasmagories, and loud-gibbering Spectral Realities,
which thou yet beholdest not, but shalt! ' *Que voulez-
vous ?* ' said De Launay, turning pale at the sight,
with an air of reproach, almost of menace. 'Monsieur',
said Thuriot, rising into the moral-sublime, 'what
mean *you*? Consider if I could not precipitate *both* of
us from this height',—say only a hundred feet,
exclusive of the walled ditch! Whereupon De Launay
fell silent. Thuriot shows himself from some pinnacle,
to comfort the multitude becoming suspicious, fremescent: then descends; departs with protest; with
warning addressed also to the Invalides,—on whom,

however, it produces but a mixed indistinct impression.
The old heads are none of the clearest; besides, it is
said, De Launay has been profuse of beverages (*pro-
digua des buissons*). They think, they will not fire,—
if not fired on, if they can help it; but must, on the
whole, be ruled considerably by circumstances.

Woe to thee, De Launay, in such an hour, if thou
canst not, taking some one firm decision, *rule* circumstances! Soft speeches will not serve; hard grapeshot
is questionable; but hovering between the two is
*un*questionable. Ever wilder swells the tide of men;
their infinite hum waxing ever louder, into imprecations,
perhaps into crackle of stray musketry,—which latter,
on walls nine feet thick, cannot do execution. The
Outer Drawbridge has been lowered for Thuriot; new
deputation of citizens (it is the third, and noisiest of all)
penetrates that way into the Outer Court: soft speeches
producing no clearance of these, De Launay gives fire;
pulls up his Drawbridge. A slight sputter;—which
has *kindled* the too combustible chaos; made it a roaring fire-chaos! Bursts forth Insurrection, at sight of
its own blood (for there were deaths by that sputter
of fire), into endless rolling explosion of musketry,
distraction, execration;—and over head, from the
Fortress, let one great gun, with its grapeshot, go
booming, to show what we *could* do. The Bastille is
besieged!

On, then, all Frenchmen, that have hearts in your
bodies! Roar with all your throats, of cartilage and
metal, ye Sons of Liberty; stir spasmodically whatsoever of utmost faculty is in you, soul, body, or spirit;
for it is the hour! Smite, thou Louis Tournay, cart-
wright of the Marais, old-soldier of the Regiment
Dauphiné; smite at that Outer Drawbridge chain,
though the fiery hail whistles round thee! Never,
over nave or felloe, did thy axe strike such a stroke.
Down with it, man; down with it to Orcus: let the
whole accursed Edifice sink thither, and Tyranny be
swallowed up for ever! Mounted, some say, on the
roof of the guard-room, some ' on bayonets stuck into

joints of the wall', Louis Tournay smites, brave Aubin
Bonnemère (also an old soldier) seconding him: the
chain yields, breaks; the huge Drawbridge slams down,
thundering (*avec fracas*). Glorious: and yet, alas, it
is still but the outworks. The Eight grim Towers, with
their Invalide musketry, their paving stones and cannon-mouths, still soar aloft intact;—Ditch yawning
impassable, stone-faced; the inner Drawbridge with
its *back* towards us: the Bastille is still to take!

To describe this Siege of the Bastille (thought to be
one of the most important in History) perhaps trans-
cends the talent of mortals. Could one but, after infinite
reading, get to understand so much as the plan of the
building! But there is open Esplanade, at the end of
the Rue Saint-Antoine; there are such Forecourts,
Cour Avancé, Cour de l'Orme, arched Gateway (where
Louis Tournay now fights); then new drawbridges,
dormant-bridges, rampart-bastions, and the grim
Eight Towers: a labyrinthic Mass, high-frowning
there, of all ages from twenty years to four hundred
and twenty;—beleaguered, in this its last hour, as we
said, by mere Chaos come again! Ordnance of all
calibres; throats of all capacities; men of all plans,
every man his own engineer: seldom since the war of
Pygmies and Cranes* was there seen so anomalous
a thing. Half-pay Elie is home for a suit of regimentals; no one would heed him in coloured clothes: half-
pay Hulin is haranguing Gardes Françaises in the Place
de Grève. Frantic Patriots pick up the grapeshots;
bear them, still hot (or seemingly so), to the Hôtel-de-
Ville:—Paris, you perceive, is to be burnt! Flesselles is
'pale to the very lips', for the roar of the multitude
grows deep. Paris wholly has got to the acme of its
frenzy; whirled, all ways, by panic madness. At
every street-barricade, there whirls simmering a minor
whirlpool,—strengthening the barricade, since God
knows what is coming; and all minor whirlpools play
distractedly into that grand Fire-Mahlstrom which is
lashing round the Bastille.

And so it lashes and it roars. Cholat the wine-merchant has become an impromptu cannoneer. See Georget, of the Marine Service, fresh from Brest, ply the King of Siam's cannon. Singular (if we were not used to the like): Georget lay, last night, taking his ease at his inn; the King of Siam's cannon also lay, knowing nothing of *him*, for a hundred years. Yet now, at the right instant, they have got together, and discourse eloquent music. For, hearing what was toward, Georget sprang from the Brest Diligence, and ran. Gardes Françaises also will be here, with real artillery : were not the walls so thick !—Upwards from the Esplanade, horizontally from all neighbouring roofs and windows, flashes one irregular deluge of musketry, without effect. The Invalides lie flat, firing compara-tively at their ease from behind stone; hardly through portholes, show the tip of a nose. We fall, shot; and make no impression !

Let conflagration rage; of whatsoever is combus-tible ! Guard-rooms are burnt, Invalides mess-rooms. A distracted ' Perukemaker with two fiery torches ' is for burning ' the saltpetres of the Arsenal ';—had not a woman run screaming; had not a Patriot, with some tincture of Natural Philosophy, instantly struck the wind out of him (butt of musket on pit of stomach), overturned barrels, and stayed the devouring element. A young beautiful lady, seized escaping in these Outer Courts, and thought falsely to be De Launay's daugh-ter, shall be burnt in De Launay's sight; she lies swooned on a paillasse: but again a Patriot, it is brave Aubin Bonnemère the old soldier, dashes in, and rescues her. Straw is burnt; three cartloads of it, hauled thither, go up in white smoke: almost to the choking of Patriotism itself; so that Elie had, with singed brows, to drag back one cart; and Réole the ' gigantic haber-dasher ' another. Smoke as of Tophet; confusion as of Babel; noise as of the Crack of Doom !*

Blood flows; the aliment of new madness. The wounded are carried into houses of the Rue Cerisaie; the dying leave their last mandate not to yield till the

accursed Stronghold fall. And yet, alas, how fall?
The walls are so thick! Deputations, three in number,
arrive from the Hôtel-de-Ville; Abbé Fauchet*(who
was of one) can say, with what almost superhuman
courage of benevolence.[1] These wave their Town-flag
in the arched Gateway; and stand, rolling their drum;
but to no purpose. In such Crack of Doom, De Launay
cannot hear them, dare not believe them: they return,
with justified rage, the whew of lead still singing in
their ears. What to do? The Firemen are here,
squirting with their fire-pumps on the Invalides
cannon, to wet the touchholes; they unfortunately
cannot squirt so high; but produce only clouds of
spray. Individuals of classical knowledge propose
catapults. Santerre, the sonorous Brewer of the Suburb
Saint-Antoine, advises rather that the place be fired,
by a 'mixture of phosphorus and oil-of-turpentine
spouted up through forcing pumps': O Spinola-
Santerre, hast thou the mixture *ready*? Every man his
own engineer! And still the fire-deluge abates not:
even women are firing, and Turks; at least one woman
(with her sweetheart), and one Turk.[2] Gardes Françaises have come: real cannon, real cannoneers. Usher
Maillard is busy; half-pay Elie, half-pay Hulin rage in
the midst of thousands.

How the great Bastille Clock ticks (inaudible) in its
Inner Court there, at its ease, hour after hour; as if
nothing special, for it or the world, were passing! It
tolled One when the firing began; and is now pointing
towards Five, and still the firing slakes not.—Far down,
in their vaults, the seven Prisoners hear muffled din
as of earthquakes; their Turnkeys answer vaguely.

Woe to thee, De Launay, with thy poor hundred
Invalides! Broglie is distant, and his ears heavy:
Besenval hears, but can send no help. One poor troop
of Hussars has crept, reconnoitring, cautiously along
the Quais, as far as the Pont Neuf. 'We are come to

---

[1] Fauchet's Narrative (Deux Amis, i. 324).
[2] Deux Amis, i. 319; Dusaulx, &c.

join you ', said the Captain; for the crowd seems
shoreless. A large-headed dwarfish individual, of
smoke-bleared aspect, shambles forward, opening his
blue lips, for there is sense in him; and croaks:
' Alight then, and give up your arms ! ' The Hussar-
Captain is too happy to be escorted to the Barriers,
and dismissed on parole. Who the squat individual
was ? Men answer, It is M. Marat, author of the
excellent pacific *Avis au Peuple !* Great truly, O thou
remarkable Dogleech, is this thy day of emergence and
new-birth : and yet this same day come four years—— !
—But let the curtains of the Future hang.

What shall De Launay do ? One thing only De
Launay could have done : what he said he would do.
Fancy him sitting, from the first, with lighted taper,
within arm's length of the Powder-Magazine ; motionless, like old Roman Senator, or Bronze Lamp-holder ;
coldly apprising Thuriot, and all men, by a slight motion
of his eye, what his resolution was :—Harmless he sat
there, while unharmed ; but the King's Fortress,
meanwhile, could, might, would, or should, in nowise
be surrendered, save to the King's Messenger : one
old man's life is worthless, so it be lost with honour ;
but think, ye brawling *canaille,* how will it be when
a whole Bastille springs skyward !—In such statuesque,
taper-holding attitude, one fancies De Launay might
have left Thuriot, the red Clerks of the Basoche, Curé
of Saint-Stephen and all the tag-rag-and-bobtail of the
world, to work their will.

And yet, withal, he could not do it. Hast thou
considered how each man's heart is so tremulously
responsive to the hearts of all men ; hast thou noted
how omnipotent is the very sound of many men ?
How their shriek of indignation palsies the strong soul ;
their howl of contumely withers with unfelt pangs ?
The Ritter Glück confessed that the ground-tone of
the noblest passage, in one of his noblest Operas,* was
the voice of the Populace he had heard at Vienna,
crying to their Kaiser : Bread ! Bread ! Great is the
combined voice of men ; the utterance of their *instincts,*

which are truer than their *thoughts* : it is the greatest
a man encounters, among the sounds and shadows
which make up this World of Time. He who can
resist that, has his footing somewhere *beyond* Time.
De Launay could not do it. Distracted, he hovers
between two ; hopes in the middle of despair ; surrenders not his Fortress ; declares that he will blow it up,
seizes torches to blow it up, and does not blow it.
Unhappy old De Launay, it is the death-agony of thy
Bastille and thee ! Jail, Jailoring and Jailor, all three,
such as they may have been, must finish.

For four hours now has the World-Bedlam roared :
call it the World-Chimera, blowing fire ! The poor
Invalides have sunk under their battlements, or rise
only with reversed muskets : they have made a white
flag of napkins : go beating the *chamade,* or seeming to
beat, for one can hear nothing. The very Swiss at the
Portcullis look weary of firing ; disheartened in the
fire-deluge : a porthole at the drawbridge is opened,
as by one that would speak. See Huissier Maillard,
the shifty man ! On his plank, swinging over the abyss
of that stone Ditch ; plank resting on parapet, balanced
by weight of Patriots,—he hovers perilous : such
a Dove towards such an Ark !* Deftly, thou shifty
Usher : one man already fell ; and lies smashed, far
down there, against the masonry ! Usher Maillard
falls not : deftly, unerring he walks, with outspread
palm. The Swiss holds a paper through his porthole ;
the shifty Usher snatches it, and returns. Terms of
surrender : Pardon, immunity to all ! Are they
accepted ?—' *Foi d'officier,* On the word of an officer ',
answers half-pay Hulin,—or half-pay Elie, for men do
not agree on it, ' they are ! ' Sinks the drawbridge,—
Usher Maillard bolting it when down ; rushes-in the
living deluge : the Bastille is fallen ! *Victoire ! La
Bastille est prise !* [1]

[1] Histoire de la Révolution, par Deux Amis de la Liberté,
i. 267–306. Besenval, iii. 410–34. Dusaulx, Prise de la
Bastille, 291–301. Bailly, Mémoires (Collection de Berville
et Barrière), i. 322 *et seqq.*

CHAPTER VII

NOT A REVOLT

WHY dwell on what follows ? Hulin's *fol d'officier* should have been kept, but could not. The Swiss stand drawn up, disguised in white canvas smocks ; the Invalides without disguise ; their arms all piled against the wall. The first rush of victors, in ecstasy that the death-peril is passed, ' leaps joyfully on their necks ' ; but new victors rush, and ever new, also in ecstasy not wholly of joy. As we said, it was a living deluge, plunging headlong : had not the Gardes Françaises, in their cool military way, ' wheeled round with arms levelled ', it would have plunged suicidally, by the hundred or the thousand, into the Bastille-ditch.

And so it goes plunging through court and corridor ; billowing uncontrollable, firing from windows—on itself ; in hot frenzy of triumph, of grief and vengeance for its slain. The poor Invalides will fare ill ; one Swiss, running off in his white smock, is driven back, with a death-thrust. Let all Prisoners be marched to the Townhall, to be judged !—Alas, already one poor Invalide has his right hand slashed off him ; his maimed body dragged to the Place de Grève, and hanged there. This same right hand, it is said, turned back De Launay from the Powder-Magazine, and saved Paris.

De Launay, ' discovered in grey frock with poppy-coloured riband ', is for killing himself with the sword of his cane. He shall to the Hôtel-de-Ville ; Hulin, Maillard and others escorting him ; Elie marching foremost ' with the capitulation-paper on his sword's point '. Through roarings and cursings ; through hustlings, clutchings, and at last through strokes ! Your escort is hustled aside, felled down ; Hulin sinks exhausted on a heap of stones. Miserable De Launay ! He shall never enter the Hôtel-de-Ville : only his ' bloody hair-queue, held up in a bloody hand ' ; that shall enter, for a sign. The bleeding trunk lies on the steps there ;

the head is off through the streets ; ghastly, aloft on a pike.

Rigorous De Launay has died ; crying out, ' O friends, kill me fast ! ' Merciful De Losme must die ; though Gratitude embraces him, in this fearful hour, and will die for him ; it avails not. Brothers, your wrath is cruel ! Your Place de Grève is become a Throat of the Tiger ; full of mere fierce bellowings, and thirst of blood. One other officer is massacred ; one other Invalide is hanged on the Lamp-iron ; with difficulty, with generous perseverance, the Gardes Françaises will save the rest. Provost Flesselles, stricken long since with the paleness of death, must descend from his seat, ' to be judged at the Palais Royal ' :—alas, to be shot dead, by an unknown hand, at the turning of the first street !—

O evening sun of July, how, at this hour, thy beams fall slant on reapers amid peaceful woody fields ; on old women spinning in cottages ; on ships far out in the silent main ; on Balls at the Orangerie of Versailles, where high-rouged Dames of the Palace are even now dancing with double-jacketed Hussar-Officers ;—and also on this roaring Hell-porch of a Hôtel-de-Ville ! Babel Tower, with the confusion of tongues, were not Bedlam added with the conflagration of thoughts, was no type of it. One forest of distracted steel bristles, endless, in front of an Electoral Committee ; points itself, in horrid radii, against this and the other accused breast. It was the Titans warring with Olympus ; and they, scarcely crediting it, have *conquered* : prodigy of prodigies ; delirious,—as it could not but be. Denunciation, vengeance ; blaze of triumph on a dark ground of terror : all outward, all inward things fallen into one general wreck of madness !

Electoral Committee ? Had it a thousand throats of brass, it would not suffice. Abbé Lefevre, in the Vaults down below, is black as Vulcan, distributing that ' five thousand-weight of Powder ' ; with what perils, these eight-and-forty hours ! Last night, a Patriot, in liquor, insisted on sitting to smoke on the

edge of one of the Powder-barrels : there smoked he,
independent of the world,—till the Abbé ' purchased
his pipe for three francs ', and pitched it far.

Elie, in the grand Hall, Electoral Committee looking
on, sits ' with drawn sword bent in three places ' ; with
battered helm, for he was of the Queen's Regiment,
Cavalry ; with torn regimentals, face singed and soiled ;
comparable, some think, to ' an antique warrior ' ;—
judging the people ; forming a list of Bastille Heroes.
O Friends, stain not with blood the greenest laurels
ever gained in this world : such is the burden of Elie's
song : could it but be listened to.　Courage, Elie !
Courage, ye Municipal Electors !　A declining sun ; the
need of victuals, and of telling news, will bring assuagement, dispersion : all earthly things must end.

Along the streets of Paris circulate Seven Bastille
Prisoners, borne shoulder-high ; seven Heads on pikes ;
the Keys of the Bastille ; and much else.　See also
the Gardes Françaises, in their steadfast military way,
marching home to their barracks, with the Invalides
and Swiss kindly enclosed in hollow square.　It is one
year and two months since these same men stood
unparticipating, with Brennus d'Agoust at the Palais
de Justice, when Fate overtook D'Espréménil ; and
now they have participated ; and will participate.
Not Gardes Françaises henceforth, but *Centre Grenadiers of the National Guard* : men of iron discipline and
humour,—not without a kind of thought in them !

Likewise ashlar stones of the Bastille continue thundering through the dusk ; its paper archives shall fly
white.　Old secrets come to view ; and long-buried
Despair finds voice.　Read this portion of an old Letter : [1] ' If for my consolation Monseigneur would grant
me, for the sake of God and the Most Blessed Trinity,
that I could have news of my dear wife ; were it only
her name on a card, to show that she is alive !　It were

---

[1] *Dated*, à la Bastille, 7 Octobre 1752 ; *signed* Quéret-
Démery.　Bastille Dévoilée ; in Linguet, Mémoires sur la
Bastille (Paris, 1821), p. 199.

the greatest consolation I could receive ; and I should
for ever bless the greatness of Monseigneur'. Poor
Prisoner, who namest thyself *Quéret-Démery*, and hast
no other history,—she is *dead*, that dear wife of thine,
and thou art dead ! 'Tis fifty years since thy breaking
heart put this question ; to be heard now first, and long
heard, in the hearts of men.

But so does the July twilight thicken ; so must
Paris, as sick children, and all distracted creatures do.
brawl itself finally into a kind of sleep. Municipal
Electors, astonished to find their heads still uppermost,
are home : only Moreau de Saint-Méry of tropical
birth and heart, of coolest judgement ; he, with two
others, shall sit permanent at the Townhall. Paris
sleeps ; gleams upward the illuminated City : patrols
go clashing, without common watchword ; there go
rumours ; alarms of war, to the extent of 'fifteen thousand men marching through the Suburb Saint-Antoine',
—who never got it marched through. Of the day's
distraction judge by this of the night : Moreau de
Saint-Méry, ' before rising from his seat, gave upwards
of three thousand orders '.[1] What a head ; comparable to Friar Bacon's Brass Head !*. Within it lies all
Paris. Prompt must the answer be, right or wrong ;
in Paris is no other authority extant. Seriously, a most
cool clear head ;—for which also thou, O brave Saint-
Méry, in many capacities, from august Senator to
Merchant's-Clerk, Book-dealer, Vice-King ; in many
places, from Virginia to Sardinia, shalt, ever as a brave
man, find employment.[2]

Besenval has decamped, under cloud of dusk, ' amid
a great affluence of people ', who did not harm him ;
he marches, with faint-growing tread, down the left
bank of the Seine, all night,—towards infinite space.
Re-summoned shall Besenval himself be ; for trial, for

[1] Dusaulx.
[2] Biographie Universelle, § Moreau Saint-Méry (by Four-
nier-Pescay).

difficult acquittal. His King's-troops, his Royal-Allemand, are gone hence for ever.

The Versailles Ball and lemonade is done; the
Orangerie is silent except for nightbirds. Over in the
Salle des Menus, Vice-president Lafayette, with unsnuffed lights, ' with some Hundred or so of Members,
stretched on tables round him ', sits erect; outwatching
the Bear. This day, a second solemn Deputation went
to his Majesty; a second and then a third: with no
effect. What will the end of these things be ?

In the Court, all is mystery, not without whisperings
of terror ; though ye dream of lemonade and epaulettes,
ye foolish women! His Majesty, kept in happy
ignorance, perhaps dreams of double-barrels and the
Woods of Meudon. Late at night, the Duke de Liancourt, having official right of entrance, gains access to
the Royal Apartments ; unfolds, with earnest clearness, in his constitutional way, the Job's-news. ' *Mais* ',
said poor Louis, ' *c'est une révolte*, Why, that is a revolt !'
— ' Sire ', answered Liancourt, ' it is not a revolt,—it
is a revolution '.

CHAPTER VIII

CONQUERING YOUR KING

ON the morrow a fourth Deputation to the Château
is on foot : of a more solemn, not to say awful character ; for, besides ' orgies in the Orangery ', it seems
' the grain-convoys are all stopped ' ; nor has Mirabeau's thunder been silent. Such Deputation is on the
point of setting out,—when lo, his Majesty himself,
attended only by his two Brothers, steps in ; quite in
the paternal manner ; announces that the troops, and
all causes of offence, are gone, and henceforth there
shall be nothing but trust, reconcilement, goodwill ;
whereof he ' permits, and even requests ', a National
Assembly to assure Paris in his name ! Acclamation.

as of men suddenly delivered from death, gives answer. The whole Assembly spontaneously rises to escort his Majesty back ; ' interlacing their arms to keep off the excessive pressure from him ' ; for all Versailles is crowding and shouting. The Château Musicians, with a felicitous promptitude, strike up the *Sein de sa Famille* (Bosom of one's Family) : the Queen appears at the Balcony with her little boy and girl, ' kissing them several times ' ; infinite *Vivats* spread far and wide ;—and suddenly there has come, as it were, a new Heaven-on-Earth.

Eighty-eight august Senators, Bailly, Lafayette and our repentant Archbishop among them, take coach for Paris, with the great intelligence ; benedictions without end on their heads. From the Place Louis Quinze, where they alight, all the way to the Hôtel-de-Ville, it is one sea of Tricolor cockades, of clear National muskets ; one tempest of huzzaings, hand-clappings, aided by ' occasional rollings ' of drum-music. Harangues of due fervour are delivered ; especially by Lally Tollendal, pious son of the ill-fated murdered Lally ; on whose head, in consequence, a civic crown (of oak or parsley) is forced,—which he forcibly transfers to Bailly's.

But surely, for one thing, the National Guard should have a General ! Moreau de Saint-Méry, he of the ' three thousand orders ', casts one of his significant glances on the Bust of Lafayette, which has stood there ever since the American War of Liberty. Whereupon, by acclamation, Lafayette is nominated. Again, in room of the slain traitor or quasi-traitor Flesselles. President Bailly shall be—Provost of the Merchants ? No : Mayor of Paris ! So be it. *Maire de Paris!* Mayor Bailly, General Lafayette ; *vive Bailly, vive Lafayette !* the universal out-of-doors multitude rends the welkin in confirmation.—And now, finally, let us to Notre-Dame for a *Te Deum.*

Towards Notre-Dame Cathedral, in glad procession, these Regenerators of the Country walk, through a jubilant people ; in fraternal manner ; Abbé Lefevre, still black with his gunpowder services, walking arm in arm

with the white-stoled Archbishop.   Poor Bailly comes
upon the Foundling Children, sent to kneel to him ;
and ' weeps '.   *Te Deum*, our Archbishop officiating,
is not only sung, but *shot* — with blank cartridges.
Our joy is boundless, as our woe ˙threatened to be.
Paris, by her own pike and musket, and the valour
of her own heart, has conquered the very war-gods,—
to the satisfaction now of Majesty itself.   A courier is,
this night, getting under way for Necker : the People's
Minister, invited back by the King, by National Assembly, and Nation, shall traverse France amid shoutings,
and the sound of trumpet and timbrel.

Seeing which course of things, Messeigneurs of the
Court Triumvirate, Messieurs of the dead-born Broglie-
Ministry, and others such, consider that their part also,
is clear : to mount and ride.   Off, ye too-royal Broglies,
Polignacs and Princes of the Blood ; off while it is yet
time !   Did not the Palais-Royal, in its late nocturnal
' violent motions ', set a specific price (place of payment
not mentioned) on each of your heads ?—With precau-
tions, with the aid of pieces of cannon and regiments
that can be depended on, Messeigneurs, between the
16th night and the 17th morning, get to their several
roads.   Not without risk !   Prince Condé has (or seems
to have) ' men galloping at full speed ' : with a view,
it is thought, to fling him into the river Oise, at Pont-
Sainte-Mayence.[1]   The Polignacs travel disguised ;
friends, not servants, on their coach-box.   Broglie has
his own difficulties at Versailles, runs his own risks at
Metz and Verdun ; does nevertheless get safe to Luxemburg, and there rests.

This is what they call the First Emigration ; determined on, as appears, in full Court-conclave ; his
Majesty assisting ; prompt he, for his share of it, to
follow any counsel whatsoever. ' Three Sons of
France, and four Princes of the blood of Saint Louis ',
says Weber, ' could not more effectually humble the

---

[1] Weber, ii. 126.

Burghers of Paris than by appearing to withdraw in
fear of their life'. Alas, the Burghers of Paris bear it
with unexpected stoicism ! The Man D'Artois indeed
is gone ; but has he carried, for example, the Land
D'Artois with him ? Not even Bagatelle the Country-
house (which shall be useful as a Tavern) ; hardly the
four-valet Breeches, leaving the Breeches-maker !—As
for old Foulon, one learns that he is dead ; at least
' a sumptuous funeral' is going on ; the undertakers
honouring him, if no other will. Intendant Berthier,
his son-in-law, is still living ; lurking : he joined
Besenval, on that Eumenides Sunday ; appearing to
treat it with levity ; and is now fled no man knows
whither.

The Emigration is not gone many miles, Prince
Condé hardly across the Oise, when his Majesty,
according to arrangement, for the Emigration also
thought it might do good,—undertakes a rather daring
enterprise : that of visiting Paris in person. With
a Hundred Members of Assembly ; with small or no
military escort, which indeed he dismissed at the
Bridge of Sèvres, poor Louis sets out ; leaving a desolate Palace ; a Queen weeping, the Present, the Past
and the Future all so unfriendly for her.

At the Barrier of Passy, Mayor Bailly, in grand gala,
presents him with the keys ; harangues him, in Academic style ; mentions that it is a great day ; that in
Henri Quatre's case, the King had to make conquest
of his People ; but in this happier case, the People
makes conquest of its King (*a conquis son Roi*). The
King, so happily conquered, drives forward, slowly,
through a steel people, all silent, or shouting only *Vive
la Nation* ; is harangued at the Townhall, by Moreau
of the three thousand orders, by King's Procureur M.
Ethys de Corny, by Lally Tollendal, and others ; knows
not what to think of it or say of it ; learns that he is
' Restorer of French Liberty ',—as a Statue of him, to
be raised on the site of the Bastille, shall testify to all
men. Finally, he is shown at the Balcony, with a Tri-

color cockade in his hat ; is greeted now, with vehement
acclamation, from Square and Street, from all windows
and roofs :—and so drives home again amid glad
mingled and, as it were, intermarried shouts, of *Vive
le Roi* and *Vive la Nation* ; wearied but safe.

It was Sunday when the red-hot balls hung over us,
in mid air : it is now but Friday, and ' the Revolution
is sanctioned '.   An august National Assembly shall
make the Constitution ; and neither foreign Pandour,
domestic Triumvirate, with levelled Cannon, Guy-Faux
powder-plots (for that too was spoken of) ; nor any
tyrannic Power on the Earth or under the Earth, shall
say to it, What dost thou ?—So jubilates the People ;
sure now of a Constitution.   Cracked Marquis Saint-
Huruge* is heard under the windows of the Château ;
murmuring sheer speculative-treason.[1]

CHAPTER IX

THE LANTERNE

The Fall of the Bastille may be said to have shaken
all France to the deepest foundations of its existence.
The rumour of these wonders flies everywhere : with
the natural speed of Rumour ; with an effect thought
to be preternatural, produced by plots.   Did D'Orléans
or Laclos, nay did Mirabeau (not overburdened with
money at this time) send riding Couriers out from Paris ;
to gallop ' on all radii ', or highways, towards all points
of France ?   It is a miracle, which no penetrating man
will call in question.[2]

Already in most Towns, Electoral Committees were
met ; to regret Necker, in harangue and resolution.
In many a Town, as Rennes, Caen, Lyons, an ebullient

---

[1] Campan, ii. 46–64.
[2] Toulongeon, i. 95 ; Weber, &c. &c.

people was already regretting him in brickbats and
musketry. But now, at every Town's-end in France,
there do arrive, in these days of terror,—'men', as
men will arrive; nay 'men on horseback', since
Rumour oftenest travels riding. These men declare,
with alarmed countenance, *The* BRIGANDS to be coming,
to be just at hand; and do then—ride on, about their
further business, be what it might! Whereupon the
whole population of such Town defensively flies to arms.
Petition is soon thereafter forwarded to National
Assembly; in such peril and terror of peril, leave to
organize yourself cannot be withheld: the armed
population becomes everywhere an enrolled National
Guard. Thus rides Rumour, careering along all radii,
from Paris outwards, to such purpose: in few days,
some say in not many hours, all France to the utmost
borders bristles with bayonets. Singular, but undeniable,—miraculous or not!—But thus may any chemical liquid, though cooled to the freezing-point, or far
lower, still continue liquid; and then, on the slightest
stroke or shake, it at once rushes wholly into ice.*
Thus has France, for long months and even years, been
chemically dealt with; brought below zero; and now,
shaken by the Fall of a Bastille, it instantaneously
congeals: into one crystallized mass, of sharp-cutting
steel! *Guai a chi la tocca*, 'Ware who touches it!

In Paris, an Electoral Committee, with a new Mayor
and General, is urgent with belligerent workmen to
resume their handicrafts. Strong Dames of the Market
(*Dames de la Halle*) deliver congratulatory harangues;
present 'bouquets to the Shrine of Sainte Geneviève'.
Unenrolled men deposit their arms,—not so readily as
could be wished: and receive 'nine francs'. With
Te Deums, Royal Visits, and sanctioned Revolution,
there is halcyon weather; weather even of preternatural
brightness; the hurricane being overblown.

Nevertheless, as is natural, the waves still run high,
hollow rocks retaining their murmur. We are but at
the 22nd of the month, hardly above a week since the

Bastille fell, when it suddenly appears that old Foulon
is alive; nay, that he is here, in early morning, in the
streets of Paris: the extortioner, the plotter, who
would make the people eat grass, and was a liar from
the beginning !—It is even so. The deceptive ' sumptuous funeral ' (of some domestic that died); the hiding-place at Vitry towards Fontainebleau, have not
availed that wretched old man. Some living domestic
or dependant, for none loves Foulon, has betrayed him
to the Village. Merciless boors of Vitry unearth him ;
pounce on him, like hell-hounds : Westward, old
Infamy ; to Paris, to be judged at the Hôtel-de-Ville !
His old head, which seventy-four years have bleached,
is bare ; they have tied an emblematic bundle of grass
on his back ; a garland of nettles and thistles is round
his neck : in this manner; led with ropes ; goaded
on with curses and menaces, must he, with his old
limbs, sprawl forward ; the pitiablest, most unpitied
of all old men.

Sooty Saint-Antoine, and every street, musters its
crowds as he passes ;—the Hall of the Hôtel-de-Ville,
the Place de Grève itself, will scarcely hold his escort
and him. Foulon must not only be judged righteously,
but judged there where he stands, without any delay.
Appoint seven judges, ye Municipals, or seventy-and-
seven ; name them yourselves, or we will name them :
but judge him ! [1] Electoral rhetoric, eloquence of
Mayor Bailly, is wasted, for hours, explaining the beauty
of the Law's delay. Delay, and still delay ! Behold,
O Mayor of the People, the morning has worn itself
into noon : and he is still unjudged !—Lafayette,
pressingly sent for, arrives ; gives voice : This Foulon,
a known man, is guilty almost beyond doubt ; but may
he not have accomplices ? Ought not the truth to be
cunningly pumped out of him,—in the Abbaye Prison ?
It is a new light ! Sansculottism claps hands ;—at
which handclapping, Foulon (in his fairness, as his
Destiny would have it) also claps. ' See ! they under-

[1] Histoire Parlementaire, ii. 146-9.

stand one another ! ' cries dark Sansculottism, blazing
into fury of suspicion.—' Friends', said 'a person in
good clothes ', stepping forward, ' what is the use of
judging this man ? Has he not been judged these
thirty years ? ' With wild yells, Sansculottism clutches
him, in its hundred hands : he is whirled across the
Place de Grève, to the ' *Lanterne* ', Lamp-iron which
there is at the corner of the *Rue de la Vannerie* ; pleading bitterly for life,—to the deaf winds. Only with the
third rope (for two ropes broke, and the quavering
voice still pleaded) can he be so much as got hanged !
His Body is dragged through the streets ; his Head
goes aloft on a pike, the mouth filled with grass : amid
sounds as of Tophet, from a grass-eating people.[1]

Surely if Revenge is a ' kind of Justice ', it is a ' wild '
kind !* O mad Sansculottism, hast thou risen, in thy
mad darkness, in thy soot and rags ; unexpectedly,
like an Enceladus, living-buried, from under his Trinacria ? They that would make grass be eaten do now
eat grass, in *this* manner ? After long dumb-groaning
generations, has the turn suddenly become thine ?—
To such abysmal overturns, and frightful instantaneous
inversions of the centre-of-gravity, are human Solecisms
all liable, if they but knew it ; the more liable, the
falser (and topheavier) they are !—

To add to the horror of Mayor Bailly and his Municipals, word comes that Berthier has also been arrested ;
that he is on his way hither from Compiègne. Berthier,
Intendant (say *Tax-levier*) of Paris ; sycophant and
tyrant ; forestaller of Corn ; contriver of Camps against
the people ;—accused of many things : is he not Foulon's son-in-law ; and, in that one point, guilty of all ?
In these hours too, when Sansculottism has its blood
up ! The shuddering Municipals send one of their
number to escort him, with mounted National Guards.
At the fall of day, the wretched Berthier, still wearing a face of courage, arrives at the Barrier ; in an open

[1] Deux Amis de la Liberté, ii. 60–6.

carriage; with the Municipal beside him; five hundred horsemen with drawn sabres; unarmed footmen enough : not without noise ! Placards go brandished round him; bearing legibly his indictment, as Sans-culottism, with unlegal brevity, 'in huge letters', draws it up.[1] Paris is come forth to meet him : with hand-clappings, with windows flung up; with dances, triumph-songs, as of the Furies. Lastly, the Head of Foulon; this also meets him on a pike. Well might his 'look become glazed', and sense fail him, at such sight !—Nevertheless, be the man's conscience what it may, his nerves are of iron. At the Hôtel-de-Ville, he will answer nothing. He says he obeyed superior orders; they have his papers; they may judge and determine : as for himself, not having closed an eye these two nights, he demands, before all things, to have sleep. Leaden sleep, thou miserable Berthier ! Guards rise with him, in motion towards the Abbaye. At the very door of the Hôtel-de-Ville, they are clutched; flung asunder, as by a vortex of mad arms; Berthier whirls towards the Lanterne. He snatches a musket; fells and strikes, defending himself like a mad lion : he is borne down, trampled, hanged, mangled : his Head too, and even his Heart, flies over the City on a pike.

Horrible, in Lands that had known equal justice ! Not so unnatural in Lands that had never known it. '*Le sang qui coule, est-il donc si pur ?*' asks Barnave; intimating that the Gallows, though by irregular methods, has its own.—Thou thyself, O Reader, when thou turnest that corner of the Rue de la Vannerie, and discernest still that same grim Bracket of old Iron, wilt not want for reflections. 'Over a grocer's shop', or otherwise; with 'a bust of Louis XIV in the niche

---

[1] '*Il a volé le Roi et la France* (He robbed the King and France)'. 'He devoured the substance of the People'. 'He was the slave of the rich, and the tyrant of the poor'. 'He drank the blood of the widow and orphan'. 'He betrayed his country'. See Deux Amis, ii. 67–73.

under it', now no longer in the niche,—*it* still sticks
there; still holding out an ineffectual light, of fish-oil;
and has seen worlds wrecked, and says nothing.

But to the eye of enlightened Patriotism, what
a thunder-cloud was this; suddenly shaping itself in
the radiance of the halcyon weather! Cloud of
Erebus blackness; betokening latent electricity without limit. Mayor Bailly, General Lafayette throw up
their commissions, in an indignant manner;—need to
be flattered back again. The cloud disappears, as
thunder-clouds do. The halcyon weather returns,
though of a greyer complexion; of a character more
and more evidently *not* supernatural.

Thus, in any case, with what rubs soever, shall the
Bastille be abolished from our Earth; and with it,
Feudalism, Despotism; and, one hopes, Scoundrelism
generally, and all hard usage of man by his brother
man. Alas, the Scoundrelism and hard usage are not
so easy of abolition! But as for the Bastille, it sinks
day after day, and month after month; its ashlars and
boulders tumbling down continually, by express order
of our Municipals. Crowds of the curious roam through
its caverns; gaze on the skeletons found walled-up,
on the *oubliettes*, iron cages, monstrous stone-blocks
with padlock chains. One day we discern Mirabeau
there; along with the Genevese Dumont.[1] Workers
and onlookers make reverent way for him; fling verses,
flowers on his path, Bastille-papers and curiosities into
his carriage, with *vivats*.

Able Editors compile Books from the *Bastille
Archives*; from what of them remain unburnt. The
Key of that Robber-Den shall cross the Atlantic; shall
lie on Washington's hall-table. The great Clock ticks
now in a private patriotic Clockmaker's apartment;
no longer measuring hours of mere heaviness. Vanished
is the Bastille, what we call vanished: the *body*, or
sandstones, of it hanging, in benign metamorphosis,
for centuries to come, over the Seine waters, as *Pont*

---

[1] Dumont, Souvenirs sur Mirabeau, p. 305.

Louis Seize ; [1] the soul of it living, perhaps still longer, in the memories of men.

So far, ye august Senators, with your Tennis-Court Oaths, your inertia and impetus, your sagacity and pertinacity, have ye brought us. ' And yet think, Messieurs', as the Petitioners justly urged, ' you who were our saviours did yourselves need saviours ',—the brave Bastillers, namely ; workmen of Paris ; many of them in straitened pecuniary circumstances ! [2] Subscriptions are opened ; Lists are formed, more accurate than Elie's ; harangues are delivered. A Body of *Bastille Heroes,* tolerably complete, did get together ; —comparable to the Argonauts ; hoping to endure like them. But in little more than a year, the whirlpool of things threw them asunder again, and they sank. So many highest superlatives achieved by man are followed by new higher; and dwindle into comparatives and positives ! The Siege of the Bastille, weighed with which, in the Historical balance, most other sieges, including that of Troy Town, are gossamer, cost, as we find, in killed and mortally wounded, on the part of the Besiegers, some Eighty-three persons : on the part of the Besieged, after all that straw-burning, fire-pumping, and deluge of musketry, One poor solitary Invalid, shot stone-dead (*roide-mort*) on the battlements ! [3] The Bastille Fortress, like the City of Jericho, was overturned by miraculous *sound.*

[1] Dulaure, Histoire de Paris, viii. 434.
[2] Moniteur, Séance du Samedi 18 Juillet 1789 (in Histoire Parlementaire, ii. 137).
[3] Dusaulx, Prise de la Bastille, p. 447, &c.

BOOK VI

CONSOLIDATION

CHAPTER I

MAKE THE CONSTITUTION

HERE perhaps is the place to fix, a little more pre
cisely, what these two words, *French Revolution*, shall
mean ; for, strictly considered, they may have as many
meanings as there are speakers of them. All things are
in revolution ; in change from moment to moment,
which becomes sensible from epoch to epoch : in this
Time-World of ours there is properly nothing else but
revolution and mutation, and even nothing else conceivable. Revolution, you answer, means *speedier*
change. Whereupon one has still to ask : How
speedy ? At what degree of speed ; in what particular points of this variable course, which varies in
velocity, but can never stop till Time itself stops, does
revolution begin and end ; cease to be ordinary mutation, and again become such ? It is a thing that will
depend on definition more or less arbitrary.

For ourselves, we answer that French Revolution
means here the open violent Rebellion, and Victory,
of disimprisoned Anarchy against corrupt worn-out
Authority : how Anarchy breaks prison ; bursts up
from the infinite Deep, and rages uncontrollable,
immeasurable, enveloping a world ; in phasis after
phasis of fever-frenzy ;—till the frenzy burning itself
out, and what elements of new Order it held (since all
Force holds such) developing themselves, the Uncontrollable be got, if not reimprisoned, yet harnessed,
and its mad forces made to work towards their object

as sane regulated ones. For as Hierarchies and
Dynasties of all kinds, Theocracies, Aristocracies, Auto-
cracies, Strumpetocracies, have ruled over the world ;
so it was appointed, in the decrees of Providence, that
this same Victorious Anarchy, Jacobinism, Sansculottism, French Revolution, Horrors of French Revolution,
or what else mortals name it, should have its turn.
The ' destructive wrath '* of Sansculottism : this is
what we speak, having unhappily no voice for singing.*

Surely a great Phenomenon : nay it is a *transcendental* one, overstepping all rules and experience ; the
crowning Phenomenon of our Modern Time. For here
again, most unexpectedly, comes antique Fanaticism
in new and newest vesture; miraculous, as all Fanaticism is. Call it the Fanaticism of ' making away with
formulas, *de humer les formules* '. The world of formulas, the *formed* regulated world, which all habitable
world is,—must needs hate such Fanaticism like death ;
and be at deadly variance with it. The world of
formulas must conquer it ; or failing that, must die
execrating it, anathematizing it ;—can nevertheless in
nowise prevent its being and its having been. The
Anathemas are there, and the miraculous Thing is
there.

Whence it cometh ? Whither it goeth ?* These are
questions ! When the age of Miracles lay faded into
the distance as an incredible tradition, and even the
age of Conventionalities was now old ; and Man's
Existence had for long generations rested on mere
formulas which were grown hollow by course of time ;
and it seemed as if no Reality any longer existed, but
only Phantasms of realities, and God's Universe were
the work of the Tailor and Upholsterer mainly, and
men were buckram masks that went about becking and
grimacing there,—on a sudden, the Earth yawns asunder, and amid Tartarean smoke, and glare of fierce
brightness, rises SANSCULOTTISM, many-headed, fire-
breathing, and asks : What think ye of *me* ? Well may
the buckram masks start together, terror-struck ; ' into
expressive well-concerted groups ' ! It is indeed,

Friends, a most singular, most fatal thing. Let whosoever is but buckram and a phantasm look to it : ill
verily may it fare with him ; here methinks he cannot
much longer be. Woe also to many a one who is not
wholly buckram, but partly real and human ! The
age of Miracles has come back ! ' Behold the World-
Phoenix,* in fire-consummation and fire-creation : wide
are her fanning wings ; loud is her death-melody, of
battle-thunders and falling towns ; skyward lashes the
funeral flame, enveloping all things : it is the Death-
Birth of a World ! '

Whereby, however, as we often say, shall one
unspeakable blessing seem attainable. This, namely :
that Man and his Life rest no more on hollowness and
a Lie, but on solidity and some kind of Truth. Welcome
the beggarliest truth, so it be one, in exchange for the
royallest sham ! Truth of any kind breeds ever new
and better truth ; thus hard granite rock will crumble
down into soil, under the blessed skyey influences ; and
cover itself with verdure, with fruitage and umbrage.
But as for Falsehood, which, in like contrary manner
grows ever falser,—what can it, or what should it do
but decease, being ripe ; decompose itself, gently or
even violently, and return to the Father of it,—too
probably in flames of fire ?

Sansculottism will burn much ; but what is incom-
bustible it will not burn. Fear not Sansculottism ;
recognize it for what it is, the portentous inevitable
end of much, the miraculous beginning of much. One
other thing thou mayst understand of it : that it too
came from God ; for has it not been ? From of old,* as
it is written, are His goings forth ; in the great Deep*
of things ; fearful and wonderful now as in the beginning :* in the whirlwind* also He speaks ; and the wrath
of men* is made to praise Him.—But to gauge and
measure this immeasurable Thing, and what is called
account for it, and reduce it to a dead logic-formula,
attempt not ! Much less shalt thou shriek thyself
hoarse, cursing it ; for that, to all needful lengths, has

been already done. As an actually existing Son of
Time, *look*, with unspeakable manifold interest, oftenest
in silence, at what the Time did bring : therewith edify,
instruct, nourish thyself, or were it but to amuse and
gratify thyself, as it is given thee.

Another question which at every new turn will rise
on us, requiring ever new reply, is this : Where the
French Revolution specially *is* ? In the King's Palace,
in his Majesty's or her Majesty's managements, and
maltreatments, cabals, imbecilities and woes, answer
some few :—whom we do not answer. In the National
Assembly, answer a large mixed multitude : who
accordingly seat themselves in the Reporter's Chair ;
and therefrom noting what Proclamations, Acts,
Reports, passages of logic-fence, bursts of parliamentary
eloquence seem notable within doors, and what tumults
and rumours of tumult become audible from without,
produce volume on volume ; and, naming it History of
the French Revolution, contentedly publish the same.
To do the like, to almost any extent, with so many
Filed Newspapers, *Choix des Rapports, Histoires Parle-
mentaires* as there are, amounting to many horseloads,
were easy for us. Easy but unprofitable. The National
Assembly, named now Constituent Assembly, goes its
course ; making the Constitution ; but the French
Revolution also goes *its* course.

In general, may we not say that the French Revolution lies in the heart and head of every violent-speak-
ing, of every violent-thinking French Man ? How the
Twenty-five Millions of such, in their perplexed combination, acting and counter-acting may give birth to
events ; which event successively is the cardinal one ;
and from what point of vision it may best be surveyed :
this is a problem. Which problem the best insight,
seeking light from all possible sources, shifting its point
of vision whithersoever vision or glimpse of vision can
be had, may employ itself in solving ; and be well content to solve in some tolerably approximate way.

As to the National Assembly, in so far as it still

towers eminent over France, after the manner of a car-borne *Carroccio*, though now no longer in the van ; and rings signals for retreat or advance,—it is and con-tinues a reality among other realities. But in so far as it sits making the Constitution, on the other hand, it is a fatuity and chimera mainly. Alas, in the never so heroic building of Montesquieu-Mably card-castles, though shouted over by the world, what interest is there ? Occupied in that way, an august National Assembly becomes for us little other than a Sanhedrim of Pedants, not of the gerund-grinding, yet of no fruit-fuller sort ; and its loud debatings and recriminations about Rights of Man, Right of Peace and War, *Veto suspensif*, *Veto absolu*, what are they but so many Pedant's-curses, ' May God confound you for your *Theory of Irregular Verbs* ! '*

A Constitution can be built, Constitutions enough *à la Sieyes* : but the frightful difficulty is, that of getting men to come and live in them ! Could Sieyes have drawn thunder and lightning out of Heaven to sanction his Constitution, it had been well : but without any thunder ? Nay, strictly considered, is it not still true that without some such celestial sanction, given visibly in thunder or invisibly otherwise, no Constitution can in the long run be worth much more than the waste-paper it is written on ? The Constitution, the set of Laws, or prescribed Habits of Acting, that men will live under, is the one which images their Convictions, —their Faith as to this wondrous Universe, and what rights, duties, capabilities they have there : which stands sanctioned, therefore, by Necessity itself ; if not by a seen Deity, then by an unseen one. Other Laws, whereof there are always enough *ready*-made, are usurpations ; which men do not obey, but rebel against, and abolish, at their earliest convenience.

The question of questions accordingly were, Who is it that, especially for rebellers and abolishers, can make a Constitution ? He that can image forth the general Belief when there is one ; that can impart one

when, as here, there is none. A most rare man ; ever,
as of old, a god-missioned man ! Here, however, in
defect of such transcendent supreme man, Time with
its infinite succession of merely superior men, each
yielding his little contribution, does much. Force
likewise (for, as Antiquarian Philosophers teach, the
royal Sceptre was from the first something of a Hammer,
to *crack* such heads as could not be convinced) will all
along find somewhat to do. And thus in perpetual
abolition and reparation, rending and mending, with
struggle and strife, with present evil, and the hope
and effort towards future good, must the Constitution,
as all human things do, build itself forward ; or unbuild
itself, and sink, as it can and may. O Sieyes, and ye
other Committee-men, and Twelve Hundred miscellaneous individuals from all parts of France ! what is
the Belief of France, and yours, if ye knew it ? Properly that there shall be no Belief ; that all formulas
be swallowed. The Constitution which will suit that ?
Alas, too clearly, a No-Constitution, an Anarchy ;—
which also, in due season, shall be vouchsafed you.

But, after all, what can an unfortunate National
Assembly do ? Consider only this, that there are
Twelve Hundred miscellaneous individuals ; not a unit
of whom but has his own thinking-apparatus, his own
speaking-apparatus ! In every unit of them is some
belief and wish, different for each, both that France
should be regenerated, and also that he individually
should do it. Twelve Hundred separate Forces, yoked
miscellaneously to any object, miscellaneously to all
sides of it ; and bidden pull for life !

Or is it the nature of National Assemblies generally
to do, with endless labour and clangour, Nothing ? Are
Representative Governments mostly at bottom Tyran-
nies too ? Shall we say, the *Tyrants*, the ambitious
contentious Persons, from all corners of the country
do, in this manner, get gathered into one place ; and
there, with motion and counter-motion, with jargon
and hubbub, *cancel* one another, like the fabulous
Kilkenny Cats ; and produce, for net-result, *zero* ;—

the country meanwhile *governing* or guiding *itself*, by such wisdom, recognized, or for most part unrecognized, as may exist in individual heads here and there ?— Nay, even that were a great improvement : for of old, with their Guelf Factions and Ghibelline*Factions, with their Red Roses and White Roses, they were wont to cancel the whole country as well. Besides they do it now in a much narrower cockpit; within the four walls of their Assembly House, and here and there an outpost of Hustings and Barrel-heads; do it with tongues too, not with swords :—all which improvements, in the art of producing zero, are they not great ? Nay, best of all, some happy Continents (as the Western one, with its Savannahs, where whosoever has four willing limbs finds food under his feet, and an infinite sky over his head) can do without governing.—What Sphinx-questions ; which the distracted world, in these very generations, must answer or die !

CHAPTER II

THE CONSTITUENT ASSEMBLY

One thing an elected Assembly of Twelve Hundred is fit for : Destroying. Which indeed is but a more decided exercise of its natural talent for Doing Nothing. Do nothing, only keep agitating, debating ; and things will destroy themselves.

So and not otherwise proved it with an august National Assembly. It took the name Constituent, as if its mission and function had been to construct or build ; which also, with its whole soul, it endeavoured to do : yet, in the fates, in the nature of things, there lay for it precisely of all functions the most opposite to that. Singular, what Gospels men will believe ; even Gospels according to Jean Jacques ! It was the fixed Faith of these National Deputies, as of all think-ing Frenchmen, that the Constitution could be *made* ;

that they, there and then, were called to make it. How, with the toughness of old Hebrews or Ishmaelite Moslem, did the otherwise light unbelieving People persist in this their *Credo quia impossibile* ;* and front the armed world with it ; and grow fanatic, and even heroic, and do exploits by it ! The Constituent Assembly's Constitution, and several others, will, being printed and not manuscript, survive to future generations, as an instructive well-nigh incredible document of the Time : the most significant Picture of the then existing France ; or at lowest, Picture of these men's Picture of it.

But in truth and seriousness, what could the National Assembly have done ? The thing to *be* done was, actually as they said, to regenerate France ; to abolish the old France, and make a new one, quietly or forcibly, by concession or by violence : this by the Law of Nature has become inevitable. With what degree of violence, depends on the wisdom of those that preside over it. With perfect wisdom on the part of the National Assembly, it had all been otherwise ; but whether, in any wise, it could have been pacific, nay other than bloody and convulsive, may still be a question.

Grant, meanwhile, that this Constituent Assembly does to the last continue to be something. With a sigh, it sees itself incessantly forced away from its infinite divine task of perfecting ' the Theory of Irregular Verbs ',—to finite terrestrial tasks, which latter have still a significance for us. It is the cynosure of revolutionary France, this National Assembly. All work of Government has fallen into its hands, or under its control; all men look to it for guidance. In the middle of that huge Revolt of Twenty-five millions, it hovers always aloft as *Carroccio* or Battle-Standard, impelling and impelled, in the most confused way : if it cannot give much guidance, it will still seem to give some. It emits pacificatory Proclamations, not a few ; with more or with less result. It authorizes the enrolment of National Guards,—lest Brigands come to devour us, and reap the unripe crops. It sends missions to quell ' effervescences ' ; to deliver men from the Lanterne. It can listen to congratulatory Addresses, which arrive daily by the sackful ; mostly in King Cambyses' vein : also to Petitions and complaints from all mortals ; so that every mortal's complaint, if it cannot get redressed, may at least hear itself complain. For the rest, an august National Assembly can produce Parliamentary Eloquence ; and appoint Committees. Committees of the Constitution, of Reports, of Researches ; and of much else : which again yield mountains of Printed Paper ; the theme of new Parliamentary Eloquence, in bursts, or in plenteous smooth-flowing floods. And so, from the waste vortex whereon all things go whirling and grinding, Organic Laws, or the similitude of such, slowly emerge.

With endless debating, we get the *Rights of Man* written down and promulgated : true paper basis of all paper Constitutions. Neglecting, cry the opponents, to declare the Duties of Man ! Forgetting, answer we, to ascertain the *Mights* of Man ;—one of the fatallest omissions !—Nay, sometimes, as on the Fourth of August, our National Assembly, fired suddenly by an almost preternatural enthusiasm, will get through whole masses of work in one night. A memorable night, this Fourth of August : Dignitaries temporal and spiritual ; Peers, Archbishops, Parlement-Presidents, each outdoing the other in patriotic devotedness, come successively to throw their now untenable possessions on the ' altar of the fatherland '. With louder and louder vivats,—for indeed it is ' after dinner ' too,—they abolish Tithes, Seignorial Dues, Gabelle, excessive preservation of Game ; nay Privilege, Immunity, Feudalism root and branch ; then appoint a *Te Deum* for it ; and so, finally, disperse about three in the morning, striking the stars with their sublime heads. Such night, unforeseen but for ever memorable, was this of the Fourth of August 1789. Miraculous, or semi-miraculous, some seem to think it. A new Night of

Pentecost,* shall we say, shaped according to the new
Time, and new Church of Jean Jacques Rousseau ?
It had its causes ; also its effects.

In such manner labour the National Deputies ; perfecting their Theory of Irregular Verbs ; governing
France, and being governed by it ; with toil and noise ;
—cutting asunder ancient intolerable bonds ; and, for
new ones, assiduously spinning ropes of sand.* Were
their labours a nothing or a something, yet the eyes of
all France being reverently fixed on them, History can
never very long leave them altogether out of sight.

For the present, if we glance into that Assembly
Hall of theirs, it will be found, as is natural, ' most
irregular '. As many as ' a hundred members are on
their feet at once ' ; no rule in making motions, or only
commencements of a rule ; Spectators' Gallery allowed
to applaud, and even to hiss ; [1] President, appointed
once a fortnight, raising many times no serene head
above the waves. Nevertheless, as in all human
Assemblages, like does begin arranging itself to like ;
the perennial rule, *Ubi homines sunt modi sunt,* proves
valid. Rudiments of Methods disclose themselves ;
rudiments of Parties. There is a Right Side (*Côté
Droit*), a Left Side (*Côté Gauche*) ; sitting on M. le President's right hand, or on his left : the *Côté Droit* con-
servative ; the *Côté Gauche* destructive. Intermediate
is Anglomaniac Constitutionalism, or Two-Chamber
Royalism ; with its Mouniers, its Lallys,—fast verging
towards nonentity. Pre-eminent, on the Right Side,
pleads and perorates Cazalès the Dragoon-captain,
eloquent, mildly fervent ; earning for himself the
shadow of a name. There also blusters Barrel-Mirabeau, the Younger Mirabeau, not without wit : dusky
D'Espréménil does nothing but sniff and ejaculate ;
might, it is fondly thought, lay prostrate the Elder
Mirabeau himself, would he but try,[2]—which he does

[1] Arthur Young, i. 111.
[2] Biographie Universelle, § D'Espréménil (by Beaulieu).

not. Last and greatest, see, for one moment, the Abbé
Maury; with his jesuitic eyes, his impassive brass
face, 'image of all the cardinal sins'. Indomitable,
unquenchable, he fights jesuitico-rhetorically; with
toughest lungs and heart; for Throne, especially for
Altar and Tithes. So that a shrill voice exclaims once,
from the Gallery: 'Messieurs of the Clergy, you *have*
to be shaved; if you wriggle too much, you will get
cut'.[1]

The Left side is also called the D'Orléans side; and
sometimes, derisively, the Palais Royal. And yet, so
confused, real-imaginary seems everything, 'it is doubtful', as Mirabeau said, 'whether D'Orléans himself
belong to that same D'Orléans party'. What can be
known and seen is, that his moon-visage does beam
forth from that point of space. There likewise sits
seagreen Robespierre; throwing in his light weight,
with decision, not yet with effect. A thin lean Puritan
and Precisian, he would make away with formulas;
yet lives, moves and has his being wholly in formulas,
of another sort. '*Peuple*', such, according to Robespierre, ought to be the Royal method of promulgating
Laws, '*Peuple*, this is the Law I have framed for thee;
dost thou accept it?'—answered, from Right Side,
from Centre and Left, by inextinguishable laughter.[2]
Yet men of insight discern that the Seagreen may by
chance go far: 'This man', observes Mirabeau, 'will
do somewhat; he believes every word he says'.

Abbé Sieyes is busy with mere Constitutional work;
wherein, unluckily, fellow-workmen are less pliable
than, with one who has completed the Science of Polity,
they ought to be. Courage, Sieyes, nevertheless!
Some twenty months of heroic travail, of contradiction
from the stupid, and the Constitution shall be built;
the top-stone of it brought out with shouting,—say
rather, the top-paper, for it is all Paper; and *thou* hast
done in it what the Earth or the Heaven could require,

[1] Dictionnaire des Hommes Marquans, ii. 519.
[2] Moniteur, No. 67 (in Hist. Parl.).

thy utmost. Note likewise this Trio; memorable for
several things; memorable were it only that their
history is written in an epigram: 'whatsoever these
Three have in hand', it is said, 'Duport thinks it,
Barnave speaks it, Lameth does it'.[1]

But royal Mirabeau ? Conspicuous among all parties,
raised above and beyond them all, this man rises more
and more. As we often say, he has an *eye*, he is
a reality; while others are formulas and eye-*glasses*.
In the Transient he will detect the Perennial; find
some firm footing even among Paper-vortexes. His
fame is gone forth to all lands; it gladdened the heart
of the crabbed old Friend of Men himself before he
died. The very Postilions of inns have heard of Mirabeau : when an impatient Traveller complains that the
team is insufficient, his Postilion answers, 'Yes, Monsieur, the wheelers are weak; but my *mirabeau* (main
horse), you see, is a right one, *mais mon mirabeau est
excellent*'.[2]

And now, Reader, thou shalt quit this noisy Discrepancy of a National Assembly; not (if thou be of
humane mind) without pity. Twelve hundred brother
men are there, in the centre of Twenty-five Millions;
fighting so fiercely with Fate and with one another;
struggling their lives out, as most sons of Adam* do,
for that which profiteth not.* Nay, on the whole, it is
admitted further to be very *dull*. 'Dull as this day's
Assembly', said some one. 'Why date, *Pourquoi
dater ?*' answered Mirabeau.

Consider that they are Twelve Hundred; that they
not only speak, but *read* their speeches; and even
borrow and steal speeches to read! With Twelve
Hundred fluent speakers, and their Noah's Deluge of
vociferous commonplace, silence unattainable may well
seem the one blessing of Life. But figure Twelve
Hundred pamphleteers; droning forth perpetual

---

[1] See Toulongeon, i. c. 3.
[2] Dumont, Souvenirs sur Mirabeau, p. 255.

pamphlets : and no man to gag them ! Neither, as in
the American Congress, do the arrangements seem
perfect. A Senator has not his own Desk and Newspaper here ; of Tobacco (much less of Pipes) there is
not the slightest provision. Conversation itself must
be transacted in a low tone, with continual interruption : only ' pencil Notes ' circulate freely ; ' in incredible numbers, to the foot of the very tribune '.[1]—Such
work is it, regenerating a Nation ; perfecting one's
Theory of Irregular Verbs !

CHAPTER III

THE GENERAL OVERTURN

Of the King's Court, for the present, there is almost
nothing whatever to be said. Silent, deserted are these
halls ; Royalty languishes forsaken of its war-god and
all its hopes, till once the Œil-de-Bœuf rally again.
The sceptre is departed*from King Louis ; is gone over
to the *Salle des Menus*, to the Paris Townhall, or one
knows not whither.   In the July days, while all ears
were yet deafened by the crash of the Bastille, and
Ministers and Princes were scattered to the four winds,
it seemed as if the very Valets had grown heavy of
hearing. Besenval, also in flight towards Infinite
Space, but hovering a little at Versailles, was addressing
his Majesty personally for an Order about post-horses ;
when, lo, ' the Valet in waiting places himself familiarly
between his Majesty and me ', stretching out his rascal
neck to learn what it was ! His Majesty, in sudden
choler, whirled round ; made a clutch at the tongs :
' I gently prevented him ; he grasped my hand in
thankfulness ; and I noticed tears in his eyes '.[2]

Poor King ; for French Kings also are men ! Louis

[1] See Dumont (pp. 159–67) ; Arthur Young, &c.
[2] Besenval, iii. 419.

Fourteenth himself once clutched the tongs, and even
smote with them; but then it was at Louvois, and
Dame Maintenon ran up.—The Queen sits weeping in her
inner apartments, surrounded by weak women: she
is ' at the height of unpopularity '; universally regarded
as the evil genius of France. Her friends and familiar
counsellors have all fled; and fled, surely, on the
foolishest errand. The Château Polignac still frowns
aloft, on its 'bold and enormous cubical rock', amid
the blooming champaigns, amid the blue girdling mountains of Auvergne: [1] but no Duke and Duchess Polignac
look forth from it; they have fled, they have ' met
Necker at Bâle '; they shall not return. That France
should see her Nobles resist the Irresistible, Inevitable,
with the face of angry men, was unhappy, not unexpected; but with the face and sense of pettish children? This was her peculiarity. They understood
nothing; would understand nothing. Does not, at
this hour, a new Polignac, first-born of these Two, sit
reflective in the Castle of Ham; [2] in an astonishment
he will never recover from; the most confused of
existing mortals?

King Louis has his new Ministry: mere Populari-
ties; Old-President Pompignan; Necker, coming back
in triumph; and other such.[3] But what will it avail
him? As was said, the sceptre, all but the wooden gilt
sceptre, has departed elsewhither. Volition, determination is not in this man: only innocence, indolence;
dependence on all persons but himself, on all circumstances but the circumstances he were lord of. So
troublous internally is our Versailles and its work.
Beautiful, if seen from afar, resplendent like a Sun;
seen near at hand, a mere Sun's-Atmosphere, hiding
darkness, confused ferment of ruin!

But over France, there goes on the indisputablest
' destruction of formulas '; transaction of realities

---

[1] Arthur Young, i. 165.   [2] A.D. 1835.
[3] Montgaillard, ii. 108.

that follow therefrom. So many millions of persons,
all gyved, and nigh strangled, with formulas; whose
Life nevertheless, at least the digestion and hunger of
it, was real enough ! Heaven has at length sent an
abundant harvest: but what profits it the poor man,
when Earth with her formulas interposes ? Industry,
in these times of insurrection, must needs lie dormant;
capital, as usual, not circulating, but stagnating
timorously in nooks. The poor man is short of work,
is therefore short of money; nay even had he money,
bread is not to be bought for it. Were it plotting of
Aristocrats, plotting of D'Orléans; were it Brigands,
preternatural terror, and the clang of Phoebus Apollo's
silver bow,—enough, the markets are scarce of grain,
plentiful only in tumult. Farmers seem lazy to thresh;
—being either ' bribed ' ; or needing no bribe, with
prices ever rising, with perhaps rent itself no longer so
pressing. Neither, what is singular, do municipal
enactments, ' That along with so many measures of
wheat you shall sell so many of rye', and other the like,
much mend the matter. Dragoons with drawn swords
stand ranked among the corn-sacks, often more
dragoons than sacks.[1] Meal-mobs abound; growing
into mobs of a still darker quality.

Starvation has been known among the French Commonalty before this; known and familiar. Did we not
see them, in the year 1775, presenting, in sallow faces,
in wretchedness and raggedness, their Petition of
Grievances; and, for answer, getting a brand-new
Gallows forty feet high ? Hunger and Darkness,
through long years ! For look back on that earlier
Paris Riot, when a Great Personage, worn out by
debauchery, was believed to be in want of Blood-baths;
and Mothers, in worn raiment, yet with living hearts
under it, ' filled the public places ' with their wild
Rachel-cries,—stilled also by the Gallows. Twenty
years ago, the Friend of Men (preaching to the deaf)
described the Limousin Peasants as wearing a pain-

---

[1] Arthur Young, i. 129, &c.

stricken (*souffre-douleur*) look, a look *past* complaint,
' as if the oppression of the great were like the hail
and the thunder, a thing irremediable, the ordinance
of Nature '.[1] And now if in some great hour, the
shock of a falling Bastille should awaken you ; and it
were found to be the ordinance of Art merely ; and
remediable, reversible !

Or has the Reader forgotten that ' flood of savages ',
which, in sight of the same Friend of Men, descended
from the mountains at Mont d'Or ?   Lank-haired
haggard faces ; shapes rawboned, in high sabots ; in
woollen jupes, with leather girdles studded with copper-
nails ! They rocked from foot to foot, and beat time
with their elbows too, as the quarrel and battle, which
was not long in beginning, went on ; shouting fiercely ;
the lank faces distorted into the similitude of a cruel
laugh. For they were darkened and hardened : long
had they been the prey of excise-men and tax-men ; of
' clerks with the cold spurt of their pen '. It was the
fixed prophecy of our old Marquis, which no man would
listen to, that ' such Government by Blind-man's-buff,
stumbling along too far, would end by the General
Overturn, the *Culbute Générale* ! '

No man would listen, each went his thoughtless
way ;—and Time and Destiny also travelled on. The
Government by Blind-man's-buff, stumbling along,
has reached the precipice inevitable for it. Dull
Drudgery, driven on, by clerks with the cold dastard
spurt of their pen, has been driven—into a Communion
of Drudges ! For now, moreover, there have come the
strangest confused tidings ; by Paris Journals with
their paper wings ; or still more portentous, where no
Journals are,[2] by rumour and conjecture : Oppression
not inevitable ; a Bastille prostrate, and the Constitution fast getting ready ! Which Constitution, if it be
something and not nothing, what can it be but bread
to eat ?

---

[1] Fils Adoptif, Mémoires de Mirabeau, i. 364-94.
[2] See Arthur Young, i. 137, 150, &c.

The Traveller, ' walking up hill bridle in hand ', over-takes ' a poor woman ' ; the image, as such commonly are, of drudgery and scarcity ; ' looking sixty years of age, though she is not yet twenty-eight '. They have seven children, her poor drudge and she : a farm, with one cow, which helps to make the children soup ; also one little horse, or garron. They have rents and quit-rents, Hens to pay to this Seigneur, Oat-sacks to that ; King's taxes, Statute-labour, Church-taxes, taxes enough ;—and think the times inexpressible. She has heard that some*where*, in some manner, some*thing* is to be done for the poor : ' God send it soon ; for the dues and taxes crush us down (*nous écrasent*) ! ' [1]

Fair prophecies are spoken, but they are not fulfilled. There have been Notables, Assemblages, turnings out and comings in. Intriguing and manœuvring ; Parle-mentary eloquence and arguing, Greek meeting Greek in high places, has long gone on ; yet still bread comes not. The harvest is reaped and garnered ; yet still we have no bread. Urged by despair and by hope, what can Drudgery do, but rise, as predicted, and produce the General Overturn ?

Fancy, then, some Five full-grown Millions of such gaunt figures, with their haggard faces (*figures hâves*) ; in woollen jupes, with copper-studded leather girths, and high sabots,—starting up to ask, as in forest-roar-ings, their washed Upper-Classes, after long unreviewed centuries, virtually this question : How have ye treated us ; how have ye taught us, fed us, and led us, while we toiled for you ? The answer can be read in flames, over the nightly summer-sky. *This* is the feeding and leading we have had of you : EMPTINESS,—of pocket, of stomach, of head and of heart. Behold there is *nothing in us* ; nothing but what Nature gives her wild children of the desert : Ferocity and Appetite ; Strength grounded on Hunger. Did ye mark among your Rights of Man, that man was not to die of starvation, while there was bread reaped by him ? It is among the Mights of Man.

[1] See Arthur Young, i. 134.

Seventy-two Châteaus have flamed aloft in the
Mâconnais and Beaujolais alone : this seems the centre
of the conflagration ; but it has spread over Dauphiné,
Alsace, the Lyonnais ; the whole South-East is in
a blaze. All over the North, from Rouen to Metz, disorder is abroad : smugglers of salt go openly in armed
bands : the barriers of towns are burnt ; toll-gatherers,
tax-gatherers, official persons put to flight. ' It was
thought ', says Young, ' the people, from hunger, would
revolt ' ; and we see they have done it. Desperate
Lackalls, long prowling aimless, now finding hope in
desperation itself, everywhere form a nucleus. They
ring the Church-bell by way of tocsin : and the Parish
turns out to the work.[1] Ferocity, atrocity ; hunger
and revenge : such work as we can imagine !

Ill stands it now with the Seigneur, who, for example,
' has walled up the only Fountain of the Township ' ;
who has ridden high on his *chartier* and parchments ;
who has preserved Game not wisely but too well.
Churches also, and Canonries, are sacked, without
mercy ; which have shorn the flock too close, forgetting
to feed it. Woe to the land over which Sansculottism,
in its day of vengeance, tramps rough-shod,—shod in
sabots ! Highbred Seigneurs, with their delicate
women and little ones, had to ' fly half-naked ', under
cloud of night : glad to escape the flames, and even
worse. You meet them at the *tables-d'hôte* of inns ;
making wise reflections or foolish, that ' rank is destroyed ' ; uncertain whither [they shall now wend.'[2]
The *métayer* will find it convenient to be slack in paying
rent. As for the Tax-gatherer, he, long hunting as
a biped of prey, may now find himself hunted as one ;
his Majesty's Exchequer will not ' fill up the Deficit ',
this season : it is the notion of many that a Patriot
Majesty, being the Restorer of French Liberty, has
abolished most taxes, though, for their private ends,
some men make a secret of it.

Where will this end ? In the Abyss, one may pro-

[1] See Hist. Parl. ii. 243–6.   [2] See Young, i. 149, &c.

phesy; whither all Delusions are, at all moments,
travelling; where this Delusion has now arrived. For
if there be a Faith, from of old, it is this, as we often
repeat, that no Lie can live for ever. The very Truth
has to change its vesture, from time to time; and be
born again. But all Lies have sentence of death written
down against them, in Heaven's Chancery itself; and,
slowly or fast, advance incessantly towards their hour.
' The sign of a Grand Seigneur being landlord ', says
the vehement plain-spoken Arthur Young, ' are wastes,
landes, deserts, ling: go to his residence, you will find
it in the middle of a forest, peopled with deer, wild
boars and wolves. The fields are scenes of pitiable
management, as the houses are of misery. To see so
many millions of hands, that would be industrious, all
idle and starving: Oh, if I were legislator of France for
one day, I would make these great lords skip again ! ' [1]
O Arthur, thou now actually beholdest them *skip* ;—
wilt thou grow to grumble at that too ?

For long years and generations it lasted; but the
time came. Featherbrain, whom no reasoning and no
pleading could touch, the glare of the firebrand had to
illuminate: there remained but that method. Consider it, look at it ! The widow is gathering nettles
for her children's dinner; a perfumed Seigneur, deli-
cately lounging in the Œil-de-Bœuf, has an alchemy
whereby he will extract from her the third nettle, and
name it Rent and Law: such an arrangement must end.
Ought it not ? But, O most fearful is *such* an ending !
Let those, to whom God, in his great mercy, has granted
time and space, prepare another and milder one.

To some it is a matter of wonder that the Seigneurs
did not do something to help themselves; say, combine
and arm: for there were a ' hundred and fifty thousand
of them ', all valiant enough. Unhappily, a hundred
and fifty thousand, scattered over wide Provinces,
divided by mutual ill-will, cannot combine. The

---

[1] Arthur Young, i. 12, 48, 84, &c.

highest Seigneurs, as we have seen, had already emigrated,—with a view of putting France to the blush.
Neither are arms now the peculiar property of Seigneurs;
but of every mortal who has ten shillings, wherewith to
buy a secondhand firelock.

Besides, those starving Peasants, after all, have not
four feet and claws, that you could keep them down
permanently in that manner. They are not even of
black colour: they are mere Unwashed Seigneurs; and
a Seigneur too has human bowels!—The Seigneurs did
what they could; enrolled in National Guards; fled,
with shrieks, complaining to Heaven and Earth. One
Seigneur, famed Memmay of Quincey, near Vesoul,
invited all the rustics of his neighbourhood to a ban-
quet; blew up his Château and them with gunpowder;
and instantaneously vanished, no man yet knows
whither.[1] Some half-dozen years after, he came back;
and demonstrated that it was by accident.

Nor are the Authorities idle; though unluckily, all
Authorities, Municipalities and such like, are in the
uncertain transitionary state; getting regenerated
from old Monarchic to new Democratic; no Official
yet knows clearly what he is. Nevertheless, Mayors
old or new do gather *Marechaussées*, National Guards,
Troops of the line; justice, of the most summary sort,
is not wanting. The Electoral Committee of Mâcon,
though but a Committee, goes the length of hanging,
for its own behoof, as many as twenty. The Prévôt of
Dauphiné traverses the country 'with a movable
column', with tipstaves, gallows-ropes; for gallows
any tree will serve, and suspend its culprit, or ' thirteen '
culprits.

Unhappy country! How is the fair gold-and-green
of the ripe bright Year defaced with horrid blackness;
black ashes of Châteaus, black bodies of gibbeted Men!
Industry has ceased in it; not sounds of the hammer
and saw, but of the tocsin and alarm-drum. The sceptre
has departed, *whither* one knows not;—breaking itself

[1] Hist. Parl. ii. 161.

in pieces : here impotent, there tyrannous. National Guards are unskilful, and of doubtful purpose ; Soldiers are inclined to mutiny : there is danger that they two may quarrel, danger that they may *agree*. Strasburg has seen riots : a Townhall torn to shreds, its archives scattered white on the winds ; drunk soldiers embracing drunk citizens for three days, and Mayor Dietrich and Marshal Rochambeau reduced nigh to desperation.[1]

Through the middle of all which phenomena is seen, on his triumphant transit, ' escorted ', through Béfort for instance, ' by fifty National Horsemen and all the military music of the place ',—M. Necker, returning from Bâle ! Glorious as the meridian ; though poor Necker himself partly guesses whither it is leading.[2] One highest culminating day, at the Paris Townhall ; with immortal vivats, with wife and daughter kneeling publicly to kiss his hand ; with Besenval's pardon granted,—but indeed revoked before sunset : one highest day, but then lower days, and ever lower, down even to lowest ! Such magic is in a name ; and in the want of a name. Like some enchanted Mambrino's Helmet,* essential to victory, comes this ' Saviour of France ' ; beshouted, becymballed by the world : alas, so soon to be *dis*enchanted, to be pitched shamefully over the lists as a Barber's Bason ! Gibbon ' could wish to show him ' (in this ejected, Barber's-Bason state) to any man of solidity, who were minded to have the soul burnt out of him, and become a *caput mortuum*, by Ambition, unsuccessful or successful.[3]

Another small phasis we add, and no more : how, in the Autumn months, our sharp-tempered Arthur has been ' pestered for some days past ', by shot, lead-drops and slugs, ' rattling five or six times into my chaise and about my ears ' ; all the mob of the country gone out to kill Game ![4] It is even so. On the Cliffs of Dover,

[1] Arthur Young, i. 141 ; Dampmartin, Evènemens qui se sont passés sous mes yeux, i. 105-127.

[2] Biographie Universelle, § Necker (by Lally-Tollendal).

[3] Gibbon's Letters.   [4] Young, i. 176.

over all the Marches of France, there appear, this
autumn, two signs on the Earth : emigrant flights of
French Seigneurs ; emigrant winged flights of French
Game ! Finished, one may say, or as good as finished,
is the Preservation of Game on this Earth ; completed
for endless Time. What part *it* had to play in the
History of Civilization is played : *plaudite ; exeat !*

In this manner does Sansculottism blaze up, illus-
trating many things ;—producing, among the rest, as
we saw, on the Fourth of August, that semi-miraculous
Night of Pentecost in the National Assembly ; semi-
miraculous, which had its causes, and its effects.
Feudalism is struck dead ; not on parchment only, and
by ink ; but in very fact, by fire ; say, by self-combustion. This conflagration of the South-East will abate ;
will be got scattered, to the West, or elsewhither :
extinguish it will not, till the *fuel* be all done.

CHAPTER IV

IN QUEUE

IF we look now at Paris, one thing is too evident :
that the Bakers' shops have got their *Queues*, or Tails ;
their long strings of purchasers, arranged *in tail*, so that
the first come be the first served,—were the shop once
open ! This waiting in tail, not seen since the early
days of July, again makes its appearance in August. In
time, we shall see it perfected by practice to the rank
almost of an art ; and the art, or quasi-art, of standing
in tail become one of the characteristics of the Parisian
People, distinguishing them from all other Peoples
whatsoever.

But consider, while work itself is so scarce, how
a man must not only realize money, but stand waiting
(if his wife is too weak to wait and struggle) for half-
days in the Tail, till he get it changed for dear bad

bread! Controversies, to the length sometimes of
blood and battery, must arise in these exasperated
Queues. Or if no controversy, then it is but one accordant *Pange Lingua* of complaint against the Powers
that be. France has begun her long Curriculum of
Hungering, instructive and productive beyond Academic Curriculums; which extends over some seven
most strenuous years. As Jean Paul says of his own
Life, ' to a great height shall the business of Hungering go ':*

Or consider, in strange contrast, the jubilee Ceremonies; for, in general, the aspect of Paris presents
these two features: jubilee ceremonials and scarcity
of victual. Processions enough walk in jubilee; of
Young Women, decked and dizened, their ribands all
tricolor; moving with song and tabor, to the Shrine
of Sainte Geneviève, to thank her that the Bastille is
down. The Strong Men of the Market, and the Strong
Women, fail not with their bouquets and speeches.
Abbé Fauchet, famed in such work (for Abbé Lefevre
could only distribute powder) blesses tricolor cloth for
the National Guard; and makes it a National Tricolor
Flag; victorious, or to be victorious, in the cause of
civil and religious liberty all over the world. Fauchet,
we say, is the man for *Te-Deums*, and public Consecra-
tions;—to which, as in this instance of the Flag, our
National Guard will ' reply with volleys of musketry ',
Church and Cathedral though it be; [1] filling Notre
Dame with such noisiest fuliginous *Amen*, significant
of several things.

On the whole, we will say our new Mayor Bailly,
our new Commander Lafayette named also ' Scipio-
Americanus ', have bought their preferment dear.
Bailly rides in gilt state-coach, with beef-eaters and
sumptuosity; Camille Desmoulins, and others, sniffing
at him for it: Scipio bestrides the ' white charger ',
and waves with civic plumes in sight of all France.
Neither of them, however, does it for nothing; but, in

[1] See Hist. Parl. iii. 20; Mercier, Nouveau Paris, &c.

truth, at an exorbitant rate. At this rate, namely:
of feeding Paris, and keeping it from fighting. Out of
the City-funds, some seventeen thousand of the utterly
destitute are employed digging on Montmartre, at ten
pence a day, which buys them, at market price, almost
two pounds of bad bread:—they look very yellow,
when Lafayette goes to harangue them. The Townhall
is in travail, night and day; it must bring forth Bread,
a Municipal Constitution, regulations of all kinds, curbs
on the Sansculottic Press; above all, Bread, Bread.

Purveyors prowl the country far and wide, with the
appetite of lions; detect hidden grain, purchase open
grain; by gentle means or forcible, must and will find
grain. A most thankless task; and so difficult, so
dangerous,—even if a man did gain some trifle by it!
On the 19th of August, there is food for one day.[1]
Complaints there are that the food is spoiled, and produces an effect on the intestines: not corn but plaster-
of-Paris! Which effect on the intestines, as well as
that ' smarting in the throat and palate ', a Townhall
Proclamation warns you to disregard, or even to consider as drastic-beneficial. The Mayor of Saint-Denis,
so black was his bread, has, by a dyspeptic populace,
been hanged on the Lanterne there. National Guards
protect the Paris Corn-Market: first ten suffice; then
six hundred.[2] Busy are ye, Bailly, Brissot de Warville,
Condorcet, and ye others!

For, as just hinted, there is a Municipal Constitution
to be made too. The old Bastille Electors, after some
ten days of psalmodying over their glorious victory,
began to hear it asked, in a splenetic tone, Who put
you there? They accordingly had to give place, not
without moanings, and audible growlings on both sides,
to a new larger Body, specially elected for that post.
Which new Body, augmented, altered, then fixed finally
at the number of Three Hundred, with the title of Town
Representatives (*Représentans de la Commune*), now

---

[1] See Bailly, Mémoires, ii. 137–409.
[2] Hist. Parl. ii. 421.

sits there; rightly portioned into Committees; assiduous making a Constitution; at all moments when not
seeking flour.

And such a Constitution; little short of miraculous:
one that shall 'consolidate the Revolution'! The
Revolution is finished then? Mayor Bailly and all
respectable friends of Freedom would fain think so.
Your Revolution, like jelly sufficiently *boiled*, needs
only to be poured into *shapes*, of Constitution, and
'consolidated' therein? Could it, indeed, contrive to
cool; which last, however, is precisely the doubtful
thing, or even the not doubtful!

Unhappy Friends of Freedom; consolidating a Revolution! They must sit at work there, their pavilion
spread on very Chaos; between two hostile worlds,
the Upper Court-world, the nether Sansculottic one;
and, beaten on by both, toil painfully, perilously,—
doing, in sad literal earnest, 'the impossible'.

CHAPTER V

THE FOURTH ESTATE

PAMPHLETEERING opens its abysmal throat wider
and wider; never to close more. Our Philosophes,
indeed, rather withdraw; after the manner of Marmontel, 'retiring in disgust the first day'. Abbé Raynal,
grown grey and quiet in his Marseilles domicile, is little
content with this work: the last literary act of the man
will again be an act of rebellion; an indignant *Letter
to the Constituent Assembly*; answered by 'the order
of the day'. Thus also Philosophe Morellet puckers
discontented brows; being indeed threatened in his
benefices by that Fourth of August: it is clearly going
too far. How astonishing that those 'haggard figures
in woollen jupes' would not rest as satisfied with
Speculation, and victorious Analysis, as we!

Alas, yes: Speculation, Philosophism, once the

ornament and wealth of the saloon, will now coin itself
into mere Practical Propositions, and circulate on
street and highway, universally; with results! A
Fourth Estate, of Able Editors, springs up; increases
and multiplies; irrepressible, incalculable. New
Printers, new Journals, and ever new (so prurient is
the world), let our Three Hundred curb and consolidate
as they can! Loustalot, under the wing of Prudhomme*
dull-blustering Printer, edits weekly his *Révolutions de
Paris*; in an acrid, emphatic manner. Acrid, corrosive, as the spirit of sloes and copperas, is Marat, *Friend
of the People*; struck already with the fact that the
National Assembly, so full of Aristocrats, 'can do
nothing', except dissolve itself, and make way for
a better; that the Townhall Representatives are little
other than babblers and imbeciles, if not even knaves.
Poor is this man; squalid, and dwells in garrets;
a man unlovely to the sense, outward and inward;
a man forbid;—and is becoming fanatical, possessed
with fixed-idea. Cruel *lusus* of Nature! Did Nature,
O poor Marat, as in cruel sport, knead thee out of her
leavings, and miscellaneous waste clay; and fling thee
forth, stepdame-like, a Distraction into this distracted
Eighteenth Century? Work is appointed thee there;
which thou shalt do. The Three Hundred have summoned and will again summon Marat: but always he
croaks forth answer sufficient; always he will defy
them, or elude them; and endure no gag.

Carra,* 'Ex-secretary of a decapitated Hospodar',
and then of a Necklace-Cardinal; likewise Pamphleteer,
Adventurer in many scenes and lands,—draws nigh
to Mercier, of the *Tableau de Paris*; and, with foam
on his lips, proposes an *Annales Patriotiques*. The
Moniteur goes its prosperous way; Barrère 'weeps',
on Paper as yet loyal; Rivarol, Royou* are not idle.*
Deep calls to deep*: your *Domine Salvum Fac Regem*
shall awaken *Pange Lingua*; with an *Ami-du-Peuple*
there is a King's-Friend Newspaper, *Ami-du-Roi*.
Camille Desmoulins has appointed himself *Procureur-
Général de la Lanterne*, Attorney-General of the Lamp-

iron ; and pleads, *not* with atrocity, under an atrocious title ; editing weekly his brilliant *Revolutions of Paris and Brabant.* Brilliant, we say ; for if, in that thick murk of Journalism, with its dull blustering, with its fixed or loose fury, any ray of genius greet thee, be sure it is Camille's. The thing that Camille touches, he with his light finger adorns : brightness plays, gentle, unexpected, amid horrible confusions ; often is the word of Camille worth reading, when no other's is. Questionable Camille, how thou glitterest with a fallen, rebellious, yet still semi-celestial light ; as is the starlight on the brow of Lucifer ! Son of the Morning,* into what times and what lands art thou fallen !

But in all things there is good ;—though it be not good for 'consolidating Revolutions'. Thousand wagon-loads of this Pamphleteering and Newspaper matter lie rotting slowly in the Public Libraries of our Europe. Snatched from the great gulf, like oysters by bibliomaniac pearl-divers, there must they first *rot*, then what was pearl, in Camille or others, may be seen as such, and continue as such.

Nor has public speaking declined, though Lafayette and his Patrols look sour on it. Loud always is the Palais Royal, loudest the Café de Foy ; such a miscellany of Citizens and Citizenesses circulating there. 'Now and then', according to Camille, 'some Citizens employ the liberty of the *press* for a private purpose ; so that this or the other Patriot finds himself short of his watch or pocket-handkerchief ! ' But for the rest, in Camille's opinion, nothing can be a livelier image of the Roman Forum. 'A Patriot proposes his motion ; if it finds any supporters, they make him mount on a chair, and speak. If he is applauded, he prospers and redacts; if he is hissed, he goes his ways '. Thus they, circulating and perorating. Tall shaggy Marquis Saint-Huruge, a man that has had losses, and has deserved them, is seen eminent, and also heard. 'Bellowing ' is the character of his voice, like that of a Bull

of Bashan ;* voice which drowns all voices, which causes
frequently the hearts of men to leap. Cracked or half-
cracked is this tall Marquis's head ; uncracked are his
lungs ; the cracked and the uncracked shall alike avail
him.

Consider further that each of the Forty-eight Districts has its own Committee ; speaking and motioning
continually ; aiding in the search for grain, in the
search for a Constitution ; checking and spurring the
poor Three Hundred of the Townhall. That Danton,
with a 'voice reverberating from the domes', is President of the Cordeliers District ; which has already
become a Goshen of Patriotism. That apart from the
'seventeen thousand utterly necessitous, digging on
Montmartre', most of whom, indeed, have got passes,
and been dismissed into Space 'with four shillings',—
there is a *strike*, or union, of Domestics out of place ;
who assemble for public speaking : next, a strike of
Tailors, for even they will strike and speak ; further,
a strike of Journeymen Cordwainers ; a strike of
Apothecaries : so dear is bread.[1] All these, having
struck, must speak ; generally under the open canopy ;
and pass resolutions ;—Lafayette and his Patrols
watching them suspiciously from the distance.

Unhappy mortals : such tugging and lugging, and
throttling of one another, to divide, in some not intolerable way, the joint Felicity of man in this Earth ; when
the whole lot to be divided is such a 'feast of *shells* !"
—Diligent are the Three Hundred ; none equals Scipio-
Americanus in dealing with mobs. But surely all these
things bode ill for the consolidating of a Revolution.

[1] Histoire Parlementaire, ii. 359, 417, 423.

BOOK VII

THE INSURRECTION OF WOMEN

CHAPTER I

PATROLLOTISM

No, Friends, this Revolution is not of the consolidating kind. Do not fires, fevers, sown seeds, chemical mixtures, men, events; all embodiments of Force that work in this miraculous Complex of Forces, named Universe—go on *growing*, through their natural phases and developments, each according to its kind; reach their height, reach their visible decline; finally sink under, vanishing, and what we call *die*? They all grow; there is nothing but what grows, and shoots forth into its special expansion,—once give it leave to spring. Observe too that each grows with a rapidity proportioned, in general, to the madness and unhealthiness there is in it: slow regular growth, though this also ends in death, is what we name health and sanity.

A Sansculottism, which has prostrated Bastilles, which has got pike and musket, and now goes burning Châteaus, passing resolutions and haranguing under roof and sky, may be said to have sprung; and, by law of Nature, must grow. To judge by the madness and diseasedness both of itself, and of the soil and element it is in, one might expect the rapidity and monstrosity would be extreme.

Many things too, especially all diseased things, grow by shoots and fits. The first grand fit and shooting forth of Sansculottism was that of Paris conquering its King; for Bailly's figure of rhetoric was all-too sad a reality. The King is conquered; going at large on

his parole; on condition, say, of absolutely good
behaviour,—which, in these circumstances, will unhappily mean no behaviour whatever. A quite untenable
position, that of Majesty put on its good behaviour!
Alas, is it not natural that whatever lives try to keep
itself living? Whereupon his Majesty's behaviour will
soon become exceptionable; and so the Second grand
Fit of Sansculottism, that of putting him in durance,
cannot be distant.

Necker, in the National Assembly, is making moan,
as usual, about his Deficit: Barriers and Customhouses
burnt; the Taxgatherer hunted, not hunting; his
Majesty's Exchequer all but empty. The remedy is
a Loan of thirty millions; then, on still more enticing
terms, a Loan of eighty millions: neither of which
Loans, unhappily, will the Stockjobbers venture to
lend. The Stockjobber has no country, except his
own black pool of *Agio*.

And yet, in those days, for men that have a country,
what a glow of patriotism burns in many a heart;
penetrating inwards to the very purse! So early as
the 7th of August, a *Don Patriotique*, 'Patriotic Gift of
jewels to a considerable extent', has been solemnly
made by certain Parisian women; and solemnly
accepted with honourable mention. Whom forthwith
all the world takes to imitating and emulating. Patriotic Gifts, always with some heroic eloquence, which
the President must answer and the Assembly listen
to, flow in from far and near: in such number that
the honourable mention can only be performed in 'lists
published at stated epochs'. Each gives what he can:
the very cordwainers have behaved munificently; one
landed proprietor gives a forest; fashionable society
gives its shoe-buckles, takes cheerfully to shoe-ties.
Unfortunate-females give what they 'have amassed in
loving'.[1] The smell of all cash, as Vespasian thought,
is good.

[1] Histoire Parlementaire, ii. 427.

Beautiful, and yet inadequate ! The Clergy must be 'invited' to melt their superfluous Church-plate,—in the Royal Mint. Nay finally, a Patriotic Contribution, of the forcible sort, has to be determined on, though unwillingly : let the fourth part of your declared yearly revenue, for this once only, be paid down ; so shall a National Assembly make the Constitution, undistracted at least by insolvency. Their own wages, as settled on the 17th of August, are but Eighteen Francs a day, each man ; but the Public Service must have sinews, must have money. To *appease* the Deficit ; not to '*combler*, or choke, the Deficit', if you or mortal could ! For withal, as Mirabeau was heard saying, ' it is the Deficit that saves us '.

Towards the end of August, our National Assembly in its constitutional labours has got so far as the question of *Veto* : shall Majesty have a Veto on the National Enactments ; or not have a Veto ? What speeches were spoken, within doors and without ; clear, and also passionate logic ; imprecations, comminations ; gone happily, for most part, to Limbo ! Through the cracked brain and uncracked lungs of Saint-Huruge, the Palais Royal rebellows with Veto. Journalism is busy, France rings with Veto. ' I shall never forget ', says Dumont, ' my going to Paris, one of those days, with Mirabeau ; and the crowd of people we found waiting for his carriage, about Le Jay the Bookseller's shop. They flung themselves before him ; conjuring him with tears in their eyes not to suffer the *Veto Absolu*. They were in a frenzy : " Monsieur le Comte, you are the People's father, you must save us ; you must defend us against those villains who are bringing back Despotism. If the King get this Veto, what is the use of National Assembly ? We are slaves ; all is done ".' [1] Friends, *if* the sky fall, there will be catching of larks ! Mirabeau, adds Dumont, was eminent on such occasions : he 'answered vaguely, with a Patrician imperturbability, and bound himself to nothing.

[1] Souvenirs sur Mirabeau, p. 156.

Deputations go to the Hôtel-de-Ville; anonymous
Letters to Aristocrats in the National Assembly,
threatening that fifteen thousand, or sometimes that
sixty thousand, 'will march to illuminate you'. The
Paris Districts are astir; Petitions signing: Saint-
Huruge sets forth from the Palais Royal with an escort
of fifteen hundred individuals, to petition in person.
Resolute, or seemingly so, is the tall shaggy Marquis,
is the Café de Foy: but resolute also is Commandant-
General Lafayette. The streets are all beset by Patrols:
Saint-Huruge is stopped at the *Barrière des Bons
Hommes*; he may bellow like the bulls of Bashan, but
absolutely must return. The brethren of the Palais
Royal 'circulate all night', and make motions, under
the open canopy; all Coffeehouses being shut. Nevertheless Lafayette and the Townhall do prevail; Saint-
Huruge is thrown into prison; *Veto Absolu* adjusts
itself into *Suspensive Veto*, prohibition not for ever, but
for a term of time; and this doom's-clamour will grow
silent, as the others have done.

So far has Consolidation prospered, though with
difficulty; repressing the Nether Sansculottic world;
and the Constitution shall be made. With difficulty:
amid jubilee and scarcity; Patriotic Gifts, Bakers'-
queues; Abbé-Fauchet Harangues, with their *Amen*
of platoon-musketry! Scipio-Americanus has deserved
thanks from the National Assembly and France. They
offer him stipends and emoluments to a handsome
extent; all which stipends and emoluments he, cove-
tous of far other blessedness than mere money, does,
in his chivalrous way, without scruple, refuse.

To the Parisian common man, meanwhile, one thing
remains inconceivable: that now when the Bastille is
down, and French Liberty restored, grain should continue so dear. Our Rights of Man are voted, Feudalism
and all Tyranny abolished; yet behold we stand *in
queue*! Is it Aristocrat forestallers; a Court still bent
on intrigues? Something is rotten,* somewhere.

And yet, alas, what to do? Lafayette, with his

Patrols, prohibits everything, even complaint. Saint-Huruge and other heroes of the *Veto* lie in durance. People's-Friend Marat was seized ; Printers of Patriotic Journals are fettered and forbidden ; the very Hawkers cannot cry, till they get licence, and leaden badges, Blue National Guards ruthlessly dissipate all groups ; scour, with levelled bayonets, the Palais Royal itself. Pass, on your affairs, along the Rue Taranne, the Patrol, presenting his bayonet, cries, *To the left !* Turn into the Rue Saint-Bénoit, he cries, *To the right !* A judicious Patriot (like Camille Desmoulins, in this instance) is driven, for quietness' sake, to take the gutter.

O much-suffering People, our glorious Revolution is evaporating in tricolor ceremonies, and complimentary harangues ! Of which latter, as Loustalot acridly calculates, ' upwards of two thousand have been delivered within the last month, at the Townhall alone '.[1] And our mouths, unfilled with bread, are to be shut, under penalties ? The Caricaturist promulgates his emblematic Tablature : *Le Patrouillotisme chassant le Patriotisme,* Patriotism driven out by Patrollotism. Ruthless Patrols ; long superfine harangues ; and scanty ill-baked loaves, more like baked Bath bricks, —which produce an effect on the intestines ! Where will this end ? In consolidation ?

CHAPTER II

O RICHARD, O MY KING*

For, alas, neither is the Townhall itself without misgivings. The Nether Sansculottic world has been suppressed hitherto : but then the Upper Court-world ! Symptoms there are that the Œil-de-Bœuf is rallying.

More than once in the Townhall Sanhedrim, often enough from those outspoken Bakers'-queues, has the

[1] Révolutions-de-Paris Newspaper (cited in Histoire Parlementaire, ii. 357).

wish uttered itself: O that our Restorer of French
Liberty were here; that he could see with his own
eyes, not with the false eyes of Queens and Cabals, and
his really good heart be enlightened! For falsehood
still environs him; intriguing Dukes de Guiche, with
Bodyguards; scouts of Bouillé; a new flight of intriguers, now that the old is flown. What else means this
advent of the *Regiment de Flandre*; entering Versailles,
as we hear, on the 23rd of September, with two pieces
of cannon? Did not the Versailles National Guard
do duty at the Château? Had they not Swiss; Hundred Swiss; *Gardes-du-Corps*, Bodyguards so-called?
Nay, it would seem, the number of Bodyguards on duty
has, by a manœuvre, been doubled: the new relieving
Battalion of them arrived at its time; but the old
relieved one does not *depart*!

Actually, there runs a whisper through the best-
informed Upper-Circles, or a nod still more portentous
than whispering, of his Majesty's flying to Metz; of
a Bond (to stand by him therein), which has been signed
by Noblesse and Clergy, to the incredible amount of
thirty, or even of sixty thousand. Lafayette coldly
whispers it, and coldly asseverates it, to Count d'Estaing
at the Dinner-table; and D'Estaing, one of the bravest
men, quakes to the core lest some lackey overhear it;
and tumbles thoughtful, without sleep, all night. [1]
Regiment de Flandre, as we said, is clearly arrived.
His Majesty, they say, hesitates about sanctioning the
Fourth of August; makes observations, of chilling
tenor, on the very Rights of Man! Likewise, may not
all persons, the Bakers'-queues themselves discern, on
the streets of Paris, the most astonishing number of
Officers on furlough, Crosses of St. Louis, and such like?
Some reckon 'from a thousand to twelve hundred'.
Officers of all uniforms; nay one uniform never before
seen by eye: green faced with red! The tricolor
cockade is not always visible: but what, in the name

---

[1] Brouillon de Lettre de M. d'Estaing à la Reine (in
Histoire Parlementaire, iii. 24).

of Heaven, may these *black* cockades, which some wear, foreshadow ?

Hunger whets everything, especially Suspicion and Indignation. Realities themselves, in this Paris, have grown unreal; preternatural. Phantasms once more stalk through the brain of hungry France. O ye laggards and dastards,* cry shrill voices from the Queues, if ye had the hearts of men, ye would take your pikes and secondhand firelocks, and look into it ; not leave your wives and daughters to be starved, murdered and worse !—Peace, women ! The heart of man is bitter and heavy*; Patriotism, driven out by Patrollotism, knows not what to resolve on.

The truth is, the Œil-de-Bœuf has rallied ; to a certain unknown extent. A changed Œil-de-Bœuf ; with Versailles National Guards, in their tricolor cockades, doing duty there ; a Court all flaring with tricolor ! Yet even to a tricolor Court men will rally. Ye loyal hearts, burnt-out Seigneurs, rally round your Queen ! With wishes ; which will produce hopes ; which will produce attempts !

For indeed self-preservation being such a law of Nature, what can a rallied Court do, but attempt and endeavour, or call it *plot*,—with such wisdom and unwisdom as it has ? They will fly, escorted, to Metz, where brave Bouillé commands ; they will raise the Royal Standard : the Bond-signatures shall become armed men. Were not the King so languid ! Their Bond, if at all signed, must be signed without his privity.—Unhappy King, *he* has but one resolution : not to have a civil war. For the rest, he still hunts, having ceased lockmaking ; he still dozes, and digests ; is clay in the hands of the potter. Ill will it fare with him, in a world where all is helping itself ; where, as has been written, ' whosoever is not hammer must be stithy ' ;* and ' the very hyssop on the wall*grows there, in that chink, because the whole Universe could not prevent its growing ! '

But as for the coming up of this Regiment de Flandre,

may it not be urged that there were Saint-Huruge
Petitions, and continual meal-mobs ? Undebauched
Soldiers, be there plot, or only dim elements of a plot,
are always good. Did not the Versailles Municipality
(an old Monarchic one, not yet refounded into a Democratic) instantly second the proposal ? Nay the very
Versailles National Guard, wearied with continual duty
at the Château, did not object ; only Draper Lecointre,
who is now Major Lecointre, shook his head.—Yes,
Friends, surely it was natural this Regiment de Flandre
should be sent for, since it could be got. It was natural
that, at sight of military bandoleers, the heart of the
rallied Œil-de-Bœuf should revive ; and Maids of
Honour, and gentlemen of honour, speak comfortable
words to epauletted defenders, and to one another.
Natural also, and mere common civility, that the Bodyguards, a Regiment of Gentlemen, should invite their
Flandre brethren to a Dinner of welcome !—Such
invitation, in the last days of September, is given and
accepted.

Dinners are defined as ' the *ultimate* act of communion ' ; men that can have communion in nothing else,
can sympathetically eat together, can still rise into
some glow of brotherhood over food and wine. The
Dinner is fixed on, for Thursday the First of October ;
and ought to have a fine effect. Further, as such
Dinner may be rather extensive, and even the Non-
commissioned and the Common man be introduced,
to see and to hear, could not his Majesty's Opera
Apartment, which has lain quite silent ever since Kaiser
Joseph was here, be obtained for the purpose ?—The
Hall of the Opera is granted ; the Salon d'Hercule
shall be drawing-room. Not only the Officers of Flandre, but of the Swiss, of the Hundred Swiss ; nay of
the Versailles National Guard, such of them as have
any loyalty, shall feast : it will be a Repast like few.

And now suppose this Repast, the solid part of it,
transacted ; and the first bottle over. Suppose the
customary loyal toasts drunk ; the King's health, the
Queen's with deafening vivats ;—that of the Nation

' omitted ', or even ' rejected '. Suppose champagne
flowing ; with pot-valorous speech, with instrumental
music ; empty featherheads growing ever the noisier,
in their own emptiness, in each other's noise. Her
Majesty, who looks unusually sad to-night (his Majesty
sitting dulled with the day's hunting), is told that
the sight of it would cheer her. Behold ! She enters
there, issuing from her State-rooms, like the Moon
from clouds, this fairest unhappy Queen of Hearts ;
royal Husband by her side, young Dauphin in her arms !
She descends from the Boxes, amid splendour and
acclaim ; walks queenlike round the Tables ; gracefully
escorted, gracefully nodding ; her looks full of sorrow,
yet of gratitude and daring, with the hope of France
on her mother-bosom ! And now, the band striking
up, *O Richard, O mon Roi, l'univers t'abandonne* (O
Richard, O my King, the world is all forsaking thee)
—could man do other than rise to height of pity, of
loyal valour ? Could featherheaded young ensigns do
other than, by white Bourbon Cockades, handed them
from fair fingers ; by waving of swords, drawn to
pledge the Queen's health ; by trampling of National
Cockades ; by scaling the Boxes, whence intrusive murmurs may come ; by vociferation, tripudiation, sound,
fury and distraction, within doors and without,—testify
what tempest-tost*state of vacuity they are in ? Till
champagne and tripudiation do their work ; and all
lie silent, horizontal ; passively slumbering with meed-
of-battle dreams !—

A natural Repast ; in ordinary times, a harmless one:
now fatal, as that of Thyestes* ; as that of Job's sons,*
when a strong wind smote the four corners of their
banquet-house ! Poor ill-advised Marie-Antoinette
with a woman's vehemence, not with a sovereign's
foresight ! It was so natural, yet so unwise. Next
day, in public speech of ceremony, her Majesty declares
herself ' delighted with the Thursday '.

The heart of the Œil-de-Bœuf glows into hope ; into
daring, which is premature. Rallied Maids of Honour,
waited on by Abbés, sew ' white cockades ' ; distribute

them, with words, with glances, to epauletted youths ;
who, in return, may kiss, not without fervour, the fair
sewing fingers.   Captains of horse and foot go swashing
with ' enormous white cockades ' ; nay one Versailles
National Captain has mounted the like, so witching
were the words and glances, and laid aside his tricolor !
Well may Major Lecointre shake his head with a look
of severity ; and speak audible resentful words.   But
now a swashbuckler, with enormous white cockade,
overhearing the Major, invites him insolently, once and
then again elsewhere, to recant ; and failing that, to
duel.   Which latter feat Major Lecointre declares that
he will not perform, not at least by any known laws
of fence ; that he nevertheless will, according to mere
law of Nature, by dirk and blade, ' exterminate ' any
' vile gladiator ' who may insult him or the Nation ;—
whereupon (for the Major is actually drawing his implement) ' they are parted ', and no weasands slit.[1]

CHAPTER III

BLACK COCKADES

But fancy what effect this Thyestes Repast, and
trampling on the National Cockade, must have had in
the *Salle des Menus* ; in the famishing Bakers'-queues
at Paris !   Nay, such Thyestes Repasts, it would seem,
continue.   Flandre has given its Counter-Dinner to
the Swiss and Hundred Swiss ; then on Saturday there
has been another.

Yes, here with us is famine ; but yonder at Versailles
is food, enough and to spare !   Patriotism stands in
queue, shivering hungerstruck, insulted by Patrollotism;
while bloodyminded Aristocrats, heated with excess of
high living, trample on the National Cockade.   Can the

[1] Moniteur (in Histoire Parlementaire, iii. 59) ; Deux
Amis, iii. 128-41 ; Campan, ii. 70-85 ; &c. &c.

atrocity be true ? Nay, look: green uniforms faced
with red ; black cockades,—the colour of Night ! Are
we to have military onfall ; and death also by starvation ? For behold the Corbeil Cornboat, which used
to come twice a-day, with its Plaster-of-Paris meal,
now comes only once. And the Townhall is deaf ; and
the men are laggard and dastard !—At the Café de Foy,
this Saturday evening, a new thing is seen, not the last
of its kind : a woman engaged in public speaking.
Her poor man, she says, was put to silence by his District ; their Presidents and Officials would not let him
speak. Wherefore she here with her shrill tongue will
speak ; denouncing, while her breath endures, the
Corbeil Boat, the Plaster-of-Paris bread, sacrilegious
Opera-dinners, green uniforms, Pirate Aristocrats, and
those black cockades of theirs !—

Truly, it is time for the black cockades at least to
vanish. Them Patrollotism itself will not protect.
Nay, sharp-tempered 'M. Tassin', at the Tuileries
parade on Sunday morning, forgets all National military
rule ; starts from the ranks, wrenches down one black
cockade which is swashing ominous there, and tramples
it fiercely into the soil of France. Patrollotism itself
is not without suppressed fury. Also the Districts
begin to stir ; the voice of President Danton reverberates in the Cordeliers : People's-Friend Marat has
flown to Versailles and back again ;—swart bird, not of
the halcyon kind.[1]

And so Patriot meets promenading Patriot, this Sunday ; and sees his own grim care reflected on the face
of another. Groups, in spite of Patrollotism, which is
not so alert as usual, fluctuate deliberative ; groups on
the Bridges, on the Quais, at the patriotic Cafés. And
ever as any black cockade may emerge, rises the many-
voiced growl and bark : *A bas*, Down ! All black
cockades are ruthlessly plucked off: one individual picks
his up again ; kisses it, attempts to refix it ; but

[1] Camille's Newspaper, Révolutions de Paris et de
Brabant (in Histoire Parlementaire, iii. 108).

a ' hundred canes start into the air ', and he desists.
Still worse went it with another individual ; doomed,
by extempore *Plebiscitum*, to the Lanterne ; saved,
with difficulty, by some active *Corps-de-Garde*.—
Lafayette sees signs of an effervescence ; which he
doubles his Patrols, doubles his diligence, to prevent.
So passes Sunday, the 4th of October 1789.

Sullen is the male heart, repressed by Patrollotism ;
vehement is the female, irrepressible. The public-
speaking woman at the Palais Royal was not the only
speaking one :—Men know not what the pantry is,
when it grows empty ; only house-mothers know. O
women, wives of men that will only calculate and not
act ! Patrollotism is strong ; but Death, by starvation and military onfall, is stronger. Patrollotism
represses male Patriotism : but female Patriotism ?
Will Guards named National thrust their bayonets into
the bosoms of women ? Such thought, or rather such
dim unshaped raw material of a thought, ferments
universally under the female night-cap ; and, by earliest
daybreak, on slight hint, will explode.

CHAPTER IV

THE MENADS[*]

IF Voltaire once, in splenetic humour, asked his countrymen : ' But you, *Gualches*,[*] what have you invented ? '
they can now answer : The Art of Insurrection. It
was an art needed in these last singular times : an art
for which the French nature, so full of vehemence, so
free from depth, was perhaps of all others the fittest.

Accordingly, to what a height, one may well say of
perfection, has this branch of human industry been
carried by France, within the last half-century ! Insurrection, which, Lafayette thought, might be ' the most
sacred of duties ', ranks now, for the French people,
among the duties which they can perform. Other mobs

are dull masses ; which roll onwards with a dull fierce
tenacity, a dull fierce heat, but emit no light-flashes of
genius as they go. The French mob, again, is among
the liveliest phenomena of our world. So rapid,
audacious ; so clear-sighted, inventive, prompt to seize
the moment ;* instinct with life to its finger-ends !
That talent, were there no other, of spontaneously
standing in queue, distinguishes, as we said, the French
People from all Peoples, ancient and modern.

Let the Reader confess too that, taking one thing
with another, perhaps few terrestrial Appearances are
better worth considering than mobs. Your mob is
a genuine outburst of Nature ; issuing from, or com-
municating with, the deepest deep of Nature. When
so much goes grinning and grimacing as a lifeless
Formality, and under the stiff buckram no heart can
be felt beating, here once more, if nowhere else, is a
Sincerity and Reality. Shudder at it ; or even shriek
over it, if thou must ; nevertheless consider it. Such
a Complex of human Forces and Individualities hurled
forth, in their transcendental mood, to act and react,
on circumstances and on one another ; to work out
what it is in them to work. The thing they will do is
known to no man ; least of all to themselves. It is
the inflammablest immeasurable Fire-work, generating,
consuming itself. With what phases, to what extent,
with what results it will burn off, Philosophy and Per-
spicacity conjecture in vain.

' Man ', as has been written, ' is for ever interesting to
man ; nay properly there is nothing else interesting '.*
In which light also, may we not discern why most
Battles have become so wearisome ?   Battles, in these
ages, are transacted by mechanism ; with the slightest
possible development of human individuality or spon-
taneity : men now even die, and kill one another, in an
artificial manner. Battles ever since Homer's time,
when they were Fighting Mobs, have mostly ceased to
be worth looking at, worth reading of or remembering.
How many wearisome bloody Battles does History
strive to represent ; or even, in a husky way, to sing :

—and she would omit or carelessly slur-over this one
Insurrection of Women ?

A thought, or dim raw-material of a thought, was
fermenting all night, universally in the female head, and
might explode.   In squalid garret, on Monday morning
Maternity awakes, to hear children weeping for bread.
Maternity must forth to the streets, to the herb-markets
and Bakers'-queues ;   meets there with hunger-stricken
Maternity, sympathetic, exasperative.   O we unhappy
women !   But, instead of Bakers'-queues, why not to
Aristocrats' palaces, the root of the matter ?   *Allons !*
Let us assemble.   To the Hôtel-de-Ville ; to Versailles ;
to the Lanterne !

In one of the Guardhouses of the Quartier Saint-
Eustache, ' a young woman ' seizes a drum,—for how
shall National Guards give fire on women, on a young
woman ?   The young woman seizes the drum ;   sets
forth, beating it, ' uttering cries relative to the dearth
of grains '.   Descend, O mothers ;   descend, ye Judiths,
to food and revenge !—All women gather and go ;
crowds storm all stairs, force out all women :   the
female Insurrectionary Force, according to Camille,
resembles the English Naval one ;   there is a universal
' Press of women '.   Robust Dames of the Halle, slim
Mantua-makers, assiduous, risen with the dawn; ancient
Virginity tripping to matins ;   the Housemaid, with
early broom ;   all must go.   Rouse ye, O women ;   the
laggard men will not act ;   they say, we ourselves may
act !

And so, like snowbreak from the mountains, for every
staircase is a melted brook, it storms ;   tumultuous,
wild-shrilling, towards the Hôtel-de-Ville.   Tumultuous ;   with or without drum-music :   for the Faubourg
Saint-Antoine also has tucked up its gown ;   and
with besom-staves, fire-irons, and even rusty pistols
(void of ammunition), is flowing on.   Sound of it flies,
with a velocity of sound, to the utmost Barriers.   By
seven o'clock, on this raw October morning, fifth of the
month, the Townhall will see wonders.   Nay, as chance

would have it, a male party are already there ; clus-
tering tumultuously round some National Patrol, and
a Baker who has been seized with short weights. They
are there ; and have even lowered the rope of the
Lanterne. So that the official persons have to smuggle
forth the short-weighing Baker by back doors, and even
send ' to all the Districts' for more force.

Grand it was, says Camille, to see so many Judiths,
from eight to ten thousand of them in all, rushing out
to search into the root of the matter !* Not unfrightful
it must have been ; ludicro-terrific, and most unmanageable. At such hour the overwatched Three
Hundred are not yet stirring : none but some Clerks,
a company of National Guards ; and M. de Gouvion,
the Major-general. Gouvion has fought in America
for the cause of civil Liberty ; a man of no inconsiderable heart, but deficient in head. He is, for the
moment, in his back apartment ; assuaging Usher
Maillard, the Bastille-sergeant, who has come, as too
many do, with ' representations '. The assuagement is
still incomplete when our Judiths arrive.

The National Guards form on the outer stairs, with
levelled bayonets ; the ten thousand Judiths press up,
resistless ; with obtestations, with outspread hands,
—merely to speak to the Mayor. The rear forces
them ; nay, from male hands in the rear, stones already
fly : the National Guard must do one of two things ;
sweep the Place de Grève with cannon, or else open to
right and left. They open ; the living deluge rushes
in. Through all rooms and cabinets, upwards to the
topmost belfry : ravenous ; seeking arms, seeking
Mayors, seeking justice ;—while, again, the better-
dressed speak kindly to the Clerks ; point out the
misery of these poor women ; also their ailments, some
even of an interesting sort.[1]

Poor M. de Gouvion is shiftless in this extremity ;—
a man shiftless, perturbed : who will one day commit
suicide. How happy for him that Usher Maillard the

[1] Deux Amis, iii. 141-66.

shifty was there, at the moment, though making
representations ! Fly back, thou shifty Maillard :
seek the Bastille Company ; and O return fast with it ;
above all, with thy own shifty head ! For, behold,
the Judiths can find no Mayor or Municipal ; scarcely,
in the topmost belfry, can they find poor Abbé Lefevre
the Powder-distributor. Him, for want of a better,
they suspend there : in the pale morning light ; over
the top of all Paris, which swims in one's failing eyes :
—a horrible end ? Nay, the rope broke, as French
ropes often did ; or else an Amazon cut it. Abbé
Lefevre falls, some twenty feet, rattling among the
leads ; and lives long years after, though always with
' a *tremblement* in the limbs '.[1]

And now doors fly under hatchets ; the Judiths have
broken the Armory ; have seized guns and cannons,
three money-bags, paper-heaps ; torches flare : in few
minutes, our brave Hôtel-de-Ville, which dates from
the Fourth Henry, will, with all that it holds, be in
flames !

CHAPTER V

USHER MAILLARD

IN flames, truly,—were it not that Usher Maillard,
swift of foot, shifty of head, has returned !

Maillard, of his own motion,—for Gouvion or the
rest would not even sanction him,—snatches a drum ;
descends the Porch-stairs, ran-tan, beating sharp, with
loud rolls, his Rogue's-march : To Versailles ! *Allons ;
à Versailles !* As men beat on kettle or warming-pan,*
when angry she-bees, or say, flying desperate wasps, are
to be hived ; and the desperate insects hear it, and
cluster round it,—simply as round *a* guidance, where
there was none : so now these Menads round shifty
Maillard, Riding-Usher of the Châtelet.   The axe pauses

[1] Dusaulx, Prise de la Bastille, note, p. 281.

uplifted ; Abbé Lefevre is left half-hanged : from the
belfry downwards all vomits itself. What rub-a-dub
is that ? Stanislas Maillard, Bastille-hero, will lead us
to Versailles ? Joy to thee, Maillard ; blessed art thou
above Riding-Ushers ! Away, then, away !

The seized cannon are yoked with seized cart-horses :
brown-locked Demoiselle Théroigne, with pike and
helmet, sits there as gunneress, ' with haughty eye and
serene fair countenance ' ; comparable, some think, to
the *Maid* of Orléans, or even recalling ' the idea of
Pallas Athene '.[1] Maillard (for his drum still rolls) is,
by heaven-rending acclamation, admitted General.
Maillard hastens the languid march. Maillard, beating
rhythmic, with sharp ran-tan, all along the Quais, leads
forward, with difficulty, his Menadic host.   Such
a host—marched not in silence ! The bargeman pauses
on the River ; all wagoners and coach-drivers fly ; men
peer from windows,—not women, lest they be pressed.
Sight of sights : Bacchantes, in these ultimate For-
malized Ages ! Bronze Henri looks on, from his Pont-
Neuf ; the Monarchic Louvre, Medicean Tuileries see
a day like none heretofore seen.

And now Maillard has his Menads in the *Champs
Elysées* (Fields *Tartarean* rather) ; and the Hôtel-de-
Ville has suffered comparatively nothing. Broken
doors ; an Abbé Lefevre, who shall never more distribute powder ; three sacks of money, most part of which
(for Sansculottism, though famishing, is not without
honour) shall be returned : [2] this is all the damage.
Great Maillard ! A small nucleus of Order is round
his drum ; but his outskirts fluctuate like the mad
Ocean : for Rascality male and female is flowing in on
him, from the four winds : guidance there is none but
in his single head and two drumsticks.

O Maillard, when, since War first was, had General
of Force such a task before him, as thou this day ?
Walter the Penniless still touches the feeling heart :
but then Walter had sanction ; had space to turn in ;

---

[1] Deux Amis, iii. 157.   [2] Hist. Parl. iii. 310.

and also his Crusaders were of the male sex. Thou, this day, disowned of Heaven and Earth, art General of Menads. Their inarticulate frenzy thou must, on the spur of the instant, render into articulate words, into actions that are not frantic. Fail in it, this way or that! Pragmatical Officiality, with its penalties and law-books, waits before thee; Menads storm behind. If such hewed off the melodious head of Orpheus, and hurled it into the Peneus waters,* what may they not make of thee,—thee rhythmic merely, with no music but a sheepskin drum !—Maillard did not fail. Remarkable Maillard, if fame were not an accident, and History a distillation of Rumour, how remarkable wert thou !

On the Elysian Fields there is pause and fluctuation ; but, for Maillard, no return. He persuades his Menads, clamorous for arms and the Arsenal, that no arms are in the Arsenal ; that an unarmed attitude, and petition to a National Assembly, will be the best: he hastily nominates or sanctions generalésses, captains of tens and fifties ;—and so, in loosest-flowing order, to the rhythm of some ' eight drums ' (having laid aside his own), with the Bastille Volunteers bringing up his rear, once more takes the road.

Chaillot, which will promptly yield baked loaves, is not plundered ; nor are the Sèvres Potteries broken. The old arches of Sèvres Bridge echo under Menadic feet ; Seine River gushes on with his perpetual murmur ; and Paris flings after us the boom of tocsin and alarm-drum,—inaudible, for the present, amid shrill-sounding hosts, and the splash of rainy weather. To Meudon, to Saint-Cloud, on both hands, the report of them is gone abroad ; and hearths, this evening, will have a topic. The press of women still continues, for it is the cause of all Eve's Daughters, mothers that are, or that ought to be. No carriage-lady, were it with never such hysterics, but must dismount, in the mud roads, in her silk shoes, and walk.[1] In this manner, amid wild

---

[1] Deux Amis, iii. 159.

October weather, they, a wild unwinged stork-flight,* through the astonished country wend their way. Travellers of all sorts they stop ; especially travellers or couriers from Paris. Deputy Lechapelier, in his elegant vesture, from his elegant vehicle, looks forth amazed through his spectacles ; apprehensive for life ;—states eagerly that he is Patriot-Deputy Lechapelier, and even Old-President Lechapelier, who presided on the Night of Pentecost, and is original member of the Breton Club. Thereupon ' rises huge shout of *Vive Lechapelier*, and several armed persons spring up behind and before to escort him '.[1]

Nevertheless, news, dispatches from Lafayette, or vague noise of rumour, have pierced through, by side roads. In the National Assembly, while all is busy discussing the order of the day ; regretting that there should be Anti-national Repasts in Opera-Halls ; that his Majesty should still hesitate about accepting the Rights of Man, and hang conditions and peradventures on them,—Mirabeau steps up to the President, experienced Mounier as it chanced to be ; and articulates, in bass under-tone : ' *Mounier, Paris marche sur nous* (Paris is marching on us)'.—' May be (*Je n'en sais rien*) ! '—' Believe it, or disbelieve it, that is not my concern ; but Paris, I say, is marching on us. Fall suddenly unwell ; go over to the Château ; tell them this. There is not a moment to lose '.—'Paris marching on us ?' responds Mounier, with an atrabiliar accent: ' Well, so much the better ! We shall the sooner be a Republic '. Mirabeau quits him, as one quits an experienced President getting blindfold into deep waters ; and the order of the day continues as before.

Yes, Paris is marching on us ; and more than the women of Paris ! Scarcely was Maillard gone, when M. de Gouvion's message to all the Districts, and such tocsin and drumming of the *générale*, began to take

[1] Deux Amis, ii. 177 ; Dictionnaire des Hommes Marquans, ii. 379.

effect. Armed National Guards from every District; especially the Grenadiers of the Centre, who are our old Gardes Françaises, arrive, in quick sequence, on the Place de Grève. An ' immense people ' is there ; Saint-Antoine, with pike and rusty firelock, is all crowding thither, be it welcome or unwelcome. The Centre Grenadiers are received with cheering: 'It is not cheers that we want', answer they gloomily; ' the Nation has been insulted ; to arms, and come with us for orders ! ' Ha, sits the wind *so* ?* Patriotism and Patrollotism are now one !

The Three Hundred have assembled ; ' all the Committees are in activity '; Lafayette is dictating dispatches for Versailles, when a Deputation of the Centre Grenadiers introduces itself to him. The Deputation makes military obeisance ; and thus speaks, not without a kind of thought in it : ' *Mon Général,* we are deputed by the Six Companies of Grenadiers. We do not think you a traitor, but we think the Government betrays you ; it is time that this end. We cannot turn our bayonets against women crying to us for bread. The people are miserable, the source of the mischief is at Versailles : we must go seek the King, and bring him to Paris. We must exterminate (*exterminer*) the *Regiment de Flandre* and the *Gardes-du-Corps,* who have dared to trample on the National Cockade. If the King be too weak to wear his crown, let him lay it down. You will crown his Son, you will name a Council of Regency : and all will go better'.[1] Reproachful astonishment paints itself on the face of Lafayette ; speaks itself from his eloquent chivalrous lips : in vain. ' My General, we would shed the last drop of our blood for you ; but the root of the mischief is at Versailles ; we must go and bring the King to Paris ; all the people wish it, *tout le peuple le veut* '.

My General descends to the outer staircase ; and harangues : once more in vain. ' To Versailles ! To Versailles ! ' Mayor Bailly, sent for through floods of

---

[1] Deux Amis, iii. 161.

Sansculottism, attempts academic oratory from his
gilt state-coach ; realizes nothing but infinite hoarse
cries of : ' Bread ! To Versailles ! '—and gladly shrinks
within doors. Lafayette mounts the white charger ;
and again harangues, and reharangues : with eloquence,
with firmness, indignant demonstration ; with all things
but persuasion. ' To Versailles ! To Versailles ! ' So
lasts it, hour after hour ;—for the space of half a day.

The great Scipio-Americanus can do nothing ; not
so much as escape. ' *Morbleu, mon Général* ', cry the
Grenadiers serrying their ranks as the white charger
makes a motion that way, ' you will not leave us, you
will abide with us ! ' A perilous juncture : Mayor
Bailly and the Municipals sit quaking within doors ;
my General is prisoner without : the Place de Grève,
with its thirty thousand Regulars, its whole irregular
Saint-Antoine and Saint-Marceau, is one minatory mass
of clear or rusty steel ; all hearts set, with a moody
fixedness, on one object. Moody, fixed are all hearts :
tranquil is no heart,—if it be not that of the white
charger, who paws there, with arched neck, composedly
champing his bit ; as if no World, with its Dynasties
and Eras, were now rushing down. The drizzly day
bends westward ; the cry is still : ' To Versailles ! '

Nay now, borne from afar, come quite sinister cries ;
hoarse, reverberating in longdrawn hollow murmurs,
with syllables too like those of ' *Lanterne !* ' Or else,
irregular Sansculottism may be marching off, of itself ;
with pikes, nay with cannon. The inflexible Scipio
does at length, by aide-de-camp, ask of the Municipals :
Whether or not he may go ? A Letter is handed out
to him, over armed heads ; sixty thousand faces flash
fixedly on his, there is stillness and no bosom breathes,
till he have read. By Heaven, he grows suddenly pale !
Do the Municipals permit ? ' Permit and even order ',
—since he can no other. Clangour of approval rends
the welkin. To your ranks, then ; let us march !

It is, as we compute, towards three in the afternoon.
Indignant National Guards may dine for once from
their haversack : dined or undined, they march with

one heart. Paris flings up her windows, claps hands,
as the Avengers, with their shrilling drums and shalms
tramp by; she will then sit pensive, apprehensive, and
pass rather a sleepless night.[1] On the white charger,
Lafayette, in the slowest possible manner, going and
coming, and eloquently haranguing among the ranks,
rolls onward with his thirty thousand. Saint-Antoine,
with pike and cannon, has preceded him; a mixed
multitude, of all and of no arms, hovers on his flanks
and skirts; the country once more pauses agape:
Paris marche sur nous.

CHAPTER VI

TO VERSAILLES

For, indeed, about this same moment, Maillard has
halted his draggled Menads on the last hill-top; and
now Versailles, and the Château of Versailles, and far
and wide the inheritance of Royalty opens to the
wondering eye. From far on the right, over Marly
and Saint-Germains-en-Laye; round towards Rambouillet, on the left: beautiful all; softly embosomed;
as if in sadness, in the dim moist weather! And
near before us is Versailles, New and Old; with that
broad frondent *Avenue de Versailles* between,—stately-
frondent, broad, three hundred feet as men reckon,
with its four Rows of Elms; and then the *Château de
Versailles*, ending in royal Parks and Pleasances, gleaming lakelets, arbours, Labyrinths, the *Ménagerie*, and
Great and Little Trianon. High-towered dwellings,
leafy pleasant places; where the gods of this lower
world abide: whence, nevertheless, black Care cannot
be excluded; whither Menadic Hunger is even now
advancing, armed with pike-thyrsi!

Yes, yonder, Mesdames, where our straight frondent

---

[1] Deux Amis, iii. 165.

Avenue, joined, as you note, by Two frondent brother
Avenues from this hand and from that, spreads out
into Place Royal and Palace Forecourt ; yonder is the
Salle des Menus. Yonder an august Assembly sits
regenerating France. Forecourt, Grand Court, Court
of Marble, Court narrowing into Court you may discern
next, or fancy: on the extreme verge of which that
glass-dome, visibly glittering like a star of hope, is the
—Œil-de-Bœuf ! Yonder, or nowhere in the world,
is bread baked for us. But, O Mesdames, were not
one thing good : That our cannons, with Demoiselle
Théroigne and all show of war, be put to the rear ?
Submission beseems petitioners of a National Assembly;
we are strangers in Versailles,—whence, too audibly,
there comes even now a sound as of tocsin and *générale* !
Also to put on, if possible, a cheerful countenance,
hiding our sorrows ; and even to sing ? Sorrow, pitied
of the Heavens, is hateful, suspicious to the Earth.—
So counsels shifty Maillard ; haranguing his Menads,
on the heights near Versailles.[1]

Cunning Maillard's dispositions are obeyed. The
draggled Insurrectionists advance up the Avenue, ' in
three columns ', among the four Elm-rows ; ' singing
Henri Quatre ', with what melody they can ; and shouting *Vive le Roi.* Versailles, though the Elm-rows are
dripping wet, crowds from both sides, with ' *Vivent
nos Parisiennes,* Our Paris ones for ever ! '

Prickers, scouts have been out towards Paris, as the
rumour deepened : whereby his Majesty, gone to shoot
in the Woods of Meudon, has been happily discovered,
and got home ; and the *générale* and tocsin set a-sound-
ing. The Bodyguards are already drawn up in front
of the Palace Grates ; and look down the Avenue de
Versailles ; sulky, in wet buckskins. Flandre too is
there, repentant of the Opera-Repast. Also Dragoons
dismounted are there. Finally Major Lecointre, and
what he can gather of the Versailles National Guard ;
—though it is to be observed, our Colonel, that same

---

[1] See Hist. Parl. iii. 70-117 ; Deux Amis, iii. 166-77, &c.

sleepless Count d'Estaing, giving neither order nor
ammunition, has vanished most improperly ; one sup-
poses, into the Œil-de-Bœuf. Red-coated Swiss stand
within the Grates, under arms. There likewise, in their
inner room, ' all the Ministers ', Saint-Priest, Lamentation Pompignan and the rest, are assembled with M.
Necker : they sit with him there ; blank, expecting
what the hour will bring.

President Mounier, though he answered Mirabeau
with a *tant mieux*, and affected to slight the matter,
had his own forebodings. Surely, for these four weary
hours he has reclined not on roses ! The order of the
day is getting forward : a Deputation to his Majesty
seems proper, that it might please him to grant
' Acceptance pure and simple ' to those Constitution-
Articles of ours ; the ' mixed qualified Acceptance ',
with its peradventures, is satisfactory to neither gods
nor men.

So much is clear. And yet there is more, which no
man speaks, which all men now vaguely understand.
Disquietude, absence of mind is on every face ; Members whisper, uneasily come and go : the order of the
day is evidently not the day's want. Till at length,
from the outer gates, is heard a rustling and justling,
shrill uproar and squabbling, muffled by walls ; which
testifies that the hour is come ! Rushing and crushing
one hears now ; then enter Usher Maillard, with
a Deputation of Fifteen muddy dripping Women,—
having, by incredible industry, and aid of all the macers,
persuaded the rest to wait out of doors. National
Assembly shall now, therefore, look its august task
directly in the face : regenerative Constitutionalism
has an unregenerate Sansculottism bodily in front of
it ; crying, ' Bread ! Bread ! '

Shifty Maillard, translating frenzy into articulation ;
repressive with the one hand, expostulative with the
other, does his best ; and really, though not bred to
public speaking, manages rather well :—In the present
dreadful rarity of grains, a Deputation of Female

Citizens has, as the august Assembly can discern, come
out from Paris to petition. Plots of Aristocrats are too
evident in the matter ; for example, one miller has
been bribed ' by a bank-note of 200 livres ' not to grind,
—name unknown to the Usher, but fact provable, at
least indubitable. Further, it seems, the National
Cockade has been trampled on ; also there are Black
Cockades, or were. All which things will not an august
National Assembly, the hope of France, take into its
wise immediate consideration ?

And Menadic Hunger, irrepressible, crying ' Black
Cockades ', crying ' Bread, bread ', adds, after such
fashion : Will it not ?—Yes, Messieurs, if a Deputation
to his Majesty, for the ' Acceptance pure and simple ',
seemed proper,—how much more now, for ' the afflicting situation of Paris ' ; for the calming of this effervescence ! President Mounier, with a speedy Deputation, among whom we notice the respectable figure of
Doctor Guillotin, gets himself forthwith on march.
Vice-President shall continue the order of the day ;
Usher Maillard shall stay by him to repress the women.
It is four o'clock, of the miserablest afternoon, when
Mounier steps out.

O experienced Mounier, what an afternoon ; the
last of thy political existence ! Better had it been to
' fall suddenly unwell ', while it was yet time. For,
behold, the Esplanade, over all its spacious expanse,
is covered with groups of squalid dripping Women ;
of lankhaired male Rascality, armed with axes, rusty
pikes, old muskets, ironshod clubs (*batons ferrés*, which
end in knives or sword-blades, a kind of extempore
billhook) ;—looking nothing but hungry revolt. The
rain pours : Gardes-du-Corps go caracoling through
the groups ' amid hisses ' ; irritating and agitating
what is but dispersed here to reunite there.

Innumerable squalid women beleaguer the President
and Deputation ; insist on going with him : has not
his Majesty himself, looking from the window, sent out
to ask, What we wanted ? ' Bread, and speech with
the King (*Du pain, et parler au Roi*) ', that was the

answer. Twelve women are clamorously added to the Deputation ; and march with it, across the Esplanade ; through dissipated groups, caracoling Bodyguards and the pouring rain.

President Mounier, unexpectedly augmented by Twelve women, copiously escorted by Hunger and Rascality, is himself mistaken for a group : himself and his Women are dispersed by caracolers ; rally again with difficulty, among the mud.[1] Finally the Grates are opened ; the Deputation gets access, with the Twelve women too in it ; of which latter, Five shall even see the face of his Majesty. Let wet Menadism, in the best spirits it can, expect their return.

CHAPTER VII

AT VERSAILLES

But already Pallas Athene (in the shape of Demoiselle Théroigne) is busy with Flandre and the dismounted Dragoons. She, and such women as are fittest, go through the ranks ; speak with an earnest jocosity ; clasp rough troopers to their patriot bosom, crush down spontoons and musketoons with soft arms : can a man, that were worthy of the name of man, attack famishing patriot women ?

One reads that Théroigne had bags of money, which she distributed over Flandre :—furnished by whom ? Alas, with money-bags one seldom sits on insurrectionary cannon. Calumnious Royalism ! Théroigne had only the limited earnings of her profession of unfortunate-female ; money she had not, but brown locks, the figure of a Heathen Goddess and an eloquent tongue and heart.

Meanwhile, Saint-Antoine in groups and troops, is continually arriving ; wetted, sulky ; with pikes and

[1] Mounier, Exposé Justificatif (cited in Deux Amis, iii. 185).

impromptu billhooks : driven thus far by popular
fixed-idea. So many hirsute figures driven hither, in
that manner : figures that have come to do they know
not what ; figures that have come to see it done !
Distinguished among all figures, who is this, of gaunt
stature, with leaden breastplate, though a small one ; [1]
bushy in red grizzled locks ; nay, with long tile-beard ?
It is Jourdan, unjust dealer in mules ; a dealer no longer,
but a Painter's Model, playing truant this day. From
the necessities of Art comes his long tile-beard ; whence
his leaden breastplate (unless indeed he were some
Hawker licensed by leaden badge) may have come,—will
perhaps remain for ever an Historical Problem. Another
Saul among the people we discern : ' *Père Adam*,
Father Adam ', as the groups name him ; to us better
known as bull-voiced Marquis Saint-Huruge ; hero of
the *Veto* ; a man that has had losses, and deserved
them. The tall Marquis, emitted some days ago from
limbo, looks peripatetically on this scene from under his
umbrella, not without interest. All which persons and
things, hurled together as we see ; Pallas Athene, busy
with Flandre ; patriotic Versailles National Guards,
short of ammunition, and deserted by D'Estaing their
Colonel, and commanded by Lecointre their Major ;
then caracoling Bodyguards, sour, dispirited, with their
buckskins wet ; and finally this flowing sea of indignant Squalor,—may they not give rise to occurrences ?

Behold, however, the Twelve She-deputies return
from the Château. Without President Mounier, indeed ;
but radiant with joy, shouting ' *Life to the King and
his House* '. Apparently the news are good, Mesdames ?
News of the best ! Five of us were admitted to the
internal splendours, to the Royal Presence. This slim
damsel, ' Louison Chabray, worker in sculpture, aged
only seventeen ', as being of the best looks and address,
her we appointed speaker. On whom, and indeed on
all of us, his Majesty looked nothing but graciousness.

----

[1] See Weber, ii. 185-231.

Nay, when Louison, addressing him, was like to faint,
he took her in his royal arms ; and said gallantly, ' It
was well worth while (*Elle en valût bien la peine*) '.
Consider, O Women, what a King ! His words were of
comfort, and that only : there shall be provision sent to
Paris, if provision is in the world ; grains shall circulate
free as air ; millers shall grind, or do worse, while their
millstones endure ; and nothing be left wrong which
a Restorer of French Liberty can right.

Good news these ; but, to wet Menads, all-too
incredible ! There seems no proof, then ? *Words* of
comfort,—they are words only ; which will feed nothing.
O miserable People, betrayed by Aristocrats, who
corrupt thy very messengers ! In his royal arms,
Mademoiselle Louison ? In his arms ? Thou shame-
less minx, worthy of a name—that shall be nameless !
Yes, thy skin is soft : ours is rough with hardship ; and
well wetted, waiting here in the rain. No children hast
thou hungry at home ; only alabaster dolls, that weep
not ! The traitress ! To the Lanterne !—And so poor
Louison Chabray, no asseveration or shrieks availing
her, fair slim damsel, late in the arms of Royalty, has
a garter round her neck, and furibund Amazons at
each end ; is about to perish so,—when two Bodyguards
gallop up, indignantly dissipating ; and rescue her.
The miscredited Twelve hasten back to the Château,
for an ' answer in writing '.

Nay, behold, a new flight of Menads, with ' M.
Brunout Bastille Volunteer ', as impressed-commandant, at the head of it. These also will advance to the
Grate of the Grand Court, and see what is toward.
Human patience, in wet buckskins, has its limits.
Bodyguard Lieutenant M. de Savonnières for one
moment lets his temper, long provoked, long pent, give
way. He not only dissipates these latter Menads ;
but caracoles and cuts, or indignantly flourishes, at
M. Brunout, the impressed-commandant ; and, finding
great relief in it, even chases him ; Brunout flying
nimbly, though in a pirouette manner, and now
with sword also drawn. At which sight of wrath and

victory, two other Bodyguards (for wrath is contagious,
and to pent Bodyguards is so solacing) do likewise give
way ; give chase, with brandished sabre, and in the air
make horrid circles. So that poor Brunout has nothing
for it but to retreat with accelerated nimbleness, through
rank after rank ; Parthian-like, fencing as he flies ;
above all, shouting lustily, ' *On nous laisse assassiner*,
They are getting us assassinated ! '

Shameful ! Three against one ! Growls come from
the Lecointrian ranks ; bellowings,—lastly shots.
Savonnières' arm is raised to strike : the bullet of
a Lecointrian musket shatters it ; the brandished sabre
jingles down harmless. Brunout has escaped, this duel
well ended : but the wild howl of war is everywhere
beginning to pipe !

The Amazons recoil ; Saint-Antoine has its cannon
pointed (full of grapeshot) ; thrice applies the lit flambeau ; which thrice refuses to catch,—the touchholes
are so wetted ; and voices cry : ' *Arrêtez, il n'est pas
temps encore*, Stop, it is not yet time ! ' [1] Messieurs of
the Garde-du-Corps, ye had orders not to fire ; nevertheless two of you limp dismounted, and one war-horse
lies slain. Were it not well to draw back out of shot-
range ; finally to file off,—into the interior ? If in so
filing off, there did a musketoon or two discharge itself,
at these armed shopkeepers, hooting and crowing,
could man wonder ? Draggled are your white cockades
of an enormous size ; would to Heaven they were got
exchanged for tricolor ones ! Your buckskins are wet,
your hearts heavy. Go, and return not !

The Bodyguards file off, as we hint ; giving and
receiving shots ; drawing no life-blood ; leaving boundless indignation. Some three times in the thickening
dusk, a glimpse of them is seen, at this or the other
Portal : saluted always with execrations, with the
whew of lead. Let but a Bodyguard show face, he is
hunted by Rascality ;—for instance, poor ' M. de
Moucheton of the Scotch Company ', owner of the slain

war-horse ; and has to be smuggled off by Versailles
Captains. Or rusty firelocks belch after him, shivering
asunder his—hat. In the end, by superior Order, the
Bodyguards, all but the few on immediate duty, disappear ; or as it were abscond ; and march, under
cloud of night, to Rambouillet.[1]

We remark also that the Versaillese have now got
ammunition : all afternoon, the official Person could
find none ; till, in these so critical moments, a patriotic
Sub-lieutenant set a pistol to his ear, and would thank
him to find some,—which he thereupon succeeded in
doing. Likewise that Flandre, disarmed by Pallas
Athene, says openly, it will not fight with citizens ; and
for token of peace has exchanged cartridges with the
Versaillese.

Sansculottism is now among mere friends ; and can
' circulate freely ' ; indignant at Bodyguards ;—complaining also considerably of hunger.

CHAPTER VIII

THE EQUAL DIET[*]

BUT why lingers Mounier ; returns not with his
Deputation ? It is six, it is seven o'clock ; and still
no Mounier, no Acceptance pure and simple.

And, behold, the dripping Menads, not now in deputation but in mass, have penetrated into the Assembly :
to the shamefullest interruption of public speaking
and order of the day. Neither Maillard nor Vice-
President can restrain them, except within wide limits ;
not even, except for minutes, can the lion-voice of
Mirabeau, though they applaud it : but ever and anon
they break in upon the regeneration of France with
cries of : ' Bread ; not so much discoursing ! Du
pain ; pas tant de longs discours ! '—So insensible were
these poor creatures to bursts of parliamentary
eloquence !

[1] Weber, ubi supra.

One learns also that the royal carriages are getting yoked, as if for Metz. Carriages, royal or not, have verily showed themselves at the back Gates. They even produced, or quoted, a written order from our Versailles Municipality,—which is a Monarchic not a Democratic one. However, Versailles Patrols drove them in again ; as the vigilant Lecointre had strictly charged them to do.

A busy man, truly, is Major Lecointre, in these hours. For Colonel d'Estaing loiters invisible in the Œil-de-Bœuf ; invisible, or still more questionably *visible* for instants : then also a too loyal Municipality requires supervision : no order, civil or military, taken about any of these thousand things ! Lecointre is at the Versailles Townhall : he is at the Grate of the Grand Court ; communing with Swiss and Bodyguards. He is in the ranks of Flandre ; he is here, he is there : studious to prevent bloodshed ; to prevent the Royal Family from flying to Metz ; the Menads from plundering Versailles.

At the fall of night, we behold him advance to those armed groups of Saint-Antoine, hovering all-too grim near the Salle des Menus. They receive him in a half-circle ; twelve speakers behind cannons with lighted torches in hand, the cannon-mouths *towards* Lecointre : a picture for Salvator !* He asks, in temperate but courageous language : What they, by this their journey to Versailles, do specially want ? The twelve speakers reply, in few words inclusive of much : ' Bread, and the end of these brabbles, *Du pain, et la fin des affaires* '. When the *affairs* will end, no Major Lecointre, nor no mortal, can say ; but as to bread, he inquires, How many are you ?—learns that they are six hundred, that a loaf each will suffice ; and rides off to the Municipality to get six hundred loaves.

Which loaves, however, a Municipality of Monarchic temper will not give. It will give two tons of rice rather,—could you but know whether it should be boiled or raw. Nay when this too is accepted, the Municipals have disappeared ;—ducked under, as the

Six-and-twenty Long-gowned of Paris did ; and, leaving not the smallest vestige of rice, in the boiled or raw state, they there vanish from History !

Rice comes not ; one's hope of food is balked ; even one's hope of vengeance : is not M. de Moucheton of the Scotch Company, as we said, deceitfully smuggled off ?   Failing all which, behold only M. de Moucheton's slain warhorse, lying on the Esplanade there ! Saint-Antoine, balked, esurient, pounces on the slain warhorse ; flays it ; roasts it, with such fuel, of paling, gates, portable timber as can be come at,—not without shouting ; *and,* after the manner of ancient Greek Heroes, *they lifted their hands to the daintily readied repast*; such as it might be.[1] Other Rascality prowls discursive ; seeking what it may devour.   Flandre will retire to its barracks ; Lecointre also with his Versaillese,—all but the vigilant Patrols, charged to be doubly vigilant.

So sink the shadows of night, blustering, rainy ; and all paths grow dark.   Strangest Night ever seen in these regions,—perhaps since the Bartholomew Night, when Versailles, as Bassompierre writes of it, was a *chétif château.* O for the Lyre of some Orpheus, to constrain, with touch of melodious strings, these mad masses into Order ! For here all seems fallen asunder, in wide-yawning dislocation.   The highest, as in down-rushing of a World, is come in contact with the lowest : the Rascality of France beleaguering the Royalty of France ; ' ironshod batons ' lifted round the diadem, not to guard it ! With denunciations of bloodthirsty Anti-national Bodyguards, are heard dark growlings against a Queenly Name.

The Court sits tremulous, powerless ; varies with the varying temper of the Esplanade, with the varying colour of the rumours from Paris.   Thick-coming rumours ; now of peace, now of war.   Necker and all the Ministers consult ; with a blank issue.   The Œil-de-Bœuf is one tempest of whispers :—We will fly to

[1] Weber ; Deux Amis, &c.

Metz; we will not fly. The royal Carriages again
attempt egress,—though for trial merely; they are
again driven in by Lecointre's Patrols. In six hours,
nothing has been resolved on; not even the Acceptance
pure and simple.

In six hours? Alas, he who, in such circumstances,
cannot resolve in six minutes, may give up the enterprise: him Fate has already resolved for. And
Menadism, meanwhile, and Sansculottism takes counsel
with the National Assembly; grows more and more
tumultuous there. Mounier returns not; Authority
nowhere shows itself: the Authority of France lies, for
the present, with Lecointre and Usher Maillard.—This
then is the abomination of desolation*; come suddenly*,
though long foreshadowed as inevitable! For, to the
blind, all things are sudden. Misery which, through
long ages, had no spokesman, no helper, will now be
its own helper and speak for itself. The dialect, one
of the rudest, is, what it could be, *this*.

At eight o'clock there returns to our Assembly not
the Deputation; but Doctor Guillotin announcing
that it will return; also that there is hope of the
Acceptance pure and simple. He himself has brought
a Royal Letter, authorizing and commanding the freest
' circulation of grains '. Which Royal Letter Menadism
with its whole heart applauds. Conformably to which
the Assembly forthwith passes a Decree; also received
with rapturous Menadic plaudits :—Only could not an
august Assembly contrive further to ' *fix* the price of
bread at eight sous the half-quartern; butchers'-meat
at six sous the pound '; which seem fair rates? Such
motion do ' a multitude of men and women ', irrepressible by Usher Maillard, now make; does an august
Assembly hear made. Usher Maillard himself is not
always perfectly measured in speech; but if rebuked,
he can justly excuse himself by the peculiarity of the
circumstances.[1]

But finally, this Decree well passed, and the disorder
continuing; and Members melting away, and no

[1] Moniteur (in Hist. Parl. iii. 105).

President Mounier returning,—what can the Vice-President do but also melt away ? The Assembly melts, under such pressure, into deliquium ; or, as it is officially called, adjourns. Maillard is dispatched to Paris, with the ' Decree concerning Grains ' in his pocket ; he and some women, in carriages belonging to the King. Thitherward slim Louison Chabray has already set forth, with that ' written answer ' which the Twelve She-deputies returned in to seek. Slim sylph, she has set forth, through the black muddy country : she has much to tell, her poor nerves so flurried ; and travels, as indeed to-day on this road all persons do, with extreme slowness. President Mounier has not come, nor the Acceptance pure and simple ; though six hours with their events have come ; though courier on courier reports that Lafayette is coming. Coming, with war or with peace ? It is time that the Château also should determine on one thing or another ; that the Château also should show itself alive, if it would continue living !

Victorious, joyful after such delay, Mounier does arrive at last, and the hard-earned Acceptance with him; which now, alas, is of small value. Fancy Mounier's surprise to find his Senate, whom he hoped to charm by the Acceptance pure and simple,—all gone ; and in its stead a Senate of Menads ! For as Erasmus's Apé mimicked, say with wooden splint, Erasmus shaving, so do these Amazons hold, in mock majesty, some confused parody of National Assembly. They make motions ; deliver speeches ; pass enactments ; productive at least of loud laughter. All galleries and benches are filled ; a Strong Dame of the Market is in Mounier's Chair. Not without difficulty, Mounier, by aid of macers and persuasive speaking, makes his way to the Female-President ; the Strong Dame, before abdicating, signifies that, for one thing, she and indeed her whole senate male and female (for what was one roasted warhorse among so many ?) are suffering very considerably from hunger.

Experienced Mounier, in these circumstances, takes

a twofold resolution : To reconvoke his Assembly
Members by sound of drum ; also to procure a supply
of food. Swift messengers fly, to all bakers, cooks,
pastrycooks, vintners, restorers ; drums beat, accompanied with shrill vocal proclamation, through all streets.
They come : the Assembly Members come ; what is
still better, the provisions come. On tray and barrow
come these latter ; loaves, wine, great store of sausages.
The nourishing baskets circulate harmoniously along
the benches ; *nor*, according to the Father of Epics,
did any soul lack a fair share of victual (δαῖτος ἐίσης,
an equal diet) ; highly desirable at the moment.[1]

Gradually some hundred or so of Assembly Members
get edged in, Menadism making way a little, round
Mounier's chair ; listen to the Acceptance pure and
simple ; and begin, what is the order of the night,
' discussion of the Penal Code '. All benches are
crowded ; in the dusky galleries, duskier with unwashed
heads, is a strange ' coruscation ',—of impromptu billhooks.[2] It is exactly five months this day since these
same galleries were filled with high-plumed jewelled
Beauty, raining bright influences ; and now ? To such
length have we got in regenerating France. Methinks
the travail-throes are of the sharpest !—Menadism will
not be restrained from occasional remarks ; asks,
' What is the use of Penal Code ? The thing we want
is Bread'. Mirabeau turns round with lion-voiced
rebuke ; Menadism applauds him ; but recommences.

Thus they, chewing tough sausages, discussing the
Penal Code, make night hideous.* What the issue will
be ? Lafayette with his thirty thousand must arrive
first : him, who cannot now be distant, all men expect,
as the messenger of Destiny.

[1] Deux Amis, iii. 208.
[2] Courrier de Provence (Mirabeau's Newspaper), No. 50,
p. 19.

CHAPTER IX

LAFAYETTE

TOWARDS midnight lights flare on the hill; Lafayette's
lights ! The roll of his drums comes up the Avenue
de Versailles. With peace, or with war ? Patience,
friends ! With neither. Lafayette is come, but not
yet the catastrophe.

He has halted and harangued so often, on the march ;
spent nine hours on four leagues of road. At Mon-
treuil, close on Versailles, the whole Host has to pause ;
and, with uplifted right hand, in the murk of Night,
to these pouring skies, swear solemnly to respect the
King's Dwelling ; to be faithful to King and National
Assembly. Rage is driven down out of sight, by the
laggard march ; the thirst of vengeance slaked in
weariness and soaking clothes. Flandre is again drawn
out under arms : but Flandre, grown so patriotic, now
needs no ' exterminating '. The wayworn Battalions
halt in the Avenue : they have, for the present, no wish
so pressing as that of shelter and rest.

Anxious sits President Mounier ; anxious the Château. There is a message coming from the Château,
that M. Mounier would please to return thither with
a fresh Deputation, swiftly ; and so at least *unite* our
two anxieties. Anxious Mounier does of himself send,
meanwhile, to apprise the General that his Majesty
has been so gracious as to grant us the Acceptance
pure and simple. The General, with a small advance
column, makes answer in passing ; speaks vaguely
some smooth words to the National President,—
glances, only with the eye, at that so mixtiform
National Assembly ; then fares forward towards the
Château. There are with him two Paris Municipals ;
they were chosen from the Three Hundred for that
errand. He gets admittance through the locked and

padlocked Grates, through sentries and ushers, to the
Royal Halls.

The Court, male and female, crowds on his passage,
to read their doom on his face ; which exhibits, say
Historians, a mixture ' of sorrow, of fervour and valour ',
singular to behold.[1] The King, with Monsieur, with
Ministers and Marshals, is waiting to receive him :
He ' is come ', in his highflown chivalrous way, ' to
offer his head for the safety of his Majesty's '. The
two Municipals state the wish of Paris : four things,
of quite pacific tenor. First, that the honour of
guarding his sacred person be conferred on patriot
National Guards ;—say, the Centre Grenadiers, who
as Gardes Françaises were wont to have that privilege.
Second, that provisions be got, if possible. Third, that
the Prisons, all crowded with political delinquents,
may have judges sent them. Fourth, *that it would
please his Majesty to come and live in Paris.* To all
which four wishes, except the fourth, his Majesty
answers readily, Yes ; or indeed may almost say that
he has already answered it. To the fourth he can
answer only, Yes or No ; would so gladly answer, Yes
and No !—But, in any case, are not their dispositions,
thank Heaven, so entirely pacific ? There is time for
deliberation. The brunt of the danger seems past !

Lafayette and D'Estaing settle the watches ; Centre
Grenadiers are to take the Guard-room they of old
occupied as Gardes Françaises ;—for indeed the Gardes-
du-Corps, its late ill-advised occupants, are gone mostly
to Rambouillet. That is the order of *this* night ;
sufficient for the night is the evil thereof. Whereupon
Lafayette and the two Municipals, with highflown
chivalry, take their leave.

So brief has the interview been, Mounier and his
Deputation were not yet got up. So brief and satis-
factory. A stone is rolled from every heart. The fair
Palace Dames publicly declare that this Lafayette,

[1] Mémoire de M. le Comte de Lally-Tollendal (Janvier
1790), pp. 161-5.

detestable though he be, is their saviour for once. Even
the ancient vinaigrous *Tantes* admit it; the King's
Aunts, ancient *Graille* and Sisterhood, known to us of
old. Queen Marie-Antoinette has been heard often
say the like. She alone, among all women and all men,
wore a face of courage, of lofty calmness and resolve,
this day. She alone saw clearly what she *meant* to do ;
and Theresa's Daughter *dares* do what she means, were
all France threatening her : abide where her children
are, where her husband is.

Towards three in the morning all things are settled :
the watches set, the Centre Grenadiers put into their
old Guard-room, and harangued ; the Swiss, and few
remaining Bodyguards harangued. The wayworn
Paris Battalions, consigned to ' the hospitality of Versailles ', lie dormant in spare-beds, spare-barracks,
coffeehouses, empty churches. A troop of them, on
their way to the Church of Saint-Louis, awoke poor
Weber, dreaming troublous, in the Rue Sartory. Weber
has had his waistcoat-pocket full of balls all day ;
' two hundred balls, and two *pears* of powder ! ' For
waistcoats were waistcoats then, and had flaps down
to mid-thigh. So many balls he has had all day ; but
no opportunity of using them : he turns over now,
execrating disloyal bandits ; swears a prayer or two,*
and straight to sleep again.

Finally the National Assembly is harangued ; which
thereupon, on motion of Mirabeau, discontinues the
Penal Code, and dismisses for this night. Menadism,
Sansculottism has cowered into guardhouses, barracks
of Flandre, to the light of cheerful fire ; failing that,
to churches, officehouses, sentry-boxes, wheresoever
wretchedness can find a lair. The troublous Day has
brawled itself to rest : no lives yet lost but that of one
warhorse. Insurrectionary Chaos lies slumbering round
the Palace, like Ocean round a Diving-bell,—no crevice
yet disclosing itself.

Deep sleep has fallen promiscuously on the high and
on the low ; suspending most things, even wrath and

famine. Darkness covers the Earth.* But, far on the
North-east, Paris flings up her great yellow gleam ; far
into the wet black Night. For all is illuminated there,
as in the old July Nights ; the streets deserted, for
alarm of war ; the Municipals all wakeful ; Patrols
hailing, with their hoarse *Who-goes*. There, as we discover, our poor slim Louison Chabray, her poor nerves
all fluttered, is arriving about this very hour. There
Usher Maillard will arrive, about an hour hence,
' towards four in the morning '. They report, successively, to a wakeful Hôtel-de-Ville what comfort they
can ; which again, with early dawn, large comfortable
Placards shall impart to all men.

Lafayette, in the Hôtel de Noailles, not far from the
Château, having now finished haranguing, sits with his
Officers consulting : at five o'clock the unanimous best
counsel is, that a man so tost and toiled for twenty-four
hours and more, fling himself on a bed, and seek some
rest.

Thus, then, has ended the First Act of the Insurrection of Women. How it will turn on the morrow ?
The morrow, as always, is with the Fates ! But his
Majesty, one may hope, will consent to come honourably to Paris ; at all events, he can visit Paris. Anti-
national Bodyguards, here and elsewhere, must take
the National Oath ; make reparation to the Tricolor ;
Flandre will swear. There may be much swearing ;
much public speaking there will infallibly be : and so,
with harangues and vows, may the matter in some
handsome way wind itself up.

Or, alas, may it not be all otherwise, *un*handsome ;
the consent not honourable, but extorted, ignominious ?
Boundless Chaos of Insurrection presses slumbering
round the Palace, like Ocean round a Diving-bell ; and
may penetrate at any crevice. Let but that accumulated insurrectionary mass find entrance ! Like the
infinite inburst of water ; or say rather, of inflammable,
self-igniting fluid ; for example, ' turpentine-and-phos-
phorus oil ',—fluid known to Spinola Santerre !

CHAPTER X

THE GRAND ENTRIES

THE dull dawn of a new morning, drizzly and chill,
had but broken over Versailles, when it pleased Destiny
that a Bodyguard should look out of window, on the
right wing of the Château, to see what prospect there
was in Heaven and in Earth. Rascality male and
female is prowling in view of him. His fasting stomach
is, with good cause, sour ; he perhaps cannot forbear
a passing malison on them ; least of all can he forbear
answering such.

Ill words breed worse : till the worst word come ;
and then the ill deed. Did the maledicent Bodyguard,
getting (as was too inevitable) better malediction than
he gave, load his musketoon, and threaten to fire ; nay
actually fire ? Were wise who wist ! It stands
asserted ; to us not credibly. But be this as it may,
menaced Rascality, in whinnying scorn, is shaking at
all Grates : the fastening of one (some write, it was
a chain merely) gives way ; Rascality is in the Grand
Court, whinnying louder still.

The maledicent Bodyguard, more Bodyguards than he
do now give fire ; a man's arm is shattered. Lecointre
will depose [1] that 'the Sieur Cardine, a National
Guard without arms, was stabbed'. But see, sure
enough, poor Jerôme l'Héritier, an unarmed National
Guard he too, 'cabinet-maker, a saddler's son, of
Paris', with the down of youthhood still on his chin,
—he reels death-stricken ; rushes to the pavement,
scattering it with his blood and brains !—Alleleu !
Wilder than Irish wakes rises the howl ; of pity, of
infinite revenge. In few moments, the Grate of the
inner and inmost Court, which they name Court of
Marble, this too is forced, or surprised, and bursts open :

---

[1] Déposition de Lecointre (in Hist. Parl. iii. 111-15).

the Court of Marble too is overflowed : up the Grand
Staircase, up all stairs and entrances rushes the living
Deluge ! Deshuttes and Varigny, the two sentry
Bodyguards, are trodden down, are massacred with
a hundred pikes. Women snatch their cutlasses, or
any weapon, and storm-in Menadic :—other women
lift the corpse of shot Jerôme ; lay it down on the
Marble steps ; there shall the livid face and smashed
head, dumb for ever, *speak*.

Woe now to all Bodyguards, mercy is none for them !
Miomandre de Sainte-Marie pleads with soft words, on
the Grand Staircase, ' descending four steps ' :—to the
roaring tornado. His comrades snatch him up, by the
skirts and belts ; literally, from the jaws of Destruction ; and slam-to their Door. This also will stand
few instants ; the panels shivering in, like potsherds.
Barricading serves not : fly fast, ye Bodyguards :
rabid Insurrection, like the Hellhound Chase,* uproaring
at your heels !

The terror-struck Bodyguards fly, bolting and barricading ; it follows. Whitherward ? Through hall on
hall : woe, now ! towards the Queen's Suite of Rooms,
in the furthest room of which the Queen is now asleep.
Five sentinels rush through that long suite ; they are
in the Anteroom knocking loud : ' Save the Queen ! '
Trembling women fall at their feet with tears : are
answered : ' Yes, we will die ; save ye the Queen ! '

Tremble not, women, but haste : for, lo, another voice
shouts far through the outermost door, ' Save the
Queen ! ' and the door is shut. It is brave Miomandre's
voice that shouts this second warning. He has stormed
across imminent death to do it ; fronts imminent death,
having done it. Brave Tardivet du Repaire, bent on
the same desperate service, was borne down with pikes ;
his comrades hardly snatched him in again alive.
Miomandre and Tardivet : let the names of these two
Bodyguards, as the names of brave men should, live
long.

Trembling Maids of Honour, one of whom from afar

caught glimpse of Miomandre as well as heard him,
hastily wrap the Queen ; not in robes of state. She
flies for her life, across the Œil-de-Bœuf ; against the
main door of which too Insurrection batters. She is
in the King's Apartment, in the King's arms ; she
clasps her children amid a faithful few. The Imperial-
hearted bursts into mother's tears : ' O my friends,
save me and my children, *O mes amis, sauvez moi et mes
enfans !* ' The battering of Insurrectionary axes clangs
audible across the Œil-de-Bœuf. What an hour !

Yes, Friends ; a hideous fearful hour ; shameful
alike to Governed and Governor ; wherein Governed
and Governor ignominiously testify that their relation is
at an end. Rage, which had brewed itself in twenty
thousand hearts for the last four-and-twenty hours,
has taken *fire* : Jerôme's brained corpse lies there as
live-coal. It is, as we said, the infinite Element bursting
in ; wild-surging through all corridors and conduits.
Meanwhile the poor Bodyguards have got hunted
mostly into the Œil-de-Bœuf. They may die there, at
the King's threshold ; they can do little to defend it.
They are heaping *tabourets* (stools of honour), benches
and all movables, against the door ; at which the axe
of Insurrection thunders.—But did brave Miomandre
perish, then, at the Queen's outer door ? No, he was
fractured, slashed, lacerated, left for dead ; he has
nevertheless crawled hither ; and shall live, honoured
of loyal France. Remark also, in flat contradiction to
much which has been said and sung, that Insurrection
did *not* burst that door he had defended ; but hurried
elsewhither, seeking new Bodyguards.[1]

Poor Bodyguards, with their Thyestes Opera-Repast !
Well for them that Insurrection has only pikes and
axes ; no right sieging-tools ! It shakes and thunders.
Must they all perish miserably, and Royalty with them ?
Deshuttes and Varigny, massacred at the first inbreak,
have been beheaded in the Marble Court ; a sacrifice

---

[1] Campan, ii. 75–87.

to Jerôme's *manes*: Jourdan with the tile-beard did
that duty willingly ; and asked, If there were no more ?
Another captive they are leading round the corpse,
with howl-chantings : may not Jourdan again tuck up
his sleeves ?

And louder and louder rages Insurrection within,
plundering if it cannot kill ; louder and louder it thunders at the Œil-de-Bœuf : what can now hinder its
bursting in ?—On a sudden it ceases ; the battering
has ceased ! Wild rushing ; the cries grow fainter ;
there is silence, or the tramp of regular steps ; then
a friendly knocking : ' We are the Centre Grenadiers,
old Gardes Françaises : Open to us, Messieurs of the
Garde-du-Corps ; we have not forgotten how you
saved us at Fontenoy ! ' [1] The door is opened ; enter
Captain Gondran and the Centre Grenadiers : there are
military embracings ; there is sudden deliverance from
death into life.—

Strange Sons of Adam ! It was to ' exterminate '
these Gardes-du-Corps that the Centre Grenadiers left
home : and now they have rushed to save them from
extermination. The memory of common peril, of old
help, melts the rough heart ; bosom is clasped to bosom,
not in war. The King shows himself, one moment,
through the door of his Apartment, with : ' Do not
hurt my Guards ! '—' *Soyons frères*, Let us be brothers ! '
cries Captain Gondran ; and again dashes off, with
levelled bayonets, to sweep the Palace clear.

Now too Lafayette, suddenly roused, not from sleep
(for his eyes had not yet closed), arrives ; with passionate popular eloquence, with prompt military word of
command. National Guards, suddenly roused, by
sound of trumpet and alarm-drum, are all arriving.
The death-melly ceases : the first sky-lambent blaze
of Insurrection is got damped down ; it burns now, if
unextinguished, yet flameless, as charred coals do, and
not inextinguishable. The King's Apartments are safe.
Ministers, Officials, and even some loyal National

[1] Toulongeon, i. 144.

Deputies are assembling round their Majesties. The
consternation will, with sobs and confusion, settle down
gradually, into plan and counsel, better or worse.

But glance now, for a moment, from the royal
windows ! A roaring sea of human heads, inundating
both Courts ; billowing against all passages : Menadic
women ; infuriated men, mad with revenge, with love
of mischief, love of plunder ! Rascality has slipped
its muzzle ; and now bays, three-throated, like the
Dog of Erebus. Fourteen Bodyguards are wounded ;
two massacred, and as we saw, beheaded ; Jourdan
asking, ' Was it worth while to come so far for two ? '
Hapless Deshuttes and Varigny ! Their fate surely
was sad. Whirled down so suddenly to the abyss ; as
men are, suddenly, by the wide thunder of the Mountain
Avalanche, awakened not by *them*, awakened far off by
others ! When the Château Clock last struck, they two
were pacing languid, with poised musketoon ; anxious
mainly that the next hour would strike. It has struck ;
to them inaudible. Their trunks lie mangled : their
heads parade, ' on pikes twelve feet long ', through the
streets of Versailles ; and shall, about noon, reach the
Barriers of Paris,—a too ghastly contradiction to the
large comfortable Placards that have been posted there !

The other captive Bodyguard is still circling the
corpse of Jerôme, amid Indian war-whooping ; bloody
Tilebeard, with tucked sleeves, brandishing his bloody
axe ; when Gondran and the Grenadiers come in sight.
' Comrades, will you see a man massacred in cold blood ? '
—' Off, butchers ! ' answer they ; and the poor Bodyguard is free. Busy runs Gondran, busy run Guards
and Captains ; scouring all corridors ; dispersing
Rascality and Robbery ; sweeping the Palace clear.
The mangled carnage is removed ; Jerôme's body to
the Townhall, for inquest : the fire of Insurrection gets
damped, more and more, into measurable, manageable
heat.

Transcendent things of all sorts, as in the general
outburst of multitudinous Passion, are huddled

together; the ludicrous, nay the ridiculous, with the horrible. Far over the billowy sea of heads, may be seen Rascality, caprioling on horses from the Royal Stud. The Spoilers these; for Patriotism is always infected so, with a proportion of mere thieves and scoundrels. Gondran snatched their prey from them in the Château; whereupon they hurried to the Stables, and took horse there. But the generous Diomedes'* steeds, according to Weber, disdained such scoundrel-burden; and, flinging up their royal heels, did soon project most of it, in parabolic curves, to a distance, amid peals of laughter; and were caught. Mounted National Guards secured the rest.

Now too is witnessed the touching last-flicker of Etiquette; which sinks not here, in the Cimmerian World-wreckage,* without a sign; as the house-cricket might still chirp in the pealing of a Trump of Doom. 'Monsieur', said some Master of Ceremonies (one hopes it might be De Brézé), as Lafayette, in these fearful moments, was rushing towards the inner Royal Apartments, ' *Monsieur, le Roi vous accorde les grandes entrées*, Monsieur, the King grants you the Grand Entries ',— not finding it convenient to refuse them ! [1]

CHAPTER XI

FROM VERSAILLES

However, the Paris National Guard, wholly under arms, has cleared the Palace, and even occupies the nearer external spaces; extruding miscellaneous Patriotism, for most part, into the Grand Court, or even into the Forecourt.

The Bodyguards, you can observe, have now of a verity ' hoisted the National Cockade ' : for they step forward to the windows or balconies, hat aloft in hand, on each hat a huge tricolor; and fling over their

[1] Toulongeon, i. App. 120.

bandoleers in sign of surrender; and shout *Vive la
Nation*. To which how can the generous heart respond
but with, *Vive le Roi*; *vivent les Gardes-du-Corps*?
His Majesty himself has appeared with Lafayette on
the balcony, and again appears: *Vive le Roi* greets him
from all throats; but also from some one throat is
heard, '*Le Roi à Paris*, The King to Paris!'

Her Majesty too, on demand, shows herself, though
there is peril in it: she steps out on the balcony, with
her little boy and girl. ' No children, *Point d'enfans!*'
cry the voices. She gently pushes back her children;
and stands alone, her hands serenely crossed on her
breast: ' should I die ', she had said, ' I will do it '.
Such serenity of heroism has its effect. Lafayette,
with ready wit, in his highflown chivalrous way, takes
that fair queenly hand, and, reverently kneeling, kisses
it: thereupon the people do shout *Vive la Reine*.
Nevertheless, poor Weber ' saw ' (or even thought he
saw; for hardly the third part of poor Weber's experiences, in such hysterical days, will stand scrutiny)
' one of these brigands level his musket at her Majesty ',
—with or without intention to shoot; for another of
the brigands ' angrily struck it down '.

So that all, and the Queen herself, nay the very
Captain of the Bodyguards, have grown National!
The very Captain of the Bodyguards steps out now
with Lafayette. On the hat of the repentant man is
an enormous tricolor; large as a soup-platter, or sun-
flower; visible to the utmost Forecourt. He takes
the National Oath with a loud voice, elevating his hat;
at which sight all the army raise their bonnets on their
bayonets, with shouts. Sweet is reconcilement to the
heart of man. Lafayette has sworn Flandre; he
swears the remaining Bodyguards, down in the Marble-
Court; the people clasp them in their arms:—O my
brothers, why would ye force us to slay you? Behold
there is joy over you, as over returning prodigal sons!
—The poor Bodyguards, now National and tricolor,
exchange bonnets, exchange arms; there shall be
peace and fraternity. And still ' *Vive le Roi* '; and

also ' *Le Roi à Paris* ', not now from one throat, but from all throats as one, for it is the heart's wish of all mortals.

Yes, *The King to Paris* : what else ? Ministers may consult, and National Deputies wag their heads : but there is now no other possibility. You have forced him to go willingly. 'At one o'clock ! ' Lafayette gives audible assurance to that purpose ; and universal Insurrection, with immeasurable shout, and a discharge of all the fire-arms, clear and rusty, great and small, that it has, returns him acceptance. What a sound ; heard for leagues : a doom-peal !—That sound too rolls away ; into the Silence of Ages. And the Château of Versailles stands ever since vacant, hushed-still ; its spacious Courts grassgrown, responsive to the hoe of the weeder. Times and generations roll on, in their confused Gulf-current ; and buildings, like builders, have their destiny.

Till one o'clock, then, there will be three parties, National Assembly, National Rascality, National Royalty, all busy enough. Rascality rejoices ; women trim themselves with tricolor. Nay motherly Paris has sent her Avengers sufficient ' cartloads of loaves ' ; which are shouted over, which are gratefully consumed. The Avengers, in return, are searching for grain-stores ; loading them in fifty wagons ; that so a National King, probable harbinger of all blessings, may be the evident bringer of plenty, for one.

And thus has Sansculottism made prisoner its King ; *revoking* his parole. The Monarchy has fallen ; and not so much as honourably : no, ignominiously ; with struggle, indeed, oft-repeated ; but then with unwise struggle ; wasting its strength in fits and paroxysms ; at every new paroxysm foiled more pitifully than before. Thus Broglie's whiff of grapeshot, which might have been something, has dwindled to the pot-valour of an Opera Repast, and *O Richard, O mon Roi*. Which again we shall see dwindle to a Favras' Conspiracy,* a thing to be settled by the hanging of one Chevalier.

Poor Monarchy! But what save foulest defeat can
await that man, who wills, and yet wills not? Apparently the King either has a right, assertible as such
to the death, before God and man; or else he has no
right. Apparently, the one or the other; could he but
know which! May heaven pity him! Were Louis
wise, he would this day abdicate.—Is it not strange so
few Kings abdicate; and none yet heard of has been
known to commit suicide? Fritz the First, of Prussia,
alone tried it; and they cut the rope.*

As for the National Assembly, which decrees this
morning that it 'is inseparable from his Majesty', and
will follow him to Paris, there may one thing be noted:
its extreme want of bodily health. After the Fourteenth of July there was a certain sickliness observable
among honourable Members; so many demanding
passports, on account of infirm health. But now, for
these following days, there is a perfect murrain: President Mounier, Lally Tollendal, Clermont Tonnere,
and all Constitutional Two-Chamber Royalists needing
change of air; as most No-Chamber Royalists had
formerly done.

For, in truth, it is the *second Emigration* this that has
now come; most extensive among Commons Deputies,
Noblesse, Clergy: so that ' to Switzerland alone there
go sixty thousand '. They will return in the day of
accounts! Yes, and have hot welcome.—But Emigration on Emigration is the peculiarity of France. One
Emigration follows another; grounded on—reasonable
fear, unreasonable hope, largely also on childish pet.
The highflyers have gone first, now the lower flyers;
and ever the lower will go, down to the crawlers.
Whereby, however, cannot our National Assembly so
much the more commodiously make the Constitution;
your Two-Chamber Anglomaniacs being all safe, distant
on foreign shores? Abbé Maury is seized and sent
back again: he, tough as tanned leather, with eloquent
Captain Cazalès and some others, will stand it out for
another year.

But here, meanwhile, the question arises: Was

Philippe d'Orléans seen, this day, 'in the Bois de
Boulogne, in grey surtout'; waiting under the wet
sere foliage, what the day might bring forth ? Alas,
yes, the Eidolon of him was,—in Weber's and other
such brains. The Châtelet shall make large inquisition
into the matter, examining a hundred and seventy
witnesses, and Deputy Chabroud publish his Report;
but disclose nothing *further*.[1] What then has caused
these two unparalleled October Days ? For surely
such dramatic exhibition never yet enacted itself without Dramatist and Machinist. Wooden Punch emerges
not, with his domestic sorrows, into the light of day,
unless the wire be pulled: how can human mobs ?
Was it not D'Orléans then, and Laclos, Marquis Sillery,
Mirabeau and the sons of confusion; hoping to drive
the King to Metz, and gather the spoil ? Nay was it
not, quite contrariwise, the Œil-de-Bœuf, Bodyguard
Colonel de Guiche, Minister Saint-Priest and highflying
Loyalists; hoping also to drive him to Metz, and try
it by the sword of civil war ? Good Marquis Toulongeon, the Historian and Deputy, feels constrained to
admit that it was *both*.[2]

Alas, my Friends, credulous incredulity*is a strange
matter. But when a whole Nation is smitten with
Suspicion, and sees a dramatic miracle* in the very
operation of the gastric juices, what help is there ?
Such Nation is already a mere hypochondriac bundle
of diseases; as good as changed into glass; atrabiliar,
decadent; and will suffer crises. Is not Suspicion itself
the one thing to be suspected, as Montaigne feared
only fear ?*

Now, however, the short hour has struck. His
Majesty is in his carriage, with his Queen, sister Elizabeth, and two royal children. Not for another hour
can the infinite Procession get marshalled and under

Rapport de Chabroud (Moniteur, du 31 Decembre
1789).
[2] Toulongeon, i. 150.

way. The weather is dim drizzling; the mind confused; the noise great.

Processional marches not a few our world has seen;
Roman triumphs and ovations, Cabiric cymbal-beatings,
Royal progresses, Irish funerals; but this of the French
Monarchy marching to its bed remained to be seen.
Miles long, and of breadth losing itself in vagueness,
for all the neighbouring country crowds to see. Slow;
stagnating along, like shoreless Lake, yet with a noise
like Niagara, like Babel and Bedlam. A splashing and
a tramping; a hurrahing, uproaring, musket-volleying;
—the truest segment of Chaos seen in these latter Ages !
Till slowly it disembogue itself, in the thickening dusk,
into expectant Paris, through a double row of faces all
the way from Passy to the Hôtel-de-Ville.

Consider this: Vanguard of National troops; with
trains of artillery; of pikemen and pikewomen, mounted
on cannons, on carts, hackney-coaches, or on foot;—
tripudiating, in tricolor ribbons from head to heel;
loaves stuck on the points of bayonets, green boughs
stuck in gun-barrels.[1] Next, as main-march, 'fifty
cart-loads of corn', which have been lent, for peace,
from the stores of Versailles. Behind which follow
stragglers of the Garde-du-Corps; all humiliated, in
Grenadier bonnets. Close on these comes the Royal
Carriage; come Royal Carriages: for there are a
Hundred National Deputies too, among whom sits Mirabeau,—his remarks not given. Then finally, pellmell,
as rearguard, Flandre, Swiss, Hundred Swiss, other
Bodyguards, Brigands, whosoever cannot get before.
Between and among all which masses, flows without
limit Saint-Antoine, and the Menadic Cohort. Menadic
especially about the Royal Carriage; tripudiating
there, covered with tricolor; singing 'allusive songs';
pointing with one hand to the Royal Carriage, which
the allusions hit, and pointing to the Provision wagons
with the other hand, and these words: ' Courage,
Friends ! We shall not want bread now; we are

---

[1] Mercier, Nouveau Paris, iii. 21.

bringing you the Baker, the Bakeress, and Baker's Boy
(*le Boulanger, la Boulangère, et le petit Mitron*)'.[1]

The wet day draggles the tricolor, but the joy is
unextinguishable. Is not all well now? '*Ah, Madame,
notre bonne Reine*', said some of these Strong-women
some days hence, ' Ah, Madame, our good Queen, don't
be a traitor any more (*ne soyez plus traître*), and we will
all love you!' Poor Weber went splashing along,
close by the Royal carriage, with the tear in his eye:
'their Majesties did me the honour', or I thought they did
it, ' to testify, from time to time, by shrugging of the
shoulders, by looks directed to Heaven, the emotions
they felt'. Thus, like frail cockle, floats the royal Life-
boat, helmless, on black deluges of Rascality.

Mercier, in his loose way, estimates the Procession
and assistants at two hundred thousand. He says it
was one boundless inarticulate Haha ;—*transcendent*
World-Laughter; comparable to the Saturnalia of the
Ancients. Why not? Here too, as we said, is Human
Nature once more human; shudder at it whoso is of
shuddering humour: yet behold it is human. It has
' swallowed all formulas '; it tripudiates even so. For
which reason they that collect Vases and Antiques, with
figures of Dancing Bacchantes ' in wild and all but
impossible positions ', may look with some interest
on it.

Thus, however, has the slow-moving Chaos, or modern
Saturnalia of the Ancients, reached the Barrier; and
must halt, to be harangued by Mayor Bailly. Thereafter it has to lumber along, between the double row
of faces, in the transcendent heaven-lashing Haha;
two hours longer, towards the Hôtel-de-Ville. Then
again to be harangued there, by several persons; by
Moreau de Saint-Méry among others; Moreau of the
Three-thousand orders, now National Deputy for St.
Domingo. To all which poor Louis, ' who seemed to
experience a slight emotion ' on entering this Townhall,

[1] Toulongeon, i. 134–61; Deux Amis, iii. c. 9; &c. &c.

can answer only that he ' comes with pleasure, with
confidence among his people '.   Mayor Bailly, in reporting it, forgets ' confidence ' : and the poor Queen says
eagerly : ' Add, with confidence '.—' Messieurs ', rejoins
Mayor Bailly, ' you are happier than if I had not forgotten '.

Finally, the King is shown on an upper balcony, by
torchlight, with a huge tricolor in his hat : ' and all the
people ', says Weber, ' grasped one another's hand ' ;—
thinking *now* surely the New Era was born.   Hardly
till eleven at night can Royalty get to its vacant, long-
deserted Palace of the Tuileries ; to lodge there, somewhat in strolling-player fashion.   It is Tuesday the
sixth of October 1789.

Poor Louis has Two other Paris Processions to make
—one ludicrous-ignominious like this ; the other not
ludicrous nor ignominious, but serious, nay sublime.

PART II
THE CONSTITUTION

Mauern seh' ich gestürzt, und Mauern seh' ich errichtet,
  Hier Gefangene, dort auch der Gefangenen viel.
Ist vielleicht nur die Welt ein großer Kerker? Und frei ist
  Wohl der Tolle, der sich Ketten zu Kränzen erkiest?

Goethe*

BOOK I

THE FEAST OF PIKES

CHAPTER I

IN THE TUILERIES

THE victim having once got his stroke-of-grace, the catastrophe can be considered as almost come. There is small interest now in watching his long low moans : notable only are his sharper agonies, what convulsive struggles he may make to cast the torture off from him ; and then finally the last departure of life itself, and how he lies extinct and ended, either wrapt like Caesar in decorous mantle-folds, or unseemly sunk together, like one that had not the force even to die.

Was French Royalty, when wrenched forth from its tapestries in that fashion, on that Sixth of October 1789, such a victim ? Universal France, and Royal Proclamation to all the Provinces, answers anxiously, *No*. Nevertheless one may fear the worst. Royalty was beforehand so decrepit, moribund, there is little life in it to heal an injury. How much of its strength, which was of the imagination merely, has fled ; Rascality having looked plainly in the King's face, and not died !* When the assembled crows can pluck up their scarecrow, and say to it, Here shalt thou stand and not there ; and can treat with it, and make it, from an infinite, a quite finite Constitutional scarecrow,—what is to be looked for ? Not in the finite Constitutional scarecrow, but in what still unmeasured, infinite-seeming force may rally round it, is there thenceforth any hope. For it is most true that all available Authority is *mystic* in its conditions, and comes ' by the grace of God '.

Cheerfuller than watching the death-struggles of Royalism will it be to watch the growth and gambollings of Sansculottism ; for, in human things, especially in human society, all death is but a death-birth*: thus if the sceptre is departing from Louis, it is only that, in other forms, other sceptres, were it even pike-sceptres, may bear sway. In a prurient element, rich with nutritive influences, we shall find that Sansculottism grows lustily, and even frisks in not ungraceful sport : as indeed most young creatures are sportful ; nay, may it not be noted further, that as the grown cat, and cat-species generally, is the cruellest thing known, so the merriest is precisely the kitten, or growing cat ?

But fancy the Royal Family risen from its truckle-beds on the morrow of that mad day : fancy the Muni-cipal inquiry, ' How would your Majesty please to lodge ?'—and then that the King's rough answer, 'Each may lodge as he can, I am well enough', is congeed and bowed away, in expressive grins, by the Townhall Func-tionaries, with obsequious upholsterers at their back ; and how the Château of the Tuileries is repainted, regarnished into a golden Royal Residence ; and La-fayette with his blue National Guards lies encompassing it, as blue Neptune (in the language of poets) does an island, wooingly. Thither may the wrecks of rehabili-tated Loyalty gather, if it will become Constitutional; for Constitutionalism thinks no evil ;* Sansculottism itself rejoices in the King's countenance. The rubbish of a Menadic Insurrection, as in this ever-kindly world all rubbish can and must be, is swept aside ; and so again, on clear arena, under new conditions, with some-thing even of a new stateliness, we begin a new course of action.

Arthur Young has witnessed the strangest scene:
Majesty walking unattended in the Tuileries Gardens;
and miscellaneous tricolor crowds, who cheer it, and
reverently make way for it: the very Queen commands
at lowest respectful silence, regretful avoidance.[1]　Simple ducks, in those royal waters, quackle for crumbs
from young royal fingers: the little Dauphin has a little
railed garden, where he is seen delving, with ruddy
cheeks and flaxen curled hair; also a little hutch to
put his tools in, and screen himself against showers.
What peaceable simplicity! Is it peace of a Father
restored to his children? Or of a Taskmaster who has
lost his whip? Lafayette and the Municipality and
universal Constitutionalism assert the former, and do
what is in them to realize it. Such Patriotism as snarls
dangerously and shows teeth, Patrollotism shall suppress; or far better, Royalty shall soothe down the
angry hair of it, by gentle pattings; and, most effectual
of all, by fuller diet. Yes, not only shall Paris be fed,
but the King's hand be seen in that work. The household goods of the Poor shall, up to a certain amount,
by royal bounty, be disengaged from pawn, and that
insatiable *Mont de Piété**shall disgorge; rides in the
city with their *Vive-le-Roi* need not fail: and so by
substance and show, shall Royalty, if man's art can
popularize it, be popularized.[2*]

Or, alas, is it neither restored Father nor diswhipped
Taskmaster that walks there; but an anomalous complex of both these, and of innumerable other heterogeneities: reducible to no rubric, if not to this newly
devised one: *King Louis Restorer of French Liberty*?
Man indeed, and King Louis like other men, lives in
this world to make rule out of the ruleless;* by his
living energy, he shall force the absurd itself to become
less absurd. But then if there *be* no living energy;
living passivity only? King Serpent, hurled into its
unexpected watery dominion, did at least bite, and

[1]　Arthur Young's Travels, i. 264–80.
[2]　Deux Amis, iii. c. 10.

assert credibly that he was there : but as for the poor
King Log,* tumbled hither and thither as thousandfold
chance and other will than his might direct, how happy
for him that he was indeed wooden ; and, doing nothing,
could also see and suffer nothing! It is a distracted
business.

For his French Majesty, meanwhile, one of the worst
things is, that he can get no hunting.   Alas, no hunting
henceforth ; only a fatal being-hunted ! Scarcely, in
the next June weeks, shall he taste again the joys of the
game-destroyer ; in next June, and never more. He
sends for his smith-tools ; gives, in the course of the
day, official or ceremonial business being ended, ' a few
strokes of the file, *quelques coups de lime*'. [1] Innocent
brother mortal, why wert thou not an obscure substantial maker of locks ; but doomed in that other far-
seen craft, to be a maker only of world-follies, unreali-
ties ; things self-destructive, which no mortal hammering could rivet into coherence !

Poor Louis is not without insight, not even without
the elements of will ; some sharpness of temper, spurt-
ing at times from a stagnating character. If harmless
inertness could save him, it were well ; but he will
slumber and painfully dream, and to *do* aught is not
given him. Royalist Antiquarians still show the rooms
where Majesty and suite, in these extraordinary circumstances, had their lodging. Here sat the Queen ;
reading,—for she had her library brought hither, though
the King refused his ; taking vehement counsel of the
vehement uncounselled ; sorrowing over altered times ;
yet with sure hope of better : in her young rosy Boy
has she not the living emblem of hope ! It is a murky,
working sky ; yet with golden gleams—of dawn, or of
deeper meteoric night ? Here again this chamber, on
the other side of the main entrance, was the King's :
here his Majesty breakfasted, and did official work ;
here daily after breakfast he received the Queen ;

[1] Le Château des Tuileries, ou récit, &c., par Roussel (in
Hist. Parl. iv. 195–219).

sometimes in pathetic friendliness ; sometimes in human sulkiness, for flesh is weak ; and when questioned
about business, would answer : ' Madame, your business
is with the children '. Nay, Sire, were it not better you,
your Majesty's self, took the children ? So asks impartial History ; scornful that the *thicker* vessel*was
not also the stronger ; pity-struck for the porcelain-
clay of humanity*rather than for the tile-clay,—though
indeed *both* were broken !

So, however, in this Medicean Tuileries,* shall the
French King and Queen now sit for one-and-forty
months ; and see a wild-fermenting France work out
its own destiny, and theirs. Months bleak, ungenial,
of rapid vicissitude ; yet with a mild pale splendour,
here and there : as of an April that were leading to
leafiest Summer ; as of an October that led only to
everlasting Frost. Medicean Tuileries, how changed
since it was a peaceful Tile-field ! Or is the ground
itself fate-stricken, accursed ; an Atreus' Palace*; for
that Louvre window is still nigh, out of which a Capet,
whipt of the Furies, fired his signal of the Säint Bartho-
lemew ! Dark is the way of the Eternal as mirrored
in this world of Time : God's way is in the sea,* and His
path in the great deep.

CHAPTER II

IN THE SALLE DE MANÉGE

To believing Patriots, however, it is now clear, that
the Constitution will march, *marcher*,—had it once legs
to stand on. Quick, then, ye Patriots, bestir yourselves
and make it ; shape legs for it ! In the *Archevêché*, or
Archbishop's Palace, his Grace himself having fled ;
and afterwards in the Riding-hall, named Manége, close
on the Tuileries : there does a National Assembly apply
itself to the miraculous work. Successfully, had there
been any heaven-scaling Prometheus among them ; not

successfully, since there was none! There, in noisy
debate, for the sessions are occasionally ' scandalous ',
and as many as three speakers have been seen in the
Tribune at once,—let us continue to fancy it wearing
the slow months.

Tough, dogmatic, long of wind is Abbé Maury; Cice-
ronian pathetic is Cazalès. Keen-trenchant, on the
other side, glitters a young Barnave; abhorrent of
sophistry; sheering, like keen Damascus sabre, all
sophistry asunder,—reckless what else he sheer with it.
Simple seemest thou, O solid Dutch-built Pétion; if
solid, surely dull. Nor lifegiving is that tone of thine,
livelier polemical Rabaut. With ineffable serenity sniffs
great Sieyes, aloft, alone; his Constitution ye may
babble over, ye may mar, but can by no possibility
mend: is not Polity a science he has exhausted? Cool,
slow, two military Lameths are visible, with their
quality sneer, or demi-sneer; they shall gallantly re-
fund their Mother's Pension, when the Red Book is
produced; gallantly be wounded in duels. A Marquis
Toulongeon, whose Pen we yet thank, sits there; in
stoical meditative humour, oftenest silent, accepts
what Destiny will send. Thouret and Parlementary
Duport produce mountains of Reformed Law; liberal,
Anglomaniac; available and unavailable. Mortals rise
and fall. Shall goose Gobel,* for example,—or Göbel,
for he is of Strasburg German breed,—be a Constitutional Archbishop?

Alone of all men there, Mirabeau may begin to discern
clearly whither all this is tending. Patriotism, accordingly, regrets that his zeal seems to be getting cool. In
that famed Pentecost-Night of the Fourth of August,
when new Faith rose suddenly into miraculous fire, and
old Feudality was burnt up, men remarked that Mirabeau took no hand in it; that, in fact, he luckily happened to be absent. But did he not defend the *Veto*,
nay *Veto Absolu*; and tell vehement Barnave that six
hundred irresponsible senators would make of all tyran-
nies the insupportablest? Again, how anxious was he
that the King's Ministers should have seat and voice

in the National Assembly;—doubtless with an eye
to being Minister himself! Whereupon the National
Assembly decides, what is very momentous, that no
Deputy shall be Minister; he, in his haughty stormful
manner, advising us to make it, 'no deputy called
Mirabeau'.[1] A man of perhaps inveterate Feudalisms;
of stratagems; too often visible leanings towards the
Royalist side: a man suspect; whom Patriotism will
unmask! Thus, in these June days, when the question, *Who shall have right to declare war?* comes on, you
hear hoarse Hawkers sound dolefully through the streets,
'Grand Treason of Count Mirabeau, price only one
sou';—because he pleads that it shall be not the
Assembly, but the King! Pleads; nay prevails: for
in spite of the hoarse Hawkers, and an endless Populace
raised by them to the pitch even of '*Lanterne*', he
mounts the Tribune next day; grim-resolute; murmuring aside to his friends that speak of danger: 'I
know it: I must come hence either in triumph, or else
torn in fragments': and it was in triumph that he
came.

A man stout of heart; whose popularity is not of the
populace, '*pas populacière*'; whom no clamour of
unwashed mobs without doors, or of washed mobs
within, can scare from his way! Dumont remembers
hearing him deliver a Report on Marseilles; 'every
word was interrupted on the part of the *Côté Droit* by
abusive epithets; calumniator, liar, assassin, scoundrel
(*scélérat*): Mirabeau pauses a moment, and, in a honeyed
tone, addressing the most furious, says: "I wait, Messieurs, till these amenities be exhausted".'[2] A man
enigmatic, difficult to unmask! For example, whence
comes his money? Can the profit of a Newspaper,
sorely eaten into by Dame Le Jay; can this, and the
eighteen francs a-day your National Deputy has, be
supposed equal to this expenditure? House in the

---

[1] Moniteur, Nos. 65, 86 (29th September, 7th November,
1789).
[2] Dumont, Souvenirs, p. 278.

Chaussée d'Antin ; Country-house at Argenteuil ; splendours, sumptuosities, orgies ; living as if he had a mint !
All saloons, barred against Adventurer Mirabeau, are
flung wide-open to King Mirabeau, the cynosure of
Europe, whom female France flutters to behold,—
though the Man Mirabeau is one and the same. As for
money, one may conjecture that Royalism furnishes
it ; which if Royalism do, will not the same be welcome, as money always is to him ?

' Sold ', whatever Patriotism thinks, he cannot readily
be : the spiritual fire which is in that man ; which
shining through such confusions is nevertheless Conviction, and makes him strong, and without which he
had no strength,—is not buyable nor saleable ; in such
transference of barter, it would vanish and not *be*.
Perhaps ' paid and not sold, *payé pas vendu* ' : as poor
Rivarol, in the unhappier converse way, calls himself
' sold and not paid ' ! A man travelling, comet-like,
in splendour and nebulosity, his wild way ; whom tele-
scopic Patriotism may long watch, but, without higher
mathematics, will not make out. A questionable, most
blameable man ; yet to us the far notablest of all.
With rich munificence, as we often say, in a most
blinkered, bespectacled, logic-chopping generation,* Nature has gifted this man with an eye. Welcome is his
word, there where he speaks and works ; and growing
ever welcomer ; for it alone goes to the heart of the
business : logical cobwebbery shrinks itself together ;
and thou seest a *thing*, how it is, how it may be worked
with.

Unhappily our National Assembly has much to do :
a France to regenerate ; and France is short of so many
requisites, short even of cash. These same Finances
give trouble enough ; no choking of the Deficit ; which
gapes ever, *Give, give !* To appease the Deficit we venture on a hazardous step, sale of the Clergy's Lands
and superfluous Edifices ; most hazardous. Nay, given
the sale, who is to buy them, ready-money having fled ?
Wherefore, on the 19th day of December, a paper-money
of ' *Assignats* ', of Bonds secured, or *assigned*, on that

Clerico-National Property, and unquestionable at least
in payment of that,—is decreed : the first of a long
series of like financial performances, which shall astonish
mankind. So that now, while old rags last, there shall
be no lack of circulating medium : whether of commo-
dities to circulate thereon, is another question. But,
after all, does not this Assignat business speak volumes
for modern science ? Bankruptcy, we may say, was
come, as the *end* of all Delusions needs must come : yet
how gently, in softening diffusion, in mild succession,
was it hereby made to fall ;—like no all-destroying
avalanche ; like gentle showers of a powdery impalpable
snow, shower after shower, till all was indeed buried,
and yet little was destroyed that could not be replaced,
be dispensed with ! To such length has modern
machinery reached. Bankruptcy, we said, was great ;
but indeed Money itself is a standing miracle.

On the whole, it is a matter of endless difficulty,
that of the Clergy. Clerical property may be made
the Nation's, and the Clergy hired servants of the State ;
but if so, is it not an altered Church ? Adjustment
enough, of the most confused sort, has become unavoidable. Old landmarks, in any sense, avail not in a new
France. Nay literally, the very Ground is new divided ;
your old parti-coloured *Provinces* become new uniform
Departments Eighty-three in number ;—whereby, as in
some sudden shifting of the Earth's axis, no mortal
knows his new latitude at once. The Twelve old Parlements too, what is to be done with them ? The old
Parlements are declared to be all ' in permanent vacation ',—till once the new equal-justice, of Departmental
Courts, National Appeal-Court, of elective Justices,
Justices of Peace, and other Thouret-and-Duport apparatus be got ready. They have to sit there, these
old Parlements, uneasily waiting ; as it were, with the
rope round their neck ; crying as they can, *Is there
none to deliver us ?** But happily the answer being, *None,
none,* they are a manageable class, these Parlements.
They can be bullied, even, into silence ; the Paris Parlement, wiser than most, has never whimpered. They

will and must sit there ; in such vacation as is fit ; their
Chamber of Vacation distributes in the interim what
little justice is going. With the rope round their neck,
their destiny may be succinct ! On the 13th of November 1790, Mayor Bailly shall walk to the Palais de Justice, few even heeding him ; and with municipal seal-
stamp and a little hot wax, seal up the Parlementary
Paper-rooms,—and the dread Parlement of Paris pass
away, into Chaos, gently as does a Dream ! So shall
the Parlements perish, succinctly ; and innumerable
eyes be dry.

Not so the Clergy. For granting even that Religion
were dead ; that it had died, half-centuries ago, with
unutterable Dubois ; or emigrated lately to Alsace, with
Necklace-Cardinal Rohan ; or that it now walked as
goblin *revenant*, with Bishop Talleyrand of Autun ; yet
does not the shadow of Religion, the Cant of Religion,
still linger ? The Clergy have means and material :
means, of number, organization, social weight ; a
material, at lowest, of public ignorance, known to be
the mother of devotion.* Nay, withal, is it incredible
that there might, in simple hearts, latent here and
there like gold-grains in the mud-beach, still dwell some
real Faith in God, of so singular and tenacious a sort
that even a Maury or a Talleyrand could still be the
symbol for it ?—Enough, the Clergy has strength, the
Clergy has craft and indignation. It is a most fatal
business this of the Clergy. A weltering hydra-coil,
which the National Assembly has stirred up about its
ears ; hissing, stinging ; which cannot be appeased,
alive ; which cannot be trampled dead ! Fatal, from
first to last ! Scarcely after fifteen months' debating,
can a *Civil Constitution of the Clergy* be so much as got
to paper ; and then for getting it into reality ? Alas,
such Civil Constitution is but an agreement to disagree.
It divides France from end to end, with a new split,
infinitely complicating all the other splits :—Catholicism, what of it there is left, with the Cant of Catholicism, raging on the one side, and sceptic Heathenism
on the other ; both, by contradiction, waxing fanatic.

What endless jarring, of Refractory hated Priests, and
Constitutional despised ones ; of tender consciences,
like the King's, and consciences hot-seared, like certain
of his People's : the whole to end in Feasts of Reason
and a War of La Vendée !* So deep-seated is Religion
in the heart of man, and holds of all infinite passions.
If the dead echo of it still did so much, what could not
the living voice of it once do ?

Finance and Constitution, Law and Gospel : this
surely were work enough ; yet this is not all. In fact,
the Ministry, and Necker himself, whom a brass inscription, ' fastened by the people over his door-lintel ',
testifies to be the ' *Ministre adoré* ', are dwindling into
clearer and clearer nullity. Execution or legislation,
arrangement or detail, from their nerveless fingers all
drops undone ; all lights at last on the toiled shoulders
of an august Representative Body. Heavy-laden
National Assembly ! It has to hear of innumerable
fresh revolts, Brigand expeditions ; of Châteaus in the
West, especially of Charter-chests, *Chartiers*, set on fire ;
for there too the overloaded Ass frightfully recalcitrates.
Of Cities in the South full of heats and jealousies ; which
will end in crossed sabres, Marseilles against Toulon,
and Carpentras beleaguered by Avignon ;—of so much
Royalist collision in a career of Freedom ; nay of
Patriot collision, which a mere difference of *velocity* will
bring about ! Of a Jourdan Coup-tête, who has skulked
thitherward, to those southern regions, from the claws
of the Châtelet ; and will raise whole scoundrel-regi-
ments.

Also it has to hear of Royalist *Camp of Jalès* : Jalès
mountain-girdled Plain, amid the rocks of the Cevennes ;
whence Royalism, as is feared and hoped, may dash
down like a mountain deluge, and submerge France !
A singular thing this Camp of Jalès ; existing mostly
on paper. For the Soldiers at Jalès, being peasants or
National Guards, were in heart sworn Sansculottes ;
and all that the Royalist Captains could do was, with
false words, to keep them, or rather keep the report of
them, drawn up there, visible to all imaginations, for

a terror and a sign,—if peradventure France might be
re-conquered by theatrical machinery, by the *picture* of
a Royalist Army done to the life ! [1] Not till the third
summer was this portent, burning out by fits and then
fading, got finally extinguished ; was the old Castle of
Jalès, no Camp being visible to the bodily eye, got blown
asunder by some National Guards.

Also it has to hear not only of Brissot and his *Friends
of the Blacks*, but by and by of a whole St. Domingo*
blazing skyward ; blazing in literal fire, and in far worse
metaphorical ; beaconing the nightly main. Also of
the shipping interest, and the landed interest, and all
manner of interests, reduced to distress. Of Industry
everywhere manacled, bewildered ; and only Rebellion
thriving. Of sub-officers, soldiers, and sailors in mutiny
by land and water. Of soldiers, at Nanci, as we shall
see, needing to be cannonaded by a brave Bouillé. Of
sailors, nay the very galley-slaves, at Brest, needing
also to be cannonaded, but with no Bouillé to do it.
For indeed, to say it in a word, in those days there was
no King in Israel,* and every man did that which was
right in his own eyes. [2]

Such things has an august National Assembly to hear
of, as it goes on regenerating France. Sad and stern :
but what remedy ? Get the Constitution ready ; and
all men will swear to it : for do not ' Addresses of
adhesion ' arrive by the cartload ? In this manner, by
Heaven's blessing, and a Constitution got ready, shall
the bottomless fire-gulf be vaulted in, with rag-paper ;
and Order will wed Freedom, and live with her there,—
till it grow too hot for them. O *Côté Gauche*, worthy
are ye, as the adhesive Addresses generally say, to ' fix
the regards of the Universe ' ; the regards of this one
poor Planet, at lowest !—

[1] Dampmartin, Evénemens, i. 208.

[2] See Deux Amis, iii. c. 14 ; iv. c. 2, 3, 4, 7, 9, 14. Ex-
pédition des Volontaires de Brest sur Lannion ; Les Lyonnais Sauveurs des Dauphinois ; Massacre au Mans ; Troubles du Maine (Pamphlets and Excerpts in Hist. Parl. iii.
251 ; iv. 162–68), &c.

Nay, it must be owned, the *Cété Droit* makes a still
madder figure. An irrational generation; irrational,
imbecile, and with the vehement obstinacy characteristic of that; a generation which will not learn.
Falling Bastilles, Insurrections of Women, thousands of
smoking Manorhouses, a country bristling with no crop
but that of Sansculottic steel: these were tolerably
didactic lessons; but them they have not taught.
There are still men, of whom it was of old written,
Bray them in a mortar !* Or, in milder language, They
have *wedded* their delusions: fire nor steel, nor any
sharpness of Experience, shall sever the bond; till
death do us part! On such may the Heavens have
mercy; for the Earth, with her rigorous Necessity, will
have none.

Admit, at the same time, that it was most natural.
Man lives by Hope: Pandora, when her box of gods'-
gifts flew all out, and became gods'-curses, still retained
Hope. How shall an irrational mortal, when his high-
place is never so evidently pulled down, and he, being
irrational, is left resourceless,—part with the belief that
it will be rebuilt ? It would make all so straight again ;
it seems so unspeakably desirable ; so reasonable,—
would you but look at it aright ! For, must not the
thing which was continue to be ; or else the solid World
dissolve ? Yes, persist, O infatuated Sansculottes of
France ! Revolt against constituted Authorities ; hunt
out your rightful Seigneurs, who at bottom so loved
you, and readily shed their blood for you,—in country's
battles as at Rossbach and elsewhere ; and, even in
preserving game, were preserving *you*, could ye but have
understood it : hunt them out, as if they were wild
wolves ; set fire to their Châteaus and Chartiers as to
wolf-dens ; and what then ? Why, then turn every
man his hand against his fellow !* In confusion, famine,
desolation, regret the days that are gone ; rueful recall
them, recall us with them. To repentant prayers we
will not be deaf.

So, with dimmer or clearer consciousness, must the
Right Side reason and act. An inevitable position

perhaps ; but a most false one for them.   Evil, be thou
our good :   this henceforth must virtually be their
prayer.   The fiercer the effervescence grows, the sooner
will it pass ;   for, after all, it is but some mad effervescence ;   the World is solid, and cannot dissolve.

For the rest, if they have any positive industry, it is
that of plots, and backstairs conclaves.   Plots which
cannot be executed ;   which are mostly theoretic on
their part ;—for which nevertheless this and the other
practical Sieur Augeard, Sieur Maillebois, Sieur Bonne
Savardin, gets into trouble, gets imprisoned, and escapes
with difficulty.   Nay there is a poor practical Chevalier
Favras, who, not without some passing reflex on Monsieur himself, gets hanged for them, amid loud uproar
of the world.   Poor Favras, he keeps dictating his last
will ' at the Hôtel-de-Ville, through the whole remainder
of the day ', a weary February day ;   offers to reveal
secrets, if they will save him ;   handsomely declines
since they will not ;   then dies, in the flare of torchlight,
with politest composure ;   remarking, rather than exclaiming, with outspread hands :   ' People, I die innocent ;   pray for me '.[1]   Poor Favras ;—type of so much
that has prowled indefatigable over France, in days now
ending ;   and, in freer field, might have *earned* instead
of prowling,—to thee it is no theory !

In the Senate-house again, the attitude of the Right
Side is that of calm unbelief.   Let an august National
Assembly make a Fourth-of-August Abolition of Feudality ;   declare the Clergy State-servants, who shall have
wages ;   vote Suspensive Vetos, new Law-Courts ;   vote
or decree what contested thing it will ;   have it
responded to from the four corners of France, nay get
King's Sanction, and what other Acceptance were
conceivable,—the Right Side, as we find, persists, with
imperturbablest tenacity, in considering, and ever and
anon shows that it still considers, all these so-called
Decrees as mere temporary whims, which indeed stand
on paper, but in practice and fact are not, and cannot

[1] See Deux Amis, iv. c. 14, 7 ;   Hist. Parl. vi. 384.

be. Figure the brass head of an Abbé Maury flooding
forth jesuitic eloquence in this strain ; dusky D'Espréménil, Barrel Mirabeau (probably in liquor), and enough
of others, cheering him from the Right ; and, for example, with what visage a seagreen Robespierre eyes
him from the Left. And how Sieyes ineffably sniffs on
him, or does not deign to sniff ; and how the Galleries
groan in spirit, or bark rabid on him : so that to escape
the Lanterne, on stepping forth, he needs presence of
mind, and a pair of pistols in his girdle ! For he is one
of the toughest of men.

Here indeed becomes notable one great difference
between our two kinds of civil war ; between the
modern *lingual* or Parliamentary-logical kind, and the
ancient or *manual* kind in the steel battlefield ;—much
to the disadvantage of the former. In the manual
kind, where you front your foe with drawn weapon,
one right stroke is final ; for, physically speaking, when
the brains are out the man does honestly die, and trouble
you no more. But how different when it is with arguments you fight ! Here no victory yet definable can
be considered as final. Beat him down with Parliamentary invective, till sense be fled ; cut him in two,
hanging one half on this dilemma-horn, the other on
that ; blow the brains or thinking-faculty quite out
of him for the time : it skills not ; he rallies and revives
on the morrow ; to-morrow he repairs his golden fires !
The thing that *will* logically extinguish him is perhaps
still a desideratum in Constitutional civilization. For
how, till a man know, in some measure, at what point
he becomes logically defunct, can Parliamentary Business be carried on, and Talk cease or slake ?

Doubtless it was some feeling of this difficulty ; and
the clear insight how little such knowledge yet existed
in the French Nation, new in the Constitutional career,
and how defunct Aristocrats would continue to walk
for unlimited periods, as Partridge the Almanac-maker
did,—that had sunk into the deep mind of People's-
friend Marat, an eminently practical mind ; and had
grown there, in that richest putrescent soil, into the

most original plan of action ever submitted to a People.
Not yet has it grown ; but it has germinated, it is growing ; rooting itself into Tartarus, branching towards
Heaven : the second season hence, we shall see it risen
out of the bottomless Darkness, full grown, into disastrous Twilight,—a Hemlock-tree, great as the world;
on or under whose boughs all the People's-friends of the
world may lodge.   ' Two hundred and Sixty thousand
Aristocrat heads ' : that is the precisest calculation,
though one would not stand on a few hundreds ; yet
we never rise as high as the round three hundred thousand.   Shudder at it, O People ; but it is as true as
that ye yourselves, and your People's-friend, are alive.
These prating Senators of yours hover ineffectual on
the barren letter, and will never save the Revolution.
A Cassandra-Marat cannot do it, with his single shrunk
arm ; but with a few determined men it were possible.
' Give me ', said the People's-friend, in his cold way,
when young Barbaroux,* once his pupil in a course of
what was called Optics, went to see him, ' Give me two
hundred Naples Bravoes, armed each with a good dirk,
and a muff on his left arm by way of shield : with them
I will traverse France, and accomplish the Revolution '.[1]
Nay, be grave, young Barbaroux ; for thou seest, there
is no jesting in those rheumy eyes, in that soot-bleared
figure, most earnest of created things ; neither indeed
is there madness, of the strait-waistcoat sort.

Such produce shall the Time ripen in cavernous Marat,
the man forbid ; living in Paris cellars, lone as fanatic
Anchorite in his Thebaid*; say, as far-seen Simon*on his
Pillar,—taking peculiar views therefrom.   Patriots may
smile ; and, using him as bandog now to be muzzled,
now to be let bark, name him, as Desmoulins does,
' Maximum of Patriotism ' and ' Cassandra-Marat ' :
but were it not singular if this dirk-and-muff plan of his
(with superficial modifications) proved to be precisely
the plan adopted ?

After this manner, in these circumstances, do august

[1] Mémoires de Barbaroux (Paris, 1822), p. 57.

Senators regenerate France. Nay, they are, in very
deed, *believed* to be regenerating it; on account of
which great fact, main fact of their history, the wearied
eye can never be permitted wholly to ignore them.

But, looking away now from these precincts of the
Tuileries, where Constitutional Royalty, let Lafayette
water it as he will, languishes too like a cut branch;
and august Senators are perhaps at bottom only perfecting their ' theory of defective verbs ',—how does
the young Reality, young Sansculottism thrive ? The
attentive observer can answer: It thrives bravely ;
putting forth new buds ; expanding the old buds into
leaves, into boughs. Is not French Existence, as before,
most prurient, all *loosened*, most nutrient for it ?
Sansculottism has the property of growing by what
other things die of: by agitation, contention, disarrangement ; nay in a word, by what is the symbol and
fruit of all these : Hunger.

In such a France as this, Hunger, as we have remarked,
can hardly fail. The Provinces, the Southern Cities
feel it in their turn ; and what it brings : Exasperation,
preternatural Suspicion. In Paris some halcyon days
of abundance followed the Menadic Insurrection, with
its Versailles grain-carts, and recovered Restorer of
Liberty ; but they could not continue. The month is
still October, when famishing Saint-Antoine, in a moment of passion, seizes a poor Baker, innocent ' François
the Baker ' ; [1] and hangs him, in Constantinople wise ;
—but even this, singular as it may seem, does not
cheapen bread ! Too clear it is, no Royal bounty, no
Municipal dexterity can adequately feed a Bastille-
destroying Paris. Wherefore, on view of the hanged
Baker, Constitutionalism in sorrow and anger demands
' *Loi Martiale* ', a kind of Riot Act ;—and indeed gets
it most readily, almost before the sun goes down.

This is that famed *Martial Law*, with its Red Flag,
its ' *Drapeau Rouge* ', in virtue of which Mayor Bailly,
or any Mayor, has but henceforth to hang out that new

---

[1] 21st October 1789 (Moniteur, No. 76).

Oriflamme of his ; then to read or mumble something
about the King's peace ; and, after certain pauses,
serve any undispersing Assemblage with musket-shot,
or whatever shot will disperse it. A decisive Law ;
and most just on one proviso : that all Patrollotism be
of God, and all mob-assembling be of the Devil ;—
otherwise not so just. Mayor Bailly, be unwilling to
use it ! Hang not out that new Oriflamme,* *flame* not
of gold but of the want of gold ! The thrice-blessed
Revolution is *done*, thou thinkest ? If so, it will be
well with thee.

But now let no mortal say henceforth that an august
National Assembly wants riot : all it ever wanted was
riot enough to balance Court-plotting ; all it now wants,
of Heaven or of Earth, is to get its theory of defective
verbs perfected.

CHAPTER III

THE MUSTER

WITH Famine and a Constitutional theory of defective
verbs going on, all other excitement is conceivable. A
universal shaking and sifting of French Existence this
is : in the course of which, for one thing, what a multitude of low-lying figures are sifted to the top, and set
busily to work there !

Dogleech Marat, now far-seen as Simon Stylites, we
already know ; him and others, raised aloft. The mere
sample these, of what is coming, of what continues
coming, upwards from the realm of Night !—Chaumette,
by and by Anaxagoras Chaumette,* one already descries :
mellifluous in street-groups ; not now a seaboy on the
high and giddy mast* : a mellifluous tribune of the common people, with long curling locks, on *bourne*stone of
the thoroughfares ; able sub-editor too ; who shall rise,
—to the very gallows. Clerk Tallien,* he also is become
sub-editor ; shall become able-editor ; and more.

Bibliopolic Momoro, Typographic Prudhomme see new
trades opening. Collot d'Herbois, tearing a passion to
rags,* pauses on the Thespian boards ; listens, with that
black bushy head, to the sound of the world's drama:
shall the Mimetic become Real ? Did ye hiss him,
O men of Lyons ?[1] Better had ye clapped !

Happy now, indeed, for all manner of *mimetic*, half-
original men ! Tumid blustering, with more or less of
sincerity, which need not be entirely sincere, yet the
sincerer the better, is like to go far. Shall we say, the
Revolution-element works itself rarer and rarer ; so
that only lighter and lighter bodies will float in it ; till
at last the mere blown-bladder is your only swimmer ?
Limitation of mind, then vehemence, promptitude,
audacity, shall all be available ; to which add only
these two : cunning and good lungs. Good fortune
must be presupposed. Accordingly, of all classes the
rising one, we observe, is now the Attorney class : witness Bazires, Carriers, Fouquier-Tinvilles, Basoche-
Captain Bourdons : more than enough. Such figures
shall Night, from her wonder-bearing bosom, emit ;
swarm after swarm. Of another deeper and deepest
swarm, not yet dawned on the astonished eye ; of pilfer-
ing Candle-snuffers, Thief-valets, disfrocked Capuchins,
and so many Héberts, Henriots, Ronsins, Rossignols,*
let us, as long as possible, forbear speaking.

Thus, over France, all stirs that has what the Physio-
logists call *irritability* in it : how much more all
wherein irritability has perfected itself into vitality,
into actual vision, and force that can will ! All stirs ;
and if not in Paris, flocks thither. Great and greater
waxes President Danton in his Cordeliers Section ; his
rhetorical tropes are all 'gigantic' : energy flashes
from his black brows, menaces in his athletic figure,
rolls in the sound of his voice ' reverberating from the
domes' : this man also, like Mirabeau, has a natural
eye, and begins to see whither Constitutionalism is
tending, though with a wish in it different from Mirabeau's.

[1] Buzot, Mémoires (Paris, 1823), p. 90.

Remark, on the other hand, how General Dumouriez
has quitted Normandy and the Cherbourg Breakwater,
to come—whither we may guess. It is his second or
even third trial at Paris, since this New Era began;
but now it is in right earnest, for he has quitted all
else. Wiry, elastic, unwearied man; whose life was
but a battle and a march ! No, *not* a creature of
Choiseul's ; ' the creature of God and of my sword ',
—he fiercely answered in old days. Overfalling Corsican batteries, in the deadly fire-hail ; wriggling
invincible from under his horse, at Closterkamp of the
Netherlands, though tethered with ' crushed stirrup-
iron and nineteen wounds ' ; tough, minatory, standing
at bay, as forlorn hope, on the skirts of Poland ;
intriguing, battling in cabinet and field ; roaming far
out, obscure, as King's spial, or sitting sealed up,
enchanted in Bastille ; fencing, pamphleteering,
scheming and struggling from the very birth of him,[1]
—the man has come thus far. How repressed, how
irrepressible ! Like some incarnate spirit in prison,
which indeed he *was* ; hewing on granite walls for
deliverance : striking fire-flashes from them. And now
has the general earthquake rent his cavern too ?
Twenty years younger, what might he not have done !
But his hair has a shade of grey ; his way of thought
is all fixed, military. He can *grow* no further, and the
new world is in such growth. We will name him, on
the whole, one of Heaven's Swiss ; without faith ;
wanting above all things work, work on *any* side.
Work also is appointed him ; and he will do it.

Not from over France only are the unrestful flocking
towards Paris ; but from all sides of Europe. Where
the carcass is, thither will the eagles gather.* Think
how many a Spanish Guzman, Martinico Fournier
named ' Fournier *l'Américain* ', Engineer Miranda
from the very Andes, were flocking or had flocked.
Walloon Pereyra might boast of the strangest parent-

---

[1] Dumouriez, Mémoires, i. 28, &c.

age: him, they say, Prince Kaunitz the Diplomatist
heedlessly dropped; like ostrich-egg, to be hatched
of Chance,—into an ostrich-*eater*! Jewish or German
Freys do business in the great Cesspool of *Agio*; which
Cesspool this *Assignat*-fiat has quickened, into a Mother
of dead dogs. Swiss Clavière could found no Socinian
Genevese Colony in Ireland; but he paused, years ago,
prophetic, before the Minister's Hôtel at Paris; and
said, it was borne on his mind that *he* one day was to
be Minister, and laughed.[1] Swiss Pache,* on the other
hand, sits sleekheaded, frugal; the wonder of his own
alley, and even of neighbouring ones, for humility of
mind, and a thought deeper than most men's: sit
there, Tartuffe,* till wanted! Ye Italian Dufournys,
Flemish Prolys, flit hither all ye bipeds of prey! Come
whosesoever head is hot; thou of mind *ungoverned*, be
it chaos as of undevelopment or chaos as of ruin; the
man who cannot get known, the man who is too well
known; if thou have any vendible faculty, nay if thou
have but edacity and loquacity, come! They come;
with hot unutterabilities in their heart; as Pilgrims
towards a miraculous shrine. Nay how many come
as vacant Strollers, aimless, of whom Europe is full,
merely towards *something*! For benighted fowls, when
you beat their bushes, rush towards any light. Thus
Frederick Baron Trenck too is here; mazed, purblind,
from the cells of Magdeburg; Minotauric cells, and his
Ariadne lost! Singular to say, Trenck, in these years,
sells wine; not indeed in bottle, but in wood.

Nor is our England without her missionaries. She
has her life-saving Needham; [2] to whom was solemnly

---

[1] Dumont, Souvenirs sur Mirabeau, p. 399.
[2] A trustworthy gentleman writes to me, three years ago,
with a feeling which I cannot but respect, that his Father,
'the late Admiral Nesham' (not *Needham*, as the French
Journalists give it) is the Englishman meant; and furthermore that the sword is 'not rusted at all', but still lies,
with the due memory attached to it, in his (the son's)
possession, at Plymouth, in a clear state. (*Note of* 1857.)

presented a 'civic sword',—long since rusted into
nothingness. Her Paine:* rebellious Staymaker;
unkempt; who feels that he, a single Needleman, did,
by his *Common Sense* Pamphlet, free America;—that
he can and will free all this World; perhaps even
the other. Price-Stanhope Constitutional Association
sends over to congratulate; [1] welcomed by National
Assembly, though they are but a London Club; whom
Burke and Toryism eye askance.

On thee too, for country's sake, O Chevalier John
Paul, be a word spent, or misspent! In faded naval
uniform, Paul Jones lingers visible here; like a wine-
skin from which the wine is all drawn. Like the ghost
of himself! Low is his once loud bruit; scarcely
audible, save, with extreme tedium, in ministerial antechambers, in this or the other charitable dining-room,
mindful of the past. What changes; culminatings
and declinings! Not now, poor Paul, thou lookest
wistful over the Solway brine, by the foot of native
Criffel, into blue mountainous Cumberland, into blue
Infinitude; environed with thrift, with humble friendliness; thyself, young fool, longing to be aloft from it,
or even to be away from it. Yes, beyond that sapphire
Promontory, which men name St. Bees, which is not
sapphire either, but dull sandstone, when one gets *close*
to it, there is a world. Which world thou too shalt taste
of!—From yonder White Haven rise his smoke-clouds;
ominous though ineffectual. Proud Forth quakes at
his bellying sails; had not the wind suddenly shifted.
Flamborough reapers, homegoing, pause on the hill-
side: for what sulphur-cloud is that that defaces the
sleek sea; sulphur-cloud spitting streaks of fire? A
sea cockfight it is, and of the hottest; where British
Serapis and French-American *Bon Homme Richard* do
lash and throttle each other, in their fashion; and lo
the desperate valour has suffocated the deliberate, and
Paul Jones too is of the Kings of the Sea!

The Euxine, the Meotian waters felt thee next, and

[1] Moniteur, 10 Novembre, 7 Decembre, 1789.

long-skirted Turks, O Paul; and thy fiery soul has
wasted itself in thousand contradictions ;—to no purpose. For, in far lands, with scarlet Nassau-Siegens,
with sinful Imperial Catherines, is not the heart broken,
even as at home with the mean ? Poor Paul ! hunger
and dispiritment track thy sinking footsteps : once or
at most twice, in this Revolution-tumult the figure of
thee emerges ; mute, ghost-like, as 'with stars dim-
twinkling through '. And then, when the light is gone
quite out, a National Legislature grants 'ceremonial
funeral ' ! As good had been the natural Presbyterian
Kirk-bell, and six feet of Scottish earth, among the
dust of thy loved ones.—*Such* world lay beyond the
Promontory of St. Bees. Such is the life of sinful
mankind here below.

But of all strangers, far the notablest for us is Baron
Jean Baptiste de Clootz*;—or, dropping baptisms and
feudalisms, World-Citizen Anacharsis Clootz, from
Cleves. Him mark, judicious Reader. Thou hast
known his Uncle, sharp-sighted thoroughgoing Cornelius de Pauw, who mercilessly cuts down cherished
illusions ; and of the finest antique Spartans will make
mere modern cut-throat Mainots.[1] The like stuff is in
Anacharsis : hot metal; full of scoriae, which should
and could have been smelted out, but which will not.
He has wandered over this terraqueous Planet ; seeking, one may say, the Paradise we lost long ago. He
has seen English Burke ; has been seen of the Portugal
Inquisition ; has roamed, and fought, and written ; is
writing, among other things, ' Evidences of the *Mahometan* Religion '. But now, like his Scythian adoptive
godfather, he finds himself in the Paris Athens ; surely,
at last, the haven of his soul. A dashing man, beloved
at Patriotic dinner-tables ; with gaiety, nay with
humour ; headlong, trenchant, of free purse ; in suitable costume ; though what mortal ever more despised
costumes ? Under all costumes Anacharsis seeks the

---

[1] De Pauw, Recherches sur les Grecs, &c.

man; not Stylites Marat will more freely trample
costumes, if they hold no man. This is the faith of
Anacharsis: That there is a Paradise discoverable;
that all costumes ought to hold men. O Anacharsis,
it is a headlong, swift-going faith. Mounted thereon,
meseems, thou art bound hastily for the City of *Nowhere*;
and wilt *arrive*! At best, we may say, arrive *in good
riding attitude*; which indeed is something.

So many new persons and new things have come
to occupy this France. Her old Speech and Thought,
and Activity which springs from these, are all changing;
fermenting towards unknown issues. To the dullest
peasant, as he sits sluggish, overtoiled, by his evening
hearth, one idea has come: that of Châteaus burnt;
of Châteaus combustible. How altered all Coffee-
houses, in Province or Capital! The *Antre de Procopé*
has now other questions than the Three Stagyrite Unities
to settle; not theatre-controversies, but a world-con-
troversy: there, in the ancient pigtail mode, or with
modern Brutus' heads, do well-frizzed logicians hold
hubbub, and Chaos umpire sits. The ever-enduring
melody of Paris Saloons has got a new ground-tone:
ever-enduring; which has been heard, and by the
listening Heaven too, since Julian the Apostate's time
and earlier; mad now as formerly.

Ex-Censor Suard, *Ex*-Censor, for we have freedom of
the Press; he may be seen there; impartial, even
neutral. Tyrant Grimm rolls large eyes, over a questionable coming Time. Atheist Naigeon, beloved-
disciple of Diderot, crows, in his small difficult way,
heralding glad dawn.[1] But on the other hand, how
many Morellets, Marmontels, who had sat all their life
hatching Philosophe eggs, cackle now, in a state bor-
dering on distraction, at the brood they have brought
out![2] It was so delightful to have one's Philosophe

[1] Naigeon, Adresse à l'Assemblée Nationale (Paris, 1790),
sur la liberté des opinions.

[2] See Marmontel, Mémoires, *passim*; Morellet, Mémoires,
&c.

Theorem demonstrated, crowned in the saloons : and now an infatuated people will not continue speculative, but have Practice ?

There also observe Preceptress Genlis,* or Sillery, or Sillery-Genlis,—for our husband is both Count and Marquis, and we have more than one title.   Pretentious, frothy ; a puritan yet creedless ; darkening counsel by words without wisdom !   For, it is in that thin element of the Sentimentalist and Distinguished-Female that Sillery-Genlis works ; she would gladly be sincere, yet can grow no sincerer thanr sincere-cant : sincere-cant of many forms, ending in the devotional form.   For the present, on a neck still of moderate whiteness, she wears as jewel a miniature Bastille, cut on mere sandstone, but then actual Bastille sandstone.   M. le Marquis is one of D'Orléans's errandmen ; in National Assembly, and elsewhere.   Madame, for her part, trains up a youthful D'Orléans generation in what superfinest morality one can ; gives meanwhile rather enigmatic account of fair Mademoiselle Pamela, the Daughter whom she has *adopted*.   Thus she, in Palais Royal saloon ; —whither, we remark, D'Orléans himself, spite of Lafayette, has returned from that English ' mission ' of his : surely no pleasant mission : for the English would not speak to him ; and Saint Hannah More* of England, so unlike Saint Sillery-Genlis of France, saw him shunned, in Vauxhall Gardens, like one peststruck,[1] and his red-blue impassive visage waxing hardly a shade bluer.

    [1] Hannah More's Life and Correspondence, ii. c. 5.

CHAPTER IV

JOURNALISM

As for Constitutionalism, with its National Guards,
it is doing what it can ; and has enough to do : it must,
as ever, with one hand wave persuasively, repressing
Patriotism ; and keep the other clenched to menace
Royalist plotters. A most delicate task ; requiring
tact.

Thus, if People's-friend Marat has to-day his writ
of ' *prise de corps*, or seizure of body ', served on him,
and dives out of sight, to-morrow he is left at large; or
is even encouraged, as a sort of bandog whose baying
may be useful. President Danton, in open Hall, with
reverberating voice, declares that, in a case like Marat's,
' force may be resisted by force '. Whereupon the
Châtelet serves Danton also with a writ ;—which however, as the whole Cordeliers District responds to it,
what Constable will be prompt to execute ? Twice
more, on new occasions, does the Châtelet launch its
writ ; and twice more in vain : the body of Danton
cannot be seized by Châtelet ; he unseized, should he
even fly for a season, shall behold the Châtelet itself
flung into limbo.

Municipality and Brissot, meanwhile, are far on with
their Municipal Constitution. The Sixty *Districts* shall
become Forty-eight *Sections* ; much shall be adjusted,
and Paris have its Constitution. A Constitution wholly
Elective ; as indeed all French Government shall and
must be. And yet, one fatal element has been introduced : that of *citoyen actif*. No man who does not
pay the *marc d'argent*, or yearly tax equal to three days'
labour, shall be other than a *passive* citizen : not the
slightest vote for him ; were he *acting*, all the year
round, with sledge-hammer, with forest-levelling axe !
Unheard of ! cry Patriot Journals. Yes truly, my
Patriot Friends, if Liberty, the passion and prayer of

all men's souls, means Liberty to send your fifty-
thousandth part of a new Tongue-fencer into National
Debating-club, then, be the gods witness, ye are hardly
entreated. Oh, if in National *Palaver**(as the Africans
name it), such blessedness is verily found, what tyrant
would deny it to Son of Adam ! Nay, might there not
be a Female Parliament too, with 'screams from the
Opposition benches', and 'the honourable Member
borne out in hysterics' ? To a Children's Parliament
would I gladly consent ; or even lower if ye wished it.
Beloved Brothers ! Liberty, one may fear, is actually,
as the ancient wise man said, of Heaven.* On this
Earth, where, thinks the enlightened public, did a brave
little Dame de Staal (not Necker's Daughter, but a
far shrewder than she) find the nearest approach to
Liberty? After mature computation, cool as Dilworth's,*
her answer is, *In the Bastille.*[1] 'Of Heaven ?' answer
many, asking. Woe that they should *ask* ; for that is
the very misery ! 'Of Heaven' means much ; share
in the National Palaver it may, or may as probably
not mean.

One Sansculottic bough that cannot fail to flourish
is Journalism. The voice of the People *being* the voice
of God, shall not such divine voice make itself heard ?
To the ends of France ; and in as many dialects as when
the *first* great Babel was to be built ! Some loud as
the lion ; some small as the sucking dove.* Mirabeau
himself has his instructive Journal or Journals, with
Geneva hodmen working in them ; and withal has
quarrels enough with Dame le Jay, his Female Bookseller, so ultra-compliant otherwise.[2]

King's-friend Royou still prints himself. Barrère
sheds tears of loyal sensibility in *Break of Day* Journal,
though with declining sale. But why is Fréron*so hot,
democratic ; Fréron, the King's-friend's Nephew ?
He has it by kind, that heat of his : *wasp* Fréron begot
him ; Voltaire's *Frélon* ; who fought stinging, while

[1] De Staal, Mémoires (Paris, 1821), i. 169–280.
[2] Dumont, Souvenirs, 6.

sting and poison-bag were left, were it only as Reviewer,
and over Printed Waste-paper. Constant,* illuminative,
as the nightly lamplighter, issues the useful *Moniteur*,
for it is now become diurnal : with facts and few commentaries ; official, safe in the middle*;—its able Editors
sunk long since, recoverably or irrecoverably, in deep
darkness. Acid Loustalot, with his ' vigour ', as of
young sloes, shall never ripen, but die untimely : his
Prudhomme, however, will not let that *Révolutions de
Paris* die ; but edit it himself, with much else,—dull-
blustering Printer though he be.

Of Cassandra-Marat we have spoken often ; yet the
most surprising truth remains to be spoken : that he
actually does not want sense ; but, with croaking gelid
throat, croaks out masses of the truth, on several things.
Nay sometimes, one might almost fancy he had a per-
ception of humour, and were laughing a little, far down
in his inner man. Camille is wittier than ever, and
more outspoken, cynical ; yet sunny as ever. A light
melodious creature ; ' born ', as he shall yet say with
bitter tears, ' to write verses ' ; light Apollo, so clear,
soft-lucent, in this war of the Titans, wherein he shall
not conquer !

Folded and hawked Newspapers exist in all countries ;
but, in such a Journalistic element as this of France,
other and stranger sorts are to be anticipated. What
says the English reader to a *Journal-Affiche*, Placard
Journal ; legible to him that has no halfpenny ; in
bright prismatic colours, calling the eye from afar ?
Such, in the coming months, as Patriot Associations,
public and private, advance, and can subscribe funds,
shall plenteously hang themselves out : *leaves*, limed
leaves, to catch what they can ! The very Government
shall have its Pasted Journal ; Louvet, busy yet with
a new ' charming romance ', shall write *Sentinelles*, and
post them with effect ; nay Bertrand de Moleville, in
his extremity, shall still more cunningly try it.[1] Great
is Journalism. Is not every Able Editor a Ruler of the

---

[1] See Bertrand-Moleville, Mémoires, ii. 100, &c.

World, being a persuader of it; though self-elected,
yet sanctioned, by the sale of his Numbers ? Whom
indeed the world has the readiest method of deposing,
should need be : that of merely doing *nothing* to him ;
which ends in starvation.

Nor esteem it small what those Bill-stickers had to
do in Paris : above Three-score of them : all with their
crosspoles, haversacks, pastepots ; nay with leaden
badges, for the Municipality licenses them. A Sacred
College, properly of World-rulers' Heralds, though not
respected as such, in an Era still incipient and raw.
They made the walls of Paris didactic, suasive, with
an ever fresh Periodical Literature, wherein he that ran
might read*: Placard Journals, Placard Lampoons,
Municipal Ordinances, Royal Proclamations ; the whole
other or vulgar Placard-department superadded,—or
omitted from contempt ! What unutterable things the
stone-walls spoke, during these five years ! But it is
all gone ; To-day swallowing Yesterday,* and then being
in its turn swallowed of To-morrow, even as Speech
ever is. Nay what, O thou immortal Man of Letters,
is Writing itself but Speech conserved for a time ?
The Placard Journal conserved it for one day ; some
Books conserve it for the matter of ten years ; nay
some for three thousand : but what then ? Why, *then*,
the years being all run, it also dies, and the world is rid
of it. Oh, were there not a spirit in the word of man,
as in man himself, that survived the audible bodied
word, and tended either Godward, or else Devilward,
for evermore, why should he trouble himself much
with the truth of it, or the falsehood of it, except for
commercial purposes ? His immortality indeed, and
whether it shall last half a lifetime or a lifetime and a
half ; is not that a very considerable thing ? Immortality, mortality :—there were certain runaways whom
Fritz the Great bullied back into the battle with a :
' R—, *wollt ihr ewig leben*, Unprintable Offscouring of
Scoundrels, would ye live for ever ! '

This is the Communication of Thought ; how happy
when there is any Thought to communicate ! Neither

let the simpler old methods be neglected, in their sphere.
The Palais-Royal Tent, a tyrannous Patrollotism has
removed; but can it remove the lungs of man?
Anaxagoras Chaumette we saw mounted on bournes-
stones, while Tallien worked sedentary at the sub-
editorial desk. In any corner of the civilized world,
a tub can be inverted, and an articulate-speaking biped
mount thereon. Nay, with contrivance, a portable
trestle, or folding-stool, can be procured, for love or
money; this the peripatetic Orator can take in his
hand, and, driven out here, set it up again there: saying mildly, with a Sage Bias, *Omnia mea mecum porto*.[*]

Such is Journalism, hawked, pasted, spoken. How
changed since One old Metra walked this same Tuileries
Garden, in gilt cocked hat, with Journal at his nose,
or held loose-folded behind his back; and was a notability of Paris, ' Metra the Newsman';[1] and Louis
himself was wont to say: *Qu'en dit Métra?* Since the
first Venetian News-sheet was sold for a *gazza*, or
farthing, and named *Gazette*! We live in a fertile
world.

CHAPTER V

CLUBBISM

WHERE the heart is full,[*] it seeks, for a thousand
reasons, in a thousand ways, to impart itself. How
sweet, indispensable, in such cases, is fellowship; soul
mystically strengthening soul! The meditative Germans, some think, have been of opinion that Enthusiasm in general means simply excessive Congregating
—*Schwärmerey*, or *Swarming*. At any rate, do we not
see glimmering half-red embers, if laid *together*, get into
the brightest white glow?

In such a France, gregarious Reunions will needs

---

[1] Dulaure, Histoire de Paris, viii. 483; Mercier, Nouveau
Paris, &c.

multiply, intensify ; French Life will step out of doors,
and, from domestic, become a public Club Life. Old
Clubs, which already germinated, grow and flourish ;
new everywhere bud forth. It is the sure symptom
of Social Unrest : in such way, most infallibly of all,
does Social Unrest exhibit itself ; find solacement, and
also nutriment. In every French head there hangs
now, whether for terror or for hope, some prophetic
picture of a New France : prophecy which brings, nay
which almost *is*, its own fulfilment ; and in all ways,
consciously and unconsciously, works towards that.

Observe, moreover, how the Aggregative Principle, let
it be but deep enough, goes on aggregating, and this
even in a geometrical progression ; how when the
whole world, in such a plastic time, is forming itself
into Clubs, some One Club, the strongest or luckiest,
shall by friendly attracting, by victorious compelling,
grow ever stronger, till it become immeasurably strong ;
and all the others, with their strength, be either
lovingly absorbed into it, or hostilely abolished by it.
This if the Club-spirit is universal ; if the time *is* plastic.
Plastic enough is the time, universal the Club-spirit :
such an all-absorbing, paramount One Club cannot be
wanting.

What a progress, since the first salient-point of the
Breton Committee ! It worked long in secret, not
languidly ; it has come with the National Assembly
to Paris ; calls itself *Club* ; calls itself, in imitation, as
is thought, of those generous Price-Stanhope English
who sent over to congratulate, *French Revolution Club* ;
but soon, with more originality, *Club of Friends of the
Constitution*. Moreover it has leased for itself, at a fair
rent, the Hall of the Jacobins Convent, one of our
' superfluous edifices ' ; and does therefrom now, in
these spring months, begin shining out on an admiring
Paris. And so, by degrees, under the shorter popular
title of *Jacobins Club*, it shall become memorable to
all times and lands. Glance into the interior : strongly
yet modestly benched and seated ; as many as Thirteen
Hundred chosen Patriots ; Assembly Members not

a few. Barnave, the two Lameths are seen there;
occasionally Mirabeau, perpetually Robespierre; also
the ferret-visage of Fouquier-Tinville with other
attorneys; Anacharsis of Prussian Scythia, and miscellaneous Patriots,—though all is yet in the most
perfectly cleanwashed state; decent, nay dignified.
President on platform, President's bell are not wanting;
oratorical Tribune high-raised; nor strangers' galleries,
wherein also sit women. Has any French Antiquarian
Society preserved that written Lease of the Jacobins
Convent Hall ? Or was it, unluckier even than Magna
Charta, *clipt**by sacrilegious Tailors ? Universal History is not indifferent to it.

These Friends of the Constitution have met mainly,
as their name may foreshadow, to look after Elections
when an Election comes, and procure fit men : but
likewise to consult generally that the Commonweal
take no damage ; one as yet sees not how. For indeed
let two or three gather together anywhere, if it be not
in Church, where all are bound to the *passive* state ;
no mortal can say accurately, themselves as little as
any, for *what* they are gathered. How often has the
broached barrel proved not to be for joy and heart-
effusion, but for duel and head-breakage ; and the
promised feast become a Feast of the Lapithae !* This
Jacobins Club, which at first shone resplendent, and
was thought to be a new celestial Sun for enlightening
the Nations, had, as things all have, to work through
its appointed phases : it burned unfortunately more
and more lurid, more sulphurous, distracted ;—and
swam at last, through the astonished Heaven, like
a Tartarean Portent, and lurid-burning Prison of Spirits
in Pain.

Its style of eloquence ? Rejoice, Reader, that thou
knowest it not, that thou canst never perfectly know.
The Jacobins published a Journal of Debates, where
they that have the heart may examine : impassioned,
dull-droning Patriotic-eloquence ; implacable, unfertile
—save for Destruction, which was indeed its work :

most wearisome, though most deadly. Be thankful
that Oblivion covers so much ; that all carrion is by
and by buried in the green Earth's bosom, and even
makes her grow the greener. The Jacobins are buried ;
but their work is not ; it continues ' making the tour
of the world ', as it can. It might be seen lately, for
instance, with bared bosom and death-defiant eye, as
far on as Greek Missolonghi*; strange enough, old
slumbering Hellas was resuscitated, into *somnambulism*
which will become clear wakefulness, by a voice from
the Rue St. Honoré ! All dies, as we often say ; except
the spirit of man, of what man *does*. Thus has not the
very House of the Jacobins vanished : scarcely lingering
in a few old men's memories ? The St. Honoré Market
has brushed it away, and now where dull-droning
eloquence, like a Trump of Doom, once shook the world,
there is pacific chaffering for poultry and greens. The
sacred National Assembly Hall itself has become common ground ; President's platform permeable to wain
and dustcart ; for the Rue de Rivoli runs there. Verily,
at Cockcrow (of this Cock or the other), *all* Apparitions
do melt and dissolve in space.

The Paris *Jacobins* became ' the Mother-Society,
Société-Mère ' ; and had as many as ' three hundred '
shrill-tongued daughters in ' direct correspondence '
with her. Of indirectly corresponding, what we may
call grand-daughters and minute progeny, she counted
' forty-four thousand ' !—But for the present we note
only two things : the first of them a mere anecdote.
One night, a couple of brother Jacobins are door-keepers;
for the members take this post of duty and honour in
rotation, and admit none that have not tickets : one
door-keeper was the worthy Sieur Laïs, a patriotic
Opera-singer, stricken in years, whose windpipe is long
since closed without result ; the other, young, and
named Louis Philippe,* D'Orléans's firstborn, has in
this latter time, after unheard-of destinies, become
Citizen-King, and struggles to rule for a season. All
flesh is grass ;* higher reedgrass or creeping herb.

The second thing we have to note is historical : that

the Mother-Society, even in this its effulgent period,
cannot content all Patriots. Already it must throw
off, so to speak, two dissatisfied swarms ; a swarm to
the right, a swarm to the left. One party, which thinks
the Jacobins lukewarm, constitutes itself into *Club of
the Cordeliers* ; a hotter Club : it is Danton's element ;
with whom goes Desmoulins. The other party, again,
which thinks the Jacobins scalding-hot, flies off to the
right, and becomes ' Club of 1789, Friends of the
Monarchic Constitution '. They are afterwards named
' *Feuillans Club* ' ; their place of meeting being the
Feuillans Convent. Lafayette is, or becomes, their
chief man ; supported by the respectable Patriot
everywhere, by the mass of Property and Intelligence,
—with the most flourishing prospects. They, in these
June days of 1790, do, in the Palais Royal, dine solemnly
with open windows ; to the cheers of the people ; with
toasts, with inspiriting songs,—with one song at least,
among the feeblest ever sung.[1] They shall, in due time,
be hooted forth, over the borders, into Cimmerian
Night.

Another expressly Monarchic or Royalist Club, ' *Club
des Monarchiens* ', though a Club of ample funds, and
all sitting on damask sofas, cannot realize the smallest
momentary cheer : realizes only scoffs and groans ;—
till, ere long, certain Patriots in disorderly sufficient
number, proceed thither, for a night or for nights, and
groan it out of pain. Vivacious alone shall the Mother-
Society and her family be. The very Cordeliers may,
as it were, return into her bosom, which will have
grown warm enough.

Fatal-looking ! Are not such Societies an incipient New Order of Society itself ? The Aggregative
Principle anew at work in a Society grown obsolete,
cracked asunder, dissolving into rubbish and primary
atoms ?

[1] Hist. Parl. vi. 334.

CHAPTER VI

JE LE JURE

WITH these signs of the times, is it not surprising
that the dominant feeling all over France was still
continually Hope ? O blessed Hope, sole boon of man :
whereby, on his strait prison-walls, are painted beautiful far-stretching landscapes ; and into the night of
very Death is shed holiest dawn ! Thou art to all an
indefeasible possession in this God's-world ; to the
wise a sacred Constantine's-banner,* written on the
eternal skies ; under which they *shall* conquer, for the
battle itself is victory : to the foolish some secular
mirage, or shadow of still waters,* painted on the parched
Earth ; whereby at least their dusty pilgrimage, if
devious, becomes cheerfuller, becomes possible.

In the death-tumults of a sinking Society, French
Hope sees only the birth-struggles of a new unspeakably
better Society ; and sings, with full assurance of faith,
her brisk Melody, which some inspired fiddler has in
these very days composed for her,—the world-famous
Ça-ira. Yes ; ' that will go ' : and then there will
come— ? All men hope ; even Marat hopes—that
Patriotism will take muff and dirk. King Louis is not
without hope : in the chapter of chances ; in a flight
to some Bouillé ; in getting popularized at Paris. But
what a hoping People he had, judge by the fact, and
series of facts, now to be noted.

Poor Louis, meaning the best, with little insight and
even less determination of his own, has to follow, in that
dim wayfaring of his, such signal as may be given him ;
by backstairs Royalism, by official or backstairs Constitutionalism, whichever for the month may have
convinced the royal mind. If flight to Bouillé, and
(horrible to think !) a *drawing* of the civil sword do
hang as theory, portentous in the background, much
nearer is this fact of these Twelve Hundred Kings, who

sit in the *Salle de Manége.* Kings uncontrollable by
him, not yet irreverent to him. Could kind management of these but prosper, how much better were it
than armed Emigrants, Turin intrigues, and the help
of Austria ! Nay, are the *two* hopes inconsistent ?
Rides in the suburbs, we have found, cost little ; yet
they always brought *vivats.*[1] Still cheaper is a soft
word ;* such as has many times turned away wrath.
In these rapid days, while France is all getting divided
into Departments, Clergy about to be remodelled,
Popular Societies rising, and Feudalism and so much
else is ready to be hurled into the melting-pot,—might
one not try ?

On the 4th of February, accordingly, M. le Président
reads to his National Assembly a short autograph,
announcing that his Majesty will step over, quite in an
unceremonious way, probably about noon. Think,
therefore, Messieurs, what it may mean ; especially,
how ye will get the Hall decorated a little. The Secretaries' Bureau can be shifted down from the platform ;
on the President's chair be slipped this cover of velvet,
' of a violet colour sprigged with gold fleur-de-lis ' ;—
for indeed M. le Président has had previous notice
underhand, and taken counsel with Doctor Guillotin.
Then some fraction of ' velvet carpet ', of like texture
and colour, cannot that be spread in front of the chair,
where the Secretaries usually sit ? So has judicious
Guillotin advised : and the effect is found satisfactory.
Moreover, as it is probable that his Majesty, in spite of
the fleur-de-lis velvet, will stand and not sit at all, the
President himself, in the interim, presides standing.
And so, while some honourable Member is discussing,
say, the division of a Department, Ushers announce :
' His Majesty ' ! In person, with small suite, enter
Majesty : the honourable Member stops short ; the
Assembly starts to its feet : the Twelve Hundred Kings
' almost all ', and the Galleries no less, do welcome the
Restorer of French Liberty with loyal shouts. His

---

[1] See Bertrand-Moleville, i. 241, &c.

Majesty's Speech, in diluted conventional phraseology,
expresses this mainly : That he, most of all Frenchmen,
rejoices to see France getting regenerated ; is sure, at
the same time, that they will deal gently with her in
the process, and not regenerate her *roughly*. Such was
his Majesty's Speech: the feat he performed was
coming to speak it, and going back again.

Surely, except to a very hoping People, there was
not much here to build upon. Yet what did they not
build ! The fact that the King has spoken, that he
has voluntarily come to speak, how inexpressibly
encouraging ! Did not the glance of his royal countenance, like concentrated sunbeams, kindle all hearts
in an august Assembly ; nay thereby in an inflammable
enthusiastic France ? To move 'Deputation of thanks',
can be the happy lot of but one man ; to go in such
Deputation the lot of not many. The Deputed have
gone, and returned with what highest-flown compliment
they could ; whom also the Queen met, Dauphin in
hand. And still do not our hearts burn with insatiable
gratitude ; and to one other man a still higher blessedness suggests itself : To move that we all renew the
National Oath.

Happiest honourable Member, with his word so in
season as word seldom was ; magic Fugleman of a whole
National Assembly, which sat there bursting to do
somewhat ; Fugleman of a whole onlooking France !
The President swears ; declares that every one shall
swear, in distinct *je le jure*. Nay the very gallery sends
him down a written slip signed, with their Oath on it ;
and as the Assembly now casts an eye that way, the
Gallery all stands up and swears again. And then out
of doors, consider at the Hôtel-de-Ville how Bailly, the
great Tennis-Court swearer, again swears, towards
nightfall, with all the Municipals, and Heads of Districts
assembled there. And ' M. Danton suggests that the
public would like to partake ' : whereupon Bailly, with
escort of Twelve, steps forth to the great outer staircase ; sways the ebullient multitude with stretched
hand ; takes their oath, with a thunder of ' rolling

drums ', with shouts that rend the welkin. And on all
streets the glad people, with moisture and fire in their
eyes, ' spontaneously formed groups, and swore one
another ',[1]—and the whole City was illuminated. This
was the Fourth of February 1790 : a day to be marked
white* in Constitutional annals.

Nor is the illumination for a night only, but partially
or totally it lasts a series of nights. For each District,
the Electors of each District will swear specially ; and
always as the District swears, it illuminates itself.
Behold them, District after District, in some open
square, where the Non-Electing People can all see and
join : with their uplifted right-hands, and *je le jure* ;
with rolling drums, with embracings, and that infinite
hurrah of the enfranchised,—which any tyrant that
there may be can consider ! Faithful to the King, to
the Law, to the Constitution which the National
Assembly *shall* make.

Fancy, for example, the Professors of Universities
parading the streets with their young France, and
swearing, in an enthusiastic manner, not without tumult.
By a larger exercise of fancy, expand duly this little
word : The like was repeated in every Town and
District in France ! Nay one Patriot Mother, in
Lagnon of Brittany, assembles her ten children ; and,
with her own aged hand, swears them all herself, the
high-souled venerable woman. Of all which, moreover,
a National Assembly must be eloquently apprised.
Such three weeks of swearing ! Saw the Sun ever such
a swearing people ? Have they been bit by a swearing
tarantula ? No : but they are men and Frenchmen ;
they have Hope ; and, singular to say, they have Faith,
were it only in the Gospel according to Jean Jacques.
O my Brothers, would to Heaven it were even as ye
think and have sworn ! But there are Lover's Oaths,
which, had they been true as love itself, *cannot* be kept ;
not to speak of Dicer's Oaths,* also a known sort.

---

[1] Newspapers (in Hist. Parl. iv. 445).

CHAPTER VII

PRODIGIES

To such length had the *Contrat Social* brought it, in
believing hearts. Man, as is well said, lives by faith ;
each generation has its own faith, more or less ; and
laughs at the faith of its predecessor,—most unwisely.
Grant indeed that this faith in the Social Contract
belongs to the stranger sorts ; that an unborn generation may very wisely, if not laugh, yet stare at it, and
piously consider. For, alas, what is *Contrat* ? If all
men were such that a mere spoken or sworn Contract
would bind them, all men were then true men, and
Government a superfluity. Not what thou and I have
promised to each other, but what the balance of our
forces can make us perform to each other : that, in so
sinful a world as ours, is the thing to be counted on.
But above all, a People and a Sovereign promising to
one another ; as if a whole People, changing from
generation to generation, nay from hour to hour, could
ever by any method be made to *speak* or promise ;
and to speak mere solecisms : ' We, be the Heavens
witness, which Heavens however do no miracles now ;
we, everchanging Millions, will *allow* thee, changeful
Unit, to *force* us or govern us ! ' The world has perhaps
seen few faiths comparable to that.

So nevertheless had the world then construed the
matter. Had they *not* so construed it, how different
had their hopes been, their attempts, their results !
But so and not otherwise did the Upper Powers will
it to be. Freedom by social Contract : such was
verily the Gospel of that Era. And all men had
believed in it, as in a Heaven's Glad-tidings men should ;
and with overflowing heart and uplifted voice clave to
it, and stood fronting Time and Eternity on it. Nay
smile not ; or only with a smile sadder than tears !
This too was a better faith than the one it had replaced ;

than faith merely in the Everlasting Nothing and man's
Digestive Power ; lower than *which* no faith can go.

Not that such universally prevalent, universally
jurant, feeling of Hope, could be a unanimous one.
Far from that. The time was ominous : social dissolution near and certain ; social renovation still a problem,
difficult and distant, even though sure. But if ominous
to some clearest onlooker, whose faith stood not with
the one side or with the other, nor in the ever-vexed
jarring of Greek with Greek at all,—how unspeakably
ominous to dim Royalist participators ; for whom
Royalism was Mankind's Palladium ; for whom, with
the abolition of Most-Christian Kingship and Most-
Talleyrand Bishopship, all loyal obedience, all religious
faith was to expire, and final Night envelop the
Destinies of Man ! On serious hearts, of that persuasion, the matter sinks down deep ; prompting, as we
have seen, to backstairs plots, to Emigration with
pledge of war, to Monarchic Clubs ; nay to still madder
things.

The Spirit of Prophecy, for instance, had been
considered extinct for some centuries : nevertheless
these last-times, as indeed is the tendency of last-times,
do revive it ; that so, of French mad things, we might
have sample also of the maddest. In remote rural
districts, whither Philosophism has not yet radiated,
where a heterodox Constitution of the Clergy is bringing
strife round the altar itself, and the very Church-bells
are getting melted into small money-coin, it appears
probable that the End of the World cannot be far off.
Deep-musing atrabiliar old men, especially old women,
hint in an obscure way that they know what they know.
The Holy Virgin, silent so long, has not gone dumb ;
—and truly now, if ever more in this world, were the
time for her to speak. One Prophetess, though careless
Historians have omitted her name, condition and
whereabout, becomes audible to the general ear ;
credible to not a few ; credible to Friar Gerle, poor
Patriot Chartreux, in the National Assembly itself !

She, in Pythoness recitative, with wildstaring eye, sings
that there shall be a Sign; that the heavenly Sun
himself will hang out a Sign, or Mock-Sun,—which,
many say, shall be stamped with the Head of hanged
Favras. List, Dom Gerle, with that poor addled poll
of thine; list, O list;—and hear nothing.[1]

Notable, however, was that 'magnetic vellum, *vélin
magnétique*', of the Sieurs d'Hozier and Petit-Jean,
Parlementeers of Rouen. Sweet young D'Hozier,
'bred in the faith of his Missal, and of parchment
genealogies', and of parchment generally; adust,
melancholic, middle-aged Petit-Jean: why came these
two to Saint-Cloud, where his Majesty was hunting,
on the festival of St. Peter and St. Paul; and waited
there, in antechambers, a wonder to whispering Swiss,
the livelong day; and even waited without the Grates,
when turned out; and had dismissed their valets to
Paris, as with purpose of endless waiting? They have
a *magnetic vellum*, these two; whereon the Virgin,
wonderfully clothing herself in Mesmerean Cagliostric
Occult-Philosophy, has inspired them to jot down
instructions and predictions for a much-straitened
King. To whom, by Higher Order, they will this day
present it; and save the Monarchy and World. Unaccountable pair of visual-objects! Ye should be men,
and of the Eighteenth Century; but your magnetic
vellum forbids us so to interpret. Say, are ye aught?
Thus ask the Guard-house Captains, the Mayor of
Saint-Cloud; nay, at great length, thus asks the
Committee of Researches, and not the Municipal, but
the National Assembly one. No distinct answer, for
weeks. At last it becomes plain that the right answer
is *negative*. Go, ye Chimeras, with your magnetic
vellum; sweet young Chimera, adust middle-aged one!
The Prison-doors are open. Hardly again shall ye
preside the Rouen Chamber of Accounts; but vanish
obscurely into Limbo.[2]

---

[1] Deux Amis, v. 7.   [2] Ibid. v. 199.

CHAPTER VIII

SOLEMN LEAGUE AND COVENANT[*]

SUCH dim masses, and specks of even deepest black,
work in that white-hot glow of the French mind, now
wholly in fusion and *con*fusion. Old women here
swearing their ten children on the new Evangel of Jean
Jacques ; old women there looking up for Favras'
Heads in the celestial Luminary : these *are* preternatural signs, prefiguring somewhat.

In fact, to the Patriot children of Hope themselves
it is undeniable that difficulties exist : emigrating
Seigneurs ; Parlements in sneaking but most malicious
mutiny (though the rope is round their neck) ; above
all, the most decided ' deficiency of grains '. Sorrowful ;
but, to a Nation that hopes, not irremediable. To
a Nation which is in fusion and ardent communion of
thought ; which, for example, on signal of one Fugleman, will lift its right-hand like a drilled regiment, and
swear and illuminate, till every village from Ardennes
to the Pyrenees has rolled its village-drum, and sent
up its little oath, and glimmer of tallow-illumination
some fathoms into the reign of Night !

If grains are defective, the fault is not of Nature
or National Assembly, but of Art and Antinational
Intriguers. Such malign individuals, of the scoundrel
species, have power to vex us, while the Constitution
is a-making. Endure it, ye heroic Patriots : nay
rather, why not cure it ? Grains do grow, they lie
extant there in sheaf or sack ; only that regraters and
Royalist plotters, to provoke the People into illegality,
obstruct the transport of grains. Quick, ye organized
Patriot Authorities, armed National Guards, meet
together ; unite your goodwill ; in union is tenfold
strength : let the concentred flash of your Patriotism
strike stealthy Scoundrelism blind, paralytic, as with
a *coup de soleil*.

Under which hat or nightcap of the Twenty-five millions, this pregnant Idea first arose, for in some one head it did rise, no man can now say. A most small idea, near at hand for the whole world : but a living one, fit ; and which waxed, whether into greatness or not, into immeasurable size. When a Nation is in this state that the Fugleman can operate on it, what will the word in season, the act in season, not do ! It will grow verily, like the Boy's Bean, in the Fairy-Tale, heaven-high, with habitations and adventures on it, in one night. It is nevertheless unfortunately still a Bean (for your long-lived Oak grows *not* so) ; and the next night, it may lie felled, horizontal, trodden into common mud.—But remark, at least, how natural to any agitated Nation, which has Faith, this business of Covenanting is. The Scotch, believing in a righteous Heaven above them, and also in a Gospel, far other than the Jean-Jacques one, swore, in their extreme need, a Solemn League and Covenant,—as Brothers on the forlorn-hope, and imminence of battle, who embrace, looking Godward : and got the whole Isle to swear it ; and even, in their tough Old-Saxon Hebrew-Presbyterian way, to keep it more or less ;—for the thing, as such things are, was heard in Heaven and partially ratified there : neither is it yet dead, if thou wilt look, nor like to die. The French too, with their Gallic-Ethnic excitability and effervescence, have, as we have seen, real Faith, of a sort ; they are hard bested, though in the middle of Hope : a National Solemn League and Covenant there may be in France too ; under how different conditions ; with how different development and issue !

Note, accordingly, the small commencement ; first spark of a mighty firework : for if the particular *hat* cannot be fixed upon, the particular District can. On the 29th day of last November, were National Guards by the thousand seen filing, from far and near, with military music, with Municipal officers in tricolor sashes, towards and along the Rhone-stream, to the little town

of Etoile. There with ceremonial evolution and
manœuvre, with fanfaronading, musketry salvoes, and
what else the Patriot genius could devise, they made
oath and obtestation to stand faithfully by one another,
under Law and King ; in particular, to have all manner
of grains, while grains there were, freely circulated, in
spite both of robber and regrater. This was the meeting of Etoile, in the mild end of November 1789.

But now, if a mere empty Review, followed by
Review-dinner, ball, and such gesticulation and flirtation as there may be, interests the happy County-town,
and makes it the envy of surrounding County-towns,
how much more might this ! In a fortnight, larger
Montélimart, half ashamed of itself, will do as good,
and better. On the Plain of Montélimart, or what is
equally sonorous, ' under the Walls of Montélimart ',
the 13th of December sees new gathering and obtestation ; six thousand strong ; and now indeed, with
these three remarkable improvements, as unanimously
resolved on there. First, that the men of Montélimart
do federate with the already federated men of Etoile.
Second, that, implying not expressing the circulation
of grain, they ' swear in the face of God and their
Country ', with much more emphasis and comprehen-
siveness, ' to obey all decrees of the National Assembly,
and see them obeyed, till death, *jusqu'à la mort* '. Third,
and most important, that official record of all this be
solemnly delivered in, to the National Assembly, to
M. de Lafayette, and ' to the Restorer of French
Liberty ' ; who shall all take what comfort from it
they can. Thus does larger Montélimart vindicate its
Patriot importance, and maintain its rank in the municipal scale.[1]

And so, with the New-year, the signal is hoisted :
for is not a National Assembly, and solemn deliverance
there, at lowest a National Telegraph ? Not only
grain shall circulate, while there is grain, on highways
or the Rhone-waters, over all that South-Eastern region,

---

[1] Hist. Parl. vii. 4.

—where also if Monseigneur d'Artois saw good to break
in from Turin, hot welcome might await him ; but
whatsoever Province of France is straitened for grain,
or vexed with a mutinous Parlement, unconstitutional
plotters, Monarchic Clubs, or any other Patriot ailment,
—can go and do likewise, or even do better. And now,
especially, when the February swearing has set them
all agog ! From Brittany to Burgundy, on most Plains
of France, under most City-walls, it is a blaring of
trumpets, waving of banners, a Constitutional manœuvring : under the vernal skies, while Nature too is
putting forth her green Hopes, under bright sunshine
defaced by the stormful East ; like Patriotism victorious, though with difficulty, over Aristocracy and
defect of grain ! There march and constitutionally
wheel, to the *ça-ira*-ing mood of fife and drum, under
their tricolor Municipals, our clear-gleaming Phalanxes ;
or halt, with uplifted right-hand, and artillery salvoes
that imitate Jove's thunder ; and all the Country, and
metaphorically all ' the Universe ', is looking on.
Wholly, in their best apparel, brave men, and beautifully dizened women, most of whom have lovers there ;
swearing, by the eternal Heavens and this green-grow-
ing all-nutritive Earth, that France is free !

Sweetest days, when (astonishing to say) mortals have
actually met together in communion and fellowship ;
and man, were it only once through long despicable
centuries, is for moments verily the brother of man !
—And then the Deputations to the National Assembly,
with high-flown descriptive harangue ; to M. de
Lafayette, and the Restorer ; very frequently moreover to the Mother of Patriotism, sitting on her stout
benches in that Hall of the Jacobins ! The general
ear is filled with Federation. New names of Patriots
emerge, which shall one day become familiar : Boyer-
Fonfrède eloquent denunciator of a rebellious Bordeaux Parlement ; Max Isnard* eloquent reporter of
the Federation of Draguignan ; eloquent pair, separated
by the whole breadth of France, who are nevertheless
to meet. Ever wider burns the flame of Federation ;

ever wider and also brighter. Thus the Brittany and
Anjou brethren mention a Fraternity of *all* true Frenchmen ; and go the length of invoking ' perdition and
death ' on any renegade : moreover, if in their National-
Assembly harangue, they glance plaintively at the *marc
d'argent* which makes so many citizens *passive*, they,
over in the Mother-Society, ask, being henceforth
themselves ' neither Bretons nor Angevins but French ',
Why all France has not one Federation, and universal
Oath of Brotherhood, once for all ? [1]   A most pertinent
suggestion ; dating from the end of March. Which
pertinent suggestion the whole Patriot world cannot
but catch, and reverberate and agitate till it become
loud ;—which in that case, the Townhall Municipals
had better take up, and meditate.

Some universal Federation seems inevitable : the
Where is given ; clearly Paris : only the When, the
How ? These also productive Time will give ; is already
giving. For always as the Federative work goes on,
it perfects itself, and Patriot genius adds contribution
after contribution. Thus, at Lyons, in the end of the
May month, we behold as many as fifty, or some say
sixty thousand, met to federate ; and a multitude
looking on, which it would be difficult to number.
From dawn to dusk ! For our Lyons Guardsmen took
rank, at five in the bright dewy morning ; came pouring
in, bright-gleaming, to the Quai de Rhone, to march
thence to the Federation-field ; amid wavings of hats
and lady-handkerchiefs ; glad shoutings of some two
hundred thousand Patriot voices and hearts ; the
beautiful and brave ! Among whom, courting no
notice, and yet the notablest of all, what queenlike
Figure is this ; with her escort of house-friends and
Champagneux the Patriot Editor ; come abroad with
the earliest ? Radiant with enthusiasm are those dark
eyes, is that strong Minerva-face, looking dignity and
earnest joy ; joyfullest she where all are joyful. It is

---

[1] Reports, &c. (in Hist. Parl. ix. 122–47).

Roland de la Platrière's Wife ! [1*] Strict elderly Roland,
King's Inspector of Manufactures here ; and now likewise, by popular choice, the strictest of our new Lyons
Municipals : a man who has gained much, if worth and
faculty be gain; but, above all things, has gained to
wife Phlipon the Paris Engraver's daughter. Reader,
mark that queenlike burgher-woman : beautiful, Ama-
zonian-graceful to the eye ; more so to the mind.
Unconscious of her worth (as all worth is), of her greatness, of her crystal clearness ; genuine, the creature of
Sincerity and Nature, in an age of Artificiality, Pollution
and Cant ; there, in her still completeness, in her still
invincibility, *she*, if thou knew it, is the noblest of all
living Frenchwomen,—and will be seen, one day. O
blessed rather while *un*seen, even of herself ! For the
present she gazes, nothing doubting, into this grand
theatricality ; and thinks her young dreams are to be
fulfilled.

From dawn to dusk, as we said, it lasts ; and truly
a sight like few. Flourishes of drums and trumpets
are something : but think of an ' artificial Rock fifty
feet high ', all cut into crag-steps, not without the
similitude of ' shrubs ' ! The interior cavity, for in
sooth it is made of deal,—stands solemn, a ' Temple of
Concord ' : on the outer summit rises ' a Statue of
Liberty ', colossal, seen for miles, with her Pike and
Phrygian Cap, and civic column ; at her feet a Country's
Altar, '*Autel de la Patrie* ' :—on all which neither deal-
timber nor lath and plaster, with paint of various
colours, have been spared. But fancy then the banners
all placed on the steps of the Rock ; high-mass chanted ;
and the civic oath of fifty thousand : with what volcanic
outburst of sound from iron and other throats, enough
to frighten back the very Saone and Rhone ; and how
the brightest fireworks, and balls, and even repasts
closed in that night of the gods ! [2] And so the Lyons
Federation vanishes too, swallowed of darkness ;—and

---

[1] Madame Roland, Mémoires, i. (Discours Préliminaire,
p. 23).

[2] Hist. Parl. xii. 274.

yet not wholly, for our brave fair Roland was there ;
also she, though in the deepest privacy, writes her
Narrative of it in Champagneux's *Courrier de Lyons* ;
a piece which ' circulates to the extent of sixty thousand ' ; which one would like now to read.

But on the whole, Paris, we may see, will have little
to devise ; will only have to borrow and apply. And
then as to the day, what day of all the calendar is fit,
if the Bastille Anniversary be not ? The particular
spot too, it is easy to see, must be the Champ-de-Mars ;
where many a Julian the Apostate has been lifted on
bucklers, to France's or the world's sovereignty ; and
iron Franks, loud-clanging, have responded to the voice
of a Charlemagne ; and from of old mere sublimities
have been familiar.

CHAPTER IX

SYMBOLIC

How natural, in all decisive circumstances, is Symbolic Representation to all kinds of men ! Nay,
what is man's whole terrestrial Life but a Symbolic
Representation, and making visible, of the Celestial
invisible Force that is in him ? By act and word he
strives to do it ; with sincerity, if possible ; failing that,
with theatricality, which latter also may have its
meaning. An Almack's Masquerade is not nothing ; in
more genial ages, your Christmas Guisings, Feasts of
the Ass, Abbots of Unreason, were a considerable something : sincere sport they were ; as Almacks may still
be sincere wish for sport. But what, on the other hand,
must not sincere earnest have been ; say, a Hebrew
Feast of Tabernacles have been ! A whole Nation
gathered, in the name of the Highest, under the eye
of the Highest ; imagination herself flagging under the
reality ; and all noblest Ceremony as yet not grown
ceremonial, but solemn, significant to the outmost

fringe ! Neither, in modern private life, are theatrical
scenes, of tearful women wetting whole ells of cambric
in concert, of impassioned bushy-whiskered youth
threatening suicide, and such like, to be so entirely
detested : drop thou a tear over them thyself rather.

At any rate, one can remark that no Nation will
throw by its work, and deliberately go out to make
a scene, without meaning something thereby. For
indeed no scenic individual, with knavish hypocritical
views, will take the trouble to *soliloquize* a scene : and
now consider, is not a scenic Nation placed precisely in
that predicament of soliloquizing ; for its own behoof
alone ; to solace its own sensibilities, maudlin or other ?
—Yet in this respect, of readiness for scenes, the difference of Nations, as of men, is very great. If our Saxon
Puritanic friends, for example, swore and signed their
National Covenant, without discharge of gunpowder,
or the beating of any drum, in a dingy Covenant-Close
of the Edinburgh High-street, in a mean room, where
men now drink mean liquor, it was consistent with their
ways so to swear it. Our Gallic-Encyclopedic friends,
again, must have a Champ-de-Mars, seen of all the
world, or universe ; and such a Scenic Exhibition, to
which the Coliseum Amphitheatre was but a stroller's
barn, as this old Globe of ours had never or hardly ever
beheld. Which method also we reckon natural, then
and there. Nor perhaps was the respective *keeping*
of these two Oaths far out of due proportion to such
respective display in taking them : inverse proportion,
namely. For the theatricality of a People goes in
a compound ratio : ratio indeed of their trustfulness,
sociability, fervency ; but then also of their excitability,
of their porosity, not *continent* ; or say, of their explo-
siveness, hot-flashing, but which does not last.

How true also, once more, is it that no man or Nation
of men, *conscious* of doing a great thing, was ever, in that
thing, doing other than a small one !* O Champ-de-
Mars Federation, with three hundred drummers, twelve
hundred wind-musicians, and artillery planted on
height after height to boom the tidings of it all over

France, in few minutes! Could no Atheist-Naigeon
contrive to discern, eighteen centuries off, those Thirteen most poor mean-dressed men, at frugal Supper,
in a mean Jewish dwelling, with no symbol but hearts
god-initiated into the ' Divine depth of Sorrow '*, and
a *Do this in remembrance of me**;—and so cease that
small difficult crowing of his, if he were not doomed
to it?

CHAPTER X

MANKIND

PARDONABLE are human theatricalities; nay, perhaps touching, like the passionate utterance of a tongue
which with sincerity *stammers*; of a head which with
insincerity *babbles*,—having gone distracted. Yet, in
comparison with unpremeditated outbursts of Nature,
such as an Insurrection of Women, how foisonless,
unedifying, undelightful; like small ale palled, like
an effervescence that has effervesced! Such scenes,
coming of forethought, were they world-great, and
never so cunningly devised, are at bottom mainly pasteboard and paint. But the others are original; emitted
from the great everliving heart of Nature herself: what
figure *they* will assume is unspeakably significant. To
us, therefore, let the French National Solemn League
and Federation be the highest recorded triumph of
the Thespian Art: triumphant surely, since the whole
Pit, which was of Twenty-five Millions, not only claps
hands, but does itself spring on the boards and passionately set to playing there. And being such, be it treated
as such: with sincere cursory admiration; with wonder
from afar. A whole Nation gone mumming deserves
so much; but deserves not that loving minuteness
a Menadic Insurrection did. Much more let prior, and
as it were, rehearsal scenes of Federation come and go,
henceforward, as they list; and, on Plains and under

City-walls, innumerable regimental bands blare off into the Inane, without note from us.

One scene, however, the hastiest reader will momentarily pause on : that of Anacharsis Clootz and the Collective sinful Posterity of Adam.—For a Patriot Municipality has now, on the 4th of June, got its plan concocted, and got it sanctioned by National Assembly ; a Patriot King assenting ; to whom, were he even free to dissent, Federative harangues, overflowing with loyalty, have doubtless a transient sweetness. There shall come Deputed National Guards, so many in the hundred, from each of the Eighty-three Departments of France. Likewise from all Naval and Military King's Forces, shall Deputed quotas come ; such Federation of National with Royal Soldier has, taking place spontaneously, been already seen and sanctioned. For the rest, it is hoped, as many as forty thousand may arrive ; expenses to be borne by the Deputing District ; of all which let District and Department take thought, and elect fit men,—whom the Paris brethren will fly to meet and welcome.

Now, therefore, judge if our Patriot Artists are busy ; taking deep counsel how to make the Scene worthy of a look from the Universe ! As many as fifteen thousand men, spademen, barrowmen, stonebuilders, rammers, with their engineers, are at work on the Champ-de-Mars ; hollowing it out into a National Amphitheatre, fit for such solemnity. For one may hope it will be annual and perennial ; a 'Feast of Pikes, *Féte des Piques*', notablest among the hightides of the year : in any case, ought not a scenic Free Nation to have some permanent National Amphitheatre ? The Champ-de-Mars is getting hollowed out ; and the daily talk and the nightly dream in most Parisian heads is of Federation, and that only. Federate Deputies are already under way. National Assembly, what with its natural work, what with hearing and answering harangues of these Federates, of this Federation, will have enough to do ! Harangue of 'American Committee ', among whom is that faint figure of Paul Jones

as ' with the stars dim-twinkling through it ',—come to
congratulate us on the prospect of such auspicious day.
Harangue of Bastille Conquerors, come to ' renounce '
any special recompense, any peculiar place at the solemnity ;—since the Centre Grenadiers rather grumble.
Harangue of ' Tennis-Court Club', who enter with
far-gleaming Brass-plate, aloft on a pole, and the
Tennis-Court Oath engraved thereon ; which far-gleaming Brass-plate they purpose to affix solemnly in the
Versailles original locality, on the 20th of this month,
which is the anniversary, as a deathless memorial, for
some years : they will then dine, as they come back,
in the Bois de Boulogne ; [1]—cannot, however, do it
without apprising the world. To such things does the
august National Assembly ever and anon cheerfully
listen, suspending its regenerative labours ; and with
some touch of impromptu eloquence, make friendly
reply ;—as indeed the wont has long been ; for it is
a gesticulating, sympathetic People, and has a heart,
and wears it on its sleeve.*

In which circumstances, it occurred to the mind of
Anacharsis Clootz, that while so much was embodying
itself into Club or Committee, and perorating applauded,
there yet remained a greater and greatest ; of which,
if *it* also took body and perorated, what might not the
effect be : Humankind namely, *le Genre Humain* itself !
In what rapt creative moment the Thought rose in
Anacharsis's soul ; all his throes, while he went about
giving shape and birth to it ; how he was sneered at by
cold worldlings ; but did sneer again, being a man of
polished sarcasm ; and moved to and fro persuasive in
coffeehouse and soirée, and dived down assiduous-
obscure in the great deep of Paris, making his Thought
a Fact : of all this the spiritual biographies of that
period say nothing. Enough that on the 19th evening
of June 1790, the sun's slant rays lighted a spectacle
such as our foolish little Planet has not often had to
show : Anacharsis Clootz entering the august Salle de

---

[1] See Deux Amis, v. 122 ; Hist. Parl. &c.

Manége, with the Human Species at his heels. Swedes,
Spaniards, Polacks ; Turks, Chaldeans, Greeks, dwellers
in Mesopotamia*; behold them all ; they have come to
claim place in the grand Federation, having an undoubted
interest in it.

' Our Ambassador titles ', said the fervid Clootz, ' are
not written on parchment, but on the living hearts of
all men '. These whiskered Polacks, long-flowing tur-
baned Ishmaelites, astrological Chaldeans, who stand
so mute here, let them plead with you, august Senators,
more eloquently than eloquence could. They are the
mute representatives of their tongue-tied, befettered,
heavy-laden Nations ; who from out of that dark bewilderment gaze wistful, amazed, with half-incredulous
hope, towards you, and this your bright light of a French
Federation : bright particular daystar, the herald of
universal day. We claim to stand there, as mute
monuments, pathetically adumbrative of much.—From
bench and gallery comes ' repeated applause ' ; for
what august Senator but is flattered even by the very
shadow of Human Species depending on him ? From
President Sieyes, who presides this remarkable fortnight,
in spite of his small voice, there comes eloquent though
shrill reply. Anacharsis and the ' Foreigners Committee ' shall have place at the Federation ; on condition
of telling their respective Peoples what they see there.
In the meantime, we invite them to the 'honours of the
sitting, *honneur de la séance* '. A long-flowing Turk,
for rejoinder, bows with Eastern solemnity, and utters
articulate sounds : but owing to his imperfect knowledge of the French dialect,[1] his words are like spilt
water ; the thought he had in him remains conjectural
to this day.

Anacharsis and Mankind accept the honours of the
sitting ; and have forthwith, as the old Newspapers
still testify, the satisfaction to see several things. First
and chief, on the motion of Lameth, Lafayette, Saint-
Fargeau and other Patriot Nobles, let the others repugn

[1] Moniteur, &c. (in Hist. Parl. xii. 283).

as they will: all Titles of Nobility, from Duke to Esquire, or lower, are henceforth *abolished*. Then, in like manner, Livery Servants, or rather the Livery of Servants. Neither, for the future, shall any man or woman, self-styled noble, be 'incensed',—foolishly fumigated with incense, in Church; as the wont has been. In a word, Feudalism being dead these ten months, why should her empty trappings and scutcheons survive? The very Coats-of-arms will require to be obliterated;—and yet Cassandra-Marat on this and the other coach-panel notices that they 'are but painted over', and threaten to peer through again.

So that henceforth De Lafayette is but the Sieur Motier, and Saint-Fargeau is plain Michel Lepelletier; and Mirabeau soon after has to say huffingly, 'With your *Riquetti* you have set Europe at cross-purposes for three days'. For his Counthood is not indifferent to this man; which indeed the admiring People treat him with to the last. But let extreme Patriotism rejoice, and chiefly Anacharsis and Mankind; for now it seems to be taken for granted that one Adam is Father of us all!—

Such was, in historical accuracy, the famed feat of Anacharsis. Thus did the most extensive of Public Bodies find a sort of spokesman. Whereby at least we may judge of one thing: what a humour the once sniffing mocking City of Paris and Baron Clootz had got into; when such exhibition could appear a propriety, next door to a sublimity. It is true, Envy did, in after times, pervert this success of Anacharsis; making him, from incidental 'Speaker of the Foreign-Nations Committee', claim to be official permanent 'Speaker, *Orateur*, of the Human Species', which he only deserved to be; and alleging, calumniously, that his astrological Chaldeans, and the rest, were a mere French tag-rag-and-bobtail disguised for the nonce; and, in short, sneering and fleering at him in *her* cold barren way: all which, however, he, the man he was, could receive on thick enough panoply, or even rebound therefrom, and also go *his* way.

Most extensive of Public Bodies, we may call it ; and
also the most unexpected : for who could have thought
to see All Nations in the Tuileries Riding-Hall ? But
so it is ; and truly as strange things may happen when
a whole People goes mumming and miming. Hast
not thou thyself perchance seen diademed Cleopatra,
daughter of the Ptolemies, pleading, almost with bended
knee, in unheroic tea-parlour, or dimlit retail-shop, to
inflexible gross Burghal Dignitary, for leave to reign
and die ; being dressed for it, and moneyless, with
small children ;—while suddenly Constables have shut
the Thespian barn, and her Antony pleaded in vain ?
Such visual spectra flit across this Earth, if the Thespian
Stage be rudely interfered with : but much more, when,
as was said, Pit jumps on Stage, then is it verily, as in
Herr Tieck's Drama, a *Verkehrte Welt*, or World
Topsyturvied !*

Having seen the Human Species itself, to have seen
the ' *Dean* of the Human Species ' ceased now to be
a miracle. Such ' *Doyen du Genre Humain*, Eldest of
Men ', had shown himself there, in these weeks : Jean
Claude Jacob, a born Serf, deputed from his native
Jura Mountains to thank the National Assembly for
enfranchising them. On his bleached worn face are
ploughed the furrowings of one hundred and twenty
years. He has heard dim *patois*-talk, of immortal
Grand-Monarch victories ; of a burned Palatinate, as
he toiled and moiled to make a little speck of this Earth
greener ; of Cevennes Dragoonings ; of Marlborough
going to the war. Four generations have bloomed out,
and loved and hated, and rustled off : he was forty-six
when Louis Fourteenth died. The Assembly, as one
man, spontaneously rose, and did reverence to the
Eldest of the World ; old Jean is to take *séance* among
them, honourably, with covered head. He gazes
feebly there, with his old eyes, on that new wonder-
scene ; dreamlike to him, and uncertain, wavering
amid fragments of old memories and dreams. For
Time is all growing unsubstantial, dreamlike ; Jean's

eyes and mind are weary, and about to close,—and
open on a far other wonder-scene, which shall be real.
Patriot Subscription, Royal Pension was got for him,
and he returned home glad ; but in two months more
he left it all, and went on his unknown way.[1]

CHAPTER XI

AS IN THE AGE OF GOLD

MEANWHILE to Paris, ever going and returning, day
after day, and all day long, towards that Field of Mars,
it becomes painfully apparent that the spadework
there cannot be got done in time.   There is such an
area of it ; three hundred thousand square feet : for
from the École Militaire (which will need to be done up
in wood with balconies and galleries) westward to the
Gate by the River (where also shall be wood, in triumphal
arches), we count some thousand yards of length ; and
for breadth, from this umbrageous Avenue of eight
rows, on the South side, to that corresponding one on
the North, some thousand feet more or less.   All this
to be scooped out, and wheeled up in slope along the
sides ; high enough ; for it must be rammed down
there, and shaped stair-wise into as many as ' thirty
ranges of convenient seats ', firm-trimmed with turf,
covered with enduring timber ;—and then our huge
pyramidal Fatherland's-Altar, *Autel de la Patrie*, in the
centre, also to be raised and stair-stepped.   Force-work
with a vengeance ; it is a World's Amphitheatre !
There are but fifteen days good : and at this languid
rate, it might take half as many weeks.   What is
singular too, the spademen seem to work lazily ; they
will not work double-tides, even for offer of more wages,
though their tide is but seven hours ; they declare
angrily that the human tabernacle requires occasional
rest !

[1] Deux Amis, iv. iii.

Is it Aristocrats secretly bribing ? Aristocrats were capable of that. Only six months since, did not evidence get afloat that subterranean Paris,—for we stand over quarries and catacombs, dangerously, as it were midway between Heaven and the Abyss, and are hollow underground,—was charged with gunpowder, which should make us ' leap ' ? Till a Cordeliers Deputation actually went to examine, and found it— carried off again ! [1] An accursed, incurable brood ; all asking for ' passports ', in these sacred days. Trouble, of rioting, château-burning, is in the Limousin and elsewhere ; for they are busy ! Between the best of Peoples and the best of Restorer Kings they would sow grudges ; with what a fiend's grin would they see this Federation, looked for by the Universe, fail !

Fail for want of spadework, however, it shall not. He that has four limbs and a French heart can do spadework ; and will ! On the first July Monday, scarcely has the signal-cannon boomed ; scarcely have the languescent mercenary Fifteen Thousand laid down their tools, and the eyes of onlookers turned sorrowfully to the still high Sun ; when this and the other Patriot, fire in his eye, snatches barrow and mattock, and himself begins indignantly wheeling. Whom scores and then hundreds follow ; and soon a volunteer Fifteen Thousand are shovelling and trundling ; with the heart of giants : and all in right order, with that extemporaneous adroitness of theirs : whereby *such* a lift has been given, worth three mercenary ones ;—which may end when the late twilight thickens, in triumph-shouts, heard or heard of beyond Montmartre !

A sympathetic population will *wait*, next day, with eagerness, till the tools are free. Or why wait ? Spades elsewhere exist ! And so now bursts forth that effulgence of Parisian enthusiasm, good-heartedness and brotherly love ; such, if Chroniclers are trustworthy, as was not witnessed since the Age of Gold. Paris,

---

[1] 23rd December 1789 (Newspapers in Hist. Parl. iv. 44).

male and female, precipitates itself towards its Southwest extremity, spade on shoulder. Streams of men,
without order ; or in order, as ranked fellow-craftsmen,
as natural or accidental reunions, march towards the
Field of Mars. Three-deep these march ; to the sound
of stringed music ; preceded by young girls with green
boughs and tricolor streamers : they have shouldered,
soldier-wise, their shovels and picks ; and with one
throat are singing *ça-ira*. Yes, *pardieu ça-ira*, cry the
passengers on the streets. All corporate Guilds, and
public and private Bodies of Citizens, from the highest
to the lowest, march ; the very Hawkers, one finds,
have ceased bawling for one day. The neighbouring
Villages turn out : their able men come marching, to
village fiddle or tambourine and triangle, under their
Mayor, or Mayor and Curate, who also walk bespaded,
and in tricolor sash. As many as one hundred and
fifty thousand workers ; nay at certain seasons, as
some count, two hundred and fifty thousand ; for, in
the afternoon especially, what mortal but, finishing his
hasty day's work, would run ! A stirring City : from
the time you reach the Place Louis-Quinze, southward
over the River, by all Avenues, it is one living throng.
So many workers ; and no mercenary mock-workers,
but real ones that lie freely to it : each Patriot *stretches*
himself against the stubborn glebe ; hews and wheels
with the whole weight that is in him.

Amiable infants, *aimables enfans* ! They do the
' *police de l'atelier* ' too, the guidance and governance,
themselves ; with that ready will of theirs, with that
extemporaneous adroitness. It is a true brethren's
work ; all distinctions confounded, abolished ; as it
was in the beginning, when Adam himself delved.*
Long-frocked tonsured Monks, with short-skirted Water-
carriers, with swallow-tailed well-frizzled *Incroyables*
of a Patriot turn ; dark Charcoalmen, meal-white
Peruke-makers ; or Peruke-wearers, for Advocate and
Judge are there, and all Heads of Districts : sober
Nuns sisterlike with flaunting Nymphs of the Opera,
and females in common circumstances named unfor-

tunate : the patriot Rag-picker, and perfumed dweller
in palaces ; for Patriotism like New-birth, and also like
Death, levels all. The Printers have come marching,
Prudhomme's all in Paper-caps with *Révolutions de
Paris* printed on them ;—as Camille notes ; wishing
that in these great days there should be a *Pacte des
Ecrivains* too, or Federation of Able Editors.[1] Beautiful to see ! The snowy linen and delicate pantaloon
alternates with the soiled check-shirt and bushel-
breeches ; for both have cast their coats, and under
both are four limbs and a set of Patriot muscles. There
do they pick and shovel ; or bend forward, yoked in
long strings to box-barrow or overloaded tumbril ;
joyous, with one mind. Abbé Sieyes is seen pulling,
wiry, vehement, if too light for draught ; by the side
of Beauharnais, who shall get Kings though he be none.*
Abbé Maury did not pull ; but the Charcoal-men
brought a mummer guised like him, and he had to pull
in effigy. Let no august Senator disdain the work :
Mayor Bailly, Generalissimo Lafayette are there ;—
and, alas, shall be there *again* another day ! The King
himself comes to see : sky-rending *Vive-le-roi !* ‘ and
suddenly with shouldered spades they form a guard of
honour round him ’. Whosoever can come*comes ; to
work, or to look, and bless the work.

Whole families have come. One whole family we
see clearly of three generations : the father picking,
the mother shovelling, the young ones wheeling assiduous ; old grandfather, hoary with ninety-three years,
holds in his arms the youngest of all : [2] frisky, not helpful this one ; who nevertheless may tell it to *his* grand-
children ; and how the Future and the Past alike
looked on, and with failing or with half-formed voice,
faltered their *ça-ira*. A vintner has wheeled in, on
Patriot truck, beverage of wine : ‘ Drink not, my
brothers, if ye are not thirsty ; that your cask may
last the longer ’ : neither did any drink but men

---

[1] See Newspapers, &c. (in Hist. Parl. vi. 381–406).
[2] Mercier, ii. 76, &c.

'evidently exhausted'. A dapper Abbé looks on,
sneering: 'To the barrow!' cry several; whom he,
lest a worse thing*befall him, obeys: nevertheless one
wiser Patriot barrowman, arriving now, interposes his
'*arrêtez*'; setting down his own barrow, he snatches
the Abbé's; trundles it fast, like an infected thing, forth
of the Champ-de-Mars circuit, and discharges it *there*.
Thus too a certain person (of some quality, or private
capital, to appearance), entering hastily, flings down
his coat, waistcoat and two watches, and is rushing to
the thick of the work: 'But your watches?' cries the
general voice.—'Does one distrust his brothers?'
answers he; nor were the watches stolen. How beautiful is noble sentiment: like gossamer gauze, beautiful
and cheap; which will stand no tear and wear!
Beautiful cheap gossamer gauze, thou film-shadow of
a raw-material of Virtue, which art *not* woven, nor
likely to be, into Duty; thou art better than nothing,
and also worse!

Young Boarding-school Boys, College Students,
shout *Vive la Nation*, and regret that they have yet
'only their sweat to give'. What say we of Boys?
Beautifullest Hebes; the loveliest of Paris, in their
light air-robes, with riband-girdle of tricolor, are there;
shovelling and wheeling with the rest; their Hebe eyes
brighter with enthusiasm, and long hair in beautiful
dishevelment; hard-pressed are their small fingers;
but they make the patriot barrow go, and even force
it to the summit of the slope (with a little tracing, which
what man's arm were not too happy to lend?)—then
bound down with it again, and go for more; with their
long locks and tricolors blown back; graceful as the
rosy Hours. O, as that evening Sun fell over the
Champ-de-Mars, and tinted with fire the thick umbrageous boscage that shelters it on this hand and on that,
and struck direct on those Domes and two-and-forty
Windows of the École Militaire, and made them all of
burnished gold,—saw he on his wide zodiac road other
such sight? A living garden spotted and dotted with
such flowerage; all colours of the prism; the beauti-

fullest blent friendly with the usefullest; all growing
and working brotherlike there, under one warm feeling,
were it but for days; once and no second time! But
Night is sinking; these Nights too, into Eternity. The
hastiest traveller Versailles-ward has drawn bridle on
the heights of Chaillot: and looked for moments over
the River; reporting at Versailles what he saw, not
without tears.[1]

Meanwhile, from all points of the compass, Federates
are arriving: fervid children of the South, ' who glory
in their Mirabeau '; considerate North-blooded Mountaineers of Jura; sharp Bretons, with their Gaelic sud-
denness; Normans, not to be overreached in bargain:
all now animated with one noblest fire of Patriotism.
Whom the Paris brethren march forth to receive; with
military solemnities, with fraternal embracing, and
a hospitality worthy of the heroic ages. They assist
at the Assembly's Debates, these Federates; the Galleries are reserved for them. They assist in the toils
of the Champ-de-Mars; each new troop will put its
hand to the spade; lift a hod of earth on the Altar
of the Fatherland. But the flourishes of rhetoric, for
it is a gesticulating People; the moral-sublime of
those Addresses to an august Assembly, to a Patriot
Restorer! Our Breton Captain of Federates kneels
even, in a fit of enthusiasm, and gives up his sword;
he wet-eyed to a King wet-eyed. Poor Louis! These,
as he said afterwards, were among the bright days of
his life.

Reviews also there must be; royal Federate-reviews,
with King, Queen, and tricolor Court looking on: at
lowest, if, as is too common, it rains, our Federate
Volunteers will file through the inner gateways, Royalty
standing dry. Nay there, should some stop occur, the
beautifullest fingers in France may take you softly by
the lapelle, and, in mild flute-voice, ask: ' Monsieur,
of what Province are you? ' Happy he who can reply,

[1] Mercier, ii. 81.

chivalrously lowering his sword's point, ' Madame, from
the Province your ancestors reigned over'. He that
happy ' Provincial Advocate ', now Provincial Federate,
shall be rewarded by a sun-smile, and such melodious
glad words addressed to a King : ' Sire, these are your
faithful Lorrainers '. Cheerier verily, in these holidays,
is this ' skyblue faced with red ' of a National Guardsman, than the dull black and grey of a Provincial
Advocate, which in workdays one was used to. For
the same thrice-blessed Lorrainer shall, this evening,
stand sentry at a Queen's door ; and feel that he could
die a thousand deaths for her : then again, at the outer
gate, and even a third time, she shall see him ; nay he
will make her do it; presenting arms with emphasis,
' making his musket jingle again ' : and in her salute
there shall again be a sun-smile, and that little blonde-
locked too hasty Dauphin shall be admonished, ' Salute
then, Monsieur, don't be unpolite ' ; and therewith she,
like a bright Sky-wanderer or Planet with her little
Moon, issues forth peculiar.[1]

But at night, when Patriot spadework is over, figure
the sacred rights of hospitality ! Lepelletier Saint-
Fargeau, a mere private senator, but with great possessions, has daily his ' hundred dinner-guests ' ; the table
of Generalissimo Lafayette may double that number.
In lowly parlour, as in lofty saloon, the wine-cup passes
round ; crowned by the smiles of Beauty ; be it of
lightly-tripping Grisette or of high-sailing Dame, for
both equally have beauty, and smiles precious to the
brave.

---

[1] Narrative by a Lorraine Federate (given in Hist. Parl.
vi. 389-91].

CHAPTER XII

SOUND AND SMOKE

AND so now, in spite of plotting Aristocrats, lazy hired spademen, and almost of Destiny itself (for there has been much rain too), the Champ-de-Mars, on the 13th of the month, is fairly ready: trimmed, rammed, buttressed with firm masonry; and Patriotism can stroll over it admiring; and as it were rehearsing, for in every head.is some unutterable image of the morrow. Pray Heaven there be not clouds. Nay what far worse cloud is this, of a misguided Municipality that talks of admitting Patriotism to the solemnity by tickets! Was it by tickets we were admitted to the work; and to what brought the work? Did we take the Bastille by tickets? A misguided Municipality sees the error; at late midnight, rolling drums announce to Patriotism starting half out of its bed-clothes, that it is to be ticketless. Pull down thy nightcap therefore; and, with demi-articulate grumble, significant of several things, go pacified to sleep again. To-morrow is Wednesday morning; unforgettable among the *fasti* of the world.

The morning comes, cold for a July one; but such a festivity would make Greenland smile. Through every inlet of that National Amphitheatre (for it is a league in circuit, cut with openings at due intervals), floods in the living throng; covers, without tumult, space after space. The École Militaire has galleries and overvaulting canopies, wherein Carpentry and Painting have vied, for the Upper Authorities; triumphal arches, at the Gate by the River, bear inscriptions, if weak, yet well-meant, and orthodox. Far aloft, over the Altar of the Fatherland, on their tall crane standards of iron, swing pensile our antique *Cassolettes* or Pans of Incense; dispensing sweet incense-fumes,—unless

for the Heathen Mythology, one sees not for whom.
Two hundred thousand Patriotic Men ; and, twice as
good, one hundred thousand Patriotic Women, all
decked and glorified as one can fancy, sit waiting in this
Champ-de-Mars.

What a picture : that circle of bright-dyed Life,
spread up there, on its thirty-seated Slope ; leaning,
one would say, on the thick umbrage of those Avenue-
Trees, for the stems of them are hidden by the height ;
and all beyond it mere greenness of Summer Earth,
with the gleams of waters, or white sparklings of stone-
edifices : little circular enamel-picture in the centre of
such a vase—of emerald ! A vase not empty : the
Invalides Cupolas want not their population, nor the
distant Windmills of Montmartre ; on remotest steeple
and invisible village belfry, stand men with spy-glasses.
On the heights of Chaillot are many-coloured undulating
groups ; round and far on, over all the circling heights
that embosom Paris, it is as one more or less peopled
Amphitheatre ; which the eye grows dim with measuring. Nay heights, as was before hinted, have cannon ;
and a floating-battery of cannon is on the Seine. When
eye fails,* ear shall serve ; and all France properly is
but one Amphitheatre ; for in paved town and unpaved
hamlet, men walk listening ; till the muffled thunder
sound audible on their horizon, that they too may begin
swearing and firing ! [1] But now, to streams of music,
come Federates enough,—for they have assembled on
the Boulevard Saint-Antoine or thereby, and come
marching through the City, with their Eighty-three
Department Banners, and blessings not loud but deep*;
comes National Assembly, and takes seat under its
Canopy ; comes Royalty, and takes seat on a throne
beside it. And Lafayette, on white charger, is here,
and all the civic Functionaries ; and the Federates
form dances, till their strictly military evolutions and
manœuvres can begin.

Evolutions and manœuvres ? Task not the pen of

[1] Deux Amis, v. 168.

mortal to describe them : truant imagination droops ;
—declares that it is not worth while.   There is wheeling
and sweeping, to slow, to quick and double-quick time :
Sieur Motier, or Generalissimo Lafayette, for they are
one and the same, and he is General of France, in the
King's stead, for four-and-twenty hours ; Sieur Motier
must step forth, with that sublime chivalrous gait of
his ; solemnly ascend the steps of the Fatherland's
Altar, in sight of Heaven and of the scarcely breathing
Earth ; and, under the creak of those swinging *Cassolettes*, ' pressing his sword's point firmly there ', pronounce the Oath, *To King, to Law, and Nation* (not to
mention ' grains ' with their circulating), in his own
name and that of armed France.   Whereat there is
waving of banners, and acclaim sufficient.   The
National Assembly must swear, standing in its place ;
the King himself audibly.   The King swears ; and now
be the welkin split with vivats : let citizens enfranchised
embrace, each smiting heartily his palm into his fellow's ;
and armed Federates clang their arms ; above all, that
floating battery speak !   It has spoken,—to the four
corners of France.   From eminence to eminence bursts
the thunder ;   faint-heard, loud-repeated.   What a
stone, cast into what a lake ; in circles that do *not*
grow fainter.   From Arras to Avignon ; from Metz to
Bayonne !   Over Orléans and Blois it rolls, in cannon-
recitative ;   Puy bellows of it amid his granite mountains ;   Pau where is the shell-cradle of Great Henri.
At far Marseilles, one can think, the ruddy evening
witnesses it ;   over the deep blue Mediterranean waters,
the Castle of If ruddy-tinted darts forth, from every
cannon's mouth, its tongue of fire ;   and all the people
shout :   Yes, France is free.   O glorious France, that
has burst out so ;   into universal sound and smoke ;   and
attained—the Phrygian *Cap* of Liberty !   In all Towns,
Trees of Liberty also may be planted ;   with or without
advantage.   Said we not, it was the highest stretch
attained by the Thespian Art on this Planet, or perhaps
attainable ?

The Thespian Art, unfortunately, one must still call

it ; for behold there, on this Field of Mars, the National
Banners, before there could be any swearing, were to
be all blessed.   A most proper operation ; since surely
without Heaven's blessing bestowed, say even, audibly
or inaudibly *sought*, no Earthly banner or contrivance
can prove victorious : but now the means of doing it ?
By what thrice-divine Franklin thunder-rod shall
miraculous fire be drawn out of Heaven ; and descend
gently, lifegiving, with health to the souls of men ?
Alas, by the simplest : by Two Hundred shaven-
crowned Individuals, ' in snow-white albs, with tricolor
girdles ', arranged on the steps of Fatherland's Altar ;
and, at their head for spokesman, Soul's-Overseer
Talleyrand-Perigord ! These shall act as miraculous
thunder-rod,—to such length as they can.   O ye deep
azure Heavens, and thou green all-nursing Earth ; ye
Streams ever-flowing ; deciduous Forests that die and
are born again, continually, like the sons of men ; stone
Mountains that die daily with every rain-shower, yet
are not dead and levelled for ages of ages, nor born
again (it seems) but with new world-explosions, and
such tumultuous seething and tumbling, steam halfway
to the Moon ; O thou unfathomable mystic All, garment
and dwelling-place of the UNNAMED ; and thou, articulate-speaking Spirit of Man, who mouldest and modellest
that Unfathomable Unnameable even as we see,—is
not *there* a miracle : That some French mortal should,
we say not have believed, but pretended to imagine
he believed that Talleyrand and Two Hundred pieces
of white Calico could do it !

Here, however, we are to remark with the sorrowing
Historians of that day, that suddenly, while Episcopus
Talleyrand, long-stoled, with mitre and tricolor belt,
was yet but hitching up the Altar-steps to do his miracle,
the material Heaven grew black ; a north-wind, moaning cold moisture, began to sing ; and there descended
a very deluge of rain.   Sad to see !   The thirty-staired
Seats, all round our Amphitheatre, get instantaneously
slated with mere umbrellas, fallacious when so thick
set : our antique *Cassolettes* become water-pots ; their

incense-smoke gone hissing, in a whiff of muddy vapour.
Alas, instead of vivats, there is nothing now but the
furious peppering and rattling. From three to four
hundred thousand human individuals feel that they
have a skin ; happily *im*pervious. The General's sash
runs water : how all military banners droop ; and will
not wave, but lazily flap, as if metamorphosed into
painted tin-banners ! Worse, far worse, these hundred
thousand, such is the Historian's testimony, of the
fairest of France ! Their snowy muslins all splashed
and draggled ; the ostrich-feather shrunk shamefully
to the backbone of a feather : all caps are ruined ;
innermost pasteboard molten into its original pap :
Beauty no longer swims decorated in her garniture,
like Love-goddess hidden-revealed in her Paphian
clouds, but struggles in disastrous imprisonment in
it, for ' the shape was noticeable ' ; and now only
sympathetic interjections, titterings, teeheeings, and
resolute good humour will avail. A deluge ; an incessant sheet or fluid-column of rain ;—such that our
Overseer's very mitre must be filled ; not a mitre, but
a filled and leaky fire-bucket on his reverend head !—
Regardless of which, Overseer Talleyrand performs his
miracle : the Blessing of Talleyrand, another than that
of Jacob,* is on all the Eighty-three departmental flags
of France ; which wave or flap, with such thankfulness
as needs. Towards three o'clock, the sun beams out
again : the remaining evolutions can be transacted
under bright heavens, though with decorations much
damaged.[1]

On Wednesday our Federation is consummated : but
the festivities last out the week, and over into the next.
Festivities such as no Bagdad Caliph, or Aladdin with
the Lamp, could have equalled. There is a Jousting
on the River ; with its water-somersets, splashing and
haha-ing : Abbé Fauchet, *Te Deum* Fauchet, preaches,
for his part, in the ' rotunda of the Corn-market ',
a funeral harangue on Franklin ; for whom the National

----

[1] Deux Amis, v. 143–79.

Assembly has lately gone three days in black. The
Motier and Lepelletier tables still groan with viands;
roofs ringing with patriotic toasts. On the fifth evening, which is the Christian Sabbath, there is a universal
Ball. Paris, out of doors and in, man, woman and
child, is jigging it, to the sound of harp and four-stringed
fiddle. The hoariest-headed man will tread one other
measure, under this nether Moon; speechless nurse-
lings, *infants* as we call them, νήπια τέκνα* crow in arms;
and sprawl out numb-plump little limbs,—impatient
for muscularity, they know not why. The stiffest balk
bends more or less; all joists creak.

Or out, on the Earth's breast itself, behold the Ruins
of the Bastille. All lamplit, allegorically decorated;
a Tree of Liberty sixty feet high; and Phrygian Cap
on it, of size enormous, under which King Arthur and
his round-table might have dined! In the depths of
the background is a single lugubrious lamp, rendering
dim-visible one of your iron cages, half-buried, and
some Prison stones,—Tyranny vanishing downwards,
all gone but the skirt: the rest wholly lamp-festoons,
trees real or of pasteboard; in the similitude of a fairy
grove; with this inscription, readable to runner:
'*Ici l'on danse*, Dancing Here'. As indeed had been
obscurely foreshadowed by Cagliostro[1] prophetic
Quack of Quacks, when he, four years ago, quitted the
grim durance;—to fall into a grimmer, of the Roman
Inquisition, and not quit it.

But, after all, what is this Bastille business to that
of the *Champs Elysées*! Thither, to these Fields well
named Elysian, all feet tend. It is radiant as day with
festooned lamps; little oil-cups, like variegated fire-
flies, daintily illume the highest leaves: trees there are
all sheeted with variegated fire, shedding far a glimmer
into the dubious wood. There, under the free sky, do
tight-limbed Federates, with fairest newfound sweethearts, elastic as Diana, and not of that coyness and
tart humour of Diana, thread their jocund mazes, all

---

[1] See his Lettre au Peuple Français (London, 1786).

through the ambrosial night; and hearts were touched
and fired; and seldom surely had our old Planet, in
that huge conic Shadow of hers 'which goes beyond
the Moon, and is named *Night*', curtained such a Ball-
room. O if, according to Seneca,* the very gods look
down on a good man struggling with adversity, and
smile; what must they think of Five-and-twenty
million indifferent ones victorious over it,—for eight
days and more?

In this way, and in such ways, however, has the
Feast of Pikes danced itself off: gallant Federates
wending homewards, towards every point of the compass, with feverish nerves, heart and head much heated;
some of them, indeed, as Dampmartin's elderly respectable friend from Strasburg, quite 'burnt out with
liquors', and flickering towards extinction.[1] The Feast
of Pikes has danced itself off, and become defunct, and
the ghost of a Feast;—nothing of it now remaining
but this vision in men's memory; and the place that
knew it (for the slope of that Champ-de-Mars is crum-
bled to half the original height [2]) now knowing it no
more. Undoubtedly one of the memorablest National
Hightides. Never or hardly ever, as we said, was Oath
sworn with such heart-effusion, emphasis and expenditure of joyance; and then it was broken irremediably
within year and day. Ah, why? When the swearing
of it was so heavenly-joyful, bosom clasped to bosom,
and Five-and-twenty million hearts all burning
together; O ye inexorable Destinies, why?—Partly
because it was sworn with such overjoyance; but
chiefly, indeed, for an older reason: that Sin had come*
into the world, and Misery by Sin! These Five-and-
twenty millions, if we will consider it, have now henceforth, with that Phrygian Cap of theirs, no force *over*
them, to bind and guide; neither *in* them, more than
heretofore, is guiding force, or rule of just living: how

[1] Dampmartin, Evénemens, i. 144-84.
[2] Dulaure, Histoire de Paris, viii. 25.

then, while they all go rushing at such a *pace*, on
unknown ways, with no bridle, towards no aim, can
hurlyburly unutterable fail ? For verily not Federa-
tion-rosepink is the colour of this Earth and her work :
not by outbursts of noble sentiment, but with far other
ammunition, shall a man front the world.

But how wise, in all cases, to ' husband your fire ' ;
to keep it deep down, rather, as genial radical-heat !
Explosions, the forciblest, and never so well directed,
are questionable ; far oftenest futile, always frightfully
wasteful : but think of a man, of a Nation of men,
spending its whole stock of fire in one artificial Fire-
work ! So have we seen fond weddings (for individuals,
like Nations, have their Hightides) celebrated with an
outburst of triumph and deray, at which the elderly
shook their heads. Better had a serious cheerfulness
been ; for the enterprise was great. Fond pair ! the
more triumphant ye feel, and victorious over terrestrial
evil, which seems all abolished, the wider-eyed will
your disappointment be to find terrestrial evil still
extant. ' And why extant ? ' will each of you cry :
' Because my false mate has played the traitor : evil
was abolished ; I, for one, meant faithfully, and did,
or would have done ! ' Whereby the over-sweet moon
of honey changes itself into long years of vinegar :
perhaps divulsive vinegar, like Hannibal's.*

Shall we say then, the French Nation has led Royalty,
or wooed and teased poor Royalty to lead *her*, to the
hymeneal Fatherland's Altar, in such over-sweet
manner ; and has, most thoughtlessly, to celebrate the
nuptials with due shine and demonstration,—burnt
her bed ?

BOOK II

NANCI

CHAPTER I

BOUILLÉ

DIMLY visible, at Metz on the North-Eastern frontier, a certain brave Bouillé, last refuge of Royalty in all straits and meditations of flight, has for many months hovered occasionally in our eye ; some name or shadow of a brave Bouillé : let us now, for a little, look fixedly at him, till he become a substance and person for us. The man himself is worth a glance ; his position and procedure there, in these days, will throw light on many things.

For it is with Bouillé as with all French Commanding Officers ; only in a more emphatic degree. The grand National Federation, we already guess, was but empty sound, or worse: a last loudest universal *Hep-hep-hurrah*, with full bumpers, in that National Lapithae-feast of Constitution-making ; as in loud denial of the palpably existing ; as if, with hurrahings, you would shut out notice of the inevitable, already knocking at the gates ! Which new National bumper, one may say, can but deepen the drunkenness ; and so, the *louder* it swears Brotherhood, will the sooner and the more surely lead to Cannibalism. Ah, under that fraternal shine and clangour, what a deep world of irreconcilable discords lie momentarily assuaged, damped down for one moment ! Respectable military Federates have barely got home to their quarters ; and the inflammablest, ' dying, burnt up with liquors, and kindness ', has

not yet got extinct; the shine is hardly out of men's
eyes, and still blazes filling all men's memories,—when
your discords burst forth again very considerably
darker than ever.   Let us look at Bouillé, and see how.

Bouillé for the present commands in the Garrison
of Metz, and far and wide over the East and North;
being indeed, by a late act of Government with sanction
of National Assembly, appointed one of our Four
supreme Generals.   Rochambeau and Mailly,* men and
Marshals of note in these days, though to us of small
moment, are two of his colleagues; tough old babbling
Lückner,* also of small moment for us, will probably be
the third.   Marquis de Bouillé is a determined Loyalist;
not indeed disinclined to moderate reform, but resolute
against immoderate.   A man long suspect to Patriotism;
who has more than once given the august Assembly
trouble; who would not, for example, take the National
Oath, as he was bound to do, but always put it off on
this or the other pretext, till an autograph of Majesty
requested him to do it as a favour.   There, in this post,
if not of honour yet of eminence and danger, he waits,
in a silent concentred manner; very dubious of the
future.   'Alone', as he says, or almost alone, of all
the old military Notabilities, he has not emigrated;
but thinks always, in atrabiliar moments, that there
will be nothing for him too but to cross the marches.
He might cross, say, to Treves or Coblentz where Exiled
Princes will be one day ranking; or say, over into
Luxemburg where old Broglie loiters and languishes.
Or is there not the great dim Deep of European Diplomacy; where your Calonnes, your Breteuils are beginning to hover, dimly discernible?

With immeasurable confused outlooks and purposes,
with no clear purpose but this of still trying to do his
Majesty a service, Bouillé waits; struggling what he
can to keep his district loyal, his troops faithful, his
garrisons furnished.   He maintains, as yet, with his
Cousin Lafayette some thin diplomatic correspondence,
by letter and messenger; chivalrous constitutional
professions on the one side, military gravity and brevity

on the other ; which thin correspondence one can see
growing ever the thinner and hollower, towards the
verge of entire vacuity.[1] A quick, choleric, sharply
discerning, stubbornly endeavouring man ; with sup-
pressed-explosive resolution, with valour, nay headlong
audacity : a man who was more in his place, lionlike
defending those Windward Isles, or, as with military
tiger-spring, clutching Nevis and Montserrat from the
English,—than here in this suppressed condition,
muzzled and fettered by diplomatic packthreads ;
looking out for a civil war, which may never arrive.
Few years ago Bouillé was to have led a French East-
Indian Expedition, and reconquered or conquered
Pondicherri and the Kingdoms of the Sun : but the
whole world is suddenly changed, and he with it ;
Destiny willed it not in that way, but in this.

CHAPTER II

ARREARS AND ARISTOCRATS

INDEED, as to the general outlook of things, Bouillé
himself augurs not well of it. The French army, ever
since those old Bastille days, and earlier, has been
universally in the questionablest state, and growing
daily worse. Discipline, which is at all times a kind
of miracle, and works by faith, broke down then ; one
sees not with what near prospect of recovering itself.
The Gardes Françaises played a deadly game ; but
how they won it, and wear the prizes of it, all men
know. In that general overturn, we saw the Hired
Fighters refuse to fight. The very Swiss of Château-
Vieux, which indeed is a kind of French Swiss, from
Geneva and the Pays de Vaud, are understood to have
declined. Deserters glided over ; Royal-Allemand

[1] Bouillé, Mémoires (London, 1797), i. c. 8.

itself looked disconsolate, though stanch of purpose.
In a word, we there saw *Military Rule,* in the shape of
poor Besenval with that convulsive unmanageable
Camp of his, pass two martyr days on the Champ-de-
Mars ; and then, veiling itself, so to speak, 'under
cloud of night', depart 'down the left bank of the
Seine', to seek refuge elsewhere ; *this* ground having
clearly become too hot for it.

But what new ground to seek, what remedy to try ?
Quarters that were 'uninfected' : this doubtless, with
judicious strictness of drilling, were the plan.   Alas,
in all quarters and places, from Paris onward to the
remotest hamlet, is infection, is seditious contagion :
inhaled, propagated by contact and converse, till the
dullest soldier catch it !   There is speech of men in
uniform with men not in uniform ; men in uniform read
journals, and even write in them.[1]   There are public
petitions or remonstrances, private emissaries and
associations ; there is discontent, jealousy, uncertainty,
sullen suspicious humour.   The whole French Army,
fermenting in dark heat, glooms ominous, boding good
to no one.

So that, in the general social dissolution and revolt,
we are to have this deepest and dismallest kind of it,
a revolting soldiery ?   Barren, desolate to look upon
is this same business of revolt under all its aspects ;
but how infinitely more so, when it takes the aspect of
military mutiny !   The very implement of rule and
restraint, whereby all the rest was managed and held
in order, has become precisely the frightfullest immeasurable implement of misrule ; like the element of Fire,
our indispensable all-ministering servant, when it gets
the *mastery,* and becomes conflagration.   Discipline
we called a kind of miracle : in fact, is it not miraculous
how one man moves hundreds of thousands ; each unit
of whom, it may be, loves him not, and singly fears
him not, yet has to obey him, to go hither or go thither,
to march and halt, to give death, and even to receive

---

[1] See Newspapers of July 1789 (in Hist. Parl. ii. 35), &c.

it, as if a Fate had spoken ; and the word-of-command
becomes, almost in the literal sense, a magic-word ?

Which magic-word, again, if it be once *forgotten* ; the
spell of it once broken ! The legions of assiduous
ministering spirits rise on you now as menacing fiends ;
your free orderly arena becomes a tumult-place of the
Nether Pit, and the hapless magician is rent limb from
limb. Military mobs are mobs with muskets in their
hands ; and also with death hanging over their heads,
for death is the penalty of disobedience, and they have
disobeyed. And now if all mobs are properly frenzies,
and work frenetically with mad fits of hot and of cold,
fierce rage alternating so incoherently with panic terror,
consider what your military mob will be, with such
a conflict of duties and penalties, whirled between
remorse and fury, and, for the hot fit, loaded fire-arms
in its hand ! To the soldier himself, revolt is frightful,
and oftenest perhaps pitiable ; and yet so dangerous,
it can only be hated, cannot be pitied. An anomalous
class of mortals these poor Hired Killers ! With
a frankness, which to the Moralist in these times seems
surprising, they have sworn to become machines ; and
nevertheless they are still partly men. Let no prudent
person in authority remind them of this latter fact ;
but always let force, let injustice above all, stop short
clearly on *this* side of the rebounding-point ! Soldiers,
as we often say, do revolt : were it not so, several
things which are transient in this world might be
perennial.

Over and above the general quarrel which all sons
of Adam maintain with their lot here below, the
grievances of the French soldiery reduce themselves to
two. First, that their Officers are Aristocrats ;
secondly, that they cheat them of their Pay. Two
grievances ; or rather we might say one, capable of
becoming a hundred ; for in that single first proposition, that the Officers are Aristocrats, what a multitude
of corollaries lie ready ! It is a bottomless ever-flowing
fountain of grievances this ; what you may call a

general raw-material of grievance, wherefrom individual
grievance after grievance will daily body itself forth.
Nay there will even be a kind of comfort in getting it,
from time to time, so embodied. Peculation of one's
Pay ! It is embodied ; made tangible, made denounce-
able ; exhalable, if only in angry words.

For unluckily that grand fountain of grievances does
exist : Aristocrats almost all our Officers necessarily
are ; they have it in the blood and bone. By the law
of the case, no man can pretend to be the pitifullest
lieutenant of militia till he have first verified, to the
satisfaction of the Lion-King, a Nobility of four
generations. Not nobility only, but four generations
of it : this latter is the improvement hit upon, in
comparatively late years, by a certain War-minister
much pressed for commissions.[1] An improvement
which did relieve the overpressed War-minister, but
which split France still further into yawning contrasts
of Commonalty and Nobility, nay of new Nobility
and old ; as if already with your new and old, and then
with your old, older and oldest, there were not contrasts
and discrepancies enough ;—the general clash whereof
men now see and hear, and in the singular whirlpool,
all contrasts gone together to the bottom ! Gone to
the bottom or going ; with uproar, without return ;
going everywhere save in the Military section of things ;
and there, it may be asked, can they hope to continue
always at the top ? Apparently, not.

It is true, in a time of external Peace, when there is
no fighting, but only drilling, this question, How you
rise from the ranks, may seem theoretical rather. But
in reference to the Rights of Man it is continually
practical. The soldier has sworn to be faithful not to
the King only, but to the Law and the Nation. Do
our commanders love the Revolution ? ask all soldiers.
Unhappily no, they hate it, and love the Counter-
Revolution. Young epauletted men, with quality-
blood in them, poisoned with quality-pride, do sniff

---

[1] Dampmartin, Evénemens, i. 89.

openly, with indignation struggling to become contempt,
at our Rights of Man, as at some newfangled cobweb,
which shall be brushed down again. Old Officers,
more cautious, keep silent, with closed uncurled lips ;
but one guesses what is passing within. Nay who
knows, how, under the plausiblest word of command,
might lie Counter-Revolution itself, sale to Exiled
Princes and the Austrian Kaiser : treacherous Aristocrats hoodwinking the small insight of us common men ?
—In such manner works that general raw-material of
grievance ; disastrous ; instead of trust and reverence,
breeding hate, endless suspicion, the impossibility of
commanding and obeying. And now when this second
more tangible grievance has articulated itself universally in the mind of the common man : Peculation of
his Pay ! Peculation of the despicablest sort does
exist, and has long existed ; but, unless the new-
declared Rights of Man, and all rights whatsoever, *be*
a cobweb, it shall no longer exist.

The French Military System seems dying a sorrowful
suicidal death. Nay more, citizen, as is natural, ranks
himself against citizen in this cause. The soldier finds
audience, of numbers and sympathy unlimited, among
the Patriot lower-classes. Nor are the higher wanting
to the officer. The officer still dresses and perfumes
himself for such sad unemigrated *soirée* as there may
still be ; and speaks his woes,—which woes, are they
not Majesty's and Nature's ? Speaks, at the same
time, his gay defiance, his firm-set resolution. Citizens,
still more Citizenesses, see the right and the wrong ;
not the Military System alone will die by suicide, but
much along with it. As was said, there is yet possible
a deeper overturn than any yet witnessed : that deepest
*up*turn of the black-burning sulphurous stratum whereon all rests and grows !

But how these things may act on the rude soldier-
mind, with its military pedantries, its inexperience of
all that lies off the parade-ground ; inexperience as of
a child, yet fierceness of a man, and vehemence of
a Frenchman ! It is long that secret communings in

mess-room and guard-room, sour looks, thousandfold
petty vexations between commander and commanded,
measure everywhere the weary military day. Ask
Captain Dampmartin ; an authentic, ingenious literary
officer of horse ; who loves the Reign of Liberty, after
a sort : yet has had his heart grieved to the quick
many times, in the hot South-Western region and
elsewhere ; and has seen riot, civil battle by daylight
and by torchlight, and anarchy hatefuller than death.
How insubordinate Troopers, with drink in their heads,
meet Captain Dampmartin and another on the ramparts, where there is no escape or side-path ; and make
military salute punctually, for we look calm on them ;
yet make it in a snappish, almost insulting manner :
how one morning they ' leave all their chamois shirts '
and superfluous buffs, which they are tired of, laid in
piles at the Captains' doors ; whereat ' we laugh ', as
the ass does eating thistles*: nay how they ' knot two
forage-cords together ', with universal noisy cursing,
with evident intent to hang the Quartermaster :—all
this the worthy Captain, looking on it through the
ruddy-and-sable of fond regretful memory, has flowingly
written down.[1] Men growl in vague discontent ;
officers fling up their commissions, and emigrate in
disgust.

Or let us ask another literary Officer ; not yet Captain ; Sub-lieutenant only, in the Artillery Regiment
La Fère : a young man of twenty-one ; not unentitled
to speak ; the name of him is *Napoleon Bonaparte*.
To such height of Sub-lieutenancy has he now got
promoted, from Brienne School, five years ago ; ' being
found qualified in mathematics by La Place '. He is
lying at Auxonne, in the West, in these months ; not
sumptuously lodged—' in the house of a Barber, to
whose wife he did not pay the customary degree of
respect ' ; or even over at the Pavillon, in a chamber
with bare walls ; the only furniture an indifferent ' bed
without curtains, two chairs, and in the recess of a

---

[1] Dampmartin, Evénemens, i. 122-46.

window a table covered with books and papers: his
Brother Louis sleeps on a coarse mattress in an adjoining
room'. However, he is doing something great: writing
his first Book or Pamphlet,—eloquent vehement *Letter
to M. Matteo Buttafuoco*, our Corsican Deputy, who is not
a Patriot, but an Aristocrat unworthy of Deputyship.
Joly of Dôle is Publisher. The literary Sub-lieutenant
corrects the proofs; ' sets out on foot from Auxonne,
every morning at four o'clock, for Dôle: after looking
over the proofs, he partakes of an extremely frugal
breakfast with Joly, and immediately prepares for
returning to his Garrison; where he arrives before
noon, having thus walked above twenty miles in the
course of the morning'.

This Sub-lieutenant can remark that, in drawing-
rooms, on streets, on highways, at inns, everywhere
men's minds are ready to kindle into a flame. That
a Patriot, if he appear in the drawing-room, or amid
a group of officers, is liable enough to be discouraged,
so great is the majority against him: but no sooner
does he get into the street, or among the soldiers, than
he feels again as if the whole Nation were with him.
That after the famous Oath, *To the King, to the Nation,
and Law*, there was a great change; that before this,
if ordered to fire on the people, he for one would have
done it in the King's name; but that after this, in the
Nation's name, he would not have done it. Likewise
that the Patriot officers, more numerous too in the
Artillery and Engineers than elsewhere, were few in
number; yet that having the soldiers on their side,
they ruled the regiment; and did often deliver the
Aristocrat brother officer out of peril and strait. One
day, for example, ' a member of our own mess roused
the mob, by singing, from the windows of our dining-
room, *O Richard, O my King*; and I had to snatch
him from their fury'.[1]

All which let the reader multiply by ten thousand;

[1] Norvins, Histoire de Napoleon, i. 47; Las Cases, Mémoires (translated into Hazlitt's Life of Napoleon, i. 23-31).

and spread it, with slight variations, over all the camps
and garrisons of France.   The French Army seems on
the verge of universal mutiny.

Universal mutiny !   There is in that what may well
make Patriot Constitutionalism and an august Assembly
shudder.   Something behoves to be done ; yet what
to do no man can tell.   Mirabeau proposes even that
the Soldiery, having come to such a pass, be forthwith
disbanded, the whole Two Hundred and Eighty
Thousand of them ; and organized anew.[1]   Impossible
this, in so sudden a manner ! cry all men.   And yet
literally, answer we, it is inevitable, in one manner or
another.   Such an army, with its four-generation
Nobles, its peculated Pay, and men knotting forage-
cords to hang their Quartermaster, cannot subsist
beside such a Revolution.   Your alternative is a slow-
pining chronic dissolution and new organization ; or
a swift decisive one ; the agonies spread over years,
or concentred into an hour.   With a Mirabeau for
Minister or Governor, the latter had been the choice ;
with no Mirabeau for Governor, it will naturally be
the former.

CHAPTER III

BOUILLÉ AT METZ

To Bouillé, in his North-Eastern circle, none of these
things are altogether hid.   Many times flight over the
marches gleams out on him as a last guidance in such
bewilderment : nevertheless he continues here ; struggling always to hope the best, not from new organization, but from happy Counter-Revolution and return
to the old.   For the rest, it is clear to him that this
same National Federation, and universal swearing and
fraternizing of People and Soldiers, has done ' incal-

[1] Moniteur, 1790, No. 233.

culable mischief'. So much that fermented secretly
has hereby got vent, and become open : National
Guards and Soldiers of the line, solemnly embracing
one another on all parade-fields, drinking, swearing
patriotic oaths, fall into disorderly street-processions,
constitutional unmilitary exclamations and hurrahings.
On which account the Regiment Picardie, for one, has
to be drawn out in the square of the barracks, here at
Metz, and sharply harangued by the General himself ;
but expresses penitence.[1]

Far and near, as accounts testify, insubordination
has begun grumbling louder and louder. Officers have
been seen shut up in their mess-rooms ; assaulted with
clamorous demands, not without menaces. The insubordinate ringleader is dismissed with ' yellow furlough ',
yellow infamous thing they call *cartouche jaune* : but
ten new ringleaders rise in his stead, and the yellow
cartouche ceases to be thought disgraceful. ' Within
a fortnight ', or at furthest a month, of that sublime
Feast of Pikes, the whole French Army, demanding
Arrears, forming Reading Clubs, frequenting Popular
Societies, is in a state which Bouillé can call by no
name but that of mutiny. Bouillé knows it as few
do ; and speaks by dire experience. Take one instance
instead of many.

It is still an early day of August, the precise date
now undiscoverable, when Bouillé, about to set out
for the waters of Aix-la-Chapelle, is once more suddenly
summoned to the barracks of Metz. The soldiers stand
ranged in fighting order, muskets loaded, the officers
all there on compulsion ; and required with many-
voiced emphasis to have their arrears paid. Picardie
was penitent ; but we see it has relapsed : the wide
space bristles and lours with mere mutinous armed
men. Brave Bouillé advances to the nearest Regiment,
opens his commanding lips to harangue ; obtains
nothing but querulous-indignant discordance, and the
sound of so many thousand livres legally due. The

[1] Bouillé, Mémoires, i. 113.

moment is trying; there are some ten thousand
soldiers now in Metz, and one spirit seems to have
spread among them.

Bouillé is firm as the adamant; but what shall he
do? A German Regiment, named of Salm, is thought
to be of better temper: nevertheless Salm too may
have heard of the precept, *Thou shalt not steal*; Salm
too may know that money is money. Bouillé walks
trustfully towards the Regiment de Salm, speaks trustful words; but here again is answered by the cry of
forty-four thousand livres odd sous. A cry waxing
more and more vociferous, as Salm's humour mounts;
which cry, as it will produce no cash or promise of cash,
ends in the wide simultaneous whirr of shouldered
muskets, and a determined quick-time march on the
part of Salm—towards its Colonel's house, in the next
street, there to seize the colours and military chest.
Thus does Salm, for its part; strong in the faith that
meum is not *tuum*, that fair speeches are not forty-four
thousand livres odd sous.

Unrestrainable! Salm tramps to military time,
quick consuming the way. Bouillé and the officers,
drawing sword, have to dash into double-quick *pas-de-
charge*, or unmilitary running; to get the start; to
station themselves on the outer staircase, and stand
there with what of death-defiance and sharp steel they
have; Salm truculently coiling itself up, rank after
rank, opposite them, in such humour as we can fancy,
which happily has not yet mounted to the murder-
pitch. There will Bouillé stand, certain at least of *one*
man's purpose: in grim calmness, awaiting the issue.
What the intrepidest of men and generals can do is
done. Bouillé, though there is a barricading picket
at each end of the street, and death under his eyes,
contrives to send for a Dragoon Regiment with orders
to charge: the dragoon officers mount; the dragoon
men will not: hope is none there for him. The street,
as we say, barricaded; the Earth all shut out, only the
indifferent heavenly Vault overhead: perhaps here or
there a timorous householder peering out of window,

with prayer for Bouillé; copious Rascality, on the
pavement, with prayer for Salm: there do the two
parties stand;—like chariots locked in a narrow
thoroughfare; like locked wrestlers at a dead-grip!
For two hours they stand: Bouillé's sword glittering
in his hand, adamantine resolution clouding his brows:
for two hours by the clocks of Metz. Moody-silent
stands Salm, with occasional clangour; but does not
fire. Rascality, from time to time, urges some grenadier to level his musket at the General; who looks on
it as a bronze General would: and always some
corporal or other strikes it up.

In such remarkable attitude, standing on that staircase for two hours, does brave Bouillé, long a shadow,
dawn on us visibly out of the dimness, and become
a person. For the rest, since Salm has not shot him
at the first instant, and since in himself there is no
variableness, the danger will diminish. The Mayor,
'a man infinitely respectable', with his Municipals
and tricolor sashes, finally gains entrance; remonstrates, perorates, promises; gets Salm persuaded
home to its barracks. Next day, our respectable
Mayor lending the money, the officers pay down the
half of the demand in ready cash. With which liqui-
dation Salm pacifies itself; and for the present all is
hushed up, as much as may be.[1]

Such scenes as this of Metz, or preparations and
demonstrations towards such, are universal over France:
Dampmartin, with his knotted forage-cords and piled
chamois-jackets, is at Strasburg in the South-East; in
these same days or rather nights, Royal Champagne is
'shouting *Vive la Nation, au diable les Aristocrates*, with
some thirty lit candles', at Hesdin, on the far North-
West. 'The garrison of Bitche', Deputy Rewbell is sorry
to state, 'went out of the town with drums beating;
deposed its officers; and then returned into the town,
sabre in hand'.[2] Ought not a National Assembly to

[1] Bouillé, i. 140-5.
[2] Moniteur (in Hist. Parl. vii. 29).

occupy itself with these objects ? Military France is
everywhere full of sour inflammatory humour, which
exhales itself fuliginously, this way or that : a whole
continent of smoking flax*; which, blown on here or
there by any angry wind, might so easily start into a
blaze, into a continent of fire.

Constitutional Patriotism is in deep natural alarm
at these things. The august Assembly sits diligently
deliberating ; dare nowise resolve, with Mirabeau, on
an instantaneous disbandment and extinction ; finds
that a course of palliatives is easier. But at least and
lowest, this grievance of the Arrears shall be rectified.
A plan, much noised of in those days, under the name
' Decree of the Sixth of August ', has been devised for
that. Inspectors shall visit all armies ; and, with
certain elected corporals and ' soldiers able to write ',
verify what arrears and peculations do lie due, and
make them good. Well, if in this way the smoky heat
be cooled down ; if it be not, as we say, ventilated
overmuch, or, by sparks and collision somewhere,
sent *up* !

CHAPTER IV

ARREARS AT NANCI

We are to remark, however, that of all districts, this
of Bouillé's seems the inflammablest. It was always
to Bouillé and Metz that Royalty would fly : Austria
lies near ; here more than elsewhere must the disunited
People look over the borders, into a dim sea of Foreign
Politics and Diplomacies, with hope or apprehension,
with mutual exasperation.

It was but in these days that certain Austrian troops,
marching peaceably across an angle of this region,
seemed an Invasion realized ; and there rushed towards
Stenai, with musket on shoulder, from all the winds,
some thirty thousand National Guards, to inquire what

the matter was.[1]   A matter of mere diplomacy it
proved ; the Austrian Kaiser, in haste to get to Belgium,
had bargained for this short cut.   The infinite dim
movement of European politics waved a skirt over
these spaces, passing on its way; like the passing
shadow of a condor ; and such a winged flight of thirty
thousand, with mixed cackling and crowing, rose in
consequence !   For, in addition to all, this people, as
we said, is much divided : Aristocrats abound ; Patriotism has both Aristocrats and Austrians to watch.
It is Lorraine, this region ; not so illuminated as old
France : it remembers ancient Feudalisms ; nay,
within man's memory it had a Court and King of its
own, or indeed the splendour of a Court and King,
without the burden.   Then, contrariwise, the Mother
Society, which sits in the Jacobins Church at Paris,
has Daughters in the Towns here ; shrill-tongued,
driven acrid : consider how the memory of good King
Stanislaus,* and ages of Imperial Feudalism, may com-
port with this New acrid Evangel, and what a virulence
of discord there may be !   In all which, the Soldiery,
officers on one side, private men on the other, takes
part, and now indeed principal part ; a Soldiery, moreover, all the hotter here as it lies the denser, the frontier
Province requiring more of it.

So stands Lorraine : but the capital City more especially so.   The pleasant City of Nanci, which faded
Feudalism loves, where King Stanislaus personally
dwelt and shone, has an Aristocrat Municipality, and
then also a Daughter Society : it has some forty
thousand divided souls of population ; and three large
Regiments, one of which is Swiss Château-Vieux, dear
to Patriotism ever since it refused fighting, or was
thought to refuse, in the Bastille days.   Here unhappily
all evil influences seem to meet concentred ; here, of
all places, may jealousy and heat evolve itself.   These
many months, accordingly, man has been set against
man, Washed against Unwashed*; Patriot Soldier

_____
[1] Moniteur, Séance du 9 Août 1790.

against Aristocrat Captain, ever the more bitterly : and
a long score of grudges has been running up.

Nameable grudges, and likewise unnameable : for
there is a punctual nature in Wrath ; and daily, were
there but glances of the eye, tones of the voice, and
minutest commissions or omissions, it will jot down
somewhat, to account, under the head of sundries,
which always swells the sum-total. For example, in
April last, in those times of preliminary Federation,
when National Guards and Soldiers were everywhere
swearing brotherhood, and all France was locally
federating, preparing for the grand National Feast of
Pikes, it was observed that these Nanci Officers threw
cold water on the whole brotherly business ; that they
first hung back from appearing at the Nanci Federation ;
then did appear, but in mere *rédingote* and undress,
with scarcely a clean shirt on ; nay that one of them,
as the National Colours flaunted by in that solemn
moment, did, without visible necessity, take occasion
to *spit*.[1]

Small ' sundries as per journal ', but then incessant
ones ! The Aristocrat Municipality, pretending to be
Constitutional, keeps mostly quiet ; not so the Daughter
Society, the five thousand adult male Patriots of the
place, still less the five thousand female : not so the
young, whiskered or whiskerless, four-generation Noblesse in epaulettes ; the grim Patriot Swiss of Château-
Vieux, effervescent infantry of Regiment du Roi, hot
troopers of Mestre-de-Camp ! Walled Nanci, which
stands so bright and trim, with its straight streets,
spacious squares, and Stanislaus' Architecture, on the
fruitful alluvium of the Meurthe ; so bright, amid the
yellow cornfields in these Reaper-Months,—is inwardly
but a den of discord, anxiety, inflammability, not far
from exploding. Let Bouillé look to it. If that
universal military heat, which we liken to a vast continent of smoking flax, do anywhere take fire, his beard,
here in Lorraine and Nanci, may the most readily of
all get singed by it.

[1] Deux Amis, v. 217.

Bouillé, for his part, is busy enough, but only with
the general superintendence ; getting his pacified Salm,
and all other still tolerable Regiments, marched out of
Metz, to southward towns and villages ; to rural Cantonments as at Vic, Marsal and thereabout, by the
still waters ; where is plenty of horse-forage, sequestered parade-ground, and the soldier's speculative
faculty can be stilled by drilling. Salm, as we said,
received only half payment of arrears ; naturally not
without grumbling. Nevertheless that scene of the
drawn sword may, after all, have raised Bouillé in the
mind of Salm ; for men and soldiers love intrepidity
and swift inflexible decision, even when they suffer by
it. As indeed is not this fundamentally the quality of
qualities for a man ? A quality which by itself is next
to nothing, since inferior animals, asses, dogs, even
mules have it ; yet, in due combination, it is the indispensable basis of all.

Of Nanci and its heats, Bouillé, commander of the
whole, knows nothing special : understands generally
that the troops in that City are perhaps the *worst*.[1]
The Officers there have it all, as they have long had it,
to themselves ; and unhappily seem to manage it ill.
' Fifty yellow furloughs ', given out in one batch, do
surely betoken difficulties. But what was Patriotism
to think of certain light-fencing Fusiliers ' set on ', or
supposed to be set on, ' to insult the Grenadier-club ',
—considerate speculative Grenadiers and that reading-
room of theirs ? With shoutings, with hootings ; till
the speculative Grenadier drew his side-arms too ; and
there ensued battery and duels ! Nay more, are not
swashbucklers of the same stamp ' sent out ' visibly,
or sent out presumably, now in the dress of Soldiers,
to pick quarrels with the Citizens ; now, disguised as
Citizens, to pick quarrels with the Soldiers ? For
a certain Roussière, expert in fence, was taken in the
very fact ; four Officers (presumably of tender years)
hounding him on, who thereupon fled precipitately !

[1] Bouillé, i. c. 9.

Fencemaster Roussière, haled to the guardhouse, had sentence of three months' imprisonment: but his comrades demanded ' yellow furlough ' for *him* of all persons; nay, thereafter they produced him on parade; capped him in paper-helmet, inscribed *Iscariot*; marched him to the gate of the City; and there sternly commanded him to vanish for evermore.

On all which suspicions, accusations and noisy procedure, and on enough of the like continually accumulating, the Officer could not but look with disdainful indignation; perhaps disdainfully express the same in words, and ' soon after fly over to the Austrians '.

So that when it here, as elsewhere, comes to the question of Arrears, the humour and procedure is of the bitterest: Regiment Mestre-de-Camp getting, amid loud clamour, some three gold louis a-man,— which have, as usual, to be borrowed from the Municipality; Swiss Château-Vieux applying for the like, but getting instead instantaneous *courrois*, or cat-o'-nine-tails, with subsequent unsufferable hisses from the women and children: Regiment du Roi, sick of hope deferred, at length seizing its military chest, and marching it to quarters, but next day marching it back again, through streets all struck silent:—unordered paradings and clamours, not without strong liquor; objurgation, insubordination; your military ranked Arrangement going all (as the Typographers say of set types, in a similar case) rapidly *to pie*! [1] Such is Nanci in these early days of August; the sublime Feast of Pikes not yet a month old.

Constitutional Patriotism, at Paris and elsewhere, may well quake at the news. War-Minister Latour du Pin runs breathless to the National Assembly, with a written message that ' all is burning, *tout brûle, tout presse* '. The National Assembly, on the spur of the instant, renders such *Decret*, and ' order to submit and repent ', as he requires; if it will avail anything. On the other hand, Journalism, through all its throats,

---

[1] Deux Amis, v. c. 8.

gives hoarse outcry, condemnatory, elegiac-applausive.
The Forty-eight Sections lift up voices; sonorous
Brewer, or call him now *Colonel* Santerre, is not silent,
in the Faubourg Saint-Antoine. For, meanwhile, the
Nanci Soldiers have sent a Deputation of Ten, furnished
with documents and proofs; who will tell another story
than the 'all-is-burning' one. Which deputed Ten,
before ever they reach the Assembly Hall, assiduous
Latour du Pin picks up, and on warrant of Mayor
Bailly, claps in prison! Most unconstitutionally; for
they had officers' furloughs. Whereupon Saint-Antoine,
in indignant uncertainty of the future, closes its shops.
Is Bouillé a traitor then, sold to Austria? In that
case, these poor private sentinels have revolted mainly
out of Patriotism?

New Deputation, Deputation of National Guardsmen
now, sets forth from Nanci to enlighten the Assembly.
It meets the old deputed Ten returning, quite unexpectedly *un*hanged; and proceeds thereupon with
better prospects; but effects nothing. Deputations,
Government Messengers, Orderlies at hand-gallop,
Alarms, thousand-voiced Rumours, go vibrating continually; backwards and forwards,—scattering distraction. Not till the last week of August does M. de
Malseigne, selected as Inspector, get down to the scene
of mutiny; with Authority, with cash, and 'Decree
of the Sixth of August'. He now shall see these Arrears
liquidated, justice done, or at least tumult quashed.

CHAPTER V

INSPECTOR MALSEIGNE

Of Inspector Malseigne we discern, by direct light,
that he is 'of Herculean stature'; and infer, with
probability, that he is of truculent moustachioed
aspect,—for *Royalist* Officers now leave the upper lip
unshaven; that he is of indomitable bull-heart; and
also, unfortunately, of thick bull-head.

On Tuesday the 24th of August 1790, he opens session
as Inspecting Commissioner; meets those 'elected
corporals, and soldiers that can write'. He finds the
accounts of Château-Vieux to be complex; to require
delay and reference: he takes to haranguing, to repri-
manding; ends amid audible grumbling. Next morning, he resumes session, not at the Townhall as prudent
Municipals counselled, but once more at the barracks.
Unfortunately Château-Vieux, grumbling all night,
will now hear of no delay or reference; from reprimand-
ing on his part, it goes to bullying,—answered with
continual cries of ' *Jugez tout de suite,* Judge it at once ';
whereupon M. de Malseigne will off in a huff. But lo,
Château-Vieux, swarming all about the barrack-court,
has sentries at every gate; M. de Malseigne, demanding
egress, cannot get it, not though Commandant Denoue
backs him; can get only ' *Jugez tout de suite* '. Here
is a nodus!

Bull-hearted M. de Malseigne draws his sword; and
will force egress. Confused splutter. M. de Malseigne's
sword breaks: he snatches Commandant Denoue's:
the sentry is wounded. M. de Malseigne, whom one is
loath to kill, does force egress,—followed by Château-
Vieux all in disarray; a spectacle to Nanci. M. de
Malseigne walks at a sharp pace, yet never runs;
wheeling from time to time, with menaces and movements of fence; and so reaches Denoue's house, unhurt;
which house Château-Vieux, in an agitated manner,
invests,—hindered as yet from entering, by a crowd
of officers formed on the staircase. M. de Malseigne
retreats by back ways to the Townhall, flustered though
undaunted; amid an escort of National Guards. From
the Townhall he, on the morrow, emits fresh orders,
fresh plans of settlement with Château-Vieux; to none
of which will Château-Vieux listen: whereupon he
finally, amid noise enough, emits order that Château-
Vieux shall march on the morrow morning, and quarter
at Sarre Louis. Château-Vieux flatly refuses marching; M. de Malseigne ' takes *act* ', due notarial protest,
of such refusal,—if happily that may avail him.

This is the end of Thursday ; and, indeed, of M. de Malseigne's Inspectorship, which has lasted some fifty hours. To such length, in fifty hours, has he unfortunately brought it. Mestre-de-Camp and Regiment du Roi hang, as it were, fluttering ; Château-Vieux is clean gone, in what way we see. Overnight, an Aide-de-Camp of Lafayette's, stationed here for such emergency, sends swift emissaries far and wide to summon National Guards. The slumber of the country is broken by clattering hoofs, by loud fraternal knockings ; everywhere the Constitutional Patriot must clutch his fighting-gear, and take the road for Nanci.

And thus the Herculean Inspector has sat all Thursday, among terror-struck Municipals, a centre of confused noise : all Thursday, Friday, and till Saturday towards noon. Château-Vieux, in spite of the notarial protest, will not march a step. As many as four thousand National Guards are dropping or pouring in ; uncertain what is expected of them, still more uncertain what will be obtained of them. For all is uncertainty, commotion and suspicion : there goes a word that Bouillé, beginning to bestir himself in the rural Cantonments eastward, is but a Royalist traitor ; that Château-Vieux and Patriotism are sold to Austria, of which latter M. de Malseigne is probably some agent. Mestre-de-Camp and Roi flutter still more questionably : Château-Vieux, far from marching, ' waves red flags out of two carriages ', in a passionate manner, along the streets ; and next morning answers its Officers : ' Pay us, then ; and we will march with you to the world's end ! '

Under which circumstances, towards noon on Saturday, M. de Malseigne thinks it were good perhaps to inspect the ramparts,—on horseback. He mounts, accordingly, with escort of three troopers. At the gate of the City, he bids two of them wait for his return ; and with the third, a trooper to be depended upon, he —gallops off for Lunéville ; where lies a certain Carbineer Regiment not yet in a mutinous state ! The two left troopers soon get uneasy ; discover how it is,

and give the alarm. Mestre-de-Camp, to the number
of a hundred, saddles in frantic haste, as if sold to
Austria ; gallops out pell-mell in chase of its Inspector.
And so they spur, and the Inspector spurs ; careering,
with noise and jingle, up the valley of the River
Meurthe, towards Lunéville and the midday sun :
through an astonished country ; indeed almost to their
own astonishment.

What a hunt ; Actaeon-like*;—which Actaeon de
Malseigne happily *gains*. To arms, ye Carbineers of
Lunéville : to chastise mutinous men, insulting your
General Officer, insulting your own quarters ;—above
all things, fire *soon*, lest there be parleying and ye refuse
to fire ! The Carbineers fire soon, exploding upon the
first stragglers of Mestre-de-Camp ; who shriek at the
very flash, and fall back hastily on Nanci, in a state
not far from distraction. Panic and fury : sold to
Austria without an *if* ; so much per regiment, the very
sums can be specified ; and traitorous Malseigne is fled !
Help, O Heaven ; help, thou Earth,—ye unwashed
Patriots ; ye too are sold like us !

Effervescent Regiment du Roi primes its firelocks,
Mestre-de-Camp saddles wholly : Commandant Denoue
is seized, is flung in prison with a ' canvas shirt (*sarreau
de toile*)' about him ; Château-Vieux bursts up the
magazines ; distributes ' three thousand fusils ' to
a Patriot people : Austria shall have a hot bargain.
Alas, the unhappy hunting-dogs, as we said, have
hunted away their huntsman ; and do now run howling
and baying, on what trail they know not ; nigh rabid !

And so there is tumultuous march of men, through
the night ; with halt on the heights of Flinval, whence
Lunéville can be seen all illuminated. Then there is
parley, at four in the morning; and reparley ; finally
there is agreement: the Carbineers gave in ; Malseigne
is surrendered, with apologies on all sides. After weary
confused hours, he is even got under way ; the Lunévillers all turning out, in the idle Sunday, to see such
departure : home-going of mutinous Mestre-de-Camp
with its Inspector captive. Mestre-de-Camp accord-

ingly marches; the Lunévillers look. See! at the
corner of the first street, our Inspector bounds off
again, bull-hearted as he is; amid the slash of sabres,
the crackle of musketry; and escapes, full gallop, with
only a ball lodged in his buff-*jerkin*. The Herculean
man! And yet it is an escape to no purpose. For the
Carbineers, to whom after the hardest Sunday's ride
on record, he has come circling back, ' stand deliberating
by their nocturnal watch-fires'; deliberating of Austria,
of traitors, and the rage of Mestre-de-Camp. So that,
on the whole, the next sight we have is that of M. de
Malseigne, on the Monday afternoon, faring bull-
hearted through the streets of Nanci; in open carriage,
a soldier standing over him with drawn sword; amid
the ' furies of the women ', hedges of National Guards,
and confusion of Babel: to the Prison beside Commandant Denoue! That finally is the lodging of
Inspector Malseigne.[1]

Surely it is time Bouillé were drawing near. The
Country all round, alarmed with watchfires, illuminated
towns, and marching and rout, has been sleepless these
several nights. Nanci, with its uncertain National
Guards, with its distributed fusils, mutinous soldiers,
black panic and red-hot ire, is not a City but a Bedlam.

CHAPTER VI

BOUILLÉ AT NANCI

HASTE with help, thou brave Bouillé: if swift help
come not, all is now verily ' burning'; and may burn,
—to what lengths and breadths! Much, in these hours,
depends on Bouillé; as it shall now fare with him, the
whole Future may be this way or be that. If, for
example, he were to loiter dubitating, and not come;

[1] Deux Amis, v. 206–51; Newspapers and Documents
(in Hist. Parl. vii. 59–162).

if he were to come, and fail: the whole Soldiery of
France to blaze into mutiny, National Guards going
some this way, some that; and Royalism to draw its
rapier, and Sansculottism to snatch its pike; and the
Spirit of Jacobinism, as yet young, girt with sun-rays,
to grow instantaneously mature, girt with hell-fire,—
as mortals, in one night of deadly crisis, have had their
heads turned grey!

Brave Bouillé is advancing fast, with the old inflexi-
bility; gathering himself, unhappily 'in small afflu-
ences', from East, from West and North; and now
on Tuesday morning, the last day of the month, he
stands all concentred, unhappily still in small force, at
the village of Frouarde, within some few miles. Son
of Adam with a more dubious task before him is not
in the world this Tuesday morning. A weltering
inflammable sea of doubt and peril, and Bouillé sure of
simply one thing, his own determination. Which one
thing, indeed, may be worth many. He puts a most
firm face on the matter: 'Submission, or unsparing
battle and destruction; twenty-four hours to make
your choice': this was the tenor of his Proclamation;
thirty copies of which he sent yesterday to Nanci:—
all which, we find, were intercepted and not posted.[1]

Nevertheless, at half-past eleven this morning,
seemingly by way of answer, there does wait on him
at Frouarde some Deputation from the mutinous
Regiments, from the Nanci Municipals, to see what
can be done. Bouillé receives this Deputation 'in
a large open court adjoining his lodging': pacified
Salm, and the rest, attend also, being invited to do it,
—all happily still in the right humour. The Mutineers
pronounce themselves with a decisiveness, which to
Bouillé seems insolence; and happily to Salm also.
Salm, forgetful of the Metz staircase and sabre, demands
that the scoundrels 'be hanged' there and then.

---

[1] Compare Bouillé, Mémoires, i. 153-76; Deux Amis,
v. 251-71; Hist. Parl. *ubi supra.*

Bouillé represses the hanging; but answers that
mutinous Soldiers have one course, and not more than
one : To liberate, with heartfelt contrition, Messieurs
Denoue and De Malseigne ; to get ready forthwith for
marching off, whither he shall order ; and 'submit and
repent', as the National Assembly has decreed, as he
yesterday did in thirty printed Placards proclaim.
These are his terms, unalterable as the decrees of
Destiny. Which terms as they, the Mutineer deputies,
seemingly do not accept, it were good for them to
vanish from this spot, and even to do it promptly;
with him too, in few instants, the word will be, Forward !
The Mutineer deputies vanish, not unpromptly ; the
Municipal ones, anxious beyond right for their own
individualities, prefer abiding with Bouillé.

Brave Bouillé, though he puts a most firm face on
the matter, knows his position full well : how at Nanci,
what with rebellious soldiers, with uncertain National
Guards, and so many distributed fusils, there rage and
roar some ten thousand fighting men ; while with himself is scarcely the third part of that number, in National
Guards also uncertain, in mere pacified Regiments,—
for the present full of rage, and clamour to march ; but
whose rage and clamour may next moment take such
a fatal *new* figure. On the top of one uncertain billow,
therewith to calm billows ! Bouillé must 'abandon
himself to Fortune' ; who is said sometimes to favour
the brave.* At half-past twelve, the Mutineer deputies
having vanished, our drums beat; we march: for
Nanci ! Let Nanci bethink itself, then ; for Bouillé
has thought and determined.

And yet how shall Nanci think : not a City but
a Bedlam ! Grim Château-Vieux is for defence to the
death ; forces the Municipality to order, by tap of
drum, all citizens acquainted with artillery to turn out,
and assist in managing the cannon. On the other
hand, effervescent Regiment du Roi is drawn up in its
barracks ; quite disconsolate, hearing the humour Salm
is in; and ejaculates dolefully from its thousand throats:
' *La loi, la loi*, Law, law ! ' Mestre-de-Camp blusters,

with profane swearing, in mixed terror and furor;
National Guards look this way and that, not knowing
what to do. What a Bedlam-City: as many plans as
heads; all ordering, none obeying: quiet none,—
except the Dead, who sleep underground, having *done*
their fighting.

And, behold, Bouillé proves as good as his word:
'at half-past two' scouts report that he is within half
a league of the gates; rattling along, with cannon, and
array; breathing nothing but destruction. A new
Deputation, Municipals, Mutineers, Officers, goes out
to meet him; with passionate entreaty for yet one
other hour. Bouillé grants an hour. Then, at the end
thereof, no Denoue or Malseigne appearing as promised,
he rolls his drums, and again takes the road. Towards
four o'clock, the terror-struck Townsmen may see him
face to face. His cannons rattle there, in their carriages; his vanguard is within thirty paces of the Gate
Stanislaus. Onward like a Planet, by appointed times,
by law of Nature! What next? Lo, flag of truce
and chamade; conjuration to halt: Malseigne and
Denoue are on the street, coming hither; the soldiers
all repentant, ready to submit and march! Adamantine Bouillé's look alters not; yet the word *Halt* is
given: gladder moment he never saw. Joy of joys!
Malseigne and Denoue do verily issue; escorted by
National Guards; from streets all frantic, with sale to
Austria and so forth: they salute Bouillé, unscathed.
Bouillé steps aside to speak with them, and with other
heads of the Town there; having already ordered by
what Gates and Routes the mutineer Regiments shall
file out.

Such colloquy with these two General Officers and
other principal Townsmen, was natural enough;
nevertheless one wishes Bouillé had postponed it, and
not stepped aside. Such tumultuous inflammable
masses, tumbling along, making way for each other;
this of keen nitrous oxide, that of sulphurous firedamp,
—were it not well to stand *between* them, keeping them
well separate, till the space be cleared? Numerous

stragglers of Château-Vieux and the rest have not
marched with their main columns, which are filing out
by the appointed Gates, taking station in the open
meadows. National Guards are in a state of nearly
distracted uncertainty; the populace, armed and
unarmed, roll openly delirious,—betrayed, sold to the
Austrians, sold to the Aristocrats. There are loaded
cannon with lit matches among them, and Bouillé's
vanguard is halted within thirty paces of the Gate.
Command dwells not in that mad inflammable mass;
which smoulders and tumbles there, in blind smoky
rage; which will not open the Gate when summoned;
says it will open the cannon's throat sooner!—Cannonade not, O Friends, or be it through my body!
cries heroic young Desilles, young Captain of *Roi*,
clasping the murderous engine in his arms, and holding
it. Château-Vieux Swiss, by main force, with oaths
and menaces, wrench off the heroic youth; who
undaunted, amid still louder oaths, seats himself on
the touch-hole. Amid still louder oaths, with ever
louder clangour,—and alas, with the loud crackle of
first one, and then of three other muskets; which
explode into his body; which roll *it* in the dust,—and
do also, in the loud madness of such moment, bring lit
cannon-match to ready priming; and so, with one
thunderous belch of grapeshot, blast some fifty of
Bouillé's vanguard into air!

Fatal! That sputter of the first musket-shot has
kindled such a cannon-shot, such a death-blaze; and
all is now red-hot madness, conflagration as of Tophet.
With demoniac rage, the Bouillé vanguard storms
through that Gate Stanislaus; with fiery sweep,
sweeps Mutiny clear away, to death, or into shelters
and cellars; from which latter, again, Mutiny continues firing. The ranked Regiments hear it in their
meadow; they rush back again through the nearest
Gate; Bouillé gallops in, distracted, inaudible;—and
now has begun, in Nanci, as in that doomed Hall of
the Nibelungen, 'a murder grim and great'.*

Miserable: such scene of dismal aimless madness as

the anger of Heaven but rarely permits among men !
From cellar or from garret, from open street in front,
from successive corners of cross-streets on each hand,
Château-Vieux and Patriotism keep up the murderous
rolling-fire, on murderous not Unpatriotic fires. Your
blue National Captain, riddled with balls, one hardly
knows on whose side fighting, requests to be laid on
the colours to die : the patriotic Woman (name not
given, deed surviving) screams to Château-Vieux that
it must *not* fire the other cannon ; and even flings
a pail of water on it, since screaming avails not.[1] Thou
shalt fight ; thou shalt not fight ; and with whom shalt
thou fight ! Could tumult awaken the old Dead, Bur-
gundian Charles the Bold might stir from under that
Rotunda of his : never since he, raging, sank in the
ditches, and lost Life and Diamond, was such a noise
heard here.

Three thousand, as some count, lie mangled, gory :
the half of Château-Vieux has been shot, without
need of Court-Martial. Cavalry, of Mestre-de-Camp
or their foes, can do little. Regiment du Roi was
persuaded to its barracks ; stands there palpitating.
Bouillé, armed with the terrors of the Law, and favoured
of Fortune, finally triumphs. In two murderous hours,
he has penetrated to the grand Squares, dauntless,
though with loss of forty officers and five hundred men :
the shattered remnants of Château-Vieux are seeking
covert. Regiment du Roi, not effervescent now, alas
no, but *having* effervesced, will offer to ground its arms ;
will ' march in a quarter of an hour '. Nay these poor
effervesced require ' escort ' to march with, and get it ;
though they are thousands strong, and have thirty
ball-cartridges a-man ! The Sun is not yet down,
when Peace, which might have come bloodless, has
come bloody : the mutinous Regiments are on march,
doleful, on their three Routes ; and from Nanci rises
wail of women and men, the voice of weeping and
desolation ; the City weeping for its slain who awaken

---

[1] Deux Amis, v. 268.

not. These streets are empty but for victorious
patrols.

Thus has Fortune, favouring the brave, dragged
Bouillé, as himself says, out of such a frightful peril
'by the hair of the head'. An intrepid adamantine
man, this Bouillé :—had *he* stood in old Broglie's place
in those Bastille days, it might have been all different !
He has extinguished mutiny, and immeasurable civil
war. Not for nothing, as we see ; yet at a rate which
he and Constitutional Patriotism consider cheap. Nay,
as for Bouillé, he, urged by subsequent contradiction
which arose, declares coldly, it was rather against his
own private mind, and more by public military rule of
duty, that he did extinguish it,[1]—immeasurable civil
war being now the only chance. Urged, we say, by
subsequent contradiction ! Civil war, indeed, is Chaos ;
and in all vital Chaos there is new Order shaping itself
free ; but what a faith this, that of all new Orders out
of Chaos and Possibility of Man and his Universe, Louis
Sixteenth and Two-Chamber Monarchy were precisely
the one that would shape itself ! It is like undertaking
to throw deuce-ace, say only five hundred successive
times, and *any* other throw to be fatal—for Bouillé.
Rather thank Fortune, and Heaven, always, thou
intrepid Bouillé ; and let contradiction go its way !
Civil war, conflagrating universally over France at this
moment, might have led to one thing or to another
thing : meanwhile, to *quench* conflagration, wheresoever one finds it, wheresoever one can ; this, in all
times, is the rule for man and General Officer.

But at Paris, so agitated and divided, fancy how it
went, when the continually vibrating Orderlies vibrated
thither at hand-gallop, with such questionable news !
High is the gratulation ; and also deep the indignation.
An august Assembly, by overwhelming majorities,
passionately thanks Bouillé ; a King's autograph, the
voices of all Loyal, all Constitutional men run to the

[1] Bouillé, i. 175.

same tenor. A solemn National funeral-service, for
the Law-defenders slain at Nanci, is said and sung in
the Champ-de-Mars ; Bailly, Lafayette and National
Guards, all except the few that protested, assist. With
pomp and circumstance, with episcopal Calicoes in
tricolor girdles, Altar of Fatherland smoking with cassolettes, or incense-kettles ; the vast Champ-de-Mars
wholly hung round with black mortcloth,—which mortcloth and expenditure Marat thinks had better have
been laid out in bread, in these dear days, and given to
the hungry living Patriot.[1] On the other hand, living
Patriotism, and Saint-Antoine, which we have seen
noisily closing its shops and such like, assembles now
' to the number of forty thousand ' ; and, with loud
cries, under the very windows of the thanking National
Assembly, demands revenge for murdered Brothers,
judgement on Bouillé, and instant dismissal of War-
Minister Latour du Pin.

At sound and sight of which things, if not War-
Minister Latour, yet ' Adored Minister ' Necker, sees
good on the 3rd of September 1790, to withdraw softly,
almost privily,—with an eye to the ' recovery of his
health '. Home to native Switzerland ; not as he last
came ; lucky to reach it alive ! Fifteen months ago,
we saw him coming, with escort of horse, with sound
of clarion and trumpet ; and now, at Arcis-sur-Aube,
while he departs, unescorted, soundless, the Populace
and Municipals stop him as a fugitive, are not unlike
massacring him as a traitor ; the National Assembly,
consulted on the matter, gives him free egress as a
nullity. Such an unstable ' drift-mould of Accident ' is
the substance of this lower world, for them that dwell in
houses of clay ; so, especially in hot regions and times,
do the proudest palaces we build of it take wings, and
become Sahara sand-palaces, spinning many-pillared
in the whirlwind, and bury us under their sand !—

In spite of the forty thousand, the National Assembly
persists in its thanks ; and Royalist Latour du Pin

---

[1] Ami du Peuple (in Hist. Parl. *ubi supra*).

continues Minister. The forty thousand assemble
next day, as loud as ever ; roll towards Latour's Hôtel ;
find cannon on the porch-steps with flambeau lit ; and
have to retire elsewhither, and digest their spleen, or
reabsorb it into the blood.

Over in Lorraine meanwhile, they of the distributed
fusils, ringleaders of Mestre-de-Camp, of Roi, have got
marked out for judgement ;—yet shall never get judged.
Briefer is the doom of Château-Vieux. Château-Vieux
is, by Swiss law, given up for instant trial in Court-
Martial of its own officers. Which Court-Martial, with
all brevity (in not many hours), has hanged some
Twenty-three, on conspicuous gibbets ; marched some
Three-score in chains to the Galleys ; and so, to
appearance, finished the matter off. Hanged men do
cease for ever from this Earth ; but out of chains and
the Galleys there may be resuscitation in triumph.
Resuscitation for the chained Hero ; and even for the
chained Scoundrel, or Semi-scoundrel ! Scottish John
Knox, such World-Hero as we know, sat once nevertheless pulling grim-taciturn at the oar of French
Galley, 'in the *Water of Lore* ' ; and even flung their
Virgin-Mary over, instead of kissing her,—as a ' *pented
bredd* ', or timber Virgin, who could naturally swim.[1]
So, ye of Château-Vieux, tug patiently, not without
hope !

But indeed at Nanci generally, Aristocracy rides
triumphant, rough. Bouillé is gone again, the second
day ; an Aristocrat Municipality, with free course, is
as cruel as it had before been cowardly. The
Daughter Society, as the mother of the whole mischief,
lies ignominiously suppressed ; the Prisons can hold
no more ; bereaved down-beaten Patriotism murmurs,
not loud but deep. Here and in the neighbouring
Towns, ' flattened balls ' picked from the streets of
Nanci are worn at buttonholes : balls flattened in
carrying death to Patriotism ; men wear them there,
in perpetual memento of revenge. Mutineer deserters

---

[1] Knox's History of the Reformation, b. i.

roam the woods ; have to demand charity at the musket's end. All is dissolution, mutual rancour, gloom
and despair :—till National Assembly Commissioners
arrive, with a steady gentle flame of Constitutionalism
in their hearts ; who gently lift up the down-trodden,
gently pull down the too uplifted ; reinstate the
Daughter Society, recall the mutineer deserter ; gradually levelling, strive in all wise ways to smooth and
soothe. With such gradual mild levelling on the one
side ; as with solemn funeral-service, cassolettes,
Courts-Martial, National thanks, on the other,—all
that Officiality can do is done. The buttonhole will
drop its flat ball ; the black ashes, so far as may be,
get green again.

This is the ' Affair of Nanci ' ; by some called the
' Massacre of Nanci ' ;—properly speaking, the unsightly
wrong-side of that thrice-glorious Feast of Pikes, the
right-side of which formed a spectacle for the very gods.
Right-side and wrong lie always so near : the one was
in July, in August the other ! Theatres, the theatres
over in London, are bright with their pasteboard
simulacrum of that ' Federation of the French people ',
brought out as Drama : this of Nanci, we may say,
though not played in any pasteboard Theatre, did for
many months enact itself, and even walk spectrally,—
in all French heads. For the news of it fly pealing
through all France : awakening, in town and village,
in clubroom, messroom, to the utmost borders, some
mimic reflex or imaginative repetition of the business ;
always with the angry questionable assertion : It was
right ; It was wrong. Whereby come controversies,
duels ; embitterment, vain jargon ; the hastening
forward, the augmenting and intensifying of whatever
new explosions lie in store for us.

Meanwhile, at this cost or at that, the mutiny, as we
say, is stilled. The French Army has neither burst up
in universal simultaneous delirium ; nor been at once
disbanded, put an end to, and made new again. It
must die in the chronic manner, through years, by

inches; with partial revolts, as of Brest Sailors or the like, which dare not spread; with men unhappy, insubordinate; officers unhappier, in Royalist moustachios, taking horse, singly or in bodies, across the Rhine: [1] sick dissatisfaction, sick disgust on both sides; the Army moribund, fit for no duty:—till it do, in that unexpected manner, Phoenix-like, with long throes, get both dead and newborn; then start forth strong, nay stronger and even strongest.

Thus much was the brave Bouillé hitherto fated to do. Wherewith let him again fade into dimness; and, at Metz or the rural Cantonments, assiduously drilling, mysteriously diplomatizing, in scheme within scheme, hover as formerly a faint shadow, the hope of Royalty.

[1] See Dampmartin, i. 249, &c. &c.

BOOK III

THE TUILERIES

CHAPTER I

EPIMENIDES*

How true, that there is nothing dead in this Universe;
that what we call dead is only changed, its forces working in inverse order! 'The leaf that lies rotting in
moist winds', says one, 'has still force; else how could
it *rot*?'* Our whole Universe is but an infinite Complex of Forces; thousandfold, from Gravitation up to
Thought and Will; man's Freedom environed with
Necessity of Nature: in all which nothing at any
moment slumbers, but all is for ever awake and busy.
The thing that lies isolated inactive thou shalt nowhere
discover; seek everywhere, from the granite mountain,
slow-mouldering since Creation, to the passing cloud-
vapour, to the living man; to the action, to the spoken
word of man. The word that is spoken, as we know,
flies irrevocable: not less, but more, the action that is
done.* 'The gods themselves', sings Pindar, 'cannot
annihilate the action that is done'. No: this, once
done, is done always; cast forth into endless Time;
and, long conspicuous or soon hidden, must verily
work and grow for ever there, an indestructible new
element in the Infinite of Things. Or, indeed, what *is*
this Infinite of Things itself, which men name Universe,
but an Action, a sum-total of Actions and Activities?
The living ready-made sum-total of these three,—which
Calculation cannot add, cannot bring on its tablets;
yet the sum, we say, is written visible: All that has
been done, All that is doing, All that will be done!

Understand it well, the Thing thou beholdest, that
Thing is an Action, the product and expression of
exerted Force : the All of Things is an infinite conju-
gation of the verb *To do*. Shoreless Fountain-Ocean
of Force, of power to *do* ; wherein Force rolls and
circles, billowing, many-streamed, harmonious ; wide
as Immensity, deep as Eternity*; beautiful and terrible,
not to be comprehended : this is what man names
Existence and Universe ; this thousand-tinted Flame-
image, at once veil and revelation, reflex such as he,
in his poor brain and heart, can paint, of One Unnameable dwelling in inaccessible light ! From beyond the
Star-galaxies, from before the Beginning of Days,* it
billows and rolls,—round *thee*, nay thyself art of it, in
this point of Space where thou now standest, in this
moment which thy clock measures.

Or apart from all Transcendentalism, is it not a plain
truth of sense, which the duller mind can even consider
as a truism, that human things wholly are in continual
movement, and action and reaction ; working continually forward, phasis after phasis, by unalterable
laws, towards prescribed issues ? How often must we
say, and yet not rightly lay to heart : The seed that
is sown, it will spring ! Given the summer's blossoming, then there is also given the autumnal withering :
so is it ordered not with seedfields only, but with transactions, arrangements, philosophies, societies, French
Revolutions, whatsoever man works with in this lower
world. The Beginning holds in it the End,* and all that
leads thereto ; as the acorn does the oak and its fortunes.
Solemn enough, did we think of it,—which unhappily,
and also happily, we do not very much ! Thou there
canst begin ; the Beginning is for thee, and there : but
where, and of what sort, and for whom will the End be ?
All grows, and seeks and endures its destinies : consider
likewise how much grows, as the trees do, whether *we*
think of it or not. So that when your Epimenides,
your somnolent Peter Klaus,* since named Rip van
Winkle, awakens again, he finds it a changed world.
In that seven-years sleep of his, so much has changed !

All that is without us will change while we think not
of it; much even that is within us. The truth that
was yesterday a restless Problem, has to-day grown
a Belief burning to be uttered : on the morrow, contradiction has exasperated it into mad Fanaticism ;
obstruction has dulled it into sick Inertness; it is
sinking towards silence, of satisfaction or of resignation. To-day is not Yesterday,* for man or for thing.
Yesterday there was the oath of Love; to-day has come
the curse of Hate. Not willingly: ah, no; but it
could not help coming. The golden radiance of youth,
would it willingly have tarnished itself into the dimness
of old age ?—Fearful : how we stand enveloped, deep-
sunk, in that Mystery of TIME ; and are Sons of Time ;
fashioned and woven out of Time ; and on us, and on
all that we have, or see, or do, is written : Rest not,
Continue not, Forward to thy doom !

But in seasons of Revolution, which indeed distin-
guish themselves from common seasons by their *velocity*
mainly, your miraculous Seven-sleeper* might, with
miracle enough, awake *sooner* : not by the century, or
seven years, need he sleep ; often not by the seven
months. Fancy, for example, some new Peter Klaus
sated with the jubilee of that Federation day, had lain
down, say directly after the Blessing of Talleyrand ;
and, reckoning it all safe *now*, had fallen composedly
asleep under the timber-work of the Fatherland's Altar ;
to sleep there, not twenty-one years, but as it were
year and day. The cannonading of Nanci, so far off,
does not disturb him ; nor does the black mortcloth,
close at hand, nor the requiems chanted, and minute-
guns, incense-pans and concourse right over his head :
none of these; but Peter sleeps through them all.
Through one circling year, as we say ; from July the
14th of 1790, till July the 17th of 1791 : but on that
latter day, no Klaus, nor most leaden Epimenides, only
the Dead could continue sleeping : and so our miraculous Peter Klaus awakens. With what eyes, O
Peter ! Earth and sky have still their joyous July

look, and the Champ-de-Mars is multitudinous with
men : but the jubilee-huzzahing has become Bedlam-
shrieking, of terror and revenge ; not blessing of Talleyrand, or any blessing, but cursing, imprecation and
shrill wail ; our cannon-salvoes are turned to sharp
shot ; for swinging of incense-pans and Eighty-three
Departmental Banners, we have waving of the one
sanguineous *Drapeau-Rouge.*—Thou foolish Klaus !
The one lay in the other, the one *was* the other *minus*
Time ; even as Hannibal's rock-rending vinegar lay
in the sweet new wine. That sweet Federation was of
last year ; this sour Divulsion is the selfsame substance,
only older by the appointed days.

No miraculous Klaus or Epimenides sleeps in these
times ; and yet, may not many a man, if of due opacity
and levity, act the same miracle in a natural way ; we
mean, with his eyes open ? Eyes has he, but he sees
not,* except what is under his nose. With a sparkling
briskness of glance, as if he not only saw but saw
through, such a one goes whisking, assiduous, in his
circle of officialities ; not dreaming but that *it* is the
whole world : as indeed, where your vision terminates,
does not inanity begin *there*, and the world's end clearly
disclose itself—to you ? Whereby our brisk-sparkling
assiduous official person (call him, for instance, Lafayette), suddenly startled, after year and day, by huge
grapeshot tumult, stares not less astonished at it than
Peter Klaus would have done. Such natural-miracle
can Lafayette perform ; and indeed not he only but
most other officials, non-officials, and generally the
whole French People can perform it ; and do bounce
up, ever and anon, like amazed Seven-sleepers awakening ; awakening amazed at the noise they themselves
make. So strangely is Freedom, as we say, environed
in Necessity*; such a singular Somnambulism, of Conscious and Unconscious, of Voluntary and Involuntary,
is this life of man. If anywhere in the world there was
astonishment that the Federation Oath went into
grapeshot, surely of all persons the French, first swearers
and then shooters, felt astonished the most.

Alas, offences must come.* The sublime Feast of
Pikes, with its effulgence of brotherly love, unknown
since the Age of Gold, has changed nothing. That
prurient heat in Twenty-five millions of hearts is not
cooled thereby; but is still hot, nay hotter. Lift off
the pressure of command from so many millions; all
pressure or binding rule, except such melodramatic
Federation Oath as they have bound *themselves* with!
For *Thou shalt* was from of old the condition of man's
being, and his weal and blessedness was in obeying
that. Woe for him when, were it on the hest of the
clearest necessity, rebellion, disloyal isolation, and
mere *I will*, becomes his rule! But the Gospel of Jean-
Jacques has come, and the first Sacrament of it has
been celebrated: all things, as we say, are got into
hot and hotter prurience; and must go on pruriently
fermenting, in continual change noted or unnoted.

'Worn out with disgusts', Captain after Captain, in
Royalist moustachios, mounts his war-horse, or his
Rozinante* war-garron, and rides minatory across the
Rhine; till all have ridden. Neither does civic
Emigration cease; Seigneur after Seigneur must, in
like manner, ride or roll; impelled to it, and even com-
pelled. For the very Peasants despise him, in that he
dare not join his order and fight.[1] Can he bear to have
a Distaff, a *Quenouille* sent to him: say in copper-plate
shadow, by post; or fixed up in wooden reality over
his gate-lintel: as if he were no Hercules, but an
Omphale?* Such scutcheon they forward to him diligently from beyond the Rhine; till he too bestir himself
and march, and in sour humour another Lord of Land
is gone, *not* taking the Land with him. Nay, what of
Captains and emigrating Seigneurs? There is not an
angry word on any of those Twenty-five million French
tongues, and indeed not an angry thought in their
hearts, but is some fraction of the great Battle. Add
many successions of angry words together, you have
the manual brawl; add brawls together, with the

[1] Dampmartin, *passim*.

festering sorrows they leave, and they rise to riots and
revolts. One reverend thing after another ceases to
meet reverence : in visible material combustion,
château after château mounts up ; in spiritual invisible
combustion, one authority after another. With noise
and glare, or noiselessly and unnoted, a whole Old
System of things is vanishing piecemeal : the morrow
thou shalt look, and it is not.

CHAPTER II

THE WAKEFUL

SLEEP who will, cradled in hope and short vision
like Lafayette, who ' always in the danger done sees
the last danger that will threaten him ',—Time is not
sleeping, nor Time's seedfield.*

That sacred Heralds'-College of a *new* Dynasty ; we
mean the Sixty and odd Billstickers with their leaden
badges, are not sleeping. Daily they, with pastepot
and cross-staff, new-clothe the walls of Paris in colours
of the rainbow : authoritative-heraldic, as we say, or
indeed almost magical-thaumaturgic ; for no Placard-
Journal that they paste but will convince some soul
or souls of men. The Hawkers bawl ; and the Ballad-
singers : great Journalism blows and blusters, through
all its throats, forth from Paris towards all corners of
France, like an Aeolus' Cave ; keeping alive all manner
of fires.

Throats or Journals there are, as men count,[1] to the
number of some Hundred and thirty-three. Of various
calibre ; from your Cheniers, Gorsases,* Camilles, down
to your Marat, down now to your incipient Hébert of
the *P're Duchesne* ; these blow, with fierce weight of
argument or quick light banter, for the Rights of Man :
Durosoys, Royous, Peltiers, Sulleaus, equally with

[1] Mercier, iii. 163.

mixed tactics (inclusive, singular to say, of much profane Parody),[1] are blowing for Altar and Throne. As
for Marat the People's-Friend, his voice is as that of
the bullfrog, or bittern by the solitary pools*; he,
unseen of men, croaks harsh thunder, and that alone
continually,—of indignation, suspicion, incurable sorrow. The People are sinking toward ruin, near starvation itself : ' My dear friends ', cries he, ' your indigence
is not the fruit of vices nor of idleness ; you have
a right to life, as good as Louis XVI, or the happiest of
the century. What man can say he has a right to dine,
when you have no bread ? ' [2] The People sinking on
the one hand : on the other hand, nothing but wretched
Sieur Motiers, treasonous Riquetti Mirabeaus ; traitors,
or else shadows and simulacra of Quacks to be seen
in high places, look where you will ! Men that go
mincing, grimacing, with plausible speech and brushed
raiment ; hollow within : Quacks political ; Quacks
scientific, academical : all with a fellow-feeling for each
other, and kind of Quack public-spirit ! Not great
Lavoisier himself, or any of the Forty can escape this
rough tongue ; which wants not fanatic sincerity, nor,
strangest of all, a certain rough caustic sense. And
then the ' three thousand gaming-houses ' that are in
Paris ; cesspools for the scoundrelism of the world ;
sinks of iniquity and debauchery,—whereas without
good morals Liberty is impossible ! There, in these
Dens of Satan, which one knows, and perseveringly
denounces, do Sieur Motier's *mouchards*[*] consort and
colleague ; battening vampire-like on a People next-
door to starvation. *'O Peuple !'* cries he ofttimes,
with heart-rending accent. Treason, delusion, vampir-
ism, scoundrelism, from Dan to Beersheba !* The soul
of Marat is sick with the sight : but what remedy ?
To erect ' Eight Hundred gibbets ', in convenient rows,
and proceed to hoisting ; 'Riquetti on the first of

---

[1] See Hist. Parl. vii. 51.
[2] Ami du Peuple, No. 306.   See other Excerpts in Hist.
Parl. viii. 139-49, 428-33 ; ix. 85-93, &c,

them ! ' Such is the brief recipe of Marat, Friend of
the People.

So blow and bluster the Hundred and thirty-three ;
nor, as would seem, are these sufficient ; for there are
benighted nooks in France, to which Newspapers do
not reach ; and everywhere is ' such an appetite for
news as was never seen in any country '. Let an
expeditious Dampmartin, on furlough, set out to return
home from Paris,[1] he cannot get along for ' peasants
stopping him on the highway ; overwhelming him with
questions ' : the *Maître de Poste* will not send out the
horses till you have wellnigh quarrelled with him, but
asks always, What news ? At Autun, in spite of the
dark night and ' rigorous frost ', for it is now January
1791, nothing will serve but you must gather your wayworn limbs and thoughts, and ' speak to the multitudes
from a window opening into the market-place '. It is
the shortest method : *This*, good Christian people, is
verily what an august Assembly seemed to me to be
doing ; this and no other is the news :

> Now my weary lips I close ;
> Leave me, leave me to repose !

The good Dampmartin !—But, on the whole, are not
Nations astonishingly true to their National character ;
which indeed runs in the blood ? Nineteen hundred
years ago, Julius Caesar, with his quick sure eye, took
note how the Gauls waylaid men. ' It is a habit of
theirs ', says he, ' to stop travellers, were it even by
constraint, and inquire whatsoever each of them may
have heard or known about any sort of matter : in
their towns, the common people beset the passing trader ;
demanding to hear from what regions he came, what
things he got acquainted with there. Excited by which
rumours and hearsays they will decide about the
weightiest matters ; and necessarily repent next
moment that they did it, on such guidance of uncertain
reports, and many a traveller answering with mere

[1] Dampmartin, i. 184.

fictions to please them, and get off '. [1] Nineteen hundred years ; and good Dampmartin, wayworn, in
winter frost, probably with scant light of stars and
fish-oil, still perorates from the Inn-window ! This
People is no longer called Gaulish ; and it has *wholly*
become *braccatus*, has got breeches, and suffered change
enough : certain fierce German *Franken* came storming
over ; and, so to speak, vaulted on the back of it ; and
always after, in their grim tenacious way, have ridden
it bridled ; for German is, by his very name, *Guerre*-
man, or man that *wars* and *gars*. And so the People,
as we say, is now called French or Frankish : nevertheless, does not the old Gaulish and Gaelic Celthood,
with its vehemence, effervescent promptitude, and
what good and ill it had, still vindicate itself little
adulterated ?—

For the rest, that in such prurient confusion, Clubbism thrives and spreads, need not be said. Already
the Mother of Patriotism, sitting in the Jacobins,
shines supreme over all ; and has paled the poor lunar
light of that Monarchic Club near to final extinction.
She, we say, shines supreme, girt with sun-light, not
yet with infernal lightning ; reverenced, not without
fear, by Municipal Authorities ; counting her Barnaves,
Lameths, Pétions, of a National Assembly ; most
gladly of all, her Robespierre. Cordeliers, again, your
Hébert, Vincent,* Bibliopolist Momoro, groan audibly
that a tyrannous Mayor and Sieur Motier harrow them
with the sharp *tribula* of Law, intent apparently to
suppress them by tribulation. How the Jacobin
Mother-Society, as hinted formerly, sheds forth
Cordeliers on this hand, and then Feuillans on that ;
the Cordeliers ' an elixir or double distillation of
Jacobin Patriotism ' ; the other a wide-spread weak
dilution thereof: how she will re-absorb the former into
her Mother-bosom, and stormfully dissipate the latter
into Nonentity : how she breeds and brings forth
Three Hundred Daughter-Societies ; her rearing of

---

[1] De Bello Gallico, lib. iv. 5.

them, her correspondence, her endeavourings and continual travail : how, under an old figure, Jacobinism
shoots forth organic filaments to the utmost corners
of confused dissolved France ; organizing it anew :—
this properly is the grand fact of the Time.

To passionate Constitutionalism, still more to
Royalism, which sees all their own Clubs fail and die,
Clubbism will naturally grow to seem the root of all
evil. Nevertheless Clubbism is not death, but rather
new organization, and life out of death : destructive,
indeed, of the remnants of the Old ; but to the New
important, indispensable. That man can co-operate
and hold communion with man, herein lies his miraculous strength. In hut or hamlet, Patriotism mourns
not now like voice in the desert :* it can walk to the
nearest Town ; and there, in the Daughter-Society,
make its ejaculation into an articulate oration, into an
action, guided forward by the Mother of Patriotism
herself. All Clubs of Constitutionalists, and such like,
fail, one after another, as shallow fountains : Jacobinism alone has gone down to the deep subterranean lake
of waters ; and may, unless *filled in*, flow there, copious,
continual, like an Artesian well. Till the Great Deep
have drained itself up ; and all be flooded and submerged, and Noah's Deluge out-deluged !

On the other hand, Claude Fauchet, preparing mankind for a Golden Age now apparently just at hand,
has opened his *Cercle Social*, with clerks, corresponding
boards, and so forth ; in the precincts of the Palais
Royal. It is *Te-Deum* Fauchet ; the same who preached
on Franklin's Death, in that huge Medicean rotunda of
the *Halle-aux-bleds*. He here, this winter, by Printing-
press and melodious Colloquy, spreads bruit of himself
to the utmost City-barriers. 'Ten thousand persons
of respectability' attend there ; and listen to this
'*Procureur-Général de la Vérité*, Attorney-General of
Truth', so has he dubbed himself ; to his sage Condorcet, or other eloquent coadjutor. Eloquent Attorney-General ! He blows out from him, better or worse,
what crude or ripe thing he holds : not without result

to himself; for it leads to a Bishopric, though only
a Constitutional one. Fauchet approves himself
a glib-tongued, strong-lunged, whole-hearted human
individual: much flowing matter there is, and really
of the better sort, about Right, Nature, Benevolence,
Progress; which flowing matter, whether 'it is pan-
theistic', or is pot-theistic, only the greener mind, in
these days, need examine. Busy Brissot was long ago
of purpose to establish precisely some such regenerative
Social Circle: nay he had tried it in 'Newman Street,
Oxford Street', of the Fog Babylon; and failed,—as
some say, surreptitiously pocketing the cash. Fauchet,
not Brissot, was fated to be the happy man; whereat,
however, generous Brissot will with sincere heart sing
a timber-toned *Nunc Domine*.[1] But 'ten thousand
persons of respectability': what a bulk have many
things in proportion to their magnitude! This *Cercle
Social*, for which Brissot chants in sincere timber-tones
such *Nunc Domine*, what is it? Unfortunately wind
and shadow. The main reality one finds in it now, is
perhaps this: that an 'Attorney-General of Truth'
did once take shape of a body, as Son of Adam, on our
Earth, though but for months or moments; and ten
thousand persons of respectability attended, ere yet
Chaos and Nox had reabsorbed him.

Hundred and thirty-three Paris Journals; regenerative Social Circle; oratory, in Mother and Daughter
Societies, from the balconies of Inns, by chimney-nook,
at dinner-table—polemical, ending many times in duel!
Add ever, like a constant growling accompaniment of
bass Discord: scarcity of work, scarcity of food. The
winter is hard and cold; ragged Bakers'-queues, like
a black tattered flag-of-distress, wave out ever and anon.
It is the third of our Hunger-years, this new year of
a glorious Revolution. The rich man when invited to
dinner, in such distress-seasons, feels bound in politeness to carry his own bread in his pocket: how the

---

[1] See Brissot, Patriote-Français Newspaper; Fauchet,
Bouche-de-Fer, &c. (excerpted in Hist. Parl. viii. ix. et seqq.)

poor dine ? And your glorious Revolution has done
it, cries one. And our glorious Revolution is subtilely,
by black traitors worthy of the Lamp-iron, *perverted* to
do it, cries another. Who will paint the huge whirlpool
wherein France, all shivered into wild incoherence,
whirls ? The jarring that went on under every French
roof, in every French heart ; the diseased things that
were spoken, done, the sum-total whereof is the French
Revolution, tongue of man cannot tell. Nor the laws
of action that work unseen in the depths of that huge
blind Incoherence ! With amazement, not with mea-
surement, men look on the Immeasurable ; not knowing its laws ; *seeing*, with all different degrees of knowledge, what new phases, and results of event, its laws
bring forth. France is as a monstrous Galvanic Mass,
wherein all sorts of far stranger than chemical galvanic
or electric forces and substances are at work ; electri-
fying one another, positive and negative ; filling with
electricity your Leyden-jars,—Twenty-five millions in
number ! As the jars get full, there will, from time to
time, be, on slight hint, an explosion.

CHAPTER III

SWORD IN HAND

On such wonderful basis, however, has Law, Royalty,
Authority, and whatever yet exists of visible Order, to
maintain itself, while it can. Here, as in that Com-
mixture of the Four Elements did the Anarch Old, has
an august Assembly spread its pavilion ; curtained by
the dark-infinite of discords ; founded on the wavering
bottomless of the Abyss ; and keeps continual hubbub.
Time is around it, and Eternity, and the Inane ; and
it does what it can, what is given it to do.

Glancing reluctantly in, once more, we discern little
that is edifying : a Constitutional Theory of Defective
Verbs struggling forward, with perseverance, amid

endless interruptions : Mirabeau, from his tribune,
with the weight of his name and genius, awing down
much Jacobin violence ; which in return vents itself
the louder over in its Jacobins Hall, and even reads him
sharp lectures there.[1] This man's path is mysterious,
questionable ; difficult, and he walks without companion in it. Pure Patriotism does not now count him
among her chosen ; pure Royalism abhors him : yet
his weight with the world is overwhelming. Let him
travel on, companionless, unwavering, whither he is
bound,—while it is yet day*with him, and the night
has not come.

But the chosen band of pure Patriot brothers is small ;
counting only some Thirty, seated now on the extreme
tip of the Left, separate from the world. A virtuous
Pétion ; an incorruptible Robespierre, most consistent,
incorruptible of thin acrid men ; Triumvirs Barnave,
Duport, Lameth, great in speech, thought, action, each
according to his kind ; a lean old Goupil de Prefeln :
on these and what will follow them has pure Patriotism
to depend.

There too, conspicuous among the Thirty, if seldom
audible, Philippe d'Orléans may be seen sitting : in
dim fuliginous bewilderment ; having, one might say,
arrived at Chaos ! Gleams there are, at once of
a Lieutenancy and Regency ; debates in the Assembly
itself, of succession to the Throne ' in case the present
Branch should fail ' ; and Philippe, they say, walked
anxiously, in silence, through the corridors, till such
high argument were done : but it came all to nothing ;
Mirabeau, glaring into the man, and through him, had
to ejaculate in strong untranslatable language : ' *Ce
j— f— ne vaut pas la peine qu'on se donne pour lui* '.
It came all to nothing ; and in the meanwhile Philippe's
money, they say, is gone ! Could he refuse a little cash
to the gifted Patriot, in want only of that ; he himself
in want of all *but* that ? Not a pamphlet can be
printed without cash ; or indeed written, without food

---

[1] Camille's Journal (in Hist. Parl. ix. 366–85).

purchasable by cash. Without cash your hopefullest
Projector cannot stir from the spot ; individual patriotic
or other Projects require cash : how much more do
widespread Intrigues, which live and exist by cash ;
lying widespread, with dragon-appetite for cash ; fit
to swallow Princedoms ! And so Prince Philippe, amid
his Sillerys, Lacloses and confused Sons of Night, has
rolled along : the centre of the strangest cloudy coil ;
out of which has visibly come, as we often say, an Epic
Preternatural Machinery of SUSPICION ; and *within*
which there has dwelt and worked,—what specialities
of treason, stratagem, aimed or aimless endeavour
towards mischief, no party living (if it be not the presiding Genius of it, Prince of the Power of the Air)*has
now any chance to know. Camille's conjecture is the
likeliest : that poor Philippe did mount up, a little way,
in treasonable speculation, as he mounted formerly in
one of the earliest Balloons ; but, frightened at the
new position he was getting into, had soon turned the
cock again, and come down. More fool than he rose !
To create Preternatural Suspicion, this was his function
in the Revolutionary Epos. But now if he have lost
his cornucopia of ready-money, what else had he to
lose ? In thick darkness, inward and outward, he
must welter and flounder on, in that piteous death-
element, the hapless man. Once, or even twice, we
shall still behold him emerged ; struggling out of the
thick death-element : in vain. For one moment, it
is the last moment, he starts aloft, or is flung aloft, even
into clearness and a kind of memorability,—to sink
then for evermore !

The *Côté Droit* persists no less ; nay with more
animation than ever, though hope has now wellnigh fled.
Tough Abbé Maury, when the obscure country Royalist
grasps his hand with transport of thanks, answers,
rolling his indomitable brazen head : ' *Hélas, Monsieur*,
all that I do here is as good as simply *nothing* '. Gallant
Faussigny, visible this one time in History, advances
frantic, into the middle of the Hall, exclaiming : ' There
is but one way of dealing with it, and that is to fall

sword in hand on those gentry there, *sabre à la main
sur ces gaillards là* ',[1] franticly indicating our chosen
Thirty on the extreme tip of the Left! Whereupon is
clangour and clamour, debate, repentance,—evapora-
tion. Things ripen towards downright incompatibility,
and what is called ' scission ': that fierce theoretic
onslaught of Faussigny's was in August 1790; next
August will not have come, till a famed Two Hundred
and Ninety-two, the chosen of Royalism, make solemn
final ' scission ' from an Assembly given up to faction ;
and depart, shaking the dust off their feet.*

Connected with this matter of sword in hand, there
is yet another thing to be noted. Of duels we have
sometimes spoken : how, in all parts of France, innumerable duels were fought; and argumentative men
and messmates, flinging down the wine-cup and weapons of reason and repartee, met in the measured field ;
to part bleeding ; or perhaps *not* to part, but to fall
mutually skewered through with iron, their wrath and
life alike ending,—and die as fools die. Long has this
lasted, and still lasts. But now it would seem as if in
an august Assembly itself, traitorous Royalism, in its
despair, had taken to a new course : that of cutting off
Patriotism by systematic duel! Bully-swordsmen,
' *Spadassins* ' of that party, go swaggering ; or indeed
they can be had for a trifle of money. ' Twelve *Spadassins* ' were *seen*, by the yellow eye of Journalism,
'arriving recently out of Switzerland '; also ' a considerable number of Assassins, *nombre considérable d'assassins*, exercising in fencing-schools and at pistol-targets '.
Any Patriot Deputy of mark can be called out; let
him escape one time, or ten times, a time there necessarily is when he must fall, and France mourn. How
many cartels has Mirabeau had; especially while he
was the People's champion ! Cartels by the hundred :
which he, since the Constitution must be made first,
and his time is precious, answers now always with

---

[1] Moniteur, Séance du 21 Août 1790.

a kind of stereotype formula : ' Monsieur, you are put
upon my List ; but I warn you that it is long, and I
grant no preferences '.

Then, in Autumn, had we not the Duel of Cazalès
and Barnave ; the two chief masters of tongue-shot
meeting now to exchange pistol-shot ? For Cazalès,
chief of the Royalists, whom we call ' Blacks or *Noirs* ',
said, in a moment of passion, ' the Patriots were sheer
Brigands ', nay in so speaking, he darted, or seemed
to dart, a fire-glance specially at Barnave ; who thereupon could not but reply by fire-glances,—by adjournment to the Bois-de-Boulogne. Barnave's second shot
took effect : on Cazalès' *hat*. The ' front nook ' of
a triangular Felt, such as mortals then wore, deadened
the ball ; and saved that fine brow from more than
temporary injury. But how easily might the lot have
fallen the other way, and Barnave's hat not been so
good ! Patriotism raises its loud denunciation of
Duelling in general ; petitions an august Assembly to
stop such Feudal barbarism by law. Barbarism and
solecism : for will it convince or convict any man to
blow half an ounce of lead through the head of him ?
Surely not.—Barnave was received at the Jacobins
with embraces, yet with rebukes.

Mindful of which, and also that his reputation in
America was that of headlong foolhardiness rather,
and want of brain not of heart, Charles Lameth does,
on the eleventh day of November, with little emotion,
decline attending some hot young Gentleman from
Artois, come expressly to challenge him : nay indeed
he first coldly engages to attend ; then coldly permits
two Friends to attend instead of him, and shame the
young Gentleman out of it, which they successfully do.
A cold procedure ; satisfactory to the two Friends, to
Lameth and the hot young Gentleman ; whereby, one
might have fancied, the whole matter was cooled down.

Not so, however : Lameth, proceeding to his senatorial duties, in the decline of the day, is met in those
Assembly corridors by nothing but Royalist *brocards* ;

sniffs, huffs, and open insults.   Human patience has its
limits :   ' Monsieur ', said Lameth, breaking silence to
one Lautrec, a man with hunchback, or natural deformity, but sharp of tongue, and a *Black* of the deepest
tint, ' Monsieur, if you were a man to be fought with ! '
—' I am one ', cries the young Duke de Castries.   Fast
as fireflash Lameth replies, ' *Tout à l'heure*, On the
instant, then ! '   And so, as the shades of dusk thicken
in that Bois-de-Boulogne, we behold two men with lion-
look, with alert attitude, side foremost, right foot
advanced ; flourishing and thrusting, stoccado and
passado, in tierce and quart ; intent to skewer one
another.   See, with most skewering purpose, headlong
Lameth, with his whole weight, makes a furious lunge ;
but deft Castries whisks aside : Lameth skewers only
the air,—and slits deep and far, on Castries' sword's-
point, his own extended left arm !   Whereupon, with
bleeding, pallor, surgeon's-lint and formalities, the
Duel is considered satisfactorily done.

But will there be no end, then ?   Beloved Lameth
lies deep-slit, not out of danger.   Black traitorous
Aristocrats kill the People's defenders, cut up not with
arguments, but with rapier-slits.   And the Twelve
Spadassins out of Switzerland, and the considerable
number of Assassins exercising at the pistol-target ?
So meditates and ejaculates hurt Patriotism, with ever-
deepening, ever-widening fervour, for the space of six-
and-thirty hours.

The thirty-six hours past, on Saturday the 13th, one
beholds a new spectacle : The Rue de Varennes, and
neighbouring Boulevard des Invalides, covered with
a mixed flowing multitude : the Castries Hôtel gone
distracted, devil-ridden, belching from every window,
' beds with clothes and curtains ', plate of silver and
gold with filigree, mirrors, pictures, images, commodes,
chiffoniers, and endless crockery and jingle : amid
steady popular cheers, absolutely without theft : for
there goes a cry, ' He shall be hanged that steals a nail '.
It is a *Plebiscitum*, or informal iconoclastic Decree of
the Common People, in the course of being executed !

—The Municipality sit tremulous; deliberating whether they will hang out the *Drapeau Rouge* and Martial Law: National Assembly, part in loud wail, part in hardly suppressed applause; Abbé Maury unable to decide whether the iconoclastic Plebs amount to forty thousand or to two hundred thousand.

Deputations, swift messengers, for it is at a distance over the River, come and go. Lafayette and National Guards, though without *Drapeau Rouge*, get under way; apparently in no hot haste. Nay, arrived on the scene, Lafayette salutes with doffed hat, before ordering to fix bayonets. What avails it? The Plebeian ' Court of *Cassation* ', as Camille might punningly name it, has done its work; steps forth, with unbuttoned vest, with pockets turned 'inside out: sack, and just ravage, not plunder! With inexhaustible patience, the Hero of two Worlds remonstrates; persuasively, with a kind of sweet constraint, though also with fixed bayonets, dissipates, hushes down: on the morrow it is once more all as usual.

Considering which things, however, Duke Castries may justly ' write to the President ', justly transport himself across the Marches; to raise a corps, or do what else is in him. Royalism totally abandons that Bobadilian*method of contest, and the twelve *Spadassins* return to Switzerland,—or even to Dreamland through the Horn-gate, whichsoever their true home is. Nay Editor Prudhomme is authorized to publish a curious thing : ' We are authorized to publish ', says he, dull-blustering Publisher, ' that M. Boyer, champion of good Patriots, is at the head of Fifty *Spadassinicide* or Bully-*killers*. His Address is : Passage du Bois-de-Boulogne, Faubourg St. Denis '.[1] One of the strangest Institutes, this of Champion Boyer and the Bully-killers ! Whose services, however, are not wanted; Royalism having abandoned the rapier-method, as plainly impracticable.

<hr/>

[1] Révolutions de Paris (in Hist. Parl. viii. 440].

CHAPTER IV

TO FLY OR NOT TO FLY

THE truth is, Royalism sees itself verging towards sad extremities ; nearer and nearer daily. From over the Rhine it comes asserted that the King in his Tuileries is not free : this the poor King may contradict, with the official mouth, but in his heart feels often to be undeniable. Civil Constitution of the Clergy ; Decree of ejectment against Dissidents from it : not even to this latter, though almost his conscience rebels, can he say Nay ; but, after two months' hesitating, signs this also. It was 'on January 21st', of this 1791, that he signed it ; to the sorrow of his poor heart yet, on *another* Twenty-first of January ! Whereby come Dissident ejected Priests ; unconquerable Martyrs according to some, incurable chicaning Traitors according to others. And so there has arrived what we once foreshadowed : with Religion, or with the Cant and Echo of Religion, all France is rent asunder in a new rupture of continuity ; complicating, embittering all the older ;—to be cured only by stern surgery, in La Vendée !

Unhappy Royalty, unhappy Majesty, Hereditary Representative, *Représentant Héréditaire*, or howsoever they may name him ; of whom much is expected, to whom little is given !* Blue National Guards encircle that Tuileries ; a Lafayette, thin constitutional Pedant ; clear, thin, inflexible, as water turned to thin ice ; whom no Queen's heart can love. National Assembly, its pavilion spread where we know, sits near by, keeping continual hubbub. From without, nothing but Nanci Revolts, sack of Castries Hôtels, riots and seditions ; riots North and South, at Aix, at Douai, at Béfort, Usez, Perpignan, at Nismes, and that incurable Avignon of the Pope's : a continual crackling and sputtering of riots from the whole face of France ;—testifying how electric it grows. Add only the hard winter, the famished *strikes* of operatives ; that continual running-bass of Scarcity, ground-tone and basis of all other Discords !

The plan of Royalty, so far as it can be said to have any fixed plan, is still, as ever, that of flying towards the frontiers. In very truth, the only plan of the smallest promise for it ! Fly to Bouillé ; bristle yourself round with cannon, served by your ' forty-thousand undebauched Germans ' : summon the National Assembly to follow you, summon what of it is Royalist, Constitutional, gainable by money ; dissolve the rest, by grapeshot if need be. Let Jacobinism and Revolt, with one wild wail, fly into Infinite Space ; driven by grapeshot. Thunder over France with the cannon's mouth ; commanding, not entreating, that this riot cease. And then to rule afterwards with utmost possible Constitutionality ; doing justice, loving mercy ; *being* Shepherd of this indigent People, not Shearer merely, and Shepherd's-similitude ! All this, if ye dare. If ye dare not, then, in Heaven's name, go to sleep : other handsome alternative seems none.

Nay, it were perhaps possible ; with a man to do it. For if such inexpressible whirlpool of Babylonish confusions (which our Era is) cannot be stilled by man, but only by Time and men, a man may moderate its paroxysms, may balance and sway, and keep himself unswallowed on the top of it,—as several men and Kings in these days do. Much is possible for a man ; men will obey a man that *kens* and *cans,* and name him reverently their *Ken-ning* or King. Did not Charlemagne rule ? Consider too whether he had smooth times of it ; hanging ' four-thousand Saxons over the Weser-Bridge ', at one dread swoop ! So likewise, who knows but, in this same distracted fanatic France, the right man may verily exist ? An olive-complexioned taciturn man ; for the present, Lieutenant in the Artillery-service, who once sat studying Mathematics at Brienne ? The same who walked in the morning to correct proof-sheets at Dôle, and enjoyed a frugal breakfast with M. Joly ?   Such a one is gone, whither also famed General Paoli his friend is gone, in these very days, to see old scenes in native Corsica, and what Democratic good can be done there.

Royalty never executes the evasion-plan, yet never abandons it; living in variable hope; undecisive, till fortune shall decide.   In utmost secrecy, a brisk Correspondence goes on with Bouillé; there is also a plot, which emerges more than once, for carrying the King to Rouen : [1] plot after plot, emerging and submerging, like *ignes fatui* in foul weather, which lead nowhither.   'About ten o'clock at night', the Hereditary Representative, in *partie quarrée*, with the Queen, with Brother Monsieur, and Madame, sits playing 'wisk', or whist.   Usher Campan enters mysteriously, with a message he only half comprehends :   How a certain Comte D'Inisdal waits anxious in the outer antechamber ; National Colonel, Captain of the watch for this night, is gained over ; post-horses ready all the way ; party of Noblesse sitting armed, determined ; will his Majesty, before midnight, consent to go ? Profound silence ; Campan waiting with upturned ear. ' Did your Majesty hear what Campan said ? ' asks the Queen.   'Yes, I heard', answers Majesty, and plays on.   ' 'Twas a pretty couplet, that of Campan's ', hints Monsieur, who at times showed a pleasant wit : Majesty, still unresponsive, plays wisk.   ' After all, one must say something to Campan ', remarks the Queen.   ' Tell M. D'Inisdal ', said the King, and the Queen puts an emphasis on it, ' That the King cannot *consent* to be forced away '.—' I see ! ' said D'Inisdal, whisking round, peaking himself into flame of irritancy : ' we have the risk ; we are to have all the blame if it fail ',[2]—and vanishes, he and his plot, as will-o'-wisps do.   The Queen sat till far in the night, packing jewels : but it

---

[1] See Hist. Parl. vii. 316 ; Bertrand-Moleville, &c.
[2] Campan, ii. 105.

came to nothing; in that peaked flame of irritancy
the will-o'-wisp had gone *out*.

Little hope there is in all this. Alas, with whom to
fly ? Our loyal *Gardes-du-Corps*, ever since the Insurrection of Women, are disbanded ; gone to their homes ;
gone, many of them, across the Rhine towards Coblentz
and Exiled Princes : brave Miomandre and brave
Tardivet, these faithful Two, have received, in nocturnal interview with both Majesties, their *viaticum* of
gold louis, of heart-felt thanks from a Queen's lips,
though unluckily ' his Majesty stood, back to fire, not
speaking ' ; [1] and do now dine through the Provinces ;
recounting hairsbreadth escapes, insurrectionary horrors. Great horrors ; to be swallowed yet of greater.
But, on the whole, what a falling off from the old
splendour of Versailles ! Here in this poor Tuileries
a National Brewer-Colonel, sonorous Santerre, parades
officially behind her Majesty's chair. Our high dignitaries all fled over the Rhine : nothing now to be gained
at Court ; but hopes, for which life itself must be risked !
Obscure busy men frequent the back stairs ; with hearsays, wind-projects, unfruitful fanfaronades. Young
Royalists, at the *Théâtre de Vaudeville*, ' sing couplets ' ;
if that could do anything. Royalists enough, Captains
on furlough, burnt-out Seigneurs, may likewise be met
with, ' in the Café de Valois, and at Méot the Restaurateur's '. There they fan one another into high loyal
glow ; drink, in such wine as can be procured, confusion
to Sansculottism ; show purchased dirks, of an improved
structure, made to order ; and, greatly daring, dine.' [2]
It is in these places, in these months, that the epithet
Sansculotte first gets applied to indigent Patriotism ;
in the last age we had Gilbert *Sansculotte*, the indigent
Poet.[3] Destitute-of-Breeches : a mournful Destitution ; which however, if Twenty millions share it, may
become more effective than most Possessions !

Meanwhile, amid this vague dim whirl of fanfaro-

[1] Campan, ii. 199–201.   [2] Dampmartin, ii. 129.
[3] Mercier, Nouveau Paris, iii. 204.

nades, wind-projects, poniards made to order, there does disclose itself one *punctum-saliens* of life and feasibility: the finger of Mirabeau! Mirabeau and the Queen of France have met; have parted with mutual trust! It is strange; secret as the Mysteries; but it is indubitable. Mirabeau took horse, one evening; and rode westward, unattended,—to see Friend Clavière in that country house of his? Before getting to Clavière's, the much-musing horseman struck aside to a back gate of the Garden of Saint-Cloud: some Duke D'Aremberg, or the like, was there to introduce him; the Queen was not far; on a ' round knoll, *rond point*, the highest of the Garden of Saint-Cloud ', he beheld the Queen's face; spake with her, alone, under the void canopy of Night. What an interview; fateful secret for us, after all searching; like the colloquies of the gods ! [1] She called him ' a Mirabeau ': elsewhere we read that she ' was charmed with him ', the wild submitted Titan; as indeed it is among the honourable tokens of this high ill-fated heart that no mind of any endowment, no Mirabeau, nay no Barnave, no Dumouriez, ever came face to face with her but, in spite of all prepossessions, she was forced to recognize it, to draw nigh to it, with trust. High imperial heart; with the instinctive attraction towards all that had any height ! ' You know not the Queen ', said Mirabeau once in confidence; ' her force of mind is prodigious; she is a man for courage '.[2]—And so, under the void Night, on the crown of that knoll, she has spoken with a Mirabeau: he has kissed loyally the queenly hand, and said with enthusiasm: ' Madame, the Monarchy is saved ! ' —Possible? The Foreign Powers, mysteriously sounded, gave favourable guarded response; [3] Bouillé is at Metz, and could find forty-thousand sure Germans. With a Mirabeau for head, and a Bouillé for hand, something verily is possible,—if Fate intervene not.

But figure under what thousandfold wrappages, and

---

[1] Campan, ii. c. 17.   [2] Dumont, p. 211.
[3] Correspondance Secrète (in Hist. Parl. viii. 169–73).

cloaks of darkness, Royalty, meditating these things,
must involve itself. There are men with 'Tickets of
Entrance'; there are chivalrous consultings, mysterious plottings. Consider also whether, involve as
it like, plotting Royalty can escape the glance of
Patriotism; lynx-eyes, by the ten thousand, fixed on
it, which see in the dark! Patriotism knows much:
knows the dirks made to order, and can specify the
shops; knows Sieur Motier's legions of *mouchards*; the
Tickets of *Entrée*, and men in black; and how plan
of evasion succeeds plan,—or may be supposed to
succeed it. Then conceive the couplets chanted at the
Théâtre de Vaudeville; or worse, the whispers, significant nods of traitors in moustachios. Conceive, on the
other hand, the loud cry of alarm that came through
the Hundred-and-Thirty Journals; the Dionysius'-Ear*
of each of the Forty-eight Sections, wakeful night and
day.

Patriotism is patient of much; not patient of all.
The *Café de Procope* has sent, visibly along the streets,
a Deputation of Patriots, 'to expostulate with bad
Editors', by trustful word of mouth: singular to see
and hear. The bad Editors promise to amend, but
do not. Deputations for change of Ministry were
many; Mayor Bailly joining even with Cordelier
Danton in such; and they have prevailed. With what
profit? Of Quacks, willing or constrained to be
Quacks, the race is everlasting: Ministers Duportail
and Dutertre will have to manage much as Ministers
Latour-du-Pin and Cicé did. So welters the confused
world.

But now, beaten on for ever by such inextricable
contradictory influences and evidences, what *is* the
indigent French Patriot, in these unhappy days, to
believe, and walk by? Uncertainty all; except that
he is wretched, indigent; that a glorious Revolution,
the wonder of the Universe, has hitherto brought
neither Bread nor Peace; being marred by traitors,
difficult to discover. Traitors that dwell in the dark,
invisible there;—or seen for moments, in pallid dubious

twilight, stealthily vanishing thither! Preternatural Suspicion once more rules the minds of men.

'Nobody here', writes Carra, of the *Annales Patriotiques*, so early as the first of February, 'can entertain a doubt of the constant obstinate project these people have on foot to get the King away; or of the perpetual succession of manœuvres they employ for that'. Nobody: the watchful Mother of Patriotism deputed two Members to her Daughter at Versailles, to examine how the matter looked there. Well, and there? Patriotic Carra continues: 'The Report of these two deputies we all heard with our own ears last Saturday. They went with others of Versailles, to inspect the King's Stables, also the stables of the whilom *Gardes-du-Corps*; they found there from seven to eight hundred horses standing always saddled and bridled, ready for the road at a moment's notice. The same deputies, moreover, saw with their own two eyes several Royal Carriages, which men were even then busy loading with large well-stuffed luggage-bags', leather *cows*, as we call them, '*vaches de cuir*; the Royal Arms on the panels almost entirely effaced'. Momentous enough! Also 'on the same day the whole *Maréchaussée*, or Cavalry Police, did assemble with arms, horses and baggage',—and disperse again. They want the King over the marches, that so Emperor Leopold* and the German Princes, whose troops are ready, may have a pretext for beginning: 'this', adds Carra, 'is the word of the riddle: this is the reason why our fugitive Aristocrats are now making levies of men on the frontiers; expecting that, one of these mornings, the Executive Chief Magistrate will be brought over to them, and the civil war commence'.[1]

If indeed the Executive Chief Magistrate, bagged, say in one of these leather *cows*, were once brought safe over to them! But the strangest thing of all is, that Patriotism, whether barking at a venture, or guided by some instinct of preternatural sagacity, is actually

----

[1] Carra's Newspaper, 1st Feb. 1791 (in Hist. Parl. ix. 39).

barking *aright* this time ; at something, not at nothing.
Bouillé's Secret Correspondence, since made public,
testifies as much.

Nay, it is undeniable, visible to all, that *Mesdames*
the King's Aunts are taking steps for departure : asking
passports of the Ministry, safe-conducts of the Municipality ; which Marat warns all men to beware of. They
will carry gold with them, ' these old *Béguines* ' ; nay
they will carry the little Dauphin, ' having nursed
a changeling, for some time, to leave in his stead ! '
Besides, they are as some light substance flung up, to
show how the wind sits ; a kind of proof-kite you fly
off to ascertain whether the grand paper-kite, Evasion
of the King, may mount !

In these alarming circumstances, Patriotism is not
wanting to itself. Municipality deputes to the King ;
Sections depute to the Municipality ; a National
Assembly will soon stir. Meanwhile, behold, on the
19th of February 1791, Mesdames, quitting Bellevue
and Versailles with all privacy, are off! Towards
Rome, seemingly ; or one knows not whither. They
are not without King's passports, countersigned ; and
what is more to the purpose, a serviceable Escort. The
Patriotic Mayor or Mayorlet of the Village of Moret
tried to detain them : but brisk Louis de Narbonne,*
of the Escort, dashed off at hand-gallop ; returned
soon with thirty dragoons, and victoriously cut them
out. And so the poor ancient women go their way ;
to the terror of France and Paris, whose nervous
excitability is become extreme. Who else would hinder
poor *Loque* and *Graille*, now grown so old, and fallen
into such unexpected circumstances, when gossip itself
turning only on terrors and horrors is no longer pleasant
to the mind, and you cannot get so much as an orthodox
confessor in peace,—from going what way soever the
hope of any solacement might lead them ?

They go, poor ancient dames,—whom the heart were
hard that did not pity : they go ; with palpitations,
with unmelodious suppressed screechings ; all France
screeching and cackling, in loud *un*suppressed terror,

behind and on both hands of them : such mutual
suspicion is among men. At Arnay le Duc, above
half-way to the frontiers, a Patriotic Municipality and
Populace again takes courage to stop them : Louis
Narbonne must now back to Paris, must consult the
National Assembly. National Assembly answers, not
without an effort, that Mesdames may go. Whereupon
Paris rises worse than ever, screeching half-distracted.
Tuileries and precincts are filled with women and men,
while the National Assembly debates this question of
questions ; Lafayette is needed at night for dispersing
them, and the streets are to be illuminated. Commandant Berthier, a Berthier before whom are great things
unknown, lies for the present under blockade at Bellevue
in Versailles. By no tactics could he get Mesdames'
Luggage stirred from the Courts there ; frantic Versaillese women came screaming about him ; his very
troops cut the wagon-traces ; he ' retired to the interior ',
waiting better times.[1]

Nay, in these same hours, while Mesdames, hardly
cut out from Moret by the sabre's edge, are driving
rapidly, to foreign parts, and not yet stopped at Arnay,
their august Nephew poor Monsieur, at Paris, has dived
deep into his cellars of the Luxembourg for shelter ;
and, according to Montgaillard, can hardly be persuaded
up again. Screeching multitudes environ that Luxembourg of his ; drawn thither by report of his departure :
but at sight and sound of Monsieur, they become
crowing multitudes ; and escort Madame and him to
the Tuileries with vivats.[2] It is a state of nervous
excitability such as few nations know.

---

[1] Campan, ii. 132.
[2] Montgaillard, ii. 282 ; Deux Amis, vi. c. 1.

CHAPTER V

THE DAY OF PONIARDS

Or, again, what means this visible reparation of the
Castle of Vincennes ?* Other Jails being all crowded
with prisoners, new space is wanted here : that is the
Municipal account. For in such changing of Judica-
tures, Parlements being abolished, and New Courts but
just set up, prisoners have accumulated. Not to say
that in these times of discord and club-law, offences
and committals are, at any rate, more numerous.
Which Municipal account, does it not sufficiently
explain the phenomenon ? Surely, to repair the Castle
of Vincennes was of all enterprises that an enlightened
Municipality could undertake, the most innocent.

Not so, however, does neighbouring Saint-Antoine
look on it : Saint-Antoine to whom these peaked
turrets and grim donjons, all too near her own dark
dwelling, are of themselves an offence. Was not
Vincennes a kind of minor Bastille ? Great Diderot
and Philosophes have lain in durance here; great
Mirabeau, in disastrous eclipse, for forty-two months.
And now when the old Bastille has become a dancing-
ground (had any one the mirth to dance), and its stones
are getting built into the Pont Louis-Seize, does this
minor, comparative insignificance of a Bastille flank
itself with fresh-hewn mullions, spread out tyrannous
wings; menacing Patriotism ? New space for prisoners : and what prisoners ? A D'Orléans, with the
chief Patriots on the tip of the Left ? It is said, there
runs 'a subterranean passage' all the way from the
Tuileries hither. Who knows ? Paris, mined with
quarries and catacombs, does hang wondrous over the
abyss; Paris was once to be blown up,—though the
powder, when we went to look, had got withdrawn.
A Tuileries, sold to Austria and Coblentz, should have
no subterranean passage. Out of which might not
Coblentz or Austria issue, some morning; and, with

cannon of long range, ' *foudroyer* ', bethunder a patriotic
Saint-Antoine into smoulder and ruin !

So meditates the benighted soul of Saint-Antoine, as
it sees the aproned workmen, in early spring, busy on
these towers. An official-speaking Municipality, a
Sieur Motier with his legions of *mouchards*, deserve no
trust at all. Were Patriot Santerre, indeed, Commander ! But the sonorous Brewer commands only our
own Battalion : of such secrets he can explain nothing,
knows nothing, perhaps suspects much.* And so the
work goes on ; and afflicted benighted Saint-Antoine
hears rattle of hammers, sees stones suspended in air.[1]

Saint-Antoine prostrated the first great Bastille :
will it falter over this comparative insignificance of
a Bastille ? Friends, what if we took pikes, firelocks,
sledgehammers ; and helped ourselves !—Speedier is
no remedy ; nor so certain. On the 28th day of
February, Saint-Antoine turns out, as it has now often
done ; and, apparently with little superfluous tumult,
moves eastward to that eye-sorrow of Vincennes. With
grave voice of authority, no need of bullying and
shouting, Saint-Antoine signifies to parties concerned
there, that its purpose is, To have this suspicious
Stronghold razed level with the general soil of the
country. Remonstrance may be proffered, with zeal ;
but it avails not. The outer gate goes up, drawbridges
tumble ; iron window-stanchions, smitten out with
sledgehammers, become iron-crowbars : it rains a rain
of furniture, stone-masses, slates : with chaotic
clatter and rattle, Demolition clatters down. And now
hasty expresses rush through the agitated streets, to
warn Lafayette, and the Municipal and Departmental
Authorities ; Rumour warns a National Assembly,
a Royal Tuileries, and all men who care to hear it :
That Saint-Antoine is up ; that Vincennes, and probably the last remaining Institution of the Country,
is coming down.[2]

[1] Montgaillard, ii. 285.

[2] Deux Amis, vi. 11-15 ; Newspapers (in Hist. Parl. ix.
111-17).

Quick, then! Let Lafayette roll his drums and fly eastward; for to all Constitutional Patriots this is again bad news. And you, ye Friends of Royalty, snatch your poniards of improved structure, made to order; your sword-canes, secret arms, and tickets of entry; quick, by backstairs passages, rally round the Son of Sixty Kings. An effervescence probably got up by D'Orléans and Company, for the overthrow of Throne and Altar: it is said her Majesty shall be put in prison, put out of the way; what then will *his* Majesty be? Clay for the Sansculottic Potter! Or were it impossible to fly this day; a brave Noblesse suddenly all rallying? Peril threatens, hope invites: Dukes de Villequier, de Duras, Gentlemen of the Chamber give Tickets and admittance; a brave Noblesse is suddenly all rallying. Now were the time to 'fall sword in hand on those gentry there', could it be done with effect.

The Hero of two Worlds is on his white charger: blue Nationals, horse and foot, hurrying eastward; Santerre, with the Saint-Antoine Battalion, is already there,— apparently indisposed to act. Heavy-laden Hero of two Worlds, what tasks are these! The jeerings, provocative gambollings of that Patriot Suburb, which is all out on the streets now, are hard to endure; unwashed Patriots jeering in sulky sport; one unwashed Patriot 'seizing the General by the boot', to unhorse him. Santerre, ordered to fire, makes answer obliquely, 'These are the men that took the Bastille'; and not a trigger stirs. Neither dare the Vincennes Magistracy give warrant of arrestment, or the smallest countenance: wherefore the General 'will take it on himself' to arrest. By promptitude, by cheerful adroitness, patience and brisk valour without limits, the riot may be again bloodlessly appeased.

Meanwhile, the rest of Paris, with more or less unconcern, may mind the rest of its business: for what is this but an effervescence, of which there are now so many? The National Assembly, in one of its stormiest moods, is debating a Law against Emigration; Mira-

beau declaring aloud, 'I swear beforehand that I will
not obey it'. Mirabeau is often at the Tribune this
day; with endless impediments from without; with
the old unabated energy from within. What can
murmurs and clamours, from Left or from Right, do
to this man; like Teneriffe or Atlas unremoved ?* With
clear thought; with strong bass-voice, though at first
low, uncertain, he claims audience, sways the storm
of men: anon the sound of him waxes, softens; he
rises into far-sounding melody of strength, triumphant,
which subdues all hearts; his rude seamed face,
desolate, fire-scathed, becomes fire-lit, and radiates:
once again men feel, in these beggarly ages, what is
the potency and omnipotency of man's word on the
souls of men. 'I will triumph or be torn in fragments',
he was once heard to say. 'Silence', he cries now, in
strong word of command, in imperial consciousness of
strength, 'Silence, the thirty voices, *Silence aux trente
voix !*'—and Robespierre and the Thirty Voices die
into mutterings; and the Law is once more as Mirabeau
would have it.

How different, at the same instant, is General
Lafayette's street-eloquence; wrangling with sonorous
Brewers, with an ungrammatical Saint-Antoine! Most
different, again, from both is the Café-de-Valois
eloquence, and suppressed fanfaronade, of this multitude of men with Tickets of Entry; who are now
inundating the Corridors of the Tuileries. Such things
can go on simultaneously in one City. How much
more in one Country; in one Planet with its discrepancies, every Day a mere crackling infinitude of
discrepancies,—which nevertheless do yield some
coherent net-product, though an infinitesimally small
one !

But be this as it may, Lafayette has saved Vincennes;
and is marching homewards with some dozen of arrested
demolitionists. Royalty is not yet saved;—nor indeed
specially endangered. But to the King's Constitutional
Guard, to these old Gardes Françaises, or Centre

Grenadiers, as it chanced to be, this affluence of men
with Tickets of Entry is becoming more and more
unintelligible.   Is his Majesty verily for Metz, then ;
to be carried off by these men, on the spur of the
instant ?   That revolt of Saint-Antoine got up by
traitor Royalists for a stalking-horse ?   Keep a sharp
outlook, ye Centre Grenadiers on duty here : good
never came from the ' men in black '.   Nay they have
cloaks, *rédingotes* ; some of them leather-breeches, boots,
—as if for instant riding !   Or what is this that sticks
visible from the lapelle of Chevalier de Court ? [1]   Too
like the handle of some cutting or stabbing instrument !
He glides and goes ; and still the dudgeon sticks from
his left lapelle.   ' Hold, Monsieur ! '—a Centre Grenadier clutches him ; clutches the protrusive dudgeon,
whisks it out in the face of the world : by Heaven,
a very dagger ; hunting-knife or whatsoever you will
call it ; fit to drink the life of Patriotism !

So fared it with Chevalier de Court, early in the day ;
not without noise ; not without commentaries.   And
now this continually increasing multitude at nightfall ?   Have they daggers too ?   Alas, with them too,
after angry parleyings, there has begun a groping and
a rummaging ; all men in black, spite of their Tickets
of Entry, are clutched by the collar, and groped.   Scandalous to think of : for always, as the dirk, sword-
cane, pistol, or were it but tailor's bodkin, is found on
him, and with loud scorn drawn forth from him, he,
the hapless man in black, is flung all too rapidly down
stairs.   Flung ;   and ignominiously descends, head
foremost ; accelerated by ignominious shovings from
sentry after sentry ; nay, as is written, by smitings,
twitchings,—spurnings *à posteriori*, not to be named.
In this accelerated way, emerges, uncertain which end
uppermost, man after man in black, through all issues,
into the Tuileries Garden.   Emerges, alas, into the
arms of an indignant multitude, now gathered and
gathering there, in the hour of dusk, to see what is

[1] Weber, ii. 286.

toward, and whether the Hereditary Representative is
carried off or not. Hapless men in black ; at last
convicted of poniards made to order ; convicted
' Chevaliers of the Poniard ! '   Within is as the burning
ship ; without is as the deep sea.   Within is no help ;
his Majesty, looking forth, one moment, from his
interior sanctuaries, coldly bids all visitors ' give up
their weapons ' ; and shuts the door again.   The
weapons given up form a heap : the convicted Chevaliers of the Poniard keep descending pellmell, with
impetuous velocity ; and at the bottom of all staircases, the mixed multitude receives them, hustles,
buffets, chases and disperses them.[1]

Such sight meets Lafayette, in the dusk of the
evening, as he returns, successful with difficulty at
Vincennes : Sansculotte Scylla hardly weathered, here
is Aristocrat Charybdis gurgling under his lee !   The
patient Hero of two Worlds almost loses temper.   He
accelerates, does not retard, the flying Chevaliers ;
delivers, indeed, this or the other hunted Loyalist of
quality, but rates him in bitter words, such as the hour
suggested ; such as no saloon could pardon.   Hero ill-
bested ; hanging, so to speak, in mid air ; hateful to
Rich divinities above ; hateful to Indigent mortals
below !   Duke de Villequier, Gentleman of the Chamber, gets such contumelious rating, in presence of all
people there, that he may see good first to exculpate
himself in the Newspapers ; then, that not prospering,
to retire over the Frontiers, and begin plotting at
Brussels.[2]   His Apartment will stand vacant ; usefuller,
as we may find, than when it stood occupied.

So fly the Chevaliers of the Poniard ; hunted of
Patriotic men, shamefully in the thickening dusk.
A dim miserable business ; born of darkness ; dying
away there in the thickening dusk and dimness.   In
the midst of which, however, let the reader discern
clearly one figure running for its life : Crispin-Catiline
d'Espréménil,—for the last time, or the last but one.

[1] Hist. Parl. ix. 139–48.   [2] Montgaillard, ii. 286.

It is not yet three years since these same Centre Grenadiers, Gardes Françaises then, marched him towards the Calypso Isles, in the grey of the May morning ; and he and they have got thus far. Buffeted, beaten down, delivered by popular Pétion, he might well answer bitterly : ' And I too, Monsieur, have been carried on the People's shoulders '.[1] A fact which popular Pétion, if he like, can meditate.

But happily, one way and another, the speedy night covers up this ignominious Day of Poniards ; and the Chevaliers escape, though maltreated, with torn coat-skirts and heavy hearts, to their respective dwelling-houses. Riot twofold is quelled ; and little blood shed, if it be not insignificant blood from the nose : Vincennes stands undemolished, reparable ; and the Hereditary Representative has not been stolen, nor the Queen smuggled into Prison. A day long remembered : commented on with loud hahas and deep grumblings ; with bitter scornfulness of triumph, bitter rancour of defeat. Royalism, as usual, imputes it to D'Orléans and the Anarchists intent on insulting Majesty : Patriotism, as usual, to Royalists, and even Constitutionalists, intent on stealing Majesty to Metz : we, also as usual, to Preternatural Suspicion, and Phoebus Apollo having made himself like the Night.

Thus, however, has the reader seen, in an unexpected arena, on this last day of February 1791, the Three long-contending elements of French Society dashed forth into singular comico-tragical collision ; acting and reacting openly to the eye. Constitutionalism, at once quelling Sansculottic riot at Vincennes, and Royalist treachery in the Tuileries, is great, this day, and prevails. As for poor Royalism, tossed to and fro in that manner, its daggers all left in a heap, what can one think of it ? Every dog, the Adage says, has its day : *has* it ; has had it ; or will have it. For the present, the day is Lafayette's and the Constitution's.

---

[1] See Mercier, ii. 40, 202.

Nevertheless Hunger and Jacobinism, fast growing fanatical, still work; their day, were they once fanatical, will come. Hitherto, in all tempests, Lafayette, like some divine Sea-ruler, raises his serene head: the upper Aeolus' blasts fly back to their caves, like foolish unbidden winds: the under sea-billows they had vexed into froth allay themselves. But if, as we often write, the *sub*marine Titanic Fire-powers came into play, the Ocean-bed from beneath being *burst* ? If they hurled Poseidon Lafayette and his Constitution out of Space; and, in the Titanic melly, sea were mixed with sky ?

CHAPTER VI

MIRABEAU

THE spirit of France waxes ever more acrid, fever-sick: towards the final outburst of dissolution and delirium. Suspicion rules all minds: contending parties cannot now commingle; stand separated sheer asunder, eyeing one another, in most aguish mood, of cold terror or hot rage. Counter-Revolution, Days of Poniards, Castries Duel; Flight of Mesdames, of Monsieur and Royalty! Journalism shrills ever louder its cry of alarm. The sleepless Dionysius's Ear of the Forty-eight Sections, how feverishly quick has it grown; convulsing with strange pangs the whole sick Body, as in such sleeplessness and sickness the ear will do!

Since Royalists get Poniards made to order, and a Sieur Motier is no better than he should be, shall not Patriotism too, even of the indigent sort, have Pikes, secondhand Firelocks, in readiness for the worst ? The anvils ring, during this March month, with hammering of Pikes. A Constitutional Municipality promulgated its Placard, that no citizen except the ' active ' or cash-citizen was entitled to have arms; but there rose, instantly responsive, such a tempest of astonishment from Club and Section, that the Constitutional Placard,

almost next morning, had to cover itself up, and die
away into inanity, in a second improved edition.[1] So
the hammering continues ; as all that it betokens does.

Mark, again, how the extreme tip of the Left is
mounting in favour, if not in its own National Hall,
yet with the Nation, especially with Paris. For in such
universal panic of doubt, the opinion that is sure of
itself, as the meagrest opinion may the soonest be, is
the one to which all men will rally. Great is Belief,
were it never so meagre ; and leads captive the doubting heart. Incorruptible Robespierre has been elected
Public Accuser in our new Courts of Judicature ;
virtuous Pétion, it is thought, may rise to be Mayor.
Cordelier Danton, called also by triumphant majorities,
sits at the Departmental Council-table ; colleague
there of Mirabeau. Of incorruptible Robespierre it
was long ago predicted that he might go far, mean
meagre mortal though he was ; for Doubt dwelt not
in him.

Under which circumstances ought not Royalty likewise to cease doubting, and begin deciding and acting ?
Royalty has always that sure trump-card in its hand :
Flight out of Paris. Which sure trump-card Royalty,
as we see, keeps ever and anon clutching at, grasping ;
and swashes it forth tentatively ; yet never tables it,
still puts it back again. Play it, O Royalty ! If there
be a chance left, this seems it, and verily the last chance ;
and now every hour is rendering this a doubtfuller.
Alas, one would so fain both fly and not fly ; play one's
card and have it to play. Royalty, in all human likelihood, will not play its trump-card till the honours, one
after one, be mainly lost ; and such trumping of it
prove to be the sudden finish of the game !

Here accordingly a question always arises ; of the
prophetic sort ; which cannot now be answered.
Suppose Mirabeau, with whom Royalty takes deep
counsel, as with a Prime Minister that cannot yet
legally avow himself as such, had got his arrangements

---

[1] Ordonnance du 17 Mars 1791 (Hist. Parl. ix. 257).

completed ? Arrangements he has ; far-stretching
plans that dawn fitfully on us, by fragments, in the
confused darkness. Thirty Departments ready to sign
loyal Addresses, of prescribed tenor : King carried out
of Paris, but only to Compiègne and Rouen, hardly to
Metz, since, once for all, no Emigrant rabble shall take
the lead in it : National Assembly consenting, by dint
of loyal Addresses, by management, by force of Bouillé,
to hear reason, and follow thither ! [1] Was it so, on
these terms, that Jacobinism and Mirabeau were then
to grapple, in their Hercules-and-Typhon*duel ; Death
inevitable for the one or the other ? The duel itself
is determined on, and sure : but on what terms ; much
more, with what issue, we in vain guess. It is vague
darkness all : unknown what is to be ; unknown even
what has already been. The giant Mirabeau walks in
darkness,* as we said ; companionless, on wild ways :
what his thoughts during these months were, no record
of Biographer, nor vague *Fils Adoptif*, will now ever
disclose.

To us, endeavouring to cast his horoscope, it of course
remains doubly vague. There is one Herculean Man ;
in internecine duel with him, there is Monster after
Monster. Emigrant Noblesse return, sword on thigh,
vaunting of their Loyalty never sullied ; descending
from the air, like Harpy-swarms* with ferocity, with
obscene greed. Earthward there is the Typhon of
Anarchy, Political, Religious ; sprawling hundred-
headed, say with Twenty-five million heads ; wide as
the area of France ; fierce as Frenzy ; strong in very
Hunger. With these shall the Serpent-queller do
battle continually, and expect no rest.

As for the King, he as usual will go wavering chame-
leonlike ; changing colour and purpose with the colour
of his environment ;—good for no Kingly use. On one
royal person, on the Queen only, can Mirabeau perhaps
place dependence. It is possible, the greatness of this
man, not unskilled too in blandishments, courtiership,

---

[1] See Fils Adoptif, vii. l. 6 ; Dumont, c. 11, 12, 14.

and graceful adroitness, might, with most legitimate
sorcery, fascinate the volatile Queen, and fix her to him.
She has courage for all noble daring; an eye and
a heart: the soul of Theresa's Daughter. '*Faut-il
donc*, Is it fated then', she passionately writes to her
Brother, ' that I with the blood I am come of, with the
sentiments I have, must live and die among such
mortals ? ' [1] Alas, poor Princess, Yes. 'She is the
only *man*', as Mirabeau observes, ' whom his Majesty
has about him'. Of one other man Mirabeau is still
surer: of himself. There lie his resources; sufficient
or insufficient.

Dim and great to the eye of Prophecy looks that
future. A perpetual life-and-death battle; confusion
from above and from below ;—mere confused darkness
for us; with here and there some streak of faint lurid
light. We see a King perhaps laid aside; not tonsured,
tonsuring is out of fashion now; but say, sent away
anywhither, with handsome annual allowance, and
stock of smith-tools. We see a Queen and Dauphin,
Regent and Minor; a Queen ' mounted on horseback ',
in the din of battles, with *Moriamur pro rege nostro*[*]!
' Such a day ', Mirabeau writes, ' may come '.

Din of battles, wars more than civil, confusion from
above and from below: in such environment the eye
of Prophecy sees Comte de Mirabeau, like some Cardinal
de Retz,[*] stormfully maintain himself; with head all-
devising, heart all-daring, if not victorious, yet unvan-
quished, while life is left him. The specialities and
issues of it, no eye of Prophecy can guess at: it is
clouds, we repeat, and tempestuous night; and in the
middle of it, now visible, far-darting, now labouring
in eclipse, is Mirabeau indomitably struggling to be
Cloud-Compeller !—One can say that, had Mirabeau
lived, the History of France and of the World had been
different. Further, that the man would have needed,
as few men ever did, the whole compass of that same
' Art of Daring, *Art d'Oser* ', which he so prized; and

[1] Fils Adoptif, *ubi supra*.

likewise that he, above all men then living, would have
practised and manifested it. Finally, that some
substantiality, and no empty simulacrum of a formula,
would have been the result realized by him : a result
you could have loved, a result you could have hated ;
by no likelihood, a result you could only have rejected
with closed lips, and swept into quick forgetfulness
for ever. Had Mirabeau lived one other year !

CHAPTER VII

DEATH OF MIRABEAU

But Mirabeau could not live another year, any more
than he could live another thousand years. Men's years
are numbered,[*] and the tale of Mirabeau's was now
complete. Important or unimportant ; to be mentioned in World-History for some centuries, or not to
be mentioned there beyond a day or two,—it matters
not to peremptory Fate. From amid the press of ruddy
busy Life, the Pale Messenger beckons silently : wide-
spreading interests, projects, salvation of French
Monarchies, what thing soever man has on hand, he
must suddenly quit it all and go. Wert thou saving
French Monarchies ; wert thou blacking shoes on the
Pont Neuf ! The most important of men cannot stay ;
did the World's History depend on an hour, that hour
is not to be given. Whereby, indeed, it comes that
these same *would-have-beens* are mostly a vanity ; and
the World's History could never in the least be what
it would, or might, or should, by any manner of poten-
tiality, but simply and altogether what it *is*.

The fierce wear and tear of such an existence has
wasted out the giant oaken strength of Mirabeau.
A fret and fever that keeps heart and brain on fire :
excess of effort, of excitement ; excess of all kinds :
labour incessant, almost beyond credibility ! 'If I

had not lived with him ', says Dumont, ' I never should
have known what a man can make of one day ; what
things may be placed within the interval of twelve
hours. A day for this man was more than a week or
a month is for others : the mass of things he guided on
together was prodigious ; from the scheming to the
executing not a moment lost '.—' Monsieur le Comte ',
said his Secretary to him once, ' what you require is
impossible '.—' Impossible ! '—answered he, starting
from his chair, ' *Ne me dites jamais ce bête de mot*, Never
name to me that blockhead of a word '.[1] And then the
social repasts ; the dinner which he gives as Commandant of National Guards, which ' cost five hundred
pounds ' ; alas, and ' the Sirens of the Opera ' ; and
all the ginger that is hot in the mouth[*]:—down what
a course is this man hurled ! Cannot Mirabeau stop ;
cannot he fly, and save himself alive ? No ! There
is a Nessus' Shirt on this Hercules ; he must storm and
burn there, without rest, till he be consumed. Human
strength, never so Herculean, has its measure. Herald
shadows flit pale across the fire-brain of Mirabeau ;
heralds of the pale repose. While he tosses and storms,
straining every nerve, in that sea of ambition and
confusion, there comes, sombre and still, a monition
that for him the issue of it will be swift death.

In January last, you might see him as President of
the Assembly ; ' his neck wrapt in linen cloths, at the
evening session ' : there was sick heat of the blood,
alternate darkening and flashing in the eyesight ; he
had to apply leeches, after the morning labour, and
preside bandaged. ' At parting he embraced me ', says
Dumont, ' with an emotion I had never seen in him :
" I am dying, my friend ; dying as by slow fire ; we
shall perhaps not meet again. When I am gone, they
will know what the value of me was. The miseries I
have held back will burst from all sides on France ".' [2]
Sickness gives louder warning ; but cannot be listened
to. On the 27th day of March, proceeding towards

[1] Dumont, p. 311.   [2] Ibid. p. 267.

the Assembly, he had to seek rest and help in Friend
de Lamarck's, by the road ; and lay there, for an hour,
half-fainted, stretched on a sofa. To the Assembly
nevertheless he went, as if in spite of Destiny itself ;
spoke, loud and eager, five several times ; then quitted
the Tribune—for ever. He steps out, utterly exhausted,
into the Tuileries Gardens ; many people press round
him, as usual, with applications, memorials ; he says
to the Friend who was with him : ' Take me out of
this ! '

And so, on the last day of March 1791, endless anxious
multitudes beset the Rue de la Chaussée d'Antin ;
incessantly inquiring ; within doors there, in that
House numbered, in our time, 42, the overwearied
giant has fallen down, to die.[1] Crowds of all parties
and kinds ; of all ranks from the King to the meanest
man ! The King sends publicly twice a-day to inquire ;
privately besides : from the world at large there is no
end of inquiring. ' A written bulletin is handed out
every three hours ', is copied and circulated ; in the
end, it is printed. The People spontaneously keep
silence ; no carriage shall enter with its noise : there
is crowding pressure ; but the Sister of Mirabeau is
reverently recognized, and has free way made for her.
The People stand mute, heart-stricken ; to all it seems
as if a great calamity were nigh : as if the last man of
France, who could have swayed these coming troubles,
lay there at hand-grips with the unearthly Power.

The silence of a whole People, the wakeful toil of
Cabanis, Friend and Physician, skills not : on Saturday,
the second day of April, Mirabeau feels that the last of
the Days has risen for him ; that on this day he has to
depart and be no more. His death is Titanic, as his life
has been ! Lit up, for the last time, in the glare of
coming dissolution, the mind of the man is all glowing
and burning ; utters itself in sayings, such as men long
remember. He longs to live, yet acquiesces in death,
argues not with the inexorable. His speech is wild and

[1] Fils Adoptif, viii. 420-79.

wondrous : unearthly Phantasms dancing now their
torch-dance round his soul ; the soul itself looking out,
fire-radiant, motionless, girt together for that great
hour ! At times comes a beam of light from him on
the world he is quitting. 'I carry in my heart the
death-dirge of the French Monarchy ; the dead remains
of it will now be the spoil of the factious'. Or again,
when he heard the cannon fire, what is characteristic
too : ' Have we the Achilles' Funeral already ? ' So
likewise, while some friend is supporting him : ' Yes,
support that head ; would I could bequeath it thee ! '
For the man dies as he has lived ; self-conscious,
conscious of a world looking on. He gazes forth on the
young Spring, which for him will never be Summer. The
Sun has risen ; he says, ' *Si ce n'est pas là Dieu, c'est
du moins son cousin germain* '.[1]—Death has mastered
the outworks ; power of speech is gone ; the citadel
of the heart still holding out : the moribund giant,
passionately, by sign, demands paper and pen ; writes
his passionate demand for opium, to end these agonies.
The sorrowful Doctor shakes his head : *Dormir*, ' To
sleep ', writes the other, passionately pointing at it !
So dies a gigantic Heathen and Titan ; stumbling
blindly, undismayed, down to his rest. At half-past
eight in the morning, Doctor Petit, standing at the
foot of the bed, says, ' *Il ne souffre plus* '. His suffering
and his working are now ended.

Even so, ye silent Patriot multitudes, all ye men of
France ; this man is rapt away from you. He has
fallen suddenly, without bending till he broke ; as
a tower falls, smitten by sudden lightning. His word
ye shall hear no more, his guidance follow no more.—
The multitudes depart, heartstruck ; spread the sad
tidings. How touching is the loyalty of men to their
Sovereign Man ! All theatres, public amusements
close ; no joyful meeting can be held in these nights,
joy is not for them : the People break in upon private

---

[1] Fils Adoptif, viii. 450 ; Journal de la maladie et de la
mort de Mirabeau, par P. J. G. Cabanis (Paris, 1803).

dancing-parties, and sullenly command that they cease.
Of such dancing-parties apparently but two came to
light; and these also have gone out. The gloom is
universal; never in this City was such sorrow for one
death; never since that old night when Louis XII
departed, 'and the *Crieurs des Corps* went sounding their bells, and crying along the streets: *Le bon
roi Louis, père du peuple, est mort,* The good King
Louis, Father of the People, is dead!'[1] King Mirabeau is now the lost King; and one may say with little
exaggeration, all the People mourns for him.

For three days there is low wide moan; weeping in
the National Assembly itself. The streets are all
mournful; orators mounted on the *bornes,* with large
silent audience, preaching the funeral sermon of the
dead. Let no coachman whip fast, distractively with
his rolling wheels, or almost at all, through these groups!
His traces may be cut; himself and his fare, as incurable Aristocrats, hurled sulkily into the kennels. The
bourne-stone orators speak as it is given them; the
Sansculottic People, with its rude soul, listens eager,
—as men will to any Sermon, or *Sermo,* when it *is*
a spoken Word meaning a Thing, and not a Babblement
meaning No-thing. In the Restaurateur's of the
Palais-Royal, the waiter remarks, 'Fine weather,
Monsieur':—'Yes, my friend', answers the ancient
Man of Letters, 'very fine; but Mirabeau is dead'.
Hoarse rhythmic threnodies come also from the throats
of ballad-singers; are sold on grey-white paper at a *sou*
each.[2] But of Portraits, engraved, painted, hewn and
written; of Eulogies, Reminiscences, Biographies, nay
Vaudevilles, Dramas and Melodramas, in all Provinces
of France, there will, through these coming months,
be the due immeasurable crop; thick as the leaves of
Spring. Nor, that a tincture of burlesque might be in
it, is Gobel's Episcopal *Mandement* wanting; goose

---

[1] Hénault, Abrégé Chronologique, p. 429.
[2] Fils Adoptif, viii. l. 10; Newspapers and Excerpts (in
Hist. Parl. ix. 366–402).

Gobel, who has just been made Constitutional Bishop
of Paris. A Mandement wherein *Ça ira* alternates
very strangely with *Nomine Domini* ; and you are, with
a grave countenance, invited to ' rejoice at possessing
in the midst of you a body of Prelates created by
Mirabeau, zealous followers of his doctrine, faithful
imitators of his virtues '.[1] So speaks, and cackles
manifold, the Sorrow of France ; wailing articulately,
inarticulately, as it can, that a Sovereign Man is
snatched away. In the National Assembly, when
difficult questions are astir, all eyes will ' turn mechani-
cally to the place where Mirabeau sat ',—and Mirabeau
is absent now.

On the third evening of the lamentation, the fourth
of April, there is solemn Public Funeral ; such as
deceased mortal seldom had. Procession of a league
in length ; of mourners reckoned loosely at a hundred
thousand. All roofs are thronged with onlookers, all
windows, lamp-irons, branches of trees. ' Sadness is
painted on every countenance ; many persons weep '.
There is double hedge of National Guards ; there is
National Assembly in a body ; Jacobin Society, and
Societies ; King's Ministers, Municipals, and all Notabilities, Patriot or Aristocrat. Bouillé is noticeable
there, ' with his hat on ' ; say, hat drawn over his brow,
hiding many thoughts ! Slow-wending, in religious
silence, the Procession of a league in length, under the
level sun-rays, for it is five o'clock, moves and marches :
with its sable plumes ; itself in a religious silence ; but,
by fits with the muffled roll of drums, by fits with some
long-drawn wail of music, and strange new-clangour
of trombones, and metallic dirge-voice ; amid the
infinite hum of men. In the Church of Saint-Eustache,
there is funeral oration by Cerutti ; and discharge of
fire-arms, which ' brings down pieces of the plaster '.
Thence, forward again to the Church of Sainte-Gene-
viève ; which has been consecrated, by supreme decree,
on the spur of this time, into a Pantheon for the Great

[1] Hist. Parl. ix. 405.

Men of the Fatherland, *Aux Grands Hommes la Patrie
réconnaissante.* Hardly at midnight is the business
done ; and Mirabeau left in his dark dwelling : first
tenant of that Fatherland's Pantheon.

Tenant, alas, who inhabits but at will, and shall be
cast out. For, in these days of convulsion and disjec-
tion, not even the dust of the dead is permitted to rest.
Voltaire's bones are, by and by, to be carried from their
stolen grave in the Abbey of Scellières, to an eager
stealing grave, in Paris his birth-city : all mortals
processioning and perorating there ; cars drawn by
eight white horses, goadsters in classical costume, with
fillets and wheat-ears enough ;—though the weather is
of the wettest.[1] Evangelist Jean Jacques too, as is
most proper, must be dug up from Ermenonville, and
processioned, with pomp, with sensibility, to the
Pantheon of the Fatherland.[2] He and others : while
again Mirabeau, we say, is cast forth from it, happily
incapable of being *replaced* ; and rests now, irrecognizable, reburied hastily at dead of night ' in the central
part of the Churchyard Sainte-Catherine, in the Suburb
Saint-Marceau ', to be disturbed no further.

So blazes out, farseen, a Man's Life, and becomes
ashes and a *caput mortuum,* in this World-Pyre, which
we name French Revolution : not the first that consumed itself there ; nor, by thousands and many
millions, the last ! A man who ' had swallowed all
formulas ' ; who, in these strange times and circumstances, felt called to live Titanically, and also to die
so. As he, for his part, had swallowed all formulas,
what Formula is there, never so comprehensive, that
will express truly the *plus* and the *minus* of him, give
us the accurate net-result of him ? There is hitherto
none such. Moralities not a few must shriek condemnatory over this Mirabeau ; the Morality by which he
could be judged has not yet got uttered in the speech

---

[1] Moniteur, du 13 Juillet 1791.
[2] Ibid. du 1 Septembre 1794.   See also du 30 Août, &c.
1791.

of men. We will say this of him again : That he is
a Reality and no Simulacrum ; a living Son of Nature
our general Mother ; not a hollow Artifice, and mechanism of Conventionalities, son of nothing, *brother* to
nothing. In which little word, let the earnest man,
walking sorrowful in a world mostly of ' Stuffed
Clothes-suits ', that chatter and grin meaningless on
him, quite *ghastly* to the earnest soul,—think what
significance there is !

Of men who, in such sense, are alive, and see with
eyes, the number is now not great : it may be well, if
in this huge French Revolution itself, with its all-
developing fury, we find some Three. Mortals driven
rabid we find ; sputtering the acridest logic ; baring
their breast to the battle-hail, their neck to the guillotine :—of whom it is so painful to say that they too are
still, in good part, manufactured Formalities, not Facts
but Hearsays !

Honour to the strong man, in these ages, who has
shaken himself loose of shams, and *is* something. For
in the way of being *worthy*, the first condition surely
is that one *be*. Let Cant cease, at all risks and at all
cost : till Cant cease, nothing else can begin. Of human
Criminals, in these centuries, writes the Moralist, I find
but one unforgivable : the Quack. ' Hateful to God ',
as divine Dante sings, ' and to the Enemies of God,

A Dio spiacente ed a' nemici sui ! *

But whoever will, with sympathy, which is the first
essential towards insight, look at this questionable
Mirabeau, may find that there lay verily in him, as
the basis of all, a Sincerity, a great free Earnestness ;
nay call it Honesty, for the man did before all things
see, with that clear flashing vision, into what *was*, into
what existed as fact ; and did, with his wild heart,
follow that and no other. Whereby on what ways
soever he travels and struggles, often enough falling,
he is still a brother man. Hate him not ; thou canst
not hate him ! Shining through such soil and tarnish,
and now victorious effulgent, and oftenest struggling

eclipsed, the light of genius itself is in this man ; which was never yet base and hateful ; but at worst was lamentable, lovable with pity. They say that he was ambitious,* that he wanted to be Minister. It is most true. And was he not simply the one man in France who could have done any good as Minister ? Not vanity alone, not pride alone ; far from that ! Wild burstings of affection were in this great heart ; of fierce lightning, and soft dew of pity. So sunk bemired in wretchedest defacements, it may be said of him, like the Magdalen of old, that he loved much : his Father, the harshest of old crabbed men, he loved with warmth, with veneration.

Be it that his falls and follies are manifold,—as himself often lamented even with tears.[1] Alas, is not the Life of every such man already a poetic Tragedy ; made up ' of Fate and of one's own Deservings ', of *Schicksal und eigene Schuld;** full of the elements of Pity and Fear ? This brother man, if not Epic for us, is Tragic ; if not great, is large ; large in his qualities, world-large in his destinies. Whom other men, recognizing him as such, may, through long times, remember, and draw nigh to examine and consider : these, in their several dialects, will say of him and sing of him, —till the right thing be said ; and so the Formula that *can* judge him be no longer an undiscovered one.

Here then the wild Gabriel Honoré drops from the tissue of our History ; not without a tragic farewell. He is gone : the flower of the wild Riquetti or Arrighetti kindred ; which seems as if in him, with one last effort, it had done its best, and then expired, or sunk down to the undistinguished level. Crabbed old Marquis Mirabeau, the Friend of Men, sleeps sound. The Bailli Mirabeau, worthy Uncle, will soon die forlorn, alone. Barrel-Mirabeau, already gone across the Rhine, his Regiment of Emigrants will drive nigh desperate. ' Barrel-Mirabeau ', says a biographer of his, ' went indignantly across the Rhine, and drilled Emigrant

[1] Dumont, p. 287.

Regiments. But as he sat one morning in his tent,
sour of stomach doubtless and of heart, meditating in
Tartarean humour on the turn things took, a certain
Captain or Subaltern demanded admittance on business.
Such Captain is refused; he again demands, with
refusal; and then again; till Colonel Viscount Barrel-
Mirabeau, blazing up into a mere burning brandy-
barrel, clutches his sword, and tumbles out on this
canaille of an intruder,—alas, on the *canaille* of an
intruder's sword-point, who had drawn with swift
dexterity; and dies, and the Newspapers name it
apoplexy and *alarming accident*'. So die the Mirabeaus.

New Mirabeaus one hears not of : the wild kindred,
as we said, is gone out with this its greatest. As families
and kindreds sometimes do; producing, after long
ages of unnoted notability, some living quintessence of
all the qualities they had, to flame forth as a man world-
noted; after whom they rest as if exhausted; the
sceptre passing to others. The chosen Last of the
Mirabeaus is gone; the chosen man of France is gone.
It was he who shook old France from its basis; and,
as if with his single hand, has held it toppling there,
still unfallen. What things depended on that one
man ! He is as a ship suddenly shivered on sunk rocks :
much swims on the waste waters, far from help.

BOOK IV

VARENNES

CHAPTER I

EASTER AT SAINT-CLOUD

THE French Monarchy may now therefore be considered as, in all human probability, lost; as struggling
henceforth in blindness as well as weakness, the last
light of reasonable guidance having gone out. What
remains of resources their poor Majesties will waste
still further, in uncertain loitering and wavering.
Mirabeau himself had to complain that they only gave
him half confidence, and always had some plan within
his plan. Had they fled frankly with him to Rouen
or anywhither, long ago! They may fly now with
chance immeasurably lessened; which will go on
lessening towards absolute zero. Decide, O Queen;
poor Louis can decide nothing: execute this Flight-
project, or at least abandon it. Correspondence with
Bouillé there has been enough; what profits consulting,
and hypothesis, while all around is in fierce activity of
practice? The Rustic sits waiting* till the river run
dry: alas, with you it is not a common river, but a
Nile Inundation; snows melting in the unseen mountains; till all, and you where you sit, be submerged.

Many things invite to flight. The voice of Journals
invites; Royalist Journals proudly hinting it as a
threat, Patriot Journals rabidly denouncing it as
a terror. Mother Society, waxing more and more emphatic, invites;—so emphatic that, as was prophesied,
Lafayette and your limited Patriots have ere long to

branch off from her, and form themselves into Feuillans;
with infinite public controversy; the victory in which,
doubtful though it look, will remain with the *unlimited*
Mother. Moreover, ever since the Day of Poniards,
we have seen unlimited Patriotism openly equipping
itself with arms. Citizens denied ' activity ', which is
facetiously made to signify a certain weight of purse,
cannot buy blue uniforms, and be Guardsmen; but
man is greater than blue cloth; man can fight, if need
be, in multiform cloth, or even almost without cloth,—
as Sansculotte. So pikes continue to be hammered,
whether those Dirks of improved structure with barbs
be ' meant for the West-India market ', or not meant.
Men beat, the wrong way, their ploughshares into
swords.* Is there not what we may call an ' Austrian
Committee ', *Comité Autrichien*, sitting daily and
nightly in the Tuileries? Patriotism, by vision and
suspicion, knows it too well! If the King fly, will
there not be Aristocrat-Austrian invasion; butchery;
replacement of Feudalism; wars more than civil? The
hearts of men are saddened and maddened.

Dissident Priests likewise give trouble enough.
Expelled from their Parish Churches, where Constitutional Priests, elected by the Public, have replaced them,
these unhappy persons resort to Convents of Nuns, or
other such receptacles; and there, on Sabbath, collecting assemblages of Anti-Constitutional individuals,
who have grown devout all on a sudden,[1] they worship
or pretend to worship in their strait-laced contumacious
manner; to the scandal of Patriotism. Dissident
Priests, passing along with their sacred wafer for the
dying, seem wishful to be massacred in the streets;
wherein Patriotism will not gratify them. Slighter
palm of martyrdom, however, shall not be denied:
martyrdom not of massacre, yet of fustigation. At
the refractory places of worship, Patriot men appear;
Patriot women with strong hazel wands, which they
apply. Shut thy eyes, O Reader; see not this misery,

[1] Toulongeon, i. 262.

peculiar to these later times,—of martyrdom without
sincerity, with only cant and contumacy ! A dead
Catholic Church is not allowed to lie dead ; no, it is
galvanized into the detestablest death-life ; whereat
Humanity, we say, shuts its eyes. For the Patriot
women take their hazel wands, and fustigate, amid
laughter of bystanders, with alacrity : broad bottom
of Priests ; alas, Nuns too, reversed and *cotillons
retroussés* ! The National Guard does what it can :
Municipality ' invokes the Principles of Toleration ' ;
grants Dissident worshippers the Church of the *Théatins*,
promising protection. But it is to no purpose : at the
door of that *Théatins* Church appears a Placard, and
suspended atop, like Plebeian Consular *fasces*,—a Bundle
of Rods ! The Principles of Toleration must do the best
they may : but no Dissident man shall worship con-
tumaciously ; there is a *Plebiscitum* to that effect ;
which, though unspoken, is like the laws of the Medes
and Persians.* Dissident contumacious Priests ought
not to be harboured, even in private, by any man : the
Club of the Cordeliers openly denounces Majesty himself
as doing it.[1]

Many things invite to flight : but probably this thing
above all others, that it has become impossible ! On
the 15th of April, notice is given that his Majesty, who
has suffered much from catarrh lately, will enjoy the
Spring weather, for a few days, at Saint-Cloud. Out at
Saint-Cloud ? Wishing to celebrate his Easter, his
Pâques or Pasch, there ; with refractory Anti-Constitutional Dissidents ?—Wishing rather to make off for
Compiègne, and thence to the Frontiers ? As were, in
good sooth, perhaps feasible, or would once have been ;
nothing but some two *chasseurs* attending you ; chasseurs easily corrupted ! It is a pleasant possibility,
execute it or not. Men say there are thirty thousand
Chevaliers of the Poniard lurking in the woods there :
lurking in the woods, and thirty thousand,—for the

[1] Newspapers of April and June 1791 (in Hist. Parl. ix.
449 ; x. 217).

human Imagination is not fettered. But now, how
easily might these, dashing out on Lafayette, snatch
off the Hereditary Representative; and roll away with
him, after the manner of a whirlblast, whither they
listed!—Enough, it were well the King did not go.
Lafayette is forewarned and forearmed: but, indeed,
is the risk his only; or his and all France's?

Monday the eighteenth of April is come; the Easter
Journey to Saint-Cloud shall take effect. National
Guard has got its orders; a First Division, as Advanced
Guard, has even marched, and probably arrived. His
Majesty's *Maison-bouche*, they say, is all busy stewing
and frying at Saint-Cloud; the King's dinner not far
from ready there. About one o'clock, the Royal
Carriage, with its eight royal blacks, shoots stately into
the Place du Carrousel; draws up to receive its royal
burden. But hark! from the neighbouring Church of
Saint-Roch, the tocsin begins ding-dong-ing. Is the
King stolen then; is he going; gone? Multitudes
of persons crowd the Carrousel: the Royal Carriage
still stands there;—and, by Heaven's strength, shall
stand!

Lafayette comes up, with aides-de-camp and oratory;
pervading the groups: '*Taisez-vous*', answer the
groups, 'the King shall not go'. Monsieur appears, at
an upper window: ten thousand voices bray and shriek,
'*Nous ne voulons pas que le Roi parte*'. Their Majesties
have mounted. Crack go the whips; but twenty
Patriot arms have seized each of the eight bridles:
there is rearing, rocking, vociferation; not the smallest
headway. In vain does Lafayette fret, indignant; and
perorate and strive: Patriots in the passion of terror
bellow round the Royal Carriage; it is one bellowing
sea of Patriot terror run frantic. Will Royalty fly off
towards Austria; like a lit rocket, towards endless
Conflagration of Civil War? Stop it, ye Patriots, in the
name of Heaven! Rude voices passionately apostrophize
Royalty itself. Usher Campan, and other the like
official persons, pressing forward with help or advice,
are clutched by the sashes, and hurled and whirled, in

a confused perilous manner ; so that her Majesty has to plead passionately from the carriage-window.

Order cannot be heard, cannot be followed ; National Guards know not how to act. Centre Grenadiers, of the Observatoire Battalion, are there ; not on duty ; alas, in quasi-mutiny ; speaking rude disobedient words ; threatening the mounted Guards with sharp shot if they hurt the people. Lafayette mounts and dismounts ; runs haranguing, panting ; on the verge of despair. For an hour and three-quarters ; ' seven quarters of an hour ', by the Tuileries Clock ! Desperate Lafayette will open a passage, were it by the cannon's mouth, if his Majesty will order. Their Majesties, counselled to it by Royalist friends, by Patriot foes, dismount ; and retire in, with heavy indignant heart ; giving up the enterprise. *Maison-bouche* may eat that cooked dinner themselves : his Majesty shall not see Saint-Cloud this day,—nor any day.[1]

The pathetic fable of imprisonment in one's own Palace has become a sad fact, then ? Majesty complains to Assembly ; Municipality deliberates, proposes to petition or address ; Sections respond with sullen brevity of negation. Lafayette flings down his Commission ; appears in civic pepper-and-salt frock ; and cannot be flattered back again ; not in less than three days ; and by unheard-of entreaty ; National Guards kneeling to him, and declaring that it is not sycophancy, that they are free men kneeling here to the *Statue of Liberty*. For the rest, those Centre Grenadiers of the Observatoire are disbanded,—yet indeed are reinlisted, all but fourteen, under a new name, and with new quarters. The King must keep his Easter in Paris ; meditating much on this singular posture of things ; but as good as determined now to fly from it, desire being whetted by difficulty.

[1] Deux Amis, vi. c. 1 ; Hist. Parl. ix. 407-14.

CHAPTER II

EASTER AT PARIS

For above a year, ever since March 1790, it would seem, there has hovered a project of Flight before the royal mind ; and ever and anon has been condensing itself into something like a purpose ; but this or the other difficulty always vaporized it again. It seems so full of risks, perhaps of civil war itself ; above all, it cannot be done without effort. Somnolent laziness will not serve : to fly, if not in a leather *vache*, one must verily stir himself. Better to adopt that Constitution of theirs ; execute it so as to show all men that it is *in*executable ? Better or not so good : surely it is *easier*. To all difficulties you need only say, There is a lion in the path,* behold your Constitution will not act ! For a somnolent person it requires no effort to counterfeit death,—as Dame de Staël and Friends of Liberty can see the King's Government long doing, *faisant la mort*.

Nay now, when desire whetted by difficulty has brought the matter to a head, and the royal mind no longer halts between two,* what can come of it ? Grant that poor Louis were safe with Bouillé, what, on the whole, could he look for there ? Exasperated Tickets of Entry answer : Much, all. But cold Reason answers : Little, almost nothing. Is not loyalty a law of Nature ? ask the Tickets of Entry. Is not love of your King, and even death for him, the glory of all Frenchmen,—except these few Democrats ? Let Democrat Constitution-builders see what they will do without their Keystone ; and France rend its hair, having lost the Hereditary Representative !

Thus will King Louis fly ; one sees not reasonably

towards what. As a maltreated Boy, shall we say, who, having a Stepmother, rushes sulky into the wide world ; and will wring the paternal heart ?—Poor Louis escapes from known unsupportable evils, to an unknown mixture of good and evil, coloured by Hope. He goes, as Rabelais did when dying, to seek a great May-be : *je vais chercher un grand Peut-être !* As not only the sulky Boy but the wise grown Man is obliged to do, so often, in emergencies.

For the rest, there is still no lack of stimulants, and stepdame maltreatments, to keep one's resolution at the due pitch. Factious disturbances cease not : as indeed how can they, unless authoritatively *conjured*, in a Revolt which is by nature bottomless ? If the ceasing of faction be the price of the King's somnolence, he may awake when he will, and take wing.

Remark, in any case, what somersets and contortions a dead Catholicism is making,—skilfully galvanized : hideous, and even piteous, to behold ! Jurant and Dissident, with their shaved crowns, argue frothing everywhere ; or are ceasing to argue, and stripping for battle. In Paris was scourging while need continued : contrariwise, in the Morbihan of Brittany, without scourging, armed Peasants are up, roused by pulpit-drum, they know not why. General Dumouriez, who has got missioned thitherward, finds all in sour heat of darkness ; finds also that explanation and conciliation will still do much.[1]

But again, consider this : that his Holiness, Pius Sixth, has seen good to excommunicate Bishop Talleyrand ! Surely, we will say then, considering it, there is no living or dead Church in the Earth that has not the indubitablest right to excommunicate Talleyrand. Pope Pius has right and might, in his way. But truly so likewise has Father Adam, *ci-devant* Marquis Saint-Huruge, in his way. Behold, therefore, on the Fourth of May, in the Palais-Royal, a mixed loud sounding multitude ; in the middle of whom, Father Adam, bull-

---

[1] Deux Amis, v. 410-21 ; Dumouriez, ii. c. 5.

voiced Saint-Huruge, in white hat, towers visible and
audible.   With him, it is said, walks Journalist Gorsas,
walk many others of the washed sort ; for no authority
will interfere.   Pius Sixth, with his plush and tiara, and
power of the Keys, they bear aloft : of natural size,—
made of lath and combustible gum.   Royou, the King's
Friend, is borne too in effigy ; with a pile of Newspaper
King's-Friends, condemned Numbers of the *Ami-du-
Roi* ; fit fuel of the sacrifice.   Speeches are spoken ;
a judgement is held, a doom proclaimed, audible in
bull-voice, towards the four winds.   And thus, amid
great shouting, the holocaust is consummated, under
the summer sky ; and our lath-and-gum Holiness, with
the attendant victims, mounts up in flame, and sinks
down in ashes ; a decomposed Pope : and right or
might, among all the parties, has better or worse
accomplished itself, as it could.[1]   But, on the whole,
reckoning from Martin Luther in the Market-place of
Wittenberg to Marquis Saint-Huruge in this Palais-
Royal of Paris, what a journey have we gone ; into
what strange territories has it carried us ! No Authority
can now interfere.   Nay Religion herself, mourning for
such things, may after all ask, What have *I* to do with
them ?*

In such extraordinary manner does dead Catholicism
somerset and caper, skilfully galvanized.   For, does the
reader inquire into the subject-matter of controversy in
this case ; what the difference between Orthodoxy or
My-doxy and Heterodoxy or *Thy-doxy**might here be ?
My-doxy is, that an august National Assembly can
equalize the extent of Bishopricks ; that an equalized
Bishop, his Creed and Formularies being left quite as
they were, can swear Fidelity to King, Law and Nation,
and so become a Constitutional Bishop.   Thy-doxy, if
thou be Dissident, is that he cannot ; but that he must
become an accursed thing.   Human ill-nature needs
but some Homoiousian*iota, or even the pretence of one ;
and will flow copiously through the eye of a needle*:

[1] Hist. Parl. x. 99–102.

thus always must mortals go jargoning and fuming,

> And, like the ancient Stoics in their porches,
> With fierce dispute maintain their churches.*

This *Auto-da-fé* of Saint-Huruge's was on the Fourth
of May 1791. Royalty sees it ; but says nothing.

CHAPTER III

COUNT FERSEN*

ROYALTY, in fact, should, by this time, be far on
with its preparations. Unhappily much preparation is
needful. Could an Hereditary Representative be carried
in leather *vache*, how easy were it ! But it is not so.

New Clothes are needed ; as usual, in all Epic transactions, were it in the grimmest iron ages ; consider
' Queen Chrimhilde,* with her sixty seamstresses ', in
that iron *Nibelungen Song* ! No Queen can stir without
new clothes. Therefore, now, Dame Campan whisks
assiduous to this mantua-maker and to that : and there
is clipping of frocks and gowns, upper clothes and under,
great and small ; such a clipping and sewing, as might
have been dispensed with. Moreover, her Majesty
cannot go a step anywhither without her *Nécessaire*;
dear *Nécessaire*, of inlaid ivory and rosewood ; cunningly
devised ; which holds perfumes, toilette-implements,
infinite small queenlike furnitures : necessary to terrestrial life. Not without a cost of some five hundred
louis, of much precious time, and difficult hoodwinking
which does not blind, can this same Necessary of life
be forwarded by the Flanders Carriers,—never to get
to hand.[1] All which, you would say, augurs ill for the
prospering of the enterprise. But the whims of women
and queens must be humoured.

---

[1] Campan, ii. c. 18.

Bouillé, on his side, is making a fortified Camp at
Montmédi ; gathering Royal-Allemand, and all manner
of other German and true French Troops thither, ' to
watch the Austrians '. His Majesty will not cross the
frontiers, unless on compulsion. Neither shall the
Emigrants be much employed, hateful as they are to all
people.[1] Nor shall old war-god Broglie have any hand
in the business; but solely our brave Bouillé; to whom,
on the day of meeting, a Marshal's Baton shall be
delivered, by a rescued King, amid the shouting of all
the troops.   In the meanwhile, Paris being so suspicious,
were it not perhaps good to write your Foreign Ambassadors an ostensible Constitutional Letter ; desiring all
Kings and men to take heed that King Louis loves the
Constitution, that he has voluntarily sworn, and does
again swear, to maintain the same, and will reckon
those his enemies who affect to say otherwise ? Such
a Constitutional Circular is dispatched by Couriers, is
communicated confidentially to the Assembly, and
printed in all Newspapers ; with the finest effect.[2]
Simulation and dissimulation mingle extensively in
human affairs.

We observe, however, that Count Fersen is often
using his Ticket of Entry ; which surely he has clear
right to do. A gallant Soldier, and Swede, devoted
to this fair Queen ;—as indeed the Highest Swede now
is. Has not King Gustav,* famed fiery *Chevalier du
Nord,* sworn himself, by the old laws of chivalry, her
Knight ? He will descend on fire-wings, of Swedish
musketry, and deliver her from these foul dragons,—if,
alas, the assassin's pistol intervene not !
But, in fact, Count Fersen does seem a likely young
soldier, of alert decisive ways : he circulates widely,
seen, unseen ; and has business on hand. Also Colonel
the Duke de Choiseul,* nephew of Choiseul the great,
of Choiseul the now deceased ; he and Engineer

[1] Bouillé, Mémoires, ii. c. 10.
[2] Moniteur, Séance du 23 Avril, 1791.

Goguelat*are passing and repassing between Metz and
the Tuileries : and Letters go in cipher,—one of them,
a most important one, hard to *de*cipher ; Fersen having
ciphered it in haste.[1] As for Duke de Villequier, he is
gone ever since the Day of Poniards ; but his Apartment is useful for her Majesty.

On the other side, poor Commandant Gouvion,
watching at the Tuileries, second in National command,
sees several things hard to interpret. It is the same
Gouvion who sat, long months ago, at the Townhall,
gazing helpless into that Insurrection of Women ;
motionless, as the brave stabled steed when conflagration rises, till Usher Maillard snatched his drum.
Sincerer Patriot there is not ; but many a shiftier. He,
if Dame Campan gossip credibly, is paying some
similitude of love-court to a certain false Chambermaid of the Palace, who betrays much to him : the
Nécessaire, the clothes, the packing of jewels,[2]—could
he understand it when betrayed. Helpless Gouvion
gazes with sincere glassy eyes into it ; stirs up his
sentries to vigilance ; walks restless to and fro ; and
hopes the best.

But, on the whole, one finds that, in the second week
of June, Colonel de Choiseul is privately in Paris ;
having come ' to see his children '. Also that Fersen
has got a stupendous new Coach built, of the kind named
Berline ; done by the first artists ; according to a
model : they bring it home to him, in Choiseul's presence ; the two friends take a proof-drive in it, along
the streets ; in meditative mood ; then send it up to
' Madame Sullivan's, in the Rue de Clichy ', far North,
to wait there till wanted. Apparently a certain Russian
Baroness de Korff, with Waiting-woman, Valet, and
two Children, will travel homewards with some state :
in whom these young military gentlemen take interest ?
A Passport has been procured for her ; and much
assistance shown, with Coach-builders and such like ;—

[1] Choiseul, Relation du Départ de Louis XVI (Paris,
1822), p. 39.   [2] Campan, ii. 141.

so helpful-polite are young military men. Fersen has likewise purchased a Chaise fit for two, at least for two waiting-maids; further, certain necessary horses: one would say, he is himself quitting France, not without outlay? We observe finally that their Majesties, Heaven willing, will assist at *Corpus-Christi Day*, this blessed Summer Solstice, in Assumption Church, here at Paris, to the joy of all the world. For which same day, moreover, brave Bouillé, at Metz, as we find, has invited a party of friends to dinner; but indeed is gone from home, in the interim, over to Montmédi.

These are of the Phenomena, or visual Appearances, of this wide-working terrestrial world: which truly is all phenomenal, what they call spectral; and never rests at any moment; one never at any moment can know why.

On Monday night, the Twentieth of June 1791, about eleven o'clock, there is many a hackney-coach, and glass-coach (*carrosse de remise*), still rumbling, or at rest, on the streets of Paris. But of all glass-coaches, we recommend this to thee, O Reader, which stands drawn up in the Rue de l'Echelle, hard by the Carrousel and out-gate of the Tuileries; in the Rue de l'Echelle that then was; 'opposite Ronsin the saddler's door', as if waiting for a fare there! Not long does it wait: a hooded Dame, with two hooded Children has issued from Villequier's door, where no sentry walks, into the Tuileries Court-of-Princes; into the Carrousel; into the Rue de l'Echelle; where the Glass-coachman readily admits them; and again waits. Not long; another Dame, likewise hooded or shrouded, leaning on a servant, issues in the same manner; bids the servant good night; and is, in the same manner, by the Glass-coachman, cheerfully admitted. Whither go so many Dames? 'Tis his Majesty's *Couchée*, Majesty just gone to bed, and all the Palace-world is retiring home. But the Glass-coachman still waits; his fare seemingly incomplete.

By and by, we note a thickset Individual, in round hat and peruke, arm-and-arm with some servant,

seemingly of the Runner or Courier sort; he also
issues through Villequier's door; starts a shoebuckle as
he passes one of the sentries, stoops down to clasp it
again; is however, by the Glass-coachman, still more
cheerfully admitted. And *now*, is his fare complete?
Not yet; the Glass-coachman still waits.—Alas! and
the false Chambermaid has warned Gouvion that she
thinks the Royal Family will fly this very night; and
Gouvion distrusting his own glazed eyes, has sent
express for Lafayette; and Lafayette's Carriage, flaring
with lights, rolls this moment through the inner Arch
of the Carrousel,—where a Lady shaded in broad gipsy-
hat, and leaning on the arm of a servant, also of the
Runner or Courier sort, stands aside to let it pass, and
has even the whim to touch a spoke of it with her
badine,—light little magic rod which she calls *badine*,
such as the Beautiful then wore. The flare of Lafayette's
Carriage rolls past: all is found quiet in the Court-of-
Princes; sentries at their post; Majesties' Apartments
closed in smooth rest. Your false Chambermaid must
have been mistaken? Watch thou, Gouvion, with
Argus' vigilance; for, of a truth, treachery is within
these walls.

But where is the Lady that stood aside in gipsy-hat,
and touched the wheel-spoke with her *badine*? O
Reader, that Lady that touched the wheel-spoke was
the Queen of France! She has issued safe through that
inner Arch, into the Carrousel itself; but not into the
Rue de l'Echelle. Flurried by the rattle and rencounter,
she took the right hand not the left; neither she nor
her Courier knows Paris; he indeed is no Courier, but
a loyal stupid *ci-devant* Bodyguard disguised as one.
They are off, quite wrong, over the Pont Royal and
River; roaming disconsolate in the Rue du Bac;
far from the Glass-coachman, who still waits. Waits,
with flutter of heart; with thoughts—which he must
button close up, under his jarvie-surtout!

Midnight clangs from all the City-steeples; one
precious hour has been spent so; most mortals are
asleep. The Glass-coachman waits; and in what

mood ! A brother jarvie drives up, enters into conversation ; is answered cheerfully in jarvie-dialect : the
brothers of the whip exchange a pinch of snuff ;[1]
decline drinking together ; and part with good night.
Be the Heavens blest ! here at length is the Queen-
lady, in gipsy-hat ; safe after perils ; who has had to
inquire her way. She too is admitted ; her Courier
jumps aloft, as the other, who is also a disguised Bodyguard, has done : and now, O Glass-coachman of a
thousand,—Count Fersen, for the Reader sees it is
thou,—drive !

Dust shall not stick to the hoofs of Fersen : crack !
crack ! the Glass-coach rattles, and every soul breathes
lighter. But is Fersen on the right road ? Northeastward, to the Barrier of Saint-Martin and Metz Highway,
thither were we bound : and lo, he drives right Northward ! The royal Individual, in round hat and peruke,
sits astonished ; but right or wrong, there is no remedy.
Crack, crack, we go incessant, through the slumbering
City. Seldom, since Paris rose out of mud, or the Longhaired Kings went in Bullock-carts, was there such a
drive. Mortals on each hand of you, close by, stretched
out horizontal, dormant ; and we alive and quaking !
Crack, crack, through the Rue de Grammont ; across
the Boulevard ; up the Rue de la Chaussée d'Antin,—
these windows, all silent, of Number 42, were Mirabeau's.
Towards the Barrier not of Saint-Martin, but of Clichy
on the utmost North ! Patience, ye royal Individuals ;
Fersen understands what he is about. Passing up the
Rue de Clichy, he alights for one moment at Madame
Sullivan's : ' Did Count Fersen's Coachman get the
Baroness de Korff's new Berline ? '—' Gone with it an
hour-and-half ago ', grumbles responsive the drowsy
Porter.—' C'est bien '. Yes, it is well ;—though had
not such hour-and-half been lost, it were still better.
Forth therefore, O Fersen, fast, by the Barrier de Clichy ;
then Eastward along the Outer Boulevard, what horses
and whipcord can do !

[1] Weber, ii. 340-2 ; Choiseul, pp. 44-56.

Thus Fersen drives, through the ambrosial night. Sleeping Paris is now all on the right-hand of him ; silent except for some snoring hum : and now he is Eastward as far as the Barrier de Saint-Martin ; looking earnestly for Baroness de Korff's Berline. This Heaven's Berline he at length does descry, drawn up with its six horses, his own German Coachman waiting on the box. Right, thou good German : now haste, whither thou knowest !—And as for us of the Glass-coach, haste too, O haste ; much time is already lost ! The august Glass-coach fare, six Insides, hastily packs itself into the new Berline ; two Bodyguard Couriers behind. The Glass-coach itself is turned adrift, its head towards the City ; to wander whither it lists,—and be found next morning tumbled in a ditch. But Fersen is on the new box, with its brave new hammer-cloths ; flourishing his whip ; he bolts forward towards Bondy. There a third and final Bodyguard Courier of ours ought surely to be, with post-horses ready-ordered. There likewise ought that purchased Chaise, with the two Waiting-maids and their band-boxes, to be ; whom also her Majesty could not travel without. Swift, thou deft Fersen, and may the Heavens turn it well !

Once more, by Heaven's blessing, it is all well. Here is the sleeping Hamlet of Bondy ; Chaise with Waiting-women ; horses all ready, and postilions with their churn-boots, impatient in the dewy dawn. Brief harnessing done, the postilions with their churn-boots vault into the saddles ; brandish circularly their little noisy whips. Fersen, under his jarvie-surtout, bends in lowly silent reverence of adieu ; royal hands wave speechless inexpressible response ; Baroness de Korff's Berline, with the Royalty of France, bounds off : for ever, as it proved. Deft Fersen dashes obliquely Northward, through the country, towards Bougret ; gains Bougret, finds his German Coachman and chariot waiting there ; cracks off, and drives undiscovered into unknown space. A deft active man, we say ; what he undertook to do is nimbly and successfully done.

And so the Royalty of France is actually fled ? This
precious night, the shortest of the year, it flies, and
drives ! *Baroness de Korff* is, at bottom, Dame de
Tourzel, Governess of the Royal Children : she who
came hooded with the two hooded little ones ; little
Dauphin ; little Madame Royale, known long afterwards as Duchesse d'Angoulême. Baroness de Korff's
Waiting-maid is the Queen in gipsy-hat. The royal
Individual in round hat and peruke, he is *Valet* for the
time being. That other hooded Dame, styled *Travelling-
companion*, is kind Sister Elizabeth*; she had sworn,
long since, when the Insurrection of Women was, that
only death should part her and them. And so they rush
there, not too impetuously, through the Wood of Bondy:
—over a Rubicon in their own and France's History.

Great ; though the future is all vague ! If we reach
Bouillé ? If we do not reach him ? O Louis ! and this
all round thee is the great slumbering Earth (and overhead, the great watchful Heaven) ; the slumbering
Wood of Bondy,—where Longhaired Childeric Donothing was struck through with iron ; [1] not unreason-
ably, in a world like ours. These peaked stone-towers
are Raincy ; towers of wicked D'Orléans. All slumbers
save the multiplex rustle of our new Berline. Loose-
skirted scarecrow of an Herb-merchant, with his ass
and early greens, toilsomely plodding, seems the only
creature we meet. But right ahead the great Northeast
sends up evermore his grey brindled dawn : from dewy
branch, birds here and there, with short deep warble,
salute the coming Sun. Stars fade out, and Galaxies ;
Street-lamps of the City of God. The Universe, O my
brothers, is flinging wide its portals for the Levée of the
GREAT HIGH KING. Thou, poor King Louis, farest
nevertheless, as mortals do, towards Orient lands of
Hope ; and the Tuileries with *its* Levées, and France
and the Earth itself, is but a larger kind of doghutch,—
occasionally going rabid.

---

[1] Hénault, Abrégé Chronologique, p. 36.

CHAPTER IV

ATTITUDE

But in Paris, at six in the morning; when some
Patriot Deputy, warned by a billet, awoke Lafayette,
and they went to the Tuileries ?—Imagination may
paint, but words cannot, the surprise of Lafayette ; or
with what bewilderment helpless Gouvion rolled glassy
Argus' eyes, discerning now that his false Chambermaid
had told true !

However, it is to be recorded that Paris, thanks to an
august National Assembly, did, on this seeming doomsday, surpass itself. Never, according to Historian eye-
witnesses, was there seen such an ' imposing attitude '.[1]
Sections all ' in permanence ' ; our Townhall too, having
first, about ten o'clock, fired three solemn alarm-cannons:
above all, our National Assembly ! National Assembly,
likewise permanent, decides what is needful; with
unanimous consent, for the *Côté Droit* sits dumb, afraid
of the Lanterne. Decides with a calm promptitude,
which rises towards the sublime. One must needs vote,
for the thing is self-evident, that his Majesty has been
abducted, or spirited away, ' *enlevé* ', by some person or
persons unknown : in which case, what will the Constitution have us do ? Let us return to first principles, as
we always say : ' *revenons aux principes* '.

By first or by second principles, much is promptly
decided : Ministers are sent for, instructed how to
continue their functions ; Lafayette is examined ; and
Gouvion, who gives a most helpless account, the best
he can. Letters are found written : one Letter, of
immense magnitude ; all in his Majesty's hand, and
evidently of his Majesty's own composition ; addressed
to the National Assembly. It details, with earnestness,
with a childlike simplicity, what woes his Majesty
has suffered. Woes great and small: A Necker seen

[1] Deux Amis, vi. 67–178 ; Toulongeon, ii. 1–38; Camille,
Prudhomme and Editors (in Hist. Parl. x. 240–4).

applauded, a Majesty not ; then insurrection ; want of
due furniture in Tuileries Palace ; want of due cash in
Civil List ; *general* want of cash, of furniture and order ;
anarchy everywhere : Deficit never yet, in the smallest,
' choked or *comblé* ' :—wherefore, in brief, his Majesty
has retired towards a place of Liberty ; and, leaving
Sanctions, Federation, and what Oaths there may be,
to shift for themselves, does now refer—to what, thinks
an august Assembly ? To that ' Declaration of the
Twenty-third of June ', with its ' *Seul il fera*, He alone
will make his People happy '. As if *that* were not buried,
deep enough, under two irrevocable Twelve-months,
and the wreck and rubbish of a whole Feudal World !
This strange autograph Letter the National Assembly
decides on printing ; on transmitting to the Eighty-
three Departments, with exegetic commentary, short
but pithy. Commissioners also shall go forth on all
sides; the People be exhorted; the Armies be increased ;
care taken that the Commonweal suffer no damage.—
And now, with a sublime air of calmness, nay of indifference, we ' pass to the order of the day ' !

By such sublime calmness, the terror of the People
is calmed. These gleaming Pike-forests, which bristled
fateful in the early sun, disappear again ; the far-
sounding Street-orators cease, or spout milder. We are
to have a civil war ; let us have it then. The King
is gone ; but National Assembly, but France and we
remain. The People also takes a great attitude ; the
People also is calm ; motionless as a couchant lion.
With but a few *broolings*, some waggings of the tail ;
to show what it *will* do ! Cazalès, for instance, was
beset by street-groups, and cries of *Lanterne* ; but
National Patrols easily delivered him. Likewise all
King's effigies and statues, at least stucco ones, get
abolished. Even King's names ; the word *Roi* fades
suddenly out of all shop-signs ; the Royal Bengal Tiger
itself, on the Boulevards, becomes the National Bengal
one, *Tigre National*.[1]

[1] Walpoliana.

How great is a calm couchant People! On the
morrow, men will say to one another: 'We have no
King, yet we slept sound enough'. On the morrow,
fervent Achille de Châtelet, and Thomas Paine the
rebellious Needleman, shall have the walls of Paris
profusely plastered with their Placard; announcing
that there must be a *Republic*.[1]—Need we add, that
Lafayette too, though at first menaced by Pikes, has
taken a great attitude, or indeed the greatest of all?
Scouts and Aides-de-camp fly forth, vague, in quest and
pursuit; young Romœuf towards Valenciennes, though
with small hope.

Thus Paris; sublimely calmed, in its bereavement.
But from the *Messageries Royales*, in all Mail-bags,
radiates forth far-darting the electric news: Our
Hereditary Representative is flown. Laugh, black
Royalists: yet be it in your sleeve only; lest Patriotism
notice, and waxing frantic, lower the Lanterne! In
Paris alone is a sublime National Assembly with its
calmness; truly, other places must take it as they can:
with open mouth and eyes; with panic cackling, with
wrath, with conjecture. How each one of those dull
leathern Diligences, with its leathern bag and 'The
King is fled', furrows up smooth France as it goes;
through town and hamlet, ruffles the smooth public
mind into quivering agitation of death-terror; then
lumbers on, as if nothing had happened! Along all
highways; towards the utmost borders; till all France
is ruffled,—roughened up (metaphorically speaking)
into one enormous, desperate-minded, red guggling
Turkey Cock!

For example, it is under cloud of night that the
leathern Monster reaches Nantes; deep sunk in sleep.
The word spoken rouses all Patriot men: General
Dumouriez, enveloped in roquelaures, has to descend
from his bedroom; finds the street covered with 'four
or five thousand citizens in their shirts'.[2] Here and
there a faint farthing rushlight, hastily kindled; and

[1] Dumont, c. 16.   [2] Dumouriez, Mémoires, ii. 109.

so many swart-featured haggard faces with nightcaps
pushed back ; and the more or less flowing drapery of
nightshirt : open-mouthed till the General say his word !
And overhead, as always, the Great Bear is turning so
quiet round Boötes ; steady, indifferent as the leathern
Diligence itself. Take comfort, ye men of Nantes ;
Boötes and the steady Bear are turning ; ancient
Atlantic still sends his brine, loud-billowing, up your
Loire-stream ; brandy shall be hot in the stomach :
this is not the Last of the Days, but one before the
Last.—The fools ! If they knew what was doing, in
these very instants, also by candlelight, in the far North-
east !

Perhaps, we may say, the most terrified man in Paris
or France is—who thinks the Reader ?—seagreen
Robespierre. Double paleness, with the shadow of
gibbets and halters, overcasts the seagreen features :
it is too clear to him that there is to be ' a Saint-
Bartholomew of Patriots ', that in four-and-twenty
hours he will not be in life. These horrid anticipations
of the soul he is heard uttering at Pétion's : by a notable
witness. By Madame Roland, namely ; her whom we
saw, last year, radiant at the Lyons Federation. These
four months, the Rolands have been in Paris ; arranging
with Assembly Committees the Municipal affairs of
Lyons, affairs all sunk in debt ;—communing, the while,
as was most natural, with the best Patriots to be found
here, with our Brissots, Pétions, Buzots, Robespierres :
who were wont to come to us, says the fair Hostess,
four evenings in the week. They, running about, busier
than ever this day, would fain have comforted the seagreen man ; spake of Achille de Châtelet's Placard ;
of a Journal to be called *The Republican* ; of preparing
men's minds for a Republic. ' A Republic ? ' said
the Seagreen, with one of his dry husky *un*sportful
laughs, ' What is that ? ' [1]   O seagreen Incorruptible,
thou shalt see !

[1] Madame Roland, ii. 70.

CHAPTER V

THE NEW BERLINE

But scouts, all this while, and aides-de-camp, have
flown forth faster than the leathern Diligences. Young
Romœuf, as we said, was off early towards Valenciennes:
distracted Villagers seize him, as a traitor with a finger
of his own in the plot ; drag him back to the Townhall ;
to the National Assembly, which speedily grants a new
passport. Nay now, that same scarecrow of an Herb-
merchant with his ass has bethought him of the grand
new Berline seen in the Wood of Bondy ; and delivered
evidence of it : [1] Romœuf, furnished with new passport,
is sent forth with double speed on a hopefuller track ;
by Bondy, Claye and Chalons, towards Metz, to track
the new Berline ; and gallops à franc étrier.

Miserable new Berline ! Why could not Royalty go
in some old Berline similar to that of other men ?
Flying for life, one does not stickle about his vehicle.
Monsieur, in a commonplace travelling-carriage is off
Northwards ; Madame, his Princess, in another, with
variation of route : they cross one another while
changing horses, without look of recognition ; and
reach Flanders, no man questioning them. Precisely
in the same manner, beautiful Princess de Lamballe
set off, about the same hour ; and will reach England
safe :—would she had continued there ! The beautiful,
the good, but the unfortunate ; reserved for a frightful
end !

All runs along, unmolested, speedy, except only the
new Berline. Huge leathern vehicle :—huge Argosy,
let us say, or Acapulco-ship*; with its heavy stern-boat
of Chaise-and-pair ; with its three yellow Pilot-boats
of Mounted Bodyguard Couriers, rocking aimless round
it and ahead of it, to bewilder, not to guide ! It lumbers

[1] Moniteur, &c. (in Hist. Parl. x. 244-53).

along, lurchingly with stress, at a snail's pace ; noted
of all the world. The Bodyguard Couriers, in their
yellow liveries, go prancing and clattering ; loyal but
stupid ; unacquainted with all things. Stoppages
occur ; and breakages, to be repaired at Etoges. King
Louis too will dismount, will walk up hills, and enjoy
the blessed sunshine :—with eleven horses and double
drink-money, and all furtherances of Nature and Art,
it will be found that Royalty, flying for life, accomplishes Sixty-nine miles in Twenty-two incessant hours.
Slow Royalty ! And yet not a minute of these hours
but is precious : on minutes hang the destinies of
Royalty now.

Readers, therefore, can judge in what humour Duke
de Choiseul might stand waiting, in the village of
Pont-de-Sommevelle, some leagues beyond Chalons,
hour after hour, now when the day bends visibly westward. Choiseul drove out of Paris, in all privity, ten
hours before their Majesties' fixed time ; his Hussars,
led by Engineer Goguelat, are here duly, come ' to
escort a Treasure that is expected ' : but, hour after
hour, is no Baroness de Korff's Berline. Indeed, over
all that North-east Region, on the skirts of Champagne
and of Lorraine, where the great Road runs, the agitation is considerable. For all along, from this Pont-de-
Sommevelle Northeastward as far as Montmédi, at
Post-villages and Towns, escorts of Hussars and
Dragoons do lounge waiting ; a train or chain of
Military Escorts ; at the Montmédi end of it our brave
Bouillé : an electric thunder-chain ; which the invisible
Bouillé, like a Father Jove, holds in his hand—for wise
purposes ! Brave Bouillé has done what man could ;
has spread out his electric thunder-chain of Military
Escorts, onwards to the threshold of Chalons : it waits
but for the new Korff Berline ; to receive it, escort it,
and, if need be, bear it off in whirlwind of military fire.
They lie and lounge there, we say, these fierce Troopers ;
from Montmédi and Stenai, through Clermont, Sainte-
Menehould to utmost Pont-de-Sommevelle, in all Post-

villages ; for the route shall avoid Verdun and great
Towns : they loiter impatient, ' till the Treasure arrive '.

Judge what a day this is for brave Bouillé : perhaps
the first day of a new glorious life ; surely the last day
of the old ! Also, and indeed still more, what a day,
beautiful and terrible, for your young full-blooded
Captains : your Dandoins, Comte de Damas, Duke de
Choiseul, Engineer Goguelat, and the like ; entrusted
with the secret !—Alas, the day bends ever more westward ; and no Korff Berline comes to sight. It is four
hours beyond the time, and still no Berline. In all
Village-streets, Royalist Captains go lounging, looking
often Paris-ward ; with face of unconcern, with heart
full of black care : rigorous Quartermasters can hardly
keep the private dragoons from *cafés* and dramshops.[1]
Dawn on our bewilderment, thou new Berline ; dawn
on us, thou Sun-Chariot of a new Berline, with the
destinies of France !

It was of his Majesty's ordering, this military array
of Escorts : a thing solacing the Royal imagination
with a look of security and rescue ; yet, in reality,
creating only alarm, and, where there was otherwise no
danger, danger without end. For each Patriot, in
these Post-villages, asks naturally : This clatter of
cavalry, and marching and lounging of troops, what
means it ? To escort a Treasure ? Why escort, when
no Patriot will steal from the Nation ; or where is your
Treasure ?—There has been such marching and counter-
marching : for it is another fatality, that certain of these
Military Escorts came out so early as yesterday ; the
Nineteenth not the Twentieth of the month being the
day *first* appointed ; which her Majesty, for some
necessity or other, saw good to alter. And now consider
the suspicious nature of Patriotism ; suspicious, above
all, of Bouillé the Aristocrat ; and how the sour doubting humour has had leave to accumulate and exacerbate
for four-and-twenty hours !

[1] Déclaration du Sieur La Gache du Regiment Royal-
Dragons (in Choiseul, pp. 125-39).

At Pont-de-Sommevelle, these Forty foreign Hussars of Goguelat and Duke Choiseul are becoming an unspeakable mystery to all men. They lounged long enough, already, at Sainte-Menehould; lounged and loitered till our National Volunteers there, all risen into hot wrath of doubt, 'demanded three hundred fusils of their Townhall', and got them. At which same moment too, as it chanced, our Captain Dandoins was just coming in, from Clermont with *his* troop, at the other end of the Village. A fresh troop; alarming enough; though happily they are only Dragoons and French! So that Goguelat with his Hussars had to ride, and even to do it fast; till here at Pont-de-Sommevelle, where Choiseul lay waiting, he found resting-place. Resting-place as on burning marle.[*] For the rumour of him flies abroad; and men run to and fro in fright and anger: Chalons sends forth exploratory pickets of National Volunteers towards this hand; which meet exploratory pickets, coming from Sainte-Menehould, on that. What is it, ye whiskered Hussars, men of foreign guttural speech; in the name of Heaven, what is it that brings you? A Treasure?—exploratory pickets shake their heads. The hungry Peasants, however, know too well what Treasure it is; Military seizure for rents, feudalities; which no Bailiff could make us pay! This they know;—and set to jingling their Parish-bell by way of tocsin; with rapid effect! Choiseul and Goguelat, if the whole country is not to take fire, must needs, be there Berline, be there no Berline, saddle and ride.

They mount; and this parish tocsin happily ceases. They ride slowly Eastward; towards Sainte-Menehould; still hoping the Sun-Chariot of a Berline may overtake them. Ah me, no Berline! And near now is that Sainte-Menehould, which expelled us in the morning, with its 'three hundred National fusils'; which looks, belike, not too lovingly on Captain Dandoins and his fresh Dragoons, though only French;—which, in a word, one dare not enter the *second* time, under pain of explosion! With rather heavy heart, our Hussar

Party strikes off to the left ; through by-ways, through
pathless hills and woods, they, avoiding Sainte-Menehould and all places which have seen them heretofore,
will make direct for the distant Village of Varennes.
It is probable they will have a rough evening-ride.

This first military post, therefore, in the long thunder-
chain, has gone off with no effect ; or with worse, and
your chain threatens to entangle itself !—The Great
Road, however, is got hushed again into a kind of
quietude, though one of the wakefullest. Indolent
Dragoons cannot, by any Quartermaster, be kept
altogether from the dramshop ; where Patriots drink,
and will even treat, eager enough for news. Captains,
in a state near distraction, beat the dusty highway,
with a face of indifference ; and no Sun-Chariot appears.
Why lingers it ? Incredible, that with eleven horses,
and such yellow Couriers and furtherances, its rate
should be under the weightiest dray-rate, some three
miles an hour ! Alas, one knows not whether it ever
even got out of Paris ;—and yet also one knows not
whether, this very moment, it is not at the Village-end !
One's heart flutters on the verge of unutterabilities.

CHAPTER VI

OLD-DRAGOON DROUET[*]

In this manner, however, has the Day bent downwards. Wearied mortals are creeping home from their
field-labour ; the village-artisan eats with relish his
supper of herbs, or has strolled forth to the village-
street for a sweet mouthful of air and human news.
Still summer-eventide everywhere ! The great Sun
hangs flaming on the utmost Northwest ; for it is his
longest day this year. The hill-tops rejoicing will ere
long be at their ruddiest, and blush Good-night. The
thrush, in green dells, on long-shadowed leafy spray,
pours gushing his glad serenade, to the babble of brooks

grown audibler; silence is stealing over the Earth.
Your dusty Mill of Valmy, as all other mills and
drudgeries, may furl its canvas, and cease swashing
and circling. The swenkt* grinders in this Treadmill
of an Earth have ground out another Day ; and lounge
there, as we say, in village-groups ; movable, or ranked
on social stone-seats; [1] their children, mischievous
imps, sporting about their feet. Unnotable hum of
sweet human gossip rises from this Village of Sainte-
Menehould, as from all other villages. Gossip mostly
sweet, unnotable ; for the very Dragoons are French
and gallant ; nor as yet has the Paris-and-Verdun
Diligence, with its leathern bag, rumbled in, to terrify
the minds of men.

One figure nevertheless we do note at the last door
of the Village : that figure in loose-flowing nightgown,
of Jean Baptiste Drouet, Master of the Post here. An
acrid choleric man, rather dangerous-looking ; still in
the prime of life, though he has served, in his time, as
a Condé Dragoon. This day, from an early hour Drouet
got his choler stirred, and has been kept fretting.
Hussar Goguelat in the morning saw good, by way of
thrift, to bargain with his own Innkeeper, not with
Drouet regular *Maître de Post*, about some gig-horse
for the sending back of his gig ; which thing Drouet
perceiving came over in red ire, menacing the Innkeeper, and would not be appeased. Wholly an un-
satisfactory day. For Drouet is an acrid Patriot too,
was at the Paris Feast of Pikes : and what do these
Bouillé soldiers mean ? Hussars,—with their gig, and
a vengeance to it !—have hardly been thrust out, when
Dandoins and his fresh Dragoons arrive from Clermont,
and stroll. For what purpose ? Choleric Drouet steps
out and steps in, with long-flowing nightgown ; looking
abroad, with that sharpness of faculty which stirred
choler gives to man.

On the other hand, mark Captain Dandoins on the
street of that same Village ; sauntering with a face of

[1] Rapport de M. Remy (in Choiseul, p. 143).

indifference, a heart eaten of black care ! For no Korff
Berline makes its appearance. The great Sun flames
broader towards setting : one's heart flutters on the
verge of dread unutterabilities.

By Heaven ! here is the yellow Bodyguard Courier ;
spurring fast, in the ruddy evening light ! Steady,
O Dandoins, stand with inscrutable indifferent face ;
though the yellow blockhead spurs past the Post-house ;
inquires to find it ; and stirs the Village, all delighted
with his fine livery.—Lumbering along with its mountains of bandboxes, and Chaise behind, the Korff
Berline rolls in ; huge Acapulco-ship with its Cockboat,
having got thus far. The eyes of the Villagers look
enlightened, as such eyes do when a coach-transit,
which is an event, occurs for them. Strolling Dragoons
respectfully, so fine are the yellow liveries, bring hand
to helmet ; and a Lady in gipsy-hat responds with a
grace peculiar to her.[1] Dandoins stands with folded
arms, and what look of indifference and disdainful
garrison-air a man can, while the heart is like leaping
out of him. Curled disdainful moustachio ; careless
glance,—which however surveys the Village-groups, and
does not like them. With his eye he bespeaks the yellow
Courier, Be quick, be quick ! Thick-headed Yellow
cannot understand the eye ; comes up mumbling, to
ask in words : seen of the village !

Nor is Post-master Drouet unobservant, all this
while : but steps out and steps in, with his long-flowing
nightgown, in the level sunlight ; prying into several
things. When a man's faculties, at the right time, are
sharpened by choler, it may lead to much. That Lady
in slouched gipsy-hat, though sitting back in the
Carriage, does she not resemble some one we have seen,
some time ;—at the Feast of Pikes, or elsewhere ? And
this *Grosse-Tête* in round hat and peruke, which, looking
rearward, pokes itself out from time to time, methinks
there are features in it—— ? Quick, Sieur Guillaume,
Clerk of the *Directoire,* bring me a new Assignat !

---

[1] Déclaration de La Gache (in Choiseul, p. 143).

Drouet scans the new Assignat ; compares the Paper-
money Picture with the Gross Head in round hat there :
by Day and Night ! you might say the one was an
attempted Engraving of the other. And this march
of Troops ; this sauntering and whispering,—I see it !

Drouet Post-master of this Village, hot Patriot,
Old-Dragoon of Condé, consider, therefore, what thou
wilt do. And fast, for behold the new Berline, expedi-
tiously yoked, cracks whipcord, and rolls away !—
Drouet dare not, on the spur of the instant, clutch the
bridles in his own two hands ; Dandoins, with broad-
sword, might hew you off. Our poor Nationals, not
one of them here, have three hundred fusils, but then
no powder ; besides one is not sure, only morally-
certain. Drouet, as an adroit Old-Dragoon of Condé,
does what is advisablest ; privily bespeaks Clerk
Guillaume, Old-Dragoon of Condé he too ; privily,
while Clerk Guillaume is saddling two of the fleetest
horses, slips over to the Townhall to whisper a word ;
then mounts with Clerk Guillaume ; and the two
bound eastward in pursuit, to *see* what can be done.

They bound eastward, in sharp trot : their moral-
certainty permeating the Village, from the Townhall
outwards, in busy whispers. Alas ! Captain Dandoins
orders his Dragoons to mount ; but they, complaining
of long fast, demand bread-and-cheese first ;—before
which brief repast can be eaten, the whole Village is
permeated ; not whispering now, but blustering and
shrieking ! National Volunteers, in hurried muster,
shriek for gunpowder ; Dragoons halt between
Patriotism and Rule of the Service, between bread-and-
cheese and fixed bayonets : Dandoins hands secretly
his Pocket-book, with its secret dispatches, to the
rigorous Quartermaster : the very Ostlers have stable-
forks and flails. The rigorous Quartermaster, half-
saddled, cuts out his way with the sword's edge, amid
levelled bayonets, amid Patriot vociferations, adjura-
tions, flail-strokes ; and rides frantic ; [1]—few or even

---

[1] Déclaration de La Gache (in Choiseul, p. 134).

none following him ; the rest, so sweetly constrained, consenting to stay there.

And thus the new Berline rolls ; and Drouet and Guillaume gallop after it, and Dandoins' Troopers or Trooper gallops after them ; and Sainte-Menehould, with some leagues of the King's Highway, is in explosion ; —and your Military thunder-chain has gone off in a self-destructive manner ; one may fear, with the frightfullest issues.

CHAPTER VII

THE NIGHT OF SPURS[*]

THIS comes of mysterious Escorts, and a new Berline with eleven horses : ' he that has a secret should not only hide it, but hide that he has it to hide '.[*] Your first Military Escort has exploded self-destructive ; and all Military Escorts, and a suspicious Country will now be up, explosive ; comparable *not* to victorious thunder. Comparable, say rather, to the first stirring of an Alpine Avalanche ; which, once stir it, as here at Sainte-Menehould, will spread,—all round, and on and on, as far as Stenai ; thundering with wild ruin, till Patriot Villagers, Peasantry, Military Escorts, new Berline and Royalty are down,—jumbling in the Abyss !

The thick shades of Night are falling. Postilions crack and whip : the Royal Berline is through Clermont, where Colonel Comte de Damas got a word whispered to it ; is safe through, towards Varennes ; rushing at the rate of double drink-money : an Unknown, '*Inconnu* on horseback ', shrieks earnestly some hoarse whisper, not audible, into the rushing Carriage-window, and vanishes, left in the night.[1] August Travellers palpitate ; nevertheless overwearied Nature sinks every one of them into a kind of sleep. Alas, and Drouet and Clerk Guillaume spur ; taking side-roads, for

[1] Campan, ii. 159.

shortness, for safety; scattering abroad that moral-
certainty of theirs; which flies, a bird of the air
carrying it !

And your rigorous Quartermaster spurs; awakening
hoarse trumpet-tone,—as here at Clermont, calling out
Dragoons gone to bed. Brave Colonel de Damas has
them mounted, in part, these Clermont men; young
Cornet Remy dashes off with a few. But the Patriot
Magistracy is out here at Clermont too; National
Guards shrieking for ball-cartridges; and the Village
'illuminates itself';—deft Patriots springing out of
bed; alertly, in shirt or shift, striking a light; sticking
up each his farthing candle, or penurious oil-cruse, till
all glitters and glimmers; so deft are they ! A *camisado*,
or shirt-tumult, everywhere: storm-bell set a-ringing;
village-drum beating furious *générale*, as here at
Clermont, under illumination; distracted Patriots
pleading and menacing ! Brave young Colonel de
Damas, in that uproar of distracted Patriotism, speaks
some fire-sentences to what Troopers he has: 'Comrades insulted at Sainte-Menehould: King and Country
calling on the brave'; then gives the fire-word, *Draw
swords*. Whereupon, alas, the Troopers only *smite*
their sword-handles, driving them further home ! 'To
me, whoever is for the King !' cries Damas in despair;
and gallops, he with some poor loyal Two, of the
Subaltern sort, into the bosom of the Night.[1]

Night unexampled in the Clermontais; shortest of
the year: remarkablest of the century: Night deserving
to be named of Spurs ! Cornet Remy, and those Few
he dashed off with, has missed his road; is galloping
for hours towards Verdun; then, for hours, across
hedged country, through roused hamlets, towards
Varennes. Unlucky Cornet Remy; unluckier Colonel
Damas, with whom there ride desperate only some
loyal Two ! More ride not of that Clermont Escort:
of other Escorts, in other Villages, not even Two may

---

[1] Procès-verbal du Directoire de Clermont (in Choiseul,
pp. 189-95).

ride ; but only all curvet and prance,—impeded by
storm-bell and your Village illuminating itself.

And Drouet rides and Clerk Guillaume ; and the
Country runs.—Goguelat and Duke Choiseul are
plunging through morasses, over cliffs, over stock and
stone, in the shaggy woods of the Clermontais ; by
tracks ; or trackless, with guides ; Hussars tumbling
into pitfalls, and lying ' swooned three quarters of an
hour ', the rest refusing to march without them. What
an evening-ride from Pont-de-Sommevelle ; what
a thirty hours, since Choiseul quitted Paris, with
Queen's-valet Leonard in the chaise by him ! Black
Care* sits behind the rider. Thus go they plunging ;
rustle the owlet from his branchy nest ; champ the
sweet-scented forest-herb, queen-of-the-meadows *spil-
ling* her spikenard ; and frighten the ear of Night.
But hark ! towards twelve o'clock, as one guesses, for
the very stars are gone out : sound of the tocsin from
Varennes ? Checking bridle, the Hussar Officer listens :
' Some fire undoubtedly ! '—yet rides on, with double
breathlessness, to verify.

Yes, gallant friends that do your utmost, it is a certain
sort of fire : difficult to quench.—The Korff Berline,
fairly ahead of all this riding Avalanche, reached the
little paltry Village of Varennes about eleven o'clock ;
hopeful, in spite of that hoarse-whispering Unknown.
Do not all Towns now lie behind us ; Verdun avoided,
on our right ? Within wind of Bouillé himself, in
a manner ; and the darkest of midsummer nights
favouring us ! And so we halt on the hill-top at the
South end of the Village ; expecting our relay ; which
young Bouillé, Bouillé's own son, with his Escort of
Hussars, was to have ready ; for in this Village is no
Post. Distracting to think of : neither horse nor
Hussar is here ! Ah, and stout horses, a proper relay
belonging to Duke Choiseul, do stand at hay, but in
the Upper Village over the Bridge ; and we know not of
them. Hussars likewise do wait, but drinking in the
taverns. For indeed it is six hours beyond the time ;
young Bouillé, silly stripling, thinking the matter over

for this night, has retired to bed. And so our yellow
Couriers, inexperienced, must rove, groping, bungling,
through a Village mostly asleep : Postilions will not,
for any money, go on with the tired horses ; not at
least without refreshment ; not they, let the Valet in
round hat argue as he likes.

Miserable ! 'For five-and-thirty minutes' by the
King's watch, the Berline is at a dead stand : Round-
hat arguing with Churn-boots ; tired horses slobbering their meal-and-water ; yellow Couriers groping,
bungling ;—young Bouillé asleep, all the while, in the
Upper Village, and Choiseul's fine team standing there
at hay. No help for it ; not with a King's ransom ;
the horses deliberately slobber, Round-hat argues,
Bouillé sleeps. And mark now, in the thick night, do
not two Horsemen, with jaded trot, come clank-
clanking; and start with half-pause, if one noticed them,
at sight of this dim mass of a Berline, and its dull
slobbering and arguing ; then prick off faster, into the
Village ? It is Drouet, he and Clerk Guillaume ! Still
ahead, they two, of the whole, riding hurly-burly ;
unshot, though some brag of having chased them.
Perilous is Drouet's errand also ; but he is an Old-
Dragoon, with his wits shaken thoroughly awake.

The Village of Varennes lies dark and slumberous ;
a most unlevel Village, of inverse saddle-shape, as men
write. It sleeps ; the rushing of the River Aire singing
lullaby to it. Nevertheless from the Golden Arm,
Bras d'Or Tavern, across that sloping Market-place,
there still comes shine of social light ; comes voice of
rude drovers, or the like, who have not yet taken the
stirrup-cup ; Boniface Le Blanc, in white apron,
serving them : cheerful to behold. To this *Bras d'Or*,
Drouet enters, alacrity looking through his eyes ; he
nudges Boniface, in all privacy, ' *Camarade, es-tu bon
Patriote*, Art thou a good Patriot ? '—' *Si je suis !* '
answers Boniface.—' In that case ', eagerly whispers
Drouet—what whisper is needful, heard of Boniface
alone.[1]

---

[1] *Deux Amis*, vi. 139-78.

And now see Boniface Le Blanc bustling, as he never did for the jolliest toper. See Drouet and Guillaume, dexterous Old-Dragoons, instantly down blocking the Bridge, with a ' furniture-wagon they find there ', with whatever wagons, tumbrils, barrels, barrows their hands can lay hold of ;—till no carriage can pass. Then swiftly, the Bridge once blocked, see them take station hard by, under Varennes Archway : joined by Le Blanc, Le Blanc's Brother, and one or two alert Patriots he has roused. Some half-dozen in all, with National muskets, they stand close, waiting under the Archway, till that same Korff Berline rumble up.

It rumbles up : *Alte là !* lanterns flash out from under coat-skirts, bridles chuck in strong fists, two National muskets level themselves fore and aft through the two Coach-doors : ' Mesdames, your Passports ? '—Alas, alas! Sieur Sausse, Procureur of the Township, Tallow-chandler also and Grocer, is there, with official grocer-politeness ; Drouet with fierce logic and ready wit :—The respected Travelling Party, be it Baroness de Korff's, or persons of still higher consequence. will perhaps please to rest itself in M. Sausse's till the dawn strike up !

O Louis ; O hapless Marie-Antoinette, fated to pass thy life with such men ! Phlegmatic Louis, art thou but lazy semi-animate phlegm then, to the centre of thee ? King, Captain-General, Sovereign Frank ! if thy heart ever formed, since it began beating under the name of heart, any resolution at all, be it now then, or never in this world :—' Violent nocturnal individuals, and if it were persons of high consequence ? And if it were the King himself ? Has the King not the power, which all beggars have, of travelling unmolested on his own Highway ? Yes : it is the King ; and tremble ye to know it ! The King has said, in this one small matter ; and in France, or under God's Throne, is no power that shall gainsay. Not the King shall ye stop here under this your miserable Archway ; but his dead body only, and answer it to Heaven and Earth. To me, Bodyguards ; Postilions, *en avant* ! '—One fancies

in that case the pale paralysis of these two Le Blanc
musketeers, the drooping of Drouet's underjaw ; and
how Procureur Sausse had melted like tallow in furnace-
heat : Louis faring on ; in some few steps awakening
Young Bouillé, awakening relays and Hussars :
triumphant entry, with cavalcading high-brandishing
Escort, and Escorts, into Montmédi ; and the whole
course of French History different !

Alas, it was not *in* the poor phlegmatic man. Had
it been in him, French History had never come under
this Varennes Archway to decide itself.—He steps out ;
all step out. Procureur Sausse gives his grocer-arms
to the Queen and Sister Elizabeth; Majesty taking the
two children by the hand. And thus they walk, coolly
back, over the Market-place, to Procureur Sausse's ;
mount into his small upper story ; where straightway his Majesty ' demands refreshments '. Demands
refreshments, as is written ; gets bread-and-cheese
with a bottle of Burgundy ; and remarks, that it is the
best Burgundy he ever drank !

Meanwhile, the Varennes Notables, and all men,
official and non-official, are hastily drawing on their
breeches ; getting their fighting gear. Mortals half-
dressed tumble out barrels, lay felled trees ; scouts
dart off to all the four winds,—the tocsin begins
clanging, ' the Village illuminates itself '. Very
singular : how these little Villages do manage, so adroit
are they, when startled in midnight alarm of war.
Like little adroit municipal rattlesnakes, suddenly
awakened : for their storm-bell rattles and rings ; their
eyes glisten luminous (with tallow-light), as in rattle-
snake ire ; and the Village will *sting*. Old-Dragoon
Drouet is our engineer and generalissimo ; valiant as
a Ruy Diaz*:—Now or never, ye Patriots, for the
soldiery is coming ; massacre by Austrians, by Aristocrats, wars more than civil, it all depends on you and
the hour !—National Guards rank themselves, half-
buttoned : mortals, we say, still only in breeches, in
under-petticoat, tumble out barrels and lumber, lay
felled trees for barricades : the Village will *sting*. Rabid

Democracy, it would seem, is *not* confined to Paris,
then ? Ah no, whatsoever Courtiers might talk ; too
clearly no. This of dying for one's King is grown into
a dying for one's self, *against* the King, if need be.

And so our riding and running Avalanche and
Hurly-burly has *reached* the Abyss, Korff Berline foremost ; and may pour itself thither, and jumble :
endless ! For the next six hours, need we ask if there
was a clattering far and wide ? Clattering and tocsin-
ing and hot tumult, over all the Clermontais, spreading
through the Three-Bishopricks ; Dragoon and Hussar
Troops galloping on roads and no-roads ; National
Guards arming and starting in the dead of night ;
tocsin after tocsin transmitting the alarm. In some
forty minutes, Goguelat and Choiseul, with their
wearied Hussars, reach Varennes. Ah, it is no fire,
then ; or a fire difficult to quench ! They leap the
tree-barricades, in spite of National sergeant ; they
enter the village, Choiseul instructing his Troopers
how the matter really is ; who respond interjectionally,
in their guttural dialect, ' *Der König ; die Königinn !* '
and seem stanch. These now, in their stanch humour,
will, for one thing, beset Procureur Sausse's house.
Most beneficial : had not Drouet stormfully ordered
otherwise ; and even bellowed, in his extremity,
' Cannoneers, to your guns ! '—two old honeycombed
Field-pieces, empty of all but cobwebs ; the rattle
whereof, as the Cannoneers with assured countenance
trundled them up, did nevertheless abate the Hussar
ardour, and produce a respectfuller ranking further
back. Jugs of wine, handed over the ranks,—for the
German throat too has sensibility,—will complete the
business. When Engineer Goguelat, some hour or so
afterwards, steps forth, the response to him is—
a hiccuping *Vive la Nation !*

What boots it ? Goguelat, Choiseul, now also Count
Damas, and all the Varennes Officiality are with the
King ; and the King can give no order, form no opinion ;
but sits there, as he has ever done, like clay on potter's

wheel; perhaps the absurdest of all pitiable and
pardonable clay-figures that now circle under the Moon.
He will go on, next morning, and take the National
Guard *with* him ; Sausse permitting ! Hapless Queen :
with her two children laid there on the mean bed,
old Mother Sausse kneeling to Heaven, with tears and
an audible prayer, to bless them; imperial Marie-
Antoinette near kneeling to Son Sausse and Wife Sausse,
amid candle-boxes and treacle-barrels,—in vain !
There are Three thousand National Guards got in ;
before long they will count Ten thousand : tocsins
spreading like fire on dry heath, or far faster.

Young Bouillé, roused by this Varennes tocsin, has
taken horse, and—fled towards his Father. Thitherward also rides, in an almost hysterically desperate
manner, a certain Sieur Aubriot, Choiseul's Orderly ;
swimming dark rivers, our Bridge being blocked ;
spurring as if the Hell-hunt were at his heels.[1] Through
the village of Dun, he galloping still on, scatters the
alarm ; at Dun, brave Captain Deslons and *his* Escort
of a Hundred saddle and ride. Deslons too gets into
Varennes ; leaving his Hundred outside, at the
tree-barricade ; offers to cut King Louis out, if he will
order it : but unfortunately ' the work *will* prove hot ' :
whereupon King Louis has ' no orders to give '.[2]

And so the tocsin clangs, and Dragoons gallop, and
can do nothing, having galloped : National Guards
stream in like the gathering of ravens : your exploding
Thunder-chain, falling Avalanche, or what else we
liken it to, does play, with a vengeance,—up now as
far as Stenai and Bouillé himself.[3] Brave Bouillé, son
of the whirlwind, he saddles Royal-Allemand ; speaks
fire-words, kindling heart and eyes ; distributes
twenty-five gold-louis a company :—Ride, Royal-
Allemand, long-famed : no Tuileries Charge and

[1] Rapport de M. Aubriot (in Choiseul, pp. 150–7).
[2] Extrait d'un Rapport de M. Deslons (in Choiseul,
pp. 164–7).
[3] Bouillé, ii. 74–6.

Necker-Orléans Bust-Procession ; a very King made
captive, and world all to win !—Such is the Night
deserving to be named of Spurs.

At six o'clock two things have happened. Lafayette's
Aide-de-camp, Romœuf, riding *à franc étrier*, on that
old Herb-merchant's route, quickened during the last
stages, has got to Varennes ; where the Ten thousand
now furiously demand, with fury of panic terror, that
Royalty shall forthwith return Paris-ward, that there
be not infinite bloodshed. Also, on the other side,
' English Tom ', Choiseul's *jokei*, flying with that
Choiseul relay, has met Bouillé on the heights of Dun ;
the adamantine brow flushed with dark thunder ;
thunderous rattle of Royal-Allemand at his heels.
English Tom answers as he can the brief question,
How it is at Varennes ?—then asks in turn, What he,
English Tom, with M. de Choiseul's horses, is to do,
and whither to ride ?—To the Bottomless Pool !
answers a thunder voice ; then again speaking and
spurring, orders Royal-Allemand to the gallop ; and
vanishes, swearing (*en jurant*).[1] 'Tis the last of our
brave Bouillé. Within sight of Varennes, he having
drawn bridle, calls a council of officers ; finds that it
is in vain. King Louis has departed, consenting : amid
the clangour of universal storm-bell ; amid the tramp
of Ten thousand armed men, already arrived ; and say,
of Sixty thousand flocking thither. Brave Deslons,
even without ' orders ', darted at the River Aire with
his Hundred ; [2] swam one branch of it, could not the
other ; and stood there, dripping and panting, with
inflated nostril ; the Ten thousand answering him with
a shout of mockery, the new Berline lumbering Paris-
ward its weary inevitable way. No help, then, in
Earth ; nor, in an age not of miracles, in Heaven !

That night, ' Marquis de Bouillé and twenty-one
more of us rode over the Frontiers : the Bernardine

---

[1] Déclaration du Sieur Thomas (in Choiseul, p. 188).
[2] Weber, ii. 386.

monks at Orval in Luxemburg gave us supper and lodgings'.[1] With little of speech, Bouillé rides; with thoughts that do not brook speech. Northward, towards uncertainty, and the Cimmerian Night: towards West-Indian Isles, for with thin Emigrant delirium the son of the whirlwind cannot act; towards England, towards premature Stoical death; not towards France any more. Honour to the Brave; who, be it in this quarrel or in that, *is* a substance and articulate-speaking piece of human Valour, not a fanfaronading hollow Spectrum and squeaking and gibbering Shadow! One of the few Royalist Chief-actors this Bouillé, of whom so much can be said.

The brave Bouillé too, then, vanishes from the tissue of our Story. Story and tissue, faint ineffectual Emblem of that grand Miraculous Tissue, and Living Tapestry named *French Revolution*, which did weave itself then in very fact, ' on the loud-sounding LOOM OF TIME '*! The old Brave drop out from it, with their strivings; and new acrid Drouets, of new strivings and colour, come in :—as is the manner of that weaving.

CHAPTER VIII

THE RETURN

So, then, our grand Royalist Plot, of Flight to Metz, has *executed* itself. Long hovering in the background, as a dread royal *ultimatum*, it has rushed forward in its terrors : verily to some purpose. How many Royalist Plots and Projects, one after another, cunningly-devised, that were to explode like powder-mines and thunder-claps; not one solitary Plot of which has issued otherwise ! Powder-mine of a *Séance Royale* on the Twenty-third of June 1789, which exploded as we then said, ' through the touchhole '; which next, your

[1] Aubriot, *ut supra*, p. 158.

wargod Broglie having reloaded it, brought a Bastille
about your ears. Then came fervent Opera-Repast,
with flourishing of sabres, and *O Richard, O my King* ;
which, aided by Hunger, produces Insurrection of
Women, and Pallas Athene in the shape of Demoiselle
Théroigne. Valour profits not ; neither has fortune
smiled on fanfaronade. The Bouillé Armament ends
as the Broglie one had done. Man after man spends
himself in this cause, only to work it quicker ruin ;
it seems a cause doomed, forsaken of Earth and Heaven.*

On the Sixth of October gone a year, King Louis,
escorted by Demoiselle Théroigne and some two hundred
thousand, made a Royal Progress and Entrance into
Paris, such as man had never witnessed ; we prophesied
him Two more such ; and accordingly another of them,
after this Flight to Metz, is now coming to pass.
Théroigne will not escort here ; neither does Mirabeau
now ' sit in one of the accompanying carriages '.
Mirabeau lies dead, in the Pantheon of Great Men.
Théroigne lies living, in dark Austrian Prison ; having
gone to Liége, professionally, and been seized there.
Bemurmured now by the hoarse-flowing Danube : the
light of her Patriot Supper-parties gone quite out ; so
lies Théroigne : she shall speak with the Kaiser face to
face, and return. And France lies—how ! Fleeting
Time shears down the great and the little ; and in two
years alters many things.

But at all events, here, we say, is a second Ignominious Royal Procession, though much altered ; to
be witnessed also by its hundreds of thousands.
Patience, ye Paris Patriots ; the Royal Berline is
returning. Not till Saturday : for the Royal Berline
travels by slow stages ; amid such loud-voiced confluent sea of National Guards, sixty thousand as they
count ; amid such tumult of all people. Three National
Assembly Commissioners, famed Barnave, famed Pétion,
generally-respectable Latour-Maubourg, have gone to
meet it ; of whom the two former ride in the Berline
itself beside Majesty, day after day. Latour, as a mere
respectability, and man of whom all men speak well,

can ride in the rear, with Dame de Tourzel and the *Soubrettes*.

So on Saturday evening, about seven o'clock, Paris by hundreds of thousands is again drawn up : not now dancing the tricolor joy-dance of hope ; nor as yet dancing in fury-dance of hate and revenge : but in silence, with vague look of conjecture, and curiosity mostly scientific. A Saint-Antoine Placard has given notice this morning that ' whosoever insults Louis shall be caned, whosoever applauds him shall be hanged '. Behold then, at last, that wonderful New Berline ; encircled by blue National sea with fixed bayonets, which flows slowly, floating it on, through the silent assembled hundreds of thousands. Three yellow Couriers sit atop bound with ropes ; Pétion, Barnave, their Majesties, with Sister Elizabeth, and the Children of France, are within.

Smile of embarrassment, or cloud of dull sourness, is on the broad phlegmatic face of his Majesty ; who keeps declaring to the successive Official persons, what is evident, ' *Eh bien, me voilà*, Well, here you have me ' ; and what is not evident, ' I do assure you I did not mean to pass the frontiers ' ; and so forth : speeches natural for that poor Royal Man ; which Decency would veil. Silent is her Majesty, with a look of grief and scorn ; natural for that Royal Woman. Thus lumbers and creeps the ignominious Royal Procession, through many streets, amid a silent-gazing people : comparable, Mercier thinks,[1] to some *Procession du Roi de Basoche* ; or say, Procession of King Crispin, with his Dukes of Sutor-mania* and royal blazonry of Cord-wainery. Except indeed that this is *not* comic ; ah no, it is comico-tragic ; with bound Couriers, and a Doom hanging over it ; most fantastic, yet most miserably real. Miserablest *flebile ludibrium** of a Pickleherring* Tragedy ! It sweeps along there, in most *un*gorgeous pall, through many streets in the dusty summer evening ; gets itself at length wriggled out of sight ;

vanishing in the Tuileries Palace—towards its doom,
of slow torture, *peine forte et dure.**

Populace, it is true, seizes the three rope-bound
yellow Couriers ; will at least massacre *them*. But our
august Assembly, which is sitting at this great moment,
sends out Deputation of rescue ; and the whole is got
huddled up. Barnave, ' all dusty ', is already there,
in the National Hall ; making brief discreet address
and report. As indeed, through the whole journey,
this Barnave has been most discreet, sympathetic ;
and has gained the Queen's trust, whose noble instinct
teaches her always who is to be trusted. Very different
from heavy Pétion ; who, if Campan speaks truth, ate
his luncheon, comfortably filled his wine-glass, in the
Royal Berline ; flung out his chicken-bones past the
nose of Royalty itself ; and, on the King's saying,
' France cannot be a Republic ', answered, ' No, it is
not ripe yet '. Barnave is henceforth a Queen's adviser,
if advice could profit : and her Majesty astonishes
Dame Campan by signifying almost a regard for Barnave ;
and that, in a day of retribution and Royal triumph,
Barnave shall *not* be executed.[1]

On Monday night Royalty went ; on Saturday
evening it returns : so much, within one short week,
has Royalty accomplished for itself. The Pickleherring Tragedy has vanished in the Tuileries Palace,
towards ' pain strong and hard '. Watched, fettered
and humbled, as Royalty never was. Watched even
in its sleeping-apartments and inmost recesses : for it
has to sleep with door set ajar, blue National Argus
watching, his eye fixed on the Queen's curtains ; nay,
on one occasion, as the Queen cannot sleep, he offers
to sit by her pillow, and converse a little ![2]

[1] Campan, ii. c. 18.   [2] Ibid. ii. 149.

CHAPTER IX

SHARP SHOT

In regard to all which, this most pressing question arises : What is to be done with it ? Depose it ! resolutely answers Robespierre and the thoroughgoing few. For, truly, with a King who runs away, and needs to be watched in his very bedroom that he may stay and govern you, what other reasonable thing can be done ? Had Philippe d'Orléans not been a *caput mortuum* ! But of him, known as one defunct, no man now dreams. Depose it not ; say that it is inviolable, that it was spirited away, was *enlevé* ; at any cost of sophistry and solecism, re-establish it ! so answer with loud vehemence all manner of Constitutional Royalists ; as all your pure Royalists do naturally likewise, with low vehemence, and rage compressed by fear, still more passionately answer. Nay Barnave and the two Lameths, and what will follow them, do likewise answer so. Answer, with their whole might : terror-struck at the unknown Abysses on the verge of which, driven thither by themselves mainly, all now reels, ready to plunge.

By mighty effort and combination, this latter course is the course fixed on ; and it shall by the strong arm, if not by the clearest logic, be made good. With the sacrifice of all their hard-earned popularity, this notable Triumvirate, says Toulongeon, 'set the Throne up again, which they had so toiled to overturn : as one might set up an overturned pyramid, on its vertex ' ; to stand so long as it is *held*.

Unhappy France ; unhappy in King, Queen and Constitution ; one knows not in which unhappiest ! Was the meaning of our so glorious French Revolution this, and no other, That when Shams and Delusions, long soul-killing, had become body-killing, and got the length of Bankruptcy and Inanition, a great People

rose and, with one voice, said, in the Name of the
Highest : *Shams shall be no more* ? So many sorrows
and bloody horrors, endured, and to be yet endured
through dismal coming centuries, were they not the
heavy price paid and payable for this same : Total
Destruction of Shams from among men ? And now,
O Barnave Triumvirate ! is it in such *double*-distilled
Delusion, and Sham even of a Sham, that an effort of
this kind will rest acquiescent ? Messieurs of the
popular Triumvirate, never !—But, after all, what can
poor popular Triumvirates, and fallible august Senators
do ? They can, when the Truth is all-too horrible, stick
their heads ostrich-like into what sheltering Fallacy is
nearest ; and wait there, *à posteriori*.

Readers who saw the Clermontais and Three-
Bishopricks gallop in the Night of Spurs ; Diligences
ruffling up all France into one terrific terrified Cock of
India ; and the Town of Nantes in its shirt,—may
fancy what an affair to settle this was. Robespierre,
on the extreme Left, with perhaps Pétion and lean old
Goupil, for the very Triumvirate has defalcated, are
shrieking hoarse ; drowned in Constitutional clamour.
But the debate and arguing of a whole Nation ; the
bellowings through all Journals, for and against ; the
reverberant voice of Danton ; the Hyperion shafts of
Camille, the porcupine-quills of implacable Marat :—
conceive all this.

Constitutionalists in a body, as we often predicted,
do now recede from the Mother Society, and become
Feuillans ; threatening her with inanition, the rank
and respectability being mostly gone. Petition after
Petition, forwarded by Post, or borne in Deputation,
comes praying for Judgement and *Déchéance*, which
is our name for Deposition ; praying, at lowest, for
Reference to the Eighty-three Departments of France.
Hot Marseillese Deputation comes declaring, among
other things : ' Our Phocean Ancestors flung a Bar of
Iron into the Bay at their first landing ; this Bar will
float again on the Mediterranean brine before we consent

to be slaves'. All this for four weeks or more, while
the matter still hangs doubtful ; Emigration streaming with double violence over the frontiers ;[1] France
seething in fierce agitation of this question and prize-
question : What is to be done with the fugitive Hereditary Representative ?

Finally, on Friday the 15th of July 1791, the National
Assembly decides ; in what negatory manner we know.
Whereupon the Theatres all close, the *Bourne*-stones
and Portable-chairs begin spouting. Municipal Placards
flaming on the walls, and Proclamations published by
sound of trumpet, ' invite to repose ' ; with small effect.
And so, on Sunday the 17th, there shall be a thing seen,
worthy of remembering. Scroll of a Petition, drawn up
by Brissots, Dantons, by Cordeliers, Jacobins ; for the
thing was infinitely shaken and manipulated, and many
had a hand in it : such Scroll lies now visible, on the
wooden framework of the Fatherland's Altar, for
signature. Unworking Paris, male and female, is
crowding thither, all day, to sign or to see. Our fair
Roland herself the eye of History can discern there,
' in the morning ' ;[2] not without interest. In few
weeks the fair Patriot will quit Paris ; yet perhaps
only to return.

But, what with sorrow of balked Patriotism, what
with closed theatres, and Proclamations still publishing
themselves by sound of trumpet, the fervour of men's
minds, this day, is great. Nay, over and above, there
has fallen out an incident, of the nature of Farce-
Tragedy and Riddle ; enough to stimulate all creatures.
Early in the day, a Patriot (or some say, it was a
Patriotess, and indeed the truth is undiscoverable),
while standing on the firm deal-board of Fatherland's
Altar, feels suddenly, with indescribable torpedo-shock
of amazement, his bootsole pricked through from below;
clutches up suddenly this electrified bootsole and foot ;
discerns next instant—the point of a gimlet or bradawl
playing up, through the firm deal-board, and now

hastily drawing itself back! Mystery, perhaps Treason?
The wooden framework is impetuously broken up ; and
behold, verily a mystery ; never explicable fully to the
end of the world !   Two human individuals, of mean
aspect, one of them with a wooden leg, lie ensconced
there, gimlet in hand : they must have come in overnight ; they have a supply of provisions,—no ' barrel
of gunpowder ' that one can *see* ; they affect to be
asleep ; look blank enough, and give the lamest account
of themselves.   ' Mere curiosity ; they were boring up,
to get an eyehole ; to see, perhaps '' with lubricity '',
whatsoever, from that *new* point of vision, could be
seen ' : —little that was edifying, one would think !
But indeed what stupidest thing may not human
Dullness, Pruriency, Lubricity, Chance and the Devil,
choosing Two out of Half-a-million idle human heads,
tempt them to ? [1]

Sure enough, the two human individuals with their
gimlet are there.   Ill-starred pair of individuals !   For
the result of it all is, that Patriotism, fretting itself,
in this state of nervous excitability, with hypotheses,
suspicions and reports, keeps questioning these two
distracted human individuals, and again questioning
them ; claps them into the nearest Guardhouse, clutches
them out again ; one hypothetic group snatching them
from another : till finally, in such extreme state of
nervous excitability, Patriotism hangs them as spies
of Sieur Motier ; and the life and secret is choked out
of them for evermore.   For evermore, alas !   Or is
a day to be looked for when these two evidently mean
individuals, who are human nevertheless, will become
Historical Riddles ; and, like him of the *Iron Mask*
(also a human individual, and evidently nothing more),
—have their Dissertations ?   To us this only is certain,
that they had a gimlet, provisions and a wooden leg ;
and have died there on the Lanterne, as the unluckiest
fools might die.

And so the signature goes on, in a still more excited

[1] Hist. Parl. xi. 104–7.

manner.   And Chaumette, for Antiquarians possess the
very Paper to this hour,[1] —has signed himself ' in a
flowing saucy hand slightly leaned ' ;   and Hébert,
detestable *Père Duchesne*, as if ' an inked spider had
dropped on the paper ' ;   Usher Maillard also has
signed, and many Crosses, which cannot write.   And
Paris, through its thousand avenues, is welling to the
Champ-de-Mars and from it, in the utmost excitability
of humour ;   central Fatherland's Altar quite heaped
with signing Patriots and Patriotesses ;   the Thirty
benches and whole internal Space crowded with onlookers, with comers and goers ;   one regurgitating
whirlpool of men and women in their Sunday clothes.
All which a Constitutional Sieur Motier sees ; and Bailly,
looking into it with his long visage made still longer.
Auguring no good ;   perhaps *Déchéance* and Deposition
after all !   Stop it, ye Constitutional Patriots ;   fire
itself is quenchable, yet only quenchable at *first*.

Stop it, truly :   but how stop it ?   Have not the first
free People of the Universe a right to petition ?—
Happily, if also unhappily, here is one proof of riot :
these two human individuals hanged at the Lanterne.
Proof, O treacherous Sieur Motier ?   Were they not
two human individuals sent thither by *thee* to be
hanged ;   to be a pretext for thy bloody *Drapeau
Rouge* ?   This question shall many a Patriot, one day,
ask ;   and answer affirmatively, strong in Preternatural
Suspicion.

Enough, towards half-past seven in the evening, the
mere natural eye can behold this thing : Sieur Motier,
with Municipals in scarf, with blue National Patrollotism, rank after rank, to the clang of drums ;   wending
resolutely to the Champ-de-Mars ;   Mayor Bailly, with
elongated visage, bearing, as in sad duty bound, the
Drapeau Rouge.   Howl of angry derision rises in
treble and bass from a hundred thousand throats, at
the sight of Martial Law ;   which nevertheless, waving
its Red sanguinary Flag, advances there, from the Gros-

[1] Hist. Parl. xi. 113, &c.

Caillou Entrance ; advances, drumming and waving, towards Altar of Fatherland. Amid still wilder howls, with objurgation, obtestation ; with flights of pebbles and mud, *saxa et faeces* ; with crackle of a pistol-shot ;— finally with volley-fire of Patrollotism ; levelled muskets ; roll of volley on volley ! Precisely after one year and three days, our sublime Federation Field is wetted, in this manner, with French blood.

Some ' Twelve unfortunately shot ', reports Bailly, counting by units ; but Patriotism counts by tens and even by hundreds. Not to be forgotten, nor forgiven ! Patriotism flies, shrieking, execrating. Camille ceases journalizing, this day ; great Danton with Camille and Fréron have taken wing, for their life ; Marat burrows deep in the Earth, and is silent. Once more Patrollotism has triumphed ; one other time ; but it is the last.

This was the Royal Flight to Varennes. Thus was the Throne overturned thereby ; but thus also was it victoriously set up again—on its vertex ; and will stand while it can be held.

END OF VOL. I

VOLUME II

PART II

THE CONSTITUTION
(Continued)

BOOK V

PARLIAMENT FIRST

CHAPTER I

GRANDE ACCEPTATION

IN the last nights of September, when the autumnal
equinox is past, and grey September fades into brown
October, why are the Champs Elysées illuminated ; why
is Paris dancing, and flinging fire-works ? They are
gala-nights, these last of September ; Paris may well
dance, and the Universe : the Edifice of the Constitution is completed ! Completed ; nay *revised*, to see
that there was nothing insufficient in it ; solemnly proffered to his Majesty ; solemnly accepted by him, to the
sound of cannon-salvoes, on the fourteenth of the month.
And now by such illumination, jubilee, dancing and fire-
working, do we joyously handsel the new Social Edifice,
and first raise heat and reek there, in the name of Hope.

The Revision, especially with a throne standing on its
vertex, has been a work of difficulty, of delicacy. In
the way of propping and buttressing, so indispensable
now, something could be done ; and yet, as is feared,
not enough. A repentant Barnave Triumvirate, our
Rabauts, Duports, Thourets, and indeed all Constitutional Deputies did strain every nerve : but the Extreme Left was so noisy ; the People were so suspicious,
clamorous to have the work ended : and then the loyal
Right Side sat feeble-petulant all the while, and as it
were pouting and petting ; unable to help, had they
even been willing. The Two Hundred and Ninety had
solemnly made scission, before that ; and departed,

shaking the dust off their feet. To such transcendency
of fret, and desperate hope that worsening of the bad
might the sooner end it and bring back the good, had
our unfortunate loyal Right Side now come ! [1]

However, one finds that this and the other little prop
has been added, where possibility allowed. Civil-list
and Privy-purse were from of old well cared for. King's
Constitutional Guard, Eighteen hundred loyal men from
the Eighty-three Departments, under a loyal Duke de
Brissac ; this, with trustworthy Swiss besides, is of
itself something. The old loyal Bodyguards are indeed
dissolved, in name as well as in fact ; and gone mostly
towards Coblentz. But now also those Sansculottic
violent Gardes Françaises, or Centre Grenadiers, shall
have their mittimus : they do ere long, in the Journals,
not without a hoarse pathos, publish their Farewell ;
' wishing all Aristocrats the graves in Paris which to
us are denied '.[2] They depart, these first Soldiers of
the Revolution ; they hover very dimly in the distance
for about another year ; till they can be remodelled,
new-named, and sent to fight the Austrians : and then
History beholds them no more. A most notable Corps
of men ; which has its place in World-History ;—though
to us, so is History written, they remain mere rubrics
of men ; nameless ; a shaggy Grenadier Mass, crossed
with buff-belts. And yet might we not ask : What
Argonauts, what Leonidas' Spartans*had done such a
work ? Think of their destiny : since that May morning, some three years ago, when they, unparticipating,
trundled off D'Espréménil to the Calypso Isles ; since
that July evening, some two years ago, when they,
participating and sacre-ing with knit brows, poured a
volley into Besenval's Prince de Lambesc ! History
waves them her mute adieu.

So that the Sovereign Power, these Sansculottic
Watchdogs, more like wolves, being leashed and led
away from his Tuileries, breathes freer. The Sovereign
Power is guarded henceforth by a loyal Eighteen Hundred,—whom Contrivance, under various pretexts, may

[1] Toulongeon, ii. 56, 59.   [2] Hist. Parl. xiii. 73.

gradually swell to Six Thousand ; who will hinder no
journey to Saint-Cloud. The sad Varennes business
has been soldered up ; cemented, even in the blood
of the Champ-de-Mars, these two months and more ;
and indeed ever since, as formerly, Majesty has had its
privileges, its ' choice of residence ', though, for good
reasons, the royal mind ' prefers continuing in Paris '.
Poor royal mind, poor Paris ; that have to go mumming ; enveloped in speciosities, in falsehood which
knows itself false ; and to enact mutually your sorrowful farce-tragedy, being bound to it ; and on the whole,
to hope always, in spite of hope !

Nay, now that his Majesty has accepted the Constitution, to the sound of cannon-salvoes, who would not
hope ? Our good King was misguided, but he meant
well. Lafayette has moved for an Amnesty, for universal forgiving and forgetting of Revolutionary faults ;
and now surely the glorious Revolution, cleared of its
rubbish, is complete ! Strange enough, and touching
in several ways, the old cry of *Vive le Roi* once more
rises round King Louis the Hereditary Representative.
Their Majesties went to the Opera ; gave money to the
Poor : the Queen herself, now when the Constitution
is accepted, hears voice of cheering. Bygone shall be
bygone ; the New Era *shall* begin ! To and fro, amid
those lamp-galaxies of the Elysian Fields, the Royal
Carriage slowly wends and rolls ; everywhere with
vivats, from a multitude striving to be glad. Louis
looks out, mainly on the variegated lamps and gay
human groups, with satisfaction enough for the hour.
In her Majesty's face, ' under that kind graceful smile
a deep sadness is legible '.[1] Brilliancies, of valour and
of wit stroll here observant : a Dame de Staël, leaning
most probably on the arm of her Narbonne. She meets
Deputies ; who have built this Constitution ; who saunter herewith vague communings,—not without thoughts
whether it will stand. But as yet melodious fiddle-
strings twang and warble everywhere, with the rhythm
of light fantastic feet ; long lamp-galaxies fling their

[1] De Staël, Considérations, i. c. 23.

coloured radiance ; and brass-lunged Hawkers elbow
and bawl, ' *Grande Acceptation, Constitution Monar-
chique* ' : it behoves the Son of Adam to hope.   Have
not Lafayette, Barnave, and all Constitutionalists set
their shoulders handsomely to the inverted pyramid of
a throne ?   Feuillans, including almost the whole Constitutional Respectability of France, perorate nightly
from their tribune ; correspond through all Post-offices ;
denouncing unquiet Jacobinism ; trusting well that *its*
time is nigh done.   Much is uncertain, questionable ;
but if the Hereditary Representative be wise and lucky,
may one not, with a sanguine Gaelic temper, hope that
he will get in motion better or worse ; that what is wanting to him will gradually be gained and added ?

For the rest, as we must repeat, in this building of
the Constitutional Fabric, especially in this Revision
of it, nothing that one could think of to give it new
strength, especially to steady it, to give it permanence,
and even eternity, has been forgotten.   Biennial Parliament, to be called Legislative, *Assemblée Législative* ;
with Seven Hundred and Forty-five Members, chosen
in a judicious manner by the ' active citizens ' alone,
and even by electing of electors still more active : this,
with privileges of Parliament, shall meet, self-authorized
if need be, and self-dissolved ; shall grant money-sup-
plies and talk ; watch over the administration and
authorities ; discharge for ever the functions of a
Constitutional Great Council, Collective Wisdom and
National Palaver—as the Heavens will enable.   Our
First biennial Parliament, which indeed has been a-
choosing since early in August, is now as good as chosen.
Nay it has mostly got to Paris : it arrived gradually ;—
not without pathetic greeting to its venerable Parent,
the now moribund Constituent ; and sat there in the
Galleries, reverently listening ; ready to begin, the
instant the ground were clear.

Then as to changes in the Constitution itself ? This,
impossible for any Legislative, or common biennial Parliament, and possible solely for some resuscitated Constituent or National Convention, is evidently one of the

most ticklish points.   The august moribund Assembly
debated it for four entire days.   Some thought a change,
or at least a reviewal and new approval, might be ad-
missible in thirty years ;   some even went lower, down
to twenty, nay to fifteen.   The august Assembly had
once decided for thirty years ;   but it revoked that, on
better thoughts ;   and did not fix any date of time, but
merely some vague outline of a posture of circumstances,
and, on the whole, left the matter hanging.[1]   Doubtless
a National Convention can be assembled even *within*
the thirty years :   yet one may hope, not ;   but that
Legislatives, biennial Parliaments of the common kind,
with their limited faculty, and perhaps quiet successive
additions thereto, may suffice, for generations, or indeed while computed Time runs.

Furthermore, be it noted that no member of this
Constituent has been, or could be, elected to the new
Legislative.   So noble-minded were these Law-makers !
cry some :   and Solon-like would banish themselves.   So
splenetic !   cry more :   each grudging the other, none
daring to be outdone in self-denial by the other.   So
unwise in either case !   answer all practical men.   But
consider this other self-denying ordinance, That none
of us can be King's Minister, or accept the smallest
Court Appointment, for the space of four, or at lowest
(and on long debate and Revision), for the space of two
years! So moves the incorruptible seagreen Robespierre;
with cheap magnanimity he ;   and none dare be outdone
by him.   It was such a law, not superfluous *then*, that
sent Mirabeau to the gardens of Saint-Cloud, under
cloak of darkness, to that colloquy of the gods ;   and
thwarted many things.   Happily and unhappily there
is no Mirabeau now to thwart.

Welcomer meanwhile, welcome surely to all right
hearts, is Lafayette's chivalrous Amnesty.   Welcome
too is that hard-wrung Union of Avignon ;* which has
cost us, first and last, ' thirty sessions of debate ', and so
much else :   may it at length prove lucky !   Rousseau's

---

[1] Choix de Rapports, &c. (Paris, 1825), vi. 239-317.

statue is decreed : virtuous Jean-Jacques, Evangelist
of the Contrat Social. Not Drouet of Varennes ; nor
worthy Lataille, master of the old world-famous Tennis-
Court in Versailles, is forgotten ; but each has his
honourable mention, and due reward in money.[1] Whereupon, things being all so neatly winded up, and the
Deputations, and Messages, and royal and other ceremonials having rustled by ; and the King having now
affectionately perorated about peace and tranquilliza-
tion, and members having answered '*Oui ! oui !*'
with effusion, even with tears,—President Thouret, he
of the Law Reforms, rises, and, with a strong voice,
utters these memorable last-words : ' The National
Constituent Assembly declares that it has finished its
mission ; and that its sittings are all ended '. Incorruptible Robespierre, virtuous Pétion are borne home
on the shoulders of the people ; with vivats heaven-
high. The rest glide quietly to their respective places
of abode. It is the last afternoon of September 1791 ;
on the morrow morning the new Legislative will begin.

So, amid glitter of illuminated streets and Champs
Elysées, and crackle of fireworks and glad deray, has
the first National Assembly vanished ; *dissolving*, as
they well say, into blank Time ; and is no more.
National Assembly is gone, its work remaining ; as all
Bodies of men go, and as man himself goes : it had its
beginning, and must likewise have its end. A Phan-
tasm-Reality born of Time, as the rest of us are ; flitting
ever backwards now on the tide of Time ; to be long
remembered of men. Very strange Assemblages, San-
hedrims, Amphictyonics, Trades-Unions, Ecumenic
Councils, Parliaments and Congresses, have met together on this Planet, and dispersed again ; but a
stranger Assemblage than this august Constituent, or
with a stranger mission, perhaps never met there. Seen
from the distance, this also will be a miracle. Twelve
Hundred human individuals, with the Gospel of Jean-

---

[1] Moniteur (in Hist. Parl. xi. 473).

Jacques Rousseau in their pocket, congregating in the
name of Twenty-five Millions, with full assurance of
faith, to 'make the Constitution': such sight, the
acme and main product of the Eighteenth Century, our
World can witness once only. For Time is rich in
wonders, in monstrosities most rich; and is observed
never to repeat himself, or any of his Gospels :—surely
least of all, this Gospel according to Jean-Jacques.
Once it was right and indispensable, since such had
become the Belief of men; but once also is enough.

They have made the Constitution, these Twelve
Hundred Jean-Jacques Evangelists; not without result. Near twenty-nine months they sat, with various
fortune; in various capacity ;—always, we may say,
in that capacity of car-borne Carroccio, and miraculous
Standard of the Revolt of Men, as a Thing high and
lifted up; whereon whosoever looked might hope healing. They have seen much, cannons levelled on them;
then suddenly, by interposition of the Powers, the cannons drawn back; and a wargod Broglie vanishing, in
thunder *not* his own, amid the dust and downrushing of
a Bastille and old Feudal France. They have suffered
somewhat: Royal Session, with rain and Oath of the
Tennis-Court; Nights of Pentecost; Insurrections of
Women. Also have they not done somewhat? Made
the Constitution, and managed all things the while;
passed, in these twenty-nine months, ' twenty-five hundred Decrees', which on the average is some three for
each day, including Sundays! Brevity, one finds, is
possible, at times: had not Moreau de St. Méry to give
three thousand orders before rising from his seat ?—
There was valour (or value) in these men; and a kind
of faith,—were it only faith in this, That cobwebs are
not cloth; that a Constitution could be made. Cobwebs and chimeras ought verily to disappear; for
a Reality there is. Let formulas, soul-killing, and now
grown body-killing, insupportable, begone, in the name
of Heaven and Earth !—Time, as we say, brought forth
these Twelve Hundred; Eternity was before them,
Eternity behind: they worked, as we all do, in the

confluence of Two Eternities; what work was given
them. Say not that it was nothing they did. Consciously they did somewhat; unconsciously how much!
They had their giants and their dwarfs, they accomplished their good and their evil; they are gone, and
return no more. Shall they not go with our blessing,
in these circumstances; with our mild farewell?

By post, by diligence, on saddle or sole; they are
gone: towards the four winds. Not a few over the
marches, to rank at Coblentz. Thither wended Maury,
among others; but in the end towards Rome,—to be
clothed there in red Cardinal plush; in falsehood as
in a garment;* pet-son (her *last* born?) of the Scarlet
Woman. Talleyrand-Perigord, excommunicated Constitutional Bishop, will make his way to London: to be
Ambassador, spite of the Self-denying Law; brisk
young Marquis Chauvelin acting as Ambassador's-
Cloak. In London too, one finds Pétion the virtuous;
harangued and haranguing, pledging the wine-cup with
Constitutional Reform-Clubs, in solemn tavern-dinner.
Incorruptible Robespierre retires for a little to native
Arras: seven short weeks of quiet; the last appointed
him in this world. Public Accuser in the Paris Department, acknowledged highpriest of the Jacobins; the
glass of incorruptible thin Patriotism, for his narrow
emphasis is loved of all the narrow,—this man seems
to be rising, somewhither? He sells his small heritage
at Arras; accompanied by a Brother and a Sister, he
returns, scheming out with resolute timidity a small
sure destiny for himself and them, to his old lodging,
at the Cabinet-maker's, in the Rue St. Honoré:—
O resolute-tremulous incorruptible seagreen man, towards *what* a destiny!

Lafayette, for his part, will lay down the command.
He retires Cincinnatus-like*to his hearth and farm; but
soon leaves them again. Our National Guard, however, shall henceforth have no one Commandant; but
all Colonels shall command in succession, month about.
Other Deputies we have met, or Dame de Staël has
met, 'sauntering in a thoughtful manner'; perhaps

uncertain what to do. Some, as Barnave, the Lameths,
and their Duport, will continue here in Paris ; watching the new biennial Legislative, Parliament the First ;
teaching it to walk, if so might be ; and the Court to
lead it.

Thus these : sauntering in a thoughtful manner ;
travelling by post or diligence,—whither Fate beckons.
Giant Mirabeau slumbers in the Pantheon of Great
Men : and .France ? and Europe ?—The brass-lunged
Hawkers sing ' Grand Acceptation, Monarchic Constitution ' through these gay crowds : the Morrow, grandson of Yesterday, must be what it can, as To-day its
father is. Our new biennial Legislative* begins to
constitute itself on the first of October 1791.

CHAPTER II

THE BOOK OF THE LAW

IF the august Constituent Assembly itself, fixing the
regards of the Universe, could, at the present distance
of time and place, gain comparatively small attention
from us, how much less can this poor Legislative ! It
has its Right Side and its Left ; the less Patriotic and
the more, for Aristocrats exist not here or now : it
spouts and speaks ; listens to Reports, reads Bills and
Laws ; works in its vocation, for a season : but the
History of France, one finds, is seldom or never there.
Unhappy Legislative, what can History do with it ; if
not drop a tear over it, almost in silence ?   First of the
two-year Parliaments of France, which, if Paper Constitution and oft-repeated National Oath could avail aught,
were to follow in softly-strong indissoluble sequence
while Time ran,—it had to vanish dolefully within *one*
year ; and there came no second like it. Alas ! your
biennial Parliaments in endless indissoluble sequence ;
they, and all that Constitutional Fabric, built with such
explosive Federation Oaths, and its top-stone brought
out with dancing and variegated radiance, went to

pieces, like frail crockery, in the crash of things ; and
already, in eleven short months, were in that Limbo
near the Moon,* with the ghosts of other Chimeras.
There, except for rare specific purposes, let them rest,
in melancholy peace.

On the whole, how unknown is a man to himself ;
or a public Body of men to itself ! Aesop's fly sat on
the chariot-wheel, exclaiming, What a dust I do raise*!
Great Governors, clad in purple with fasces and insignia, are governed by their valets, by the pouting of
their women and children ; or, in Constitutional countries, by the paragraphs of their Able Editors. Say
not, I am this or that ; I am doing this or that ! For
thou knowest *it* not;* thou knowest only the name it as
yet goes by. A purple Nebuchadnezzar rejoices to feel
himself now verily Emperor of this great Babylon which
he has builded*; and *is* a nondescript biped-quadruped,
on the eve of a seven-years course of grazing ! These
Seven Hundred and Forty-five elected individuals doubt
not but they are the first biennial Parliament, come to
govern France by parliamentary eloquence : and they
are what ? And they have come to do what ? Things
foolish and not wise !

It is much lamented by many that this First Biennial
had no members of the old Constituent in it, with their
experience of parties and parliamentary tactics ; that
such was their foolish Self-denying Law. Most surely,
old members of the Constituent had been welcome to us
here. But, on the other hand, what old or what new
members of any Constituent under the Sun could have
effectually profited ? There are first biennial Parliaments so postured as to be, in a sense, *beyond* wisdom ;
where wisdom and folly differ only in degree, and wreckage and dissolution are the appointed issue for both.

Old-Constituents, your Barnaves, Lameths and the
like, for whom a special Gallery has been set apart,
where they may sit in honour and listen, are in the
habit of sneering at these new Legislators ; [1] but let not

---

[1] Dumouriez, ii. 150, &c.

us ! The poor Seven Hundred and Forty-five, sent together by the active citizens of France, are what they
could be : do what is fated them. That they are of
Patriot temper we can well understand. Aristocrat Noblesse had fled over the marches, or sat brooding silent
in their unburnt Châteaus ; small prospect had they in
Primary Electoral Assemblies. What with Flights to
Varennes, what with Days of Poniards, with plot after
plot, the People are left to themselves ; the People
must needs choose Defenders of the People, such as can
be had. Choosing, as *they* also will ever do, ' if not
the ablest man, yet the man ablest to be chosen ! '* Fervour of character, decided Patriot-Constitutional feeling ; these are qualities : but free utterance, mastership
in tongue-fence ; this is the quality of qualities. Accordingly one finds, with little astonishment, in this First
Biennial, that as many as Four hundred Members are
of the Advocate or Attorney species. Men who can
speak, if there be aught to speak : nay here are men
also who can think, and even act. Candour will say of
this ill-fated First French Parliament, that it wanted not
its modicum of talent, its modicum of honesty ; that it,
neither in the one respect nor in the other, sank below
the average of Parliaments, but rose above the average.
Let average Parliaments, whom the world does *not*
guillotine, and cast forth to long infamy, be thankful
not to themselves but to their stars !

France, as we say, has once more done what it could :
fervid men have come together from wide separation ;
for strange issues. Fiery Max Isnard is come, from the
utmost Southeast ; fiery Claude Fauchet, Te-Deum
Fauchet Bishop of Calvados, from the utmost Northwest. No Mirabeau now sits here, who had swallowed
formulas : our only Mirabeau now is Danton, working
as yet out of doors ; whom some call ' Mirabeau of the
Sansculottes '.

Nevertheless we have our gifts,—especially of speech
and logic. An eloquent Vergniaud* we have ; most
mellifluous yet most impetuous of public speakers ;
from the region named Gironde, of the Garonne : a man

unfortunately of indolent habits; who will sit playing
with your children, when he ought to be scheming and
perorating. Sharp-bustling Guadet*; considerate grave
Gensonné*; kind-sparkling mirthful young Ducos; Valazé*doomed to a sad end : all these likewise are of that
Gironde or Bourdeaux region : men of fervid Constitutional principles; of quick talent, irrefragable logic,
clear respectability ; who will have the Reign of Liberty
establish itself, but only by respectable methods.
Round whom others of like temper will gather ; known
by and by as *Girondins,* to the sorrowing wonder of the
world. Of which sort note Condorcet, Marquis and
Philosopher ; who has worked at much, at Paris Municipal Constitution, Differential Calculus, Newspaper
Chronique de Paris, Biography, Philosophy; and now
sits here as two-years Senator : a notable Condorcet,
with stoical Roman face, and fiery heart; 'volcano
hid under snow ' ; styled likewise, in irreverent language, '*mouton enragé*', peaceablest of creatures bitten
rabid ! Or note, lastly, Jean-Pierre Brissot; whom
Destiny, long working noisily with him, has hurled
hither, say, to have done with him. A biennial Senator
he too; nay, for the present, the king of such. Restless,
scheming, scribbling Brissot; who took to himself the
style *de Warville,* heralds know not in the least why ;
—unless it were that the father of him did, in an un-
exceptionable manner, perform Cookery and Vintnery
in the Village of *Ouar*ville ? A man of the windmill
species, that grinds always, turning towards all winds ;
not in the steadiest manner.

In all these men there is talent, faculty to work ;
and they will do it : working and shaping, not *without*
effect, though alas not in marble, only in quicksand !—
But the highest faculty of them all remains yet to be
mentioned ; or indeed has yet to unfold itself for mention : Captain Hippolyte Carnot,* sent hither from the
Pas de Calais ; with his cold mathematical head, and
silent stubbornness of will : iron Carnot, far-planning,
imperturbable, unconquerable ; who, in the hour of
need, shall not be found wanting. His hair is yet

black ; and it shall grow grey, under many kinds of
fortune, bright and troublous ; and with iron aspect
this man shall face them all.

Nor is *Côté Droit*, and band of King's friends, wanting : Vaublanc, Dumas, Jaucourt the honoured Chevalier ; who love Liberty, yet with Monarchy over it ; and
speak fearlessly according to that faith ;—whom the
thick-coming hurricanes will sweep away. With them,
let a new military Theodore Lameth be named ;—were
it only for his two Brothers' sake, who look down on
him, approvingly there, from the Old-Constituents' Gallery. Frothy professing Pastorets, honey-mouthed conciliatory Lamourettes, and speechless nameless individuals sit plentiful, as Moderates, in the middle. Still
less is a *Côté Gauche* wanting : extreme Left ; sitting
on the topmost benches, as if aloft on its speculatory
Height or *Mountain*, which will become a practical
fulminatory Height, and make the name of Mountain
famous-infamous to all times and lands.

Honour waits not on this Mountain ; nor as yet even
loud dishonour. Gifts it boasts not, nor graces, of
speaking or of thinking ; solely this one gift of assured
faith, of audacity that will defy the Earth and the
Heavens. Foremost here are the Cordelier Trio : hot
Merlin* from Thionville, hot Bazire, Attorneys both ;
Chabot,* disfrocked Capuchin, skilful in agio. Lawyer
Lacroix, who wore once as subaltern the single epaulette,
has loud lungs and a hungry heart. There too is Couthon,* little dreaming *what* he is ;—whom a sad chance
has paralysed in the lower extremities. For, it seems,
he sat once a whole night, not warm in his true-love's
bower (who indeed was by law another's), but sunken
to the middle in a cold peat-bog, being hunted out from
her ; quaking for his life, in the cold quaking morass ; [1]
and goes now on crutches to the end. Cambon likewise, in whom slumbers undeveloped such a finance-
talent for printing of Assignats ; Father of Paper-
money ; who, in the hour of menace, shall utter this

---

[1] Dumouriez, ii. 370.

stern sentence, 'War to the Manorhouse, peace to the
Hut, *Guerre aux Châteaux, paix aux Chaumières !*' [1]
Lecointre, the intrepid Draper of Versailles, is welcome
here; known since the Opera-Repast and Insurrection
of Women. Thuriot too; Elector Thuriot, who stood in
the embrasures of the Bastille, and saw Saint-Antoine
rising in mass; who has many other things to see.
Last and grimmest of all, note old Ruhl, with his brown
dusky face and long white hair; of Alsatian Lutheran
breed; a man whom age and book-learning have not
taught; who, haranguing the old men of Rheims, shall
hold up the Sacred *Ampulla**(Heaven-sent, wherefrom
Clovis and all Kings have been anointed) as a mere
worthless oil-bottle, and dash it to sherds on the pavement there; who, alas, shall dash much to sherds, and
finally his own wild head by pistol-shot, and *so* end it.

Such lava welters redhot in the bowels of this Mountain; unknown to the world and to itself! A mere
commonplace Mountain hitherto; distinguished from
the Plain chiefly by its superior *barrenness*, its baldness
of look: at the utmost it may, to the most observant,
perceptibly *smoke*. For as yet all lies so solid, peaceable; and doubts not, as was said, that it will endure
while Time runs. Do not all love Liberty and the Constitution? All heartily;—and yet with degrees. Some,
as Chevalier Jaucourt and his Right Side, may love
Liberty less than Royalty, were the trial made; others,
as Brissot and his Left Side, may love it more than
Royalty. Nay again, of these latter some may love
Liberty more than Law itself; others not more. Parties *will* unfold themselves; no mortal as yet knows
how. Forces work within these men and without: dissidence grows opposition; ever widening; waxing into
incompatibility and internecine feud; till the strong is
abolished by a´stronger; himself in his turn by a
strongest! Who can help it? Jaucourt and his Mon-
archists, Feuillans, or Moderates; Brissot and his Brissotins, Jacobins, or Girondins; these, with the Cordelier

---

[1] Choix de Rapports, xi. 25.

Trio, and all men, must work what is appointed them, and in the way appointed them.

And to think what fate these poor Seven Hundred and Forty-five are assembled, most unwittingly, to meet! Let no heart be so hard as not to pity them. Their soul's wish was to live and work as the First of the French Parliaments; and make the Constitution march. Did they not, at their very instalment, go through the most affecting Constitutional ceremony, almost with tears? The Twelve eldest are sent solemnly to fetch the Constitution itself, the printed Book of the Law. Archivist Camus, an Old-Constituent appointed Archivist, he and the Ancient Twelve, amid blare of military pomp and clangour, enter, bearing the divine Book: and President and all Legislative Senators, laying their hand on the same, successively take the Oath, with cheers and heart-effusion, universal three-times-three.[1] In this manner they begin their Session. Unhappy mortals! For, that same day, his Majesty having received their Deputation of welcome, as seemed, rather drily, the Deputation cannot but feel slighted, cannot but lament such slight: and thereupon our cheering swearing First Parliament sees itself, on the morrow, obliged to explode into fierce retaliatory sputter of anti-royal Enactment as to how they, for their part, will receive Majesty; and how Majesty shall not be called Sire any more, except they please: and then, on the following day, to recall this Enactment of theirs, as too hasty, and a mere sputter, though not unprovoked.

An effervescent well-intentioned set of Senators; too combustible, where continual sparks are flying! Their History is a series of sputters and quarrels; true desire to do their function, fatal impossibility to do it. Denunciations, reprimandings of King's Ministers, of traitors supposed and real; hot rage and fulmination against fulminating Emigrants; terror of Austrian

[1] Moniteur, Séance du 4 Octobre 1791.

Kaiser, of ' Austrian Committee ' in the Tuileries itself ;
rage and haunting terror, haste and doubt and dim
bewilderment !—Haste, we say ; and yet the Constitution had provided against haste.   No Bill can be passed
till it have been printed, till it have been thrice read,
with intervals of eight days ;—' unless the Assembly
shall beforehand decree that there is urgency '.   Which,
accordingly, the Assembly, scrupulous of the Constitution, never omits to do : Considering this, and also considering that, and then that other, the Assembly decrees
always ' *qu'il y a urgence* ' ; and thereupon ' the Assembly, having decreed that there is urgence ', is free to
decree—what indispensable distracted thing seems best
to it.   Two thousand and odd decrees, as men reckon,
within Eleven months ! [1]   The haste of the Constituent
seemed great ; but this is treble-quick.   For the time
itself is rushing treble-quick ; and they have to keep
pace with that.   Unhappy Seven Hundred and Forty-
five : true-patriotic, but so combustible ; being fired,
they must needs fling fire : Senate of touchwood and
rockets, in a world of smoke-storm, with sparks wind-
driven continually flying !

Or think, on the other hand, looking forward some
months, of that scene they call *Baiser de Lamourette !*
The dangers of the country are now grown imminent,
immeasurable ; National Assembly, hope of France, is
divided against itself.   In such extreme circumstances,
honey-mouthed Abbé Lamourette, new Bishop of Lyons,
rises, whose name, *l'amourette*, signifies *the sweetheart*,
or Delilah doxy,*—he rises, and, with pathetic honeyed
eloquence, calls on all august Senators to forget mutual
griefs and grudges, to swear a new oath, and unite as
brothers.   Whereupon they all, with vivats, embrace
and swear ; Left Side confounding itself with Right ;
barren Mountain rushing down to fruitful Plain, Pas-
toret into the arms of Condorcet, injured to the breast
of injurer, with tears : and all swearing that whosoever
wishes either Feuillant Two-Chamber Monarchy or Ex-

---

[1] Montgaillard, iii. 1, 237.

treme-Jacobin Republic, or anything but the Constitution and that only, shall be anathema maranatha:[1]
Touching to behold! For, literally on the morrow
morning, they must again quarrel, driven by Fate; and
their sublime reconcilement is called derisively the
Baiser de L'amourette, or Delilah Kiss.

Like fated Eteocles-Polynices* Brothers, embracing,
though in vain; weeping that they must not love, that
they must hate only, and die by each other's hands!
Or say, like doomed Familiar Spirits; ordered, by Art
Magic under penalties, to do a harder than twist ropes
of sand: 'to make the Constitution march'. If the
Constitution would but march! Alas, the Constitution
will not stir. It falls on its face; they tremblingly lift
it on end again: march, thou gold Constitution! The
Constitution will not march.—'He shall march, by
—— !'* said kind Uncle Toby, and even swore. The
Corporal answered mournfully: 'He will never march
in this world'.

A Constitution, as we often say, will march when it
images, if not the old Habits and Beliefs of the Constituted; then accurately their Rights, or better indeed
their Mights;—for these two, well-understood, are they
not one and the same? The old Habits of France are
gone: her new Rights and Mights are not yet ascer-
tained, except in Paper-theorem; nor can be, in any
sort, till she have *tried*. Till she have measured herself,
in fell death-grip, and were it in utmost preternatural
spasm of madness, with Principalities and Powers,* with
the upper and the under, internal and external; with
the Earth and Tophet and the very Heaven! Then
will she know.—Three things bode ill for the marching
of this French Constitution: the French People; the
French King; thirdly, the French Noblesse and an
assembled European World.

[1] Moniteur, Séance du 6 Juillet 1792.

CHAPTER III

AVIGNON

But quitting generalities, what strange Fact is this,
in the far Southwest, towards which the eyes of all men
do now, in the end of October, bend themselves ? A
tragical combustion, long smoking and smouldering
unluminous, has now burst into flame there.

Hot is that Southern Provençal blood : alas, col-
lisions, as was once said, must occur in a career of
Freedom ; different directions will produce such ; nay
different *velocities* in the same direction will ! To much
that went on there, History, busied elsewhere, would
not specially give heed : to troubles of Uzez,* troubles
of Nismes,* Protestant and Catholic, Patriot and Aristocrat ; to troubles of Marseilles, Montpellier,* Arles*; to
Aristocrat Camp of Jalès, that wondrous real-imaginary
Entity, now fading pale-dim, then always again glowing
forth deep-hued (in the imagination mainly) ;—ominous
magical, ' an Aristocrat *picture* of war done naturally ! '
All this was a tragical deadly combustion, with plot and
riot, tumult by night and by day ; but a *dark* combustion, not luminous, not noticed ; which now, however,
one cannot help noticing.

Above all places, the unluminous combustion in
Avignon and the Comtat Venaissin was fierce. Papal
Avignon, with its Castle rising sheer over the Rhone-
stream ; beautifullest Town, with its purple vines and
gold-orange groves ; why must foolish old rhyming
Réné,* the last Sovereign of Provence, bequeath it to
the Pope and Gold Tiara, not rather to Louis Eleventh
with the Leaden Virgin in his hatband ? For good and
for evil ! Popes, Antipopes, with their pomp, have
dwelt in that Castle of Avignon rising sheer over the
Rhone-stream : there Laura de Sade* went to hear mass ;
her Petrarch twanging and singing by the Fountain of

Vaucluse hard by, surely in a most melancholy manner.
This was in the old days.

And now in these new days such issues do come
from a squirt of the pen by some foolish rhyming Réné,
after centuries,—this is what we have : Jourdan *Coupe-
tête*, leading to siege and warfare an Army, from three
to fifteen thousand strong, called the Brigands of Avignon ; which title they themselves accept, with the addition of an epithet, ' The *brave* Brigands of Avignon ! '
It is even so.   Jourdan the Headsman fled hither from
that Châtelet Inquest, from that Insurrection of Women ;
and began dealing in madder ; but the scene was rife
in other than dye-stuffs ; so Jourdan shut his madder-
shop, and has risen, for he was the man to do it.   The
tile-beard of Jourdan is shaven off ; his fat visage has
got coppered and studded with black carbuncles ; the
Silenus-trunk is swollen with drink and high living : he
wears blue National uniform with epaulettes, ' an enormous sabre, two horse-pistols crossed in his belt, and
other two smaller sticking from his pockets ' ; styles
himself General, and is the tyrant of men.[1]   Consider
this one fact, O Reader ; and what sort of facts must
have preceded it, must accompany it !   Such things
come of old Réné ; and of the question which has risen,
Whether Avignon cannot now cease wholly to be Papal,
and become French and free ?

For some twenty-five months the confusion has
lasted.   Say three months of arguing ; then seven of
raging ; then finally some fifteen months now of fighting, and even of hanging.   For already in February
1790, the Papal Aristocrats had set up four gibbets, for
a sign ; but the People rose in June, in retributive
frenzy ; and, forcing the public Hangman to act,
hanged four Aristocrats, on each Papal gibbet a Papal
Haman.   Then were Avignon Emigrations, Papal Aristocrats emigrating over the Rhone River ; demission
of Papal Consul, flight, victory : re-entrance of Papal
Legate, truce, and new onslaught ; and the various

[1] Dampmartin, Evénemens, i. 267.

turns of war. Petitions there were to National Assembly; Congresses of Townships; three-score and odd Townships voting for French Reunion, and the blessings of Liberty; while some twelve of the smaller, manipulated by Aristocrats, gave vote the other way: with shrieks and discord! Township against Township, Town against Town: Carpentras, long jealous of Avignon, is now turned out in open war with it;—and Jourdan *Coupe-tête*, your first General being killed in mutiny, closes his dye-shop; and does there visibly, with siege-artillery, above all with bluster and tumult, with the ' brave Brigands of Avignon', beleaguer the rival Town, for two months, in the face of the world.

Feats were done, doubt it not, far-famed in Parish History; but to Universal History unknown. Gibbets we see rise, on the one side and on the other; and wretched carcasses swinging there, a dozen in the row; wretched Mayor of Vaison buried before dead.[1] The fruitful seedfields lie unreaped, the vineyards trampled down; there is red cruelty, madness of universal choler and gall. Havoc and anarchy everywhere; a combustion most fierce, but *unlucent*, not to be noticed here! —Finally, as we saw, on the 14th of September last, the National Constituent Assembly,—having sent Commissioners and heard them;[2] having heard Petitions, held Debates, month after month ever since August 1789; and on the whole ' spent thirty sittings ' on this matter,—did solemnly decree that Avignon and the Comtat were incorporated with France, and his Holiness the Pope should have what indemnity was reasonable.

And so hereby all is amnestied and finished ? Alas, when madness of choler has gone through the blood of

[1] Barbaroux, Mémoires, p. 26.
[2] Lescène Desmaisons, Compte rendu à l'Assemblée Nationale 10 Septembre 1791 (Choix des Rapports, vii. 273-93).

men, and gibbets have swung on this side and on that,
what will a parchment Decree and Lafayette Amnesty
do ? Oblivious Lethe flows not *above* ground ! Papal
Aristocrats and Patriot Brigands are still an eye-sorrow
to each other ; suspected, suspicious, in what they do
and forbear. The august Constituent Assembly is gone
but a fortnight, when, on Sunday the Sixteenth morning
of October 1791, the unquenched combustion suddenly
becomes luminous. For Anti-constitutional Placards
are up, and the Statue of the Virgin is said to have
shed tears, and grown red.[1] Wherefore, on that morning, Patriot l'Escuyer, one of our ' six leading Patriots ',
having taken counsel with his brethren and General
Jourdan, determines on going to Church, in company
with a friend or two : not to hear mass, which he values
little ; but to meet all the Papalists there in a body, nay
to meet that same weeping Virgin, for it is the Cordeliers Church ; and give them a word of admonition.
Adventurous errand ; which has the fatallest issue !
What L'Escuyer's word of admonition might be, no
History records ; but the answer to it was a shrieking
howl from the Aristocrat Papal worshippers, many of
them women. A thousand-voiced shriek and menace ;
which, as L'Escuyer did not fly, became a thousand-
handed hustle and jostle ; a thousand-footed kick, with
tumblings and tramplings, with the pricking of seam-
stress stilettoes, scissors and female pointed instruments.
Horrible to behold ; the ancient Dead, and Petrarchan
Laura, sleeping round it there : [2] high Altar and burning
tapers looking down on it ; the Virgin quite tearless,
and of the natural stone-colour !—L'Escuyer's friend
or two rush off, like Job's Messengers, for Jourdan and
the National Force. But heavy Jourdan will seize the
Town-Gates first ; does not run treble-fast, as he might :
on arriving at the Cordeliers Church, the Church is
silent, vacant ; L'Escuyer, all alone, lies there, swimming in his blood, at the foot of the high Altar ; pricked

[1] Procès-verbal de la Commune d'Avignon, &c. (in Hist.
Parl. xii. 419–23).
[2] Ugo Foscolo, Essay on Petrarch, p. 35.

with scissors, trodden, massacred;—gives one dumb sob, and gasps out his miserable life for evermore.*

Sight to stir the heart of any man ; much more of many men, self-styled Brigands of Avignon ! The corpse of L'Escuyer, stretched on a bier, the ghastly head girt with laurel, is borne through the streets ; with many-voiced unmelodious *Nenia* ; funeral-wail still deeper than it is loud ! The copper-face of Jourdan, of bereft Patriotism, has grown black. Patriot Municipality dispatches official Narrative and tidings to Paris ; orders numerous or innumerable arrestments for inquest and perquisition. Aristocrats male and female are haled to the Castle ; lie crowded in subterranean dungeons there, bemoaned by the hoarse rushing of the Rhone ; cut out from help.

So lie they ; waiting inquest and perquisition. Alas ! with a Jourdan Headsman for Generalissimo, with his copper-face grown black, and armed Brigand Patriots chanting their *Nenia*, the inquest is likely to be brief. On the next day and the next, let Municipality consent or not, a Brigand Court-Martial establishes itself in the subterranean stories of the Castle of Avignon ; Brigand Executioners, with naked sabre, waiting at the door for a Brigand verdict. Short judgement, no appeal ! There is Brigand wrath and vengeance ; not unrefreshed by brandy. Close by is the dungeon of the *Glacière*, or Ice-Tower : there may be deeds done— ? For which language has no name !—Darkness and the shadow of horrid cruelty envelopes these Castle Dungeons, that *Glacière* Tower : clear only that many have entered, that few have returned. Jourdan and the Brigands, supreme now over Municipals, over all authorities Patriot or Papal, reign in Avignon, waited on by Terror and Silence.

The result of all which is, that, on the 15th of November 1791, we behold Friend Dampmartin, and subalterns beneath him, and General Choisi above him, with Infantry and Cavalry, and proper cannon-carriages rattling in front, with spread banners, to the sound of fife and drum, wend, in a deliberate formidable manner,

towards that sheer Castle Rock, towards those broad
Gates of Avignon; three new National-Assembly Commissioners following at safe distance in the rear.[1] Avignon, summoned in the name of Assembly and Law,
flings its Gates wide open; Choisi with the rest, Dampmartin and the ' *Bons Enfans*, Good Boys, of *Baufre-
mont* ',—so they name these brave Constitutional
Dragoons, known to them of old,—do enter, amid
shouts and scattered flowers. To the joy of all honest
persons; to the terror only of Jourdan Headsman and
the Brigands. Nay next we behold carbuncled swollen
Jourdan himself show copper-face, with sabre and four
pistols; affecting to talk high; engaging, meanwhile,
to surrender the Castle that instant. So the Choisi
Grenadiers enter with him there. They start and stop,
passing that *Glacière*, snuffing its horrible breath; with
wild yell, with cries of ' Cut the Butcher down ! '—and
Jourdan has to whisk himself through secret passages,
and instantaneously vanish.

Be the mystery of iniquity laid bare then ! A Hundred and Thirty Corpses, of men, nay of women and
even children (for the trembling mother, hastily seized,
could not leave her infant), lie heaped in that *Glacière*;
putrid, under putridities : the horror of the world. For
three days there is mournful lifting out, and recognition;
amid the cries and movements of a passionate Southern
people, now kneeling in prayer, now storming in wild
pity and rage : lastly there is solemn sepulture, with
muffled drums, religious requiem, and all the people's
wail and tears. Their Massacred rest now in holy
ground; buried in one grave.

And Jourdan *Coupe-tête* ? Him also we behold again,
after a day or two : in flight, through the most romantic
Petrarchan hill-country; vehemently spurring his nag;
young Ligonnet, a brisk youth of Avignon, with Choisi
Dragoons, close in his rear ! With such swollen mass
of a rider no nag can run to advantage. The tired nag,
spur-driven, does take the River Sorgue; but sticks in
the middle of it; firm on that *chiaro fondo di Sorga**;

[1] Dampmartin, i. 251-94.

and will proceed no further for spurring ! Young
Ligonnet dashes up ; the Copper-face menaces and
bellows, draws pistol, perhaps even snaps it ; is nevertheless seized by the collar ; is tied firm, ankles under
horse's belly, and ridden back to Avignon, hardly to be
saved from massacre on the streets there.[1]

Such is the combustion of Avignon and the Southwest, when it becomes luminous. Long loud debate
is in the august Legislative, in the Mother-Society, as
to what now shall be done with it. Amnesty, cry eloquent Vergniaud and all Patriots : let there be mutual
pardon and repentance, restoration, pacification, and, if
so might anyhow be, an end ! Which vote ultimately
prevails. So the Southwest smoulders and welters again
in an ' Amnesty ', or Non-remembrance, which alas
cannot *but* remember, no Lethe flowing above ground !
Jourdan himself remains unhanged ; gets loose again,
as one not yet gallows-ripe ; nay, as we transiently discern from the distance, is ' carried in triumph through
the cities of the South '.[2] What things men carry !

With which transient glimpse, of a Copper-faced
Portent faring in this manner through the cities of
the South, we must quit these regions ;—and let them
smoulder. They want not their Aristocrats ; proud old
Nobles, not yet emigrated. Arles has its ' *Chiffonne* ', so
in symbolical cant, they name that Aristocrat Secret-
Association ; Arles has its pavements piled up, by and
by, into Aristocrat barricades. Against which Rebecqui, the hot-clear Patriot, must lead Marseillese with
cannon. The Bar of Iron has not yet risen to the top
in the Bay of Marseilles ; neither have these hot Sons
of the Phoceans submitted to be slaves. By clear management and hot instance, Rebecqui dissipates that
Chiffonne, without bloodshed ; restores the pavement
of Arles. He sails in Coast-barks, this Rebecqui, scrutinizing suspicious Martello-towers, with the keen eye of
Patriotism ; marches overland with dispatch, singly,

[1] Dampmartin, *ubi suprà*.
[2] Deux Amis, vii. (Paris, 1797), pp. 59–71.

or in force; to City after City; dim scouring far and
wide; [1]—argues, and if it must be, fights. For there
is much to do; Jalès itself is looking suspicious. So
that Legislator Fauchet, after debate on it, has to
propose Commissioners and a Camp on the Plain of
Beaucaire; with or without result.

Of all which, and much else, let us note only this
small consequence, that young Barbaroux, Advocate,
Town-Clerk of Marseilles, being charged to have these
things remedied, arrives at Paris in the month of February 1792. The beautiful and brave: young Spartan,
ripe in energy, not ripe in wisdom; over whose black
doom there shall flit nevertheless a certain ruddy fervour, streaks of bright Southern tint, not wholly swallowed of Death! Note also that the Rolands of Lyons
are again in Paris; for the second and final time. King's
Inspectorship is abrogated at Lyons, as elsewhere: Roland has his retiring-pension to claim, if attainable; has
Patriot friends to commune with; at lowest, has a Book
to publish. That young Barbaroux and the Rolands
came together; that elderly Spartan Roland liked, or
even loved the young Spartan, and was loved by him,
one can fancy: and Madame —— ? Breathe not, thou
poison-breath, Evil-speech! That soul is taintless, clear
as the mirror-sea. And yet if they two did look into
each other's eyes, and each, in silence, in tragical re-
nunciance, did find that the other was all-too lovely?
Honi soit![*] She calls him ' beautiful as Antinous '*: he
' will speak elsewhere of that astonishing woman '.—
A Madame d'Udon (or some such name, for Dumont
does not recollect quite clearly) gives copious Breakfast
to the Brissotin Deputies and us Friends of Freedom, at
her House in the Place Vendôme; with temporary
celebrity, with graces and wreathed smiles; not without cost. There, amid wide babble and jingle, our plan
of Legislative Debate is settled for the day, and much
counselling held. Strict Roland is seen there, but does
not go often.[2]

[1] Barbaroux, p. 21; Hist. Parl. xiii. 421-4.
[2] Dumont, Souvenirs, p. 374.

CHAPTER IV

NO SUGAR

SUCH are our inward troubles; seen in the Cities
of the South; extant, seen or unseen, in all cities
and districts, North as well as South. For in all are
Aristocrats, more or less malignant; watched by
Patriotism; which again, being of various shades, from
light Fayettist-Feuillant down to deep-sombre Jacobin,
has to watch even *itself*.

Directories of Departments, what we call County
Magistracies, being chosen by Citizens of a too ' active '
class, are found to pull one way; Municipalities, Town
Magistracies, to pull the other way. In all places
too are Dissident Priests; whom the Legislative will
have to deal with: contumacious individuals, working
on that angriest of passions; plotting, enlisting for
Coblentz; or suspected of plotting: fuel of a universal
unconstitutional heat. What to do with them ? They
may be conscientious as well as contumacious: gently
they should be dealt with, and yet it must be speedily.
In unilluminated La Vendée the simple are like to be
seduced by them; many a simple peasant, a Cathelineau
the wooldealer wayfaring meditative with his wool-
packs, in these hamlets, dubiously shakes his head! Two
Assembly Commissioners went thither last Autumn;
considerate Gensonné, not yet called to be a senator;
Gallois, an editorial man. These Two, consulting with
General Dumouriez, spake and worked, softly, with
judgement; they have hushed down the irritation, and
produced a soft Report,—for the time.

The General himself doubts not in the least but he
can keep peace there; being an able man. He passes
these frosty months among the pleasant people of Niort,
occupies ' tolerably handsome apartments in the
Castle of Niort', and tempers the minds of men.[1] Why

[1] Dumouriez, ii. 129.

is there but one Dumouriez? Elsewhere you find,
South or North, nothing but untempered obscure
jarring; which breaks forth ever and anon into open
clangour of riot. Southern Perpignan has its tocsin,
by torchlight; with rushing and onslaught: Northern
Caen not less, by daylight; with Aristocrats ranged
in arms at Places of Worship; Departmental compromise proving impossible; breaking into musketry
and a Plot discovered ![1] Add Hunger too: for bread,
always dear, is getting dearer: not so much as Sugar
can be had; for good reasons. Poor Simoneau,
Mayor of Etampes, in this Northern region, hanging
out his Red Flag in some riot of grains, is trampled
to death by a hungry exasperated People. What
a trade this of Mayor, in these times! Mayor of
Saint-Denis hung at the Lanterne, by Suspicion and
Dyspepsia, as we saw long since; Mayor of Vaison, as
we saw lately, buried before dead; and now this poor
Simoneau the Tanner, of Etampes,—whom legal Constitutionalism will not forget.

With factions, suspicions, want of bread and sugar,
it is verily what they call *déchiré*, torn asunder, this
poor country: France and all that is French. For,
over seas too come bad news. In black Saint-Domingo,
before that variegated Glitter in the Champs Elysées
was lit for an Accepted Constitution, there had risen,
and was burning contemporary with it, quite another
variegated Glitter and nocturnal Fulgor, had we known
it: of molasses and ardent-spirits; of sugar-boileries,
plantations, furniture, cattle and men: sky-high; the
Plain of Cap Français one huge whirl of smoke and
flame!

What a change here, in these two years; since that
first 'Box of Tricolor Cockades' got through the Cus-
tom-house, and atrabiliar Creoles too rejoiced that
there was a levelling of Bastilles! Levelling is comfortable, as we often say: levelling, yet only down to oneself. Your pale-white Creoles have their grievances:

[1] Hist. Parl. xii. 131, 141; xiii. 114, 417.

—and your yellow Quarteroons ? And your dark-
yellow Mulattoes ? And your Slaves soot-black ?
Quarteroon Ogé, Friend of our Parisian-Brissotin
Friends of the Blacks, felt for his share too, that Insurrection was the most sacred of duties. So the tricolor
Cockades had fluttered and swashed only some three
months on the Creole hat, when Ogé's signal-con-
flagrations went aloft ; with the voice of rage and
terror. Repressed, doomed to die, he took black
powder or seedgrains in the hollow of his hand, this
Ogé ; sprinkled a film of white ones on the top, and
said to his Judges, ' Behold they are white ' ; then
shook his hand, and said, ' Where are the whites, *Où
sont les blancs ?* '

So now, in the Autumn of 1791, looking from the
sky-windows of Cap Français, thick clouds of smoke
girdle our horizon, smoke in the day, in the night fire ;
preceded by fugitive shrieking white women, by Terror
and Rumour. Black demonized squadrons are massacring and harrying, with nameless cruelty. They
fight and fire ' from behind thickets and coverts ', for
the Black man loves the Bush ; they rush to the attack,
thousands strong, with brandished cutlasses and fusils,
with caperings, shoutings and vociferation,—which, if
the White Volunteer Company stands firm, dwindle
into staggerings, into quick gabblement, into panic
flight at the first volley, perhaps before it.[1] Poor Ogé
could be broken on the wheel ; this fire-whirlwind too
can be abated, driven up into the Mountains : but
Saint-Domingo is *shaken*, as Ogé's seedgrains were ;
shaking, writhing in long horrid death-throes, it is
Black without remedy ; and remains, as African Haiti,
a monition to the world.

O my Parisian Friends, is not *this*, as well as Regraters and Feuillant Plotters, one cause of the astonishing dearth of Sugar ! The Grocer, palpitant, with
drooping lip, sees his Sugar *taxé* ; weighed out by
female Patriotism, in instant retail, at the inadequate

---

[1] Deux Amis, x. 157.

rate of twenty-five sous, or thirteen pence a pound.
' Abstain from it ? ' Yes, ye Patriot Sections, all ye
Jacobins, abstain ! Louvet and Collot-d'Herbois so
advise ; resolute to make the sacrifice ; though ' how
shall literary men do without coffee ? ' Abstain, with
an oath ; that is the surest ! [1]

Also, for like reason, must not Brest and the Shipping
Interest languish ? Poor Brest languishes, sorrowing,
not without spleen ; denounces an Aristocrat Bertrand-Moleville, traitorous Aristocrat Marine-Minister.
Do not her Ships and King's Ships lie rotting piecemeal
in harbour ; Naval Officers mostly fled, and on furlough
too, with pay? Little stirring there; if it be not the
Brest Galleys, whip-driven, with their Galley-Slaves,
—alas, with some Forty of our hapless Swiss Soldiers
of Château-Vieux, among others ! These Forty Swiss,
too mindful of Nanci, do now, in their red wool caps,
tug sorrowfully at the oar ; looking into the Atlantic
brine, which reflects only their own sorrowful shaggy
faces ; and seem forgotten of Hope.

But, on the whole, may we not say, in figurative
language, that the French Constitution which shall
march is very *rheumatic,* full of shooting internal pains,
in joint and muscle ; and will not march without
difficulty ?

CHAPTER V

KINGS AND EMIGRANTS

EXTREMELY rheumatic Constitutions have been
known to march, and keep on their feet, though in a
staggering sprawling manner, for long periods, in virtue
of one thing only : that the *Head* were healthy. But
this Head of the French Constitution ! What King
Louis is and cannot help being, Readers already know.

[1] Débats des Jacobins, &c. (Hist. Parl. xiii. 171, 92-8).

A King who cannot take the Constitution, nor reject
the Constitution : nor do anything at all, but miserably
ask, What shall I do ? A King environed with endless
confusions ; in whose own mind is no germ of order.
Haughty implacable remnants of Noblesse struggling
with humiliated repentant Barnave-Lameths ; struggling in that obscure element of fetchers and carriers, of
Half-pay braggarts from the Café Valois, of Chamber-
maids, whisperers, and subaltern officious persons ;
fierce Patriotism looking on all the while, more and
more suspicious, from without : what, in such struggle,
can they do ? At best, *cancel* one another, and produce
zero. Poor King ! Barnave and your Senatorial Jau-
courts speak earnestly into this ear ; Bertrand-Moleville, and Messengers from Coblentz,* speak earnestly
into that : the poor Royal head turns to the one side
and to the other side ; can turn itself fixedly to no
side. Let Decency drop a veil over it : sorrier misery
was seldom enacted in the world. This one small fact,
does it not throw the saddest light on much ? The
Queen is lamenting to Madame Campan : ' What am
I to do ? When they, these Barnaves, get us advised
to any step which the Noblesse do not like, then I am
pouted at ; nobody comes to my card-table ; the King's
Couchee is solitary '.[1]   In such a case of dubiety, what
is one to do ? Go inevitably to the ground !

The King has accepted this Constitution, knowing
beforehand that it will not serve : he studies it, and
executes it in the hope mainly that it will be found in-
executable. King's Ships lie rotting in harbour, their
officers gone; the Armies disorganized ; robbers scour
the Highways, which wear down unrepaired ; all Public
Service lies slack and waste : the Executive makes no
effort, or an effort only to throw the blame on the Constitution. Shamming death, ' *faisant la mort !* ' What
Constitution, use it in this manner, can march ? ' Grow
to disgust the Nation ', it will truly,'[2]—unless *you*
first grow to disgust the Nation ! It is Bertrand de

---

[1] Campan, ii. 177, 202.   [2] Bertrand-Moleville, i. c. 4.

Moleville's plan, and his Majesty's; the best they can
form.

Or if, after all, this best-plan proved too slow;
proved a failure? Provident of that too, the Queen,
shrouded in deepest mystery, ' writes all day, in cipher,
day after day, to Coblentz '; Engineer Goguelat, he of
the *Night of Spurs*, whom the Lafayette Amnesty has
delivered from Prison, rides and runs. Now and then,
on fit occasion, a Royal familiar visit can be paid to
that Salle de Manége, an affecting encouraging Royal
Speech (sincere, doubt it not, for the moment) can be
delivered there, and the Senators all cheer and almost
weep;—at the same time Mallet du Pan has visibly
ceased editing, and invisibly bears abroad a King's
Autograph, soliciting help from the Foreign Potentates.[1]
Unhappy Louis, *do* this thing or else that other,—if thou
couldst!

The thing which the King's Government did do was
to stagger distractedly from contradiction to contradiction; and wedding Fire to Water, envelope itself in
hissing, and ashy steam. Danton and needy corrup-
tible Patriots are sopped with presents of cash: they
accept the sop; they rise refreshed by it, and—travel
their own way.[2] Nay, the King's Government did
likewise hire Hand-clappers, or *claqueurs*, persons to
applaud. Subterranean Rivarol has Fifteen Hundred
Men in King's pay, at the rate of some £10,000 sterling
per month; what he calls ' a staff of genius ': Para-
graph-writers, Placard Journalists; ' two hundred and
eighty Applauders, at three shillings a day ': one of
the strangest Staffs ever commanded by man. The
muster-rolls and account-books of which still exist.[3]
Bertrand-Moleville himself, in a way he thinks very
dexterous, contrives to pack the Galleries of the Legislative; gets Sansculottes hired to go thither, and
applaud at a signal given, they fancying it was Pétion
that bade them: a device which was not detected for
almost a week. Dexterous enough; as if a man, finding

[1] Moleville, i. 370.   [2] Ibid. i. c. 17.
[3] Montgaillard, iii. 41.

the Day fast decline, should determine on altering the Clock-hands : *that* is a thing possible for him.

Here too let us note an unexpected apparition of Philippe d'Orléans at Court : his last at the Levée of any King. D'Orléans, sometime in the winter months seemingly, has been appointed to that old first-coveted rank of Admiral,—though only over ships rotting in port. The wished-for comes too late ! However, he waits on Bertrand-Moleville to give thanks : nay to state that he would willingly thank his Majesty in person ; that, in spite of all the horrible things men have said and sung, he is far from being his Majesty's enemy ; at bottom, how far ! Bertrand delivers the message, brings about the royal Interview, which does pass to the satisfaction of his Majesty ; D'Orléans seeming clearly repentant, determined to turn over a new leaf. And yet, next Sunday, what do we see ? 'Next Sunday', says Bertrand, ' he came to the King's Levée ; but the Courtiers ignorant of what had passed, the Crowd of Royalists who were accustomed to resort thither on that day specially to pay their court, gave him the most humiliating reception. They came pressing round him ; managing, as if by mistake, to tread on his toes, to elbow him towards the door, and not let him enter again. He went downstairs to her Majesty's Apartments, where cover was laid ; so soon as he showed face, sounds rose on all sides, " *Messieurs, take care of the dishes* ", as if he had carried poison in his pockets. The insults, which his presence everywhere excited, forced him to retire without having seen the Royal Family : the crowd followed him to the Queen's staircase ; in descending, he received a spitting (*crachat*) on the head, and some others on his clothes. Rage and spite were seen visibly painted on his face ' : [1] as indeed how could they miss to be ? He imputes it all to the King and Queen, who know nothing of it, who are even much grieved at it ; and so descends to his Chaos again. Bertrand was there at the Château that day himself, and an eye-witness to these things.

[1] Bertrand-Moleville, i. 177.

For the rest, Non-jurant Priests, and the repression of them, will distract the King's conscience ; Emigrant Princes and Noblesse will force him to double-dealing : there must be *veto* on *veto* ; amid the ever-waxing indignation of men. For Patriotism, as we said, looks on from without, more and more suspicious. Waxing tempest, blast after blast, of Patriotic indignation, from without ; dim inorganic whirl of Intrigues, Fatuities, within ! Inorganic, fatuous ; from which the eye turns away. De Staël intrigues for her so gallant Narbonne, to get him made War-Minister ; and ceases not, having got him made. The King shall fly to Rouen ; shall there, with the gallant Narbonne, properly ' modify the Constitution '. This is the same brisk Narbonne, who, last year, cut out from their entanglement, by force of dragoons, those poor fugitive Royal Aunts : men say he is at bottom their Brother, or even *more*, so scandalous is scandal. He drives now, with his De Staël, rapidly to the Armies, to the Frontier Towns ; produces rose-coloured Reports, not too credible ; perorates, gesticulates ; wavers poising himself on the top, for a moment, seen of men ; then tumbles, dismissed, washed away by the Time-flood.

Also the fair Princess de Lamballe intrigues, bosom-friend of her Majesty : to the angering of Patriotism. Beautiful Unfortunate, why did she ever return from England ? Her small silver-voice, what can it profit in that piping of the black World-tornado ? Which will whirl *her*, poor fragile Bird of Paradise, against grim rocks. Lamballe and De Staël intrigue visibly, apart or together : but who shall reckon how many others, and in what infinite ways, invisibly ! Is there not what one may call an ' Austrian Committee ', sitting invisible in the Tuileries ; centre of an invisible Anti-National Spiderweb, which, for we sleep among mysteries, stretches its threads to the ends of the Earth ? Journalist Carra has now the clearest certainty of it : to Brissotin Patriotism ; and France generally, it is growing more and more probable.

O Reader, hast thou no pity for this Constitution ?

Rheumatic shooting pains in its members ; pressure of
hydrocephale and hysteric vapours on its Brain : a Constitution divided against itself*; which will never march,
hardly even stagger ! Why were not Drouet and Procureur Sausse in their beds, that unblessed Varennes
Night ! Why did they not, in the name of Heaven, let
the Korff Berline go whither it listed ! Nameless inco-
herency, incompatibility, perhaps prodigies at which
the world still shudders, had been spared.

But now comes the third thing that bodes ill for the
marching of this French Constitution : besides the
French People, and the French King, there is thirdly—
the assembled European World. It has become necessary now to look at that also. Fair France is so luminous : and round and round it, is troublous Cimmerian
Night. Calonnes, Breteuils hover dim, far-flown ;
overnetting Europe with intrigues. From Turin to
Vienna ; to Berlin, and utmost Petersburg in the
frozen North ! Great Burke has raised his great voice
long ago ; eloquently demonstrating that the end of
an Epoch is come, to all appearance the end of Civilized
Time. Him many answer : Camille Desmoulins, Clootz
Speaker of Mankind, Paine the rebellious Needleman,
and honourable Gaelic Vindicators in that country
and in this : but the great Burke remains unanswer-
able ; 'the Age of Chivalry *is* gone';* and could not but
go, having now produced the still more indomitable
Age of Hunger. Altars enough, of the Dubois-Rohan
sort, changing to the Gobel-and-Talleyrand sort, are
faring by rapid transmutations to—shall we say, the
right Proprietor of them ? French Game and French
Game-Preservers did alight on the Cliffs of Dover, with
cries of distress. Who will say that the end of much
is not come ? A set of mortals has risen, who believe
that Truth is not a printed Speculation, but a practical
Fact ; that Freedom and Brotherhood are possible in
this Earth, supposed always to be Belial's, which ' the
Supreme Quack ' was to inherit ! Who will say that
Church, State, Throne, Altar are not in danger ; that

the sacred Strongbox itself, last Palladium of effete
Humanity, may not be blasphemously blown upon, and
its padlocks undone ?

The poor Constituent Assembly might act with what
delicacy and diplomacy it would ; declare that it ab-
jured meddling with its neighbours, foreign conquest,
and so forth ; but from the first this thing was to be
predicted : that old Europe and new France could not
subsist *together*. A Glorious Revolution, oversetting
State-Prisons and Feudalism ; publishing, with outburst of Federative Cannon, in face of all the Earth, that
Appearance is not Reality, how shall it subsist amid
Governments which, if Appearance is *not* Reality, are—
one knows not what ? In death-feud, and internecine
wrestle and battle, it shall subsist with them ; not
otherwise.

Rights of Man, printed on Cotton Handkerchiefs, in
various dialects of human speech, pass over to the
Frankfort Fair.[1] What say we, Frankfort Fair ? They
have crossed Euphrates, and the fabulous Hydaspes ;
wafted themselves beyond the Ural, Altai, Himmalayah ;
struck off from wood stereotypes, in angular Picture-
writing, they are jabbered and jingled of in China and
Japan. Where will it stop ? Kien-Lung* smells mischief ; not the remotest Dalai-Lama shall now knead
his dough-pills in peace.—Hateful to us, as is the Night !
Bestir yourselves, ye Defenders of Order ! They do bestir
themselves : all Kings and Kinglets, with their spiritual
temporal array, are astir ; their brows clouded with
menace. Diplomatic emissaries fly swift ; Conventions,
privy Conclaves assemble ; and wise wigs wag, taking
what counsel they can.

Also, as we said, the Pamphleteer draws pen, on this
side and that : zealous fists beat the Pulpit-drum.
Not without issue ! Did not iron Birmingham, shouting
' Church and King ', itself knew not why, burst out, last
July, into rage, drunkenness and fire ; and your
Priestleys,* and the like, dining there on that Bastille

---

[1] Toulongeon, i. 256.

day, get the maddest singeing: scandalous to consider!
In which same days, as we can remark, High Potentates, Austrian and Prussian, with Emigrants, were
faring towards Pilnitz in Saxony; there, on the 27th
of August, they, keeping to themselves what further
'secret Treaty' there might or might not be, did publish
their hopes and their threatenings, their Declaration
that it was 'the common cause of Kings'.

Where a will to quarrel is, there is a way. Our
readers remember that Pentecost-Night, Fourth of
August 1789, when Feudalism fell in a few hours? The
National Assembly, in abolishing Feudalism, promised
that 'compensation' should be given; and did endeavour to give it. Nevertheless the Austrian Kaiser
answers that his German Princes, for their part, cannot
be unfeudalized; that they have Possessions in French
Alsace, and Feudal Rights secured to them, for which
no conceivable compensation will suffice. So this of
the Possessioned Princes, *Princes Possessionés*, is
bandied from Court to Court; covers acres of diplomatic paper at this day: a weariness to the world.
Kaunitz argues from Vienna; Delessart responds from
Paris, though perhaps not sharply enough. The Kaiser
and his Possessioned Princes will too evidently come and
take compensation,—so much as they can get. Nay
might one not *partition* France, as we have done Poland,
and are doing; and so pacify it with a vengeance?

From South to North! For actually it is 'the common cause of Kings'. Swedish Gustav, sworn Knight
of the Queen of France, will lead Coalized Armies;—
had not Ankarström treasonously shot him; for,
indeed, there were griefs nearer home.[1] Austria and
Prussia speak at Pilnitz;* all men intensely listening.
Imperial Rescripts have gone out from Turin; there
will be secret Convention at Vienna. Catherine of
Russia beckons approvingly; will help, were she
ready. Spanish Bourbon stirs amid his pillows; from
him too, even from him, shall there come help. Lean
Pitt,* 'the Minister of Preparatives', looks out from

[1] 30th March 1792 (Annual Register, p. 11).

his watch-tower in Saint James's, in a suspicious manner. Councillors plotting, Calonnes dim-hovering ;—
alas, Sergeants rub-a-dubbing openly through all
manner of German market-towns, collecting ragged
valour ! [1] Look where you will, immeasurable Obscurantism is girdling this fair France ; which, again, will
not be girdled by it. Europe is in travail ; pang after
pang ; what a shriek was that of Pilnitz ! The birth
will be : WAR.

Nay the worst feature of the business is this last,
still to be named ; the Emigrants at Coblentz. So
many thousands ranking there, in bitter hate and menace : King's Brothers, all Princes of the Blood except
wicked D'Orléans ; your duelling De Castries, your
eloquent Cazalès ; bull-headed Malseignes, a wargod
Broglie ; Distaff Seigneurs, insulted Officers, all that
have ridden across the Rhine-stream ;—D'Artois
welcoming Abbé Maury with a kiss, and clasping him
publicly to his own royal heart ! Emigration, flowing
over the Frontiers, now in drops, now in streams, in
various humours of fear, of petulance, rage and hope,
ever since those first Bastille days when D'Artois went,
'to shame the citizens of Paris',—has swollen to the
size of a Phenomenon for the world. Coblentz is
become a small extra-national Versailles ; a Versailles
in partibus: briguing, intriguing, favouritism, strum-
petocracy itself, they say, goes on there ; all the old
activities, on a small scale, quickened by hungry
Revenge.

Enthusiasm, of loyalty, of hatred and hope, has
risen to a high pitch ; as, in any Coblentz tavern you
may hear, in speech and in singing. Maury assists in
the interior Council ; much is decided on : for one
thing, they keep lists of the dates of your emigrating ;
a month sooner, or a month later, determines your
greater or your less right to the coming Division of the
Spoil. Cazalès himself, because he had occasionally

---

[1] Toulongeon, ii. 100–117.

spoken with a Constitutional tone, was looked on coldly
at first: so pure are our principles.[1] And arms are
a-hammering at Liége; 'three thousand horses'
ambling hitherward from the Fairs of Germany:
Cavalry enrolling; likewise Foot-soldiers, 'in blue
coat, red waistcoat and nankeen trousers'.[2] They
have their secret domestic correspondences, as their
open foreign: with disaffected Crypto-Aristocrats, with
contumacious Priests, with Austrian Committee in the
Tuileries. Deserters are spirited over by assiduous
crimps; Royal-Allemand is gone almost wholly. Their
route of march, towards France and the Division of the
Spoil, is marked out, were the Kaiser once ready.
'It is said, they mean to poison the sources; but',
adds Patriotism making report of it, 'they will not
poison the source of Liberty'; whereat 'on applaudit',
we cannot but applaud. Also they have manufactories
of False Assignats; and men that circulate in the
interior, distributing and disbursing the same; one of
these we denounce now to Legislative Patriotism: 'a
man Lebrun by name; about thirty years of age, with
blonde hair and in quantity; has', only for the time
being surely, 'a black-eye, œil poché; goes in a wiski
with a black horse',[3]—always keeping his Gig!

Unhappy Emigrants, it was their lot, and the lot of
France! They are ignorant of much that they should
know: of themselves, of what is around them. A
Political Party that knows not when it is beaten, may
become one of the fatallest of things, to itself, and to
all. Nothing will convince these men that they cannot
scatter the French Revolution at the first blast of their
war-trumpet; that the French Revolution is other
than a blustering Effervescence, of brawlers and
spouters, which, at the flash of chivalrous broadswords,

---

[1] Montgaillard, iii. 5-17. Toulongeon, ubi suprà.

[2] See Hist. Parl. xiii. 11-38, 41-61, 358, &c.

[3] Moniteur, Séance du 2 Novembre 1791 (Hist. Parl. xii.
212).

at the rustle of gallows-ropes, will burrow itself, in dens the deeper the welcomer. But, alas, what man does know and measure himself, and the things that are round him ;—else where were the need of physical fighting at all ? Never, till they are cleft asunder, can these heads believe that a Sansculottic arm has any vigour in it : cleft asunder, it will be too late to believe.

One may say, without spleen against his poor erring brothers of any side, that above all other mischiefs, this of the Emigrant Nobles acted fatally on France. Could they have known, could they have understood! In the beginning of 1789, a splendour and a terror still surrounded them : the Conflagration of their Châteaus, kindled by months of obstinacy, went out after the Fourth of August ; and might have continued out, had they at all known what to defend, what to relinquish as indefensible. They were still a graduated Hierarchy of Authorities, or the accredited similitude of such : they sat there, uniting King with Commonalty ; transmitting and translating *gradually*, from degree to degree, the command of the one into the obedience of the other ; rendering command and obedience still possible. Had they understood their place, and what to do in it, this French Revolution, which went forth explosively in years and in months, might have spread itself over generations ; and not a torture-death but a quiet euthanasia have been provided for many things.

But they were proud and high, these men ; they were not wise to consider. They spurned all from them in disdainful hate, they drew the sword and flung away the scabbard.* France has not only no Hierarchy of Authorities, to translate command into obedience ; its Hierarchy of Authorities has fled to the enemies of France ; calls loudly on the enemies of France to interfere armed, who want but a pretext to do that. Jealous Kings and Kaisers might have looked on long, meditating interference, yet afraid and ashamed to interfere : but now do not the King's Brothers, and all French Nobles, Dignitaries and Authorities that are free to speak, which the King himself is not,—passionately invite us,

in the name of Right and of Might? Ranked at
Coblentz, from Fifteen to Twenty thousand stand
now brandishing their weapons, with the cry: On, on!
Yes, Messieurs, you shall on;—and divide the spoil
according to your dates of emigrating.

Of all which things a poor Legislative Assembly,
and Patriot France, is informed: by denunciant friend,
by triumphant foe. Sulleau's Pamphlets, of the Rivarol
Staff of Genius, circulate; heralding supreme hope.
Durosoy's Placards tapestry the walls; *Chant du Coq*
crows day, pecked at by Tallien's *Ami des Citoyens*.
King's-Friend Royou, *Ami du Roi*, can name, in exact
arithmetical ciphers, the contingents of the various
Invading Potentates; in all, Four hundred and nineteen thousand Foreign fighting men, with Fifteen
thousand Emigrants. Not to reckon these your daily
and hourly desertions, which an Editor must daily
record, of whole Companies, and even Regiments,
crying *Vive le Roi, Vive la Reine*, and marching over
with banners spread:¹—lies all, and wind; yet to
Patriotism not wind; nor, alas, one day, to Royou!
Patriotism, therefore, may brawl and babble yet a little
while: but its hours are numbered: Europe is coming
with Four hundred and nineteen thousand and the
Chivalry of France; the gallows, one may hope, will
get its own.

¹ Ami-du-Roi Newspaper (in Hist. Parl. xiii. 175).

CHAPTER VI

BRIGANDS AND JALÈS

WE shall have War, then; and on what terms ! With an Executive ' pretending ', really with less and less deceptiveness now, ' to be dead ' ; casting even a wishful eye towards the enemy : on such terms we shall have War.

Public Functionary in vigorous action there is none ; if it be not Rivarol with his Staff of Genius and Two hundred and eighty Applauders. The Public Service lies waste ; the very Taxgatherer has forgotten his cunning : in this and the other Provincial Board of Management (*Directoire de Département*) it is found advisable to *retain* what Taxes you can gather, to pay your own inevitable expenditures. Our Revenue is Assignats ; emission on emission of Paper-money. And the Army ; our Three grand Armies, of Rochambeau, of Lückner, of Lafayette ? Lean, disconsolate hover these Three grand Armies, watching the Frontiers there ; three Flights of long-necked Cranes in moulting time ;—wrecked, disobedient, disorganized ; who never saw fire ; the old Generals and Officers gone across the Rhine. War-Minister Narbonne, he of the rose-coloured Reports, solicits recruitments, equipments, money, always money ; threatens, since he can get none, to ' take his sword ', which belongs to himself, and go serve his country with that.[1]

The question of questions is : What shall be done ? Shall we, with a desperate defiance which Fortune sometimes favours,'draw the sword at once, in the face of this in-rushing world of Emigration and Obscurantism ; or wait, and temporize and diplomatize, till, if possible, our resources mature themselves a little ?

---

[1] *Moniteur, Séance du 23 Janvier 1792* ; *Biographie des Ministres*, § Narbonne.

And yet again, are our resources growing towards maturity; or growing the *other* way? Dubious: the ablest Patriots are divided; Brissot and his Brissotins, or Girondins, in the Legislative, cry aloud for the former defiant plan; Robespierre, in the Jacobins, pleads as loud for the latter dilatory one: with responses, even with mutual reprimands; distracting the Mother of Patriotism. Consider also what agitated Breakfasts there may be at Madame d'Udon's in the Place Vendôme! The alarm of all men is great. Help, ye Patriots; and O at least agree; for the hour presses. Frost was not yet gone, when in that 'tolerably handsome apartment of the Castle of Niort', there arrived a Letter: General Dumouriez must to Paris. It is War-Minister Narbonne that writes; the General shall give counsel about many things.[1] In the month of February 1792, Brissotin friends welcome their Dumouriez *Polymetis*,*—comparable really to an antique Ulysses in modern costume; quick, elastic, shifty, insuppressible, a 'many-counselled man'.

Let the Reader fancy this fair France with a whole Cimmerian Europe girdling her, rolling in on her, black, to burst in red thunder of War; fair France herself hand-shackled and foot-shackled in the weltering complexities of this Social Clothing, or Constitution, which they have made for her; a France that, in such Constitution, cannot march! And Hunger too; and plotting Aristocrats, and excommunicating Dissident Priests: 'the man Lebrun by name' urging his black *wiski*, visible to the eye; and, still more terrible in his invisibility, Engineer Goguelat, with Queen's cipher, riding and running!

The excommunicatory Priests give new trouble in the Maine and Loire; La Vendée, nor Cathelineau the wool-dealer, has not ceased grumbling and rumbling. Nay behold Jalès itself once more: how often does that real-imaginary Camp of the Fiend require to be extin-

---

[1] Dumouriez, ii. c. 6.

guished! For near two years now, it has waned faint
and again waxed bright, in the bewildered soul of
Patriotism : actually, if Patriotism knew it, one of the
most surprising products of Nature working with Art.
Royalist Seigneurs, under this or the other pretext, assemble the simple people of these Cevennes Mountains ;
men not unused to revolt, and with heart for fighting,
could their poor heads be got persuaded. The Royalist
Seigneur harangues ; harping mainly on the religious
string : 'True Priests maltreated, false Priests in-
truded, Protestants (once dragooned) now triumphing,
things sacred given to the dogs' ; and so produces,
from the pious Mountaineer throat, rough growlings :—
'Shall we not testify, then, ye brave hearts of the
Cevennes ; march to the rescue ? Holy Religion ; duty
to God and the King ?'—'*Si fait, si fait*, Just so, just
so', answer the brave hearts always : '*Mais il y a de
bien bonnes choses dans la Révolution*, But there are
main good things in the Revolution too ! '—And so the
matter, cajole as we may, will only turn on its axis, not
stir from the spot, and remains theatrical merely.[1]

Nevertheless deepen your cajolery, harp quick and
quicker, ye Royalist Seigneurs ; with a dead-lift effort
you may bring it to that. In the month of June next,
this *Camp of Jalès* will step forth as a theatricality suddenly become real ; Two thousand strong, and with the
boast that it is Seventy thousand : most strange to see ;
with flags flying, bayonets fixed ; with Proclamation,
and D'Artois Commission of civil war ! Let some
Rebecqui, or other the like hot-clear Patriot ; let some
'Lieutenant-Colonel Aubry'; if Rebecqui is busy elsewhere, raise instantaneous National Guards, and disperse and dissolve it ; and blow the Old Castle asunder,[2]
that so, if possible, we hear of it no more !

In the Months of February and March, it is recorded,
the terror, especially of rural France, had risen even to
the transcendental pitch : not far from madness   In

[1] Dampmartin, i. 201.
[2] Moniteur, Séance du 15 Juillet 1792.

Town and Hamlet is rumour, of war, massacre : that
Austrians, Aristocrats, above all, that *The Brigands* are
close by. Men quit their houses and huts ; rush fugitive, shrieking, with wife and child, they know not
whither. Such a terror, the eye-witnesses say, never
fell on a Nation ; nor shall again fall, even in Reigns of
Terror expressly so-called. The Countries of the Loire,
all the Central and Southeast regions, start up distracted,
' simultaneously as by an electric shock ' ;—for indeed
grain too gets scarcer and scarcer. ' The people barricade the entrances of Towns, pile stones in the upper
stories, the women prepare boiling water; from moment
to moment, expecting the attack. In the Country, the
alarm-bell rings incessant ; troops of peasants, gathered
by it, scour the highways, seeking an imaginary enemy.
They are armed mostly with scythes stuck in wood ;
and, arriving in wild troops at the barricaded Towns,
are themselves sometimes taken for Brigands '.[1]

So rushes old France : old France is rushing *down*.
What the end will be is known to no mortal ; that the
end is near all mortals may know.

CHAPTER VII

CONSTITUTION WILL NOT MARCH

To all which our poor Legislative, tied up by an unmarching Constitution, can oppose nothing, by way of
remedy, but mere bursts of parliamentary eloquence[*]!
They go on, debating, denouncing, objurgating : loud
weltering Chaos, which devours *itself*.

But their two thousand and odd Decrees ? Reader,
these happily concern not thee, nor me. Mere Occa-
sional-Decrees, foolish and not foolish ; sufficient for
that day was its own evil ! Of the whole two thousand
there are not now half a score, and these mostly blighted

---

[1] Newspapers, &c. (in Hist. Parl. xiii. 325).

in the bud by royal *Veto*, that will profit or disprofit us. On the 17th of January, the Legislative, for one thing, got its High Court, its *Haute Cour*, set up at Orléans. The theory had been given by the Constituent, in May last, but this is the reality : a Court for the trial of Political Offences ; a Court which cannot want work. To this it was decreed that there needed no royal Acceptance, therefore that there could be no *Veto*. Also Priests can now be married ; ever since last October. A patriotic adventurous Priest had made bold to marry himself then ; and not thinking this enough, came to the bar with his new spouse ; that the whole world might hold honeymoon with him, and a Law be obtained.

Less joyful are the Laws against Refractory Priests ; and yet not less needful ! Decrees on Priests and Decrees on Emigrants : these are the two brief Series of Decrees, worked out with endless debate, and then cancelled by *Veto*, which mainly concern us here. For an august National Assembly must needs conquer these Refractories, Clerical or Laic, and thumbscrew them into obedience : yet, behold, always as you turn your legislative thumbscrew, and will press and even crush till Refractories give way,—King's *Veto* steps in with magical paralysis ; and your thumbscrew, hardly squeezing, much less crushing, does not act !

Truly a melancholy Set of Decrees, a pair of Sets ; paralysed by *Veto* ! First, under date the 28th of October 1791, we have Legislative Proclamation, issued by herald and bill-sticker ; inviting Monsieur, the King's Brother, to return within two months, under penalties. To which invitation Monsieur replies nothing ; or indeed replies by Newspaper Parody, inviting the august Legislative ' to return to common sense within two months ', under penalties. Whereupon the Legislative must take stronger measures. So, on the 9th of November, we declare all Emigrants to be ' suspect of conspiracy ' ; and, in brief, to be ' outlawed ', if they have not returned at Newyear's-day :— Will the King say *Veto* ? That ' triple impost ' shall be levied on these men's Properties, or even their Pro-

perties be ' put in sequestration ', one can understand.
But further, on Newyear's-day itself, not an individual
having ' returned ', we declare, and with fresh emphasis
some fortnight later again declare, That Monsieur is
déchu, forfeited of his eventful Heirship to the Crown ;
nay more, that Condé, Calonne, and a considerable List
of others are accused of high treason; and shall be
judged by our High Court of Orléans : *Veto !*—Then
again as to Non-jurant Priests : it was decreed, in November last, that they should forfeit what Pensions
they had; be ' put under inspection, under *surveillance* ',
and, if need were, be banished : *Veto !* A still sharper
turn is coming; but to this also the answer will be, *Veto.*

Veto after *Veto* ; your thumbscrew paralysed ! Gods
and men may see that the Legislative is in a false position. As, alas, who is in a true one ? Voices already
murmur for a ' National Convention '.[1] This poor
Legislative, spurred and stung into action by a whole
France and a whole Europe, cannot act ; can only
objurgate and perorate ; with stormy ' motions ', and
motion in which is no *way* ; with effervescence, with
noise and fuliginous fury !

What scenes in that National Hall ! President
jingling his inaudible bell ; or, as utmost signal of distress, clapping on his hat ; ' the tumult subsiding in
twenty minutes ', and this or the other indiscreet Member sent to the Abbaye Prison for three days ! Suspected Persons must be summoned and questioned ;
old M. de Sombreuil of the *Invalides* has to give account
of himself, and why he leaves his Gates open. Unusual
smoke rose from the Sèvres Pottery, indicating conspiracy ; the Potters explained that it was Necklace-
Lamotte's *Mémoires*, bought up by her Majesty, which
they were endeavouring to suppress by fire,[2]—which
nevertheless he that runs may still read.

Again, it would seem, Duke de Brissac and the
King's Constitutional-Guard are ' making cartridges

---

[1] December 1791 (Hist. Parl. xii. 257).
[2] Moniteur, Séance du 28 Mai 1792 ; Campan, ii. 196.

secretly in the cellars ' : a set of Royalists, pure and
impure ; black cut-throats many of them, picked out of
gaming-houses and sinks ; in all Six thousand instead
of Eighteen hundred ; who evidently gloom on us every
time we enter the Château.[1] Wherefore, with infinite
debate, let Brissac and King's Guard be *disbanded*.
Disbanded accordingly they are ; after only two months
of existence, for they did not get on foot till March of
this same year. So ends briefly the King's new Constitutional *Maison Militaire* ; he must now be guarded
by mere Swiss and blue Nationals again. It seems
the lot of Constitutional things. New Constitutional
Maison Civile he would never even establish, much as
Barnave urged it ; old resident Duchesses sniffed at it,
and held aloof ; on the whole her Majesty thought it
not worth while, the Noblesse would so soon be back
triumphant.[2]

Or, looking still into this National Hall and its scenes,
behold Bishop Torné, a Constitutional Prelate, not of
severe morals, demanding that ' religious costumes and
such caricatures ' be abolished. Bishop Torné warms,
catches fire ; finishes by untying, and indignantly
flinging on the table, as if for gage or bet, his own
pontifical cross. Which cross, at any rate, is instantly
covered by the cross of *Te-Deum* Fauchet, then by other
crosses, and insignia, till all are stripped ; this clerical
Senator clutching off his skull-cap, that other his frill-
collar,—lest Fanaticism return on us.[3]

Quick is the movement here ! And then so confused,
unsubstantial, you might call it almost *spectral* : pallid,
dim, inane, like the Kingdoms of Dis ! Unruly Linguet,
shrunk to a kind of spectre for us, pleads here some
cause that he has ; amid rumour and interruption,
which excel human patience : he ' tears his papers,
and withdraws ', the irascible adust little man. Nay
honourable Members will tear their papers, being

[1] Dumouriez, ii. 168.
[2] Campan, ii. c. 19.
[3] Moniteur, du 7 Avril 1792 ; Deux Amis, vii. 111.

effervescent : Merlin of Thionville tears his papers, crying : ' So, the People cannot be saved by *you* ! ' Nor are Deputations wanting : Deputations of Sections ; generally with complaint and denouncement, always with Patriot fervour of sentiment : Deputation of Women, pleading that they also may be allowed to take Pikes, and exercise in the Champ-de-Mars. Why not, ye Amazons, if it be in you ? Then occasionally, having done our message and got answer, we ' defile through the Hall, singing *ça-ira* ' ; or rather roll and whirl through it, ' dancing our *ronde patriotique* the while ',— our new *Carmagnole,* or Pyrrhic war-dance and liberty-dance. Patriot Huguenin,* Ex-Advocate, Ex-Carbineer, Ex-Clerk of the Barriers, comes deputed, with Saint Antoine at his heels ; denouncing Anti-patriotism, Famine, Forestalment and Man-eaters ; asks an august Legislative : ' Is there not a *tocsin in your hearts* against these *mangeurs d'hommes* ! ' [1]

But above all things, for this is a continual business, the Legislative has to reprimand the King's Ministers. Of his Majesty's Ministers we have said hitherto, and say, next to nothing. Still more spectral these ! Sorrowful ; of no permanency any of them, none at least since Montmorin vanished : the ' eldest of the King's Council ' is occasionally not ten days old.[2] Feuillant-Constitutional, as your respectable Cahier de Gerville, as your respectable unfortunate Delessarts ; or Royalist-Constitutional, as Montmorin last Friend of Necker ; or Aristocrat, as Bertrand-Moleville : they flit there phantom-like, in the huge simmering confusion ; poor shadows, dashed in the racking winds ; powerless, without meaning ;—whom the human memory need not charge itself with.

But how often, we say, are these poor Majesty's Ministers summoned over ; to be questioned, tutored ; nay threatened, almost bullied ! They answer what, with adroitest simulation and casuistry, they can : of

---

[1] See Moniteur, Séances (in Hist. Parl. xiii. xiv.].

[2] Dumouriez, ii. 137.

which a poor Legislative knows not what to make.
One thing only is clear, That Cimmerian Europe is
girdling us in ; that France (not actually dead, surely ?)
cannot march. Have a care, ye Ministers ! Sharp
Guadet transfixes you with cross-questions, with sudden
Advocate-conclusions ; the sleeping tempest that is in
Vergniaud can be awakened. Restless Brissot brings
up Reports, Accusations, endless thin Logic ; it is the
man's highday even now. Condorcet redacts, with his
firm pen, our ' Address of the Legislative Assembly to
the French Nation '.[1] Fiery Max Isnard, who, for the
rest, will ' carry not Fire and Sword ' on those Cimmerian Enemies ' but Liberty ',—is for declaring ' that
we hold Ministers responsible ; and that by responsibility we mean death, *nous entendons la mort* '.

For verily it grows serious : the time presses, and
traitors there are. Bertrand-Moleville has a smooth
tongue, the known Aristocrat; gall in his heart. How
his answers and explanations flow ready ; jesuitic,
plausible to the ear ! But perhaps the notablest is this,
which befell once when Bertrand had done answering
and was withdrawn. Scarcely had the august Assembly
begun considering what was to be done with him, when
the Hall fills with *smoke*. Thick sour smoke: no oratory, only wheezing and barking ;—irremediable ; so
that the august Assembly has to adjourn ! [2] A miracle ?
Typical miracle ? One knows not: only this one seems
to know, that ' the Keeper of the Stoves *was appointed*
by Bertrand ' or by some underling of his !—O fuliginous confused Kingdom of Dis, with thy Tantalus-Ixion
toils, with thy angry Fire-floods, and Streams named
of Lamentation, why hast thou not thy Lethe too, that
so one might *finish* ?

---

[1] 16th February 1792 (Choix des Rapports, viii. 375–92).
[2] Courrier-de-Paris, 14 Janvier 1792 (Gorsas's Newspaper), in Hist. Parl. xiii. 83.

CHAPTER VIII

THE JACOBINS

NEVERTHELESS let not Patriotism despair. Have we
not, in Paris at least, a virtuous Pétion, a wholly Patriotic Municipality ? Virtuous Pétion, ever since November, is Mayor of Paris : in our Municipality, the Public,
for the Public is now admitted too, may behold an
energetic Danton ; further an epigrammatic slow-sure
Manuel*; a resolute unrepentant Billaud-Varennes,* of
Jesuit breeding ; Tallien able-editor ; and nothing but
Patriots, better or worse. So ran the November Elections : to the joy of most citizens ; nay the very Court
supported Pétion rather than Lafayette. And so Bailly
and his Feuillants, long waning like the Moon, had to
withdraw then, making some sorrowful obeisance,[1] into
extinction :—or indeed into worse, into lurid half-light,
grimmed by the shadow of that Red Flag of theirs, and
bitter memory of the Champ-de-Mars. How swift is
the progress of things and men ! Not now does Lafayette,
as on that Federation-day, when *his* noon was, ' press
his sword firmly on the Fatherland's Altar ', and swear
in sight of France : ah no ; he, waning and setting ever
since that hour, hangs now, disastrous, on the edge of
the horizon ; commanding one of those Three moulting
Crane-flights of Armies, in a most suspected, unfruitful,
uncomfortable manner.

But, at worst, cannot Patriotism, so many thousands
strong in this Metropolis of the Universe, help itself ?
Has it not right-hands, pikes ? Hammering of Pikes,
which was not to be prohibited by Mayor Bailly, has
been sanctioned by Mayor Pétion ; sanctioned by
Legislative Assembly. How not, when the King's so-
called Constitutional Guard ' was making cartridges in

---

[1] Discours de Bailly, Réponse de Pétion (Moniteur du
20 Novembre 1791).

secret' ? Changes are necessary for the National Guard
itself; this whole Feuillant-Aristocrat Staff of the
Guard must be disbanded. Likewise, citizens without
uniform may surely rank in the Guard, the pike beside
the musket, in such a time : the ' active ' citizen and
the passive who can fight for us, are they not both
welcome ?—O my Patriot friends, indubitably Yes !
Nay the truth is, Patriotism throughout, were it never so
white-frilled, logical, respectable, must either lean itself
heartily on Sansculottism, the black, bottomless ; or
else vanish, in the frightfullest way, to Limbo ! Thus
some, with upturned nose, will altogether sniff and
disdain Sansculottism ; others will lean heartily on it ;
nay others again will lean what we call *heartlessly* on
it : three sorts ; each sort with a destiny corresponding.

In such point of view, however, have we not for the
present a Volunteer Ally, stronger than all the rest ;
namely, Hunger ? Hunger ; and what rushing of Panic
Terror this and the sum-total of our other miseries may
bring ! For Sansculottism grows by what all other
things die of. Stupid Peter Baille almost made an
epigram, though unconsciously, and with the Patriot
world laughing not at it but at him, when he wrote :
' *Tout va bien ici, le pain manque,* All goes well here,
food is not to be had '.[1]

Neither, if you knew it, is Patriotism without her
Constitution that *can* march ; her *not* impotent Parliament ; or call it, Ecumenic Council, and General-
Assembly of the Jean-Jacques Churches : the MOTHER-
SOCIETY, namely ! Mother-Society with her three-
hundred full-grown Daughters ; with what we can call
little Grand-daughters trying to walk, in every village
of France, numerable, as Burke thinks, by the hundred
thousand. This is the true Constitution ; made not by
Twelve-Hundred august Senators, but by Nature herself ; and has grown, unconsciously, out of the wants
and the efforts of these Twenty-five Millions of men.
They are ' Lords of the Articles ', our Jacobins ; they

[1] Barbaroux, p. 94.

originate debates for the Legislative ; discuss Peace and
War ; settle beforehand what the Legislative is to do.
Greatly to the scandal of philosophical men, and of
most Historians ;—who do in that judge naturally, and
yet not wisely. A Governing Power must exist : your
other powers here are simulacra ; this power is *it.*

Great is the Mother-Society : she has had the honour
to be denounced by Austrian Kaunitz ;[1] and is all the
dearer to Patriotism. By fortune and valour she has
extinguished Feuillantism itself, at least the Feuillant
Club. This latter, high as it once carried its head,
she, on the 18th of February, has the satisfaction to
see shut, extinct ; Patriots having gone thither, with
tumult, to hiss it out of pain. The Mother-Society has
enlarged her locality, stretches now over the whole nave
of the Church. Let us glance in, with the worthy Toulongeon, our old Ex-Constituent Friend, who happily
has eyes to see. ' The nave of the Jacobins Church ',
says he, ' is changed into a vast Circus, the seats of
which mount up circularly like an amphitheatre to the
very groin of the domed roof. A high Pyramid of black
marble, built against one of the walls, which was formerly a funeral monument, has alone been left standing:
it serves now as back to the Office-bearers' Bureau.
Here on an elevated Platform sit President and Secretaries, behind and above them the white Busts of Mirabeau, of Franklin, and various others, nay finally of
Marat. Facing this is the Tribune, raised till it is midway between floor and groin of the dome, so that the
speaker's voice may be in the centre. From that point
thunder the voices which shake all Europe : down
below, in silence, are forging the thunderbolts and the
firebrands. Penetrating into this huge circuit, where
all is out of measure, gigantic, the mind cannot repress
some movement of terror and wonder ; the imagination
recalls those dread temples which Poetry, of old, had
consecrated to the Avenging Deities '.[2]

---

[1] Moniteur, Séance du 29 Mars 1792.
[2] Toulongeon, ii. 124.

Scenes too are in this Jacobin Amphitheatre,—had
History time for them. Flags of the ' Three Free
Peoples of the Universe ', trinal brotherly flags of England, America, France, have been waved here in concert;
by London Deputation, of Whigs or *Wighs* and their
Club, on this hand, and by young French Citoyennes
on that ; beautiful sweet-tongued Female Citizens,
who solemnly send over salutation and brotherhood,
also Tricolor stitched by their own needle, and finally
Ears of Wheat ; while the dome rebellows with *Vivent
les trois peuples libres !* from all throats :—a most dramatic scene. Demoiselle Théroigne recites, from that
Tribune in mid air, her persecutions in Austria ; comes
leaning on the arm of Joseph Chénier, Poet Chénier, to
demand Liberty for the hapless Swiss of Château-Vieux.[1]
Be of hope, ye forty Swiss ; tugging there, in the Brest
waters ; *not* forgotten !

Deputy Brissot perorates from that Tribune ; Desmoulins, our wicked Camille, interjecting audibly from
below, ' *Coquin !* ' Here, though oftener in the Cordeliers, reverberates the lion-voice of Danton ; grim
Billaud-Varennes is here ; Collot d'Herbois, pleading
for the Forty Swiss ; tearing a passion to rags. Apoph-
thegmatic Manuel winds up in this pithy way : ' A
Minister must perish ! '—to which the Amphitheatre
responds : ' *Tous, Tous*, All, All ! ' But the Chief
Priest and Speaker of this place, as we said, is Robespierre, the long-winded incorruptible man. What spirit
of Patriotism dwelt in men in those times, this one
fact, it seems to us, will evince : that fifteen hundred
human creatures, not bound to it, sat quiet under the
oratory of Robespierre ; nay, listened nightly, hour
after hour, applausive ; and gaped as for the word of
life. More insupportable individual, one would say,
seldom opened his mouth in any Tribune. Acrid, im-
placable-impotent ; dull-drawling, barren as the Harmattan-wind.* He pleads, in endless earnest-shallow
speech, against immediate War, against Woollen Caps

---

[1] Débats des Jacobins (Hist. Parl. xiii. 259, &c.).

or *Bonnets Rouges*, against many things; and is the
Trismegistus*and Dalai-Lama of Patriot men. Whom
nevertheless a shrill-voiced little man, yet with fine eyes,
and a broad beautifully sloping brow, rises respectfully
to controvert; he is, say the Newspaper Reporters,
'M. Louvet, Author of the charming Romance of *Faublas*'. Steady, ye Patriots! Pull not *yet* two ways;
with a France rushing panic-stricken in the rural districts, and a Cimmerian Europe storming in on you!

CHAPTER IX

MINISTER ROLAND

ABOUT the vernal equinox, however, one unexpected
gleam of hope does burst forth on Patriotism: the
appointment of a thoroughly Patriot Ministry. This
also his Majesty, among his innumerable experiments
of wedding fire to water, will try. *Quod bonum sit.*
Madame d'Udon's Breakfasts have jingled with a new
significance; not even Genevese Dumont but had a
word in it. Finally, on the 15th and onwards to the
23rd day of March, 1792, when all is negotiated,—this
is the blessed issue; this Patriot Ministry that we see.

General Dumouriez, with the Foreign Portfolio, shall
ply Kaunitz and the Kaiser, in another style than did
poor Delessarts; whom indeed we have sent to our High
Court of Orléans for his sluggishness. War-Minister
Narbonne is washed away by the Time-flood; poor
Chevalier de Grave, chosen by the Court, is fast washing
away: then shall austere Servan, able Engineer-Officer,
mount suddenly to the War Department. Genevese
Clavière sees an omen realized: passing the Finance
Hôtel, long years ago, as a poor Genevese exile, it was
borne wondrously on his mind that *he* was to be Finance-
Minister; and now he is it;—and his poor Wife, given
up by the Doctors, rises and walks, not the victim of

nerves but their vanquisher.[1] And above all, our
Minister of the Interior ? Roland de la Platrière, he of
Lyons ! So have the Brissotins, public or private
Opinion, and Breakfasts in the Place Vendôme, decided
it. Strict Roland, compared to a *Quaker endimanché*,
or Sunday Quaker, goes to kiss hands at the Tuileries, in
round hat and sleek hair, his shoes tied with mere riband
or ferrat. The Supreme Usher twitches Dumouriez
aside : ' *Quoi, Monsieur !* No buckles to his shoes ? '
—' Ah, Monsieur ', answers Dumouriez, glancing towards the ferrat : ' All is lost, *Tout est perdu* '.[2]

And so our fair Roland removes from her upper-
floor in the Rue Saint-Jacques, to the sumptuous saloons once occupied by Madame Necker. Nay still
earlier, it was Calonne that did all this gilding ; it was
he who ground these lustres, Venetian mirrors ; who
polished this inlaying, this veneering and or-moulu ;
and made it, by rubbing of the proper *lamp*, an Aladdin's
Palace :—and now behold, he wanders dim-flitting over
Europe ; half-drowned in the Rhine-stream, scarcely
saving his Papers ! *Vos non vobis.*—The fair Roland,
equal to either fortune, has her public Dinner on Fri-
days, the Ministers all there in a body : she withdraws
to her desk (the cloth once removed), and seems busy
writing ; nevertheless loses no word : if, for example,
Deputy Brissot and Minister Clavière get too hot in
argument, she, not without timidity, yet with a cunning gracefulness, will interpose. Deputy Brissot's
head, they say, is getting giddy, in this sudden height ;
as feeble heads do.

Envious men insinuate that the Wife Roland is
Minister, and not the Husband : it is happily the worst
they have to charge her with. For the rest, let whose
head soever be getting giddy, it is not this brave
woman's. Serene and queenly here, as she was of old
in her own hired garret of the Ursulines Convent ! She
who has quietly shelled French-beans for her dinner ;
being led to that, as a young maiden, by quiet insight

---

[1] Dumont, c. 20, 21.　　[2] Madame Roland, ii. 80-115.

and computation; and knowing what that was, and
what she was: such a one will also look quietly on
or-moulu and veneering, not ignorant of these either.
Calonne did the veneering: he gave dinners here, old
Besenval diplomatically whispering to him; and was
great: yet Calonne we saw at last 'walk with long
strides'. Necker next: and where now is Necker?
Us also a swift change has brought hither; a swift
change will send us hence. Not a Palace but a Caravansera!

So wags and wavers this unrestful World, day after
day, month after month. The Streets of Paris, and all
Cities, roll daily their oscillatory flood of men; which
flood does nightly disappear, and lie hidden horizontal
in beds and trucklebeds; and awakes on the morrow
to new perpendicularity and movement. Men go their
roads, foolish or wise;—Engineer Goguelat to and fro,
bearing Queen's cipher. A Madame de Staël is busy;
cannot clutch her Narbonne from the Time-flood: a
Princess de Lamballe is busy; cannot help her Queen.
Barnave, seeing the Feuillants dispersed, and Coblentz
so brisk, begs by way of final recompense to kiss her
Majesty's hand; 'augers not well of her new course';
and retires home to Grenoble, to wed an heiress there.
The Café Valois and Méot the Restaurateur's hear daily
gasconade; loud babble of Half-pay Royalists, with or
without poniards. Remnants of Aristocrat saloons call
the new Ministry *Ministère-Sansculotte*. A Louvet, of
the Romance *Faublas*, is busy in the Jacobins. A
Cazotte, of the Romance *Diable Amoureux*, is busy
elsewhere: better wert thou quiet, old Cazotte; it is a
world, this, of magic become *real*! All men are busy;
doing they only half guess what:—flinging seeds, of
tares mostly, into the 'Seed-field of TIME': this, by
and by, will declare wholly what.

But Social Explosions have in them something dread,
and as it were mad and magical; which indeed Life
always secretly has: thus the dumb Earth (says Fable),
if you pull her mandrake-roots,*will give a daemonic mad-

making *moan*. These Explosions and Revolts ripen,
break forth like dumb dread Forces of Nature ; and
yet they are Men's forces ; and yet *we* are part of them :
the Daemonic that is in man's life has burst out on us,
will sweep us too away !—One day here is like another,
and yet it is not like but different.   How much is growing, silently resistless, at all moments !   Thoughts are
growing ; forms of Speech are growing, and Customs
and even Costumes ; still more visibly are actions and
transactions growing, and that doomed Strife of France
with herself and with the whole world.

The word *Liberty* is never named now except in con-
junction with another ; *Liberty* and *Equality*.   In like
manner, what, in a reign of Liberty and Equality, can
these words, 'Sir', 'Obedient Servant', 'Honour to
be', and such like, signify ?   Tatters and fibres of old
Feudality ; which, were it only in the Grammatical
province, ought to be rooted out !   The Mother-Society
has long since had proposals to that effect : these she
could not entertain ; not, at the moment.   Note too
how the Jacobin Brethren are mounting new Symbolical
head-gear : the Woollen Cap or Nightcap, *bonnet de
laine*, better known as *bonnet rouge*, the colour being *red*.
A thing one wears not only by way of Phrygian Cap-of-
Liberty,* but also for convenience'-sake, and then also
in compliment to the Lower-class Patriots and Bastille-
Heroes ; for the Red Nightcap combines all the three
properties.   Nay cockades themselves begin to be made
of wool, of tricolor yarn : the riband-cockade, as a
symptom of Feuillant Upper-class temper, is becoming
suspicious.   Signs of the times.

Still more, note the travail-throes of Europe : or
rather, note the birth she brings ; for the successive
throes and shrieks, of Austrian and Prussian Alliance,
of Kaunitz Antijacobin Dispatch, of French Ambassadors cast out, and so forth, were long to note.
Dumouriez corresponds with Kaunitz, Metternich,*
or Cobentzel,* in another style than Delessarts did.
Strict becomes stricter ; categorical answer, as to this
Coblentz work and much else, shall be given.   Failing

which ? Failing which, on the 20th day of April 1792,
King and Ministers step over to the Salle de Manége ;
promulgate how the matter stands ; and poor Louis,
' with tears in his eyes ', proposes that the Assembly
do now decree War. After due eloquence, War is
decreed that night.

War, indeed ! Paris came all crowding, full of expectancy, to the morning, and still more to the evening,
session. D'Orléans with his two sons is there ; looks
on, wide-eyed, from the opposite gallery.[1] Thou canst
look, O Philippe : it is a War big with issues, for thee
and for all men. Cimmerian Obscurantism and this
thrice-glorious Revolution shall wrestle for it, then :
some Four-and-twenty years; in immeasurable Briareus
wrestle ; trampling and tearing ; before they can come
to any, not agreement, but compromise, and approximate ascertainment each of what is in the other.

Let our Three Generals on the Frontiers look to it,
therefore ; and poor Chevalier de Grave, the War-
Minister, consider what he will do. What is in the
three Generals and Armies we may guess. As for poor
Chevalier de Grave, he, in this whirl of things all coming
to a press and pinch upon him, loses head, and merely
whirls with them, in a totally distracted manner ; signing himself at last, ' De Grave, *Mayor of Paris* ' ; whereupon he demits, returns over the Channel, to walk in
Kensington Gardens ;[2] and austere Servan, the able
Engineer-Officer, is elevated in his stead. To the post
of Honour ? To that of Difficulty, at least.

[1] Deux Amis, vii. 146-66.   [2] Dumont, c. 19, 21.

CHAPTER X

PÉTION-NATIONAL-PIQUE

AND yet, how, on dark bottomless Cataracts there plays the foolishest fantastic-coloured spray and shadow; hiding the Abyss under vapoury rainbows ! Alongside of this discussion as to Austrian-Prussian War, there goes on not less but more vehemently a discussion, Whether the Forty or Two-and-forty Swiss of Château-Vieux shall be liberated from the Brest Galleys ? And then, Whether, being liberated, they shall have a public Festival, or only private ones ?

Théroigne, as we saw, spoke ; and Collot took up the tale. Has not Bouillé's final display of himself, in that final Night of Spurs, stamped your so-called ' Revolt of Nanci ' into a ' Massacre of Nanci ', for all Patriot judgements ? Hateful is that massacre ; hateful the Lafayette-Feuillant ' public thanks ' given for it ! For indeed, Jacobin Patriotism and dispersed Feuillantism are now at death-grips ; and do fight with all weapons, even with scenic shows. The walls of Paris, accordingly, are covered with Placard and Counter-Placard, on the subject of Forty Swiss blockheads. Journal responds to Journal ; Player Collot to Poetaster Roucher ; Joseph Chénier the Jacobin, squire of Théroigne, to his Brother André the Feuillant ; Mayor Pétion to Dupont de Nemours : and for the space of two months, there is nowhere peace for the thought of man,—till this thing be settled.

Gloria in excelsis ! The Forty Swiss are at last got ' amnestied '. Rejoice ye Forty ; doff your greasy wool Bonnets, which shall become Caps of Liberty. The Brest Daughter-Society welcomes you from on board, with kisses on each cheek : your iron Handcuffs are disputed as Relics of Saints ; the Brest Society indeed can have one portion, which it will beat into Pikes, a sort of Sacred Pikes ; but the other portion

must belong to Paris, and be suspended from the dome
there, along with the Flags of the Three Free Peoples !
Such a goose is man ; and cackles over plush-velvet
Grand Monarques and woollen Galley-slaves ; over
everything and over nothing,—and will cackle with his
whole soul, merely if others cackle !

On the ninth morning of April, these Forty Swiss
blockheads arrive. From Versailles; with *vivats* heaven-
high ; with the affluence of men and women. To the
Townhall we conduct them ; nay to the Legislative itself, though not without difficulty. They are harangued,
bedinnered, begifted,—the very Court, *not* for conscience'-sake, contributing something ; and their Public
Festival shall be next Sunday. Next Sunday accordingly it is.[1] They are mounted into a ' triumphal Car
resembling a ship ' ; are carted over Paris, with the
clang of cymbals and drums, all mortals assisting
applausive ; carted to the Champ-de-Mars and Fatherland's Altar ; and finally carted, for Time always brings
deliverance,—into invisibility for evermore.

Whereupon dispersed Feuillantism, or that Party
which loves Liberty yet *not* more than Monarchy, will
likewise have its Festival : Festival of Simonneau, unfortunate Mayor of Etampes, who died for the Law ;
most surely for the Law, though Jacobinism disputes :
being trampled down with his Red Flag in the riot
about grains. At which Festival the Public again
assists, *un*applausive : not we.

On the whole, Festivals are not wanting ; beautiful
rainbow-spray when all is now rushing treble-quick
towards its Niagara Fall. National Repasts there are ;
countenanced by Mayor Pétien ; Saint-Antoine, and
the Strong Ones of the Halles defiling through Jacobin
Club, ' their felicity ', according to Santerre, ' not
perfect otherwise ' ; singing many-voiced their *ça-ira*,
dancing their *ronde patriotique*. Among whom one is

---

[1] Newspapers of February, March, April 1792 ; Iambe
d'André Chénier sur la Fête des Suisses ; &c, &c. (in Hist.
Parl. xiii. xiv.).

glad to discern Saint-Huruge, expressly ' in white hat ',
the Saint-Christopher*of the Carmagnole. Nay a certain *Tambour*, or National Drummer, having just been
presented with a little daughter, determines to have
the new Frenchwoman christened, on Fatherland's
Altar, then and there. Repast once over, he accordingly has her christened ; Fauchet the Te-Deum Bishop
acting in chief, Thuriot and honourable persons standing gossips : by the name, Pétion-National-Pique ![1]
Does this remarkable Citizeness, now past the meridian
of life, still walk the Earth ? Or did she die perhaps
of teething ? Universal History is not indifferent.

CHAPTER XI

THE HEREDITARY REPRESENTATIVE

AND yet it is not by carmagnole-dances, and singing
of *ça-ira*, that the work can be done. Duke Brunswick*
is not dancing carmagnoles, but has his drill-sergeants
busy.

On the Frontiers, our Armies, be it treason or not,
behave in the worst way. Troops badly commanded,
shall we say ? Or troops intrinsically bad ? Unap-
pointed, undisciplined, mutinous ; that, in a thirty-
years peace, have never seen fire ? In any case, Lafayette's and Rochambeau's little clutch, which they
made at Austrian Flanders, has prospered as badly as
clutch need do : soldiers starting at their own shadow ;
suddenly shrieking, ' *On nous trahit* ', and flying off
in wild panic, at or before the first shot ;—managing
only to hang some two or three prisoners they had
picked up, and massacre their own Commander, poor
Theobald Dillon, driven into a granary by them in the
Town of Lille.

[1] Patriote-Français (Brissot's Newspaper), in Hist. Parl.
xiii. 451.

And poor Gouvion: he who sat shiftless in that Insurrection of Women! Gouvion quitted the Legislative Hall and Parliamentary duties, in disgust and despair, when those Galley-slaves of Château-Vieux were admitted there. He said, 'Between the Austrians and the Jacobins there is nothing but a soldier's death for it';[1] and so, 'in the dark stormy night', he has flung himself into the throat of the Austrian cannon, and perished in the skirmish at Maubeuge on the ninth of June. Whom Legislative Patriotism shall mourn, with black mort-cloths and melody in the Champ-de-Mars: many a Patriot shiftier, truer none. Lafayette himself is looking altogether dubious; in place of beating the Austrians, is about writing to denounce the Jacobins. Rochambeau, all disconsolate, quits the service: there remains only Lückner, the babbling old Prussian Grenadier.

Without Armies, without Generals! And the Cimmerian Night *has* gathered itself; Brunswick preparing his proclamation; just about to march! Let a Patriot Ministry and Legislative say, what in these circumstances it will do? Suppress internal enemies, for one thing, answers the Patriot Legislative; and proposes, on the 24th of May, its Decree for the Banishment of Priests. Collect also some nucleus of determined internal friends, adds War-Minister Servan; and proposes, on the 7th of June, his Camp of Twenty-thousand. Twenty-thousand National Volunteers; Five out of each Canton, picked Patriots, for Roland has charge of the Interior: they shall assemble here in Paris; and be for a defence, cunningly devised, against foreign Austrians and domestic *Austrian Committee* alike. So much can a Patriot Ministry and Legislative do.

Reasonable and cunningly devised as such Camp may, to Servan and Patriotism, appear, it appears not so to Feuillantism; to that Feuillant-Aristocrat Staff of the Paris Guard; a Staff, one would say again, which will need to be *dissolved*. These men see, in this proposed

---

[1] Toulongeon, ii. 149.

Camp of Servan's, an offence ; and even, as they pretend to say, an insult. Petitions there come, in consequence, from blue Feuillants in epaulettes ; ill received. Nay, in the end, there comes one Petition, called ' of the Eight-thousand National Guards ' : so many names are on it, including women and children. Which famed Petition of the Eight-thousand is indeed received : and the Petitioners, all under arms, are admitted to the honours of the sitting,—if honours or even if sitting there be ; for the instant their bayonets appear at the one door, the Assembly ' adjourns ', and begins to flow out at the other.[1]

Also, in these same days, it is lamentable to see how National Guards, escorting *Fête-Dieu*, or *Corpus-Christi* ceremonial, do collar and smite down any Patriot that does not uncover as the Hostie passes. They clap their bayonets to the breast of Cattle-butcher Legendre,* a known Patriot ever since the Bastille days ; and threaten to butcher him ; though he sat quite respectfully, he says, in his Gig, at a distance of fifty paces, waiting till the thing were by. Nay, orthodox females were shrieking to have down the *Lanterne* on him.[2]

To such height has Feuillantism gone in this Corps. For indeed, are not their Officers creatures of the chief Feuillant, Lafayette ? The Court too has, very naturally, been tampering with them ; caressing them, ever since that dissolution of the so-called Constitutional Guard. Some Battalions are altogether ' *pétris*, kneaded full ' of Feuillantism, mere Aristocrats at bottom : for instance, the Battalion of the *Filles-Saint-Thomas*, made up of your Bankers, Stockbrokers, and other Full-purses of the Rue Vivienne. Our worthy old Friend Weber, Queen's Foster-brother Weber, carries a musket in that Battalion,—one may judge with what degree of Patriotic intention.

Heedless of all which, or rather heedful of all which, the Legislative, backed by Patriot France and the feel-

<hr/>

[1] Moniteur, Séance du 10 Juin 1792.
[2] Débats des Jacobins (in Hist. Parl. xiv. 429).

ing of Necessity, decrees this Camp of Twenty-thousand.
Decisive though conditional Banishment of malign
Priests it has already decreed.

It will now be seen, therefore, Whether the Hereditary Representative is for us or against us ? Whether
or not, to all our other woes, this intolerablest one is to
be added ; which renders us not a menaced Nation in
extreme jeopardy and need, but a paralytic Solecism of
a Nation ; sitting wrapped as in dead cerements, of a
Constitutional-Vesture that were no other than a winding-sheet ; our right hand glued to our left : to wait
there, writhing and wriggling, unable to stir from the
spot, till in Prussian rope we mount to the gallows ?
Let the Hereditary Representative consider it well :
The Decree of Priests ? The Camp of Twenty-thousand ?—By Heaven, he answers, *Veto ! Veto !*—Strict
Roland hands in his *Letter to the King ;* or rather it
was Madame's Letter, who wrote it all at a sitting ; one
of the plainest-spoken Letters ever handed in to any
King. This plain-spoken Letter King Louis has the
benefit of reading overnight. He reads, inwardly digests ; and next morning, the whole Patriot Ministry
finds itself turned out. It is the 13th of June 1792.[1]

Dumouriez, the many-counselled, he, with one Du-
ranthon, called Minister of Justice, does indeed linger
for a day or two ; in rather suspicious circumstances ;
speaks with the Queen, almost weeps with her : but in
the end, he too sets off for the Army ; leaving what
Un-Patriot or Semi-Patriot Ministry and Ministries can
now accept the helm, to accept it. Name them not ;
new quick-changing Phantasms, which shift like magic-
lantern figures ; more spectral than ever !

Unhappy Queen, unhappy Louis ! The two *Vetos*
were so natural : are not the Priests martyrs ; also
friends ? This Camp of Twenty-thousand, could it be
other than of stormfullest Sansculottes ? Natural ;
and yet, to France, unendurable. Priests that co-
operate with Coblentz must go elsewhither with their

---

[1] Madame Roland, ii. 115.

martyrdom : stormful Sansculottes, these and no other
kind of creatures will drive back the Austrians. If thou
prefer the Austrians, then for the love of Heaven go
join them. If not, join frankly with what will oppose
them to the death. Middle course is none.

Or, alas, what extreme course was there left now for
a man like Louis ? Underhand Royalists, Ex-Minister
Bertrand-Moleville, Ex-Constituent Malouet, and all
manner of unhelpful individuals, advise and advise.
With face of hope turned now on the Legislative Assembly, and now on Austria and Coblentz, and round
generally on the Chapter of Chances, an ancient Kingship is reeling and spinning, one knows not whitherward, on the flood of things.

CHAPTER XII

PROCESSION OF THE BLACK BREECHES

BUT is there a thinking man in France who, in these
circumstances, can persuade himself that the Constitution will march ? Brunswick is stirring ; *he*, in few
days now, will march. Shall France sit still, wrapped
in dead cerements and grave-clothes, its right hand
glued to its left, till the Brunswick Saint-Bartholomew
arrive ; till France be as Poland, and its Rights of Man
become a Prussian Gibbet ?

Verily it is a moment frightful for all men. National
Death ; or else some preternatural convulsive outburst of National Life ;—that same *daemonic* outburst !
Patriots whose audacity has limits had, in truth, better
retire like Barnave ; court private felicity at Grenoble.
Patriots whose audacity has no limits must sink down
into the obscure ; and, daring and defying all things,
seek salvation in stratagem, in Plot of Insurrection.
Roland and young Barbaroux have spread out the Map
of France before them, Barbaroux says ' with tears ' :

they consider what Rivers, what Mountain-ranges are
in it : they will retire behind this Loire-stream, defend
these Auvergne stone-labyrinths ; save some little
sacred Territory of the Free ; die at least in their last
ditch. Lafayette indites his emphatic Letter to the
Legislative against Jacobinism ; [1] which emphatic Letter will not heal the unhealable.

Forward, ye Patriots whose audacity has no limits ;
it is you now that must either do or die ! The Sections
of Paris sit in deep counsel ; send out Deputation after
Deputation to the Salle de Manége, to petition and
denounce. Great is their ire against tyrannous *Veto,
Austrian Committee*, and the combined Cimmerian
Kings. What boots it ? Legislative listens to the
' tocsin in our hearts ' ; grants us honours of the sitting,
sees us defile with jingle and fanfaronade ; but the
Camp of Twenty-thousand, the Priest-Decree, bevetoed
by Majesty, are become impossible for Legislative.
Fiery Isnard says, ' We will have Equality, should we
descend for it to the tomb '. Vergniaud utters, hypothetically, his stern Ezekiel-visions of the fate of Anti-
national Kings. But the question is : Will hypothetic
prophecies, will jingle and fanfaronade demolish the
Veto ; or will the Veto, secure in its Tuileries Château,
remain undemolishable by these ? Barbaroux, dashing
away his tears, writes to the Marseilles Municipality,
that they must send him ' Six-hundred men who know
how to die, *qui savent mourir* '. [2] No wet-eyed message
this, but a fire-eyed one ;—which will be obeyed !

Meanwhile the Twentieth of June is nigh, anniversary
of that world-famous Oath of the Tennis-Court : on
which day, it is said, certain citizens have in view to
plant a *Mai* or Tree of Liberty in the Tuileries Terrace
of the Feuillants ; perhaps also to petition the Legislative and Hereditary Representative about these Vetos ;
—with such demonstration, jingle and evolution, as may

---

[1] Moniteur, Séance du 18 Juin 1792.
[2] Barbaroux, p. 40.

seem profitable and practicable. Sections have gone
singly, and jingled and evolved : but if they all went,
or great part of them, and there, planting their *Mai*
in these alarming circumstances, sounded the tocsin in
their hearts ?

Among King's Friends there can be but one opinion
as to such a step : among Nation's Friends there may
be two. On the one hand, might it not by possibility
scare away these unblessed Vetos ? Private Patriots
and even Legislative Deputies may have each his own
opinion, or own no-opinion : but the hardest task falls
evidently on Mayor Pétion and the Municipals, at once
Patriots and Guardians of the public Tranquillity.
Hushing the matter down with the one hand ; tickling
it up with the other ! Mayor Pétion and Municipality
may lean this way ; Department-Directory with Procureur-Syndic Roederer, having a Feuillant tendency,
may lean that. On the whole, each man must act according to his one opinion or to his two opinions ; and
all manner of influences, official representations cross
one another in the foolishest way. Perhaps after all,
the Project, desirable and yet not desirable, will dissipate itself, being run athwart by so many complexities ;
and come to nothing ?

Not so ; on the Twentieth morning of June, a large
Tree of Liberty, Lombardy Poplar by kind, lies visibly
tied on its car, in the Suburb Saint-Antoine. Suburb
Saint-Marceau too, in the uttermost Southeast, and
all that remote Oriental region, Pikemen and Pikewomen, National Guards, and the unarmed curious
are gathering,—with the peaceablest intentions in the
world. A tricolor Municipal arrives ; speaks. Tush, it is
all peaceable, we tell thee, in the way of Law : are not
Petitions allowable, and the Patriotism of *Mais* ? The
tricolor Municipal returns without effect : your Sansculottic rills continue flowing, combining into brooks :
towards noontide, led by tall Santerre in blue uniform,
by tall Saint-Huruge in white hat, it moves westward,
a respectable river, or complication of still-swelling
rivers.

What Processions have we not seen : *Corpus-Christi*
and Legendre waiting in his Gig ; Bones of Voltaire
with bullock-chariots, and goadsmen in Roman Costume ; Feasts of Château-Vieux and Simonneau ; Gouvion Funerals, Rousseau Sham-funeral, and the Baptism
of Pétion-National-Pike ! Nevertheless this Procession
has a character of its own. Tricolor ribands streaming
aloft from Pike-heads ; ironshod batons ; and emblems
not a few ; among which see specially these two, of the
tragic and the untragic sort : a Bull's Heart transfixed
with iron, bearing this epigraph, ' *Cœur d'Aristocrate*,
Aristocrat's heart ' ; and, more striking still, properly
the standard of the host, a pair of old Black Breeches
(silk, they say), extended on cross-staff, high overhead,
with these memorable words : ' *Tremblez tyrans, voilà
les Sansculottes*, Tremble tyrants, here are the Sans-
indispensables ! ' Also, the Procession trails two cannons.

Scarfed tricolor Municipals do now again meet it,
in the Quai Saint-Bernard ; and plead earnestly, having
called halt. Peaceable, ye virtuous tricolor Municipals,
peaceable are we as the sucking dove. Behold our
Tennis-Court *Mai*. Petition is legal ; and as for arms,
did not an august Legislative receive the so-called Eight-
thousand in arms, Feuillants though they were ? Our
Pikes, are they not of National iron ? Law is our father
and mother, whom we will not dishonour ; but Patriotism is our own soul. Peaceable, ye virtuous Municipals ;—and on the whole, limited as to time ! Stop we
cannot ; march ye with us.—The Black Breeches agitate
themselves, impatient ; the cannon-wheels grumble :
the many-footed Host tramps on.

How it reached the Salle de Manége, like an ever-
waxing river ; got admittance after debate ; read its
Address ; and defiled, dancing and *ça-ira*-ing, led by
tall sonorous Santerre and tall sonorous Saint-Huruge :
how it flowed, not now a waxing river but a shut
Caspian lake, round all Precincts of the Tuileries ; the
front Patriot squeezed by the rearward against barred
iron Grates, like to have the life squeezed out of him,

and looking too into the dread throat of cannon, for
National Battalions stand ranked within : how tricolor
Municipals ran assiduous, and Royalists with Tickets of
Entry ; and both Majesties sat in the interior sur-
rounded by men in black : all this the human mind shall
fancy for itself, or read in old Newspapers, and Syndic
Roederer's *Chronicle of Fifty Days.*[1]

Our *Mai* is planted ; if not in the Feuillants Terrace,
whither is no ingate, then in the Garden of the Capuchins, as near as we could get. National Assembly has
adjourned till the Evening Session : perhaps this shut
lake, finding no ingate, will retire to its sources again ;
and disappear in peace ? Alas, not yet : rearward still
presses on ; rearward knows little what pressure is in
the front. One would wish at all events, were it possible, to have a word with his Majesty first !

The shadows fall longer, eastward ; it is four o'clock :
will his Majesty not come out ? Hardly he ! In that
case, Commandant Santerre, Cattle-butcher Legendre,
Patriot Huguenin with the tocsin in his heart ; they,
and others of authority, will enter *in*. Petition and
request to wearied uncertain National Guard ; louder
and louder petition ; backed by the rattle of our two
cannons ! The reluctant Grate opens : endless Sansculottic multitudes flood the stairs ; knock at the wooden
guardian of your privacy. Knocks, in such case, grow
strokes, grow smashings : the wooden guardian flies
in shivers. And now ensues a Scene over which the
world has long wailed ; and not unjustly ; for a sorrier
spectacle, of Incongruity fronting Incongruity, and as
it were recognizing themselves incongruous, and staring
stupidly in each other's face, the world seldom saw.

King Louis, his door being beaten on, opens it ;
stands with free bosom ; asking, ' What do you want ? '
The Sansculottic flood recoils awestruck ; returns how-
ever, the rear pressing on the front, with cries of ' Veto !
Patriot Ministers ! Remove Veto ! '—which things,
Louis valiantly answers, this is not the time to do, nor

---

[1] Roederer, &c. &c. (in Hist. Parl. xv. 98–194).

this the way to ask him to do. Honour what virtue
is in a man. Louis does not want courage; he has even
the higher kind called moral-courage, though only the
passive-half of that. His few National Grenadiers
shuffle back with him, into the embrasure of a window:
there he stands, with unimpeachable passivity, amid
the shouldering and the braying; a spectacle to men.
They hand him a red Cap of Liberty; he sets it quietly
on his head, forgets it there. He complains of thirst;
half-drunk Rascality offers him a bottle, he drinks of it.
'Sire, do not fear', says one of his Grenadiers. 'Fear?'
answers Louis: 'feel then', putting the man's hand
on his heart. So stands Majesty in Red woollen Cap;
black Sansculottism weltering round him, far and wide,
aimless, with inarticulate dissonance, with cries of
'Veto! Patriot Ministers!'

For the space of three hours or more! The National
Assembly is adjourned; tricolor Municipals avail almost nothing: Mayor Pétion tarries absent; Authority
is none. The Queen with her Children and Sister Elizabeth, in tears and terror not for themselves only, are
sitting behind barricaded tables and Grenadiers, in an
inner room. The Men in black have all wisely disappeared. Blind lake of Sansculottism welters stagnant
through the King's Château, for the space of three hours.

Nevertheless all things do end. Vergniaud arrives
with Legislative Deputation, the Evening Session
having now opened. Mayor Pétion has arrived; is
haranguing, 'lifted on the shoulders of two Grenadiers'.
In this uneasy attitude and in others, at various places
without and within, Mayor Pétion harangues; many
men harangue; finally Commandant Santerre defiles;
passes out, with his Sansculottism, by the opposite side
of the Château. Passing through the room where the
Queen, with an air of dignity and sorrowful resignation,
sat among the tables and Grenadiers, a woman offers her
too a Red Cap; she holds it in her hand, even puts it
on the little Prince Royal. 'Madame', said Santerre,
'this People loves you more than you think'.[1]—About

[1] Toulongeon, ii. 173; Campan, ii. c. 20.

eight o'clock the Royal Family fall into each other's arms amid 'torrents of tears'. Unhappy Family! Who would not weep for it, were there not a whole world to be wept for ?

Thus has the Age of Chivalry gone, and that of Hunger come. Thus does all-needing Sansculottism look in the face of its *Roi*, Regulator, King or Able-man; and find that *he* has nothing to give it. Thus do the two Parties, brought face to face after long centuries, stare stupidly at one another, *This, it is I ; but, good Heaven, is that Thou ?*—and depart, not knowing what to make of it. And yet, Incongruities having recognized themselves to be incongruous, something must be made of it. The Fates know what.

This is the world-famous Twentieth of June, more worthy to be called the *Procession of the Black Breeches*. With which, what we had to say of this First French biennial Parliament, and its products and activities, may perhaps fitly enough terminate.

BOOK VI

THE MARSEILLESE

CHAPTER I

EXECUTIVE THAT DOES NOT ACT

How could your paralytic National Executive be put 'in action', in any measure, by such a Twentieth of June as this ? Quite contrariwise : a large sympathy for Majesty so insulted arises everywhere ; expresses itself in Addresses, Petitions, ' Petition of the Twenty-thousand inhabitants of Paris ', and such like, among all Constitutional persons ; a decided rallying round the throne.

Of which rallying it was thought King Louis might have made something. However, he does make nothing of it, or attempt to make ; for indeed his views are lifted beyond domestic sympathy and rallying, over to Coblentz mainly. Neither in itself is this same sympathy worth much. It is sympathy of men who believe still that the Constitution can march. Wherefore the old discord and ferment, of Feuillant sympathy for Royalty, and Jacobin sympathy for Fatherland, acting against each other from within ; with terror of Coblentz and Brunswick acting from without :—this discord and ferment must hold on its course, till a catastrophe do ripen and come. One would think, especially as Brunswick is near marching, such catastrophe cannot now be distant. Busy, ye Twenty-five French Millions ; ye foreign Potentates, minatory Emigrants, German drill-sergeants; each do what his hand findeth!* Thou, O Reader, at such safe distance, wilt see what they make of it among them.

Consider, therefore, this pitiable Twentieth of June

as a futility; no catastrophe, rather a *catastasis*, or
heightening. Do not its Black Breeches wave there,
in the Historical Imagination, like a melancholy flag of
distress; soliciting help, which no mortal can give ?
Soliciting pity, which thou wert hard-hearted not to
give freely, to one and all ! Other such flags, or what
are called Occurrences, and black or bright symbolic
Phenomena, will flit through the Historical Imagination;
these, one after one, let us note, with extreme brevity.

The first phenomenon is that of Lafayette at the Bar
of the Assembly; after a week and day. Promptly,
on hearing of this scandalous Twentieth of June,
Lafayette has quitted his Command on the North Frontier, in better or worse order; and got hither, on the
28th, to repress the Jacobins: not by letter now; but by
oral Petition, and weight of character, face to face.
The august Assembly finds the step questionable;
invites him meanwhile to the honours of the sitting.[1]
Other honour, or advantage, there unhappily came
almost none; the Galleries all growling; fiery Isnard
glooming; sharp Guadet not wanting in sarcasms.

And out of doors, when the sitting is over, Sieur
Resson, keeper of the Patriot *Café* in these regions,
hears in the street a hurlyburly; steps forth to look, he
and his Patriot customers: it is Lafayette's carriage,
with a tumultuous escort of blue Grenadiers, Cannoneers,
even Officers of the Line, hurrahing and capering round
it. They make a pause opposite Sieur Resson's door;
wag their plumes at him; nay shake their fists, bellowing *A bas les Jacobins*; but happily pass on without
onslaught. They pass on, to plant a *Mai* before the
General's door, and bully considerably. All which the
Sieur Resson cannot but report with sorrow, that night,
in the Mother-Society.[2] But what no Sieur Resson nor
Mother-Society can do more than guess is this, That a
council of rank Feuillants, your unabolished Staff of the

[1] Moniteur, Séance du 28 Juin 1792.
[2] Débats des Jacobins (Hist. Parl. xv. 235).

Guard and who else has status and weight, is in these very moments privily deliberating at the General's : Can we not put down the Jacobins by force ? Next day, a Review shall be held, in the Tuileries Garden, of such as will turn out, and try. Alas, says Toulongeon, hardly a hundred turned out. Put it off till to-morrow, then, to give better warning. On the morrow, which is Saturday, there turn out ' some thirty ' ; and depart shrugging their shoulders ! [1] Lafayette promptly takes carriage again ; returns musing on many things.

The dust of Paris is hardly off his wheels, the summer Sunday is still young, when Cordeliers in deputation pluck up that *Mai* of his : before sunset, Patriots have burnt him in effigy. Louder doubt and louder rises, in Section, in National Assembly, as to the legality of such unbidden Antijacobin visit on the part of a General : doubt swelling and spreading all over France, for six weeks or so ; with endless talk about usurping soldiers, about English Monk, nay about Cromwell : O thou poor *Grandison*-Cromwell !—What boots it ? King Louis himself looked coldly on the enterprise : colossal Hero of two Worlds, having weighed himself in the balance,* finds that he is become a gossamer Colossus, only some thirty turning out.

In a like sense, and with a like issue, works our Department-Directory here at Paris ; who, on the 6th of July, take upon them to suspend Mayor Pétion and Procureur Manuel from all civic functions, for their conduct, replete, as is alleged, with omissions and commissions, on that delicate Twentieth of June. Virtuous Pétion sees himself a kind of martyr, or pseudomartyr, threatened with several things ; drawls out due heroical lamentation ; to which Patriot Paris and Patriot Legislative duly respond. King Louis and Mayor Pétion have already had an interview on that business of the Twentieth ; an interview and dialogue, distinguished by frankness on both sides ; ending on

---

[1] Toulongeon, ii. 180. See also Dampmartin, ii. 161.

King Louis's side with the words ' *Taisez-vous*, Hold
your peace '.

For the rest, this of suspending our Mayor does seem
a mistimed measure. By ill chance, it came out precisely on the day of that famous *Baiser de l'amourette*,
or miraculous reconciliatory Delilah-Kiss, which we
spoke of long ago. Which Delilah-Kiss was thereby
quite hindered of effect. For now his Majesty has to
write, almost that same night, asking a reconciled
Assembly for advice ! The reconciled Assembly will
not advise ; will not interfere. The King confirms the
suspension ; then perhaps, but not till then will the
Assembly interfere, the noise of Patriot Paris getting
loud. Whereby your Delilah-Kiss, such was the destiny
of Parliament First, becomes a Philistine Battle !*

Nay there goes a word that as many as Thirty of our
chief Patriot Senators are to be clapped in prison, by
mittimus and indictment of Feuillant Justices, *Juges
de Paix*; who here in Paris were well capable of such
a thing. It was but in May last that *Juge-de-Paix
Larivière*, on complaint of Bertrand-Moleville touching
that *Austrian Committee*, made bold to launch his mittimus against three heads of the Mountain, Deputies
Bazire, Chabot, Merlin, the Cordelier Trio ; summoning
them to appear before *him*, and show where that
Austrian Committee was, or else suffer the consequences.
Which mittimus the Trio, on their side, made bold to
fling in the fire : and valiantly pleaded privilege of
Parliament. So that, for his zeal without knowledge,
poor Justice Larivière now sits in the prison of Orléans,
waiting trial from the *Haute Cour* there. Whose
example, may it not deter other rash Justices ; and
so this word of the Thirty arrestments continue a word
merely ?

But on the whole, though Lafayette weighed so
light, and has had his *Mai* plucked up, Official Feuillantism falters not a whit ; but carries its head high,
strong in the letter of the Law. Feuillants all of these
men ; a Feuillant Directory ; founding on high character, and such like ; with Duke de la Rochefoucault

for President,—a thing which may prove dangerous for him ! Dim now is the once bright Anglomania of these admired Noblemen. Duke de Liancourt offers, out of Normandy where he is Lord-Lieutenant, not only to receive his Majesty, thinking of flight thither, but to lend him money to enormous amounts. Sire, it is not a Revolt, it is a Revolution ; and truly no rose-water one ! Worthier Noblemen were not in France nor in Europe than those two : but the Time is crooked,* quick-shifting, perverse ; what straightest course will lead to any goal, in *it* ?

Another phasis which we note, in these early July days, is that of certain thin streaks of Federate National Volunteers wending from various points towards Paris, to hold a new Federation-Festival, or Feast of Pikes, on the Fourteenth there. So has the National Assembly wished it, so has the Nation willed it. In this way, perhaps, may we still have our Patriot Camp in spite of *Veto*. For cannot these Fédérés, having celebrated their Feast of Pikes, march on to Soissons ; and, there being drilled and regimented, rush to the Frontiers, or whither we like ? Thus were the one *Veto* cunningly eluded !

As indeed the other *Veto*, about Priests, is also like to be eluded ; and without much cunning. For Provincial Assemblies, in Calvados as one instance, are proceeding, on their own strength, to judge and banish Antinational Priests. Or still worse, without Provincial Assembly, a desperate People, as at Bourdeaux, can ' hang two of them on the Lanterne ', on the way towards judgement.[1] Pity for the spoken *Veto*, when it cannot become an acted one !

It is true, some ghost of a War-minister, or Home-minister, for the time being, ghost whom we do not name, does write to Municipalities and King's Commanders, that they shall, by all conceivable methods, obstruct this Federation, and even turn back the

---

[1] Hist. Parl. xvi. 259.

Fédérés by force of arms: a message which scatters
mere doubt, paralysis and confusion; irritates the poor
Legislature; reduces the Fédérés, as we see, to thin
streaks. But being questioned, this ghost and the other
ghosts, What it is then that they propose to do for
saving the country?—they answer, That they cannot
tell; that indeed they, for their part, have, this morning,
resigned in a body; and do now merely respectfully
take leave of the helm altogether. With which words
they rapidly walk out of the Hall, *sortent brusquement
de la salle*, the ' Galleries cheering loudly', the poor
Legislature sitting 'for a good while in silence' ! [1] Thus
do Cabinet-ministers themselves, in extreme cases,
strike work; one of the strangest omens. Other complete Cabinet-ministry there will not be; only fragments, and these changeful, which never get completed; spectral Apparitions that cannot so much as
appear! King Louis writes that he now views this
Federation Feast with approval; and will himself have
the pleasure to take part in the same.

And so these thin streaks of Fédérés wend Paris-
ward through a paralytic France. Thin grim streaks;
not thick joyful ranks, as of old to the first Feast of
Pikes ! No: these poor Federates march now towards
Austria and Austrian Committee, towards jeopardy and
forlorn hope; men of hard fortune and temper, not rich
in the world's goods. Municipalities, paralysed by
War-minister, are shy of affording cash; it may be,
your poor Federates cannot arm themselves, cannot
march, till the Daughter-Society of the place open her
pocket, and subscribe. There will not have arrived, at
the set day, Three-thousand of them in all. And yet,
thin and feeble as these streaks of Federates seem, they
are the only thing one discerns moving with any clearness of aim, in this strange scene. Angry buzz and
simmer; uneasy tossing and moaning of a huge France,
all enchanted, spell-bound by unmarching Constitution,
into frightful conscious and unconscious Magnetic-sleep;

[1] Moniteur, Séance du 10 Juillet 1792

which frightful Magnetic-sleep must now issue soon in
one of two things : Death or Madness ! The Fédérés
carry mostly in their pocket some earnest cry and Petition, to have the ' National Executive put in action ' ;
or as a step towards that, to have the King's *Déchéance*,
King's Forfeiture, or at least his Suspension, pronounced.
They shall be welcome to the Legislative, to the Mother
of Patriotism ; and Paris will provide for their lodging.

Déchéance, indeed : and, what next ? A France spell-
free, a Revolution saved ; and anything, and all things
next ! so answer grimly Danton and the unlimited
Patriots, down deep in their subterranean region of
Plot, whither they have now dived. *Déchéance*, answers
Brissot with the limited : and if next the little Prince
Royal were crowned, and some Regency of Girondins
and recalled Patriot Ministry set over him ? Alas, poor
Brissot ; looking, as indeed poor man does always, on
the nearest morrow as his peaceable promised land ;
deciding what must reach to the world's end, yet with
an insight that reaches not beyond his own nose ! Wiser
are the unlimited subterranean Patriots, who with light
for the hour itself, leave the rest to the gods.

Or were it not, as we now stand, the probablest
issue of all, that Brunswick, in Coblentz, just gathering
his huge limbs towards him to rise, might arrive first ;
and stop both *Déchéance*, and theorizing on it ? Brunswick is on the eve of marching ; with Eighty-thousand,
they say ; fell Prussians, Hessians, feller Emigrants :
a General of the Great Frederick, with such an Army.
And our Armies ? And our Generals ? As for Lafayette,
on whose late visit a Committee is sitting and all
France is jarring and censuring, he seems readier to
fight *us* than fight Brunswick. Lückner and Lafayette
pretend to be interchanging corps, and are making
movements, which Patriotism cannot understand. This
only is very clear, that their corps go marching and
shuttling, in the interior of the country ; much nearer
Paris than formerly ! Lückner has ordered Dumouriez
down to him ; down from Maulde, and the Fortified
Camp there. Which order the many-counselled Du-

mouriez, with the Austrians hanging close on him, he busy meanwhile training a few thousands to stand fire and be soldiers, declares that, come of it what will, he cannot obey.[1] Will a poor Legislative, therefore, sanction Dumouriez; who applies to it, 'not knowing whether there is any War-ministry'? Or sanction Lückner and these Lafayette movements?

The poor Legislative knows not what to do. It decrees, however, that the Staff of the Paris Guard, and indeed all such Staffs, for they are Feuillants mostly, shall be broken and replaced. It decrees earnestly in what manner one can declare that the *Country is in Danger*. And finally, on the 11th of July, the morrow of that day when the Ministry struck work, it decrees that *the Country be*, with all dispatch, *declared in Danger*. Whereupon let the King sanction; let the Municipality take measures: if such Declaration will do service, *it* need not fail.

In Danger, truly, if ever Country was! Arise, O Country; or be trodden down to ignominious ruin! Nay, are not the chances a hundred to one that no rising of the Country will save it; Brunswick, the Emigrants, and Feudal Europe drawing nigh?

CHAPTER II

LET US MARCH

BUT, to our minds, the notablest of all these moving phenomena is that of Barbaroux's 'Six hundred Marseillese who know how to die'.

Prompt to the request of Barbaroux, the Marseilles Municipality has got these men together: on the fifth morning of July, the Townhall says, '*Marchez, abattez le Tyran*, March, strike down the Tyrant';[2] and they, with grim appropriate '*Marchons*', are marching.

---

[1] Dumouriez, ii. 1, 5.   [2] Dampmartin, ii. 183.

Long journey, doubtful errand ; *Enfans de la Patrie*, may a good genius guide you ! Their own wild heart and what faith it has will guide them : and is not that the monition of some genius, better or worse ? Five-hundred and Seventeen able men, with Captains of fifties and tens ; well armed all, musket on shoulder, sabre on thigh : nay they drive three pieces of cannon ; for who knows what obstacles may occur ? Municipalities there are, paralysed by War-minister ; Commandants with orders to stop even Federation Volunteers : good, when sound arguments will not open a Town-gate, if you have a petard to shiver it ! They have left their sunny Phocean City and Sea-haven, with its bustle and its bloom : the thronging *Course*, with high-frondent Avenues, pitchy dockyards, almond and olive groves, orange-trees on house-tops, and white glittering *bastides* that crown the hills, are all behind them. They wend on their wild way, from the extremity of French land, through unknown cities, toward an unknown destiny ; with a purpose that they know.

Much wondering at this phenomenon, and how, in a peaceable trading City, so many householders or hearth-holders do severally fling down their crafts and indus-trial tools ; gird themselves with weapons of war, and set out on a journey of six-hundred miles, to ' strike down the tyrant ',—you search in all Historical Books, Pamphlets and Newspapers, for some light on it : un-happily without effect. Rumour and Terror precede this march ; which still echo on you ; the march itself an unknown thing.   Weber, in the backstairs of the Tuileries, has understood that they were *Forçats*, Galley-slaves and mere scoundrels, these Marseillese ; that, as they marched through Lyons, the people shut their shops ;—also that the number of them was some Four *Thousand*. Equally vague is Blanc Gilli, who likewise murmurs about *Forçats* and danger of plunder.[1] *Forçats* they were not ; neither was there plunder, or danger of it.   Men of regular life, or of the best-filled purse, they

---

[1] See Barbaroux, Mémoires (Note in p. 40, 1).

could hardly be; the one thing needful in them was
that they 'knew how to die'. Friend Dampmartin
saw them, with his own eyes, march 'gradually'
through his quarters at Villefranche in the Beaujolais:
but saw in the vaguest manner; being indeed preoccupied, and himself minded for marching just then—
across the Rhine. Deep was his astonishment to think
of such a march, without appointment or arrangement,
station or ration; for the rest, it was 'the same men
he had seen formerly' in the troubles of the South;
'perfectly civil'; though his soldiers could not be kept
from talking a little with them.[1]

So vague are all these; *Moniteur, Histoire Parlementaire* are as good as silent: garrulous History, as is
too usual, will say nothing where you most wish her to
speak! If enlightened Curiosity ever get sight of the
Marseilles Council-Books, will it not perhaps explore
this strangest of Municipal procedures; and feel called
to fish up what of the Biographies, creditable or discre-
ditable, of these Five-hundred and Seventeen, the
stream of Time has not yet irrevocably swallowed?

As it is, these Marseillese remain inarticulate, un-
distinguishable in feature; a blackbrowed Mass, full of
grim fire, who wend there, in the hot sultry weather:
very singular to contemplate. They wend; amid the
infinitude of doubt and dim peril; they not doubtful:
Fate and Feudal Europe, having decided, come girdling
in from without; they, having also decided, do march
within. Dusty of face, with frugal refreshment, they
plod onwards; unweariable, not to be turned aside.
Such march will become famous. The Thought, which
works voiceless in this blackbrowed mass, an inspired
Tyrtaean*Colonel, Rouget de Lille, whom the Earth still
holds,[2] has translated into grim melody and rhythm;
into his *Hymn* or March *of the Marseillese*: luckiest
musical-composition ever promulgated. The sound of
which will make the blood tingle in men's veins; and
whole Armies and Assemblages will sing it, with eyes

---

[1] Dampmartin, *ubi suprà*.   [2] A.D. 1836.

weeping and burning, with hearts defiant of Death,
Despot and Devil.

One sees well, these Marseillese will be too late for
the Federation Feast. In fact, it is not Champ-de-Mars
Oaths that they have in view. They have quite another
feat to do : a paralytic National Executive to set in
action. They must 'strike down' whatsoever 'Tyrant',
or Martyr-Fainéant, there may be who paralyses it ;
strike and be struck ; and on the whole prosper, and
know how to die.

CHAPTER III

SOME CONSOLATION TO MANKIND

OF the Federation Feast itself we shall say almost
nothing. There are Tents pitched in the Champ-de-
Mars ; tent for National Assembly ; tent for Hereditary
Representative,—who indeed is there too early, and has
to wait long in it. There are Eighty-three symbolic
Departmental Trees-of-Liberty ; trees and *mais* enough :
beautifullest of all, there is one huge *mai,* hung round
with effete Scutcheons, Emblazonries and Genealogy-
books, nay better still, with Lawyers'-bags, ' *sacs de pro-
cédure* ' ; which shall be burnt. The Thirty seat-rows
of that famed Slope are again full ; we have a bright
Sun ; and all is marching, streamering and blaring : but
what avails it ? Virtuous Mayor Pétion, whom Feuillantism had suspended, was reinstated only last night,
by Decree of the Assembly. Men's humour is of the
sourest. Men's hats have on them, written in chalk,
' *Vive Pétion* ' ; and even, ' Pétion or Death, *Pétion ou la
Mort* '.

Poor Louis, who has waited till five o'clock before
the Assembly would arrive, swears the National Oath
this time, with a quilted cuirass under his waistcoat
which will turn pistol-bullets.[1] Madame de Staël,

---

[1] Campan, ii. c. 20 ; De Staël, ii. c. 7.

from that Royal Tent, stretches out the neck in a kind
of agony, lest the waving multitude which receive him
may not render him back alive.   No cry of *Vive le Roi*
salutes the ear ; cries only of *Vive Pétion* ; *Pétion ou la
Mort.* The National Solemnity is as it were huddled
by ; each cowering off almost before the evolutions are
gone through.   The very *Mai* with its Scutcheons and
Lawyers'-bags is forgotten, stands unburnt ; till ' certain Patriot Deputies ', called by the people, set a
torch to it, by way of voluntary after-piece.   Sadder
Feast of Pikes no man ever saw.

Mayor Pétion, named on hats, is at his zenith in
this Federation ; Lafayette again is close upon his
nadir.   Why does the storm-bell of Saint-Roch speak
out, next Saturday ; why do the citizens shut their
shops ? [1] It is Sections defiling, it is fear of effervescence.
Legislative Committee, long deliberating on Lafayette
and that Antijacobin visit of his, reports, this day, that
there is ' *not* ground for Accusation ' ! Peace, ye
Patriots, nevertheless ; and let that tocsin cease : the
Debate is not finished, nor the Report accepted ; but
Brissot, Isnard and the Mountain will sift it, and resift
it, perhaps for some three weeks longer.
So many bells, storm-bells and noises do ring ;—
scarcely audible ; one drowning the other.   For example : in this same Lafayette tocsin, of Saturday,
was there not withal some faint bob-minor, and Deputation of Legislative, ringing the Chevalier Paul Jones
to his long rest ; tocsin or dirge now all one to him !
Not ten days hence Patriot Brissot, beshouted this day
by the Patriot Galleries, shall find himself begroaned
by them, on account of his limited Patriotism ; nay
pelted at while perorating, and ' hit with two prunes '. [2]
It is a distracted empty-sounding world ; of bob-minors
and bob-majors, of triumph and terror, of rise and fall !
The more touching is this other Solemnity, which

---

[1] Moniteur, Séance du 21 Juillet 1792.
[2] Hist. Parl. xvi. 185.

happens on the morrow of the Lafayette tocsin: Proclamation that the *Country is in Danger*. Not till the present Sunday could such Solemnity be. The Legislative decreed it almost a fortnight ago; but Royalty and the ghost of a Ministry held back as they could. Now however, on this Sunday, 22nd day of July 1792, it will hold back no longer; and the Solemnity in very deed is. Touching to behold! Municipality and Mayor have on their scarfs; cannon-salvo booms alarm from the Pont-Neuf, and single-gun at intervals all day. Guards are mounted, scarfed Notabilities, Halberdiers and a Cavalcade; with streamers, emblematic flags; especially with one huge Flag, flapping mournfully: *Citoyens, la Patrie est en Danger*. They roll through the streets, with stern-sounding music, and slow rattle of hoofs; pausing at set stations, and with doleful blast of trumpet, singing out through Herald's throat, what the Flag says to the eye: ' Citizens, our Country is in Danger ! '

Is there a man's heart that hears it without a thrill ? The many-voiced responsive hum or bellow of these multitudes is not of triumph; and yet it is a sound deeper than triumph. But when the long Cavalcade and Proclamation ended ; and our huge Flag was fixed on the Pont-Neuf, another like it on the Hôtel-de-Ville, to wave there till better days ; and each Municipal sat in the centre of his Section, in a Tent raised in some open square, Tents surmounted with flags of *Patrie en Danger*, and topmost of all a Pike and *Bonnet Rouge* ; and, on two drums in front of him, there lay a plank-table, and on this an open Book, and a Clerk sat, like recording-angel, ready to write the lists, or as we say to enlist ! O, then, it seems, the very gods might have looked down on it. Young Patriotism, Culottic and Sansculottic, rushes forward emulous: That is my name ; name, blood and life is all my country's ; why have I nothing more ! Youths of short stature weep that they are below size. Old men come forward, a son in each hand. Mothers themselves will grant the son of their travail ; send him, though with tears. And

the multitude bellows *Vive la Patrie*, far reverberating.
And fire flashes in the eyes of men ;—and at eventide,
your Municipal returns to the Townhall followed by
his long train of Volunteer valour ; hands in his List ;
says proudly, looking round, This is my day's harvest.[1]
They will march, on the morrow, to Soissons ; small
bundle holding all their chattels.

So, with *Vive la Patrie, Vive la Liberté*, stone Paris
reverberates like Ocean in his caves ; day after day,
Municipals enlisting in tricolor Tent ; the Flag flapping
on Pont-Neuf and Townhall, *Citoyens, la Patrie est en
Danger.* Some Ten-thousand fighters, without discipline but full of heart, are on march in few days. The
like is doing in every Town of France.—Consider, therefore, whether the Country will want defenders, had we
but a National Executive ? Let the Sections and Primary Assemblies, at any rate, become Permanent! They
do become Permanent, and sit continually in Paris, and
over France, by Legislative Decree, dated Wednesday
the 25th.[2]

Mark contrariwise how, in these very hours, dated
the 25th, Brunswick ' shakes himself, *s'ébranle* ', in
Coblentz ; and takes the road ! Shakes himself indeed ;
one spoken word becomes such a shaking. Successive,
simultaneous *dirl* of thirty-thousand muskets shouldered ; prance and jingle of ten-thousand horsemen,
fanfaronading Emigrants in the van ; drum, kettledrum ; noise of weeping, swearing ; and the immeasurable lumbering clank of baggage-wagons and camp-
kettles that groan into motion : all this is Brunswick
shaking himself ; not without all this does the one man
march, ' covering a space of forty miles '. Still less without his Manifesto, dated, as we say, the 25th ; a State-
Paper worthy of attention !

By this Document, it would seem great things are
in store for France. The universal French People shall
now have permission to rally round Brunswick and his

---

[1] Tableau de la Révolution, § *Patrie en Danger.*
[2] Moniteur, Séance du 25 Juillet 1792.

Emigrant Seigneurs ; tyranny of a Jacobin Faction
shall oppress them no more ; but they shall return, and
find favour with their own good King ; who, by Royal
Declaration (three years ago) of the Twenty-third of
June, said that he would himself make them happy.
As for National Assembly, and other Bodies of Men
invested with some temporary shadow of authority,
they are charged to maintain the King's Cities and
Strong Places intact, till Brunswick arrive to take de-
livery of them. Indeed, quick submission may extenuate
many things ; but to this end it must be quick.   Any
National Guard or other unmilitary person found resisting in arms shall be ' treated as a traitor ' ; that is
to say, hanged with promptitude.   For the rest, if Paris,
before Brunswick gets thither, offer any insult to the
King ; or, for example, suffer a Faction to carry the
King away elsewhither ; in that case, Paris shall be
blasted asunder with cannon-shot and ' military execution '.   Likewise all other Cities, which may witness,
and not resist to the uttermost, such forced-march of
his Majesty, shall be blasted asunder ; and Paris and
every City of them, starting-place, course and goal of
said sacrilegious forced-march, shall, as rubbish and
smoking ruin, lie there for a sign.   Such vengeance
were indeed signal, ' an *insigne vengeance* ' :—O Brunswick, what words thou writest and blusterest ! In this
Paris, as in old Nineveh, are so many score thousands
that know not the right hand from the left, and also
much cattle.   Shall the very milk-cows, hard-living
cadgers'-asses, and poor little canary-birds die ?

Nor is Royal and Imperial Prussian-Austrian Declaration wanting : setting forth, in the amplest
manner, their Sanssouci-Schönbrunn* version of this
whole French Revolution, since the first beginning of
it ; and with what grief these high heads have seen such
things done under the Sun.   However, ' as some small
consolation to mankind ',[1] they do now dispatch
Brunswick ; regardless of expense, as one might say,

[1] Annual Register (1792), 236.

or of sacrifices on their own part ; for is it not the first
duty to console men ?

Serene Highnesses, who sit there protocolling and
manifestoing, and consoling mankind ! how were it if,
for once in the thousand years, your parchments, formularies and reasons of state were blown to the four
winds ; and Reality Sans-indispensables stared you,
even you, in the face ; and Mankind said for itself what
the thing was that would console it ?—

CHAPTER IV

SUBTERRANEAN

But judge if there was comfort in this to the Sections
all sitting permanent ; deliberating how a National
Executive could be put in action !

High rises the response, not of cackling terror but of
crowing counter-defiance, and *Vive la Nation* ; young
Valour streaming towards the Frontiers ; *Patrie en Danger* mutely beckoning on the Pont-Neuf. Sections are
busy, in their permanent Deep ; and down, lower still,
works unlimited Patriotism, seeking salvation in plot.
Insurrection, you would say, becomes once more the
sacredest of duties ? Committee, self-chosen, is sitting
at the Sign of the Golden Sun ; Journalist Carra, Camille Desmoulins, Alsatian Westermann*friend of Danton, American Fournier of Martinique ;—a Committee
not unknown to Mayor Pétion, who, as an official person, must sleep with one eye open. Not unknown to
Procureur Manuel ; least of all to Procureur-Substitute
Danton ! He, wrapped in darkness, being also official,
bears it on his giant shoulders ; cloudy invisible Atlas
of the whole.

Much is invisible ; the very Jacobins have their reti-
cences. Insurrection is to be : but when ? This only
we can discern, that such Fédérés as are not yet gone

to Soissons, as indeed are not inclined to go yet, ' for
reasons ', says the Jacobin President, ' which it may be
interesting not to state ',—have got a *Central Committee*
sitting close by, under the roof of the Mother-Society
herself. Also, what in such ferment and danger of
effervescence is surely proper, the Forty-eight Sections
have got their Central Committee; intended ' for
prompt communication '. To which Central Committee
the Municipality, anxious to have it at hand, could not
refuse an Apartment in the Hôtel-de-Ville.

Singular City ! For overhead of all this, there is the
customary baking and brewing ; Labour hammers and
grinds. Frilled promenaders saunter under the trees ;
white-muslin promenaderess, in green parasol, leaning
on your arm. Dogs dance, and shoeblacks polish, on
that Pont-Neuf itself, where Fatherland is in danger.
So much goes its course ; and yet the course of all things
is nigh altering and ending.

Look at that Tuileries and Tuileries Garden. Silent
all as Sahara ; none entering save by ticket ! They shut
their Gates, after the Day of the Black Breeches ; a
thing they had the liberty to do. However, the National Assembly grumbled something about Terrace of
the Feuillants, how said Terrace lay contiguous to the
back-entrance to their Salle, and was partly *National*
Property ; and so now National Justice has stretched
a Tricolor Riband athwart it, by way of boundary-line ;
respected with splenetic strictness by all Patriots.
It hangs there that Tricolor boundary-line; carries
'satirical inscriptions on cards', generally in verse; and
all beyond this is called *Coblentz*, and remains vacant;
silent as a fateful Golgotha*; sunshine and umbrage
alternating on it in vain. Fateful Circuit : what hope
can dwell in it ? Mysterious Tickets of Entry introduce
themselves ; speak of Insurrection very imminent.
Rivarol's Staff of Genius had better purchase blunderbusses ; Grenadier bonnets, red Swiss uniforms may
be useful. Insurrection will come ; but likewise will
it not be met ? Staved off, one may hope, till Brunswick arrive ?

But consider withal if the Bourne-stones and Port-able-chairs remain silent; if the Heralds' College of Bill-Stickers sleep! Louvet's *Sentinel* warns gratis on all walls; Sulleau is busy; *People's-Friend* Marat and *King's-Friend* Royou croak and counter-croak. For the man Marat, though long hidden since that Champ-de-Mars Massacre, is still alive. He has lain, who knows in what cellars; perhaps in Legendre's; fed by a steak of Legendre's killing: but, since April, the bull-frog voice of him sounds again; hoarsest of earthly cries. For the present, black terror haunts him: O brave Barbaroux, wilt thou not smuggle me to Marseilles, 'disguised as a jockey'?[1] In Palais-Royal and all public places, as we read, there is sharp activity; private individuals haranguing that Valour may enlist; haranguing that the Executive may be put in action. Royalist Journals ought to be solemnly burnt: argument thereupon; debates, which generally end in single-stick, *coups de cannes.*[2] Or think of this; the hour midnight; place Salle de Manége; august Assembly just adjourning; ' Citizens of both sexes enter in a rush, exclaiming, *Vengeance; they are poisoning our Brothers*'; —baking brayed glass among their bread at Soissons! Vergniaud has to speak soothing words, How Commissioners are already sent to investigate this brayed glass, and do what is needful therein;—till the rush of Citizens ' makes profound silence '; and goes home to its bed.

Such is Paris; the heart of a France like to it. Preternatural suspicion, doubt, disquietude, nameless anticipation, from shore to shore:—and those blackbrowed Marseillese marching, dusty, unwearied, through the midst of it; not doubtful they. Marching to the grim music of their hearts, they consume continually the long road, these three weeks and more; heralded by Terror and Rumour. The Brest Fédérés arrive on the 26th;

[1] Barbaroux, p. 60.
[2] Newspapers, Narratives, and Documents (Hist. Parl. xv. 240; xvi. 399).

through hurrahing streets. Determined men are these also, bearing or not bearing the Sacred Pikes of Château-Vieux ; and on the whole decidedly disinclined for Soissons as yet. Surely the Marseillese Brethren do draw nigher all days.

CHAPTER V

AT DINNER

It was a bright day for Charenton, that 29th of the month, when the Marseillese Brethren actually came in sight. Barbaroux, Santerre and Patriots have gone out to meet the grim Wayfarers. Patriot clasps dusty Patriot to his bosom ; there is footwashing and refection: 'dinner of twelve-hundred covers at the Blue Dial, *Cadran Bleu* ' ; and deep interior consultation, that one wots not of.[1] Consultation indeed which comes to little ; for Santerre, with an open purse, with a loud voice, has almost no head. Here, however, we repose this night : on the morrow is public entry into Paris.

Of which public entry the Day-Historians, *Diurnalists*, or Journalists as they call themselves, have preserved record enough. How Saint-Antoine male and female, and Paris generally, gave brotherly welcome, with bravo and hand-clapping, in crowded streets ; and all passed in the peaceablest manner ;—except it might be our Marseillese pointed out here and there a riband-cockade, and beckoned that it should be snatched away, and exchanged for a wool one ; which was done. How the Mother-Society in a body has come as far as the Bastille-ground, to embrace you. How you then wend onwards, triumphant, to the Townhall, to be embraced by Mayor Pétion ; to put down your muskets in the Barracks of Nouvelle France, not far off ;—then towards

[1] Deux Amis, viii. 90–101.

the appointed Tavern in the Champs Elysées, to enjoy
a frugal Patriot repast.[1]

Of all which the indignant Tuileries may, by its
Tickets of Entry, have warning. Red Swiss look
doubly sharp to their Château-Grates ;—though surely
there is no danger ? Blue Grenadiers of the Filles-
Saint-Thomas Section are on duty there this day : men
of Agio, as we have seen ; with stuffed purses, riband-
cockades ; among whom serves Weber. A party of
these latter, with Captains, with sundry Feuillant Notabilities, Moreau de Saint-Méry of the three-thousand
orders, and others, have been dining, much more re-
spectably, in a Tavern hard by. They have dined,
and are now drinking Loyal-Patriotic toasts ; while
the Marseillese, *National*-Patriotic merely, are about
sitting down to their frugal covers of delf. How it
happened remains to this day undemonstrable ; but the
external fact is, certain of these Filles-Saint-Thomas
Grenadiers do issue from their Tavern ; perhaps
touched, surely not yet muddled with any liquor they
have had ;—issue in the professed intention of testifying to the Marseillese, or to the multitude of Paris
Patriots who stroll in these spaces, That they, the Filles-
Saint-Thomas men, if well seen into, are not a whit less
Patriotic than any other class of men whatever.

It was a rash errand ! For how can the strolling
multitude credit such a thing ; or do other indeed than
hoot at it, provoking and provoked ?—till Grenadier
sabres stir in the scabbard, and thereupon a sharp shriek
rises : ' *À nous, Marseillais*, Help, Marseillese ! ' Quick
as lightning, for the frugal repast is not yet served, that
Marseillese Tavern flings itself open : by door, by window ; running, bounding, vault forth the Five-hundred
and Seventeen undined Patriots ; and, sabre flashing
from thigh, are on the scene of controversy. Will ye
parley, ye Grenadier Captains and official Persons ;
' with faces grown suddenly pale ', the Deponents say ?[2]

[1] Hist. Parl. xvi. 196. See Barbaroux, pp. 51–5.

[2] Moniteur, Séances du 30, du 31 Juillet 1792 (Hist. Parl.
xvi. 197–210).

Advisabler were instant moderately swift retreat ! The
Filles-Saint-Thomas men retreat, back foremost ; then,
alas, face foremost, at treble-quick time ; the Marseillese, according to a Deponent, ' clearing the fences and
ditches after them, like lions : Messieurs, it was an
imposing spectacle '.

Thus they retreat, the Marseillese following. Swift
and swifter, towards the Tuileries : where the Drawbridge receives the bulk of the fugitives ; and, then
suddenly drawn up, saves them ; or else the green mud
of the Ditch does it. The bulk of them ; not all ; ah,
no ! Moreau de Saint-Méry for example, being too fat,
could not fly fast ; he got a stroke, *flat*-stroke only, over
the shoulder-blades, and fell prone ;—and disappears
there from the History of the Revolution. Cuts also
there were, pricks in the posterior fleshy parts ; much
rending of skirts, and other discrepant waste. But poor
Sub-lieutenant Duhamel, innocent Change-broker, what
a lot for him ! He turned on his pursuer, or pursuers,
with a pistol ; he fired and missed ; drew a second
pistol, and again fired and missed ; then ran : unhappily
in vain. In the Rue Saint-Florentin, they clutched
him ; thrust him through, in red rage : that was
the end of the New Era, and of all Eras, to poor
Duhamel.

Pacific readers can fancy what sort of grace-before-
meat this was to frugal Patriotism. Also how the Battalion of the Filles-Saint-Thomas ' drew out in arms ',
luckily without further result ; how there was accusation at the Bar of the Assembly, and counter-accusation
and defence ; Marseillese challenging the sentence of a
free jury-court,—which never got empanelled. We ask
rather, What the upshot of all these distracted wildly
accumulating things may, by probability, be ? Some
upshot ; and the time draws nigh ! Busy are Central
Committees, of Fédérés at the Jacobins Church, of Sections at the Townhall ; Reunion of Carra, Camille and
Company at the Golden Sun. Busy ; like submarine
deities, or call them mud-gods, working there in deep
murk of waters ; till the thing be ready.

And how your National Assembly, like a ship water-logged, helmless, lies tumbling ; the Galleries, of shrill Women, of Fédérés with sabres, bellowing down on it, not unfrightful ;—and waits where the waves of chance may please to strand it ; suspicious, nay on the Left-side, conscious, what submarine Explosion is meanwhile a-charging ! Petition for King's Forfeiture rises often there : Petition from Paris Section, from Provincial Pa-triot Towns ; ' from Alençon, Briançon, and the Traders at the Fair of Beaucaire'. Or what of these ? On the 3rd of August, Mayor Pétion and the Municipality come petitioning for Forfeiture : they openly, in their tricolor Municipal scarfs. Forfeiture is what all Patriots now want and expect. All Brissotins want Forfeiture ; with the little Prince Royal for King, and us for Pro-tector over him. Emphatic Fédérés ask the Legisla-ture : ' Can you save us, or not ? ' Forty-seven Sec-tions have agreed to Forfeiture ; only that of the Filles-Saint-Thomas pretending to disagree. Nay Section Mauconseil declares Forfeiture to be, properly speaking, come ; Mauconseil, for one, ' does from this day ', the last of July, ' cease allegiance to Louis', and take minute of the same before all men. A thing blamed aloud ; but which will be praised aloud ; and the name *Mauconseil*, of Ill-counsel, be thenceforth changed to *Bonconseil*, of Good-counsel.

President Danton, in the Cordeliers Section, does another thing : invites all Passive Citizens to take place among the Active in Section-business, one peril threat-ening all. Thus he, though an official person ; cloudy Atlas of the whole. Likewise he manages to have that blackbrowed Battalion of Marseillese shifted to new Barracks, in his own region of the remote Southeast. Sleek Chaumette, cruel Billaud, Deputy Chabot the Disfrocked, Huguenin with the tocsin in his heart, will welcome them there. Wherefore, again and again : ' O Legislators, can you save us or not ? ' Poor Legis-lators ; with their Legislature water-logged, volcanic Explosion charging under it ! Forfeiture shall be de-bated on the ninth of August ; that miserable business of Lafayette may be expected to terminate on the eighth.

Or will the humane Reader glance into the Levée-day of Sunday the fifth ? The last Levée ! Not for a long time, 'never', says Bertrand-Moleville, had a Levée been so brilliant, at least so crowded. A sad presaging interest sat on every face ; Bertrand's own eyes were filled with tears. For, indeed, outside of that Tricolor Riband on the Feuillants Terrace, Legislature is debating, Sections are defiling, all Paris is astir this very Sunday, demanding *Déchéance*.[1] Here, however, within the riband, a grand proposal is on foot, for the hundredth time, of carrying his Majesty to Rouen and the Castle of Gaillon. Swiss at Courbevoye are in readiness ; much is ready ; Majesty himself seems almost ready. Nevertheless, for the hundredth time, Majesty, when near the point of action, draws back ; writes, after one has waited, palpitating, an endless summer day, that ' he has reason to believe the Insurrection is not so ripe as you suppose '. Whereat Bertrand-Moleville breaks forth ' into extremity at once of spleen and despair, *d'humeur et de désespoir* '.[2]

CHAPTER VI

THE STEEPLES AT MIDNIGHT

FOR, in truth, the Insurrection is just about ripe. Thursday is the ninth of the month August : if Forfeiture be not pronounced by the Legislature that day, we must pronounce it ourselves.

Legislature ? A poor water-logged Legislature can pronounce nothing. On Wednesday the eighth, after endless oratory once again, they cannot even pronounce Accusation against Lafayette ; but absolve him,—hear

[1] Hist. Parl. xvi. 337-9.
[2] Bertrand-Moleville, Mémoires, ii. 129.

it, Patriotism !—by a majority of two to one. Patriotism hears it ; Patriotism, hounded on by Prussian
Terror, by Preternatural Suspicion, roars tumultuous
round the Salle de Manége, all day ; insults many leading Deputies, of the absolvent Right-side ; nay chases
them, collars them with loud menace : Deputy Vaublanc, and others of the like, are glad to take refuge in
Guard-houses, and escape by the back window. And
so, next day, there is infinite complaint ; Letter after
Letter from insulted Deputy ; mere complaint, debate
and self-cancelling jargon : the sun of Thursday sets
like the others, and no Forfeiture pronounced. Wherefore in fine, To your tents, O Israel !*

The Mother-Society ceases speaking ; groups cease
haranguing : Patriots, with closed lips now, ' take one
another's arm ' ; walk off, in rows, two and two, at
a brisk business-pace ; and vanish afar in the obscure
places of the East.[1] Santerre is ready ; or we will make
him ready. Forty-seven of the Forty-eight Sections are
ready ; nay, Filles-Saint-Thomas itself turns up the
Jacobin side of it, turns down the Feuillant side of it,
and is ready too. Let the unlimited Patriot look to his
weapon, be it pike, be it firelock; and the Brest brethren,
—above all, the blackbrowed Marseillese prepare themselves for the extreme hour ! Syndic Roederer knows,
and laments or not as the issue may turn, that ' five-
thousand ball-cartridges, within these few days, have
been distributed to Fédérés, at the Hôtel-de-Ville '.[2]

And ye likewise, gallant gentlemen, defenders of
Royalty, crowd ye on your side to the Tuileries. Not
to a Levée : no, to a Couchée ; where much will be put
to bed. Your Tickets of Entry are needful ; needfuller
your blunderbusses !—They come and crowd, like gallant men who also know how to die : old Maillé the
Camp-Marshal has come, his eyes gleaming once again,
though dimmed by the rheum of almost fourscore years.

---

[1] Deux Amis, viii. 129–88.
[2] Roederer à la Barre (Séance du 9 Août, in Hist. Parl.
xvi. 393).

Courage, Brothers! We have a thousand red Swiss; men stanch of heart, steadfast as the granite of their Alps. National Grenadiers are at least friends of Order; Commandant Mandat breathes loyal ardour, will ' answer for it on his head '. Mandat will, and his Staff; for the Staff, though there stands a doom and Decree to that effect, is happily never yet dissolved.

Commandant Mandat has corresponded with Mayor Pétion; carries a written Order from him these three days, to repel force by force. A squadron on the Pont-Neuf with cannon shall turn back these Marseillese coming across the River: a squadron at the Townhall shall cut Saint-Antoine in two, ' as it issues from the Arcade Saint-Jean '; drive one half back to the obscure East, drive the other half forward ' through the Wickets of the Louvre '. Squadrons not a few, and mounted squadrons; squadrons in the Palais-Royal, in the Place Vendôme: all these shall charge, at the right moment; sweep this street, and then sweep that. Some new Twentieth of June we shall have; only still more in-effectual? Or probably the Insurrection will not dare to rise at all? Mandat's Squadrons, Horse-Gendar-merie and blue Guards march, clattering, tramping; Mandat's Cannoneers rumble. Under cloud of night; to the sound of his *générale*, which begins drumming when men should go to bed. It is the 9th night of August 1792.

On the other hand, the Forty-eight Sections corre-spond by swift messengers; are choosing each their ' three Delegates with full powers '. Syndic Roederer, Mayor Pétion are sent for to the Tuileries: courageous Legislators, when the drum beats danger, should repair to their Salle. Demoiselle Théroigne has on her grena-dier-bonnet, short-skirted riding-habit; two pistols garnish her small waist, and sabre hangs in baldric by her side.

Such a game is playing in this Paris Pandemonium, or City of All the Devils!—And yet the Night, as Mayor Pétion walks here in the Tuileries Garden, ' is beautiful

and calm ' ; Orion and the Pleiades*glitter down quite
serene. Pétion has come forth, the ' heat ' inside was
so oppressive.[1] Indeed, his Majesty's reception of him
was of the roughest ; as it well might be. And now
there is no outgate ; Mandat's blue Squadrons turn
you back at every Grate ; nay the Filles-Saint-Thomas
Grenadiers give themselves liberties of tongue, How
a virtuous Mayor ' shall pay for it, if there be mischief ',
and the like ; though others again are full of civility.
Surely if any man in France is in straits this night, it
is Mayor Pétion : bound, under pain of death, one may
say, to smile dexterously with the one side of his face,
and weep with the other ;—death if he do it not dexterously enough ! Not till four in the morning does
a National Assembly, hearing of his plight, summon
him over ' to give account of Paris ' ; of which he knows
nothing : whereby, however, he shall get home to bed,
and only his gilt coach be left. Scarcely less delicate
is Syndic Roederer's task ; who must wait whether he
will lament or not, till he see the issue. Janus Bifrons,*
or *Mr. Facing-both-ways,* as vernacular Bunyan has it !
They walk there, in the meanwhile, these two Januses,
with others of the like double conformation ; and ' talk
of indifferent matters '.

Roederer, from time to time, steps in ; to listen, to
speak ; to send for the Department-Directory itself,
he their Procureur Syndic not seeing how to act. The
Apartments are all crowded ; some seven-hundred
gentlemen in black elbowing, bustling ; red Swiss standing like rocks ; ghost, or partial-ghost of a Ministry, with
Roederer and advisers, hovering round their Majesties ;
old Marshal Maillé kneeling at the King's feet to say,
He and these gallant gentlemen are come to die for him.
List ! through the placid midnight ; clang of the distant
storm-bell ! So, in very sooth : steeple after steeple
takes up the wondrous tale. Black Courtiers listen at
the windows, opened for air ; discriminate the steeple-

---

[1] Roederer, Chronique de Cinquante Jours ; Récit de
Pétion ; Townhall Records, &c. (in Hist. Parl. xvi. 399-466).

bells : [1] this is the tocsin of Saint-Roch ; that again, is it not Saint-Jacques, named *de la Boucherie* ? Yes, Messieurs! Or even Saint-Germain l'Auxerrois, hear ye *it* not? The same metal that rang storm, two hundred and twenty years ago ; but by a Majesty's order then ; on Saint Bartholomew's Eve ! [2]—So go the steeple-bells ; which Courtiers can discriminate. Nay, meseems, there is the Townhall itself ; we know it by its sound ! Yes, Friends, that is the Townhall ; discoursing *so*, to the Night. Miraculously ; by miraculous metal-tongue and man's-arm : Marat himself, if you knew it, is pulling at the rope there ! Marat is pulling ; Robespierre lies deep, invisible for the next forty hours ; and some men have heart, and some have as good as none, and not even frenzy will give them any.

What struggling confusion, as the issue slowly draws on; and the doubtful Hour, with pain and blind struggle, brings forth its Certainty, never to be abolished !— The Full-power Delegates, three from each Section, a Hundred and forty-four in all, got gathered at the Townhall, about midnight. Mandat's Squadron, stationed there, did not hinder their entering: are they not the ' Central Committee of the Sections ' who sit here usually ; though in greater number to-night ? They are there : presided by Confusion, Irresolution, and the Clack of Tongues. Swift scouts fly ; Rumour buzzes, of Black Courtiers, red Swiss, of Mandat and his Squadrons that shall charge. Better put off the Insurrection ? Yes, put it off. Ha, hark ! Saint-Antoine booming out eloquent tocsin, of its own accord !—Friends, no : ye cannot put off the Insurrection ; but must put it on, and live with it, or die with it.

Swift now, therefore : let these actual Old Municipals, on sight of the Full-powers, and mandate of the Sovereign elective People, lay down their functions ; and this New Hundred and Forty-four take them up ! Will ye nill ye, worthy Old Municipals, go ye must. Nay is it not a happiness for many a Municipal that he can

---

[1] Roederer, *ubi supra*.   [2] 24th August 1572.

wash his hands of such a business ; and sit there paralysed, unaccountable, till the Hour do bring forth ; or
even go home to his night's rest ? [1] Two only of the
Old, or at most three, we retain : Mayor Pétion, for
the present walking in the Tuileries ; Procureur Manuel ;
Procureur-Substitute Danton, invisible Atlas of the
whole.   And so, with our Hundred and Forty-four,
among whom are a Tocsin-Huguenin, a Billaud, a Chaumette ; and Editor-Talliens, and Fabre d'Eglantines,
Sergents, Panises*; and in brief, either emergent, or else
emerged and full-blown, the entire Flower of unlimited
Patriotism : have we not, as by magic, made a New
Municipality ; ready to act in the unlimited manner ;
and declare itself roundly, ' in a State of Insurrection ! '
—First of all, then, be Commandant Mandat sent for,
with that Mayor's-Order of his ; also let the New Municipals visit those Squadrons that were to charge ; and
let the storm-bell ring its loudest ;—and, on the whole,
Forward, ye Hundred and Forty-four ; retreat is now
none for you !

Reader, fancy not, in thy languid way, that Insurrection is easy. Insurrection is difficult : each individual uncertain even of his next neighbour ; totally
uncertain of his distant neighbours, what strength is
with him, what strength is against him ; certain only
that, in case of failure, his individual portion is the
gallows ! Eight hundred thousand heads, and in each
of them a separate estimate of these uncertainties, a
separate theorem of action conformable to that : out of
so many uncertainties, does the certainty, and inevitable
net-result never to be abolished, go on, at all moments,
bodying itself forth ;—leading thee also towards civic-
crowns or an ignominious noose.

Could the Reader take an Asmodeus' Flight,* and
waving open all roofs and privacies, look down from
the Tower of Notre-Dame, what a Paris were it ! Of
treble-voice whimperings or vehemence, of bass-voice

---

[1] Section Documents, Townhall Documents (Hist. Parl.
ubi supra).

growlings, dubitations ; Courage screwing itself to desperate defiance ; Cowardice trembling silent within
barred doors;—and all round, Dullness calmly snoring;
for much Dullness, flung on its mattresses, always sleeps.
O, between the clangour of these high-storming tocsins
and that snore of Dullness, what a gamut : of trepidation, excitation, desperation ; and above it mere Doubt,
Danger, Atropos*and Nox !

Fighters of this Section draw out ; hear that the
next Section does not ; and thereupon draw in.   Saint-
Antoine, on this side the River, is uncertain of Saint-
Marceau on that.   Steady only is the snore of Dullness,
are the Six-hundred Marseillese that know how to die.
Mandat, twice summoned to the Townhall, has not
come.   Scouts fly incessant, in distracted haste ; and
the many-whispering voices of Rumour.   Théroigne and
unofficial Patriots flit, dim-visible, exploratory, far and
wide ; like Night-birds on the wing.   Of Nationals some
Three-thousand have followed Mandat and his *générale* ;
the rest follow each his own theorem of the uncertainties :   theorem, that one should march rather with Saint-
Antoine ; innumerable theorems, that in such a case
the wholesomest were *sleep*.   And so the drums beat,
in mad fits, and the storm-bells peal.   Saint-Antoine
itself does but draw out and draw in ;   Commandant
Santerre, over there, cannot believe that the Marseillese
and Saint-Marceau will march.   Thou laggard sonorous
Beer-vat, with the loud voice and timber-head, is it
time now to palter ?   Alsatian Westermann clutches
him by the throat with drawn sabre :   whereupon the
Timber-headed believes.   In this manner wanes the
slow night ;   amid fret, uncertainty and tocsin ;   all
men's humour rising to the hysterical pitch ;   and
nothing done.

However, Mandat, on the third summons, does come ;
—come, unguarded ;   astonished to find the Municipality *new*.   They question him straitly on that Mayor's
Order to resist force by force ;   on that strategic scheme
of cutting Saint-Antoine in two halves :   he answers
what he can :   they think it were right to send this

strategic National Commandant to the Abbaye Prison,
and let a Court of Law decide on him. Alas, a Court
of Law, not Book-Law but primeval Club-Law, crowds
and jostles out of doors ; all fretted to the hysterical
pitch ; cruel as Fear, blind as the Night : such Court
of Law, and no other, clutches poor Mandat from his
constables ; beats him down, massacres him, on the
steps of the Townhall. Look to it, ye new Municipals ;
ye People, in a state of Insurrection ! Blood is shed,
blood must be answered for ;—alas, in such hysterical
humour, more blood will flow : for it is as with the
Tiger in that ; he has only to begin.

Seventeen Individuals have been seized in the
Champs Elysées, by exploratory Patriotism ; they flitting
dim-visible, by it flitting dim-visible. Ye have pistols,
rapiers, ye Seventeen ? One of those accursed ' false
Patrols ' ; that go marauding, with Anti-National intent ; seeking what they can spy, what they can spill !
The Seventeen are carried to the nearest Guard-house ;
eleven of them escape by back passages. ' How is
this ? ' Demoiselle Théroigne appears at the front
entrance, with sabre, pistols and a train ; denounces
treasonous connivance ; demands, seizes, the remaining
six, that the justice of the People be not trifled with.
Of which six two more escape in the whirl and debate
of the Club-Law Court ; the last unhappy Four are
massacred, as Mandat was : Two Ex-Bodyguards ; one
dissipated Abbé ; one Royalist Pamphleteer, Sulleau,
known to us by name, Able Editor, and wit of all
work. Poor Sulleau : his *Acts of the Apostles*, and brisk
Placard-Journals (for he was an able man) come to
Finis, in this manner ; and questionable jesting issues
suddenly in horrid earnest ! Such doings usher in the
dawn of the Tenth of August 1792.

Or think what a night the poor National Assembly
has had : sitting there, ' in great paucity ', attempting
to debate ;—quivering and shivering ; pointing towards
all the thirty-two azimuths at once, as the magnet-
needle does when thunderstorm is in the air ! If the
Insurrection come ? If it come, and fail ? Alas, in

that case, may not black Courtiers with blunderbusses, red Swiss with bayonets rush over, flushed with victory, and ask us :   Thou undefinable, waterlogged, self-distractive, self-destructive Legislative, what dost thou here *unsunk* ?—Or figure the poor National Guards, bivouacking in ' temporary tents ' there ; or standing ranked, shifting from leg to leg, all through the weary night ;   New tricolor Municipals ordering one thing, old Mandat Captains ordering another.   Procureur Manuel has ordered the cannons to be withdrawn from the Pont-Neuf ;   none ventured to disobey him.   It seems certain, then, the old Staff, so long doomed, has finally been dissolved, in these hours ;   and Mandat is not our Commandant now, but Santerre ?   Yes, friends :   Santerre henceforth,—surely Mandat no more !   The Squadrons that were to charge see nothing certain, except that they are cold, hungry, worn down with watching ;   that it were sad to slay French brothers ;   sadder to be slain by them.   Without the Tuileries Circuit, and within it, sour uncertain humour sways these men :   only the red Swiss stand steadfast.   Them their officers refresh now with a slight wetting of brandy ;   wherein the Nationals, too far gone for brandy, refuse to participate.

King Louis meanwhile had laid him down for a little sleep ;   his wig when he reappeared had lost the powder on one side.[1]   Old Marshal Maillé and the gentlemen in black rise always in spirits, as the Insurrection does not rise :   there goes a witty saying now, ' *Le tocsin ne rend pas* '.   The tocsin, like a dry milk-cow, does not yield.   For the rest, could not one proclaim Martial Law ?   Not easily ;   for now, it seems, Mayor Pétion is gone.   On the other hand, our Interim Commandant, poor Mandat being off ' to the Hôtel-de-Ville ', complains that so many Courtiers in black encumber the service, are an eyesorrow to the National Guards.   To which her Majesty answers with emphasis, That they will obey all, will suffer all, that they are sure men these.

[1] Roederer, *ubi supra*.

And so the yellow lamplight dies out in the grey of morning, in the King's Palace, over such a scene. Scene of jostling, elbowing, of confusion, and indeed conclusion, for the thing is about to end. Roederer and spectral Ministers jostle in the press; consult, in side-cabinets, with one or with both Majesties. Sister Elizabeth takes the Queen to the window: ' Sister, see what a beautiful sunrise ', right over the Jacobins Church and that quarter ! How happy if the tocsin did not yield ! But Mandat returns not; Pétion is gone: much hangs wavering in the invisible Balance. About five o'clock, there rises from the Garden a kind of sound; as of a shout which had become a howl, and instead of *Vive le Roi* were ending in *Vive la Nation*. '*Mon Dieu !*' ejaculates a spectral Minister, ' what is he doing down there ? ' For it is his Majesty, gone down with old Marshal Maillé to review the troops; and the nearest companies of them answer *so*. Her Majesty bursts into a stream of tears. Yet on stepping from the cabinet, her eyes are dry and calm, her look is even cheerful. ' The Austrian lip, and the aquiline nose, fuller than usual, gave to her countenance ', says Peltier,[1] ' something of majesty, which they that did not see her in these moments cannot well have an idea of '. O thou Theresa's Daughter !

King Louis enters, much blown with the fatigue; but for the rest with his old air of indifference. Of all hopes now, surely the joyfullest were, that the tocsin did not yield.

[1] In Toulongeon, ii. 241.

CHAPTER VII

THE SWISS

UNHAPPY Friends, the tocsin does yield, has yielded !
Lo ye, how with the first sunrays its Ocean-tide, of pikes
and fusils, flows glittering from the far East ;—immeasurable ; born of the Night ! They march there, the
grim host ; Saint-Antoine on this side the River ; Saint-
Marceau on that, the blackbrowed Marseillese in the
van. With hum, and grim murmur, far-heard ; like
the Ocean-tide, as we say : drawn up, as if by Luna and
Influences, from the great Deep of Waters, they roll
gleaming on ; no King, Canute*or Louis, can bid them
roll back. Wide-eddying side-currents, of onlookers,
roll hither and thither, unarmed, not voiceless ; they,
the steel host, roll on. New-Commandant Santerre,
indeed, has taken seat at the Townhall ; rests there, in
his halfway-house. Alsatian Westermann, with flashing sabre, does not rest ; nor the Sections, nor the Marseillese, nor Demoiselle Théroigne ; but roll continually
on.

And now, where are Mandat's Squadrons that were
to charge ? Not a Squadron of them stirs : or they stir
in the wrong direction, out of the way ; their officers
glad that they will even do that. It is to this hour uncertain whether the Squadron on the Pont-Neuf made
the shadow of resistance, or did not make the shadow :
enough, the blackbrowed Marseillese, and Saint-Marceau following them, do cross without let ; do cross, in
sure hope now of Saint-Antoine and the rest ; do billow
on, towards the Tuileries, where their errand is. The
Tuileries, at sound of them, rustles responsive : the
red Swiss look to their priming ; Courtiers in black draw
their blunderbusses, rapiers, poniards, some have even
fire-shovels ; every man his weapon of war.

Judge if, in these circumstances, Syndic Roederer
felt easy ! Will the kind Heavens open no middle-

course of refuge for a poor Syndic who halts between
two ?   If indeed his Majesty would consent to go over
to the Assembly !   His Majesty, above all her Majesty,
cannot agree to that.   Did her Majesty answer the proposal with a ' *Fi donc* ' ; did she say even, she would
be nailed to the walls sooner ?   Apparently not.   It is
written also that she offered the King a pistol ; saying,
Now or else never was the time to show himself.   Close
eye-witnesses did not see it, nor do we.   They saw only
that she was queenlike, quiet ; that she argued not,
upbraided not, with the Inexorable ; but, like Caesar in
the Capitol,* wrapped her mantle, as it beseems Queens
and Sons of Adam to do.   But thou, O Louis ! of what
stuff art thou at all ?   Is there no stroke in thee, then,
for Life and Crown ?   The silliest hunted deer dies
not so.   Art thou the languidest of all mortals ; or the
mildest-minded ?   Thou art the worst-starred.

The tide advances ; Syndic Roederer's and all men's
straits grow straiter and straiter.   Fremescent clangour
comes from the armed Nationals in the Court ; far and
wide is the infinite hubbub of tongues.   What counsel ?
And the tide is now nigh !   Messengers, forerunners
speak hastily through the outer Grates ; hold parley
sitting astride the walls.   Syndic Roederer goes out and
comes in.   Cannoneers ask him : Are we to fire against
the people ?   King's Ministers ask him : Shall the
King's House be forced ?   Syndic Roederer has a hard
game to play.   He speaks to the Cannoneers with eloquence, with fervour ; such fervour as a man can, who
has to blow hot and cold in one breath.   Hot and cold,
O Roederer ?   We, for our part, cannot live *and* die !
The Cannoneers, by way of answer, fling down their
linstocks.—Think of this answer, O King Louis, and
King's Ministers ; and take a poor Syndic's safe middle-
course, towards the Salle de Manége.   King Louis sits,
his hands leant on his knees, body bent forward ; gazes
for a space fixedly on Syndic Roederer ; then answers,
looking over his shoulder to the Queen : *Marchons !*
They march ; King Louis, Queen, Sister Elizabeth, the
two royal children and governess : these, with Syndic

Roederer, and Officials of the Department; amid a
double rank of National Guards. The men with blunderbusses, the steady red Swiss gaze mournfully, reproachfully; but hear only these words from Syndic
Roederer: 'The King is going to the Assembly; make
way'. It has struck eight, on all clocks, some minutes
ago: the King has left the Tuileries—for ever.

O ye stanch Swiss, ye gallant gentlemen in black,
for what a cause are ye to spend and be spent !* Look
out from the western windows, ye may see King Louis
placidly hold on his way; the poor little Prince Royal
' sportfully kicking the fallen leaves '. Fremesçent multitude on the Terrace of the Feuillants whirls parallel
to him; one man in it, very noisy, with a long pole:
will they not obstruct the outer Staircase, and back-
entrance of the Salle, when it comes to that ? King's
Guards can go no further than the bottom step there.
Lo, Deputation of Legislators come out; he of the long
pole is stilled by oratory; Assembly's Guards join themselves to King's Guards, and all may mount in this case
of necessity; the outer Staircase is free, or passable.
See, Royalty ascends; a blue Grenadier lifts the poor
little Prince Royal from the press; Royalty has entered
in. Royalty has vanished for ever from your eyes.—
And ye? Left standing there, amid the yawning abysses,
and earthquake of Insurrection; without course; without command: if ye perish, it must be as more than
martyrs, as martyrs who are now without a cause ! The
black Courtiers disappear mostly; through such issues
as they can. The poor Swiss know not how to act: one
duty only is clear to them, that of standing by their
post; and they will perform that.

But the glittering steel tide has arrived; it beats
now against the Château barriers, and eastern Courts;
irresistible, loud-surging far and wide;—breaks in, fills
the Court of the Carrousel, blackbrowed Marseillese in
the van. King Louis gone, say you; over to the Assembly ! Well and good : but till the Assembly pronounce
Forfeiture of him, what boots it ? Our post is in that
Château or stronghold of his; there till then must we

continue. Think, ye stanch Swiss, whether it were good
that grim murder began, and brothers blasted one
another in pieces for a stone edifice ?—Poor Swiss !
they know not how to act : from the southern windows,
some fling cartridges, in sign of brotherhood ; on the
eastern outer staircase, and within through long stairs
and corridors, they stand firm-ranked, peaceable and
yet refusing to stir. Westermann speaks to them in
Alsatian German ; Marseillese plead, in hot Provençal
speech and pantomime ; stunning hubbub pleads and
threatens, infinite, around. The Swiss stand fast, peaceable and yet immovable ; red granite pier in that waste-
flashing sea of steel.

Who can help the inevitable issue ; Marseillese and
all France on this side ; granite Swiss on that ? The
pantomime grows hotter and hotter ; Marseillese sabres
flourishing by way of action ; the Swiss brow also clouding itself, the Swiss thumb bringing its firelock to the
cock. And hark ! high thundering above all the din,
three Marseillese cannon from the Carrousel, pointed
by a gunner of bad aim, come rattling over the roofs !
Ye Swiss, therefore : *Fire !* The Swiss fire ; by volley,
by platoon, in rolling-fire : Marseillese men not a few,
and ' a tall man that was louder than any ', lie silent,
smashed upon the pavement ;—not a few Marseillese,
after the long dusty march, have made halt *here.* The
Carrousel is void ; the black tide recoiling ; ' fugitives
rushing as far as Saint-Antoine before they stop '. The
Cannoneers without linstock have squatted invisible,
and left their cannon ; which the Swiss seize.

Think what a volley : reverberating doomful to the
four corners of Paris, and through all hearts ; like the
clang of Bellona's thongs !* The blackbrowed Marseil-
lese, rallying on the instant, have become black Demons
that know how to die. Nor is Brest behindhand ; nor
Alsatian Westermann ; Demoiselle Théroigne is Sibyl
Théroigne : Vengeance, *Victoire ou la mort !* From all
Patriot artillery, great and small ; from Feuillants
Terrace, and all terraces and places of the widespread
Insurrectionary sea, there roars responsive a red blazing

whirlwind. Blue Nationals, ranked in the Garden,
cannot help their muskets going off, *against* Foreign
murderers. For there is a sympathy in muskets, in
heaped masses of men : nay, are not Mankind, in whole,
like tuned strings, and a cunning infinite concordance
and unity ; you smite one string, and all strings will
begin sounding,—in soft sphere-melody, in deafening
screech of madness ! Mounted Gendarmerie gallop distracted ; are fired on merely as a thing running ; galloping over the Pont Royal, or one knows not whither.
The brain of Paris, brain-fevered in the centre of it here,
has gone mad ; what you call, taken fire.

Behold, the fire slackens not ; nor does the Swiss
rolling-fire slacken from within. Nay they clutched
cannon, as we saw ; and now, from the other side, they
clutch three pieces more ; alas, cannon without linstock;
nor will the steel-and-flint answer, though they try it.[1]
Had it chanced to answer ! Patriot onlookers have their
misgivings ; one strangest Patriot onlooker thinks that
the Swiss, had they a commander, would beat. He is
a man not unqualified to judge ; the name of him
Napoleon Bonaparte.[2] And onlookers, and women,
stand gazing, and the witty Dr. Moore* of Glasgow
among them, on the other side of the River : cannon
rush rumbling past them ; pause on the Pont Royal ;
belch out their iron entrails there, against the Tuileries ;
and at every new belch, the women and onlookers
' shout and clap hands '.[3] City of all the Devils ! In
remote streets, men are drinking breakfast-coffee ; following their affairs ; with a start now and then, as some
dull echo reverberates a note louder. And here ? Marseillese fall wounded ; but Barbaroux has surgeons ;
Barbaroux is close by, managing, though underhand,
and under cover. Marseillese fall death-struck ; bequeath their firelock, specify in which pocket are the cartridges ; and die, murmuring, ' Revenge me, Revenge

[1] Deux Amis, viii. 179–88.
[2] See Hist. Parl. xvii. 56 ; Las Cases, &c.
[3] Moore, Journal during a Residence in France (Dublin,
1793), i. 26.

thy country ! ' Brest Fédéré Officers, galloping in red
coats, are shot as Swiss. Lo you, the Carrousel has
burst into flame !—Paris Pandemonium ! Nay the
poor City, as we said, is in fever-fit and convulsion :
such crisis has lasted for the space of some half hour.

But what is this that, with Legislative Insignia, ventures through the hubbub and death-hail, from the back-
entrance of the Manége ? Towards the Tuileries and
Swiss : written Order from his Majesty to cease firing !
O ye hapless Swiss, why was there no order not to begin
it ? Gladly would the Swiss cease firing : but who will
bid mad Insurrection cease firing ? To Insurrection
you cannot speak ; neither can it, hydraheaded, hear.
The dead and dying, by the hundred, lie all around ;
are borne bleeding through the streets, towards help ;
the sight of them, like a torch of the Furies, kindling
Madness. Patriot Paris roars ; as the bear bereaved
of her whelps. On, ye Patriots : Vengeance ! Victory
or death ! There are men seen, who rush on, armed
only with walking-sticks.[1] Terror and Fury rule the
hour.

The Swiss, pressed on from without, paralysed from
within, have ceased to shoot ; but not to be shot. What
shall they do ? Desperate is the moment. Shelter or
instant death : yet How, Where ? One party flies
out by the Rue de l'Echelle ; is destroyed utterly, ' en
entier '. A second, by the other side, throws itself into
the Garden ; ' hurrying across a keen fusillade ' ; rushes
suppliant into the National Assembly ; finds pity and
refuge in the back benches there. The third, and
largest, darts out in column, three hundred strong,
towards the Champs Elysées : Ah, could we but reach
Courbevoye, where other Swiss are ! Woe ! see, in such
fusillade the column ' soon breaks itself by diversity of
opinion ', into distracted segments, this way and that ;
—to escape in holes, to die fighting from street to street.

---

[1] Hist. Parl. *ubi supra* ; Rapport du Capitaine des
Canonniers, Rapport du Commandant, &c. (Ibid. xvii.
300-18).

The firing and murdering will not cease; not yet for long. The red Porters of Hôtels are shot at, be they *Suisse* by nature, or *Suisse* only in name. The very Firemen, who pump and labour on that smoking Carrousel, are shot at: why should the Carrousel *not* burn? Some Swiss take refuge in private houses; find that mercy too does still dwell in the heart of man. The brave Marseillese are merciful, late so wroth; and labour to save. Journalist Gorsas pleads hard with infuriated groups. Clemence, the Wine-merchant, stumbles forward to the Bar of the Assembly, a rescued Swiss in his hand; tells passionately how he rescued him with pain and peril, how he will henceforth support him, being childless himself; and falls a-swoon round the poor Swiss's neck: amid plaudits. But the most are butchered, and even mangled. Fifty (some say Fourscore) were marched as prisoners, by National Guards, to the Hôtel-de-Ville: the ferocious people bursts through on them, in the Place-de-Grève; massacres them to the last man. '*O Peuple*, envy of the universe!' *Peuple*, in mad Gaelic effervescence!

Surely few things in the history of carnage are painfuller. What ineffaceable red streak, flickering so sad in the memory, is that, of this poor column of red Swiss ' breaking itself in the confusion of opinions '; dispersing, into blackness and death! Honour to you, brave men; honourable pity, through long times! Not martyrs were ye; and yet almost more. He was no King of yours, this Louis; and he forsook you like a King of shreds and patches*: ye were but sold to him for some poor sixpence a-day; yet would ye work for your wages, keep your plighted word. The work now was to die; and ye did it. Honour to you, O Kinsmen; and may the old Deutsch *Biederkeit* and *Tapferkeit*,* and Valour which is *Worth* and *Truth*, be they Swiss, be they Saxon, fail in no age! Not bastards; true-born were these men: sons of the men of Sempach, of Murten,* who knelt, but not to thee, O Burgundy!—Let the traveller, as he passes through Lucerne, turn aside to look a little at their monumental Lion; not for Thorwaldsen's*sake

alone. Hewn out of living rock, the Figure rests there,
by the still Lake-waters, in lullaby of distant-tinkling
rance-des-vaches, the granite Mountains dumbly keeping
watch all round ; and, though inanimate, speaks.

CHAPTER VIII

CONSTITUTION BURST IN PIECES

THUS is the Tenth of August won and lost. Patriotism
reckons its slain by the thousand on thousand, so deadly
was the Swiss fire from these windows ; but will finally
reduce them to some Twelve-hundred. No child's-play
was it ;—nor is it ! Till two in the afternoon the massacring, the breaking and the burning has not ended ;
nor the loose Bedlam shut itself again.

How deluges of frantic Sansculottism roared through
all passages of this Tuileries, ruthless in vengeance ; how
the Valets were butchered, hewn down ; and Dame
Campan saw the Marseillese sabre flash over her head,
but the Blackbrowed said, '*Va-t-en*, Get thee gone',
and flung her from him unstruck ; [1] how in the cellars
wine-bottles were broken, wine-butts were staved in and
drunk ; and, upwards to the very garrets, all windows
tumbled out their precious royal furnitures : and, with
gold mirrors, velvet curtains, down of ripped featherbeds, and dead bodies of men, the Tuileries was like no
Garden of the Earth :—all this let him who has a taste
for it see amply in Mercier, in acrid Montgaillard,* or
Beaulieu of the *Deux Amis*. A hundred and eighty
bodies of Swiss lie piled there ; naked, unremoved till
the second day. Patriotism has torn their red coats
into snips ; and marches with them at the Pike's point :
the ghastly bare corpses lie there, under the sun and
under the stars ; the curious of both sexes crowding to
look. Which let not us do. Above a hundred carts,

[1] Campan, ii. c. 21.

heaped with Dead, fare towards the Cemetery of Sainte-
Madeleine ; bewailed, bewept ; for all had kindred, all
had mothers, if not here, then there. It is one of those
Carnage-fields, such as you read of by the name 'Glorious
Victory ', brought home in this case to one's own door.

But the blackbrowed Marseillese have struck down
the tyrant of the Château. He is struck down ; low,
and hardly again to rise. What a moment for an august
Legislative was that when the Hereditary Representative entered, under such circumstances ; and the Grenadier, carrying the little Prince Royal out of the press, set
him down on the Assembly-table ! A moment,—which
one had to smooth off with oratory ; waiting what the
next would bring ! Louis said few words : ' He was
come hither to prevent a great crime ; he believed himself safer nowhere than here '. President Vergniaud
answered briefly, in vague oratory as we say, about
'defence of Constituted Authorities ', about dying at
our post.[1] And so King Louis sat him down ; first here,
then there ; for a difficulty arose, the Constitution not
permitting us to debate while the King is present :
finally he settles himself with his Family in the ' Loge
of the Logographe', in the Reporter's-Box of a Journalist;
which is beyond the enchanted Constitutional Circuit,
separated from it by a rail. To such Lodge of the Logographe, measuring some ten feet square, with a small
closet at the entrance of it behind, is the King of
broad France now limited : here can he and his sit pent,
under the eyes of the world, or retire into their closet at
intervals ; for the space of sixteen hours. Such quite
peculiar moment has the Legislative lived to see.

But also what a moment was that other, few minutes
later, when the three Marseillese cannon went off, and
the Swiss rolling-fire and universal thunder, like the
crack of Doom, began to rattle ! Honourable Members
start to their feet ; stray bullets singing epicedium even
here, shivering in with window-glass and jingle. ' No,

[1] Moniteur, Séance du 10 Août 1792.

this is our post; let us die here!' They sit therefore,
like stone Legislators. But may not the Loge of the
Logographe be forced from behind? Tear down the
railing that divides it from the enchanted Constitutional
Circuit! Ushers tear and tug; his Majesty himself
aiding from within: the railing gives way; Majesty and
Legislative are united in place, unknown Destiny hovering over both.

Rattle, and again rattle, went the thunder; one
breathless wide-eyed messenger rushing in after another:
King's order to the Swiss went out. It was a fearful
thunder; but, as we know, it ended. Breathless messengers, fugitive Swiss, denunciatory Patriots, trepidation; finally tripudiation!—Before four o'clock much
has come and gone.

The New Municipals have come and gone; with
Three Flags, *Liberté, Egalité, Patrie,* and the clang of
vivats. Vergniaud, he who as President few hours ago
talked of dying for Constituted Authorities, has moved,
as Committee-Reporter, that the Hereditary Representative *be suspended*; that a NATIONAL CONVENTION do
forthwith assemble to say what further! An able Report; which the President must have had ready in his
pocket? A President, in such cases, must have much
ready, and yet not ready; and Janus-like look before
and after.

King Louis listens to all; retires about midnight ' to
three little rooms on the upper floor '; till the Luxembourg be prepared for him, and ' the safeguard of the
Nation '. Safer if Brunswick were once here! Or, alas,
not so safe? Ye hapless discrowned heads! Crowds
came, next morning, to catch a glimpse of them, in their
three upper rooms. Montgaillard says the august
Captives wore an air of cheerfulness, even of gaiety;
that the Queen and Princess Lamballe, who had joined
her overnight, looked out of the opened window,
' shook powder from their hair on the people below and
laughed '.[1] He is an acrid distorted man.

---

[1] Montgaillard, ii. 135–67.

For the rest, one may guess that the Legislative, above all that the New Municipality continues busy. Messengers, Municipal or Legislative, and swift dispatches rush off to all corners of France; full of triumph, blended with indignant wail, for Twelve-hundred have fallen. France sends up its blended shout responsive; the Tenth of August shall be as the Fourteenth of July, only bloodier and greater. The Court has conspired? Poor Court: the Court has been vanquished; and will have both the scath to bear and the scorn. How the statues of Kings do now all fall! Bronze Henri himself, though he wore a cockade once, jingles down from the Pont Neuf, where *Patrie* floats *in Danger*. Much more does Louis Fourteenth, from the Place Vendôme, jingle down; and even breaks in falling. The curious can remark, written on his horse's shoe: ' 12 *Août* 1692 '; a Century and a Day.

The Tenth of August was Friday. The week is not done, when our old Patriot Ministry is recalled, what of it can be got: strict Roland, Genevese Clavière; add heavy Monge the Mathematician, once a stone-hewer; and, for Minister of Justice,—Danton, 'led hither', as himself says, in one of his gigantic figures, ' through the breach of Patriot cannon! ' These, under Legislative Committees, must rule the wreck as they can: confusedly enough; with an old Legislative water-logged, with a new Municipality so brisk. But National Convention will get itself together; and *then* ! Without delay, however, let a new Jury-Court and Criminal Tribunal be set up in Paris, to try the crimes and conspiracies of the Tenth. High Court of Orléans is distant, slow: the blood of the Twelve-hundred Patriots, whatever become of other blood, shall be inquired after. Tremble, ye Criminals and Conspirators; the Minister of Justice is Danton! Robespierre too, after the victory, sits in the New Municipality; insurrectionary ' improvised Municipality ', which calls itself Council General of the Commune.

For three days now, Louis and his Family have

heard the Legislative Debates in the Lodge of the
Logographe ; and retired nightly to their small upper
rooms. The Luxembourg and safeguard of the Nation
could not be got ready : nay, it seems the Luxembourg
has too many cellars and issues ; no Municipality can
undertake to watch it. The compact Prison of the
Temple, not so elegant indeed, were much safer. To
the Temple, therefore ! On Monday, 13th day of August
1792, in Mayor Pétion's carriage, Louis and his sad
suspended Household fare thither ; all Paris out to
look at them. As they pass through the Place Vendôme, Louis Fourteenth's Statue lies broken on the
ground. Pétion is afraid the Queen's looks may be
thought scornful, and produce provocation ; she casts
down her eyes, and does not look at all. The ' press is
prodigious ', but quiet : here and there, it shouts *Vive
la Nation* ; but for most part gazes in silence. French
Royalty vanishes within the gates of the Temple : these
old peaked Towers, like peaked Extinguisher or *Bon-
soir*, do cover it up ;—from which same Towers, poor
Jacques Molay* and his Templars were burnt out, by
French Royalty, five centuries since. Such are the
turns of Fate below. Foreign Ambassadors, English
Lord Gower have all demanded passports ; are driving
indignantly towards their respective homes.

So, then, the Constitution is over ? For ever and a
day !* Gone is that wonder of the Universe ; First biennial Parliament, water-logged, waits only till the Convention come ; and will then sink to endless depths.
One can guess the silent rage of Old-Constituents, Constitution-builders, extinct Feuillants, men who thought
the Constitution would march ! Lafayette rises to the
altitude of the situation ; at the head of his Army.
Legislative Commissioners are posting towards him
and it, on the Northern Frontier, to congratulate and
perorate : he orders the Municipality of Sedan to arrest
these Commissioners, and keep them strictly in ward
as Rebels, till he say further. The Sedan Municipals
obey.

The Sedan Municipals obey: but the Soldiers of the
Lafayette Army ? The Soldiers of the Lafayette Army
have, as all Soldiers have, a kind of dim feeling that
they themselves are Sansculottes in buff belts ; that the
victory of the Tenth of August is also a victory for
them. They will not rise and follow Lafayette to
Paris ; they will rise and *send* him thither ! On the
18th, which is but next Saturday, Lafayette, with some
two or three indignant Staff-officers, one of whom is
Old-Constituent Alexandre de Lameth, having first put
his Lines in what order he could,—rides swiftly over
the Marches, towards Holland. Rides, alas, swiftly
into the claws of Austrians ! He, long wavering, trembling on the verge of the Horizon, has set, in Olmutz
Dungeons ; this History knows him no more. Adieu,
thou Hero of two Worlds ; thinnest, but compact
honour-worthy man ! Through long rough night of captivity, through other tumults, triumphs and changes,
thou wilt swing well, ' fast-anchored to the Washington
Formula ' ; and be the Hero and Perfect-character,
were it only of one idea. The Sedan Municipals repent
and protest ; the Soldiers shout *Vive la Nation.* Dumouriez Polymetis, from his Camp at Maulde, sees
himself made Commander-in-Chief.

And, O Brunswick ! what sort of ' military execution ' will Paris merit now ? Forward, ye well-drilled
exterminatory men ; with your artillery-wagons, and
camp-kettles jingling. Forward, tall chivalrous King
of Prussia ; fanfaronading Emigrants and war-god
Broglie, ' for some consolation to mankind ', which verily
is not without need of some.

PART III
THE GUILLOTINE

Alle Freiheits-Apostel, sie waren mir immer zuwider;
　Willkür suchte doch nur Jeder am Ende für sich.
Willst du Viele befrein, so wag' es Vielen zu dienen.
　Wie gefährlich das sey, willst du es wissen? Versuch's!

Goethe.*

BOOK I

SEPTEMBER

CHAPTER I

THE IMPROVISED COMMUNE

YE have roused her, then, ye Emigrants and Despots of the world; France is roused! Long have ye been lecturing and tutoring this poor Nation, like cruel uncalled-for pedagogues, shaking over her your ferulas of fire and steel: it is long that ye have pricked and fillipped and affrighted her, there as she sat helpless in her dead cerements of a Constitution, you gathering in on her from all lands, with your armaments and plots, your invadings and truculent bullyings;—and lo now, ye have pricked her to the quick, and she is up, and her blood is up. The dead cerements are rent into cobwebs, and she fronts you in that terrible strength of Nature, which no man has measured, which goes down to Madness and Tophet: see now how ye will deal with her.

This month of September 1792, which has become one of the memorable months of History, presents itself under two most diverse aspects; all of black on the one side, all of bright on the other. Whatsoever is cruel in the panic frenzy of Twenty-five million men, whatsoever is great in the simultaneous death-defiance of Twenty-five million men, stand here in abrupt contrast, near by one another. As indeed is usual when a man, how much more when a Nation of men, is hurled suddenly beyond the limits. For Nature, as green as

she looks, rests everywhere on dread foundations, were
we further down ; and Pan, to whose music the Nymphs*
dance, has a cry in him that can drive all men distracted.

Very frightful it is when a Nation, rending asunder
its Constitutions and Regulations which were grown
dead cerements for it, becomes *trans*cendental ; and
must now seek its wild way through the New, Chaotic,—
where Force is not yet distinguished into Bidden and
Forbidden, but Crime and Virtue welter unseparated,—
in that domain of what is called the Passions ; of what
we call the Miracles and the Portents ! It is thus that,
for some three years to come, we are to contemplate
France, in this final Third Volume of our History.
Sansculottism reigning in all its grandeur and in all its
hideousness : the Gospel (God's-Message) of Man's
Rights, Man's *mights* or strengths, once more preached
irrefragably abroad ; along with this, and still louder
for the time, the fearfullest Devil's-Message of Man's
weaknesses and sins ;—and all on such a scale, and under
such aspect : cloudy ' death-birth of a world ' : huge
smoke-cloud, streaked with rays as of heaven on one
side ; girt on the other as with hell-fire ! History tells
us many things : but for the last thousand years and
more, what thing has she told us of a sort like this ?
Which therefore let us two, O Reader, dwell on willingly,
for a little ; and from its endless significance endeavour
to extract what may, in present circumstances, be
adapted for us.

It is unfortunate, though very natural, that the history of this Period has so generally been written in
hysterics. Exaggeration abounds, execration, wailing ;
and, on the whole, darkness. But thus too, when foul
old Rome had to be swept from the Earth, and those
Northmen, and other horrid sons of Nature, came in,
' swallowing formulas ' as the French now do, foul old
Rome screamed execratively her loudest ; so that the
true shape of many things is lost for us. Attila's Huns
had arms of such length that they could lift a stone
without stooping. Into the body of the poor Tatars
execrative Roman History intercalated an alphabetic

letter ; and so they continue Tartars, of fell Tartarean nature, to this day. Here, in like manner, search as we will in these multiform innumerable French Records, darkness too frequently covers, or sheer distraction bewilders. One finds it difficult to imagine that the Sun shone in this September month, as he does in others. Nevertheless it is an indisputable fact that the Sun did shine ; and there was weather and work,—nay, as to that, very bad weather for harvest-work ! An unlucky Editor may do his utmost ; and after all, require allowances.

He had been a wise Frenchman, who, looking close at hand on this waste aspect of France all stirring and whirling, in ways new, untried, had been able to discern where the cardinal movement lay ; which tendency it was that had the rule and primary direction of it then ! But at forty-four years' distance, it is different. To all men now, two cardinal movements or grand tendencies, in the September whirl, have become discernible enough : that stormful effluence towards the Frontiers ; that frantic crowding towards Townhouses and Council-halls in the interior. Wild France dashes, in desperate death-defiance, towards the Frontiers, to defend itself from foreign Despots ; crowds towards Townhalls and Election Committee-rooms, to defend itself from domestic Aristocrats. Let the Reader conceive well these two cardinal movements ; and what side-currents and endless vortexes might depend on these. He shall judge too, whether, in such sudden wreckage of all old Authorities, such a pair of cardinal movements, half-frantic in themselves, could be of soft nature ? As in dry Sahara, when the winds waken, and lift and winnow the immensity of sand ! The air itself (Travellers say) is a dim sand-air ; and dim looming through it, the wonderfullest uncertain colonnades of Sand-Pillars rush whirling from this side and from that, like so many mad Spinning-Dervishes, of a hundred feet in stature ; and dance their huge Desert-waltz there !—

Nevertheless, in all human movements, were they

but a day old, there is order, or the beginning of order. Consider two things in this Sahara-waltz of the French Twenty-five millions ; or rather one thing, and one hope of a thing ; the *Commune* (Municipality) of Paris, which is already here ; the National Convention,* which shall in few weeks be here. The Insurrectionary Commune, which, improvising itself on the eve of the Tenth of August, worked this ever-memorable Deliverance by explosion, must needs rule over it,—till the Convention meet. This Commune, which they may well call a spontaneous or 'improvised' Commune, is, for the present, sovereign of France. The Legislative, deriving its authority from the Old, how can *it* now have authority when the Old is exploded by insurrection ? As a floating piece of wreck, certain things, persons and interests may still cleave to it : volunteer defenders, riflemen or pikemen in green uniform, or red nightcap (of *bonnet rouge*), defile before it daily, just on the wing towards Brunswick ; with the brandishing of arms ; always with some touch of Leonidas-eloquence, often with a fire of daring that threatens to outherod Herod;* —the Galleries, ' especially the Ladies, never done with applauding '.[1] Addresses of this or the like sort can be received and answered, in the hearing of all France ; the Salle de Manége is still useful as a place of proclamation. For which use, indeed, it now chiefly serves. Vergniaud delivers spirit-stirring orations ; but always with a prophetic sense only, looking towards the coming Convention. ' Let our memory perish ', cries Vergniaud, 'but let France be free !'—whereupon they all start to their feet, shouting responsive : ' Yes, yes, *périsse notre mémoire, pourvu que la France soit libre !* '[2] Disfrocked Chabot adjures Heaven that at least we may ' have done with Kings ' ; and fast as powder under spark, we all blaze up once more, and with waved hats shout and swear : ' Yes, *nous le jurons ; plus de rois !* '[3] All which, as a method of proclamation, is very convenient.

[1] Moore's Journal, i. 85.   [2] Hist. Parl. xvii. 467.
[3] Ibid. xvii. 437.

For the rest, that our busy Brissots, rigorous Rolands,
men who once had authority, and now have less and
less ; men who love law, and will have even an Explosion explode itself as far as possible according to rule,
do find this state of matters most unofficial-unsatis-
factory,—is not to be denied. Complaints are made ;
attempts are made : but without effect. The attempts
even recoil ; and must be desisted from, for fear of
worse : the sceptre has departed from this Legislative
once and always. A poor Legislative, so hard was fate,
had let itself be hand-gyved, nailed to the rock like an
Andromeda,* and could only wail there to the Earth and
Heavens ; miraculously a winged Perseus (or Improvised Commune) has dawned out of the void Blue, and
cut her loose : but whether now is it she, with her
softness and musical speech, or is it he, with his hard-
ness and sharp falchion and aegis, that shall have cast-
ing-vote ? Melodious *agreement* of vote ; this were the
rule ! But if otherwise, and votes diverge, then surely
Andromeda's part is to weep,—if possible, tears of gratitude alone.

Be content, O France, with this Improvised Commune, such as it is ! It has the implements, and has
the hands : the time is not long. On Sunday the
twenty-sixth of August, our Primary Assemblies shall
meet, begin electing of Electors ; on Sunday the second
of September (may the day prove lucky !) the Electors
shall begin electing Deputies ; and so an all-healing
National Convention will come together. No *marc
d'argent,* or distinction of Active and Passive, now insults
the French Patriot : but there is universal suffrage, unlimited liberty to choose. Old-Constituents, Present-
Legislators, all France is eligible. Nay, it may be
said, the flower of all the Universe (*de l'Univers*) is
eligible; for in these very days we, by Act of Assembly,
'naturalize' the chief Foreign Friends of Humanity :
Priestley, burnt out for us in Birmingham ; Klopstock,*
genius of all countries ; Jeremy Bentham,* a useful Juris-
consult; distinguished Paine, the rebellious Needleman;
—some of whom may be chosen. As is most fit; for

a Convention of this kind. In a word, Seven-hundred and Forty-five unshackled sovereigns, admired of the universe, shall replace this hapless impotency of a Legislative,—out of which, it is likely, the best Members, and the Mountain in mass, may be re-elected. Roland is getting ready the *Salle des Cent Suisses*, as preliminary rendezvous for them; in that void Palace of the Tuileries, now void and National, and not a Palace, but a Caravansera.

As for the Spontaneous Commune, one may say that there never was on Earth a stranger Town-Council. Administration, not of a great City, but of a great Kingdom in a state of revolt and frenzy, this is the task that has fallen to it. Enrolling, provisioning, judging; devising, deciding, doing, endeavouring to do: one wonders the human brain did not give way under all this, and reel. But happily human brains have such a talent of taking up simply what they can carry, and ignoring all the rest; leaving all the rest, as if it were not there! Whereby somewhat is verily shifted for; and much shifts for itself. This Improvised Commune walks along, nothing doubting; promptly making front, without fear or flurry, at what moment soever, to the wants of the moment. Were the world on fire, one improvised tricolor Municipal has but one life to lose. They are the elixir and chosen-men of Sansculottic Patriotism; promoted to the forlorn-hope; unspeakable victory or a high gallows, this is their meed. They sit there, in the Townhall, these astonishing tricolor Municipals; in Council General; in Committee of Watchfulness (*de Surveillance*,* which will even become *de Salut Public*, of Public Salvation), or what other Committees and Subcommittees are needful;—managing infinite Correspondence; passing infinite Decrees: one hears of a Decree being 'the ninety-eighth of the day'. Ready! is the word. They carry loaded pistols in their pocket; also some improvised luncheon by way of meal. Or indeed, by and by, *traiteurs* contract for the supply of repasts, to be eaten on the spot,—too lavishly, as it was afterwards grumbled. Thus they: girt in their tricolor sashes; Municipal note-paper in the one hand, fire-arms in the other. They have their Agents out all over France; speaking in townhouses, market-places, high-ways and byways; agitating, urging to arm; all hearts tingling to hear. Great is the fire of Anti-Aristocrat eloquence: nay some, as Bibliopolic Momoro, seem to hint afar off at something which smells of Agrarian Law, and a surgery of the overswoln dropsical strongbox itself;—whereat indeed the bold Bookseller runs risk of being hanged, and Ex-Constituent Buzot has to smuggle him off.[1]

Governing Persons, were they never so insignificant intrinsically, have for most part plenty of Memoir-writers; and the curious, in after-times, can learn minutely their goings out and comings in: which, as men always love to know their fellow-men in singular situations, is a comfort, of its kind. Not so with these Governing Persons, now in the Townhall! And yet what most original fellow-man, of the Governing sort, high-chancellor, king, kaiser, secretary of the home or the foreign department, ever showed such a phasis as Clerk Tallien, Procureur Manuel, future Procureur Chaumette, here in this Sand-waltz of the Twenty-five millions now do? O brother mortals,—thou Advocate Panis, friend of Danton, kinsman of Santerre; Engraver Sergent, since called *Agate*-Sergent; thou Huguenin, with the tocsin in thy heart! But, as Horace says, they wanted the sacred memoir-writer (*sacro vate*)*; and we know them not. Men bragged of August and its doings, publishing them in high places; but of this September none now or afterwards would brag. The September world remains dark, fuliginous, as Lapland witch-midnight;—from which, indeed, very strange shapes will evolve themselves.

Understand this, however: that incorruptible Robes-pierre is not wanting, now when the brunt of battle is past; in a stealthy way the seagreen man sits there, his feline eyes excellent in the twilight. Also understand

[1] Mémoires de Buzot (Paris, 1823), p. 88.

this other, a single fact worth many: that Marat is not
only there, but has a seat of honour assigned him, a
tribune particulière. How changed for Marat; lifted
from his dark cellar into this luminous 'peculiar tribune'! All dogs have their day; even rabid dogs.
Sorrowful, incurable Philoctetes*Marat; without whom
Troy cannot be taken! Hither, as a main element of
the Governing Power, has Marat been raised. Royalist
types, for we have 'suppressed' innumerable Durosoys,
Royous, and even clapt them in prison,—Royalist types
replace the worn types often snatched from a People's-
Friend in old ill days. In our 'peculiar tribune' we
write and redact: Placards, of due monitory terror;
Amis-du-Peuple (now under the name of *Journal de la
République*); and sit obeyed of men. 'Marat', says
one, 'is the conscience of the Hôtel-de-Ville'. *Keeper*,
as some call it, of the Sovereign's Conscience; which
surely, in such hands, will not lie hid in a napkin !*

Two great movements, as we said, agitate this distracted National mind: a rushing against domestic
Traitors, a rushing against foreign Despots. Mad movements both, restrainable by no known rule; strongest
passions of human nature driving them on: love,
hatred, vengeful sorrow, braggart Nationality also
vengeful,—and pale Panic over all! Twelve-hundred
slain Patriots, do they not, from their dark catacombs
there, in Death's dumb-show, plead (O ye Legislators)
for vengeance? Such was the destructive rage of these
Aristocrats on the ever-memorable Tenth. Nay, apart
from vengeance, and with an eye to Public Salvation
only, are there not still, in this Paris (in round numbers)
'Thirty-thousand Aristocrats', of the most malignant
humour; driven now to their last trump-card?—Be
patient, ye Patriots: our New High Court, 'Tribunal
of the Seventeenth', sits; each Section has sent Four
Jurymen; and Danton, extinguishing improper judges,
improper practices wheresoever found, is 'the same
man you have known at the Cordeliers'. With such a
Minister of Justice, shall not Justice be done?—Let

it be swift then, answers universal Patriotism; swift and sure !—

One would hope, this Tribunal of the Seventeenth is swifter than most. Already on the 21st, while our Court is but four days old, Collenot d'Angremont, 'the Royalist enlister' (crimp, *embaucheur*), dies by torch-light. For, lo, the great *Guillotine*, wondrous to behold, now stands there; the Doctor's *Idea* has become Oak and Iron; the huge cyclopean axe 'falls in its grooves like the ram of the Pile-engine', swiftly snuffing out the light of men ! ' *Mais vous, Gualches,* what have you invented ? ' *This ?*—Poor old Laporte, Intendant of the Civil List, follows next; quietly, the mild old man. Then Durosoy, Royalist Placarder, 'cashier of all the Anti-Revolutionists of the interior': he went rejoicing ; said that a Royalist like him ought to die, of all days, on this day, the 25th or Saint Louis's Day. All these have been tried, cast,—the Galleries shouting approval ; and handed over to the Realized Idea, within a week. Besides those whom we have acquitted, the Galleries murmuring, and have dismissed; or even have per-sonally guarded back to Prison, as the Galleries took to howling, and even to menacing and elbowing.[1] Languid this Tribunal is not.

Nor does the other movement slacken ; the rushing against foreign Despots. Strong forces shall meet in death-grip; drilled Europe against mad undrilled France ; and singular conclusions will be tried.— Conceive therefore, in some faint degree, the tumult that whirls in this France, in this Paris! Placards from Section, from Commune, from Legislative, from the individual Patriot, flame monitory on all walls. Flags of Danger to Fatherland wave at the Hôtel-de-Ville ; on the Pont Neuf—over the prostrate Statues of Kings. There is universal enlisting, urging to enlist; there is tearful-boastful leave-taking; irregular marching on the Great Northeastern Road. Marseillese sing their wild *To Arms*, in chorus ; which now all men, all women

[1] Moore's Journal, i. 159–68.

and children have learnt, and sing chorally, in Theatres, Boulevards, Streets; and the heart burns in every bosom: *Aux armes ! Marchons !*—Or think how your Aristocrats are skulking into covert; how Bertrand-Moleville lies hidden in some garret 'in Aubry-le-boucher Street, with a poor surgeon who had known me'! Dame de Staël has secreted her Narbonne, not knowing what in the world to make of him. The Barriers are sometimes open, oftenest shut; no passports to be had; Townhall Emissaries, with the eyes and claws of falcons, flitting watchful on all points of your horizon! In two words: Tribunal of the Seventeenth, busy under howling Galleries; Prussian Brunswick, 'over a space of forty miles', with his war-tumbrils, and sleeping thunders, and Briarean 'sixty-six thousand'[1] right hands,—coming, coming!

O Heavens, in these latter days of August, he is come! Durosoy was not yet guillotined when news had come that the Prussians were harrying and ravaging about Metz; in some four days more, one hears that Longwi, our first strong-place on the borders, is fallen 'in fifteen hours'. Quick, therefore, O ye improvised Municipals; quick, and ever quicker!—The improvised Municipals make front to this also. Enrolment urges itself; and clothing, and arming. Our very officers have now 'wool epaulettes'; for it is the reign of Equality, and also of Necessity. Neither do men now *monsieur* and *sir* one another; *citoyen* (citizen) were suitabler; we even say *thou*, as 'the free peoples of Antiquity did': so have Journals and the Improvised Commune suggested; which shall be well.

Infinitely better, meantime, could we suggest, where arms are to be found. For the present, our *Citoyens* chant chorally *To arms*; and have no arms! Arms are searched for; passionately; there is joy over any musket. Moreover, entrenchments shall be made round Paris: on the slopes of Montmartre men dig and shovel; though even the simple suspect this to be desperate. They dig; Tricolor sashes speak encouragement and

[1] See Toulongeon, Hist. de France, ii. c. 5.

well-speed-ye. Nay finally 'twelve Members of the
Legislative go daily', not to encourage only, but to bear
a hand, and delve : it was decreed with acclamation.
Arms shall either be provided ; or else the ingenuity of
man crack itself, and become fatuity.   Lean Beaumarchais, thinking to serve the Fatherland, and do a stroke
of trade in the old way, has commissioned sixty-thousand stand of good arms out of Holland : would to
Heaven, for Fatherland's sake and his, they were come !
Meanwhile railings are torn up ; hammered into pikes ;
chains themselves shall be welded together into pikes.
The very coffins of the dead are raised ; for melting into
balls.   All Church-bells must down into the furnace to
make cannon ; all Church-plate into the mint to make
money.   Also behold the fair swan-bevies of *Citoyennes*
that have alighted in Churches, and sit there with swan-
neck,—sewing tents and regimentals ! Nor are Patriotic
Gifts wanting, from those that have aught left ; nor
stingily given : the fair Villaumes, mother and daughter,
Milliners in the Rue St.-Martin, give a 'silver thimble,
and a coin of fifteen *sous* (sevenpence halfpenny) ', with
other similar effects ; and offer, at least the mother
does, to mount guard.   Men who have not even a
thimble, give a thimbleful,—were it but of invention.
One Citoyen has wrought out the scheme of a wooden
cannon ; which France shall exclusively profit by, in
the first instance.   It is to be made of *staves*, by the
coopers ;—of almost boundless calibre, but uncertain
as to strength ! Thus they : hammering, scheming,
stitching, founding, with all their heart and with all
their soul.   Two bells only are to remain in each Parish,
—for tocsin and other purposes.

But mark also, precisely while the Prussian batteries
were playing their briskest at Longwi in the North-
east, and our dastardly Lavergne saw nothing for it but
surrender,—southwestward, in remote, patriarchal La
Vendée, that sour ferment about Nonjuring Priests,
after long working, is ripe, and explodes : at the wrong
moment for us !   And so we have 'eight-thousand
Peasants at Châtillon-sur-Sèvre ' who will not be bal-

loted for soldiers ; will not have their Curates molested.
To whom Bonchamps, Larochejaquelins, and Seigneurs
enough of a Royalist turn, will join themselves ; with
Stofflets and Charettes ; with Heroes and Chouan*
Smugglers ; and the loyal warmth of a simple people,
blown into flame and fury by theological and seignorial
bellows ! So that there shall be fighting from behind
ditches, death-volleys bursting out of thickets and
ravines of rivers ; huts burning, feet of the pitiful
women hurrying to refuge with their children on their
back ; seed-fields fallow, whitened with human bones ;
—' eighty-thousand, of all ages, ranks, sexes, flying at
once across the Loire ', with wail borne far on the
winds : and in brief, for years coming, such a suite of
scenes as glorious war has not offered in these late ages,
not since our Albigenses* and Crusadings were over,—
save indeed some chance Palatinate,* or so, we might
have to ' burn ', by way of exception. The ' eight-
thousand at Châtillon ' will be got dispelled for the
moment ; the fire scattered, not extinguished. To the
dints and bruises of outward battle there is to be added
henceforth a deadlier internal gangrene.

This rising in La Vendée reports itself at Paris on
Wednesday the 29th of August ;—just as we had got
our Electors elected ; and, in spite of Brunswick and
Longwi, were hoping still to have a National Convention, if it pleased Heaven. But indeed otherwise this
Wednesday is to be regarded as one of the notablest
Paris had yet seen : gloomy tidings come successively,
like Job's messengers ; are met by gloomy answers. Of
Sardinia* rising to invade the Southeast, and Spain
threatening the South, we do not speak. But are not
the Prussians masters of Longwi (treacherously yielded,
one would say) ; and preparing to besiege Verdun*?
Clairfait and his Austrians are encompassing Thionville ; darkening the North. Not Metzland now, but
the Clermontais is getting harried ; flying hulans and
hussars have been seen on the Chalons Road, almost
as far as Sainte-Menehould.* Heart, ye Patriots ; if
ye lose heart, ye lose all !

It is not without a dramatic emotion that one reads in the Parliamentary Debates of this Wednesday evening ' past seven o'clock ', the scene with the military fugitives from Longwi. Wayworn, dusty, disheartened, these poor men enter the Legislative, about sunset or after ; give the most pathetic detail of the frightful pass they were in : Prussians billowing round by the myriad, volcanically spouting fire for fifteen hours : we, scattered sparse on the ramparts, hardly a cannoneer to two guns ; our dastard Commandant Lavergne nowhere showing face ; the priming would not catch ; there was no powder in the bombs,—what could we do ? ' *Mourir*, Die ! ' answer prompt voices ; [1] and the dusty fugitives must shrink elsewhither for comfort.— Yes, *Mourir*, that is now the word. Be Longwi a proverb and a hissing*among French strong-places : let it (says the Legislative) be obliterated rather, from the shamed face of the Earth ;—and so there has gone forth Decree, that Longwi shall, were the Prussians once out of it, ' be razed ', and exist only as ploughed ground.

Nor are the Jacobins milder ; as how could they, the flower of Patriotism ? Poor Dame Lavergne, wife of the poor Commandant, took her parasol one evening, and escorted by her Father came over to the Hall of the mighty Mother ; and ' reads a memoir tending to justify the Commandant of Longwi '. *Lafarge, Président*, makes answer : ' Citoyenne, the Nation will judge Lavergne ; the Jacobins are bound to tell him the truth. He would have ended his course there (*terminé sa carrière*), if he had loved the honour of his country '.[2]

[1] Hist. Parl xvii. 148.   [2] Ibid. xix. 300.

CHAPTER II

DANTON

But better than razing of Longwi, or rebuking poor
dusty soldiers or soldiers' wives, Danton had come over,
last night, and demanded a Decree to *search* for arms,
since they were not yielded voluntarily.   Let ' Domiciliary visits ', with rigour of authority, be made to this
end.   To search for arms ; for horses,—Aristocratism
rolls in its carriage, while Patriotism cannot trail its
cannon.   To search generally for munitions of war, ' in
the houses of persons suspect ',—and even, if it seem
proper, to seize and imprison the suspect persons themselves !   In the Prisons their plots will be harmless ;
in the Prisons they will be as hostages for us, and not
without use.   This Decree the energetic Minister of
Justice demanded last night, and got ; and this same
night it is to be executed ; it is being executed at the
moment when these dusty soldiers get saluted with
Mourir.   Two-thousand stand of arms, as they count,
are foraged in this way ; and some four-hundred head
of new Prisoners ; and, on the whole, such a terror and
damp is struck through the Aristocrat heart, as all but
Patriotism, and even Patriotism were it out of this
agony, might pity.   Yes, Messieurs ! if Brunswick blast
Paris to ashes, he probably will blast the Prisons of
Paris too : pale Terror,* if we have got it, we will also
give it, and the depth of horrors that lie in it ; the same
leaky bottom, in these wild waters, bears us all.

One can judge what stir there was now among the
' thirty-thousand Royalists ' : how the Plotters, or the
accused of Plotting, shrank each closer into his lurking-
place,—like Bertrand-Moleville, looking eager towards
Longwi, hoping the weather would keep fair.   Or how
they dressed themselves in valets' clothes, like Narbonne, and ' got to England as Dr. Bollman's famulus ' :
how Dame de Staël bestirred herself, pleading with

Manuel as a Sister in Literature, pleading even with
Clerk Tallien ; a prey to nameless chagrins ! [1] Royalist
Peltier, the Pamphleteer, gives a touching Narrative
(not deficient in height of colouring) of the terrors of that
night.　From five in the afternoon, a great city is struck
suddenly silent ; except for the beating of drums,
for the tramp of marching feet ; and ever and anon the
dread thunder of the knocker at some door, a Tricolor
Commissioner with his blue Guards (*black*-guards !)
arriving.　All Streets are vacant, says Peltier ; beset
by Guards at each end : all Citizens are ordered to be
within doors.　On the River float sentinel barges, lest
we escape by water : the Barriers hermetically closed.
Frightful !　The Sun shines ; serenely westering, in
smokeless mackerel-sky ; Paris is as if sleeping, as if
dead :—Paris is holding its breath, to see what stroke
will fall on it.　Poor Peltier !　*Acts of Apostles*, and all
jocundity of Leading-Articles, are gone out, and it is
become bitter earnest instead ; polished satire changed
now into coarse pike-points (hammered out of railing) ;
all logic reduced to this one primitive thesis, An eye for
an eye, a tooth for a tooth !*—Peltier, dolefully aware
of it, ducks low ; escapes unscathed to England ; to
urge there the inky war anew ;—to have Trial by Jury,
in due season, and deliverance by young Whig eloquence, world-celebrated for a day.

Of ' thirty-thousand ', naturally, great multitudes
were left unmolested : but, as we said, some four-hundred, designated as ' persons suspect ', were seized ; and
an unspeakable terror fell on all.　Woe to him who is
guilty of Plotting, of Anticivism, Royalism, Feuillantism ; who, guilty or not guilty, has an enemy in his
Section to call him guilty !　Poor old M. de Cazotte is
seized ; his young loved Daughter with him, refusing
to quit him.　Why, O Cazotte, wouldst thou quit
romancing and *Diable Amoureux*, for such reality as
this ?　Poor old M. de Sombreuil, he of the *Invalides*,
is seized ; a man seen askance by Patriotism ever since

---

[1] De Staël, Considérations sur la Révolution, ii. 67–81.

the Bastille days; whom also a fond Daughter will
not quit. With young tears hardly suppressed, and
old wavering weakness rousing itself once more,—
O my brothers, O my sisters !

The famed and named go; the nameless, if they
have an accuser. Necklace Lamotte's Husband is in
these Prisons (*she* long since squelched on the London
Pavements); but gets delivered. Gross de Morande,
of the *Courrier de l'Europe*, hobbles distractedly to and
fro there : but they let him hobble out; on right nimble
crutches ;—his hour not being yet come. Advocate
Maton de la Varenne, very weak in health, is snatched
off from mother and kin; Tricolor Rossignol (journeyman goldsmith and scoundrel lately, a risen man now)
remembers an old Pleading of Maton's ! Jourgniac de
Saint-Méard goes; the brisk frank soldier : he was in
the Mutiny of Nancy, in that ' effervescent Regiment
du Roi ',—on the wrong side. Saddest of all : Abbé
Sicard goes; a Priest who could not take the Oath, but
who could teach the Deaf and Dumb : in his Section
one man, he says, had a grudge at him; one man, at
the fit hour, launches an arrest against him; which
hits. In the Arsenal quarter, there are dumb hearts
making wail, with signs, with wild gestures; he their
miraculous healer and speech-bringer is rapt away.

What with the arrestments on this night of the
Twenty-ninth, what with those that have gone on more
or less, day and night, ever since the Tenth, one may
fancy what the Prisons now were. Crowding and confusion; jostle, hurry, vehemence and terror ! Of the
poor Queen's Friends, who had followed her to the
Temple, and been committed elsewhither to Prison,
some, as Governess de Tourzelle, are to be let go : one,
the poor Princess de Lamballe, is not let go; but waits
in the strong-rooms of La Force there, what will betide
further.

Among so many hundreds whom the launched arrest
hits, who are rolled off to Townhall or Section-hall, to
preliminary Houses of Detention, and hurled in thither

as into cattle-pens, we must mention one other : Caron
de Beaumarchais, Author of *Figaro*; vanquisher of
Maupeou Parlements and Goezman helldogs; once
numbered among the demigods; and now— ? We
left him in his culminant state ; what dreadful decline
is this, when we again catch a glimpse of him ! 'At
midnight' (it was but the 12th of August yet), 'the
servant, in his shirt', with wide-staring eyes, enters
your room :—Monsieur, rise ; all the people are come
to seek you ; they are knocking, like to break in the
door ! 'And they were in fact knocking in a terrible
manner (*d'une façon terrible*). I fling on my coat,
forgetting even the waistcoat, nothing on my feet but
slippers ; and say to him '—And *he*, alas, answers mere
negatoryincoherences, panicinterjections. And through
the shutters and crevices, in front or rearward, the dull
street-lamps disclose only streetfuls of haggard countenances ; clamorous, bristling with pikes : and you rush
distracted for an outlet, finding none ;—and have to
take refuge in the crockery-press, down stairs ; and
stand there, palpitating, in that imperfect costume,
lights dancing past your key-hole, tramp of feet overhead, and the tumult of Satan, 'for four hours and
more' ! And old ladies, of the quarter, started up (as
we hear next morning) ; rang for their *bonnes* and cor-
dial-drops, with shrill interjections: and old gentlemen,
in their shirts, 'leapt garden-walls' ; flying while none
pursued ; one of whom unfortunately broke his leg.[1]
Those sixty-thousand stand of Dutch Arms (which
never arrive), and the bold stroke of trade, have turned
out so ill !—

Beaumarchais escaped for this time ; but not for
the next time, ten days after. On the evening of the
Twenty-ninth he is still in that chaos of the Prisons, in
saddest wrestling condition ; unable to get justice, even
to get audience ; 'Panis scratching his head' when you
speak to him, and making off. Nevertheless let the

[1] Beaumarchais' Narrative, Mémoires sur les Prisons
(Paris, 1823), i. 179-90.

lover of Figaro know that Procureur Manuel, a Brother in Literature, found him, and delivered him once more. But how the lean demigod, now shorn of his splendour, had to lurk in barns, to roam over harrowed fields, panting for life ; and to wait under eavesdrops, and sit in darkness ' on the Boulevarde amid paving-stones and boulders ', longing for one word of any Minister, or Minister's Clerk, about those accursed Dutch muskets, and getting none,—with heart fuming in spleen, and terror, and suppressed canine-madness ; alas, how the swift sharp hound, once fit to be Diana's, breaks his old teeth now, gnawing mere whinstones ; and must ' fly to England ' ; and, returning from England, must creep into the corner, and lie quiet, toothless (moneyless),— all this let the lover of Figaro fancy, and weep for. We here, without weeping, not without sadness, wave the withered tough fellow-mortal our farewell. His Figaro has returned to the French stage ; nay is, at this day, sometimes named the best piece there. And indeed, so long as Man's Life can ground itself only on artificiality and aridity ; each new Revolt and Change of Dynasty turning up only a new stratum of *dry-rubbish*, and no *soil* yet coming to view,—may it not be good to protest against such a Life, in many ways, and even in the Figaro way ?

CHAPTER III

DUMOURIEZ

SUCH are the last days of August 1792 ; days gloomy, disastrous and of evil omen. What will become of this poor France ? Dumouriez rode from the Camp of Maulde, eastward to Sedan, on Tuesday last, the 28th of the month; reviewed that so-called Army left forlorn there by Lafayette : the forlorn soldiers gloomed on him ; were heard growling on him, ' This is one of them, *ce b—e là*, that made War be declared '.[1] Un-

[1] Dumouriez, Mémoires, ii. 383.

promising Army! Recruits flow in, filtering through
Dépôt after Dépôt; but recruits merely: in want of
all; happy if they have so much as arms.   And Longwi
has fallen basely; and Brunswick, and the Prussian
King, with his sixty-thousand, will beleaguer Verdun;
and Clairfait and Austrians press deeper in, over the
Northern marches: ' a hundred and fifty thousand ' as
fear counts, ' eighty-thousand ' as the returns show, do
hem us in; Cimmerian Europe behind them.   There
is Castries-and-Broglie chivalry; Royalist foot ' in red
facing and nankeen trousers '; breathing death and
the gallows.*

And lo, finally! at Verdun on Sunday the 2nd of
September 1792, Brunswick is here.   With his King
and sixty-thousand, glittering over the heights, from
beyond the winding Meuse River, he looks down on us,
on our ' high citadel ' and all our confectionery-ovens
(for we are celebrated for confectionery); has sent
courteous summons, in order to spare the effusion
of blood!—Resist him to the death?   Every day of
retardation precious?   How, O General Beaurepaire
(asks the amazed Municipality) shall we resist him?
We, the Verdun Municipals, see no resistance possible.
Has he not sixty-thousand, and artillery without end?
Retardation, Patriotism is good; but so likewise is
peaceable baking of pastry, and sleeping in whole
skin.—Hapless Beaurepaire stretches out his hands, and
pleads passionately, in the name of country, honour, of
Heaven and of Earth: to no purpose.   The Municipals
have, by law, the power of ordering it;—with an Army
officered by Royalism or Crypto-Royalism, such a Law
seemed needful: and they order it, as pacific Pastry-
cooks, not as heroic Patriots would,—To surrender!
Beaurepaire strides home, with long steps: his valet,
entering the room, sees him ' writing eagerly ', and
withdraws.   His valet hears then, in few minutes, the
report of a pistol: Beaurepaire is lying dead; his eager
writing had been a brief suicidal farewell.   In this manner died Beaurepaire, wept of France; buried in the
Pantheon, with honourable Pension to his Widow, and

for Epitaph these words, *He chose Death rather than yield to Despots.* The Prussians, descending from the heights, are peaceable masters of Verdun.

And so Brunswick advances, from stage to stage : who shall now stay him,—covering forty miles of country ? Foragers fly far ; the villages of the Northeast are harried ; your Hessian forager has only ' three sous a-day ' : the very Emigrants, it is said, will take silver-plate,—by way of revenge. Clermont, Sainte-Mene-hould, Varennes especially, ye Towns of the *Night of Spurs,* tremble ye ! Procureur Sausse and the Magistracy of Varennes have fled ; brave Boniface Le Blanc of the *Bras d'Or* is to the woods : Mrs. Le Blanc, a young woman fair to look upon, with her young infant, has to live in greenwood, like a beautiful Bessy Bell of Song,* her bower thatched with rushes ;—catching premature rheumatism.[1] Clermont may ring the tocsin now, and illuminate itself ! Clermont lies at the foot of its *Cow* (or *Vache,* so they name that Mountain), a prey to the Hessian spoiler : its fair women, fairer than most, are robbed ; not of life, or what is dearer, yet of all that is cheaper and portable ; for Necessity, on three half-pence a-day, has no law. At Sainte-Menehould the enemy has been expected more than once,—our Nationals all turning out in arms ; but was not yet seen. Postmaster Drouet, he is not in the woods, but minding his Election ; and will sit in the Convention, notable King-taker, and bold Old-Dragoon as he is.

Thus on the Northeast all roams and runs ; and on a set day, the *date* of which is irrecoverable by History, Brunswick ' has engaged to dine in Paris ',—the Powers willing. And at Paris, in the centre, it is as we saw ; and in La Vendée Southwest, it is as we saw ; and Sardinia is in the Southeast, and Spain is in the South, and Clairfait with Austria and sieged Thionville is in the North ;—and all France leaps distracted, like the winnowed Sahara waltzing in sand-colonnades ! More

---

[1] Helen Maria Williams, Letters from France (London, 1791–1793), iii. 96.

desperate posture no country ever stood in. A country,
one would say, which the Majesty of Prussia (if it so
pleased him) might partition and clip in pieces, like a
Poland ; flinging the remainder to poor Brother Louis,
—with directions to keep it quiet, or else *we* will keep
it for him !

Or perhaps the Upper Powers, minded that a new
Chapter in Universal History shall begin here and not
further on, may have ordered it all otherwise ? In that
case, Brunswick will not dine in Paris on the set day ;
nor, indeed, one knows not when !—Verily, amid this
wreckage, where poor France seems grinding itself down
to dust and bottomless ruin, who knows what miraculous salient-point of Deliverance and New-life may
have already come into existence there ; and be already
working there, though as yet human eye discern it not !
On the night of that same twenty-eighth of August,
the unpromising Review-day in Sedan, Dumouriez
assembles a Council of War at his lodgings there. He
spreads out the map of this forlorn war-district ; Prussians here, Austrians there ; triumphant both, with
broad highway, and little hindrance, all the way to
Paris : we scattered, helpless, here and here : what to
advise ? The Generals, strangers to Dumouriez, look
blank enough ; know not well what to advise,—if it be
not retreating, and retreating till our recruits accumulate ; till perhaps the chapter of chances turn up some
leaf for us ; or Paris, at all events, be sacked at the
latest day possible. The Many-counselled, who ' has
not closed an eye for three nights ', listens with little
speech to these long cheerless speeches ; merely watching the speaker, that he may know him ; then wishes
them all good-night ;—but beckons a certain young
Thouvenot, the fire of whose looks had pleased him, to
wait a moment. Thouvenot waits : *Voilà*, says Polymetis, pointing to the map ! That is the Forest of
Argonne,* that long strip of rocky Mountain and wild
Wood ; forty miles long ; with but five, or say even
three practicable Passes through it : this, for they have
forgotten it, might one not still seize, though Clairfait

sits so nigh ? Once seized;—the Champagne called the Hungry (or worse, Champagne *Pouilleuse*) on their side of it ; the fat Three Bishoprics, and willing France, on ours ; and the Equinox-rains not far ;—this Argonne ' might be the Thermopylae of France ! ' [1]

O brisk Dumouriez Polymetis with thy teeming head, may the gods grant it !—Polymetis, at any rate, folds his map together, and flings himself on bed ; resolved to try, on the morrow morning. With astucity, with swiftness, with audacity ! One had need to be a lion-fox, and have luck on one's side.

CHAPTER IV

SEPTEMBER IN PARIS

At Paris, by lying Rumour which proved prophetic and veridical, the fall of Verdun was known some hours *before* it happened. It is Sunday the second of September ; handiwork hinders not the speculations of the mind. Verdun gone (though some still deny it) ; the Prussians in full march, with gallows-ropes, with fire and faggot ! Thirty-thousand Aristocrats within our own walls ; and but the merest quarter-tithe of them yet put in Prison ! Nay there goes a word that even these will revolt. Sieur Jean Julien, wagoner of Vaugirard,[2] being set in the Pillory last Friday, took all at once to crying, That he would be well revenged ere long ; that the King's Friends in Prison would burst out, force the Temple, set the King on horseback, and, joined by the unimprisoned, ride roughshod over us all. This the unfortunate wagoner of Vaugirard did bawl, at the top of his lungs: when snatched off to the Town-hall, he persisted in it, still bawling ; yesternight, when they guillotined him, he died with the froth of it on his lips.[3] For a man's mind, padlocked to the Pillory, may

---

[1] Dumouriez, ii. 391.   [2] Moore, i. 178.
[3] Hist. Parl. xvii. 409.

go mad ; and all men's minds may go mad, and ' believe him ', as the frenetic will do, ' *because* it is impossible '.

So that apparently the knot of the crisis and last agony of France is come ? Make front to this, thou Improvised Commune, strong Danton, whatsoever man is strong ! Readers can judge whether the Flag of Country in Danger flapped soothingly or distractively on the souls of men, that day.

But the Improvised Commune, but strong Danton is not wanting, each after his kind. Huge Placards are getting plastered to the walls ; at two o'clock the storm-bell shall be sounded, the alarm-cannon fired ; all Paris shall rush to the Champ-de-Mars, and have itself en-rolled. Unarmed, truly, and undrilled ; but desperate, in the strength of frenzy. Haste, ye men ; ye very women, offer to mount guard and shoulder the brown musket : weak clucking-hens, in a state of desperation, will fly at the muzzle of the mastiff ; and even conquer him,—by vehemence of character ! Terror itself, when once grown transcendental, becomes a kind of courage ; as frost sufficiently intense, according to Poet Milton, will *burn*.—Danton, the other night, in the Legislative Committee of General Defence, when the other Minis-ters and Legislators had all opined, said, It would not do to quit Paris, and fly to Saumur ; that they must abide by Paris ; and take such attitude as would put their enemies in fear,—*faire peur ;* a word of his which has been often repeated, and reprinted—in italics.[1]

At two of the clock, Beaurepaire, as we saw, has shot himself at Verdun ; and, over Europe, mortals are going in for afternoon sermon. But at Paris, all steeples are clangouring not for sermon ; the alarm-gun booming from minute to minute ; Champ-de-Mars and Father-land's Altar boiling with desperate terror-courage : what a *miserere* going up to Heaven from this once Capital of the Most Christian King ! The Legislative sits in alternate awe and effervescence ; Vergniaud proposing that Twelve shall go and dig personally on Montmartre ; which is decreed by acclaim.

[1] Biographie des Ministres (Bruxelles, 1826), p. 96.

But better than digging personally with acclaim, see Danton enter ;—the black brows clouded, the colossus-figure tramping heavy ; grim energy looking from all features of the rugged man ! Strong is that grim Son of France and Son of Earth ; a Reality and not a Formula he too : and surely now if ever, being hurled *low* enough, it is on the Earth and on Realities that he rests. 'Legislators!' so speaks the stentor-voice, as the Newspapers yet preserve it for us, ' it is not the alarm-cannon that you hear : it is the *pas-de-charge* against our enemies. To conquer them, to hurl them back, what do we require ? *Il nous faut de l'audace, et encore de l'audace, et toujours de l'audace,* To dare, and again to dare, and without end to dare !' [1]—Right so, thou brawny Titan ; there is nothing left for thee but that. Old men, who heard it, will still tell you how the reverberating voice made all hearts swell, in that moment; and braced them to the sticking-place ; and thrilled abroad over France, like electric virtue, as a word spoken in season.

But the Commune, enrolling in the Champ-de-Mars ? But the Committee of Watchfulness, become now Committee of Public Salvation ; whose conscience is Marat ? The Commune enrolling enrolls many; provides Tents for them in that Mars'-Field, that they may march with dawn on the morrow : praise to this part of the Commune ! To Marat and the Committee of Watchfulness not praise ;—not even blame, such as could be meted out in these insufficient dialects of ours ; expressive silence rather ! Lone Marat, the man forbid, meditating long in his Cellars of refuge, on his Stylites Pillar, could see salvation in one thing only : in the fall of 'two hundred and sixty thousand Aristocrat heads'. With so many score of Naples Bravoes, each a dirk in his right-hand, a muff on his left, he would traverse France, and do it. But the world laughed, mocking the severe-benevolence of a People's-Friend ; and his idea could not become an action, but only a fixed-idea.

---

[1] Moniteur (in Hist. Parl. xvii. 347).

Lo, now, however, he has come down from his Stylites
Pillar, to a *Tribune particulière*; here now, without the
dirks, without the *muffs* at least, were it not grown
possible,—now in the knot of the crisis, when salvation
or destruction hangs in the hour !

The Ice-Tower of Avignon was noised of sufficiently,
and lives in all memories; but the authors were not punished : nay we saw Jourdan Coupe-tête, borne on men's
shoulders, like a copper Portent, ' traversing the cities
of the South '.—What phantasms, squalid-horrid, shaking their dirk and muff, may dance through the brain of
a Marat, in this dizzy pealing of tocsin-miserere and universal frenzy, seek not to guess, O Reader ! Nor what
the cruel Billaud ' in his short brown coat ' was thinking ; nor Sergent, not yet *Agate*-Sergent ; nor Panis the
confidant of Danton ;—nor, in a word, how gloomy
Orcus does breed in her gloomy womb, and fashion her
monsters and prodigies of Events, which thou seest her
visibly bear ! Terror is on these streets of Paris ; terror
and rage, tears and frenzy : tocsin-miserere pealing
through the air ; fierce desperation rushing to battle ;
mothers, with streaming eyes and wild hearts, sending
forth their sons to die. ' Carriage-horses are seized by
the bridle ', that they may draw cannon ; ' the traces
cut, the carriages left standing '. In such tocsin-miserere, and murky bewilderment of Frenzy, are not
Murder, Até and all Furies near at hand ? On slight
hint—who knows on how slight ?—may not Murder
come ; and, with *her* snaky-sparkling head, illuminate
this murk !

How it was and went, what part might be premedi-
tated, what was improvised and accidental, man will
never know, till the great Day of Judgement make it
known. But with a Marat for keeper of the Sovereign's
Conscience—And we know what the *ultima ratio** of
Sovereigns, when they are driven to it, is ! In this
Paris there are as wicked men, say a hundred or more,
as exist in all the Earth : to be hired, and set on ; to
set on, of their own accord, unhired.—And yet we will
remark that premeditation itself is not performance, is

not surety of performance ; that it is perhaps, at most, surety of *letting* whosoever wills perform. From the purpose of crime*to the act of crime there is an abyss ; wonderful to think of. The finger lies on the pistol ; but the man is not yet a murderer : nay, his whole nature staggering at such consummation, is there not a confused pause rather,—one last instant of possibility for him ? Not yet a murderer ; it is at the mercy of light trifles whether the most fixed idea may not yet become unfixed. One slight twitch of a muscle, the death-flash bursts ; and he is it, and will for Eternity be it ;—and Earth has become a penal Tartarus for him ; his horizon girdled now not with golden hope, but with red flames of remorse ; voices from the depths of Nature sounding, Woe, woe on him !

Of such stuff are we all made ; on such powder-mines of bottomless guilt and criminality,—' if God restrained not ', as is well said,—does the purest of us walk. There are depths in man that go the length of lowest Hell, as there are heights that reach highest Heaven ;—for are not both Heaven and Hell made out of him, made by him, everlasting Miracle and Mystery as he is ?—But looking on this Champ-de-Mars, with its tent-buildings and frantic enrolments ; on this murky-simmering Paris, with its crammed Prisons (supposed about to burst), with its tocsin-miserere, its mothers' tears, and soldiers' farewell shoutings,—the pious soul might have prayed, that day, that God's grace would restrain, and greatly restrain ; lest on slight hest or hint, Madness, Horror and Murder rose, and this Sabbathday of September became a Day black in the Annals of men.

The tocsin is pealing its loudest, the clocks inaudibly striking *Three*, when poor Abbé Sicard, with some thirty other Nonjurant Priests, in six carriages, fare along the streets, from their preliminary House of Detention at the Townhall, westward towards the Prison of the Abbaye. Carriages enough stand deserted on the streets ; these six move on,—through angry multitudes, cursing

as they move. Accursed Aristocrat Tartuffes, this is the
pass ye have brought us to! And now ye will break
the Prisons, and set Capet Veto*on horseback to ride
over us? Out upon you, Priests of Beelzebub and
Moloch; of Tartuffery, Mammon and the Prussian
Gallows,—which ye name Mother-Church and God!—
Such reproaches have the poor Nonjurants to endure,
and worse; spoken in on them by frantic Patriots, who
mount even on the carriage-steps; the very Guards
hardly refraining. Pull up your carriage-blinds?—No!
answers Patriotism, clapping its horny paw on the
carriage-blind, and crushing it down again. Patience in
oppression has limits: we are close on the Abbaye, it
has lasted long: a poor Nonjurant, of quicker temper,
smites the horny paw with his cane; nay, finding
solacement in it, smites the unkempt head, sharply and
again more sharply, twice over,—seen clearly of us and
of the world. It is the last that we see clearly. Alas,
next moment, the carriages are locked and blocked in
endless raging tumults; in yells deaf to the cry for
mercy, which answer the cry for mercy with sabre-
thrusts through the heart.[1] The thirty Priests are torn
out, are massacred about the Prison-Gate, one after one,
—only the poor Abbé Sicard, whom one Moton a watchmaker, knowing him, heroically tried to save and secrete
in the Prison, escapes to tell;—and it is Night and
Orcus, and Murder's snaky-sparkling head *has* risen in
the murk!—

From Sunday afternoon (exclusive of intervals and
pauses not final) till Thursday evening, there follow con-
secutively a Hundred Hours. Which hundred hours
are to be reckoned with the hours of the Bartholomew
Butchery, of the Armagnac Massacres,* Sicilian Vespers,
or whatsoever is savagest in the annals of this world.
Horrible the hour when man's soul, in its paroxysm,
spurns asunder the barriers and rules; and shows what

---

[1] Félémhesi (anagram for Méhée Fils), La Vérité tout
entière, sur les vrais auteurs de la journée du 2 Septembre
1792 (reprinted in Hist. Parl. xviii. 156–81), p. 167.

dens and depths are in it! For Night and Orcus, as
we say, as was long prophesied, have burst forth, here
in this Paris, from their subterranean imprisonment:
hideous, dim-confused; which it is painful to look on;
and yet which cannot, and indeed which should not, be
forgotten.

The Reader, who looks earnestly through this dim
Phantasmagory of the Pit, will discern few fixed certain
objects; and yet still a few. He will observe, in this
Abbaye Prison, the sudden massacre of the Priests being
once over, a strange Court of Justice, or call it Court
of Revenge and Wild-Justice, swiftly fashion itself, and
take seat round a table, with the Prison-Registers spread
before it;—Stanislas Maillard, Bastille-hero, famed
Leader of the Menads, presiding. O Stanislas, one
hoped to meet thee elsewhere than here; thou shifty
Riding-Usher, with an inkling of Law! This work also
thou hadst to do; and then—to depart for ever from
our eyes. At *La Force*, at the *Châtelet*, the *Conciergerie*,
the like Court forms itself, with the like accompani-
ments: the thing that one man does, other men can do.
There are some Seven Prisons in Paris, full of Aristocrats with conspiracies;—nay not even *Bicêtre* and *Salpêtrière* shall escape, with their Forgers of Assignats:
and there are seventy times seven hundred Patriot
hearts in a state of frenzy. Scoundrel hearts also there
are; as perfect, say, as the Earth holds,—if such are
needed. To whom, in this mood, law is as no-law; and
killing, by what name soever called, is but work to be
done.

So sit these sudden Courts of Wild-Justice, with the
Prison-Registers before them; unwonted wild tumult
howling all round; the Prisoners in dread expectancy
within. Swift: a name is called; bolts jingle, a
Prisoner is there. A few questions are put; swiftly
this sudden Jury decides: Royalist Plotter or not?
Clearly not; in that case, Let the Prisoner be enlarged
with *Vive la Nation*. Probably yea; then still, Let
the Prisoner be enlarged, but without *Vive la Nation*;
or else it may run, Let the Prisoner be conducted to La

Force. At La Force again their formula is, Let the
Prisoner be conducted to the Abbaye.—' To La Force
then ! ' Volunteer bailiffs seize the doomed man ; he
is at the outer gate ; ' enlarged ', or ' conducted ', not
into La Force, but into a howling sea ; forth, under an
arch of wild sabres, axes and pikes ; and sinks, hewn
asunder. And another sinks, and another ; and there
forms itself a piled heap of corpses, and the kennels
begin to run red. Fancy the yells of these men, their
faces of sweat and blood ; the crueller shrieks of these
women, for there are women too ; and a fellow-mortal
hurled naked into it all ! Jourgniac de Saint-Méard has
seen battle, has seen an effervescent Regiment du Roi
in mutiny ; but the bravest heart may quail at this.
The Swiss Prisoners, remnants of the Tenth of August,
' clasped each other spasmodically, and hung back ;
grey veterans crying : "Mercy, Messieurs ; ah, mercy!"
But there was no mercy. Suddenly, however, one of
these men steps forward. He had on a blue frock coat ;
he seemed about thirty, his stature was above common,
his look noble and martial. " I go first ", said he,
" since it must be so : adieu ! " Then dashing his hat
sharply behind him : " Which way ? " cried he to the
Brigands : " Show it me, then ". They open the fold-
ing gate ; he is announced to the multitude. He stands
a moment motionless ; then plunges forth among the
pikes, and dies of a thousand wounds '.[1]

Man after man is cut down ; the sabres need sharpen-
ing, the killers refresh themselves from wine-jugs. Onward and onward goes the butchery ; the loud yells
wearying down into bass growls. A sombre-faced
shifting multitude looks on ; in dull approval, or dull
disapproval ; in dull recognition that it is Necessity.
' An *Anglais* in drab greatcoat ' was seen, or seemed to
be seen, serving liquor from his own dram-bottle ;—for
what purpose, ' if not set on by Pitt ', Satan and himself
know best ! Witty Dr. Moore grew sick on approaching, and turned into another street.[2]—Quick enough

[1] Félémhesi, La Vérité tout entière (*ut supra*), p. 173.
[2] Moore's Journal, i. 185–95.

goes this Jury-Court; and rigorous. The brave are
not spared, nor the beautiful, nor the weak. Old M. de
Montmorin, the Minister's Brother, was acquitted by
the Tribunal of the Seventeenth; and conducted back,
elbowed by howling galleries; but is not acquitted here.
Princess de Lamballe has lain down on bed: 'Madame,
you are to be removed to the Abbaye'. 'I do not wish
to remove; I am well enough here'. There is a need-
be for removing. She will arrange her dress a little,
then; rude voices answer, 'You have not far to go'.
She too is led to the hell-gate; a manifest Queen's-
Friend. She shivers back, at the sight of bloody sabres;
but there is no return: Onwards! That fair hind head
is cleft with the axe; the neck is severed. That fair
body is cut in fragments; with indignities, and obscene
horrors of moustachio *grands-lèvres*, which human
nature would fain find incredible,—which shall be read
in the original language only. She was beautiful, she
was good, she had known no happiness. Young hearts,
generation after generation, will think with themselves:
O worthy of worship, thou king-descended, god-de-
scended, and poor sister-woman! why was not I there;
and some Sword Balmung or Thor's Hammer*in my
hand? Her head is fixed on a pike; paraded under the
windows of the Temple; that a still more hated, a Marie
Antoinette, may see. One Municipal, in the Temple
with the Royal Prisoners at the moment, said, 'Look
out'. Another eagerly whispered, 'Do not look'. The
circuit of the Temple is guarded, in these hours, by
a long stretched tricolor riband: terror enters, and the
clangour of infinite tumult; hitherto not regicide,
though that too may come.

But it is more edifying to note what thrillings of
affection, what fragments of wild virtues turn up in this
shaking asunder of man's existence; for of these too
there is a proportion. Note old Marquis Cazotte: he
is doomed to die; but his young Daughter clasps him
in her arms, with an inspiration of eloquence, with a
love which is stronger than very death: the heart of
the killers themselves is touched by it; the old man is

spared. Yet he was guilty, if plotting for his King is
guilt: in ten days more, a Court of Law condemned
him, and he had to die elsewhere; bequeathing his
Daughter a lock of his old grey hair.   Or note old M. de
Sombreuil, who also had a Daughter :—My Father is
not an Aristocrat: O good gentlemen, I will swear it,
and testify it, and in all ways prove it ; we are not ; we
hate Aristocrats ! 'Wilt thou drink Aristocrats' blood ?'
The man lifts blood (if universal Rumour can be
credited) ;[1] the poor maiden does drink.   'This Sombreuil is innocent then ! '   Yes, indeed,—and now note,
most of all, how the bloody pikes, at this news, do rattle
to the ground ; and the tiger-yells become bursts of
jubilee over a brother saved ; and the old man and his
daughter are clasped to bloody bosoms, with hot tears ;
and borne home in triumph of *Vive la Nation*, the killers
refusing even money !   Does it seem strange, this temper of theirs ?   It seems very certain, well proved by
Royalist testimony in other instances ;[2] and very
significant.

CHAPTER V

A TRILOGY

As all Delineation, in these ages, were it never so
Epic, 'speaking itself and not singing itself', must either
found on Belief and provable Fact, or have no foundation at all (nor, except as floating cobweb, any existence
at all),—the Reader will perhaps prefer to take a glance
with the very eyes of eye-witnesses ; and see, in that
way, for himself, how it was.   Brave Jourgniac, innocent Abbé Sicard, judicious Advocate Maton, these,
greatly compressing themselves, shall speak, each an
instant.   Jourgniac's *Agony of Thirty-eight hours* went

[1] Dulaure, Esquisses historiques des principaux événemens de la Révolution, ii. 206 (cited in Montgaillard, iii. 205).
[2] Bertrand-Moleville (Mém. particuliers, ii. 213), &c. &c.

through ' above a hundred editions ', though intrinsically a poor work. Some portion of it may here go through above the hundred-and-first, for want of a better.

' *Towards seven o'clock* ' (Sunday night at the Abbaye; for Jourgniac goes by dates): ' We saw two men enter, their hands bloody and armed with sabres ; a turnkey, with a torch, lighted them ; he pointed to the bed of the unfortunate Swiss, Reding. Reding spoke with a dying voice. One of them paused ; but the other cried, *Allons donc* ; lifted the unfortunate man ; carried him out on his back to the street. He was massacred there.

' We all looked at one another in silence, we clasped each other's hands. Motionless, with fixed eyes, we gazed on the pavement of our prison ; on which lay the moonlight, checkered with the triple stancheons of our windows '.

' *Three in the morning :* They were breaking in one of the prison-doors. We at first thought they were coming to kill us in our room ; but heard, by voices on the staircase, that it was a room where some Prisoners had barricaded themselves. They were all butchered there, as we shortly gathered '.

' *Ten o'clock :* The Abbé Lenfant and the Abbé de Chapt-Rastignac appeared in the pulpit of the Chapel, which was our prison ; they had entered by a door from the stairs. They said to us that our end was at hand ; that we must compose ourselves, and receive their last blessing. An electric movement, not to be defined, threw us all on our knees, and we received it. These two whitehaired old men, blessing us from their place above ; death hovering over our heads, on all hands environing us ; the moment is never to be forgotten. Half an hour after, they were both massacred, and we heard their cries '.[1]—Thus Jourgniac in his *Agony* in the Abbaye.

[1] Jourgniac Saint-Méard, Mon Agonie de Trente-huit heures (reprinted in Hist. Parl. xviii. 103-35).

But now let the good Maton speak, what he, over in
La Force, in the same hours, is suffering and witnessing.
This *Résurrection* by him is greatly the best, the least
theatrical of these Pamphlets ; and stands testing by
documents :

'Towards seven o'clock', on Sunday night, 'prisoners
were called frequently, and they did not reappear.
Each of us reasoned, in his own way, on this singularity :
but our ideas became calm, as we persuaded ourselves
that the Memorial I had drawn up for the National
Assembly was producing effect'.

'At one in the morning, the grate which led to our
quarter opened anew.   Four men in uniform, each with
a drawn sabre and blazing torch, came up to our corridor, preceded by a turnkey ; and entered an apartment
close to ours, to investigate a box there, which we heard
them break up.   This done, they stepped into the
gallery and questioned the man Cuissa, to know where
Lamotte' (Necklace's Widower) 'was. Lamotte, they
said, had some months ago, under pretext of a treasure
he knew of, swindled a sum of three-hundred livres from
one of them, inviting him to dinner for that purpose.
The wretched Cuissa, now in their hands, who indeed
lost his life this night, answered trembling, That he
remembered the fact well, but could not tell what was
become of Lamotte.   Determined to find Lamotte and
confront him with Cuissa, they rummaged, along with
this latter, through various other apartments ; but
without effect, for we heard them say : " Come search
among the corpses then ; for, *nom de Dieu !* we must
find where he is ".

'At this same time, I heard Louis Bardy, the Abbé
Bardy's name called : he was brought out ; and directly
massacred, as I learnt.   He had been accused, along
with his concubine, five or six years before, of having
murdered and cut in pieces his own Brother, Auditor
of the *Chambre des Comptes* of Montpelier ; but had
by his subtlety, his dexterity, nay his eloquence, outwitted the judges, and escaped.

'One may fancy what terror these words, " Come

search among the corpses then", had thrown me into.
I saw nothing for it now but resigning myself to die.
I wrote my last will; concluding it by a petition and
adjuration, that the paper should be sent to its address.
Scarcely had I quitted the pen, when there came two
other men in uniform; one of them, whose arm and
sleeve up to the very shoulder, as well as his sabre,
were covered with blood, said, He was as weary as a
hodman that had been beating plaster'.

'Baudin de la Chenaye was called; sixty years of
virtues could not save him. They said, A l'Abbaye: he
passed the fatal outer-gate; gave a cry of terror, at
sight of the heaped corpses; covered his eyes with his
hands, and died of innumerable wounds. At every
new opening of the grate, I thought I should hear my
own name called, and see Rossignol enter'.

'I flung off my night-gown and cap; I put on a
coarse unwashed shirt, a worn frock without waistcoat,
an old round hat; these things I had sent for, some
days ago, in the fear of what might happen.

'The rooms of this corridor had been all emptied but
ours. We were four together; whom they seemed to
have forgotten: we addressed our prayers in common
to the Eternal to be delivered from this peril'.

'Baptiste the turnkey came up by himself, to see
us. I took him by the hands; I conjured him to save
us; promised him a hundred louis, if he would conduct
me home. A noise coming from the grates made him
hastily withdraw.

'It was the noise of some dozen or fifteen men, armed
to the teeth; as we, lying flat to escape being seen,
could see from our windows. "Up stairs!" said they:
"Let not one remain". I took out my penknife; I considered where I should strike myself',—but reflected
'that the blade was too short', and also 'on religion'.

Finally, however, between seven and eight o'clock in
the morning, enter four men with bludgeons and sabres!
—'To one of whom Gérard my comrade whispered,
earnestly, apart. During their colloquy I searched
everywhere for shoes, that I might lay off the Advocate

pumps (*pantoufles de Palais*) I had on', but could find
none.—' Constant, called le Sauvage, Gérard, and a
third whose name escapes me, they let clear off : as for
me, four sabres were crossed over my breast, and they
led me down. I was brought to their bar ; to the
Personage with the scarf, who sat as judge there. He
was a lame man, of tall lank stature. He recognized
me on the streets and spoke to me, seven months
after. I have been assured that he was son of a retired
attorney, and named Chepy. Crossing the Court called
Des Nourrices, I saw Manuel haranguing in tricolor
scarf'. The trial, as we see, ends in acquittal and
resurrection.[1]

Poor Sicard, from the *violon* of the Abbaye, shall say
but a few words ; true-looking, though tremulous.
Towards three in the morning, the killers bethink them
of this little *violon* ; and knock from the court. ' I
tapped gently, trembling lest the murderers might hear
on the opposite door, where the Section Committee was
sitting : they answered gruffly, that they had no key.
There were three of us in this *violon* ; my companions
thought they perceived a kind of loft overhead. But
it was very high ; only one of us could reach it by
mounting on the shoulders of both the others. One of
them said to me, that my life was usefuller than theirs :
I resisted, they insisted : no denial ! I fling myself
on the neck of these two deliverers ; never was scene
more touching. I mount on the shoulders of the first,
then on those of the second, finally on the loft ; and
address to my two comrades the expression of a soul
overwhelmed with natural emotions '.[2]

The two generous companions, we rejoice to find, did
not perish. But it is time that Jourgniac de Saint-
Méard should speak his last words, and end this singular
trilogy. The night had become day ; and the day has

---

[1] Maton de la Varenne, Ma Résurrection (in Hist. Parl.
xviii. 135-56).

[2] Abbé Sicard, Relation adressée à un de ses amis (Hist.
Parl. xviii. 98-103).

again become night.   Jourgniac, worn down with uttermost agitation, was fallen asleep, and had a cheering
dream : he has also contrived to make acquaintance
with one of the volunteer bailiffs, and spoken in native
Provençal with him.   On Tuesday, about one in the
morning, his *Agony* is reaching its crisis.

'By the glare of two torches, I now descried the
terrible tribunal, where lay my life or my death.   The
President, in grey coat, with a sabre at his side, stood
leaning with his hands against a table, on which were
papers, an inkstand, tobacco-pipes and bottles.   Some
ten persons were around, seated or standing; two of
whom had jackets and aprons: others were sleeping
stretched on benches.   Two men, in bloody shirts,
guarded the door of the place; an old turnkey had
his hand on the lock.   In front of the President three
men held a Prisoner, who might be about sixty' (or
seventy: he was old Marshal Maillé, of the Tuileries
and August Tenth).   'They stationed me in a corner ;
my guards crossed their sabres on my breast.   I looked
on all sides for my Provençal: two National Guards,
one of them drunk, presented some appeal from the
Section of Croix Rouge in favour of the Prisoner ; the
Man in Grey answered : "They are useless, these appeals for traitors".   Then the Prisoner exclaimed : "It
is frightful; your judgement is a murder".   The President answered : "My hands are washed of it; take
M. Maillé away".   They drove him into the street;
where, through the opening of the door, I saw him
massacred.

'The President sat down to write ; registering, I suppose, the name of this one whom they had finished;
then I heard him say : "Another, *A un autre !* "

'Behold me then haled before this swift and bloody
judgement-bar, where the best protection was to have
no protection, and all resources of ingenuity became
null if they were not founded on truth.   Two of my
guards held me each by a hand, the third by the collar
of my coat.   "Your name, your profession ? " said
the President.   "The smallest lie ruins you", added

one of the Judges.—" My name is Jourgniac Saint-
Méard ; I have served, as an officer, twenty years : and
I appear at your tribunal with the assurance of an
innocent man, who therefore will not lie ".—" We shall
see that ", said the President : " Do you know why
you are arrested ? "—" Yes, Monsieur le Président ;
I am accused of editing the Journal *De la Cour et de
la Ville.* But I hope to prove the falsity " '.—

But no ; Jourgniac's proof of the falsity, and defence
generally, though of excellent result as a defence, is not
interesting to read. It is longwinded ; there is a loose
theatricality in the reporting of it, which does not
amount to unveracity, yet which tends that way. We
shall suppose him successful, beyond hope, in proving
and disproving ; and skip largely,—to the catastrophe
almost at two steps.

' " But after all ", said one of the Judges, " there is
no smoke without kindling ; tell us why they accuse
you of that ".—" I was about to do so " '—Jourgniac
does so ; with more and more success.

' " Nay ", continued I, " they accuse me even of
recruiting for the Emigrants ! " At these words there
arose a general murmur. " O Messieurs, Messieurs ",
I exclaimed, raising my voice, " it is my turn to speak ;
I beg M. le Président to have the kindness to maintain
it for me ; I never needed it more ".—" True enough,
true enough ", said almost all the Judges with a laugh :
" Silence ! "

' While they were examining the testimonials I had
produced, a new Prisoner was brought in, and placed
before the President. " It was one Priest more ", they
said, " whom they had ferreted out of the Chapelle ".
After very few questions : " *A la Force !* " He flung
his breviary on the table ; was hurled forth, and massacred. I reappeared before the tribunal.

' " You tell us always ", cried one of the Judges, with
a tone of impatience, " that you are not this, that you
are not that ; what are you then ? "—" I was an open
Royalist ".—There arose a general murmur ; which was
miraculously appeased by another of the men, who had

seemed to take an interest in me : " We are not here to judge opinions ", said he, " but to judge the results of them ". Could Rousseau and Voltaire both in one, pleading for me, have said better ?—" Yes, Messieurs ", cried I, " always till the Tenth of August I was an open Royalist. Ever since the Tenth of August that cause has been finished. I am a Frenchman, true to my country. I was always a man of honour " '.

' " My soldiers never distrusted me. Nay, two days before that business of Nanci, when their suspicion of their officers was at its height, they chose me for commander, to lead them to Lunéville, to get back the prisoners of the Regiment Mestre-de-Camp, and seize General Malseigne " '. Which fact there is, most luckily, an individual present who by a certain token can confirm.

' The President, this cross-questioning being over, took off his hat and said : " I see nothing to suspect in this man : I am for granting him his liberty. Is that your vote ? " To which all the Judges answered : " *Oui, Oui ;* it is just ! " '

And there arose vivats within doors and without ; ' escort of three', amid shoutings and embracings : thus Jourgniac escaped from jury-trial and the jaws of death.[1] Maton and Sicard did, either by trial and no bill found, lank President Chepy finding ' absolutely nothing '; or else by evasion, and new favour of Moton the brave watchmaker, likewise escape ; and were embraced and wept over ; weeping in return, as they well might.

Thus they three, in wondrous trilogy, or triple soliloquy : uttering simultaneously, through the dread night-watches, their Night-thoughts,—grown audible to us ! They Three are become audible : but the other ' Thousand and Eighty-nine, of whom Two-hundred and two were Priests '; who also had Night-thoughts, remain inaudible ; choked for ever in black Death. Heard only of President Chepy and the Man in Grey !—

[1] Mon Agonie (*ut supra*, Hist. Parl. xviii. 128).

CHAPTER VI

THE CIRCULAR

But the Constituted Authorities, all this while? The Legislative Assembly; the Six Ministers; the Town-hall; Santerre with the National Guard?—It is very curious to think what a City is. Theatres, to the number of some twenty-three, were open every night during these prodigies; while right-arms here grew weary with slaying, right-arms there were twiddledeeing on melodious catgut: at the very instant when Abbé Sicard was clambering up his second pair of shoulders, three-men high, five hundred thousand human individuals were lying horizontal, as if nothing were amiss.

As for the poor Legislative, the sceptre had departed from it. The Legislative did send Deputation to the Prisons, to these Street-Courts; and poor M. Dusaulx did harangue there; but produced no conviction whatsoever: nay at last, as he continued haranguing, the Street-Court interposed, not without threats; and he had to cease, and withdraw. This is the same poor worthy old M. Dusaulx who told, or indeed almost sang (though with cracked voice), the *Taking of the Bastille*, to our satisfaction, long since. He was wont to announce himself, on such and on all occasions, as *the Translator of Juvenal*. ' Good Citizens, you see before you a man who loves his country, who is the Translator of Juvenal ', said he once.—' Juvenal ? ' interrupts Sansculottism : ' Who the devil is Juvenal ? One of your *sacrés Aristocrates* ? To the *Lanterne* ! ' From an orator of this kind, conviction was not to be expected. The Legislative had much ado to save one of its own Members, or Ex-Members, Deputy Jounneau, who chanced to be lying in arrest for mere Parliamentary delinquencies, in these Prisons. As for poor old Dusaulx and Company, they returned to the Salle de

Manége, saying, 'It was dark; and they could not
see well what was going on '.[1]

Roland writes indignant messages, in the name of
Order, Humanity and the Law; but there is no Force
at his disposal. Santerre's National Force seems lazy
to rise : though he made requisitions, he says,—which
always dispersed again. Nay did not we, with Advocate Maton's eyes, see ' men in uniform ' too, with their
' sleeves bloody to the shoulder ' ? Pétion goes in tricolor scarf ; speaks ' the austere language of the law ' :
the killers give up, while he is there ; when his back
is turned, recommence. Manuel too in scarf we, with
Maton's eyes, transiently saw haranguing, in the Court
called of Nurses, *Cour des Nourrices*. On the other
hand, cruel Billaud, likewise in scarf, ' with that small
puce coat and black wig we are used to on him ',[2] audibly
delivers, ' standing among corpses', at the Abbaye, a
short but ever-memorable harangue, reported in various
phraseology, but always to this purpose : ' Brave Citizens, you are extirpating the Enemies of Liberty ; you
are at your duty. A grateful Commune and Country
would wish to recompense you adequately ; but cannot, for you know its want of funds. Whoever shall
have worked (*travaillé*) in a Prison shall receive a draft
of one louis, payable by our cashier. Continue your
work '.[3] The Constituted Authorities are of yesterday:
all pulling different ways : there is properly no Constituted Authority, but every man is his own King*; and
all are kinglets, belligerent, allied, or armed-neutral,
without king over them.

' O everlasting infamy ', exclaims Montgaillard, ' that
Paris stood looking on in stupor for four days, and did
not interfere ! ' Very desirable indeed that Paris had
interfered ; yet not unnatural that it stood even so,
looking on in stupor. Paris is in death-panic, the enemy
and gibbets at its door: whosoever in Paris has the

[1] Moniteur, Debate of 2nd September 1792.
[2] Méhée Fils (*ut suprà*, in Hist. Parl. xviii. p. 189).
[3] Montgaillard, iii. 191.

heart to front death, finds it more pressing to do it
fighting the Prussians, than fighting the killers of Aristocrats. Indignant abhorrence, as in Roland, may be
here; gloomy sanction, premeditation or not, as in
Marat and Committee of Salvation, may be there; dull
disapproval, dull approval, and acquiescence in Necessity and Destiny, is the general temper. The Sons of
Darkness, 'two-hundred or so', risen from their lurk-
ing-places, have scope to do their work. Urged on by
fever-frenzy of Patriotism, and the madness of Terror;
—urged on by lucre, and the gold louis of wages? Nay,
not lucre; for the gold watches, rings, money of the
Massacred, are punctually brought to the Townhall,
by Killers sans-indispensables, who higgle afterwards
for their twenty shillings of wages; and Sergent sticking an uncommonly fine agate on his finger (fully 'meaning to account for it') becomes *Agate*-Sergent. But
the temper, as we say, is dull acquiescence. Not till
the Patriotic or Frenetic part of the work is finished
for want of material; and Sons of Darkness, bent
clearly on lucre alone, begin wrenching watches and
purses, brooches from ladies' necks, 'to equip volunteers', in daylight, on the streets,—does the temper
from dull grow vehement; does the Constable raise
his truncheon, and striking heartily (like a cattle-driver
in earnest) beat the 'course of things' back into its old
regulated drove-roads. The *Garde-Meuble** itself was
surreptitiously plundered, on the 17th of the month,
to Roland's new horror; who anew bestirs himself, and
is, as Sieyès says, 'the veto of scoundrels', Roland *veto
des coquins.*[1]—

This is the September Massacre, otherwise called
'Severe Justice of the People'. These are the Septemberers (*Septembriseurs*); a name of some note and
lucency,—but lucency of the Nether-fire sort; very
different from that of our Bastille Heroes, who shone,
disputable by no Friend of Freedom, as in Heavenly
light-radiance: to such phasis of the business have we

---

[1] Helen Maria Williams, iii. 27.

advanced since then! The numbers massacred are, in
the Historical *fantasy*, ' between two and three thousand'; or indeed they are ' upwards of six thousand ',
for Peltier (in vision) saw them massacring the very
patients of the Bicêtre Madhouse ' with grape-shot ';
nay finally they are ' twelve thousand' and odd hundreds,—not more than that.[1] In Arithmetical ciphers,
and Lists drawn up by accurate Advocate Maton, the
number, including two-hundred and two priests, three
' persons unknown', and ' one thief killed at the Ber-
nardins ', is, as above hinted, a Thousand and Eighty-
nine,—not less than that.

A thousand and eighty-nine lie dead, ' two-hundred
and sixty heaped carcasses on the Pont au Change '
itself ;—among which, Robespierre pleading afterwards
will ' nearly weep' to reflect that there was said to be
one slain innocent.[2] One ; not two, O thou seagreen
Incorruptible ? If so, Themis Sansculotte must be
lucky ; for she was brief !—In the dim Registers of the
Townhall, which are preserved to this day, men read,
with a certain sickness of heart, items and entries not
usual in Town Books : ' To workers employed in preserving the salubrity of the air in the Prisons, and persons who presided over these dangerous operations ', so
much,—in various items, nearly seven hundred pounds
sterling. To carters employed to ' the Burying-grounds
of Clamart, Montrouge and Vaugirard ', at so much
a journey, per cart ; this also is an entry. Then so
many francs and odd sous ' for the necessary quantity
of quick-lime ' ![3] Carts go along the streets ; full of
stript human corpses, thrown pellmell ; limbs sticking
up :—seest thou that cold Hand sticking up, through
the heaped embrace of brother corpses, in its yellow
paleness, in its cold rigour ; the palm opened towards

[1] See Hist. Parl. xvii. 421, 22.

[2] Moniteur of 6th November (Debate of 5th November
1793).

[3] État des sommes payées par la Commune de Paris (Hist.
Parl. xviii. 231).

Heaven, as if in dumb prayer, in expostulation *de pro-fundis*; Take pity on the Sons of Men !—Mercier saw it, as he walked down ' the Rue Saint-Jacques from Mont-rouge, on the morrow of the Massacres ' : but not a Hand ; it was a Foot,—which he reckons still more significant, one understands not well why.   Or was it as the Foot of one *spurning* Heaven ?   Rushing, like a wild diver, in disgust and despair, towards the depths of Annihilation ?   Even there shall His hand find thee, and His right-hand hold thee,—surely for right not for wrong, for good not evil !   ' I saw that Foot ', says Mercier ;   ' I shall know it again at the great Day of Judgement, when the Eternal, throned on his thunders, shall judge both Kings and Septemberers '.[1]

That a shriek of inarticulate horror rose over this thing, not only from French Aristocrats and Moderates, but from all Europe, and has prolonged itself to the present day, was most natural and right.   The thing lay done, irrevocable ;   a thing to be counted beside some other things, which lie very black in our Earth's Annals, yet which will not erase therefrom.   For man, as was remarked, has transcendentalisms in him ;   standing, as he does, poor creature, every way ' in the confluence of Infinitudes ' ;   a mystery to himself and others :   in the centre of two Eternities, of three Immensities,—in the intersection of primaeval Light with the everlasting Dark !—Thus have there been, especially by vehement tempers reduced to a state of desperation, very miser-able things done.   Sicilian Vespers, and ' eight thousand slaughtered in two hours ', are a known thing.   Kings themselves, not in desperation, but only in difficulty, have sat hatching, for year and day (nay De Thou says for seven years), their Bartholomew Business ;   and then, at the right moment, also on an Autumn Sunday, this very Bell (they say it is the identical metal) of Saint-Germain l'Auxerrois was set a-pealing—with effect.[2]

[1] Mercier, Nouveau Paris, vi. 21.

[2] 9th to 13th September 1572 (Dulaure, Hist. de Paris, iv. 289).

Nay the same black boulder-stones of these Paris Prisons
have seen Prison-massacres before now; men massacring
countrymen, Burgundies massacring Armagnacs, whom
they had suddenly imprisoned, till, as now, there were
piled heaps of carcasses, and the streets ran red;—the
Mayor Pétion of the time speaking the austere language
of the law, and answered by the Killers, in old French
(it is some four hundred years old): ' *Maugré bieu, Sire,*
—Sir, God's malison on your "justice", your "pity",
your "right reason". Cursed be of God whoso shall
have pity on these false traitorous Armagnacs, English;
dogs they are; they have destroyed us, wasted this
realm of France, and sold it to the English '.[1] And so
they slay, and fling aside the slain, to the extent of
' fifteen hundred and eighteen, among whom are found
four Bishops of false and damnable counsel, and two
Presidents of Parlement'. For though it is not Satan's
world this that we live in, Satan always has his place
in it (underground properly); and from time to time
bursts up. Well may mankind shriek, inarticulately
anathematizing as they can. There are actions of such
emphasis that no shrieking can be too emphatic for
them. Shriek ye; acted have they.

Shriek who might in this France, in this Paris Legislative or Paris Townhall, there are Ten Men who do
not shriek. A Circular goes out from the Committee
of *Salut Public,* dated 3rd of September 1792; directed
to all Townhalls: a State-paper too remarkable to be
overlooked. ' A part of the ferocious conspirators detained in the Prisons', it says, ' have been put to death
by the People; and we cannot doubt but the whole
Nation, driven to the edge of ruin by such endless
series of treasons, will make haste to adopt *this* means
of public salvation; and all Frenchmen will cry as the
men of Paris: We go to fight the enemy; but we will
not leave robbers behind us, to butcher our wives and
children'. To which are legibly appended these signatures: Panis; Sergent; Marat, Friend of the People;[2]

---

[1] Dulaure, iii. 494.   [2] Hist. Parl. xvii. 433.

with Seven others ;—carried down thereby, in a strange
way, to the late remembrance of Antiquarians.   We
remark, however, that their Circular rather recoiled on
themselves.   The Townhalls made no use of it ; even
the distracted Sansculottes made little ; they only
howled and bellowed, but did not bite.   At Rheims
' about eight persons ' were killed ; and two afterwards
were hanged for doing it.   At Lyons, and a few other
places, some attempt was made ; but with hardly any
effect, being quickly put down.

Less fortunate were the Prisoners of Orléans ; was
the good Duke de La Rochefoucault. He journeying,
by quick stages, with his Mother and Wife, towards
the Waters of Forges, or some quieter country, was
arrested at Gisors ; conducted along the streets, amid
effervescing multitudes, and killed dead ' by the stroke
of a paving-stone hurled through the coach-window '.
Killed as a once Liberal now Aristocrat ; Protector of
Priests, Suspender of virtuous Pétions, and most unfortunate Hot-grown-cold, detestable to Patriotism.   He
dies lamented of Europe ; his blood spattering the
cheeks of his old Mother, ninety-three years old.

As for the Orléans Prisoners, they are State Criminals :
Royalist Ministers, Delessarts, Montmorins ; who have
been accumulating on the High Court of Orléans, ever
since that Tribunal was set up.   Whom now it seems
good that we should get transferred to our new Paris
Court of the Seventeenth ; which proceeds far quicker.
Accordingly hot Fournier from Martinique, Fournier
l'Américain, is off, missioned by Constituted Authority ;
with stanch National Guards, with Lazouski the Pole ;
sparingly provided with road-money.   These, through
bad quarters, through difficulties, perils, for Authorities
cross each other in this time,—do triumphantly bring
off the Fifty or Fifty-three Orléans Prisoners, towards
Paris ; where a swifter Court of the Seventeenth will
do justice on them.[1]   But lo, at Paris, in the interim,
a still swifter and swiftest Court of the *Second*, and of

[1] Hist. Parl. xvii. 434.

September, has instituted itself : enter not Paris, or that will judge you !—What shall hot Fournier do ? It was his duty, as volunteer Constable, had he been a perfect character, to guard those men's lives never so Aristocratic, at the expense of his own valuable life never so Sansculottic, till some Constituted Court had disposed of them. But he was an imperfect character and Constable; perhaps one of the more imperfect.

Hot Fournier, ordered to turn thither by one Authority, to turn thither by another Authority, is in a perplexing multiplicity of orders; but finally he strikes off for Versailles. His Prisoners fare in tumbrils, or open carts, himself and Guards riding and marching around : and at the last village, the worthy Mayor of Versailles comes to meet him, anxious that the arrival and locking-up were well over. It is Sunday, the ninth day of the month. Lo, on entering the Avenue of Versailles, what multitudes, stirring, swarming in the September sun, under the dull-green September foliage ; the Four-rowed Avenue all humming and swarming, as if the Town had emptied itself ! Our tumbrils roll heavily through the living sea; the Guards and Fournier making way with ever more difficulty; the Mayor speaking and gesturing his persuasivest; amid the inarticulate growling hum, which growls ever the deeper even by hearing itself growl, not without sharp yelpings here and there :—Would to God we were out of this strait place, and wind and separation had cooled the heat, which seems about igniting here !

And yet if the wide Avenue is too strait, what will the Street *de Surintendance* be, at leaving of the same ? At the corner of Surintendance Street, the compressed yelpings become a continuous yell: savage figures spring on the tumbril-shafts; first spray of an endless coming tide ! The Mayor pleads, pushes, half-desperate; is pushed, carried off in men's arms : the savage tide has entrance, has mastery. Amid horrid noise, and tumult as of fierce wolves, the Prisoners sink massacred,—all but some eleven, who escaped into houses, and found mercy. The Prisons, and what other Prisoners they

held, were with difficulty saved.   The stript clothes are
burnt in bonfire ;   the corpses lie heaped in the ditch
on the morrow morning.[1]   All France, except it be the
Ten Men of the Circular and their people, moans and
rages, inarticulately shrieking ;   all Europe rings.

But neither did Danton shriek ;   though, as Minister
of Justice, it was more his part to do so.   Brawny Danton is in the breach, as of stormed Cities and Nations ;
amid the sweep of Tenth-of-August cannon, the rustle
of Prussian gallows-ropes, the smiting of September
sabres ;   destruction all round him, and the rushing-
down of worlds :   Minister of Justice is his name ;   but
Titan of the Forlorn Hope, and *Enfant Perdu* of the
Revolution, is his quality,—and the man acts according to that.   ' We must put our enemies in fear ! '
Deep fear, is it not, as of its own accord, falling on our
enemies ?   The Titan of the Forlorn Hope, he is not the
man that would swiftest of all prevent its so falling.
Forward, thou lost Titan of an *Enfant Perdu* ;   thou
must dare, and again dare, and without end dare ;
there is nothing left for thee but that !   ' *Que mon nom
soit flétri*, Let my name be blighted ' :   what am I ?
The Cause alone is great ;   and shall live, and not
perish.—So, on the whole, here too is a Swallower of
Formulas ;   of still wider gulp than Mirabeau :   this
Danton, Mirabeau of the Sansculottes.   In the September days, this Minister was not heard of as co-
operating with strict Roland ;   his business might lie
elsewhere,—with Brunswick and the Hôtel-de-Ville.
When applied to by an official person, about the
Orléans Prisoners, and the risks they ran, he answered
gloomily, twice over, ' Are not these men guilty ? '—
When pressed, he ' answered in a terrible voice ', and
turned his back.[2]   A thousand slain in the Prisons ;
horrible if you will :   but Brunswick is within a day's
journey of us ;   and there are Five-and-twenty Millions

---

[1] Pièces officielles relatives au massacre des Prisonniers à
Versailles (in Hist. Parl. xviii. 236–49).

[2] Biographie des Ministres, p. 97.

yet, to slay or to save. Some men have tasks,—frightfuller than ours! It seems strange, but is not strange,
that this Minister of Moloch-Justice,* when any suppliant for a friend's life got access to him, was found
to have human compassion; and yielded and granted
'always'; neither did one personal enemy of Danton
perish in these days'.[1]

To shriek, we say, when certain things are acted,
is proper and unavoidable. Nevertheless, articulate
speech, not shrieking, is the faculty of man: when
speech is not yet possible, let there be, with the shortest
delay, at least—silence. Silence, accordingly, in this
forty-fourth year of the business, and eighteen hundred
and thirty-sixth of an ' Era called Christian as *lucus
à non* ', is the thing we recommend and practise. Nay,
instead of shrieking more, it were perhaps edifying to
remark, on the other side, what a singular thing Customs (in Latin, *Mores*) are; and how fitly the Virtue,
Vir-tus, Manhood or Worth, that is in a man, is called
his *Morality* or *Customariness*. Fell Slaughter, one of
the most authentic products of the Pit you would say,
once give it Customs, becomes War, with Laws of War;
and is Customary and Moral enough; and red individuals
carry the tools of it girt round their haunches, not
without an air of pride,—which do thou nowise blame.
While, see! so long as it is but dressed in hodden or
russet; and Revolution, less frequent than War, has
not yet got its Laws of Revolution, but the hodden
or russet individuals are Uncustomary—O shrieking
beloved brother blockheads of Mankind, let us close
those wide mouths of ours; let us cease shrieking, and
begin considering!

[1] Biographie des Ministres, p. 103.

CHAPTER VII

SEPTEMBER IN ARGONNE

PLAIN, at any rate, is one thing : that the *fear*, whatever of fear those Aristocrat enemies might need, has been brought about. The matter is getting serious then ! Sansculottism too has become a Fact, and seems minded to assert itself as such ? This huge mooncalf of Sansculottism, staggering about, as young calves do, is not mockable only, and soft like another calf ; but terrible too, if you prick it ; and, through its hideous nostrils, blows fire !—Aristocrats, with pale panic in their hearts, fly towards covert ; and a light rises to them over several things ; or rather a confused transition towards light, whereby for the moment darkness is only darker than ever. But what will become of this France ? Here is a question ! France is dancing its desert-waltz, as Sahara does when the winds waken ; in whirlblasts twenty-five millions in number ; waltzing towards Townhalls, Aristocrat Prisons and Election Committee-rooms ; towards Brunswick and the frontiers ;—towards a New Chapter of Universal History ; if indeed it be not the *Finis*, and winding-up of that !

In Election Committee-rooms there is now no dubiety ; but the work goes bravely along. The Convention is getting chosen,—really in a decisive spirit ; in the Townhall we already date *First year of the Republic*. Some Two-hundred of our best Legislators may be re-elected, the Mountain bodily : Robespierre, with Mayor Pétion, Buzot, Curate Grégoire, Rabaut, some three-score Old-Constituents ; though we once had only ' thirty voices '. All these ; and along with them, friends long known to Revolutionary fame : Camille Desmoulins, though he stutters in speech ; Manuel, Tallien and Company ; Journalists Gorsas, Carra,

Mercier, Louvet of *Faublas*; Clootz, Speaker of Mankind; Collot d'Herbois, tearing a passion to rags; Fabre
d'Eglantine, speculative Pamphleteer; Legendre, the
solid Butcher; nay Marat, though rural France can
hardly believe it, or even believe that there *is* a Marat,
except in print. Of Minister Danton, who will lay down
his Ministry for a Membership, we need not speak.
Paris is fervent; nor is the Country wanting to itself.
Barbaroux, Rebecqui, and fervid Patriots are coming
from Marseilles. Seven-hundred and forty-five men
(or indeed forty-nine, for Avignon now sends Four)
are gathering: so many are to meet; not so many
are to part!

Attorney Carrier from Aurillac, Ex-Priest Lebon from
Arras, these shall both gain a *name*. Mountainous
Auvergne re-elects her Romme; hardy tiller of the soil,
once Mathematical Professor; who, unconscious, carries
in petto a remarkable *New Calendar*, with Messidors,
Pluvioses, and such like;—and having given it well
forth, shall depart by the death they call Roman.
Sieyès, Old-Constituent, comes; to make new Constitutions as many as wanted: for the rest, peering out of
his clear cautious eyes, he will cower low in many an
emergency, and find silence safest. Young Saint-Just
is coming, deputed by Aisne in the North; more like
a Student than a Senator; not four-and-twenty yet;
who has written Books; a youth of slight stature, with
mild mellow voice, enthusiast olive-complexion and long
black hair. Féraud, from the far valley D'Aure in the
folds of the Pyrenees, is coming; an ardent Republican;
doomed to fame, at least in death.

All manner of Patriot men are coming: Teachers,
Husbandmen, Priests and Ex-Priests, Traders, Doctors;
above all, Talkers, or the Attorney-species. Man-mid-
wives, as Levasseur of the Sarthe, are not wanting. Nor
Artists: gross David,* with the swoln cheek, has long
painted, with genius in a state of convulsion; and will
now legislate. The swoln cheek, choking his words in
the birth, totally disqualifies him as an orator; but his
pencil, his head, his gross hot heart, with genius in

a state of convulsion, will be there.   A man bodily and
mentally swoln-cheeked, disproportionate ; flabby-large,
instead of great ; weak withal as in a state of convulsion, not strong in a state of composure : so let him play
his part.   Nor are naturalized Benefactors of the Species
forgotten : Priestley, elected by the Orne Department,
but declining ; Paine the rebellious Needleman, by the
Pas de Calais, who accepts.

Few Nobles come, and yet not none.   Paul-François
Barras,* ' noble as the Barrases, old as the rocks of Provence ' ; he is one.   The reckless, shipwrecked man :
flung ashore on the coast of the Maldives long ago, while
sailing and soldiering as Indian Fighter : flung ashore
since then, as hungry Parisian Pleasure-hunter and
Half-pay, on many a Circe Island, with temporary
enchantment, temporary conversion into beasthood and
hoghood ;—the remote Var Department has now sent
him hither.   A man of heat and haste ; defective in
utterance ; defective indeed in anything to utter ; yet
not without a certain rapidity of glance, a certain swift
transient courage ; who in these times, Fortune favouring, may go far.   He is tall, handsome to the eye, ' only
the complexion a little yellow ' ; but ' with a robe of
purple, with a scarlet cloak and plume of tricolor, on
occasions of solemnity ', the man will look well.[1]   Lepelletier Saint-Fargeau, Old-Constituent, is a kind of
noble, and of enormous wealth ; he too has come hither :
—to have the Pain of Death *abolished* ?   Hapless Ex-
Parlementeer ! Nay, among our Sixty Old-Constituents,
see Philippe d'Orléans, a Prince of the Blood ! Not
now *D'Orléans* : for, Feudalism being swept from the
world, he demands of his worthy friends the Electors
of Paris, to have a new name of their choosing ; whereupon Procureur Manuel, like an antithetic literary man,
recommends *Equality*, Égalité.   A Philippe Égalité
therefore will sit ; seen of the Earth and Heaven.

Such a Convention is gathering itself together.   Mere
angry poultry in moulting season ; whom Brunswick's

---

[1] Dictionnaire des Hommes Marquans, § Barras.

grenadiers and cannoneers will give short account of.
Would the weather, as Bertrand is always praying, only
mend a little ! [1]

In vain, O Bertrand! The weather will not mend
a whit: nay even if it did? Dumouriez Polymetis,
though Bertrand knows it not, started from brief slumber at Sedan, on that morning of the 29th of August;
with stealthiness, with promptitude, audacity. Some
three mornings after that, Brunswick, opening wide
eyes, perceives the Passes of the Argonne all seized;
blocked with felled trees, fortified with camps; and
that it is a most shifty swift Dumouriez this, who has
outwitted him !

The manœuvre may cost Brunswick 'a loss of three
weeks', very fatal in these circumstances. A Mountain-
wall of forty miles lying between him and Paris: which
he should have preoccupied;—which how now to get
possession of ? Also the rain it raineth every day; and
we are in a hungry Champagne Pouilleuse, a land flowing only with ditchwater. How to cross this Mountain-
wall of the Argonne; or what in the world to do with
it ?—There are marchings and wet splashings by steep
paths, with *sackerments* and guttural interjections;
forcings of Argonne Passes,—which unhappily will not
force. Through the woods, volleying War reverberates,
like huge gong-music, or Moloch's kettledrum, borne
by the echoes; swoln torrents boil angrily round the
foot of rocks, floating pale carcasses of men. In vain!
Islettes Village, with its church-steeple, rises intact in the
Mountain-pass, between the embosoming heights; your
forced marchings and climbings have become forced
slidings, and tumblings back. From the hill-tops thou
seest nothing but dumb crags, and endless wet moaning woods; the Clermont *Vache* (huge Cow that she is)
disclosing herself [2] at intervals; flinging off her cloud-
blanket, and soon taking it on again, drowned in the

---

[1] Bertrand-Moleville, Mémoires, ii. 225.
[2] See Helen Maria Williams, Letters, iii. 79-81.

pouring Heaven. The Argonne Passes will not force : you must *skirt* the Argonne : go round by the end of it.

But fancy whether the Emigrant Seigneurs have not got their brilliancy dulled a little ; whether that ' Foot Regiment in red-facings with nankeen trousers ' could be in field-day order ! In place of gasconading, a sort of desperation, and hydrophobia from *excess* of water, is threatening to supervene. Young Prince de Ligne, son of that brave literary De Ligne the Thundergod of Dandies, fell backwards ; shot dead in Grand-Pré, the Northmost of the Passes : Brunswick is skirting and rounding, laboriously, by the extremity of the South. Four days ; days of a rain as of Noah,—without fire, without food ! For fire you cut down green trees, and produce smoke ; for food you eat green grapes, and pro- duce colic, pestilential dysentery, ὀλέκοντο δὲ λαοί.* And the Peasants assassinate us, they do not join us ; shrill women cry shame on us, threaten to draw their very scissors on us ! O ye hapless dulled-bright Seig- neurs, and hydrophobic splashed Nankeens ;—but O, ten times more, ye poor *sackerment*ing ghastly-visaged Hessians and Hulans, fallen on your backs ; who had no call to die there, except compulsion and three-half- pence a-day ! Nor has Mrs. Le Blanc of the Golden Arm a good time of it, in her bower of dripping rushes. Assassinating Peasants are hanged ; Old-Constituent Honourable Members, though of venerable age, ride in carts with their hands tied : these are the woes of war.

Thus they ; sprawling and wriggling, far and wide, on the slopes and passes of the Argonne ;—a loss to Brunswick of five-and-twenty disastrous days. There is wriggling and struggling ; facing, backing and right- about facing ; as the positions shift, and the Argonne gets partly rounded, partly forced:—but still Dumouriez, force him, round him as you will, sticks like a rooted fixture on the ground ; fixture with many *hinges* ; wheeling now this way, now that; showing always new front, in the most unexpected manner : nowise consent- ing to take himself away. Recruits stream up on him : full of heart ; yet rather difficult to deal with. Behind

Grand-Pré, for example, Grand-Pré which is on the wrong-side of the Argonne, for we are now forced and rounded,—the full heart, in one of those wheelings and showings of new front, did as it were overset itself, as full hearts are liable to do; and there rose a shriek of *sauve qui peut*, and a death-panic which had nigh ruined all! So that the General had to come galloping; and, with thunder-words, with gesture, stroke of drawn sword even, check and rally, and bring back the sense of shame; [1]—nay to seize the first shriekers and ring-leaders; 'shave their heads and eyebrows', and pack them forth into the world as a sign. Thus too (for really the rations are short, and wet camping with hungry stomach brings bad humour) there is like to be mutiny. Whereupon again Dumouriez 'arrives at the head of their line, with his staff, and an escort of a hundred hussars. He had placed some squadrons behind them, the artillery in front; he said to them: "As for you, for I will neither call you citizens, nor soldiers, nor my men (*ni mes enfans*), you see before you this artillery, behind you this cavalry. You have dishonoured yourselves by crimes. If you amend, and grow to behave like this brave Army which you have the honour of belonging to, you will find in me a good father. But plunderers and assassins I do not suffer here. At the smallest mutiny I will have you shivered in pieces (*hacher en pièces*). Seek out the scoundrels that are among you, and dismiss them yourselves; I hold you responsible for them"'.[2]

Patience, O Dumouriez! This uncertain heap of shriekers, mutineers, were they once drilled and inured, will become a phalanxed mass of Fighters; and wheel and whirl, to order, swiftly like the wind or the whirl-wind: tanned moustachio-figures; often barefoot, even bare-backed; with sinews of iron; who require only bread and gunpowder: very Sons of Fire, the adroitest, hastiest, hottest ever seen perhaps since Attila's time.

[1] Dumouriez, Mémoires, iii. 29.
[2] Ibid., iii. 55.

They may conquer and overrun amazingly, much as
that same Attila did;—whose Attila's-Camp and Battlefield thou now seest, on this very ground ; [1] who, after
sweeping bare the world, was, with difficulty, and days
of tough fighting, checked *here* by Roman Aetius and
Fortune ; and his dust-cloud made to vanish in the
East again !—

Strangely enough, in this shrieking Confusion of a
Soldiery, which we saw long since fallen all suicidally
out of square, in suicidal collision,—at Nanci, or on the
streets of Metz, where brave Bouillé stood with drawn
sword ; and which has collided and ground itself to
pieces worse and worse ever since, down now to such
a state : in this shrieking Confusion, and not elsewhere,
lies the first germ of returning Order for France ! Round
which, we say, poor France, nearly all ground down
suicidally likewise into rubbish and Chaos, will be glad
to rally ; to begin growing, and new-shaping her inorganic dust ; very slowly, through centuries, through
Napoleons, Louis-Philippes, and other the like media
and phases,—into a new, infinitely preferable France,
we can hope !—

These wheelings and movements in the region of
the Argonne, which are all faithfully described by
Dumouriez himself, and more interesting to us than
Hoyle's* or Philidor's best Game of Chess,* let us nevertheless, O Reader, entirely omit;—and hasten to remark
two things : the first a minute private, the second a
large public thing. Our minute private thing is : the
presence, in the Prussian host, in that war-game of the
Argonne, of a certain Man, belonging to the sort called
Immortal ; who, in days since then, is becoming visible
more and more in that character, as the Transitory more
and more vanishes : for from of old it was remarked
that when the Gods appear among men, it is seldom in
recognizable shape ; thus Admetus's neatherds give
Apollo* a draught of their goatskin whey-bottle (well if

---

[1] Helen Maria Williams, iii. 32.

they do not give him strokes with their ox-rungs), not dreaming that he is the Sungod ! This man's name is *Johann Wolfgang von Goethe.* He is Herzog Weimar's Minister, come with the small contingent of Weimar; to do insignificant unmilitary duty here; very irrecognizable to nearly all ! He stands at present, with drawn bridle, on the height near Sainte-Menehould, making an experiment on the ' cannon-fever '; having ridden thither against persuasion, into the dance and firing of the cannon-balls, with a scientific desire to understand what that same cannon-fever may be : ' The sound of them ', says he, ' is curious enough ; as if it were compounded of the humming of tops, the gurgling of water, and the whistle of birds. By degrees you get a very uncommon sensation ; which can only be described by similitude. It seems as if you were in some place extremely hot, and at the same time were completely penetrated by the heat of it ; so that you feel as if you and this element you are in were perfectly on a par. The eyesight loses nothing of its strength or distinctness; and yet it is as if all things had got a kind of brown-red colour, which makes the situation and the objects still more impressive on you '.[1]

This is the cannon-fever, as a World-Poet feels it. —A man entirely irrecognizable ! In whose irrecognizable head, meanwhile, there verily is the spiritual counterpart (and call it complement) of this same huge Death-Birth of the World ; which now effectuates itself, outwardly in the Argonne, in such cannon-thunder; inwardly, in the irrecognizable head, quite otherwise than by thunder ! Mark that man, O Reader, as the memorablest of all the memorable in this Argonne Campaign. What we say of him is not dream, nor flourish of rhetoric, but scientific historic fact ; as many men, now at this distance, see or begin to see.

But the large public thing we had to remark is this : That the Twentieth of September 1792 was a raw morning covered with mist ; that from three in the

---

[1] Goethe, Campagne in Frankreich (Werke, xxx. 73).

morning, Sainte-Menehould, and those Villages and
homesteads we know of old, were stirred by the rumble
of artillery-wagons, by the clatter of hoofs and many-
footed tramp of men : all manner of military, Patriot
and Prussian, taking up positions, on the Heights of
La Lune and other Heights ; shifting and shoving,—
seemingly in some dread chess-game ; which may the
Heavens turn to good ! The Miller of Valmy has fled
dusty under ground ; his Mill, were it never so windy,
will have rest to-day. At seven in the morning the mist
clears off : see Kellermann, Dumouriez' second in command, with ' eighteen pieces of cannon ', and deep-ser-
ried ranks, drawn up round that same silent Windmill,
on his knoll of strength ; Brunswick, also with serried
ranks and cannon, glooming over to him from the Height
of La Lune : only the little brook and its little dell now
parting them.

So that the much-longed-for has come at last ! Instead of hunger and dysentery, we shall have sharp shot ;
and then !—Dumouriez, with force and firm front, looks
on from a neighbouring height ; can help only with his
wishes, in silence. Lo, the eighteen pieces do bluster
and bark, responsive to the bluster of La Lune ; and
thunder-clouds mount into the air ; and echoes roar
through all dells, far into the depths of Argonne Wood
(deserted now) ; and limbs and lives of men fly dissipated, this way and that. Can Brunswick make an
impression on them ? The dulled-bright Seigneurs stand
biting their thumbs ; these Sansculottes seem *not* to fly
like poultry ! Towards noontide a cannon-shot blows
Kellermann's horse from under him ; there bursts a
powder-cart high into the air, with knell heard over all :
some swagging and swaying observable ;—Brunswick
will try ! ' *Camarades* ', cries Kellermann, ' *Vive la
Patrie ! Allons vaincre pour elle*, Come let us conquer
for her '. ' Live the Fatherland ! ' rings responsive to
the welkin, like rolling-fire from side to side : our ranks
are as firm as rocks ; and Brunswick may recross the
dell, ineffectual ; regain his old position on La Lune ;
not unbattered by the way. And so, for the length of

a September day,—with bluster and bark ; with bellow
far-echoing ! The cannonade lasts till sunset ; and no
impression made. · Till an hour after sunset, the few
remaining Clocks of the District striking Seven ; at this
late time of day Brunswick tries again. With not a
whit better fortune ! He is met by rock-ranks, by shout
of *Vive la Patrie* ; and driven back, not unbattered.
Whereupon he ceases ; retires ' to the Tavern of La
Lune ' ; and sets to raising a redoute lest *he* be attacked !

Verily so, ye dulled-bright Seigneurs, make of it what
ye may. Ah, and France does not rise round us in
mass ; and the Peasants do not join us, but assassinate
us : neither hanging nor any persuasion will induce
them ! They have lost their old distinguishing love of
King, and King's-cloak,—I fear, altogether ; and will
even fight to be rid of it : that seems now their humour.
Nor does Austria prosper, nor the siege of Thionville.
The Thionvillers, carrying their insolence to the epigrammatic pitch, have put a Wooden Horse on their
walls, with a bundle of Hay hung from him, and this
Inscription : ' When I finish my hay, you will take
Thionville '. [1] To such height has the frenzy of mankind risen.

The trenches of Thionville may shut ; and what
though those of Lille open ? The Earth smiles not on
us, nor the Heaven ; but weeps and blears itself, in sour
rain, and worse. Our very friends insult us ; we are
wounded in the house of our friends : ' His Majesty of
Prussia had a greatcoat, when the rain came ; and (contrary to all known laws) he put it on, though our two
French Princes, the hope of their country, had none ! '
To which indeed, as Goethe admits, what answer could
be made ? [2]—Cold and Hunger and Affront, Colic and
Dysentery and Death ; and we here, cowering *redouted*,
most unredoubtable, amid the ' tattered corn-shocks
and deformed stubble ', on the splashy Height of La
Lune, round the mean Tavern de la Lune !—

---

[1] Hist. Parl. xix. 177.   [2] Goethe, xxx. 49.

This is the Cannonade of Valmy ; wherein the World-Poet experimented on the cannon-fever ; wherein the French Sansculottes did not fly like poultry. Precious to France ! Every soldier did his duty, and Alsatian Kellermann (how preferable to old Lückner the dismissed !) began to become greater ; and *Égalité Fils,* Equality Junior, a light gallant Field-Officer, distinguished himself by intrepidity :—it is the same intrepid individual who now, as Louis-Philippe, without the Equality, struggles, under sad circumstances, to be called King of the French for a season.

CHAPTER VIII

EXEUNT

BUT this Twentieth of September is otherwise a great day. For, observe, while Kellermann's horse was flying blown from under him at the Mill of Valmy, our new National Deputies, that shall be a NATIONAL CONVENTION, are hovering and gathering about the Hall of the Hundred Swiss : with intent to constitute themselves !

On the morrow, about noontide, Camus the Archivist is busy ' verifying their powers ' ; several hundreds of them already here. Whereupon the Old Legislative comes solemnly over, to merge its old ashes Phoenix-like in the body of the new ;—and so forthwith, returning all solemnly back to the Salle de Manége, there sits a National Convention, Seven-hundred and Forty-nine complete, or complete enough ; presided by Pétion ; — which proceeds directly to do business. Read that reported afternoon's-debate, O Reader ; there are few debates like it : dull reporting *Moniteur* itself becomes more dramatic than a very Shakespeare. For epigrammatic Manuel rises, speaks strange things ; how the President shall have a guard of honour, and lodge in the Tuileries :—*rejected.* And Danton rises and speaks ; and Collot d'Herbois rises, and Curate Grégoire, and

lame Couthon of the Mountain rises; and in rapid
Meliboean*stanzas, only a few lines each, they propose
motions not a few: That the corner-stone of our new
Constitution is, Sovereignty of the People; that our
Constitution shall be accepted by the People or be null;
further that the People ought to be avenged, and have
right Judges; that the Imposts must continue till new
order; that Landed and other Property be sacred for
ever; finally that ' Royalty from this day is abolished
in France ':—*Decreed* all, before four o'clock strike, with
acclamation of the world![1]   The tree was all so ripe;
only shake it, and there fall such yellow cart-loads.

And so over in the Valmy Region, as soon as the
news come, what stir is this, audible, visible from our
muddy Heights of La Lune?[2]   Universal shouting of
the French on their opposite hill-side; caps raised on
bayonets: and a sound as of *République*; *Vive la Ré-*
publique borne dubious on the winds !—On the morrow
morning, so to speak, Brunswick slings his knapsacks
before day, lights any fires he has; and marches without tap of drum.   Dumouriez finds ghastly symptoms
in that camp; ' *latrines* full of blood' ![3]   The chivalrous King of Prussia; for he, as we saw, is here in person,
may long rue the day; may look colder than ever on
these dulled-bright Seigneurs, and French Princes their
Country's hope;—and, on the whole, put on his great·
coat without ceremony, happy that he has one.   They
retire, all retire with convenient dispatch, through a
Champagne trodden into a quagmire, the wild weather
pouring on them: Dumouriez, through his Keller-
manns and Dillons, pricking them a little in the hinder
parts.   A little, not much; now pricking, now negotiating: for Brunswick has his eyes opened; and the
Majesty of Prussia is a repentant Majesty.

Nor has Austria prospered, nor the Wooden Horse of
Thionville bitten his hay; nor Lille City surrendered

[1] Hist. Parl. xix. 19.   [2] Williams, iii. 71.
[3] 1st October 1792: Dumouriez, iii. 73.

itself.   The Lille trenches opened, on the 29th of the
month ; with balls and shells, and redhot balls ; as if
not trenches but Vesuvius and the Pit had opened.   It
was frightful, say all eye-witnesses ; but it is ineffectual.
The Lillers have risen to such temper ; especially after
these news from Argonne and the East.   Not a Sans-
indispensables in Lille that would surrender for a King's
ransom.   Redhot balls rain, day and night; 'six-
thousand', or so, and bombs 'filled internally with oil of
turpentine which splashes up in flame' ; —mainly on
the dwellings of the Sansculottes and Poor ; the streets
of the Rich being spared.   But the Sansculottes get
water-pails ; form quenching-regulations : 'The ball is
in Peter's house!'   'The ball is in John's!'   They
divide their lodging and substance with each other ;
shout *Vive la République* ; and faint not in heart.   A ball
thunders through the main chamber of the Hôtel-de-
Ville while the Commune is there assembled : 'We are
in permanence', says one, coldly, proceeding with his
business ; and the ball remains permanent too, sticking in the wall, probably to this day.[1]

The Austrian Archduchess (Queen's Sister) will herself see red artillery fired : in their over-haste to satisfy
an Archduchess, 'two mortars explode and kill thirty
persons'.   It is in vain ; Lille, often burning, is always
quenched again ; Lille will not yield.   The very boys
deftly wrench the matches out of fallen bombs:
'a man clutches a rolling ball with his hat, which takes
fire ; when cool, they crown it with a *bonnet rouge*'.
Memorable also be that nimble Barber, who when the
bomb burst beside him, snatched up a sherd of it, introduced soap and lather into it, crying, '*Voilà mon
plat à barbe*, My new shaving-dish !' and shaved 'fourteen people' on the spot.   Bravo, thou nimble Shaver ;
worthy to shave old spectral Redcloak, and find trea-
sures !—On the eighth day of this desperate siege, the
sixth day of October, Austria finding it fruitless,
draws off, with no pleasurable consciousness ; rapidly,

[1] Bombardement de Lille (in Hist. Parl. xx. 63–71).

Dumouriez tending thitherward ; and Lille too, black
with ashes and smoulder, but jubilant sky-high, flings
its gates open. The *Plat à barbe* became fashionable ;
' no Patriot of an elegant turn ', says Mercier several
years afterwards, ' but shaves himself out of the
splinter of a Lille bomb '.

Quid multa, Why many words ? The Invaders are
in flight ; Brunswick's Host, the third part of it gone to
death, staggers disastrous along the deep highways of
Champagne ; spreading out also into ' the fields of a
tough spongy red-coloured clay ' :—' like Pharaoh
through a Red Sea of mud ', says Goethe ; ' for here
also lay broken chariots, and riders and foot seemed
sinking around '.[1] On the eleventh morning of October, the World-Poet, struggling Northwards out of
Verdun, which he had entered Southwards, some five
weeks ago, in quite other order, discerned the following
Phenomenon and formed part of it :

' Towards three in the morning, without having had
any sleep, we were about mounting our carriage, drawn
up at the door ; when an insuperable obstacle disclosed
itself : for there rolled on already, between the pave-
ment-stones which were crushed up into a ridge on each
side, an uninterrupted column of sick-wagons through
the Town, and all was trodden as into a morass. While
we stood waiting what could be made of it, our Landlord the Knight of Saint-Louis pressed past us, without
salutation '. He had been a Calonne's Notable in 1787,
an Emigrant since ; had returned to his home, jubilant,
with the Prussians ; but must now forth again into the
wide world, ' followed by a servant carrying a little
bundle on his stick '.

' The activity of our alert Lisieux shone eminent, and
on this occasion too brought us on : for he struck into
a small gap of the wagon-row ; and held the advancing team back till we, with our six and our four horses,
got intercalated ; after which, in my light little coach-

---

[1] Campagne in Frankreich, p. 103.

let, I could breathe freer. We were now under way;
at a funeral pace, but still under way. The day
broke; we found ourselves at the outlet of the
Town, in a tumult and turmoil without measure. All
sorts of vehicles, few horsemen, innumerable foot-
people, were crossing each other on the great esplanade
before the Gate. We turned to the right, with our
Column, towards Estain, on a limited highway, with
ditches at each side. Self-preservation, in so monstrous a press, knew now no pity, no respect of aught.
Not far before us there fell down a horse of an ammu-
nition-wagon; they cut the traces, and let it lie. And
now as the three others could not bring their load along,
they cut them also loose, tumbled the heavy-packed
vehicle into the ditch; and with the smallest retardation, we had to drive on right over the horse, which was
just about to rise; and I saw too clearly how its legs,
under the wheels, went crashing and quivering.

'Horse and foot endeavoured to escape from the
narrow laborious highway into the meadows: but these
too were rained to ruin; overflowed by full ditches, the
connexion of the footpaths everywhere interrupted.
Four gentlemanlike, handsome, well-dressed French
soldiers waded for a time beside our carriage; wonderfully clean and neat: and had such art of picking their
steps, that their foot-gear testified no higher than the
ankle to the muddy pilgrimage these good people found
themselves engaged in.

'That under such circumstances one saw, in ditches,
in meadows, in fields and crofts, dead horses enough,
was natural to the case: by and by, however, you
found them also flayed, the fleshy parts even cut away;
sad token of the universal distress.

'Thus we fared on; every moment in danger, at
the smallest stoppage on our own part, of being ourselves tumbled overboard; under which circumstances,
truly, the careful dexterity of our Lisieux could not be
sufficiently praised. The same talent showed itself at
Estain; where we arrived towards noon; and descried,
over the beautiful well-built little Town, through streets

and on squares, around and beside us, one sense-con-
fusing tumult : the mass rolled this way and that ; and,
all struggling forward, each hindered the other.   Unexpectedly our carriage drew up before a stately house
in the market-place ; master and mistress of the mansion saluted us in reverent distance '.   Dexterous
Lisieux, though we knew it not, had said we were the
King of Prussia's Brother !

' But now, from the ground-floor windows, looking
over the whole market-place, we had the endless
tumult lying, as it were, palpable.   All sorts of walkers,
soldiers in uniform, marauders, stout but sorrowing
citizens and peasants, women and children, crushed and
jostled each other, amid vehicles of all forms : ammu-
nition-wagons,   baggage-wagons ;   carriages,   single,
double, and multiplex ; such hundredfold miscellany
of teams, requisitioned or lawfully owned, making way,
hitting together, hindering each other, rolled here to
right and to left.   Horned-cattle too were struggling
on ; probably herds that had been put in requisition.
Riders you saw few ; but the elegant carriages
of the Emigrants, many-coloured, lackered, gilt and
silvered, evidently by the best builders, caught your
eye.[1]

' The crisis of the strait, however, arose further on
a little ; where the crowded market-place had to introduce itself into a street,—straight indeed and good,
but proportionably far too narrow.   I have, in my life,
seen nothing like it : the aspect of it might perhaps
be compared to that of a swoln river which has been
raging over meadows and fields, and is now again
obliged to press itself through a narrow bridge, and
flow on in its bounded channel.   Down the long street,
all visible from our windows, there swelled continually
the strangest tide : a high double-seated travelling
coach towered visible over the flood of things.   We
thought of the fair French-women we had seen in the

---

[1] See Hermann und Dorothea (also by Goethe), Buch
Kalliope.

morning. It was not they, however; it was Count
Haugwitz; him you could look at, with a kind of sardonic malice, rocking onwards, step by step, there '.[1]

In such untriumphant Procession has the Brunswick
Manifesto issued! Nay in worse, ' in Negotiation with
these miscreants ',—the first news of which produced
such a revulsion in the Emigrant nature, as put our
scientific World-Poet ' in fear for the wits of several '.[2]
There is no help : they must fare on, these poor Emigrants, angry with all persons and things, and making
all persons angry in the hapless course they struck into.
Landlord and landlady testify to you, at *tables d'hôte*,
how insupportable these Frenchmen are : how, in spite
of such humiliation, of poverty and probable beggary,
there is ever the same struggle for precedence, the same
forwardness and want of discretion.   High in honour,
at the head of the table, you with your own eyes observe
not a Seigneur, but the automaton of a Seigneur fallen
into dotage ; still worshipped, reverently waited on and
fed.   In miscellaneous seats is a miscellany of soldiers,
commissaries, adventurers ; consuming silently their
barbarian victuals.   ' On all brows is to be read a hard
destiny ; all are silent, for each has his own sufferings
to bear, and looks forth into misery without bounds '.
One hasty wanderer, coming in, and eating without
ungraciousness what is set before him, the landlord lets
off almost scot-free.   ' He is ', whispered the landlord
to me, ' the first of these cursed people I have seen
condescend to taste our German black bread '.[3]

And Dumouriez is in Paris ; lauded and feasted ;
paraded in glittering saloons, floods of beautifullest
blonde-dresses and broadcloth-coats flowing past him,
endless, in admiring joy.   One night, nevertheless, in
the splendour of one such scene, he sees himself suddenly apostrophized by a squalid unjoyful Figure, who

---

[1] Campagne in Frankreich, Goethe's Werke (Stuttgart,
1829), xxx. 133-7.
[2] Ibid. 152.   [3] Ibid. 210-12.

has come in *uninvited*, nay despite of all lackeys ; an
unjoyful Figure ! The Figure is come ' in express mission from the Jacobins ', to inquire sharply, better then
than later, touching certain things : ' Shaven eyebrows
of Volunteer Patriots, for instance ? ' Also, ' your
threats of shivering in pieces ? ' Also, ' why you have
not chased Brunswick hotly enough ? ' Thus, with
sharp croak, inquires the Figure.—' *Ah, c'est vous qu'on
appelle Marat*, You are he they call Marat ! ' answers
the General, and turns coldly on his heel.[1]—' Marat ! '
The blonde-gowns quiver like aspens ; the dress-coats
gather round ; Actor Talma (for it is his house), Actor
Talma, and almost the very chandelier-lights, are blue :
till this obscene Spectrum, swart unearthly Visual-
Appearance, vanish, back into its native Night.

General Dumouriez, in few brief days, is gone again,
towards the Netherlands ; will attack the Netherlands,
winter though it be. And General Montesquiou, on
the Southeast, has driven in the Sardinian Majesty ;
nay, almost without a shot fired, has taken Savoy from
him, which longs to become a piece of the Republic. And
General Custine,* on the Northeast, has dashed forth on
Spires and its Arsenal ; and then on Electoral Mentz,
not uninvited, wherein are German Democrats and no
shadow of an Elector now : so that in the last days of
October, Frau Forster, a daughter of Heyne's, somewhat democratic, walking out of the Gate of Mentz*with
her Husband, finds French Soldiers playing at bowls
with cannon-balls there. Forster*trips cheerfully over
one iron bomb, with ' Live the Republic ! ' A black-
bearded National Guard answers: ' *Elle vivra bien sans
vous*, It will probably live independently of you '.[2]

[1] Dumouriez, iii. 115. Marat's account, in the Débats
des Jacobins and Journal de la République (Hist. Parl. xix.
317–21), agrees to the turning on the heel ; but strives to
interpret it differently.

[2] Johann Georg Forster's Briefwechsel (Leipzig, 1829).
i. 88.

BOOK II

REGICIDE

CHAPTER I

THE DELIBERATIVE

FRANCE therefore has done two things very completely: she has hurled back her Cimmerian Invaders far over the marches; and likewise she has shattered her own internal Social Constitution, even to the minutest fibre of it, into wreck and dissolution. Utterly it is all altered: from King down to Parish Constable, all Authorities, Magistrates, Judges, persons that bore rule, have had, on the sudden, to alter themselves, so far as needful; or else, on the sudden, and not without violence, to be altered; a Patriot 'Executive Council of Ministers', with a Patriot Danton in it, and then a whole Nation and National Convention, have taken care of that. Not a Parish Constable, in the farthest hamlet, who has said *De par le Roi*, and shown loyalty, but must retire, making way for a new improved Parish Constable who can say *De par la République*.

It is a change such as History must beg her readers to imagine, *un*described. An instantaneous change of the whole body-politic, the soul-politic being all changed; such a change as few bodies, politic or other, can experience in this world. Say, perhaps, such as poor Nymph Semele's body did experience, when she would needs, with woman's humour, see her Olympian Jove as very Jove;—and so stood, poor Nymph, this moment Semele, next moment not Semele, but Flame and a Statue of red-hot Ashes! France has looked upon

Democracy; seen it face to face.—The Cimmerian Invaders will rally, in humbler temper, with better or worse luck: the wreck and dissolution must reshape itself into a social Arrangement as it can and may. But as for this National Convention, which is to settle everything, if it do, as Deputy Paine and France generally expects, get all finished 'in a few months', we shall call it a most deft Convention.

In truth, it is very singular to see how this mercurial French People plunges suddenly from *Vive le Roi* to *Vive la République*; and goes simmering and dancing, shaking off daily (so to speak), and trampling into the dust, its old social garnitures, ways of thinking, rules of existing; and cheerfully dances towards the Ruleless, Unknown, with such hope in its heart, and nothing but *Freedom, Equality and Brotherhood* in its mouth. Is it two centuries, or is it only two years, since all France roared simultaneously to the welkin, bursting forth into sound and smoke at its *Feast of Pikes,* 'Live the Restorer of French Liberty'? Three short years ago there was still Versailles and an Œil-de-Bœuf: now there is that watched Circuit of the Temple, girt with dragon-eyed Municipals, where, as in its final limbo, Royalty lies extinct. In the year 1789, Constituent Deputy Barrère 'wept', in his *Break-of-Day* Newspaper, at sight of a reconciled King Louis; and now in 1792, Convention Deputy Barrère, perfectly tearless, may be considering, whether the reconciled King Louis shall be guillotined or not!

Old garnitures and social vestures drop off (we say) so fast, being indeed quite decayed, and are trodden under the National dance. And the new vestures, where are they; the new modes and rules? Liberty, Equality, Fraternity: not vestures, but the wish for vestures! The Nation is for the present, figuratively speaking, *naked*; it has no rule or vesture; but is naked,—a Sansculottic Nation.

So far therefore, and in such manner, have our Patriot Brissots, Guadets triumphed. Vergniaud's Ezekiel-visions*of the fall of thrones and crowns, which

he spake hypothetically and prophetically in the Spring
of the year, have suddenly come to fulfilment in the
Autumn.   Our eloquent Patriots of the Legislative, like
strong Conjurers, by the word of their mouth, have
swept Royalism with its old modes and formulas to the
winds ; and shall now govern a France free of formulas.
Free of formulas ! And yet man lives not except with
formulas ; with customs, *ways* of doing and living : no
text truer than this ; which will hold true from the
Tea-table and Tailor's shopboard up to the High Senate-
houses, Solemn Temples ; nay through all provinces
of Mind and Imagination, onwards to the outmost con-
fines of articulate Being,—*Ubi homines sunt modi sunt*.
There are modes wherever there are men.   It is the
deepest law of man's nature ; whereby man is a craftsman and 'tool-using animal'*; not the slave of Impulse,
Chance and brute Nature, but in some measure their
lord.   Twenty-five millions of men, suddenly stripped
bare of their *modi*, and dancing them down in that
manner, are a terrible thing to govern !

Eloquent Patriots of the Legislative, meanwhile,
have precisely this problem to solve.   Under the name
and nickname of ' statesmen, *hommes d'état* ', of ' moderate men, *modérantins* ', of Brissotins, Rolandins, finally
of *Girondins*, they shall become world-famous in solving
it.   For the Twenty-five millions are Gallic effervescent
too ;—filled both with hope of the unutterable, of universal Fraternity and Golden Age ; and with terror of
the unutterable, Cimmerian Europe all rallying on us.
It is a problem like few.   Truly, if man, as the Philosophers brag, did to any extent look before and after,*
what, one may ask, in many cases would become of
him ? What, in this case, would become of these Seven-
hundred and Forty-nine men ? The Convention, seeing
clearly before and after, were a paralysed Convention.
Seeing clearly to the length of its own nose, it is not
paralysed.

To the Convention itself neither the work nor the
method of doing it is doubtful ! To make the Constitution ; to defend the Republic till that be made.

Speedily enough, accordingly, there has been a 'Committee of the Constitution' got together. Sieyès, Old-
Constituent, Constitution-builder by trade ; Condorcet,
fit for better things ; Deputy Paine, foreign Benefactor
of the Species, with that 'red carbuncled face and the
black beaming eyes' ; Hérault de Séchelles,* Ex-Parle-
menteer, one of the handsomest men in France : these,
with inferior guild-brethren, are girt cheerfully to the
work ; will once more 'make the Constitution' ; let
us hope, more effectually than last time. For that the
Constitution can be made, who doubts,—unless the
Gospel of Jean Jacques came into the world in vain ?
True, our last Constitution did tumble within the year,
so lamentably. But what then ; except sort the rubbish and boulders, and build them up again better ?
'Widen your basis', for one thing,—to Universal Suffrage, if need be ; exclude rotten materials, Royalism
and such like, for another thing. And in brief, *build*,
O unspeakable Sieyès and Company, unwearied !
Frequent perilous downrushing of scaffolding and
rubble-work, be that an irritation, no discouragement.
Start ye always again, clearing aside the wreck ; if with
broken limbs, yet with whole hearts; and build, we say,
in the name of Heaven,—till either the work do stand ;
or else mankind abandon it, and the Constitution-
builders be paid off, with laughter and tears ! One good
time, in the course of Eternity, it was appointed that this
of Social Contract too should try itself out. And so the
Committee of Constitution shall toil : with hope and
faith ;—with no disturbance from any reader of these
pages.

To make the Constitution, then, and return home
joyfully in a few months ; this is the prophecy our
National Convention gives of itself ; by this scientific
programme shall its operations and events go on. But
from the best scientific programme, in such a case, to the
actual fulfilment, what a difference ! Every reunion of
men, is it not, as we often say, a reunion of incalculable
Influences ; every unit of it a microcosm of Influences ;
—of which how shall Science calculate or prophesy ?

Science, which cannot, with all its calculuses, differential, integral and of variations, calculate the Problem of Three gravitating Bodies,* ought to hold her peace here, and say only : In this National Convention there are Seven-hundred and Forty-nine very singular Bodies, that gravitate and do much else ;—who, probably in an amazing manner, will work the appointment of Heaven.

Of National Assemblages, Parliaments, Congresses, which have long sat ; which are of saturnine temperament ; above all, which are not ' dreadfully in earnest ', something may be computed or conjectured : yet even these are a kind of Mystery in progress,—whereby accordingly we see the Journalist Reporter find livelihood : even these jolt madly out of the ruts, from time to time. How much more a poor National Convention, of French vehemence ; urged on at such velocity ; without routine, without rut, track, or landmark ; and dreadfully in earnest every man of them ! It is a Parliament literally such as there was never elsewhere in the world. Themselves are new, unarranged ; they are the Heart and presiding centre of a France fallen wholly into maddest disarrangement. From all cities, hamlets, from the utmost ends of this France with its Twenty-five million vehement souls, thick-streaming influences storm in on that same Heart, in the Salle de Manége, and storm out again : such fiery venous-arterial circulation is the function of that Heart. Seven-hundred and Forty-nine human individuals, we say, never sat together on our Earth under more original circumstances. Common individuals most of them, or not far from common : yet in virtue of the position they occupied, so notable. How, in this wild piping of the whirlwind of human passions, with death, victory, terror, valour, and all height and all depth pealing and piping, these men, left to their own guidance, will speak and act ?

Readers know well that this French National Convention (quite contrary to its own Programme) became the astonishment and horror of mankind ; a kind of Apocalyptic Convention, or black *Dream become real*; concerning which History seldom speaks except in the

way of interjection : how it covered France with woe,
delusion and delirium ; and from its bosom there went
forth Death on the pale Horse.* To hate this poor
National Convention is easy ; to praise and love it has
not been found impossible. It is, as we say, a Parliament in the most original circumstances. To us, in
these pages, be it as a fuliginous fiery mystery, where
Upper has met Nether, and in such alternate glare and
blackness of darkness poor bedazzled mortals know not
which is Upper, which is Nether ; but rage and plunge
distractedly, as mortals in that case will do. A Convention which has to consume itself, suicidally ; and
become dead ashes—with its World ! Behoves us, not
to enter exploratively its dim embroiled deeps ; yet to
stand with unwavering eyes, looking how it welters ;
what notable phases and occurrences it will successively
throw up.

One general superficial circumstance we remark
with praise : the force of Politeness. To such depth
has the sense of civilization penetrated man's life ; no
Drouet, no Legendre, in the maddest tug of war, can
altogether shake it off. Debates of Senates dreadfully
in earnest are seldom given frankly to the world ; else
perhaps they would surprise it. Did not the Grand
Monarque himself once chase his Louvois*with a pair
of brandished tongs ? But reading long volumes of
these Convention Debates, all in a foam with furious
earnestness, earnest many times to the extent of life and
death, one is struck rather with the degree of continence
they manifest in speech ; and how in such wild ebulli-
tion, there is still a kind of polite rule struggling for
mastery, and the forms of social life never altogether
disappear. These men, though they menace with
clenched right-hands, do not clutch one another by the
collar ; they draw no daggers, except for oratorical purposes, and this not often : profane swearing is almost
unknown, though the Reports are frank enough ; we
find only one or two oaths, oaths by Marat, reported
in all.

For the rest, that there is 'effervescence' who
doubts ? Effervescence enough ; Decrees passed by acclamation to-day, repealed by vociferation to-morrow;
temper fitful, most rotatory-changeful, always headlong ! The 'voice of the orator is covered with rumours;
a hundred 'honourable Members rush with menaces
towards the Left side of the Hall'; President has
' broken three bells in succession ',—claps on his hat,
as signal that the country is near ruined. A fiercely
effervescent Old-Gallic Assemblage !—Ah, how the loud
sick sounds of Debate, and of Life, which is a *debate*,
sink silent one after another : so loud now, and in a little
while so low! Brennus, and those antique Gael Captains,
in their way to Rome, to Galatia and such places,
whither they were in the habit of marching in the most
fiery manner, had Debates as effervescent, doubt it not;
though no *Moniteur* has reported them. They scolded
in Celtic Welsh, those Brennuses ; neither were they
Sansculotte ; nay rather breeches (*braccae*, say of felt
or rough-leather) were the only thing they had ; being,
as Livy testifies,* naked down *to* the haunches :—and,
see, it is the same sort of work and of men still, now when
they have got coats, and speak nasally a kind of broken
Latin ! But, on the whole, does not TIME envelope
this present National Convention ; as it did those
Brennuses, and ancient august Senates in felt breeches ?
Time surely ; and also Eternity. Dim dusk of Time,—
or noon which will be dusk ; and then there is night,
and silence ; and Time with all its sick noises is swallowed in the still sea. Pity thy brother, O son of Adam !
The angriest frothy jargon that he utters, is it not
properly the whimpering of an infant which cannot
speak what ails it, but is in distress clearly, in the
inwards of it ; and so must squall and whimper continually, till its Mother take it, and it get—to sleep !

This Convention is not four days old, and the
melodious Meliboean stanzas that shook down Royalty
are still fresh in our ear, when there bursts out a new
diapason,—unhappily, of Discord, this time. For speech

has been made of a thing difficult to speak of well : the
September Massacres.   How deal with these September Massacres ; with the Paris Commune that presided
over them ? A Paris Commune hateful-terrible ; before
which the poor effete Legislative had to quail, and sit
quiet.   And now if a young omnipotent Convention
will not so quail and sit, what steps shall it take ? Have
a Departmental Guard in its pay, answer the Girondins,
and Friends of Order ! A Guard of National Volunteers, missioned from all the Eighty-three or Eighty-
five Departments, for that express end ; these will keep
Septemberers, tumultuous Communes in a due state of
submissiveness, the Convention in a due state of sovereignty.   So have the Friends of Order answered, sitting in Committee, and reporting ; and even a Decree
has been passed of the required tenor.   Nay certain
Departments, as the Var or Marseilles, in mere expectation and assurance of a Decree, have their contingent
of Volunteers already on march ; brave Marseillese,
foremost on the Tenth of August, will not be hindmost
here ; ' fathers gave their sons a musket and twenty-
five louis ', says Barbaroux, ' and bade them march '.

Can anything be properer ? A Republic that will
found itself on justice must needs investigate September Massacres ; a Convention calling itself National,
ought it not to be guarded by a National force ?—Alas,
Reader, it seems so to the eye : and yet there is much
to be said and argued.   Thou beholdest here the small
beginning of a Controversy, which mere logic will not
settle.   Two small well-springs, September, Departmental Guard, or rather at bottom they are but one and
the same small well-spring ; all manner of subsidiary
streams and brooks of bitterness flowing in, from this
side and that ; till it become a wide river of bitterness,
of rage and separation,—which can subside only into the
Catacombs.   This Departmental Guard, decreed by
overwhelming majorities, and then repealed for peace's
sake, and not to insult Paris, is again decreed more than
once ; nay it is partially executed, and the very men

that are to be of it are seen visibly parading the Paris
streets,—shouting once, being overtaken with liquor:
'*A bas Marat*, Down with Marat!'[1] Nevertheless,
decreed never so often, it is repealed just as often; and
continues, for some seven months, an angry noisy
Hypothesis only: a fair Possibility struggling to become
a Reality, but which shall never be one; which, after
endless struggling, shall, in February next, sink into
sad rest,—dragging much along with it. So singular
are the ways of men and honourable Members.

But on this fourth day of the Convention's existence,
as we said, which is the 25th of September 1792, there
comes Committee Report on that Decree of the Departmental Guard, and speech of repealing it; there come
denunciations of Anarchy, of a Dictatorship,—which
let the incorruptible Robespierre consider: there come
denunciations of a certain *Journal de la République*,
once called *Ami du Peuple*; and so thereupon there
comes, visibly stepping up, visibly standing aloft on
the Tribune, ready to speak,—the Bodily Spectrum of
People's-Friend Marat! Shriek, ye Seven-hundred and
Forty-nine; it is verily Marat, he and not another.
Marat is no phantasm of the brain, or mere lying impress
of Printer's Types; but a thing material, of joint and
sinew, and a certain small stature; ye behold him
there, in his blackness, in his dingy squalor, a living
fraction of Chaos and Old Night; visibly incarnate,
desirous to speak. 'It appears', says Marat to the
shrieking Assembly, 'that a great many persons here
are enemies of mine'.—'All! all!' shriek hundreds
of voices: enough to drown any People's-Friend. But
Marat will not drown: he speaks and croaks explanation; croaks with such reasonableness, air of sincerity,
that repentant pity smothers anger, and the shrieks
subside, or even become applauses. For this Convention
is unfortunately the crankest of machines: it shall be
pointing eastward with stiff violence, this moment; and
then do but touch some spring dexterously, the whole

[1] Hist. Parl. xx. 184.

machine, clattering and jerking seven-hundredfold,
will whirl with huge crash, and, next moment, is pointing westward ! Thus Marat, absolved and applauded,
victorious in this turn of fence, is, as the Debate goes
on, pricked at again by some dexterous Girondin ; and
then the shrieks rise anew, and Decree of Accusation is
on the point of passing ; till the dingy People's-Friend
bobs aloft once more ; croaks once more persuasive stillness, and the Decree of Accusation sinks. Whereupon
he draws forth—a Pistol ; and setting it to his Head,
the seat of such thought and prophecy, says : ' If they
had passed their Accusation Decree, he, the People's-
Friend, would have blown his brains out '. A People's-
Friend has that faculty in him. For the rest, as to this
of the two-hundred and sixty-thousand Aristocrat
Heads, Marat candidly says, ' *C'est là mon avis*, Such is
my opinion '. Also is it not indisputable : ' No power
on Earth can prevent me from seeing into traitors, and
unmasking them',—by my superior originality of mind ?[1]
An honourable member like this Friend of the People
few terrestrial Parliaments have had.

We observe, however, that this first onslaught by
the Friends of Order, as sharp and prompt as it was,
has failed. For neither can Robespierre, summoned
out by talk of Dictatorship, and greeted with the like
rumour on showing himself, be thrown into Prison, into
Accusation ; not though Barbaroux openly bear testimony against him, and sign it on paper. With such
sanctified meekness does the Incorruptible lift his seagreen cheek to the smiter ; lift his thin voice, and with
jesuitic dexterity plead, and prosper ; asking at last,
in a prosperous manner : ' But what witnesses has the
Citoyen Barbaroux to support his testimony ? ' ' *Moi !*'
cries hot Rebecqui, standing up, striking his breast
with both hands, and answering ' Me ! '[2] Nevertheless

---

[1] Moniteur Newspaper, Nos. 271, 280, 294, Année première;
Moore's Journal, ii. 21, 157, &c. (which, however, may
perhaps, as in similar cases, be only a copy of the Newspaper).
[2] Moniteur, *ut supra* : Séance du 25 Septembre.

the Seagreen pleads again, and makes it good: the long hurlyburly, 'personal merely', while so much public matter lies fallow, has ended in the order of the day. O Friends of the Gironde, why will you occupy our august sessions with mere paltry Personalities, while the grand Nationality lies in such a state?—The Gironde has touched, this day, on the foul black-spot of its fair Convention Domain; has trodden on it, and yet *not* trodden it down. Alas, it is a *well-spring*, as we said, this black-spot; and will not tread down!

CHAPTER II

THE EXECUTIVE

MAY we not conjecture therefore that round this grand enterprise of Making the Constitution, there will, as heretofore, very strange embroilments gather, and questions and interests complicate themselves; so that after a few or even several months, the Convention will not have settled everything? Alas, a whole tide of questions comes rolling, boiling; growing ever wider, without end! Among which, apart from this question of September and Anarchy, let us notice three, which emerge oftener than the others, and promise to become Leading Questions: Of the Armies; of the Subsistences; thirdly, of the Dethroned King.

As to the Armies, Public Defence must evidently be put on a proper footing; for Europe seems coalizing itself again; one is apprehensive even England will join it. Happily Dumouriez prospers in the North;—nay, what if he should prove *too* prosperous, and become *Liberticide*, Murderer of Freedom!—Dumouriez prospers, through this winter season; yet not without lamentable complaints. Sleek Pache, the Swiss Schoolmaster, he that sat frugal in his Alley, the wonder of neighbours, has got lately—whither thinks the Reader?

To be Minister of War! Madame Roland, struck with
his sleek ways, recommended him to her husband as
Clerk; the sleek Clerk had no need of salary, being
of true Patriotic temper; he would come with a bit
of bread in his pocket, to save dinner and time; and
munching incidentally, do three men's work in a day;
punctual, silent, frugal,—the sleek Tartuffe that he was.
Wherefore Roland, in the late Overturn, recommended
him to be War-Minister. And now, it would seem, he
is secretly undermining Roland; playing into the hands
of your hotter Jacobins and September Commune; and
cannot, like strict Roland, be the *Veto des Coquins*![1]

How the sleek Pache might mine and undermine, one
knows not well; this however one does know: that his
War-Office has become a den of thieves and confusion,
such as all men shudder to behold. That the Citizen
Hassenfratz,* as Head-Clerk, sits there in *bonnet rouge*,
in rapine, in violence, and some Mathematical calculation; a most insolent, red-nightcapped man. That
Pache munches his pocket-loaf, amid head-clerks and
sub-clerks, and has spent all the War-Estimates. That
Furnishers scour in gigs, over all districts of France, and
drive bargains. And lastly that the Army gets next to
no furniture: no shoes, though it is winter; no clothes;
some have not even arms; ' in the Army of the South',
complains an honourable Member, ' there are thirty-
thousand pairs of breeches wanting',—a most scandalous want.

Roland's strict soul is sick to see the course things
take: but what can he do? Keep his own Department strict; rebuke, and repress wheresoever possible;
at lowest, complain. He can complain in Letter after
Letter, to a National Convention, to France, to Posterity, the Universe; grow ever more querulous-indignant;—till at last, may he not grow wearisome? For
is not this continual text of his, at bottom, a rather
barren one: How astonishing that in a time of Revolt
and abrogation of all Law but Cannon Law, there should

[1] Madame Roland, Mémoires, ii. 237, &c.

be such Unlawfulness ? Intrepid Veto-of-Scoundrels,
narrow-faithful, respectable, methodic man, work thou
in that manner, since happily it is thy manner, and
wear thyself away; though ineffectual, not profitless in
it—then nor *now* !—The brave Dame Roland, bravest
of all French women, begins to have misgivings : The
figure of Danton has too much of the ' Sardanapalus
character '* at a Republican Rolandin Dinner-table :
Clootz, Speaker of Mankind, proses sad stuff about
a Universal Republic, or union of all Peoples and
Kindreds in one and the same Fraternal Bond ; of
which Bond, how it is to be *tied*, one unhappily sees
not.

It is also an indisputable, unaccountable or account-
able fact, that Grains are becoming scarcer and scarcer.
Riots for grain, tumultuous Assemblages demanding to
have the price of grain fixed, abound far and near.   The
Mayor of Paris and other poor Mayors are like to have
their difficulties.   Pétion was re-elected Mayor of Paris;
but has declined ; being now a Convention Legislator.
Wise surely to decline : for, besides this of Grains and
all the rest, there is in these times an Improvised
Insurrectionary Commune passing into an Elected
legal one ; getting their accounts settled,—not without irritancy ! Pétion has declined : nevertheless many
do covet and canvass.   After months of scrutinizing,
balloting, arguing and jargoning, one Doctor Chambon
gets the post of honour : who will not long keep it ;
but be, as we shall see, literally *crushed* out of it.[1]

Think also if the private Sansculotte has not his
difficulties, in a time of dearth ! Bread, according to
the People's-Friend, may be some ' six sous per pound,
a day's wages some fifteen ' ; and grim winter here.
How the Poor Man continues living, and so seldom
starves ; by miracle ! Happily, in these days, he can
enlist, and have himself shot by the Austrians, in an
unusually satisfactory manner : for the Rights of Man.
—But Commandant Santerre, in this so straitened

---

[1] Dictionnaire des Hommes Marquans, § Chambon.

condition of the flour-market, and state of Equality
and Liberty, proposes, through the Newspapers, two
remedies, or at least palliatives: *First*, that all classes of
men should live two days of the week on potatoes ; then
second, that every man should hang his dog. Hereby,
as the Commandant thinks, the saving, which indeed he
computes to so many sacks, would be very considerable.
Cheerfuller form of inventive-stupidity than Commandant Santerre's dwells in no human soul. Inventive-
stupidity, imbedded in health, courage and good nature:
much to be commended. ' My whole strength', he
tells the Convention once, ' is, day and night, at the
service of my fellow-Citizens : if they find me worthless,
they will dismiss me ; I will return, and brew beer '.[1]

Or figure what correspondences a poor Roland,
Minister of the Interior, must have, on this of Grains
alone ! Free-trade in Grain, impossibility to fix the
Prices of Grain ; on the other hand, clamour and necessity to fix them ; Political Economy lecturing from
the Home Office, with demonstration clear as Scripture;
—ineffectual for the empty National Stomach. The
Mayor of Chartres, like to be eaten himself, cries to the
Convention ; the Convention sends honourable Members in Deputation ; who endeavour to feed the multitude by miraculous spiritual methods ; but cannot.
The multitude, in spite of all Eloquence, come bellowing
round ; will have the Grain-Prices fixed, and at a
moderate elevation; or else—the honourable Deputies
hanged on the spot! The honourable Deputies
reporting this business, admit that, on the edge of
horrid death, they did fix, or affect to fix the Price of
Grain : for which, be it also noted, the Convention, a
Convention that will not be trifled with, sees good to
reprimand them.[2]

But as to the origin of these Grain-Riots, is it not
most probably your secret Royalists again ? Glimpses
of Priests were discernible in this of Chartres,—to the

---

[1] Moniteur (in Hist. Parl. xx. 412).
[2] Hist. Parl. xx. 431-40.

eye of Patriotism. Or indeed may not ' the root of it all lie in the Temple Prison, in the heart of a perjured King ', well as we guard him ? [1] Unhappy perjured King !—And so there shall be Bakers' Queues, by and by, more sharp-tempered than ever : on every Baker's door-rabbet an iron ring, and coil of rope ; whereon, with firm grip, on this side and that, we form our Queue : but mischievous deceitful persons cut the rope, and our Queue becomes a ravelment ; wherefore the coil must be made of iron chain.[2] Also there shall be Prices of Grain well fixed ; but then no grain purchasable by them : bread not to be had except by Ticket from the Mayor, few ounces per mouth daily ; after long swaying, with firm grip, on the chain of the Queue. And Hunger shall stalk direful ; and Wrath and Suspicion, whetted to the Preternatural pitch, shall stalk ; as those other preternatural ' shapes of Gods in their wrathfulness ' were discerned stalking, ' in glare and gloom of that fire-ocean ', when Troy Town fell !*—

CHAPTER III

DISCROWNED

But the question more pressing than all on the Legislator, as yet, is this third : What shall be done with King Louis ?

King Louis, now King and Majesty to his own family alone, in their own Prison Apartment alone, has been Louis Capet and the Traitor Veto with the rest of France. Shut in his Circuit of the Temple, he has heard and seen the loud whirl of things ; yells of September Massacres, Brunswick war-thunders dying off in disaster and discomfiture ; he passive, a spectator merely ; waiting whither it would please to whirl with him. From the neighbouring windows, the curious, not

[1] Hist. Parl. xx. 409.　　　　[2] Mercier, Nouveau Paris.

without pity, might see him walk daily, at a certain hour, in the Temple Garden, with his Queen, Sister and two Children, all that now belongs to him in this Earth.[1] Quietly he walks and waits ; for he is not of lively feelings, and is of a devout heart. The wearied Irresolute has, at least, no need of resolving now. His daily meals, lessons to his Son, daily walk in the Garden, daily game at ombre or draughts, fill up the day : the morrow will provide for itself.*

The morrow indeed ; and yet How ? Louis asks, How ? France, with perhaps still more solicitude, asks, How ? A King dethroned by insurrection is verily not easy to dispose of. Keep him prisoner, he is a secret centre for the Disaffected, for endless plots, attempts and hopes of theirs. Banish him, he is an open centre for them ; his royal war-standard, with what of divinity it has, unrolls itself, summoning the world. Put him to death ? A cruel questionable extremity that too : and yet the likeliest in these extreme circumstances, of insurrectionary men, whose own life and death lies staked : accordingly it is said, from the last step of the throne to the first of the scaffold there is short distance.

But, on the whole, we will remark here that this business of Louis looks altogether different now, as seen over Seas and at the distance of forty-four years, from what it looked then, in France, and struggling confused all round one. For indeed it is a most lying thing that same Past Tense always : so beautiful, sad, almost Elysian-sacred, ' in the moonlight of Memory ', it seems ; and *seems* only. For observe, always one most important element is surreptitiously (we not noticing it) withdrawn from the Past Time : the haggard element of Fear ! Not *there* does Fear dwell, nor Uncertainty, nor Anxiety ; but it dwells *here* ; haunting us, tracking us ; running like an accursed ground-discord through all the music-tones of our Existence ; —making the Tense a mere Present one ! Just so is it

---

[1] Moore, i. 123 ; ii. 224, &c.

with this of Louis. Why smite the fallen? asks
Magnanimity, out of danger now. He is fallen so low
this once-high man; no criminal nor traitor, how far
from it; but the unhappiest of Human Solecisms:
whom if abstract Justice had to pronounce upon, she
might well become concrete Pity, and pronounce only
sobs and dismissal!

So argues retrospective Magnanimity: but Pusilla-
nimity, present, prospective? Reader, thou hast
never lived, for months, under the rustle of Prussian
gallows-ropes; never wert thou portion of a National
Sahara-waltz, Twenty-five millions running distracted
to fight Brunswick! Knights Errant themselves, when
they conquered Giants, usually slew the Giants: quarter
was only for other Knights Errant, who knew courtesy
and the laws of battle. The French Nation, in simultaneous, desperate dead-pull, and as if by miracle of
madness, has pulled down the most dread Goliath, huge
with the growth of ten centuries; and cannot believe,
though his giant bulk, covering acres,* lies prostrate,
bound with peg and packthread, that he will not rise
again, man-devouring; that the victory is not partly
a dream. Terror has its scepticism; miraculous
victory its rage of vengeance. Then as to criminality,
is the prostrated Giant, who will devour us if he rise, an
innocent Giant? Curate Grégoire, who indeed is now
Constitutional Bishop Grégoire, asserts, in the heat of
eloquence, that Kingship by the very nature of it is a
crime capital; that Kings' Houses are as wild-beasts'
dens.[1] Lastly consider this: that there is on record a
Trial of Charles First! This printed *Trial of Charles
First* is sold and read everywhere at present:[2] —*Quelle
spectacle!* Thus did the English People judge their
Tyrant, and become the first of Free Peoples: which
feat, by the grace of Destiny, may not France now rival?
Scepticism of terror, rage of miraculous victory, sublime
spectacle to the universe,—all things point one fatal way.

[1] Moniteur, Séance du 21 Septembre, An 1er (1792).
[2] Moore's Journal, ii. 165.

Such leading questions, and their endless incidental ones,—of September Anarchists and Departmental Guard ; of Grain-Riots, plaintive Interior Ministers ; of Armies, Hassenfratz dilapidations ; and what is to be done with Louis,—beleaguer and embroil this Convention ; which would so gladly make the Constitution rather. All which questions too, as we often urge of such things, are in *growth* ; they grow in every French head ; and can be *seen* growing also, very curiously, in this mighty welter of Parliamentary Debate, of Public Business which the Convention has to do. A question emerges, so small at first ; is put off, submerged ; but always re-emerges bigger than before. It is a curious, indeed an indescribable sort of growth which such things have.

We perceive, however, both by its frequent re-emergence and by its rapid enlargement of bulk, that this Question of King Louis will take the lead of all the rest. And truly, in that case, it will take the *lead* in a much deeper sense. For as Aaron's Rod swallowed all the other serpents ; so will the Foremost Question, which-ever may get foremost, absorb all other questions and interests ; and from it and the decision of it will they all, so to speak, be *born*, or new-born, and have shape, physiognomy and destiny corresponding. It was appointed of Fate that, in this wide-weltering, strangely growing, monstrous stupendous imbroglio of Convention Business, the grand First-Parent of all the questions, controversies, measures and enterprises which were to be evolved there to the world's astonishment, should be this Question of King Louis.

CHAPTER IV

THE LOSER PAYS*

THE Sixth of November 1792 was a great day for the Republic : outwardly, over the Frontiers ; inwardly, in the *Salle de Manége*.

Outwardly: for Dumouriez, overrunning the Nether-lands, did, on that day, come in contact with Saxe-Teschen and the Austrians; Dumouriez wide-winged, they wide-winged ; at and around the village of Jemappes, near Mons. And fire-hail is whistling far and wide there, the great guns playing, and the small ; so many green Heights getting fringed and maned with red Fire. And Dumouriez is swept back on this wing, and swept back on that, and is like to be swept back utterly ; when he rushes up in person, the prompt Polymetis ; speaks a prompt word or two ; and then, with clear tenor-pipe, ' uplifts the Hymn of the Marseillese, *entonna la Mar-seillaise* ',[1] ten-thousand tenor or bass pipes joining ; or say, some Forty-thousand in all ; for every heart leaps at the sound ; and so with rhythmic march-melody, waxing ever quicker, to double and to treble quick, they rally, they advance, they rush, death-defying, man-devouring ; carry batteries, redoutes, whatsoever is to be carried ; and, like the fire-whirlwind, sweep all manner of Austrians from the scene of action.   Thus, through the hands of Dumouriez, may Rouget de Lille, in figurative speech, be said to have gained, miraculously, like another Orpheus, by his Marseillese fiddle-strings (*fidibus canoris*),* a Victory of Jemappes ; and con-quered the Low Countries.

Young General Égalité, it would seem, shone brave among the bravest on this occasion.   Doubtless a brave Égalité ;—whom however does not Dumouriez rather talk of oftener than need were ? The Mother-Society has her own thoughts. As for the Elder Égalité, he flies

[1] Dumouriez, Mémoires, iii. 174.

low at this time ; appears in the Convention for some
half-hour daily, with rubicund, preoccupied, or impassive quasi-contemptuous countenance ; and then takes
himself away.[1] The Netherlands are conquered, at
least overrun. Jacobin missionaries, your Prolys,
Pereiras, follow in the train of the Armies ; also Convention Commissioners, melting church-plate, revo-
lutionizing and remodelling,—among whom Danton,
in brief space, does immensities of business ; not
neglecting his own wages and trade-profits, it is thought.
Hassenfratz dilapidates at home ; Dumouriez grumbles
and they dilapidate abroad : within the walls there is
sinning, and without the walls there is sinning.

But in the Hall of the Convention, at the same hour
with this victory of Jemappes, there went another thing
forward : Report, of great length, from the proper
appointed Committee, on the Crimes of Louis. The
Galleries listen breathless ; take comfort, ye Galleries :
Deputy Valazé, Reporter on this occasion, thinks Louis
very criminal ; and that, if convenient, he should be
tried ;—poor Girondin Valazé, who may be tried himself, one day ! Comfortable so far. Nay here comes
a second Committee-reporter, Deputy Mailhe, with a
Legal Argument, very prosy to read now, very refreshing
to hear then, That, by the Law of the Country, Louis
Capet was only called Inviolable by a figure of rhetoric ;
but at bottom was perfectly violable, triable ; that
he can, and even should be tried. This Question of
Louis, emerging so often as an angry confused possibility, and submerging again, has emerged now in an
articulate shape.

Patriotism growls indignant joy. The so-called reign
of Equality is not to be a mere name, then, but a thing !
Try Louis Capet ? scornfully ejaculates Patriotism :
Mean criminals go to the gallows for a purse cut ; and
this chief criminal, guilty of a France cut ; of a France
slashed asunder with Clotho-scissors* and Civil war ;
with his victims ' twelve-hundred on the Tenth of

---

[1] Moore, ii. 148.

August alone' lying low in the Catacombs, fattening the passes of Argonne₃Wood, of Valmy and far Fields ; *he*, such chief criminal, shall not even come to the bar ? —For, alas, O Patriotism ! add we, it was from of old said, *The loser pays!* It is he who has to pay *all* scores, run up by whomsoever; on him must all breakages and charges fall ; and the twelve-hundred on the Tenth of August are not rebel traitors, but victims and martyrs : such is the law of quarrel.

Patriotism, nothing doubting, watches over this Question of the trial, now happily emerged in an articulate shape ; and will see it to maturity, if the gods permit. With a keen solicitude Patriotism watches ; getting ever keener, at every new difficulty, as Girondins and false brothers interpose delays ; till it get a keenness as of fixed-idea, and will have this Trial and no earthly thing instead of it,—if Equality be not a name. Love of Equality ; then scepticism of terror, rage of victory, sublime spectacle to the universe : all these things are strong.

But indeed this Question of the Trial, is it not to all persons a most grave one ; filling with dubiety many a Legislative head ! Regicide ? asks the Gironde Respectability : To kill a king, and become the horror of respectable nations and persons ? But then also, to save a king ; to lose one's footing with the decided Patriot ; the undecided Patriot, though never so respectable, being mere hypothetic froth and no footing ?—The dilemma presses sore ; and between the horns of it you wriggle round and round. Decision is nowhere, save in the Mother-Society and her Sons. These have decided, and go forward : the others wriggle round uneasily within their dilemma-horns, and make way nowhither.

CHAPTER V

STRETCHING OF FORMULAS

But how this Question of the Trial grew laboriously, through the weeks of gestation, now that it has been articulated or conceived, were superfluous to trace here. It emerged and submerged among the infinite of questions and embroilments. The Veto of Scoundrels writes plaintive Letters as to Anarchy; 'concealed Royalists', aided by Hunger, produce Riots about Grain. Alas, it is but a week ago, these Girondins made a new fierce onslaught on the September Massacres!

For, one day, among the last of October, Robespierre, being summoned to the tribune by some new hint of that old calumny of the Dictatorship, was speaking and pleading there, with more and more comfort to himself; till rising high in heart, he cried out valiantly: Is there any man here that dare specifically accuse me? '*Moi!*' exclaimed one. Pause of deep silence: a lean angry little Figure, with broad bald brow, strode swiftly towards the tribune, taking papers from its pocket: 'I accuse thee, Robespierre',—I, Jean Baptiste Louvet! The Seagreen became tallowgreen; shrinking to a corner of the tribune: Danton cried, 'Speak, Robespierre, there are many good citizens that listen'; but the tongue refused its office. And so Louvet, with a shrill tone, read and recited crime after crime: dictatorial temper, exclusive popularity, bullying at elections, mob-retinue, September Massacres;—till all the Convention shrieked again, and had almost indicted the Incorruptible there on the spot. Never did the Incorruptible run such a risk. Louvet, to his dying day, will regret that the Gironde did not take a bolder attitude, and extinguish him there and then.

Not so, however: the Incorruptible, about to be indicted in this sudden manner, could not be refused a week of delay. That week he is not idle; nor is the

Mother-Society idle,—fierce-tremulous for her chosen
son. He is ready at the day with his written Speech;
smooth as a Jesuit Doctor's; and convinces some.
And now? Why now lazy Vergniaud does *not* rise with
Demosthenic thunder; poor Louvet, unprepared, can
do little or nothing: Barrère proposes that these comparatively despicable 'personalities' be dismissed by
order of the day! Order of the day it accordingly is.
Barbaroux cannot even get a hearing; not though he
rush down to the Bar, and demand to be heard there as
a petitioner.[1] The Convention, eager for public business (with that first articulate emergence of the Trial
just coming on), dismisses these comparative *misères*
and despicabilities: splenetic Louvet must digest his
spleen, regretfully for ever: Robespierre, dear to Patriotism, is dearer for the dangers he has run.

This is the second grand attempt by our Girondin
Friends of Order, to extinguish that black-spot in their
domain; and we see they have made it far blacker and
wider than before! Anarchy, September Massacre: it
is a thing that lies hideous in the general imagination;
very detestable to the undecided Patriot, of Respectability: a thing to be harped on as often as need is.
Harp on it, denounce it, trample it, ye Girondin
Patriots:—and yet behold, the black-spot will not
trample down; it will only, as we say, trample blacker
and wider: fools, it is no black-spot of the surface, but
a well-spring of the deep! Consider rightly, it is the
Apex of the everlasting Abyss, this black-spot, looking
up as water through thin ice;—say, as the region of
Nether Darkness through your thin film of Gironde
Regulation and Respectability: trample it *not*, lest the
film break, and then—!

The truth is, if our Gironde Friends had an understanding of it, where were French Patriotism, with all
its eloquence, at this moment, had *not* that same great

---

[1] Louvet, *Mémoires* (Paris, 1823), p. 52; Moniteur
(Séances, 29 Octobre, 5 Novembre, 1792); Moore, ii. 178,
&c.

Nether Deep, of Bedlam, Fanaticism and Popular
wrath and madness, risen unfathomable on the Tenth
of August ? French Patriotism were an eloquent
Reminiscence ; swinging on Prussian gibbets. Nay,
where, in few months, were it still, should the same
great Nether Deep subside ?—Nay, as readers of Newspapers pretend to recollect, this hatefulness of the
September Massacre is itself partly an afterthought :
readers of Newspapers can quote Gorsas and various
Brissotins approving of the September Massacre, at
the time it happened ; and calling it a salutary vengeance.[1] So that the real grief, after all, were not so
much righteous horror, as grief that one's own power
was departing ? Unhappy Girondins !

In the Jacobin Society, therefore, the decided Patriot
complains that here are men who with their private
ambitions and animosities will ruin Liberty, Equality
and Brotherhood, all three : they check the spirit of
Patriotism ; throw stumbling-blocks in its way ; and
instead of pushing on, all shoulders at the wheel, will
stand idle there, spitefully clamouring what foul ruts
there are, what rude jolts we give ! To which the
Jacobin Society answers with angry roar ;—with angry
shriek, for there are Citoyennes too, thick crowded in
the galleries here. Citoyennes who bring their seam
with them, or their knitting-needles ; and shriek or
knit as the case needs ; famed *Tricoteuses*, Patriot
Knitters ; *Mère Duchesse*, or the like Deborah* and
Mother of the Faubourgs, giving the key-note. It is
a changed Jacobin Society ; and a still changing.
Where Mother Duchess now sits, authentic Duchesses
have sat. High-rouged dames went once in jewels
and spangles ; now, instead of jewels, you may take
the knitting-needles and leave the rouge : the rouge
will gradually give place to natural brown, clean washed
or even unwashed : and Demoiselle Théroigne herself
get scandalously fustigated. Strange enough ; it is

---

[1] See Hist. Parl. xvii. 401 ; Newspapers by Gorsas and
others (cited *ibid.* 428).

the same tribune raised in mid-air, where a high Mirabeau, a high Barnave and Aristocrat Lameths once
thundered ; whom gradually your Brissots, Guadets,
Vergniauds, a hotter style of Patriots in *bonnet rouge*,
did displace ; red heat, as one may say, superseding
light. And now your Brissots in turn, and Brissotins,
Rolandins, Girondins, are becoming supernumerary ;
must desert the sittings, or be expelled : the light of
the Mighty Mother is burning not red but blue !—
Provincial Daughter-Societies loudly disapprove these
things ; loudly demand the swift reinstatement of such
eloquent Girondins, the swift ' erasure of Marat,
radiation de Marat'. The Mother-Society, so far as
natural reason can predict, seems ruining herself.
Nevertheless she has at all crises seemed so ; she has
a *preter*natural life in her, and will not ruin.

But, in a fortnight more, this great Question of the
Trial, while the fit Committee is assiduously but
silently working on it, receives an unexpected stimulus.
Our readers remember poor Louis's turn for smith-
work ; how, in old happier days, a certain Sieur Gamain
of Versailles was wont to come over and instruct him in
lock-making ;—often scolding him, they say, for his
numbness. By whom, nevertheless, the royal Apprentice had learned something of that craft. Hapless
Apprentice ; perfidious Master-Smith ! For now, on
this 20th of November 1792, dingy Smith Gamain
comes over to the Paris Municipality, over to Minister
Roland, with hints that he, Smith Gamain, knows a
thing ; that, in May last, when traitorous Correspondence was so brisk, he and the royal Apprentice fabricated an ' Iron Press, *Armoire de Fer*', cunningly
inserting the same in a wall of the royal chamber in the
Tuileries ; invisible under the wainscot ; where doubtless it still sticks ! Perfidious Gamain, attended by the
proper Authorities, finds the wainscot panel which none
else can find ; wrenches it up ; discloses the Iron
Press,—full of Letters and Papers ! Roland clutches
them out ; conveys them over in towels to the fit

assiduous Committee, which sits hard by. In towels,
we say, and without notarial inventory; an oversight
on the part of Roland.

Here, however, are Letters enough: which disclose
to a demonstration the Correspondence of a traitorous
self-preserving Court; and this not with Traitors only,
but even with Patriots, so-called! Barnave's treason,
of Correspondence with the Queen, and friendly advice
to her, ever since that Varennes Business, is hereby
manifest: how happy that we have him, this Barnave,
lying safe in the Prison of Grenoble, since September
last, for he had long been suspect! Talleyrand's
treason, many a man's treason, if not manifest hereby,
is next to it. Mirabeau's treason: wherefore his Bust
in the Hall of the Convention 'is veiled with gauze',
till we ascertain. Alas, it is too ascertainable! His
Bust in the Hall of the Jacobins, denounced by Robespierre from the tribune in mid-air, is not veiled, it is
instantly broken to sherds; a Patriot mounting
swiftly with a ladder, and shivering it down on the
floor;—it and others: amid shouts.[1] Such is *their*
recompense and amount of wages, at this date: on
the principle of supply and demand. Smith Gamain,
inadequately recompensed for the present, comes,
some fifteen months after, with a humble Petition;
setting forth that no sooner was that important Iron
Press finished off by him, than (as he now bethinks
himself) Louis gave him a large glass of wine. Which
large glass of wine did produce in the stomach of Sieur
Gamain the terriblest effects, evidently tending towards
death, and was then brought up by an emetic; but
has, notwithstanding, entirely ruined the constitution of
Sieur Gamain; so that he cannot work for his family
(as he now bethinks himself). The recompense of
which is 'Pension of Twelve-hundred Francs', and
'honourable mention'. So different is the ratio of
demand and supply at different times.

[1] Journal des Débats des Jacobins (in Hist. Parl. xxii.
296).

Thus, amid obstructions and stimulating furtherances, has the Question of the Trial to grow; emerging and submerging; fostered by solicitous Patriotism. Of the Orations that were spoken on it, of the painfully devised Forms of Process for managing it, the Law Arguments to prove it lawful, and all the infinite floods of Juridical and other ingenuity and oratory, be no syllable reported in this History. Lawyer ingenuity is good: but what can it profit here? If the truth must be spoken, O august Senators, the only Law in this case is: *Vae victis,* The loser pays! Seldom did Robespierre say a wiser word than the hint he gave to that effect, in his oration, That it was needless to speak of Law; that here, if never elsewhere, our Right was Might. An oration admired almost to ecstasy, by the Jacobin Patriot: who shall say that Robespierre is not a thorough-going man; bold in Logic at least? To the like effect, or still more plainly, spake young Saint-Just, the black-haired, mild-toned youth. Danton is on mission, in the Netherlands, during this preliminary work. The rest, far as one reads, welter amid Law of Nations, Social Contract, Juristics, Syllogistics; to us barren as the East wind. In fact, what can be more unprofitable than the sight of Seven-hundred and Forty-nine ingenious men struggling with their whole force and industry, for a long course of weeks, to do at bottom this: To stretch out the old Formula and Law Phraseology, so that it may cover the new, contradictory, entirely *un*coverable Thing? Whereby the poor Formula does but *crack,* and one's honesty along with it! The thing that is palpably *hot,* burning, wilt thou prove it, by syllogism, to be a freezing mixture? This of stretching out Formulas till they crack, is, especially in times of swift change, one of the sorrowfullest tasks poor Humanity has.

CHAPTER VI

AT THE BAR

MEANWHILE, in a space of some five weeks, we have got to another emerging of the Trial, and a more practical one than ever.

On Tuesday, eleventh of December, the King's Trial has *emerged*, very decidedly : into the streets of Paris ; in the shape of that green Carriage of Mayor Chambon, within which sits the King himself, with attendants, on his way to the Convention Hall ! Attended, in that green carriage, by Mayors Chambon, Procureurs Chaumette ; and outside of it by Commandants Santerre, with cannon, cavalry and double row of infantry ; all Sections under arms, strong Patrols scouring all streets ; so fares he, slowly through the dull drizzling weather : and about two o'clock we behold him, ' in walnut-coloured greatcoat, *redingote noisette*', descending through the Place Vendôme, towards that Salle de Manége ; to be indicted, and judicially interrogated. The mysterious Temple Circuit has given up its secret ; which now, in this walnut-coloured coat, men behold with eyes. The same bodily Louis who was once Louis the Desired, fares there : hapless King, he is getting now towards port ; his deplorable farings and voyagings draw to a close. What duty remains to him henceforth, that of placidly enduring, he is fit to do.

The singular Procession fares on ; in silence, says Prudhomme, or amid growlings of the Marseillese Hymn ; in silence, ushers itself into the Hall of the Convention, Santerre holding Louis's arm with his hand. Louis looks round him, with composed air, to see what kind of Convention and Parliament it is. Much changed indeed :—since February gone two years, when our Constituent, then busy, spread fleur-de-lis velvet for us ; and we came over to say a kind word here, and they all started up swearing Fidelity ; and all France started up swearing, and made it a Feast of Pikes ; which has

ended in this! Barrère, who once 'wept' looking up
from his Editor's Desk, looks down now from his
President's-Chair, with a list of Fifty-seven Questions;
and says, dry-eyed : ' Louis, you may sit down '. Louis
sits down : it is the very seat, they say, same timber
and stuffing, from which he accepted the Constitution,
amid dancing and illumination, autumn gone a year.
So much woodwork remains identical; so much else is
not identical. Louis sits and listens, with a composed
look and mind.

Of the Fifty-seven Questions we shall not give so
much as one. They are questions captiously embracing
all the main Documents seized on the Tenth of August,
or found lately in the Iron Press; embracing all the
main incidents of the Revolution History; and they
ask, in substance, this : Louis, who wert King, art
thou not guilty to a certain extent, by act and written
document, of trying to continue King ? Neither in the
Answers is there much notable. Mere quiet negations,
for most part; an accused man standing on the simple
basis of *No* : I do not recognize that document; I did
not do that act; or did it according to the law that then
was. Whereupon the Fifty-seven Questions, and Documents to the number of a Hundred and Sixty-two, being
exhausted in this manner, Barrère finishes, after some
three hours, with his : ' Louis, I invite you to withdraw '.

Louis withdraws, under Municipal escort, into a
neighbouring Committee-room; having first, in leaving
the bar, demanded to have Legal Counsel. He declines
refreshment, in this Committee-room; then, seeing
Chaumette busy with a small loaf which a grenadier
had divided with him, says, he will take a bit of bread.
It is five o'clock; and he had breakfasted but slightly,
in a morning of such drumming and alarm. Chaumette
breaks his half-loaf : the King eats of the crust; mounts
the green Carriage, eating; asks now, What he shall do
with the crumb ? Chaumette's clerk takes it from him;
flings it out into the street. Louis says, It is pity to
fling out bread, in a time of dearth. ' My grandmother ',

remarks Chaumette, 'used to say to me, Little boy,
never waste a crumb of bread; you cannot make one'.
'Monsieur Chaumette', answers Louis, 'your grandmother seems to have been a sensible woman'.[1] Poor
innocent mortal; so quietly he waits the drawing of
the lot;—fit to do this at least well; Passivity alone,
without Activity, sufficing for it! He talks once of
travelling over France by and by, to have a geographical
and topographical view of it; being from of old fond of
geography.—The Temple Circuit again receives him,
closes on him; gazing Paris may retire to its hearths
and coffeehouses, to its clubs and theatres: the damp
Darkness has sunk, and with it the drumming and
patrolling of this strange Day.

Louis is now separated from his Queen and Family;
given up to his simple reflections and resources. Dull
lie these stone walls round him; of his loved ones none
with him. 'In this state of uncertainty', providing
for the worst, he writes his Will: a Paper which can
still be read; full of placidity, simplicity, pious sweetness. The Convention, after debate, has granted him
Legal Counsel, of his own choosing. Advocate Target
feels himself 'too old', being turned of fifty-four; and
declines. He had gained great honour once, defending
Rohan the Necklace-Cardinal; but will gain none here.
Advocate Tronchet, some ten years older, does not
decline. Nay behold, good old Malesherbes steps
forward voluntarily; to the last of his fields, the good
old hero! He is grey with seventy years: he says,
'I was twice called to the Council of him who was my
Master, when all the world coveted that honour; and
I owe him the same service now, when it has become
one which many reckon dangerous'. These two, with
a younger Desèze, whom they will select for pleading,
are busy over that Fifty-and-sevenfold Indictment,
over the Hundred and Sixty-two Documents; Louis
aiding them as he can.

[1] Prudhomme's Newspaper (in Hist. Parl. xxi. 314).

A great Thing is now therefore in open progress ; all men, in all lands, watching it. By what Forms and Methods shall the Convention acquit itself, in such manner that there rest not on it even the suspicion of blame ? Difficult that will be ! The Convention, really much at a loss, discusses and-deliberates. All day from morning to night, day after day, the Tribune drones with oratory on this matter ; one must stretch the old Formula to cover the new Thing. The Patriots of the Mountain, whetted ever keener, clamour for dispatch above all ; the only good Form will be a swift one. Nevertheless the Convention deliberates ; the Tribune drones,—drowned indeed in tenor, and even in treble, from time to time ; the whole Hall shrilling up round it into pretty frequent wrath and provocation. It has droned and shrilled wellnigh a fortnight, before we can decide, this shrillness getting ever shriller, That on Wednesday 26th of December, Louis shall appear and plead. His Advocates complain that it is fatally soon ; which they well might as Advocates : but without remedy ; to Patriotism it seems endlessly late.

On Wednesday therefore, at the cold dark hour of eight in the morning, all Senators are at their post. Indeed they warm the cold hour, as we find, by a violent effervescence, such as is too common now ; some Louvet or Buzot attacking some Tallien, Chabot ; and so the whole Mountain effervescing against the whole Gironde. Scarcely is this done, at nine, when Louis and his three Advocates, escorted by the clang of arms and Santerre's National force, enter the Hall.

Desèze unfolds his papers ; honourably fulfilling his perilous office, pleads for the space of three hours. An honourable Pleading, ' composed almost overnight ' ; courageous yet discreet ; not without ingenuity, and soft pathetic eloquence : Louis fell on his neck, when they had withdrawn, and said with tears, ' *Mon pauvre Desèze !* ' Louis himself, before withdrawing, had added a few words, ' perhaps the last he would utter to them ' : how it pained his heart, above all things, to be held guilty of that bloodshed on the Tenth of August ; or

of ever shedding or wishing to shed French blood. So
saying, he withdrew from that Hall;—having indeed
finished his work there. Many are the strange errands
he has had thither; but this strange one is the last.

And now, why will the Convention loiter? Here is
the Indictment and Evidence; here is the Pleading:
does not the rest follow of itself? The Mountain, and
Patriotism in general, clamours still louder for dispatch;
for Permanent-session, till the task be done. Nevertheless a doubting, apprehensive Convention decides
that it will still deliberate first; that all Members, who
desire it, shall have leave to speak.—To your desks, therefore, ye eloquent Members! Down with your thoughts,
your echoes and hearsays of thoughts; now is the time
to show oneself; France and the Universe listens!
Members are not wanting: Oration, spoken Pamphlet
follows spoken Pamphlet, with what eloquence it can:
President's List swells ever higher with names claiming
to speak; from day to day, all days and all hours, the
constant Tribune drones;—shrill Galleries supplying,
very variably, the tenor and treble. It were a dull tone
otherwise.

The Patriots, in Mountain and Galleries, or taking
counsel nightly in Section-house, in Mother-Society,
amid their shrill *Tricoteuses*, have to watch lynx-eyed;
to give voice when needful; occasionally very loud.
Deputy Thuriot, he who was Advocate Thuriot, who
was Elector Thuriot, and from the top of the Bastille
saw Saint-Antoine rising like the ocean; this Thuriot
can stretch a Formula as heartily as most men. Cruel
Billaud is not silent, if you incite him. Nor is cruel
Jean-Bon* silent; a kind of Jesuit he too;—write him
not, as the Dictionaries too often do, *Jambon*, which
signifies mere *Ham*!

But, on the whole, let no man conceive it possible
that Louis is not guilty. The only question for a
reasonable man is, or was: Can the Convention judge
Louis? Or must it be the whole People; in Primary
Assembly, and with delay? Always delay, ye Girondins,

false *hommes d'état* ! so bellows Patriotism, its patience
almost failing.—But indeed, if we consider it, what
shall these poor Girondins do ? Speak their conviction
that Louis is a Prisoner of War ; and cannot be put to
death without injustice, solecism, peril ? Speak such
conviction ; and lose utterly your footing with the
decided Patriot ! Nay properly it is not even a conviction, but a conjecture and dim puzzle. How many
poor Girondins are sure of but one thing : That a man
and Girondin ought to *have* footing somewhere, and to
stand firmly on it ; keeping well with the Respectable
Classes ! *This* is what conviction and assurance of faith
they have. They must wriggle painfully between their
dilemma-horns.[1]

Nor is France idle, nor Europe. It is a Heart this
Convention, as we said, which sends out influences, and
receives them. A King's Execution, call it Martyrdom,
call it Punishment, were an influence !—Two notable influences this Convention has already sent forth over all
Nations ; much to its own detriment. On the 19th of
November, it emitted a Decree, and has since confirmed
and unfolded the details of it, That any Nation which
might see good to shake off the fetters of Despotism
was thereby, so to speak, the Sister of France, and should
have help and countenance. A Decree much noised
of by Diplomatists, Editors, International Lawyers ;
such a Decree as no living Fetter of Despotism, nor
Person in Authority anywhere, can approve of ! It was
Deputy Chambon the Girondin who propounded this
Decree ;—at bottom perhaps as a flourish of rhetoric.

The second influence we speak of had a still poorer
origin : in the restless loud-rattling slightly-furnished
head of one Jacob Dupont from the Loire country.
The Convention is speculating on a plan of National
Education : Deputy Dupont in his speech says, ' I am
free to avow, M. le Président, that I for my part am an

[1] See Extracts from their Newspapers, in Hist. Parl.
xxi. 1–38, &c.

Atheist ', [1]—thinking the world might like to know that.
The French world received it without commentary ; or
with no audible commentary, so *loud* was France otherwise.   The Foreign world received it with confutation,
with horror and astonishment ; [2] a most miserable
influence this ! And now if to these two were added a
third influence and sent pulsing abroad over all the
Earth : that of Regicide ?

Foreign Courts interfere in this Trial of Louis ; Spain,
England : not to be listened to ; though they come, as
it were, at least Spain comes, with the olive-branch in
one hand, and the sword without scabbard in the other.
But at home too, from out of this circumambient Paris
and France, what influences come thick-pulsing !
Petitions flow in ; pleading for equal justice, in a reign
of so-called Equality. The living Patriot pleads ;—
O ye National Deputies, do not the dead Patriots plead ?
The Twelve-hundred that lie in cold obstruction, do
not they plead ; and petition, in Death's dumb-show,
from their narrow house there, more eloquently than
speech ? Crippled Patriots hop on crutches round the
Salle de Manége, demanding justice.   The Wounded
of the Tenth of August, the Widows and Orphans of
the Killed petition in a body ; and hop and defile,
eloquently mute, through the Hall : one wounded
Patriot, unable to hop, is borne on his bed thither, and
passes shoulder-high, in the horizontal posture. [3] The
Convention Tribune, which has paused at such sight,
commences again,—droning mere Juristic Oratory. But
out of doors Paris is piping ever higher. Bull-voiced
St.-Huruge is heard ; and the hysteric eloquence of
Mother Duchess ; ' Varlet, Apostle of Liberty ', with
pike and red cap, flies hastily, carrying his oratorical
folding-stool. Justice on the Traitor ! cries all the
Patriot world. Consider also this other cry, heard loud

---

[1] Moniteur, Séance du 14 Decembre 1792.

[2] Mrs. Hannah More, Letter to Jacob Dupont (London,
1793) ; &c. &c.

[3] Hist. Parl. xxii. 131 ; Moore, &c.

on the streets : ' Give us Bread, or else kill us ! ' Bread
and Equality ; Justice on the Traitor, that we may
have Bread !

The Limited or undecided Patriot is set against the
Decided. Mayor Chambon heard of dreadful rioting at
the *Théâtre de la Nation* : it had come to rioting, and
even to fist-work, between the Decided and the Undecided, touching a new Drama called *Ami des Lois*[*](Friend
of the Laws). One of the poorest Dramas ever written ;
but which had didactic applications in it ; wherefore
powdered wigs of Friends of Order and black hair of
Jacobin heads are flying there ; and Mayor Chambon
hastens with Santerre, in hopes to quell it. Far from
quelling it, our poor Mayor gets so ' squeezed ', says
the Report, and likewise so blamed and bullied, say
we,—that he, with regret, quits the brief Mayoralty
altogether, ' his lungs being affected '. This miserable
Ami des Lois is debated of in the Convention itself ; so
violent, mutually-enraged, are the Limited Patriots and
the Unlimited.[1]

Between which two classes, are not Aristocrats
enough, and Crypto-Aristocrats, busy ? Spies running
over from London with important Packets ; spies pretending to run ! One of these latter, Viard was the
name of him, pretended to accuse Roland, and even the
Wife of Roland : to the joy of Chabot and the Mountain.
But the Wife of Roland came, being summoned, on the
instant, to the Convention Hall ; came, in her high
clearness ; and, with few clear words, dissipated this
Viard into despicability and air ; all Friends of Order
applauding.[2] So, with Theatre-riots, and ' Bread, or
else kill us ' ; with Rage, Hunger, preternatural Suspicion, does this wild Paris pipe. Roland grows ever
more querulous, in his Messages and Letters ; rising
almost to the hysterical pitch. Marat, whom no power
on Earth can prevent seeing into traitors and Rolands,
takes to bed for three days ; almost dead, the invaluable

[1] Hist. Parl. xxiii. 31, 48, &c.
[2] Moniteur, Séance du 7 Decembre 1792.

People's-Friend, with heartbreak, with fever and head-ache : ' *O Peuple babillard, si tu savais agir,* People of Babblers, if thou couldst but *act* ! '

To crown all, victorious Dumouriez, in these New-year's days, is arrived in Paris ;—one fears, for no good. He pretends to be complaining of Minister Pache, and Hassenfratz dilapidations ; to be concerting measures for the spring Campaign : one finds him much in the company of the Girondins. Plotting with them against Jacobinism, against Equality, and the Punishment of Louis ? We have Letters of his to the Convention itself. Will he act the old Lafayette part, this new victorious General ? Let him withdraw again ; not undenounced.[1]

And still, in the Convention Tribune, it drones continually, mere Juristic Eloquence, and Hypothesis without Action ; and there are still fifties on the President's List. Nay these Gironde Presidents give their own party preference : we suspect they play foul with the List ; men of the Mountain cannot be heard. And still it drones, all through December into January and a New year ; and there is no end ! Paris pipes round it ; multitudinous ; ever higher, to the note of the whirl-wind. Paris will ' bring cannon from Saint-Denis ' ; there is talk of ' shutting the Barriers ',—to Roland's horror.

Whereupon, behold, the Convention Tribune sud-denly ceases droning : we cut short, be on the List who likes ; and *make* end. On Tuesday next, the Fifteenth of January 1793, it shall go to the Vote, name by name ; and one way or other, this great game play itself out !

---

[1] Dumouriez, Mémoires, iii. c. 4.

CHAPTER VII

THE THREE VOTINGS

Is Louis Capet guilty of conspiring against Liberty ?
Shall our Sentence be itself final, or need ratifying by
Appeal to the People ? If guilty, what Punishment ?
This is the form agreed to, after uproar and ' several
hours of tumultuous indecision ' : these are the Three
successive Questions, whereon the Convention shall
now pronounce. Paris floods round their Hall ; multitudinous, many-sounding. Europe and all Nations
listen for their answer. Deputy after Deputy shall
answer to his name : Guilty or Not guilty ?

As to the Guilt, there is, as above hinted, no doubt in
the mind of Patriot men. Overwhelming majority
pronounces Guilt ; the unanimous Convention votes
for Guilt, only some feeble twenty-eight voting not
Innocence, but refusing to vote at all. Neither does
the Second Question prove doubtful, whatever the
Girondins might calculate. Would not Appeal to the
People be another name for civil war ? Majority of two
to one answers that there shall be no Appeal : this also
is settled. Loud Patriotism, now at ten o'clock, may
hush itself for the night ; and retire to its bed not without hope. Tuesday has gone well. On the morrow
comes, What Punishment ? On the morrow is the tug
of war.

Consider therefore if, on this Wednesday morning,
there is an affluence of Patriotism ; if Paris stands
a-tiptoe, and all Deputies are at their post ! Seven-
hundred and Forty-nine honourable Deputies ; only
some twenty absent on mission, Duchâtel and some
seven others absent by sickness. Meanwhile expectant
Patriotism and Paris standing a-tiptoe, have need of
patience. For this Wednesday again passes in debate
and effervescence; Girondins proposing that a 'majority

of three-fourths' shall be required; Patriots fiercely
resisting them. Danton, who has just got back from
mission in the Netherlands, does obtain 'order of the
day' on this Girondin proposal; nay he obtains further
that we decide *sans désemparer*, in Permanent-session,
till we have done.

And so, finally, at eight in the evening this Third
stupendous Voting, by roll-call or *appel nominal*, does
begin. What Punishment? Girondins undecided,
Patriots decided, men afraid of Royalty, men afraid of
Anarchy, must answer here and now. Infinite Patriotism, dusky in the lamp-light, floods all corridors, crowds
all galleries; sternly waiting to hear. Shrill-sounding
Ushers summon you by Name and Department; you
must rise to the Tribune, and say.

Eye-witnesses have represented this scene of the Third
Voting, and of the votings that grew out of it; a scene
protracted, like to be endless, lasting, with few brief
intervals, from Wednesday till Sunday morning,—as
one of the strangest seen in the Revolution. Long
night wears itself into day, morning's paleness is spread
over all faces; and again the wintry shadows sink, and
the dim lamps are lit: but through day and night and
the vicissitudes of hours, Member after Member is
mounting continually those Tribune-steps; pausing
aloft there, in the clearer upper light, to speak his Fate-
word; then diving down into the dusk and throng again.
Like Phantoms in the hour of midnight; most spectral,
pandemonial! Never did President Vergniaud, or any
terrestrial President, superintend the like. A King's
Life, and so much else that depends thereon, hangs
trembling in the balance. Man after man mounts; the
buzz hushes itself till he have spoken: Death; Banishment; Imprisonment till the Peace. Many say, Death;
with what cautious well-studied phrases and paragraphs
they could devise, of explanation, of enforcement, of
faint recommendation to mercy. Many too say,
Banishment; something short of Death. The balance
trembles, none can yet guess whitherward. Whereat
anxious Patriotism bellows; irrepressible by Ushers.

The poor Girondins, many of them, under such fierce
bellowing of Patriotism, say Death; justifying, *moti-*
vant, that most miserable word of theirs by some brief
casuistry and jesuitry. Vergniaud himself says, Death;
justifying by jesuitry. Rich Lepelletier Saint-Fargeau
had been of the Noblesse, and then of the Patriot Left
Side, in the Constituent; and had argued and reported,
there and elsewhere, not a little, *against* Capital Punishment: nevertheless he now says, Death; a word which
may cost him dear. Manuel did surely rank with the
Decided in August last; but he has been sinking and
backsliding ever since September and the scenes of
September. In this Convention, above all, no word he
could speak would find favour; he says now, Banishment; and in mute wrath quits the place for ever,—
much hustled in the corridors. Philippe Égalité votes,
in his soul and conscience, Death: at the sound of
which and of whom, even Patriotism shakes its head;
and there runs a groan and shudder through this Hall
of Doom. Robespierre's vote cannot be doubtful; his
speech is long. Men see the figure of shrill Sieyes
ascend; hardly pausing, passing merely, this figure
says, ' *La Mort sans phrase,* Death without phrases';
and fares onward and downward. Most spectral, pandemonial!

And yet if the Reader fancy it of a funereal, sorrowful
or even grave character, he is far mistaken: ' the Ushers
in the Mountain quarter', says Mercier, ' had become
as Box-keepers at the Opera'; opening and shutting
of Galleries for privileged persons, for ' D'Orléans
Égalité's mistresses ', or other high-dizened women of
condition, rustling with laces and tricolor. Gallant
Deputies pass and repass thitherward, treating them
with ices, refreshments and small-talk; the high-
dizened heads beck responsive; some have their card
and pin, pricking down the Ayes and Noes, as at a game
of *Rouge-et-Noir.* Further aloft reigns Mère Duchesse
with her unrouged Amazons; she cannot be prevented
making long *Hahas,* when the vote is not *La Mort.* In
these Galleries there is refection, drinking of wine and

brandy ' as in open tavern, *en pleine tabagie* '. Betting
goes on in all coffee-houses of the neighbourhood. But
within doors, fatigue, impatience, uttermost weariness
sits now on all visages ; lighted up only from time to
time by turns of the game. Members have fallen asleep ;
Ushers come and awaken them to vote : other Members
calculate whether they shall not have time to run and
dine. Figures rise, like phantoms, pale in the dusky
lamp-light ; utter from this Tribune, only one word :
Death. ' *Tout est optique* ', says Mercier, ' The world
is all an optical shadow '.[1] Deep in the Thursday night,
when the Voting is done, and Secretaries are summing
it up, sick Duchâtel, more spectral than another, comes
borne on a chair, wrapt in blankets, in ' nightgown and
nightcap ', to vote for Mercy : one vote it is thought
may turn the scale.

Ah no ! In profoundest silence, President Vergniaud,
with a voice full of sorrow, has to say : ' I declare, in
the name of the Convention, that the punishment it
pronounces on Louis Capet is that of Death '. Death
by a small majority of Fifty-three. Nay, if we deduct
from the one side, and add to the other, a certain
Twenty-six, who said Death but coupled some faintest
ineffectual surmise of mercy with it, the majority will
be but *One*.

Death is the sentence : but its execution ? It is not
executed yet ! Scarcely is the vote declared when
Louis's Three Advocates enter ; with Protest in his
name, with demand for Delay, for Appeal to the People.
For this do Desèze and Tronchet plead, with brief
eloquence : brave old Malesherbes pleads for it with
eloquent want of eloquence, in broken sentences, in
embarrassment and sobs ; that brave time-honoured
face, with its grey strength, its broad sagacity and
honesty, is mastered with emotion, melts into dumb
tears.[2]—They reject the Appeal to the People ; that

[1] Mercier, Nouveau Paris, vi. 156–9 ; Montgaillard, iii.
348-87 ; Moore, &c.

[2] Moniteur (in Hist. Parl. xxiii. 210). See Boissy d'Anglas, Vie de Malesherbes, ii. 139.

having been already settled.   But as to the Delay, what
they call *Sursis*, it *shall* be considered ; shall be voted
for to-morrow : at present we adjourn.   Whereupon
Patriotism ' hisses ' from the Mountain : but a ' tyrannical majority ' has so decided, and adjourns.

There is still this *fourth* Vote then, growls indignant
Patriotism :—this vote, and who knows what other
votes, and adjournments of voting ; and the whole
matter still hovering hypothetical ! And at every new
vote those Jesuit Girondins, even they who voted for
Death, would so fain find a loophole ! Patriotism must
watch and rage.   Tyrannical adjournments there have
been ; one, and now another at midnight on plea of
fatigue,—all Friday wasted in hesitation and higgling :
in *re*-counting of the votes, which are found correct
as they stood ! Patriotism bays fiercer than ever ;
Patriotism, by long watching, has become red-eyed,
almost rabid.

' Delay : yes or no ? ' men do vote it finally, all
Saturday, all day and night.   Men's nerves are worn
out, men's hearts are desperate ; now it shall end.
Vergniaud, spite of the baying, ventures to say Yes,
Delay ; though he had voted Death.   Philippe Égalité
says, in his soul and conscience, No.   The next Member
mounting : ' Since Philippe says No, I for my part
say Yes, *moi je dis Oui* '.   The balance still trembles.
Till finally, at three o'clock on Sunday morning, we
have : *No Delay*, by a majority of Seventy ; *Death
within four-and-twenty hours !*

Garat, Minister of Justice, has to go to the Temple
with this stern message : he ejaculates repeatedly,
' *Quelle commission affreuse*, What a frightful function !'[1]
Louis begs for a Confessor ; for yet three days of life,
to prepare himself to die.   The Confessor is granted ;
the three days and all respite are refused.

There is no deliverance, then ?   Thick stone walls
answer, None.   Has King Louis no friends ?   Men of

[1] Biographie des Ministres, p. 157.

action, of courage grown desperate, in this his extreme need ? King Louis's friends are feeble and far. Not even a voice in the coffee-houses rises for him. At Méot the Restaurateur's no Captain Dampmartin now dines ; or sees death-doing whiskerandoes on furlough exhibit daggers of improved structure. Méot's gallant Royalists on furlough are far across the marches ; they are wandering distracted over the world : or their bones lie whitening Argonne Wood. Only some weak Priests ' leave Pamphlets on all the bourne-stones ', this night, calling for a rescue : calling for the pious women to rise ; or are taken distributing Pamphlets, and sent to prison.[1]

Nay there is one death-doer, of the ancient Méot sort, who, with effort, has done even less and worse : slain a Deputy, and set all the Patriotism of Paris on edge ! It was five on Saturday evening when Lepelletier St. Fargeau, having given his vote, *No Delay,* ran over to Février's in the Palais-Royal to snatch a morsel of dinner. He had dined, and was paying. A thickset man ' with black hair and blue beard ', in a loose kind of frock, stepped up to him ; it was, as Février and the bystanders bethought them, one Pâris of the old King's-Guard. ' Are you Lepelletier ? ' asks he.—' Yes '.— ' You voted in the King's Business - - ? '—' I voted Death '.—' *Scélérat,* take that ! ' cries Pâris, flashing out a sabre from under his frock, and plunging it deep in Lepelletier's side. Février clutches him : but he breaks off ; is gone.

The voter Lepelletier lies dead ; he has expired in great pain, at one in the morning ;—two hours before that Vote of *No Delay* was fully summed up. Guardsman Pâris is flying over France ; cannot be taken ; will be found some months after, self-shot in a remote inn.[2]—Robespierre sees reason to think that Prince

---

[1] See Prudhomme's Newspaper, Révolutions de Paris (in Hist. Parl. xxiii. 318).
[2] Hist. Parl. xxiii. 275, 318. Félix Lepelletier, Vie de Michel Lepelletier son Frère, p. 61, &c. : Félix, with due

d'Artois himself is privately in Town ; that the Convention will be butchered in the lump. Patriotism sounds mere wail and vengeance : Santerre doubles and trebles all his patrols. Pity is lost in rage and fear ; the Convention has refused the three days of life and all respite.

CHAPTER VIII

PLACE DE LA RÉVOLUTION

To this conclusion, then, hast thou come, O hapless Louis ! The Son of Sixty Kings is to die on the Scaffold by form of Law. Under Sixty Kings this same form of Law, form of Society, has been fashioning itself together, these thousand years ; and has become, one way and other, a most strange Machine. Surely, if needful, it is also frightful, this Machine ; dead, blind ; not what it should be ; which, with swift stroke, or by cold slow torture, has wasted the lives and souls of innumerable men. And behold now a King himself, or say rather Kinghood in his person, is to expire here in cruel tortures ;—like a Phalaris*shut in the belly of his own red-heated Brazen Bull ! It is ever so ; and thou shouldst know it, O haughty tyrannous man : injustice breeds injustice ; curses and falsehoods do verily return 'always *home*', wide as they may wander. Innocent Louis bears the sins of many generations : he too experiences that man's tribunal is not in this Earth ; that if he had no Higher one, it were not well with him.

A King dying by such violence appeals impressively to the imagination ; as the like must do, and ought to do. And yet at bottom it is not the King dying, but the man ! Kingship is a coat : the grand loss is of the skin. The man from whom you take his Life, to him

love of the miraculous, will have it that the Suicide in the inn was not Pàris, but some *double-ganger* of his.

can the whole combined world do *more* ?   Lally went
on his hurdle ; his mouth filled with a gag.   Miserablest
mortals, doomed for picking pockets, have a whole five-
act Tragedy in them, in that dumb pain, as they go to
the gallows, unregarded ; they consume the cup of
trembling down to the lees.   For Kings and for Beggars,
for the justly doomed and the unjustly, it is a hard
thing to die.   Pity them all : thy utmost pity, with all
aids and appliances and throne-and-scaffold contrasts,
how far short is it of the thing pitied !

A Confessor has come ; Abbé Edgeworth, of Irish
extraction, whom the King knew by good report, has
come promptly on this solemn mission.   Leave the
Earth alone, then, thou hapless King ; it with its malice
will go its way, thou also canst go thine.   A hard scene
yet remains : the parting with our loved ones.   Kind
hearts, environed in the same grim peril with us ; to be
left *here* !   Let the Reader look with the eyes of Valet
Cléry, through these glass-doors, where also the Municipality watches ; and see the cruellest of scenes :
    ' At half-past eight, the door of the ante-room opened:
the Queen appeared first, leading her Son by the hand ;
then Madame Royale and Madame Elizabeth : they all
flung themselves into the arms of the King.   Silence
reigned for some minutes ; interrupted only by sobs.
The Queen made a movement to lead his Majesty
towards the inner room, where M. Edgeworth was waiting unknown to them : " No ", said the King, " let us
go into the dining-room, it is there only that I can see
you ".   They entered there ; I shut the door of it, which
was of glass.   The King sat down, the Queen on his left
hand, Madame Elizabeth on his right, Madame Royale
almost in front ; the young Prince remained standing
between his Father's legs.   They all leaned towards
him, and often held him embraced.   This scene of woe
lasted an hour and three quarters ; during which we
could hear nothing ; we could see only that always
when the King spoke, the sobbings of the Princesses
redoubled, continued for some minutes ; and that then

the King began again to speak '. [1]—And so our meetings
and our partings do now end ! The sorrows we gave
each other ; the poor joys we faithfully shared, and all
our lovings and our sufferings, and confused toilings
under the earthly Sun, are over. Thou good soul, I shall
never, never through all ages of Time, see thee any
more !—NEVER ! O Reader, knowest thou that hard
word ?

For nearly two hours this agony lasts ; then they
tear themselves asunder. 'Promise that you will see
us on the morrow'. He promises :—Ah yes, yes ; yet
once ; and go now, ye loved ones ; cry to God for yourselves and me !—It was a hard scene, but it is over. He
will not see them on the morrow. The Queen, in passing
through the ante-room, glanced at the Cerberus Municipals ; and, with woman's vehemence, said through
her tears, ' *Vous êtes tous des scélérats* '.

King Louis slept sound, till five in the morning, when
Cléry, as he had been ordered, awoke him. Cléry dressed
his hair : while this went forward, Louis took a ring
from his watch, and kept trying it on his finger ; it was
his wedding-ring, which he is now to return to the Queen
as a mute farewell. At half-past six, he took the Sacrament ; and continued in devotion, and conference with
Abbé Edgeworth. He will not see his Family : it were
too hard to bear.

At eight, the Municipals enter : the King gives them
his Will, and messages and effects ; which they, at first,
brutally refuse to take charge of : he gives them a roll
of gold pieces, a hundred and twenty-five louis ; these
are to be returned to Malesherbes, who had lent them.
At nine, Santerre says the hour is come. The King
begs yet to retire for three minutes. At the end of
three minutes, Santerre again says the hour is come.
' Stamping on the ground with his right foot, Louis
answers : " *Partons*, Let us go" '.—How the rolling of
those drums comes in, through the Temple bastions

[1] Cléry's Narrative (London, 1798), cited in Weber, iii.
312.

and bulwarks, on the heart of a queenly wife ; soon to
be a widow ! He is gone, then, and has not seen us ?
A Queen weeps bitterly ; a King's Sister and Children.
Over all these Four does Death also hover : all shall
perish miserably save one ; she, as Duchesse d'Angoulême,* will live,—not happily.

At the Temple Gate were some faint cries, perhaps
from voices of pitiful women : ' *Grâce ! Grâce !* '
Through the rest of the streets there is silence as of the
grave. No man not armed is allowed to be there : the
armed, did any even pity, dare not express it, each man
overawed by all his neighbours. All windows are down,
none seen looking through them. All shops are shut.
No wheel-carriage rolls, this morning, in these streets
but one only. Eighty-thousand armed men stand
ranked, like armed statues of men ; cannons bristle,
cannoneers with match burning, but no word or movement : it is as a city enchanted into silence and stone :
one carriage with its escort, slowly rumbling, is the only
sound. Louis reads, in his Book of Devotion, the
Prayers of the Dying : clatter of this death-march falls
sharp on the ear, in the great silence ; but the thought
would fain struggle heavenward, and forget the
Earth.

As the clocks strike ten, behold the Place de la Révolution, once Place de Louis Quinze : the Guillotine,
mounted near the old Pedestal where once stood the
Statue of that Louis ! Far round, all bristles with cannons and armed men : spectators crowding in the rear ;
D'Orléans Égalité there in cabriolet. Swift messengers,
hoquetons, speed to the Townhall, every three minutes :
near by is the Convention sitting,—vengeful for Lepelletier. Heedless of all, Louis reads his Prayers of the
Dying ; not till five minutes yet has he finished ; then
the Carriage opens. What temper he is in ? Ten
different witnesses will give ten different accounts of
it. He is in the collision of all tempers ; arrived now
at the black Mahlstrom and descent of Death : in
sorrow, in indignation, in resignation struggling to be
resigned. 'Take care of M. Edgeworth', he straitly

charges the Lieutenant who is sitting with them : then they two descend.

The drums are beating : ' *Taisez-vous,* Silence ! ' he cries ' in a terrible voice, *d'une voix terrible* '. He mounts the scaffold, not without delay ; he is in puce coat, breeches of grey, white stockings. He strips off the coat ; stands disclosed in a sleeve-waistcoat of white flannel. The Executioners approach to bind him : he spurns, resists ; Abbé Edgeworth has to remind him how the Saviour, in whom men trust, submitted to be bound. His hands are tied, his head bare ; the fatal moment is come. He advances to the edge of the Scaffold, ' his face very red ', and says : ' Frenchmen, I die innocent : it is from the Scaffold and near appear-ing before God that I tell you so. I pardon my enemies ; I desire that France——' A General on horseback, Santerre or another, prances out, with uplifted hand : ' *Tambours !* ' The drums drown the voice. ' Execu-tioners, do your duty ! ' The Executioners, desperate lest themselves be murdered (for Santerre and his Armed Ranks will strike, if they do not), seize the hapless Louis : six of them desperate, him singly desperate, struggling there ; and bind him to their plank. Abbé Edgeworth, stooping, bespeaks him : ' Son of Saint Louis, ascend to Heaven '. The Axe clanks down ; a King's Life is shorn away. It is Monday the 21st of January 1793. He was aged Thirty-eight years four months and twenty-eight days.[1]

Executioner Samson shows the Head : fierce shout of *Vive la République* rises, and swells ; caps raised on bayonets, hats waving : students of the College of Four Nations take it up, on the far Quais ; fling it over Paris. D'Orléans drives off in his cabriolet : the Townhall Councillors rub their hands, saying, ' It is done, It is done '. There is dipping of handkerchiefs, of pike-points in the blood. Headsman Samson, though he

---

[1] Newspapers, Municipal Records, &c. &c. (in Hist. Parl. xxiii. 298-349) ; Deux Amis, ix. 369-73 ; Mercier, Nou-veau Paris, iii. 3-8.

afterwards denied it,[1] sells locks of the hair : fractions
of the puce coat are long after worn in rings.[2]—And so,
in some half-hour it is done ; and the multitude has all
departed. Pastry-cooks, coffee-sellers, milkmen sing
out their trivial quotidian cries : the world wags on,
as if this were a common day. In the coffee-houses that
evening, says Prudhomme, Patriot shook hands with
Patriot in a more cordial manner than usual. Not till
some days after, according to Mercier, did public men
see what a grave thing it was.

A grave thing it indisputably is ; and will have consequences. On the morrow morning, Roland, so long
steeped to the lips in disgust and chagrin, sends in his
demission. His accounts lie all ready, correct in black-
on-white to the uttermost farthing : these he wants
but to have audited, that he might retire to remote
obscurity, to the country and his books. They will
never be audited, those accounts ; he will never get
retired thither.

It was on Tuesday that Roland demitted. On Thursday comes Lepelletier St. Fargeau's Funeral, and passage to the Pantheon of Great Men. Notable as the
wild pageant of a winter day. The Body is borne aloft,
half-bare ; the winding-sheet disclosing the death-
wound : sabre and bloody clothes parade themselves ;
a ' lugubrious music ' wailing harsh *naeniae*. Oak-
crowns shower down from windows; President Vergniaud walks there, with Convention, with Jacobin
Society, and all Patriots of every colour, all mourning
brotherlike.

Notable also for another thing, this Burial of Lepelletier : it was the last act these men ever did with concert ! All Parties and figures of Opinion, that agitate
this distracted France and its Convention, now stand,
as it were, face to face, and dagger to dagger ; the
King's Life, round which they all struck and battled,

---

[1] His Letter in the Newspapers (Hist. Parl. *ubi supra*).
[2] Forster's Briefwechsel, i. 473.

being hurled down. Dumouriez, conquering Holland,
growls ominous discontent, at the head of Armies. Men
say Dumouriez will have a King ; that young D'Orléans
Égalité shall be his King. Deputy Fauchet, in the
Journal des Amis, curses his day, more bitterly than
Job did*; invokes the poniards of Regicides, of ' Arras
Vipers' or Robespierres, of Pluto Dantons, of horrid
Butchers Legendre and Simulacra d'Herbois, to send
him swiftly to another world than *theirs*.[1] This is *Te-
Deum* Fauchet, of the Bastille Victory, of the *Cercle
Social*. Sharp was the death-hail rattling round one's
Flag-of-truce, on that Bastille day : but it was soft to
such wreckage of High Hope as this ; one's New Golden
Era going down in leaden dross, and sulphurous black
of the Everlasting Darkness !

At home this Killing of a King has divided all friends ;
and abroad it has united all enemies. Fraternity of
Peoples, Revolutionary Propagandism ; Atheism, Regicide ; total destruction of social order in this world !
All Kings, and lovers of Kings, and haters of Anarchy,
rank in coalition ; as in a war for life. England signifies to Citizen Chauvelin, the Ambassador or rather
Ambassador's-Cloak, that he must quit the country in
eight days. Ambassador's-Cloak and Ambassador,
Chauvelin and Talleyrand, depart accordingly.[2] Talleyrand, implicated in that Iron Press of the Tuileries,
thinks it safest to make for America.

England has cast out the Embassy : England declares
war,—being shocked principally, it would seem, at the
condition of the River Scheldt.* Spain declares war ;
being shocked principally at some other thing ; which
doubtless the Manifesto indicates.[3] Nay we find it was
not England that declared war first, or Spain first ; but
that France herself declared war first on both of them ; [4]

---

[1] Hist. Parl. *ubi supra*.
[2] Annual Register of 1793, pp. 114–28.
[3] 23rd March (ibid. p. 161).
[4] 1st February ; 7th March (Moniteur of these dates).

—a point of immense Parliamentary and Journalistic
interest in those days, but which has become of no
interest whatever in these. They all declare war. The
sword is drawn, the scabbard thrown away. It is even
as Danton said, in one of his all-too gigantic figures :
' The coalized Kings threaten us ; we hurl at their feet,
as gage of battle, the Head of a King '.

BOOK III

THE GIRONDINS

CHAPTER I

CAUSE AND EFFECT

THIS huge Insurrectionary Movement, which we liken
to a breaking out of Tophet and the Abyss, has swept
away Royalty, Aristocracy, and a King's life. The
question is, What will it next do ; how will it henceforth
shape itself ? Settle down into a reign of Law and
Liberty ; according as the habits, persuasions and
endeavours of the educated, moneyed, respectable class
prescribe ? That is to say : the volcanic lava-flood,
bursting up in the manner described, will explode and
flow according to Girondin Formula and pre-established
rule of Philosophy ? If so, for our Girondin friends it
will be well.

Meanwhile were not the prophecy rather, that as no
external force, Royal or other, now remains which could
control this Movement, the Movement will follow a
course of its own ; probably a very original one ?
Further, that whatsoever man or men can best interpret
the inward tendencies it has, and give them voice and
activity, will obtain the lead of it ? For the rest, that
as a thing *without* order, a thing proceeding from beyond
and beneath the region of order, it must work and
welter, not as a Regularity but as a Chaos ; destructive
and self-destructive ; always till something that *has*
order arise, strong enough to bind it into subjection
again ? Which something, we may further conjecture,
will not be a Formula, with philosophical propositions

and forensic eloquence; but a Reality, probably with a sword in its hand!

As for the Girondin Formula, of a respectable Republic for the Middle Classes, all manner of Aristocracies being now sufficiently demolished, there seems little reason to expect that the business will stop there. *Liberty, Equality, Fraternity*, these are the words; enunciative and prophetic. Republic for the respectable washed Middle Classes, how can that be the fulfilment thereof? Hunger and nakedness, and nightmare oppression lying heavy on Twenty-five million hearts; this, not the wounded vanities or contradicted philosophies of philosophical Advocates, rich Shopkeepers, rural Noblesse, was the prime mover in the French Revolution; as the like will be in all such Revolutions, in all countries. Feudal Fleur-de-lis had become an insupportably bad marching-banner, and needed to be torn and trampled: but Moneybag of Mammon (for that, in these times, is what the respectable Republic for the Middle Classes will signify) is a still worse, while it lasts. Properly, indeed, it is the worst and basest of all banners, and symbols of dominion among men; and indeed is possible only in a time of general Atheism, and Unbelief in anything save in brute Force and Sensualism; pride of birth, pride of office, any known kind of pride being a degree better than purse-pride. Freedom, Equality, Brotherhood: not in the Money-bag, but far elsewhere, will Sansculottism seek these things.

We say therefore that an Insurrectionary France, loose of control from without, destitute of supreme order from within, will form one of the most tumultuous Activities ever seen on this Earth; such as no Girondin Formula can regulate. An immeasurable force, made up of forces manifold, heterogeneous, compatible and incompatible. In plainer words, this France must needs split into Parties; each of which seeking to make itself good, contradiction, exasperation will arise; and Parties on Parties find that they cannot work together, cannot exist together.

As for the number of Parties, there will, strictly

counting, be as many Parties as there are opinions.
According to which rule, in this National Convention
itself, to say nothing of France generally, the number
of Parties ought to be Seven-hundred and Forty-nine;
for every unit entertains his opinion. But now, as
every unit has at once an individual nature or necessity
to follow his own road, and a gregarious nature or necessity to see himself travelling by the side of others,—
what can there be but dissolutions, precipitations, endless turbulence of attracting and repelling; till once
the master-element get evolved, and this wild alchemy
arrange itself again?

To the length of Seven-hundred and Forty-nine Parties, however, no Nation was ever yet seen to go. Nor
indeed much beyond the length of Two Parties; two
at a time;—so invincible is man's tendency to unite,
with all the invincible divisiveness he has! Two Parties, we say, are the usual number at one time: let
these two fight it out, all minor shades of party rallying
under the shade likest them; when the one has fought
down the other, then it, in its turn, may divide, self-
destructive; and so the process continue, as far as
needful. This is the way of Revolutions, which spring
up as the French one has done; when the so-called
Bonds of Society snap asunder; and all Laws that are
not Laws of Nature become naught and Formulas
merely.

But, quitting these somewhat abstract considerations,
let History note this concrete reality which the streets of
Paris exhibit, on Monday the 25th of February 1793.
Long before daylight that morning, these streets are
noisy and angry. Petitioning enough there has been;
a Convention often solicited. It was but yesterday
there came a Deputation of Washerwomen with Petition; complaining that not so much as soap could be
had; to say nothing of bread, and condiments of bread.
The cry of women, round the Salle de Manége, was heard
plaintive: ' *Du pain et du savon*, Bread and soap '.[1]

[1] Moniteur, &c. (Hist. Parl. xxiv. 332–48).

And now from six o'clock, this Monday morning, one perceives the Bakers' Queues unusually expanded, angrily agitating themselves. Not the Baker alone, but two Section Commissioners to help him, manage with difficulty the daily distribution of loaves. Soft-spoken assiduous, in the early candle-light, are Baker and Commissioners: and yet the pale chill February sunrise discloses an unpromising scene. Indignant Female Patriots, partly supplied with bread, rush now to the shops, declaring that they will have groceries. Groceries enough: sugar-barrels rolled forth into the street, Patriot Citoyennes weighing it out at a just rate of elevenpence a pound; likewise coffee-chests, soap-chests, nay cinnamon and cloves-chests, with *aquavitae* and other forms of alcohol, —at a just rate, which some do not pay; the pale-faced Grocer silently wringing his hands! What help? The distributive Citoyennes are of violent speech and gesture, their long Eumenides-hair hanging out of curl; nay in their girdles pistols are seen sticking: some, it is even said, have *beards,*—male Patriots in petticoats and mob-cap. Thus, in the street of Lombards, in the street of Five-Diamonds, street of Pulleys, in most streets of Paris does it effervesce, the livelong day; no Municipality, no Mayor Pache, though he was War-Minister lately, sends military against it, or aught against it but persuasive-eloquence, till seven at night, or later.

On Monday gone five weeks, which was the twenty-first of January, we saw Paris, beheading its King, stand silent, like a petrified City of Enchantment: and now on this Monday it is so noisy, selling sugar! Cities, especially Cities in Revolution, are subject to these alternations; the secret courses of civic business and existence effervescing and efflorescing, in this manner, as a concrete Phenomenon to the eye. Of which Pheno-menon, when secret existence becoming public efflorescces on the street, the philosophical cause and effect is not so easy to find. What, for example, may be the accu-rate philosophical meaning, and meanings, of this sale of sugar? These things that have become visible in

the street of Pulleys and over Paris, whence are they,
we say ; and whither ?—

That Pitt has a hand in it, the gold of Pitt : so much,
to all reasonable Patriot men, may seem clear. But
then, through what agents of Pitt ? Varlet, Apostle
of Liberty, was discerned again of late, with his pike
and red nightcap. Deputy Marat published in his
Journal, this very day, complaining of the bitter
scarcity, and sufferings of the people, till he seemed to
get wroth : ' If your Rights of Man were anything but
a piece of written paper, the plunder of a few shops,
and a forestaller or two hung up at the door-lintels,
would put an end to such things '.[1] Are not these, say
the Girondins, pregnant indications ? Pitt has bribed
the Anarchists ; Marat is the agent of Pitt : hence this
sale of sugar. To the Mother-Society, again, it is clear
that the scarcity is factitious ; is the work of Girondins,
and such like ; a set of men sold partly to Pitt ; sold
wholly to their own ambitions, and hard-hearted pedantries ; who will not fix the grain-prices, but prate
pedantically of free-trade ; wishing to starve Paris into
violence, and embroil it with the Departments : *hence*
this sale of sugar.

And, alas, if to these two notabilities, of a Phenomenon and such Theories of a Phenomenon, we add this
third notability, That the French Nation has believed,
for several years now, in the possibility, nay certainty
and near advent, of a universal Millennium, or reign of
Freedom, Equality, Fraternity, wherein man should be
the brother of man, and sorrow and sin flee away ?* Not
bread to eat, nor soap to wash with ; and the reign of
Perfect Felicity ready to arrive, due always since the
Bastille fell ! How did our hearts burn within us,* at
that Feast of Pikes, when brother flung himself on
brother's bosom ; and in sunny jubilee, Twenty-five
millions burst forth into sound and cannon-smoke !
Bright was our Hope then, as sunlight ; red-angry is

---

[1] Hist. Parl. xxiv. 353-6.

our Hope grown now, as consuming fire. But, O
Heavens, what enchantment is it, or devilish legerde-
main, of such effect, that Perfect Felicity, always
within arm's length, could never be laid hold of, but
only in her stead Controversy and Scarcity ? This set
of traitors after that set ! Tremble, ye traitors ; dread
a People which calls itself patient, long-suffering ; but
which cannot always submit to have its pocket picked,
in this way,—of a Millennium !

Yes, Reader, here is the miracle. Out of that
putrescent rubbish of Scepticism, Sensualism, Sentimentalism, hollow Machiavelism, such a Faith has verily
risen ; flaming in the heart of a People. A whole
People, awakening as it were to consciousness in deep
misery, believes that it is within reach of a Fraternal
Heaven-on-Earth. With longing arms, it struggles to
embrace the Unspeakable ; cannot embrace it, owing
to certain causes.—Seldom do we find that a whole
People can be said to have any Faith at all ; except in
things which it can eat and handle. Whensoever it
gets any Faith, its history becomes spirit-stirring, noteworthy. But since the time when steel Europe shook
itself simultaneously at the word of Hermit Peter,* and
rushed towards the Sepulchre where God had lain, there
was no universal impulse of Faith that one could note.
Since Protestantism went silent, no Luther's voice, no
Zisca's drum* any longer proclaiming that God's truth
was *not* the Devil's Lie ; and the Last of the Cameronians*(Renwick was the name of him ; honour to the
name of the brave !) sank, shot, on the Castle-hill of
Edinburgh, there was no partial impulse of Faith among
Nations. Till now, behold, once more, this French
Nation believes ! Herein, we say, in that astonishing
Faith of theirs, lies the miracle. It is a Faith un-
doubtedly of the more prodigious sort, even among
Faiths ; and will embody itself in prodigies. It is the
soul of that world-prodigy named French Revolution ;
whereat the world still gazes and shudders.

But, for the rest, let no man ask History to explain
by cause and effect how the business proceeded hence-

forth.   This battle of Mountain and Gironde, and what
follows, is the battle of Fanaticisms and Miracles ; unsuitable for cause and effect.   The sound of it, to the
mind, is as a hubbub of voices in distraction ; little of
articulate is to be gathered by long listening and studying ; only battle-tumult, shouts of triumph, shrieks of
despair.   The Mountain has left no Memoirs ; the
Girondins have left Memoirs, which are too often little
other than long-drawn Interjections, of *Woe is me*, and
Cursed be ye.   So soon as History can philosophically
delineate the conflagration of a kindled Fireship, she
may try this other task.   Here lay the bitumen-stratum,
there the brimstone one ; so ran the vein of gunpowder,
of nitre, terebinth and foul grease : this, were she
inquisitive enough, History might partly know.   But
how they acted and reacted below decks, one fire-
stratum playing into the other, by its nature and the
art of man, now when all hands ran raging, and the
flames lashed high over shrouds and topmast : this let
not History attempt.

The Fireship is old France, the old French Form of
Life ; her crew a Generation of men.   Wild are their
cries and their ragings there, like spirits tormented in
that flame.   But, on the whole, are they not *gone*, O
Reader ?   Their Fireship and they, frightening the
world, have sailed away ; its flames and its thunders
quite away, into the Deep of Time.   One thing therefore History will do : pity them all ; for it went hard
with them all.   Not even the seagreen Incorruptible
but shall have some pity, some human love, though it
takes an effort.   And now, so much once thoroughly
attained, the rest will become easier.   To the eye of
equal brotherly pity, innumerable perversions dissipate
themselves ; exaggerations and execrations fall off, of
their own accord.   Standing wistfully on the safe
shore, we will look, and see, what is of interest to us,
what is adapted to us.

CHAPTER II

CULOTTIC AND SANSCULOTTIC

GIRONDE and Mountain are now in full quarrel; their
mutual rage, says Toulongeon, is growing a ' pale ' rage.
Curious, lamentable: all these men have the word
Republic on their lips; in the heart of every one of them is
a passionate wish for something which he calls Republic:
yet see their death-quarrel! So, however, are men
made. Creatures who live in confusion; who, once
thrown together, can readily fall into that confusion of
confusions which quarrel is, simply because their confusions differ from one another; still more because
they seem to differ! Men's words are a poor exponent
of their thought; nay their thought itself is a poor
exponent of the inward unnamed Mystery, wherefrom
both thought and action have their birth. No man can
explain himself, can get himself explained; men see not
one another, but distorted phantasms which they call
one another; which they hate and go to battle with:
for all battle is well said to be *misunderstanding*.

But indeed that similitude of the Fireship; of our
poor French brethren, so fiery themselves, working also
in an *element* of fire, was not insignificant. Consider it
well, there is a shade of the truth in it. For a man,
once committed headlong to republican or any other
Transcendentalism, and fighting and fanaticizing amid
a Nation of his like, becomes as it were enveloped in
an ambient atmosphere of Transcendentalism and
Delirium: his individual self is lost in something that is
not himself, but foreign though inseparable from him.
Strange to think of, the man's cloak still seems to hold
the same man: and yet the man is not there, his volition is not there; nor the source of what he will do and
devise; instead of the man and his volition there is
a piece of Fanaticism and Fatalism incarnated in the
shape of him. He, the hapless incarnated Fanaticism,

goes his road ; no man can help him, he himself least of all. It is a wonderful, tragical predicament ;—such as human language, unused to deal with these things, being contrived for the uses of common life, struggles to shadow out in figures. The ambient element of material fire is not wilder than this of Fanaticism ; nor, though visible to the eye, is it more real. Volition bursts forth involuntary-voluntary ; rapt along ; the movement of free human minds becomes a raging tornado of fatalism, blind as the winds ; and Mountain and Gironde, when they recover themselves, are alike astounded to see *where* it has flung and dropped them. To such height of miracle can men work on men ; the Conscious and the Unconscious blended inscrutably in this our inscrutable Life ; endless Necessity environing Freewill !

The weapons of the Girondins are Political Philosophy, Respectability and Eloquence. Eloquence, or call it rhetoric, really of a superior order ; Vergniaud, for instance, turns a period as sweetly as any man of that generation. The weapons of the Mountain are those of mere Nature : Audacity and Impetuosity which may become Ferocity, as of men complete in their determination, in their conviction ; nay of men, in some cases, who as Septemberers must either prevail or perish. The ground to be fought for is Popularity : further you may either seek Popularity with the friends of Freedom and Order, or with the friends of Freedom Simple ; to seek it with both has unhappily become impossible. With the former sort, and generally with the Authorities of the Departments, and such as read Parliamentary Debates, and are of Respectability, and of a peace-loving moneyed nature, the Girondins carry it. With the extreme Patriot again, with the indigent Millions, especially with the Population of Paris who do not read so much as hear and see, the Girondins altogether lose it, and the Mountain carries it.

Egoism, nor meanness of mind, is not wanting on either side. Surely not on the Girondin side ; where in fact the instinct of self-preservation, too prominently

unfolded by circumstances, cuts almost a sorry figure;
where also a certain finesse, to the length even of
shuffling and shamming, now and then shows itself.
They are men skilful in Advocate-fence. They have
been called the Jesuits of the Revolution;[1] but that
is too hard a name. It must be owned likewise that
this rude blustering Mountain has a sense in it of what
the Revolution means; which these eloquent Girondins
are totally void of. Was the Revolution made, and
fought for, against the world, these four weary years,
that a Formula might be substantiated; that Society
might become *methodic*, demonstrable by logic; and
the old Noblesse with their pretensions vanish? Or
ought it not withal to bring some glimmering of light
and alleviation to the Twenty-five Millions, who sat in
darkness, heavy-laden, till they rose with pikes in their
hands? At least and lowest, one would think, it should
bring them a proportion of bread to live on? There is
in the Mountain here and there; in Marat People's-
friend; in the incorruptible Seagreen himself, though
otherwise so lean and formulary, a heartfelt knowledge
of this latter fact;—without which knowledge all other
knowledge here is naught, and the choicest forensic
eloquence is as sounding brass and a tinkling cymbal.
Most cold, on the other hand, most patronizing,
unsubstantial is the tone of the Girondins towards ' our
poorer brethren';—those brethren whom one often
hears of under the collective name of ' the masses ', as
if they were not persons at all, but mounds of combustible explosive material, for blowing down Bastilles
with! In very truth, a Revolutionist of this kind, is he
not a Solecism? Disowned by Nature and Art;
deserving only to be erased, and disappear! Surely, to
our poorer brethren of Paris, all this Girondin patronage
sounds deadening and killing: if fine-spoken and
incontrovertible in logic, then all the falser, all the hatefuller in fact.

Nay doubtless, pleading for Popularity, here among

---

[1] Dumouriez, Mémoires, iii. 314.

our poorer brethren of Paris, the Girondin has a hard
game to play. If he gain the ear of the Respectable
at a distance, it is by insisting on September and such
like ; it is at the expense of this Paris where he dwells
and perorates.   Hard to perorate in such an auditory !
Wherefore the question arises : Could we not get ourselves out of this Paris ? Twice or oftener such an
attempt is made. If not we ourselves, thinks Guadet,
then at least our *Suppléans* might do it.   For every
Deputy has his *Suppléant*, or Substitute, who will take
his place if need be : might not these assemble, say at
Bourges, which is a quiet episcopal Town, in quiet
Berri, forty good leagues off ? In that case, what profit
were it for the Paris Sansculottery to insult us ; our
Suppléans sitting quiet in Bourges, to whom we could
run ? Nay, even the Primary electoral Assemblies,
thinks Guadet, might be re-convoked, and a New Convention got, with new orders from the Sovereign People ;
and right glad were Lyons, were Bordeaux, Rouen,
Marseilles, as yet Provincial Towns, to welcome us in
their turn, and become a sort of Capital Towns ; and
teach these Parisians reason.

Fond schemes ; which all misgo ! If decreed, in heat
of eloquent logic, to-day, they are repealed, by clamour
and passionate wider considerations, on the morrow.[1]
Will you, O Girondins, parcel us into separate Republics,
then ; like the Swiss, like your Americans ; so that
there be no Metropolis or indivisible French Nation
any more ? Your Departmental Guard seemed to point
that way ! Federal Republic ? Federalist ? Men and
Knitting-women repeat *Fédéraliste*, with or without
much Dictionary-meaning ; but go on repeating it, as
is usual in such cases, till the meaning of it becomes
almost magical, fit to designate all mystery of Iniquity ;
and *Fédéraliste* has grown a word of Exorcism and
Apage-Satanas.   But furthermore, consider what
' poisoning of public opinion ' in the Departments, by
these Brissot, Gorsas, Caritat-Condorcet Newspapers !

[1] Moniteur, 1793, No. 140, &c.

And then also what counter-poisoning, still feller in
quality, by a *Père Duchesne* of Hébert, brutallest Newspaper yet published on Earth ; by a *Rougiff* of Guffroy*;
by the ' incendiary leaves of Marat ' ! More than once,
on complaint given and effervescence rising, it is decreed
that a man cannot both be Legislator and Editor ; that
he shall choose between the one function and the other.[1]
But this too, which indeed could help little, is revoked
or eluded ; remains a pious wish mainly.

Meanwhile, as the sad fruit of such strife, behold,
O ye National Representatives, how between the
friends of Law and the friends of Freedom everywhere,
mere heats and jealousies have arisen ; fevering the
whole Republic ! Department, Provincial Town is
set against Metropolis, Rich against Poor, Culottic
against Sansculottic, man against man. From
the Southern Cities come Addresses of an almost
inculpatory character ; for Paris has long suffered
Newspaper calumny. Bourdeaux demands a reign of
Law and Respectability, meaning Girondism, with
emphasis. With emphasis Marseilles demands the like.
Nay, from Marseilles there come *two* Addresses : one
Girondin ; one Jacobin Sansculottic. Hot Rebecqui,
sick of this Convention-work, has given place to his
Substitute, and gone home ; where also, with such
jarrings, there is work to be sick of.

Lyons, a place of Capitalists and Aristocrats, is in still
worse state ; almost in revolt. Chalier the Jacobin
Town-Councillor has got, too literally, to daggers-
drawn with Nièvre-Chol the *Modérantin* Mayor ; one
of your Moderate, perhaps Aristocrat, Royalist or
Federalist Mayors ! Chalier,* who pilgrimed to Paris ' to
behold Marat and the Mountain', has verily kindled
himself at their sacred urn : for on the 6th of February
last, History or Rumour has seen him haranguing his
Lyons Jacobins in a quite transcendental manner, with
a drawn dagger in his hand ; recommending (they say)
sheer September methods, patience being worn out ;

[1] Hist. Parl. xxv. 25, &c.

and that the Jacobin Brethren should, impromptu,
work the Guillotine themselves ! One sees him still, in
Engravings : mounted on a table ; foot advanced, body
contorted ; a bald, rude, slope-browed, infuriated
visage of the canine species, the eyes starting from their
sockets ; in his puissant right-hand the brandished
dagger, or horse-pistol, as some give it ; other dog-
visages kindling under him :—a man not likely to end
well ! However, the Guillotine was *not* got together
impromptu, that day, ' on the Pont Saint-Clair ', or
elsewhere ; but indeed continued lying rusty in its
loft : [1] Nièvre-Chol with military went about, rumbling
cannon, in the most confused manner ; and the ' nine-
hundred prisoners ' received no hurt. So distracted
is Lyons grown, with its cannons rumbling. Convention Commissioners must be sent thither forthwith : if
even they can appease it, and keep the Guillotine in its
loft ?

Consider finally if, on all these mad jarrings of the
Southern Cities, and of France generally, a traitorous
Crypto-Royalist class is not looking and watching ;
ready to strike in, at the right season ! Neither is there
bread ; neither is there soap : see the Patriot women
selling out sugar, at a just rate of twenty-two sous per
pound ! Citizen Representatives, it were verily well
that your quarrels finished, and the reign of Perfect
Felicity began.

CHAPTER III

GROWING SHRILL

On the whole, one cannot say that the Girondins are
wanting to themselves, so far as goodwill might go.
They prick assiduously into the sore-places of the
Mountain ; from principle, and also from Jesuitism.

Besides September, of which there is now little to be
made except effervescence, we discern two sore-places

[1] Hist. Parl. xxiv. 385–93 ; xxvi. 229, &c.

where the Mountain often suffers : Marat, and Orléans
Égalité. Squalid Marat, for his own sake and for the
Mountain's, is assaulted ever and anon ; held up to
France, as a squalid bloodthirsty Portent, inciting to the
pillage of shops ; of whom let the Mountain have the
credit ! The Mountain murmurs, ill at ease : this
'Maximum of Patriotism', how shall they either own
him or disown him ? As for Marat personally, he, with
his fixed-idea, remains invulnerable to such things ;
nay the People's-friend is very evidently rising in
importance, as his befriended People rises. No shrieks
now, when he goes to speak ; occasional applauses
rather, furtherance which breeds confidence. The
day when the Girondins proposed to 'decree him
accused' (*décréter d'accusation*, as they phrase it) for
that February Paragraph, of 'hanging up a Forestaller
or two at the door-lintels', Marat proposes to have
them 'decreed insane' ; and, descending the Tribune-
steps, is heard to articulate these most unsenatorial
ejaculations : ' *Les cochons, les imbécilles*, Pigs, idiots ! '
Oftentimes he croaks harsh sarcasm, having really
a rough rasping tongue, and a very deep fund of contempt for fine outsides ; and once or twice, he even
laughs, nay 'explodes into laughter, *rit aux éclats*', at
the gentilities and superfine airs of these Girondin
'men of statesmanship', with their pedantries, plausi-
bilities, pusillanimities : 'these two years', says he,
'you have been whining about attacks, and plots, and
danger from Paris ; and you have not a scratch to
show for yourselves '.[1]—Danton gruffly rebukes him,
from time to time : a Maximum of Patriotism, whom
one can neither own nor disown !

But the second sore-place of the Mountain is this
anomalous Monseigneur Equality Prince d'Orléans.
Behold these men, says the Gironde ; with a whilom
Bourbon Prince among them : they are creatures of the
D'Orléans Faction ; they will have Philippe made
King ; one King no sooner guillotined than another

[1] Moniteur, Séance du 20 Mai 1793.

made in his stead ! Girondins have moved, Buzot
moved long ago, from principle and also from jesuitism,
that the whole race of Bourbons should be marched
forth from the soil of France ; this Prince Égalité to
bring up the rear. Motions which might produce some
effect on the public ;—which the Mountain, ill at ease,
knows not what to do with.

And poor Orléans Égalité himself, for one begins to
pity even him, what does he do with them ? The disowned of all parties, the rejected and foolishly bedrifted
hither and thither, to what corner of Nature can he now
drift with advantage ? Feasible hope remains not for
him : unfeasible hope, in pallid doubtful glimmers,
there may still come, bewildering, not cheering or
illuminating,—from the Dumouriez quarter ; and how,
if not the time-wasted Orléans Égalité, then perhaps
the young unworn Chartres Égalité might rise to be
a kind of King ? Sheltered, if shelter it be, in the clefts
of the Mountain, poor Égalité will wait : one refuge
in Jacobinism, one in Dumouriez and Counter-
Revolution, are there not two chances ? However, the
look of him, Dame Genlis says, is grown gloomy ; sad
to see. Sillery also, the Genlis's Husband, who hovers
about the Mountain, not on it, is in a bad way. Dame
Genlis has come to Raincy, out of England and Bury
St. Edmunds, in these days ; being summoned by
Égalité, with her young charge, Mademoiselle Égalité,—*
that so Mademoiselle might not be counted among
Emigrants and hardly dealt with. But it proves a
ravelled business : Genlis and charge find that they
must retire to the Netherlands ; must wait on the
Frontiers, for a week or two ; till Monseigneur, by
Jacobin help, get it wound up. ' Next morning ', says
Dame Genlis, ' Monseigneur, gloomier than ever, gave
me his arm, to lead me to the carriage. I was greatly
troubled ; Mademoiselle burst into tears ; her Father
was pale and trembling. After I had got seated, he
stood immovable at the carriage-door, with his eyes
fixed on me ; his mournful and painful look seemed
to implore pity ;—" *Adieu, Madame !* " said he.   The

altered sound of his voice completely overcame me ;
unable to utter a word, I held out my hand ; he grasped
it close ; then turning, and advancing sharply towards
the postilions, he gave them a sign, and we rolled away'.[1]

Nor are Peace-makers wanting ; of whom likewise
we mention two ; one fast on the crown of the Mountain,
the other not yet alighted anywhere : Danton and
Barrère. Ingenious Barrère, Old-Constituent and
Editor, from the slopes of the Pyrenees, is one of the
usefullest men of this Convention, in his way. Truth
may lie on both sides, on either side, or on neither side ;
my friends, ye must give and take : for the rest, success
to the winning side ! This is the motto of Barrère.
Ingenious, almost genial ; quick-sighted, supple, graceful ; a man that will prosper. Scarcely Belial in the
assembled Pandemonium* was plausibler to ear and
eye. An indispensable man : in the great *Art of
Varnish* he may be said to seek his fellow. Has there
an explosion arisen, as many do arise, a confusion,
unsightliness, which no tongue can speak of, nor eye
look on ; give it to Barrère ; Barrère shall be
Committee-Reporter of it ; you shall see it transmute
itself into a regularity, into the very beauty and improvement that was needed. Without one such man,
we say, how were this Convention bested ? Call him
not, as exaggerative Mercier does, ' the greatest liar in
France ' : nay it may be argued there is not truth
enough in him to make a real lie of. Call him, with
Burke, Anacreon of the Guillotine,* and a man serviceable to this Convention.

The other Peace-maker whom we name is Danton.
Peace, O peace with one another ! cries Danton often
enough : Are we not alone against the world ; a little
band of brothers ? Broad Danton is loved by all the
Mountain ; but they think him too easy-tempered,
deficient in suspicion : he has stood between Dumouriez
and much censure, anxious not to exasperate our only

[1] Genlis, Mémoires (London, 1825), iv. 118.

General : in the shrill tumult Danton's strong voice reverberates, for union and pacification. Meetings there are ; dinings with the Girondins : it is so pressingly essential that there be union. But the Girondins are haughty and respectable : this Titan Danton is not a man of Formulas, and there rests on him a shadow of September. 'Your Girondins have no confidence in me' : this is the answer a conciliatory Meillan gets from him ; to all the arguments and pleadings this conciliatory Meillan can bring, the repeated answer is, '*Ils n'ont point de confiance*'.[1]—The tumult will get ever shriller ; rage is growing pale.

In fact, what a pang is it to the heart of a Girondin, this first withering probability that the despicable unphilosophic anarchic Mountain, after all, may triumph ! Brutal Septemberers, a fifth-floor Tallien, 'a Robespierre without an idea in his head', as Condorcet says, 'or a feeling in his heart' : and yet we, the flower of France, cannot stand against them ; behold the sceptre departs from us ; from us and goes to them ! Eloquence, Philosophism, Respectability avail not : 'against Stupidity the very gods fight to no purpose,

'*Mit der Dummheit kämpfen Götter selbst vergebens !*'*

Shrill are the plaints of Louvet ; his thin existence all acidified into rage, and preternatural insight of suspicion. Wroth is young Barbaroux ; wroth and scornful. Silent, like a Queen with the aspic on her bosom,* sits the wife of Roland ; Roland's Accounts never yet got audited, his name become a byword. Such is the fortune of war, especially of revolution. The great gulf of Tophet, and Tenth of August, opened itself at the magic of your eloquent voice ; and lo now, it will not close at your voice ! It is a dangerous thing such magic. The Magician's Famulus* got hold of the forbidden Book, and summoned a goblin : *Plait-il*, What is your will ? said the goblin. The Famulus, somewhat

---

[1] Mémoires de Meillan, Représentant du Peuple (Paris, 1823), p. 51.

struck, bade him fetch water : the swift goblin fetched
it, pail in each hand ; but lo, would not cease fetching
it ! Desperate, the Famulus shrieks at him, smites at
him, cuts him in two ; lo, *two* goblin water-carriers ply ;
and the house will be swum away in Deucalion*Deluges.

CHAPTER IV

FATHERLAND IN DANGER

Or rather we will say, this Senatorial war might have
lasted long ; and Party tugging and throttling with
Party might have suppressed and smothered one another,
in the ordinary bloodless Parliamentary way ; on one
condition : that France had been at least able to exist,
all the while. But this Sovereign People has a digestive
faculty, and cannot do without bread. Also we are
at war, and must have victory ; at war with Europe,
with Fate and Famine : and behold, in the spring of
the year, all victory deserts us.

Dumouriez had his outposts stretched as far as Aix-
la-Chapelle, and the beautifullest plan for pouncing on
Holland, by stratagem, flat-bottomed boats and rapid
intrepidity ; wherein too he had prospered so far ; but
unhappily could prosper no further. Aix-la-Chapelle
is lost ; Maestricht*will not surrender to mere smoke
and noise : the flat-bottomed boats must launch themselves again, and return the way they came. Steady
now, ye rapidly intrepid men ; retreat with firmness,
Parthian-like ! Alas, were it General Miranda's fault ;
were it the War-minister's fault ; or were it Dumouriez's
own fault and that of Fortune : enough, there is nothing
for it but retreat,—well if it be not even flight ; for
already terror-stricken cohorts and stragglers pour off,
not waiting for order ; flow disastrous, as many as ten
thousand of them, without halt till they see France
again.[1] Nay worse : Dumouriez himself is perhaps

[1] Dumouriez, iv. 16–73.

secretly turning traitor ? Very sharp is the tone in which he writes to our Committees. Commissioners and Jacobin Pillagers have done such incalculable mischief ; Hassenfratz sends neither cartridges nor clothing ; shoes we have, deceptively ' soled with wood and pasteboard '. Nothing in short is right. Danton and Lacroix, when it was they that were Commissioners, would needs join Belgium to France ;—of which Dumouriez might have made the prettiest little Duchy for his own secret behoof ! With all these things the General is wroth ; and writes to us in a sharp tone. Who knows what this hot little General is meditating ? Dumouriez Duke of Belgium or Brabant ; and say, Égalité the Younger King of France : there were an end for our Revolution !—Committee of Defence gazes, and shakes its head : who except Danton, defective in suspicion, could still struggle to be of hope ?

And General Custine is rolling back from the Rhine Country ; conquered Mentz will be reconquered, the Prussians gathering round to bombard it with shot and shell. Mentz may resist, Commissioner Merlin, the Thionviller, 'making sallies, at the head of the besieged' ; —resist to the death ; but not longer than that. How sad a reverse for Mentz ! Brave Forster, brave Lux[*] planted Liberty-trees, amid *ça-ira*-ing music, in the snow-slush of last winter, there ; and made Jacobin Societies ; and got the Territory incorporated with France ; they came hither to Paris, as Deputies or Delegates, and have their eighteen francs a-day : but see, before once the Liberty-tree is got rightly in leaf, Mentz is changing into an explosive crater ; vomiting fire, bevomited with fire !

Neither of these men shall again see Mentz ; they have come hither only to die. Forster has been round the Globe ; he saw Cook[*] perish under Owyhee clubs ; but like this Paris he has yet seen or suffered nothing. Poverty escorts him : from home there can nothing come, except Job's-news ; the eighteen daily francs, which we here as Deputy or Delegate with difficulty ' touch ', are in paper *assignats*, and sink fast in value.

Poverty, disappointment, inaction, obloquy; the brave
heart slowly breaking! Such is Forster's lot. For the
rest, Demoiselle Théroigne smiles on you in the Soirées;
'a beautiful brownlocked face', of an exalted temper;
and contrives to keep her carriage. Prussian Trenck,
the poor subterranean Baron, jargons and jangles in an
unmelodious manner. Thomas Paine's face is red-
pustuled, 'but the eyes uncommonly bright'. Convention Deputies ask you to dinner: very courteous; and
'we all play at *plumpsack*'.[1] 'It is the Explosion and
New-creation of a World', says Forster; 'and the
actors in it, such small mean objects, buzzing round one
like a handful of flies '.—

Likewise there is war with Spain. Spain will advance
through the gorges of the Pyrenees; rustling with
Bourbon banners, jingling with artillery and menace.
And England has donned the red coat; and marches,
with Royal Highness of York,*—whom some once spake
of inviting to be our King. Changed that humour now:
and ever more changing; till no hatefuller thing walk
this Earth than a denizen of that tyrannous Island;
and Pitt be declared and decreed, with effervescence,
'*L'ennemi du genre humain*, The enemy of mankind ';
and, very singular to say, you make order that no
Soldier of Liberty give quarter to an Englishman.
Which order, however, the Soldier of Liberty does but
partially obey. We will take no Prisoners then, say
the Soldiers of Liberty; they shall all be 'Deserters '
that we take.[2] It is a frantic order; and attended
with inconvenience. For surely, if you give no quarter,
the plain issue is that you will get none; and so the
business become as broad as it was long.—Our 'recruitment of Three-hundred Thousand men ', which was
the decreed force for this year, is like to have work
enough laid to its hand.

So many enemies come wending on; penetrating
through throats of mountains, steering over the salt

[1] Forster's Briefwechsel, ii. 514, 460, 631.
[2] See Dampmartin, Evénemens, ii. 213–30.

sea ; towards all points of our territory ; rattling chains
at us. Nay, worst of all : there is an enemy within our
own territory itself. In the early days of March, the
Nantes Postbags do not arrive; there arrive only instead
of them Conjecture, Apprehension, bodeful wind of
Rumour. The bodefullest proves true. Those fanatic
Peoples of La Vendée will no longer keep under : their
fire of insurrection, heretofore dissipated with difficulty,
blazes out anew, after the King's Death, as a wide
conflagration ; not riot, but civil war. Your Cathe-
lineaus, your Stofflets, Charettes, are other men than
was thought: behold how their Peasants, in mere russet
and hodden, with their rude arms, rude array, with their
fanatic Gaelic frenzy and wild-yelling battle-cry of *God
and the King*, dash at us like a dark whirlwind ; and
blow the best-disciplined Nationals we can get into panic
and *sauve-qui-peut* ! Field after field is theirs ; one sees
not where it will end. Commandant Santerre may be
sent there ; but with non-effect ; he might as well have
returned and brewed beer.

It has become peremptorily necessary that a National
Convention cease arguing, and begin acting. Yield one
party of you to the other, and do it swiftly. No theoretic
outlook is here, but the close certainty of ruin ; the very
day that is passing over us must be provided for.

It was Friday the Eighth of March when this Job's-
post from Dumouriez, thickly preceded and escorted
by so many other Job's-posts, reached the National
Convention. Blank enough are most faces. Little will
it avail whether our Septemberers be punished or go
unpunished ; if Pitt and Cobourg*are coming in, with
one punishment for us all ; nothing now between Paris
itself and the Tyrants but a doubtful Dumouriez, and
hosts in loose-flowing loud retreat !—Danton the Titan
rises in this hour, as always in the hour of need. Great
is his voice, reverberating from the domes :—Citizen-
Representatives, shall we not, in such crisis of Fate, lay
aside discords ? Reputation : O what is the reputation
of this man or of that ? ' *Que mon nom soit flétri ; que*

la France soit libre : Let my name be blighted ; let
France be free ! ' It is necessary now again that France
rise, in swift vengeance, with her million right-hands,
with her heart as of one man. Instantaneous recruitment in Paris ; let every Section of Paris furnish its
thousands ; every Section of France ! Ninety-six Commissioners of us, two for each Section of the Forty-eight,
they must go forthwith, and tell Paris what the Country
needs of her. Let Eighty more of us be sent, post-
haste, over France ; to spread the fire-cross, to call
forth the might of men. Let the Eighty also be on the
road, before this sitting rise. Let them go, and think
what their errand is. Speedy Camp of Fifty-thousand
between Paris and the North-Frontier ; for Paris will
pour forth her volunteers ! Shoulder to shoulder ; one
strong universal death-defiant rising and rushing ; we
shall hurl back these Sons of Night yet again ; and
France, in spite of the world, be free ! [1]—So sounds the
Titan's voice : into all Section-houses ; into all French
hearts. Sections sit in Permanence, for recruitment,
enrolment, that very night. Convention Commissioners,
on swift wheels, are carrying the fire-cross from Town
to Town, till all France blaze.

And so there is Flag of *Fatherland in Danger* waving
from the Townhall, Black Flag from the top of Notre-
Dame Cathedral ; there is Proclamation, hot eloquence ;
Paris rushing out once again to strike its enemies down.
That, in such circumstances, Paris was in no mild
humour can be conjectured. Agitated streets ; still
more agitated round the Salle de Manége ! Feuillans-
Terrace crowds itself with angry Citizens, angrier
Citizenesses ; Varlet perambulates with portable chair :
ejaculations of no measured kind, as to perfidious fine-
spoken *Hommes d'état*, friends of Dumouriez, secret-
friends of Pitt and Cobourg, burst from the hearts and
lips of men. To fight the enemy ? Yes, and even to
' freeze him with terror, *glacer d'effroi* ' : but first to
have domestic Traitors punished ! Who are they that,

----

[1] Moniteur (in Hist. Parl. xxv. 6).

carping and quarrelling, in their jesuitic most *moderate*
way, seek to shackle the Patriotic movement ? That
divide France against Paris, and poison public opinion
in the Departments? That when we ask for bread, and
a Maximum fixed-price, treat us with lectures on Free-
trade in grains ? Can the human stomach satisfy itself
with lectures on Free-trade ; and are we to fight the
Austrians in a moderate manner, or in an immoderate ?
This Convention must be *purged.*

  ' Set up a swift Tribunal for Traitors, a Maximum for
Grains': thus speak with energy the Patriot Volunteers,
as they defile through the Convention Hall, just on the
wing to the Frontiers ;—perorating in that heroical
Cambyses' vein of theirs : beshouted by the Galleries
and Mountain ; bemurmured by the Right-side and
Plain. Nor are prodigies wanting : lo, while a Captain
of the Section Poissonnière perorates with vehemence
about Dumouriez, Maximum and Crypto-Royalist
Traitors, and his troop beat chorus with him, waving
their Banner overhead, the eye of a Deputy discerns,
in this same Banner, that the *cravates* or streamers of it
have Royal fleurs-de-lis ! The Section-Captain shrieks ;
his troop shriek, horror-struck, and 'trample the Banner
under foot' : seemingly the work of some Crypto-
Royalist Plotter ? Most probable : [1]—or perhaps at
bottom, only the *old* Banner of the Section, manufactured prior to the Tenth of August, when such streamers
were according to rule ! [2]

History, looking over the Girondin Memoirs, anxious
to disentangle the truth of them from the hysterics, finds
these days of March, especially this Sunday the Tenth
of March, play a great part. Plots, plots ; a plot for
murdering the Girondin Deputies ; Anarchists and
Secret-Royalists plotting, in hellish concert, for that
end ! The far greater part of which is hysterics. What
we do find indisputable is, that Louvet and certain

[1] Choix des Rapports, xi. 277.
[2] Hist. Parl. xxv. 72.

Girondins were apprehensive they might be murdered
on Saturday, and did not go to the evening sitting; but
held council with one another, each inciting his fellow
to do something resolute, and end these Anarchists;
to which, however, Pétion, opening the window, and
finding the night very wet, answered only, '*Ils ne
feront rien*', and 'composedly resumed his violin', says
Louvet;[1] thereby, with soft Lydian tweedledeeing, to
wrap himself against eating cares. Also that Louvet
felt especially liable to being killed; that several Girondins went abroad to seek beds: liable to being killed;
but were not. Further that, in very truth, Journalist
Deputy Gorsas, poisoner of the Departments, he and his
Printer had their houses broken into (by a tumult of
Patriots, among whom redcapped Varlet, American
Fournier loom forth, in the darkness of the rain and
riot); had their wives put in fear; their presses, types
and circumjacent equipments beaten to ruin; no
Mayor interfering in time; Gorsas himself escaping,
pistol in hand, 'along the coping of the back wall'.
Further that Sunday, the morrow, was not a workday;
and the streets were more agitated than ever: Is it a
new September, then, that these Anarchists intend?
Finally, that no September came;—and also that
hysterics, not unnaturally, had reached almost their
acme.[2]

Vergniaud denounces and deplores; in sweetly turned
periods. Section Bonconseil, *Good-counsel* so-named,
not Mauconseil or *Ill-counsel* as it once was,—does a far
notabler thing: demands that Vergniaud, Brissot,
Guadet, and other denunciatory fine-spoken Girondins,
to the number of Twenty-two, be put under arrest!
Section Good-counsel, so named ever since the Tenth of
August, is sharply rebuked, like a Section of Ill-counsel:[3]
but its word is spoken, and will not fall to the ground.

In fact, one thing strikes us in these poor Girondins:

---

[1] Louvet, Mémoires, p. 72.
[2] Meillan, pp. 23, 24; Louvet, pp. 71-80.
[3] Moniteur (Séance du 12 Mars), 15 Mars.

their fatal shortness of vision ; nay fatal poorness of character, for that is the root of it. They are as strangers to the People they would govern ; to the thing they have come to work in. Formulas, Philosophies, Respectabilities, what has been written in Books, and admitted by the Cultivated Classes : *this* inadequate *Scheme* of Nature's working is all that Nature, let her work as she will, can reveal to these men. So they perorate and speculate ; and call on the Friends of Law, when the question is not Law or No-Law, but Life or No-Life. Pedants of the Revolution, if not Jesuits of it ! Their Formalism is great ; great also is their Egoism. France rising to fight Austria has been raised only by plot of the Tenth of March, to kill Twenty-two of *them* ! This Revolution Prodigy, unfolding itself into terrific stature and articulation, by its own laws and Nature's, not by the laws of Formula, has become unintelligible, incredible as an impossibility, the ' waste chaos of a Dream '. A Republic founded on what they call the Virtues ; on what we call the Decencies and Respectabilities : this they will have, and nothing but this. Whatsoever other Republic Nature and Reality send, shall be considered as not sent ; as a kind of Nightmare Vision, and thing non-extant ; disowned by the Laws of Nature, and of Formula. Alas ! dim for the best eyes is this Reality ; and as for these men, they will not look at it with eyes at all, but only through ' facetted spectacles '*of Pedantry, wounded Vanity ; which yield the most portentous fallacious spectrum. Carping and complaining for ever of Plots and Anarchy, they will do one thing ; prove, to demonstration, that the Reality will not translate into their Formula ; that they and their Formula are incompatible with the Reality : and, in its dark wrath, the Reality will extinguish it and them ! What a man *kens* he *cans*. But the beginning of a man's doom is, that vision be withdrawn from him* ; that he see not the reality, but a false spectrum of the reality ; and following that, step darkly, with more or less velocity, downwards to the utter Dark ; to Ruin, which is the

great Sea of Darkness, whither all falsehoods, winding
or direct, continually flow !

This Tenth of March we may mark as an epoch in the
Girondin destinies ; the rage so exasperated itself, the
misconception so darkened itself. Many desert the
sittings ; many come to them armed.[1]   An honourable
Deputy, setting out after breakfast, must now, besides
taking his Notes, see whether his Priming is in order.

Meanwhile with Dumouriez in Belgium it fares ever
worse.   Were it again General Miranda's fault, or some
other's fault, there is no doubt whatever but the ' Battle
of Nerwinden ', on the 18th of March, is lost ; and our
rapid retreat has become a far too rapid one. Victorious
Cobourg, with his Austrian prickers, hangs like a dark
cloud on the rear of us : Dumouriez never off horseback
night or day ; engagement every three hours ; our
whole discomfited Host rolling rapidly inwards, full
of rage, suspicion and *sauve-qui-peut* ! And then Dumouriez himself, what his intents may be ? Wicked
seemingly and not charitable !   His dispatches to
Committee openly denounce a factious Convention, for
the woes it has brought on France and him.   And
his speeches—for the General has no reticence !   The
execution of the Tyrant this Dumouriez calls the Murder
of the King.   Danton and Lacroix, flying thither as
Commissioners once more, return very doubtful ; even
Danton now doubts.

Three Jacobin Missionaries, Proly, Dubuisson, Pereyra,
have flown forth ; sped by a wakeful Mother Society :
they are struck dumb to hear the General speak.   The
Convention, according to this General, consists of three-
hundred scoundrels and four-hundred imbeciles: France
cannot do without a King. ' But we have executed
our King '.   ' And what is it to me ', hastily cries Dumouriez, a General of no reticence, ' whether the King's
name be *Ludovicus* or *Jacobus* ? '   ' Or *Philippus* ! '
rejoins Proly ;—and hastens to report progress.   Over
the Frontiers such hope is there.

[1] Meillan, Mémoires, pp. 85, 24.

CHAPTER V

SANSCULOTTISM ACCOUTRED

LET us look, however, at the grand internal Sansculottism and Revolution Prodigy, whether it stirs and waxes : there and not elsewhere may hope still be for France. The Revolution Prodigy, as Decree after Decree issues from the Mountain, like creative *fiats*, accordant with the nature of the Thing,—is shaping itself rapidly, in these days, into terrific stature and articulation, limb after limb. Last March, 1792, we saw all France flowing in blind terror ; shutting town-barriers, boiling pitch for Brigands : happier, this March, that it is a seeing terror ; that a creative Mountain exists, which can say *fiat*! Recruitment proceeds with fierce celerity : nevertheless our Volunteers hesitate to set out, till Treason be punished at home ; they do not fly to the frontiers ; but only fly hither and thither, demanding and denouncing. The Mountain must speak new *fiat*, and new *fiats*.

And does it not speak such ? Take, as first example, those *Comités Révolutionnaires* for the arrestment of Persons Suspect. Revolutionary Committee, of Twelve chosen Patriots, sits in every Township of France ; examining the Suspect, seeking arms, making domiciliary visits and arrestments ;—caring, generally, that the Republic suffer no detriment. Chosen by universal suffrage, each in its Section, they are a kind of elixir of Jacobinism ; some Forty-four Thousand of them awake and alive over France ! In Paris and all Towns, every house-door must have the names of the inmates legibly printed on it, ' at a height not exceeding five feet from the ground ' ; every Citizen must produce his certificatory *Carte de Civisme*, signed by Section-President ; every man be ready to give account of the faith that is in him. Persons Suspect had as well depart this soil

of Liberty ! And yet departure too is bad : all Emigrants are declared Traitors, their property become
National ; they are ‘ dead in Law ’,—save indeed that
for *our* behoof they shall ‘ live yet fifty years in Law ’,
and what heritages may fall to them in that time become
National too ! A mad vitality of Jacobinism, with
Forty-four Thousand centres of activity, circulates
through all fibres of France.

Very notable also is the *Tribunal Extraordinaire* : [1]
decreed by the Mountain ; some Girondins dissenting,
for surely such a Court contradicts every formula ;—
other Girondins assenting, nay co-operating, for do not
we all hate Traitors, O ye people of Paris ?—Tribunal
of the Seventeenth, in Autumn last, was swift ; but
this shall be swifter. Five Judges ; a standing Jury,
which is named from Paris and the Neighbourhood, that
there be not delay in naming it : they are subject to no
Appeal ; to hardly any Law-forms, but must ‘ get themselves convinced ’ in all readiest ways ; and for security
are bound ‘ to vote audibly ’ ; audibly, in the hearing
of a Paris Public. This is the *Tribunal Extraordinaire* ;
which, in few months, getting into most lively action,
shall be entitled *Tribunal Révolutionnaire*; as indeed
it from the very first has entitled itself: with a Herman or
a Dumas for Judge President, with a Fouquier-Tinville
for Attorney-General, and a Jury of such as Citizen
Leroi, who has surnamed himself *Dix-Août*, ‘ Leroi
August-Tenth ’, it will become the wonder of the world.
Herein has Sansculottism fashioned for itself a Sword
of Sharpness*: a weapon magical ; tempered in the
Stygian hell-waters ; to the edge of it all armour, and
defence of strength or of cunning shall be soft ; it shall
mow down Lives and Brazen-gates ; and the waving of
it shed terror through the souls of men.

But speaking of an amorphous Sansculottism taking
form, ought we not, above all things, to specify how the
Amorphous gets itself a Head ? Without metaphor,
this Revolution Government continues hitherto in a very

---

[1] *Moniteur*, No. 70 (du 11 Mars), No. 76, &c.

anarchic state. Executive Council of Ministers, Six in
number, there is : but they, especially since Roland's
retreat, have hardly known whether they were Ministers
or not. Convention Committees sit supreme over them ;
but then each Committee as supreme as the others :
Committee of Twenty-one, of Defence, of General Surety ;
simultaneous or successive, for specific purposes. The
Convention alone is all-powerful,—especially if the Commune go with it ; but is too numerous for an adminis-
trative body. Wherefore, in this perilous quick-whirl-
ing condition of the Republic, before the end of March
we obtain our small *Comité de Salut Public* ; [1] as it
were, for miscellaneous accidental purposes requiring
dispatch ;—as it proves, for a sort of universal supervision, and universal subjection. They are to report
weekly, these new Committee-men ; but to deliberate
in secret. Their number is Nine, firm Patriots all,
Danton one of them ; renewable every month ;—yet
why not re-elect them if they turn out well ? The
flower of the matter is, that they are but nine ; that
they sit in secret. An insignificant-looking thing at
first, this Committee ; but with a principle of growth
in it ! Forwarded by fortune, by internal Jacobin
energy, it will reduce all Committees and the Convention itself to mute obedience, the Six Ministers to Six
assiduous Clerks ; and work its will on the Earth
and under Heaven, for a season. A ' Committee of
Public Salvation ', whereat the world still shrieks and
shudders.

If we call that Revolutionary Tribunal a Sword, which
Sansculottism has provided for itself, then let us call
the ' Law of the Maximum ', a Provender-scrip, or
Haversack, wherein, better or worse, some ration of
bread may be found. It is true, Political Economy,
Girondin free-trade, and all law of supply and demand,
are hereby hurled topsyturvy : but what help ? Patriotism must live ; the ' cupidity of farmers ' seems to
have no bowels.* Wherefore this Law of the Maximum,

[1] Moniteur, No. 83 (du 24 Mars 1793), Nos. 86, 98, 99, 100.

fixing the highest price of grains, is, with infinite effort,
got passed; [1] and shall gradually extend itself into
a Maximum for all manner of *comestibles* and commodi-
ties: with such scrambling and topsyturvying as may
be fancied! For now if, for example, the farmer will
not sell? The farmer shall be forced to sell. An accurate Account of what grain he has shall be delivered in
to the Constituted Authorities: let him see that he say
not too much; for in that case, his rents, taxes and
contributions will rise proportionally: let him see that
he say not too little; for, on or before a set day, we
shall suppose in April, *less* than one-third of this declared quantity must remain in his barns, more than
two-thirds of it must have been thrashed and sold.
One can denounce him, and raise penalties.

By such inextricable overturning of all Commercial
relations will Sansculottism keep life in; since not
otherwise. On the whole, as Camille Desmoulins says
once, ' while the Sansculottes fight, the Monsieurs must
pay'. So there come *Impôts Progressifs*, Ascending
Taxes; which consume, with fast-increasing voracity,
the ' superfluous-revenue ' of men: beyond fifty-pounds
a-year you are not exempt; rising into the hundreds,
you bleed freely; into the thousands and tens of thousands, you bleed gushing. Also there come Requisitions; there comes ' Forced-Loan of a Milliard ', some
Fifty-Millions Sterling; which of course they that *have*
must lend. Unexampled enough; it has grown to be
no country for the Rich, this; but a country for the
Poor! And then if one fly, what steads it? Dead in
Law; nay kept alive fifty years yet, for *their* accursed
behoof! In this manner therefore it goes; topsyturvying, *ça-ira*-ing;—and withal there is endless sale
of Emigrant National-Property, there is Cambon with
endless cornucopia of Assignats. The Trade and
Finance of Sansculottism; and how, with Maximum
and Bakers'-queues, with Cupidity, Hunger, Denunciation and Paper-money, it led its galvanic-life, and began

[1] Moniteur (du 20 Avril, &c. to 20 Mai, 1793).

and ended,—remains the most interesting of all Chapters in Political Economy : still to be written.

All which things, are they not clean against Formula ? O Girondin Friends, it is not a Republic of the Virtues we are getting ; but only a Republic of the Strengths, virtuous and other !

CHAPTER VI

THE TRAITOR

But Dumouriez, with his fugitive Host, with his King *Ludovicus* or King *Philippus* ? There lies the crisis ; there hangs the question : Revolution Prodigy, or Counter-Revolution ?—One wide shriek covers that North-east region. Soldiers, full of rage, suspicion and terror, flock hither and thither ; Dumouriez, the many-counselled, never off horseback, knows now no counsel that were not worse than none : the counsel, namely, of joining himself with Cobourg ; marching to Paris, extinguishing Jacobinism, and, with some new King Ludovicus or King Philippus, restoring the Constitution of 1791 ! [1]

Is wisdom quitting Dumouriez ; the herald of Fortune*quitting him ?   Principle, faith political or other, beyond a certain faith of mess-rooms, and honour of an officer, had him not to quit. At any rate his quarters in the Burgh of Saint-Amand ; his headquarters in the Village of Saint-Amand des Boues, a short way off, —have become a Bedlam. National Representatives, Jacobin Missionaries are riding and running ; of the ' three Towns ', Lille, Valenciennes or even Condé, which Dumouriez wanted to snatch for himself, not one can be snatched ; your Captain is admitted, but the Town-gate is closed on him, and then alas the Prison-gate, and ' his men wander about the ramparts '.

[1] Dumouriez, Mémoires, iv. c. 7-c. 10.

Couriers gallop breathless ; men wait, or seem waiting,
to assassinate, to be assassinated ; Battalions nigh
frantic with such suspicion and uncertainty, with *Vive-
la-République* and *Sauve-qui-peut*, rush this way and
that ;—Ruin and Desperation in the shape of Cobourg
lying entrenched close by.

Dame Genlis and her fair Princess d'Orléans find
this Burgh of Saint-Amand no fit place for them ;
Dumouriez's protection is grown worse than none.
Tough Genlis, one of the toughest women; a woman, as
it were, with nine lives in her ; whom nothing will beat:
she packs her bandboxes ; clear for flight in a private
manner. Her beloved Princess she will—leave here,
with the Prince Chartres Égalité her Brother. In the
cold grey of the April morning, we find her accordingly
established in her hired vehicle, on the street of Saint-
Amand ; postilions just cracking their whips to go,—
when behold the young Princely Brother, struggling
hitherward, hastily calling ; bearing the Princess in
his arms ! Hastily he has clutched the poor young
lady up, in her very night-gown, nothing saved of her
goods except the watch from the pillow : with brotherly
despair he flings her in, among the bandboxes, into
Genlis's chaise, into Genlis's arms : Leave her not, in
the name of Mercy and Heaven ! A shrill scene, but
a brief one :—the postilions crack and go. Ah, whither ?
Through by-roads and broken hill-passes ; seeking their
way with lanterns after nightfall ; through perils, and
Cobourg Austrians, and suspicious French Nationals:
finally, into Switzerland ; safe though nigh moneyless.[1]
The brave young Égalité has a most wild Morrow to
look for ; but now only himself to carry through it.

For indeed over at that Village named *of the Mud-
baths*, Saint-Amand des Boues, matters are still worse.
At four o'clock on Tuesday afternoon, the 2nd of April
1793, two Couriers come galloping as if for life :
Mon Général ! Four National Representatives, War-

---

[1] Genlis, iv. 139.

Minister at their head, are posting hitherward from
Valenciennes ; are close at hand,—with what intents
one may guess ! While the Couriers are yet speaking,
War-Minister and National Representatives, old Camus
the Archivist for chief speaker of them, arrive. Hardly
has *Mon Général* had time to order out the Hussar
Regiment de Berchigny ; that it take rank and wait
near by, in case of accident. And so, enter War-
Minister Beurnonville, with an embrace of friendship,
for he is an old friend ; enter Archivist Camus and the
other three following him.

They produce Papers, invite the General to the bar
of the Convention : merely to give an explanation or
two. The General finds it unsuitable, not to say impossible, and that ' the service will suffer '. Then comes
reasoning ; the voice of the old Archivist getting loud.
Vain to reason loud with this Dumouriez ; he answers
mere angry irreverences. And so, amid plumed staff-
officers, very gloomy-looking ; in jeopardy and uncertainty, these poor National messengers debate and consult, retire and re-enter, for the space of some two hours:
without effect. Whereupon Archivist Camus, getting
quite loud, proclaims, in the name of the National Convention, for he has the power to do it, That General
Dumouriez is *arrested* : ' Will you obey the National
mandate, General? '—' *Pas dans ce moment-ci*, Not at
this particular moment', answers the General also aloud;
then glancing the other way, utters certain unknown
vocables, in a mandatory manner ; seemingly a German
word-of-command.[1] Hussars clutch the Four National
Representatives, and Beurnonville the War-Minister ;
pack them out of the apartment ; out of the Village,
over the lines to Cobourg, in two chaises that very
night,—as hostages, prisoners ; to lie long in Maestricht and Austrian strongholds ! [2] *Jacta est alea.*

This night Dumouriez prints his ' Proclamation ' ;

---

[1] Dumouriez, iv. 159, &c.

[2] Their Narrative, written by Camus (in Toulongeon, iii.
app. 60–87).

this night and the morrow the Dumouriez Army, in
such darkness visible, and rage of semi-desperation as
there is, shall meditate what the General is doing, what
they themselves will do in it. Judge whether this
Wednesday was of halcyon nature, for any one ! But
on the Thursday morning, we discern Dumouriez with
small escort, with Chartres Égalité and a few staff-
officers, ambling along the Condé Highway : perhaps
they are for Condé, and trying to persuade the Garrison
there ; at all events, they are for an interview with
Cobourg, who waits in the woods by appointment, in
that quarter. Nigh the Village of Doumet, three
National Battalions, a set of men always full of Jacobinism, sweep past us ; marching rather swiftly,—seemingly in mistake, by a way we had not ordered. The
General dismounts, steps into a cottage, a little from
the wayside ; will give them right order in writing.
Hark ! what strange growling is heard ; what barkings
are heard, loud yells of ' Traitors ', of ' Arrest ' : the
National Battalions have wheeled round, are emitting
shot ! Mount, Dumouriez, and spring for life ! Dumouriez and Staff strike the spurs in, deep ; vault over
ditches, into the fields, which prove to be morasses ;
sprawl and plunge for life ; bewhistled with curses and
lead. Sunk to the middle, with or without horses,
several servants killed, they escape out of shot-range,
to General Mack the Austrian's quarters. Nay they
return on the morrow, to Saint-Amand and faithful
foreign Berchigny ; but what boots it ? The Artillery
has all revolted, is jingling off to Valenciennes ; all have
revolted, are revolting; except only foreign Berchigny,
to the extent of some poor fifteen hundred, none will
follow Dumouriez against France and Indivisible Republic : Dumouriez's occupation 's gone.[1]

Such an instinct of Frenchhood and Sansculottism
dwells in these men : they will follow no Dumouriez
nor Lafayette, nor any mortal on such, errand. Shriek
may be of *Sauve-qui-peut*, but will also be of *Vive-la*-

---

[1] Mémoires, iv. 162–80.

République. New National Representatives arrive; new General Dampierre, soon killed in battle; new General Custine: the agitated Hosts draw back to some Camp of Famars; make head against Cobourg as they can.

And so Dumouriez is in the Austrian quarters; his drama ended, in this rather sorry manner. A most shifty, wiry man; one of Heaven's Swiss; that wanted only work. Fifty years of unnoticed toil and valour; one year of toil and valour, not unnoticed, but seen of all countries and centuries; then thirty other years again unnoticed, of Memoir-writing, English Pension, scheming and projecting to no purpose: Adieu, thou Swiss of Heaven, worthy to have been something else!

His Staff go different ways. Brave young Égalité reaches Switzerland and the Genlis Cottage; with a strong crabstick in his hand, a strong heart in his body: his Princedom is now reduced to that. Égalité the Father sat playing whist, in his Palais Égalité, at Paris, on the 6th day of this same month of April, when a catchpole entered: Citoyen Égalité is wanted at the Convention Committee![1] Examination, requiring Arrestment; finally requiring Imprisonment, transference to Marseilles and the Castle of If! Orléansdom has sunk in the black waters; Palais Égalité, which was Palais Royal, is like to become Palais National.

CHAPTER VII

IN FIGHT

OUR Republic, by paper Decree, may be 'One and Indivisible'; but what profits it while these things are? Federalists in the Senate, renegades in the Army, traitors everywhere! France, all in desperate recruitment since the Tenth of March, does not fly to the frontier, but only flies hither and thither. This defection of contemptuous diplomatic Dumouriez falls

[1] See Montgaillard, iv. 144.

heavy on the fine-spoken high-sniffing *Hommes d'état*
whom he consorted with; forms a second epoch in
their destinies.

Or perhaps more strictly we might say, the second
Girondin epoch, though little noticed then, began on the
day when, in reference to this defection, the Girondins
broke with Danton. It was the first day of April;
Dumouriez had not yet plunged across the morasses
to Cobourg, but was evidently meaning to do it, and
our Commissioners were off to arrest him; when what
does the Girondin Lasource* see good to do, but rise,
and jesuitically question and insinuate at great length,
whether a main accomplice of Dumouriez had not
probably been—Danton! Gironde grins sardonic assent; Mountain holds its breath. The figure of
Danton, Levasseur says, while this speech went on, was
noteworthy. He sat erect with a kind of internal convulsion struggling to keep itself motionless; his eye
from time to time flashing wilder, his lip curling in
Titanic scorn.[1] Lasource, in a fine-spoken attorney-
manner, proceeds: there is this probability to his mind,
and there is that: probabilities which press painfully
on him, which cast the Patriotism of Danton under
a painful shade;—which painful shade, he, Lasource,
will hope that Danton may find it not impossible to
dispel.

'*Les Scélérats!*' cries Danton, starting up, with
clenched right-hand, Lasource having done; and descends from the Mountain, like a lava-flood: his answer
not unready. Lasource's probabilities fly like idle dust;
but leave a result behind them. 'Ye were right, friends
of the Mountain', begins Danton, 'and I was wrong:
there is no peace possible with these men. Let it bo
war then! They will not save the Republic with us:
it shall be saved without them; saved in spite of them'.
Really a burst of rude Parliamentary eloquence this;
which is still worth reading, in the old *Moniteur*. With
fire-words the exasperated rude Titan rives and smites

---

[1] Mémoires de Réné Levasseur (Bruxelles, 1830), i. 164.

these Girondins; at every hit the glad Mountain utters
chorus; Marat, like a musical *bis*, repeating the last
phrase.[1] Lasource's probabilities are gone; but Danton's pledge of battle remains lying.

A third epoch, or scene in the Girondin Drama, or
rather it is but the completion of this second epoch, we
reckon from the day when the patience of virtuous
Pétion finally boiled over; and the Girondins, so to
speak, took up this battle-pledge of Danton's, and
decreed Marat accused.   It was the eleventh of the
same month of April, on some effervescence rising, such
as often rose; and President had covered himself, mere
Bedlam now ruling; and Mountain and Gironde were
rushing on one another with clenched right-hands, and
even with pistols in them; when, behold, the Girondin
Duperret*drew a sword! Shriek of horror rose, instantly
quenching all other effervescence, at sight of the clear
murderous steel; whereupon Duperret returned it to
the leather again;—confessing that he did indeed draw
it, being instigated by a kind of sacred madness, ' *sainte
fureur* ', and pistols held at him; but that if he parri-
cidally had chanced to scratch the outmost skin of
National Representation with it, he too carried pistols,
and would have blown his brains out on the spot.[2]

But now in such posture of affairs, virtuous Pétion
rose, next morning, to lament these effervescences, this
endless Anarchy invading the Legislative Sanctuary
itself; and here, being growled at and howled at by
the Mountain, his patience, long tried, did, as we say,
boil over; and he spake vehemently, in high key, with
foam on his lips; ' whence ', says Marat, ' I concluded
he had got *la rage* ', the rabidity, or dog-madness.
Rabidity smites others rabid: so there rises new foam-
lipped demand to have Anarchists extinguished; and
specially to have Marat put under Accusation.   Send a
representative to the Revolutionary Tribunal? Violate

---

[1] Séance du 1ᵉʳ Avril 1793 (in Hist. Parl. xxv. 24-35).
[2] Ibid. xv. 397.

the inviolability of a Representative ? Have a care,
O Friends ! This poor Marat has faults enough ; but
against Liberty or Equality, what fault ? That he has
loved and fought for it, not wisely but too well.* In
dungeons and cellars, in pinching poverty, under anathema of men ; even so, in such fight, has he grown so
dingy, bleared ; even so has his head become a Stylites
one ! Him you will fling to your Sword of Sharpness ;
while Cobourg and Pitt advance on us, fire-spitting ?

The Mountain is loud, the Gironde is loud and deaf ;
all lips are foamy. With ' Permanent-Session of twenty-
four hours ', with vote by rollcall, and a deadlift effort,
the Gironde carries it : Marat is ordered to the Revolutionary Tribunal, to answer for that February Paragraph of Forestallers at the door-lintel, with other
offences ; and, after a little hesitation, he obeys.[1]

Thus is Danton's battle-pledge taken up ; there is,
as he said there would be, ' war without truce or treaty,
ni trève ni composition'. Wherefore, close now with
one another, Formula and Reality, in death-grips, and
wrestle it out ; both of you cannot live, but only one !

CHAPTER VIII

IN DEATH-GRIPS

It proves what strength, were it only of inertia, there
is in established Formulas, what weakness in nascent
Realities, and illustrates several things, that this death-
wrestle should still have lasted some six weeks or more.
National business, discussion of the Constitutional Act,
for our Constitution should decidedly be got ready,
proceeds along with it. We even change our Locality ;
we shift, on the Tenth of May, from the old Salle de
Manége into our new Hall, in the Palace, once a King's
but now the Republic's, of the Tuileries. Hope and

---

[1] Moniteur (du 16 Avril 1793, *et seqq.*).

ruth, flickering against despair and rage, still struggle
in the minds of men.

It is a most dark confused death-wrestle, this of the
six weeks. Formalist frenzy against Realist frenzy;
Patriotism, Egoism, Pride, Anger, Vanity, Hope and
Despair, all raised to the frenetic pitch: Frenzy meets
Frenzy, like dark clashing whirlwinds; neither understands the other; the weaker, one day, will understand
that *it* is verily swept down! Girondism is strong as
established Formula and Respectability: do not as many
as Seventy-two of the Departments, or say respectable
Heads of Departments, declare for us? Calvados,
which loves its Buzot, will even rise in revolt, so hint
the Addresses; Marseilles, cradle of Patriotism, will
rise; Bourdeaux will rise, and the Gironde Department, as one man; in a word, who will *not* rise, were
our *Représentation Nationale* to be insulted, or one hair
of a Deputy's head harmed! The Mountain, again, is
strong as Reality and Audacity. To the Reality of the
Mountain are not all furthersome things possible?
A new Tenth of August, if needful; nay a new Second
of September!—

But, on Wednesday afternoon, Twenty-fourth day of
April, year 1793, what tumult as of fierce jubilee is this?
It is Marat returning from the Revolutionary Tribunal!
A week or more of death-peril: and now there is triumphant acquittal; Revolutionary Tribunal can find no
accusation against this man. And so the eye of History
beholds Patriotism, which had gloomed unutterable
things all week, break into loud jubilee, embrace its
Marat; lift him into a chair of triumph, bear him
shoulder-high through the streets. Shoulder-high is the
injured People's-friend, crowned with an oak-garland;
amid the wavy sea of red nightcaps, carmagnole
jackets, grenadier bonnets and female mob-caps; far-
sounding like a sea! The injured People's-friend has
here reached his culminating-point; he too strikes the
stars with his sublime head.

But the Reader can judge with what face President

Lasource, he of the 'painful probabilities', who presides in this Convention Hall, might welcome such
jubilee-tide, when it got thither, and the Decreed of
Accusation floating on the top of it! A National
Sapper, spokesman on the occasion, says, the People
know their Friend, and love his life as their own;
'whosoever wants Marat's head must get the Sapper's
first'.[1] Lasource answered with some vague painful
mumblement,—which, says Levasseur, one could not
help tittering at.[2] Patriot Sections, Volunteers not yet
gone to the Frontiers, come demanding the 'purgation
of traitors from your own bosom'; the expulsion, or
even the trial and sentence, of a factious Twenty-two.

Nevertheless the Gironde has got its Commission of
Twelve; a Commission specially appointed for investi-
gating these troubles of the Legislative Sanctuary: let
Sansculottism say what it will, Law shall triumph.
Old-Constituent Rabaut Saint-Etienne presides over
this Commission: 'it is the last plank whereon a
wrecked Republic may perhaps still save herself'.
Rabaut and they therefore sit, intent; examining witnesses; launching arrestments; looking out into a
waste dim sea of troubles,—the womb of *Formula*, or
perhaps her grave! Enter not that sea, O Reader!
There are dim desolation and confusion; raging women
and raging men. Sections come demanding Twenty-
two; for the *number* first given by Section Bonconseil
still holds, though the names should even vary. Other
Sections, of the wealthier kind, come denouncing such
demand; nay the same Section will demand to-day, and
denounce the demand to-morrow, according as the
wealthier sit, or the poorer. Wherefore, indeed, the
Girondins decree that all Sections shall close 'at ten
in the evening'; before the working people come:
which Decree remains without effect. And nightly the
Mother of Patriotism wails doleful; doleful, but her
eye kindling! And Fournier l'Américain is busy, and

---

[1] Séance (in Moniteur, No. 116, du 26 Avril, An 1er).
[2] Levasseur, Mémoires, i. c. 6.

the two banker Freys, and Varlet Apostle of Liberty;
the bull-voice of Marquis St.-Huruge is heard.   And
shrill women vociferate from all Galleries, the Convention ones and downwards.   Nay a 'Central Committee'
of all the Forty-eight Sections looms forth huge and
dubious; sitting dim in the *Archevêché*, sending Resolutions, receiving them: a Centre of the Sections; in
dread deliberation as to a New Tenth of August!

One thing we will specify, to throw light on many:
the aspect under which, seen through the eyes of these
Girondin Twelve, or even seen through one's own eyes,
the Patriotism of the softer sex presents itself.   There
are Female Patriots, whom the Girondins call Megaeras,
and count to the extent of eight thousand; with serpent hair, all out of curl; who have changed the distaff
for the dagger.   They are of 'the Society called Brotherly', *Fraternelle*, say *Sisterly*, which meets under the
roof of the Jacobins.   'Two thousand daggers', or *so*,
have been ordered,—doubtless for them.   They rush
to Versailles, to raise more women; but the Versailles
women will not rise.[1]

Nay behold, in National Garden of Tuileries,—Demoiselle Théroigne herself is become as a brownlocked Diana
(were that possible) attacked by her own dogs, or she-
dogs!   The Demoiselle, keeping her carriage, is for
Liberty indeed, as she has full well shown; but then
for Liberty with Respectability: whereupon these ser-
pent-haired Extreme She-Patriots do now fasten on her,
tatter her, shamefully fustigate her, in their shameful
way; almost fling her into the Garden-ponds, had not
help intervened.   Help, alas, to small purpose.   The
poor Demoiselle's head and nervous-system, none of
the soundest, is so tattered and fluttered that it will
never recover; but flutter worse and worse, till it
crack; and within year and day we hear of her in
madhouse and strait-waistcoat, which proves perma-

---

[1] Buzot, Mémoires, pp. 69, 84; Meillan, Mémoires, pp.
192, 195, 196.   See Commission des Douze (in Choix des
Rapports, xii. 69-131).

nent !—Such brownlocked Figure did flutter, and inarticulately jabber and gesticulate, little able to *speak*
the obscure meaning it had, through some segment of
the Eighteenth Century of Time. She disappears here
from the Revolution and Public History for evermore.[1]

Another thing we will not again specify, yet again
beseech the Reader to imagine : the reign of Fraternity
and Perfection. Imagine, we say, O Reader, that the
Millennium were struggling on the threshold, and yet not
so much as groceries could be had,—owing to traitors.
With what impetus would a man strike traitors, in that
case ! Ah, thou canst not imagine it ; thou hast thy
groceries safe in the shops, and little or no hope of a
Millennium ever coming !—But indeed, as to the temper
there was in men and women, does not this one fact
say enough : the height SUSPICION had risen to ? Preternatural we often called it ; seemingly in the language
of exaggeration : but listen to the cold deposition of
witnesses. Not a musical Patriot can blow himself
a snatch of melody from the French Horn, sitting mildly
pensive on the housetop, but Mercier will recognize it
to be a signal which one Plotting Committee is making
to another. Distraction has possessed Harmony herself ; lurks in the sound of *Marseillaise* and *Ça-ira*.[2]
Louvet, who can see as deep into a millstone as the
most, discerns that we shall be invited back to our old
Hall of the Manége, by a Deputation ; and then the
Anarchists will massacre Twenty-two of us, as we walk
over. It is Pitt and Cobourg ; the gold of Pitt.—Poor
Pitt ! They little know what work he has with his own
Friends of the People ; getting them bespied, beheaded,
their habeas-corpuses suspended, and his own Social
Order and strong-boxes kept tight,—to fancy him
raising mobs among his neighbours !

---

[1] Deux Amis, vii. 77–80 ; Forster, i. 514 ; Moore, i. 70.
She did not die till 1817 ; in the Salpêtrière, in the most
abject state of insanity : see Esquirol, Des Maladies Men-
tales (Paris, 1838), i. 445–50.

[2] Mercier, Nouveau Paris, vi. 63.

But the strangest fact connected with French or indeed with human Suspicion, is perhaps this of Camille Desmoulins. Camille's head, one of the clearest in France, has got itself so saturated through every fibre with Preternaturalism of Suspicion, that looking back on that Twelfth of July 1789, when the thousands rose round him, yelling responsive at his word in the Palais-Royal Garden, and took cockades, he finds it explicable only on this hypothesis, That they were all hired to do it, and set on by the Foreign and other Plotters. ' It was not for nothing ', says Camille with insight, ' that this multitude burst up round me when I spoke ! ' No, not for nothing. Behind, around, before, it is one huge Preternatural Puppet-play of Plots ; Pitt pulling the wires.[1] Almost I conjecture that I, Camille myself, am a Plot, and wooden with wires.—The force of insight could no further go.

Be this as it will, History remarks that the Commission of Twelve, now clear enough as to the Plots ; and luckily having ' got the threads of them all by the end ', as they say,—are launching Mandates of Arrest rapidly in these May days ; and carrying matters with a high hand ; resolute that the sea of troubles shall be restrained. What chief Patriot, Section-President even, is safe ? They can arrest him ; tear him from his warm bed, because he has made irregular Section Arrestments ! They arrest Varlet Apostle of Liberty. They arrest Procureur-Substitute Hébert, *Père Duchesne* ; a Magistrate of the People, sitting in Townhall ; who, with high solemnity of martyrdom, takes leave of his colleagues ; prompt he, to obey the Law ; and solemnly acquiescent, disappears into prison.

The swifter fly the Sections, energetically demanding him back ; demanding not arrestment of Popular Magistrates, but of a traitorous Twenty-two. Section comes flying after Section ;—defiling energetic, with their

[1] See Histoire des Brissotins, par Camille Desmoulins (a Pamphlet of Camille's, Paris, 1793).

Cambyses-vein of oratory: nay the Commune itself
comes, with Mayor Pache at its head; and with question not of Hébert and the Twenty-two alone, but with
this ominous old question made new, 'Can you save
the Republic, or must we do it?' To whom President
Max Isnard makes fiery answer: If by fatal chance, in
any of those tumults which since the Tenth of March
are ever returning, Paris were to lift a sacrilegious finger
against the National Representation, France would rise
as one man, in never-imagined vengeance, and shortly
'the traveller would ask, on which side of the Seine
Paris had stood!'[1] Whereat the Mountain bellows
only louder, and every Gallery; Patriot Paris boiling
round.

And Girondin Valazé has nightly conclaves at his
house; sends billets, 'Come punctually, and well armed,
for there is to be business'. And Megaera women
perambulate the streets, with flags, with lamentable
alleleu.[2] And the Convention-doors are obstructed by
roaring multitudes: fine-spoken *Hommes d'état* are
hustled, maltreated, as they pass; Marat will apostrophize you, in such death-peril, and say, Thou too art of
them. If Roland ask leave to quit Paris, there is
order of the day. What help? Substitute Hébert,
Apostle Varlet, must be given back; to be crowned
with oak-garlands. The Commission of Twelve, in
a Convention overwhelmed with roaring Sections, is
broken; then on the morrow, in a Convention of rallied
Girondins, is reinstated. Dim Chaos, or the sea of
troubles, is struggling through all its elements; writhing
and chafing towards some Creation.

[1] Moniteur, Séance du 25 Mai 1793.
[2] Meillan, Mémoires, p. 195; Buzot, pp. 69, 84.

CHAPTER IX

EXTINCT

ACCORDINGLY, on Friday, the Thirty-first of May 1793, there comes forth into the summer sunlight one of the strangest scenes. Mayor Pache with Municipality arrives at the Tuileries Hall of Convention ; sent for, Paris being in visible ferment ; and gives the strangest news.

How, in the grey of this morning, while we sat Permanent in Townhall, watchful for the commonweal, there entered, precisely as on a Tenth of August, some Ninety-six extraneous persons ; who declared themselves to be in a state of Insurrection ; to be plenipotentiary Commissioners from the Forty-eight Sections, sections or members of the Sovereign People, all in a state of Insurrection ; and further that we, in the name of said Sovereign in Insurrection, were dismissed from office. How we thereupon laid off our sashes, and withdrew into the adjacent Saloon of Liberty. How, in a moment or two, we were called back ; and reinstated ; the Sovereign pleasing to think us still worthy of confidence. Whereby, having taken new oath of office, we on a sudden find ourselves Insurrectionary Magistrates with extraneous Committee of Ninety-six sitting by us ; and a Citoyen Henriot, one whom some accuse of Septemberism, is made Generalissimo of the National Guard ; and, since six o'clock, the tocsins ring, and the drums beat :—Under which peculiar circumstances, what would an august National Convention please to direct us to do ? [1]

Yes, there is the question ! ' Break the Insurrectionary Authorities ', answer some with vehemence, Vergniaud at least will have ' the National Represen-

---

[1] Débats de la Convention (Paris, 1828), iv. 187–223 ; Moniteur, Nos. 152, 3, 4, An 1ᵉʳ.

tatives all die at their post'; this is sworn to, with
ready loud acclaim. But as to breaking the Insurrectionary Authorities,—alas, while we yet debate, what
sound is that? Sound of the Alarm-Cannon on the
Pont Neuf; which it is death by the Law to fire without
order from us!

It does boom off there, nevertheless; sending a
stound through all hearts. And the tocsins discourse
stern music; and Henriot with his Armed Force has
enveloped us! And Section succeeds Section, the livelong day; demanding with Cambyses-oratory, with the
rattle of muskets, That traitors, Twenty-two or more,
be punished; that the Commission of Twelve be
irrecoverably broken. The heart of the Gironde dies
within it; distant are the Seventy-two respectable
Departments, this fiery Municipality is near! Barrère
is for a middle course; granting something. The Commission of Twelve declares that, not waiting to be
broken, it hereby breaks itself, and is no more. Fain
would Reporter Rabaut speak his and its last-words;
but he is bellowed off. Too happy that the Twenty-
two are still left unviolated!—Vergniaud, carrying the
laws of refinement to a great length, moves, to the
amazement of some, that 'the Sections of Paris have
deserved well of their country'. Whereupon, at a late
hour of the evening, the deserving Sections retire to
their respective places of abode. Barrère shall report
on it. With busy quill and brain he sits, secluded;
for him no sleep to-night. Friday the last of May has
ended in this manner.

The Sections have deserved well: but ought they not
to deserve better? Faction and Girondism is struck
down for the moment, and consents to be a nullity; but
will it not, at another favourabler moment, rise, still
feller; and the Republic have to be saved in spite of it?
So reasons Patriotism, still Permanent; so reasons the
Figure of Marat, visible in the dim Section-world, on
the morrow. To the conviction of men!—And so at
eventide of Saturday, when Barrère had just got the

thing all varnished by the labour of a night and day,
and his Report was setting off in the evening mail-bags,
tocsin peals out *again*. *Générale* is beating; armed
men taking station in the Place Vendôme and elsewhere,
for the night; supplied with provisions and liquor.
There, under the summer stars, will they wait, this
night, what is to be seen and to be done, Henriot and
Townhall giving due signal.

The Convention, at sound of *générale*, hastens back
to its Hall; but to the number only of a Hundred;
and does little business, puts off business till the morrow.
The Girondins do not stir out thither, the Girondins are
abroad seeking beds.—Poor Rabaut, on the morrow
morning, returning to his post, with Louvet and some
others, through streets all in ferment, wrings his
hands, ejaculating, ' *Illa suprema dies!* ' [1]* It has
become Sunday, the second day of June, year 1793,
by the old style; by the new style, year One of Liberty,
Equality, Fraternity. We have got to the last scene
of all, that ends this history of the Girondin Senator-
ship.

It seems doubtful whether any terrestrial Convention had ever met in such circumstances as this National
one now does. Tocsin is pealing; Barriers shut; all
Paris is on the gaze, or under arms. As many as a
Hundred Thousand under arms they count: National
Force; and the Armed Volunteers, who should have
flown to the Frontiers and La Vendée; but would not,
treason being unpunished; and only flew hither and
thither! So many, steady under arms, environ the
National Tuileries and Garden. There are horse, foot,
artillery, sappers with beards: the artillery one can
see with their camp-furnaces in this National Garden,
heating bullets red, and their match is lighted. Henriot
in plumes rides, amid a plumed Staff: all posts and
issues are safe; reserves lie out, as far as the Wood of
Boulogne; the choicest Patriots nearest the scene.

---

[1] Louvet, *Mémoires*, p. 89.

One other circumstance we will note: that a careful
Municipality, liberal of camp-furnaces, has not forgotten provision-carts. No member of the Sovereign
need now go home to dinner; but can keep rank,—
plentiful victual circulating unsought. Does not this
People understand Insurrection? Ye, *not* uninventive,
Gualches!—

Therefore let a National Representation, 'manda-
tories of the Sovereign', take thought of it. Expulsion
of your Twenty-two, and your Commission of Twelve:
we stand here till it be done! Deputation after Deputation, in ever stronger language, comes with that message. Barrère proposes a middle course:—Will not
perhaps the inculpated Deputies consent to withdraw
voluntarily; to make a generous demission, and self-
sacrifice for the sake of one's country? Isnard, repentant of that search on which river-bank Paris stood,
declares himself ready to demit. Ready also is *Te-
Deum* Fauchet; old Dusaulx of the Bastille, '*vieux
radoteur*, old dotard', as Marat calls him, is still readier.
On the contrary, Lanjuinais*the Breton declares that
there is one man who never will demit voluntarily; but
will protest to the uttermost, while a voice is left him.
And he accordingly goes on protesting; amid rage and
clangour; Legendre crying at last: 'Lanjuinais, come
down from the Tribune, or I will fling thee down, *ou je
te jette en bas*!' For matters are come to extremity.
Nay they do clutch hold of Lanjuinais, certain zealous
Mountain-men; but cannot fling him down, for he
'cramps himself on the railing'; and 'his clothes get
torn'. Brave Senator, worthy of pity! Neither will
Barbaroux demit; he 'has sworn to die at his post,
and will keep that oath'. Whereupon the Galleries
all rise with explosion; brandishing weapons, some of
them; and rush out, saying: '*Allons*, then; we must
save our country!' Such a Session is this of Sunday
the second of June.

Churches fill, over Christian Europe, and then empty
themselves; but this Convention empties not, the
while: a day of shrieking contention, of agony, humilia-

tion and tearing of coat-skirts ; *illa suprema dies!*
Round stand Henriot and his Hundred Thousand,
copiously refreshed from tray and basket : nay he is
' distributing five francs a-piece ', we Girondins saw it
with our eyes ; five francs to keep them in heart ! And
distraction of armed riot encumbers our borders, jangles
at our Bar ; we are prisoners in our own Hall : Bishop
Grégoire could not get out for a *besoin actuel* without
four gendarmes to wait on him ! What is the character
of a National Representative become ? And now the
sunlight falls yellower on western windows, and the
chimney-tops are flinging longer shadows ; the refreshed
Hundred Thousand, nor their shadows, stir not ! What
to resolve on ? Motion rises, superfluous one would
think, That the Convention go forth in a body ; ascertain with its own eyes whether it is free or not. Lo,
therefore, from the Eastern Gate of the Tuileries, a
distressed Convention issuing ; handsome Hérault
Séchelles at their head ; he with hat on, in sign of
public calamity, the rest bareheaded,—towards the Gate
of the Carrousel ; wondrous to see: towards Henriot and
his plumed staff. ' In the name of the National Convention, make way ! '   Not an inch of way does Henriot
make : ' I receive no orders, till the Sovereign, yours
and mine, have been obeyed '.   The Convention presses
on ; Henriot prances back, with his staff, some fifteen
paces, ' To arms ! Cannoneers, to your guns ! '—flashes
out his puissant sword, as the Staff all do, and the
Hussars all do. Cannoneers brandish the lit match ;
Infantry present arms,—alas, in the level way, as if for
firing ! Hatted Hérault leads his distressed flock,
through their pinfold of a Tuileries again ; across the
Garden, to the Gate on the opposite side. Here is
Feuillans-Terrace, alas, there is our old Salle de Manége ;
but neither at this Gate of the Pont Tournant is there
egress. Try the other ; and the other : no egress ! We
wander disconsolate through armed ranks ; who indeed
salute with *Live the Republic*, but also with *Die the
Gironde*. Other such sight, in the year One of Liberty,
the westering sun never saw.

And now behold Marat meets us ; for he lagged in this Suppliant Procession of ours : he has got some hundred elect Patriots at his heels ; he orders us, in the Sovereign's name, to return to our place, and do as we are bidden and bound. The Convention returns. ' Does not the Convention ', says Couthon with a singular power of face, ' see that it is free ',—none but friends round it ? The Convention, overflowing with friends and armed Sectioners, proceeds to vote as bidden. Many will not vote, but remain silent ; some one or two protest, in words, the Mountain has a clear unanimity. Commission of Twelve, and the denounced Twenty-two, to whom we add Ex-Ministers Clavière and Lebrun : these, with some slight extempore alterations (this or that orator proposing, but Marat disposing), are voted to be under ' Arrestment in their own houses '. Brissot, Buzot, Vergniaud, Guadet, Louvet, Gensonné, Barbaroux, Lasource, Lanjuinais, Rabaut,—Thirty-two, by the tale ; all that we have known as Girondins, and more than we have known. They, ' under the safeguard of the French People ' ; by and by, under the safeguard of two Gendarmes each, shall dwell peaceably in their own houses ; as Non-Senators ; till further order. Herewith ends *Séance* of Sunday the second of June 1793.

At ten o'clock, under mild stars, the Hundred Thousand, their work well finished, turn homewards. Already yesterday, Central Insurrection Committee had arrested Madame Roland ; imprisoned her in the Abbaye. Roland has fled, no man knows whither.

Thus fell the Girondins, by Insurrection ; and became extinct as a Party : not without a sigh from most Historians. The men were men of parts, of Philosophic culture, decent behaviour ; not condemnable, but most unfortunate. They wanted a Republic of the Virtues, wherein themselves should be head ; and they could only get a Republic of the Strengths, wherein others than they were head.

For the rest, Barrère shall make Report of it. The

night concludes with a 'civic promenade by torch-light':[1] surely the true reign of Fraternity is now not far ?

[1] Buzot, Mémoires, p. 310. See Pièces Justificatives, of Narratives, Commentaries, &c. in Buzot, Louvet, Meillan, Documens Complémentaires in Hist. Parl. xxviii. 1–78.

BOOK IV

TERROR

CHAPTER I

CHARLOTTE CORDAY

IN the leafy months of June and July, several French
Departments germinate a set of rebellious *paper*-leaves,
named Proclamations, Resolutions, Journals, or Diur-
nals, ' of the Union for Resistance to Oppression '.   In
particular, the Town of Caen* in Calvados, sees its
paper-leaf of *Bulletin de Caen* suddenly bud, suddenly
establish itself as Newspaper there ; under the Editor-
ship of Girondin National Representatives !

For among the proscribed Girondins are certain of
a more desperate humour.   Some, as Vergniaud, Valazé,
Gensonné, ' arrested in their own houses ', will await
with stoical resignation what the issue may be.   Some,
as Brissot, Rabaut, will take to flight, to concealment ;
which, as the Paris Barriers are opened again in a day
or two, is not yet difficult.   But others there are who
will rush, with Buzot, to Calvados ; or far over France,
to Lyons, Toulon, Nantes and elsewhither, and then
rendezvous at Caen : to awaken as with war-trumpet
the respectable Departments ;   and strike down an
anarchic Mountain Faction ;   at least not yield without
a stroke at it.   Of this latter temper we count some
score or more, of the Arrested, and of the Not-yet-
arrested : a Buzot, a Barbaroux, Louvet, Guadet,
Pétion, who have escaped from Arrestment in their own
homes ; a Salles, a Pythagorean Valady, a Duchâtel, the

Duchâtel that came in blanket and nightcap to vote for
the life of Louis, who have escaped from danger and
likelihood of Arrestment.   These, to the number at one
time of Twenty-seven, do accordingly lodge here, at the
'*Intendance*, or Departmental Mansion ', of the town of
Caen in Calvados ; welcomed by Persons in Authority ;
welcomed and defrayed, having no money of their
own.   And the *Bulletin de Caen* comes forth, with the
most animating paragraphs : How the Bordeaux
Department, the Lyons Department, this Department
after the other is declaring itself ; sixty, or say sixty-
nine, or seventy-two [1] respectable Departments either
declaring, or ready to declare.   Nay Marseilles, it seems,
will march on Paris by itself, if need be.   So has Marseilles Town said, That she will march.   But on the
other hand, that Montélimart Town has said, No
thoroughfare ; and means even to ' bury herself ' under
her own stone and mortar first,—of this be no mention
in *Bulletin de Caen*.

Such animating paragraphs we read in this new
Newspaper; and fervours and eloquent sarcasm: tirades
against the Mountain, from the pen of Deputy Salles ;
which resemble, say friends, Pascal's *Provincials*.* What
is more to the purpose, these Girondins have got
a General in chief, one Wimpfen, formerly under
Dumouriez ; also a secondary questionable General
Puisaye;* and others ; and are doing their best to raise
a force for war.   National Volunteers, whosoever is of
right heart : gather in, ye national Volunteers, friends
of Liberty ; from our Calvados Townships, from the
Eure, from Brittany, from far and near : forward to
Paris, and extinguish Anarchy !   Thus at Caen, in the
early July days, there is a drumming and parading, a
perorating and consulting : Staff and Army ; Council;
Club of *Carabots*, Antijacobin friends of Freedom, to
denounce atrocious Marat.   With all which, and the
editing of *Bulletins*, a National Representative has his
hands full.

[1] Meillan, pp. 72, 73 ; Louvet, p. 129.

At Caen it is most animated ; and, as one hopes, more or less animated in the ' Seventy-two Departments that adhere to us '. And in a France begirt with Cimmerian invading Coalitions, and torn with an internal La Vendée, *this* is the conclusion we have arrived at : To put down Anarchy by Civil War ! *Durum et durum*, the Proverb says, *non faciunt murum*.* La Vendée burns : Santerre can do nothing there ; he may return home and brew beer. Cimmerian bombshells fly all along the North. That Siege of Mentz is become famed ; —lovers of the Picturesque (as Goethe will testify), washed country-people of both sexes, stroll thither on Sundays, to see the artillery work and counterwork ; ' you only duck a little while the shot whizzes past '.[1] Condé is capitulating to the Austrians ; Royal Highness of York, these several weeks, fiercely batters Valenciennes. For, alas, our fortified Camp of Famars was stormed ; General Dampierre was killed ; General Custine was blamed,—and indeed is now come to Paris to give ' explanations '.

Against all which the Mountain and atrocious Marat must even make head as they can. They, anarchic Convention as they are, publish Decrees, expostulatory, explanatory, yet not without severity ; they ray forth Commissioners, singly or in pairs, the olive-branch in one hand, yet the sword in the other. Commissioners come even to Caen ; but without effect. Mathematical Romme, and Prieur named of the Côte d'Or, venturing thither, with their olive and sword, are packed into prison : there may Romme lie, under lock and key, ' for fifty days ' ; and meditate his New Calendar, if he please. Cimmeria, La Vendée, and Civil War ! Never was Republic One and Indivisible at a lower ebb.—

Amid which dim ferment of Caen and the World, History specially notices one thing : in the lobby of the Mansion *de l'Intendance*, where busy Deputies are

---

[1] Belagerung von Mainz (Goethe's Werke, xxx. 278–334).

coming and going, a young Lady with an aged valet,
taking grave graceful leave of Deputy Barbaroux.[1]
She is of stately Norman figure ; in her twenty-fifth
year ; of beautiful still countenance : her name is
Charlotte Corday, heretofore styled D'Armans, while
Nobility still was. Barbaroux has given her a Note
to Deputy Duperret,—him who once drew his sword
in the effervescence. Apparently she will to Paris on
some errand ? 'She was a Republican before the
Revolution, and never wanted energy'. A completeness, a decision is in this fair female Figure : ' by energy
she means the spirit that will prompt one to sacrifice
himself for his country '. What if she, this fair young
Charlotte, had emerged from her secluded stillness,
suddenly like a Star ; cruel-lovely, with half-angelic,
half-daemonic splendour ; to gleam for a moment, and
in a moment be extinguished : to be held in memory,
so bright complete was she, through long centuries !—
Quitting Cimmerian Coalitions without, and the dim-
simmering Twenty-five millions within, History will
look fixedly at this one fair Apparition of a Charlotte
Corday ; will note whither Charlotte moves, how the
little Life burns forth so radiant, then vanishes swallowed of the Night.

With Barbaroux's Note of Introduction, and slight
stock of luggage, we see Charlotte on Tuesday the ninth
of July seated in the Caen Diligence, with a place for
Paris. None takes farewell of her, wishes her Good-
journey : her Father will find a line left, signifying that
she is gone to England, that he must pardon her, and
forget her. The drowsy Diligence lumbers along ; amid
drowsy talk of Politics, and praise of the Mountain ; in
which she mingles not : all night, all day, and again
all night. On Thursday, not long before noon, we are
at the bridge of Neuilly ; here is Paris with her thousand black domes, the goal and purpose of thy journey !
Arrived at the Inn de la Providence in the Rue des
Vieux Augustins, Charlotte demands a room ; hastens

---

[1] Meillan, p. 75 ; Louvet, p. 114.

to bed; sleeps all afternoon and night, till the morrow
morning.

On the morrow morning, she delivers her Note to
Duperret. It relates to certain Family Papers which
are in the Minister of the Interior's hand ; which a Nun
at Caen, an old Convent-friend of Charlotte's, has
need of ; which Duperret shall assist her in getting :
this then was Charlotte's errand to Paris ? She
has finished this, in the course of Friday ;—yet says
nothing of returning. She has seen and silently investigated several things. The Convention, in bodily
reality, she has seen ; what the Mountain is like. The
living physiognomy of Marat she could not see ; he is
sick at present, and confined to home.

About eight on the Saturday morning, she purchases
a large sheath-knife in the Palais Royal ; then straightway, in the Place des Victoires, takes a hackney-coach :
' To the Rue de l'Ecole de Médecine, No. 44 '. It is the
residence of the Citoyen Marat !—The Citoyen Marat
is ill, and cannot be seen ; which seems to disappoint
her much. Her business is with Marat, then ? Hapless
beautiful Charlotte ; hapless squalid Marat ! From
Caen in the utmost West, from Neuchâtel in the utmost
East, they two are drawing nigh each other ; they two
have, very strangely, business together.—Charlotte, returning to her Inn, dispatches a short Note to Marat ;
signifying that she is from Caen, the seat of rebellion ;
that she desires earnestly to see him, and ' will put it
in his power to do France a great service '. No answer.
Charlotte writes another Note, still more pressing ; sets
out with it by coach, about seven in the evening, herself.
Tired day-labourers have again finished their Week ;
huge Paris is circling and simmering, manifold, according to its vague wont : this one fair Figure has decision
in it ; drives straight,—towards a purpose.

It is yellow July evening, we say, the thirteenth of
the month ; eve of the Bastille day,—when ' M. Marat ',
four years ago, in the crowd of the Pont Neuf, shrewdly
required of that Besenval Hussar-party, which had such
friendly dispositions, ' to dismount, and give up their

arms, then'; and became notable among Patriot men.
Four years: what a road he has travelled;—and sits
now, about half-past seven of the clock, stewing in
slipper-bath; sore afflicted; ill of Revolution Fever,—
of what other malady this History had rather not name.
Excessively sick and worn, poor man: with precisely
eleven-pence-halfpenny of ready money, in paper; with
slipper-bath; strong three-footed stool for writing on,
the while; and a squalid—Washerwoman, one may
call her: that is his civic establishment in Medical-
School Street; thither and not elsewhither has his road
led him. Not to the reign of Brotherhood and Perfect
Felicity; yet surely on the way towards that?—Hark,
a rap again! A musical woman's voice, refusing to be
rejected: it is the Citoyenne who would do France
a service. Marat, recognizing from within, cries, Admit
her. Charlotte Corday is admitted.

Citoyen Marat, I am from Caen the seat of rebellion,
and wished to speak with you.—Be seated, *mon enfant*.
Now what are the Traitors doing at Caen? What
Deputies are at Caen?—Charlotte names some Deputies. 'Their heads shall fall within a fortnight', croaks
the eager People's-friend, clutching his tablets to write:
Barbaroux, Pétion, writes he with bare shrunk arm,
turning aside in the bath: *Pétion*, and *Louvet*, and—
Charlotte has drawn her knife from the sheath; plunges
it, with one sure stroke, into the writer's heart. '*A moi,
chère amie*, Help, dear!' no more could the Death-
choked say or shriek. The helpful Washerwoman running in, there is no Friend of the People, or Friend of
the Washerwoman left; but his life with a groan gushes
out, indignant, to the shades below.[1]*

And so Marat People's-friend is ended; the lone
Stylites has got hurled down suddenly from his Pillar
—*whitherward* He that made him knows.* Patriot Paris
may sound triple and tenfold, in dole and wail; re-
echoed by Patriot France; and the Convention, 'Chabot

[1] Moniteur, Nos. 197, 8, 9; Hist. Parl. xxviii. 301-5;
Deux Amis, x. 368-74.

pale with terror, declaring that they are to be all assassinated', may decree him Pantheon Honours, Public
Funeral, Mirabeau's dust making way for him ; and
Jacobin Societies, in lamentable oratory, summing up
his character, parallel him to One, whom they think
it honour to call ' the good Sansculotte ',—whom we
name not here ; [1] also a Chapel may be made, for the
urn that holds his Heart, in the Place du Carrousel ; and
new-born children be named Marat ; and Lago-di-
Como Hawkers bake mountains of stucco into unbeauti-
ful Busts ; and David paint his Picture, or Death-
Scene ; and such other Apotheosis take place as the
human genius, in these circumstances, can devise : but
Marat returns no more to the light of this Sun.   One
sole circumstance we have read with clear sympathy,
in the old *Moniteur* Newspaper : how Marat's Brother
comes from Neuchâtel to ask of the Convention, ' that
the deceased Jean-Paul Marat's musket be given him '.[2]
For Marat too had a brother, and natural affections ;
and was wrapt once in swaddling-clothes, and slept safe
in a cradle like the rest of us.   Ye children of men !—
A sister of his, they say, lives still to this day in Paris.

As for Charlotte Corday, her work is accomplished ;
the recompense of it is near and sure.   The *chère amie*,
and neighbours of the house, flying at her, she ' overturns some movables ', entrenches herself till the gendarmes arrive ; then quietly surrenders ; goes quietly
to the Abbaye Prison : she alone quiet, all Paris sounding, in wonder, in rage or admiration, round her.
Duperret is put in arrest, on account of her; his Papers
sealed,—which may lead to consequences.   Fauchet, in
like manner ; though Fauchet had not so much as heard
of her.   Charlotte, confronted with these two Deputies,
praises the grave firmness of Duperret, censures the
dejection of Fauchet.

On Wednesday morning, the thronged Palais de

---

[1] See Eloge funèbre de Jean-Paul Marat, prononcé à
Strasbourg (in Barbaroux, p. 125–31); Mercier, &c.

[2] Séance du 16 Septembre 1793.

Justice and Revolutionary Tribunal can see her face ;
beautiful and calm : she dates it 'fourth day of the
Preparation of Peace '. A strange murmur ran through
the Hall, at sight of her ; you could not say of what
character.[1] Tinville has his indictments and tape-
papers : the cutler of the Palais Royal will testify that
he sold her the sheath-knife ; ' All these details are
needless ', interrupted Charlotte ; ' it is I that killed
Marat '. By whose instigation ?—' By no one's '. What
tempted you, then ? His crimes. ' I killed one man ',
added she, raising her voice extremely (*extrémement*),
as they went on with their questions, ' I killed one man
to save a hundred thousand ; a villain to save innocents ;
a savage wild-beast to give repose to my country.
I was a Republican before the Revolution ; I never
wanted energy '. There is therefore nothing to be said.
The public gazes astonished : the hasty limners sketch
her features, Charlotte not disapproving : the men of
law proceed with their formalities. The doom is Death
as a murderess. To her Advocate she gives thanks ; in
gentle phrase, in high-flown classical spirit. To the
Priest they send her she gives thanks ; but needs not
any shriving, any ghostly or other aid from him.

On this same evening therefore, about half-past seven
o'clock, from the gate of the Conciergerie, to a City all
on tiptoe, the fatal Cart issues ; seated on it a fair
young creature, sheeted in red smock of Murderess ;
so beautiful, serene, so full of life ; journeying towards
death,—alone amid the World. Many take off their
hats, saluting reverently ; for what heart but must be
touched ?[2] Others growl and howl. Adam Lux, of
Mentz, declares that she is greater than Brutus ; that
it were beautiful to die with her : the head of this
young man seems turned. At the Place de la Révolution, the countenance of Charlotte wears the same still
smile. The executioners proceed to bind her feet ; she

---

[1] Procès de Charlotte Corday, &c. (Hist. Parl. xxviii.
311–38).
[2] Deux Amis, x. 374–84.

resists, thinking it meant as an insult ; on a word of explanation, she submits with cheerful apology. As the last act, all being now ready, they take the necker-chief from her neck ; a blush of maidenly shame over-spreads that fair face and neck ; the cheeks were still tinged with it when the executioner lifted the severed head, to show it to the people. ' It is most true ', says Forster, ' that he struck the cheek insultingly ; for I saw it with my eyes : the Police imprisoned him for it '.[1]

In this manner have the Beautifullest and the Squalidest come in collision, and extinguished one another. Jean-Paul Marat and Marie-Anne Charlotte Corday both, suddenly, are no more. ' Day of the Preparation of Peace ' ? Alas, how were peace possible or preparable, while, for example, the hearts of lovely Maidens, in their convent-stillness, are dreaming not of Love-paradises, and the light of Life ; but of Codrus'-sacrifices, and Death well-earned ? That Twenty-five million hearts have got to such temper, this *is* the Anarchy ; the soul of it lies in this : whereof not peace can be the embodiment ! The death of Marat, whetting old animosities tenfold, will be worse than any life. O ye hapless Two, mutually extinctive, the Beautiful and the Squalid, sleep ye well,—in the Mother's bosom that bore you both !

This is the History of Charlotte Corday ; most definite, most complete ; angelic-daemonic : like a Star ! Adam Lux goes home, half-delirious ; to pour forth his Apotheosis of her, in paper and print ; to propose that she have a statue with this inscription, *Greater than Brutus*. Friends represent his danger ; Lux is reckless ; thinks it were beautiful to die with her.

---

[1] Briefwechsel, i. 508.

CHAPTER II

IN CIVIL WAR

But during these same hours, another guillotine is at work, on another : Charlotte, for the Girondins, dies at Paris to-day; Chalier, by the Girondins, dies at Lyons to-morrow.

From rumbling of cannon along the streets of that City, it has come to firing of them, to rabid fighting : Nièvre Chol and the Girondins triumph ;—behind whom there is, as everywhere, a Royalist Faction waiting to strike in. Trouble enough at Lyons ; and the dominant party carrying it with a high hand ! For, indeed, the whole South is astir ; incarcerating Jacobins ; arming for Girondins : wherefore we have got a 'Congress of Lyons' ; also a 'Revolutionary Tribunal of Lyons', and Anarchists shall tremble. So Chalier was soon found guilty, of Jacobinism, of murderous Plot, 'address with drawn dagger on the sixth of February last ' ; and, on the morrow, he also travels his final road, along the streets of Lyons, ' by the side of an ecclesiastic, with whom he seems to speak earnestly ',—the axe now glittering nigh. He could weep, in old years, this man, and 'fall on his knees on the pavement ', blessing Heaven at sight of Federation Programmes or the like ; then he pilgrimed to Paris, to worship Marat and the Mountain : now Marat and he are both gone ;—we said he could not end well. Jacobinism groans inwardly, at Lyons ; but dare not outwardly. Chalier, when the Tribunal sentenced him, made answer : ' My death will cost this City dear '.

Montélimart Town is not buried under its ruins ; yet Marseilles is actually marching, under order of a ' Lyons Congress ' ; is incarcerating Patriots ; the very Royalists now showing face. Against which a General Cartaux fights, though in small force ; and with him an

Artillery Major, of the name of—Napoleon Bonaparte. This Napoleon, to prove that the Marseillese have no chance ultimately, not only fights but writes ; publishes his *Supper of Beaucaire*,* a Dialogue which has become curious.[1] Unfortunate Cities, with their actions and their reactions ! Violence to be paid with violence in geometrical ratio ; Royalism and Anarchism both striking in ;—the final net-amount of which geometrical series, what man shall sum ?

The Bar of Iron has never yet floated in Marseilles Harbour ; but the Body of Rebecqui was found floating, self-drowned there. Hot Rebecqui, seeing how confusion deepened, and Respectability grew poisoned with Royalism, felt that there was no refuge for a Republican but death. Rebecqui disappeared : no one knew whither ; till, one morning, they found the empty case or body of him risen to the top, tumbling on the salt waves ;[2] and perceived that Rebecqui had withdrawn for ever.—Toulon likewise is incarcerating Patriots ; sending delegates to Congress ; intriguing, in case of necessity, with the Royalists and English. Montpellier, Bordeaux, Nantes : all France, that is not under the swoop of Austria and Cimmeria, seems rushing into madness, and suicidal ruin. The Mountain labours ; like a volcano in a burning volcanic Land. Convention Committees, of Surety, of Salvation, are busy night and day : Convention Commissioners whirl on all highways ; bearing olive-branch and sword, or now perhaps sword only. Chaumette and Municipals come daily to the Tuileries demanding a Constitution : it is some weeks now since he resolved, in Townhall, that a Deputation ' should go every day ', and demand a Constitution, till one were got ;[3] whereby suicidal France might rally and pacify itself ; a thing inexpressibly desirable.

This then is the fruit your Anti-anarchic Girondins have got from that Levying of War in Calvados ? This

---

[1] See Hazlitt, ii. 529–41.   [2] Barbaroux, p. 29.
[3] Deux Amis, x. 345.

fruit, we may say; and no other whatsoever. For indeed, before either Charlotte's or Chalier's head had fallen, the Calvados War itself had, as it were, vanished, dreamlike, in a shriek! With 'seventy-two Departments' on our side, one might have hoped better things. But it turns out that Respectabilities, though they will vote, will not fight. Possession always is nine points in Law; but in Lawsuits of *this* kind, one may say, it is ninety-and-nine points. Men do what they were wont to do; and have immense irresolution and inertia: they obey him who has the symbols that claim obedience. Consider what, in modern society, this one fact means: the Metropolis is with our enemies! Metropolis, *Mother-city*; rightly so named: all the rest are but as her children, her nurslings. Why, there is not a leathern Diligence, with its post-bags and luggage-boots, that lumbers out from her, but is as a huge life-pulse; she is the heart of all. Cut short that one leathern Diligence, how much is cut short!—General Wimpfen, looking practically into the matter, can see nothing for it but that one should fall back on Royalism; get into communication with Pitt! Dark innuendoes he flings out, to that effect: whereat we Girondins start, horror-struck. He produces as his Second in command a certain '*Ci-devant*', one Comte Puisaye; entirely unknown to Louvet; greatly suspected by him.

Few wars, accordingly, were ever levied of a more insufficient character than this of Calvados. He that is curious in such things may read the details of it in the Memoirs of that same *Ci-devant* Puisaye, the much-enduring man and Royalist: How our Girondin National forces, marching off with plenty of wind-music, were drawn out about the old Château of Brécourt, in the wood-country near Vernon, to meet the Mountain National forces advancing from Paris. How on the fifteenth afternoon of July, they did meet;—and, as it were, shrieked mutually, and took mutually to flight, without loss. How Puisaye thereafter,—for the Mountain Nationals fled first, and we thought ourselves the victors,—was roused from his warm bed in the Castle

of Brécourt ; and had to gallop without boots ; our
Nationals, in the night-watches, having fallen unexpectedly into *sauve-qui-peut*:—and in brief the Calvados
War had burnt priming ; and the only question now
was, Whitherward to vanish, in what hole to hide
oneself ! [1]

The National Volunteers rush homewards, faster than
they came. The Seventy-two Respectable Departments, says Meillan, ' all turned round and forsook us,
in the space of four-and-twenty hours '. Unhappy
those who, as at Lyons for instance, have gone too far
for turning ! ' One morning ', we find placarded on
our Intendance Mansion, the Decree of Convention
which casts us *Hors la loi*, into Outlawry ; placarded
by our Caen Magistrates ;—clear hint that we also are
to vanish. Vanish indeed : but whitherward ? Gorsas
has friends in Rennes ; he will hide there,—unhappily
will not lie hid. Guadet, Lanjuinais are on cross
roads ; making for Bordeaux. To Bordeaux! cries the
general voice, of Valour alike and of Despair. Some
flag of Respectability still floats there, or is thought to
float.

Thitherward therefore ; each as he can ! Eleven of
these ill-fated Deputies, among whom we may count as
twelfth, Friend Riouffe the Man of Letters, do an original
thing : Take the uniform of National Volunteers, and
retreat southward with the Breton Battalion, as private
soldiers of that corps. These brave Bretons had stood
truer by us than any other. Nevertheless, at the end
of a day or two, they also do now get dubious, self-
divided ; we must part from them ; and, with some
half-dozen as convoy or guide, retreat by ourselves,—
a solitary marching detachment, through waste regions
of the West.[2]

---

[1] Mémoires de Puisaye (London, 1803), ii. 142-67.
[2] Louvet, pp. 101-37 ; Meillan, pp. 81, 241-70.

CHAPTER III

RETREAT OF THE ELEVEN

IT is one of the notablest Retreats, this of the Eleven, that History presents : The handful of forlorn Legislators retreating there, continually, with shouldered firelock and well-filled cartridge-box, in the yellow autumn ; long hundreds of miles between them and Bordeaux ; the country all getting hostile, suspicious of the truth ; simmering and buzzing on all sides, more and more. Louvet has preserved the Itinerary of it ; a piece worth all the rest he ever wrote.

O virtuous Pétion, with thy early-white head, O brave young Barbaroux, has it come to this ? Weary ways, worn shoes, light purse ;—encompassed with perils as with a sea ! Revolutionary Committees are in every Township ; of Jacobin temper ; our friends all cowed, our cause the losing one. In the Borough of Moncontour, by ill chance, it is market-day : to the gaping public such transit of a solitary Marching Detachment is suspicious ; we have need of energy, of promptitude and luck, to be allowed to march through. Hasten, ye weary pilgrims ! The country is getting up ; noise of you is bruited day after day, a solitary Twelve retreating in this mysterious manner : with every new day, a wider wave of inquisitive pursuing tumult is stirred up till the whole West will be in motion. 'Cussy is tormented with gout, Buzot is too fat for marching'. Riouffe, blistered, bleeding, marches only on tiptoe ; Barbaroux limps with sprained ankle, yet ever cheery, full of hope and valour. Light Louvet glances hare-eyed, not hare-hearted : only virtuous Pétion's serenity 'was but once seen ruffled'.[1] They lie in straw-lofts, in woody brakes ; rudest paillasse on the floor of a secret friend is luxury. They are seized in the dead

[1] Meillan, pp. 119–37.

of night by Jacobin mayors and tap of drum ; get off
by firm countenance, rattle of muskets, and ready wit.

Of Bordeaux, through fiery La Vendée and the long
geographical spaces that remain, it were madness to
think : well, if you can get to Quimper on the sea-coast,
and take shipping there. Faster, ever faster ! Before
the end of the march, so hot has the country grown,
it is found advisable to march all night. They do it ;
under the still night-canopy they plod along ;—and yet
behold, Rumour has outplodded them. In the paltry
Village of Carhaix (be its thatched huts and bottomless
peat-bogs long notable to the Traveller), one is astonished to find light still glimmering : citizens are awake,
with rushlights burning, in that nook of the terrestrial
Planet ; as we traverse swiftly the one poor street, a
voice is heard saying, ' There they are, *Les voilà qui
passent* ! ' [1] Swifter, ye doomed lame Twelve : speed
ere they can arm ; gain the Woods of Quimper before
day, and lie squatted there !

The doomed Twelve do it ; though with difficulty,
with loss of road, with peril and the mistakes of a
night. In Quimper are Girondin friends, who perhaps
will harbour the homeless, till a Bordeaux ship weigh.
Wayworn, heartworn, in agony of suspense, till Quimper
friendship get warning, they lie there, squatted under
the thick wet boscage ; suspicious of the face of man.
Some pity to the brave ; to the unhappy ! Unhappiest
of all Legislators, O when ye packed your luggage,
some score or two-score months ago, and mounted this
or the other leathern vehicle, to be Conscript Fathers
of a regenerated France, and reap deathless laurels,—did
ye think your journey was to lead *hither* ? The Quimper
Samaritans find them squatted ; lift them up to help
and comfort ; will hide them in sure places. Thence
let them dissipate gradually ; or there they can lie
quiet, and write *Memoirs*, till a Bordeaux ship sail.

And thus, in Calvados all is dissipated ; Romme is

[1] Louvet, pp. 138-64.

out of prison, meditating his Calendar ; ringleaders are
locked in his room. At Caen the Corday family mourns
in silence : Buzot's House is a heap of dust and demolition ; and amid the rubbish sticks a Gallows ; with
this inscription, *Here dwelt the Traitor Buzot who conspired against the Republic.* Buzot and the other
vanished Deputies are *hors la loi,* as we saw ; their lives
free to take where they can be found. The worse fares
it with the poor Arrested visible Deputies at Paris.
' Arrestment at home ' threatens to become ' Confinement in the Luxembourg ' ; to end : *where ?* For
example, what pale-visaged thin man is this, journeying towards Switzerland as a Merchant of Neuchâtel,
whom they arrest in the town of Moulins ? To Revolutionary Committee he is suspect. To Revolutionary
Committee, on probing the matter, he is evidently :
Deputy Brissot ! Back to thy Arrestment, poor Brissot ; or indeed to strait confinement,—whither others
are fated to follow. Rabaut has built himself a
false-partition, in a friend's house ; lives, in invisible
darkness, between two walls. It will end, this same
Arrestment business, in Prison, and the Revolutionary
Tribunal.

Nor must we forget Duperret, and the seal put on his
papers by reason of Charlotte. One Paper is there, fit
to breed woe enough : A secret solemn Protest against
that *suprema dies* of the Second of June ! This Secret
Protest our poor Duperret had drawn up, the same
week, in all plainness of speech ; waiting the time for
publishing it : to which Secret Protest his signature,
and that of other honourable Deputies not a few, stands
legibly appended. And now, if the seals were once
broken, the Mountain still victorious ? Such Protesters, your Merciers, Bailleuls, Seventy-three by the
tale, what yet remains of Respectable Girondism in the
Convention, may tremble to think !—These are the
fruits of levying civil war.

Also we find, that in these last days of July, the famed
Siege of Mentz is *finished* : the Garrison to march out
with honours of war ; not to serve against the Coalition

for a year. Lovers of the Picturesque, and Goethe
standing on the Chaussée of Mentz, saw, with due
interest, the Procession issuing forth, in all solemnity :

' Escorted by Prussian horse came first the French
Garrison. Nothing could look stranger than this latter ;
a column of Marseillese, slight, swarthy, parti-coloured,
in patched clothes, came tripping on ;—as if King Edwin
had opened the Dwarf Hill, and sent out his nimble
Host of Dwarfs. Next followed regular troops ; serious,
sullen ; not as if downcast or ashamed. But the remarkablest appearance, which struck every one, was
that of the Chasers (*Chasseurs*) coming out mounted :
they had advanced quite silent to where we stood, when
their Band struck up the *Marseillaise*. This revolutionary *Te-Deum* has in itself something mournful and
bodeful, however briskly played ; but at present they
gave it in altogether slow time, proportionate to the
creeping step they rode at. It was piercing and fearful,
and a most serious-looking thing, as these cavaliers,
long, lean men, of a certain age, with mien suitable to
the music, came pacing on : singly you might have
likened them to Don Quixote ; in mass, they were
highly dignified.

' But now a single troop became notable : that of
the Commissioners or *Représentans*. Merlin of Thionville, in hussar uniform, distinguishing himself by wild
beard and look, had another person in similar costume
on his left ; the crowd shouted out, with rage, at sight
of this latter, the name of a Jacobin Townsman and
Clubbist ; and shook itself to seize him. Merlin drew
bridle ; referred to his dignity as French Representative,
to the vengeance that should follow any injury done ;
he would advise every one to compose himself, for this
was not the *last time* they would see him here.' [1] Thus
rode Merlin ; threatening in defeat. But what now
shall stem that tide of Prussians setting-in through the
opened Northeast ? Lucky if fortified Lines of Weissembourg, and impassabilities of Vosges Mountains

---

[1] Belagerung von Mainz (Goethe's Werke, xxx. 315).

confine it to French Alsace, keep it from submerging
the very heart of the country !

Furthermore, precisely in the same days, Valenciennes Siege is finished, in the Northwest :—fallen,
under the red hail of York ! Condé fell some fortnight
since. Cimmerian Coalition presses on. What seems
very notable too, on all these captured French Towns
there flies not the Royalist fleur-de-lis, in the name of
a new Louis the Pretender ; but the Austrian flag flies ;
as if Austria meant to keep them for herself ! Perhaps
General Custine, still in Paris, can give some explanation of the fall of these strong-places ? Mother-Society,
from tribune and gallery, growls loud that he ought
to do it ;—remarks, however, in a splenetic manner that
' the *Monsieurs* of the Palais Royal' are calling Long-
life to this General.

The Mother-Society, purged now, by successive ' scru-
tinies or *épurations* ', from all taint of Girondism, has
become a great Authority : what we can call shield-
bearer, or bottle-holder, nay call it fugleman, to the
purged National Convention itself. The Jacobins Debates are reported in the *Moniteur*, like Parliamentary
ones.

CHAPTER IV

O NATURE

But looking more specially into Paris City, what is
this that History, on the 10th of August, Year One of
Liberty, ' by old-style, year 1793 ', discerns there ?
Praised be the Heavens, a new Feast of Pikes !

For Chaumette's ' Deputation every day ' has worked
out its result : a Constitution. It was one of the
rapidest Constitutions ever put together ; made, some
say in eight days, by Hérault Séchelles and others ;
probably a workmanlike, roadworthy Constitution
enough ;—on which point, however, we are, for some

reasons, little called to form a judgement. Workmanlike or not, the Forty-four Thousand Communes of
France, by overwhelming majorities, did hasten to
accept it ; glad of any Constitution whatsoever. Nay
Departmental Deputies have come, the venerablest
Republicans of each Department, with solemn message
of Acceptance ; and now what remains but that our
new Final Constitution be proclaimed, and sworn to, in
Feast of Pikes ? The Departmental Deputies, we say,
are come some time ago ; Chaumette very anxious about
them, lest Girondin *Monsieurs*, Agio-jobbers, or were it
even *Filles de joie* of a Girondin temper, corrupt their
morals.[1] Tenth of August, immortal Anniversary,
greater almost than Bastille July, is the Day.

Painter David has not been idle. Thanks to David
and the French genius, there steps forth into the sunlight, this day, a Scenic Phantasmagory unexampled :
—whereof History, so occupied with Real Phantasmagories, will say but little.

For one thing, History can notice with satisfaction,
on the ruins of the Bastille, a *Statue of Nature* ; gigantic,
spouting water from her two *mammelles*. Not a dream
this ; but a fact, palpable visible. There she spouts,
great Nature ; dim, before daybreak. But as the
coming Sun ruddies the East, come countless Multitudes, regulated and unregulated ; come Departmental
Deputies, come Mother Society and Daughters ; comes
National Convention, led on by handsome Hérault; soft
wind-music breathing note of expectation. Lo, as great
Sol scatters his first fire-handful, tipping the hills and
chimney-heads with gold, Hérault is at great Nature's
feet (she is Plaster of Paris merely) ; Hérault lifts, in
an iron saucer, water spouted from the sacred breasts ;
drinks of it, with an eloquent Pagan Prayer, beginning,
' O Nature ! ' and all the Departmental Deputies drink,
each with what best suitable ejaculation or prophetic-
utterance is in him ;—amid breathings, which become
blasts, of wind-music ; and the roar of artillery and

[1] Deux Amis, xi. 73.

human throats: finishing well the first act of this solemnity.

Next are processionings along the Boulevards: Deputies or Officials bound together by long indivisible tricolor riband; general 'members of the Sovereign' walking pell-mell, with pikes, with hammers, with the tools and emblems of their crafts; among which we notice a Plough, and ancient Baucis and Philemon[*] seated on it, drawn by their children. Many-voiced harmony and dissonance filling the air. Through Triumphal Arches enough: at the basis of the first of which, we descry—whom thinkest thou ?—the Heroines of the Insurrection of Women. Strong Dames of the Market, they sit there (Théroigne too ill to attend, one fears), with oak-branches, tricolor bedizenment; firm seated on their Cannons. To whom handsome Hérault, making pause of admiration, addresses soothing eloquence; whereupon they rise and fall into the march.

And now mark, in the Place de la Révolution, what other august Statue may this be; veiled in canvas,— which swiftly we shear off by pulley and cord ? The *Statue of Liberty* ! She too is of plaster, hoping to become of metal; stands where a Tyrant Louis Quinze once stood. 'Three thousand birds' are let loose, into the whole world, with labels round their necks, *We are free; imitate us.* Holocaust of Royalist and *ci-devant* trumpery, such as one could still gather, is burnt; pontifical eloquence must be uttered, by handsome Hérault, and Pagan orisons offered up.

And then forward across the River; where is new enormous Statuary; enormous plaster Mountain; Hercules-*Peuple,* with uplifted all-conquering club; 'many-headed Dragon of Girondin Federalism rising from fetid marsh':—needing new eloquence from Hérault. To say nothing of Champ-de-Mars, and Fatherland's Altar there; with urn of slain Defenders, Carpenter's-level of the Law; and such exploding, gesticulating and perorating, that Hérault's lips must be growing white, and his tongue cleaving to the roof of his mouth.[1*]

[1] Choix des Rapports, xii. 432–42.

Towards six o'clock let the wearied President, let Paris Patriotism generally sit down to what repast, and social repasts, can be had ; and with flowing tankard or light mantling glass, usher in this New and Newest Era. In fact, is not Romme's New Calendar getting ready ? On all housetops flicker little tricolor Flags, their flagstaff a Pike and Liberty-Cap. On all house-walls, for no Patriot, not suspect, will be behind another, there stand printed these words : *Republic one and indivisible, Liberty, Equality, Fraternity, or Death.*

As to the New Calendar, we may say here rather than elsewhere that speculative men have long been struck with the inequalities and incongruities of the Old Calendar ; that a New one has long been as good as determined on. Maréchal the Atheist, almost ten years ago, proposed a New Calendar, free at least from super-stition : this the Paris Municipality would now adopt, in defect of a better ; at all events, let us have either this of Maréchal's or a better,—the New Era being come. Petitions, more than once, have been sent to that effect ; and indeed, for a year past, all Public Bodies, Journalists, and Patriots in general, have dated *First Year of the Republic.* It is a subject not without difficulties. But the Convention has taken it up ; and Romme, as we say, has been meditating it ; not Maré-chal's New Calendar, but a better New one of Romme's and our own. Romme, aided by a Monge, a Lagrange and others, furnishes mathematics ; Fabre d'Eglantine furnishes poetic nomenclature : and so, on the 5th of October 1793, after trouble enough, they bring forth this New Republican Calendar of theirs, in a complete state ; and by Law, get it put in action.

Four equal Seasons, Twelve equal Months of Thirty days each ; this makes three hundred and sixty days; and five odd days remain to be disposed of. The five odd days we will make Festivals, and name the five *Sansculottides,* or Days without Breeches. Festival of Genius ; Festival of Labour ; of Actions ; of Rewards ; of Opinion: these are the five Sansculottides. Whereby

the great Circle, or Year, is made complete: solely every
fourth year, whilom called Leap-year, we introduce a
sixth Sansculottide : and name it Festival of the Revolution. Now as to the day of commencement, which
offers difficulties, is it not one of the luckiest coinci-
dences that the Republic herself commenced on the
21st of September ; close on the Autumnal Equinox ?
Autumnal Equinox, at midnight for the meridian of Paris,
in the year whilom Christian 1792, from that moment
shall the New Era reckon itself to begin. *Vendémiaire,
Brumaire, Frimaire ;* or as one might say, in mixed
English, *Vintagearious, Fogarious, Frostarious* : these
are our three Autumn months. *Nivose, Pluviose, Ventose,* or say, *Snowous, Rainous, Windous,* make our
Winter season. *Germinal, Floréal, Prairial,* or *Buddal,
Floweral, Meadowal,* are our Spring season. *Messidor,
Thermidor, Fructidor,* that is to say (*dor* being Greek
for *gift*) *Reapidor, Heatidor, Fruitidor,* are Republican
Summer. These Twelve, in a singular manner, divide
the Republican Year. Then as to minuter subdivisions,
let us venture at once on a bold stroke : adopt your
decimal subdivision ; and instead of the world-old
Week, or *Se'ennight,* make it a *Tennight,* or *Décade ;*—
not without results. There are three Decades, then,
in each of the months ; which is very regular ; and
the *Décadi,* or Tenth-day, shall always be the ' Day
of Rest '. And the Christian Sabbath, in that case ?
Shall shift for itself !

This, in brief, is the New Calendar of Romme and
the Convention ; calculated for the meridian of Paris,
and Gospel of Jean Jacques : not one of the least
afflicting occurrences for the actual British reader of
French History ;—confusing the soul with *Messidors,
Meadowals* ; till at last, in self-defence, one is forced to
construct some ground-scheme, or rule of Commutation
from New-style to Old-style, and have it lying by him.
Such ground-scheme, almost worn out in our service,
but still legible and printable, we shall now, in a Note,
present to the reader. For the Romme Calendar, in
so many Newspapers, Memoirs, Public Acts, has

stamped itself deep into that section of Time : a New
Era that lasts some Twelve years and odd is not to be
despised.[1] Let the Reader, therefore, with such ground-
scheme, help himself where needful, out of New-style
into Old-style, called also ' slave-style, *stile-esclave* ';—
whereof we, in these pages, shall as much as possible
use the latter only.

Thus with new Feast of Pikes, and New Era or New
Calendar, did France accept her New Constitution : the
most Democratic Constitution ever committed to paper.
How it will work in practice ? Patriot Deputations,
from time to time, solicit fruition of it ; that it be set
a-going. Always, however, this seems questionable ;
for the moment, unsuitable. Till, in some weeks, *Salut
Public*, through the organ of Saint-Just, makes report,

[1] September 22nd of 1792 is Vendémiaire 1st of Year One,
and the new months are all of 30 days each ; therefore :

To the number of the day in		ADD	We have the number of the day in		DAYS
	Vendémiaire .	. 21		September	. 30
	Brumaire .	. 21		October .	. 31
	Frimaire .	. 20		November	. 30
	Nivose .	. 20		December .	. 31
	Pluviose .	. 19		January .	. 31
	Ventose .	. 18		February .	. 28
	Germinal .	. 20		March .	. 31
	Floréal .	. 19		April .	. 30
	Prairial .	. 19		May .	. 31
	Messidor .	. 18		June .	. 30
	Thermidor .	. 18		July .	. 31
	Fructidor .	. 17		August .	. 31

There are 5 Sansculottides, and in leap-year a sixth, to be
added at the end of Fructidor.

The New Calendar ceased on the 1st of January 1806.
See Choix des Rapports, xiii. 83–99 ; xix. 199.

that, in the present alarming circumstances, the state
of France is Revolutionary; that her 'Government
must be Revolutionary till the Peace'! Solely as
Paper, then, and as a Hope, must this poor new Constitution exist;—in which shape we may conceive it lying,
even now, with an infinity of other things, in that Limbo
near the Moon. Further than paper it never got, nor
ever will get.

CHAPTER V

SWORD OF SHARPNESS

IN fact it is something quite other than paper
theorems, it is iron and audacity that France now
needs.

Is not La Vendée still blazing;—alas too literally;
rogue Rossignol burning the very corn-mills? General
Santerre could do nothing there; General Rossignol,
in blind fury, often in liquor, can do less than nothing.
Rebellion spreads, grows ever madder. Happily those
lean Quixote-figures, whom we saw retreating out of
Mentz, 'bound not to serve against the Coalition for
a year', have got to Paris. National Convention packs
them into post-vehicles and conveyances; sends them
swiftly, by post, into La Vendée. There valiantly struggling, in obscure battle and skirmish, under rogue
Rossignol, let them, unlaurelled, save the Republic,
and 'be cut down gradually to the last man'.[1]

Does not the Coalition, like a fire-tide, pour in;
Prussia through the opened Northeast; Austria, England through the Northwest? General Houchard prospers no better there than General Custine did: let him
look to it! Through the Eastern and the Western
Pyrenees Spain has deployed itself; spreads, rustling
with Bourbon banners, over the face of the South.

[1] Deux Amis, xi. 147; xiii. 160–92, &c.

Ashes and embers of confused Girondin civil war
covered that region already. Marseilles is damped
down, not quenched ; to be quenched in blood. Toulon,
terrorstruck, too far gone for turning, has flung itself,
ye righteous Powers,—into the hands of the English !
On Toulon Arsenal there flies a flag,—nay not even
the Fleur-de-lis of a Louis Pretender ; there flies that
accursed St. George's Cross of the English and Admiral
Hood ! What remnant of sea-craft, arsenals, roperies,
war-navy France had, has given itself to these enemies
of human nature, ' *ennemis du genre humain* '. Beleaguer it, bombard it, ye Commissioners Barras, Fréron,
Robespierre Junior*; thou General Cartaux, General
Dugommier ; above all, thou remarkable Artillery-
Major, Napoleon Bonaparte ! Hood is fortifying himself, victualling himself ; means, apparently, to make
a new Gibraltar of it.

But lo, in the Autumn night, late night, among the
last of August, what sudden red sunblaze is this that
has risen over Lyons City ; with a noise to deafen the
world ? It is the Powder-tower of Lyons, nay the
Arsenal with four Powder-towers, which has caught fire
in the Bombardment ; and sprung into the air, carrying ' a hundred and seventeen houses ' after it. With
a light, one fancies, as of the noon sun ; with a roar
second only to the Last Trumpet ! All living sleepers
far and wide it has awakened. What a sight was that,
which the eye of History saw, in the sudden nocturnal
sunblaze ! The roofs of hapless Lyons, and all its
domes and steeples made momentarily clear ; Rhone
and Saone streams flashing suddenly visible ; and
height and hollow, hamlet and smooth stubblefield, and
all the region round ;—heights, alas, all scarped and
counterscarped, into trenches, curtains, redoubts ;
blue Artillery-men, little Powder-devilkins, plying
their hell-trade, there through the *not* ambrosial night !
Let the darkness cover it again ; for it pains the
eye. Of a truth, Chalier's death is costing the City
dear. Convention Commissioners, Lyons Congresses

have come and gone ; and action there was and reaction ; bad ever growing worse ; till it has come to this ;
Commissioner Dubois-Crancé, ' with seventy-thousand
men, and all the Artillery of several Provinces ', bombarding Lyons day and night.

Worse things still are in store. Famine is in Lyons,
and ruin and fire. Desperate are the sallies of the
besieged ; brave Précy, their National Colonel and
Commandant, doing what is in man : desperate but
ineffectual. Provisions cut off ; nothing entering our
city but shot and shells ! The Arsenal has roared aloft ;
the very Hospital will be battered down, and the sick
buried alive. A black Flag hung on this latter noble
Edifice, appealing to the pity of the besiegers ; for
though maddened, were they not still our brethren ?
In their blind wrath, they took it for a flag of defiance,
and aimed thitherward the more. Bad is growing ever
worse here : and how will the worse stop, till it have
grown worst of all ? Commissioner Dubois will listen
to no pleading, to no speech, save this only, We surrender at discretion. Lyons contains in it subdued
Jacobins ; dominant Girondins ; secret Royalists. And
now, mere deaf madness and cannon-shot enveloping
them, will not the desperate Municipality fly, at last,
into the arms of Royalism itself ? Majesty of Sardinia was to bring help, but it failed. Emigrant
d'Autichamp, in name of the Two Pretender Royal
Highnesses,* is coming through Switzerland with help ;
coming, not yet come : Précy hoists the Fleur-de-lis !

At sight of which, all true Girondins sorrowfully fling
down their arms :—Let our Tricolor brethren storm us,
then, and slay us in their wrath ; with *you* we conquer
not. The famishing women and children are sent forth :
deaf Dubois sends them back ;—rains in mere fire and
madness. Our ' redoubts of cotton-bags ' are taken,
retaken ; Précy under his Fleur-de-lis' is valiant as
Despair. What will become of Lyons ? It is a siege
of seventy days.[1]

[1] Deux Amis, xi. 80–143.

Or see, in these same weeks, far in the Western waters: breasting through the Bay of Biscay, a greasy dingy little Merchant-ship, with Scotch skipper; under hatches whereof sit, disconsolate,—the last forlorn nucleus of Girondism, the Deputies from Quimper ! Several have dissipated themselves, whithersoever they could. Poor Riouffe fell into the talons of Revolutionary Committee and Paris Prison. The rest sit here under hatches ; reverend Pétion with his grey hair, angry Buzot, suspicious Louvet, brave young Barbaroux, and others. They have escaped from Quimper, in this sad craft ; are now tacking and struggling ; in danger from the waves, in danger from the English, in still worse danger from the French ;—banished by Heaven and Earth to the greasy belly of this Scotch skipper's Merchant-vessel, unfruitful Atlantic raving round. They are for Bordeaux, if peradventure hope yet linger there. Enter not Bordeaux, O Friends ! Bloody Convention Representatives, Tallien and such like, with their Edicts, with their Guillotine, have arrived there ; Respectability is driven under ground ; Jacobinism lords it on high. From that Réole landing-place, or *Beak of Ambès*, as it were, pale Death, waving his Revolutionary Sword of Sharpness, waves you elsewhither !

On one side or the other of that Bec d'Ambès, the Scotch Skipper with difficulty moors, a dexterous greasy man ; with difficulty lands his Girondins ;—who, after reconnoitring, must rapidly burrow in the Earth ; and so, in subterranean ways, in friends' back-closets, in cellars, barn-lofts, in caves of Saint-Emilion and Libourne, stave off cruel Death.[1] Unhappiest of all Senators !

----

[1] Louvet, pp. 180–199.

CHAPTER VI

RISEN AGAINST TYRANTS

AGAINST all which incalculable impediments, horrors
and disasters, what can a Jacobin Convention oppose ?
The uncalculating Spirit of Jacobinism, and Sansculottic
sans-formulistic Frenzy ! Our Enemies press in on us,
says Danton, but they shall not conquer us, ' we will
burn France to ashes rather, *nous brûlerons la France* '.
Committees, of *Sûreté*, of *Salut*, have raised themselves, ' *à la hauteur*, to the height of circumstances '.
Let all mortals raise themselves *à la hauteur*. Let the
Forty-four thousand Sections and their Revolutionary
Committees stir every fibre of the Republic ; and every
Frenchman feel that he is to do or die. They are the
life-circulation of Jacobinism, these Sections and Committees : Danton, through the organ of Barrère and
Salut Public, gets decreed, That there be in Paris, by
law, two meetings of Section weekly ; also, that the
Poorer Citizen be *paid* for attending, and have his day's-
wages of Forty Sous.[1] This is the celebrated ' Law of
the Forty Sous ' ; fiercely stimulant to Sansculottism,
to the life-circulation of Jacobinism.

On the twenty-third of August, Committee of Public
Salvation, as usual through Barrère, had promulgated,
in words not unworthy of remembering, their Report,
which is soon made into a Law, of *Levy in Mass*.* ' All
France, and whatsoever it contains of men or resources,
is put under requisition ', says Barrère ; really in Tyrtaean words, the best we know of his. ' The Republic
is one vast besieged city '. Two-hundred and fifty
Forges shall, in these days, be set up in the Luxembourg
Garden, and round the outer wall of the Tuileries ; to
make gun-barrels ; in sight of Earth and Heaven ! From
all hamlets, towards their Departmental Town ; from

[1] Moniteur, Séance du 5 Septembre 1793.

all Departmental Towns, towards the appointed Camp and seat of war, the Sons of Freedom shall march ; their banner is to bear : ' *Le Peuple Français debout contre les Tyrans,* The French People risen against Tyrants. The young men shall go to the battle ; it is their task to conquer : the married men shall forge arms, transport baggage and artillery ; provide subsistence : the women shall work at soldiers' clothes, make tents ; serve in the hospitals : the children shall scrape old-linen into surgeon's-lint : the aged men shall have themselves carried into public places ; and there, by their words, excite the courage of the young ; preach hatred to Kings and unity to the Republic '.[1] Tyrtaean words ; which tingle through all French hearts.

In this humour, then, since no other serves, will France rush against its enemies. Headlong, reckoning no cost or consequence ; heeding no law or rule but that supreme law, Salvation of the People ! The weapons are, all the iron that is in France ; the strength is, that of all the men, women and children that are in France. There, in their two-hundred and fifty shed-smithies, in Garden of Luxembourg or Tuileries, let them forge gun-barrels, in sight of Heaven and Earth.

Nor with heroic daring against the Foreign foe, can black vengeance against the Domestic be wanting. Life-circulation of the Revolutionary Committees being quickened by that *Law of the Forty Sous,* Deputy Merlin, not the Thionviller, whom we saw ride out of Mentz, but Merlin of Douai, named subsequently Merlin *Suspect,*—comes, about a week after, with his world-famous *Law of the Suspect*; ordering all Sections, by their Committees, instantly to arrest all Persons Suspect; and explaining withal who the Arrestable and Suspect specially are. ' Are suspect ', says he, ' all who by their actions, by their connexions, speakings, writings have ' —in short become Suspect.[2] Nay Chaumette, illumi-

---

[1] Débats, Séance du 23 Août 1793.
[2] Moniteur, Séance du 17 Septembre 1793.

nating the matter still further, in his Municipal Placards
and Proclamations, will bring it about that you may
almost recognize a Suspect on the streets, and clutch
him there,—off to Committee, and Prison.   Watch well
your words, watch well your looks : if Suspect of
nothing else, you may grow, as came to be a saying,
' Suspect of being Suspect ! ' For are we not in a State
of Revolution ?

No frightfuller Law ever ruled in a Nation of men.
All Prisons and Houses of Arrest in French land are getting crowded to the ridge-tile : Forty-four thousand
Committees, like as many companies of reapers or
gleaners, gleaning France, are gathering their harvest,
and storing it in these Houses.   Harvest of Aristocrat
tares ! Nay lest the Forty-four thousand, each on its
own harvest-field, prove insufficient, we are to have an
ambulant ' Revolutionary Army' : six-thousand strong,
under right captains, this shall perambulate the country
at large, and strike in wherever it finds such harvest-
work slack.   So have Municipality and Mother-Society
petitioned ; so has Convention decreed.[1]   Let Aristocrats, Federalists, Monsieurs vanish, and all men
tremble : ' the Soil of Liberty shall be purged ',—with
a vengeance !

Neither hitherto has the Revolutionary Tribunal
been keeping holyday.   Blanchelande, for losing Saint-
Domingo; 'Conspirators of Orléans ', for ' assassinating',
for assaulting the sacred Deputy Léonard-Bourdon :
these with many Nameless, to whom life was sweet,
have died.   Daily the great Guillotine has its due.   Like
a black Spectre, daily at eventide, glides the Death-
tumbril through the variegated throng of things.   The
variegated street shudders at it, for the moment ; next
moment forgets it : The Aristocrats ! They were
guilty against the Republic ; their death, were it only
that their goods are confiscated, will be useful to the
Republic ; *Vive la République !*

In the last days of August fell a notabler head :

----

[1] Moniteur, Séances du 5, 9, 11 Septembre.

General Custine's. Custine was accused of harshness, of
unskilfulness, perfidiousness; accused of many things:
found guilty, we may say, of one thing, unsuccessfulness.
Hearing his unexpected Sentence, 'Custine fell down
before the Crucifix', silent for the space of two hours:
he fared, with moist eyes and a look of prayer, towards
the Place de la Révolution; glanced upwards at the
clear suspended axe; then mounted swiftly aloft,[1]
swiftly was struck away from the lists of the Living.
He had fought in America; he was a proud, brave man;
and his fortune led him *hither*.

On the 2nd of this same month, at three in the morning,
a vehicle rolled off, with closed blinds, from the Temple
to the Conciergerie. Within it were two Municipals;
and Marie-Antoinette, once Queen of France! There
in that Conciergerie, in ignominious dreary cell, she,
secluded from children, kindred, friend and hope, sits
long weeks; expecting when the end will be.[2]

The Guillotine, we find, gets always a quicker motion,
as other things are quickening. The Guillotine, by its
speed of going, will give index of the general velocity of
the Republic. The clanking of its huge axe, rising and
falling there, in horrid systole-diastole, is portion of
the whole enormous Life-movement and pulsation of
the Sansculottic System!—'Orléans Conspirators' and
Assaulters had to die, in spite of much weeping and
entreating; so sacred is the person of a Deputy. Yet
the sacred can become desecrated: your very Deputy
is not greater than the Guillotine. Poor Deputy
Journalist Gorsas: we saw him hide at Rennes, when
the Calvados War burnt priming. He stole, afterwards,
in August, to Paris; lurked several weeks about the
Palais *ci-devant* Royal; was seen there, one day; was
clutched, identified, and without ceremony, being
already 'out of the Law', was sent to the Place de la

[1] Deux Amis, xi. 148-88.
[2] See Mémoires Particuliers de la Captivité à la Tour du
Temple (by the Duchesse d'Angoulême, Paris, 21 Janvier
1817).

Révolution. He died, recommending his wife and
children to the pity of the Republic. It is the ninth
day of October 1793. Gorsas is the first Deputy that
dies on the scaffold ; he will not be the last.

Ex-Mayor Bailly is in Prison ; Ex-Procureur Manuel,
Brissot and our poor Arrested Girondins have become
Incarcerated Indicted Girondins ; universal Jacobinism
clamouring for their punishment. Duperret's Seals are
broken ! Those Seventy-three Secret Protesters, suddenly one day, are reported upon, are decreed accused ;
the Convention-doors being ' previously shut ', that
none implicated might escape. They were marched,
in a very rough manner, to Prison that evening.
Happy those of them who chanced to be absent ! Condorcet has vanished into darkness ; perhaps, like
Rabaut, sits between two walls, in the house of a
friend.

CHAPTER VII

MARIE-ANTOINETTE

On Monday the Fourteenth of October 1793, a Cause
is pending in the Palais de Justice, in the new Revolutionary Court, such as these old stone-walls never
witnessed : the Trial of Marie-Antoinette. The once
brightest of Queens, now tarnished, defaced, forsaken,
stands here at Fouquier-Tinville's Judgement-bar ;
answering for her life. The Indictment was delivered
her last night.[1] To such changes of human fortune
what words are adequate ? Silence alone is adequate.

There are few Printed things one meets with of such
tragic, almost ghastly, significance as those bald Pages
of the *Bulletin du Tribunal Révolutionnaire*, which bear
title, *Trial of the Widow Capet*. Dim, dim, as if in
disastrous eclipse ; like the pale kingdoms of Dis !

[1] Procès de la Reine (Deux Amis, xi. 251–381).

Plutonic Judges, Plutonic Tinville; encircled, nine
times, with Styx and Lethe, with Fire-Phlegethon and
Cocytus named of Lamentation! The very witnesses
summoned are like Ghosts: exculpatory, inculpatory,
they themselves are all hovering over death and doom;
they are known, in our imagination, as the prey of the
Guillotine. Tall *ci-devant* Count d'Estaing, anxious to
show himself Patriot, cannot escape; nor Bailly, who,
when asked If he knows the Accused, answers with a
reverent inclination towards her, 'Ah, yes, I know
Madame'. Ex-Patriots are here, sharply dealt with,
as Procureur Manuel; Ex-Ministers, shorn of their
splendour. We have cold Aristocratic impassivity,
faithful to itself even in Tartarus; rabid stupidity, of
Patriot Corporals, Patriot Washerwomen, who have
much to say of Plots, Treasons, August Tenth, old
Insurrection of Women. For all now has become a
crime, in her who has *lost*.

Marie-Antoinette, in this her utter abandonment, and
hour of extreme need, is not wanting to herself, the imperial woman. Her look, they say, as that hideous
Indictment was reading, continued calm; 'she was
sometimes observed moving her fingers, as when one
plays on the piano'. You discern, not without interest,
across that dim Revolutionary Bulletin itself, how she
bears herself queenlike. Her answers are prompt,
clear, often of Laconic brevity; resolution, which has
grown contemptuous without ceasing to be dignified,
veils itself in calm words. 'You persist, then, in denial?'
—'My plan is not denial: it is the truth I have said, and
I persist in that'. Scandalous Hébert has borne his
testimony as to many things: as to one thing, concerning Marie-Antoinette and her little Son,—wherewith
Human Speech had better not further be soiled. She
has answered Hébert; a Juryman begs to observe
that she has not answered as to *this*. 'I have not
answered', she exclaims with noble emotion, 'because
Nature refuses to answer such a charge brought against
a Mother. I appeal to all the Mothers that are here'.
Robespierre, when he heard of it, broke out into some-

thing almost like swearing at the brutish blockheadism of this Hébert ; [1] on whose foul head his foul lie has recoiled. At four o'clock on Wednesday morning, after two days and two nights of interrogating, jury-charging, and other darkening of counsel, the result comes out : sentence of Death. 'Have you anything to say ?' The Accused shook her head, without speech. Night's candles are burning out ; and with her too Time is finishing, and it will be Eternity and Day. This Hall of Tinville's is dark, ill-lighted except where she stands. Silently she withdraws from it, to die.

Two Processions, or Royal Progresses, three-and-twenty years apart, have often struck us with a strange feeling of contrast. The first is of a beautiful Arch-duchess and Dauphiness, quitting her Mother's City, at the age of Fifteen ; towards hopes such as no other Daughter of Eve then had : 'On the morrow', says Weber an eye-witness, 'the Dauphiness left Vienna. The whole city crowded out ; at first with a sorrow which was silent. She appeared : you saw her sunk back into her carriage ; her face bathed in tears ; hiding her eyes now with her handkerchief, now with her hands ; several times putting out her head to see yet again this Palace of her Fathers, whither she was to return no more. She motioned her regret, her gratitude to the good Nation, which was crowding here to bid her farewell. Then arose not only tears ; but piercing cries, on all sides. Men and women alike abandoned themselves to such expression of their sorrow. It was an audible sound of wail, in the streets and avenues of Vienna. The last Courier that followed her disappeared, and the crowd melted away'.[2]

The young imperial Maiden of Fifteen has now become a worn discrowned Widow of Thirty-eight ; grey before her time : this is the last Procession : 'Few minutes after the Trial ended, the drums were beating

[1] Villate, Causes secrètes de la Révolution de Thermidor (Paris, 1825), p. 179.
[2] Weber, i. 6.

to arms in all Sections ; at sunrise the armed force was on foot, cannons getting placed at the extremities of the Bridges, in the Squares, Crossways, all along from the Palais de Justice to the Place de la Révolution. By ten o'clock, numerous patrols were circulating in the Streets ; thirty thousand foot and horse drawn up under arms. At eleven, Marie-Antoinette was brought out. She had on an undress of *piqué blanc* : she was led to the place of execution, in the same manner as an ordinary criminal ; bound, on a Cart ; accompanied by a Constitutional Priest in Lay dress ; escorted by numerous detachments of infantry and cavalry. These, and the double row of troops all along her road, she appeared to regard with indifference. On her countenance there was visible neither abashment nor pride. To the cries of *Vive la République* and *Down with Tyranny,* which attended her all the way, she seemed to pay no heed. She spoke little to her Confessor. The tricolor Streamers on the housetops occupied her attention, in the Streets du Roule and Saint-Honoré ; she also noticed the Inscriptions on the house-fronts. On reaching the Place de la Révolution, her looks turned towards the *Jardin National,* whilom Tuileries ; her face at that moment gave signs of lively emotion. She mounted the Scaffold with courage enough ; at a quarter past Twelve, her head fell ; the Executioner showed it to the people, amid universal long-continued cries of *Vive la République* '.[1]

[1] Deux Amis, xi. 301.

CHAPTER VIII

THE TWENTY-TWO

WHOM next, O Tinville! The next are of a different colour: our poor Arrested Girondin Deputies. What of them could still be laid hold of; our Vergniaud, Brissot, Fauchet, Valazé, Gensonné; the once flower of French Patriotism, Twenty-two by the tale: *hither*, at Tinville's Bar, onward from ' safeguard of the French People ', from confinement in the Luxembourg, imprisonment in the Conciergerie, have they now, by the course of things, arrived. Fouquier-Tinville must give what account of them he can.

Undoubtedly this Trial of the Girondins is the greatest that Fouquier has yet had to do. Twenty-two, all chief Republicans, ranged in a line there; the most eloquent in France; Lawyers too; not without friends in the auditory. How will Tinville prove these men guilty of Royalism, Federalism, Conspiracy against the Republic? Vergniaud's eloquence awakes once more; ' draws tears ', they say. And Journalists report, and the Trial lengthens itself out day after day; ' threatens to become eternal ', murmur many. Jacobinism and Municipality rise to the aid of Fouquier. On the 28th of the month, Hébert and others come in deputation to inform a Patriot Convention that the Revolutionary Tribunal is quite ' shackled by Forms of Law '; that a Patriot Jury ought to have ' the power of cutting short, of *terminer les débats*, when they feel themselves convinced '. Which pregnant suggestion, of cutting short, passes itself, with all dispatch, into a Decree.

Accordingly, at ten o'clock on the night of the 30th of October, the Twenty-two, summoned back once more, receive this information, That the Jury feeling themselves convinced have cut short, have brought in their verdict; that the Accused are found guilty, and the

Sentence on one and all of them is, Death with confis-
cation of goods.

Loud natural clamour rises among the poor Girondins; tumult; which can only be repressed by the
gendarmes. Valazé stabs himself; falls down dead
on the spot. The rest, amid loud clamour and confusion, are driven back to their Conciergerie; Lasource
exclaiming, 'I die on the day when the People have
lost their reason; ye will die when they recover it'.[1]
No help! Yielding to violence, the Doomed uplift the
Hymn of the Marseillese; return singing to their dungeon.

Riouffe, who was their Prison-mate in these last days,
has lovingly recorded what death they made. To our
notions, it is not an edifying death. Gay satirical *Pot-
pourri* by Ducos*; rhymed Scenes of Tragedy, wherein
Barrère and Robespierre discourse with Satan; death's
eve spent in 'singing' and 'sallies of gaiety', with
'discourses on the happiness of peoples': these things,
and the like of these, we have to accept for what they
are worth. It is the manner in which the Girondins
make *their* Last Supper. Valazé, with bloody breast,
sleeps cold in death; hears not the singing. Vergniaud
has his dose of poison; but it is not enough for his
friends, it is enough only for himself; wherefore he
flings it from him; presides at this Last Supper of the
Girondins, with wild coruscations of eloquence, with
song and mirth. Poor human Will struggles to assert
itself; if not in this way, then in that.[2]

But on the morrow morning all Paris is out; such
a crowd as no man had seen. The Death-carts, Valazé's
cold corpse stretched among the yet living Twenty-one,
roll along. Bareheaded, hands bound; in their shirt-
sleeves, coat flung loosely round the neck: so fare the

[1] Δημοσθένους εἰπόντος, Ἀποκτενοῦσί σε Ἀθηναῖοι, Φωκίων·
Ἂν μανῶσιν, εἶπε σὲ δ', ἐὰν σωφρονῶσι.—Plut. *Opp.* t. iv.
p. 310, ed. Reiske, 1776.

[2] Mémoires de Riouffe (in Mémoires sur les Prisons, Paris,
1823), pp. 48–55.

eloquent of France ; bemurmured, beshouted.   To the
shouts of *Vive la République*, some of them keep answering with counter-shouts of *Vive la République*.   Others,
as Brissot, sit sunk in silence.   At the foot of the
scaffold they again strike up, with appropriate variations, the Hymn of the Marseillese.   Such an act of
music ; conceive it well !   The yet Living chant there ;
the chorus so rapidly wearing weak !   Samson's axe is
rapid ; one head per minute, or little less.   The chorus
is wearing weak ; the chorus is worn *out* ;—farewell
for evermore, ye Girondins.   Te-Deum Fauchet has
become silent ; Valazé's dead head is lopped : the
sickle of the Guillotine has reaped the Girondins all
away.   'The eloquent, the young, the beautiful and
brave !' exclaims Riouffe.   O Death, what feast is
toward in thy ghastly Halls ?

Nor, alas, in the far Bordeaux region will Girondism
fare better.   In caves of Saint-Emilion, in loft and cellar,
the weariest months roll on ; apparel worn, purse
empty ; wintry November come ; under Tallien and
his Guillotine, all hope now gone.   Danger drawing ever
nigher, difficulty pressing ever straiter, they determine
to separate.   Not unpathetic the farewell ; tall Barbaroux, cheeriest of brave men, stoops to clasp his Louvet :
'In what place soever thou findest my Mother', cries he,
' try to be instead of a son to her : no resource of mine
but I will share with thy Wife, should chance ever lead
me where she is '.[1]

Louvet went with Guadet, with Salles and Valadi ;
Barbaroux with Buzot and Pétion.   Valadi soon went
southward, on a way of his own.   The two friends and
Louvet had a miserable day and night ; the 14th of the
November month, 1793.   Sunk in wet, weariness and
hunger, they knock, on the morrow, for help, at a
friend's country-house ; the fainthearted friend refuses
to admit them.   They stood therefore under trees, in
the pouring rain.   Flying desperate, Louvet thereupon
will to Paris. He sets forth, there and then, splashing the

---

[1] Louvet, p. 213.

mud on each side of him, with a fresh strength gathered
from fury or frenzy.   He passes villages, finding ' the
sentry asleep in his box in the thick rain ' ; he is gone,
before the man can call after him.   He bilks Revolutionary Committees ; rides in carriers' carts, covered
carts and open ; lies hidden in one, under knapsacks
and cloaks of soldiers' wives on the Street of Orléans,
while men search for him ; has hairbreadth escapes
that would fill three romances : finally he gets to Paris
to his fair Helpmate ; gets to Switzerland, and waits
better days.

Poor Guadet and Salles were both taken, ere long ;
they died by the Guillotine in Bordeaux ;   drums
beating to drown their voice.   Valadi also is caught,
and guillotined.   Barbaroux and his two comrades
weathered it longer, into the summer of 1794 ; but
not long enough.   One July morning, changing their
hiding-place, as they have often to do, ' about a league
from Saint-Emilion, they observe a great crowd of
country-people' : doubtless Jacobins come to take
them ? Barbaroux draws a pistol, shoots himself dead.
Alas, and it was not Jacobins ; it was harmless villagers
going to a village wake.   Two days afterwards, Buzot
and Pétion were found in a Cornfield, their bodies half-
eaten by dogs.[1]

Such was the end of Girondism.   They arose to
regenerate France, these men ; and have accomplished
this.   Alas, whatever quarrel we had with them, has not
their cruel fate abolished it ? Pity only survives.   So
many excellent souls of heroes sent down to Hades ;
they themselves given as a prey of dogs and all manner
of birds !* But, here too, the will of the Supreme Power
was accomplished.   As Vergniaud said : ' The Revolution, like Saturn, is devouring its own children'.

[1] Recherches Historiques sur les Girondins (in Mémoires
de Buzot), p. 107.

BOOK V

TERROR THE ORDER
OF THE DAY

CHAPTER I

RUSHING DOWN

We are now, therefore, got to that black precipitous
Abyss; whither all things have long been tending;
where, having now arrived on the giddy verge, they
hurl down, in confused ruin; headlong, pellmell, down,
down;—till Sansculottism have consummated itself;
and in this wondrous French Revolution, as in a
Doomsday, a World have been rapidly, if not born
again, yet destroyed and engulfed. Terror has long been
terrible: but to the actors themselves it has now
become manifest that their appointed course is one of
Terror; and they say, Be it so. ' *Que la Terreur soit
à l'ordre du jour* '.

So many centuries, say only from Hugh Capet
downwards, had been adding together, century transmitting it with increase to century, the sum of Wicked-
ness, of Falsehood, Oppression of man by man. Kings
were sinners, and Priests were, and People. Open
Scoundrels rode triumphant, bediademed, becoroneted,
bemitred; or the still fataller species of Secret-Scoun-
drels, in their fair-sounding formulas, speciosities,
respectabilities, hollow within: the race of Quacks was
grown many as the sands of the sea.* Till at length
such a sum of Quackery had accumulated itself as, in
brief, the Earth and the Heavens were weary of.
Slow seemed the Day of Settlement; coming on, all
imperceptible, across the bluster and fanfaronade of

Courtierisms, Conquering-Heroisms, Most Christian *Grand Monarque*-isms, Well-beloved Pompadourisms : yet behold it was always coming ; behold it has come, suddenly, unlooked for by any man ! The harvest of long centuries was ripening and whitening*so rapidly of late ; and now it is grown *white,* and is reaped rapidly, as it were, in one day. Reaped, in this Reign of Terror ; and carried home, to Hades and the Pit !—Unhappy Sons of Adam : it is ever so ; and never do they know it, nor will they know it. With cheerfully smoothed countenances, day after day, and generation after generation, they, calling cheerfully to one another, Well-speed-ye, are at work, *sowing the wind.* And yet, as God lives, they *shall reap the whirlwind* ; no* other thing, we say, is possible,—since God is a Truth and His World is a Truth.

History, however, in dealing with this Reign of Terror, has had her own difficulties. While the Phenomenon continued in its primary state, as mere ' Horrors of the French Revolution ', there was abundance to be said and shrieked. With and also without profit. Heaven knows, there were terrors and horrors enough : yet that was not all the Phenomenon ; nay, more properly, that was not the Phenomenon at all, but rather was the *shadow* of it, the negative part of it. And now, in a new stage of the business, when History, ceasing to shriek, would try rather to include under her old Forms of speech or speculation this new amazing Thing ; that so some accredited scientific Law of Nature might suffice for the unexpected Product of Nature, and History might get to speak of it articulately, and draw inferences and profit from it ; in this new stage, History, we must say, babbles and flounders perhaps in a still painfuller manner. Take, for example, the latest Form of speech we have seen propounded on the subject as adequate to it, almost in these months, by our worthy M. Roux, in his *Histoire Parlementaire.** The latest and the strangest : that the French Revolution was a dead-lift effort, after eighteen hundred years of preparation, to realize—the Christian Religion ! [1] *Unity, Indivisibility, Brotherhood or Death,* did indeed stand printed on all Houses of the Living ; also, on Cemeteries, or Houses of the Dead, stood printed, by order of Procureur Chaumette, *Here is Eternal Sleep*: [2] but a Christian Religion realized by the Guillotine and Death-Eternal 'is suspect to me', as Robespierre was wont to say, '*m'est suspecte*'.

Alas, no, M. Roux ! A Gospel of Brotherhood, not according to any of the Four old Evangelists, and calling on men to repent, and amend *each his own* wicked existence, that they might be saved ; but a Gospel rather, as we often hint, according to a new Fifth Evangelist Jean-Jacques, calling on men to amend *each the whole world's* wicked existence, and be saved by making the Constitution. A thing different and distant *toto coelo,* as they say : the whole breadth of the sky, and further if possible !—It is thus, however, that History, and indeed all human Speech and Reason does yet, what Father Adam began life by doing : strive to *name* the new Things it sees of Nature's producing,—often helplessly enough.

But what if History were to admit, for once, that all the Names and Theorems yet known to her fall short? That this grand Product of Nature was even grand, and new, in that it came not to range itself under old recorded Laws of Nature at all, but to disclose new ones ? In that case, History renouncing the pretension to *name* it at present, will *look* honestly at it, and name what she can of it ! Any approximation to the right Name has value : were the right Name itself once here, the Thing is known henceforth ; the Thing is then ours, and can be dealt with.

Now surely not realization, of Christianity, or of aught earthly, do we discern in this Reign of Terror, in this French Revolution of which it is the consummating. Destruction rather we discern,—of all that was destructible. It is as if Twenty-five millions, risen at length into

---

[1] Hist. Parl. (Introd.), i. 1 *et seqq.*　　[2] Deux Amis, xii. 78.

the Pythian mood, had stood up simultaneously to say, with a sound which goes through far lands and times, that this Untruth of an Existence had become insupportable. O ye Hypocrisies and Speciosities, Royal mantles, Cardinal plush-cloaks, ye Credos, Formulas, Respectabilities, fair-painted Sepulchres full of dead men's bones,*—behold, ye appear to us to be altogether a Lie. Yet our Life is not a Lie ; yet our Hunger and Misery is not a Lie ! Behold we lift up, one and all, our Twenty-five million right-hands; and take the Heavens, and the Earth and also the Pit of Tophet to witness, that either ye shall be abolished, or else we shall be abolished !

· No inconsiderable Oath, truly ; forming, as has been often said, the most remarkable transaction in these last thousand years. Wherefrom likewise there follow, and will follow, results. The fulfilment of this Oath ; that is to say, the black desperate battle of Men against their whole Condition and Environment,—a battle, alas, withal, against the Sin and Darkness that was in themselves as in others : this is the Reign of Terror. Transcendental despair was the purport of it, though not consciously so. False hopes, of Fraternity, Political Millennium, and what not, we have always seen : but the unseen heart of the whole, the transcendental despair, was not false ; neither has it been of no effect. Despair, pushed far enough, completes the circle, so to speak ; and becomes a kind of genuine productive hope again.

Doctrine of Fraternity, out of old Catholicism, does, it is true, very strangely in the vehicle of a Jean-Jacques Evangel, suddenly plump down out of its cloud-firmament ; and from a theorem determine to make itself a practice. But just so do all creeds, intentions, customs, knowledges, thoughts and things, which the French have, suddenly plump down ; Catholicism, Classicism, Sentimentalism, Cannibalism : all *isms* that make up Man in France, are rushing and roaring in that gulf ; and the theorem has become a practice, and whatsoever cannot swim sinks. Not Evangelist Jean-

Jacques alone ; there is not a Village Schoolmaster but
has contributed his quota : do we not *thou* one another
according to the Free Peoples of Antiquity ? The
French Patriot, in red Phrygian night-cap of Liberty,
christens his poor little red infant Cato,—Censor, or else
of Utica.* Gracchus has become Baboeuf,* and edits
Newspapers ; Mutius Scaevola,* Cordwainer of that ilk,
presides in the Section Mutius-Scaevola : and in brief,
there is a world wholly jumbling itself, to try what will
swim.

Wherefore we will, at all events, call this Reign of
Terror a very strange one. Dominant Sansculottism
makes, as it were, free arena ; one of the strangest
temporary states Humanity was ever seen in. A nation
of men, full of wants and void of habits ! The old habits
are gone to wreck because they were old : men, driven
forward by Necessity and fierce Pythian Madness, have,
on the spur of the instant, to devise for the want the
way of satisfying it. The Wonted tumbles down ; by
imitation, by invention, the Unwonted hastily builds
itself up. What the French National head has in it
comes out : if not a great result, surely one of the
strangest.

Neither shall the Reader fancy that it was all black,
this Reign of Terror : far from it. How many hammer-
men and squaremen, bakers and brewers, washers and
wringers, over this France, must ply their old daily
work, let the Government be one of Terror or one of
Joy ! In this Paris there are Twenty-three Theatres
nightly; some count as many as Sixty Places of Dancing.[1]
The Playwright manufactures,—pieces of a strictly
Republican character. Ever fresh Novel-garbage, as
of old, fodders the Circulating Libraries.[2] The ' Cesspool of *Agio* '* now in a time of Paper Money, works
with a vivacity unexampled, unimagined ; exhales
from itself ' sudden fortunes ', like Aladdin-Palaces :
really a kind of miraculous Fata-Morganas,* since you

---

[1] Mercier, ii. 124.
[2] Moniteur of these months, *passim.*

can live in them, for a time.   Terror is as a sable ground, on which the most variegated of scenes paints itself. In startling transitions, in colours all intensated, the sublime, the ludicrous, the horrible succeed one another; or rather, in crowding tumult, accompany one another.

Here, accordingly, if anywhere, the 'hundred tongues'*, which the old Poets often clamour for, were of supreme service ! In defect of any such organ on our part, let the Reader stir up his own imaginative organ : let us snatch for him this or the other significant glimpse of things, in the fittest sequence we can.

CHAPTER II

DEATH

In the early days of November, there is one transient glimpse of things that is to be noted : the last transit to his long home of Philippe d'Orléans Égalité. Philippe was ' decreed accused ', along with the Girondins, much to his and their surprise ; but not tried along with them. They are doomed and dead, some three days, when Philippe, after his long half-year of durance at Marseilles, arrives in Paris. It is, as we calculate, the third of November 1793.

On which same day, two notable Female Prisoners are also put in ward there : Dame Dubarry, and Josephine Beauharnais.* Dame whilom Countess Dubarry, Unfortunate-female, had returned from London ; they snatched her, not only as Ex-harlot of a whilom Majesty, and therefore suspect ; but as having ' furnished the Emigrants with money '. Contemporaneously with whom there comes the wife Beauharnais, soon to be the widow : she that is Josephine Tascher Beauharnais ; that shall be Josephine Empress Bonaparte,—for a black Divineress of the Tropics prophesied long since that she should be a Queen and more. Likewise, in the

same hours, poor Adam Lux, nigh turned in the head,
who, according to Forster, 'has taken no food these
three weeks', marches to the Guillotine for his Pamphlet
on Charlotte Corday: he 'sprang to the scaffold';
said 'he died for her with great joy'. Amid such
fellow-travellers does Philippe arrive. For, be the
month named Brumaire year 2 of Liberty, or November
year 1793 of Slavery, the Guillotine goes always, *Guillotine va toujours*.

Enough, Philippe's indictment is soon drawn, his jury
soon convinced. He finds himself made guilty of
Royalism, Conspiracy and much else; nay, it is a guilt
in him that he voted Louis's Death, though he answers,
'I voted in my soul and conscience'. The doom he
finds is death forthwith; this present sixth dim day
of November is the last day that Philippe is to see.
Philippe, says Montgaillard, thereupon called for breakfast: sufficiency of 'oysters, two cutlets, best part of
an excellent bottle of claret'; and consumed the same
with apparent relish. A Revolutionary Judge, or some
official Convention Emissary, then arrived, to signify
that he might still do the State some service by revealing
the truth about a plot or two. Philippe answered that,
on him, in the pass things had come to, the State had,
he thought, small claim; that nevertheless, in the
interest of Liberty, he, having still some leisure on his
hands, was willing, were a reasonable question-asked
him, to give a reasonable answer. And so, says Montgaillard, he leant his elbow on the mantel-piece, and
conversed in an undertone, with great seeming composure; till the leisure was done, or the Emissary went
his ways.

At the door of the Conciergerie, Philippe's attitude
was erect and easy, almost commanding. It is five
years, all but a few days, since Philippe, within these
same stone walls, stood up with an air of graciosity, and
asked King Louis, 'Whether it was a Royal Session,
then, or a Bed of Justice?' O Heaven!—Three poor
blackguards were to ride and die with him: some say,
they objected to such company, and had to be flung in,

neck and heels; [1] but it seems not true. Objecting
or not objecting, the gallows-vehicle gets under way.
Philippe's dress is remarked for its elegance ; green
frock, waistcoat of white *piqué*, yellow buckskins, boots
clear as Warren : his air, as before, entirely composed,
impassive, not to say easy and Brummellean-polite.
Through street after street ; slowly, amid execrations ;
—past the Palais Égalité, whilom Palais Royal ! The
cruel Populace stopped him there, some minutes : Dame
de Buffon, it is said, looked out on him, in Jezebel headtire*; along the ashlar Wall there ran these words in
huge tricolor print, REPUBLIC ONE AND INDIVISIBLE ;
LIBERTY, EQUALITY, FRATERNITY OR DEATH : *National
Property*. Philippe's eyes flashed hell-fire, one instant ;
but the next instant it was gone, and he sat impassive,
Brummellean-polite. On the scaffold, Samson was for
drawing off his boots : ' Tush ', said Philippe, ' they will
come better off *after* ; let us have done, *dépêchons-nous*! '

So Philippe was not without virtue, then ? God forbid
that there should be any living man without it ! He
had the virtue to keep living for five-and-forty years ;—
other virtues perhaps more than we know of. But
probably no mortal ever had such things recorded of
him : such facts, and also such lies. For he was a
Jacobin Prince of the Blood ; consider what a combination ! Also, unlike any Nero, any Borgia, he lived in
the Age of Pamphlets. Enough for us : Chaos *has*
reabsorbed him ; may it late or never bear his like
again !—Brave young Orléans Égalité, deprived of
all, only not deprived of himself, is gone to Coire in
the Grisons, under the name of Corby, to teach Mathematics. The Égalité Family is at the darkest depths
of the Nadir.

A far nobler Victim follows ; one who will claim
remembrance from several centuries : Jeanne-Marie
Phlipon, the Wife of Roland. Queenly, sublime in her un-
complaining sorrow, seemed she to Riouffe in her Prison.
' Something more than is usually found in the looks of

---

[1] Forster, ii. 628 ; Montgaillard, iv. 141-57.

women painted itself', says Riouffe,[1] 'in those large
black eyes of hers, full of expression and sweetness.
She spoke to me often, at the Grate : we were all attentive round her, in a sort of admiration and astonishment ; she expressed herself with a purity, with a harmony and prosody that made her language like music,
of which the ear could never have enough. Her conversation was serious, not cold ; coming from the mouth
of a beautiful woman, it was frank and courageous as that
of a great man'. 'And yet her maid said : ".Before
you, she collects her strength ; but in her own room,
she will sit three hours sometimes leaning on the window, and weeping " '. She has been in Prison, liberated
once, but recaptured the same hour, ever since the first
of June : in agitation and uncertainty ; which has
gradually settled down into the last stern certainty,
that of death. In the Abbaye Prison, she occupied
Charlotte Corday's apartment. Here in the Conciergerie, she speaks with Riouffe, with Ex-Minister
Clavière ; calls the beheaded Twenty-two ' *Nos amis,*
our Friends ',—whom we are soon to follow. During
these five months, those *Memoirs* of hers were written,
which all the world still reads.

But now, on the 8th of November, ' clad in white ',
says Riouffe, ' with her long black hair hanging down
to her girdle ', she is gone to the Judgement-bar. She
returned with a quick step ; lifted her finger, to signify
to us that she was doomed : her eyes seemed to have
been wet. Fouquier-Tinville's questions had been
' brutal ' ; offended female honour flung them back on
him, with scorn, not without tears. And now, short
preparation soon done, she too shall go her last road.
There went with her a certain Lamarche, ' Director of
Assignat-printing ' ; whose dejection she endeavoured
to cheer. Arrived at the foot of the scaffold, she asked
for pen and paper, ' to write the strange thoughts that
were rising in her ' :[2] a remarkable request ; which was

[1] Mémoires (Sur les Prisons, i.), pp. 55–7.
[2] Mémoires de Madame Roland (Introd.), i, 68.

refused. Looking at the Statue of Liberty which stands there, she says bitterly : ' O Liberty, what things are done in thy name ! ' For Lamarche's sake, she will die first ; show him how easy it is to die : ' Contrary to the order ', said Samson.—' Pshaw, you cannot refuse the last request of a Lady ' ; and Samson yielded.

Noble white Vision, with its high queenly face, its soft proud eyes, long black hair flowing down to the girdle ; and as brave a heart as ever beat in woman's bosom ! Like a white Grecian Statue, serenely complete, she shines in that black wreck of things ;—long memorable. Honour to great Nature who, in Paris City, in the Era of Noble-Sentiment and Pompadourism, can make a Jeanne Phlipon, and nourish her to clear perennial Womanhood, though but on Logics, *Encyclopédies*, and the Gospel according to Jean-Jacques ! Biography will long remember that trait of asking for a pen ' to write the strange thoughts that were rising in her '. It is as a little light-beam, shedding softness, and a kind of sacredness, over all that preceded : so in her too there was an Unnameable ; she too was a Daughter of the Infinite ; there were mysteries which Philosophism had not dreamt of !—She left long written counsels to her little Girl ; she said her Husband would not survive her.

Still crueller was the fate of poor Bailly, First National President, First Mayor of Paris : doomed now for Royalism, Fayettism ; for that Red-Flag Business of the Champ-de-Mars ;—one may say in general, for leaving his Astronomy to meddle with Revolution. It is the 10th of November 1793, a cold bitter drizzling rain, as poor Bailly is led through the streets ; howling Populace covering him with curses, with mud ; waving over his face a burning or smoking mockery of a Red Flag. Silent, unpitied, sits the innocent old man. Slow faring through the sleety drizzle, they have got to the Champ-de-Mars : Not there ! vociferates the cursing Populace ; such Blood ought not to stain an Altar of the Fatherland : not there ; but on that dung-heap by the Riverside ! So vociferates the cursing Populace ; Officiality gives ear to them. The Guillotine is taken down, though with hands numbed by the sleety drizzle; is carried to the River-side; is there set up again, with slow numbness; pulse after pulse still counting itself out in the old man's weary heart. For hours long; amid curses and bitter frost-rain! 'Bailly, thou tremblest', said one. '*Mon ami*, it is for cold', said Bailly, '*c'est de froid*'. Crueller end had no mortal.[1]

Some days afterwards, Roland, hearing the news of what happened on the 8th, embraces his kind Friends at Rouen, leaves their kind house which had given him refuge; goes forth, with farewell too sad for tears. On the morrow morning, 16th of the month, 'some four leagues from Rouen, Paris-ward, near Bourg-Baudoin, in M. Normand's Avenue', there is seen sitting leant against a tree the figure of a rigorous wrinkled man; stiff now in the rigour of death; a cane-sword run through his heart; and at his feet this writing: 'Whoever thou art that findest me lying, respect my remains: they are those of a man who consecrated all his life to being useful; and who has died as he lived, virtuous and honest'. 'Not fear, but indignation, made me quit my retreat, on learning that my Wife had been murdered. I wished not to remain longer on an Earth polluted with crimes'.[2]

Barnave's appearance at the Revolutionary Tribunal was of the bravest; but it could not stead him. They have sent for him from Grenoble; to pay the common smart. Vain is eloquence, forensic or other, against the dumb Clotho-shears of Tinville. He is still but two-and-thirty, this Barnave, and has known such changes. Short while ago, we saw him at the top of Fortune's wheel, his word a law to all Patriots: and now surely he is at the *bottom* of the wheel; in stormful altercation with a Tinville Tribunal, which is dooming him to die![3] And Pétion, once also of the Extreme

---

[1] Vie de Bailly (in Mémoires, i.), p. 29.
[2] Mémoires de Madame Roland (Introd.), i. 88.
[3] Forster, ii. 629.

Left, and named *Pétion Virtue*, where is he ?   Civilly
dead ; in the Caves of Saint-Emilion ; to be devoured
of dogs.   And Robespierre, who rode along with him
on the shoulders of the people, is in Committee of *Salut* ;
civilly alive : not to live always.   So giddy-swift whirls
and spins this immeasurable *tormentum* of a Revolution ;
wild-booming ; not to be followed by the eye.   Barnave,
on the Scaffold, stamped with his foot ; and looking
upwards was heard to ejaculate, ' This then is my
reward ? '

Deputy Ex-Procureur Manuel is already gone ; and
Deputy Osselin, famed also in August and September,
is about to go : and Rabaut, discovered treacherously
between his two walls, and the Brother of Rabaut.
National Deputies not a few !   And Generals : the
memory of General Custine cannot be defended by his
Son ; his Son is already guillotined.   Custine the Ex-
Noble was replaced by Houchard the Plebeian : he too
could not prosper in the North ; for him too there was
no mercy ; he has perished in the Place de la Révolution, after attempting suicide in Prison.   And Generals
Biron, Beauharnais, Brunet, whatsoever General prospers not ; tough old Lückner, with his eyes grown
rheumy ; Alsatian Westermann, valiant and diligent
in La Vendée : *none of them can*, as the Psalmist sings,
his soul from death deliver.

How busy are the Revolutionary Committees ; Sections with their Forty Halfpence a-day !   Arrestment
on arrestment falls quick, continual ; followed by death.
Ex-Minister Clavière has killed himself in Prison.
Ex-Minister Lebrun, seized in a hayloft, under the disguise of a working man, is instantly conducted to death.[1]
Nay, withal, is it not what Barrère calls ' coining money
on the Place de la Révolution ' ?   For always the
' property of the guilty, if property he have', is confiscated.   To avoid accidents, we even make a Law that
suicide shall not defraud us ; that a criminal who kills

[1] Moniteur, 11, 30 Décembre, 1793 ; Louvet, p. 287.

himself does not the less incur forfeiture of goods. Let the guilty tremble, therefore, and the suspect, and the rich, and in a word all manner of Culottic men! Luxembourg Palace, once Monsieur's, has become a huge loathsome Prison; Chantilly Palace too, once Condé's: —And their Landlords are at Blankenberg, on the wrong side of the Rhine. In Paris are now some Twelve Prisons; in France some Forty-four Thousand: thither-ward, thick as brown leaves in Autumn, rustle and travel the suspect; shaken down by Revolutionary Committees, they are swept thitherward, as into their storehouse,—to be consumed by Samson and Tinville. ' The Guillotine goes not ill, *La Guillotine ne va pas mal*'.

CHAPTER III

DESTRUCTION

THE suspect may well tremble; but how much more the open rebels;—the Girondin Cities of the South! Revolutionary Army is gone forth, under Ronsin the Playwright; six thousand strong; ' in red nightcap, in tricolor waistcoat, in black-shag trousers, black-shag spencer, with enormous moustachios, enormous sabre, —in *carmagnole complète* '; [1] and has portable guillo-tines. Representative Carrier has got to Nantes, by the edge of blazing La Vendée, which Rossignol has literally set on fire: Carrier will try what captives you make; what accomplices they have, Royalist or Giron-din: his guillotine goes always, *va toujours*; and his wool-capped ' Company of Marat '. Little children are guillotined, and aged men. Swift as the machine is, it will not serve; the Headsman and all his valets sink, worn down with work; declare that the human muscles can no more. [2] Whereupon you must try fusillading; to which perhaps still frightfuller methods may succeed.

---

[1] See Louvet, p. 301.   [2] Deux Amis, xii. 249-51.

In Brest, to like purpose, rules Jean-Bon Saint-André; with an Army of Red Nightcaps. In Bordeaux rules Tallien, with his Isabeau and henchmen; Guadets, Cussys, Salleses, many fall; the bloody Pike and Nightcap bearing supreme sway; the Guillotine coining money. Bristly fox-haired Tallien, once Able Editor, still young in years, is now become most gloomy, potent; a Pluto on Earth, and has the keys of Tartarus. One remarks, however, that a certain Senhorina Cabarus,* or call her rather *Senhora* and wedded not yet widowed *Dame de Fontenai*, brown beautiful woman, daughter of Cabarus the Spanish Merchant,—has softened the red bristly countenance; pleading for herself and friends; and prevailing. The keys of Tartarus, or any kind of power, are something to a woman; gloomy Pluto himself is not insensible to love. Like a new Proserpine,* she, by this red gloomy Dis, is gathered; and, they say, softens his stone heart a little.

Maignet, at Orange in the South; Lebon, at Arras in the North, become world's wonders. Jacobin Popular Tribunal, with its National Representative, perhaps where Girondin Popular Tribunal had lately been, rises here and rises there; wheresoever needed. Fouchés, Maignets, Barrases, Frérons scour the Southern Departments; like reapers, with their guillotine-sickle. Many are the labourers, great is the harvest. By the hundred and the thousand, men's lives are cropped; cast like brands into the burning.*

Marseilles is taken, and put under martial law: lo, at Marseilles, what one besmutted red-bearded corn-ear is this which they cut;—one gross Man, we mean, with copper-studded face; plenteous beard, or beard-stubble, of a tile-colour? By Nemesis and the Fatal Sisters, it is Jourdan Coupe-tête! Him they have clutched, in these martial-law districts; him too, with their 'national razor', their *rasoir national*, they sternly shave away. Low now is Jourdan the Headsman's own head;—low as Deshuttes's and Varigny's, which he sent on pikes, in the Insurrection of Women! No more shall he, as a copper Portent, be seen gyrating through

the Cities of the South ; no more sit judging, with pipes
and brandy, in the Ice-tower of Avignon. The all-
hiding Earth has received him, the bloated Tilebeard :
may we never look upon his like again !—Jourdan one
names ; the other Hundreds are not named. Alas,
they, like confused faggots, lie massed together for us ;
counted by the cart-load : and yet not an individual
faggot-twig of them but had a Life and History ; and
was cut, not without pangs as when a Kaiser dies !

Least of all cities can Lyons escape. Lyons, which
we saw in dread sunblaze, that Autumn night when the
Powder-tower sprang aloft, was clearly verging towards
a sad end. Inevitable : what could desperate valour
and Précy do ; Dubois-Crancé, deaf as Destiny, stern
as Doom, capturing their ' redoubts of cotton-bags ' ;
hemming them in, ever closer, with his Artillery-lava ?
Never would that *ci-devant* D'Autichamp arrive ; never
any help from Blankenberg. The Lyons Jacobins were
hidden in cellars ; the Girondin Municipality waxed
pale, in famine, treason and red fire. Précy drew his
sword, and some Fifteen Hundred with him ; sprang to
saddle, to cut their way to Switzerland. They cut
fiercely ; and were fiercely cut, and cut down ; not
hundreds, hardly units of them ever saw Switzerland.[1]
Lyons, on the 9th of October, surrenders at discretion ;
it is become a devoted Town. Abbé Lamourette, now
Bishop Lamourette, whilom Legislator, he of the old
Baiser-l'Amourette or Delilah-Kiss, is seized here ; is
sent to Paris to be guillotined : ' he made the sign of
the cross ', they say, when Tinville intimated his death-
sentence to him ; and died as an eloquent Constitutional Bishop. But woe now to all Bishops, Priests,
Aristocrats and Federalists that are in Lyons ! The
manes of Chalier are to be appeased ; the Republic,
maddened to the Sibylline pitch, has bared her right
arm. Behold ! Representative Fouché, it is Fouché
of Nantes, a name to become well known ; he with a

---

[1] Deux Amis, xi. 145.

Patriot company goes duly, in wondrous Procession,
to raise the corpse of Chalier. An Ass housed in Priest's
cloak, with a mitre on his head, and trailing the Mass-
Books, some say the very Bible, at its tail, paces through
Lyons streets : escorted by multitudinous Patriotism,
by clangour as of the Pit ; towards the grave of Martyr
Chalier. The body is dug up, and burnt : the ashes
are collected in an Urn ; to be worshipped of Paris
Patriotism. The Holy Books were part of the funeral
pile ; their ashes are scattered to the wind. Amid cries
of ' Vengeance ! Vengeance ! '—which, writes Fouché,
shall be satisfied.[1]

Lyons in fact is a Town to be abolished ; not
Lyons henceforth, but ' *Commune Affranchie*, Township
Freed ': the very name of it shall perish. It is to be razed,
this once great City, if Jacobinism prophesy right ; and
a Pillar to be erected on the ruins, with this Inscription,
Lyons rebelled against the Republic ; Lyons is no more.
Fouché, Couthon, Collot, Convention Representatives
succeed one another : there is work for the hangman ;
work for the hammerman, *not* in building. The very
Houses of Aristocrats, we say, are doomed. Paralytic
Couthon, borne in a chair, taps on the wall, with emblematic mallet, saying, ' *La Loi te frappe*, The Law
strikes thee ' ; masons, with wedge and crowbar, begin
demolition. Crash of downfall, dim ruin and dust-clouds
fly in the winter wind. Had Lyons been of soft stuff,
it had all vanished in those weeks, and the Jacobin
prophecy had been fulfilled. But Towns are not built
of soap-froth ; Lyons Town is built of stone. Lyons,
though it rebelled against the Republic, *is* to this day.

Neither have the Lyons Girondins all one neck, that
you could dispatch it at one swoop. Revolutionary
Tribunal here, and Military Commission, guillotining,
fusillading, do what they can : the kennels of the Place
des Terreaux run red ; mangled corpses roll down the
Rhone. Collot d'Herbois, they say, was once hissed on
the Lyons stage : but with what sibilation, of world-

---

[1] Moniteur (du 17 Novembre 1793), &c.

catcall or hoarse Tartarean Trumpet, will ye hiss him
now, in this his new character of Convention Representative,—not to be repeated! Two-hundred and
nine men are marched forth over the River, to be shot
in mass, by musket and cannon, in the Promenade of
the Brotteaux. It is the second of such scenes; the
first was of some Seventy. The corpses of the first were
flung into the Rhone, but the Rhone stranded some;
so these now, of the second lot, are to be buried on land.
Their one long grave is dug; they stand ranked, by the
loose mould-ridge; the younger of them singing the
Marseillaise. Jacobin National Guards give fire; but
have again to give fire, and again; and to take the
bayonet and the spade, for though the doomed all fall,
they do not all die;—and it becomes a butchery too
horrible for speech. So that the very Nationals, as they
fire, turn away their faces. Collot, snatching the musket
from one such National, and levelling it with unmoved
countenance, says, ' It is thus a Republican ought to
fire '.

This is the second Fusillade, and happily the last: it
is found too hideous; even inconvenient. There were
Two-hundred and nine marched out; one escaped at
the end of the Bridge: yet behold, when you count the
corpses, they are Two-hundred and *ten*. Rede us this
riddle, O Collot? After long guessing, it is called to
mind that two individuals, here in the Brotteaux ground,
did attempt to leave the rank, protesting with agony
that they were not condemned men, that they were
Police Commissaries: which two we repulsed, and dis-
believed, and shot with the rest![1] Such is the vengeance of an enraged Republic. Surely this, according
to Barrère's phrase, is Justice ' under rough forms, *sous
des formes acerbes* '. But the Republic, as Fouché says,
must ' march to Liberty over corpses '. Or again, as
Barrère has it: ' None but the dead do not come back,
Il n'y a que les morts qui ne reviennent pas '. Terror
hovers far and wide: ' the Guillotine goes not ill '.

[1] Deux Amis, xii. 251-62.

But before quitting those Southern regions, over which History can cast only glances from aloft, she will alight for a moment, and look fixedly at one point: the Siege of Toulon. Much battering and bombarding, heating of balls in furnaces or farm-houses, serving of artillery well and ill, attacking of Ollioules Passes, Forts Malbosquet, there has been: as yet to small purpose. We have had General Cartaux here, a whilom Painter elevated in the troubles of Marseilles; General Doppet, a whilom Medical man elevated in the troubles of Piemont, who, under Crancé, took Lyons, but cannot take Toulon. Finally we have General Dugommier, a pupil of Washington. Convention *Représentans* also we have had; Barrases, Salicettis, Robespierres the Younger:—also an Artillery *Chef de brigade*, of extreme diligence, who often takes his nap of sleep among the guns; a short, taciturn, olive-complexioned young man, not unknown to us, by name Bonaparte; one of the best Artillery-officers yet met with. And still Toulon is not taken. It is the fourth month now; December, in slave-style; *Frostarious* or *Frimaire*, in new-style: and still their cursed Red-Blue Flag flies there. They are provisioned from the Sea; they have seized all heights, felling wood, and fortifying themselves; like the coney, they have built their nest in the rocks.*

Meanwhile, *Frostarious* is not yet become *Snowous* or *Nivose*, when a Council of War is called; Instructions have just arrived from Government and *Salut Public*. Carnot, in *Salut Public*, has sent us a plan of siege: on which plan General Dugommier has this criticism to make, Commissioner Salicetti has that; and criticisms and plans are very various; when that young Artillery-Officer ventures to speak; the same whom we saw snatching sleep among the guns, who has emerged several times in this History,—the name of him Napoleon Bonaparte. It is his humble opinion, for he has been gliding about with spy-glasses, with thoughts, That a certain Fort l'Eguillette can be clutched, as with lion-spring, on the sudden; wherefrom, were it once ours, the very heart of Toulon might be battered;

the English Lines were, so to speak, turned inside out,
and Hood and our Natural Enemies must next day
either put to sea, or be burnt to ashes. Commissioners
arch their eyebrows, with negatory sniff: who is this
young gentleman with more wit than we all ? Brave
veteran Dugommier, however, thinks the idea worth
a word; questions the young gentleman; becomes
convinced; and there is for issue, Try it.

On the taciturn bronze-countenance therefore, things
being now all ready, there sits a grimmer gravity than
ever, compressing a hotter central-fire than ever. Yonder, thou seest, is Fort l'Eguillette; a desperate lion-
spring, yet a possible one ; this day to be tried !—Tried
it is ; and found *good.* By stratagem and valour, stealing through ravines, plunging fiery through the fire-
tempest, Fort l'Eguillette is clutched at, is carried ; the
smoke having cleared, we see the Tricolor fly on it: the
bronze-complexioned young man was right. Next
morning, Hood, finding the interior of his lines exposed,
his defences turned inside out, makes for his shipping.
Taking such Royalists as wished it on board with him,
he weighs anchor ; on this 19th of December 1793,
Toulon is once more the Republic's !

Cannonading has ceased at Toulon ; and now the
guillotining and fusillading may begin. Civil horrors,
truly : but at least that infamy of an English domination
is purged away. Let there be Civic Feast universally
over France : so reports Barrère, or Painter David ; and
the Convention assist in a body.[1] Nay, it is said, these
infamous English (with an attention rather to their own
interests than to ours) set fire to our store-houses,
arsenals, warships in Toulon Harbour, before weighing ;
some score of brave war-ships, the only ones we now
had ! However, it did not prosper, though the flame
spread far and high ; some two ships were burned, not
more ; the very galley-slaves ran with buckets to
quench. These same proud Ships, Ship *l'Orient* and
the rest, have to carry this same young Man to Egypt

[1] Moniteur, 1793, Nos. 101 (31 Décembre), 95, 96, 98, &c.

first: not yet can they be changed to ashes, or to Sea-
Nymphs; not yet to sky-rockets, O ship *l'Orient*; nor
become the prey of England,—before their time!

And so, over France universally, there is Civic Feast
and high-tide: and Toulon sees fusillading, grape-
shotting in mass, as Lyons saw; and 'death is poured
out in great floods, *vomie à grands flots*'; and Twelve-
thousand Masons are requisitioned from the neighbouring country, to raze Toulon from the face of the Earth.
For it is to be razed, so reports Barrère; all but the
National Shipping Establishments; and to be called
henceforth not Toulon, but *Port of the Mountain*. There
in black death-cloud we must leave it;—hoping only
that Toulon too is built of stone; that perhaps even
Twelve-thousand Masons cannot pull it down, till the
fit pass.

One begins to be sick of 'death vomited in great
floods'. Nevertheless, hearest thou not, O Reader (for
the sound reaches through centuries), in the dead
December and January nights, over Nantes Town,—
confused noises, as of musketry and tumult, as of rage
and lamentation; mingling with the everlasting moan
of the Loire waters there? Nantes Town is sunk in
sleep; but *Représentant* Carrier is not sleeping, the wool-
capped Company of Marat is not sleeping. Why un-
moors that flatbottomed craft, that *gabarre*; about
eleven at night; with Ninety Priests under hatches?
They are going to Belle Isle? In the middle of the
Loire stream, on signal given, the gabarre is scuttled;
she sinks with all her cargo. 'Sentence of Deportation',
writes Carrier, 'was executed *vertically*'. The Ninety
Priests, with their gabarre-coffin, lie deep! It is the
first of the *Noyades*,* what we may call *Drownages*, of
Carrier; which have become famous for ever.

Guillotining there was at Nantes, till the Headsman
sank worn out: then fusillading 'in the Plain of Saint-
Mauve'; little children fusilladed, and women with
children at the breast; children and women, by the
hundred and twenty; and by the five hundred, so hot
is La Vendée: till the very Jacobins grew sick, and all

but the Company of Marat cried, Hold ! Wherefore now we have got Noyading ; and on the 24th night of *Frostarious* year 2, which is 14th of December 1793, we have a second Noyade ; consisting of ' a Hundred and Thirty-eight persons '.[1]

Or why waste a gabarre, sinking it with them ? Fling them out ; fling them out, with their hands tied : pour a continual hail of lead over all the space, till the last struggler of them be sunk ! Unsound sleepers of Nantes, and the Sea-Villages thereabouts, hear the musketry amid the night-winds ; wonder what the meaning of it is. And women were in that gabarre ; whom the Red Nightcaps were stripping naked ; who begged, in their agony, that their smocks might not be stripped from them. And young children were thrown in, their mothers vainly pleading : ' Wolflings ', answered the Company of Marat, ' who would grow to be wolves '.

By degrees, daylight itself witnesses Noyades : women and men are tied together, feet and feet, hands and hands ; and flung in : this they call *Mariage Républicain*, Republican Marriage. Cruel is the panther of the woods, the she-bear bereaved of her whelps*: but there is in man a hatred crueller than that. Dumb, out of suffering now, as pale swoln corpses, the victims tumble confusedly seaward along the Loire stream ; the tide rolling them back : clouds of ravens darken the River ; wolves prowl on the shoal-places : Carrier writes, ' *Quel torrent révolutionnaire*, What a torrent of Revolution ! ' For the man is rabid ; and the Time is rabid. These are the Noyades of Carrier ; twenty-five by the tale, for what is done in darkness comes to be investigated in sunlight : [2] not to be forgotten for centuries.—We will turn to another aspect of the Consummation of Sansculottism ; leaving this as the blackest.

But indeed men are all rabid ; as the Time is. Representative Lebon, at Arras, dashes his sword into the blood flowing from the Guillotine ; exclaims, ' How

---

[1] Deux Amis, xii. 266–72 ; Moniteur, du 2 Janvier 1794.
[2] Procès de Carrier (4 tomes, Paris, 1795).

I like it!' Mothers, they say, by his order, have to stand by while the Guillotine devours their children: a band of music is stationed near; and, at the fall of every head, strikes up its *Ça ira*.[1] In the Burgh of Bedouin, in the Orange region, the Liberty-tree has been cut down overnight. Representative Maignet, at Orange, hears of it; burns Bedouin Burgh to the last dog-hutch; guillotines the inhabitants, or drives them into the caves and hills.[2] Republic One and Indivisible! She is the newest Birth of Nature's waste inorganic Deep, which men name Orcus, Chaos, primaeval Night; and knows one law, that of self-preservation. *Tigresse Nationale*: meddle not with a whisker of her! Swift-rending is her stroke; look what a paw she spreads;—pity has not entered into her heart.

Prudhomme, the dull-blustering Printer and Able Editor, as yet a Jacobin Editor, will become a renegade one, and publish large volumes, on these matters, *Crimes of the Revolution*; adding innumerable lies withal, as if the truth were not sufficient. We, for our part, find it more edifying to know, one good time, that this Republic and National Tigress *is* a New-Birth; a Fact of Nature among Formulas, in an Age of Formulas; and to look, oftenest in silence, how the so genuine Nature-Fact will demean itself among these. For the Formulas are partly genuine, partly delusive, supposititious: we call them, in the language of metaphor, regulated modelled *shapes*; some of which have bodies and life still in them; most of which, according to a German Writer, have only emptiness, ' glass-eyes glaring on you with a ghastly affectation of life, and in their interior unclean accumulation of beetles and spiders!'* But the Fact, let all men observe, is a genuine and sincere one; the sincerest of Facts; terrible in its sincerity, as very Death. Whatsoever is equally sincere may front it, and beard it; but whatsoever is *not*?—

---

[1] Les Horreurs des Prisons d'Arras (Paris, 1823).
[2] Montgaillard, iv. 200.

CHAPTER IV

CARMAGNOLE COMPLETE

SIMULTANEOUSLY with this Tophet-black aspect, there unfolds itself another aspect, which one may call a Tophet-red aspect, the Destruction of the Catholic Religion ; and indeed, for the time being, of Religion itself. We saw Romme's New Calendar establish its *Tenth* Day of Rest ; and asked, what would become of the Christian Sabbath ? The Calendar is hardly a month old, till all this is set at rest. Very singular, as Mercier observes : last *Corpus-Christi* Day 1792 the whole world, and Sovereign Authority itself, walked in religious gala, with a quite devout air ;—Butcher Legendre, supposed to be irreverent, was like to be massacred in his Gig, as the thing went by. A Gallican Hierarchy, and Church, and Church Formulas seemed to flourish, a little brown-leaved or so, but not browner than of late years or decades ; to flourish far and wide, in the sympathies of an unsophisticated People ; defying Philosophism, Legislature and the Encyclopédie. Far and wide, alas, like a brown-leaved Vallombrosa : which waits but one whirl-blast of the November wind, and in an hour stands bare ! Since that *Corpus-Christi* Day, Brunswick has come, and the Emigrants, and La Vendée, and eighteen months of Time : to all flourishing, especially to brown-leaved flourishing, there comes, were it never so slowly, an end.

On the 7th of November, a certain Citoyen Parens, Curate of Boissise-le-Bertrand, writes to the Convention that he has all his life been preaching a lie, and is grown weary of doing it ; wherefore he will now lay down his Curacy and stipend, and begs that an august Convention would give him something else to live upon. '*Mention honorable*', shall we give him ? Or 'reference to Committee of Finances' ? Hardly is this got decided, when goose Gobel, Constitutional Bishop of Paris, with his

Chapter, with Municipal and Departmental escort in
red nightcaps, makes his appearance, to do as Parens
has done. Goose Gobel will now acknowledge 'no
Religion but Liberty'; therefore he doffs his Priest-
gear, and receives the Fraternal embrace. To the joy
of Departmental Momoro, of Municipal Chaumettes and
Héberts, of Vincent and the Revolutionary Army!
Chaumette asks, Ought there not, in these circumstances, to be among our intercalary Days Sans-breeches,
a Feast of Reason?[1] Proper surely! Let Atheist
Maréchal, Lalande,* and little Atheist Naigeon rejoice;
let Clootz, Speaker of Mankind, present to the Convention his *Evidences of the Mahometan Religion*, ' a work
evincing the nullity of all Religions ',—with thanks.
There shall be Universal Republic now, thinks Clootz;
and ' one God only, *Le Peuple* '.

The French Nation is of gregarious imitative nature;
it needed but a fugle-motion in this matter; and goose
Gobel, driven by Municipality and force of circumstances, has given one. What Curé will be behind him
of Boissise; what Bishop behind him of Paris? Bishop
Grégoire, indeed, courageously declines; to the sound
of ' We force no one; let Grégoire consult his conscience '; but Protestant and Romish by the hundred
volunteer and assent. From far and near, all through
November into December, till the work is accomplished,
come Letters of renegation, come Curates who ' are
learning to be Carpenters ', Curates with their new-
wedded Nuns : has not the day of Reason dawned, very
swiftly, and become noon? From sequestered Townships come Addresses, stating plainly, though in Patois
dialect, That ' they will have no more to do with the
black animal called Curay, *animal noir appelé Curay* '.[2]

Above all things, there come Patriotic Gifts, of
Church-furniture. The remnant of bells, except for
tocsin, descend from their belfries, into the National
melting-pot to make cannon. Censers and all sacred

---

[1] Moniteur, Séance du 17 Brumaire (7th November), 1793.
[2] Analyse du Moniteur (Paris, 1801), ii. 280.

vessels are beaten broad; of silver, they are fit for the
poverty-stricken Mint; of pewter, let them become
bullets, to shoot the ' enemies *du genre humain* '. Dal-
matics of plush make breeches for him who had none;
linen stoles will clip into shirts for the Defenders of the
Country: old-clothesmen, Jew or Heathen, drive the
briskest trade. Chalier's Ass-Procession, at Lyons, was
but a type of what went on, in those same days, in all
Towns. In all Towns and Townships as quick as the
guillotine may go, so quick goes the axe and the wrench:
sacristies, lutrins, altar-rails are pulled down; the
Mass-Books torn into cartridge-papers: men dance the
Carmagnole all night about the bonfire. All highways
jingle with metallic Priest-tackle, beaten broad; sent
to the Convention, to the poverty-stricken Mint. Good
Sainte Geneviève *Chasse* is let down: alas, to be burst
open, this time, and burnt on the Place de Grève. Saint
Louis's Shirt is burnt;—might not a Defender of the
Country have had it? At Saint-Denis Town, no longer
Saint-Denis but *Franciade,* Patriotism has been down
among the Tombs, rummaging; the Revolutionary
Army has taken spoil. This, accordingly, is what the
streets of Paris saw:

' Most of these persons were still drunk, with the
brandy they had swallowed out of chalices;—eating
mackerel on the patenas! Mounted on Asses, which
were housed with Priests' cloaks, they reined them
with Priests' stoles; they held clutched with the same
hand communion-cup and sacred wafer. They stopped
at the doors of Dramshops; held out ciboriums: and
the landlord, stoop in hand, had to fill them thrice.
Next came Mules high laden with crosses, chandeliers,
censers, holy-water vessels, hyssops;—recalling to mind
the Priests of Cybele, whose panniers, filled with the
instruments of their worship, served at once as storehouse, sacristy, and temple. In such equipage did these
profaners advance towards the Convention. They enter
there, in an immense train, ranged in two rows; all
masked like mummers in fantastic sacerdotal vestments;
bearing on hand-barrows their heaped plunder,—

ciboriums, suns, candelabras, plates of gold and silver '.[1]

The Address we do not give; for indeed it was in strophes, sung *vivâ voce*, with all the parts ;—Danton glooming considerably, in his place; and demanding that there be prose and decency in future.[2] Nevertheless the captors of such *spolia opima**crave, not untouched with liquor, permission to dance the Carmagnole also on the spot: whereto an exhilarated Convention cannot but accede. Nay 'several Members', continues the exaggerative Mercier, who was not there to witness, being in Limbo now, as one of Duperret's *Seventy-three*, 'several Members, quitting their curule chairs, took the hand of girls flaunting in Priests' vestures, and danced the Carmagnole along with them'. Such Old-Hallowtide have they, in this year, once named of Grace 1793.

Out of which strange fall of Formulas, tumbling there in confused welter, betrampled by the Patriotic dance, is it not passing strange to see a *new* Formula arise ? For the human tongue is not adequate to speak what 'triviality run distracted' there is in human nature. Black Mumbo-Jumbo of the woods, and most Indian Wau-waus, one can understand : but this of Procureur *Anaxagoras*, whilom John-Peter, Chaumette ? We will say only : Man is a born idol-worshipper, *sight*-worshipper, so sensuous-imaginative is he ; and also partakes much of the nature of the ape.

For the same day, while this brave Carmagnole-dance has hardly jigged itself out, there arrive Procureur Chaumette and Municipals and Departmentals, and with them the strangest freightage : a New Religion ! Demoiselle Candeille, of the Opera ; a woman fair to look upon, when well rouged ; she, borne on palanquin shoulder high ; with red woollen nightcap ; in azure

[1] Mercier, iv. 134. See Moniteur, Séance du 10 Novembre

[2] See also Moniteur, Séance du 26 Novembre.

mantle ; garlanded with oak ; holding in her hand the Pike of the Jupiter-*Peuple*, sails in : heralded by white young women girt in tricolor. Let the world consider it ! This, O National Convention wonder of the universe, is our New Divinity ; *Goddess of Reason*, worthy, and alone worthy of revering. Her henceforth we adore. Nay, were it too much to ask of an august National Representation that it also went with us to the *ci-devant* Cathedral called of Notre-Dame, and executed a few strophes in worship of her ?

President and Secretaries give Goddess Candeille, borne at due height round their platform, successively the Fraternal kiss ; whereupon she, by decree, sails to the right-hand of the President and there alights. And now, after due pause and flourishes of oratory, the Convention, gathering its limbs, does get under way in the required procession towards Notre-Dame ;—Reason, again in her litter, sitting in the van of them, borne, as one judges, by men in the Roman costume ; escorted by wind-music, red nightcaps, and the madness of the world. And so, straightway, Reason taking seat on the high-altar of Notre-Dame, the requisite worship or quasi-worship is, say the Newspapers, *executed* ; National Convention chanting ' the *Hymn to Liberty*, words by Chénier, music by Gossec '. It is the first of the *Feasts of Reason* ; first communion-service of the New Religion of Chaumette.

' The corresponding Festival in the Church of Saint-Eustache ', says Mercier, ' offered the spectacle of a great tavern. The interior of the choir represented a landscape decorated with cottages and boskets of trees. Round the choir stood tables overloaded with bottles, with sausages, pork-puddings, pastries and other meats. The guests flowed in and out through all doors : whosoever presented himself took part of the good things : children of eight, girls as well as boys, put hand to plate, in sign of Liberty ; they drank also of the bottles, and their prompt intoxication created laughter. Réason sat in azure mantle aloft, in a serene manner, Cannoneers, pipe in mouth, serving her as acolytes.

And out of doors', continues the exaggerative man, 'were mad multitudes dancing round the bonfire of Chapel-balustrades, of Priests' and Canons' stalls; and the dancers,—I exaggerate nothing,—the dancers nigh bare of breeches, neck and breast naked, stockings down, went whirling and spinning, like those Dust-vortexes, forerunners of Tempest and Destruction '.[1] At Saint-Gervais Church, again, there was a terrible 'smell of herrings'; Section or Municipality having provided no food, no condiment, but left it to chance. Other mysteries, seemingly of a Cabiric or even Paphian character, we leave under the Veil, which appropriately stretches itself 'along the pillars of the aisles',—not to be lifted aside by the hand of History.

But there is one thing we should like almost better to understand than any other: what Reason herself thought of it, all the while. What articulate words poor Mrs. Momoro, for example, uttered; when she had become ungoddessed again, and the Bibliopolist and she sat quiet at home, at supper ? For he was an earnest man, Bookseller Momoro; and had notions of Agrarian Law. Mrs. Momoro, it is admitted, made one of the best Goddesses of Reason; though her teeth were a little defective.—And now if the Reader will represent to himself that such visible Adoration of Reason went on 'all over the Republic', through these November and December weeks, till the Church woodwork was burnt out, and the business otherwise completed, he will perhaps feel sufficiently what an adoring Republic it was, and without reluctance quit this part of the subject.

Such gifts of Church-spoil are chiefly the work of the *Armée Révolutionnaire**; raised, as we said, some time ago. It is an army with portable guillotine: commanded by Playwright Ronsin in terrible moustachios; and even by some uncertain shadow of Usher Maillard, the old Bastille Hero, Leader of the Menads, September

[1] Mercier, iv. 127–46.

Man in Grey ! Clerk Vincent of the War Office, one of
Pache's old Clerks, ' with a head heated by the ancient
orators ', had a main hand in the appointments, at least
in the staff-appointments.

But of the marchings and retreatings of these Six-
thousand no Xenophon* exists. Nothing, but an inarticulate hum, of cursing, and sooty frenzy, surviving
dubious in the memory of ages ! They scour the country
round Paris ; seeking Prisoners ; raising Requisitions ;
seeing that Edicts are executed, that the Farmers have
thrashed sufficiently ; lowering Church-bells or metallic
Virgins. Detachments shoot forth dim, towards remote
parts of France ; nay new Provincial Revolutionary
Armies rise dim, here and there, as Carrier's Company
of Marat, as Tallien's Bordeaux Troop ; like sympathetic clouds in an atmosphere all electric. Ronsin,
they say, admitted, in candid moments, that his troops
were the elixir of the Rascality of the Earth. One sees
them drawn up in market-places ; travel-splashed,
rough-bearded, in *carmagnole complète* : the first exploit
is to prostrate what Royal or Ecclesiastical monument,
crucifix or the like, there may be : to plant a cannon at
the steeple ; fetch down the bell without climbing for
it, bell and belfry together. This, however, it is said,
depends somewhat on the size of the town : if the town
contains much population, and these perhaps of a
dubious choleric aspect, the Revolutionary Army will
do its work gently, by ladder and wrench ; nay perhaps
will take its billet without work at all ; and, refreshing
itself with a little liquor and sleep, pass on to the next
stage.[1] Pipe in cheek, sabre on thigh ; in Carmagnole
complete !

Such things have been ; and may again be. Charles
Second* sent out his Highland Host over the Western
Scotch Whigs ; Jamaica Planters got Dogs from the
Spanish Main to hunt their Maroons* with ; France too
is bescoured with a Devil's Pack, the baying of which,
at this distance of half a century, still sounds in the
mind's ear.

[1] Deux Amis, xii. 62-5,

CHAPTER V

LIKE A THUNDER-CLOUD

BUT the grand, and indeed substantially primary and generic aspect of the Consummation of Terror remains still to be looked at; nay blinkard History has for most part all but *over*looked this aspect, the soul of the whole; that which makes it terrible to the Enemies of France. Let Despotism and Cimmerian Coalitions consider. All French men and French things are in a State of Requisition; Fourteen Armies are got on foot; Patriotism, with all that it has of faculty in heart or in head, in soul or body or breeches-pocket, is rushing to the Frontiers, to prevail or die! Busy sits Carnot, in *Salut Public*; busy, for his share, in 'organizing victory'. Not swifter pulses that Guillotine, in dread systole-diastole in the Place de la Révolution, than smites the Sword of Patriotism, smiting Cimmeria back to its own borders, from the sacred soil.

In fact, the Government is what we can call Revolutionary; and some men are '*à la hauteur*', on a level with the circumstances; and others are not *à la hauteur*, —so much the worse for them. But the Anarchy, we may say, has *organized* itself: Society is literally overset; its old forces working with mad activity, but in the inverse order; destructive and self-destructive.

Curious to see how all still refers itself to some head and fountain; not even an Anarchy but must have a centre to revolve round. It is now some six months since the Committee of *Salut Public* came into existence; some three months since Danton proposed that all power should be given it, and 'a sum of fifty millions', and the 'Government be declared Revolutionary'. He himself, since that day, would take no hand in it, though again and again solicited; but sits private in his place on the Mountain. Since that day, the Nine, or if they should even rise to Twelve, have become permanent,

always re-elected when their term runs out; *Salut
Public, Sûreté Générale** have assumed their ulterior
form and mode of operating.

Committee of Public Salvation, as supreme; of
General Surety, as subaltern: these, like a Lesser and
Greater Council, most harmonious hitherto, have
become the centre of all things. They ride this
Whirlwind; they, raised by force of circumstances,
insensibly, very strangely, thither to that dread height;
—and guide it, and seem to guide it. Stranger set of
Cloud-Compellers the Earth never saw. A Robespierre,
a Billaud, a Collot, Couthon, Saint-Just; not to mention
still meaner Amars, Vadiers,* in *Sûreté Générale*: these
are your Cloud-Compellers. Small intellectual talent
is necessary: indeed where among them, except in the
head of Carnot, busied organizing victory, would you
find any? The talent is one of instinct rather. It is
that of divining aright what this great dumb Whirlwind
wishes and wills; that of willing, with more frenzy than
any one, what all the world wills. To stand at no
obstacles; to heed no considerations, human or divine;
to know well that, of divine or human, there is one
thing needful, Triumph of the Republic, Destruction of
the Enemies of the Republic! With this one spiritual
endowment, and so few others, it is strange to see how
a dumb inarticulately storming Whirlwind of things
puts, as it were, its reins into your hand, and invites
and compels you to be leader of it.

Hard by, sits a Municipality of Paris; all in red
nightcaps since the fourth of November last: a set of
men fully 'on a level with circumstances', or even
beyond it. Sleek Mayor Pache, studious to be safe in
the middle; Chaumettes, Héberts, Varlets, and Henriot
their great Commandant; not to speak of Vincent the
War-clerk, of Momoros, Dobsents* and such like: all
intent to have Churches plundered, to have Reason
adored, Suspects cut down, and the Revolution triumph.
Perhaps carrying the matter *too* far? Danton was
heard to grumble at the civic strophes; and to recommend prose and decency. Robespierre also grumbles

that, in overturning Superstition, we did not mean to
make a religion of Atheism. In fact, your Chaumette
and Company constitute a kind of Hyper-Jacobinism,
or rabid 'Faction *des Enragés*'; which has given
orthodox Patriotism some umbrage, of late months. To
'know a Suspect on the streets'; what is this but
bringing the *Law of the Suspect* itself into ill odour?
Men half-frantic, men zealous overmuch,—they toil
there, in their red nightcaps, restlessly, rapidly, accom-
plishing what of Life is allotted them.

And the Forty-four Thousand other Townships, each
with Revolutionary Committee, based on Jacobin
Daughter-Society; enlightened by the spirit of
Jacobinism; quickened by the Forty Sous a-day!—
The French Constitution spurned always at anything
like Two Chambers; and yet behold, has it not verily
got Two Chambers? National Convention, elected, for
one; Mother of Patriotism, self-elected, for another!
Mother of Patriotism has her Debates reported in
the *Moniteur*, as important state-procedures; which
indisputably they are. A Second Chamber of Legislature we call this Mother-Society;—if perhaps it were
not rather comparable to that old Scotch Body named
Lords of the Articles, without whose origination, and
signal given, the so-called Parliament could introduce
no bill, could do no work? Robespierre himself, whose
words are a law, opens his incorruptible lips copiously
in the Jacobins Hall. Smaller Council of *Salut Public*,
Greater Council of *Sûreté Générale*, all active Parties,
come here to plead; to shape beforehand what decision
they must arrive at, what destiny they have to expect.
Now if a question arose, Which of those Two Chambers,
Convention, or Lords of the Articles, was the *stronger*?
Happily they as yet go hand in hand.

As for the National Convention, truly it has become
a most composed Body. Quenched now the old
effervescence; the Seventy-three locked in ward;
once noisy Friends of the Girondins sunk all into silent
men of the Plain, called even 'Frogs of the Marsh',
Crapauds du Marais! Addresses come, Revolutionary

Church-plunder comes; Deputations, with prose or strophes: these the Convention receives. But beyond this, the Convention has one thing mainly to do: to listen what *Salut Public* proposes, and say, Yea.

Bazire followed by Chabot, with some impetuosity, declared, one morning, that this was not the way of a Free Assembly. 'There ought to be an Opposition side, a *Côté Droit*', cried Chabot: 'if none else will form it, I will. People say to me, You will all get guillotined in your turn, first you and Bazire, then Danton, then. Robespierre himself'.[1] So spake the Disfrocked, with a loud voice: next week, Bazire and he lie in the Abbaye; wending, one may fear, towards Tinville and the Axe; and 'people say to me'— what seems to be proving true! Bazire's blood was all inflamed with Revolution Fever; with coffee and spasmodic dreams.[2] Chabot, again, how happy with his rich Jew-Austrian wife, late Fräulein Frey! But he lies in Prison; and his two Jew-Austrian Brothers-in-Law, the Bankers Frey, lie with him; waiting the urn of doom. Let a National Convention, therefore, take warning, and know its function. Let the Convention, all as one man, set its shoulder to the work; not with bursts of Parliamentary eloquence, but in quite other and serviceabler ways!

Convention Commissioners, what we ought to call Representatives, '*Représentans* on mission', fly, like the Herald Mercury,* to all points of the Territory; carrying your behests far and wide. In their 'round hat, plumed with tricolor feathers, girt with flowing tricolor taffeta; in close frock, tricolor sash, sword and jackboots', these men are powerfuller than King or Kaiser. They say to whomso they meet, Do; and he must do it: all men's goods are at their disposal; for France is as one huge City in Siege. They smite with Requisitions, and Forced-loan; they have the power of life and death. Saint-Just and Lebas* order the rich

[1] Débats, du 10 Novembre 1793.
[2] Dictionnaire des Hommes Marquans, i. 115.

classes of Strasburg to ' strip off their shoes ', and send
them to the Armies, where as many as ' ten-thousand
pairs ' are needed. Also, that within four-and-twenty
hours, ' a thousand beds ' be got ready ; [1] wrapped in
matting, and sent under way. For the time presses !—
Like swift bolts, issuing from the fuliginous Olympus
of *Salut Public*, rush these men, oftenest in pairs ;
scatter your thunder-orders over France ; make France
one enormous Revolutionary thunder-cloud.

CHAPTER VI

DO THY DUTY

ACCORDINGLY, alongside of these bonfires of Church-
balustrades, and sounds of fusillading and noyading,
there rise quite another sort of fires and sounds : Smithy-
fires and Proof-volleys for the manufacture of arms.

Cut off from Sweden and the world, the Republic must
learn to make steel for itself ; and, by aid of Chemists,
she has learnt it. Towns that knew only iron, now
know steel : from their new dungeons at Chantilly,
Aristocrats may hear the rustle of our new steel furnace
there. Do not bells transmute themselves into cannon ;
iron stanchions into the white-weapon (*arme blanche*),
by sword-cutlery ? The wheels of Langres scream, amid
their sputtering fire-halo ; grinding mere swords. The
stithies of Charleville ring with gun-making. What
say we, Charleville ? Two-hundred and fifty-eight
Forges stand in the open spaces of Paris itself ; a
hundred and forty of them in the Esplanade of the
Invalides, fifty-four in the Luxembourg Garden : so
many Forges stand ; grim Smiths beating and forging
at lock and barrel there. The Clockmakers have come,
requisitioned, to do the touch-holes, the hard-solder
and file-work. Five great Barges swing at anchor on

[1] Moniteur du 27 Novembre 1793.

the Seine Stream, loud with boring; the great press-drills grating harsh thunder to the general ear and heart. And deft Stock-makers do gouge and rasp; and all men bestir themselves, according to their cunning:—in the language of hope, it is reckoned that ' a thousand finished muskets can be delivered daily '.[1] Chemists of the Republic have taught us miracles of swift tanning:[2] the cordwainer bores and stitches ;—*not* of ' wood and pasteboard ', or he shall answer it to Tinville ! The women sew tents and coats, the children scrape surgeon's-lint, the old men sit in the market-places; able men are on march; all men in requisition: from Town to Town flutters, on the Heaven's winds, this Banner, THE FRENCH PEOPLE RISEN AGAINST TYRANTS.

All which is well. But now arises the question: What is to be done for saltpetre ? Interrupted Commerce and the English Navy shut us out from saltpetre ; and without saltpetre there is no gunpowder. Republican Science again sits meditative; discovers that saltpetre exists here and there, though in attenuated quantity ; that old plaster of walls holds a sprinkling of it ;—that the earth of the Paris Cellars holds a sprinkling of it, diffused through the common rubbish ; that were these dug up and washed, saltpetre might be had. Whereupon, swiftly, see ! the Citoyens, with upshoved *bonnet rouge,* or with doffed bonnet, and hair toil-wetted, digging fiercely, each in his own cellar, for saltpetre. The Earth-heap rises at every door ; the Citoyennes with hod and bucket carrying it up ; the Citoyens, pith in every muscle, shovelling and digging: for life and saltpetre. Dig, my *braves* ; and right well speed ye ! What of saltpetre is essential the Republic shall not want.

Consummation of Sansculottism has many aspects and tints : but the brightest tint, really of a solar or stellar brightness, is this which the Armies give it.

[1] Choix des Rapports. xiii. 189.   [2] Ibid. xv. 360.

That same fervour of Jacobinism, which internally fills
France with hatreds, suspicions, scaffolds, and Reason-
worship, does, on the Frontiers, show itself as a glorious
Pro patria mori.* Ever since Dumouriez's defection,
three Convention Representatives attend every General.
Committee of *Salut* has sent them; often with this
Laconic order only: ' Do thy duty, *Fais ton devoir* '.
It is strange, under what impediments the fire of Jacobinism, like other such fires, will burn. These Soldiers
have shoes of wood and pasteboard, or go booted in
hay-ropes, in dead of winter; they skewer a bast mat
round their shoulders, and are destitute of most things.
What then ? It is for Rights of Frenchhood, of Manhood, that they fight: the unquenchable spirit, here
as elsewhere, works miracles. ' With steel and bread ',
says the Convention Representative, ' one may get to
China '. The Generals go fast to the guillotine; justly
and unjustly. From which what inference ? This,
among others : That ill-success is death ; that in victory
alone is life ! To conquer or die is no theatrical palabra,
in these circumstances, but a practical truth and necessity. All Girondism, Halfness, Compromise is swept
away. Forward, ye Soldiers of the Republic, captain
and man ! Dash, with your Gaelic impetuosity, on
Austria, England, Prussia, Spain, Sardinia ; Pitt,
Cobourg, York, and the Devil and the World ! Behind
us is but the Guillotine; before us is Victory, Apotheosis
and Millennium without end !

See, accordingly, on all Frontiers, how the Sons of
Night, astonished after short triumph, do recoil ;—the
Sons of the Republic flying at them, with wild *Ça-ira* or
Marseillese *Aux armes*, with the temper of cat-o'-moun-
tain, or demon incarnate ; which no Son of Night
can stand ! Spain, which came bursting through the
Pyrenees, rustling with Bourbon banners, and went
conquering here and there for a season, falters at such
cat-o'-mountain welcome ; draws itself in again ; too
happy now were the Pyrenees impassable. Not only
does Dugommier, conqueror of Toulon, drive Spain
back ; he invades Spain. General Dugommier invades

it by the Eastern Pyrenees ; General Müller shall invade
it by the Western. *Shall*, that is the word : Committee
of *Salut Public* has said it ; Representative Cavaignac[*]
on mission there, must see it done. Impossible ! cries
Müller.—Infallible ! answers Cavaignac. Difficulty,
impossibility, is to no purpose. 'The Committee is
deaf on that side of its head', answers Cavaignac,
'*n'entend pas de cette oreille là*. How many wantest
thou, of men, of horses, cannons ? Thou shalt have them.
Conquerors, conquered or hanged, forward we must '.[1]
Which things also, even as the Representatives spake
them, were *done*. The Spring of the new Year sees
Spain invaded : and redoubts are carried, and Passes
and Heights of the most scarped description ; Spanish
Field-officerism struck mute at such cat-o'-mountain
spirit, the cannon forgetting to fire.[2] Swept are the
Pyrenees ; Town after Town flies open, burst by terror
or the petard. In the course of another year, Spain
will crave Peace ; acknowledge its sins and the Republic ;
nay, in Madrid, there will be joy as for a victory, that
even Peace is got.

Few things, we repeat, can be notabler than these
Convention Representatives, with their power more
than kingly. Nay at bottom are they not Kings, *Able-
men*, of a sort ; chosen from the Seven-hundred and
Forty-nine French Kings ; with this order, Do thy
duty ? Representative Levasseur, of small stature, by
trade a mere pacific Surgeon-Accoucheur, has mutinies
to quell ; mad hosts (mad at the Doom of Custine)
bellowing far and wide ; he alone amid them, the one
small Representative,—small, but as hard as flint,
which also carries *fire* in it ! So too, at Hondschooten,
far in the afternoon, he declares that the Battle is not

---

[1] There is, in *Prudhomme*, an atrocity *à la* Captain-Kirk[*]
reported of this Cavaignac ; which has been copied into
Dictionaries, of *Hommes Marquans*, of *Biographie Universelle*, &c. ; which not only has no truth in it, but, much
more singular, is still capable of being proved to have none.

[2] Deux Amis, xiii. 205-30 ; Toulongeon, &c.

lost ; that it must be gained ; and fights, himself, with
his own obstetric hand ;—horse shot under him, or say
on foot, ' up to the haunches in tide-water ' ; cutting
stoccado and passado there, in defiance of Water,
Earth, Air and Fire, the choleric little Representative
that he was ! Whereby, as natural, Royal Highness of
York had to withdraw,—occasionally at full gallop ; like
to be swallowed by the tide : and his Siege of Dunkirk
became a dream, realizing only much loss of beautiful
siege-artillery and of brave lives.[1]

General Houchard, it would appear, stood behind a
hedge on this Hondschooten occasion ; wherefore they
have since guillotined him. A new General Jourdan,
late Sergeant Jourdan, commands in his stead : he, in
long-winded Battles of Watigny, ' murderous artillery-
fire mingling itself with sound of Revolutionary battle-
hymns ', forces Austria behind the Sambre again ; has
hopes of purging the soil of Liberty. With hard
wrestling, with artillerying and *ça-ira*-ing, it shall be
done. In the course of a new Summer, Valenciennes
will see itself beleaguered ; Condé beleaguered ; whatsoever is yet in the hands of Austria beleaguered and
bombarded : nay, by Convention Decree, we even
summon them *all* ' either to surrender in twenty-four
hours, or else be put to the sword ' ;—a high saying,
which, though it remains unfulfilled, may show what
spirit one is of.

Representative Drouet, as an Old-dragoon, could
fight by a kind of second nature : but he was unlucky.
Him, in a night-foray at Maubeuge, the Austrians took
alive, in October last. They stripped him almost naked,
he says ; making a show of him, as King-taker of
Varennes. They flung him into carts ; sent him far into
the interior of Cimmeria, to ' a Fortress called Spitzberg ' on the Danube River ; and left him there, at an
elevation of perhaps a hundred and fifty feet, to his
own bitter reflections. Reflections ; and also devices !
For the indomitable Old-dragoon constructs wing-

machinery, of Paperkite; saws window-bars; determines to fly down.   He will seize a boat, will follow the River's course; land somewhere in Crim Tartary, in the Black-Sea or Constantinople region: *à la* Sindbad! Authentic History, accordingly, looking far into Cimmeria, discerns dimly a phenomenon.   In the dead night-watches, the Spitzberg sentry is near fainting with terror:—Is it a huge vague Portent descending through the night-air ?   It is a huge National Representative Old-dragoon, descending by Paperkite; too rapidly, alas!   For Drouet had taken with him ' a small provision-store, twenty pounds weight or thereby '; which proved accelerative: so he fell, fracturing his leg; and lay there, moaning, till day dawned, till you could discern clearly that he was not a Portent but a Representative.[1]

Or see Saint-Just, in the Lines of Weissembourg, though physically of a timid apprehensive nature, how he charges with his ' Alsatian Peasants armed hastily ' for the nonce; the solemn face of him blazing into flame; his black hair and tricolor hat-taffeta flowing in the breeze!   These our Lines of Weissembourg were indeed forced, and Prussia and the Emigrants rolled through: but we *re*-force the Lines of Weissembourg; and Prussia and the Emigrants roll back again still faster,—hurled with bayonet-charges and fiery *ça-ira*-ing.

Ci-devant Sergeant Pichegru, *ci-devant* Sergeant Hoche, risen now to be Generals, have done wonders here.   Tall Pichegru was meant for the Church; was Teacher of Mathematics once, in Brienne School,—his remarkablest Pupil there was the Boy Napoleon Bonaparte.   He then, not in the sweetest humour, enlisted, exchanging ferula for musket; and had got the length of the halberd, beyond which nothing could be hoped; when the Bastille barriers falling made passage for him, and he is here.   Hoche bore a hand at the literal overturn of the Bastille; he was, as we saw,

[1] His Narrative (in Deux Amis, xiv. 177–86).

a Sergeant of the *Gardes Françaises*, spending his pay
in rushlights and cheap editions of books. How the
Mountains are burst, and many an Enceladus is disimprisoned ; and Captains founding on Four parchments
of Nobility are blown with their parchments across the
Rhine, into Lunar Limbo !

What high feats of arms, therefore, were done in these
Fourteen Armies ; and how, for love of Liberty and hope
of Promotion, lowborn valour cut its desperate way to
Generalship ; and, from the central Carnot in *Salut
Public* to the outmost drummer on the Frontiers, men
strove for their Republic, let Readers fancy. The
snows of Winter, the flowers of Summer continue to be
stained with warlike blood.   Gaelic impetuosity mounts
ever higher with victory ; spirit of Jacobinism weds
itself to national vanity : the Soldiers of the Republic
are becoming, as we prophesied, very Sons of Fire.
Barefooted, barebacked : but with bread and iron you
can get to China ! It is one Nation against the whole
world ; but the Nation has that within her which the
whole world will not conquer.   Cimmeria, astonished,
recoils faster or slower ; all round the Republic there
rises fiery, as it were, a magic ring of musket-volleying
and *ça-ira*-ing. Majesty of Prussia, as Majesty of Spain,
will by and by acknowledge his sins and the Republic ;
and make a Peace of Bâle.

Foreign Commerce, Colonies, Factories in the East
and in the West, are fallen or falling into the hands of
sea-ruling Pitt, enemy of human nature.   Nevertheless
what sound is this that we hear, on the first of June
1794 ; sound as of war-thunder borne from the Ocean
too, of tone most piercing ? War-thunder from off the
Brest waters : Villaret-Joyeuse and English Howe,
after long manœuvring, have ranked themselves there ;
and are belching fire.   The enemies of human nature
are on their own element ; cannot be conquered ;
cannot be kept from conquering.   Twelve hours of
raging cannonade ; sun now sinking westward through
the battle-smoke : six French Ships taken, the Battle

lost; what Ship soever can still sail, making off! But
how is it, then, with that *Vengeur* Ship, she neither
strikes nor makes off? She is lamed, she cannot make
off; strike she will not. Fire rakes her fore and aft
from victorious enemies; the *Vengeur* is sinking.
Strong are ye, Tyrants of the sea; yet we also, are we
weak? Lo! all flags, streamers, jacks, every rag of
tricolor that will yet run on rope, fly rustling aloft: the
whole crew crowds to the upper deck; and with universal soul-maddening yell, shouts *Vive la République*,—
sinking, sinking. She staggers, she lurches, her last
drunk whirl; Ocean yawns abysmal: down rushes the
Vengeur, carrying *Vive la République* along with her,
unconquerable, into Eternity.[1] Let foreign Despots
think of that. There is an Unconquerable in man,
when he stands on his Rights of Man: let Despots and
Slaves and all people know this, and only them that
stand on the Wrongs of Man tremble to know it.—So
has History written, nothing doubting, of the sunk
Vengeur.

——Reader! Mendez Pinto, Münchäusen, Cagliostro,
Psalmanazar have been great*; but they are not the
greatest. O Barrère, Barrère, Anacreon of the Guillotine! must inquisitive pictorial History, in a new
edition, ask again, 'How *is* it with the *Vengeur*', in
this its glorious suicidal sinking; and, with resentful
brush, dash a bend-sinister of contumelious lampblack
through thee and it? Alas, alas! The *Vengeur*, after
fighting bravely, did sink altogether as other ships do,
her captain and above two-hundred of her crew escaping gladly in British boats; and this same enormous
inspiring Feat, and rumour ' of sound most piercing ',
turns out to be an enormous inspiring Non-entity, extant
nowhere save, as falsehood, in the brain of Barrère!
Actually so.[2] Founded, like the World itself, on
Nothing; proved by Convention Report, by solemn

---

[1] Compare Barrère (Choix des Rapports, xiv. 416–21);
Lord Howe (Annual Register of 1794, p. 86), &c.
[2] Carlyle's Miscellanies, § *Sinking of the Vengeur*.

Convention Decree and Decrees, and wooden '*Model of the Vengeur*'; believed, bewept, besung by the whole French People to this hour, it may be regarded as Barrère's masterpiece; the largest, most inspiring piece of *blague* manufactured, for some centuries, by any man or nation. As such, and not otherwise, be it henceforth memorable.

CHAPTER VII

FLAME-PICTURE

In this manner, mad-blazing with flame of all imaginable tints, from the red of Tophet to the stellar-bright, blazes off this Consummation of Sansculottism.

But the hundredth part of the things that were done, and the thousandth part of the things that were projected and decreed to be done, would tire the tongue of History. Statue of the *Peuple Souverain*, high as Strasburg Steeple; which shall fling its shadow from the Pont Neuf over Jardin National and Convention Hall; —enormous, in Painter David's Head! With other the like enormous Statues not a few: realized in paper Decree. For, indeed, the Statue of Liberty herself is still but Plaster, in the Place de la Révolution. Then Equalization of Weights and Measures, with decimal division; Institutions, of Music and of much else; Institute in general; School of Arts, School of Mars, *Elèves de la Patrie*, Normal Schools: amid such Gun-boring, Altar-burning, Saltpetre-digging, and miraculous improvements in Tannery!

What, for example, is this that Engineer Chappe is doing, in the Park of Vincennes? In the Park of Vincennes; and onwards, they say, in the Park of Lepelletier Saint-Fargeau the assassinated Deputy; and still onwards to the Heights of Ecouen and further, he has scaffolding set up, has posts driven in; wooden arms with elbow joints are jerking and fugling in the air,

in the most rapid mysterious manner ! Citoyens ran up,
suspicious. Yes, O Citoyens, we are signalling : it is
a device this, worthy of the Republic ; a thing for what
we will call *Far-writing* without the aid of postbags ; in
Greek it shall be named Telegraph.—*Télégraphe sacré !*
answers Citoyenism : For writing to Traitors, to
Austria ?—and tears it down. Chappe had to escape,
and get a new Legislative Decree. Nevertheless he has
accomplished it, the indefatigable Chappe : this his
Far-writer, with its wooden arms and elbow-joints, can
intelligibly signal ; and lines of them are set up, to the
North Frontiers and elsewhither. On an Autumn
evening of the Year Two, Far-writer having just written
that Condé Town has surrendered to us, we send from
the Tuileries Convention-Hall this response in the
shape of Decree : ' The name of Condé is changed to
Nord-Libre, North-Free. The Army of the North
ceases not to merit well of the country '.—To the
admiration of men ! For lo, in some half hour, while the
Convention yet debates, there arrives this new answer :
' I inform thee, *je t'annonce*, Citizen President, that the
Decree of Convention, ordering change of the name
Condé into *North-Free* ; and the other, declaring that
the Army of the North ceases not to merit well of the
country ; are transmitted and acknowledged by
Telegraph. I have instructed my Officer at Lille to
forward them to North-Free by express. *Signed*,
CHAPPE '.[1]

Or see, over Fleurus in the Netherlands, where
General Jourdan, having now swept the soil of Liberty,
and advanced thus far, is just about to fight, and
sweep or be swept, hangs there not in the Heaven's
Vault, some Prodigy, seen by Austrian eyes and spy-
glasses : in the similitude of an enormous Windbag,
with netting and enormous Saucer depending from it ?
A Jove's Balance, O ye Austrian spy-glasses ? One
saucer-scale of a Jove's Balance ; *your* poor Austrian
scale having kicked itself quite aloft, out of sight ?

----

[1] Choix des Rapports, xv. 378, 384.

By Heaven, answer the spy-glasses, it is a Montgolfier,
a Balloon, and they are making signals! Austrian
cannon-battery barks at this Montgolfier; harmless
as dog at the Moon*: the Montgolfier makes its signals;
detects what Austrian ambuscade there may be, and
descends at its ease.[1]—What will not these devils incarnate contrive?

On the whole, is it not, O Reader, one of the strangest
Flame-Pictures that ever painted itself; flaming off
there, on its ground of Guillotine-black? And the
nightly Theatres are Twenty-three; and the *Salons
de danse* are Sixty; full of mere *Égalité, Fraternité* and
Carmagnole. And Section Committee-rooms are Forty-
eight; redolent of tobacco and brandy; vigorous with
twenty-pence a-day, coercing the Suspect. And the
Houses of Arrest are Twelve, for Paris alone; crowded
and even crammed. And at all turns, you need your
'Certificate of Civism'; be it for going out, or for
coming in; nay without it you cannot, for money, get
your daily ounces of bread. Dusky red-capped Bakers'-
queues; wagging themselves; not in silence! For we
still live by Maximum, in all things; waited on by these
two, Scarcity and Confusion. The faces of men are
darkened with suspicion; with suspecting, or being
suspect. The streets lie unswept; the ways unmended.
Law has shut her Books; speaks little, save impromptu,
through the throat of Tinville. Crimes go unpunished;
not crimes against the Revolution.[2] 'The number of
foundling children', as some compute, 'is doubled'.

How silent now sits Royalism; sits all Aristocratism;
Respectability that kept its Gig! The honour now, and
the safety, is to Poverty, not to Wealth. Your Citizen,
who would be fashionable, walks abroad, with his Wife
on his arm, in red wool nightcap, black-shag spencer,
and carmagnole complete. Aristocratism crouches low,
in what shelter is still left; submitting to all requisitions, vexations; too happy to escape with life.

[1] 26th June 1794 (see Rapport de Guyton-Morveau sur
les aérostats, in Moniteur du 6 Vendémiaire, An 2).

[2] Mercier, v. 25; Deux Amis, xii. 142–99.

Ghastly châteaus stare on you by the wayside; disroofed, diswindowed; which the National Housebroker is peeling for the lead and ashlar. The old tenants hover disconsolate, over the Rhine with Condé; a spectacle to men. *Ci-devant* Seigneur, exquisite in palate, will become an exquisite Restaurateur Cook in Hamburg; *Ci-devant* Madame, exquisite in dress, a successful *Marchande des Modes* in London. In Newgate-Street, you meet M. le Marquis, with a rough deal on his shoulder, adze and jack-plane under arm; he has taken to the joiner trade; it being necessary to live (*faut vivre*).[1]—Higher than all Frenchmen the domestic Stock-jobber flourishes,—in a day of Paper-money. The Farmer also flourishes: 'Farmers' houses', says Mercier, 'have become like Pawnbrokers' shops'; all manner of furniture, apparel, vessels of gold and silver accumulate themselves there: bread is precious. The Farmer's rent is Paper-money, and he alone of men has bread: Farmer is better than Landlord, and will himself become Landlord.

And daily, we say, like a black Spectre, silently through that Life-tumult, passes the Revolution Cart; writing on the walls its MENE, MENE, *Thou art weighed, and found wanting!* A Spectre with which one has grown familiar. Men have adjusted themselves: complaint issues not from that Death-tumbril. Weak women and *ci-devants*, their plumage and finery all tarnished, sit there; with a silent gaze, as if looking into the Infinite Black. The once light lip wears a curl of irony, uttering no word; and the Tumbril fares along. They may be guilty before Heaven, or not; they are guilty, we suppose, before the Revolution. Then, does not the Republic 'coin money' of them, with its great axe? Red Nightcaps howl dire approval: the rest of Paris looks on; if with a sigh, that is much: Fellow-creatures whom sighing cannot help; whom black Necessity and Tinville have clutched.

[1] See Deux Amis, xv. 189-92; Mémoires de Genlis; Founders of the French Republic, &c. &c.

One other thing, or rather two other things, we will still mention ; and no more : The Blond Perukes ; the Tannery at Meudon. Great talk is of these *Perruques blondes* : O Reader, they are made from the Heads of Guillotined women ! The locks of a Duchess, in this way, may come to cover the scalp of a Cordwainer ; her blonde German Frankism his black Gaelic poll, if it be bald. Or they may be worn affectionately, as relics ; rendering one suspect ? [1] Citizens use them, not without mockery ; of a rather cannibal sort.

Still deeper into one's heart goes that Tannery at Meudon ; not mentioned among the other miracles of tanning ! 'At Meudon ', says Montgaillard with considerable calmness, ' there was a Tannery of Human Skins ; such of the Guillotined as seemed worth flaying : of which perfectly good wash-leather was made ' ; for breeches, and other uses. The skin of the men, he remarks, was superior in toughness (*consistance*) and quality to shamoy ; that of the women was good for almost nothing, being so soft in texture ! [2]—History looking back over Cannibalism, through *Purchas's Pilgrims* and all early and late Records, will perhaps find no terrestrial Cannibalism of a sort, on the whole, so detestable. It is a manufactured, soft-feeling, quietly elegant sort ; a sort *perfide* ! Alas then, is man's civilization only a wrappage, through which the savage nature of him can still burst, infernal as ever ? Nature still makes him ; and has an Infernal in her as well as a Celestial.

[1] Mercier, ii. 134.   [2] Montgaillard, iv. 290.

BOOK VI

THERMIDOR

CHAPTER I

THE GODS ARE ATHIRST

WHAT then is this Thing, called *La Révolution*, which,
like an Angel of Death, hangs over France, noyading,
fusillading, fighting, gun-boring, tanning human skins ?
La Révolution is but so many Alphabetic Letters ; a
thing nowhere to be laid hands on, to be clapped under
lock and key : where is it ? what is it ? It is the Madness that dwells in the hearts of men. In this man it
is, and in that man ; as a rage or as a terror, it is in all
men. Invisible, impalpable ; and yet no black Azrael,
with wings spread over half a continent, with sword
sweeping from sea to sea, could be a truer Reality.

To explain, what is called explaining, the march of
this Revolutionary Government, be no task of ours.
Man cannot explain it. A paralytic Couthon, asking in
the Jacobins, ' What hast thou done to be hanged if
Counter-Revolution should arrive ? ' a sombre Saint-
Just, not yet six-and-twenty, declaring that ' for Revolutionists there is no rest but in the tomb ' ; a seagreen
Robespierre converted into vinegar and gall ; much
more an Amar and Vadier, a Collot and Billaud : to
inquire what thoughts, predetermination or prevision,
might be in the head of these men ! Record of their
thought remains not ; Death and Darkness have swept
it out utterly. Nay, if we even had their thought, all
that they could have articulately spoken to us, how
insignificant a fraction were that of the Thing which
realized itself, which decreed itself, on signal given by

them ! As has been said more than once, this Revolutionary Government is not a self-conscious but a blind
fatal one.   Each man, enveloped in his ambient-atmo-
sphere of revolutionary fanatic Madness, rushes on,
impelled and impelling ;   and has become a blind brute
Force ; no rest for him but in the grave ! Darkness and
the mystery of horrid cruelty cover it for us, in History ;
as they did in Nature.   The chaotic Thunder-cloud,
with its pitchy black, and its tumult of dazzling jagged
fire, in a world all electric :   thou wilt not undertake to
show how that comported itself,—what the secrets of
its dark womb were ; from what sources, with what
specialties, the lightning it held did, in confused brightness of terror, strike forth, destructive and self-destructive, till it ended ? Like a Blackness naturally of Erebus,
which by will of Providence had for once mounted itself
into dominion and the Azure :   is not this properly the
nature of Sansculottism consummating itself ?   Of
which Erebus Blackness be it enough to discern that
this and the other dazzling fire-bolt, dazzling fire-
torrent, does by small Volition and great Necessity,
verily issue,—in such and such succession ; destructive
so and so, self-destructive so and so :   till it end.

Royalism is extinct ; ' sunk ', as they say, ' in the mud
of the Loire ' ;   Republicanism dominates without and
within :   what, therefore, on the 15th day of March
1794, is this ?   Arrestment, sudden really as a bolt out
of the Blue, has hit strange victims : Hébert *Père*
Duchesne, Bibliopolist Momoro, Clerk Vincent, General
Ronsin ; high Cordelier Patriots, redcapped Magistrates
of Paris, Worshippers of Reason, Commanders of
Revolutionary Army ! Eight short days ago, their Cordelier Club was loud, and louder than ever, with Patriot
denunciations.   Hébert *Père Duchesne* had ' held his
tongue and his heart these two months, at sight of
Moderates, Crypto-Aristocrats, Camilles, *Scélérats* in
the Convention itself : but could not do it any longer ;
would, if other remedy were not, invoke the sacred right
of Insurrection '.   So spake Hébert in Cordelier Session ;

with vivats, till the roofs rang again.[1] Eight short days
ago ; and now already ! They rub their eyes : it is no
dream ; they find themselves in the Luxembourg.
Goose Gobel too ; and they that burnt Churches !
Chaumette himself, potent Procureur, *Agent National*
as they now call it, who could ' recognize the Suspect by
the very face of them ', he lingers but three days ; on
the third day he too is hurled in. Most chopfallen, blue,
enters the National Agent this Limbo whither he has
sent so many. Prisoners crowd round, jibing and
jeering ; 'Sublime National Agent', says one, 'in
virtue of thy immortal Proclamation, lo there ! I am
suspect, thou art suspect, he is suspect, we are suspect,
ye are suspect, they are suspect ! '

The meaning of these things ? Meaning ! It is a Plot ;
Plot of the most extensive ramifications ; which, however, Barrère holds the threads of. Such Church-
burning and scandalous masquerades of Atheism, fit to
make the Revolution odious : where indeed could they
originate but in the gold of Pitt ? Pitt indubitably, as
Preternatural Insight will teach one, did hire this
Faction of *Enragés*, to play their fantastic tricks ; to
roar in their Cordeliers Club about Moderatism ; to
print their *Père Duchesne* ; worship skyblue Reason
in red nightcap ; rob all Altars,—and bring the spoil
to *us* !

Still more indubitable, visible to the mere bodily
sight, is this : that the Cordeliers Club sits pale, with
anger and terror ; and has ' veiled the Rights of Man ',
—without effect. Likewise that the Jacobins are in
considerable confusion ; busy ' purging themselves,
s'épurant ', as in times of Plot and public Calamity
they have repeatedly had to do. Not even Camille
Desmoulins but has given offence : nay there have
risen murmurs against Danton himself ; though he
bellowed them down, and Robespierre finished the
matter by ' embracing him in the Tribune '.

Whom shall the Republic and a jealous Mother-

[1] Moniteur, du 17 Ventose (7th March) 1794.

Society trust ? In these times of temptation, of Preternatural Insight ! For there are Factions of the Stranger,
'*de l'étranger*', Factions of Moderates, of Enraged; all
manner of Factions : we walk in a world of Plots ;
strings universally spread, of deadly gins and falltraps,
baited by the gold of Pitt ! Clootz, Speaker of Mankind
so-called, with his *Evidences of Mahometan Religion*,
and babble of Universal Republic, him an incorruptible
Robespierre has purged away. Baron Clootz, and
Paine rebellious Needleman lie, these two months, in
the Luxembourg ; limbs of the Faction *de l'étranger*.
Representative Phélippeaux is purged out : he came
back from La Vendée with an ill report in his mouth
against rogue Rossignol, and our method of warfare
there. Recant it, O Phélippeaux,* we entreat thee !
Phélippeaux will not recant ; and is purged out.
Representative Fabre d'Eglantine, famed Nomenclator
of Romme's Calendar, is purged out ; nay, is cast into
the Luxembourg : accused of Legislative Swindling
' in regard to moneys of the India Company '. There
with his Chabots, Bazires, guilty of the like, let Fabre
wait his destiny. And Westermann friend of Danton,
he who led the Marseillese on the Tenth of August, and
fought well in La Vendée, but spoke not well of rogue
Rossignol, is purged out. Lucky, if he too go not to
the Luxembourg. And your Prolys, Guzmans, of the
Faction of the Stranger, they have gone ; Pereyra,
though he fled, is gone, ' taken in the disguise of a
Tavern Cook '. I am suspect, thou art suspect, he is
suspect !—

The great heart of Danton is weary of it. Danton
is gone to native Arcis, for a little breathing-time of
peace : Away, black Arachne-webs, thou world of
Fury, Terror and Suspicion ; welcome, thou everlasting
Mother, with thy spring greenness, thy kind household
loves and memories ; true art thou, were all else untrue !
The great Titan walks silent, by the banks of the
murmuring Aube, in young native haunts that knew
him when a boy ; wonders what the end of these things
may be,

But strangest of all, Camille Desmoulins is purged
out. Couthon gave as a test in regard to Jacobin
purgation the question, 'What hast thou done to be
hanged if Counter-Revolution should arrive?' Yet
Camille, who could so well answer this question, is
purged out! The truth is, Camille, early in December
last, began publishing a new Journal, or Series of Pamphlets, entitled the *Vieux Cordelier*, Old Cordelier.
Camille, not afraid at one time to 'embrace Liberty on
a heap of dead bodies', begins to ask now, Whether
among so many arresting and punishing Committees,
there ought not to be a 'Committee of Mercy'? Saint-
Just, he observes, is an extremely solemn young
Republican, who 'carries his head as if it were a *Saint-
Sacrement*', adorable Hostie, or divine Real-Presence!
Sharply enough, this *old* Cordelier,—Danton and he
were of the earliest primary Cordeliers,—shoots his
glittering war-shafts into your *new* Cordeliers, your
Héberts, Momoros, with their brawling brutalities and
despicabilities; say, as the Sun-god (for poor Camille
is a Poet) shot into that Python Serpent,* sprung of
mud.

Whereat, as was natural, the Hébertist Python did
hiss and writhe amazingly; and threaten 'sacred right
of Insurrection';—and, as we saw, get cast into Prison.
Nay, with all the old wit, dexterity and light graceful
poignancy, Camille, translating 'out of *Tacitus*, from
the Reign of Tiberius', pricks into the *Law of the Suspect*
itself; making it odious! Twice, in the Decade, his
wild Leaves issue; full of wit, nay of humour, of
harmonious ingenuity and insight,—one of the strangest
phenomena of that dark time; and smite, in their
wild-sparkling way, at various monstrosities, Saint-
Sacrament heads, and Juggernaut idols, in a rather
reckless manner. To the great joy of Josephine
Beauharnais, and the other Five-thousand and odd
Suspect, who fill the Twelve Houses of Arrest; on
whom a ray of hope dawns! Robespierre, at first appro-
batory, knew not at last what to think; then thought,
with his Jacobins, that Camille must be expelled.

A man of true Revolutionary spirit, this Camille ; but
with the unwisest sallies ; whom Aristocrats and
Moderates have the art to corrupt ! Jacobinism is in
uttermost crisis and struggle ; enmeshed wholly in plots,
corruptibilities, neck-gins and baited falltraps of Pitt
Ennemi du Genre Humain. Camille's First Number
begins with ' *O Pitt !* '—his last is dated 15 Pluviose
Year 2, 3rd February 1794 ; and ends with these words
of Montezuma's,* ' *Les dieux ont soif*, The gods are
athirst '.

Be this as it may, the Hébertists lie in Prison only
some nine days. On the 24th of March, therefore, the
Revolution Tumbrils carry through that Life-tumult
a new cargo : Hébert, Vincent, Momoro, Ronsin, Nineteen of them in all ; with whom, curious enough, sits
Clootz Speaker of Mankind. They have been massed
swiftly into a lump, this miscellany of Nondescripts ;
and travel now their last road. No help. They too
must ' look through the little window ' ; they too
must ' sneeze into the sack ', *éternuer dans le sac* ; as
they have done to others, so is it done to them. *Sainte-*
Guillotine, meseems, is worse than the old Saints of
Superstition ; a man-devouring Saint ? Clootz, still
with an air of polished sarcasm, endeavours to jest, to
offer cheering ' arguments of Materialism ' ; he requested
to be executed last, ' in order to establish certain
principles ',—which hitherto, I think, Philosophy has
got no good of. General Ronsin too, he still looks forth
with some air of defiance, eye of command : the rest are
sunk in a stony paleness of despair. Momoro, poor
Bibliopolist, no Agrarian Law yet realized,—they might
as well have hanged thee at Evreux, twenty months
ago, when Girondin Buzot hindered them. Hébert
Père Duchesne shall never in this world rise in sacred
right of insurrection ; he sits there low enough, head
sunk on breast ; Red Nightcaps shouting round him, in
frightful parody of his Newspaper Articles, ' Grand
choler of the Père Duchesne ! ' Thus perish they ; the
sack receives all their heads. Through some section of

History, Nineteen spectre-chimeras shall flit, squeaking
and gibbering ; till Oblivion swallow them.

In the course of a week, the Revolutionary Army
itself is disbanded ; the General having become spectral.
This Faction of Rabids, therefore, is also purged from
the Republican soil ; here also the baited falltraps of
that Pitt have been wrenched up harmless ; and anew
there is joy over a Plot discovered. The Revolution,
then, is verily devouring its own children ? All Anarchy,
by the nature of it, is not only destructive but *self*-
destructive.

CHAPTER II

DANTON, NO WEAKNESS

DANTON, meanwhile, has been pressingly sent for
from Arcis : he must return instantly, cried Camille,
cried Phélippeaux and Friends, who scented danger in
the wind. Danger enough ! A Danton, a Robespierre,
chief-products of a victorious Revolution, are now
arrived in immediate front of one another ; must
ascertain how they will live together, rule together.
One conceives easily the deep mutual incompatibility
that divided these two : with what terror of feminine
hatred the poor seagreen Formula looked at the
monstrous colossal Reality, and grew greener to
behold him ;—the Reality, again, struggling to think
no ill of a chief-product of the Revolution ; yet feeling
at bottom that such chief-product was little other than
a chief windbag, blown large by Popular air ; not a
man, with the heart of a man, but a poor spasmodic
incorruptible pedant, with a logic-formula instead of
heart ; of Jesuit or Methodist-Parson nature ; full of
sincere-cant, incorruptibility, of virulence, poltroonery ;
barren as the eastwind ! Two such chief-products are
too much for one Revolution.

Friends, trembling at the results of a quarrel on their

part, brought them to meet. ' It is right ', said Danton,
swallowing much indignation, ' to repress the Royalists :
but we should not strike except where it is useful to the
Republic ; we should not confound the innocent and
the guilty '.—' And who told you ', replied Robespierre
with a poisonous look, ' that one innocent person had
perished ? '—' *Quoi* ', said Danton, turning round to
Friend Pâris self-named Fabricius,* Juryman in the
Revolutionary Tribunal : ' *Quoi*, not one innocent ?
What sayest thou of it, Fabricius ! ' [1]—Friends, Westermann, this Pâris and others urged him to show himself,
to ascend the Tribune and act. The man Danton was
not prone to show himself ; to act, or uproar for his
own safety. A man of careless, large, hoping nature ;
a large nature that could rest : he would sit whole
hours, they say, hearing Camille talk, and liked nothing
so well. Friends urged him to fly ; his Wife urged
him : ' Whither fly ? ' answered he : ' If freed France
cast me out, there are only dungeons for me elsewhere.
One carries not his country with him at the sole of his
shoe ! ' The man Danton sat still. Not even the arrestment of Friend Hérault, a member of *Salut*, yet arrested
by *Salut*, can rouse Danton.—On the night of the 30th
of March Juryman Pâris came rushing in ; haste
looking through his eyes : A clerk of the *Salut* Committee had told him Danton's warrant was made out,
he is to be arrested this very night ! Entreaties there
are and trepidation, of poor Wife, of Pâris and Friends :
Danton sat silent for a while ; then answered, ' *Ils
n'oseraient*, They dare not ' ; and would take no
measures. Murmuring ' They dare not ', he goes to
sleep as usual.

And yet, on the morrow morning, strange rumour
spreads over Paris City : Danton, Camille, Phélippeaux,
Lacroix have been arrested overnight ! It is verily so :
the corridors of the Luxembourg were all crowded,
Prisoners crowding forth to see this giant of the Revolution enter among them. ' Messieurs ', said Danton

[1] Biographie des Ministres, § Danton.

politely, ' I hoped soon to have got you all out of this :
but here I am myself ; and one sees not where it will
end '.—Rumour may spread over Paris : the Convention clusters itself into groups ; wide-eyed, whispering,
' Danton arrested ! ' Who then is safe ? Legendre,
mounting the Tribune, utters, at his own peril, a feeble
word for him ; moving that he be heard at that Bar
before indictment; but Robespierre frowns him down :
' Did you hear Chabot, or Bazire ? Would you have
two weights and measures ? ' Legendre cowers low :
Danton, like the others, must take his doom.

Danton's Prison-thoughts were curious to have ;
but are not given in any quantity : indeed few such
remarkable men have been left so obscure to us as this
Titan of the Revolution. He was heard to ejaculate :
' This time twelvemonth, I was moving the creation of
that same Revolutionary Tribunal. I crave pardon
for it of God and man. They are all Brothers Cain ;
Brissot would have had me guillotined as Robespierre
now will. I leave the whole business in a frightful
welter (*gâchis épouvantable*) : not one of them understands anything of government. Robespierre will
follow me ; I drag down Robespierre. O, it were
better to be a poor fisherman than to meddle with
governing of men '.—Camille's young beautiful Wife,
who had made him rich not in money alone, hovers
round the Luxembourg, like a disembodied spirit, day
and night. Camille's stolen letters to her still exist ;
stained with the mark of his tears.[1] ' I carry my head
like a Saint-Sacrament ? ' so Saint-Just was heard
to mutter : ' perhaps he will carry his like a Saint-
Dennis '.*

Unhappy Danton, thou still unhappier light Camille,
once light *Procureur de la Lanterne,* ye also have arrived,
then, at the Bourne of Creation, where, like Ulysses
Polytlas*at the limit and utmost Gades of his voyage,

---

[1] Aperçus sur Camille Desmoulins (in Vieux Cordelier,
Paris, 1825), pp. 1-29.

gazing into that dim Waste beyond Creation, a man
does see *the Shade of his Mother*, pale, ineffectual ;—and
days when his Mother nursed and wrapped him are
all too sternly contrasted with this day ! Danton,
Camille, Hérault, Westermann, and the others, very
strangely massed up with Bazires, Swindler Chabots,
Fabre d'Eglantines, Banker Freys, a most motley Batch,
'*Fournée*' as such things will be called, stand ranked
at the Bar of Tinville. It is the 2nd of April 1794.
Danton has had but three days to lie in Prison ; for the
time presses.

What is your name ? place of abode ? and the like,
Fouquier asks ; according to formality. ' My name is
Danton ', answers he ; ' a name tolerably known in the
Revolution : my abode will soon be Annihilation (*dans
le Néant*) ; but I shall live in the Pantheon of History '.
A man will endeavour to say something forcible, be it
by nature or not ! Hérault mentions epigrammatically
that he ' sat in this Hall, and was detested of Parlementeers '. Camille makes answer, ' My age is that of the
bon Sansculotte Jésus ; an age fatal to Revolutionists '.
O Camille, Camille ! And yet in that Divine Transaction,
let us say, there did lie, among other things, the fatallest
Reproof ever uttered here below to Worldly Right-
honourableness ; ' the highest fact ', so devout Novalis
calls it, ' in the Rights of Man '.* Camille's real age,
it would seem, is thirty-four. Danton is one year
older.

Some five months ago, the Trial of the Twenty-two
Girondins was the greatest that Fouquier had then
done. But here is a still greater to do ; a thing which
tasks the whole faculty of Fouquier ; which makes the
very heart of him waver. For it is the voice of Danton
that reverberates now from these domes ; in passionate
words, piercing with their wild sincerity, winged with
wrath.* Your best Witnesses he shivers into ruin at
one stroke. He demands that the Committee-men
themselves come as Witnesses, as Accusers ; he ' will
cover them with ignominy '. He raises his huge
stature, he shakes his huge black head, fire flashes from

the eyes of him,—piercing to all Republican hearts:
so that the very Galleries, though we filled them by
ticket, murmur sympathy; and are like to burst down,
and raise the People, and deliver him! He complains
loudly that he is classed with Chabots, with swindling
Stockjobbers; that his Indictment is a list of platitudes
and horrors. ' Danton hidden on the 10th of August ? '
reverberates he, with the roar of a lion in the toils:
' where are the men that had to press Danton to show
himself, that day ? Where are these high-gifted souls of
whom he borrowed energy ? Let them appear, these
Accusers of mine: I have all the clearness of my self-
possession when I demand them. I will unmask the
three shallow scoundrels ', *les trois plats coquins*, Saint-
Just, Couthon, Lebas, 'who fawn on Robespierre, and lead
him towards his destruction. Let them produce themselves here; I will plunge them into Nothingness, out of
which they ought never to have risen '. The agitated
President agitates his bell; enjoins calmness, in a
vehement manner: ' What is it to thee how I defend
myself ? ' cries the other: ' the right of *dooming* me is
thine always. The voice of a man speaking for his
honour and his life may well drown the jingling of thy
bell! ' Thus Danton, higher and higher; till the lion-
voice of him ' dies away in his throat ': speech will
not utter what is in that man. The Galleries murmur
ominously; the first day's Session is over.

O Tinville, President Herman, what will ye do ? They
have two days more of it, by strictest Revolutionary
Law. The Galleries already murmur. If this Danton
were to burst your meshwork!—Very curious indeed
to consider. It turns on a hair: and what a Hoitytoity
were *there*, Justice and Culprit changing places; and
the whole History of France running changed! For
in France there is this Danton only that could still try
to govern France. He only, the wild amorphous Titan;
—and perhaps that other olive-complexioned individual,
the Artillery-Officer at Toulon, whom we left pushing
his fortune in the South ?

On the evening of the second day, matters looking

not better but worse and worse, Fouquier and Herman,
distraction in their aspect, rush over to *Salut Public*.
What is to be done ? *Salut Public* rapidly concocts a
new Decree ; whereby if men 'insult Justice', they
may be 'thrown out of the Debates'. For indeed,
withal, is there not ' a Plot in the Luxembourg Prison ' ?
Ci-devant General Dillon, and others of the Suspect,
plotting with Camille's Wife to distribute *assignats* ;
to force the Prisons, overset the Republic ? Citizen
Laflotte, himself Suspect but desiring enfranchisement,
has reported said Plot for us :—a report that may bear
fruit ! Enough, on the morrow morning, an obedient
Convention passes this Decree. *Salut* rushes off with it
to the aid of Tinville, reduced now almost to extremities.
And so, *Hors de Débats*, Out of the Debates, ye insolents !
Policemen do your duty ! In such manner, with a
dead-lift effort, *Salut*, Tinville, Herman, Leroi *Dix-Août*,
and all stanch jurymen setting heart and shoulder to
it, the Jury becomes 'sufficiently instructed' ; Sentence is passed, is sent by an Official, and torn and
trampled on : *Death this day*. It is the 5th of April
1794. Camille's poor Wife may cease hovering about
this Prison. Nay, let her kiss her poor children ; and
prepare to enter it, and to follow !—

Danton carried a high look in the Death-cart. Not
so Camille : it is but one week, and all is so topsyturvied ;
angel Wife left weeping ; love, riches, Revolutionary
fame, left all at the Prison-gate ; carnivorous Rabble
now howling round. Palpable, and yet incredible ; like
a madman's dream ! Camille struggles and writhes ;
his shoulders shuffle the loose coat off them, which
hangs knotted, the hands tied : 'Calm, my friend ',
said Danton ; 'heed not that vile canaille (*laissez là
cette vile canaille*) '. At the foot of the Scaffold, Danton
was heard to ejaculate : ' O my Wife, my well-beloved,
I shall never see thee more then ! '—but, interrupting
himself : ' Danton, no weakness ! ' He said to Hérault-
Séchelles stepping forward to embrace him : ' Our
heads will meet *there* ', in the Headsman's sack. His
last words were to Samson the Headsman himself :

' Thou wilt show my head to the people ; it is worth showing '.

So passes, like a gigantic mass, of valour, ostentation, fury, affection and wild revolutionary force and manhood, this Danton, to his unknown home. He was of Arcis-sur-Aube ; born of ' good farmer-people ' there. He had many sins ; but one worst sin he had not, that of Cant. No hollow Formalist, deceptive and self-deceptive, *ghastly* to the natural sense, was this ; but a very Man : with all his dross he was a Man ; fiery-real, from the great fire-bosom of Nature herself. He saved France from Brunswick ; he walked straight his own wild road, whither it led him. He may live for some generations in the memory of men.

CHAPTER III

THE TUMBRILS

NEXT week, it is still but the 10th of April, there comes a new Nineteen ; Chaumette, Gobel, Hébert's Widow, the Widow of Camille : these also roll their fated journey ; black Death devours them. Mean Hébert's Widow was weeping, Camille's Widow tried to speak comfort to her. O ye kind Heavens, azure, beautiful, eternal behind your tempests and Time-clouds, is there not pity in store for all ! Gobel, it seems, was repentant ; he begged absolution of a Priest ; died as a Gobel best could. For Anaxagoras Chaumette, the sleek head now stript of its *bonnet rouge*, what hope is there ? Unless Death *were* ' an eternal sleep ' ? Wretched Anaxagoras, God shall judge thee, not I.

Hébert, therefore, is gone, and the Hébertists ; they that robbed Churches, and adored blue Reason in red nightcap. Great Danton, and the Dantonists ; they also are gone. Down to the catacombs ; they are become silent men ! Let no Paris Municipality, no Sect or Party of this hue or that, resist the will of Robespierre and *Salut*. Mayor Pache, not prompt

enough in denouncing these Pitt Plots, may congratulate
about them now. Never so heartily ; it skills not !
His course likewise is to the Luxembourg. We appoint
one Fleuriot-Lescot* Interim-Mayor in his stead : an
' architect from Belgium ', they say, this Fleuriot ; he
is a man one can depend on. Our new Agent-National
is Payan, lately Juryman ; whose cynosure also is
Robespierre.

Thus then, we perceive, this confusedly electric
Erebus-cloud of Revolutionary Government has altered
its shape somewhat. Two masses, or wings, belonging
to it ; an over-electric mass of Cordelier Rabids, and
an under-electric of Dantonist Moderates and Clemency-
men,—these two masses, shooting bolts at one another,
so to speak, have annihilated one another. For the
Erebus-cloud, as we often remark, is of suicidal nature ;
and, in jagged irregularity, darts its lightning withal
into itself. But now these two discrepant masses being
mutually annihilated, it is as if the Erebus-cloud had
got to internal composure ; and did only pour its hell-
fire lightning on the World that lay under it. In plain
words, Terror of the Guillotine was never terrible till
now. Systole, diastole, swift and ever swifter goes the
Axe of Samson. Indictments cease by degrees to have
so much as plausibility : Fouquier chooses from the
Twelve Houses of Arrest what he calls Batches, ' *Fournées* ', a score or more at a time ; his Jurymen are
charged to make *feu de file*, file-firing till the ground be
clear. Citizen Laflotte's report of Plot in the Luxembourg is verily bearing fruit ! If no speakable charge
exist against a man, or Batch of men, Fouquier has
always this : a Plot in the Prison. Swift and ever
swifter goes Samson ; up, finally, to three score and
more at a Batch. It is the highday of Death : none
but the Dead return not.

O dusky D'Espréménil, what a day is this, the 22nd of
April, thy last day ! The Palais Hall here is the same
stone Hall, where thou, five years ago, stoodest
perorating, amid endless pathos of rebellious Parlement,
in the grey of the morning ; bound to march with

D'Agoust to the Isles of Hières.   The stones are the
same stones : but the rest, Men, Rebellion, Pathos,
Peroration, see ! it has all fled, like a gibbering troop
of ghosts, like the phantasms of a dying brain.   With
D'Espréménil, in the same line of Tumbrils, goes the
mournfullest medley.   Chapelier goes, *ci-devant* popular
President of the Constituent ; whom the Menads and
Maillard met in his carriage, on the Versailles Road.
Thouret likewise, *ci-devant* President, father of Constitutional Law-acts ; he whom we heard saying, long
since, with a loud voice, ' The Constituent Assembly
has fulfilled its mission !' And the noble old Malesherbes,
who defended Louis and could not speak, like a grey old
rock dissolving into sudden water : he journeys here
now, with his kindred, daughters, sons and grandsons,
his   Lamoignons,   Châteaubriands ;   silent,   towards
Death.—One young Châteaubriand alone is wandering
amid the Natchez, by the roar of Niagara Falls, the
moan of endless forests : Welcome thou great Nature,
savage, but not false, not unkind, unmotherly ;   no
Formula thou, or rabid jangle of Hypothesis, Parliamentary   Eloquence,   Constitution-building   and   the
Guillotine ; speak thou to me, O Mother, and sing my
sick heart thy mystic everlasting lullaby-song, and let
all the rest be far !—

Another row of Tumbrils we must notice : that which
holds Elizabeth, the Sister of Louis.   Her Trial was
like the rest ; for Plots, for Plots.   She was among the
kindliest, most innocent of women.   There sat with her,
amid four-and-twenty others, a once timorous Mar-
chioness de Crussol ; courageous now ; expressing towards
her the liveliest loyalty.   At the foot of the Scaffold,
Elizabeth with tears in her eyes thanked this Mar-
chioness ; said she was grieved she could not reward her.
' Ah, Madame, would your Royal Highness deign to
embrace me, my wishes were complete ! '—' Right
willingly, Marquise de Crussol, and with my whole
heart '.[1]   Thus they : at the foot of the Scaffold.   The

[1] Montgaillard, iv. 200.

Royal Family is now reduced to two : a girl and a little
boy.* The boy, once named Dauphin, was taken from
his Mother while she yet lived ; and given to one
Simon, by trade a Cordwainer, on service then about
the Temple-Prison, to bring him up in principles of
Sansculottism. Simon taught him to drink, to swear,
to sing the *carmagnole*. Simon is now gone to the
Municipality : and the poor boy, hidden in a tower of
the Temple, from which in his fright and bewilderment
and early decrepitude he wishes not to stir out, lies
perishing, ' his shirt not changed for six months ' ;
amid squalor and darkness, lamentably,[1]—so as none but
poor Factory Children and the like are wont to perish,
and *not* be lamented !

The Spring sends its green leaves and bright weather,
bright May, brighter than ever : Death pauses not.
Lavoisier, famed Chemist, shall die and not live*:
Chemist Lavoisier was Farmer-General Lavoisier too,
and now ' all the Farmers-General are arrested ' ; all, and
shall give an account* of their moneys and incomings ;
and die for ' putting water in the tobacco ' they sold.[2]
Lavoisier begged a fortnight more of life, to finish some
experiments : but ' the Republic does not need such ' ;
the axe must do its work. Cynic Chamfort, reading
these inscriptions of *Brotherhood or Death*, says ' it is
a Brotherhood of Cain ' : arrested, then liberated ; then
about to be arrested again, this Chamfort cuts and
slashes himself with frantic uncertain hand ; gains, not
without difficulty, the refuge of death. Condorcet has
lurked deep, these many months ; Argus-eyes watching
and searching for him. His concealment is become
dangerous to others and himself ; he has to fly again,
to skulk, round Paris, in thickets and stone-quarries.
And so at the Village of Clamars, one bleared May
morning, there enters a Figure, ragged, rough-bearded,

[1] Duchesse d'Angoulême, Captivité à la Tour du Temple,
pp. 37–71.

[2] Tribunal Révolutionnaire, du 8 Mai 1794 (Moniteur,
No. 231).

hunger-stricken ; asks breakfast in the tavern there.
Suspect, by the look of him ! 'Servant out of place,
sayest thou ?' Committee-President of Forty-Sous
finds a Latin Horace on him : 'Art thou not one of
those *Ci-devants* that were wont to keep servants ?
Suspect !' He is haled forthwith, breakfast unfinished,
towards Bourg-la-Reine, on foot : he faints with exhaus-
tion ; is set on a peasant's horse ; is flung into his
damp prison-cell : on the morrow, recollecting him,
you enter ; Condorcet lies dead on the floor. They
die fast, and disappear : the Notabilities of France
disappear, one ofter one, like lights in a Theatre, which
you are snuffing out.

Under which circumstances, is it not singular, and
almost touching, to see Paris City drawn out, in the
meek May nights, in civic ceremony, which they call
'*Souper Fraternel*', Brotherly Supper ? Spontaneous ;
or partially spontaneous, in the twelfth, thirteenth,
fourteenth nights of this May month, it is seen. Along
the Rue Saint-Honoré, and main Streets and Spaces,
each Citoyen brings forth what of supper the stingy
Maximum has yielded him, to the open air ; joins it
to his neighbour's supper ; and with common table,
cheerful light burning frequent, and what due modicum
of cut-glass and other garnish and relish is convenient,
they eat frugally together, under the kind stars.[1] See
it, O Night ! With cheerfully pledged wine-cup, hobnobbing to the Reign of Liberty, Equality, Brotherhood,
with their wives in best ribands, with their little ones
romping round, the Citoyens, in frugal Love-feast, sit
there. Night in her wide empire sees nothing similar.
O my brothers, why is the reign of Brotherhood *not*
come ! It is come, it shall have come, say the Citoyens
frugally hobnobbing.—Ah me ! these everlasting stars,
do they not look down 'like glistening eyes, bright
with immortal pity, over the lot of man' !—*

----

[1] Tableaux de la Révolution, § Soupers Fraternels ;
Mercier, ii. 150.

One lamentable thing, however, is, that individuals will attempt assassination—of Representatives of the People. Representative Collot, Member even of *Salut*, returning home, ' about one in the morning ', probably touched with liquor, as he is apt to be, meets on the stairs the cry ' *Scélérat !* ' and also the snap of a pistol : which latter flashes in the pan ; disclosing to him, momentarily, a pair of truculent saucer-eyes, swart grim-clenched countenance ; recognizable as that of our little fellow-lodger, Citoyen Amiral, formerly ' a clerk in the Lotteries ' ! Collot shouts *Murder*, with lungs fit to awaken all the *Rue Favart* ; Amiral snaps a second time ; a second time flashes in the pan ; then darts up into his apartment ; and, after there firing, still with inadequate effect, one musket at himself and another at his captor, is clutched and locked in Prison.[1] An indignant little man this Amiral, of Southern temper and complexion, of ' considerable muscular force '. He denies not that he meant to ' purge France of a Tyrant '; nay avows that he had an eye to the Incorruptible himself, but took Collot as more convenient !

Rumour enough hereupon ; heaven-high congratulation of Collot, fraternal embracing, at the Jacobins and elsewhere. And yet, it would seem, the assassin mood proves catching. Two days more, it is still but the 23rd of May, and towards nine in the evening, Cécile Rénault, Paper-dealer's daughter, a young woman of soft blooming look, presents herself at the Cabinetmaker's in the Rue Saint-Honoré ; desires to see Robespierre. Robespierre cannot be seen ; she grumbles irreverently. They lay hold of her. She has left a basket in a shop hard by : in the basket are female change of raiment and two knives ! Poor Cécile, examined by Committee, declares she ' wanted to see what a tyrant was like ' : the change of raiment was ' for my own use in the place I am surely going to '.— ' What place ? '—' Prison ; and then the Guillotine ', answered she.—Such things come of Charlotte Corday ;

---

[1] Riouffe, p. 73 ; Deux Amis, xii. 298–302.

in a people prone to imitation, and monomania ! Swart
choleric men try Charlotte's feat, and their pistols miss
fire ; soft blooming young women try it, and, only half-
resolute, leave their knives in a shop.

O Pitt, and ye Faction of the Stranger, shall the
Republic never have rest ; but be torn continually by
baited springes, by wires of explosive spring-guns ?
Swart Amiral, fair young Cécile, and all that knew
them, and many that did not know them, lie locked,
waiting the scrutiny of Tinville.

CHAPTER IV

MUMBO-JUMBO

BUT on the day they call *Décadi*, New-Sabbath,
20 *Prairial*, 8th June by old style, what thing is this
going forward in the Jardin National, whilom Tuileries
Garden ?

All the world is there, in holyday clothes :[1] foul
linen went out with the Hébertists ; nay Robespierre,
for one, would never once countenance that ; but went
always elegant and frizzled, not without vanity even,—
and had his room hung round with seagreen Portraits
and Busts. In holyday clothes, we say, are the innumerable Citoyens and Citoyennes : the weather is of the
brightest ; cheerful expectation lights all countenances.
Juryman Vilate*gives breakfast to many a Deputy, in
his official Apartment, in the Pavillon *ci-devant* of
Flora ; rejoices in the bright-looking multitudes, in the
brightness of leafy June, in the auspicious *Décadi*, or
New-Sabbath. This day, if it please Heaven, we are
to have, on improved Anti-Chaumette principles : a
New Religion.

Catholicism being burned out, and Reason-worship
guillotined, was there not need of one ? Incorruptible

---

[1] Vilate, *Causes Secrètes de la Révolution du 9 Thermidor.*

Robespierre, not unlike the Ancients, as Legislator of
a free people, will now also be Priest and Prophet. He
has donned his sky-blue coat, made for the occasion ;
white silk waistcoat broidered with silver, black silk
breeches, white stockings, shoe-buckles of gold. He
is President of the Convention ; he has made the Convention *decree*, so they name it, *décréter* the ' Existence
of the Supreme Being ', and likewise ' *ce principe con-
solateur* of the Immortality of the Soul '. These consolatory principles, the basis of rational Republican
Religion, are getting decreed ; and here, on this blessed
Décadi, by help of Heaven and Painter David, is to be
our first act of worship.

See, accordingly, how after Decree passed, and what
has been called ' the scraggiest Prophetic Discourse ever
uttered by man ',—Mahomet Robespierre, in sky-blue
coat and black breeches, frizzled and powdered to
perfection, bearing in his hand a bouquet of flowers and
wheat-ears, issues proudly from the Convention Hall ;
Convention following him, yet, as is remarked, with
an interval. Amphitheatre has been raised, or at least
Monticule or Elevation ; hideous Statues of Atheism,
Anarchy and such like, thanks to Heaven and Painter
David, strike abhorrence into the heart. Unluckily,
however, our Monticule is too small. On the top of it
not half of us can stand ; wherefore there arises indecent
shoving, nay treasonous irreverent growling. Peace,
thou Bourdon de l'Oise ; peace, or it may be worse for
thee !

The seagreen Pontiff takes a torch, Painter David
handing it ; mouths some other froth-rant of vocables,
which happily one cannot hear ; strides resolutely
forward, in sight of expectant France ; sets his torch
to Atheism and Company, which are but made of pasteboard steeped in turpentine. They burn up rapidly ;
and, from within, there rises ' by machinery ', an incom-
bustible Statue of Wisdom, which, by ill hap, gets
besmoked a little ; but does stand there visible in as
serene attitude as it can.

And then ? Why, then, there is other Processioning,
scraggy Discoursing, and—this *is* our Feast of the *Être
Suprême*; our new Religion, better or worse, is come !
—Look at it one moment, O Reader, not two. The
shabbiest page of Human Annals : or is there, that thou
wottest of, one shabbier ? Mumbo-Jumbo of the African
woods to me seems venerable beside this new Deity of
Robespierre; for this is a *conscious* Mumbo-Jumbo,
and *knows* that he is machinery. O seagreen Prophet,
unhappiest of windbags blown nigh to bursting, what
distracted Chimera among realities art thou growing to !
This then, this common pitch-link for artificial fire-
works of turpentine and pasteboard ; *this* is the miraculous Aaron's Rod thou wilt stretch over a hag-ridden
hell-ridden France, and bid her plagues cease ? Vanish,
thou and it !—' *Avec ton Être Suprême* ', said Billaud,
' *tu commences m'embêter :* With thy *Être Suprême* thou
beginnest to be a bore to me '.[1]

Catherine Théot, on the other hand, ' an ancient serv-
ing-maid seventy-nine years of age ', inured to Prophecy
and the Bastille from of old, sits in an upper room in
the Rue de Contrescarpe, poring over the Book of
Revelations, with an eye to Robespierre ; finds that
this astonishing thrice-potent Maximilien really is the
Man spoken of by Prophets, who is to make the Earth
young again. With her sit devout old Marchionesses,
ci-devant honourable women ; among whom Old-
Constituent Dom Gerle, with his addle head, cannot be
wanting. They sit there, in the Rue de Contrescarpe ;
in mysterious adoration : Mumbo is Mumbo, and Robespierre is his Prophet. A conspicuous man .this Robespierre. He has his volunteer Bodyguard of *Tappe-durs*,
let us say *Strike-sharps*, fierce Patriots with feruled
sticks ; and Jacobins kissing the hem of his garment.
He enjoys the admiration of many, the worship of some ;
and is well worth the wonder of one and all.

[1] See Vilate, Causes Secrètes. (Vilate's Narrative is
very curious ; but is not to be taken as true, without
sifting ; being, at bottom, in spite of its title, not a Narrative but a Pleading.)

The grand question and hope, however, is : Will not
this Feast of the Tuileries Mumbo-Jumbo be a sign
perhaps that the Guillotine is to abate ? Far enough
from that ! Precisely on the second day after it,
Couthon, one of the ' three shallow scoundrels ', gets
himself lifted into the Tribune ; produces a bundle of
papers. Couthon proposes that, as Plots still abound,
the *Law of the Suspect* shall have extension, and
Arrestment new vigour and facility. Further that, as
in such case business is like to be heavy, our Revolutionary Tribunal too shall have extension ; be divided,
say, into Four Tribunals, each with its President, each
with its Fouquier or Substitute of Fouquier, all labouring
at once, and any remnant of shackle or dilatory formality
be struck off : in this way it may perhaps still overtake
the work. Such is Couthon's *Decree of the Twenty-
second Prairial,** famed in those times. At hearing of
which Decree, the very Mountain gasped, awestruck ;
and one Ruamps ventured to say that if it passed without adjournment and discussion, he, as one Representative, ' would blow his brains out '. Vain saying ! The
Incorruptible knit his brows ; spoke a prophetic fateful
word or two : the *Law of Prairial* is Law ; Ruamps
glad to leave his rash brains where they are. Death
then, and always Death ! Even so. Fouquier is enlarg-
ing his borders ; making room for Batches of a Hundred
and fifty at once ;—getting a Guillotine set up of
improved velocity, and to work under cover, in the
apartment close by. So that *Salut* itself has to intervene, and forbid him : ' Wilt thou *demoralize* the
Guillotine', asks Collot, reproachfully, '*démoraliser le
supplice !* '

There is indeed danger of that ; were not the Republican faith great, it were already done. See, for
example, on the 17th of June, what a *Batch*, Fifty-four
at once ! Swart Amiral is here, he of the pistol that
missed fire ; young Cécile Rénault, with her father,
family, entire kith and kin ; the Widow of D'Espréménil ; old M. de Sombreuil of the Invalides, with his
Son,—poor old Sombreuil, seventy-three years old, his

Daughter saved him in September, and it was but for *this*. Faction of the Stranger, fifty-four of them! In red shirts and smocks, as Assassins and Faction of the Stranger, they flit along there; red baleful Phantasmagory, towards the land of Phantoms.

Meanwhile will not the people of the Place de la Révolution, the inhabitants along the Rue Saint-Honoré as these continual Tumbrils pass, begin to look gloomy? Republicans too have bowels. The Guillotine is shifted, then again shifted; finally set up at the remote extremity of the Southeast:[1] Suburbs Saint-Antoine and Saint-Marceau, it is to be hoped, if they have bowels, have very tough ones.

CHAPTER V

THE PRISONS

It is time now, however, to cast a glance into the Prisons. When Desmoulins moved for his Committee of Mercy, these Twelve Houses of Arrest held five-thousand persons. Continually arriving since then, there have now accumulated twelve-thousand. They are Ci-devants, Royalists; in far greater part, they are Republicans, of various Girondin, Fayettish, Un-Jacobin colour. Perhaps no human Habitation or Prison ever equalled in squalor, in noisome horror, these Twelve Houses of Arrest. There exist records of personal experience in them, *Mémoires sur les Prisons*; one of the strangest Chapters in the Biography of Man.

Very singular to look into it: how a kind of order rises up in all conditions of human existence; and wherever two or three are gathered together, there are formed modes of existing together, habitudes, observances, nay gracefulnesses, joys! Citoyen Coittant will explain fully how our lean dinner, of herbs and carrion,

---

[1] Montgaillard, iv. 237.

was consumed not without politeness and *place-aux-dames*: how Seigneur and Shoeblack, Duchess and Doll-Tearsheet,* flung pell-mell into a heap, ranked themselves according to method: at what hour 'the Citoyennes took to their needlework'; and we, yielding the chairs to them, endeavoured to talk gallantly in a standing posture, or even to sing and harp more or less. Jealousies, enmities, are not wanting; nor flirtations, of an effective character.

Alas, by degrees, even needlework must cease: Plot in the Prison rises, by Citoyen Laflotte and Preternatural Suspicion. Suspicious Municipality snatches from us all implements; all money and possession, of means or metal, is ruthlessly searched for, in pocket, in pillow and paillasse, and snatched away; red-capped Commissaries entering every cell. Indignation, temporary desperation, at robbery of its very thimble, fills the gentle heart. Old Nuns shriek shrill discord; demand to be killed forthwith. No help from shrieking! Better was that of the two shifty male Citizens, who, eager to preserve an implement or two, were it but a pipe-picker, or needle to darn hose with, determined to defend themselves: by tobacco. Swift then, as your fell Red Caps are heard in the Corridor rummaging and slamming, the two Citoyens light their pipes, and begin smoking. Thick darkness envelops them. The Red Nightcaps, opening the cell, breathe but one mouthful; burst forth into chorus of barking and coughing. '*Quoi, Messieurs*', cry the two Citoyens, 'you don't smoke? Is the pipe disagreeable? *Est-ce que vous ne fumez pas?*' But the Red Nightcaps have fled, with slight search: '*Vous n'aimez pas la pipe?*' cry the Citoyens, as their door slams-to again.[1] My poor brother Citoyens, O surely, in a reign of Brotherhood, you are not the two I would guillotine!

Rigour grows, stiffens into horrid tyranny; Plot in the Prison getting ever rifer. This Plot in the Prison,

---

[1] Maison d'Arrêt de Port-Libre, par Coittant, &c. (Mémoires sur les Prisons, ii.).

as we said, is now the stereotype formula of Tinville : against whomsoever he knows no crime, this is a ready-made crime. His Judgement-bar has become unspeakable ; a recognized mockery ; known only as the wicket one passes through, towards Death. His Indictments are drawn out in blank ; you insert the Names after. He has his *moutons*, detestable traitor jackals, who report and bear witness ; that they themselves may be allowed to live,—for a time. His *Fournées*, says the reproachful Collot, ' shall in no case exceed threescore ' ; that is his *maximum*. Nightly come his Tumbrils to the Luxembourg, with the fatal Roll-call ; list of the *Fournée* of to-morrow. Men rush towards the Grate ; listen, if their name be in it ? One deep-drawn breath, when the name is not in ; we live still one day ! And yet some score or scores of names were in. Quick these, they clasp their loved ones to their heart, one last time ; with brief adieu, wet-eyed or dry-eyed, they mount, and are away. This night to the Conciergerie ; through the Palais misnamed *of Justice*, to the Guillotine, to-morrow.

Recklessness, defiant levity, the Stoicism if not of strength yet of weakness, has possessed all hearts. Weak women and *Ci-devants*, their locks not yet made into blond perukes, their skins not yet tanned into breeches, are accustomed to ' act the Guillotine ' by way of pastime. In fantastic mummery, with towel-turbans, blanket-ermine, a mock Sanhedrim of Judges sits, a mock Tinville pleads ; a culprit is doomed, is guillotined by the oversetting of two chairs. Sometimes we carry it further : Tinville himself, in his turn, is doomed, and not to the Guillotine alone. With blackened face, hirsute, horned, a shaggy Satan snatches him not unshrieking ; shows him, with outstretched arm and voice, the fire that is not quenched, the worm that dies not ; the monotony of Hell-pain, and the *What hour ?* answered by, *It is Eternity.*[1]

And still the Prisons fill fuller, and still the Guillotine

---

[1] Montgaillard, iv. 218 ; Riouffe, p. 273.

goes faster. On all high roads march flights of Prisoners,
wending towards Paris. Not *Ci-devants* now ; they, the
noisy of them, are mown down; it is Republicans
now. Chained two and two they march; in exasperated
moments singing their *Marseillaise*. A hundred and
thirty-two men of Nantes, for instance, march towards
Paris, in these same days : Republicans, or say even
Jacobins to the marrow of the bone ; but Jacobins who
had not approved Noyading.[1] *Vive la République* rises
from them in all streets of towns : they rest by night in
unutterable noisome dens, crowded to choking ; one or
two dead on the morrow. They are wayworn, weary
of heart ; can only shout : *Live the Republic* ; we, as
under horrid enchantment, dying in this way for it !

Some Four-hundred Priests, of whom also there is
record, ride at anchor, ' in the roads of the Isle of Aix ',
long months ; looking out on misery, vacuity, waste
Sands of Oleron and the ever-moaning brine. Ragged,
sordid, hungry ; wasted to shadows : eating their unclean ration on deck, circularly, in parties of a dozen,
with finger and thumb ; beating their scandalous
clothes between two stones ; choked in horrible mias-
mata, closed under hatches, seventy of them in a berth,
through night ; so that the ' aged Priest is found lying
dead in the morning, in the attitude of prayer ' ![2]—
How long, O Lord !*

Not for ever; no. All Anarchy, all Evil, Injustice,
is, by the nature of it, *dragon's-teeth*; suicidal, and
cannot endure.

[1] Voyage de Cent Trente-deux Nantais (Prisons, ii. 288–
335).

[2] Relation de ce qu'ont souffert pour la Religion les
Prêtres déportés en 1794, dans la rade de l'île d'Aix (Prisons,
ii. 387–485).

CHAPTER VI

TO FINISH THE TERROR

It is very remarkable, indeed, that since the *Être-Suprême* Feast, and the sublime continued harangues on it, which Billaud feared would become a bore to him, Robespierre has gone little to Committee; but held himself apart, as if in a kind of pet. Nay they have made a Report on that old Catherine Théot, and her Regenerative Man spoken of by the Prophets; not in the best spirit. This Théot mystery they affect to regard as a Plot; but have evidently introduced a vein of satire, of irreverent banter, not against the Spinster alone, but obliquely against her Regenerative Man! Barrère's light pen was perhaps at the bottom of it: read through the solemn snuffling organs of old Vadier of the *Sûreté Générale*, the Théot Report had its effect; wrinkling the general Republican visage into an iron grin. Ought these things to be?

We note further, that among the Prisoners in the Twelve Houses of Arrest, there is one whom we have seen before. Senhora Fontenai, *born* Cabarus, the fair Proserpine whom Representative Tallien Pluto-like did gather at Bordeaux, not without effect on himself! Tallien is home, by recall, long since, from Bordeaux; and in the most alarming position. Vain that he sounded, louder even than ever, the note of Jacobinism, to hide past shortcomings: the Jacobins purged him out; two times has Robespierre growled at him words of omen from the Convention Tribune. And now his fair Cabarus, hit by denunciation, lies Arrested, Suspect, in spite of all he could do!—Shut in horrid pinfold of death, the Senhora smuggles out to her red-gloomy Tallien the most pressing entreaties and conjurings: Save me; save thyself. Seest thou not that thy own head is doomed; thou with a too fiery audacity; a Dantonist withal; against whom lie grudges?

Are ye not all doomed, as in the Polyphemus Cavern*:
the fawningest slave of you will be but eaten last !—
Tallien feels with a shudder that it is true. Tallien has
had words of omen, Bourdon has had words, Fréron is
hated and Barras : each man ' feels his head if it yet
stick on his shoulders '.

Meanwhile Robespierre, we still observe, goes little
to Convention, not at all to Committee ; speaks nothing
except to his Jacobin House of Lords, amid his bodyguard of *Tappe-durs*. These ' forty-days ', for we are
now far in July, he has not showed face in Committee ;
could only work there by his three shallow scoundrels,
and the terror there was of him. The Incorruptible
himself sits apart ; or is seen stalking in solitary places
in the fields, with an intensely meditative air ; some
say, ' with eyes red-spotted ',[1] fruit of extreme bile :
the lamentablest seagreen Chimera that walks the
Earth that July ! O hapless Chimera ; for thou too
hadst a life, and heart of flesh,—what is this that the
stern gods, seeming to smile all the way, have led and
let thee to ! Art not thou he, who, few years ago, was
a young Advocate of promise ; and gave up the Arras
Judgeship rather than sentence one man to die ?—

What his thoughts might be ? His plans for finishing
the Terror ? One knows not. Dim vestiges there flit
of Agrarian Law ; a victorious Sansculottism become
Landed Proprietor ; old Soldiers sitting in National
Mansions, in Hospital Palaces of Chambord and Chantilly ; peace bought by victory ; breaches healed by
Feast of *Être Suprême* ;—and so, through seas of blood,
to Equality, Frugality, worksome Blessedness, Fraternity, and Republic of the virtues. Blessed shore, of
such a sea of Aristocrat blood : but how to land on it ?
Through one last wave : blood of corrupt Sansculot-
tists ; traitorous or semi-traitorous Conventionals, rebellious Talliens, Billauds, to whom with my *Être
Suprême* I have become a bore ; with my Apocalyptic
Old Woman a laughing-stock !—So stalks he, this poor

[1] Deux Amis, xii. 347–73.

Robespierre, like a seagreen ghost, through the blooming July. Vestiges of schemes flit dim. But *what* his schemes or his thoughts were will never be known to man.

New Catacombs, some say, are digging for a huge simultaneous butchery. Convention to be butchered, down to the right pitch, by General Henriot and Company: Jacobin House of Lords made dominant; and Robespierre Dictator.[1] There is actually, or else there is not actually, a List made out; which the Hairdresser has got eye on, as he frizzled the Incorruptible locks. Each man asks himself, Is it I ?

Nay, as Tradition and rumour of Anecdote still convey it, there was a remarkable bachelor's dinner, one hot day, at Barrère's. For doubt not, O Reader, this Barrère and others of them gave dinners; had ' country-house at Clichy ', with elegant enough sumptuosities, and pleasures high-rouged.[2] But at this dinner we speak of, the day being so hot, it is said, the guests all stript their coats, and left them in the drawing-room: whereupon Carnot glided out; groped in Robespierre's pocket; found a list of Forty, his own name among them; and tarried not at the wine-cup that day !*— Ye must bestir yourselves, O Friends; ye dull Frogs of the Marsh, mute ever since Girondism sank under, even you now must croak or die ! Councils are held, with word and beck; nocturnal, mysterious as death. Does not a feline Maximilien stalk there; voiceless as yet; his green eyes red-spotted; back bent, and hair up ? Rash Tallien, with his rash temper and audacity of tongue; he shall *bell the cat.** Fix a day; and be it soon, lest never !

Lo, before the fixed day, on the day which they call Eighth of Thermidor, 26th July 1794, Robespierre himself reappears in Convention; mounts to the Tribune ! The biliary face seems clouded with new gloom : judge whether your Talliens, Bourdons, listened with interest. It is a voice bodeful of death or of life. Long-winded,

---

[1] Deux Amis, xii. 350–8.   [2] See Vilate.

unmelodious as the screech-owl's, sounds that prophetic
voice : Degenerate condition of Republican spirit ; corrupt Moderatism ; *Sûreté*, *Salut* Committees themselves infected ; backsliding on this hand and on that ;
I, Maximilien, alone left incorruptible, ready to die at
a moment's warning. For all which what remedy is
there ? The Guillotine ; new vigour to the all-healing
Guillotine ; death to traitors of every hue ! So sings
the prophetic voice ; into its Convention sounding-
board. The old song this : but to-day, O Heavens !
has the sounding-board ceased to act ? There is not
resonance in this Convention ; there is, so to speak,
a gasp of silence ; nay a certain grating of one knows
not what !—Lecointre, our old Draper of Versailles, in
these questionable circumstances, sees nothing he can
do so safe as rise, ' insidiously ' or not insidiously, and
move, according to established wont, that the Robespierre Speech be ' printed and sent to the Departments '.
Hark : gratings, even of dissonance ! Honourable Members hint dissonance ; Committee-Members, inculpated
in the Speech, utter dissonance, demand ' delay in
printing '. Ever higher rises the note of dissonance ;
inquiry is even made by Editor Fréron : ' What has
become of the Liberty of Opinions in this Convention ? '
The Order to print and transmit, which had got passed,
is rescinded. Robespierre, greener than ever before, has
to retire, foiled ; discerning that it is mutiny, that evil
is nigh !

Mutiny is a thing of the fatallest nature in all enterprises whatsoever ; a thing so incalculable, swift-fright-
ful : not to be dealt with in *fright*. But mutiny in a
Robespierre Convention, above all,—it is like fire seen
sputtering in the ship's powder-room ! One death-
defiant plunge at it, this moment, and you may still
tread it out : hesitate till next moment,—ship and
ship's captain, crew and cargo are shivered far ; the
ship's voyage has suddenly ended between sea and sky.
If Robespierre can, to-night, produce his Henriot and
Company, and get his work done by them, he and Sans-

culottism may still subsist some time ; if not, probably
not. Oliver Cromwell, when that Agitator Sergeant
stept forth from the ranks, with plea of grievances, and
began gesticulating and demonstrating, as the mouth-
piece of Thousands expectant there,—discerned, with
those truculent eyes of his, how the matter lay ; plucked
a pistol from his holsters ; blew Agitator and Agitation
instantly out. Noll was a man fit for such things.*

Robespierre, for his part, glides over at evening to
his Jacobin House of Lords ; unfolds there, instead of
some adequate resolution, his woes, his uncommon
virtues, incorruptibilities ; then, secondly, his rejected
screech-owl Oration ;—reads this latter over again ; and
declares that he is ready to die at a moment's warning.
Thou shalt not die ! shouts Jacobinism from its thousand throats. 'Robespierre, I will drink the hemlock
with thee ', cries Painter David, ' *Je boirai la cigue avec
toi* ' ;—a thing not essential to *do*, but which, in the fire
of the moment, can be said.

Our Jacobin sounding-board, therefore, does act !
Applauses heaven-high cover the rejected Oration ; fire-
eyed fury lights all Jacobin features : Insurrection a
sacred duty ; the Convention to be purged ; Sovereign
People under Henriot and Municipality ; we will make
a new June-Second of it : To your tents, O Israel ! In
this key pipes Jacobinism ; in sheer tumult of revolt.
Let Tallien and all Opposition men make off. Collot
d'Herbois, though of the supreme *Salut*, and so lately
near shot, is elbowed, bullied ; is glad to escape alive.
Entering Committee-room of *Salut*, all dishevelled, he
finds sleek sombre Saint-Just there, among the rest ;
who in his sleek way asks, 'What is passing at the
Jacobins ? '—' What is passing ? ' repeats Collot, in the
unhistrionic Cambyses' vein : ' What is passing ? Nothing but revolt and horrors are passing. Ye want our
lives ; ye shall not have them '. Saint-Just stutters at
such Cambyses-oratory ; takes his hat to withdraw.
That *Report* he had been speaking of, Report on Republican Things in General we may say, which is to be read
in Convention on the morrow, he cannot show it them,

at this moment: a friend has it; he, Saint-Just, will
get it, and send it, were he once home. Once home, he
sends not it, but an answer that he will not send it; that
they will hear it from the Tribune to-morrow.

Let every man, therefore, according to a well-known
good-advice, 'pray to Heaven, and keep his powder
dry'!* Paris, on the morrow, will see a thing. Swift
scouts fly dim or invisible, all night, from *Sûreté* and
Salut; from conclave to conclave; from Mother-
Society to Townhall. Sleep, can it fall on the eyes of
Talliens, Frérons, Collots? Puissant Henriot, Mayor
Fleuriot, Judge Coffinhal, Procureur Payan, Robespierre and all the Jacobins are getting ready.

CHAPTER VII

GO DOWN TO

TALLIEN'S eyes beamed bright, on the morrow, Ninth
of Thermidor 'about nine o'clock', to see that the
Convention had actually met. Paris is in rumour: but
at least we are met, in Legal Convention here; we have
not been snatched seriatim; treated with a *Pride's
Purge**at the door. '*Allons*, brave men of the Plain',
late Frogs of the Marsh! cried Tallien with a squeeze
of the hand, as he passed in; Saint-Just's sonorous
voice being now audible from the Tribune, and the game
of games begun.

Saint-Just is verily reading that Report of his; green
Vengeance, in the shape of Robespierre, watching nigh.
Behold, however, Saint-Just has read but few sentences,
when interruption rises, rapid *crescendo*; when Tallien
starts to his feet, and Billaud, and this man starts and
that,—and Tallien, a second time, with his: 'Citoyens,
at the Jacobins last night, I trembled for the Republic.
I said to myself, if the Convention dare not strike the
Tyrant, then I myself dare; and with this I will do it,
if need be', said he, whisking out a clear-gleaming

Dagger, and brandishing it there; the Steel of Brutus, as we call it. Whereat we all bellow, and brandish, impetuous acclaim. 'Tyranny! Dictatorship! Triumvirate!' And the *Salut* Committee-men accuse, and all men accuse, and uproar, and impetuously acclaim. And Saint-Just is standing motionless, pale of face; Couthon ejaculating, 'Triumvir?' with a look at his paralytic legs. And Robespierre is struggling to speak, but President Thuriot is jingling the bell against him, but the Hall is sounding against him like an Aeolus-Hall: and Robespierre is mounting the Tribune-steps and descending again; going and coming, like to choke with rage, terror, desperation:—and mutiny is the order of the day! [1]

O President Thuriot, thou that wert Elector Thuriot, and from the Bastille battlements sawest Saint-Antoine rising like the Ocean-tide, and hast seen much since, sawest thou ever the like of this? Jingle of bell, which thou jinglest against Robespierre, is hardly audible amid the Bedlam-storm; and men rage for life. 'President of Assassins', shrieks Robespierre, 'I demand speech of thee for the last time!' It cannot be had. 'To you, O virtuous men of the Plain', cries he, finding audience one moment, 'I appeal to you!' The virtuous men of the Plain sit silent as stones. And Thuriot's bell jingles, and the Hall sounds like Aeolus's Hall. Robespierre's frothing lips are grown 'blue'; his tongue dry, cleaving to the roof of his mouth. 'The blood of Danton chokes him', cry they. 'Accusation! Decree of Accusation!' Thuriot swiftly puts that question. Accusation passes; the incorruptible Maximilien is decreed Accused.

'I demand to share my Brother's fate, as I have striven to share his virtues', cries Augustin, the Younger Robespierre: Augustin also is decreed. And Couthon, and Saint-Just, and Lebas, they are all decreed; and packed forth,—not without difficulty, the Ushers almost

[1] Moniteur, Nos. 311, 312; Débats, iv. 421-42; Deux Amis, xii. 390-411.

trembling to obey. Triumvirate and Company are
packed forth, into *Salut* Committee-room ; their tongue
cleaving to the roof of their mouth. You have but to
summon the Municipality ; to cashier Commandant
Henriot, and launch Arrest at him ; to regulate formalities ; hand Tinville his victims. It is noon : the
Aeolus-Hall has delivered itself ; blows now victorious,
harmonious, as one irresistible wind.

And so the work is finished ? One thinks so : and
yet it is not so. Alas, there is yet but the first-act
finished ; three or four other acts still to come ; and an
uncertain catastrophe ! A huge City holds in it so many
confusions : seven hundred thousand human heads ;
not one of which knows what its neighbour is doing,
nay not what itself is doing.—See, accordingly, about
three in the afternoon, Commandant Henriot, how in-.
stead of sitting cashiered, arrested, he gallops along the
Quais, followed by Municipal Gendarmes, ' trampling
down several persons ! ' For the Townhall sits deliberating, openly insurgent : Barriers to be shut ; no Jailor
to admit any Prisoner this day ;—and Henriot is galloping towards the Tuileries, to deliver Robespierre. On
the Quai de la Ferraillerie, a young Citoyen, walking
with his wife, says aloud : ' Gendarmes, that man is not
your Commandant ; he is under arrest '. The Gendarmes strike down the young Citoyen with the flat of
their swords.[1]

Representatives themselves (as Merlin the Thionviller), who accost him, this puissant Henriot flings into
guardhouses. He bursts towards the Tuileries Committee-room, ' to speak with Robespierre ' : with difficulty, the Ushers and Tuileries Gendarmes, earnestly
pleading and drawing sabre, seize this Henriot ; get the
Henriot Gendarmes persuaded not to fight ; get Robespierre and Company packed into hackney-coaches, sent
off under escort, to the Luxembourg and other Prisons.
This then *is* the end ? May not an exhausted Conven-

---

[1] Précis des événemens du Neuf Thermidor ; par C. A.
Méda, ancien Gendarme (Paris, 1825).

tion adjourn now, for a little repose and sustenance, ' at five o'clock ' ?

An exhausted Convention did it ; and repented it. The end was not come ; only the end of the *second-act.* Hark, while exhausted Representatives sit at victuals, —tocsin bursting from all steeples, drums rolling, in the summer evening : Judge Coffinhal is galloping with new Gendarmes, to deliver Henriot from Tuileries Committee-room ; and does deliver him ! Puissant Henriot vaults on horseback ; sets to haranguing the Tuileries Gendarmes ; corrupts the Tuileries Gendarmes too ; trots off with them to Townhall. Alas, and Robespierre is not in Prison : the Jailor showed his Municipal order, durst not, on pain of his life, admit any Prisoner ; the Robespierre hackney-coaches, in this confused jangle and whirl of uncertain Gendarmes, have floated safe— into the Townhall ! There sit Robespierre and Company, embraced by Municipals and Jacobins, in sacred right of Insurrection ; redacting Proclamations ; sounding tocsins ; corresponding with Sections and Mother-Society. Is not here a pretty enough third-act of a *natural* Greek Drama ; catastrophe more uncertain than ever ?

The hasty Convention rushes together again, in the ominous nightfall : President Collot, for the chair is his, enters with long strides, paleness on his face ; claps on his hat ; says with solemn tone : ' Citoyens, armed Villains have beset the Committee-rooms, and got possession of them. The hour is come, to die at our post ! ' ' *Oui* ', answer one and all : ' We swear it ! ' It is no rhodomontade, this time, but a sad fact and necessity ; unless we *do* at our posts, we must verily die. Swift therefore, Robespierre, Henriot, the Municipality, are declared Rebels ; put *Hors la Loi*, Out of Law. Better still, we appoint Barras Commandant of what Armed-force is to be had ; send Missionary Representatives to all Sections and quarters, to preach, and raise force ; will die at least with harness on our back.*

What a distracted City ; men riding and running, reporting and hearsaying ; the Hour clearly in travail,

—child not to be *named* till born ! The poor Prisoners
in the Luxembourg hear the rumour ; tremble for a new
September. They see men making signals to them, on
skylights and roofs, apparently signals of hope ; cannot
in the least make out what it is.[1] We observe, however,
in the eventide, as usual, the Death-tumbrils faring
Southeastward, through Saint-Antoine, towards their
Barrier du Trône. Saint-Antoine's tough bowels melt ;
Saint-Antoine surrounds the Tumbrils ; says, It shall
not be. O Heavens, why should it ! Henriot and Gendarmes, scouring the streets that way, bellow, with
waved sabres, that it must. Quit hope, ye poor Doomed !
The Tumbrils move on.

But in this set of Tumbrils there are two other things
notable : one notable person ; and one want of a notable
person. The notable person is Lieutenant-General
Loiserolles, a nobleman by birth and by nature ; laying
down his life here for his son. In the Prison of Saint-
Lazare, the night before last, hurrying to the Grate to
hear the Death-list read, he caught the name of his son.
The son was asleep at the moment. ' I am Loiserolles ',
cried the old man : at Tinville's bar, an error in the
Christian name is little ; small objection was made.—
The want of the notable person, again, is that of
Deputy Paine ! Paine has sat in the Luxembourg since
January ; and seemed forgotten ; but Fouquier had
pricked him at last. The Turnkey, List in hand, is mark-
ing with chalk the outer doors of to-morrow's *Fournée.*
Paine's outer door happened to be open, turned back
on the wall ; the Turnkey marked it on the side next
him, and hurried on : another Turnkey came, and shut
it ; no chalk-mark now visible, the *Fournée* went without Paine. Paine's life lay not there.—

Our fifth-act, of this natural Greek Drama, with its
natural unities, can only be painted in gross ; somewhat
as that antique Painter, driven desperate, did the *foam.*[*]
For through this blessed July night, there is clangour,
confusion very great, of marching troops ; of Sections
going this way, Sections going that ; of Missionary

[1] Mémoires sur les Prisons, ii. 277.

Representatives reading Proclamations by torchlight; Missionary Legendre, who has raised force somewhere, emptying out the Jacobins, and flinging their key on the Convention table: ' I have locked their door; it shall be Virtue that reopens it '. Paris, we say, is set against itself, rushing confused, as Ocean-currents do; a huge Mahlstrom, sounding there, under cloud of night. Convention sits permanent on this hand; Municipality most permanent on that. The poor prisoners hear tocsin and rumour; strive to bethink them of the signals apparently of hope. Meek continual Twilight streaming up, which will be Dawn and a To-morrow, silvers the Northern hem of Night; it wends and wends there, that meek brightness, like a silent prophecy, along the great ring-dial of the Heaven. So still, eternal! and on Earth all is confused shadow and conflict; dissidence, tumultuous gloom and glare; and ' Destiny as yet sits wavering, and shakes her doubtful urn '*

About three in the morning, the dissident Armed Forces have *met*. Henriot's Armed Force stood ranked in the Place de Grève; and now Barras's, which he has recruited, arrives there; and they front each other, cannon bristling against cannon. Citoyens! cries the voice of Discretion loudly enough, Before coming to bloodshed, to endless civil-war, hear the Convention Decree read: ' Robespierre and all rebels Out of Law ! ' —Out of Law ? There is terror in the sound. Unarmed Citoyens disperse rapidly home. Municipal Cannoneers, in sudden whirl, anxiously unanimous, range themselves on the Convention side, with shouting. At which shout, Henriot descends from his upper room, far gone in drink as some say; finds his Place de Grève empty; the cannons' mouth turned *towards* him; and on the whole, —that it is now the catastrophe !

Stumbling in again, the wretched drunk-sobered Henriot announces: ' All is lost ! ' ' *Misérable*, it is thou that hast lost it ! ' cry they; and fling him, or else he flings himself, out of window: far enough down; into masonwork and horror of cesspool; not into death but worse. Augustin Robespierre follows him; with the like fate. Saint-Just, they say, called on Lebas to kill him ; who would not. Couthon crept under a table ; attempting to kill himself ; not doing it.—On entering that Sanhedrim of Insurrection, we find all as good as extinct ; undone, ready for seizure. Robespierre was sitting on a chair, with pistol-shot blown through not his head but his under-jaw ; the suicidal hand had failed.[1] With prompt zeal, not without trouble, we gather these wrecked Conspirators ; fish up even Henriot and Augustin, bleeding and foul ; pack them all, rudely enough, into carts ; and shall, before sunrise, have them safe under lock and key. Amid shoutings and embracings.

Robespierre lay in an anteroom of the Convention Hall, while his Prison-escort was getting ready ; the mangled jaw bound up rudely with bloody linen : a spectacle to men. He lies stretched on a table, a deal-box his pillow ; the sheath of the pistol is still clenched convulsively in his hand. Men bully him, insult him : his eyes still indicate intelligence ; he speaks no word. ' He had on the sky-blue coat he had got made for the Feast of the *Être Suprême*'—O Reader, can thy hard heart hold out against that ? His trousers were nankeen ; the stockings had fallen down over the ankles. He spake no word more in this world.

And so, at six in the morning, a victorious Convention adjourns. Report flies over Paris as on golden wings ; penetrates the Prisons ; irradiates the faces of those that were ready to perish : turnkeys and *moutons*, fallen from their high estate, look mute and blue. It is the 28th day of July, called 10th of Thermidor, year 1794.

Fouquier had but to identify ; his Prisoners being already Out of Law. At four in the afternoon, never before were the streets of Paris seen so crowded. From

---

[1] Méda, p. 384. (Méda asserts that it was he who, with infinite courage, though in a lefthanded manner, shot Robespierre. Méda got promoted for his services of this night ; and died General and Baron. Few credited Méda, in what was otherwise incredible.)

the Palais de Justice to the Place de la Révolution, for *thither* again go the Tumbrils this time, it is one dense stirring mass ; all windows crammed ; the very roofs and ridge-tiles budding forth human Curiosity, in strange gladness. The Death-tumbrils, with their motley Batch of Outlaws, some Twenty-three or so, from Maximilien to Mayor Fleuriot and Simon the Cordwainer, roll on. All eyes are on Robespierre's Tumbril, where he, his jaw bound in dirty linen, with his half-dead Brother, and half-dead Henriot, lie shattered ; their ' seventeen hours ' of agony about to end. The Gendarmes point their swords at him, to show the people which is he. A woman springs on the Tumbril ; clutching the side of it with one hand ; waving the other Sibyl-like ; and exclaims : ' The death of thee gladdens my very heart, *m'enivre de joie* ' ; Robespierre opened his eyes ; ' *Scélérat*, go down to Hell, with the curses of all wives and mothers ! '—At the foot of the scaffold, they stretched him on the ground till his turn came. Lifted aloft, his eyes again opened ; caught the bloody axe. Samson wrenched the coat off him ; wrenched the dirty linen from his jaw : the jaw fell powerless, there burst from him a cry ;—hideous to hear and see. Samson, thou canst not be too quick !

Samson's work done, there bursts forth shout on shout of applause. Shout, which prolongs itself not only over Paris, but over France, but over Europe, and down to this generation. Deservedly, and also undeservedly. O unhappiest Advocate of Arras, wert thou worse than other Advocates ? Stricter man, according to his Formula, to his Credo and his Cant, of probities, benevolences, pleasures-of-virtue, and such like, lived not in that age. A man fitted, in some luckier settled age, to have become one of those incorruptible barren Pattern-Figures, and have had marble-tablets and funeral-sermons. His poor landlord, the Cabinet-maker in the Rue Saint-Honoré, loved him ; his Brother died for him. May God be merciful to him, and to us !

This is the end of the Reign of Terror ; new glorious

Revolution named *of Thermidor*; of Thermidor 9th, year 2; which being interpreted into old slave-style means 27th of July 1794. Terror is ended; and death in the Place de la Révolution, were the ' *Tail* of Robespierre' once executed; which service Fouquier in large Batches is swiftly managing.

BOOK VII

VENDÉMIAIRE

CHAPTER I

DECADENT

How little did any one suppose that here was the end not of Robespierre only, but of the Revolution System itself! Least of all did the mutinying Committee-men suppose it; who had mutinied with no view whatever except to continue the National Regeneration with their own heads on their shoulders. And yet so it verily was. The insignificant stone they had struck out, so insignificant anywhere else, proved to be the Keystone; the whole arch-work and edifice of Sansculottism began to loosen, to crack, to yawn; and tumbled piecemeal, with considerable rapidity, plunge after plunge; till the Abyss had swallowed it all, and in this upper world Sansculottism was no more.

For despicable as Robespierre himself might be, the death of Robespierre was a signal at which great multitudes of men, struck dumb with terror heretofore, rose out of their hiding-places; and, as it were, saw one another, how multitudinous they were; and began speaking and complaining. They are countable by the thousand and the million; who have suffered cruel wrong. Ever louder rises the plaint of such a multitude; into a universal sound, into a universal continuous peal, of what they call Public Opinion. Camille had demanded a ‘ Committee of Mercy ’, and could not get it; but now the whole Nation resolves itself into a Committee of Mercy: the Nation has tried Sansculottism, and

is weary of it. Force of Public Opinion ! What King
or Convention can withstand it ? You in vain struggle :
the thing that is rejected as ' calumnious ' to-day must
pass as veracious with triumph another day : gods and
men have declared that Sansculottism cannot be. Sansculottism, on that Ninth night of Thermidor suicidally
' fractured its under-jaw ' ; and lies writhing, never to
rise more.

Through the next fifteen months, it is what we may
call the death-agony of Sansculottism. Sansculottism,
Anarchy of the Jean-Jacques Evangel, having now got
deep enough, is to perish in a new singular system of
Culottism and Arrangement. For Arrangement is indispensable to man ; Arrangement, were it grounded
only on that old primary Evangel of Force, with Sceptre
in the shape of Hammer ! Be there method, be there
order, cry all men ; were it that of the Drill-sergeant*!
More tolerable is the drilled Bayonet-rank, than that
undrilled Guillotine, incalculable as the wind.—How
Sansculottism, writhing in death-throes, strove some
twice, or even three times, to get on its feet again ; but
fell always, and was flung resupine, the next instant ;
and finally breathed out the life of it, and stirred no
more : this we are now, from a due distance, with due
brevity, to glance at ; and then—O Reader !—Courage,
I see land !

Two of the first acts of the Convention, very natural
for it after this Thermidor, are to be specified here : the
first is, renewal of the Governing Committees. Both
Sûreté Générale and *Salut Public*, thinned by the Guillotine, need filling up : we naturally fill them up with
Talliens, Frérons, victorious Thermidorian men. Still
more to the purpose, we appoint that they shall, as
Law directs, not in name only but in deed, be renewed
and changed from period to period ; a fourth part of
them going out monthly. The Convention will no more
lie under bondage of Committees, under terror of death ;
but be a free Convention ; free to follow its own judgement, and the Force of Public Opinion. Not less natural

is it to enact that Prisoners and Persons under Accusation shall have right to demand some ' Writ of Accusation ', and see clearly what they are accused of. Very natural acts : the harbingers of hundreds not less so.

For now Fouquier's trade, shackled by Writ of Accusation, and legal proof, is as good as gone ; effectual only against Robespierre's Tail. The Prisons give up their Suspect ; emit them faster and faster. The Committees see themselves besieged with Prisoners' friends ; complain that they are hindered in their work : it is as with men rushing out of a crowded place ; and obstructing one another. Turned are the tables : Prisoners pouring out in floods ; Jailors, *Moutons* and the Tail of Robespierre going now whither they were wont to send !— The Hundred and thirty-two Nantese Republicans, whom we saw marching in irons, have arrived ; shrunk to Ninety-four, the fifth man of them choked by the road. They arrive : and suddenly find themselves not pleaders for life, but denouncers to death. Their Trial is for acquittal, and more. As the voice of a trumpet, their testimony sounds far and wide, mere atrocities of a Reign of Terror. For a space of nineteen days ; with all solemnity and publicity. Representative Carrier, Company of Marat ; Noyadings, Loire Marriages, things done in darkness, come forth into light : clear is the voice of these poor resuscitated Nantese ; and Journals, and Speech, and universal Committee of Mercy reverberate it loud enough, into all ears and hearts. Deputation arrives from Arras ; denouncing the atrocities of Representative Lebon. A tamed Convention loves its own life : yet what help ? Representative Lebon, Representative Carrier must wend towards the Revolutionary Tribunal ; struggle and delay as we will, the cry of a Nation pursues them louder and louder. Them also Tinville must abolish ;—if indeed Tinville himself be not abolished.

We must note moreover the decrepit condition into which a once omnipotent Mother-Society has fallen. Legendre flung her keys on the Convention table, that Thermidor night ; her President was guillotined with

Robespierre. The once mighty Mother came, some
time after, with a subdued countenance, begging back
her keys : the keys were restored her ; but the strength
could not be restored her ; the strength had departed
for ever. Alas, one's day is done. Vain that the Tribune
in mid-air sounds as of old : to the general ear it has
become a horror, and even a weariness. By and by,
Affiliation is prohibited : the mighty Mother sees herself suddenly childless ; mourns as so hoarse a Rachel
may.*

The Revolutionary Committees, without Suspects to
prey upon, perish fast ; as it were, of famine. In Paris
the old Forty-eight of them are reduced to Twelve ;
their *Forty sous* are abolished : yet a little while, and
Revolutionary Committees are no more. *Maximum*
will be abolished ; let Sansculottism find food where it
can.[1] Neither is there now any Municipality ; any
centre at the Townhall. Mayor Fleuriot and Company
perished ; whom we shall not be in haste to replace.
The Townhall remains in a broken submissive state ;
knows not well what it is growing to ; knows only that
it is grown weak, and must obey. What if we should
split Paris into, say, a Dozen separate Municipalities ;
incapable of concert ! The Sections were thus rendered
safe to act with :—or indeed might not the Sections
themselves be abolished ? You had then merely your
Twelve manageable pacific Townships, without centre
or subdivision ;[2] and sacred right of Insurrection fell
into abeyance !

So much is getting abolished ; fleeting swiftly into
the Inane. For the Press speaks, and the human tongue ;
Journals, heavy and light, in Philippic and Burlesque :
a renegade Fréron, a renegade Prudhomme, loud they
as ever, only the contrary way. And *Ci-devants* show
themselves, almost parade themselves ; resuscitated as
from death-sleep ; publish what death-pains they have
had. The very Frogs of the Marsh croak with emphasis.

[1] 24th December 1794 (Moniteur, No. 97).
[2] October 1795 (Dulaure, viii. 454–6).

Your protesting Seventy-three shall, with a struggle, be emitted out of Prison, back to their seats; your Louvets, Isnards, Lanjuinais, and wrecks of Girondism, recalled from their haylofts, and caves in Switzerland, will resume their place in the Convention:[1] natural foes of Terror!

Thermidorian Talliens, and mere foes of Terror, rule in this Convention, and out of it. The compressed Mountain shrinks silent more and more. Moderatism rises louder and louder: not as a tempest, with threatenings; say rather, as the rushing of a mighty organblast, and melodious deafening Force of Public Opinion, from the Twenty-five million windpipes of a Nation all in Committee of Mercy: which how shall any detached body of individuals withstand?

CHAPTER II

LA CABARUS

How, above all, shall a poor National Convention withstand it? In this poor National Convention, broken, bewildered by long terror, perturbations and guillotinement, there is no Pilot, there is not now even a Danton, who could undertake to steer you anywhither, in such press of weather. The utmost a bewildered Convention can do, is to veer, and trim, and try to keep itself steady; and rush, undrowned, before the wind. Needless to struggle; to fling helm a-lee, and make 'bout ship! A bewildered Convention sails not in the teeth of the wind; but is rapidly blown round again. So strong is the wind, we say; and so changed; blowing fresher and fresher, as from the sweet Southwest; your devastating Northeasters, and wild Tornado-gusts of Terror, blown utterly out! All Sansculottic things are passing away*; all things are becoming Culottic.

---

[1] Deux Amis, xiii. 3-39.

Do but look at the cut of clothes ; that light visible
Result, significant of a thousand things which are not
so visible.   In winter 1793, men went in red nightcap ;
Municipals themselves in *sabots* ; the very Citoyennes
had to petition against such headgear.   But now in this
winter 1794, where is the red nightcap ?   With the
things beyond the Flood.   Your moneyed Citoyen pon-
ders in what elegantest style he shall dress himself ;
whether he shall not even dress himself as the Free
Peoples of Antiquity.   The more adventurous Citoyenne
has already done it.   Behold her, that beautiful adventurous Citoyenne : in costume of the Ancient Greeks,
such Greek as Painter David could teach ;   her sweeping
tresses snooded by glittering antique fillet ;   bright-dyed
tunic of the Greek women ;   her little feet naked, as in
Antique Statues, with mere sandals, and winding-strings
of riband,—defying the frost !

There is such an effervescence of Luxury.   For your
Emigrant *Ci-devants* carried not their mansions and
furnitures out of the country with them ;   but left them
standing here :   and in the swift changes of property,
what with money coined on the Place de la Révolution,
what with Army-furnishings, sales of Emigrant Do-
mains and Church Lands and King's Lands, and then
with the Aladdin's-lamp of Agio in a time of Paper-
money, such mansions have found new occupants.
Old wine, drawn from *Ci-devant* bottles, descends new
throats.   Paris has swept herself, relighted herself ;
Salons, Soupers not Fraternal, beam once more with
suitable effulgence, very singular in colour.   The fair
Cabarus is come out of Prison ;   wedded to her red-
gloomy Dis, whom they say she treats too loftily :   fair
Cabarus gives the most brilliant soirées.   Round her is
gathered a new Republican Army, of Citoyennes in
sandals ;   *Ci-devants* or other :   what remnants soever
of the old grace survive are rallied there.   At her right-
hand, in this cause, labours fair Josephine the Widow
Beauharnais, though in straitened circumstances :   intent, both of them, to blandish down the grimness of
Republican austerity, and recivilize mankind.

Recivilize, even as of old they were civilized: by
witchery of the Orphic fiddle-bow, and Euterpean
rhythm; by the Graces, by the Smiles! Thermidorian
Deputies are there in those soirées: Editor Fréron,
Orateur du Peuple; Barras, who has known other dances
than the Carmagnole. Grim Generals of the Republic
are there; in enormous horse-collar neckcloth, good
against sabre-cuts; the hair gathered all into one knot,
'flowing down behind, fixed with a comb'. Among
which latter do we not recognize, once more, that little
bronze-complexioned Artillery-Officer of Toulon, home
from the Italian Wars! Grim enough; of lean, almost
cruel aspect: for he has been in trouble, in ill health;
also in ill favour, as a man promoted, deservingly or
not, by the Terrorists and Robespierre Junior. But
does not Barras know him? Will not Barras speak a
word for him? Yes,—if at any time it will serve Barras
so to do. Somewhat forlorn of fortune, for the present,
stands that Artillery-Officer; looks, with those deep
earnest eyes of his, into a future as waste as the most.
Taciturn; yet with the strangest utterances in him,
if you awaken him, which smite home, like light or
lightning;—on the whole, rather dangerous? A 'dissocial' man? Dissocial enough; a natural terror
and horror to all Phantasms, being himself of the
genus Reality! He stands here, without work or
outlook, in this forsaken manner;—glances nevertheless, it would seem, at the kind glance of Josephine
Beauharnais; and, for the rest, with severe countenance, with open eyes, and closed lips, waits what will
betide.

That the Balls, therefore, have a new figure this
winter, we can see. Not Carmagnoles, rude 'whirlblasts of rags', as Mercier called them, 'precursors of
storm and destruction': no, soft Ionic motions*; fit
for the light sandal, and antique Grecian tunic! Efflo-
rescence of Luxury has come out: for men have wealth;
nay new-got wealth; and under the Terror you durst
not dance, except in rags. Among the innumerable

kinds of Balls, let the hasty reader mark only this single
one : the kind they call Victim Balls, *Bals à Victime*.
The dancers, in choice costume, have all crape round
the left arm : to be admitted, it needs that you be a
Victime ; that you have lost a relative under the Terror.
Peace to the Dead ; let us *dance* to their memory ! For
in all ways one must dance.

It is very remarkable, according to Mercier, under
what varieties of figure this great business of dancing
goes on. 'The women', says he, 'are Nymphs, Sul-
tanas ; sometimes Minervas, Junos, even Dianas. In
lightly-unerring gyrations they swim there ; with such
earnestness of purpose ; with perfect silence, so absorbed are they. What is singular', continues he, ' the
onlookers are as it were mingled with the dancers ; form,
as it were, a circumambient element round the different
contre-dances, yet without deranging them. It is rare,
in fact, that a Sultana in such circumstances experiences
the smallest collision. Her pretty foot darts down, an
inch from mine ; she is off again ; she is as a flash of
light : but soon the measure recalls her to the point she
set out from. Like a glittering comet she travels her
ellipse ; revolving on herself, as by a double effect of
gravitation and attraction '.[1] Looking forward a little
way, into Time, the same Mercier discerns *Merveilleuses*
in ' flesh-coloured drawers ' with gold circlets ; mere
dancing Houris of an artificial Mahomet's-Paradise*:
much too Mahometan. Montgaillard, with his splenetic
eye, notes a no less strange thing ; that every fashionable Citoyenne you meet is in an interesting situation.
Good Heavens, *every* ? Mere pillows and stuffing ! adds
the acrid man ;—such in a time of depopulation by war
and guillotine, being the fashion.[2] No further seek its
merits to disclose.*

Behold also, instead of the old grim *Tappe-durs* of
Robespierre, what new street-groups are these ? Young
men habited not in black-shag Carmagnole spencer, but

---

[1] Mercier, *Nouveau Paris*, iii. 138, 153.
[2] Montgaillard, iv. 436–42.

in superfine *habit carré*, or spencer with rectangular tail
appended to it; 'square-tailed coat', with elegant
anti-guillotinish specialty of collar; 'the hair plaited
at the temples', and knotted back, long-flowing, in
military wise: young men of what they call the *Muscadin* or Dandy species! Fréron, in his fondness, names
them *Jeunesse Dorée*, Golden or Gilt Youth. They have
come out, these Gilt Youths, in a kind of resuscitated
state; they wear crape round the left arm, such of
them as were *Victims*. More, they carry clubs loaded
with lead; in an angry manner: any *Tappe-dur*, or
remnant of Jacobinism they may fall in with, shall fare
the worse. They have suffered much: their friends
guillotined; their pleasures, frolics, superfine collars
ruthlessly repressed: 'ware now the base Red Nightcaps who did it! Fair Cabarus and the Army of Greek
sandals smile approval. In the Théâtre Feydeau, young
Valour in square-tailed coat eyes Beauty in Greek sandals, and kindles by her glances: Down with Jacobinism! No Jacobin hymn or demonstration, only Thermidorian ones, shall be permitted here: we beat down
Jacobinism with clubs loaded with lead.

But let any one who has examined the Dandy nature,
how petulant it is, especially in the gregarious state,
think what an element, in sacred right of insurrection,
this Gilt Youth was! Broils and battery; war without
truce or measure! Hateful is Sansculottism, as Death
and Night. For indeed is not the Dandy *culottic*, habi-
latory, by law of existence; 'a cloth-animal; one that
lives, moves and has his being in cloth'?

So goes it, waltzing, bickering; fair Cabarus, by
Orphic witchery, struggling to recivilize mankind. Not
unsuccessfully, we hear. What utmost Republican
grimness can resist Greek sandals, in Ionic motion, the
very toes covered with gold rings?[1] By degrees the
indisputablest new-politeness rises; grows, with vigour.
And yet, whether, even to this day, that inexpressible

[1] Montgaillard, Mercier (*ubi suprà*).

tone of society known under the old Kings, when Sin had ' lost all its deformity ' (with or without advantage to us), and airy Nothing had obtained such a local habitation and establishment as she never had,—be recovered ?   Or even, whether it be not lost beyond recovery ? [1]—Either way, the world must contrive to struggle on.

CHAPTER III

QUIBERON [*]

BUT indeed do not these long-flowing hair-queues of a *Jeunesse Dorée* in semi-military costume betoken, unconsciously, another still more important tendency ? The Republic, abhorrent of her Guillotine, loves her Army.

And with cause. For, surely, if good fighting be a kind of honour, as it is in its season ; and be with the vulgar of men, even the chief kind of honour ; then here is good fighting, in good season, if there ever was. These Sons of the Republic, they rose, in mad wrath, to deliver her from Slavery and Cimmeria. And have they not done it ?   Through Maritime Alps, through gorges of Pyrenees, through Low Countries, Northward along the Rhine-valley, far is Cimmeria hurled back from the sacred Motherland. Fierce as fire, they have carried her Tricolor over the faces of all her enemies ; —over scarped heights, over cannon-batteries, it has flown victorious, winged with rage. She has ' Eleven hundred-thousand fighters on foot ', this Republic : ' at one particular moment she had ', or supposed she had, ' Seventeen-hundred thousand '.[2] Like a ring of light-ning, they, volleying and *ça-ira*-ing, begirdle her from shore to shore. Cimmerian Coalition of Despots recoils, smitten with astonishment and strange pangs.

[1] De Staël, Considérations, iii. c. 10, &c.
[2] Toulongeon, iii. c. 7 ; v. c. 10 (p. 194).

Such a fire is in these Gaelic Republican men ; high-blazing ; which no Coalition can withstand ! Not scutcheons, with four degrees of nobility ; but *ci-devant* Sergeants, who have had to clutch Generalship out of the cannon's throat, a Pichegru, a Jourdan, a Hoche lead them on. They have bread, they have iron ; ' with bread and iron you can get to China '.—See Pichegru's soldiers, this hard winter, in their looped and windowed destitution, in their ' straw-rope shoes and cloaks of bast-mat ', how they overrun Holland, like a demon-host, the ice having bridged all waters ; and rush shout-ing from victory to victory ! Ships in the Texel are taken by hussars on horseback : fled is York ; fled is the Stadtholderi glad to escape to England, and leave Holland to fraternize.[1] Such a Gaelic fire, we say, blazes in this People, like the conflagration of grass and dry-jungle ; which no mortal can withstand—for the moment.

And even so it will blaze and run, scorching all things ; and, from Cadiz to Archangel, mad Sansculottism drilled now into Soldiership, led on by some ' armed Soldier of Democracy ' (say, that monosyllabic Artil-lery-Officer), will set its foot cruelly on the necks of its enemies ; and its shouting and their shrieking shall fill the world !—Rash Coalized Kings, such a fire have ye kindled ; yourselves fireless, *your* fighters animated only by drill-sergeants, mess-room moralities, and the drum-mer's cat ! However, it is begun, and will not end : not for a matter of twenty years. So long, this Gaelic fire, through its successive changes of colour and charac-ter, will blaze over the face of Europe, and afflict and scorch all men :—till it provoke all men ; till it kindle another kind of fire, the Teutonic kind, namely ; and be swallowed up, so to speak, in a day ! For there is a fire comparable to the burning of dry-jungle and grass ; most sudden, high-blazing : and another fire which we liken to the burning of coal, or even of anthra-cite coal ; difficult to kindle, but then which no known

[1] 19th January 1795 (Montgaillard, iv. 287–311).

thing will put out. The ready Gaelic fire, we can remark further,—and remark not in Pichegrus only, but in innumerable Voltaires, Racines, Laplaces, no less ; for a man, whether he fight, or sing, or think, will remain the same unity of a man,—is admirable for roasting eggs,* in every conceivable sense. The Teutonic anthracite again, as we see in Luthers, Leibnizes, Shakespeares, is preferable for smelting metals. How happy is our Europe that has both kinds !—

But be this as it may, the Republic is clearly triumphing. In the spring of the year, Mentz Town again sees itself besieged ; will again change master : did not Merlin the Thionviller, ' with wild beard and look ', say it was not for the last time they saw him there ? The Elector of Mentz circulates among his brother Potentates this pertinent query, Were it not advisable to treat of Peace ? Yes ! answers many an Elector from the bottom of his heart. But, on the other hand, Austria hesitates ; finally refuses, being subsidied by Pitt. As to Pitt, whoever hesitate, he, suspending his Habeas-corpus, suspending his Cash-payments, stands inflexible,—spite of foreign reverses ; spite of domestic obstacles, of Scotch National Conventions and English Friends of the People, whom he is obliged to arraign, to hang, or even to see acquitted with jubilee : a lean inflexible man. The Majesty of Spain, as we predicted, makes Peace ; also the Majesty of Prussia : and there is a Treaty of Bâle.[1] Treaty with black Anarchists and Regicides ! Alas, what help ? You cannot hang this Anarchy ; it is like to hang you : you must needs treat with it.

Likewise, General Hoche has even succeeded in pacificating La Vendée. Rogue Rossignol and his ' Infernal Columns ' have vanished : by firmness and justice, by sagacity and industry, General Hoche has done it. Taking ' Movable Columns ', not infernal ; girdling-in the Country ; pardoning the submissive, cutting down the resistive, limb after limb of the Revolt is brought

---

[1] 5th April 1795 (Montgaillard, iv. 319).

under. La Rochejacquelin, last of our Nobles, fell in battle ; Stofflet himself makes terms ; Georges-Cadoudal is back to Brittany, among his Chouans : the frightful gangrene of La Vendée seems veritably extirpated. It has cost, as they reckon in round numbers, the lives of a Hundred-thousand fellow-mortals ; with noyadings, conflagratings by infernal column, which defy arithmetic. This is the La Vendée War.[1]

Nay in few months, it does burst up once more, but once only ;—blown upon by Pitt, by our Ci-devant Puisaye of Calvados, and others. In the month of July 1795, English Ships will ride in Quiberon roads. There will be debarkation of chivalrous Ci-devants, of volunteer Prisoners-of-war—eager to desert ; of fire-arms, Proclamations, clothes-chests, Royalists and specie. Whereupon also, on the Republican side, there will be rapid stand-to-arms ; with ambuscade marchings by Quiberon beach, at midnight ; storming of Fort Penthièvre ; war-thunder mingling with the roar of the nightly main ; and such a morning light as has seldom dawned : debarkation hurled back into its boats, or into the devouring billows, with wreck and wail ;—in one word, a Ci-devant Puisaye as totally ineffectual here as he was in Calvados, when he rode from Vernon Castle without boots.[2]

Again, therefore, it has cost the lives of many a brave man. Among whom the whole world laments the brave Son of Sombreuil.* Ill-fated family ! The father and younger son went to the guillotine ; the heroic daughter languishes, reduced to want, hides her woes from History : the elder son perishes here ; shot by military tribunal as an Emigrant ; Hoche himself cannot save him. If all wars, civil and other, are misunderstandings, what a thing must right-understanding be !

[1] Histoire de la Guerre de la Vendée, par M. le Comte de Vauban ; Mémoires de Madame de la Rochejacquelin, &c.
[2] Deux Amis, xiv. 94–106 ; Puisaye, Mémoires, iii.–vii.

CHAPTER IV

LION NOT DEAD

THE Convention, borne on the tide of Fortune towards foreign Victory, and driven by the strong wind
of Public Opinion towards Clemency and Luxury, is
rushing fast; all skill of pilotage is needed, and more
than all, in such a velocity.

Curious to see, how we veer and whirl, yet must ever
whirl round again, and scud before the wind. If, on the
one hand, we re-admit the Protesting Seventy-three,
we, on the other hand, agree to consummate the Apotheosis of Marat; lift his body from the Cordeliers Church,
and transport it to the Pantheon of Great Men,—flinging
out Mirabeau to make room for him. To no purpose:
so strong blows Public Opinion! A Gilt Youthhood,
in plaited hair-tresses, tears down his Busts from the
Théâtre Feydeau; tramples them under foot; scatters
them, with vociferation, into the Cesspool of Montmartre.[1] Swept is his Chapel from the Place du Carrousel; the Cesspool of Montmartre will receive his
very dust. Shorter godhood had no divine man. Some
four months in this Pantheon, Temple of All the Immortals; then to the Cesspool, grand *Cloaca* of Paris
and the World! 'His Busts at one time amounted to
four thousand'. Between Temple of All the Immortals
and Cloaca of the World, how are poor human creatures
whirled!

Furthermore the question arises, When will the Con-
stitution of *Ninety-three*, of 1793, come into action?
Considerate heads surmise, in all privacy, that the
Constitution of Ninety-three will never come into action.
Let them busy themselves to get ready a better.

Or, again, where now are the Jacobins? Childless,
most decrepit, as we saw, sat the mighty Mother;

[1] Moniteur, du 25 Septembre 1794, du 4 Février 1795.

gnashing not teeth, but empty gums, against a traitorous Thermidorian Convention and the current of things.
Twice were Billaud, Collot and Company accused in
Convention, by a Lecointre, by a Legendre; and the
second time, it was not voted calumnious.   Billaud
from the Jacobin tribune says, ' The lion is not dead,
he is only sleeping '.   They ask him in Convention,
What he means by the awakening of the lion ?   And
bickerings, of an extensive sort, arose in the Palais-
Égalité between *Tappe-durs* and the Gilt Youthhood;
cries of ' Down with the Jacobins, the *Jacoquins* ',
coquin meaning scoundrel !   The Tribune in mid-air
gave battle-sound ; answered only by silence and uncertain gasps.   Talk was, in Government Committees,
of ' suspending ' the Jacobin Sessions.   Hark, there !
—it is in Allhallow-time, or on the Hallow-eve itself,
month *ci-devant* November, year once named of Grace
1794, sad eve for Jacobinism,—volley of stones dashing through our windows, with jingle and execration !
The female Jacobins, famed *Tricoteuses* with knitting-
needles, take flight ; are met at the doors by a Gilt
Youthhood and ' mob of four thousand persons ' ; are
hooted, flouted, hustled ; fustigated, in a scandalous
manner, *cotillons retroussés* ;—and vanish in mere hysterics. Sally out, ye male Jacobins ! The male Jacobins
sally out ; but only to battle, disaster and confusion.
So that armed Authority has to intervene : and again
on the morrow to intervene ; and suspend the Jacobin
Sessions for ever and a day.[1]—Gone are the Jacobins ;
into invisibility ; in a storm of laughter and howls.
Their Place is made a Normal School, the first of the
kind seen ; it then vanishes into a ' Market of Thermidor Ninth ' ; into a Market of Saint-Honoré, where is
now peaceable chaffering for poultry and greens.   The
solemn temples, the great globe itself ; the baseless
fabric !   Are not we such stuff, we and this world of
ours, as Dreams are made of ?[*]

Maximum being abrogated, Trade was to take its own

[1] Moniteur, Séances du 10-12 Novembre 1794 ; Deux
Amis, xiii. 43-49.

free course. Alas, Trade, shackled, topsyturvied in the
way we saw, and now suddenly let go again, can for
the present take no course at all; but only reel and
stagger. There is, so to speak, no Trade whatever for
the time being. Assignats, long sinking, emitted in
such quantities, sink now with an alacrity beyond
parallel. ' *Combien ?* ' said one, to a Hackney-coachman, ' What fare ? ' ' Six thousand livres ', answered
he: some three hundred pounds sterling, in Paper-
money.[1] Pressure of Maximum withdrawn, the things
it compressed likewise withdraw. ' Two ounces of
bread per day ' is the modicum allotted: wide-waving,
doleful are the Bakers' Queues; Farmers' houses are
become pawnbrokers' shops.

One can imagine, in these circumstances, with what
humour Sansculottism growled in its throat, ' *La Cabarus* '; beheld Ci-devants return dancing, the Thermidor
effulgence of recivilization, and Balls in flesh-coloured
drawers. Greek tunics and sandals; hosts of *Muscadins* parading, with their clubs loaded with lead;—and
we here, cast out, abhorred, ' picking offals from the
street ';[2] agitating in Baker's Queue for our two ounces
of bread! Will the Jacobin lion, which they say is
meeting secretly ' at the Archevêché, in *bonnet rouge*
with loaded pistols ', not awaken? Seemingly, not.
Our Collot, our Billaud, Barrère, Vadier, in these last
days of March 1795, are found worthy of *Déportation*,
of Banishment beyond seas; and shall, for the present,
be trundled off to the Castle of Ham. The lion is dead;
—or writhing in death-throes!

Behold, accordingly, on the day they call Twelfth of
Germinal (which is also called First of April, not a lucky
day), how lively are these streets of Paris once more!
Floods of hungry women, of squalid hungry men;

[1] Mercier, ii. 94. (' 1st February 1796: at the Bourse
of Paris, the gold louis ', of 20 francs in silver, ' costs
5,300 francs in assignats '. Montgaillard, iv. 419).
[2] Fantin Desodoards, Histoire de la Révolution, vii. c. 4.

ejaculating: 'Bread, Bread, and the Constitution of Ninety-three!' Paris has risen, once again, like the Ocean-tide; is flowing towards the Tuileries, for Bread and a Constitution. Tuileries Sentries do their best; but it serves not: the Ocean-tide sweeps them away; inundates the Convention Hall itself; howling, 'Bread and the Constitution!'

Unhappy Senators, unhappy People, there is yet, after all toils and broils, no Bread, no Constitution. '*Du pain, pas tant de longs discours,* Bread, not bursts of Parliamentary eloquence!' so wailed the Menads of Maillard, five years ago and more; so wail ye to this hour. The Convention, with unalterable countenance, with what thought one knows not, keeps its seat in this waste howling chaos; rings its storm-bell from the Pavilion of Unity. Section Lepelletier, old *Filles Saint-Thomas,* who are of the money-changing species; these and Gilt Youthhood fly to the rescue: sweep chaos forth again, with levelled bayonets. Paris is declared 'in a state of siege'. Pichegru, Conqueror of Holland, who happens to be here, is named Commandant, till the disturbance end. He, in one day so to speak, ends it. He accomplishes the transfer of Billaud, Collot and Company; dissipating all opposition 'by two cannon-shots', blank cannon-shots, and the terror of his name; and thereupon, announcing, with a Laconicism which should be imitated, 'Representatives, your decrees are executed',[1] lays down his Commandantship.

This Revolt of Germinal, therefore, has passed, like a vain cry. The Prisoners rest safe in Ham, waiting for ships; some nine-hundred 'chief Terrorists of Paris' are disarmed. Sansculottism, swept forth with bayonets, has vanished, with its misery, to the bottom of Saint-Antoine and Saint-Marceau.—Time was when Usher Maillard with Menads could alter the course of Legislation; but that time is not. Legislation seems to have got bayonets; Section Lepelletier takes its fire-

[1] Moniteur, Séance du 13 Germinal (2nd April), 1795.

lock, not for us ! We retire to our dark dens ; our cry of hunger is called a Plot of Pitt ; the Saloons glitter, the flesh-coloured Drawers gyrate as before. It was for ' *The Cabarus* ' then, and her *Muscadins* and Money-changers that we fought ? It was for Balls in flesh-coloured drawers that we took Feudalism by the beard, and did, and dared, shedding our blood like water ? Expressive Silence, muse thou their praise !—

CHAPTER V

LION SPRAWLING ITS LAST

REPRESENTATIVE Carrier went to the Guillotine, in December last ; protesting that he acted by orders. The Revolutionary Tribunal, after all it has devoured, has now only, as Anarchic things do, to devour itself. In the early days of May, men see a remarkable thing : Fouquier-Tinville pleading at the Bar once his own. He and his chief Jurymen, Leroi *August-Tenth*, Jury-man Vilate, a Batch of Sixteen ; pleading hard, pro-testing that they acted by orders : but pleading in vain. Thus men break the axe with which they have done hateful things ; the axe itself having grown hateful. For the rest Fouquier died hard enough : ' Where are thy Batches ? ' howled the people.—' Hungry *canaille* ', asked Fouquier, ' is thy Bread cheaper, wanting them ? '

Remarkable Fouquier ; once but as other Attorneys and Law-beagles, which hunt ravenous on this Earth, a well-known phasis of human nature ; and now thou art and remainest the most remarkable Attorney that ever lived and hunted in the Upper Air ! For, in this terrestrial Course of Time, there was to be an *Avatar* of Attorneyism ; the Heavens had said, Let there be an Incarnation, not divine, of the venatory Attorney-spirit which keeps its eye on the bond only ;—and lo, this was it ; and they have attorneyed it in its turn. Vanish, then, thou rat-eyed Incarnation of Attorneyism ; who at bottom wert but as other Attorneys, and too hungry sons of Adam ! Juryman Vilate had striven hard for life, and published, from his Prison, an ingenious Book, not unknown to us ; but it would not stead : he also had to vanish ; and this his Book of the *Secret Causes of Thermidor*, full of lies, with particles of truth in it undiscoverable otherwise, is all that remains of him.

Revolutionary Tribunal has done ; but vengeance has not done. Representative Lebon, after long struggling, is handed over to the ordinary Law Courts, and by them guillotined. Nay at Lyons and elsewhere, resuscitated Moderatism, in its vengeance, will not wait the slow process of Law ; but bursts into the Prisons, sets fire to the Prisons : burns some threescore imprisoned Jacobins to dire death, or chokes them ' with the smoke of straw '. There go vengeful truculent ' Companies of Jesus ', ' Companies of the Sun ' ; slaying Jacobinism wherever they meet with it ; flinging it into the Rhone-stream ; which once more bears seaward a horrid cargo.[1] Whereupon, at Toulon, Jacobinism rises in revolt ; and is like to hang the National Representatives.—With such action and reaction, is not a poor National Convention hard bested ? It is like the settlement of winds and waters, of seas long tornadobeaten ; and goes on with jumble and with jangle. Now flung aloft, now sunk in trough of the sea, your Vessel of the Republic has need of all pilotage and more.

What Parliament that ever sat under the Moon had such a series of destinies as this National Convention of France ? It came together to make the Constitution ; and instead of that, it has had to make nothing but destruction and confusion : to burn up Catholicisms, Aristocratisms ; to worship Reason and dig Saltpetre ; to fight Titanically with itself and with the whole world. A Convention decimated by the Guillotine ; above the tenth man has bowed his neck to the axe. Which has seen Carmagnoles danced before it, and patriotic strophes

---

[1] *Moniteur, du 27 Juin, du 31 Août, 1795* ; Deux Amis, xiii. 121-9.

sung amid Church-spoils ; the wounded of the Tenth
of August defile in handbarrows ; and, in the Pandemonial Midnight, Égalité's dames in tricolor drink
lemonade, and spectrum of Sieyes mount, saying, *Death
sans phrase.* A Convention which has effervesced, and
which has congealed ; which has been red with rage,
and also pale with rage ; sitting with pistols in its
pocket, drawing sword (in a moment of effervescence) :
now storming to the four winds, through a Danton-
voice, Awake, O France, and smite the tyrants ; now
frozen mute under its Robespierre, and answering his
dirge-voice by a dubious gasp. Assassinated, decimated ;
stabbed at, shot at, in baths, on streets and staircases ;
which has been the nucleus of Chaos. Has it not heard
the chimes at midnight ? It has deliberated, beset by
a Hundred-thousand armed men with artillery-furnaces
and provision-carts. It has been betocsined, bestormed ;
overflooded by black deluges of Sansculottism ; and
has heard the shrill cry, *Bread and Soap.* For, as we
say, it was the nucleus of Chaos : it sat as the centre of
Sansculottism ; and had spread its pavilion on the
waste Deep, where is neither path nor landmark, neither
bottom nor shore. In intrinsic valour, ingenuity, fidelity, and general force and manhood, it has perhaps not
far surpassed the average of Parliaments ; but in frankness of purpose, in singularity of position, it seeks its
fellow. One other Sansculottic submersion, or at most
two, and this wearied vessel of a Convention reaches
land.

Revolt of Germinal Twelfth ended as a vain cry ;
moribund Sansculottism was swept back into invisibility. There it has lain moaning, these six weeks :
moaning, and also scheming. Jacobins disarmed, flung
forth from their Tribune in mid-air, must needs try to
help themselves, in secret conclave under ground. Lo
therefore, on the First day of the Month *Prairial,** 20th
of May 1795, sound of the *générale* once more ; beating
sharp, ran-tan, To arms, To arms !
Sansculottism has risen, yet again, from its death-

lair ; waste, wild-flowing, as the unfruitful Sea. Saint-
Antoine is afoot : ' Bread and the Constitution of
Ninety-three ', so sounds it ; so stands it written with
chalk on the hats of men. They have their pikes, their
firelocks ; Paper of Grievances ; standards ; printed
Proclamation, drawn up in quite official manner,—considering this, and also considering that, they, a much-
enduring Sovereign People, are in Insurrection ; will
have Bread and the Constitution of Ninety-three. And
so the Barriers are seized, and the *générale* beats, and
tocsins discourse discord. Black deluges overflow the
Tuileries ; spite of sentries, the Sanctuary itself is invaded : enter, to our Order of the Day, a torrent of
dishevelled women, wailing, ' Bread ! Bread ! ' President may well cover himself ; and have his own tocsin
rung in ' the Pavilion of Unity ' ; the ship of the State
again labours and leaks ; overwashed, near to swamp-
ing, with unfruitful brine.

What a day, once more ! Women are driven out :
men storm irresistibly in ; choke all corridors, thunder
at all gates. Deputies, putting forth head, obtest, conjure ; Saint-Antoine rages, ' Bread and Constitution '.
Report has risen that the ' Convention is assassinating
the women ' : crushing and rushing, clangour and furor !
The oak doors have become as oak tambourines, sounding under the axe of Saint-Antoine ; plaster-work
crackles, wood-work booms and jingles ; door starts
up ;—bursts-in Saint-Antoine with frenzy and vociferation, with Rag-standards, printed Proclamation, drum-
music : astonishment to eye and ear. Gendarmes, loyal
Sectioners charge through the other door ; they are
recharged ; musketry exploding : Saint-Antoine cannot be expelled. Obtesting Deputies obtest vainly :
Respect the President ; approach not the President !
Deputy Féraud, stretching out his hands, baring his
bosom scarred in the Spanish wars, obtests vainly ;
threatens and resists vainly. Rebellious Deputy of the
Sovereign, if thou have fought, have not we too ? We
have no Bread, no Constitution ! They wrench poor
Féraud ; they tumble him, trample him, wrath waxing

to see itself work : they drag him into the corridor,
dead or near it ; sever his head, and fix it on a pike.
Ah, did an unexampled Convention want this variety
of destiny, too, then ? Féraud's bloody head goes on
a pike. Such a game has begun ; Paris and the Earth
may wait how it will end.

And so it billows free through all Corridors ; within
and without, far as the eye reaches, nothing but Bedlam, and the great Deep broken loose ! President
Boissy d'Anglas sits like a rock : the rest of the Convention is floated ' to the upper benches ' ; Sectioners
and Gendarmes still ranking there to form a kind of
wall for them. And Insurrection rages ; rolls its drums ;
will read its Paper of Grievances, will have this decreed,
will have that. Covered sits President Boissy ; un-
yielding ; like a rock in the beating of seas. They
menace him, level muskets at him, he yields not ; they
hold up Féraud's bloody head to him, with grave stern
air he bows to it, and yields not.

And the Paper of Grievances cannot get itself read
for uproar : and the drums roll, and the throats bawl ;
and Insurrection, like sphere-music, is inaudible for
very noise : Decree us this, Decree us that. One man
we discern bawling ' for the space of an hour at all
intervals ', ' *Je demande l'arrestation des coquins et des
lâches* '. Really one of the most comprehensive Petitions ever put up ; which indeed, to this hour, includes
all that you can reasonably ask Constitution of the
Year One, Rotten-Borough, Ballot-Box, or other miraculous Political Ark of the Covenant to do for you to
the end of the world ! I also *demand arrestment of the
Knaves and Dastards*, and nothing more whatever.—
National Representation, deluged with black Sansculottism, glides out ; for help elsewhere, for safety elsewhere ; here is no help.

About four in the afternoon, there remain hardly
more than some Sixty Members : mere friends, or even
secret-leaders ; a remnant of the Mountain-crest, held
in silence by Thermidorian thraldom. Now is the time
for them ; now or never let them descend, and speak !

They descend, these Sixty, invited by Sansculottism :
Romme of the New Calendar, Ruhl of the Sacred Phial,
Goujon, Duquesnoy, Soubrany, and the rest.   Glad
Sansculottism forms a ring for them ; Romme takes
the President's chair ; they begin resolving and decreeing.   Fast enough now comes Decree after Decree, in
alternate brief strains, or strophe and antistrophe,—
what will cheapen bread, what will awaken the dormant
lion.   And at every new decree, Sansculottism shouts
' Decreed, decreed ! ' and rolls its drums.

Fast enough ; the work of months in hours,—when
see, a Figure enters, whom in the lamp-light we recognize to be Legendre ; and utters words : fit to be hissed
out !   And then see, Section Lepelletier or other Muscadin Section enters, and Gilt Youth, with levelled
bayonets, countenances screwed to the sticking-place !
Tramp, tramp, with bayonets gleaming in the lamp-
light : what can one do, worn down with long riot,
grown heartless, dark, hungry, but roll back, but rush
back, and escape who can ?   The very windows need
to be thrown up, that Sansculottism may escape fast
enough.   Money-changer Sections and Gilt Youth sweep
them forth, with steel besom, far into the depths of
Saint-Antoine.   Triumph once more !   The Decrees of
that Sixty are not so much as rescinded ; they are
declared null and non-extant.   Romme, Ruhl, Goujon
and the ringleaders, some thirteen in all, are decreed
Accused.   Permanent-session ends at three in the morning.[1]   Sansculottism, once more flung resupine, lies
sprawling ; sprawling its *last.*

Such was the First of Prairial, 20th of May 1795.
Second and Third of Prairial, during which Sansculottism still sprawled, and unexpectedly rang its tocsin,
and assembled in arms, availed Sansculottism nothing.
What though with our Rommes and Ruhls, accused but
not yet arrested, we make a new ' True National Convention ' of our own, over in the East ; and put the
others Out of Law ?   What though we rank in arms

[1] Deux Amis, xiii. 129-46.

and march ? Armed Force and Muscadin Sections,
some thirty-thousand men, environ that old False Convention : we can but bully one another ; bandying
nicknames, ' *Muscadins* ', against ' Blood-drinkers, *Bu-
veurs de Sang* '. Féraud's Assassin, taken with the red
hand, and sentenced, and now near to Guillotine and
Place de Grève, is retaken ; is carried back into Saint-
Antoine :—to no purpose. Convention Sectionaries and
Gilt Youth come, according to Decree, to seek him ; nay
to disarm Saint-Antoine ! And they do disarm it : by
rolling of cannon, by springing upon enemy's cannon ;
by military audacity, and terror of the Law. Saint-
Antoine surrenders its arms ; Santerre even advising
it, anxious for life and brewhouse. Féraud's Assassin
flings himself from a high roof : and all is lost.[1]

Discerning which things, old Ruhl shot a pistol
through his old white head ; dashed his life in pieces,
as he had done the Sacred Phial of Rheims. Romme,
Goujon and the others stand ranked before a swiftly-
appointed, swift Military Tribunal. Hearing the sentence, Goujon drew a knife, struck it into his breast,
passed it to his neighbour Romme ; and fell dead.
Romme did the like ; and another all-but did it ;
Roman-death rushing on there, as in electric-chain,
before your Bailiffs could intervene ! The Guillotine
had the rest.

They were the *Ultimi Romanorum.* Billaud, Collot
and Company are now ordered to be tried for life ; but
are found to be already off, shipped for Sinamarri, and
the hot mud of Surinam. There let Billaud surround
himself with flocks of tame parrots ; Collot take the
yellow fever, and drinking a whole bottle of brandy,
burn up his entrails.[2] Sansculottism sprawls no more.
The dormant lion has become a dead one ; and now, as
we see, any hoof may smite him.

---

[1] Toulongeon, v. 297 ; Moniteur, Nos. 244, 5, 6.
[2] Dictionnaire des Hommes Marquans, §§ Billaud, Collot.

CHAPTER VI

GRILLED HERRINGS

So dies Sansculottism, the *body* of Sansculottism ; or is changed. Its ragged Pythian Carmagnole-dance has transformed itself into a Pyrrhic, into a dance of Cabarus Balls. Sansculottism is dead ; extinguished by new *isms* of that kind, which were its own natural progeny ; and is buried, we may say, with such deafening jubilation and disharmony of funeral-knell on their part, that only after some half-century or so does one begin to learn clearly why it ever was alive.

And yet a meaning lay in it : Sansculottism verily was alive, a New-Birth of TIME ; nay it still lives, and is not dead but changed. The *soul* of it still lives ; still works far and wide, through one bodily shape into another less amorphous, as is the way of cunning Time with his New-Births :—till, in some perfected shape, it embrace the whole circuit of the world ! For the wise man may now everywhere discern that he must found on his manhood, not on the garnitures of his manhood. He who, in these Epochs of our Europe, founds on garnitures, formulas, culottisms of what sort soever, is founding on old cloth and sheepskin, and cannot endure. But as for the body of Sansculottism, that is dead and buried,—and, one hopes, need not reappear, in primary amorphous shape, for another thousand years.

It was the frightfullest thing ever born of Time ? One of the frightfullest. This Convention, now grown Antijacobin, did, with an eye to justify and fortify itself, publish Lists of what the Reign of Terror had perpetrated : Lists of Persons Guillotined. The Lists, cries splenetic Abbé Montgaillard, were not complete. They contain the names of, How many persons thinks the Reader ?—Two-thousand all but a few. There were above Four-thousand, cries Montgaillard : so many were guillotined, fusilladed, noyaded, done to dire death; of whom Nine-hundred were women.[1] It is a horrible sum of human lives, M. l'Abbé:—some ten times as many shot rightly on a field of battle, and one might have had his Glorious-Victory with *Te-Deum*. It is not far from the two-hundredth part of what perished in the entire Seven-Years War. By which Seven-Years War, did not the great Fritz wrench Silesia* from the great Theresa; and a Pompadour, stung by epigrams, satisfy herself that she could not be an Agnes Sorel?* The head of man is a strange vacant sounding-shell, M. l'Abbé; and studies Cocker to small purpose.

But what if History somewhere on this Planet were to hear of a Nation, the third soul of whom had not, for thirty weeks each year, as many third-rate potatoes as would sustain him?[2] History, in that case, feels bound to consider that starvation is starvation; that starvation from age to age presupposes much; History ventures to assert that the French Sansculotte of Ninety-three, who, roused from long death-sleep, could rush at once to the frontiers, and die fighting for an immortal Hope and Faith of Deliverance for him and his, was but the *second*-miserablest of men! The Irish Sans-potato, had he not senses then, nay a soul! In his frozen darkness, it was bitter for him to die famishing; bitter to see his children famish. It was bitter for him to be a beggar, a liar and a knave. Nay, if that dreary Greenland-wind of benighted Want, perennial from sire to son, had frozen him into a kind of torpor and numb callosity, so that he saw not, felt not,—was this, for a creature with a soul in it, some assuagement; or the cruellest wretchedness of all?*

Such things were; such things are; and they go on in silence peaceably:—and Sansculottisms follow them. History, looking back over this France through long times, back to Turgot's time for instance, when dumb Drudgery staggered up to its King's Palace, and in wide expanse of sallow faces, squalor and winged ragged-ness, presented hieroglyphically its Petition of Griev-

[1] Montgaillard, iv. 241.

[2] Report of the Irish Poor-Law Commission, 1836.

ances ; and for answer got hanged on a 'new gallows
forty feet high ',—confesses mournfully that there is
no period to be met with, in which the general Twenty-
five Millions of France suffered *less* than in this period
which they name Reign of Terror ! But it was not the
Dumb Millions that suffered here ; it was the Speaking
Thousands, and Hundreds and Units ; who shrieked
and published, and made the world ring with their wail,
as they could and should : that is the grand peculiarity.
The frightfullest Births of Time are never the loud-
speaking ones, for these soon die ; they are the silent
ones, which can live from century to century ! Anarchy,
hateful as Death, is abhorrent to the whole nature of
man ; and so must itself soon die.

Wherefore let all men know what of depth and of
height is still revealed in man ; and, with fear and
wonder, with just sympathy and just antipathy, with
clear eye and open heart, contemplate it and appropriate it ; and draw innumerable inferences from it.
This inference, for example, among the first : That ' if
the gods of this lower world will sit on their glittering
thrones, indolent as Epicurus' gods, with the living
Chaos of Ignorance and Hunger weltering uncared-for
at their feet, and smooth Parasites preaching, Peace,
peace,* when there is no peace ', then the dark Chaos,
it would seem, will rise ;—has risen, and O Heavens !
has it not tanned their skins into breeches for itself ?
That there be no second Sansculottism in our Earth
for a thousand years, let us understand well what the
first was ; and let Rich and Poor of us go and do *otherwise*.—But to our tale.

The Muscadin Sections greatly rejoice ; Cabarus Balls
gyrate : the well-nigh insoluble problem, *Republic without Anarchy*, have we not solved it ?—Law of Fraternity
or Death is gone : chimerical *Obtain-who-need* has
become practical *Hold-who-have*. To anarchic Republic
of the Poverties there has succeeded orderly Republic
of the Luxuries ; which will continue as long as it
can.

On the Pont au Change, on the Place de Grève, in long sheds, Mercier, in these summer evenings, saw working men at their repast. One's allotment of daily bread has sunk to an ounce and a half. ' Plates containing each three grilled herrings, sprinkled with shorn onions, wetted with a little vinegar ; to this add some morsel of boiled prunes, and lentils swimming in a clear sauce : at these frugal tables, the cook's gridiron hissing near by, and the pot simmering on a fire between two stones, I have seen them ranged by the hundred ; consuming, without bread, their scant messes, far too moderate for the keenness of their appetite, and the extent of their stomach '.[1] Seine water, rushing plenteous by, will supply the deficiency.

O Man of Toil, thy struggling and thy daring, these six long years of insurrection and tribulation, thou hast profited nothing by it then ? Thou consumest thy herring and water, in the blessed gold-red evening. O why was the Earth so beautiful, becrimsoned with dawn and twilight, if man's dealings with man were to make it a vale of scarcity, of tears, not even soft tears ? Destroying of Bastilles, discomfiting of Brunswicks, fronting of Principalities and Powers, of Earth and Tophet, all that thou hast dared and endured,—it was for a Republic of the Cabarus Saloons ? Patience : thou must have patience : the end is not yet.

CHAPTER VII

THE WHIFF OF GRAPESHOT*

In fact, what can be more natural, one may say inevitable, as a Post-Sansculottic transitionary state, than even this ? Confused wreck of a Republic of the Poverties, which ended in Reign of Terror, is arranging itself into such composure as it can. Evangel of Jean-Jacques, and most other Evangels, becoming incredible, what is

[1] Nouveau Paris, iv. 118.

there for it but return to the old Evangel of Mammon ?
Contrat-Social is true or untrue, Brotherhood is Brotherhood or Death ; but money always will buy money's
worth : in the wreck of human dubitations, this remains indubitable, that Pleasure is pleasant.   Aristocracy of Feudal Parchment has passed away with a
mighty rushing ; and now, by a natural course, we
arrive at Aristocracy of the Moneybag.   It is the course
through which all European Societies are, at this hour,
travelling.   Apparently a still baser sort of Aristocracy ?
An infinitely baser ; the basest yet known.*

In which, however, there is this advantage, that, like
Anarchy itself, it cannot continue.   Hast thou considered how Thought is stronger than Artillery-parks,
and (were it fifty years after death and martyrdom, or
were it two thousand years) writes and unwrites Acts of
Parliament, removes mountains ; models the World
like soft clay ?   Also how the beginning of all Thought,
worth the name, is Love ; and the wise head never yet
was, without first the generous heart ?   The Heavens
cease not their bounty ; they send us generous hearts
into every generation.   And now what generous heart
can pretend to itself, or be hoodwinked into believing,
that Loyalty to the Moneybag is a noble Loyalty ?
Mammon, cries the generous heart out of all ages and
countries, is the basest of known Gods, even of known
Devils.   In him what glory is there, that ye should
worship him ?   No glory discernible ; not even terror :
at best, detestability, ill-matched with despicability !
—Generous hearts, discerning, on this hand, wide-
spread Wretchedness, dark without and within, mois-
tening its ounce-and-half of bread with tears ; and, on
that hand, mere Balls in flesh-coloured drawers, and
inane or foul glitter of such sort,—cannot but ejaculate,
cannot but announce : Too much, O divine Mammon ;
somewhat too much !—The voice of these, once announcing itself, carries *fiat* and *pereat* in it, for all things
here below.

Meanwhile we will hate Anarchy as Death, which it
is ; and the things worse than Anarchy shall be hated

more. Surely Peace alone is fruitful. Anarchy is destruction ; a burning up, say, of Shams and Insup-
portabilities ; but which leaves Vacancy behind. Know
this also, that out of a world of Unwise nothing but an
Unwisdom can be made. Arrange it, constitution-build
it, sift it through ballot-boxes as thou wilt, it is and
remains an Unwisdom,—the new prey of new quacks
and unclean things, the latter end of it slightly better
than the beginning. Who can bring a wise thing out
of men unwise ? Not one. And so Vacancy and general
Abolition having come for this France, what can
Anarchy do more ? Let there be Order, were it under
the Soldier's Sword ; let there be Peace, that the bounty
of the Heavens be not spilt ; that what of Wisdom they
do send us bring fruit in its season !—It remains to be
seen how the quellers of Sansculottism were themselves
quelled, and sacred right of Insurrection was blown
away by gunpowder ; wherewith this singular eventful
History called *French Revolution* ends.

The Convention, driven such a course by wild wind,
wild tide, and steerage and non-steerage, these three
years, has become weary of its own existence, sees all
men weary of it ; and wishes heartily to finish. To the
last, it has to strive with contradictions : it is now
getting fast ready with a Constitution, yet knows no
peace. Sieyes, we say, is making the Constitution once
more ; has as good as made it. Warned by experience,
the great Architect alters much, admits much. Distinction of Active and Passive Citizen, that is, Money-
qualification for Electors : nay Two Chambers, ' Council of Ancients ', as well as ' Council of Five-hundred ' ;
to that conclusion have we come ! In a like spirit,
eschewing that fatal self-denying ordinance of your Old
Constituents, we enact not only that actual Convention
Members are re-eligible, but that Two-thirds of them
must be re-elected. The Active Citizen Electors shall
for this time have free choice of only One-third of their
National Assembly. Such enactment, of Two-thirds
to be re-elected, we append to our Constitution ; we

submit our Constitution to the Townships of France,
and say, Accept *both*, or reject both. Unsavoury as this
appendix may be, the Townships, by overwhelming
majority, accept and ratify. With Directory of Five;
with Two good Chambers, double-majority of them
nominated by ourselves, one hopes this Constitution
may prove final. *March* it will; for the legs of it, the
re-elected Two-thirds, are already here, able to march.
Sieyes looks at his paper-fabric with just pride.

But now see how the contumacious Sections, Lepelletier foremost, kick against the pricks !* Is it not
manifest infraction of one's Elective Franchise, Rights
of Man, and Sovereignty of the People, this appendix
of re-electing *your* Two-thirds ? Greedy tyrants who
would perpetuate yourselves !—For the truth is, victory over Saint-Antoine, and long right of Insurrection,
has spoiled these men. Nay spoiled all men. Consider
too how each man was free to hope what he liked; and
now there is to be no hope, there is to be fruition,
fruition of *this*.

In men spoiled by long right of Insurrection, what
confused ferments will rise, tongues once begun wagging ! Journalists declaim, your Lacretelles, Laharpes;
Orators spout. There is Royalism traceable in it, and
Jacobinism. On the West Frontier, in deep secrecy,
Pichegru, durst he trust his Army, is treating with
Condé : in these Sections, there spout wolves in sheep's
clothing, masked Emigrants and Royalists.[1] All men,
as we say, had hoped, each that the Election would do
something for his own side : and now there is no Election, or only the third of one. Black is united with
white against this clause of the Two-thirds; all the
Unruly of France, who see their trade thereby near
ending.

Section Lepelletier, after Addresses enough, finds that
such clause is a manifest infraction; that it, Lepelletier,
for one, will simply not conform thereto; and invites

[1] Napoleon, Las Cases (in Choix des Rapports, xvii. 398–
411).

all other free Sections to join it, ' in central Committee ',
in resistance to oppression.[1] The Sections join it, nearly
all ; strong with their Forty-thousand fighting men.
The Convention therefore may look to itself ! Lepelletier, on this 12th day of Vendémiaire, 4th of October
1795, is sitting in open contravention, in its Convent of
Filles Saint-Thomas, Rue Vivienne, with guns primed.
The Convention has some Five-thousand regular troops
at hand ; Generals in abundance ; and a Fifteen-hun-
dred of miscellaneous persecuted Ultra-Jacobins, whom
in this crisis it has hastily got together and armed, under
the title *Patriots of Eighty-nine*. Strong in Law, it
sends its General Menou to disarm Lepelletier.

General Menou marches accordingly, with due summons and demonstration ; with no result. General
Menou, about eight in the evening, finds that he is
standing ranked in the Rue Vivienne, emitting vain
summonses ; with primed guns pointed out of every
window at him ; and that he cannot disarm Lepelletier.
He has to return, with whole skin, but without success ;
and be thrown into arrest, as ' a traitor '. Whereupon
the whole Forty-thousand join this Lepelletier which
cannot be vanquished : to what hand shall a quaking
Convention now turn ? Our poor Convention, after
such voyaging, just entering harbour, so to speak, has
struck on the bar ;—and labours there frightfully, with
breakers roaring round it, Forty-thousand of them, like
to wash it, and its Sieyes Cargo and the whole future of
France, into the deep ! Yet one last time, it struggles,
ready to perish.

Some call for Barras to be made Commandant ; he
conquered in Thermidor. Some, what is more to the
purpose, bethink them of the Citizen Bonaparte, un-
employed Artillery-Officer, who took Toulon. A man
of head, a man of action : Barras is named Commandant's-Cloak ; this young Artillery-Officer is named
Commandant. He was in the Gallery at the moment,
and heard it ; he withdrew, some half-hour, to consider

---

[1] Deux Amis, xiii. 375–406.

with himself : after a half-hour of grim compressed considering, to be or not to be, he answers *Yea*.

And now, a man of head being at the centre of it, the whole matter gets vital. Swift, to Camp of Sablons ; to secure the Artillery, there are not twenty men guarding it ! A swift Adjutant, Murat is the name of him, gallops ; gets thither some minutes within time, for Lepelletier was also on march that way : the Cannon are ours. And now beset this post, and beset that ; rapid and firm : at Wicket of the Louvre, in Cul-de-sac Dauphin, in Rue Saint-Honoré, from Pont-Neuf all along the north Quays, southward to Pont *ci-devant* Royal,—rank round the Sanctuary of the Tuileries, a ring of steel discipline ; let every gunner have his match burning, and all men stand to their arms !

Thus there is Permanent-session through the night ; and thus at sunrise of the morrow, there is seen sacred Insurrection once again : vessel of State labouring on the bar ; and tumultuous sea all round her, beating *générale*, arming and sounding,—not ringing tocsin, for we have left no tocsin but our own in the Pavilion of Unity. It is an imminence of shipwreck, for the whole world to gaze at. Frightfully she labours, that poor ship, within cable-length of port ; huge peril for her. However, she has a man at the helm. Insurgent messages, received and not received ; messenger admitted blindfolded ; counsel and counter-counsel : the poor ship labours !—Vendémiaire 13th, year 4 : curious enough, of all days, it is the fifth day of October, eve of the anniversary of that Menad-march, six years ago ; by sacred right of Insurrection we are got thus far.

Lepelletier has seized the Church of Saint-Roch ; has seized the Pont-Neuf, our piquet there retreating without fire. Stray shots fall from Lepelletier ; rattle down on the very Tuileries Staircase. On the other hand, women advance dishevelled, shrieking, Peace ; Lepelletier behind them waving its hat in sign that we shall fraternize. Steady ! The Artillery-Officer is steady as bronze ; can, if need were, be quick as lightning. He sends eight-hundred muskets with ball-cartridges to the

Convention itself ; honourable Members shall act with
these in case of extremity : whereat they look grave
enough. Four of the afternoon is struck.[1] Lepelletier,
making nothing by messengers, by fraternity or hat-
waving, bursts out, along the Southern Quai Voltaire,
along streets and passages, treble-quick, in huge veri-
table onslaught ! Whereupon, thou bronze Artillery-
Officer— ? 'Fire !' say the bronze lips. And roar
and thunder, roar and again roar, continual, volcano-
like, goes his great gun, in the Cul-de-sac Dauphin
against the Church of Saint-Roch ; go his great guns
on the Pont-Royal ; go all his great guns ;—blow to
air some two-hundred men, mainly about the Church
of Saint-Roch ! Lepelletier cannot stand such horse-
play ; no Sectioner can stand it ; the Forty-thousand
yield on all sides, scour towards covert. 'Some hundred or so of them gathered about the Théâtre de la
République ; but', says he, 'a few shells dislodged
them. It was all finished at six '.

The Ship is *over* the bar, then ; free she bounds shore-
ward,—amid shouting and vivats ! Citoyen Bonaparte is 'named General of the Interior, by acclamation ' ; quelled Sections have to disarm in such humour
as they may ; sacred right of Insurrection is gone for
ever ! The Sieyes Constitution can disembark itself,
and begin marching. The miraculous Convention Ship
has got to land ;—and is there, shall we figuratively
say, changed, as Epic Ships are wont,* into a kind of
Sea Nymph, never to sail more ; to roam the waste
Azure, a Miracle in History !

' It is false ', says Napoleon, ' that we fired first with
blank charge ; it had been a waste of life to do that '.
Most false : the firing was with sharp and sharpest
shot : to all men it was plain that here was no sport ;
the rabbets and plinths of Saint-Roch Church show
splintered by it to this hour.—Singular : in old Bróglie's
time, six years ago, this Whiff of Grapeshot was promised ; but it could not be given then ; could not have

---

[1] Moniteur, Séance du 5 Octobre 1795.

profited then. Now, however, the time is come for it,
and the man*; and behold, you have it ; and the thing
we specifically call *French Revolution* is blown into space
by it, and become a thing that was !—

CHAPTER VIII

FINIS

HOMER'S EPOS, it is remarked, is like a Bas-Relief
sculpture : it does not conclude, but merely ceases.
Such, indeed, is the Epos of Universal History itself.
Directorates, Consulates, Emperorships, Restorations,
Citizen-Kingships succeed this Business in due series,
in due genesis one out of the other. Nevertheless the
First-parent of all these may be said to have gone to
air in the way we see. A Babœuf Insurrection, next
year, will die in the birth ; stifled by the Soldiery.
A Senate, if tinged with Royalism, can be purged by
the Soldiery ; and an Eighteenth of Fructidor*transacted by the mere show of bayonets.[1] Nay Soldiers'
bayonets can be used *à posteriori* on a Senate, and make
it leap out of window,—still bloodless ; and produce
an Eighteenth of Brumaire.[2] Such changes must happen : but they are managed by intriguings, caballings,
and then by orderly word of command ; almost like
mere changes of Ministry. Not in general by sacred
right of Insurrection, but by milder methods growing
ever milder, shall the events of French History be henceforth brought to pass.

It is admitted that this Directorate, which owned, at
its starting, these three things, an ' old table, a sheet of
paper, and an inkbottle ', and no visible money or
arrangement whatever,[3] did wonders : that France,
since the Reign of Terror hushed itself, has been a new

[1] Moniteur, du 4 Septembre 1797.
[2] 9th November 1799 (Choix des Rapports, xvii. 1–96).
[3] Bailleul, Examen critique des Considérations de Madame de Staël, ii. 275.

France, awakened like a giant out of torpor ; and has gone on, in the Internal Life of it, with continual progress. As for the External form and forms of Life, what can we say, except that out of the Eater* there comes Strength ; out of the Unwise there comes *not* Wisdom !—Shams are burnt up ; nay, what as yet is the peculiarity of France, the very Cant of them is burnt up. The new Realities are not yet come : ah no, only Phantasms, Paper models, tentative Prefigurements of such ! In France there are now Four Million Landed Properties ; that black portent of an Agrarian Law is, as it were, *realized.* What is still stranger, we understand all Frenchmen have ' the right of duel ' ; the Hackney-coachman with the Peer, if insult be given : such is the law of Public Opinion. Equality at least in death ! The Form of Government is by Citizen King, frequently shot at, not yet shot.

On the whole, therefore, has it not been fulfilled what was prophesied, *ex-post facto* indeed, by the Arch-quack Cagliostro, or another ? He, as he looked in rapt vision and amazement into these things, thus spake : [1*] ' Ha ! What is *this* ? Angels, Uriel, Anachiel, and ye other Five ; Pentagon of Rejuvenescence ; Power that destroyedst Original Sin ; Earth, Heaven, and thou Outer Limbo, which men name Hell ! Does the EMPIRE OF IMPOSTURE waver ! Burst there, in starry sheen updarting, Light-rays from out of *its* dark foundations ; as it rocks and heaves, not in travail-throes but in death-throes ? Yea, Light-rays, piercing, clear, that salute the Heavens,—lo, they *kindle* it ; their starry clearness becomes as red Hellfire !

' IMPOSTURE is in flames, Imposture is burnt up : one red sea of Fire, wild-bellowing, enwraps the World ; with its fire-tongue licks at the very Stars. Thrones are hurled into it, and Dubois Mitres, and Prebendal Stalls that drop fatness, and—ha ! what see I ?—all the *Gigs* of Creation : all, all ! Woe is me ! Never since Pharaoh's Chariots, in the Red Sea of water, was there

[1] Diamond Necklace (Carlyle's Miscellanies).

wreck of Wheel-vehicles like this in the Sea of Fire. Desolate, as ashes, as gases, shall they wander in the wind.

'Higher, higher yet flames the Fire-Sea; crackling with new dislocated timber; hissing with leather and prunella. The metal Images are molten; the marble Images become mortar-lime; the stone Mountains sulkily explode. RESPECTABILITY, with all her collected Gigs inflamed for funeral pyre, wailing, leaves the Earth: not to return save under new Avatar. Imposture how it burns, through generations: how it is burnt up; for a time. The World is black ashes;—which, ah, when will they grow green? The Images all run into amorphous Corinthian brass*; all Dwellings of men destroyed; the very mountains peeled and riven, the valleys black and dead: it is an empty World! Woe to them that shall be born then !— — A King, a Queen (ah me !) were hurled in; did rustle once; flew aloft, crackling, like paper-scroll. Iscariot Égalité was hurled in; thou grim de Launay, with thy grim Bastille; whole kindreds and peoples; five millions of mutually destroying Men. For it is the End of the dominion of IMPOSTURE (which is Darkness and opaque Firedamp); and the burning up, with unquenchable fire, of all the Gigs that are in the Earth'. This Prophecy, we say, has it not been fulfilled, is it not fulfilling ?

And so here, O Reader, has the time come for us two to part. Toilsome was our journeying together; not without offence; but it is done. To me thou wert as a beloved shade, the disembodied or not yet embodied spirit of a Brother. To thee I was but as a Voice. Yet was our relation a kind of sacred one; doubt not that ! For whatsoever once sacred things become hollow jargons, yet while the Voice of Man speaks with Man, hast thou not there the living fountain* out of which all sacrednesses sprang, and will yet spring ? Man, by the nature of him, is definable as ' an incarnated Word'. Ill stands it with me if I have spoken falsely : thine also it was to hear truly. Farewell.

EXPLANATORY NOTES

These notes are necessarily selective and do not normally include words to be found in standard dictionaries, nor some proper names. Other names are identified in the index, and cross-referencing has been reduced on the assumption that readers will make use of it.

Abbreviations

CA	Constituent Assembly
CL	*Collected Letters*, Duke–Edinburgh edition (1970–)
CGS	Committee of General Safety
CPS	Committee of Public Safety
EG	Estates General
FR	*The French Revolution*
F.R.	French Revolution
LA	Legislative Assembly
NC	National Convention
NLS	National Library of Scotland
PL	*Paradise Lost*
PP	Paris Parlement
TC	Thomas Carlyle
Works	Carlyle, Centenary edition, 30 vols. (1896–99); citations are to this edition, usually just by volume and page.

VOLUME I

title page: Arrian, *The Discourses of Epictetus* II. xviii.28: 'Great is the struggle, divine the task; the prize is a kingdom, freedom, serenity, peace.'

Marcus Aurelius Antoninus, *Meditations* IX. xxix: 'For who can alter another's conviction? Failing a change of conviction we merely get men pretending to be persuaded and chafing like slaves under coercion.'

xxxiii Goethe, *Venezianische Epigramme* (1791): 'To this stithy I liken the land, the hammer its ruler, / And the people that plate, beaten between them that writhes: / Woe to the plate, when nothing but wilful bruises on bruises / Hit it at random; and made, cometh no Kettle to view!' (trans. by TC)

3 *Hénault*: C. J. F. (1685–1770), man of fashion, scholar, president of the PP, manager of the Queen's household.

Little Trianon: one of two small palaces built for Louis XV betweem 1762 and 1768; belonged first to Mme du Barry and later to Marie Antoinette.

4 *Dubarry*: M. J. A. de V., comtesse (1743–93), last official mistress of Louis XV, guillotined.

Aiguillon: E. A. de V du P. de R., duc d' (1720–88), governor of Brittany whose part in the victory at St Cast, Sept. 1758, was disputed by the Bretons; they later indicted him on a number of charges.

Maupeou: R. N. C. A. de (1714–92), chancellor, engineered the demise of the PP, exiling its members and replacing them with royal appointees.

Richelieu: L. F. A. D. de (1696–1788), marshal, statesman, libertine, grand-nephew of A. J. du P. de Richelieu (1585–1642), cardinal, statesman.

Choiseul: E. F., duc de (1719–75), foreign minister, dismissed, 1770.

5 *Dumouriez*: general C. F. du P. (1739–1823), later foreign minister, minister of war.

Terray: J. M., abbé (1715–78), comptroller-general 1769, preached austerity and efficiency but spent lavishly at court.

Domdaniel: infernal cavern in Southey's *Thalaba the Destroyer* (1801).

Armida-Palace: A., grieving sorceress in Tasso's *Gerusalemme liberata* (1581) who burns her palace on losing her lover.

6 *Chateauroux*: M. A. N., duchesse de (1717–44), see intro.; Louis XV's mistress, ordered to leave him after his serious illness at Metz, 1744.

Pompadour: J. A. P., marquise de (1721–64), Louis XV's beloved mistress, whose enemies tried to banish her from court after a mentally disturbed footman, R. Damiens (1714–57) wounded the king, 1757.

Rossbach: where Frederick II's Prussian army defeated French and Austrian troops, 1757.

Lettres de Cachet: sealed royal letters authorizing arbitrary imprisonment.

7 *Bicêtre Hospital*: men's hospital on the Fontainebleau road, mainly for the mentally ill, paralytics, epileptics.

Regrater of Bread: profiteering middleman; later shown to be untrue.

'brings means of seeing': echoing Goethe, *Zahme Xenien* 3; repeated, 'Varnhagen Von Ense's Memoirs' (xix.106).

Newton's Dog Diamond: which upset a candle on his master's desk, destroying the result of many year's experiments, making him exclaim, 'thou little knowest the mischief thou hast done!'

8 Maison-Bouche *and* Valetaille: 'house channel', 'flunkeydom'.

Not we: TC echoes J. G. Fichte (1762–1814), whose *das Nicht Ich* ('the not me') referred to the mind's power to perceive material creation as a spiritual phenomenon.

9 *'reckons itself real'!*: a favourite notion of TC's that time is what Teufelsdröckh in *Sartor* calls a 'world-embracing Phantasm' (i.203).

Merovingian Kings: first dynasty governing the kingdom of the Franks.

Charlemagne: (*c*.742–814), king of France and Holy Roman Emperor, buried at Aix-la-Chapelle; confused here with Frederick Barbarossa.

Charles the Hammer, Pepin Bow-legged: (1) C. Martel (*c*.688–741), united the Frankish kingdom under his rule. (2) P. III the Short (d. 768), C. M.'s son, first king of the Carolingian dynasty and father of Charlemagne.

Rollo: (d. 917? 923?), one of the fiercest Norman chiefs to invade France in the 9th and 10th centuries.

Towhead: Childeric II (*c*.649–75), proclaimed ruler of Austrasia, 662.

Taillefer: troubadour and warrior, inspired the Normans at the Battle of Hastings.

Fredegonda . . . Brunhilda: (1) (d. 597), queen consort of the Merovingian king Chilperic I. (2) (d. 613), wife of C. I's rival, sought to rule Austrasia and Burgundy, murdered by F.'s son.

Nesle: dame de; according to legend, she lured gallants to the Tour de N., entertained them, and had them thrown in the Seine.

10 Bibliothèque du Roi: founded by Charles V, the collection became part of the B. Nationale after the F.R.

11 *'conflux of Eternities'*: from J. P. F. Richter, *Blumen- Frucht- und Dornenstücke* (1818), first used by TC, 'Signs of the Times' (xxvii.59).

Henri Fourths: (1553–1610), first Bourbon king of France, brought unity and prosperity after religious wars; assassinated.

12 *Clovis*: Clodoveus, (*c*.466–511) king of the Franks; the story is told by St Gregory of Tours, *History of the Franks*, Bk. 3.

13 *penance-shirt*: referring to Emperor Henry IV's penance before Gregory VII (Hildebrand), 1077.

Sorbonne: the Faculty of Theology in the Univ. of Paris, founded by Robert de Sorbon, *c*.1257.

14 *Fronde*: the civil war (1648) between Mazarin and a group of populist nobles and their followers; the word means 'a sling'.

Tiberius and Commodus: Emperors of Rome (42 BC–AD 37 and AD 161–92), whose reigns were marked by tyranny and bloodshed.

15 *taillable et corvéable*: the taille was a property tax on commoners; the corvée imposed unpaid labour on peasants.

Gabelle: the government's salt monopoly ensured its high price, particularly in poorer regions.

naked wretches!: *King Lear*, III.iv.

16 *horror of great darkness*: Gen. 15:12.

cup of trembling: Zech. 12:2.

'faculty of Thought': *Sartor* (i.95).

17 *Chesterfield*: Philip Stanhope, Lord (1694–1773), author of *Letters to His Son* (1774).

18 *Parc-aux-cerfs*: a district in the town of Versailles, formerly a deer park, where Louis XV bought a house for his pleasures, 1755.

Jansenists: influential dissident religious group named after its founder Cornelius Jansen (1585–1638), the bishop of Ypres.

Roche-Aymon: C.'A. de la (1692–1777), cardinal and archbishop of Rheims, grand almoner of France.

Oeil de Boeuf: antechamber of the King's apartment at Versailles, with a circular window or 'bull's eye'.

19 *Sansculottic*: 'without breeches', referring to poorer Parisians, wearing trousers rather than knee-breeches; extreme republicans or revolutionaries.

right hand from your left: Jonah 4:11.

Condé: L. J. de Bourbon, prince de (1736–1818), Louis XV's cousin, governor of Burgundy, general, counter-revolutionary leader.

Chartres: L. P. J., duc d'Orléans (1747–93), named 'Egalité', Bourbon prince, deputy to NC, alleged conspirator against both King and F. R., guillotined.

Dauphin: title of eldest son of the kings of France; Louis XVI took the title in 1765 after the deaths of his father and two elder brothers.

jacta est alea: 'the die is cast', Caesar's words on crossing the Rubicon.

20 *Besenval*: P. V. baron de (1722–91), commander of troops, reputedly exercised political influence over M. Antoinette.

all is Vanity!: Eccles. 1:2.

21 *King of Terrors*: Job 18:14.

22 *Quebec*: fell to the British, 1759.

an epigram: legendary tale that an insulting epigram by Frederick the Great provoked France to declare war.

23 *flattering unction*: Hamlet, III.iv.

'*imprisoned into Time!*': a Fichtean notion; Teufelsdröckh remarks in *Sartor*, 'only in the transitory Time-Symbol is the ever-motionless Eternity we stand on made manifest' (i.91).

'*Dead Dogs*': the Fleet ditch, an open sewer; see Pope, *Dunciad* II. 271 ff.

24 Mayor of the Palace: title of Pepin of Herstal (d. 714), who defended the autonomy of Austrasia and ensured the continuation of the Merovingian kings.

25 *knows her no more*: Ps. 103:16.

in coming years: Mme Can.pan recalls in her *Mémoires* (1822) that once when strolling with the Queen in the park at Versailles she caught sight again of du Barry.

26 *out of the windows*: Eccles. 12:3.

cistern-wheel: Eccles. 12:6.

27 *Artois*: C. P. comte d' (1757–1836), Louis XVI's brother, émigré, later Charles X, king of France, 1824–30.

by a film!: cf. *Sartor* (i.43).

Campan: J. L. H. G. Mme. (1752–1822), M. Antoinette's femme de chambre and defender.

29 *ASTRAEA REDUX*: Sibylline prophecy of a new golden age to follow the return of A. or Justice, told by Virgil, *Eclogues*, iv.

Montesquieu's: C. L. de S. baron de (1689–1755), *philosophe*, author of *Lettres Persannes* (1721), *Esprit des Lois* (1748).

'*annals are vacant*': attrib. to Montesquieu, used again by TC, *Frederick* (xvi.196); the 'paradoxical philosopher' may be Cesare Beccaria, often quoted as saying much the same in the intro. to *Dei delitti e delle pene* (1764).

'*Silence is divine*': a Carlylean and Goethean expression; cf. *Sartor* (1:174).

30 *Attila . . . Thirty-Years' Wars*: (1) king of the Huns, 434–53; (2) *Walter-the-Penniless*: one of the leaders of the French peasant crusade in 1096, renowned for courage and disciplinary skills. (3) *Sicilian Vespers*: Sicilian massacre of the French, 1282, began at first toll of vespers bell. (4) 1618–48, began with the claim of Frederick the Elector Palatine to the throne of Bohemia and ended with Treaty of Westphalia.

grows and dies: cf. Eccles. 3:1.

31 *required of thee!*: Luke 12:20.

Parlement of Paris: supreme court of justice, est. 1345, became a vehicle of opposition to royal despotism.

32 *Turgot*: A. R. J. (1727–81), economist, *philosophe*, Louis XVI's comptroller-general.

Maurepas: J. F. P., comte de (1701–81), minister of state, Louis XVI's chief adviser, opponent of Necker and Turgot.

'*losing all its deformity*': mocking Burke's panegyric in *Reflections on the Revolution in France* (1790) of Louis XIV's dignified reign, 'under which vice itself lost half of its evil by losing all its grossness' (*Works*, 1887 edn., iv.332).

Voltaire . . . Raynals: (1) (1694–1778), for TC, the patron-saint of '*philosophism*'. (2) *Diderot*: D. (1713–84), editor of the *Encyclopédie*. (3) *Alembert*: J. le R. d' (1717–83), mathematician, scientist, *philosophe*. (4) *Marmontels*: J. F. (1723–99), critic, poet, man of letters. (5) *Morellets*: A. (1729–1819), republican economist. (6) *Chamforts*: S. R. N. (1741–94), playwright, committed suicide. (7) G. (1713–96), abbé, republican convert.

Farmer-General: name for speculators who bought the right to levy taxes.

suppers of the gods: Horace, *Satires*, II.vi.65.

'*Age of Revolutions approaches*': Rousseau, *Émile* (1762), Bk.3: 'Nous approchons de l'état de crise et du siècle des révolutions.'

down the eastern steeps: Gray, 'The Progress of Poesy' (1757), 53.

33   *stomach that is empty*: an ironic version of Virgil's picture of the golden age, *Eclogues*, iv.40–5.

not grievous, but joyous: Heb. 12:11.

Gratuitous Tailors: possibly a reference to F. C. M. Fourier (1772–1837), a Besançon clothier's son and leading socialist theorist.

Redeunt Saturnia regna: Virgil, *Eclogues*, iv.6.

Sufficient for the day: Matt. 6:34.

34   *Weber*: J. (1755–1822?), intimate of M. Antoinette, royalist, émigré.

Polignac: Y. M. G., duchesse de (*c*.1749–93), royal governess, financial adviser to the queen, emigrated after the fall of the Bastille.

Lamballe: M. T. L. de S. C., princesse de (1748–92), companion of the queen, massacred.

St. Cloud: Louis XVI purchased it from the duc d'Orléans for 7,700,000 francs.

Sardinian Sisters-in-law: daughters of the King of Sardinia married the king's brothers, the comte de *Provence*, later Louis XVIII (1755–1824) and the comte d'*Artois*.

35 *Grätz*: where Charles X died; now Gonzia, Italy.

Three Days: 27–9 July 1830, when the Parisian masses overthrew Charles X.

prick him, he will bleed: cf. *Merchant of Venice*, III.i.

36 *hieroglyphic writing*: nature as the hieroglyphic expression of divinity was a favourite theme of Novalis, Schelling, and Schiller.

37 *beatings of the wind!*: cf. 1 Cor. 9:26.

Mirabeau: V. R., marquis de (1715–89), political economist, author of *Ami des hommes* (1756).

38 *world keeps wagging*: cf. *As You Like It*, II.vii.

painted on it: cf. TC's poem, 'Cui Bono', xxvi.470.

unbelieving people: cf. Ps. 78:22.

39 *King Popinjay*: a parrot, figuratively, a coxcomb.

Loménie [de] Brienne: E. C. (1727–94), archbishop, cardinal, president of the CA, Calonne's successor as minister of finance, 1787.

Holbach's: P. H. T., baron d' (1723–89), materialist philosopher, strident anti-Christian.

Jezebel: Ahab's wife, who turned against God and killed his prophets; see 1 Kgs 18:4.

40 *'every man . . . mad-man'*: Sartor (i.207).

41 *still other Lies?*: cf. John 8:44.

worse than the beginning: cf. Luke 11:26.

Innovation and Conservation: cf. Coleridge, *On the Constitution of Church and State* (1829), Ch. 2: 'the two antagonist powers . . . under which all other state interests are comprised, are those of PERMANENCE and of PROGRESSION.'

'Amazons': mythical tribe of female warriors who lived in Asia minor and fought on the side of the Trojans; TC may be recalling *Aeneid*, xi.648 ff.

Enceladus . ˙. Trinacria: (1) one of the hundred-headed giants that fought against the gods, buried under Aetna; when he stirred the mountain shook, and when he breathed, it erupted. (2) ancient name for Sicily.

'Man is based on Hope': Sartor (i.129).

42 *'Nestor'*: sage and pious king of Pylos in the *Iliad*.

Montgolfier: J. M. (1740–1810) and J. E. (1745–99), brothers, developed the first passenger balloon.

'*Despotism tempered by Epigrams*': TC was either recalling the well-known phrase of a Russian nobleman on the killing of the emperor, 1801: 'Despotism tempered by assassination, that is our Magna Carta', or S. R. N. Chamfort, *Maximes* (1795), no. 486: 'L'histoire des peuples soumis au despotisme n'est qu'un recueil d'anecdotes.'

43 *confusion of tongues*: at Babel; see Gen. 11:1–8.

many-toned sound: cf. *Odyssey*, ii.150.

Fortunatus: hero of a sixteenth-century French tale, who had an inexhaustible purse and a wishing cap to transport him wherever he wished.

Augean Stable: as one of twelve labours required by Zeus, Hercules had to clean stables left unattended for thirty years.

44 *Hope then is deferred?*: Prov. 13:12.

'*glittering like carbuncles*': cf. *PL* ix.500.

45 *Beaumarchais*: P. A. C. de (1732–99), financier, polemic and dramatic writer, sent to America during the War of Independence, author of *Le Marriage de Figaro* (1784).

46 *Deane . . . Franklin*: (1) S. (1737–89), diplomat. (2) B. (1706–90), philosopher, diplomat, scientist, and author in France from 1776; greatly esteemed by the French.

Kaiser Joseph: Joseph II (1741–90), emperor, enlightened despot.

Jones: J. P. (1747–92), American naval officer, born in SW Scotland; his ship 'Bonhomme Richard' was named in compliment to Franklin's *Poor Richard's Almanack* (1758).

47 *Rochambeaus . . . Lafayette*: (1) J. B. D. de V., comte de (1725–1807), general, marshal. (2) *Bouillé*: F. C. A., marquis de (1739–1800), general, governor of West Indies, American Revolutionary hero, led repression of the Nancy mutiny, helped Louis XVI's flight to Varennes. (3) *Lameths*: [3 brothers] (*a*) A. T. V., comte de (1760–1829), (*b*) C. M. F., comte de (1757–1832), and (*c*) T., comte de (1756–1854), all American volunteers. (4) M. J. P. du M., marquis de [Mons.

Motier] (1757–1832), general, deputy to EG, CA, commander of the Parisian national guard.

Ushant: naval battle, 1778; the duc de Chartres was charged with failing to obey signals.

call endless: cf. *Iliad*, i.2–3.

Jalès: in Languedoc, where a counter-revolutionary plot was formed in Sept. 1790 to overthrow the CA.

48 *Gibraltar*: Spain blockaded the fortress from 1779 to 1782, without taking it.

Pacte de Famille: Choiseul's compact linking Bourbon sovereigns.

Calpe: one of the pillars of Hercules.

49 *Necker*: J. (1732–1804), born at Geneva, Louis XVI's finance minister, moderate constitutionalist.

Celadon: comparing Edward Gibbon (1737–94) to the platonic, sentimental lover in H. d'Urfée's romance *Astrée* (1610); G. broke off his engagement to Susane Curchod (later Mme Necker and de Staël) because his father disapproved.

Staël: A. L. G. Necker, baronne de S.-Holstein (1766–1817), writer, author of *Corinne* (1807), *de l'Allemagne* (1813).

Compte Rendu: 'Account rendered', a hypothetical budget published by Necker, 1791, misled public opinion about the condition of the economy.

'*vectigal of Parsimony*': cf. Cicero, *Paradoxa*, 49.

50 Tenebris: masses in Holy Week.

51 *neither have ye found it*: cf. Prov. 3:13.

reap the whirlwind: Hos. 8:7.

sin is death?: Rom. 6:23.

Longchamp: racecourse between the Seine and Bois de Boulogne.

Liancourt, de la Rochefoucault: F. A. F., duc de la R.-L. (1747–1827), philanthropist, statesman.

'*butter and eggs*': *1 Henry IV*, II.i.

fervid wheels: PL, vii.224.

52 Marat: J. P. (1743–93), revolutionary leader and writer.

advocate of one-man dictatorship, was made physician to Artois' guards, 1777.

Eon: C. de B. d', chevalier (1728–1810), secret agent, pensioned by French government, 1774, on condition of his wearing women's clothes; at death found to be a man.

Dodd: W. (1729–77), pleasure-seeking clergymen, author, hanged for forgery.

Philidor: F. A. D. (1726–95), composer, one of a famous musical family, who studied with and defeated Légal, France's leading chess player, at the Café de la Régence.

54 *Pilâtre-like*: [P. de R.] J. F. (1756–85), physicist, aeronaut, died when his hydrogen balloon exploded while crossing the English Channel.

Mesmer: F. A. (1734–1815), Austrian exponent of animal magnetism, earned large sums after visiting Paris, 1788; investigated by the Academy, fell into disrepute, and withdrew.

infidel-faith!: cf. Matt. 15:28.

Duport . . . Berthollet: (1) A. J. F. (1759–98), lawyer, magistrate, deputy to CA. (2) *Bergasse*: N. (1750–1832), writer, lawyer, deputy to EG. (3) *Espréménil*: J. J. D. d' (1746–94), deputy to EG, leading opponent of the queen, guillotined. (4) C. L., comte (1748–1822), chemist, commissioner of the national mint during the F.R.

Baillys . . . Lavoisiers: (1) J. S. (1736–93), astronomer, politician. (2) *Franklin*: see i.46. (3) A. L. (1743–94), scientist, regarded as founder of modern chemistry.

55 *CONTRAT SOCIAL*: In *Du contrat social* (1762), Rousseau argued that rulers should govern in accordance with the people's general will.

Rohan: L. R., Prince de (1734–1803), cardinal, leading figure in the Necklace affair.

56 *Mablys*: G. B., abbé de (1709–85), political theorist, historian.

and even false: Carlylean notion; see, e.g., TC's 1838 lecture in *Transcripts and Studies* (1887), ed. E. Dowden, 3–4.

57 *cunningly-devised deception*: 2 Pet. 1:16.

58 *Linguet*: S. N. H. (1736–94), satirist who feuded with both court and revolutionaries; guillotined.

59 *Mirabeau*: H. G. R., comte de (1749–91), statesman, orator, politician, and author, for TC the true hero of the F. R., the only man who could have prevented the violence and chaos; later historians have challenged this view, arguing that M.'s role in a royal conspiracy weakened his popular support and made him untrustworthy.

Cagliostro: A. Balsamo (1743–95), Italian alchemist and arch imposter, the subject of TC's 'Count Cagliostro' (*Works* xxviii. 249–318) in *Frazer's Magazine* (1833), he was involved in the complicated swindle of 'The Diamond Necklace' (*Works* xxviii. 324–402) (told by TC in *Fraser's* Magazine, 1837) in which Cardinal Rohan was tricked into paying for the necklace by the Countess Lamotte meaning to acquire it on behalf of Marie Antoinette. TC intended to tell it as a kind of prelude to the *FR*, 'with the strictest fidelity; yet in a kind of musical way' (*CL* 7:61). The account also opens with an attack on the 'dignity of history'.

Walpurgis Dance: in German folklore, a celebration of the powers of darkness.

Satan's Invisible World displayed: a popular work on witchcraft by Professor George Sinclair (d. 1696) of Glasgow, mentioned in *Sartor* (i.35). Cf. 53 above.

smoke of its torment: cf. Rev. 19:3.

60 *'obedience that made men free'*: cf. *Sartor* (i.200): 'whoso cannot obey cannot be free.'

(écraser l'infame)?: Voltaire to d'Alembert, letter of 28 Nov. 1762.

61 *account-day has come*: cf. Rom. 2:6.

day of wrath: Rom. 2:5.

Doom-Book of a God!: cf. Rev. 20:12.

nothing left but Hope: Latin proverb, 'Dum spiro, spero.'

Pandora's Box: in Greek mythology, a box containing the world's evils, opened by Pandora, the first woman. The evils escaped, leaving only Hope.

62 *Saint-Pierre's*: J. H. B. de (1737–1814), author of *Paul et Virginie* (1789), a novel in which primitivism and natural simplicity are exalted over civilization.

Louvet's: [de C.] J. B. (1760–97), Girondist, author of *Les*

Amours du Chevalier de Faublas (1787–89), about the numerous love affairs of his heroine Lodoïska.

65 *material fire*: described by Gibbon, *Decline and Fall*, Ch. 40.

66 *Malesherbes*.... *Sabatiers*: (1) C. G. de L. de (1721–94), Louis XVI's last chancellor. (2) *D'Espréménil*: see i.54. (3) *Lepelletiers*: [L. de St.-F.] M. (1760–93), Parisian deputy to EG, murdered by royalists. (4) *Lamoignons*: C. F. de (1735–89), judge, reformist keeper of the seals, assistant to Brienne, supporter of the PP, later of the king. (5) *Duports*: see i.54. (6) *Fréteaus*: [F. de St.-J.] E. M. J. P. (1745–94), judge, leader of the PP in opposition, deputy to EG, CA. (7) [S. de C.] abbé (d. 1816), clerical counsellor of the PP, supporter of F. de St.-J.

ambrosial curls!: Olympus quaked when Zeus shook his locks; see *Iliad*, i.528–30.

67 *thick as autumnal leaves*: *PL*, i.302.

Polignac: J., comte de (d.1817), postmaster-general, emigrated 1789.

68 *Coigny*: M. F., duc de (1737–1821), marshal, commander of royalist armies, 1791.

Ormesson: H. F. d' (1751–1807), blundering successor to J. de F., 1783.

70 *Calonne*: C. A. de (1734–1802), statesman, lawyer, comptroller-general, 1783.

Foulons, Berthiers: (1) J. F. (1715–89), director of the army during the Seven Years War, candidate for the comptroller-ship. (2) [B. de S.] L. B. F. (1737–89), F.'s son-in-law, intendant of Paris; both violently killed by a Parisian mob.

71 *rough places plain*: Luke 3:5.

73 *la Motte*: J. de St.-R., comtesse de (1756–91), architect of the Necklace affair, imprisoned in the Salpêtrière, 1786.

74 *Aaron's Rod*: Exod. 4:2.

75 *Talleyrand*: [T.-P.] C. M., comte de (1754–1838), bishop, deputy to the EG, NC, statesman, diplomat.

76 *Orpheus*: in Greek mythology a musician, the sound of whose lyre persuaded Pluto to release his wife Eurydice from the underworld.

78 *Cave of the Winds*: where Aeolus keeper of the winds in Greek mythology tamed their passions.

80 *vacant interlunar cave*: Milton, *Samson Agonistes*, 89.

Breteuil . . . Montmorin: (1) L. A. Le T., baron de (1730–1807), minister of the king's house, émigré diplomat. (2) [de S. H.] A. M., comte de (1745–92), foreign minister in 1787, supporter of Necker, violently killed by a Parisian mob.

83 *'States-General?'*: þody composed of representatives of the clergy, nobility, and third estate, assembled 5 May 1789 to propose solutions to the national deficit.

84 *vain jangling*: cf. *PL*, xii.55.

85 *Neptuno-Plutonic*: theory stating that geological formations came from both the action of water and intense heat, advanced by James Hutton, *Theory of the Earth* (1785).

fool says in his heart: Ps. 14:1.

to-morrow be as yesterday: cf. Isa. 56:12.

86 *Weisshaupt*: A. (1748–1830), mystic, founder of the Illuminati, an anti-clerical and republican secret society.

Harmodius and Aristogiton: Athenian champions of liberty.

Nemean Lion: overcome by Hercules as his first labour.

87 *'all things but death'*: Sancho Panza, in *Don Quixote*, ii. Ch.43: 'Paro todo hay remedio sino par la muerte.'

sound and fury: *Macbeth*, v.v.

Bed of Justice: a special session of the PP at which the King could compel its members to register his decrees, named after the King's bed-shaped throne in parliament.

88 *Greek meeting Greek*: common version of Nathaniel Lee, *The Rival Queens* (1667): 'Greek joyn'd Greek.'

his sublime head: cf. Horace, *Odes*, I.i.34–6.

90 *Vulcan's-panoply*: Roman god of the smithy.

murdered Lally: T. A., comte de L.-T. (1702–66), beheaded in Paris for surrendering to the English in India, 1761.

91 *young Lally*: T. G., marquis de L.-T. (1751–1830), Parisian deputy to EG, moderate constitutionalist.

94 *Stadtholder*: William V (1748–1806), last stadtholder, or leader of Netherlands union, English sympathizer, exiled 1795.

95 *enterprises of pith*: cf. *Measure for Measure*, I.iv.

sphere answering sphere: *PL*, vi.315.

96 *confusions of confusions*: cf. *PL*, ii.996.

97 *Buffon*: M. F. de St.-B., Mme. de (1732–69), wife of the naturalist G. L. Leclerc, comte de B. (1707–88).

99 *Rivarol*: A., comte de (1753–1801), royalist writer.

100 *Horse in the Fable*: Aesop's.

101 *measure of the Inquity*: cf. Job 4:8.

set against man: cf. Gen. 16:12.

102 *fruit . . . within clutch*: cf. *Odyssey*, xi.588–92.

103 *Danaë*: visited by Zeus in a shower of gold; see Horace, *Odes*, III.xvi.1–11.

104 *cockatrice-egg*: Isa. 59:5.

106 *Brennus*: according to tradition, the leader of the Gauls who captured Rome, 390 BC.

108 *Calypso's Island*: where the shipwrecked Odysseus is kindly received, *Odyssey*, xii.

spectacle to gods and men: cf. 1 Cor. 4:9.

109 *Bertrand de Moleville*: A. F., marquis de (1744–1818), minister of the navy, royalist, historian, emigrated 1792.

Jacobins' Society: the most influential political group of the F. R., began as the Breton club at Versailles 1789, later moved to Paris, founded in the convent of the Jacobin friars, 1791; closed Nov. 1795.

110 *Mounier, a Barnave*: (1) J. J., baron (1752–1810), general, member of the Directorate, 1799. (2) A. P. J. M. (1761–93), deputy to the CA, historian.

Broglie: V. F., duc de (1718–1804), general, minister of war.

111 *wreck-storm of* Paul et Virginie: see note i.62, and *P. et V.* (1825 edn.), 162–3.

112 *BONAPARTE!*: N. (1769–1821), later general, first consul, emperor.

Nessus'-shirt: the centaur's poisoned shirt that burnt Hercules' flesh.

121 *Fénelon*: F. de S. de la M., archbishop (1651–1715), mystical theologian, liberal.

potter may shape: cf. Isa. 64:8.

123 *Aintrigues*: [Antraigues] E. L. H. de L., comte d' (1755–1812), deputy to the EG, radical converted to the émigré cause, assassinated in London.

Sieyes: E. J. abbé (1748–1836), writer, constitutional theorist.

Laclos: P. A. B. C. de (1741–1803), major-general, author of the *Liaisons Dangereuses* (1782).

127 *Bailliages, by Seneschalsies*: 'tribunal of a bailiff'; 'seneschal's jurisdiction'. Almost all men over 25 whose names were on the taxation rolls had a vote.

Cahier: a valuable source for modern historians unavailable to TC.

128 *sleep no more!*: *Macbeth*, II.ii.

130 *thorn in its nose*: cf. Ezek. 8:17.

Behemoth-Briareus: Behemoth, large animal described in Job 40:15; Briareus, a hundred-headed giant.

131 *Gracchi*: Tiberius and Caius Sempronius, tribunes of Rome, 2nd century BC.

Achilles . . . killed mutton: *Iliad*, ix. 205–10.

132 *Guillotin*: Dr J. I. (1738–1814), professor of anatomy, physiology, and pathology at the Univ. of Paris, deputy to EG, CA; his machine was considered to benefit mankind as it was quicker than previous methods of execution, and meant for criminals of all classes.

Brigands: armed hordes that terrorized the French countryside and provoked the 'Great Fear', said to be in the service of aristocrats and foreign countries.

133 (νυκτὶ ἐοικώς)!: *Iliad*, i.47.

Immortals fighting: cf. *Aeneid*, ii.622–3.

134 *Dampmartin*: captain A. H. C. de (1755–1820), commander of the Strasbourg garrison at the outbreak of the F.R., writer.

Réveillon: wealthy wallpaper manufacturer whose premises were stormed and ransacked by workers, 28 April, in spite of military protection; there were heavy casualties, though widely varying estimates. TC's account agrees closely with George Rudé, *The Crowd in the French Revolution* (1967).

135 *'Communion of Drudges'*: a Carlylean expression.

137 *evil is his good*: *PL*, iv.110.

Diana in the shape of Hunger?: cf. Butler, *Hudibras* (1663), I.ii. 781–4.

Dioscuri: twin sons of Zeus.

138 *Brézé*: H. E., marquis de D.-B. (1762–1829), grand master of ceremonies under Louis XVI, XVIII, and Charles X.

139 *Xerxes*: who wept at the destruction of the Persian army in Aeschylus's *Persai*.

140 *September Massacres* ... *Lodi*: (1) see ii.148–64. (2) where Bonaparte's troops charged Austrian defences, 1792.

Peterloos ... *Tarbarrels*: (1) violent dispersal of a radical meeting, Manchester, 16 Aug. 1819. (2) *Tenpound Franchises*: introduced in 1832 Reform Bill. (3) ignited in political disturbances, cf. *Latter-Day Pamphlets* (xx.2), 'leading-articles and tar-barrels'.

'be your help!': misquoting Luther at the Diet of Worms.

Grecian birds might drop dead: Bacon, *Sylva Sylvarum* (1627), no. 127: 'It hath been anciently reported ... that extreme applauses and shouting of people assembled in great multitudes, have so rarified and broken the air, that birds flying over have fallen down, the air not being able to support them.'

142 *Malebranche*: N. (1638–1715), theologian, Cartesian philosopher.

Théroigne?: [Terwagne], A. J. (1762–1817), heroine of the F.R., leader of the women's march on Versailles, Oct. 1789, died insane.

Valadi: J. G. C. (d. 1793), abolitionist, follower of the English Quaker and vegetarian ('Pythagorean'), Robert Pigott (1736–94), guillotined.

Brissot: J. P. [B. de W.] (1754–93), abolitionist, leading Girondist, deputy to NC, guillotined.

Condorcet: M. J. A. N. Caritat, marquis de (1743–94), *philosophe*, mathematician, revolutionary.

Clavière: E. (1735–93), French finance minister 1792, Girondist, killed himself in prison.

'*Moniteur Newspaper*': founded, 1789, by C. J. Panckoucke (1736–98), periodical magnate.

Maillard: S. M., (1763–94), Parisian political figure, took part in the storming of the Bastille, the women's march, and the Sept. massacres.

Hulin: captain P. A. (1758–1841), Bastille victor, later general.

Jourdan: M. (1749–94), feared ruffian, executioner ('*coup-tête*'), executed.

143 *Lecointre*: L. (1750–1805), Versailles draper, successively Dantonist, Montagnard, Thermidorean.

Santerre: A. J. (1752–1809), Bastille, victor, commander of the Parisian national guard, Vendée general, 1793.

Danton: G. J. (1759–94), militant, orator, deputy to CA, NC, member of the CPS, accused on conspiracy, guillotined.

Desmoulins: L. C. S. (Camille), (1760–94), revolutionary and journalist, allied with Dantonists, executed.

fellow of infinite shrewdness: cf. *Hamlet*, V.i.

Cordeliers District: whose citizens, under the direction of Danton, Marat, and Desmoulins, founded the militant Cordeliers club (1790–5), which rivalled the Jacobins in influence until the CPS moved against it, March 1794.

145 *lion's whelp*: Shakespearian expression, as *1 Henry IV*, III.iii.

sinned against and sinning: cf. *King Lear*, III.ii.

146 *Ali's admiration*: reported by Gibbon, *Decline and Fall*, Ch. 50.

147 '(humé, *swallowed) all* Formulas': a phrase congenial to TC in 'Fils Adoptif', *Mémoires biographiques* (1834–5), iii.151–2.

148 Robespierre: M. (1758–94), lawyer, revolutionary leader.

149 Cazalès: captain J. A. M. de (1758–1805), deputy to the EG, orator of the rightist opposition in the CA, royalist émigré.

Pétion: [P. de V.] J. (1756–94), Jacobin, mayor of Paris, federalist, executed by Jacobins.

Rabaut-St.-Etienne: J. P. (1743–93), Protestant minister, deputy to the CA, NC, executed by Jacobins.

151 *not so miserable*: cf. *PL*, i.157.

Astolpho: English knight who gets possession of a hippogriff in Ariosto's *Orlando Furioso* (1532).

Dumont: P. E. L. (1759–1829), Benthamite theorist, writer.

152 *victorious cause* . . . (victa Catoni): Lucan, *Civil Wars* i.128.

    Cromwell-Grandison: Mirabeau's term for Lafayette, seeing him as a combination of Richardson's faultless gentlemanly hero and the Protector.

    Crispin-Catiline: Mirabeau's term for d'E., comparing him to the debauched Roman conspirator and to Le Sage's farcical character in the play of the same name.

153 Younger *Mirabeau*: A. B. L. de R., vicomte de (1754–92), M.'s younger brother, defender of absolute monarchy.

    Reeds shaken in the wind!: Matt. 11:7.

    become least: cf. Luke 9:48.

    Grégoire: H. B. (1750–1831), republican cleric, deputy to NC, abolitionist, church reformer.

154 Maury: J. S., abbé (1746–1817), counter-revolutionary.

    Mercier: L. S. (1740–1814), writer, deputy to NC.

    O Tempus ferax rerum!: cf. Ovid, *Metamorphoses*, xv.234.

155 *Some towards honour*: 2 Tim. 2:20.

159 *faith and obedience*: cf. Rom. 16:26.

    Carroccio: waggon with a bell, described by Gibbon, *Decline and Fall*, Ch. 49.

160 *Resist the beginnings!*: Ovid, *Remediorum Amoris*, 91.

161 'system of inertia': P. J. B. Buchez and P. C. Roux-L., *Histoire parlementaire* (1834–38), i.425.

    harmless as doves: Matt. 10:16.

    Eros-egg: in Greek myth Eros was born from the cosmic egg, produced by Chaos (or Night); see *Sartor* (i.194), 'one day to be hatched into a Universe!'

168 National Assembly!: (June 1789–30 Sept. 1791), legislative body during the first period of the F.R; became the CA on 9 July 1789 after the king agreed to allow the third estate to join in meetings with the clergy and nobility.

170 *cranes on wing*: echoing Schiller's poem 'Die Kraniche von Ibykus' (1797) and possibly *Iliad*, iii.1–5.

171 *wheresoever two or three*: Matt. 18:20.

    Abdiel: loyal though dissenting angel; *PL*, v.805–9.

172 *bitter rain too*: cf. Rev. 8:11.

173 *word in season*: Prov. 15:23.

    moment is the mother of ages!: cf. Voltaire, *Dictionnaire philosophique* (1764) vii.571: 'La présent accouche, dit-on, de l'avenir.'

174 *respect of persons*: Col. 3:25.

    Sunt lachrymae rerum: *Aeneid*, i.462.

    seas . . . multitudinous: *Macbeth*, II.ii.

178 *universal hubbub*: *PL*, ii.951, in Chaos.

179 *bone of his bone*: Gen. 2:23.

    'dead i' the spital': *Henry V*, v.i.

181 *Pride . . . before a fall*: Prov. 16:18.

    hardened their hearts: biblical expression, as Exod. 14:17.

182 *Flesselles*: J. de (1721–89), lord mayor of the Parisian council, murdered at the Hotel de Ville.

183 *Job's-news*: unwelcome news; Job 3:25.

    choked in the water-works: cf. Mark 5:13.

185 guingette *tabernacles*: country taverns where Parisians went on Sundays; see Lev. 24:1–9 for the 'feast of tabernacles'.

186 *Eumenides*: demonic avengers of the Gods, as in Aeschylus.

188 *Venice wine-glass*: said to burst if poison placed in it.

192 *naphtha-lighted*: main ingredient of Greek fire, which the residents of Constantinople exploded to frighten off invading Barbarians; see Gibbon, *Decline and Fall*, Ch. 52.

    fearful and wonderful: Ps. 139:14.

    deep silence: *Aeneid*, x.63.

    flame-girt Sinai: Exod. 19:18 ff.

    fire by night!: Exod. 13:21.

193 *no abiding*: 1 Chron. 29:15.

194 *Sombreuil*: C. F. V., marquis de (1727–94), general, governor of the Hotel des Invalides.

    Tophet: cf. Isa. 30:33.

195 *quit you like men*: 1 Cor. 16:13.

    do or die: Burns, 'Scots Wha Hae' (1794).

196 *one thing needful*: Luke 10:42.

Priam's curtains!: *2 Henry IV*, I.i.

197 *Clerks of the Basoche*: law clerks.

200 *Pygmies and Cranes*: Greek legend describes the pygmies, tiny dwellers on the southern shores of Ocean, being warred on by migrating cranes.

201 *Crack of Doom!*: *Macbeth*, IV.i.

202 *Fauchet*: C., abbé (1774–93), Bastille negotiator, deputy to LA, NC, founder of *Cercle Social*, a radical club and publishing group.

Spinola-Santerre: comparing the brewer to Ambrogio S. (1569–1630), Spanish general who captured the Dutch fortress of Breda, 1625, after a long siege.

203 *noblest Operas*: *Iphigénie en Aulide* (1774), when Agamemnon laments the required sacrifice of his daughter.

204 *Dove towards . . . Ark!*: Gen. 8:10.

206 *steel bristles*: Cf. *PL*, i.547.

208 *Bacon's Brass Head!*: legendary talking head.

213 *Saint-Huruge*: marquis de (d. 1810), aristocrat, Palais-Royal demagogue, called *Père Adam*, led the insurrection at the Tuileries, 1792.

214 *wholly into ice*: a metaphor used in *Sartor* (i.8); possibly indebted to Robert Boyle's *New Experiments . . . Touching Cold* (1665), 119–23.

216 *a 'wild' kind!*: Bacon, 'Of Revenge', *Essays* (1597).

222 *'destructive wrath'*: *Iliad*, i.1.

no voice for singing: cf. *Aeneid*, i.1.

Whither it goeth?: John 3:8.

223 *World-Phoenix*: *Sartor* (i.194).

From of old: Mic. 5:2.

great Deep: Gen. 7:11.

as in the beginning: Gen. 1:1.

in the whirlwind: cf. Job 38:1.

wrath of men: Ps. 76:10.

225 'Irregular Verbs!': a favourite Carlylean expression, taken

from Isaac D'Israeli, *Curiosities of Literature* (9th edn., 1834), ii.97.

227 *Guelf ... and Ghibelline*: twelfth- and thirteenth-century feuding Italian parties.

228 Credo quia impossibile: Tertullian, *De Carne Christi*, Chap. 5.

229 *King Cambyses' vein*: *1 Henry IV*, II.iv.

230 *Night of Pentecost*: Acts 2:1.

ropes of sand: Bacon, *Promus* (*c*.1594), no. 778.

sunt modi sunt: Proverb, 'Where men are, are established things.'

231 *has his being*: Acts 17:28.

inextinguishable laughter: cf. *Iliad*, i.599.

232 *sons of Adam*: Deut. 32:8.

profiteth not: cf. Job 34:9.

233 *sceptre is departed*: Gen. 49:10.

241 *Mambrino's Helmet*: enchanted gold headpiece described in Ariosto's *Orlando Furioso* Bk. 1; a barber's basin as seen by Don Quixote.

243 *'Hungering go'*: 'Jean Paul Friedrich Richter Again' (xxvii. 122).

246 *Prudhomme*: L. M. (1752–1832), bookseller, revolutionary writer.

Carra: J. L. (1743–93), secretary to the Hospadar of Moldavia and later to Cardinal Rohan, deputy to NC, executed.

Barrère ... Rivarol, Royou: (1) [B. de V.] B. (1755–1841), deputy to CA, NC, secretary of CPS. (2) see i.99. (3) T. M., Royau abbé (*c*.1745–92), editor, royalist writer.

Deep calls to deep: Ps. 42:7.

Domine Salvum Fac Regem: 'Make safe the King, O Lord,' inscription on French coins.

247 *Son of the Morning*: Isa. 14:12.

248 *Bull of Bashan*: Ps. 22:12.

'feast of shells!': Ossian, 'Finegal' (1762), Bk. 3: 'He sent Ullin of the songs to bid him to the f. of shs'; see also 'Biography' (xxviii.47).

250 *gives what he can*: Tobit 4:8: 'If thou hast abundance, give alms accordingly: if thou have but a little, be not afraid to give according to that little.'

Vespasian: Roman emperor renowned for his love of money; for the 'smell of . . . cash', see Suetonius, *Lives of the Caesars*, viii. 23.

252 *Something is rotten*: *Hamlet*, I.iv.

253 *O MY KING*: Michel Jean Sedaine, *Richard Coeur-de-Lion* (1784), Blondel's song.

254 *Estaing*: C. H., comte d' (1729–94), naval officer, commander of the Versailles national guard, executed.

255 *laggards and dastards*: cf. Scott, *Marmion*, V.xii. 2 ('Lochinvar').

bitter and heavy: cf. Prov. 14:10, 12:25.

'*hammer must be stithy*': cf. Goethe, *Der Gross-Cophta* (1791), Act 2: 'Thou must . . . be either anvil or hammer.'

'*hyssop on the wall*': 1 Kgs 4:33.

257 *tempest-tost*: *Macbeth*, I.iii.

Thyestes: who unknowingly feasted on the bodies of his sons.

Job's sons: Job 1:18–19.

260 *THE MENADS*: frantic priestesses of Bacchus.

'Gualches': reactionary self-satisfied Frenchmen.

261 *seize the moment*: cf. Goethe, *Faust*, Pt. 1, *Studierzimmer* (1806): 'He who seizes on the moment, he is the right man.'

'*nothing else interesting*': *Sartor* (i.59–60), quoting Goethe, *Wilhelm Meisters Lehrjahre*.

262 *Judiths*: See Judith 16:2–6.

263 *root of the matter!*: Job 19:28.

264 *warming-pan*: cf. Daniel Hilman, *Tusser Redivivus* (1710), 62: 'The tinkling after them with a Warming-Pan . . . or Kettle, is of good Use to let the Neighbours know you have a Swarm in the Air.'

265 *blessed art thou*: ironically biblical, as Matt. 16:17, Luke 1:28.

266 *Peneus waters*: mistaken by TC for the Hebrus.

267 *stork-flight*: see *Iliad*, ii.459–64.

268 *sits the wind* so?: *Much Ado About Nothing*, II.iii.

278 *THE EQUAL DIET*: *Iliad*, xxiii.57.

279 *Salvator*: S. Rosa (1615–73), painter of the Neopolitan school.

280 readied repast: *Odyssey*, iv.67.

all paths grow dark: Homeric phrase, *Odyssey*, ii.388, iii.487, 497.

Bartholomew Night: massacre of Huguenots, St. B.'s Day, 24 Aug. 1572.

Bassompierre: F. de (1579–1646), marshal, diplomat, writer.

281 *abomination of desolation*: Matt. 24:15.

come suddenly: cf. Jer. 6:26, Isa. 47:11.

282 *Erasmus's Ape*: possibly a ref. to E.'s adage, 'An ape is an ape, although he weare badges of golde.'

283 *make night hideous*: *Hamlet*, I.iv.

286 *swears a prayer or two*: *Romeo and Juliet*, I.iv.

287 *Darkness covers the Earth*: cf. Gen. 1:2.

289 *Hellhound Chase*: cf. *PL*, ii.653–6.

293 *Diomedes'*: fed his horses on human flesh.

Cimmerian World-wreckage: repeated Homeric epithet from Cimmeria, land of darkness, *Odyssey*, xi.19.

295 *Favras' Conspiracy*: Thomas de Mahy, marquis de F. (1744–90), implicated in schemes for the escape of Louis XVI from Paris, hanged.

296 *cut the rope*: TC added as a '*Note of* 1868': 'Calumnious rumour, current long since, in loose vehicles (*Edinburgh Review* on *Mémoires de Bastille*, for example), concerning Friedrich Wilhelm and his ways, then so mysterious and miraculous to many;—not the least truth in it!'

297 *credulous incredulity*: Pascal, *Pensées*, Pt. 2, Art. 18, No. 120: 'The incredulous are the most credulous.'

dramatic miracle: perhaps recalling TC's description of the Athos monks' navel-gazing, *Sartor* (i.220).

feared only fear: *Essays* (1580), Bk. 1, Ch. 17: 'That of which I stand most in fear is fear.'

298 *Cabiric*: the Cabiri were deities held in great veneration in the ancient Greek world.

302 *Epigraph*: Goethe, *Weissagungen des Bakis* (1798), no. 14: 'Walls I can see tumbled down, walls I see also a-building; / Here sit prisoners, there likewise do prisoners sit: / Is the world, then, itself a huge prison? Free only the madman, / His chains knitting still up into some graceful festoon?' (trans. by TC).

303 *and not died!*: cf. Exod. 33:20.

304 *death-birth*: *Sartor* (i.189).

thinks no evil: 1 Cor. 13:5.

305 Mont de Piété: pawn depots to advance small loans to the poor, started by Pope Leo X.

be popularized: echoing Peel's phrase to the Tories, *Fraser's Magazine* (July 1835), xii.37: 'that to preserve their power they must popularise themselves.'

out of the ruleless: cf. Aristotle, *Politics* I.ii.8: 'Men are marked out from the moment of birth to rule or be ruled.'

306 *King Serpent . . . Log*: a version of Aesop's fable of the frogs asking Jupiter for a king; when they refuse his offer of a log, he sends a serpent that devours them.

307 thicker *vessel*: cf. 1 Peter 3:7.

porcelain-clay of humanity: cf. Byron, *Don Juan*, IV.xi.

Medicean Tuileries: purchased by the royal family, 1518, the palace was begun by Catherine de Medicis.

Atreus' Palace: where Thyestes ate his 'fatal repast' (see i.257).

is in the sea: Ps. 77:19.

308 *Toulongeon . . . Gobel*: (1) F. E., vicomte de (1748–1812), deputy to EG, distinguished soldier, author of *Histoire de France depuis la Revolution* (1801). (2) *Thouret*: J. G. (1746–94), legal reformer, executed. (3) *Duport*: (see i.54). (4) J. B. J. (1727–94), bishop, Jacobin sympathizer, sanctioned clerical marriage, executed. Strasbourg is famous for its geese.

310 *logic-chopping generation*: TC's favourite term for Utilitarians and *philosophes*.

311 none to deliver us?: cf. Deut. 32:39.

312 *mother of devotion*: Burton, *Anatomy of Melancholy* (1621), Pt. 3, Sec. 4, Mem. 1, Subs. 2.

313 *Feasts of Reason . . . La Vendée*: (1) celebrations of dechristian-

ization; (2) insurrection and wars south of the Loire, which first broke out March 1793.

314 *St. Domingo*: French colony, West Indies. France gave mulattos full civil rights, soon revoked, and the CA abolished slavery, May 1791, to be met by a revolt of the planters. The violence and disorder that followed largely justify TC's cynicism.

no King *in Israel*: Judg. 17:6.

315 *Bray them in a mortar!*: cf. Provs. 27:22.

hand against his fellow!: cf. Judg. 7:22.

317 *brains are out*: *Macbeth*, III.iv.

318 *Barbaroux*: C. J. M. (1767–94), scientist, administrator, deputy to NC, Girondist, guillotined.

in his Thebaid: hermit in part of upper Egypt.

Simon: S. Stylites, fifth-century ascetic who lived on top of a column.

320 Oriflamme: the old ensign of France.

Chaumette: P. G. (1763–94), dechristianizer, *procureur* of the Paris Commune, guillotined; calling himself Anaxagoras after the rationalist Greek philosopher.

high and giddy mast: cf. *2 Henry IV*, III.i.

321 *Tallien . . . Rossignols*: (1) J. L. (1767–1820), Jacobin, member of the CGS, right-wing Thermidorean, opponent of Robespierre. (2) *Momoro*: A. F. (1756–94), leading member of the Cordeliers, dechristianizer, executed. (3) *Prudhomme*: see i.246: (4) *Collot d'Herbois*: J. M. (1749–96), actor, terrorist, member of the CPS. (5) *Bazires*: C. (1764–94), deputy to NC, executed. (6) *Carriers*: J. B. (1756–94), terrorist, guillotined. (7) *Fouquier-Tinvilles*: A. Q. (1746–95), public prosecutor, inventor of the Hébertist conspiracy theory, guillotined. (8) *Bourdons*: F. L. (1758–98), *procureur* of the PP, deputy to NC, deported by Directory, 4 Sept. 1797. (9) *Héberts*: J. R. (1757–94), leader of the Parisian Sansculottes, member of the Paris Commune, dechristianizer, later deputy to NC, accused of plotting a conspiracy, executed. (10) *Henriots*: F. (1761–94), took part in 10 Aug. insurrection and Sept. massacres, commander of Commune forces, guillotined with Robespierre. (11) *Ronsins*: general C. P. (1752–94), Jacobin dramatist,

executed. (12) general J. A. (1759–1802), Jacobin dramatist, deported.

passion to rags: *Hamlet*, III.ii.

322 *eagles gather*: Matt. 24:28.

323 *Guzman . . . Pache*: (1) A. M. (1752–94), Spanish militant, member of the Paris Commune, guillotined. (2) *Fournier*: C. (1745–1825), commander of Parisian national guard during Sept. massacres. (3) *Miranda*: general F. de (1750–1816), Spanish exile, Girondist, accused of incompetence at the Battle of Neerwinden, deported. (4) *Pereyra*: [Pereira] J. (d. 1794), Jacobin, diplomat, suspected Hebertist, guillotined. (5) *Freys*: [Frei] E. J. (d. 1794) and S. G. (*c*.1760–94), Austrian Jews, bankers, army contractors, accused of being spies, guillotined. (6) *Clavière*: see i.142. (7) *Pache*: J. N. (1746–1823), political functionary during ancien régime and Revolution, minister of war in 1793, mayor of Paris, Mar. 1793–Apr. 1794.

Tartuffe: hypocrite, as in Molière's play, produced 1667.

324 *Paine*: T. (1737–1809), author of 'Common Sense' (1776), *Rights of Man* (1791).

325 *Clootz*: J. B., baron (1755–94), dechristianizer, Jacobin, member of the NC, took the name of the Scythian sage Anacharsis.

326 Antre de Procope: Parisian café, leading resort of intellectuals and radicals.

Julian the Apostate's: (332–63), on accession as emperor he proclaimed toleration and announced his conversion to paganism.

327 *Preceptress Genlis*: F. D., comtesse de (1746–1830), companion of the duc d'Orléans, supposed mother of his daughter 'Mademoiselle Pamela'; wife of A. B., marquis de, comte de G.-S. (1737–93), deputy to NC, guillotined.

Hannah More: (1745–1833), English religious writer.

329 *National* Palaver: TC's term for democracy; see *Past and Present* (x.219).

Liberty . . . of Heaven: cf. 2 Cor. 3:17.

Dilworth's: author of a popular arithmetic book, *The Schoolmaster's Assistant* (1760).

sucking dove: *Midsummer Night's Dream*, I.ii.

Fréron: L. M. S. (1754–1802), son of Voltaire's opponent, deputy to NC, radical editor, Thermidorean, turncoat terrorist and reactionary; his father was depicted satirically as 'Wasp' ('Frélon') in V.'s comedy, *Le Café; ou L'Ecossaise* (1760).

330 *Constant*: [C. de R.] H. B. (1767–1830), Franco-Swiss novelist, political writer, journalist.

safe in the middle: Ovid, *Metamorphoses*, ii.137: 'Medio tutissimus ibis'.

331 *that ran might read*: Hab. 2:2.

To-day swallowing Yesterday: cf. Job 8:9.

332 Omnia mea mecum porto: Cicero, *Paradoxa*, i.1.

heart is full: cf. James Kelly, *Scottish Proverbs* (1721), 356: 'When the heart is full the tongue will speak.'

334 *Magna Charta* clipt: the parchment was said to have been discovered as it was about to be cut up by a tailor.

Feast of the Lapithae: the marriage feast of Hippodamia, at which the Centaurs were defeated by the Thessalians.

335 *Missolonghi*: siege of M., 1825–26, war of freedom in which Byron died in 1824.

Louis Philippe: duc d'Orleans, de Chartres (1773–1850), general, king of France, 1830–48.

All flesh is grass: Isa. 40:6.

337 *Constantine's-banner*: on which was printed 'In hoc signo vinces.'

still waters: Ps. 23:2.

338 *a soft word*: cf. Prov. 15:1.

340 *marked white*: the Romans marked lucky days in the calendar with chalk.

Dicer's Oaths: *Hamlet*, III,iv.

343 *Ye should be men*: cf. *Macbeth*, I.iii.

344 *SOLEMN LEAGUE AND COVENANT*: Agreed with the English in alliance against Charles I and in support of presbyterianism in Britain (see 345). The National Covenant (351) was signed in Greyfriars churchyard, Edinburgh, 28

Feb. 1638, and renewed soon after when a copy was placed for signature in a mansion, later Covenant House, Covenant Close (162 High St.), which TC would have known in his day as a tavern. The allusion is apocryphal, therefore.

347 *Isnard*: M. (1751–1830), merchant, manufacturer, Girondist, deputy to LA, NC.

349 *Roland de la Platrière's Wife*: (1) [husband] J. M. (1734–93), civil servant, minister of the interior, Girondist, committed suicide. (2) [wife] *Phlipon*: M. J. (1754–93), writer, Girondist, guillotined.

351 *a small one!*: cf. 'Characteristics' (xxviii.16–18).

352 '*Divine depth of Sorrow*': a Goethe-inspired expression; see *Sartor* (i.151).

in remembrance of me: 1 Cor. 11:24.

354 *wears it on its sleeve*: *Othello*, I.i.

355 *dwellers in Mesopotamia*: Acts 2:9.

357 *Topsyturvied!*: *Verkehrte Welt*, published in *Peter Leberrechts Volksmährchen* (1797); see *German Romance* (xxi.258–59).

360 *Adam himself delved*: echoing John Ball's words at Blackheath, 1381: 'When Adam dolve / And Eve span / Who was then the gentleman?'

361 *though he be none*: cf. *Macbeth*, I.iii.

Whosoever can come: cf. Rev. 22:17.

362 *lest a worst thing*: John 5:14.

366 *When eye fails*: reversing *1 Henry VI*, I.iv: 'though thy speech doth fail, / one eye thou hast.'

not loud but deep: *Macbeth*, V.iii.

369 *that of Jacob*: see Gen. 49.

370 νήπια τέκνα: 'little children'; *Iliad*, ii.136.

371 *according to Seneca*: *Moral Essays*, I.ii.9: 'a contest worthy of God,—a brave man matched against ill-fortune.'

Sin had come: cf. Rom. 5:12.

372 *Hannibal's*: Hannibal, on crossing the Alps, cut a passage through solid rock by first heating and then pouring vinegar on it; see Livy, *Historiae*, XXI.xxxvii.1–6.

374 *Mailly*: A. J. de., marquis d'Haucourt (1708–94), marshal

defended Tuileries during 10th Aug. insurrection, executed.

Lückner: N., comte de (1722–94), Bavarian soldier, marshal, commander of Rhine army, executed.

380 *ass does eating thistles*: proverb which provoked Marcus Crassus to laugh for the only time in his life; see Cicero, *De Finibus*, V.xxx.92.

386 *smoking flax*: Isa. 42:3.

387 *Stanislaus*: S. Leszczynski (1677–1766), titular King of Poland, father-in-law of Louis XV; Lorraine was passed to France after his death.

Washed against Unwashed: 'the great unwashed,' the lower orders, as attrib. to Lord Brougham.

394 *Actaeon-like*: hunter changed to a stag and eaten by his own hounds.

397 *favour the brave*: cf. *Aeneid*, x.284.

399 *'grim and great'*: 'The Nibelungen Lied' (xxvii.263).

401 *in all vital Chaos*: See 'Organic Filaments', *Sartor* (i.195).

407 *EPIMENIDES*: sixth century BC Cretan prophet, slept in a cave for fifty-seven years.

'how could it rot?: *Sartor* (i.56).

'action that is done': *Olympian Odes*, ii.16.

408 *deep as Eternity*: cf. 'Characteristics' (xxviii.4).

Beginning of Days: Heb. 7:3.

holds in it the End: cf. Rev. 22:13.

Peter Klaus: hero of a German folk-legend which was the source of Washington Irving's *Rip Van Winkle*; they both sleep in a cave for twenty years and return to a world they do not recognize.

409 *To-day is not Yesterday*: 'Characteristics' (xxviii.39).

Seven-sleeper[s]: who escaped persecution by hiding in a cave, where they slept for two hundred years.

410 *but he sees not*: cf. Ps. 115:5.

environed in Necessity: cf. *Sartor* (1.78).

411 *offences must come*: Matt. 18:7.

Rozinante: Don Quixote's horse.

Quenouille: a staff used in spinning sent from émigrés to inactive colleagues in France.

Omphale?: in Greek legend, a Lydian queen who bought Hercules as a slave and set him to women's work.

412 *Time's seedfield*: Goethe, *West-Östlicher Divan*, VI: *Buch der Sprüche* (1819); used as a motto for *Sartor*.

Gorsases: A. J. (1752–93), deputy to the NC, journalist, guillotined.

413 *by the solitary pools*: cf. Isa. 14:23.

mouchards: Lafayette's spies.

Dan to Beersheba: biblical expression, as Judg. 20:1.

415 *Vincent*: F. N. (1767–94), leading Hébertist, executed.

416 *voice in the desert*: cf. Isa. 40:3.

419 *while it is yet day*: John 9:4.

420 *(Power of the Air)*: Eph. 2:2.

421 *dust off their feet*: Matt. 10:14.

424 *Bobadilian*: like the braggart in Ben Jonson's *Every Man in His Humour* (1598).

425 *to whom little is given!*: cf. Luke 12:48.

426 *loving mercy*: cf. Mic. 6:8.

430 *Dionysius'-Ear*: an ear-shaped cave used by D. the first to eavesdrop on his court.

431 *Leopold*: [L. II] (1747–92), archduke of Austria, king of Hungary, Holy Roman Emperor, 1790.

432 *Narbonne*: [N.-L.] L., comte de (1755–1813), general, diplomat, minister of war.

434 *Vincennes*: just beyond the Porte St Antoine, residence of medieval kings of France, first used as a state prison by Louis XI.

435 *suspects much*: Santerre's battalion was largely composed of 'victors of the Bastille', barred from the scene by Lafayette.

437 *Teneriffe or Atlas unremoved?*: *PL*, iv.987.

443 *Hercules-and-Typhon*: TC seems to confuse Hercules with Zeus, who eventually vanquished the monster after a long battle.

walks in darkness: cf. 1 John 1:6.

Harpy-swarms: in Greek myth, foul predatory creatures, half women and half bird, ministers of divine vengeance.

444 Moriamur pro rege nostro!: 'Let us die for our king.' Acclamation with which Maria Theresa, her infant son in her hands, is supposed to have been given by the Hungarian Diet, Presburg, Sept. 1741, in the war with Frederick II.

Retz: J. F. P. de G., cardinal de (1613–79), politician, statesman, conspirator against Richelieu.

Cloud-Compeller: Homeric epithet for Zeus.

445 *Men's years are numbered*: cf. Ps. 90:10.

446 *hot in the mouth*: *Twelfth Night*, II.iii.

452 *ed a' nemici sui!*: *Inferno* iii.63.

453 *he was ambitious*: cf. *Julius Caesar* III.ii.

Schicksal und eigene Schuld: cf. Goethe, *Die Leiden des jungen Werthers* (1774), preface to Bk. 1, where he tells his readers, 'und lab das Büchlein deiner Freund sein, wenn du ans Geschick oder eigener Schuld keinen nähern finden kannst.'

455 *Rustic sits waiting*: Horace, *Epistles*, I.ii.41–2.

456 *ploughshares into swords*: Mic. 4:3.

457 *Medes and Persians*: unalterable laws; see Dan. 6:8.

460 *lion in the path*: cf. Prov. 26:13.

halts between two: cf. 1 Kgs 18:21.

461 un grand Peut-être!: Rabelais, F. (*c*.1438–1553).

Pius Sixth: (1717–99), pope from 1775–99.

462 *to do with them?*: biblical expression as Matt. 8:29.

My-Doxy . . . Thy-doxy: attrib. to Bishop Joseph Butler (1692–1752).

Homoiousian: the iota ι is the difference of the single letter between Homoiousians and Homoousians, who differed sharply about whether Christ was the same as or similar to the Father.

eye of a needle: Matt. 19:24.

463 *maintain their churches*: Butler, *Hudibras* II.ii.15–16.

FERSEN: H. A. von, Count (1755–1810), Swedish officer, diplomat, killed by a mob.

'*Queen Chrimhilde*': See 'Nibelungen Lied' (xxvii.241).

464 *Gustav*: Gustavus III (1746–92), king of Sweden from 1771, opponent of the F.R., assassinated by royalists.

Choiseul: C. A. G., duc de (1760–1838), military man.

465 *Goguelat*: general F. (1746–1831), confidant of the King, counter-revolutionary.

470 *Elizabeth*: [de France] P. M. H., Mme de (1764–94), Louis XVI's youngest sister, condemned as a traitor, guillotined.

475 *Argosy . . . Acapulco-ship*: (1) the galley of Jason and the Argonauts, who went in search of the golden fleece. (2) resort of Manilla galleons.

476 *Sixty-nine miles*: In fact 142 miles, or 228 km; it is hard to believe that TC was not aware of the mistake when he passed later editions for publication, though it destroys his argument.

478 *burning marle*: cf. *PL* i.296.

479 *DROUET*: J. B. (1763–1824), future deputy; see ii.368–9.

480 *swenkt*: Old English, 'toil-worn'.

483 *NIGHT OF SPURS*: recalling the Battle of Spurs, 1513, when the English, Germans, and Swiss so frightened the French cavalry that they spurred their horses to flight.

'*has it to hide*': attrib. to TC.

485 *Black Care*: Horace, *Odes*, III.i.40: 'Post equitem sedet atra Cura.'

488 *Ruy Diaz*: El Cid, eleventh-century national hero of Spain.

492 '*LOOM OF TIME!*': Goethe, *Faust*, i.508.

493 *of Earth and Heaven*: cf. Matt. 27:46.

494 *Crispin . . . Sutor-mania*: (1) patron saint of shoe-making. (2) Souters (Scots, cobblers) known for noisy celebrations.

flebile ludibrium: 'deplorable mockery'.

Pickleherring: a buffoon.

495 *forte et dure*: 'intense and severe', a kind of torture for felons who refused to plead, abolished, 1772.

499 *Iron Mask*: a mysterious prisoner in Louis XIV's reign

VOLUME II

4 *Leonidas' Spartans*: L., king of Sparta, who defended Thermopylae against the Persians, 480 BC.

7 *Solon-like*: S. (*c*.638–*c*.558 BC), admired moderate Plutarchian lawgiver, who resigned his office of legislator when his work was done, and retired from Athens.

Union of Avignon: territory under Papal possession since the fourteenth century, to be joined with France.

10 *as in a garment*: cf. Ps. 109:18.

Cincinnatus-like: Roman hero of 500–400 BC, who after delivering his country from danger, returned to his plough.

11 *Legislative [Assembly]*: (1 Oct. 1791–20 Sept. 1792), est. under the const. of 1791, responsible for taxes, expenditures, new statutes, military salaries, wars and treaties; dissolved as a result of the 10th Aug. insurrection.

12 *Limbo near the Moon*: a paradise of fools, where everything wasted on earth is treasured; see *PL*, iii.496.

dust I do raise!: fable of 'The Fly and the Draught-Mule'.

knowest it *not*: cf. Isa. 55:5.

which he has builded: cf. Dan. 4:30.

13 *'ablest to be chosen!'*: cf. 'On History Again' (xxviii.171).

Vergniaud: P. V. (1753–93), lawyer, deputy to the LA, NC, leader of the Girondins, executed.

14 *Guadet*: M. E. (1755–94), barrister, deputy to NC, guillotined.

Gensonné: A. (1758–93), deputy to LA, NC, executed.

Valazé: C. E. du F. de (1751–93), lieutenant, barrister, deputy to NC, committed suicide.

Carnot: L. N. M. (1753–1823), deputy to LA, deputy to NC, military man, savant, 'organizer of Victory', Year II.

15 *Merlin*: [de T.] A. C. (1762–1833), deputy to the LA, NC, military man, opponent of Robespierre and the Jacobins at Thermidor.

Chabot: F. (1756–94), Capuchin friar, converted to Jacobinism, deputy to NC, executed.

Couthon: G. (1755–94), barrister, deputy to NC, member of CPS, supporter of Robespierre, guillotined.

16 Ampulla: [Ampoule], said to have been wrought by an angel at the prayer of St Remi for the anointing of Clovis, broken by Ruhl, 7 July 1793.

18 *Delilah doxy*: false woman like D. see Judg. 16.

19 *anathema maranatha*: accursed, 1 Cor. 16:22.

Eteocles-Polynices: warring rulers of Thebes, who killed one another in combat.

'He shall march, by—!': Sterne, *Tristram Shandy*, Vol. 6, Bk. 8.

Principalities and Powers: Col. 1:16.

20 *Uzez*: diocese in the Massif Central, hub of brigandage and counter-revolutionary activity.

Nismes: [Nîmes], centre of terrorist activity.

Marseilles, Montpellier: where a power struggle broke out between the Jacobins and national guard, 1790–2.

Arles: where an army from Marseilles overthrew the counter-revolutionary Chiffonists, 1792.

Réné: duc d'A. (1409–80), king of Sicily, Jerusalem; Joanna I of Naples, in fact, sold Avignon to Pope Clement VI, 1348.

Louis Eleventh: (1423–83), son of Charles VII and Marie d'Anjou.

Laura de Sade: first seen by *Petrarch* (1304–74) at an Avignon church, an event which he claimed made him a poet.

21 *Silenus*: drunken attendant, nurse of Bacchus, represented as a fat, jovial old man riding on an ass.

24 *life for evermore*: Homeric.

25 di Sorga: Petrarch, *Canzoniere*, cclxxxi.10.

26 *Phoceans*: who gave orders to have their women and children burnt if they failed to defeat the Thessalians.

27 Honi soit!: the motto of the Order of the Garter, 'Evil be to him who evil thinks'.

'*Antinous*': model of manly beauty, companion of Hadrian.

32 *Coblentz*: small fortified city at the junction of the Rhine and Moselle rivers, centre of counter-revolution.

36 *divided against itself*: Mark 3:25.

'*Age of Chivalry* is *gone*': *Reflections, Works* (1887 edn.) iv.331.

37 *Kien-Lung*: [Ch'ien-Lung], the emperor of China, 1710–99.

Priestleys: J. (1733–1804), theologian, man of science; rioters destroyed his house after the radical dinner.

38 *Pilnitz*: The Holy Roman Emperor Leopold II and Frederick William II, king of Prussia, on 27 Aug. 1791, threatened intervention against the F.R.

Pitt: W. [the younger] (1759–1806), prime minister, 1783–1801, 1804–06.

39 in partibus: '*i. p. infidelium*', 'in the region of the faithless,' in the R.C. church, applied to bishops without a diocese.

41 *flung away the scabbard*: cf. Clarendon, *History of the Rebellion* (1674), Vol. 4, Bk. 7: 'When he [Hampden] first drew his sword, he threw away the scabbard.'

44 Polymetis: Greek, 'of many wiles,' Homer's epithet for Odysseus, e.g. *Odyssey*, ii.173.

45 '*Aubry*': possibly A. de la Boucharderie, C. C. (1773–1813), lieutenant of artillery, later general.

46 *bursts of parliamentary eloquence!*: favourite Carlylean expression; see *CL* vi.350.

50 *Huguenin*: S. (*c.*1750–*c.*1803), lawyer, president of the 9–10 Aug. insurrectionary commune, later accused of peculation.

52 *Manuel*: L. P. (1751–93), *procureur-syndic* of the Paris Commune, deputy to NC, guillotined.

Billaud-Varennes: J. N. (1762–1819), radical political leader, member of CPS.

54 *Kaunitz*: W. A., Prince Von (1711–94), Austrian foreign minister during the early years of the F.R.

55 *Harmattan-wind*: a dry wind from the desert in W. Africa.

56 *Trismegistus*: Hermes, 'thrice-greatest,' Greek name of the all-accomplished Egyptian god, Thoth.

Quod bonum sit: cf. Cicero, *De Divinatione*, I.xlv.102.

57 Vos non vobis: 'Thus ye labour, but not for yourselves', attrib. to Virgil.

58 *mandrake-roots*: resembling the human form, fabled to utter a
     deadly shriek when pulled from the ground.

59 *Phrygian Cap-of-Liberty*: supposedly worn by enemies of des-
     potism in ancient Greece and Rome.

     Metternich: [-Winneburg] C. W. L. (1773–1859), Austrian
     statesman, diplomatist.

     Cobentzel: J. P. Graf von (1741–1810), Austrian statesman and
     chancellor, advocated co-operation with Prussia in order to
     absorb Bavaria in exchange for the Austrian Netherlands.

63 *Saint-Christopher*: perhaps ironically referring to the legendary
     giant who bore the Christ-child over a brook.

     Brunswick: K. W. F., Duke of (1735–1806), German general,
     commander of Prussian and Austrian forces, 1792.

65 *Legendre*: L. (1755?–97), Bastille victor, deputy to NC,
     member of the CGS.

75 *his hand findeth!*: cf. Eccles. 9:10.

77 *weighed himself in the balance*: cf. Dan. 5:27.

78 *Philistine Battle!*: Delilah (cf. ii.18) was corrupted by the P.'s
     and betrayed Samson; see Judg. 16.

79 *Time is crooked*: cf. *Hamlet*, I.v.

84 *Tyrtaean*: Tyrtaeus (650 BC) inspired the Spartans with his
     war-songs.

89 *Sanssouci-Schönbrunn*: (1) palace of Frederick the Great at
     Potsdam. (2) palace at Vienna.

90 *Westermann*: general F. J. (1751–94), soldier, revolutionary
     military, guillotined with Danton.

91 *Golgotha*: 'the place of a skull', of the crucifixion.

98 *To your tents, O Israel!*: 1 Kgs 12:16.

100 *Orion and the Pleiades*: Job 9:9.

     Janus Bifrons: Roman deity of two faces, keeper of Heaven; see
     Aeneid, vii.180, xii.198.

     Mr. Facing-both-ways: of the town of Fair-speech, in Bunyan's
     Pilgrim's Progress.

101 *doubtful Hour*: *1 Henry IV*, IV.i.

102 *Fabre d'Eglantines . . . Panises*: (1) (1750–94), poet. satirist.
     deputy to NC, guillotined. (2) *Sergents*: A. F. (1751–1847),

deputy to NC, police administrator, participant in Sept. massacres. (3) E. J. (1757–1833), deputy to NC, member of CGS, CPS, adversary of Robespierre.

Asmodeus' Flight: A., evil demon in Le Sage's *Le Diable Boiteux* (1707) who opens the roofs of houses beneath him to show the interiors to his companion Don Cleofas.

103 *Atropos*: in Greek myth, eldest of the three Fates, who severs the thread of life.

107 *Canute*: (*c.*955–1035), king of England and Denmark.

108 *Caesar in the Capitol*: cf. *Julius Caesar*, III.ii.

109 *spend and be spent!*: 2 Cor. 12:15.

110 *Bellona's thongs!*: cf. *PL*, ii.922.

111 *Moore*: Dr J. (1729–1802), writer, physician.

113 *King of shreds and patches*: *Hamlet*, III.iv.

Biederkeit *and* Tapferkeit: (1) honesty. (2) bravery.

Sempach, of Murten: (1) decisive victory won by the Swiss in their struggle with the Austrian Hapsburgs, 9 July 1386. (2) where the Swiss defeated the troops of Charles the Bold of Burgundy, 1476.

Thorwaldsen's: B. (1768?–1844), Danish sculptor.

114 *Montgaillard*: G. H. R. abbé de (1772–1825), historian, author of *Histoire de France* (1826–7).

118 *Molay*: J. de (1243–1314), last grand master of the Knights Templars, burnt as a lapsed heretic by Philip IV's officers.

ever and a day!: *As You Like It*, IV.i.

122 *Epigraph*: Goethe, *Venezianische Epigramme*: 'No Apostle-of-Liberty much to my heart ever found I; / License, each for himself, this was at bottom their want. / Liberator of many! first dare to be Servant of many: / What a business is that, wouldst thou know it, go try!' (trans. by TC)

124 *Pan . . . the Nymphs*: god of the country, emblem of fecundity and lust; origin of *panic* fear.

126 *National Convention*: (1792–95) elected to draft a new constitution after the fall of the monarchy. Of five million eligible to vote not more than one million voted.

outherod Herod: *Hamlet*, III.ii.

127 *Andromeda*: beauty chained to a rock by a sea-monster, rescued by Perseus.

   Klopstock: G. F. (1724–1803), German poet.

   Bentham: J. (1748–1832), his utilitarian philosophy was detested by TC.

128 *Committee* ... de Surveillance: (1792–5) local revolutionary organizations established under popular pressure for the arrest and punishment of suspects; gradually controlled by the Jacobins and absorbed into the two main committees of central government, the CGS (17 Oct. 1792) and later the CPS (Apr. 1793).

129 *Buzot*: F. N. L. (1760–94), deputy to EG, NC, Girondist, committed suicide.

   (sacro vate): *Odes*, IV.ix.28.

130 *Philoctetes*: wounded while carrying Hercules' fabled arrows to Troy; his arrival in the last year of the siege ensured the city's destruction; presumably from Sophocles' *Philoctetes*

   hid in a napkin!: cf. Luke 19:20.

132 *Longwi*: French fortress captured 23 Aug. 1792.

134 *Chouan*: Breton insurgents.

   Albigenses: twelfth-century reformers or heretics of mid-France, against whom Innocent III ordered massacres and crusades of 1204 and 1219.

   Palatinate: German state ravaged by France in the war of the P., 1688–97.

   Sardinia: allied with Austria against France, 1792.

   Verdun: fortress captured by Austrians, 2 Sept. 1792.

   Chalons Road ... *Sainte-Menehould*: southern points of the Prussian advance.

135 *proverb and a hissing*: cf. Jer. 25:18.

136 *pale Terror*: Homeric, e.g. *Odyssey*, xi.633.

137 *tooth for a tooth!*: Deut. 19:21.

141 *death and the gallows*: cf. *Iliad*, iii.8.

142 *Bessy Bell of Song*: In the ballad 'Bessy Bell and Mary Gray', Bessy builds a shelter on the hillside to escape the plague. See *Scottish Song*, ed. M. C. Aitken (TC's niece) (1874), 20.

143 *Forest of Argonne*: near Valmy, where Dumouriez's heavily
    outnumbered army decisively defeated Brunswick's Prussian
    forces.

145 *to Poet Milton*: *PL*, ii.595.

147 ultima ratio: according to Richelieu, inscribed on some of
    Louis XVI's cannons.

148 *From the purpose of crime*: cf. *Julius Caesar*, II.i.

149 *Capet Veto*: ancient royal prerogative, named after H. Capet
    (938–96), founder of the French dynasty of the same
    name.

    Armagnac Massacres: 12 June 1418, when the leaders of the
    comte d'A.'s party were massacred by the populace.

152 *Sword Balmung or Thor's Hammer*: (1) Siegfried's sword, see
    'Nibelungen Lied' (xxvii.233). (2) Scandinavian god of war,
    whose weapon typified thunder and lightning.

160 *'were Priests'*: Between 1,100 and 1,400 prisoners were killed;
    in fact, only a quarter of them were priests, nobles, or
    'politicals', and most were ordinary thieves, prostitutes,
    forgers, and vagrants.

162 *every man is his own King*: cf. Judg. 17:6.

163 Garde-Meuble: royal armoury.

165 de profundis: 'out of the depths,' opening words of Ps. 130,
    crying for mercy.

    Thou: J. A. de (1553–1617), statesman, bibliophile, histori-
    ographer.

170 *Moloch-Justice*: involving the sacrifice of what is dear; see 2 Kgs
    23:10.

172 *Carrier . . . David*: (1) J. B. (1756–94), deputy to NC, terrorist,
    helped to organize the conspiracy that overthrew Robespierre,
    guillotined. (2) *Lebon*: G. F. J. (1765–95), deputy to NC,
    member of CGS, representative on mission, guillotined. (3)
    Romme: G. G. (1750–95), deputy to LA, NC, committed
    suicide. (4) *Saint-Just*: L. A. L. de (1767–94), deputy to LA,
    NC, Jacobin, leading spokesman for CPS, guillotined.
    (5) *Féraud*: J. B. (1754–95), deputy to NC, murdered in the
    Convention chamber. (6) *Levasseur*: [de la S.] R. (1747–1834),
    surgeon, deputy to NC. (7) J. L. (1748–1825), painter,
    neoclassicist.

173 *Barras*: P. F. N. vicomte de (1755–1829), terrorist, member of the Directory.

175 ὀλέχοντο δέ λαοί: *Iliad*, i.10.

177 *Hoyle's*: E. (1672–1709) writer on games.

Game of Chess: TC had noted in his journal after reading Thiers' *Histoire* (1823–7) that war was like 'Philidor's chess games', but his interest in battles was not yet developed: 'Why should the learner trouble himself . . .? War must and will one day become obsolete: the sooner the less we need it.'

Admetus's . . . Apollo: see Euripides, *Alcestis* 1–10.

178 *Goethe*: (1749–1832), the great poet and writer, so admired by TC; epigraphs from his poems set the tone for each vol. of the *FR*; he disliked both royalists and revolutionaries.

Weimar's: K. A., grand duke ('Herzog') of S.-W.-E. (1758–1828), Goethe's patron, liberal, enlightened ruler.

182 *Meliboean*: answering each other; from Meliboeus in Virgil's first eclogue.

King of Prussia: Frederick William II (1786–97).

188 *Custine*: A. P., comte de (1740–93), deputy to EG, general, guillotined.

Mentz: [Mainz] on the Rhine, annexed by France, besieged June 1793.

Forster [husband]: J. G. A. (1754–94), German revolutionary, naturalist.

190 *Ezekiel-visions*: cf. Ezek. 1:1 ff.

191 *'tool-using animal'*: *Sartor* (i.32).

before and after: *Hamlet*, IV.iv.

192 *Hérault de Séchelles*: M. J. (1759–94), member of CPS, expelled Girondists from NC, guillotined.

193 *Three gravitating Bodies*: a reference to Condorcet's *Du calcul intégral* (1765).

194 *Death on the pale Horse*: Rev. 6:8.

Louvois: F. M. L., marquis de (1639–91), Louis XIV's adviser and secretary of state for war; the story is told in the *Biographie universelle* xxv.360.

195 *Livy testifies*: *Historiae* V.xxxvi–xxxviii.

200 *Hassenfratz*: J. H. (1755–1827), chemist, member of CPS.

201 *'Sardanapalus-character'*: Greek name of Asurbanipal, or Asnapper, extravagant tyrant described in Ezra 4:10.

203 *Troy Town fell!*: cf. *Iliad*, xx.1–75.

204 *provide for itself*: cf. Matt. 6:34.

205 *covering acres*: TC may identify Goliath with Tityus, son of Zeus and Gaea, whose body covered nine acres.

207 *THE LOSER PAYS*: 'vae victis', Livy V.xlviii.9.

   (fidibus canoris): Horace, *Odes*. I.xii.11.

208 *Clotho-scissors*: one of the three destinies spinning the thread of life.

212 *Deborah*: who judged Israel, Judg. 4:4.

220 *Jean-Bon*: [St.-A.] J. (1749–1813), organizer of the revolutionary navy, member of CPS.

222 *'Varlet'*: J. F. (1764–1832), orator, activist, deputy to NC, egalitarian theorist.

223 Ami des Lois: anti-Jacobin play by J. L. Laya (1761–1833), staged 2 Jan. 1792, suspended 11 Jan.

231 *Phalaris*: tyrant of Agrigentum.

234 *Angoulême*: [Mme Royale] M. T. C. de B., duchesse d' (1778–1851), Louis XVI's surviving daughter.

237 *more bitterly than Job did*: Job 3:1 ff.

   River Scheldt: reopened to trade in spite of the treaty of Utrecht, 1713.

243 *sorrow and sin flee away?*: Isa. 51:11.

   burn within us: Luke 24:32.

244 *Hermit Peter*: (*c.*1050–1115), preacher; the legend that Christ appeared to P. in the Church of the Holy Sepulchre, Jerusalem, inspiring him to lead the first crusade.

   'Zisca's drum: John of Trocznov (1360–1424), Bohemian noble who ordered his skin after death to be made into drum-heads.

   Cameronians: followers of Richard Cameron (1648–80), founder of Reformed Presbyterian Church.

248 *tinkling cymbal*: 1 Cor. 13:1.

249 Apage-Satanas: 'Get thee behind me, Satan'; Matt. 16:23.

250 *Guffroy*: A. B. J. (1742–1801), deputy to NC, member of CGS, founder of *Rougiff*, the title being an anagram of his name.

Chalier: M. J. (1747–93), Montagnard militant, federalist, guillotined, proclaimed by Jacobins as a martyr of the F.R.

253 *Mademoiselle Égalité*: [Adelaide, Mme d'Orleans] E. L. (1777–1847), sister and confidante of L. Philippe.

254 *assembled Pandemonium*: *PL*, i.756.

Anacreon of the Guillotine: comparing Barrère to the Greek lyric poet, a popular title which TC attributes to Burke.

255 'Götter selbst vergebens!': Schiller, *Die Jungfrau von Orleans* (1801) III.vi. see 'Schiller' (xxvii.208).

aspic on her bosom: as in *Antony and Cleopatra*, v.ii.

Magician's Famulus: Goethe, 'Der Zauberlehrling' ('The Magician's Apprenticeship'), in *Balladen* (1815).

256 *Deucalion*: Greek counterpart of Noah, son of Prometheus, built an ark to save himself and wife from Zeus's deluge.

Aix-la-Chapelle . . . Maestricht: (1) where Westermann and the French were halted by Austrian forces, Feb. 1793. (2) siege led by Miranda, Feb. 1793.

257 *Lux*: A. (1766–93), deputy for Mainz to NC, sought to incorporate the German electorate with France, guillotined.

Cook: Captain J. (1728–79), navigator, killed by Hawaiian natives.

258 *York*: F. A. Duke of (1763–1827), second son of George III, commander of the British forces, 1793.

259 *Cobourg*: [S.-C.] F. J. Duke of (1737–1815), commander of Austrian forces.

263 *'facetted spectacles'*: Carlylean expression.

vision be withdrawn from him: echoing Prov. 29:18: 'Where there is no vision, the people perish.'

266 Tribunal Extraordinaire . . . Révolutionnaire: special high court for crimes against the Republic, 1793.

Sword of Sharpness: cf. Rev. 1:16.

267 *no bowels*: cf. 1 John 3:17.

269 *wisdom . . . herald of Fortune*: cf. Juvenal, *Satires* xiii.20: 'Victrix fortunae sapientia.'

272 *Dumouriez's occupation's gone*: cf. *Othello*, III.iii.

274 *Lasource*: M. D. A. (1763–93), deputy to LA, NC, guillotined.

275 *Duperret*: C. R. L. (1747–93), deputy to LA, NC, guillotined.

276 *not wisely, but too well*: *Othello*, V.ii.

285 'Illa suprema dies!': 'the last day,' Tacitus, *Annales* i.53.

   last scene of all: *As You Like It*, II.vii.

286 *Lanjuinais*: J. D., comte (1753–1827), deputy to NC, moderate.

291 *Caen*: chief city in Normandy, centre of federalist revolt, made the capital of the dept. of Calvados, 1793.

292 *Pascal's* Provincials: *Lettres Provinciales* (1656).

   Puisaye: J. G., comte de (1755–1827), deputy to CA, royalist commander in Brittany, 1794–98.

293 non faciunt murum: 'Hard and hard will not make a wall.'

296 *to the shades below*: Homeric, e.g. *Iliad* iv.525–6.

   He that made him knows: cf. Jer. 1:5.

299 *Codrus'-sacrifices*: last king of Athens, who gave his life for the good of his country.

301 Supper of Beaucaire: *Le Souper de Beaucaire* (1793), championed the Jacobins against the Girondins.

310 *Baucis and Philemon*: rustics who entertained the gods and were saved from destruction by being turned into trees, types of aged and virtuous contentment.

   the roof of his mouth: Ezek. 3:26.

315 *Robespierre Junior*: A. B. J. de (1763–94), called R. the Younger, deputy to NC, representative on mission, guillotined.

316 *Pretender Royal Highnesses*: Charles Emmanuel IV (1751–1819) and Victor Emmanuel I (1759–1824), of Savoy, future kings of Sardinia.

317 *unfruitful Atlantic*: cf. *Iliad*, i.316.

318 Levy in Mass: primarily conscripted bachelors and childless widowers of the 18–25 age group, although other groups were mobilized.

319 Law of the Suspect: act taken by the NC to provide a legal basis for punishing suspected counter revolutionaries, 17 Sept. 1793.

327 Pot-pourri *by Ducos*: satirical poems, printed in Riouffe, *Mémoires d'un détenu* (1795).

329 *all manner of birds!*: *Iliad*, i.3–4.

331 *sands of the sea*: biblical expression as in Gen. 32:12.

332 *harvest . . . whitening*: cf. John 4:35.

   God is a Truth: cf. Deut. 32:4.

   Histoire Parlementaire: TC appreciatively reviewed the *Histoire*, 23 vols. (Paris, 1833–6), 'Parliamentary History of the French Revolution', *London and Westminster Review*, 27 (April 1837): 233–47, but with the same objections and regretting Roux' prefaces on the 'Progress of the Species . . . and what not' (xxix.1–21).

333 *calling on men to repent*: cf. Acts 3:19.

   toto coelo: 'By the whole heaven's width.' A thing different in distance by the whole heaven's width.

   name *the new Things*: cf. Gen. 2:20.

334 *dead men's bones*: Matt. 23:27.

335 *Cato,—Censor, or else of Utica*: (1) Marcus Porcius the elder (234–149 BC), statesman, orator. (2) Marcus Porcius Uticensis (95–46 BC), great grandson of C., killed himself at Utica.

   Babœuf: F. N. (1760–97), leader of the communist movement against the Directory in 1796, publisher of *Tribun du peuple* in which he took the name of Caius Gracchus, executed.

   Mutius Scaevola: section and its leather-working leader [cordwainer] named after the Roman soldier who put his hand in the fire prepared for his execution to show his disregard of death.

   '*Cesspool of* Agio': Carlylean expression for financial speculation.

   Fata-Morganas: striking mirage seen in the straits of Messina.

336 '*hundred tongues*': *Aeneid*, vi.625.

   Josephine Beauharnais: [M. J. R. T. de La P.] (1763–1814), future wife of Napoleon, Empress of France.

338 *Jezebel headtire*: 2 Kgs 9:30.

342 tormentum: an engine for hurling missiles

   from death deliver: cf. Ps. 33:19

344 *Cabarus*: [Cabarrus] J. M. I. T. ('Theresia') (1773–1835), leader of fashionable society during the Thermidorean reaction and the Directory, divorced from J. J. de *Fontenay*, counsellor in PP, remarried Tallien.

Proserpine: daughter of Ceres abducted by *Pluto*, the god of Hell, while gathering flowers.

brands into the burning: cf. Amos 4:11.

348 *nest in the rocks*: Prov. 30:26.

350 Noyades: of Catholic and royalist supporters by local radicals; though not directly involved in the executions, Carrier was guilty of neglect.

351 *bereaved of her whelps*: Hos. 13:8.

352 '*beetles and spiders*': TC quotes from himself in the guise of Teufelsdröckh, *Sartor* (i.172), where the context shows that the formulas there are 'Church' ones. He is mocking, or self-mocking, as only readers of *Fraser's Magazine* in Britain could have seen the allusion.

354 *Lalande*: J. J. le F de (1732–1807), astronomer, atheist, collaborator of Maréchal in the *Dictionaire des Athées* (1800).

356 spolia opima: 'richest spoils', taken by a Roman general from the enemy leader he had killed in single combat.

358 Armée Révolutionnaire: paramilitary forces organized under popular pressure to enforce policies of the revolutionary government in the interior of France, 1793–4.

359 *Xenophon*: (431–*c*.350 BC), who describes the retreat of ten thousand Greeks in the *Anabasis*.

Charles Second: (1630–85), king of Gt. Britain and Ireland; his troops brutally persecuted Scottish rebels (Covenanters) who refused to accept episcopacy.

hunt their Maroons: in the Maroon wars planters waged hostilities against fugitive negroes throughout the eighteenth century.

361 Sûreté Générale: [CGS] committee of the NC, administered arrests, inquiries, passports, and reports; dissolved 1795.

Amars, Vadiers: (1) J. A. (1755–1816), terrorist, member of CGS. (2) M. G. A. (1736–1828), deputy to EG, president of CGS.

Dobsents: C. E. (1742–1811), president of the Central Revolutionary Committee, which organized the overthrow of the Girondins, 2 June 1793.

363 *Herald Mercury*: *Richard III*, IV.iii.

Lebas: P. F. J. (1764–94), deputy to NC, member of CGS, Robespierrist, committed suicide.

366 Pro patria mori: Horace, *Odes*, III. ii.13.

367 *Cavaignac*: J. B., baron de Lalande (1763–1829), father of TC's great friend Godefroy, the exiled revolutionary at the time of TC's writing the *FR*, who accused him of 'impartiality' and remained an unrepentant Robespierrist.

à la *Captain-Kirk*: P. (1646?–91), English general stationed at Tangier, returned in 1685 to crush rebellion against James II in Somerset, renowned for his ruthlessness.

369 *Pichegru*: J. C. (1761–1804), general accused of treason, found strangled, possibly on Bonaparte's orders.

371 *have been great*: i.e. liars; (1) *Mendez Pinto*: F. (*c.*1510–83), storyteller, adventurer. (2) *Münchhäusen*: K. F. H., F. von (1720–97), soldier, raconteur. (3) *Cagliostro*: see i.59. (4) *Psalmanazar*: G. (*c.*1679–1763), French literary imposter, forged books on Formosa.

373 *Jove's Balance*: cf. *Iliad*, xxii where Achilles' and Hector's lots are weighed by Zeus.

374 *dog at the moon*: cf. *Julius Caesar*, IV.ii.

376 Purchas's Pilgrims: S. Purchas (*c.*1577–1626), traveller, author with Hakluyt of *Purchas his Pilgrimes* (1625).

380 *Phélippeaux*: [Philippeaux] P. N. (1759–94), lawyer, Jacobin, deputy to NC, Dantonist, executed.

381 *Sun-god . . . Python Serpent*: Apollo slew the monster serpent at Delphi.

382 *Montezuma's*: (1466–1520), last Aztec emperor.

384 *Fabricius*: [Caius Luscinus] (d. *c.*270 BC), Roman consul noted for courage and austere incorruptibility.

385 *Saint-Dennis*: (d. 272), first bishop of Paris, apostle of France, beheaded for his faith, represented in legend as rising and taking his head under his arm.

Ulysses Polytlas: 'much-enduring Odysseus', *Odyssey*, vii.344.

386 Shade of his Mother: cf. *Odyssey*, xi.84–9.

'*in the Rights of Man*': 'Die Christenheit oder Europa', in *Novalis Schriften* (1826); see 'Novalis' (xxvii.43).

winged with wrath: cf. *Iliad*, i.201.

390 *Fleuriot-Lescot*: J. B. E. (1761–94), mayor of Paris, Montagnard, guillotined.

392 *little boy*: [Louis XVII] (1785–95), second son of Louis XVI, declared king by the comte de Provence after his father's execution, died in the Temple prison.

die and not live: Ps. 118:17.

give an account: Romans 14:12.

393 '*lot of man*'!: Another half-mocking self-quotation, from Teufelsdröckh, *Sartor* (i.145).

395 *Vilate*: J. (1768–95), abbé, Robespierrist, juror on the revolutionary tribunal, executed.

398 Decree of the Twenty-second Prairial: passed by the NC 10 June 1794, to increase the number of suspects brought before the revolutionary tribunal.

400 *Doll-Tearsheet*: courtesan, *2 Henry IV*.

402 *How long, O Lord!*: Ps. 13:1.

dragon's teeth: attacked while sewing a dragon's teeth, Cadmus threw a stone among his assailants who then fought and killed each other; the same story is told of Jason.

404 *Polyphemus Cavern*: home of the Cyclops, *Odyssey*, ix.

405 *at the wine-cup that day!*: cf. Prov. 23:30.

bell the cat: name for Archibald Douglas, fifth Earl of Angus (*c*.1449–1513) who undertook to rid the kingdom of the upstart Earl of Mar; from the fable of the mice who tried to tie a bell to the neck of a cat, which would warn of its approach.

407 *fit for such things*: Not traced, probably incorrect, and not repeated in TC's *Cromwell* (cf. vi.294).

408 '*keep his powder dry*'!: poetically ascribed to Cromwell.

Pride's Purge: the excluding of parliamentarians from the House of Commons by Colonel T. Pride, and the establishing of the 'Rump', 6 Dec. 1648.

411 *harness on our back*: *Macbeth*, v.v.

412 *did the* foam: Apelles, unable to paint the foam on the mouth of Alexander's horse, threw his brush at the canvass and did so accidentally.

413 *'shakes her doubtful urn'*: Horace, *Odes*, II.iii.26.

418 *Drill-sergeant!*: cf. 'Shooting Niagara' (xxx.41): 'I often say, The One Official Person . . . is the Drill-Sergeant who is master of his work, and who will perform it.'

420 *a Rachel may*: cf. Matt. 2:18.

421 *passing away*: cf. 2 Cor. 5:17.

423 *Euterpean*: muse of music, patron of wind instruments.

      Ionic motions: Horace, *Odes*, III.vi.21.

424 *Houris . . . Mahomet's Paradise*: According to Mohammedan faith, an intercourse with the virgins of paradise is the chief delight to the faithful.

      merits to disclose: Gray, *Elegy* (1751), Epitaph.

426 *QUIBERON*: peninsula on the SW coast of Brittany where a British-backed émigré expedition was routed, July 1795.

428 *roasting eggs*: Bacon, 'Of Wisdom For A Man's Self', *Essays* (1609).

429 *Son of Sombreuil*: C. (1769–95), commander of a battalion in the Quiberon expedition, executed.

431 *Dreams are made of?*: cf. *Tempest*, IV.i.

436 *Month* Prairial: insurrection by Sansculotte militants against the NC, 1–4 Prairial Year III (20–3 May 1795).

440 Ultimi Romanorum: 'The last of the Romans', *Julius Caesar*, V.iii.

442 *Fritz wrench Silesia*: Maria Theresa's (1717–80) rejection of Frederick's claim to the Silesian duchies led to his invasion 1741.

      Agnes Sorel: (1422?–50), influential mistress of Charles VII.

      wretchedness of all: In Feb. 1836 parliament debated the report of a royal commission on the Irish Poor Law. In Nov. a further report was made by a Mr G. Nicholls; and in 1838 a new and unsatisfactory bill was passed. TC kept an enlightened interest in its action, and visited Ireland in 1846 and 1849 to see the results.

443 *Peace, peace*: Jer. 8:11.

444 *WHIFF OF GRAPESHOT*: TC's own trans. of 'salve de canons'.

445 *basest yet known*: the impression of such historians as A. Cobban that TC did not understand that the F.R. was bourgeois is highly questionable; his comments can be sustained historically.

447 *kick against the pricks!*: Acts 9:5.

450 *as Epic ships are wont*: cf. *Odyssey*, xiii.160–3.

451 *for it, and the man*: cf. Scott, *Guy Mannering* (1815), Ch. 54: 'Because the Hour's come, and the Man.'

  Eighteenth of Fructidor: *coup d'état* removing moderates from the Directory, 4 Sept. 1797.

452 *out of the Eater*: Judg. 14:14.

  thus spake: TC repeats the 'prophecy' of 'death-rebirth' that he voiced through the false 'arch-quack' Cagliostro in 'The Diamond Necklace' (xxviii.399–400).

453 *Corinthian brass*: When Mummius set fire to Corinth, the heat was so great that it melted the metal, which ran down the streets in streams.

  living fountain: cf. Jer. 2:13.

INDEX

The index is selective but identifies many figures omitted from the Notes. Authors' works (and usually characters), allusions, etc., are indexed under authors' names, except for the Bible which is indexed only for characters; place-names are given sparingly; and some repeated allusions (e.g. 'Cimmeria') only on the first or selected occasions. TC's footnote citations are not usually indexed.